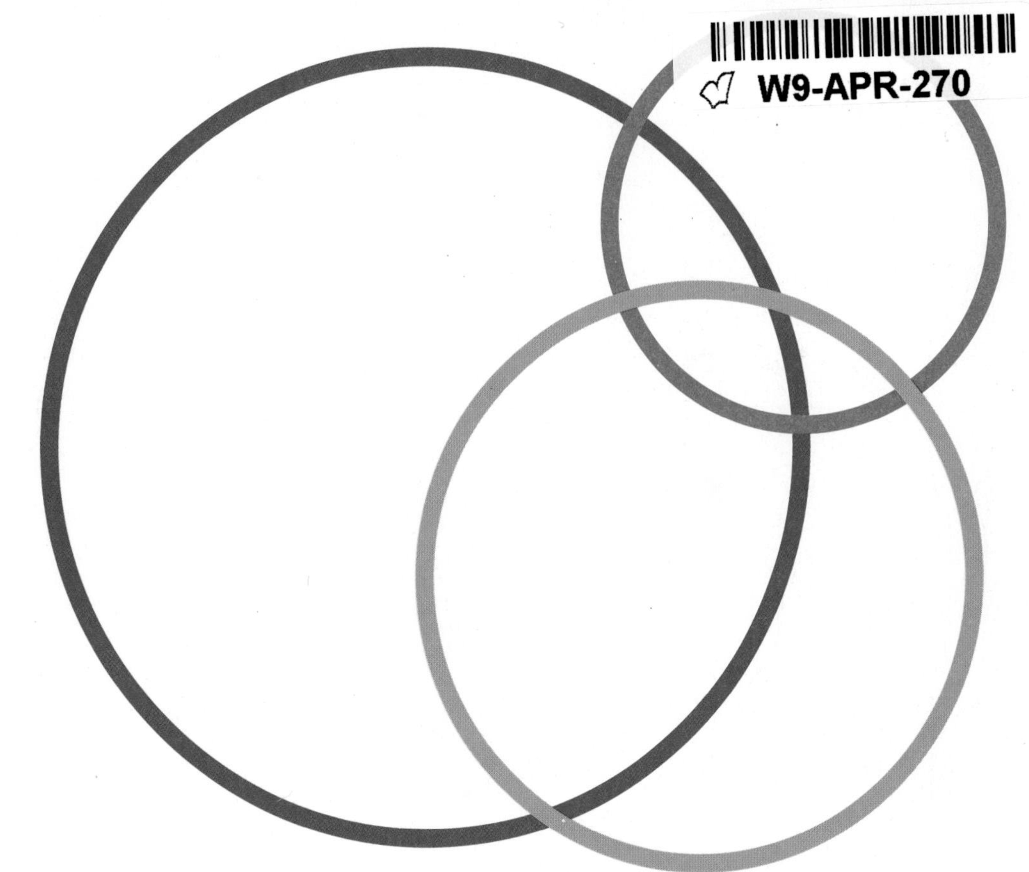

Global Business Today

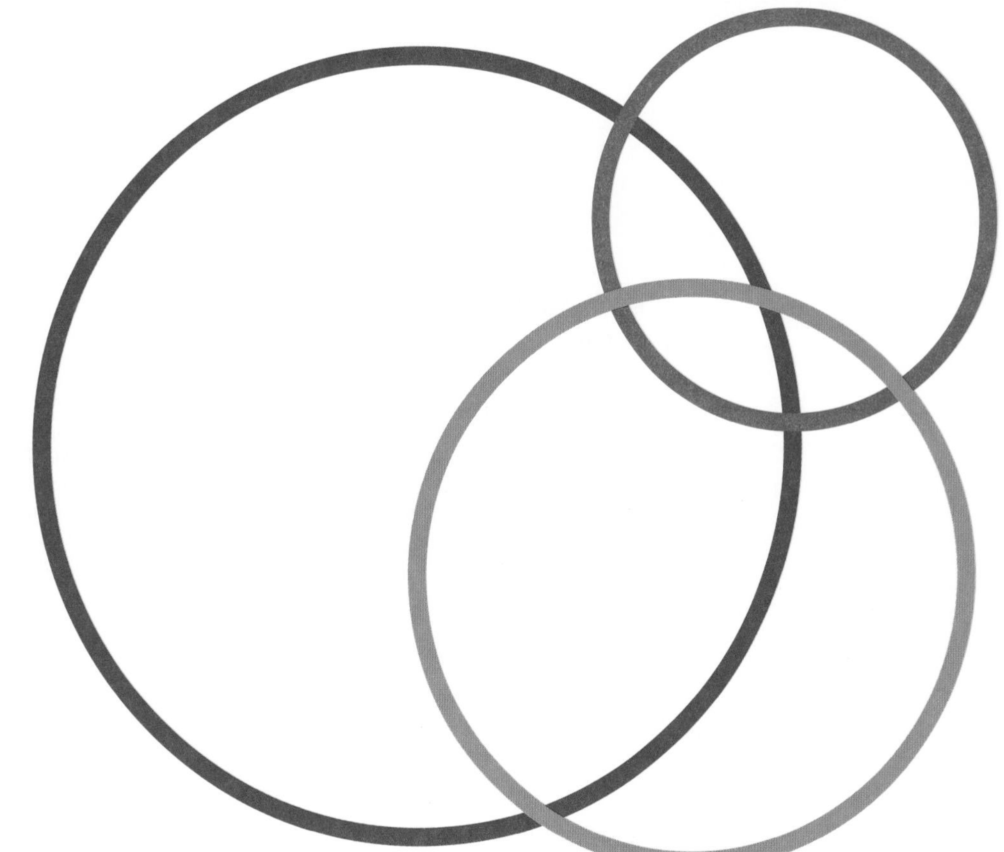

fifth edition

Global Business Today

Charles W. L. Hill

University of Washington

Boston Burr Ridge, IL Dubuque, IA Madison, WI New York San Francisco St. Louis
Bangkok Bogotá Caracas Kuala Lumpur Lisbon London Madrid Mexico City
Milan Montreal New Delhi Santiago Seoul Singapore Sydney Taipei Toronto

GLOBAL BUSINESS TODAY
Published by McGraw-Hill/Irwin, a business unit of The McGraw-Hill Companies, Inc., 1221 Avenue of the Americas, New York, NY, 10020.

Some ancillaries, including electronic and print components, may not be available to customers outside the United States.

This book is printed on acid-free paper.

2 3 4 5 6 7 8 9 0 DOW/DOW 0 9 8 7

ISBN 978-0-07-321054-4
MHID 0-07-321054-4

Editorial director: *John E. Biernat*
Development editor I : *Kirsten Guidero*
Associate marketing manager : *Margaret A. Beamer*
Media producer: *Lynn Bluhm*
Project manager: *Jim Labeots*
Senior production spervisor: *Carol Bielski*
Senior designer: *Kami Carter*
Photo research coordinator: *Kathy Shive*
Photo researcher: *Teri Stratford*
Senior media project manager: *Susan Lombardi*
Cover design: *Mary Kazak*
Interior design: *Mary Kazak*
Typeface: *10/12 Janson Text Roman*
Compositor: *Techbooks*
Printer: *R. R. Donnelley*

Library of Congress Cataloging-in-Publication Data

Hill, Charles W. L.
Global business today / Charles W. L. Hill. — 5th ed.
p. cm.
Includes index.
ISBN-13: 978-0-07-321054-4 (alk. paper)
ISBN-10: 0-07-321054-4 (alk. paper)
1. International business enterprises—Management. 2. International trade.
3. Investments, Foreign. 4. Capital market. I. Title.
HD62.4.H548 2008
658′.049—dc22

2006100722

www.mhhe.com

For June and Mike Hill, my parents

about the author

Charles W. L. Hill is the Hughes M. Blake Professor of International Business at the School of Business, University of Washington. Professor Hill received his PhD in industrial organization economics in 1983 from the University of Manchester's Institute of Science and Technology (UMIST) in Great Britain. In addition to his position at the University of Washington, he has served on the faculties of UMIST, Texas A&M University, and Michigan State University.

Professor Hill has published more than 40 articles in peer-reviewed academic journals. He has also published four college textbooks, one on strategic management, one on principles of management, and the other two on international business (one of which you are now holding). He serves on the editorial boards of several academic journals and previously served as consulting editor at the *Academy of Management Review.*

Professor Hill teaches in the MBA and executive MBA programs at the University of Washington and has received awards for teaching excellence in both programs. He has also taught in several customized executive programs. He lives in Seattle with his wife Lane and children.

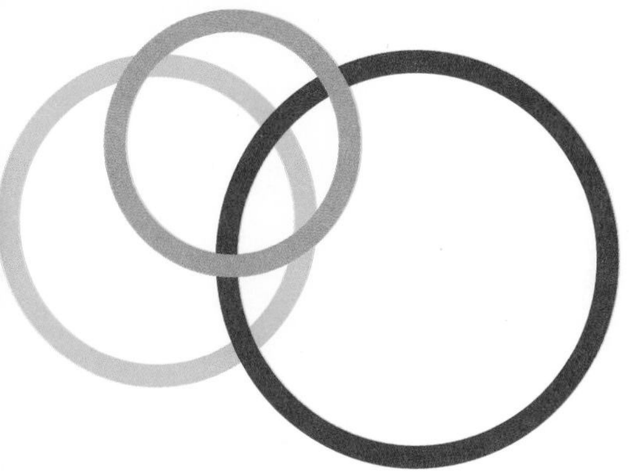

brief contents

contents

preface

Global Business Today is intended for the first international business course at either the undergraduate or MBA level. My goal in writing this book has been to set a new standard for international business textbooks. I have attempted to write a book that

1. Is comprehensive and up-to-date.
2. Goes beyond an uncritical presentation and shallow explanation of the body of knowledge.
3. Maintains a tight, integrated flow between chapters.
4. Focuses on managerial implications.
5. Makes important theories accessible and interesting to students.
6. Incorporates ancillary resources that enliven the text and make it easier to teach.

Over the years, and through now five editions, I have worked hard to adhere to these goals. It has not always been easy. An enormous amount has happened over the last decade, both in the real world of economics, politics, and business, and in the academic world of theory and empirical research. Often I have had to significantly rewrite chapters, scrap old examples, bring in new ones, incorporate new theory and evidence into the book, and phase out older theories that are increasingly less relevant to the modern and dynamic world of international business. That process continues in the current edition. As noted below, there have been significant changes in this edition, and that will no doubt continue to be the case in the future. In deciding what changes to make, I have been guided not only by my own reading, teaching, and research, but also by the invaluable feedback I receive from professors and students around the world who use the book, from reviewers, and from the editorial staff at McGraw-Hill/Irwin. My thanks go out to all of them.

Comprehensive and Up-to-Date

To be comprehensive, an international business textbook must

- Explain how and why the world's countries differ.
- Present a thorough review of the economics and politics of international trade and investment.
- Explain the functions and form of the global monetary system.
- Examine the strategies and structures of international businesses.
- Assess the special roles of an international business's various functions.

I have always endeavored to do all of these things. Too many other texts have paid insufficient attention to the strategies and structures of international businesses and to the implications of international business for firms' various functions. This omission has been a serious deficiency. Many of the students in these international business courses will soon be working in international businesses, and they will be expected to understand the implications of international business for their organization's strategy, structure, and functions. This book pays close attention to these issues.

Comprehensiveness and relevance also require coverage of the major theories. It has always been my goal to incorporate the insights gleaned from recent academic work into the text. Consistent with this goal, over the last four editions I have added insights from the following research:

- The new trade theory and strategic trade policy.
- The work of Nobel Prize–winning economist Amartya Sen on economic development.
- The work of Hernando de Soto on the link between property rights and economic development.
- Samuel Huntington's influential thesis on the "clash of civilizations."
- The new growth theory of economic development championed by Paul Romer and Gene Grossman.
- Empirical work by Jeffery Sachs and others on the relationship between international trade and economic growth.
- Michael Porter's theory of the competitive advantage of nations.
- Robert Reich's work on national competitive advantage.
- The work of Nobel Prize–winner Douglas North and others on national institutional structures and the protection of property rights.
- The market imperfections approach to foreign direct investment that has grown out of Ronald Coase and Oliver Williamson's work on transaction cost economics.
- Bartlett and Ghoshal's research on the transnational corporation.
- The writings of C. K. Prahalad and Gary Hamel on core competencies, global competition, and global strategic alliances.
- Insights for international business strategy that can be derived from the resource-based view of the firm.

In addition to including leading-edge theory, in light of the fast-changing nature of the international business environment, I have made every effort to ensure that the book was as up-to-date as possible when it went to press. A significant amount has happened in the world since I first began work on this book. The Uruguay Round of GATT negotiations were successfully concluded and the World Trade Organization was established. In 2001, the WTO embarked upon another major round of talks aimed to reduce barriers to trader, the Doha Round. The European Union moved forward with its post-1992 agenda to achieve a closer economic and monetary union, including the establishment of a common currency in January 1999. The North American Free Trade Agreement passed into law, and Chile indicated its desire to become the next member of the free trade area. The Asian Pacific Economic Cooperation forum emerged as the kernel of a possible future Asia Pacific free trade area. The former Communist states of Eastern Europe and Asia continued on the road to economic and political reform. As they did, the euphoric mood that followed the collapse of communism in 1989 was slowly replaced with a growing sense of realism about the hard path ahead for many of these countries. The global money market continued its meteoric growth. By 2006, more than $1.5 trillion per day was flowing across national borders. The size of such flows fueled concern about the ability of short-term speculative shifts in global capital markets to destabilize the world economy. The World Wide Web emerged from nowhere to become the backbone of an emerging global network for electronic commerce. The world continued to become more global. Several Asian Pacific economies, most notably China, continued to grow their economies at a rapid rate. Outsourcing of service functions to places like China and India emerged as a major issue in developed Western nations. New multinationals continued to emerge from developing nations in addition to the world's established industrial powers. Increasingly, the globalization of the world economy affected a wide range of firms of all sizes, from the very large to the very small. And unfortunately, in the wake of the terrorist attacks on the United States that took place on September 11, 2001, global terrorism and the attendant geopolitical risks emerged as a threat to global economic integration and activity.

To reflect this rapid change, in this edition of the book I have tried to ensure that all material and statistics are as up-to-date as possible as of 2006.

What's New in the Fifth Edition

The success of the first four editions of *Global Business Today* was based in part upon the incorporation of leading-edge research into the text, the use of the up-to-date examples and statistics to illustrate global trends and enterprise strategy, and the discussion of current events within the context of the appropriate theory. Building on these strengths, my goals for the fifth revision have been threefold:

1. Incorporate new insights from recent scholarly research wherever appropriate.
2. Make sure the content of the text covers all appropriate issues.
3. Make sure the text is as up-to-date as possible with regard to current events, statistics, and examples.

As part of the overall revision process, *changes have been made to every chapter in the book.* All statistics have been updated to incorporate the most recently available data. New examples, cases, and boxes have been added and older examples updated to reflect new developments. New material has been inserted wherever appropriate to reflect recent academic work or important current events. See below for three primary examples.

A New Round of Talks: Doha Antidumping actions, trade in agricultural products, better enforcement of intellectual property laws, and expanded market access were four of the issues the WTO wanted to tackle at the 1999 meetings in Seattle, but those meetings were derailed. In late 2001, the WTO tried again to launch a new round of talks between member states aimed at further liberalizing the global trade and investment framework. For this meeting, it picked the remote location of Doha in the Persian Gulf state of Qatar, no doubt with an eye on the difficulties that antiglobalization protesters would have in getting there. Unlike the Seattle meetings, at Doha, the member states of the WTO agreed to launch a new round of talks and staked out an agenda. The talks were originally scheduled to last three years, although they have already gone on longer and may not be concluded for a while.

Chapter 6 has been updated to discuss progress on the current round of talks sponsored by the WTO aimed at reducing barriers to trade, particularly in agriculture (the Doha Round). See pages 215–220 for the rest of this section.

TRENDS IN FDI The past 30 years have seen a marked increase in both the flow and stock of FDI in the world economy. The average yearly outflow of FDI increased from \$25 billion in 1975 to a record \$1.2 trillion in 2000, before falling back to an estimated \$897 billion in 2005 (see Figure 7.1).[2] Over this period, the flow of FDI accelerated faster than the growth in world trade and world output. For example, between 1992 and 2005, the total flow of FDI from all countries increased more than fivefold while world trade by value grew by some 140 percent and world output by around 40 percent.[3] As a result of the strong FDI flow, by 2004 the global stock of FDI exceeded \$9 trillion. At least 70,000 parent companies had 690,000 affiliates in foreign markets that collectively employed more than 50 million people abroad and generated value accounting for about one-tenth of global GDP. The foreign affiliates of multinationals had an estimated \$19 trillion in global sales, much higher than the value of global exports, which stood at close to \$11 trillion.[4]

Chapter 7 now includes updated statistics on trends in foreign direct investment flows that took place in the 2001–04 period. See pages 229–230 for the rest of this section.

Additionally, at several places in the book, there is extended discussion of the outsourcing of service activities, from software testing and diagnosis of MRI scans to telephone call centers and billing functions, to developing nations such as India. The implications of this development for international business are explored.

ENLARGEMENT OF THE EUROPEAN UNION A major issue facing the EU over the past few years has been that of enlargement. Enlargement of the EU into Eastern Europe has been a possibility since the collapse of communism at the end of the 1980s, and by the end of the 1990s, 13 countries had applied to become EU members. To qualify for EU membership, the applicants had to privatize state assets, deregulate markets, restructure industries, and tame inflation. They also had to incorporate complex EU laws into their own systems, establish stable democratic governments, and respect human rights.[18] In December 2002, the EU formally agreed to accept the applications of 10 countries, and they joined on May 1, 2004. The new members include the Baltic countries, the Czech Republic, and the larger nations of Hungary and Poland. The only new members not in Eastern Europe are the Mediterranean island nations of Malta and Cyprus. Their inclusion in the EU expanded the union to 25 states, stretching from the Atlantic to the borders of Russia; added 23 percent to the landmass of the EU; brought 75 million new citizens into the EU, building an EU with a population of 450 million people; and created a single continental economy with a GDP of close to €11 trillion.

The section on the European Union in Chapter 8 has been revised to reflect the fact that 10 more member states were admitted on May 1, 2004. See page 277 for the rest of this section.

However, being absolutely up-to-date is impossible because change is always with us. What is current today may be outdated tomorrow. Accordingly, this edition is accompanied by two programs created to help instructors stay in touch with current events and issues:

Enhanced Course Cartridge

We have also created an enhanced course cartridge for this text, which walks students through each chapter with remedial activities, quizzes that report directly to an instructor gradebook, and interactive review exercises to help students master the concepts presented in the book. (www.mhhe.com/hillgbt5e)

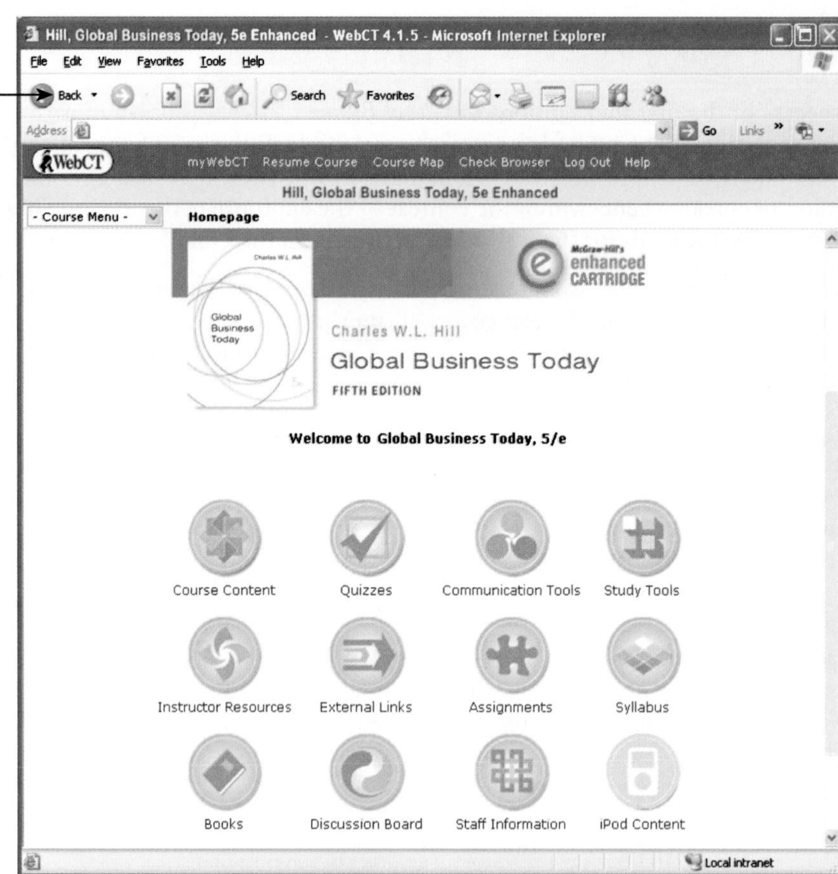

Revised and Expanded DVD

Finally, a revised and expanded DVD accompanies this text to help spark classroom discussions. Classic footage joins new stories to help you engage your students in international business topics. The Instructor's Manual includes notes on how to use the videos with each chapter.

Beyond Uncritical Presentation and Shallow Explanation

Many issues in international business are complex and thus necessitate considerations of pros and cons. To demonstrate this to students, I have adopted a critical approach that presents the arguments for and against economic theories, government policies, business strategies, organizational structures, and so on.

Related to this, I have attempted to explain the complexities of the many theories and phenomena unique to international business so the student might fully comprehend the statements of a theory or the reasons a phenomenon is the way it is. I believe that these theories and phenomena are explained in more depth in this book than they are in competing textbooks, which seem to use the rationale that a shallow explanation is little better than no explanation. In international business, a little knowledge is indeed a dangerous thing.

To help students go a step farther in expanding their understanding of international business, each chapter incorporates two globalEDGE research tasks designed and written by Tunga Kiyuk and the team at Michigan State University's globalresearch.com site to dovetail with the content just covered.

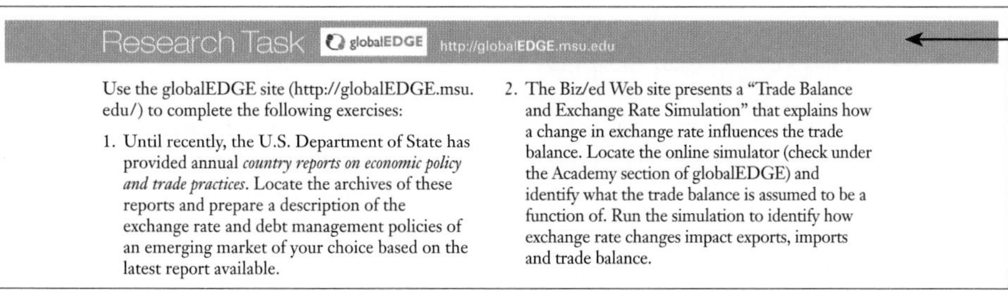

Research Task globalEDGE http://globalEDGE.msu.edu

Use the globalEDGE site (http://globalEDGE.msu.edu/) to complete the following exercises:

1. Until recently, the U.S. Department of State has provided annual *country reports on economic policy and trade practices*. Locate the archives of these reports and prepare a description of the exchange rate and debt management policies of an emerging market of your choice based on the latest report available.
2. The Biz/ed Web site presents a "Trade Balance and Exchange Rate Simulation" that explains how a change in exchange rate influences the trade balance. Locate the online simulator (check under the Academy section of globalEDGE) and identify what the trade balance is assumed to be a function of. Run the simulation to identify how exchange rate changes impact exports, imports and trade balance.

GlobalEDGE

The globalEDGE task for Chapter 10 focuses on learning how to research the U.S. Department of State's statistics on other countries' economic policies and trade practices, as well as on discovering how exchange rates affect trade balances. See page 356 for more details.

Integrated Progression of Topics

A weakness of many texts is that they lack a tight, integrated flow of topics from chapter to chapter. In Chapter 1 of this book, students will learn how the book's topics are related to each other. I've achieved integration by organizing the material so that each chapter builds on the material of the previous ones in a logical fashion.

PART ONE Chapter 1 provides an overview of the key issues to be addressed and explains the plan of the book.

PART TWO Chapters 2 and 3 focus on national differences in political economy and culture, and Chapter 4 examines ethical issues in international business. Most international business textbooks place this material at a later point, but I believe it is vital to discuss national differences first. After all, many of the central issues in international trade and investment, the global monetary system, international business strategy and structure, and international business operations arise out of national differences in political economy and culture. To fully understand these issues, students must first appreciate the differences in countries and cultures. Ethical issues are dealt with at this juncture primarily because many ethical dilemmas flow out of national differences in political systems, economic systems, and culture.

PART THREE Chapters 5 through 8 investigate the political economy of international trade and investment. The purpose of this part is to describe and explain the trade and investment environment in which international business occurs.

PART FOUR Chapters 9 and 10 describe and explain the global monetary system, laying out in detail the monetary framework in which international business transactions are conducted.

PART FIVE In Chapters 11 through 16, attention shifts from the environment to the firm. Here the book examines the strategies that firms adopt to compete effectively in the international business environment and explains how firms can perform key functions—production, marketing, R&D, human resource management, accounting, and finance—in order to compete and succeed in the international business environment.

Throughout the book, the relationship of new material to topics discussed in earlier chapters is pointed out to the students to reinforce their understanding of how the material comprises an integrated whole.

Focus on Managerial Implications

I have always believed that it is important to show students how the material covered in the text is relevant to the actual practice of international business. This is explicit in the later chapters of the book, which focus on the practice of international business, but it is not always obvious in the first half of the book, which considers many macroeconomic and political issues, from international trade theory and foreign direct investment flows to the IMF and the influence of inflation rates on foreign exchange quotations. Accordingly, at the end of each chapter in Parts Two, Three, and Four—where the focus is on the environment of international business, as opposed to particular firms—there is a section titled "Focus on Managerial Implications." In this section, the managerial implications of the material discussed in the chapter are clearly explained.

Focus on Managerial Implications

For example, Chapter 5, "International Trade Theory," ends with a detailed discussion of the various trade theories' implications for international business management. See pages 183–185 for the rest of this feature.

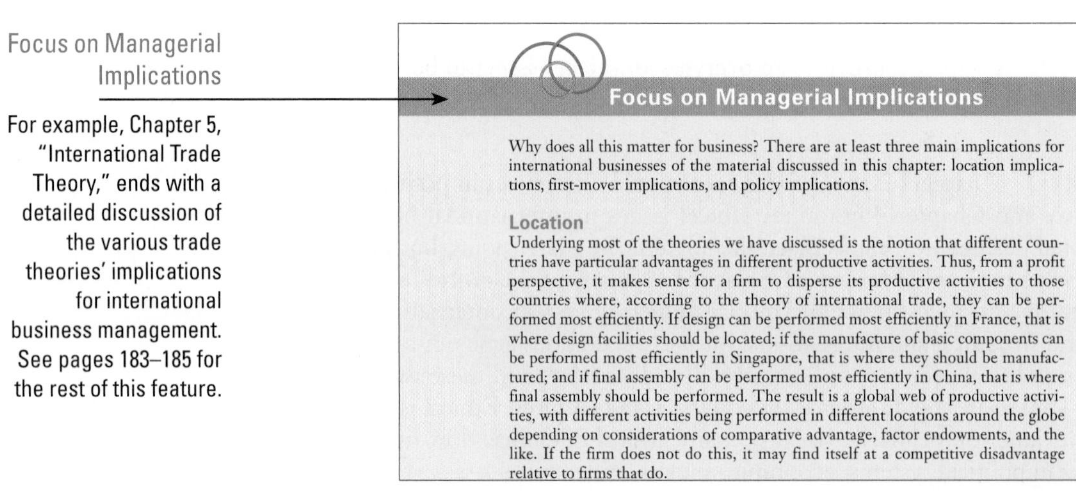

Focus on Managerial Implications

Why does all this matter for business? There are at least three main implications for international businesses of the material discussed in this chapter: location implications, first-mover implications, and policy implications.

Location

Underlying most of the theories we have discussed is the notion that different countries have particular advantages in different productive activities. Thus, from a profit perspective, it makes sense for a firm to disperse its productive activities to those countries where, according to the theory of international trade, they can be performed most efficiently. If design can be performed most efficiently in France, that is where design facilities should be located; if the manufacture of basic components can be performed most efficiently in Singapore, that is where they should be manufactured; and if final assembly can be performed most efficiently in China, that is where final assembly should be performed. The result is a global web of productive activities, with different activities being performed in different locations around the globe depending on considerations of comparative advantage, factor endowments, and the like. If the firm does not do this, it may find itself at a competitive disadvantage relative to firms that do.

In addition, each chapter begins with an **opening case** that sets the stage for the chapter content and familiarizes students with how real international companies conduct business.

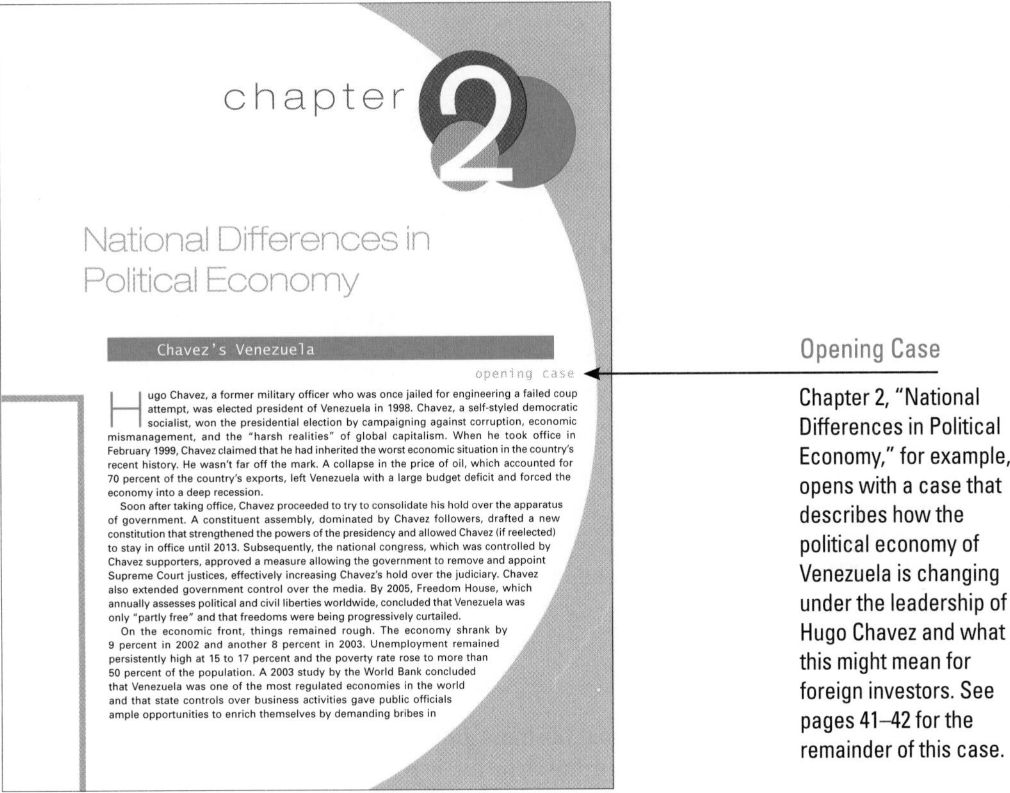

chapter 2

National Differences in Political Economy

Chavez's Venezuela

opening case

Hugo Chavez, a former military officer who was once jailed for engineering a failed coup attempt, was elected president of Venezuela in 1998. Chavez, a self-styled democratic socialist, won the presidential election by campaigning against corruption, economic mismanagement, and the "harsh realities" of global capitalism. When he took office in February 1999, Chavez claimed that he had inherited the worst economic situation in the country's recent history. He wasn't far off the mark. A collapse in the price of oil, which accounted for 70 percent of the country's exports, left Venezuela with a large budget deficit and forced the economy into a deep recession.

Soon after taking office, Chavez proceeded to try to consolidate his hold over the apparatus of government. A constituent assembly, dominated by Chavez followers, drafted a new constitution that strengthened the powers of the presidency and allowed Chavez (if reelected) to stay in office until 2013. Subsequently, the national congress, which was controlled by Chavez supporters, approved a measure allowing the government to remove and appoint Supreme Court justices, effectively increasing Chavez's hold over the judiciary. Chavez also extended government control over the media. By 2005, Freedom House, which annually assesses political and civil liberties worldwide, concluded that Venezuela was only "partly free" and that freedoms were being progressively curtailed.

On the economic front, things remained rough. The economy shrank by 9 percent in 2002 and another 8 percent in 2003. Unemployment remained persistently high at 15 to 17 percent and the poverty rate rose to more than 50 percent of the population. A 2003 study by the World Bank concluded that Venezuela was one of the most regulated economies in the world and that state controls over business activities gave public officials ample opportunities to enrich themselves by demanding bribes in

Opening Case

Chapter 2, "National Differences in Political Economy," for example, opens with a case that describes how the political economy of Venezuela is changing under the leadership of Hugo Chavez and what this might mean for foreign investors. See pages 41–42 for the remainder of this case.

I have also added a **closing case** to each chapter. These cases are also designed to illustrate the relevance of chapter material for the practice of international business as well as to provide continued insight into how real companies handle those issues.

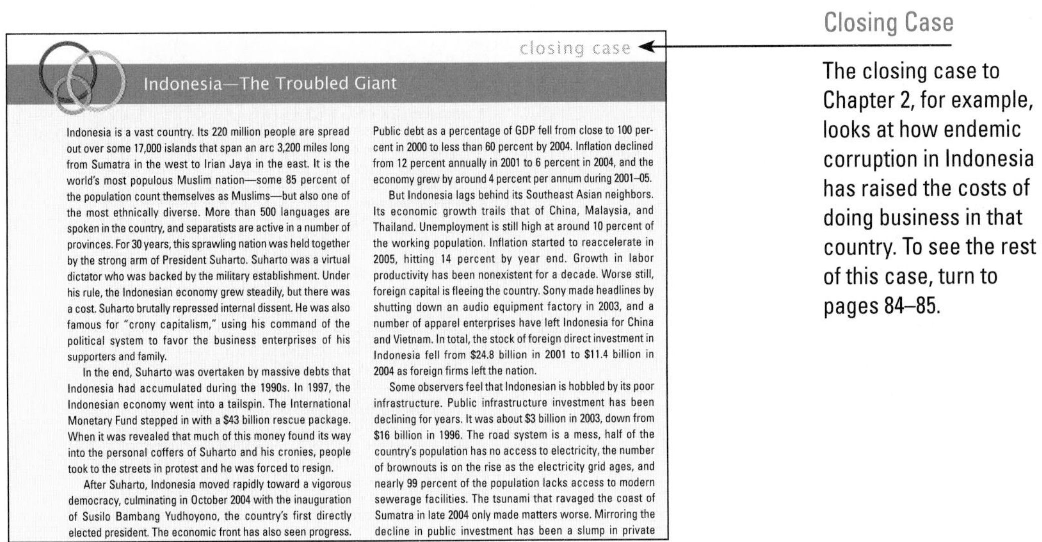

closing case

Indonesia—The Troubled Giant

Indonesia is a vast country. Its 220 million people are spread out over some 17,000 islands that span an arc 3,200 miles long from Sumatra in the west to Irian Jaya in the east. It is the world's most populous Muslim nation—some 85 percent of the population count themselves as Muslims—but also one of the most ethnically diverse. More than 500 languages are spoken in the country, and separatists are active in a number of provinces. For 30 years, this sprawling nation was held together by the strong arm of President Suharto. Suharto was a virtual dictator who was backed by the military establishment. Under his rule, the Indonesian economy grew steadily, but there was a cost. Suharto brutally repressed internal dissent. He was also famous for "crony capitalism," using his command of the political system to favor the business enterprises of his supporters and family.

In the end, Suharto was overtaken by massive debts that Indonesia had accumulated during the 1990s. In 1997, the Indonesian economy went into a tailspin. The International Monetary Fund stepped in with a $43 billion rescue package. When it was revealed that much of this money found its way into the personal coffers of Suharto and his cronies, people took to the streets in protest and he was forced to resign.

After Suharto, Indonesia moved rapidly toward a vigorous democracy, culminating in October 2004 with the inauguration of Susilo Bambang Yudhoyono, the country's first directly elected president. The economic front has also seen progress. Public debt as a percentage of GDP fell from close to 100 percent in 2000 to less than 60 percent by 2004. Inflation declined from 12 percent annually in 2001 to 6 percent in 2004, and the economy grew by around 4 percent per annum during 2001–05.

But Indonesia lags behind its Southeast Asian neighbors. Its economic growth trails that of China, Malaysia, and Thailand. Unemployment is still high at around 10 percent of the working population. Inflation started to reaccelerate in 2005, hitting 14 percent by year end. Growth in labor productivity has been nonexistent for a decade. Worse still, foreign capital is fleeing the country. Sony made headlines by shutting down an audio equipment factory in 2003, and a number of apparel enterprises have left Indonesia for China and Vietnam. In total, the stock of foreign direct investment in Indonesia fell from $24.8 billion in 2001 to $11.4 billion in 2004 as foreign firms left the nation.

Some observers feel that Indonesian is hobbled by its poor infrastructure. Public infrastructure investment has been declining for years. It was about $3 billion in 2003, down from $16 billion in 1996. The road system is a mess, half of the country's population has no access to electricity, the number of brownouts is on the rise as the electricity grid ages, and nearly 99 percent of the population lacks access to modern sewerage facilities. The tsunami that ravaged the coast of Sumatra in late 2004 only made matters worse. Mirroring the decline in public investment has been a slump in private

Closing Case

The closing case to Chapter 2, for example, looks at how endemic corruption in Indonesia has raised the costs of doing business in that country. To see the rest of this case, turn to pages 84–85.

Another tool that I have used to focus on managerial implications are **Management Focus** boxes. There is at least one Management Focus in most chapters. Like the opening cases, the purpose of these boxes is to illustrate the relevance of chapter material for the practice of international business.

Management Focus

The Management Focus in Chapter 2, for example, looks at how Starbucks won an important battle its intellectual property in China. This box illustrates the important role that national differences in the protection of intellectual property rights can play in international business. See page 57 for the rest of this Focus.

Management FOCUS

Starbucks Wins Key Trademark Case in China

Starbucks has big plans for China. It believes the fast-growing nation will become the company's second-largest market after the United States. Starbucks entered the country in 1999, and by the end of 2005 it had 209 stores open. But in China, copycats of well-established Western brands are commonplace. Starbucks too faced competition from a look alike, Shanghai Xing Ba Ke Coffee Shop, whose stores closely matched the Starbucks format, right down to a green and white Xing Ba Ke circular logo that mimics Starbuck's ubiquitous logo. Moreover, the name mimics the standard Chinese translation for Starbucks. *Xing* means "star" and *Ba Ke* sounds like "bucks."

In 2003, Starbuck decided to sue Xing Ba Ke in Chinese court for trademark violations. Xing Ba Ke's general manager responded by claiming that it was just an accident that the logo and name were so similar to that of Starbucks. Moreover, he claimed the right to use the logo and name because Xing Ba Ke had registered as a company in Shanghai in 1999, before Starbucks entered the city. "I hadn't heard of Starbucks at the time," claimed the manager, "so how could I imitate its brand and logo?"

However, in January 2006 a Shanghai court ruled that Starbucks had precedence, in part because it had registered its Chinese name in 1998. The Court stated that Xing Ba Ke's use of the name and similar logo was "clearly malicious" and constituted improper competition. The court ordered Xing Ba Ke to stop using the name and to pay Starbucks $62,000 in compensation. While the money involved here may be small, the precedent is not. In a country where violation of trademarks has been commonplace, the courts seem to be signaling that a shift toward greater protection of intellectual property rights may be in progress. This is perhaps not surprising, since foreign governments and the World Trade Organization have been pushing China hard recently to start respecting intellectual property rights.

Sources: M. Dickie, "Starbucks Wins Case against Chinese Copycat," *Financial Times*, January 3, 2006, p. 1; "Starbucks: Chinese Court Backs Company over Trademark Infringement," *The Wall Street Journal*, January 2, 2006, p. A11; and "Starbucks Calls China Its Top Growth Focus," *The Wall Street Journal*, February 14, 2006, p.1.

Accessible and Interesting

The international business arena is fascinating and exciting, and I have tried to communicate my enthusiasm for it to the student. Learning is easier and better if the subject matter is communicated in an interesting, informative, and accessible manner. One technique I have used to achieve this is weaving interesting anecdotes into the narrative of the text, that is, stories that illustrate theory. The use of **Another Perspective** boxes also serves to provide additional context for the chapter topics.

Another Perspective

For example, this Another Perspective box in Chapter 12 illustrates further how mode of entry and freedom of information caused conflict for Microsoft in China. See page 399 for the rest of the picture.

Another Perspective

Microsoft in China: Where Does Freedom of Information Fit into Modes of Entry?

The almost meteoric rise of information on the Internet presents decisions and challenges that extend to human rights issues.

Microsoft says it was simply ifacing realityî when it agreed to shut down the MSN Spaces Web site, a demand made by the Chinese government, in order to gain access to the 103 million Chinese Internet usersóand that figure is growing wildly. China added almost 10 million new Internet users in the first six months of 2005. Microsoftís official statement about the site shutdown in China was:

> Microsoft does business in many countries around the world. While different countries have different standards, Microsoft and other multinational companies have to ensure that our products and services comply with local laws, norms and industry standards.

Reporters Without Borders, a group in Paris that tracks censorship around the world, vehemently protested Microsoftís actions. They call on all corporations to uphold the free flow of information and even recommend that Western governments take action against corporations that restrict the flow of information. They see it as a loss of freedom for Chinese Web users and a fundamental human rights issue.

In addition to the Management Focus feature, most chapters also have a **Country Focus** box that provides background on the political, economic, social, or cultural aspects of countries grappling with an international business issue.

Country FOCUS

Corruption in Nigeria

When Nigeria gained independence from Great Britain in 1960, there were hopes that the country might emerge as an economic heavyweight in Africa. Not only was Nigeria Africa's most populous country, but it also was blessed with abundant natural resources, particularly oil, from which the country earned over $400 billion between 1970 and 2005. Despite this, Nigeria remains one of the poorest countries in the world. According to the 2005 Human Development Index compiled by the United Nations, Nigeria ranked 158 out of 177 countries covered. Gross national income per capita was just $430, 32 percent of the adult population was illiterate, and life expectancy at birth was only 43 years.

What went wrong? Although there is no simple answer, a number of factors seem to have conspired to damage economic activity in Nigeria. The country is composed of several competing ethnic, tribal, and religious groups, and the conflict among them has limited political stability and led to political strife, including a brutal civil war in the 1970s. With the legitimacy of the government always in question, political leaders often purchased support by legitimizing bribes and by raiding the national treasury to reward allies. Civilian rule after independence was followed by a series of military dictatorships, each of which seemed more corrupt and inept than the last (the country returned to civilian rule in 1999).

During the 1990s, the military dictator, Sani Abacha, openly and systematically plundered the state treasury for his own personal gain. His most blatant scam was the Petroleum Trust Fund, which he set up in the mid-1990s ostensibly to channel extra revenue from an increase in fuel prices into much-needed infrastructure projects and other investments. The fund was not independently audited, and almost none of the money that passed through it was properly accounted for. It was, in fact, a vehicle for Abacha and his supporters to spend at will a sum that in 1996 was equivalent to some 25 percent of the total federal budget. Abacha, aware of his position as an unpopular and unelected leader, lavished money on personal security and handed out bribes to those whose support he coveted. With examples like this at the very top of the government, it is not surprising that corruption could be found throughout the political and bureaucratic apparatus.

Some of the excesses were simply astounding. In the 1980s an aluminum smelter was built on the orders of the government, which wanted to industrialize Nigeria. The cost of the smelter was $2.4 billion, some 60 to 100 percent higher than the cost of comparable plants elsewhere in the developed world. This high cost was widely interpreted to reflect the bribes that had to be paid to local politicians by the international contractors that built the plant. The smelter has never operated at more than a fraction of its intended capacity.

Has the situation in Nigeria improved since the country returned to civilian rule in 1999? In 2003, Olusegun Obasanjo was elected president on a platform that included a promise to fight corruption. By some accounts, progress has been seen. His anticorruption chief, Nuhu Ribadu, has claimed that whereas 70 percent of the country's oil revenues were being stolen or wasted in 2002, by 2004 the figure was "only" 40 percent. But in its most recent survey, Transparency International still ranked Nigeria among the most corrupt countries in the world in 2005 (see Figure 2.1), suggesting that the country still has long way to go. Mr. Ribadu has suggested that the problem lies with state governments, who are still riddled with corruption.

Sources: "A Tale of Two Giants," *The Economist*, January 15, 2000, p. 5; J. Coolidge and S. Rose Ackerman, "High Level Rent Seeking and Corruption in African Regimes," World Bank policy research working paper no. 1780, June 1997; D. L. Bevan, P. Collier, and J. W. Gunning, *Nigeria and Indonesia: The Political Economy of Poverty, Equity and Growth* (Oxford: Oxford University Press, 1999); "Democracy and Its Discontents," *The Economist*, January 29, 2005, p. 55; and A. Field. "Can Reform Save Nigeria?" *Journal of Commerce*, November 21, 2005, p. 1.

Country Focus

In Chapter 2, for example, one Country Focus box discusses the steps that India has taken over the last decade to build a dynamic, market-based economic system. See page 55 for more on India's transformation.

Ancillary Resources That Enliven the Text and Make It Easier to Teach

For instructors, this text offers a number of materials to help them keep their students active and engaged in the learning process. In addition to the course cartridge and International Business DVD, the **Instructor's Resource CD-ROM** is a one-stop place for several key instructor aids, including the following:

- **Instructor's Manual.** The Instructor's Manual, prepared by Veronica Horton, contains course outlines; chapter teaching resources, including chapter overviews and outlines, teaching suggestions, chapter objectives, teaching suggestions for opening cases, lecture outlines, answers to critical discussion questions, teaching suggestions for the closing case, and two student activities (some with Internet components); and expanded Video Notes with discussion questions for each video. The answers to globalEDGE research tasks will also be included here.
- **Test Bank.** The test bank was prepared by Amit Shah of Frostburg State University and contains approximately 100 true-false, multiple-choice, and essay questions per chapter. New to this edition, the test bank questions are also categorized by Bloom's taxonomy levels of learning and how they meet various AACSB objectives.
- **EZ Test.** A computerized version of the test bank is available, allowing the instructor to generate random tests and to add his or her own questions.

- **PowerPoint®.** Recreated for this edition by Veronica Horton, the PowerPoint program consists of approximately 500 slides featuring original materials not found in the text in addition to reproductions and illuminations of key text figures, tables, and maps. Quiz questions to keep students on their toes during classroom presentations are also included, along with instructor notes.

Finally, the book's **Online Learning Center (www.mhhe.com/hillgbt5e)** is available for all adopters of *Global Business Today*. The password-protected instructor version grants access to the Instructor's Manual, PowerPoints, Video Cases, and globalEDGE answers. Instructors can also view student resources to make more effective supplementary assignments.

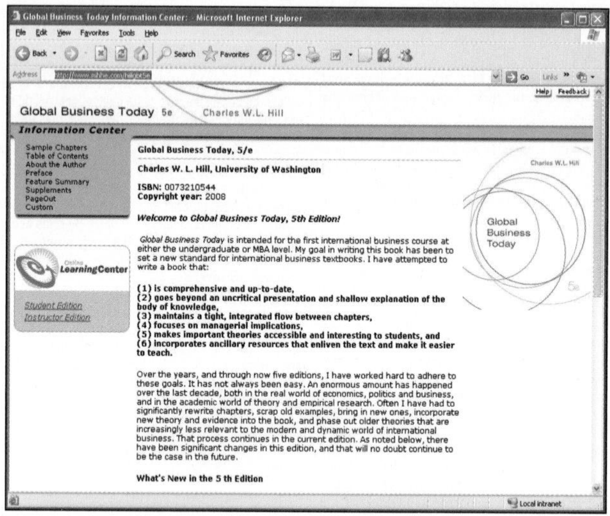

For students, this book also provides rich interactive resources to help them learn how to practice international business.

The Online Learning Center (www.mhhe.com/hillgbt5e) for students includes chapter quizzes, student PowerPoints, and chapter overviews. Students can also access the text glossary as well as all *Global Business Today* interactive modules, including the following:

Concept Exercises

Concept Exercises help students learn how to solve realistic problems by exploring Flash modules, linked to the appropriate chapter, of the Hofstede study, absolute and comparative advantage, foreign direct investment, balance of payments, purchasing power parity and inflation, historical exchange rates, and export and import financing.

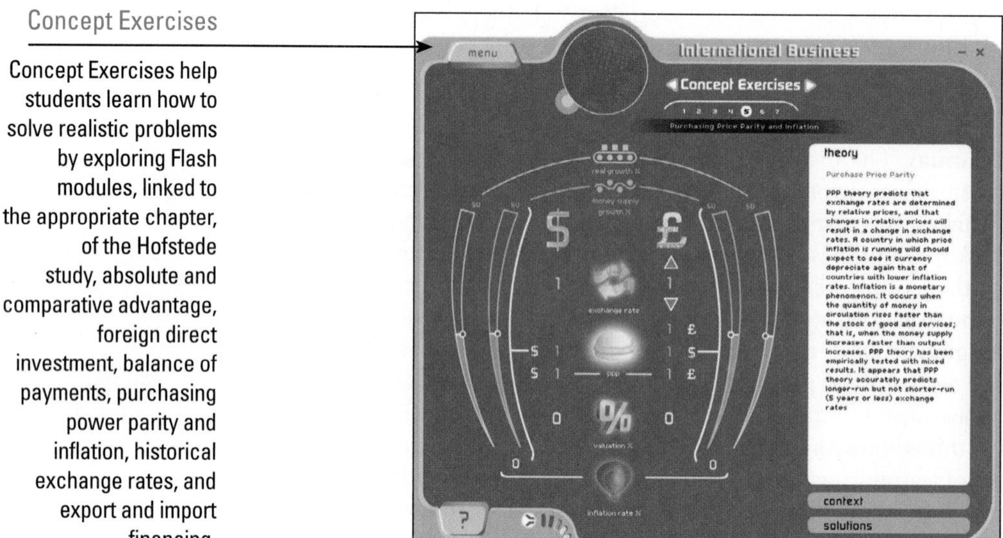

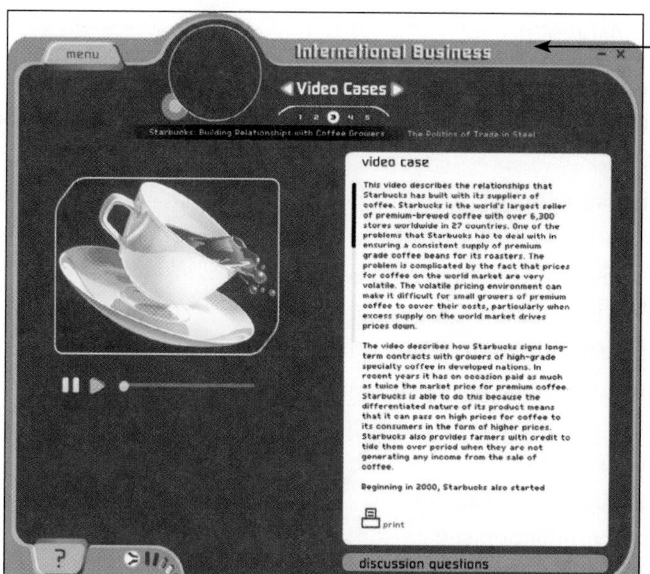

Concept Videos

The eight Concept Videos, complemented by cases and discussion questions written by Charles Hill, are also exclusive to these online activities. Students can watch and learn more when they access this activity for the appropriate chapter.

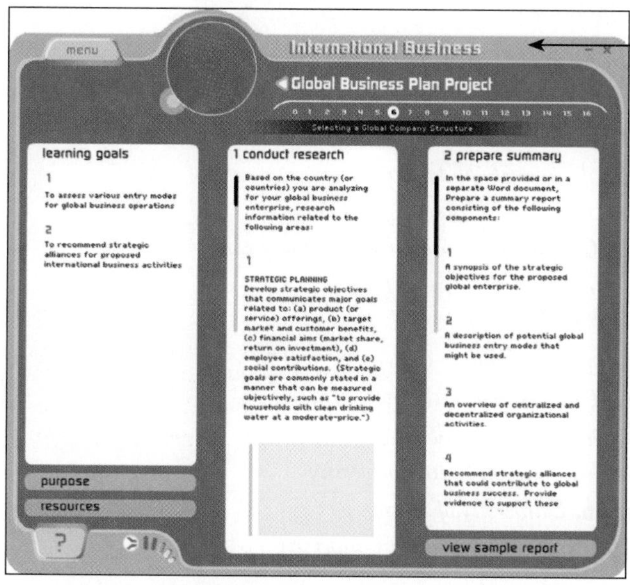

Global Business Plan

The Global Business Plan helps students take it one step further into applications, allowing them to build their own business plan one section at a time to prepare for entering a foreign market.

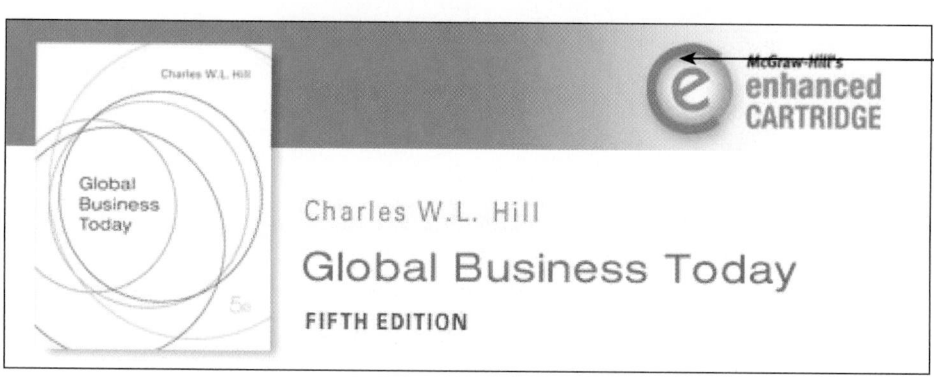

Enhanced Cartridge

The enhanced cartridge, already mentioned above, allows students access to additional remedial activities that capture grades for instructors and promotes greater accountability for student engagement with the course.

Acknowledgments

Numerous people deserve to be thanked for their assistance in preparing this book. First, I want to thank all the people at McGraw-Hill/Irwin who have worked with me on this project:

John E. Biernat, editorial director
Ryan Blankenship, senior sponsoring editor
Kirsten L. Guidero, developmental editor
Meg Beamer, marketing manager
Damian Moshak and Lynn Bluhm, media producers
Susan Lombardi, media project manager
Laura Griffin and Jim Labeots, project managers
Kami Carter, senior designer
Mary Kazak, freelance designer
Carol Bielski, production supervisor
Kathy Shive, photo research coordinator

Second, my thanks go to the reviewers, who provided good feedback that helped shape this edition of the book:

R. Apana, *University of Cincinnati*
David Bruce, *Georgia State University*
Bruce Keillor, *University of Akron*
Anthony Koh, *University of Toledo*
Joseph Leonard, *Miami University of Ohio*
Mingfang Li, *California State University Northridge*
Hoon Park, *University of Central Florida*
Janis Petronis, *Tarleton University*
Lee Pickler, *Baldwin-Wallace College*
Gary Shantz, *University of LaVerne*
Charlie Shi, *Diablo Valley College*
Len Trevino, *Washington State University*
Tim Wilkinson, *University of Akron*
Andrzej Wlodarczyk, *Lindenwood University*

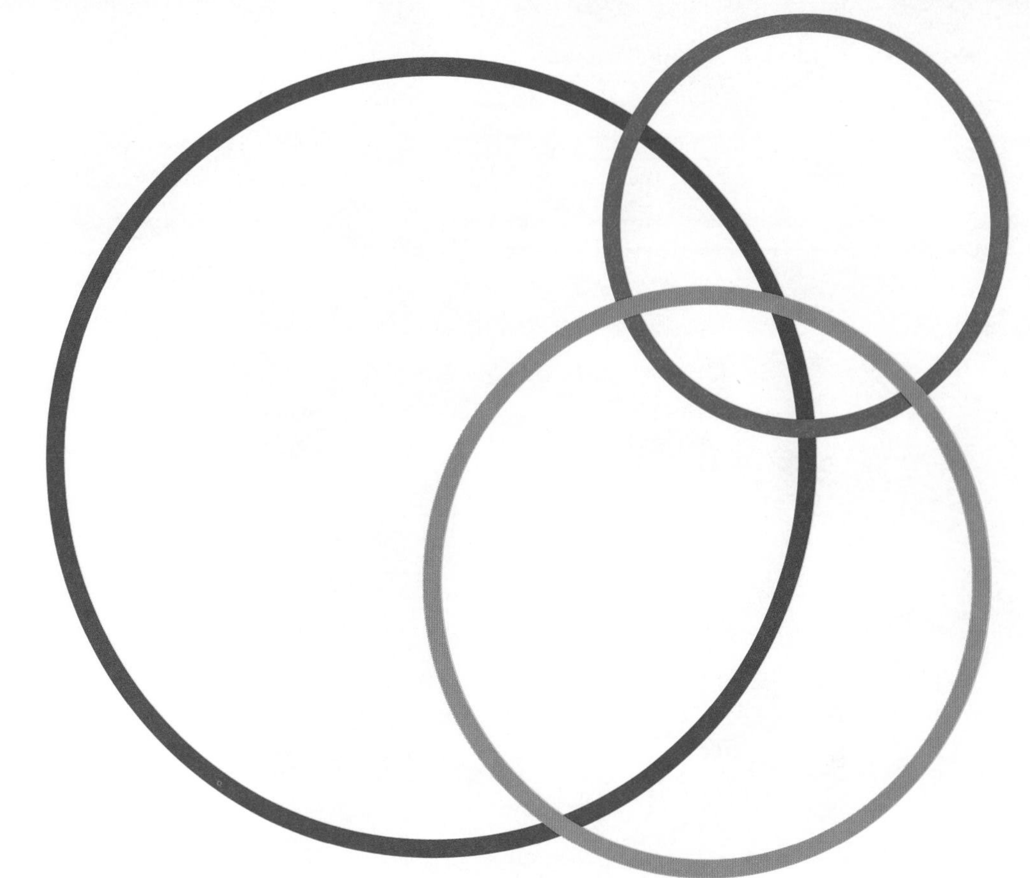

Global Business Today

part 1 Introduction and Overview

LEARNING OBJECTIVES

1. Understand what is meant by the term *globalization.*
2. Be familiar with the main drivers of globalization.
3. Appreciate the changing nature of the global economy.
4. Understand the main arguments in the debate over the impact of globalization.
5. Appreciate how the process of globalization is creating opportunities and challenges for business managers.

chapter 1

Globalization

IKEA–The Global Retailer

opening case

IKEA may be the world's most successful global retailer. Established by Ingvar Kamprad in Sweden in 1943 when he was just 17 years old, the home-furnishing superstore has grown into a global cult brand with 230 stores in 33 countries that host 410 million shoppers a year and generated sales of €14.8 billion ($17.7 billion) in 2005. Kamprad himself, who still owns the private company, is rumored to be the world's richest man.

IKEA's target market is the global middle class who are looking for low-priced but attractively designed furniture and household items. The company applies the same basic formula worldwide: Open large warehouse stores festooned in the blue and yellow colors of the Swedish flag that offer 8,000 to 10,000 items, from kitchen cabinets to candlesticks. Use wacky promotions to drive traffic into the stores. Configure the interior of the stores so that customers have to pass through each department to get to the checkout. Add restaurants and child care facilities so that shoppers stay as long as possible. Price the items as low as possible. Make sure that product design reflects the simple, clean Swedish lines that have become IKEA's trademark. And then watch the results–customers who enter the store planning to buy a $40 coffee table and end up spending $500 on everything from storage units to kitchenware.

IKEA aims to reduce the price of its offerings by 2 to 3 percent per year, which requires relentless attention to cost cutting. With a network of 1,300 suppliers in 53 countries, IKEA devotes considerable attention to finding the right manufacturer for each item. Consider the company's best-selling Klippan love seat. Designed in 1980, the Klippan, with its clean lines, bright colors, simple legs, and compact size, has sold some 1.5 million units since its introduction. IKEA originally manufactured the product in Sweden but soon transferred production to lower-cost suppliers in Poland. As demand for the Klippan grew, IKEA then decided that it made more sense to work with suppliers in each of the company's big markets to avoid the costs associated with shipping the product all over the world. Today there are five suppliers of the frames in Europe, plus three in the United States and two in China. To reduce the cost of the cotton slipcovers, IKEA has concentrated production in four core suppliers in China and Europe. The resulting efficiencies from these global sourcing decisions enabled IKEA to reduce the price of the Klippan by some 40 percent between 1999 and 2005.

Despite its standard formula, to achieve global success IKEA had to adapt its offerings to the tastes and preferences of consumers in different nations. IKEA first discovered this in the early 1990s when it entered the United States. The company soon found that its European-style offerings didn't always resonate with American consumers. Beds were measured in centimeters, not the king, queen, and twin sizes with which Americans are familiar. Sofas weren't big enough, wardrobe drawers were not deep enough, glasses were too small, curtains too short, and kitchens didn't fit U.S. size appliances. Since then, IKEA has redesigned its U.S. offerings to appeal to American consumers, which has resulted in stronger sales. The same process is now unfolding in China, where the company plans to establish 10 stores by 2010. The store layout in China reflects the layout of many Chinese apartments, and since many Chinese apartments have balconies, IKEA's Chinese stores include a balcony section. IKEA also has had to adapt its locations in China, where car ownership is still not widespread. In the West, IKEA stores are generally located in suburban areas and have lots of parking space. In China, stores are located near public transportation, and IKEA offers delivery services so that Chinese customers can get their purchases home.

Sources: K. Capell, A. Sains, C. Lindblad, and A.T. Palmer, "IKEA," *BusinessWeek,* November 14, 2005, pp. 96–101; K. Capell et al., "What a Sweetheart of a Love Seat," *BusinessWeek,* November 14, 2005, p. 101; P.M. Miller, "IKEA with Chinese Characteristics," *Chinese Business Review,* July–August 2004, pp. 36–69; and C. Daniels, "Create IKEA, Make Billions, Take Bus," *Fortune,* May 3, 2004, p. 44.

Introduction

A fundamental shift is occurring in the world economy. We are moving away from a world in which national economies were relatively self-contained entities, isolated from each other by barriers to cross-border trade and investment; by distance, time zones, and language; and by national differences in government regulation, culture, and business systems. And we are moving toward a world in which barriers to cross-border trade and investment are declining; perceived distance is shrinking due to advances in transportation and telecommunications technology; material culture is starting to look similar the world over; and national economies are merging into an interdependent, integrated global economic system. The process by which this is occurring is commonly referred to as *globalization.*

In this interdependent global economy, an American might drive to work in a car designed in Germany that was assembled in Mexico by DaimlerChrysler from components made in the United States and Japan that were fabricated from Korean steel and Malaysian rubber. She may have filled the car with gasoline at a BP service station owned by a British multinational company. The gasoline could have been made from oil pumped out of a well off the coast of Africa by a French oil company that transported it to the United States in a ship owned by a Greek shipping line. While driving to work, the American might talk to her stockbroker on a Nokia cell phone that was designed in Finland and assembled in Texas using chip sets produced in Taiwan that were designed by Indian engineers working for Texas Instruments. She could tell the stockbroker to purchase shares in Deutsche Telekom, a German telecommunications firm that was transformed from a former state-owned monopoly into a global company by an energetic Israeli CEO. She may turn on the car radio, which was made in Malaysia by a Japanese firm, to hear a popular hip-hop song composed by a Swede and sung by a group of Danes in English who signed a record contract with a French music company to promote their record in America. The driver might pull into a drive-through coffee shop run by a Korean immigrant and order a "single, tall, nonfat latte" and chocolate-covered biscotti. The coffee beans came from Brazil and the chocolate from Peru, while the biscotti was made locally using an old Italian recipe. After the song ends, a news announcer might inform the American listener that antiglobalization protests at a meeting of the World Economic Forum in Davos, Switzerland, have turned violent. One protester has been killed. The announcer then turns to the next item, a story about how fear of interest rate hikes in the United States has sent Japan's Nikkei stock market index down sharply.

This is the world in which we live. It is a world where the volume of goods, services, and investment crossing national borders has expanded faster than world output consistently for more than half a century. It is a world where more than $1.2 billion in foreign exchange transactions are made every day, where $10.41 trillion of goods and $2.41 trillion of services were sold across national borders in 2005.[1] It is a world in which international institutions such as the World Trade Organization and gatherings of leaders from the world's most powerful economies have called for even lower barriers to cross-border trade and investment. It is a world where the symbols of material and popular culture are increasingly global: from Coca-Cola and Starbucks to Sony PlayStations, Nokia cell phones, MTV shows, Disney films, and IKEA stores. It is a world in which products are made from inputs that come from all over the world. It is a world in which an economic crisis in Asia can cause a recession in the United States, and the threat of higher interest rates in the United States really did help drive Japan's Nikkei index down in the spring of 2006. It is also a world in which vigorous and vocal groups protest against globalization, which they blame for a list of ills, from unemployment in developed nations to environmental degradation and the Americanization of popular culture. And yes, these protests have on occasion turned violent.

For businesses, this process has produced many opportunities. Firms can expand their revenues by selling around the world and reduce their costs by producing in nations where key inputs, including labor, are cheap. As we saw in the opening case, this is exactly what the Swedish retailer, IKEA, has done. IKEA generates only 8 percent of its revenues from its home country, Sweden, and now has stores in 32 other nations. The company uses the same basic retailing formula worldwide to sell its merchandise—big stores offering a wide selection of well-designed products sold at a low price.

Another Perspective

The United States in Perspective

The United States has the highest level of output in the world, with the GDP valued at more than $12.5 trillion in 2005. The U.S. GDP per capita is $42,129. With around 4.6 percent of the world's population, the United States produces about 20.4 percent of the global GDP. (*The Economist,* May 1, 2006; Factsheet, CIA Factbook)

Making profits at a low price point requires IKEA to source merchandise from low-cost locations around the globe.

The expansion of enterprises like IKEA has been facilitated by favorable political and economic trends. Since the collapse of communism at the end of the 1980s, the pendulum of public policy in nation after nation has swung toward the free market end of the economic spectrum. Regulatory and administrative barriers to doing business in foreign nations have come down, while those nations have often transformed their economies, privatizing state-owned enterprises, deregulating markets, increasing competition, and welcoming investment by foreign businesses. This has allowed businesses both large and small, from both advanced nations and developing nations, to expand internationally. Thus, IKEA now has six stores in Russia, four in China, and seven in Poland, all countries that were off limits to Western enterprises for much of the second half of the twentieth century.

At the same time, globalization has created new threats for businesses accustomed to dominating their domestic markets. Foreign companies have entered many formerly protected industries in developing nations, increasing competition and driving down prices. For three decades, U.S. automobile companies have been battling foreign enterprises, as Japanese, European, and now Korean companies have taken business from them. General Motors has seen its market share decline from more than 50 percent to about 28 percent, while Japan's Toyota has passed Chrysler, now DaimlerChrysler, to become the second-largest automobile company in America behind GM and ahead of Ford.

As globalization unfolds, it is transforming industries and creating anxiety among those who believed their jobs were protected from foreign competition. Historically, while many workers in manufacturing industries worried about the impact foreign competition might have on their jobs, workers in service industries felt more secure. Now this too is changing. Advances in technology, lower transportation costs, and the rise of skilled workers in developing countries imply that many services no longer need to be performed where they are delivered. The outsourcing trend is even hitting health services. An MRI scan, transmitted over the Internet, might now be interpreted by a radiologist living in Bangalore. Similar trends can be seen in many other service industries. Accounting work is being outsourced from America to India. In 2005, some 400,000 individual tax returns were compiled in India. Indian accountants, trained in U.S. tax rules, perform work for U.S. accounting firms.[2] They access individual tax returns stored on computers in the United States, perform routine calculations, and save their work so that it can be inspected by a U.S. accountant, who then bills clients. As the best-selling author Thomas Friedman has recently argued, the world is becoming flat.[3] People living in developed nations no longer have the playing field tilted in their favor. Increasingly, enterprising individuals based in India, China, or Brazil have the same opportunities to better themselves as those living in Western Europe, the United States, or Canada.

In this book we will take a close look at the issues introduced here, and at many more besides. We will explore how changes in regulations governing international trade and investment, when coupled with changes in political systems and technology, have dramatically altered the competitive playing field confronting many businesses. We will discuss the resulting opportunities and threats and review the different strategies that managers can pursue to exploit the opportunities and counter the threats. We will consider whether globalization benefits or harms national economies. We will look at what economic theory has to say about the outsourcing of manufacturing and service jobs to places such as India and China, and at the benefits and costs of outsourcing, not just to business firms and their employees, but also to entire economies. First, though, we need to get a better overview of the nature and process of globalization, and that is the function of the current chapter.

What Is Globalization?

As used in this book, **globalization** refers to the shift toward a more integrated and interdependent world economy. Globalization has several facets, including the globalization of markets and the globalization of production.

LEARNING OBJECTIVE 1
Understand what is meant by the term *globalization*.

THE GLOBALIZATION OF MARKETS The **globalization of markets** refers to the merging of historically distinct and separate national markets into one huge global marketplace. Falling barriers to cross-border trade have made it easier to sell internationally. It has been argued for some time that the tastes and preferences of consumers in different nations are beginning to converge on some global norm, thereby helping to create a global market.[4] Consumer products such as Citigroup credit cards, Coca-Cola soft drinks, Sony PlayStation video games, McDonald's hamburgers, Starbucks coffee, and IKEA furniture are frequently held up as prototypical examples of this trend. Firms such as those just cited are more than just benefactors of this trend; they are also facilitators of it. By offering the same basic product worldwide, they help to create a global market.

Globalization
The shift toward a more integrated and interdependent world economy.

Globalization of Markets
The merging of historically distinct and separate national markets into one huge global marketplace.

A company does not have to be the size of these multinational giants to facilitate, and benefit from, the globalization of markets. In the United States, for example, nearly 90 percent of firms that export are small businesses employing less than 100 people, and their share of total U.S. exports has grown steadily over the last decade to now exceed 20 percent.[5] Firms with less than 500 employees accounted for 97 percent of all U.S. exporters and almost 30 percent of all exports by value.[6] Typical of these is Hytech, a New York–based manufacturer of solar panels that generates 40 percent of its $3 million in annual sales from exports to five countries, or B&S Aircraft Alloys, another New York company whose exports account for 40 percent of its $8 million annual revenues.[7] The situation is similar in several other nations. In Germany, for example, which is the world's largest exporter, a staggering 98 percent of small and mid-sized companies have exposure to international markets, either via exports or international production.[8]

Despite the global prevalence of Citigroup credit cards, McDonald's hamburgers, Starbucks coffee, and IKEA stores, it is important not to push too far the view that national markets are giving way to the global market. As we shall see in later chapters, significant differences still exist among national markets along many relevant dimensions, including consumer tastes and preferences, distribution channels, culturally embedded value systems, business systems, and legal regulations. These differences frequently require companies to customize marketing strategies, product features, and operating practices to best match conditions in a particular country. In the opening case, for example, we saw how IKEA has had to alter its merchandise and location strategy to take national differences into account. Similarly, automobile companies will promote different car models in different nations, depending on a range of factors such as local fuel costs, income levels, traffic congestion, and cultural values.

The most global markets currently are not markets for consumer products—where national differences in tastes and preferences are still often important enough to act as a brake on globalization—but markets for industrial goods and materials that serve a universal need the world over. These include the markets for commodities such as aluminum, oil, and wheat; for industrial products such as microprocessors, DRAMs (computer memory chips), and commercial jet aircraft; for computer software; and for financial assets from U.S. Treasury bills to eurobonds and futures on the Nikkei index or the Mexican peso.

In many global markets, the same firms frequently confront each other as competitors in nation after nation. Coca-Cola's rivalry with PepsiCo is a global one, as are the rivalries between Ford and Toyota, Boeing and Airbus, Caterpillar and Komatsu in earthmoving equipment, and Sony, Nintendo, and Microsoft in video games. If a firm moves into a nation not currently served by its rivals, many of those rivals are sure to follow to prevent their competitor from gaining an advantage.[9] As firms follow each other around the world, they bring with them many of the assets that served them well in other national markets—including their products, operating strategies, marketing strategies, and brand names—creating some homogeneity across markets. Thus, greater uniformity replaces diversity. In an increasing number of industries, it is no longer meaningful to talk about "the German market," "the American market," "the Brazilian market," or "the Japanese market"; for many firms there is only the global market.

Globalization of Production
Sourcing goods and services from locations around the globe to take advantage of national differences in the cost and quality of various factors of production.

Factors of Production
Components of production such as labor, energy, land, and capital.

THE GLOBALIZATION OF PRODUCTION The **globalization of production** refers to the sourcing of goods and services from locations around the globe to take advantage of national differences in the cost and quality of **factors of production** (such as labor, energy, land, and capital). By doing this, companies hope to lower their overall cost structure or improve the quality or functionality of their product offering, thereby allowing them to compete more effectively. Consider the Boeing's 777, a commercial jet airliner. Eight Japanese suppliers make parts for the fuselage, doors, and wings; a supplier in Singapore makes the doors for the nose landing gear; three suppliers in Italy manufacture wing flaps; and so on.[10] In total, some 30 percent of the 777, by value, is built by foreign companies. For its next jet airliner, the 787, Boeing is pushing this trend even further, with some 65 percent of the total value of the aircraft scheduled to be outsourced to foreign companies, 35 percent of which will go to three major Japanese companies.[11]

Part of Boeing's rationale for outsourcing so much production to foreign suppliers is that these suppliers are the best in the world at their particular activity. A global web of suppliers yields a better final product, which enhances the chances of Boeing winning a greater share of total orders for aircraft than its global rival Airbus Industrie. Boeing also outsources some production to foreign countries to increase the chance that it will win significant orders from airlines based in that country.

For another example of a global web of activities, consider the example of the Lenovo ThinkPad laptop computer.[12] Lenovo, a Chinese company, acquired IBM's personal computer operations in 2005. The ThinkPad is designed in the United States because Lenovo believes that the country is the best location in the world to do the basic design work. However, the case, keyboard, and hard drive are made in Thailand; the display screen and memory in South Korea; the built-in wireless card in Malaysia; and the microprocessor in the United States. In deciding on where to manufacture each component, Lenovo assessed both the production and transportation costs involved in each location. These components are then shipped to a plant in Mexico where the product is assembled before being shipped to the United States for final sale. Lenovo located the assembly of the ThinkPad in Mexico because of low labor costs in the country. The marketing and sales strategy for North America was developed in the United States, primarily because Lenovo believes that U.S. personnel possess better knowledge of the local marketplace than people based elsewhere (for more on Lenovo, see the Management Focus feature later in this chapter).

Early outsourcing efforts were primarily confined to manufacturing enterprises, such as those undertaken by Boeing and Lenovo; increasingly, however, companies are taking advantage of modern communications technology, particularly the Internet, to outsource service activities to low-cost producers in other nations. The Internet has allowed hospitals to outsource some radiology work to India, where images from MRI scans and the like are read at night while U.S. physicians sleep and the results are ready for them in the morning. Similarly, in December 2003, IBM announced it would move the work of some 4,300 software engineers from the United States to India and China (software production is counted as a service activity).[13] Many software companies now use Indian engineers to perform maintenance functions on software designed in the United States. The time difference allows Indian engineers to run debugging tests on software written in the United States when U.S. engineers sleep, transmitting the corrected code back to the United States over secure Internet connections so it is ready for U.S. engineers to work on the following day. Dispersing value-creation activities in this way can compress the time and lower the costs required to develop new software programs. Other companies, from computer makers to banks, are outsourcing customer service functions, such as customer call centers, to developing nations where labor is cheaper.

Robert Reich, who served as secretary of labor in the Clinton administration, has argued that as a consequence of the trend exemplified by companies such as Boeing and IBM, in many cases it is becoming irrelevant to talk about American products, Japanese products, German products, or Korean products. Increasingly, according to Reich, the outsourcing of productive activities to different suppliers results in the creation of products that are global in nature, that is, "global products."[14] But as with the globalization of markets, companies must be careful not to push the globalization of production too far. As we will see in later chapters, substantial impediments still make it difficult for firms to achieve the optimal dispersion of their productive activities to locations around the globe. These impediments include formal and informal barriers to trade between countries, barriers to foreign direct investment, transportation costs, and issues associated with economic and political risk. For example, government regulations ultimately limit the ability of hospitals to outsource the process of interpreting MRI scans to developing nations where radiologists are cheaper.

Nevertheless, the globalization of markets and production will continue. Modern firms are important actors in this trend, their very actions fostering increased globalization. These firms, however, are merely responding in an efficient manner to changing conditions in their operating environment—as well they should.

The Emergence of Global Institutions

As markets globalize and an increasing proportion of business activity transcends national borders, institutions are needed to help manage, regulate, and police the global marketplace, and to promote the establishment of multinational treaties to govern the global business system. Over the past half century, a number of important global institutions have been created to help perform these functions, including the **General Agreement on Tariffs and Trade (GATT)** and its successor, the World Trade Organization (WTO); the International Monetary Fund (IMF) and its sister institution, the World Bank; and the United Nations (UN). All these institutions were created by voluntary agreement between individual nation-states, and their functions are enshrined in international treaties.

General Agreement on Tariffs and Trade (GATT)
International treaty that committed signatories to lowering barriers to the free flow of goods across national borders; led to the WTO.

The **World Trade Organization** (like the GATT before it) is primarily responsible for policing the world trading system and making sure nation-states adhere to the rules laid down in trade treaties signed by WTO member states. As of 2006, 149 nations that collectively accounted for 97 percent of world trade were WTO members, thereby giving the organization enormous scope and influence. The WTO

World Trade Organization
The organization that succeeded the General Agreement on Tariffs and Trade and now acts to police the world trading system.

is also responsible for facilitating the establishment of additional multinational agreements between WTO member states. Over its entire history, and that of the GATT before it, the WTO has promoted the lowering of barriers to cross-border trade and investment. In doing so, the WTO has been the instrument of its member states, which have sought to create a more open global business system unencumbered by barriers to trade and investment between countries. Without an institution such as the WTO, the globalization of markets and production is unlikely to have proceeded as far as it has. However, as we shall see in this chapter and in Chapter 6 when we look closely at the WTO, critics charge that the organization is usurping the national sovereignty of individual nation-states.

International Monetary Fund
International institution set up to maintain order in the international monetary system.

The **International Monetary Fund** and the **World Bank** were both created in 1944 by 44 nations that met at Bretton Woods, New Hampshire. The IMF was established to maintain order in the international monetary system; the World Bank was set up to promote economic development. In the 60 years since their creation, both institutions have emerged as significant players in the global economy. The World Bank is the less controversial of the two sister institutions. It has focused on making low-interest loans to cash-strapped governments in poor nations that wish to undertake significant infrastructure investments (such as building dams or roads).

World Bank
International organization set up to promote economic development, primarily by offering low-interest loans to cash-strapped governments of poorer nations.

The IMF is often seen as the lender of last resort to nation-states whose economies are in turmoil and currencies are losing value against those of other nations. Repeatedly during the past decade, for example, the IMF has lent money to the governments of troubled states, including Argentina, Indonesia, Mexico, Russia, South Korea, Thailand, and Turkey. IMF loans come with strings attached, however; in return for loans, the IMF requires nation-states to adopt specific economic policies aimed at returning their troubled economies to stability and growth. These requirements have sparked controversy. Some critics charge that the IMF's policy recommendations are often inappropriate; others maintain that by telling national governments what economic policies they must adopt, the IMF, like the WTO, is usurping the sovereignty of nation-states. We shall look at the debate over the role of the IMF in Chapter 10.

United Nations
An international organization made up of 191 countries charged with keeping international peace, developing cooperation between nations, and promoting human rights.

The **United Nations** was established October 24, 1945, by 51 countries committed to preserving peace through international cooperation and collective security. Today nearly every nation in the world belongs to the United Nations; membership now totals 191 countries. When states become members of the United Nations, they agree to accept the obligations of the UN Charter, an international treaty that establishes basic principles of international relations. According to the charter, the UN has four purposes: to maintain international peace and security, to develop friendly relations among nations, to cooperate in solving international problems and in promoting respect for human rights, and to be a center for harmonizing the actions of nations. Although the UN is perhaps best known for its peacekeeping role, one of the organization's central mandates is the promotion of higher standards of living, full employment, and conditions of economic and social progress and development—all issues that are central to the creation of a vibrant global economy. As much as 70 percent of the work of the UN system is devoted to accomplishing this mandate. To do so, the UN works closely with other international institutions such as the World Bank. Guiding the work is the belief that eradicating poverty and improving the well-being of people everywhere are necessary steps in creating conditions for lasting world peace.[15]

The United Nations has the important goal of improving the well being of people around the world. *Mario Tama/Getty Images*

Drivers of Globalization

Two macro factors seem to underlie the trend toward greater globalization.[16] The first is the decline in barriers to the free flow of goods, services, and capital that has occurred since the end of World War II. The second factor is technological change, particularly the dramatic developments in recent years in communication, information processing, and transportation technologies.

LEARNING OBJECTIVE 2
Be familiar with the main drivers of globalization.

DECLINING TRADE AND INVESTMENT BARRIERS During the 1920s and 30s, many of the world's nation-states erected formidable barriers to international trade and foreign direct investment. **International trade** occurs when a firm exports goods or services to consumers in another country. **Foreign direct investment (FDI)** occurs when a firm invests resources in business activities outside its home country. Many of the barriers to international trade took the form of high tariffs on imports of manufactured goods. The typical aim of such tariffs was to protect domestic industries from foreign competition. One consequence, however, was "beggar thy neighbor" retaliatory trade policies, with countries progressively raising trade barriers against each other. Ultimately, this depressed world demand and contributed to the Great Depression of the 1930s.

International Trade
Occurs when a firm exports goods or services to consumers in another country.

Foreign Direct Investment (FDI)
Occurs when a firm invests resources in business activities outside its home country.

Having learned from this experience, the advanced industrial nations of the West committed themselves after World War II to removing barriers to the free flow of goods, services, and capital between nations.[17] This goal was enshrined in the General Agreement on Tariffs and Trade. Under the umbrella of GATT, eight rounds of negotiations among member states (now numbering 149) have worked to lower barriers to the free flow of goods and services. The most recent round of negotiations, known as the Uruguay Round, was completed in December 1993. The Uruguay Round further reduced trade barriers; extended GATT to cover services as well as manufactured goods; provided enhanced protection for patents, trademarks, and copyrights; and established the World Trade Organization to police the international trading system.[18] Table 1.1 summarizes the impact of GATT agreements on average tariff rates for manufactured goods. As can be seen, average tariff rates have fallen significantly since 1950 and now stand at about 4 percent.

In late 2001, the WTO launched a new round of talks aimed at further liberalizing the global trade and investment framework. For this meeting, it picked the remote location of Doha in the Persian Gulf state of Qatar. At Doha, the member states of

table 

Average Tariff Rates on Manufactured Products as Percent of Value

	1913	1950	1990	2005
France	21%	18%	5.9%	3.9%
Germany	20	26	5.9	3.9
Italy	18	25	5.9	3.9
Japan	30	—	5.3	2.3
Holland	5	11	5.9	3.9
Sweden	20	9	4.4	3.9
Great Britain	—	23	5.9	3.9
United States	44	14	4.8	3.2

Source: 1913–1990 data are from "Who Wants to Be a Giant?" *The Economist: A Survey of the Multinationals,* June 24, 1995, pp. 3–4. The 2005 data are from World Trade Organization, *2005 World Trade Report* (Geneva: WTO, 2006). Used by permission.

the WTO staked out an agenda. The talks were scheduled to last three years, although it now looks as if they may go on significantly longer. The agenda includes cutting tariffs on industrial goods, services, and agricultural products; phasing out subsidies to agricultural producers; reducing barriers to cross-border investment; and limiting the use of antidumping laws. The biggest gain may come from discussion on agricultural products; average agricultural tariff rates are still about 40 percent, and rich nations spend some $300 billion a year in subsidies to support their farm sectors. The world's poorer nations have the most to gain from any reduction in agricultural tariffs and subsidies; such reforms would give them access to the markets of the developed world.[19]

In addition to reducing trade barriers, many countries have also been progressively removing restrictions to foreign direct investment. According to the United Nations, some 93 percent of the 2,156 changes made worldwide between 1991 and 2004 in the laws governing foreign direct investment created a more favorable environment for FDI.[20] The desire of governments to facilitate FDI also has been reflected in a dramatic increase in the number of bilateral investment treaties designed to protect and promote investment between two countries. As of 2004, 2,392 such treaties involved more than 160 countries, a 12-fold increase from the 181 treaties that existed in 1980.[21]

Such trends have been driving both the globalization of markets and the globalization of production. The lowering of barriers to international trade enables firms to view the world, rather than a single country, as their market. The lowering of trade and investment barriers also allows firms to base production at the optimal location for that activity. Thus, a firm might design a product in one country, produce component parts in two other countries, assemble the product in yet another country, and then export the finished product around the world.

The data summarized in Figure 1.1 imply several things. First, more firms are doing what Boeing does with the 777 and 787 and Lenovo with the ThinkPad:

figure 1.1

Volume of World Trade and World Production, 1950–2005

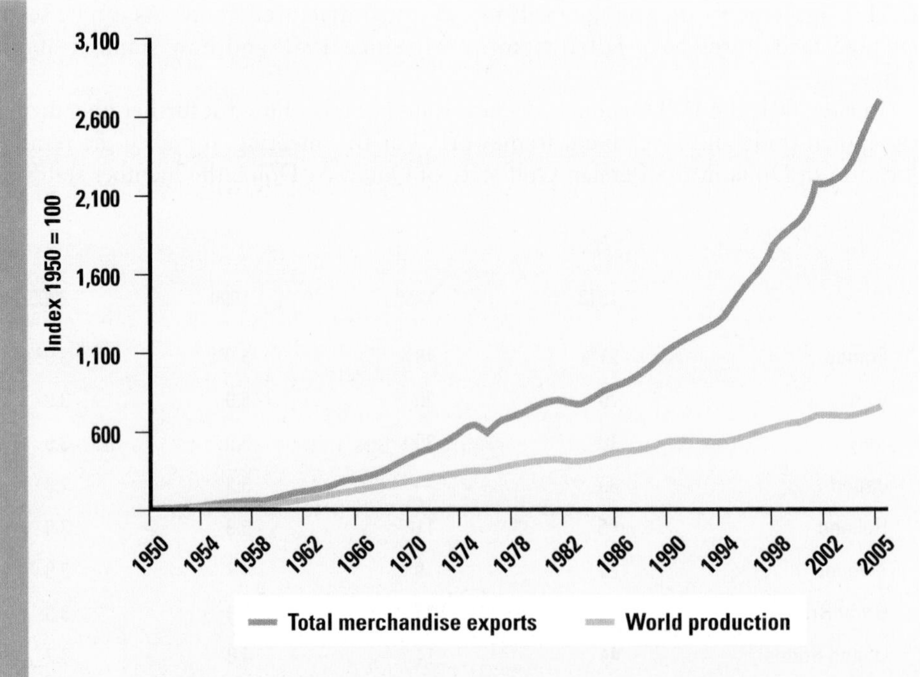

dispersing parts of their production process to different locations around the globe to drive down production costs and increase product quality. Second, the economies of the world's nation-states are becoming more intertwined. As trade expands, nations are becoming increasingly dependent on each other for important goods and services. Third, the world has become significantly wealthier since 1950, and the implication is that rising trade is the engine that has helped to pull the global economy along.

According to WTO data, the volume of world merchandise trade has grown faster than the world economy since 1950 (see Figure 1.1).[22] From 1970 to 2005, the volume of world merchandise trade expanded 27-fold, outstripping the expansion of world production, which grew about 7.5 times in real terms. (World merchandise trade includes trade in manufactured goods, agricultural goods, and mining products, but *not* services. World production and trade are measured in real, or inflation-adjusted, dollars.) As suggested by Figure 1.1, due to falling barriers to cross-border trade and investment, the growth in world trade seems to have accelerated since the early 1980s.

What Figure 1.1 does not show is that since the mid-1980s the value of international trade in services has grown robustly. Trade in services now accounts for almost 20 percent of the value of all international trade. Increasingly, international trade in services has been driven by advances in communications, which allow corporations to outsource service activities to different locations around the globe (see the opening case). Thus, as noted earlier, many corporations in the developed world outsource customer service functions, from software maintenance activities to customer call centers, to developing nations where labor costs are lower.

The evidence also suggests that foreign direct investment is playing an increasing role in the global economy as firms increase their cross-border investments. The average yearly outflow of FDI increased from $25 billion in 1975 to a record $1.2 trillion in 2000, before falling back to an estimated $897 billion in 2005.[23] Over this period, the flow of FDI accelerated faster than the growth in world trade and world output. For example, between 1992 and 2005, the total flow of FDI from all countries increased more than fivefold while world trade by value grew by some 140 percent and world output by around 40 percent.[24] As a result of the strong FDI flow, by 2004 the global stock of FDI exceeded $9 trillion. At least 70,000 parent companies had 690,000 affiliates in foreign markets that collectively employed more than 50 million people abroad and generated value accounting for about one-tenth of global GDP. The foreign affiliates of multinationals had an estimated $19 trillion in global sales, much higher than the value of global exports, which stood at close to $11 trillion.[25]

The globalization of markets and production and the resulting growth of world trade, foreign direct investment, and imports all imply that firms are finding their home markets under attack from foreign competitors. This is true in Japan, where U.S. companies such as Kodak, Procter & Gamble, and Merrill Lynch are expanding their presence. It is true in the United States, where Japanese automobile firms have taken market share away from General Motors and Ford. And it is true in Europe, where the once-dominant Dutch company Philips has seen its market share in the consumer electronics industry taken by Japan's JVC, Matsushita, and Sony, and Korea's Samsung and LG. The growing integration of the world economy into a single, huge marketplace is increasing the intensity of competition in a range of manufacturing and service industries.

However, declining barriers to cross-border trade and investment cannot be taken for granted. As we shall see in subsequent chapters, demands for "protection" from foreign competitors are still often heard in countries around the world, including the United

States. Although a return to the restrictive trade policies of the 1920s and 30s is unlikely, it is not clear whether the political majority in the industrialized world favors further reductions in trade barriers. If trade barriers decline no further, at least for the time being, this will put a brake upon the globalization of both markets and production.

THE ROLE OF TECHNOLOGICAL CHANGE The lowering of trade barriers made globalization of markets and production a theoretical possibility. Technological change has made it a tangible reality. Since the end of World War II, the world has seen major advances in communication, information processing, and transportation technology, including the explosive emergence of the Internet and World Wide Web. Telecommunications is creating a global audience. Transportation is creating a global village. From Buenos Aires to Boston, and from Birmingham to Beijing, ordinary people are watching MTV, they're wearing blue jeans, and they're listening to iPods as they commute to work.

Microprocessors and Telecommunications Perhaps the single most important innovation has been development of the microprocessor, which enabled the explosive growth of high-power, low-cost computing, vastly increasing the amount of information that can be processed by individuals and firms. The microprocessor also underlies many recent advances in telecommunications technology. Over the past 30 years, global communications have been revolutionized by developments in satellite, optical fiber, and wireless technologies, and now the Internet and the World Wide Web (WWW). These technologies rely on the microprocessor to encode, transmit, and decode the vast amount of information that flows along these electronic highways. The cost of microprocessors continues to fall, while their power increases (a phenomenon known as **Moore's Law,** which predicts that the power of microprocessor technology doubles and its cost of production falls in half every 18 months).[26] As this happens, the cost of global communications plummets, which lowers the costs of coordinating and controlling a global organization. Thus, between 1930 and 1990, the cost of a three-minute phone call between New York and London fell from $244.65 to $3.32.[27] By 1998, it had plunged to just 36 cents for consumers, and much lower rates were available for businesses.[28] Indeed, by using the Internet, the cost of an international phone call is rapidly plummeting toward just a few cents per minute.

Moore's Law
The premise that the power of microprocessor technology doubles and its cost of production drops in half every 18 months.

The Internet and World Wide Web The rapid growth of the World Wide Web is the latest expression of this development. In 1990, fewer than 1 million users were connected to the Internet. By 1995, the figure had risen to 50 million. By 2007, the Internet may have more than 1.47 billion users, or about 25 percent of the world's population.[29] The WWW has developed into the information backbone of the global economy. Web-based transactions hit $657 billion in 2000, up from nothing in 1994, and reached some $6.8 trillion in 2004.[30]

Included in the expanding volume of Web-based traffic is a growing percentage of cross-border trade. Viewed globally, the Web is emerging as an equalizer. It rolls back some of the constraints of location, scale, and time zones.[31] The Web makes it much easier for buyers and sellers to find each other, wherever they may be located and whatever their size. It allows businesses, both small and large, to expand their global presence at a lower cost than ever before.

Transportation Technology In addition to developments in communication technology, several major innovations in transportation technology have occurred since World War II. In economic terms, the most important are probably the development

Before the advent of containerization, it could take several days and several hundred longshoremen to unload a ship and reload goods onto trucks and trains. *Digital Vision/Punchstock/DIL*

of commercial jet aircraft and super-freighters and the introduction of containerization, which simplifies transshipment from one mode of transport to another. The advent of commercial jet travel, by reducing the time needed to get from one location to another, has effectively shrunk the globe. In terms of travel time, New York is now "closer" to Tokyo than it was to Philadelphia in the Colonial days.

Containerization has revolutionized the transportation business, significantly lowering the costs of shipping goods over long distances. Before the advent of containerization, moving goods from one mode of transport to another was very labor intensive, lengthy, and costly. It could take days and several hundred longshoremen to unload a ship and reload goods onto trucks and trains. With the advent of widespread containerization in the 1970s and 1980s, the whole process can now be executed by a handful of longshoremen in a couple of days. Since 1980, the world's containership fleet has more than quadrupled, reflecting in part the growing volume of international trade and in part the switch to this mode of transportation. As a result of the efficiency gains associated with containerization, transportation costs have plummeted, making it much more economical to ship goods around the globe, thereby helping to drive the globalization of markets and production. Between 1920 and 1990, the average ocean freight and port charges per ton of U.S. export and import cargo fell from $95 to $29 (in 1990 dollars).[32] The cost of shipping freight per ton-mile on railroads in the United States fell from 3.04 cents in 1985 to 2.3 cents in 2000, largely as a result of efficiency gains from the widespread use of containers.[33] An increased share of cargo now goes by air. Between 1955 and 1999, average air transportation revenue per ton-kilometer fell by more than 80 percent.[34] Reflecting the falling cost of airfreight, by the early 2000s air shipments accounted for 28 percent of the value of U.S. trade, up from 7 percent in 1965.[35]

Implications for the Globalization of Production

As transportation costs associated with the globalization of production declined, dispersal of production to geographically separate locations became more economical. As a result of the technological innovations discussed above, the real costs of information processing and communication have fallen dramatically in the past two decades. These developments make it possible for a firm to create and then manage a globally dispersed production system, further facilitating the globalization of production. A worldwide communications network has become essential for many international businesses. For example, Dell uses the Internet to coordinate and control a globally dispersed production system to such an extent that it holds only three days' worth of inventory at its assembly locations. Dell's Internet-based system records orders for computer equipment as they are submitted by customers via the company's Web site, then immediately transmits the resulting orders for components to various suppliers around the world, which have a real-time look at Dell's order flow and can adjust their production schedules accordingly. Given the low cost of airfreight, Dell can use air transportation to speed up the delivery of critical components to meet unanticipated demand shifts without delaying the shipment of final product to consumers. Dell also has used modern communications technology to outsource its customer service operations to India. When U.S. customers call Dell with a service inquiry, they are routed to Bangalore in India, where English-speaking service personnel handle the call.

The Internet has been a major force facilitating international trade in services. It is the Web that allows hospitals in Chicago to send MRI scans to India for analysis, accounting offices in San Francisco to outsource routine tax preparation work to accountants living in the Philippines, and software testers in India to debug code written by developers in Redmond, Washington, the headquarters of Microsoft. We are probably still in the early stages of this development. As Moore's Law continues to advance and telecommunications bandwidth continues to increase, almost any work processes that can be digitalized will be, and this will allow that work to be performed wherever in the world it is most efficient and effective to do so.

The development of commercial jet aircraft has also helped knit together the worldwide operations of many international businesses. Using jet travel, an American manager need spend a day at most traveling to his or her firm's European or Asian operations. This enables the manager to oversee a globally dispersed production system.

Implications for the Globalization of Markets In addition to the globalization of production, technological innovations have also facilitated the globalization of markets. Low-cost global communications networks such as the World Wide Web are helping to create electronic global marketplaces. As noted above, low-cost transportation has made it more economical to ship products around the world, thereby helping to create global markets. For example, due to the tumbling costs of shipping goods by air, roses grown in Ecuador can be cut and sold in New York two days later while they are still fresh. This has given rise to an industry in Ecuador that did not exist 20 years ago and now supplies a global market for roses (see the accompanying Country Focus). In addition, low-cost jet travel has resulted in the mass movement of people between countries. This has reduced the cultural distance between countries and is bringing about some convergence of consumer tastes and preferences. At the same time, global communication networks and global media are creating a worldwide culture. U.S. television networks such as CNN, MTV, and HBO are now received in many countries, and Hollywood films are shown the world over. In any society, the media are primary conveyors of culture; as global media develop, we must expect the evolution of something akin to a global culture. A logical result of this evolution is the emergence of global markets for consumer products. The first signs of this are already apparent. It is now as easy to find a McDonald's restaurant in Tokyo as it is in New York, to buy an iPod in Rio as it is in Berlin, and to buy Gap jeans in Paris as it is in San Francisco.

Despite these trends, we must be careful not to overemphasize their importance. While modern communication and transportation technologies are ushering in the

Country FOCUS

Ecuadorean Valentine Roses

It is 6:20 a.m. February 7, in the Ecuadorean town of Cayambe, and Maria Pacheco has just been dropped off for work by the company bus. She pulls on thick rubber gloves, wraps an apron over her white, traditional embroidered dress, and grabs her clippers, ready for another long day. Any other time of year, Maria would work until 2 p.m., but it's a week before Valentine's Day, and Maria along with her 84 coworkers at the farm are likely to be busy until 5 p.m. By then, Maria will have cut more than 1,000 rose stems.

A few days later, after they have been refrigerated and shipped via aircraft, the roses Maria cut will be selling for premium prices in stores from New York to London. Ecuadorean roses are quickly becoming the Rolls-Royce of roses. They have huge heads and unusually vibrant colors, including 10 different reds, from bleeding heart crimson to a rosy lover's blush.

Most of Ecuador's 460 or so rose farms are located in the Cayambe and Cotopaxi regions, 10,000 feet up in the Andes about an hour's drive from the capital, Quito. The rose bushes are planted in huge flat fields at the foot of snowcapped volcanoes that rise to more than 20,000 feet. The bushes are protected by 20-foot-high canopies of plastic sheeting. The combination of intense sunlight, fertile volcanic soil, an equatorial location, and high altitude makes for ideal growing conditions, allowing roses to flower almost year-round.

Ecuador's rose industry started some 20 years ago and has been expanding rapidly since. Ecuador is now the world's fourth-largest producer of roses. Roses are the nation's fifth-largest export, with customers all over the world. Rose farms generate $240 million in sales and support tens of thousands of jobs. In Cayambe, the population has increased in 10 years from 10,000 to 70,000, primarily as a result of the rose industry. The revenues and taxes from rose growers have helped to pave roads, build schools, and construct sophisticated irrigation systems. In 2003, construction was to begin on an international airport between Quito and Cayambe from which Ecuadorean roses will begin their journey to flower shops all over the world.

Maria works Monday to Saturday, and earns $210 a month, which she says is an average wage in Ecuador and substantially above the country's $120 a month minimum wage. The farm also provides her with health care and a pension. By employing women such as Maria, the industry has fostered a social revolution in which mothers and wives have more control over their family's spending, especially on schooling for their children.

For all of the benefits that roses have bought to Ecuador, where the gross national income per capita is only $1,080 a year, the industry has come under fire from environmentalists. Large growers have been accused of misusing a toxic mixture of pesticides, fungicides, and fumigants to grow and export unblemished pest-free flowers. Reports claim that workers often fumigate roses in street clothes without protective equipment. Some doctors and scientists claim that many of the industry's 50,000 employees have serious health problems as a result of exposure to toxic chemicals. A study by the International Labor Organization claimed that women in the industry had more miscarriages than average and that some 60 percent of all workers suffered from headaches, nausea, blurred vision, and fatigue. Still, the critics acknowledge that their studies have been hindered by a lack of access to the farms, and they do not know what the true situation is. The International Labor Organization has also claimed that some rose growers in Ecuador use child labor, a claim that has been strenuously rejected by both the growers and Ecuadorean government agencies.

In Europe, consumer groups have urged the European Union to press for improved environmental safeguards. In response, some Ecuadorean growers have joined a voluntary program aimed at helping customers identify responsible growers. The certification signifies that the grower has distributed protective gear, trained workers in using chemicals, and hired doctors to visit workers at least weekly. Other environmental groups have pushed for stronger sanctions, including trade sanctions, against Ecuadorean rose growers that are not environmentally certified by a reputable agency. On February 14, however, most consumers are oblivious to these issues; they simply want to show their appreciation to their wives and girlfriends with a perfect bunch of roses.

Sources: G. Thompson, "Behind Roses' Beauty, Poor and Ill Workers," *The New York Times,* February 13, 2003, pp. A1, A27; J. Stuart, "You've Come a Long Way Baby," *The Independent,* February 14, 2003, p. 1; V. Marino, "By Any Other Name, It's Usually a Rosa," *The New York Times,* May 11, 2003, p. A9; A. DePalma, "In Trade Issue, the Pressure Is on Flowers," *The New York Times,* January 24, 2002, p. 1; and "The Search for Roses without Thorns," *The Economist,* February 18, 2006, p. 38.

"global village," significant national differences remain in culture, consumer preferences, and business practices. A firm that ignores differences between countries does so at its peril. We shall stress this point repeatedly throughout this book and elaborate on it in later chapters.

The Changing Demographics of the Global Economy

LEARNING OBJECTIVE 3
Appreciate the changing nature of the global economy.

Hand in hand with the trend toward globalization has been a fairly dramatic change in the demographics of the global economy over the past 30 years. As late as the 1960s, four stylized facts described the demographics of the global economy. The first was U.S. dominance in the world economy and world trade picture. The second was U.S. dominance in world foreign direct investment. Related to this, the third fact was the dominance of large, multinational U.S. firms on the international business scene. The fourth was that roughly half the globe—the centrally planned economies of the Communist world—were off-limits to Western international businesses. As will be explained below, all four of these qualities either have changed or are now changing rapidly.

THE CHANGING WORLD OUTPUT AND WORLD TRADE PICTURE In the early 1960s, the United States was still by far the world's dominant industrial power. In 1963 the United States accounted for 40.3 percent of world output. By 2005, the United States accounted for 20.1 percent of world output, still by far the world's largest industrial power but down significantly in relative size since the 1960s (see Table 1.2). Nor was the United States the only developed nation to see its relative standing slip. The same occurred to Germany, France, and the United Kingdom, all nations that were among the first to industrialize. This change in the U.S. position was not an absolute decline, since the U.S. economy grew at a robust average annual rate of more than 3 percent from 1963 to 2005 (the economies of Germany, France, and the United Kingdom also grew during this time). Rather, it was a relative decline, reflecting the faster economic growth of several other economies, particularly in Asia. For example, as can be seen from Table 1.2, from 1963 to 2005, China's share of world output increased from a trivial amount to 15.4 percent. Other countries that markedly increased their share of world output included Japan, Thailand, Malaysia, Taiwan, and South Korea.

By the end of the 1980s, the U.S. position as the world's leading exporter was threatened. Over the past 30 years, U.S. dominance in export markets has waned as Japan, Germany, and a number of newly industrialized countries such as South Korea and China have taken a larger share of world exports. During the 1960s, the United States routinely accounted for 20 percent of world exports of manufactured goods. But as Table 1.2 shows, the U.S. share of world exports of goods and services had slipped to 10.1 percent by 2005. Despite the fall, the United States still remained the world's

table 1.2

The Changing Demographics of World Output and Trade

Sources: IMF, *World Economic Outlook*, April 2006. Data for 1963 are from N. Hood and J. Young, *The Economics of the Multinational Enterprise* (New York: Longman, 1973). The GDP data are based on purchasing power parity figures, which adjust the value of GDP to reflect the cost of living in various economies.

Country	Share of World Output, 1963	Share of World Output, 2005	Share of World Exports, 2005
United States	40.3%	20.1%	10.1%
Germany	9.7	4.1	9.0
France	6.3	3.0	4.4
Italy	3.4	2.7	3.6
United Kingdom	6.5	3.0	4.5
Canada	3.0	1.8	3.4
Japan	5.5	6.4	5.3
China	NA	15.4	6.7

largest exporter, ahead of Germany, Japan, France, and the fast-rising economic power, China.

As emerging economies such as China, India, and Brazil continue to grow, a further relative decline in the share of world output and world exports accounted for by the United States and other long-established developed nations seems likely. By itself, this is not bad. The relative decline of the United States reflects the growing economic development and industrialization of the world economy, as opposed to any absolute decline in the health of the U.S. economy, which by many measures is stronger than ever.

Most forecasts now predict a rapid rise in the share of world output accounted for by developing nations such as China, India, Indonesia, Thailand, South Korea, Mexico, and Brazil, and a commensurate decline in the share enjoyed by rich industrialized countries such as Great Britain, Germany, Japan, and the United States. If current trends continue, by 2020 the Chinese economy could be larger than that of the United States, while the economy of India will approach that of Germany (see the Another Perspective box at right for details). The World Bank has estimated that today's developing nations may account for more than 60 percent of world economic activity by 2020, while today's rich nations, which currently account for more than 55 percent of world economic activity, may account for only about 38 percent. Forecasts are not always correct, but these suggest that a shift in the economic geography of the world is now underway, although the magnitude of that shift is not totally evident. For international businesses, the implications of this changing economic geography are clear: Many of tomorrow's economic opportunities may be found in the developing nations of the world, and many of tomorrow's most capable competitors will probably also emerge from these regions.

Another Perspective

India's Tech Export Business Surges and EMC Gains

India's computer-software and services industry, which started out about 20 years ago, undertaking routine outsourced office functions for companies based in the United States and United Kingdom, has extended its scope of operations and grown into a $23.6 billion export business. The industry employed 1.3 million people in 2006, according to the National Association of Software and Service Companies (Nasscom), India's lobbying group. They estimate 382,000 students will graduate with engineering qualifications in 2006–2007.

EMC Corp, the world's biggest maker of storage computers and software, plans to more than double its investment in India to $500 million by 2010 to expand sales, research, and the local market. Research will account for most of EMC's spending because India's primary draw is the quality of the country's technology professionals. Wages are about one-sixth of those in the united States. However, EMC says there are countries lower in cost than India and that the company is going for quality investment. What do you think? (Ashok Bhattacharjee, *Bloomberg News,* June 21, 2006)

THE CHANGING FOREIGN DIRECT INVESTMENT PICTURE Reflecting the dominance of the United States in the global economy, U.S. firms accounted for 66.3 percent of worldwide foreign direct investment flows in the 1960s. British firms were second, accounting for 10.5 percent, while Japanese firms were a distant eighth, with only 2 percent. The dominance of U.S. firms was so great that books were written about the economic threat posed to Europe by U.S. corporations.[36] Several European governments, most notably France, talked of limiting inward investment by U.S. firms.

However, as the barriers to the free flow of goods, services, and capital fell, and as other countries increased their shares of world output, non-U.S. firms increasingly began to invest across national borders. The motivation for much of this foreign direct investment by non-U.S. firms was the desire to disperse production activities to optimal locations and to build a direct presence in major foreign markets. Thus, beginning in the 1970s, European and Japanese firms began to shift labor-intensive manufacturing operations from their home markets to developing nations where labor costs were lower. In addition, many Japanese firms invested in North America and Europe—often as a hedge against unfavorable currency movements and the possible

figure 1.2

Percentage Share of Total FDI Stock, 1980–2004

Source: Calculated by author from data in United Nations, *World Investment Report, 2005* (Geneva: United Nations, 2005).

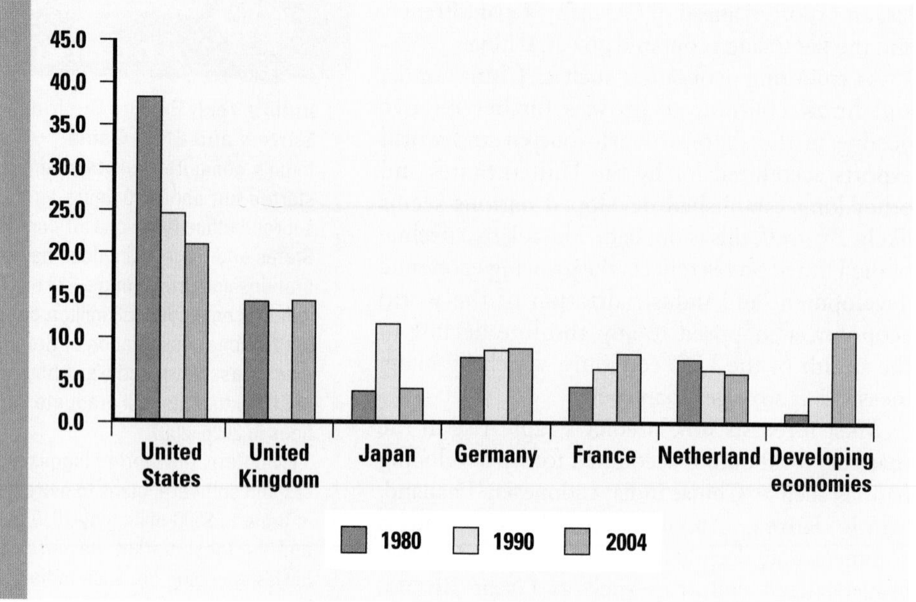

imposition of trade barriers. For example, Toyota, the Japanese automobile company, rapidly increased its investment in automobile production facilities in the United States and Europe during the late 1980s and early 1990s. Toyota executives believed that an increasingly strong Japanese yen would price Japanese automobile exports out of foreign markets; therefore, production in the most important foreign markets, as opposed to exports from Japan, made sense. Toyota also undertook these investments to head off growing political pressures in the United States and Europe to restrict Japanese automobile exports into those markets.

One consequence of thease developments is illustrated in Figure 1.2, which shows how the stock of foreign direct investment by the world's six most important national sources—the United States, the United Kingdom, Germany, the Netherlands, France, and Japan—changed between 1980 and 2003. (The **stock of foreign direct investment** refers to the total cumulative value of foreign investments.) Figure 1.2 also shows the stock accounted for by firms from developing economies. The share of the total stock accounted for by U.S. firms declined from about 38 percent in 1980 to 21 percent in 2004. Meanwhile, the shares accounted for by France and the world's developing nations increased markedly. The rise in the share of FDI stock accounted for by developing nations reflects a growing trend for firms from these countries to invest outside their borders. In 2004, firms based in developing nations accounted for 10.6 percent of the stock of foreign direct investment, up from only 1.1 percent in 1980. Firms based in Hong Kong, South Korea, Singapore, Taiwan, and mainland China accounted for much of this investment.

Stock of Foreign Direct Investment
The total accumulated value of foreign-owned assets at a given time.

Figure 1.3 illustrates two other important trends—the sustained growth in cross-border flows of foreign direct investment that occurred during the 1990s and the importance of developing nations as the destination of foreign direct investment. Throughout the 1990s, the amount of investment directed at both developed and developing nations increased dramatically, a trend that reflects the increasing internationalization of business corporations. A surge in foreign direct investment from 1998 to 2000 was followed by a slump from 2001 to 2003 associated with a slowdown in global economic activity after the collapse of the financial bubble of the late 1990s and 2000. However, the growth of foreign direct investment resumed in 2004 and continued through 2005. Among

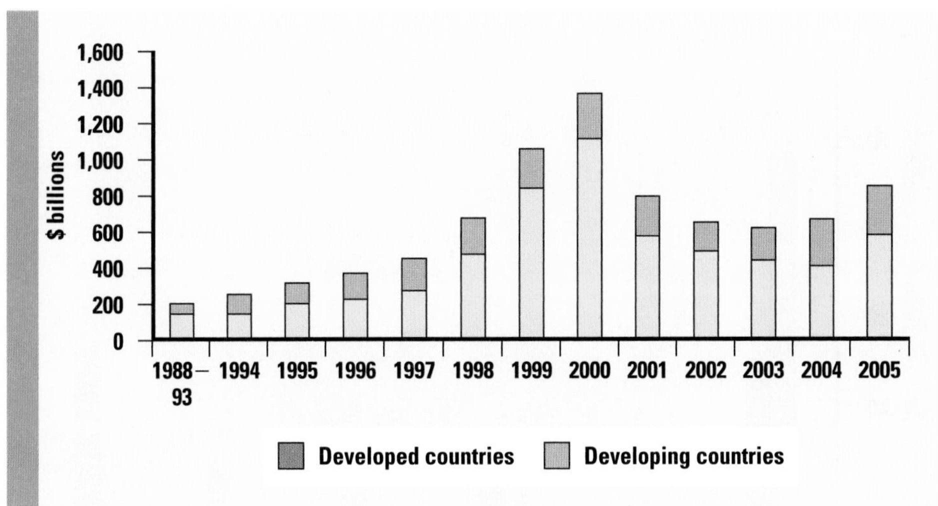

figure 1.3

FDI Inflows 1988–2005

Source: Calculated by author from data in United Nations, *World Investment Report, 2005* (Geneva: United Nations, 2005). Data for 2005 are from United Nations Conference on Trade and Development, "Data Shows Foreign Direct Investment Climbed Sharply in 2005," press release, January 23, 2006.

developing nations, the largest recipient of foreign direct investment has been China, which in 2004 and 2005 received $61 billion a year in inflows. As we shall see later in this book, the sustained flow of foreign investment into developing nations is an important stimulus for economic growth in those countries, which bodes well for the future of countries such as China, Mexico, and Brazil, all leading beneficiaries of this trend.

THE CHANGING NATURE OF THE MULTINATIONAL ENTERPRISE

A **multinational enterprise** (MNE) is any business that has productive activities in two or more countries. Since the 1960s, two notable trends in the demographics of the multinational enterprise have been (1) the rise of non-U.S. multinationals and (2) the growth of mini-multinationals.

Multinational Enterprise (MNE)
Any business that has productive activities in two or more countries.

Non-U.S. Multinationals

In the 1960s, global business activity was dominated by large U.S. multinational corporations. With U.S. firms accounting for about two-thirds of foreign direct investment during the 1960s, one would expect most multinationals to be U.S. enterprises. According to the data summarized in Figure 1.4 (see page 22), in 1973, 48.5 percent of the world's 260 largest multinationals were U.S. firms. The second-largest source country was the United Kingdom, with 18.8 percent of the largest multinationals. Japan accounted for 3.5 percent of the world's largest multinationals at the time. The large number of U.S. multinationals reflected U.S. economic dominance in the three decades after World War II, while the large number of British multinationals reflected that country's industrial dominance in the early decades of the twentieth century.

By 2004 things had shifted significantly. Some 25 of the world's 100 largest nonfinancial multinationals were now U.S. enterprises; 14 were French; 14, German; 12, British; and 9, Japanese. In terms of the global stock of foreign direct investment, 21 percent belonged to U.S. firms, 14 percent to British, 8 percent to French firms, 8.5 percent to German firms, 5.6 percent to Dutch firms, and 4 percent to Japanese.[37] Although the 1973 data are not strictly comparable with the later data, they illustrate the trend (the 1973 figures are based on the largest 260 firms, whereas the later figures are based on the largest 100 multinationals). The globalization of the world economy has resulted in a relative decline in the dominance of U.S. firms in the global marketplace.

According to UN data, the ranks of the world's largest 100 multinationals are still dominated by firms from developed economies.[38] However, four firms from developing economies entered the UN's list of the 100 largest multinationals. They were Hutchison

figure 1.4

National Origin of Largest Multinational Enterprises, 1973 and 2004

Source: Calculated by author from data in United Nations, *World Investment Report, 2005* (New York & Geneva: United Nations, 2005). The 1970 data are from N. Hood and J. Young, *The Economics of the Multinational Enterprise* (New York: Longman, 1973).

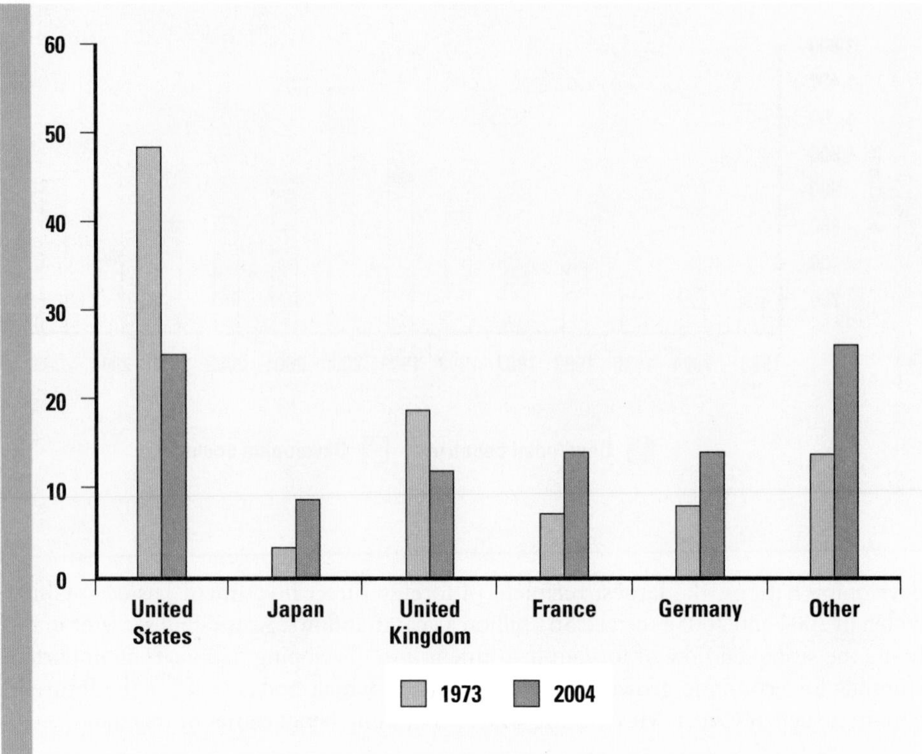

Whampoa of Hong Kong, China, which ranked 16 in terms of foreign assets; Singtel of Singapore, which was ranked 66; Petronas of Malaysia; and Samsung of Korea.[39] The growth in the number of multinationals from developing economies is evident when we look at smaller firms. By 2004, the largest 50 multinationals from developing economies had foreign sales of $202 billion out of total sales of $512 billion and employed 1.08 million people outside of their home countries. Some 60 percent of these companies came from China or countries with large ethnic Chinese population (20 percent from Hong Kong, 18 percent from Singapore, 16 percent from Taiwan, and 6 percent from mainland China). Other nations with multiple entries on the list included South Korea, Brazil, Mexico and Malaysia. We can reasonably expect more growth of new multinational enterprises from the world's developing nations. Firms from developing nations can be expected to emerge as important competitors in global markets, further shifting the axis of the world economy away from North America and Western Europe and threatening the long dominance of Western companies. One such rising competitor, Lenovo of China, is profiled in the accompanying Management Focus.

The Rise of Mini-Multinationals

Another trend in international business has been the growth of medium-size and small multinationals (mini-multinationals).[40] When people think of international businesses, they tend to think of firms such as Exxon, General Motors, Ford, Fuji, Kodak, Matsushita, Procter & Gamble, Sony, and Unilever—large, complex multinational corporations with operations that span the globe. Although most international trade and investment is still conducted by large firms, many medium-size and small businesses are becoming increasingly involved in international trade and investment.

For another example, consider Lubricating Systems, Inc., of Kent, Washington. Lubricating Systems, which manufactures lubricating fluids for machine tools, employs

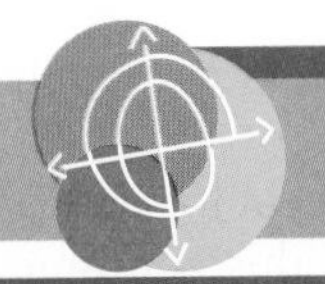

Management FOCUS

China's Lenovo Acquires IBM's PC Operations

In late 2004, the Chinese personal computer manufacturer Lenovo stunned the business world when it announced that it would acquire IBM's PC operations for $1.25 billion. Lenovo, formerly known as Legend, was founded in 1984 by a group of young Chinese scientists with government financing. The company started as a distributor of computers and printers, selling IBM, ACT, and Hewlett-Packard brands. In the late 1980s, however, the company moved into manufacturing and began to design, make, and sell its own personal computers. Taking advantage of China's low labor costs, Lenovo quickly emerged as a low-cost provider.

By 2004, the company led the PC market in China, where it had a 26 percent share. But for Lenovo's founders, this was not enough. They were worried about the entry of efficient foreign competitors, such as Dell, into the Chinese market. Lenovo might have low labor costs, but its 2.3 percent share of global PC sales left it trailing far behind Dell and Hewlett-Packard, which held 18.3 percent and 15.7 percent of the global market, respectively. Dell and HP could realize substantial economies of scale from their global volume. As a result, increasingly they were able to match Lenovo on costs. At the same time, Lenovo's managers wondered whether it was time to expand internationally and turn Lenovo into a global brand. To deal with Dell at home, and expand into the global marketplace, Lenovo's managers realized that they needed to do two things: (1) attain greater scale economies to further lower costs, which meant more sales volume, and (2) match Western companies on product innovation, differentiation, and brand.

Their solution was to acquire IBM's PC business, which held 6 percent of the global market in 2004. The IBM purchase not only gave Lenovo potential scale economies and global reach, but it also brought Lenovo IBM's renowned engineering skills, exemplified by the company's best-selling line of ThinkPad laptop computers, and IBM's extensive sales force and long-established customers. Top executives at Lenovo were smart enough to realize that the acquisition would have little value if IBM's managers and engineers left the company, so they made another surprising decision—they moved Lenovo's global headquarters to New York! Moreover, the former head of IBM's PC division, Stephen Ward, was appointed CEO of Lenovo, while Yang Yuanqing, the former CEO of Lenovo, will become chairman, and Lenovo's Mary Ma will be CFO. The 30-member top management team is split down the middle—half Chinese, half American—and boasts more women than men. English has been declared the company's new business language. The goal, according to Yang, is to transform Lenovo into a truly global corporation capable of going head-to-head with Dell in the battle for dominance in the global PC business.

Sources: D. Barboza, "An Unknown Giant Flexes Its Muscles," *The New York Times,* December 4, 2004, pp. B1, B3; D. Roberts and L. Lee, "East Meets West," *BusinessWeek,* May 9, 2005, pp. 1–4; and C. Forelle, "How IBM's Ward Will Lead China's Largest PC Company," *The Wall Street Journal,* April 21, 2005, p. B1.

25 people and generates sales of $6.5 million. It's hardly a large, complex multinational, yet more than $2 million of the company's sales are generated by exports to a score of countries, including Japan, Israel, and the United Arab Emirates. Lubricating Systems also has set up a joint venture with a German company to serve the European market.[41] Consider also Lixi, Inc., a small U.S. manufacturer of industrial X-ray equipment; 70 percent of Lixi's $4.5 million in revenues comes from exports to Japan.[42] Or take G.W. Barth, a manufacturer of cocoa-bean roasting machinery based in Ludwigsburg, Germany. Employing just 65 people, this small company has captured 70 percent of the global market for cocoa-bean roasting machines.[43] See the Management Focus box above for a look at how Lenovo is entering the global PC market. International business is conducted not just by large firms but also by medium-size and small enterprises.

THE CHANGING WORLD ORDER Between 1989 and 1991 a series of remarkable democratic revolutions swept the Communist world. For reasons that are explored in more detail in Chapter 2, in country after country throughout Eastern Europe and eventually in the Soviet Union itself, Communist Party governments collapsed like the shells of rotten eggs. The Soviet Union is now receding into history, having been replaced by 15 independent republics. Czechoslovakia has divided itself into two states, while Yugoslavia dissolved into a bloody civil war, now thankfully over, among its five successor states.

Many of the former Communist nations of Europe and Asia seem to share a commitment to democratic politics and free market economics. If this continues, the opportunities for international businesses may be enormous. For half a century, these countries were essentially closed to Western international businesses. Now they present a host of export and investment opportunities. Just how this will play out over the next 10 to 20 years is difficult to say. The economies of many of the former Communist states are still relatively undeveloped, and their continued commitment to democracy and free market economics cannot be taken for granted. Disturbing signs of growing unrest and totalitarian tendencies continue to be seen in several Eastern European and Central Asian states, including Russia, which under the government of Vladimir Putin has shown signs of shifting back toward greater state involvement in economic activity.[44] Thus, the risks involved in doing business in such countries are high, but so may be the returns.

In addition to these changes, more quiet revolutions have been occurring in China and Latin America. Their implications for international businesses may be just as profound as the collapse of communism in Eastern Europe. China suppressed its own pro-democracy movement in the bloody Tiananmen Square massacre of 1989. Despite this, China continues to move progressively toward greater free market reforms. If what is occurring in China continues for two more decades, China may move from Third World to industrial superpower status even more rapidly than Japan did. If China's gross domestic product (GDP) per capita grows by an average of 6 to 7 percent, which is slower than the 8 percent growth rate achieved during the last decade, then by 2020 this nation of 1.273 billion people could boast an average income per capita of about $13,000, roughly equivalent to that of Spain's today.

The potential consequences for international business are enormous. On the one hand, with more than 1 billion people, China represents a huge and largely untapped market. Reflecting this, between 1983 and 2005, annual foreign direct investment in China increased from less than $2 billion to $61 billion. On the other hand, China's new firms are proving to be very capable competitors, and they could take global market share away from Western and Japanese enterprises (for example, see the Management Focus about Lenovo). Thus, the changes in China are creating both opportunities and threats for established international businesses.

Another Perspective

Economic Freedom and Globalization: A Different Picture

The Frasier Institute's *Economic Freedom of the World Report*, which measures economic freedom using 38 variables, indicates a strong correlation between economic freedom, per capita growth, and life expectancy. In the 2005 report, Hong Kong has the highest rating for economic freedom (8.7 of 10) closely followed by Singapore (8.5). New Zealand, Switzerland, and the United States tied for third with ratings of 8.2. Botswana's ranking of 30 is the highest-ranking African economy and ranks higher than France (38) and Italy (54). See the 2005 report results and data at www.freetheworld.com.

As for Latin America, both democracy and free market reforms also seem to have taken hold. For decades, most Latin American countries were ruled by dictators, many of whom seemed to view Western international businesses as instruments of imperialist domination. Accordingly, they restricted direct investment by foreign firms. In addition, the poorly managed economies of Latin America were characterized by low growth, high debt, and hyperinflation—all of which discouraged investment by international businesses. In the last two decades much of this had changed. Throughout most of Latin America, debt and inflation are down, governments have sold state-owned enterprises to private investors, foreign investment is welcomed, and the region's economies have expanded. Brazil, Mexico, and Chile have led the way here. These changes have increased the attractiveness of Latin America, both as a market for exports and as a site for foreign direct investment. At the same time, given the long history of economic mismanagement in Latin America, there is no guarantee that these favorable trends will continue. Indeed, in Bolivia and Venezuela there have been shifts back toward greater state involvement in industry in the last few years, and foreign investment is now less welcome than it was during the 1990s. In both nations, the government has seized control of oil and gas fields from foreign investors and has limited the rights of foreign energy companies to extract oil and gas from their nations. Thus, as in the case of Eastern Europe, substantial opportunities are accompanied by substantial risks.

THE GLOBAL ECONOMY OF THE TWENTY-FIRST CENTURY As discussed, the past quarter century has seen rapid changes in the global economy. Barriers to the free flow of goods, services, and capital have been coming down. The volume of cross-border trade and investment has been growing more rapidly than global output, indicating that national economies are becoming more closely integrated into a single, interdependent, global economic system. As their economies advance, more nations are joining the ranks of the developed world. A generation ago, South Korea and Taiwan were viewed as second-tier developing nations. Now they boast large economies, and their firms are major players in many global industries, from shipbuilding and steel to electronics and chemicals. The move toward a global economy has been further strengthened by the widespread adoption of liberal economic policies by countries that had firmly opposed them for two generations or more. Thus, in keeping with the normative prescriptions of liberal economic ideology, in country after country we have seen state-owned businesses privatized, widespread deregulation adopted, markets opened to more competition, and commitment increased to removing barriers to cross-border trade and investment. This suggests that over the next few decades, countries such as the Czech Republic, Mexico, Poland, Brazil, China, India, and South Africa may build powerful market-oriented economies. In short, current trends indicate that the world is moving rapidly toward an economic system that is more favorable for international business.

But it is always hazardous to use established trends to predict the future. The world may be moving toward a more global economic system, but globalization is not inevitable. Countries may pull back from the recent commitment to liberal economic ideology if their experiences do not match their expectations. Periodic signs, for example, indicate a retreat from liberal economic ideology in Russia. Russia has experienced considerable economic pain as it tries to shift from a centrally planned economy to a market economy. If Russia's hesitation were to become more permanent and widespread, the liberal vision of a more prosperous global economy based on free market principles might not occur as quickly as many hope. Clearly, this would be a tougher world for international businesses.

Also, greater globalization brings with it risks of its own. This was starkly demonstrated in 1997 and 1998 when a financial crisis in Thailand spread first to other East Asian nations and then in 1998 to Russia and Brazil. Ultimately, the crisis threatened to plunge the economies of the developed world, including the United States, into a recession. We explore the causes and consequences of this and other similar global financial crises in Chapter 10. Even from a purely

Another Perspective

Globalization and Complexity

Another way to understand globalization is to think of it as the result of our increasing ability to deal with complexity. Some cultures such as the Chinese, Japanese, and Middle Eastern (see Chapter 3 for high context and high power distance) are inclined to work well with complexity. Will these cultural traits serve as a comparative advantage as globalization proceeds?

economic perspective, globalization is not all good. The opportunities for doing business in a global economy may be significantly enhanced, but as we saw in 1997–98, the risks associated with global financial contagion are also greater. Still, as explained later in this book, firms can exploit the opportunities associated with globalization, while at the same time reducing the risks through appropriate hedging strategies.

The Globalization Debate

LEARNING OBJECTIVE 4
Understand the main arguments in the debate over the impact of globalization.

Is the shift toward a more integrated and interdependent global economy a good thing? Many influential economists, politicians, and business leaders seem to think so.[45] They argue that falling barriers to international trade and investment are the twin engines driving the global economy toward greater prosperity. They say increased international trade and cross-border investment will result in lower prices for goods and services. They believe that globalization stimulates economic growth, raises the incomes of consumers, and helps to create jobs in all countries that participate in the global trading system. The arguments of those who support globalization are covered in detail in Chapters 5, 6, and 7. As we shall see, there are good theoretical reasons for believing that declining barriers to international trade and investment do stimulate economic growth, create jobs, and raise income levels. As described in Chapters 6 and 7, empirical evidence lends support to the predictions of this theory. However, despite the existence of a compelling body of theory and evidence, globalization has its critics.[46] Some of these critics have become increasingly vocal and active, taking to the streets to demonstrate their opposition to globalization. Here we look at the rising tide of protests against globalization and briefly review the main themes of the debate concerning the merits of globalization. In later chapters we elaborate on many of the points mentioned below.

ANTIGLOBALIZATION PROTESTS Street demonstrations against globalization date to December 1999, when more than 40,000 protesters blocked the streets of Seattle in an attempt to shut down a World Trade Organization meeting being held in the city. The demonstrators were protesting against a wide range of issues, including job losses in industries under attack from foreign competitors, downward pressure on the wage rates of unskilled workers, environmental degradation, and the cultural imperialism of global media and multinational enterprises, which was seen as being dominated by what some protesters called the "culturally impoverished" interests and values of the United States. All of these ills, the demonstrators claimed, could be laid at the feet of globalization. The World Trade Organization was meeting to try to launch a new round of talks to cut barriers to cross-border trade and investment. As such, it was seen as a promoter of globalization and a legitimate target for the antiglobalization protesters. The protests turned violent, transforming the normally placid streets of Seattle into a running battle between "anarchists" and Seattle's bemused and poorly prepared police department. Pictures of brick-throwing protesters and armored police wielding their batons were duly recorded by the global media, which then circulated the images around the world. Meanwhile, the World Trade Organization meeting failed to reach agreement, and although the protests outside the meeting halls had little to do with that failure, the impression took hold that the demonstrators had succeeded in derailing the meetings.

Emboldened by the experience in Seattle, antiglobalization protesters now turn up at almost every major meeting of a global institution. Smaller scale protests have occurred in several countries, such as France, where antiglobalization activists destroyed a McDonald's restaurant in August 1999 to protest the impoverishment of French culture by American imperialism (see the Country Focus, "Protesting Globalization in

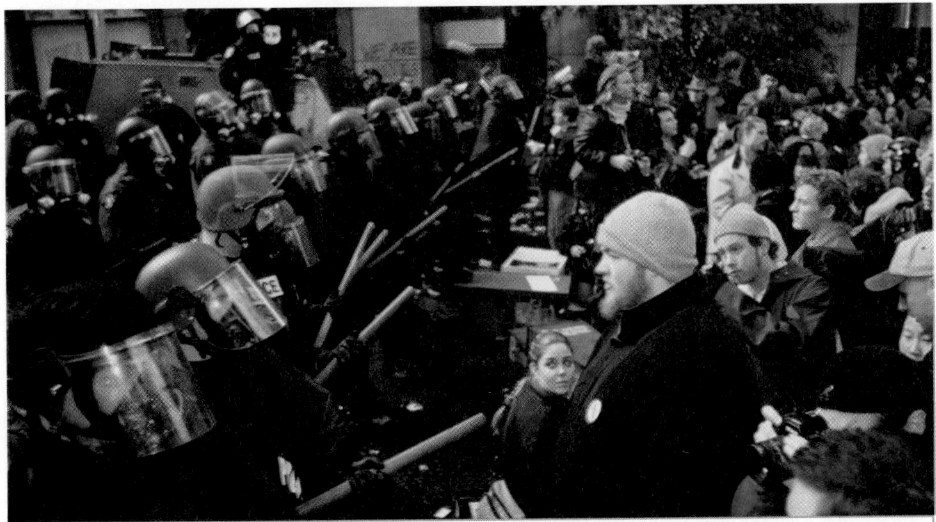

Demonstrators at the WTO meeting in Seattle in December 1999 began looting and rioting in the city's downtown area. Why do you think they felt that behavior was necessary? *Daniel Sheehan/Getty Images*

France," for details). While violent protests may give the antiglobalization effort a bad name, it is clear from the scale of the demonstrations that support for the cause goes beyond a core of anarchists. Large segments of the population in many countries believe that globalization has detrimental effects on living standards and the environment, and the media have often fed on this fear. In 2004 and 2005, for example, CNN news anchor Lou Dobbs ran a series that was highly critical of the trend by American companies to take advantage of globalization and "export jobs" overseas. Both theory and evidence suggest that many of these fears are exaggerated, but this may not have been communicated clearly and both politicians and businesspeople need to do more to counter these fears. Many protests against globalization are tapping into a general sense of loss at the passing of a world in which barriers of time and distance, and vast differences in economic institutions, political institutions, and the level of development of different nations, produced a world rich in the diversity of human cultures. This world is now passing into history. However, while the rich citizens of the developed world may have the luxury of mourning the fact that they can now see McDonald's restaurants and Starbucks coffeehouses on their vacations to exotic locations such as Thailand, fewer complaints are heard from the citizens of those countries, who welcome the higher living standards that progress brings.

GLOBALIZATION, JOBS, AND INCOME One concern frequently voiced by globalization opponents is that falling barriers to international trade destroy manufacturing jobs in wealthy advanced economies such as the United States and the United Kingdom. The critics argue that falling trade barriers allow firms to move manufacturing activities to countries where wage rates are much lower.[47] D.L. Bartlett and J.B. Steele, two journalists for the *Philadelphia Inquirer* who gained notoriety for their attacks on free trade, cite the case of Harwood Industries, a U.S. clothing manufacturer that closed its U.S. operations, where it paid workers $9 per hour, and shifted manufacturing to Honduras, where textile workers receive 48 cents per hour.[48] Because of moves such as this, argue Bartlett and Steele, the wage rates of poorer Americans have fallen significantly over the past quarter of a century.

Country FOCUS

Protesting Globalization in France

One night in August 1999, 10 men under the leadership of local sheep farmer and rural activist Jose Bove crept into the town of Millau in central France and vandalized a McDonald's restaurant under construction, causing an estimated $150,000 damage. These were no ordinary vandals, however, at least according to their supporters, for the "symbolic dismantling" of the McDonald's outlet had noble aims, or so it was claimed. The attack was initially presented as a protest against unfair American trade policies. The European Union had banned imports of hormone-treated beef from the United States, primarily because of fears that it might lead to health problems (although EU scientists had concluded there was no evidence of this). After a careful review, the World Trade Organization stated the EU ban was not allowed under trading rules that the EU and United States were party to, and that the EU would have to lift it or face retaliation. The EU refused to comply, so the U.S. government imposed a 100 percent tariff on imports of certain EU products, including French staples such as foie gras, mustard, and Roquefort cheese. On farms near Millau, Bove and others raised sheep whose milk was used to make Roquefort. They felt incensed by the American tariff and decided to vent their frustrations on McDonald's.

Bove and his compatriots were arrested and charged. They quickly became a focus of the antiglobalization movement in France that was protesting everything from a loss of national sovereignty and "unfair" trade policies that were trying to force hormone-treated beef on French consumers, to the invasion of French culture by alien American values, so aptly symbolized by McDonald's. Lionel Jospin, France's prime minister, called the cause of Jose Bove "just." Allowed to remain free pending his trial, Bove traveled to Seattle in December to protest against the World Trade Organization, where he was feted as a hero of the antiglobalization movement. In France, Bove's July 2000 trial drew some 40,000 supporters to the small town of Millau, where they camped outside the courthouse and waited for the verdict. Bove was found guilty and sentenced to three months in jail, far less than the maximum possible sentence of five years. His supporters wore T-shirts claiming, "The world is not merchandise, and neither am I."

About the same time in the Languedoc region of France, California winemaker Robert Mondavi had reached agreement with the mayor and council of the village of Aniane and regional authorities to turn 125 acres of wooded hillside belonging to the village into a vineyard. Mondavi planned to invest $7 million in the project and hoped to produce top-quality wine that would sell in Europe and the United States for $60 a bottle. However, local environmentalists objected to the plan, which they claimed would destroy the area's unique ecological heritage. Jose Bove, basking in sudden fame, offered his support to the opponents, and the protests started. In May 2001, the Socialist mayor who had approved the project was defeated in local elections in which the Mondavi project had become the major issue. He was replaced by a Communist, Manuel Diaz, who denounced the project as a capitalist plot designed to enrich wealthy U.S. shareholders at the cost of his villagers and the environment. Following Diaz's victory, Mondavi announced he would pull out of the project. A spokesman noted, "It's a huge waste, but there are clearly personal and political interests at play here that go way beyond us."

So are the French opposed to foreign investment? The experience of McDonald's and Mondavi seems to suggest so, as does the associated news coverage, but look closer and a different reality seems to emerge. McDonald's has more than 800 restaurants in France and continues to do very well there. In fact, France is one of the most profitable markets for McDonald's. France has long been one of the most favored locations for inward foreign direct investment, receiving over $100 billion of foreign investment between 2003 and 2005, more than any other European nation with the exception of Britain. American companies have always accounted for a significant percentage of this investment. Moreover, French enterprises have also been significant foreign investors; some 1,100 French multinationals account for around 8 percent of the global stock of foreign direct investment.

Sources: "Behind the Bluster," *The Economist,* May 26, 2001; "The French Farmers' Anti-global Hero," *The Economist,* July 8, 2000; C. Trueheart, "France's Golden Arch Enemy?" *Toronto Star,* July 1, 2000; J. Henley, "Grapes of Wrath Scare Off U.S. Firm," *The Economist,* May 18, 2001, p. 11; and United Nations, *World Investment Report, 2005* (New York and Geneva: United Nations, 2005).

In the last few years, the same fears have been applied to services, which have increasingly been outsourced to nations with lower labor costs. The popular feeling is that when corporations such as Dell, IBM, or Citigroup outsource service activities to lower-cost foreign suppliers—as all three have done—they are "exporting jobs" to low-wage nations and contributing to higher unemployment and lower living standards in their home nations (in this case, the United States). Some lawmakers in the

United States have responded by calling for legal barriers to job outsourcing.

By outsourcing its customer service call centers to India, Dell can reduce its cost structure and pass on the savings to their customers. *STR/AFP/Getty Images*

Supporters of globalization reply that critics of these trends miss the essential point about free trade—the benefits outweigh the costs.[49] They argue that free trade will result in countries specializing in the production of those goods and services that they can produce most efficiently, while importing goods and services that they cannot produce as efficiently. When a country embraces free trade, there is always some dislocation—lost textile jobs at Harwood Industries, or lost call center jobs at Dell—but the whole economy is better off as a result. According to this view, it makes little sense for the United States to produce textiles at home when they can be produced at a lower cost in Honduras or China (which, unlike Honduras, is a major source of U.S. textile imports). Importing textiles from China leads to lower prices for clothes in the United States, which enables consumers to spend more of their money on other items. At the same time, the increased income generated in China from textile exports increases income levels in that country, which helps the Chinese to purchase more products produced in the United States, such as pharmaceuticals from Amgen, Boeing jets, Intel-based computers, Microsoft software, and Cisco routers.

The same argument can be made to support the outsourcing of services to low-wage countries. By outsourcing its customer service call centers to India, Dell can reduce its cost structure, and thereby its prices for PCs. U.S. consumers benefit from this development. As prices for PCs fall, Americans can spend more of their money on other goods and services. Moreover, the increase in income levels in India allows Indians to purchase more U.S. goods and services, which helps to create jobs in the United States. In this manner, supporters of globalization argue that free trade benefits *all* countries that adhere to a free trade regime.

Nevertheless, some supporters of globalization concede that the wage rate enjoyed by unskilled workers in many advanced economies may have declined in recent years.[50] However, the evidence on this is decidedly mixed.[51] A U.S. Federal Reserve study found that in the seven years preceding 1996, the earnings of the best-paid 10 percent of U.S. workers rose in real terms by 0.6 percent annually while the earnings of the 10 percent at the bottom of the heap fell by 8 percent. In some areas, the fall was much greater.[52] Another study of long-term trends in income distribution concluded,

> Nationwide, from the late 1970s to the late 1990s, the average income of the lowest-income families fell by over 6 percent after adjustment for inflation, and the average real income of the middle fifth of families grew by about 5 percent. By contrast, the average real income of the highest-income fifth of families increased by over 30 percent.[53]

While globalization critics argue that the decline in unskilled wage rates is due to the migration of low-wage manufacturing jobs offshore and a corresponding reduction in demand for unskilled workers, supporters of globalization see a more complex picture. They maintain that the apparent decline in real wage rates of unskilled workers owes far more to a technology-induced shift within advanced economies away from jobs where the only qualification was a willingness to turn up for work every day and toward jobs that require significant education and skills. They point out that many advanced economies report a shortage of highly skilled workers and an excess supply of unskilled workers. Thus, growing income inequality is a result of the wages for skilled workers being bid up by the labor market and the wages for unskilled workers being discounted. If one agrees with this logic, a solution to the problem of declining incomes is to be found not in limiting free trade and globalization, but in increasing society's investment in education to reduce the supply of unskilled workers.[54]

Some research also suggests that the evidence of growing income inequality may be suspect. Robert Lerman of the Urban Institute believes that the finding of inequality is based on inappropriate calculations of wage rates. Reviewing the data using a different methodology, Lerman has found that far from income inequality increasing, an index of wage rate inequality for all workers actually fell by 5.5 percent between 1987 and 1994.[55] A 2002 study by the Organization for Economic Cooperation and Development, whose members include the 20 richest economies in the world, also suggests a more complex picture. The study noted that while the gap between the poorest and richest segments of society in some OECD countries had widened, this trend was by no means universal.[56] In the United States, for example, the OECD study found that while income inequality increased from the mid-1970s to the mid-1980s, it did not widen further in the next decade. The report also notes that in almost all countries, real income levels rose over the 20-year period looked at in the study, including the incomes of the poorest segment of most OECD societies. To add to the mixed research results, a 2002 U.S. study that included data from 1990 to 2000 concluded that during those years, falling unemployment rates brought gains to low-wage workers and fairly broad-based wage growth, especially in the latter half of the 1990s. The income of the worst-paid 10 percent of the population actually rose twice as fast as that of the average worker during 1998–2000.[57] If such trends continued into the 2000s—and they may not have—the argument that globalization leads to growing income inequality may lose some of its punch.

GLOBALIZATION, LABOR POLICIES, AND THE ENVIRONMENT A second source of concern is that free trade encourages firms from advanced nations to move manufacturing facilities to less developed countries that lack adequate regulations to protect labor and the environment from abuse by the unscrupulous.[58] Globalization critics often argue that adhering to labor and environmental regulations significantly increases the costs of manufacturing enterprises and puts them at a competitive disadvantage in the global marketplace vis-à-vis firms based in developing nations that do not have to comply with such regulations. Firms deal with this cost disadvantage, the theory goes, by moving their production facilities to nations that do not have such burdensome regulations or that fail to enforce the regulations they have.

If this were the case, one might expect free trade to lead to an increase in pollution and result in firms from advanced nations exploiting the labor of less developed nations.[59] This argument was used repeatedly by those who opposed the 1994 formation of the North American Free Trade Agreement (NAFTA) between Canada, Mexico, and the United States. They painted a picture of U.S. manufacturing firms moving to Mexico in droves so that they would be free to pollute the environment, employ child labor, and ignore workplace safety and health issues, all in the name of higher profits.[60]

Supporters of free trade and greater globalization express doubts about this scenario. They argue that tougher environmental regulations and stricter labor standards go hand in hand with economic progress.[61] In general, as countries get richer, they enact tougher environmental and labor regulations.[62] Because free trade enables developing countries to increase their economic growth rates and become richer, this should lead to tougher environmental and labor laws. In this view, the critics of free trade have got it backward—free trade does not lead to more pollution and labor exploitation, it leads to less. By creating wealth and incentives for enterprises to produce technological innovations, the free market system and free trade could make it easier for the world to cope with pollution and population growth. Indeed, while pollution levels are rising

Income Levels and Environmental Pollution

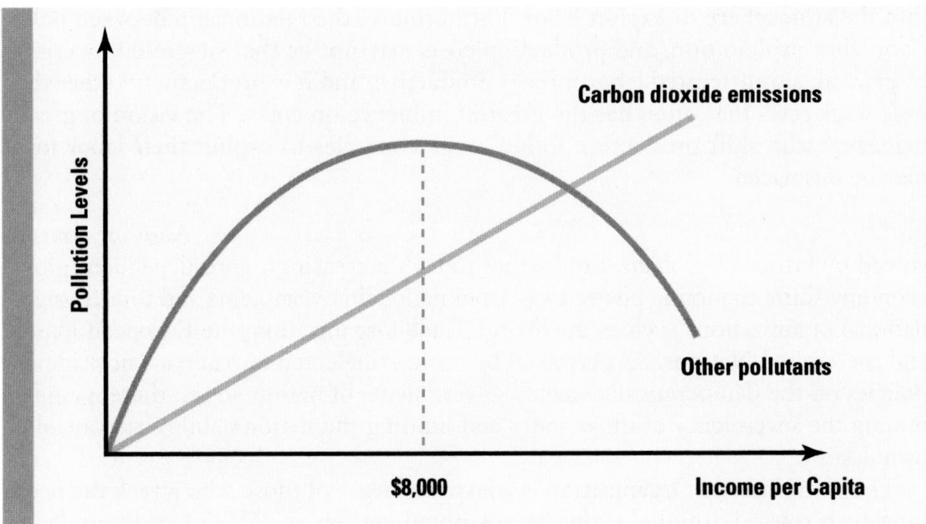

in the world's poorer countries, they have been falling in developed nations. In the United States, for example, the concentration of carbon monoxide and sulphur dioxide pollutants in the atmosphere decreased by 60 percent between 1978 and 1997, while lead concentrations decreased by 98 percent—and these reductions have occurred against a background of sustained economic expansion.[63]

A number of econometric studies have found consistent evidence of a hump-shaped relationship between income levels and pollution levels (see Figure 1.5).[64] As an economy grows and income levels rise, initially pollution levels also rise. However, past some point, rising income levels lead to demands for greater environmental protection, and pollution levels then fall. A seminal study by Grossman and Krueger found that the turning point generally occurred before per capita income levels reached $8,000.[65]

While the hump-shaped relationship depicted in Figure 1.5 seems to hold across a wide range of pollutants—from sulphur dioxide to lead concentrations and water quality—carbon dioxide emissions are an important exception, rising steadily with higher income levels. Given that increased atmospheric carbon dioxide concentrations are implicated in global warming, this should be a concern. The solution to the problem, however, is probably not to roll back the trade liberalization efforts that have fostered economic growth and globalization, but to get the nations of the world to agree to tougher standards on limiting carbon emissions. Although UN-sponsored talks have had this as a central aim since the 1992 Earth Summit in Rio de Janeiro, there has been little success in moving toward the ambitious goals for reducing carbon emissions laid down in the Earth Summit and subsequent talks in Kyoto, Japan, in part because the largest emitter of carbon dioxide, the United States, has refused to sign global agreements that it claims would unreasonably retard economic growth.

Supporters of free trade also point out that it is possible to tie free trade agreements to the implementation of tougher environmental and labor laws in less developed countries. NAFTA, for example, was passed only after side agreements had been negotiated that committed Mexico to tougher enforcement of environmental protection regulations. Thus, supporters of free trade argue that factories based in Mexico are now cleaner than they would have been without the passage of NAFTA.[66]

They also argue that business firms are not the amoral organizations that critics suggest. While there may be some rotten apples, most business enterprises are staffed by managers who are committed to behave in an ethical manner and would be unlikely to move production offshore just so they could pump more pollution into the atmosphere or exploit labor. Furthermore, the relationship between pollution, labor exploitation, and production costs may not be that suggested by critics. In general, a well-treated labor force is productive, and it is productivity rather than base wage rates that often has the greatest influence on costs. The vision of greedy managers who shift production to low-wage countries to exploit their labor force may be misplaced.

GLOBALIZATION AND NATIONAL SOVEREIGNTY Another concern voiced by critics of globalization is that today's increasingly interdependent global economy shifts economic power away from national governments and toward supranational organizations such as the World Trade Organization, the European Union, and the United Nations. As perceived by critics, unelected bureaucrats now impose policies on the democratically elected governments of nation-states, thereby undermining the sovereignty of those states and limiting the nation's ability to control its own destiny.[67]

The World Trade Organization is a favorite target of those who attack the headlong rush toward a global economy. As noted earlier, the WTO was founded in 1994 to police the world trading system established by the General Agreement on Tariffs and Trade. The WTO arbitrates trade disputes between the 149 states that are signatories to the GATT. The arbitration panel can issue a ruling instructing a member state to change trade policies that violate GATT regulations. If the violator refuses to comply with the ruling, the WTO allows other states to impose appropriate trade sanctions on the transgressor. As a result, according to one prominent critic, U.S. environmentalist, consumer rights advocate, and presidential candidate Ralph Nader:

> Under the new system, many decisions that affect billions of people are no longer made by local or national governments but instead, if challenged by any WTO member nation, would be deferred to a group of unelected bureaucrats sitting behind closed doors in Geneva (which is where the headquarters of the WTO are located). The bureaucrats can decide whether or not people in California can prevent the destruction of the last virgin forests or determine if carcinogenic pesticides can be banned from their foods; or whether European countries have the right to ban dangerous biotech hormones in meat. . . . At risk is the very basis of democracy and accountable decision making.[68]

In contrast to Nader's rhetoric, many economists and politicians maintain that the power of supranational organizations such as the WTO is limited to what nation-states collectively agree to grant. They argue that bodies such as the United Nations and the WTO exist to serve the collective interests of member states, not to subvert those interests. Supporters of supranational organizations point out that the power of these bodies rests largely on their ability to persuade member states to follow a certain action. If these bodies fail to serve the collective interests of member states, those states will withdraw their support and the supranational organization will quickly collapse. In this view, real power still resides with individual nation-states, not supranational organizations.

GLOBALIZATION AND THE WORLD'S POOR Critics of globalization argue that despite the supposed benefits associated with free trade and investment, over the past hundred years or so the gap between the rich and poor nations of the world has gotten wider. In 1870, the average income per capita in the world's 17 richest nations was 2.4 times that of all other countries. In 1990, the same group was 4.5 times as rich as the rest.[69] While recent history has shown that some of the world's poorer nations are capable of rapid periods of economic growth— witness the transformation that has occurred in some Southeast Asian nations such as South Korea, Thailand, and Malaysia—there appear to be strong forces for stagnation among the world's poorest nations. A quarter of the countries with a GDP per capita of less than $1,000 in 1960 had growth rates of less than zero from 1960 to 1995, and a third had growth rates of less than 0.05 percent.[70] Critics argue that if globalization is such a positive development, this divergence between the rich and poor should not have occurred.

Although the reasons for economic stagnation vary, several factors stand out, none of which have anything to do with free trade or globalization.[71] Many of the world's poorest countries have suffered from totalitarian governments, economic policies that destroyed wealth rather than facilitated its creation, endemic corruption, scant protection for property rights, and war. Such factors help explain why countries such as Afghanistan, Cambodia, Cuba, Haiti, Iraq, Libya, Nigeria, Sudan, Vietnam, and Zaire have failed to improve the economic lot of their citizens during recent decades. A complicating factor is the rapidly expanding populations in many of these countries. Without a major change in government, population growth may exacerbate their problems. Promoters of free trade argue that the best way for these countries to improve their lot is to lower their barriers to free trade and investment and to implement economic policies based on free market economics.[72]

Many of the world's poorer nations are being held back by large debt burdens. Of particular concern are the 40 or so "highly indebted poorer countries" (HIPCs), which are home to some 700 million people. Among these countries, the average government debt burden is equivalent to 85 percent of the value of the economy, as measured by gross domestic product, and the annual costs of serving government debt consumes 15 percent of the country's export earnings.[73] Servicing such a heavy debt load leaves the governments of these countries with little left to invest in important public infrastructure projects, such as education, health care, roads, and power. The result is the HIPCs are trapped in a cycle of poverty and debt that inhibits economic development. Free trade alone, some argue, is a necessary but not sufficient prerequisite to help these countries bootstrap themselves out of poverty. Instead, large-scale debt relief is needed for the world's poorest nations to give them the opportunity to restructure their economies and start the long climb toward prosperity. Supporters of debt relief also argue that new democratic governments in poor

Even as India makes strides towards economic development, it continues to carry a high budget deficit that cannot meet the needs of its soaring population. *Dr. Parvinder Sethi/DIL*

Another Perspective

A Question of Debt in Emerging, Poor Economies

The Group of Eight Nations (G-8)—United States, Russia, France, Japan, Germany, Italy, Canada, and the United Kingdom—canceled about $60 billion of debt owed them in 2005 by the world's poorest countries, known as the highly indebted poor countries, or HIPCs. However, in 2006, emerging lenders such as China, India, Brazil, and South Korea are offering preferential loans and export credits to these same poor nations. The emerging lenders want to sell infrastructure-related exports into the HIPCs. China has announced $10 billion in these loans and credits.

These loans and credits don't sit too well with the G-8 finance ministers who have just issued debt relief to these same poor countries. They take the position that it is imperative to prevent the buildup of unsustainable debt in HIPCs. A World Bank study found that eight former HIPCs—including Uganda, Bolivia, Nicaragua. and Ethiopia—are again facing debt problems. The challenge continues: Will this continued debt activity help or hinder HIPC economies? (Michael. Phillips, "G8 Warns China about Loans to Poorest Nations," *The Wall Street Journal,* June 12, 2006, http://online.wsj.com/article/SB115005845957077212.html)

nations should not be forced to honor debts that were incurred and mismanaged long ago by their corrupt and dictatorial predecessors.

In the late 1990s, a debt relief movement began to gain ground among the political establishment in the world's richer nations.[74] Fueled by high-profile endorsements from Irish rock star Bono (who has been a tireless and increasingly effective advocate for debt relief), Pope John Paul II, the Dalai Lama, and influential Harvard economist Jeffrey Sachs, the debt relief movement was instrumental in persuading the United States to enact legislation in 2000 that provided $435 million in debt relief for HIPCs. More important perhaps, the United States also backed an IMF plan to sell some of its gold reserves and use the proceeds to help with debt relief. The IMF and World Bank have now picked up the banner and have embarked on a systematic debt relief program (see Another Perspective box at left).

For such a program to have a lasting effect, however, debt relief must be matched by wise investment in public projects that boost economic growth (such as education) and by the adoption of economic policies that facilitate investment and trade. The rich nations of the world also can help by reducing barriers to the importation of products from the world's poorer nations, particularly tariffs on imports of agricultural products and textiles. High tariff barriers and other impediments to trade make it difficult for poor countries to export more of their agricultural production. The World Trade Organization has estimated that if the developed nations of the world eradicated subsidies to their agricultural producers and removed tariff barriers to trade in agriculture this would raise global economic welfare by $128 billion, with $30 billion of that going to developing nations, many of which are highly indebted. The faster growth associated with expanded trade in agriculture could reduce the number of people living in poverty by as much as 13 percent by 2015, according to the WTO.[75]

Debt relief is not new; it has been tried before.[76] Too often in the past, however, the short-term benefits were squandered by corrupt governments who used their newfound financial freedom to make unproductive investments in military infrastructure or grandiose projects that did little to foster long-run economic development. Developed nations contributed to past failures by refusing to open their markets to the products of poor nations. If such a scenario can be avoided this time, the entire world will benefit.

Managing in the Global Marketplace

LEARNING OBJECTIVE 5
Appreciate how the process of globalization is creating opportunities and challenges for business managers.

Much of this book is concerned with the challenges of managing in an international business. An **international business** is any firm that engages in international trade or investment. A firm does not have to become a multinational enterprise, investing directly in operations in other countries, to engage in international business, although multinational enterprises are international businesses. All a firm has to do is export or import products from other countries. As the world shifts toward a truly integrated global economy, more firms, both large and small, are becoming international businesses. What does this shift toward a global economy mean for managers within an international business?

International Business
Any firm that engages in international trade or investment.

As their organizations increasingly engage in cross-border trade and investment, managers need to recognize that the task of managing an international business differs from that of managing a purely domestic business in many ways. At the most fundamental level, the differences arise from the simple fact that countries are different. Countries differ in their cultures, political systems, economic systems, legal systems, and levels of economic development. Despite all the talk about the emerging global village, and despite the trend toward globalization of markets and production, as we shall see in this book, many of these differences are very profound and enduring.

Differences between countries require that an international business vary its practices country by country. Marketing a product in Brazil may require a different approach from marketing the product in Germany; managing U.S. workers might require different skills than managing Japanese workers; maintaining close relations with a particular level of government may be very important in Mexico and irrelevant in Great Britain; the business strategy pursued in Canada might not work in South Korea; and so on. Managers in an international business must not only be sensitive to these differences, but they must also adopt the appropriate policies and strategies for coping with them. Much of this book is devoted to explaining the sources of these differences and the methods for successfully coping with them.

A further way in which international business differs from domestic business is the greater complexity of managing an international business. In addition to the problems that arise from the differences between countries, a manager in an international business is confronted with a range of other issues that the manager in a domestic business never confronts. The managers of an international business must decide where in the world to site production activities to minimize costs and to maximize value added. They must decide whether it is ethical to adhere to the lower labor and environmental standards found in many less-developed nations. Then they must decide how best to coordinate and control globally dispersed production activities (which, as we shall see later in the book, is not a trivial problem). The managers in an international business also must decide which foreign markets to enter and which to avoid. They must choose the appropriate mode for entering a particular foreign country. Is it best to export its product to the foreign country? Should the firm allow a local company to produce its product under license in that country? Should the firm enter into a joint venture with a local firm to produce its product in that country? Or should the firm set up a wholly owned subsidiary to serve the market in that country? As we shall see, the choice of entry mode is critical because it has major implications for the long-term health of the firm.

Conducting business transactions across national borders requires understanding the rules governing the international trading and investment system. Managers in an international business must also deal with government restrictions on international trade and investment. They must find ways to work within the limits imposed by specific governmental interventions. As this book explains, even though many governments are nominally committed to free trade, they often intervene to regulate cross-border trade and investment. Managers within international businesses must develop strategies and policies for dealing with such interventions.

Cross-border transactions also require that money be converted from the firm's home currency into a foreign currency and vice versa. Because currency exchange rates vary in response to changing economic conditions, managers in an international business must develop policies for dealing with exchange rate movements. A firm that adopts a wrong policy can lose large amounts of money, whereas one that adopts the right policy can increase the profitability of its international transactions.

In sum, managing an international business is different from managing a purely domestic business for at least four reasons: (1) countries are different, (2) the range of problems confronted by a manager in an international business is wider and the problems themselves more complex than those confronted by a manager in a domestic business, (3) an international business must find ways to work within the limits imposed by government intervention in the international trade and investment system, and (4) international transactions involve converting money into different currencies.

In this book we examine all these issues in depth, paying close attention to the different strategies and policies that managers pursue to deal with the various challenges created when a firm becomes an international business. Chapters 2 and 3 explore how countries differ from each other with regard to their political, economic, legal, and cultural institutions. Chapter 4 takes a detailed look at the ethical issues that arise in international business. Chapters 5 to 8 look at the international trade and investment environment within which international businesses must operate. Chapters 9 and 10 review the international monetary system. These chapters focus on the nature of the foreign exchange market and the emerging global monetary system. Chapters 11 and 12 explore the strategy of international businesses. Chapters 13 to 16 look at the management of various functional operations within an international business, including production, marketing, and human relations. By the time you complete this book, you should have a good grasp of the issues that managers working within international business have to grapple with on a daily basis, and you should be familiar with the range of strategies and operating policies available to compete more effectively in today's rapidly emerging global economy.

Key Terms

globalization, p. 7

globalization of markets, p. 7

globalization of production, p. 8

factors of production, p. 8

General Agreement on Tariffs and Trade (GATT), p. 9

World Trade Organization, p. 9

International Monetary Fund, p. 10

World Bank, p. 10

United Nations, p. 10

international trade, p. 11

foreign direct investment (FDI), p. 11

Moore's Law, p. 14

stock of foreign direct investment, p. 20

multinational enterprise (MNE), p. 21

international business, p. 34

Summary

This chapter sets the scene for the rest of the book. It shows how the world economy is becoming more global and reviews the main drivers of globalization, arguing that they seem to be thrusting nation-states toward a more tightly integrated global economy. We looked at how the nature of international business is changing in response to the changing global economy; we discussed some concerns raised by rapid globalization; and we reviewed implications of rapid globalization for individual managers. The chapter made the following points:

1. Over the past two decades, we have witnessed the globalization of markets and production.
2. The globalization of markets implies that national markets are merging into one huge marketplace. However, it is important not to push this view too far.
3. The globalization of production implies that firms are basing individual productive activities at the optimal world locations for the particular activities. As a consequence, it is increasingly irrelevant to talk about American products, Japanese products, or German products, since these are being replaced by "global" products.
4. Two factors seem to underlie the trend toward globalization: declining trade barriers and changes in communication, information, and transportation technologies.
5. Since the end of World War II, barriers to the free flow of goods, services, and capital have

been lowered significantly. More than anything else, this has facilitated the trend toward the globalization of production and has enabled firms to view the world as a single market.

6. As a consequence of the globalization of production and markets, in the last decade world trade has grown faster than world output, foreign direct investment has surged, imports have penetrated more deeply into the world's industrial nations, and competitive pressures have increased in industry after industry.
7. The development of the microprocessor and related developments in communication and information processing technology have helped firms link their worldwide operations into sophisticated information networks. Jet air travel, by shrinking travel time, has also helped to link the worldwide operations of international businesses. These changes have enabled firms to achieve tight coordination of their worldwide operations and to view the world as a single market.
8. In the 1960s, the U.S. economy was dominant in the world, U.S. firms accounted for most of the foreign direct investment in the world economy, U.S. firms dominated the list of large multinationals, and roughly half the world—the centrally planned economies of the Communist world—was closed to Western businesses.
9. By the mid-1990s, the U.S. share of world output had been cut in half, with major shares now being accounted for by Western European and Southeast Asian economies. The U.S. share of worldwide foreign direct investment had also fallen, by about two-thirds. U.S. multinationals were now facing competition from a large number of Japanese and European multinationals. In addition, the emergence of mini-multinationals was noted.
10. One of the most dramatic developments of the past 20 years has been the collapse of communism in Eastern Europe, which has created enormous long-run opportunities for international businesses. In addition, the move toward free market economies in China and Latin America is creating opportunities (and threats) for Western international businesses.
11. The benefits and costs of the emerging global economy are being hotly debated among businesspeople, economists, and politicians. The debate focuses on the impact of globalization on jobs, wages, the environment, working conditions, and national sovereignty.
12. Managing an international business is different from managing a domestic business for at least four reasons: (*i*) countries are different, (*ii*) the range of problems confronted by a manager in an international business is wider and the problems themselves more complex than those confronted by a manager in a domestic business, (*iii*) managers in an international business must find ways to work within the limits imposed by governments' intervention in the international trade and investment system, and (*iv*) international transactions involve converting money into different currencies.

Critical Thinking and Discussion Questions

1. Describe the shifts in the world economy over the past 30 years. What are the implications of these shifts for international businesses based in Great Britain? North America? Hong Kong?
2. "The study of international business is fine if you are going to work in a large multinational enterprise, but it has no relevance for individuals who are going to work in small firms." Evaluate this statement.
3. How have changes in technology contributed to the globalization of markets and production? Would the globalization of production and markets have been possible without these technological changes?
4. "Ultimately, the study of international business is no different from the study of domestic business. Thus, there is no point in having a separate course on international business." Evaluate this statement.
5. How might the Internet and the associated World Wide Web affect international business activity and the globalization of the world economy?
6. If current trends continue, China may be the world's largest economy by 2020. Discuss the possible implications of such a development for (*a*) the world trading system, (*b*) the world monetary system, (*c*) the business strategy of

today's European and U.S.-based global corporations, and (*d*) global commodity prices.

7. Read the Country Focus in this chapter on the Ecuadorean rose industry, then answer the following questions:
   a. How has participation in the international rose trade helped Ecuador's economy and its people? How has the rise of Ecuador as a center for rose growing benefited consumers in developed nations who purchase the roses? What do the answers to these questions tell you about the benefits of international trade?
   b. Why do you think that Ecuador's rose industry only began to take off 20 years ago? Why do you think it has grown so rapidly?
   c. To what extent can the alleged health problems among workers in Ecuador's rose industry be laid at the feet of consumers in the developed world and their desire for perfect Valentine's Day roses?
   d. Do you think governments in the developed world should place trade sanctions on Ecuador roses if reports of health issues among Ecuadorean rose workers are verified? What else might they do to improve the situation in Ecuador?

Research Task  http://globalEDGE.msu.edu

Use the globalEDGE site (http://globalEDGE.msu.edu/) to complete the following exercises:

1. Your company has developed a new product that is expected to achieve high penetration rates in all the countries in which it is introduced, regardless of the average income status of the local population. Considering the costs of the product launch, the management team has decided to initially introduce the product only in countries that have a sizeable population base. Using the *Population Reference Bureau* as a resource, you are required to prepare a preliminary report with the top 10 countries of the world in terms of population size. Since growth opportunities are another major concern, the average population growth rates should be listed for management's consideration.
2. Being sensitive to appropriate behavior in public is an important element of business relationships and developing an internal handbook on cultural sensitivity for your firm. Given that your organization is implementing a strategy that focuses on developing economies, learning more about the countries in which your firm has operations is imperative. By identifying and using a resource that explains in detail proper *business customs and etiquette*, prepare a brief report that outlines unacceptable public conduct in the three main countries your firm has facilities: Colombia, India, and Malaysia.

closing case

The Globalization of Health Care

Conventional wisdom holds that health care is one of the industries least vulnerable to dislocation from globalization. After all, like many service businesses, health care is delivered where it is purchased, right? If an American goes to a hospital for an MRI scan, won't that scan be read by a local radiologist? And if the MRI scan shows that surgery is required, surely the surgery will be done at a local hospital in the United States. Until recently, this was true, but we are now witnessing the beginnings of globalization in this traditionally most local of industries.

Consider the MRI scan: The United States has a shortage of radiologists, the doctors who specialize in reading and interpreting diagnostic medical images, including X-rays, CT scans, MRI scans, and ultrasounds. Demand for radiologists is reportedly growing twice as fast as the rate at which medical schools are graduating radiologists with the skills and qualifications required to read medical images. This imbalance between supply and demand means that radiologists are expensive; an American radiologist can earn as much as $350,000 a year. In 2002, an Indian radiologist working at the prestigious Massachusetts General Hospital, Dr. Sanjay Saini, thought he had found a clever way to deal with the shortage and expense—beam images over the Internet to India where they could be interpreted by radiologists. This would reduce the workload on America's radiologists and also cut costs. A radiologist in India might earn one-tenth of his or her U.S. counterpart. Plus, because India is on the opposite side of the globe, the images could be interpreted while it was nighttime in the United States and be ready for the attending physician when he or she arrived for work the following morning.

As for the surgery, here too we are witnessing the beginnings of an outsourcing trend. In October 2004, for example, Howard Staab, a 53-year-old uninsured self-employed carpenter from North Carolina had surgery to repair a leaking heart valve—in India! Mr. Staab flew to New Delhi, had the operation, and afterward toured the Taj Mahal, the price of which was bundled with that of the surgery. The cost, including airfare, totaled $10,000. If Mr. Staab's surgery had been performed in the United States, the cost would have been $60,000 and there would have been no visit to the Taj Mahal.

Howard Staab is not alone. Some 170,000 foreigners visited India in 2004 for medical treatments. That number is projected to rise by 15 percent a year for the next several years. According to the management consultancy McKinsey & Co., medical tourism (overseas trips to have medical procedures performed) could be a $2.3 billion industry in India by 2012. In another example, after years of living in pain, Robert Beeney, a 64-year-old from San Francisco, was advised to get his hip joint replaced, but after doing some research on the Internet, Mr. Beeney elected instead for joint resurfacing, which was not covered by his insurance. Instead of going to a nearby hospital, he flew to Hyderabad in southern India and had the surgery done for $6,600, a fraction of the $25,000 the procedure would have cost in the United States.

Mr. Beeney had his surgery performed at a branch of the Apollo hospital chain. Apollo, which was founded by Dr. Prathap C. Reddy, a surgeon trained at Massachusetts General Hospital, runs a chain of 18 state-of-the-art hospitals throughout Asia. Between 2001 and 2004, Apollo treated 43,000 foreigners, mainly from nations in Southeast Asia and the Persian Gulf, although a growing number are from Western Europe and North America. In 2004, 7 percent of its revenue came from foreigners. With 200 U.S.-trained doctors on his staff, Dr. Reddy reckons that he can offer medical care equivalent to that in the United States, but at a fraction of the cost. Nor is he alone; Mr. Staab's surgery was performed by Dr. Naresh Trehan, a cardiac surgeon who was trained at New York University School of Medicine and worked there for a decade. Dr. Trehan returned home to India and opened his own cardiac hospital, which now conducts 4,000 heart surgeries a year, with a 0.8 percent mortality rate and 0.3 percent infection rate, on par with the best of the world's hospitals.

So will demand for American health services soon collapse as work moves offshore to places like India? That seems unlikely. Regulations, personal preferences, and practical considerations mean that the majority of health services will always be performed in the country where the patient resides. Consider the MRI scan: To safeguard patient care, U.S. regulations require that a radiologist be licensed in the state where the image was made and that he or she be certified by the hospital where care is being given. Given that not many radiologists in India have these qualifications, no more than a small fraction of images can be interpreted overseas. Another complication is that the U.S. government-sponsored medical insurance program, Medicare, will not pay for services done outside of the country. Nor will many private insurance plans. . . or not yet anyway. Moreover, most people would prefer to have care delivered close to home, and only in exceptional cases, such as when the procedure is not covered by their medical plan, are they likely to consider the foreign option. Still, most experts believe that the trends now in place will continue. Given that health care costs in America are the highest in the world, it seems likely that increasingly, a small but significant percentage of medical service will be performed in a country that is different from the one where the patient resides. The trend will certainly get a big boost if insurance companies start to offer enrollees the option of getting treatment abroad for expensive surgeries, as some are rumored to be considering.

Sources: G. Colvin, "Think Your Job Can't Be Sent to India?" *Fortune,* December 13, 2004, p. 80; A. Pollack, "Who's Reading Your X-Ray," *The New York Times,* November 16, 2003, pp. 1, 9; S. Rai, "Low Costs Lure Foreigners to India for Medical Care," *The New York Times,* April 7, 2005, p. C6; J. Solomon, "Traveling Cure: India's New Coup in Outsourcing," *The Wall Street Journal,* April 26, 2004, p. A1; J. Slater, "Increasing Doses in India," *Far Eastern Economic Review,* February 19, 2004, pp. 32–35; and U. Kher, "Outsourcing Your Heart," *Time,* May 29, 2006, pp. 44–47.

Case Discussion Questions

1. A decade ago the idea that medical procedures might move offshore was unthinkable. Today it is a reality. What trends have facilitated this process?
2. Is the globalization of health care good or bad for patients?
3. Is the globalization of health care good or bad for the American economy?
4. Who might benefit from the globalization of health care? Who might lose?
5. Do you think that the U.S. government should restrict the outsourcing of medical procedures to developing nations? What if physicians in those countries are certified by U.S. medical institutions?

Pedro Lara/AP Wide World

part 2 Country Differences

LEARNING OBJECTIVES

1. Understand how the Political systems of countries differ.
2. Understand how the economic systems of countries differ.
3. Understand how the legal systems of countries differ.
4. Be able to explain what determines the level of economic development of a nation.
5. Discuss the macro-political and economic changes taking place worldwide.
6. Describe how transition economies are moving toward market-based systems.
7. Articulate the implications for management practice of national differences in political economy.

chapter 

National Differences in Political Economy

Chavez's Venezuela

opening case

Hugo Chavez, a former military officer who was once jailed for engineering a failed coup attempt, was elected president of Venezuela in 1998. Chavez, a self-styled democratic socialist, won the presidential election by campaigning against corruption, economic mismanagement, and the "harsh realities" of global capitalism. When he took office in February 1999, Chavez claimed that he had inherited the worst economic situation in the country's recent history. He wasn't far off the mark. A collapse in the price of oil, which accounted for 70 percent of the country's exports, left Venezuela with a large budget deficit and forced the economy into a deep recession.

Soon after taking office, Chavez proceeded to try to consolidate his hold over the apparatus of government. A constituent assembly, dominated by Chavez followers, drafted a new constitution that strengthened the powers of the presidency and allowed Chavez (if reelected) to stay in office until 2013. Subsequently, the national congress, which was controlled by Chavez supporters, approved a measure allowing the government to remove and appoint Supreme Court justices, effectively increasing Chavez's hold over the judiciary. Chavez also extended government control over the media. By 2005, Freedom House, which annually assesses political and civil liberties worldwide, concluded that Venezuela was only "partly free" and that freedoms were being progressively curtailed.

On the economic front, things remained rough. The economy shrank by 9 percent in 2002 and another 8 percent in 2003. Unemployment remained persistently high at 15 to 17 percent and the poverty rate rose to more than 50 percent of the population. A 2003 study by the World Bank concluded that Venezuela was one of the most regulated economies in the world and that state controls over business activities gave public officials ample opportunities to enrich themselves by demanding bribes in return for permission to expand operations, or enter new lines of business. Indeed, despite Chavez's anticorruption rhetoric, Transparency International, which ranks the world's nations according to the extent of public corruption, has noted that corruption has increased under Chavez. In 2005, Transparency International ranked Venezuela 130 out of 158 nations, down from 114 a year earlier. Consistent with his socialist rhetoric, Chavez has progressively taken various enterprises into state ownership and has required that other enterprises be restructured as "workers' cooperatives" in return for government loans. In addition, the government has begun to seize large rural farms and ranches that Chavez claims are not sufficiently productive, turning them into state-owned cooperatives.

In 2004, the world oil market bailed Chavez out of mounting economic difficulties. Oil prices started to surge from the low $20s, reaching $70 a barrel by the spring of 2006, and Venezuela, the world's fifth-largest producer, started to reap a bonanza. On the back of surging oil exports, the economy grew by 18 percent in 2004 and another 9 percent in 2005. Chavez's reaction to the oil price increase was to extend government control over foreign oil producers doing business in Venezuela, which he accused of making outsized profits at the expense of a poor nation. In 2005, he announced an increase in the royalties that the government would take from oil sales from 1 percent to 30 percent, and he increased the tax rate on sales from 34 to 50 percent. In April 2006, he announced plans to reduce the stakes held by foreign companies in oil projects in the Orinoco regions and to give the state-run oil company, Petroleos de Venezuela SA, a majority position.

Sources: D. Luhnow and P. Millard, "Chavez Plans to Take More Control of Oil away from Foreign Firms," *The Wall Street Journal*, April 24, 2006, p. A1; R. Gallego, "Chavez's Agenda Takes Shape," *The Wall Street Journal*, December 27, 2005, p. A12; "The Sickly Stench of Corruption: Venezuela," *The Economist*, April 1, 2006, p. 50; and "Chavez Squeezes the Oil Firms," *The Economist*, November 12, 2005, p. 61.

Introduction

International business is much more complicated than domestic business because countries differ in many ways. Countries have different political, economic, and legal systems. Cultural practices can vary dramatically, as can the education and skill level of the population, and countries are at different stages of economic development. All these differences can and do have major implications for the practice of international business. They have a profound impact on the benefits, costs, and risks associated with doing business in different countries; the way in which operations in different countries should be managed; and the strategy international firms should pursue in different countries. A main function of this chapter and the next is to develop an awareness of and appreciation for the significance of country differences in political systems, economic systems, legal systems, and national culture. Another function of the two chapters is to describe how the political, economic, legal, and cultural systems of many of the world's nation-states are evolving and to draw out the implications of these changes for the practice of international business.

The opening case illustrates some of the issues covered in this chapter. Under the leadership of Hugo Chavez, Venezuela has shifted to the left. The state has become more involved in business activity, regulation has expanded, and private enterprise is on the defensive, which has hurt economic growth. Corruption, long a problem in the country, has if anything gotten worse, despite the fact that Chavez originally came to power running on an anticorruption platform. As we shall see in this chapter, corruption also tends to depress economic growth. Moreover, Chavez has unilaterally rewritten the contracts with foreign oil companies that have invested in Venezuela, raising royalty rates and taxes and demanding that the state-run oil company be given a majority stake in all oil projects. While this may increase the government's take in the short run, if foreign enterprises respond by reducing their investments in Venezuela, as some are now doing, this could further constrain the country's economic growth down the road.

This chapter focuses on how the political, economic, and legal systems of countries differ. Collectively we refer to these systems as constituting the political economy of a country. We use the term **political economy** to stress that the political, economic, and legal systems of a country are interdependent; they interact and influence each other, and in doing so they affect the level of economic well-being. In addition to reviewing these systems, we also explore how differences in political economy influence the benefits, costs, and risks associated with doing business in different countries, and how they affect management practice and strategy. In the next chapter, we will look at how differences in culture influence the practice of international business. As noted, the political economy and culture of a nation are not independent of each other. As will become apparent in Chapter 3, culture can exert an impact on political economy—on political, economic, and legal systems in a nation—and the converse can also hold true.

Political Economy
The interdependent combination of a country's political, economic, and legal systems.

Political Systems

LEARNING OBJECTIVE 1
Understand how the political systems of countries differ.

The political system of a country shapes its economic and legal systems.[1] As such, we need to understand the nature of different political systems before discussing economic and legal systems. By **political system** we mean the system of government in a nation. Political systems can be assessed according to two dimensions. The first is the degree to which they emphasize collectivism as opposed to individualism. The second is the degree to which they are democratic or totalitarian. These dimensions are interrelated; systems that emphasize collectivism tend toward totalitarian, whereas those that place a high value on individualism tend to be democratic. However, a large gray area exists in the middle. It is possible to have democratic societies that emphasize a mix of collectivism and individualism. Similarly, it is possible to have totalitarian societies that are not collectivist.

Political System
The system of government in any nation.

COLLECTIVISM AND INDIVIDUALISM

Collectivism refers to a political system that stresses the primacy of collective goals over individual goals.[2] When collectivism is emphasized, the needs of society as a whole are generally viewed as being more important than individual freedoms. In such circumstances, an individual's right to do something may be restricted on the grounds that it runs counter to "the good of society" or to "the common good." Advocacy of collectivism can be traced to the ancient Greek philosopher Plato (427–347 BC), who in *The Republic* argued that individual rights should be sacrificed for the good of the majority and that property

Collectivism
A political system that stresses the primacy of collective goals over individual goals.

should be owned in common. Plato did not equate collectivism with equality; he believed that society should be stratified into classes, with those best suited to rule (which for Plato, naturally, were philosophers and soldiers) administering society for the benefit of all. In modern times, the collectivist mantle has been picked up by socialists.

Socialism
The political system that believes in state ownership of a country's means of production, distribution, and exchange so that all can benefit.

Socialism Modern **socialists** trace their intellectual roots to Karl Marx (1818–83), although socialist thought clearly predates Marx (elements of it can be traced to Plato). Marx argued that the few benefit at the expense of the many in a capitalist society where individual freedoms are not restricted. While successful capitalists accumulate considerable wealth, Marx postulated that the wages earned by the majority of workers in a capitalist society would be forced down to subsistence levels. He argued that capitalists expropriate for their own use the value created by workers, while paying workers only subsistence wages in return. According to Marx, the pay of workers does not reflect the full value of their labor. To correct this perceived wrong, Marx advocated state ownership of the basic means of production, distribution, and exchange (i.e., businesses). His logic was that if the state owned the means of production, the state could ensure that workers were fully compensated for their labor. Thus, the idea is to manage state-owned enterprise to benefit society as a whole, rather than individual capitalists.[3]

Communists
Those who believe that socialism can only be realized through violent revolution and totalitarian dictatorship.

Social Democrats
Those who believed in achieving socialism through democratic means.

In the early twentieth century, the socialist ideology split into two broad camps. The **communists** believed that socialism could be achieved only through violent revolution and totalitarian dictatorship, whereas the **social democrats** committed themselves to achieving socialism by democratic means, turning their backs on violent revolution and dictatorship. Both versions of socialism waxed and waned during the twentieth century. The communist version of socialism reached its high point in the late 1970s, when the majority of the world's population lived in communist states. The countries under Communist Party rule at that time included the former Soviet Union; its Eastern European client nations (e.g., Poland, Czechoslovakia, Hungary); China; the Southeast Asian nations of Cambodia, Laos, and Vietnam; various African nations (e.g., Angola and Mozambique); and the Latin American nations of Cuba and Nicaragua. By the mid-1990s, however, communism was in retreat worldwide. The Soviet Union had collapsed and had been replaced by a collection of 15 republics, many of which were at least nominally structured as democracies. Communism was swept out of Eastern Europe by the largely bloodless revolutions of 1989. Although China is still nominally a communist state with substantial limits to individual political freedom, in the economic sphere the country has moved sharply away from strict adherence to communist ideology. Other than China, communism hangs on only in some small fringe states, such as North Korea and Cuba.

Social democracy also seems to have passed a high-water mark, although the ideology may prove to be more enduring than communism. Social democracy has had perhaps its greatest influence in a number of democratic Western nations, including Australia, France, Germany, Great Britain, Norway, Spain, and Sweden, where Social Democratic parties have often held political power. Other countries where social democracy has had an important influence include India and Brazil. Consistent with their Marxists roots, many social democratic governments after World War II nationalized private companies in certain industries, transforming them into state-owned enterprises to be run for the "public good rather than private profit." In Great Britain by the end of the 1970s, for example, state-owned companies had a monopoly in the telecommunications, electricity, gas, coal, railway, and shipbuilding industries, as well as substantial interests in the oil, airline, auto, and steel industries.

However, experience demonstrated that state ownership of the means of production ran counter to the public interest. In many countries, state-owned companies performed poorly. Protected from competition by their monopoly position and guaranteed government financial support, many became increasingly inefficient. Individuals paid for the luxury of state ownership through higher prices and higher taxes. As a consequence, a number of Western democracies voted many Social Democratic parties out of office in the late 1970s and early 1980s. They were succeeded by political parties, such as Britain's Conservative Party and Germany's Christian Democratic Party, that were more committed to free market economics. These parties sold state-owned enterprises to private investors (a process referred to as **privatization**). Even where Social Democratic parties have regained the levers of power, as in Great Britain in 1997 when the left-leaning Labor Party won control of the government, they too now seem committed to continued private ownership.

Privatization
The sale of state-owned enterprises to private investors.

Individualism

The opposite of collectivism, **individualism** refers to a philosophy that an individual should have freedom in his or her economic and political pursuits. In contrast to collectivism, individualism stresses that the interests of the individual should take precedence over the interests of the state. Like collectivism, individualism can be traced to an ancient Greek philosopher, in this case Plato's disciple Aristotle (384–322 BC). In contrast to Plato, Aristotle argued that individual diversity and private ownership are desirable. In a passage that might have been taken from a speech by contemporary politicians who adhere to a free market ideology, he argued that private property is more highly productive than communal property and will thus stimulate progress. According to Aristotle, communal property receives little care, whereas property that is owned by an individual will receive the greatest care and therefore be most productive.

Individualism
The philosophy that an individual should have freedom in his or her economic and political pursuits.

Individualism was reborn as an influential political philosophy in the Protestant trading nations of England and the Netherlands during the sixteenth century. The philosophy was refined in the work of a number of British philosophers, including David Hume (1711–76), Adam Smith (1723–90), and John Stuart Mill (1806–73). Individualism exercised a profound influence on those in the American colonies who sought independence from Great Britain. Indeed, the concept underlies the ideas expressed in the Declaration of Independence. In more recent years, several Nobel Prize–winning economists, including Milton Friedman, Friedrich von Hayek, and James Buchanan, have championed the philosophy.

Individualism is built on two central tenets. The first is an emphasis on the importance of guaranteeing individual freedom and self-expression. As John Stuart Mill put it,

> The sole end for which mankind are warranted, individually or collectively, in interfering with the liberty of action of any of their number is self-protection. . . . The only purpose for which power can be rightfully exercised over any member of a civilized community, against his will, is to prevent harm to others. His own good, either physical or moral, is not a sufficient warrant. . . . The only part of the conduct of any one, for which he is amenable to society, is that which concerns others. In the part which merely concerns himself, his independence is, of right, absolute. Over himself, over his own body and mind, the individual is sovereign.[4]

The second tenet of individualism is that the welfare of society is best served by letting people pursue their own economic self-interest, as opposed to some collective

Another Perspective

More on Aristotle

In addition to believing that the means of production should be privately owned, Aristotle thought that if we were to abolish private property, we would do moral harm to ourselves. Without private property, there would be no need to exercise generosity. "Without private property, no man will be seen to be liberal and no man will ever do any act of liberality; for only in the use of money is liberality made effective." (*The Politics*, Book 2, Ch. 5, trans. T.A. Sinclair).

The Peruvian economist Hernando De Soto develops Aristotle's point in the argument that the underlying, basic source of poverty and underdevelopment is the lack of a legal system that allows for transferable, titled, private property. (*The Mystery of Capital: Why Capitalism Triumphs in the West and Fails Everywhere Else,* Basic Books, 2000).

body (such as government) dictating what is in society's best interest. Or as Adam Smith put it in a famous passage from *The Wealth of Nations*, an individual who intends his own gain is

> led by an invisible hand to promote an end which was no part of his intention. Nor is it always worse for the society that it was no part of it. By pursuing his own interest he frequently promotes that of the society more effectually than when he really intends to promote it. I have never known much good done by those who effect to trade for the public good.[5]

The central message of individualism, therefore, is that individual economic and political freedoms are the ground rules on which a society should be based. This puts individualism in conflict with collectivism. Collectivism asserts the primacy of the collective over the individual; individualism asserts the opposite. This underlying ideological conflict shaped much of the recent history of the world. The Cold War, for example, was in many respects a war between collectivism, championed by the former Soviet Union, and individualism, championed by the United States.

In practical terms, individualism translates into an advocacy for democratic political systems and free market economics. Since the late 1980s, the waning of collectivism has been matched by the ascendancy of individualism. Democratic ideals and free market economics have swept away socialism and communism in many states. The changes of the past 20 years go beyond the revolutions in Eastern Europe and the former Soviet Union to include a move toward greater individualism in Latin America and many of the social democratic states of the West (e.g., Great Britain and Sweden). This is not to claim that individualism has finally won a long battle with collectivism. It has clearly not (indeed, during 2005 and into 2006 there were signs of a swing back toward left-leaning social democratic ideas in several countries, most notably in Latin America). But as a guiding political philosophy, individualism has been on the ascendant. This is good news for international business because the pro-business and pro-free trade values of individualism create a favorable environment within which international business can thrive.

Democracy
A political system in which government is by the people, exercised either directly or through elected representatives.

Totalitarianism
A political system in which one person or political party exercises absolute control over all spheres of human life and prohibits opposing political parties.

DEMOCRACY AND TOTALITARIANISM Democracy and totalitarianism are at different ends of a political dimension. **Democracy** refers to a political system in which government is by the people, exercised either directly or through elected representatives. **Totalitarianism** is a form of government in which one person or political party exercises absolute control over all spheres of human life and prohibits opposing political parties. The democratic–totalitarian dimension is not independent of the collectivism–individualism dimension. Democracy and individualism go hand in hand, as do the communist versions of collectivism and totalitarianism. However, gray areas exist; it is possible to have a democratic state in which collective values predominate, and it is possible to have a totalitarian state that is hostile to collectivism and in which some degree of individualism—particularly in the economic sphere—is encouraged. For example, China has seen a move toward greater individual freedom in the economic sphere, but the country is still ruled by a totalitarian dictatorship that constrains political freedom.

Democracy The pure form of democracy, as originally practiced by several city-states in ancient Greece, is based on a belief that citizens should be directly involved in decision making. In complex, advanced societies with populations in the tens or hundreds of millions this is impractical. Most modern democratic states practice **representative democracy.** In a representative democracy, citizens periodically elect individuals to represent them. These elected representatives then form a government, whose function is to make decisions on behalf of the electorate. In a representative democracy, elected representatives who fail to perform this job adequately will be voted out of office at the next election.

To guarantee that elected representatives can be held accountable for their actions by the electorate, an ideal representative democracy has a number of safeguards that are typically enshrined in constitutional law. These include (1) an individual's right to freedom of expression, opinion, and organization; (2) a free media; (3) regular elections in which all eligible citizens are allowed to vote; (4) universal adult suffrage; (5) limited terms for elected representatives; (6) a fair court system that is independent from the political system; (7) a nonpolitical state bureaucracy; (8) a nonpolitical police force and armed service; and (9) relatively free access to state information.[6]

Representative Democracy
A democracy in which citizens periodically elect individuals to represent them in government functions.

Totalitarianism In a totalitarian country, all the constitutional guarantees on which representative democracies are built—an individual's right to freedom of expression and organization, a free media, and regular elections—are denied to the citizens. In most totalitarian states, political repression is widespread, free and fair elections are lacking, media are heavily censored, basic civil liberties are denied, and those who question the right of the rulers to rule find themselves imprisoned, or worse.

Four major forms of totalitarianism exist in the world today. Until recently, the most widespread was **communist totalitarianism.** Communism, however, is in decline worldwide, and most of the Communist Party dictatorships have collapsed since 1989. Exceptions to this trend (so far) are China, Vietnam, Laos, North Korea, and Cuba, although all these states exhibit clear signs that the Communist Party's monopoly on political power is retreating. In many respects, the governments of China, Vietnam, and Laos are communist in name only since those nations now adhere to market-based economic reforms. They remain, however, totalitarian states that deny many basic civil liberties to their populations.

A second form of totalitarianism might be labeled **theocratic totalitarianism.** Theocratic totalitarianism is found in states where political power is monopolized by a party, group, or individual that governs according to religious principles. The most common form of theocratic totalitarianism is based on Islam and is exemplified by states such as Iran and Saudi Arabia. These states limit freedom of political and religious expression with laws based on Islamic principles.

A third form of totalitarianism might be referred to as **tribal totalitarianism.** Tribal totalitarianism has arisen from time to time in African countries such as Zimbabwe, Tanzania, Uganda, and Kenya. The borders of most African states reflect the administrative boundaries drawn by the old European colonial powers rather than tribal realities. Consequently, the typical African country contains a number of tribes. Tribal totalitarianism occurs when a political party that represents the interests of a particular tribe (and not always the majority tribe) monopolizes power. Such one-party states still exist in Africa.

A fourth major form of totalitarianism might be described as **right-wing totalitarianism.** Right-wing totalitarianism generally permits some individual economic freedom but restricts individual political freedom, frequently on the

Communist Totalitarianism
A version of collectivism advocating that socialism can only be achieved through a totalitarian dictatorship.

Theocratic Totalitarianism
A political system in which political power is monopolized by a party, group, or individual that governs according to religious principles.

Tribal Totalitarianism
A political system in which a party, group, or individual that represents the interests of a particular tribe monopolizes political power.

Right-Wing Totalitarianism
A political system in which political power is monopolized by a party, group, or individual that generally permits individual economic freedom but restricts individual political freedom, including free speech, often on the grounds that it would lead to the rise of communism.

Communist totalitarianism is still the political system in Vietnam, where red banners in the Hanoi marketplace remind citizens and visitors of the government's control. *Tim Hall/Getty Images/DIL*

grounds that it would lead to the rise of communism. A common feature of many right-wing dictatorships is an overt hostility to socialist or communist ideas. Many right-wing totalitarian governments are backed by the military, and in some cases the government may be made up of military officers. The fascist regimes that ruled Germany and Italy in the 1930s and 1940s were right-wing totalitarian states. Until the early 1980s, right-wing dictatorships, many of which were military dictatorships, were common throughout Latin America. They were also found in several Asian countries, particularly South Korea, Taiwan, Singapore, Indonesia, and the Philippines. Since the early 1980s, however, this form of government has been in retreat. Most Latin American countries are now genuine multiparty democracies. Similarly, South Korea, Taiwan, and the Philippines have all become functioning democracies, as has Indonesia (see the closing case).

Economic Systems

LEARNING OBJECTIVE 2
Understand how the economic systems of countries differ.

It should be clear from the previous section that political ideology and economic systems are connected. In countries where individual goals are given primacy over collective goals, we are more likely to find free market economic systems. In contrast, in countries where collective goals are given preeminence, the state may have taken control over many enterprises; markets in such countries are likely to be restricted rather than free. We can identify three broad types of economic systems—a market economy, a command economy, and a mixed economy.

Market Economy
An economic system in which the interaction of supply and demand determines the quantity in which goods and services are produced.

MARKET ECONOMY

In a pure **market economy,** all productive activities are privately owned, as opposed to being owned by the state. The goods and services that a country produces are not planned by anyone. Production is determined by the interaction of supply and demand and signaled to producers through the price system. If demand for a product exceeds supply, prices will rise, signaling producers to produce more. If supply exceeds demand, prices will fall, signaling producers to produce less. In this system consumers are sovereign. The purchasing patterns of consumers, as signaled to producers through the mechanism of the price system, determine what is produced and in what quantity.

For a market to work in this manner, supply must not be restricted. A supply restriction occurs when a single firm monopolizes a market. In such circumstances, rather than increase output in response to increased demand, a monopolist might restrict output and let prices rise. This allows the monopolist to take a greater profit margin on each unit it sells. Although this is good for the monopolist, it is bad for the consumer, who has to pay higher prices. It also is probably bad for the welfare of society. Since a monopolist has no competitors, it has no incentive to search for ways to lower production costs. Rather, it can simply pass on cost increases to consumers in the form of higher prices. The net result is that the monopolist is likely to become increasingly inefficient, producing high-priced, low-quality goods, and society suffers as a consequence.

Given the dangers inherent in monopoly, the role of government in a market economy is to encourage vigorous free and fair competition between private producers. Governments do this by outlawing monopolies and restrictive business practices designed to monopolize a market (antitrust laws serve this function in the United States). Private ownership also encourages vigorous competition and economic efficiency. Private ownership ensures that entrepreneurs have a right to the profits generated by their own efforts. This gives entrepreneurs an incentive to search for better ways of serving consumer needs. That may be through introducing new products, by developing more efficient production processes, by pursuing better marketing and after-sale service, or simply through managing their businesses more efficiently than their competitors. In turn, the constant improvement in product and process that results from such an incentive has been argued to have a major positive impact on economic growth and development.[7]

COMMAND ECONOMY In a pure **command economy,** the government plans the goods and services that a country produces, the quantity in which they are produced, and the prices at which they are sold. Consistent with the collectivist ideology, the objective of a command economy is for government to allocate resources for "the good of society." In addition, in a pure command economy, all businesses are state owned, the rationale being that the government can then direct them to make investments that are in the best interests of the nation as a whole rather than in the interests of private individuals. Historically, command economies were found in communist countries where collectivist goals were given priority over individual goals. Since the demise of communism in the late 1980s, the number of command economies has fallen dramatically. Some elements of a command economy were also evident in a number of democratic nations led by socialist-inclined governments. France and India both experimented with extensive government planning and state ownership, although government planning has fallen into disfavor in both countries.

Command Economy
An economic system in which the government plans the allocation of resources, including determination of what goods and services should be produced and in what quantity.

While the objective of a command economy is to mobilize economic resources for the public good, the opposite seems to have occurred. In a command economy, state-owned enterprises have little incentive to control costs and be efficient, because they cannot go out of business. Also, the abolition of private ownership means there is no incentive for individuals to look for better ways to serve consumer needs; hence, dynamism and innovation are absent from command economies. Instead of growing and becoming more prosperous, such economies tend to stagnate.

Mixed Economy An economic system in which certain sectors are left to private ownership and free market mechanisms, while other sectors have significant government ownership and government planning.

MIXED ECONOMY Between market economies and command economies can be found mixed economies. In a **mixed economy,** certain sectors of the economy are left to private ownership and free market mechanisms while other sectors have significant state ownership and government planning. Mixed economies were once common throughout much of the world, although they are becoming much less so. Not long ago, Great Britain, France, and Sweden were mixed economies, but extensive privatization has reduced state ownership of businesses in all three nations. A similar trend can be observed in many other countries where there was once a large state sector, such as Brazil, Italy, and India.

In mixed economies, governments also tend to take into state ownership troubled firms whose continued operation is thought to be vital to national interests. Consider, for example, the French automobile company Renault. The government took over the company when it ran into serious financial problems. The French government reasoned that the social costs of the unemployment that might result if Renault collapsed were unacceptable, so it nationalized the company to save it from bankruptcy. Renault's competitors weren't thrilled by this move because they had to compete with a company whose costs were subsidized by the state.

Legal Systems

LEARNING OBJECTIVE 3 Understand how the legal systems of countries differ.

Legal System Rules that regulate behavior and the processes by which the laws of a country are enforced and through which redress of grievance is obtained.

The **legal system** of a country refers to the rules, or laws, that regulate behavior along with the processes by which the laws are enforced and through which redress for grievances is obtained. The legal system of a country is of immense importance to international business. A country's laws regulate business practice, define the manner in which business transactions are to be executed, and set down the rights and obligations of those involved in business transactions. The legal environments of countries differ in significant ways. As we shall see, differences in legal systems can affect the attractiveness of a country as an investment site or market.

Like the economic system of a country, the legal system is influenced by the prevailing political system (although it is also strongly influenced by historical tradition). The government of a country defines the legal framework within which firms do business—and often the laws that regulate business reflect the rulers' dominant political ideology. For example, collectivist-inclined totalitarian states tend to enact laws that severely restrict private enterprise, whereas the laws enacted by governments in democratic states where individualism is the dominant political philosophy tend to be pro-private enterprise and pro-consumer.

Here we focus on several issues that illustrate how legal systems can vary—and how such variations can affect international business. First, we look at some basic differences in legal systems. Next we look at contract law. Third, we look at the laws governing property rights with particular reference to patents, copyrights, and trademarks. Then we discuss protection of intellectual property. Finally, we look at laws covering product safety and product liability.

DIFFERENT LEGAL SYSTEMS There are three main types of legal systems—or legal tradition—in use around the world: common law, civil law, and theocratic law.

Common Law A system of law based on tradition, precedent, and custom, which is flexibly interpreted by judges as it applies to the unique circumstances of each case.

Common Law

The common law system evolved in England over hundreds of years. It is now found in most of Great Britain's former colonies, including the United States. **Common law** is based on tradition, precedent, and custom. *Tradition* refers to a country's legal history, *precedent* to cases that have come before the courts in the past, and *custom* to the ways in which laws are applied in specific situations. When law courts interpret common law, they do so with regard to these characteristics. This gives a common law system a degree of flexibility that other systems lack. Judges in a common law system have the power to interpret the law so that it applies to the unique circumstances of an individual case. In turn, each new interpretation sets a precedent that may be followed in future cases. As new precedents arise, laws may be altered, clarified, or amended to deal with new situations.

Civil Law System
A system of law based on a detailed set of written laws and codes.

Civil Law A **civil law system** is based on a detailed set of laws organized into codes. When law courts interpret civil law, they do so with regard to these codes. More than 80 countries, including Germany, France, Japan, and Russia, operate with a civil law system. A civil law system tends to be less adversarial than a common law system, since the judges rely upon detailed legal codes rather than interpreting tradition, precedent, and custom. Judges under a civil law system have less flexibility than those under a common law system. Judges in a common law system have the power to interpret the law, whereas judges in a civil law system have the power only to apply the law.

Theocratic Law System
A system of law based on religious teachings.

Theocratic Law A **theocratic law system** is one in which the law is based on religious teachings. Islamic law is the most widely practiced theocratic legal system in the modern world, although usage of both Hindu and Jewish law persisted into the twentieth century. Islamic law is primarily a moral rather than a commercial law and is intended to govern all aspects of life.[8] The foundation for Islamic law is the holy book of Islam, the Koran, along with the Sunnah, or decisions and sayings of the Prophet Muhammad, and the writings of Islamic scholars who have derived rules by analogy from the principles established in the Koran and the Sunnah. Because the Koran and Sunnah are holy documents, the basic foundations of Islamic law cannot be changed. However, in practice Islamic jurists and scholars are constantly debating the application of Islamic law to the modern world. In reality, many Muslim countries have legal systems that are a blend of Islamic law and a common or civil law system.

Although Islamic law is primarily concerned with moral behavior, it has been extended to cover certain commercial activities. An example is the payment or receipt of interest, which is considered usury and outlawed by the Koran. To the devout Muslim, acceptance of interest payments is seen as a grave sin; the giver and the taker are equally damned. This is not just a matter of theology; in several Islamic states it has also become a matter of law. In the 1990s, for example, Pakistan's Federal Shariat Court, the highest Islamic lawmaking body in the country, pronounced interest to be un-Islamic and therefore illegal and demanded that the government amend all financial laws accordingly. In 1999, Pakistan's Supreme Court ruled that Islamic banking methods should be used in the country after July 1, 2001.[9] By 2005, some 300 Islamic financial institutions in the world collectively managed more than $250 billion in assets. In addition to Pakistan, Islamic financial institutions are found in many of the Gulf states, Egypt, and Malaysia.[10]

Another Perspective

No Interest in Islamic Banking? Why?
How can a banking system operate without interest (*riba* in Arabic)? The basic economic idea is that commercial risk should be shared. In the Western approach, interest guarantees the banker a return, so on a collateralized loan, the banker avoids much of the commercial risk that's inherent in business. No matter what happens to the business, the banker gets a return. In contrast, Islam requires that the banker share this commercial risk. If the business venture is successful, the banker shares the profit. If the venture doesn't do well, neither does the banker. The value of community in Islam is stronger than the value of individual profit. See Chapter 3 for more on this point.

Contract A document that specifies the conditions under which an exchange is to occur and details the rights and obligations of the parties involved.

Contract Law The body of law that governs contract enforcement.

United Nations Convention on Contracts for the International Sale of Goods (CIGS) A set of rules governing certain aspects of the making and performance of commercial contracts between sellers and buyers who have their places of businesses in different nations.

Property Rights The bundle of legal rights over the use to which a resource is put and over the use made of any income that may be derived from that resource.

DIFFERENCES IN CONTRACT LAW

The difference between common law and civil law systems can be illustrated by the approach of each to contract law (remember, most theocratic legal systems also have elements of common or civil law). A **contract** is a document that specifies the conditions under which an exchange is to occur and details the rights and obligations of the parties involved. Some form of contract regulates many business transactions. **Contract law** is the body of law that governs contract enforcement. The parties to an agreement normally resort to contract law when one party feels the other has violated either the letter or the spirit of an agreement.

Because common law tends to be relatively ill specified, contracts drafted under a common law framework tend to be very detailed with all contingencies spelled out. In civil law systems, however, contracts tend to be much shorter and less specific because many of the issues are already covered in a civil code. Thus, it is more expensive to draw up contracts in a common law jurisdiction, and resolving contract disputes can be very adversarial in common law systems. But common law systems have the advantage of greater flexibility and allow for judges to interpret a contract dispute in light of the prevailing situation. International businesses need to be sensitive to these differences; approaching a contract dispute in a state with a civil law system as if it had a common law system may backfire, and vice versa.

When contract disputes arise in international trade, there is always the question of which country's laws to apply. To resolve this issue, a number of countries, including the United States, have ratified the **United Nations Convention on Contracts for the International Sale of Goods (CIGS).** The CIGS establishes a uniform set of rules governing certain aspects of the making and performance of everyday commercial contracts between sellers and buyers who have their places of business in different nations. By adopting the CIGS, a nation signals to other adopters that it will treat the convention's rules as part of its law. The CIGS applies automatically to all contracts for the sale of goods between different firms based in countries that have ratified the convention, unless the parties to the contract explicitly opt out. One problem with the CIGS, however, is that fewer than 70 nations have ratified the convention (the CIGS went into effect in 1988).[11] Many of the world's larger trading nations, including Japan and the United Kingdom, have not ratified the CIGS.

When firms do not wish to accept the CIGS, they often opt for arbitration by a recognized arbitration court to settle contract disputes. The most well known of these courts is the International Court of Arbitration of the International Chamber of Commerce in Paris. In 2004, this court handled some 561 requests for arbitration involving 1,682 parties from 116 countries.[12] Almost 60 percent of disputes involved sums in excess of $1 million.

PROPERTY RIGHTS AND CORRUPTION

In a legal sense, the term *property* refers to a resource over which an individual or business holds a legal title; that is, a resource that it owns. Resources include land, buildings, equipment, capital, mineral rights, businesses, and intellectual property (ideas, which are protected by patents, copyrights, and trademarks). **Property rights** refer to the legal rights over the use to which a resource is put and over the use made of any income that may be derived from that resource.[13] Countries differ in the extent to which their legal systems define and protect property rights. Although almost all countries have laws on their books that protect property rights, in many countries these laws are not enforced by the authorities and property rights are violated. Property rights can be violated in two ways—through private action and through public action.

Private Action Theft, piracy, blackmail, and the like by private individuals or groups.

Private Action In this context, **private action** refers to theft, piracy, blackmail, and the like by private individuals or groups. Although theft occurs in all countries, a weak legal system allows for a much higher level of criminal action in some than in others. For example, in Russia in the chaotic period following the collapse of communism, an outdated legal system, coupled with a weak police force and judicial system, offered both domestic and foreign businesses scant protection from blackmail by the "Russian Mafia." Successful business owners in Russia often had to pay "protection money" to the Mafia or face violent retribution, including bombings and assassinations (about 500 contract killings of businessmen occurred in 1995 and again in 1996).[14]

Russia is not alone in having Mafia problems (and the situation in Russia has improved significantly since the mid-1990s). The Mafia has a long history in the United States (Chicago in the 1930s was similar to Moscow in the 1990s). In Japan, the local version of the Mafia, known as the *yakuza*, runs protection rackets, particularly in the food and entertainment industries.[15] However, there was a big difference between the magnitude of such activity in Russia in the 1990s and its limited impact in Japan and the United States. This difference arose because the legal enforcement apparatus, such as the police and court system, was so weak in Russia following the collapse of communism. Many other countries from time to time have had problems similar to or even greater than those experienced by Russia.

Public Action The extortion of income or resources from property holders by public officials, such as politicians and government bureaucrats.

Public Action and Corruption **Public action** to violate property rights occurs when public officials, such as politicians and government bureaucrats, extort income, resources, or the property itself from property holders (see the opening case for an example). This can be done through legal mechanisms such as levying excessive taxation, requiring expensive licenses or permits from property holders, taking assets into state ownership without compensating the owners, or redistributing assets without compensating the prior owners. It can also be done through illegal means, or corruption, by demanding bribes from businesses in return for the rights to operate in a country, industry, or location.[16]

Corruption has been well documented in every society, from the banks of the Congo River to the palace of the Dutch royal family, from Japanese politicians to Brazilian bankers, and from Indonesian government officials to the New York City Police Department. The government of the late Ferdinand Marcos in the Philippines was famous for demanding bribes from foreign businesses wishing to set up operations in that country.[17] The same was true of government officials in Indonesia under the rule of former president Suharto. No society is immune to corruption. However, there are systematic differences in the extent of corruption. In some countries, the rule of law minimizes corruption. Corruption is seen and treated as illegal, and when discovered, violators are punished by the full force of the law. In other countries, the rule of law is weak and corruption by bureaucrats and politicians is rife. Corruption is so endemic in some countries that politicians and bureaucrats regard it as a perk of office and openly flout laws against corruption.

According to Transparency International, an independent nonprofit organization dedicated to exposing and fighting corruption, businesses and individuals spend some $400 billion a year worldwide on bribes related to government procurement contracts alone.[18] Transparency International has also measured the level of corruption among public officials in different countries.[19] As can be seen in Figure 2.1, the organization rated countries such as Finland and New Zealand as clean; it rated others, such as Russia, India, Indonesia, and Zimbabwe, as corrupt. Bangladesh ranked last out of all 158 countries in the survey, and Finland ranked first.

Rankings of Corruption by Country, 2005

Source: Transparency International, "Global Corruption Report," 2006.

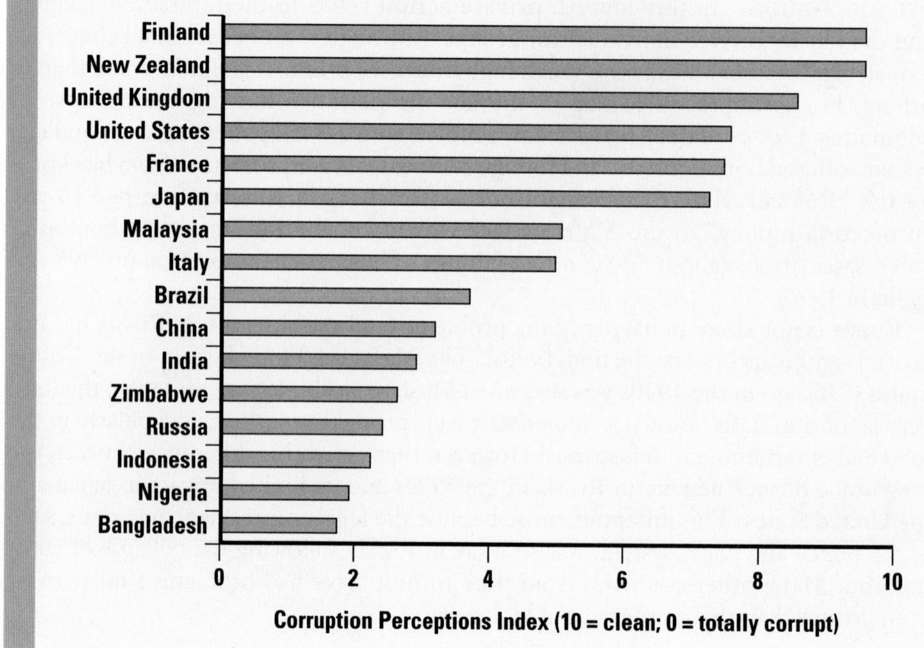

Economic evidence suggests that high levels of corruption significantly reduce the foreign direct investment, level of international trade, and economic growth rate in a country.[20] By siphoning off profits, corrupt politicians and bureaucrats reduce the returns to business investment and, hence, reduce the incentive of both domestic and foreign businesses to invest in that country. The lower level of investment that results hurts economic growth. Thus, we would expect countries such as Indonesia, Nigeria, and Russia to have a much lower rate of economic growth than might otherwise have been the case. A detailed example of the negative effect that corruption can have on economic progress is given in the accompanying Country Focus, which looks at the impact of corruption on economic growth in Nigeria.

Foreign Corrupt Practices Act
U.S. law regulating behavior regarding the conduct of international business in the taking of bribes and other unethical actions.

Foreign Corrupt Practices Act

In the 1970s, the United States passed the **Foreign Corrupt Practices Act** following revelations that U.S. companies had bribed government officials in foreign countries in an attempt to win lucrative contracts. This law makes it illegal to bribe a foreign government official to obtain or maintain business over which that foreign official has authority, and it requires all publicly traded companies (whether or not they are involved in international trade) to keep detailed records that would reveal whether a violation of the act has occurred. Along the same lines, in 1997 trade and finance ministers from the member states of the Organization for Economic Cooperation and Development (OECD), an association of the world's 30 most powerful economies, adopted the Convention on Combating Bribery of Foreign Public Officials in International Business Transactions.[21] The convention obliges member states to make the bribery of foreign public officials a criminal offense.

However, both the U.S. law and OECD convention include language that allows for exceptions known as facilitating or expediting payments (also called *grease payments*

Country FOCUS

Corruption in Nigeria

When Nigeria gained independence from Great Britain in 1960, there were hopes that the country might emerge as an economic heavyweight in Africa. Not only was Nigeria Africa's most populous country, but it also was blessed with abundant natural resources, particularly oil, from which the country earned over $400 billion between 1970 and 2005. Despite this, Nigeria remains one of the poorest countries in the world. According to the 2005 Human Development Index compiled by the United Nations, Nigeria ranked 158 out of 177 countries covered. Gross national income per capita was just $430, 32 percent of the adult population was illiterate, and life expectancy at birth was only 43 years.

What went wrong? Although there is no simple answer, a number of factors seem to have conspired to damage economic activity in Nigeria. The country is composed of several competing ethnic, tribal, and religious groups, and the conflict among them has limited political stability and led to political strife, including a brutal civil war in the 1970s. With the legitimacy of the government always in question, political leaders often purchased support by legitimizing bribes and by raiding the national treasury to reward allies. Civilian rule after independence was followed by a series of military dictatorships, each of which seemed more corrupt and inept than the last (the country returned to civilian rule in 1999).

During the 1990s, the military dictator, Sani Abacha, openly and systematically plundered the state treasury for his own personal gain. His most blatant scam was the Petroleum Trust Fund, which he set up in the mid-1990s ostensibly to channel extra revenue from an increase in fuel prices into much-needed infrastructure projects and other investments. The fund was not independently audited, and almost none of the money that passed through it was properly accounted for. It was, in fact, a vehicle for Abacha and his supporters to spend at will a sum that in 1996 was equivalent to some 25 percent of the total federal budget. Abacha, aware of his position as an unpopular and unelected leader, lavished money on personal security and handed out bribes to those whose support he coveted. With examples like this at the very top of the government, it is not surprising that corruption could be found throughout the political and bureaucratic apparatus.

Some of the excesses were simply astounding. In the 1980s an aluminum smelter was built on the orders of the government, which wanted to industrialize Nigeria. The cost of the smelter was $2.4 billion, some 60 to 100 percent higher than the cost of comparable plants elsewhere in the developed world. This high cost was widely interpreted to reflect the bribes that had to be paid to local politicians by the international contractors that built the plant. The smelter has never operated at more than a fraction of its intended capacity.

Has the situation in Nigeria improved since the country returned to civilian rule in 1999? In 2003, Olusegun Obasanjo was elected president on a platform that included a promise to fight corruption. By some accounts, progress has been seen. His anticorruption chief, Nuhu Ribadu, has claimed that whereas 70 percent of the country's oil revenues were being stolen or wasted in 2002, by 2004 the figure was "only" 40 percent. But in its most recent survey, Transparency International still ranked Nigeria among the most corrupt countries in the world in 2005 (see Figure 2.1), suggesting that the country still has long way to go. Mr. Ribadu has suggested that the problem lies with state governments, which are still riddled with corruption.

Sources: "A Tale of Two Giants," *The Economist*, January 15, 2000, p. 5; J. Coolidge and S. Rose Ackerman, "High Level Rent Seeking and Corruption in African Regimes," World Bank policy research working paper no. 1780, June 1997; D. L. Bevan, P. Collier, and J. W. Gunning, *Nigeria and Indonesia: The Political Economy of Poverty, Equity and Growth* (Oxford: Oxford University Press, 1999); "Democracy and Its Discontents," *The Economist*, January 29, 2005, p. 55; and A. Field. "Can Reform Save Nigeria?" *Journal of Commerce*, November 21, 2005, p. 1.

or *speed money*), the purpose of which is to expedite or to secure the performance of a routine governmental action.[22] For example, they allow for small payments made to speed up the issuance of permits or licenses, process paperwork, or just get vegetables off the dock and on their way to market. The explanation for this exception to general antibribery provisions is that while grease payments are, technically, bribes, they are distinguishable from (and, apparently, less offensive than) bribes used to obtain or

Intellectual Property Property that is the product of intellectual activity.

Patent A legal device that grants the inventor of a new product or process exclusive rights for a defined period to the manufacture, use, or sale of that invention.

Copyrights Exclusive legal rights of authors, composers, playwrights, artists, and publishers to publish and dispose of their work as they see fit.

Trademarks Designs and names, often officially registered, by which merchants or manufacturers designate and differentiate their products.

World Intellectual Property Organization An international organization whose members sign treaties to agree to protect intellectual property.

maintain business, because they merely facilitate performance of duties that the recipients are already obligated to perform.

THE PROTECTION OF INTELLECTUAL PROPERTY

Intellectual property refers to property that is the product of intellectual activity, such as computer software, a screenplay, a music score, or the chemical formula for a new drug. Patents, copyrights, and trademarks establish ownership rights over intellectual property. A **patent** grants the inventor of a new product or process exclusive rights for a defined period to the manufacture, use, or sale of that invention. **Copyrights** are the exclusive legal rights of authors, composers, playwrights, artists, and publishers to publish and disperse their work as they see fit. **Trademarks** are designs and names, often officially registered, by which merchants or manufacturers designate and differentiate their products (e.g., Christian Dior clothes). In the high-technology "knowledge" economy of the twenty-first century, intellectual property has become an increasingly important source of economic value for businesses. Protecting intellectual property has also become increasingly problematic, particularly if it can be rendered in a digital form and then copied and distributed at very low cost via pirated CDs or over the Internet (e.g., computer software, music and video recordings).[23]

The philosophy behind intellectual property laws is to reward the originator of a new invention, book, musical record, clothes design, restaurant chain, and the like, for his or her idea and effort. Such laws stimulate innovation and creative work. They provide an incentive for people to search for novel ways of doing things, and they reward creativity. For example, consider innovation in the pharmaceutical industry. A patent will grant the inventor of a new drug a 20-year monopoly in production of that drug. This gives pharmaceutical firms an incentive to undertake the expensive, difficult, and time-consuming basic research required to generate new drugs (it can cost $800 million in R&D and take 12 years to get a new drug on the market). Without the guarantees provided by patents, companies would be unlikely to commit themselves to extensive basic research.[24]

The protection of intellectual property rights differs greatly from country to country. Although many countries have stringent intellectual property regulations on their books, the enforcement of these regulations has often been lax. This has been the case even among many of the 183 countries that are now members of the **World Intellectual Property Organization,** all of which have signed international treaties designed to protect intellectual property, including the oldest such treaty, the **Paris Convention for the Protection of Industrial Property,** which dates to 1883 and has been signed by some 169 nations as of 2006. Weak enforcement encourages the piracy (theft) of intellectual property. China and Thailand have recently been among the worst offenders in Asia. Pirated computer software is widely available in China. Similarly, the streets of Bangkok, Thailand's capital, are lined with stands selling pirated copies of Rolex watches, Levi Strauss jeans, videotapes, and computer software.

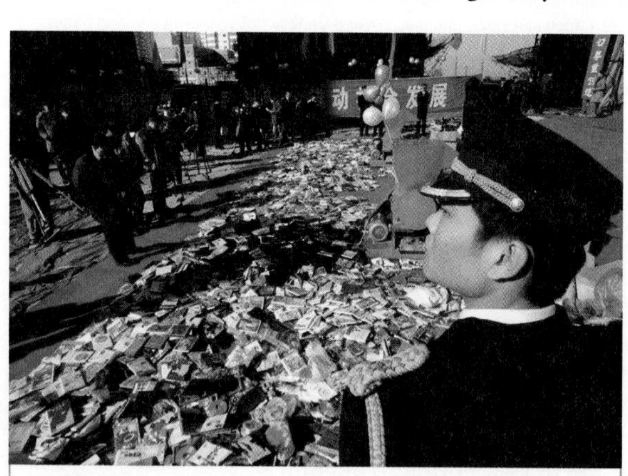
A security guard stands near a pile of pirated CDs and DVDs before they were destroyed at a ceremony in Beijing on Saturday, February 26, 2005. Thousands of pirated items were destroyed in the event. *AP/Wide World Photos*

Piracy in music recordings is rampant. The International Federation of the Phonographic Industry claims that about one-third of all recorded

Management FOCUS

Starbucks Wins Key Trademark Case in China

Starbucks has big plans for China. It believes the fast-growing nation will become the company's second-largest market after the United States. Starbucks entered the country in 1999, and by the end of 2005 it had 209 stores open. But in China, copycats of well-established Western brands are commonplace. Starbucks too faced competition from a look alike, Shanghai Xing Ba Ke Coffee Shop, whose stores closely matched the Starbucks format, right down to a green and white Xing Ba Ke circular logo that mimics Starbuck's ubiquitous logo. Moreover, the name mimics the standard Chinese translation for Starbucks. *Xing* means "star" and *Ba Ke* sounds like "bucks."

In 2003, Starbuck decided to sue Xing Ba Ke in Chinese court for trademark violations. Xing Ba Ke's general manager responded by claiming that it was just an accident that the logo and name were so similar to that of Starbucks. Moreover, he claimed the right to use the logo and name because Xing Ba Ke had registered as a company in Shanghai in 1999, before Starbucks entered the city. "I hadn't heard of Starbucks at the time," claimed the manager, "so how could I imitate its brand and logo?"

However, in January 2006 a Shanghai court ruled that Starbucks had precedence, in part because it had registered its Chinese name in 1998. The Court stated that Xing Ba Ke's use of the name and similar logo was "clearly malicious" and constituted improper competition. The court ordered Xing Ba Ke to stop using the name and to pay Starbucks $62,000 in compensation. While the money involved here may be small, the precedent is not. In a country where violation of trademarks has been commonplace, the courts seem to be signaling that a shift toward greater protection of intellectual property rights may be in progress. This is perhaps not surprising, since foreign governments and the World Trade Organization have been pushing China hard recently to start respecting intellectual property rights.

Sources: M. Dickie, "Starbucks Wins Case against Chinese Copycat," *Financial Times*, January 3, 2006, p. 1; "Starbucks: Chinese Court Backs Company over Trademark Infringement," *The Wall Street Journal*, January 2, 2006, p. A11; and "Starbucks Calls China Its Top Growth Focus," *The Wall Street Journal*, February 14, 2006, p.1.

music products sold worldwide in 2005 were pirated (illegal) copies, suggesting that piracy costs the industry more than $4.5 billion annually.[25] The computer software industry also suffers from lax enforcement of intellectual property rights. Estimates suggest that violations of intellectual property rights cost personal computer software firms revenues equal to $35 billion in 2005.[26] According to the Business Software Alliance, a software industry association, in 2005 some 35 percent of all software applications used in the world was pirated. The worst region was Latin America, where the piracy rate was 68 percent (see Figure 2.2). One of the worst countries was

Paris Convention for the Protection of Industrial Property
The oldest international treaty concerning protection of intellectual property, which has been signed by 169 nations.

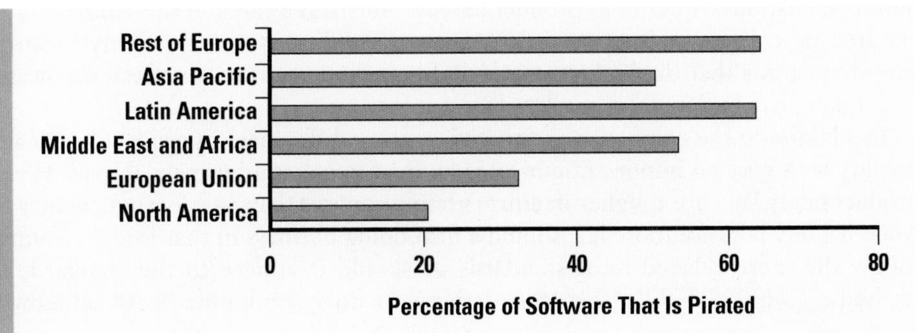

figure 

Regional Piracy Rates for Software, 2005

China, where the piracy rate in 2005 ran at 86 percent and cost the industry more than $3.9 billion in lost sales, up from $444 million in 1995. The piracy rate in the United States was much lower at 21 percent; however, the value of sales lost was more significant because of the size of the U.S. market, reaching an estimated $6.9 billion in 2005.[27]

International businesses have a number of possible responses to violations of their intellectual property. They can lobby their respective governments to push for international agreements to ensure that intellectual property rights are protected and that the law is enforced. Partly as a result of such actions, international laws are being strengthened. As we shall see in Chapter 6, the most recent world trade agreement, signed in 1994, for the first time extends the scope of the General Agreement on Tariffs and Trade to cover intellectual property. Under the new agreement, known as the Trade Related Aspects of Intellectual Property Rights (or TRIPS), as of 1995 a council of the World Trade Organization is overseeing enforcement of much stricter intellectual property regulations. These regulations oblige WTO members to grant and enforce patents lasting at least 20 years and copyrights lasting 50 years. Rich countries had to comply with the rules within a year. Poor countries, in which such protection generally was much weaker, had five years of grace, and the very poorest have 10 years.[28] (For further details of the TRIPS agreement, see Chapter 6.)

In addition to lobbying governments, firms can file lawsuits on their own behalf. For example, Starbucks recently won a landmark trademark copyright case in China against a copycat (see the Management Focus feature for details). Firms may also choose to stay out of countries where intellectual property laws are lax, rather than risk having their ideas stolen by local entrepreneurs. Firms also need to be on the alert to ensure that pirated copies of their products produced in countries with weak intellectual property laws don't turn up in their home market or in third countries. U.S. computer software giant Microsoft, for example, discovered that pirated Microsoft software, produced illegally in Thailand, was being sold worldwide as the real thing.

Product Safety Laws
Laws that set certain safety standards to which a product must adhere.

Product Liability
Involves holding a firm and its officers responsible when a product causes injury, death, or damage to its users.

PRODUCT SAFETY AND PRODUCT LIABILITY **Product safety laws** set certain safety standards to which a product must adhere. **Product liability** involves holding a firm and its officers responsible when a product causes injury, death, or damage. Product liability can be much greater if a product does not conform to required safety standards. Both civil and criminal product liability laws exist. Civil laws call for payment and monetary damages. Criminal liability laws result in fines or imprisonment. Both civil and criminal liability laws are probably more extensive in the United States than in any other country, although many other Western nations also have comprehensive liability laws. Liability laws are typically least extensive in less developed nations. A boom in product liability suits and awards in the United States resulted in a dramatic increase in the cost of liability insurance. Many business executives argue that the high costs of liability insurance make American businesses less competitive in the global marketplace.

In addition to the competitiveness issue, country differences in product safety and liability laws raise an important ethical issue for firms doing business abroad. When product safety laws are tougher in a firm's home country than in a foreign country or when liability laws are more lax, should a firm doing business in that foreign country follow the more relaxed local standards or should it adhere to the standards of its home country? While the ethical thing to do is undoubtedly to adhere to home-country standards, firms have been known to take advantage of lax safety and liability laws to do business in a manner that would not be allowed at home.

The Determinants of Economic Development

LEARNING OBJECTIVE 4
Explain what determines the level of economic development of a nation.

The political, economic, and legal systems of a country can have a profound impact on the level of economic development and hence on the attractiveness of a country as a possible market or production location for a firm. Here we look first at how countries differ in their level of development. Then we look at how political economy affects economic progress.

DIFFERENCES IN ECONOMIC DEVELOPMENT Different countries have dramatically different levels of economic development. One common measure of economic development is a country's **gross national income (GNI)** per head of population. GNI is regarded as a yardstick for the economic activity of a country; it measures the total annual income received by residents of a nation. Map 2.1 summarizes the GNI per capita of the world's nations in 2004. As can be seen, countries such as Japan, Sweden, Switzerland, and the United States are among the richest on this measure, whereas the large countries of China and India are among the poorest. Japan, for example, had a 2004 GNI per capita of $37,050, but China achieved only $1.50 and India, $620.[29]

Gross National Income (GNI)
The yardstick for measuring economic activity of a country, this measures the total annual income of a nation's residents.

GNI per person figures can be misleading because they don't consider differences in the cost of living. For example, although the 2004 GNI per capita of Switzerland, at $49,600, exceeded that of the United States, which was $41,400, the higher cost of living in Switzerland meant that U.S. citizens could actually afford more goods and services than Swiss citizens. To account for differences in the cost of living, one can adjust GNI per capita by purchasing power. Referred to as a **purchasing power parity (PPP)** adjustment, it allows for a more direct comparison of living standards in different countries. The base for the adjustment is the cost of living in the United States. The PPP for different countries is then adjusted (up or down) depending upon whether the cost of living is lower or higher than in the United States. For example, in 2004 the GNI per capita for China was $1,500, but the PPP per capita was $5,885, suggesting that the cost of living was lower in China and that $1,500 in China would buy as much as $5,885 in the United States. Table 2.1 gives the GNI per capita measured at PPP in 2004 for a selection of countries, along with their GNI per capita and their growth rate in gross domestic product (GDP) from 1994 to 2004. Map 2.2 summarizes the GNI PPP per capita in 2004 for the nations of the world.

Purchasing Power Parity (PPP)
An adjustment in gross domestic product per capita to reflect differences in the cost of living.

As can be seen, there are striking differences in the standards of living between countries. Table 2.1 suggests that the average Indian citizen can afford to consume only 8 percent of the goods and services consumed by the average U.S. citizen on a PPP basis. Given this, one might conclude that, despite having a population of 1 billion, India is unlikely to be a very lucrative market for the consumer products produced by many Western international businesses. However, this would be incorrect because India has a fairly wealthy middle class of close to 100 million people, despite its large number of very poor. Moreover, in absolute terms the Indian economy is now larger than that of Brazil, Poland, and Russia (see Table 2.1).

The GNI and PPP data give a static picture of development. They tell us, for example, that China is much poorer than the United States, but they do not tell us if China is closing the gap. To assess this, we have to look at the economic growth rates achieved by countries. Table 2.1 gives the rate of growth in gross domestic product

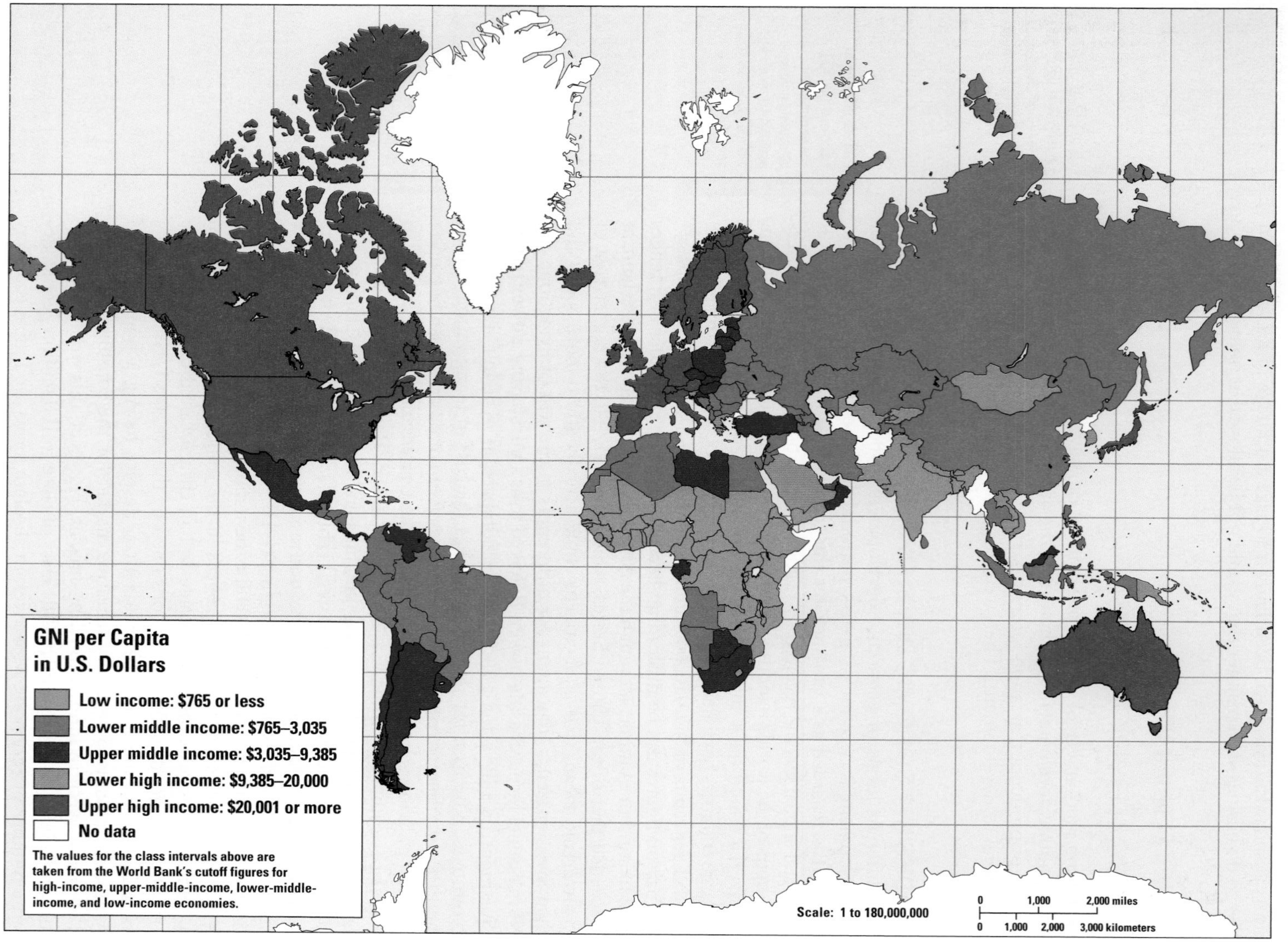

map 2.1 Gross National Income per Capita, 2004

Source: Data from World Bank, *World Development Indicators Online,* 2003. Reprinted by permission from the International Bank for Reconstruction and Development. © 2003 by the World Bank.

Country	GNI per Capita, 2004	GNI PPP per Capita, 2004	GDP Growth Rate, 1994–2004	Size of Economy GDP, 2004 ($ billions)
Brazil	$ 3,000	$ 7,935	2.7%	$ 600
China	1,500	5,885	9.5	1,930
Germany	30,690	28,168	1.6	2,740
India	620	3,116	6.3	691
Japan	37,050	29,814	1.2	4,620
Nigeria	430	966	3.5	72
Poland	6,100	12,723	4.5	242
Russia	3,400	9,683	1.5	581
Switzerland	49,600	35,661	1.3	358
United Kingdom	33,630	31,431	3.0	2120
United States	41,440	39,823	3.4	11,700

table 2.1

Economic Data for Select Countries

Source: World Development Indicators Online, 2006.

(GDP) achieved by a number of countries between 1994 and 2004. Map 2.3 summarizes the growth rate in GDP from 1994 to 2004. Although countries such as China and India are currently poor, their economies are already large in absolute terms and growing more rapidly than those of many advanced nations. They are already huge markets for the products of international businesses. If it maintains its growth rates, China in particular will be larger than all but that of the United States within a decade, and India too will be among the largest economies in the world. Given that potential, many international businesses are trying to gain a foothold in these markets now. Even though their current contributions to an international firm's revenues might be relatively small, their future contributions could be much larger.

BROADER CONCEPTIONS OF DEVELOPMENT: AMARTYA SEN

The Nobel Prize–winning economist Amartya Sen has argued that development should be assessed less by material output measures such as GNI per capita and more by the capabilities and opportunities that people enjoy (see Another Perspective box at right).[30] According to Sen, development should be seen as a process of expanding the real freedoms that people experience. Hence, development requires the removal of major impediments to freedom: poverty as well as tyranny, poor economic opportunities as well as systematic social deprivation, neglect of public facilities as well as the intolerance of repressive states. In Sen's view, development is not just an economic process, but it is a political one too, and to succeed requires the "democratization" of political communities to give citizens a voice in the important decisions made for the community. This perspective leads Sen to emphasize basic health care, especially for children, and basic education, especially for women. Not only are

Another Perspective

If We Were a Community of 100 People

To get a good sense of the scale of economic and demographic measures that this chapter describes, if we were a community of 100, 61 of us would be Asian, 12 European, 14 North and South American, 13 African, 1 Australian. Six of us would own 59 percent of the community's wealth. Thirteen would be hungry, 14 would not read, and 7 would be educated (secondary level). Thirty would have bank accounts and 25 would live on $1.00 a day or less. To learn more and see the video that puts these measures into a meaningful ratio, visit the online version of *The Miniature Earth* (www.miniature-earth.com).

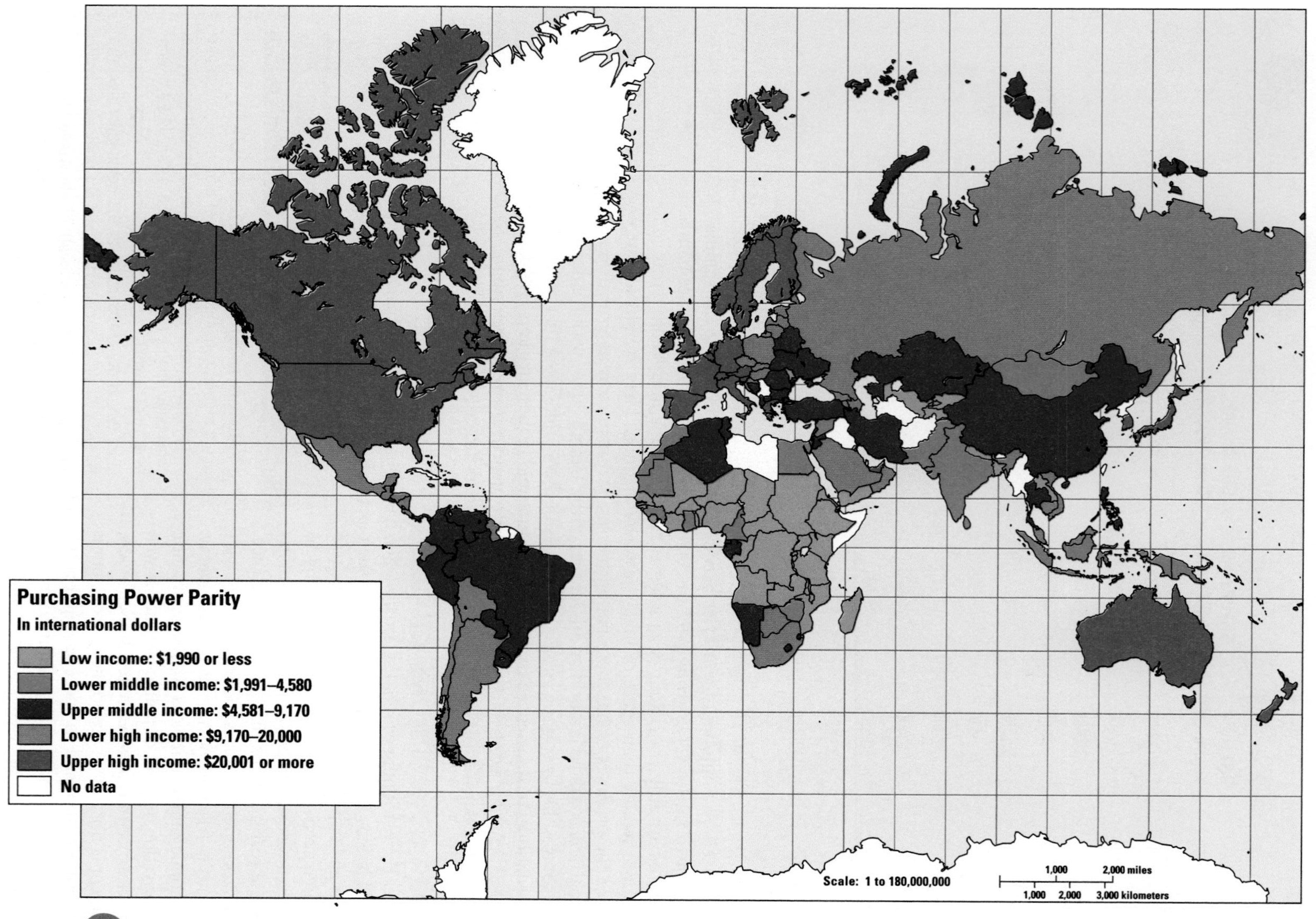

map 2.2 Purchasing Power Parity, 2004

Source: Data from World Bank, *World Development Indicators Online*, 2003. Reprinted by permission from the International Bank for Reconstruction and Development. © 2003 by the World Bank.

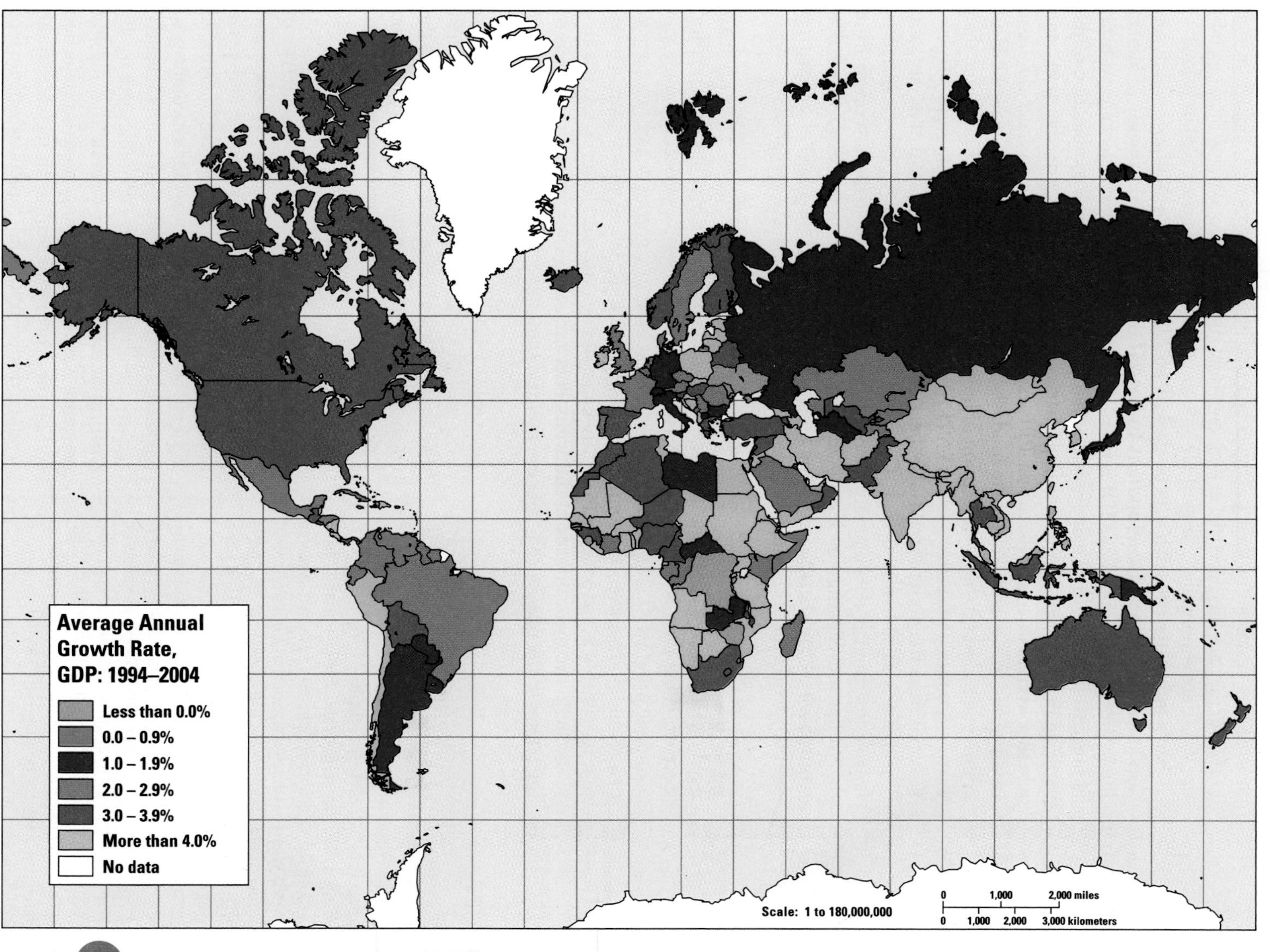

map 2.3 Growth in Gross Domestic Product, 1994–2004

Source: Data from World Bank, *World Development Indicators Online*, 2005. Reprinted by permission from the International Bank for Reconstruction and Development. © 2003 by the World Bank.

these factors desirable for their instrumental value in helping to achieve higher income levels, but they are also beneficial in their own right. People cannot develop their capabilities if they are chronically ill or woefully ignorant (see Another Perspective box below).

Human Development Index (HDI) An attempt by the UN to assess the impact of a number of factors on the quality of human life in a country.

Sen's influential thesis has been picked up by the United Nations, which has developed the **Human Development Index (HDI)** to measure the quality of human life in different nations. The HDI is based on three measures: life expectancy at birth (a function of health care), educational attainment (measured by a combination of the adult literacy rate and enrollment in primary, secondary, and tertiary education), and whether average incomes, based on PPP estimates, are sufficient to meet the basic needs of life in a country (adequate food, shelter, and health care). As such, the HDI comes much closer to Sen's conception of how development should be measured than narrow economic measures such as GNI per capita—although Sen's thesis suggests that political freedoms should also be included in the index, and they are not. The HDI is scaled from 0 to 1. Countries scoring less than 0.5 are classified as having low human development (the quality of life is poor); those scoring from 0.5 to 0.8 are classified as having medium human development; and those that score above 0.8 are classified as having high human development. Map 2.4 summarizes the HDI scores for 2003, the most recent year for which data are available.

Innovation Development of new products, processes, organizations, management practices, and strategies.

Entrepreneurs Those who first commercialize innovations.

POLITICAL ECONOMY AND ECONOMIC PROGRESS It is often argued that a country's economic development is a function of its economic and political systems. What then is the nature of the relationship between political economy and economic progress? This question has been the subject of vigorous debate among academics and policymakers for some time. Despite the long debate, this remains a question for which it is not possible to give an unambiguous answer. However, it is possible to untangle the main threads of the arguments and make a few generalizations as to the nature of the relationship between political economy and economic progress.

Another Perspective

A Powerful "Sen" Example: From "Untouchable" to Entrepreneur

Inspired by a Dalit woman, Bishu Maya Pariyar—who defied a more than 2,000-year-old caste system to become an educated woman—the Association of Dalit Women of Nepal, now called Empower Dalit Women of Nepal (EDWON), was born. The organization teaches women literacy and basic math skills and then gives them seed loans to start their own businesses. For $20 in seed money, a woman can purchase three goats or other livestock, seeds, or inventory for a tea stall. These newly empowered women lead their business ventures with the joint purpose of also educating and inspiring other Dalit women through similar micro-finance groups. More than 1,500 women in 20 communities have participated in EDWON, and more than 700 children have been awarded scholarships to secondary schools. Repayment is 100 percent because of the strong solidarity in the group. This educational and economic empowerment takes development to a new level by breaking down the rigid Hindu caste system of Nepal. Visit www.EDWON.org for a closer look.

Innovation and Entrepreneurship Are the Engines of Growth There is wide agreement that innovation and entrepreneurial activity are the engines of long-run economic growth.[31] Those who make this argument define **innovation** broadly to include not just new products but also new processes, new organizations, new management practices, and new strategies. Thus, the Toys "R" Us strategy of establishing large warehouse-style toy stores and then engaging in heavy advertising and price discounting to sell the merchandise can be classified as an innovation because it was the first company to pursue this strategy. Innovation and entrepreneurial activity helps to increase economic activity by creating new products and markets that did not previously exist. Moreover, innovations in production and business processes lead to an increase in the productivity of labor and capital, which further boosts economic growth rates.[32]

Innovation is also seen as the product of entrepreneurial activity. Often, **entrepreneurs** first commercialize innovative new products and processes, and entrepreneurial activity provides much of the dynamism in an economy. For example,

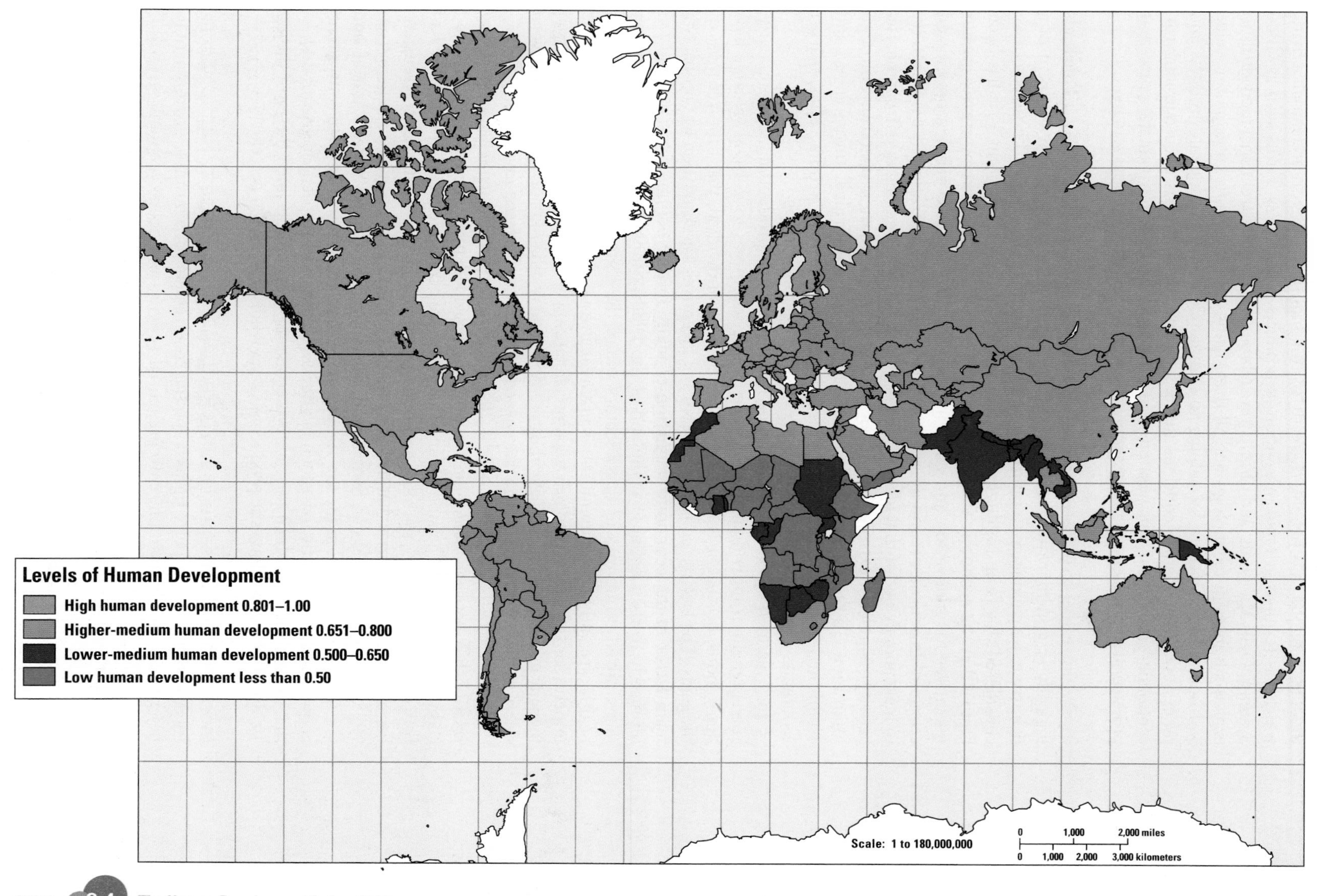

map 2.4 The Human Development Index, 2003

Source: Data from United Nations, *Human Development Report, 2004, Human Development Index, 2003.*

the U.S. economy has benefited greatly from a high level of entrepreneurial activity, which has resulted in rapid innovation in products and process. Firms such as Cisco Systems, Dell, Microsoft, and Oracle were all founded by entrepreneurial individuals to exploit advances in technology, and all these firms created significant economic value and boosted productivity by helping to commercialize innovations in products and processes. Thus, one can conclude that if a country's economy is to sustain long-run economic growth, the business environment must be conducive to the consistent production of product and process innovations and to entrepreneurial activity.

Innovation and Entrepreneurship Require a Market Economy This leads logically to a further question: What is required for the business environment of a country to be conducive to innovation and entrepreneurial activity? Those who have considered this issue highlight the advantages of a market economy.[33] It has been argued that the economic freedom associated with a market economy creates greater incentives for innovation and entrepreneurship than either a planned or a mixed economy. In a market economy, any individual who has an innovative idea is free to try to make money out of that idea by starting a business (by engaging in entrepreneurial activity). Similarly, existing businesses are free to improve their operations through innovation. To the extent that they are successful, both individual entrepreneurs and established businesses can reap rewards in the form of high profits. Thus, market economies contain enormous incentives to develop innovations.

In a planned economy, the state owns all means of production. Consequently, entrepreneurial individuals have few economic incentives to develop valuable new innovations, because it is the state, rather than the individual, that captures most of the gains. The lack of economic freedom and incentives for innovation was probably a main factor in the economic stagnation of many former communist states and led ultimately to their collapse at the end of the 1980s. Similar stagnation occurred in many mixed economies in those sectors where the state had a monopoly (such as health care and telecommunications in Great Britain). This stagnation provided the impetus for the widespread privatization of state-owned enterprises that we witnessed in many mixed economies during the mid-1980s and is still going on today (*privatization* refers to the process of selling state-owned enterprises to private investors).

A study of 102 countries over a 20-year period provided evidence of a strong relationship between economic freedom (as provided by a market economy) and economic growth.[34] The study found that the more economic freedom a country had between 1975 and 1995, the more economic growth it achieved and the richer its citizens became. The six countries that had persistently high ratings of economic freedom from 1975 to 1995 (Hong Kong, Switzerland, Singapore, the United States, Canada, and Germany) were also all in the top 10 in terms of economic growth rates. In contrast, no country with persistently low economic freedom achieved a respectable growth rate. In the 16 countries for which the index of economic freedom declined the most during 1975 to 1995, gross domestic product fell at an annual rate of 0.6 percent.

Innovation and Entrepreneurship Require Strong Property Rights Strong legal protection of property rights is another requirement for a business environment to be conducive to innovation, entrepreneurial activity, and hence economic growth.[35] Both individuals and businesses must be given the opportunity to profit from innovative ideas. Without strong property rights protection, businesses and individuals run the risk that the profits from their innovative efforts will be expropriated, either by criminal elements or by the state. The state can expropriate the profits from innovation through legal means, such as excessive taxation, or through illegal means, such as demands from state bureaucrats for kickbacks in return for granting an individual or firm a license to do business in a certain area (i.e., corruption). According to the Nobel Prize–winning economist Douglass North, throughout history many governments have displayed a tendency to engage in such behavior. Inadequately enforced property rights reduce the incentives for innovation and entrepreneurial activity—because the profits from such activity are "stolen"—and hence reduce the rate of economic growth.

The influential Peruvian development economist Hernando de Soto has argued that much of the developing world will fail to reap the benefits of capitalism until property rights are better defined and protected.[36] De Soto's arguments are interesting because he claims that the key problem is not the risk of expropriation but the chronic inability of property owners to establish legal title to the property they own. As an example of the scale of the problem, he cites the situation in Haiti where individuals must take 176 steps over 19 years to own land legally. Because most property in poor countries is informally "owned," the absence of legal proof of ownership means that property holders cannot convert their assets into capital, which could then be used to finance business ventures. Banks will not lend money to the poor to start businesses because the poor possess no proof that they own property, such as farmland, that can be used as collateral for a loan. By de Soto's calculations, the total value of real estate held by the poor in Third World and former communist states amounted to more than $9.3 trillion in 2000. If those assets could be converted into capital, the result could be an economic revolution that would allow the poor to bootstrap their way out of poverty.

The Required Political System Much debate surrounds which kind of political system best achieves a functioning market economy with strong protection for property rights.[37] People in the West tend to associate a representative democracy with a market economic system, strong property rights protection, and economic progress. Building on this, we tend to argue that democracy is good for growth. However, some totalitarian regimes have fostered a market economy and strong property rights protection and have experienced rapid economic growth. Five of the fastest-growing economies of the past 30 years—China, South Korea, Taiwan, Singapore, and Hong Kong—had one thing in common at the start of their economic growth: undemocratic governments. At the same time, countries with stable democratic governments, such as India, experienced sluggish economic growth for long periods. In 1992, Lee Kuan Yew, Singapore's leader for many years, told an audience, "I do not believe that democracy necessarily leads to development. I believe that a country needs to develop discipline more than democracy. The exuberance of democracy leads to undisciplined and disorderly conduct which is inimical to development."[38]

However, those who argue for the value of a totalitarian regime miss an important point: If dictators made countries rich, then much of Africa, Asia, and Latin America should have been growing rapidly during 1960 to 1990, and this was not the case. Only a totalitarian regime that is committed to a free market system and strong protection of property rights is capable of promoting economic growth. Also, there is no guarantee that a dictatorship will continue to pursue such progressive policies. Dictators are rarely so benevolent. Many are tempted to use the apparatus of the state to further their own private ends, violating property rights and stalling economic growth. Given this, it seems likely that democratic regimes are far more conducive to long-term economic growth than are dictatorships, even benevolent ones. Only in a well-functioning, mature democracy are property rights truly secure.[39] Nor should we forget Amartya Sen's arguments that we reviewed earlier. Totalitarian states, by limiting human freedom, also suppress human development and therefore are detrimental to progress.

Economic Progress Begets Democracy While it is possible to argue that democracy is not a necessary precondition for a free market economy in which property rights are protected, subsequent economic growth often leads to establishment of a democratic regime. Several of the fastest-growing Asian economies adopted more democratic governments during the past two decades, including South Korea and Taiwan. Thus, although democracy may not always be the cause of initial economic progress, it seems to be one consequence of that progress.

A strong belief that economic progress leads to adoption of a democratic regime underlies the fairly permissive attitude that many Western governments have adopted toward human rights violations in China. Although China has a totalitarian government in which human rights are violated, many Western countries have been hesitant to criticize the country too much for fear that this might hamper the country's march toward a free market system. The belief is that once China has a free market system, greater individual freedoms and democracy will follow. Whether this optimistic vision comes to pass remains to be seen.

GEOGRAPHY, EDUCATION, AND ECONOMIC DEVELOPMENT

While a country's political and economic systems are probably the big engine driving its rate of economic development, other factors are also important. One that has received attention recently is geography.[40] But the belief that geography can influence economic policy, and hence economic growth rates, goes back to Adam Smith. The influential Harvard University economist Jeffrey Sachs argues

> that throughout history, coastal states, with their long engagements in international trade, have been more supportive of market institutions than landlocked states, which have tended to organize themselves as hierarchical (and often military) societies. Mountainous states, as a result of physical isolation, have often neglected market-based trade. Temperate climes have generally supported higher densities of population and thus a more extensive division of labor than tropical regions.[41]

Sachs's point is that by virtue of favorable geography, certain societies were more likely to engage in trade than others and were thus more likely to be open to and develop market-based economic systems, which in turn would promote faster economic growth. He also argues that, irrespective of the economic and political institutions a country adopts, adverse geographical conditions, such as the high rate of disease, poor soils, and hostile climate that afflict many tropical countries, can have a negative impact on development. Together with colleagues at Harvard's Institute for International Development, Sachs tested for the impact of geography on a country's economic growth rate between 1965 and 1990. He found that landlocked countries grew more slowly than coastal economies and that being entirely landlocked reduced a country's growth rate by roughly 0.7 percent per year. He also found that tropical countries grew 1.3 percent more slowly each year than countries in the temperate zone.

Education emerges as another important determinant of economic development (a point that Amartya Sen emphasizes). The general assertion is that nations that invest more in education will have higher growth rates because an educated population is a more productive population. Anecdotal comparisons suggest this is true. In 1960, Pakistanis and South Koreans were on equal footing economically. However, just 30 percent of Pakistani children were enrolled in primary schools, while 94 percent of South Koreans were. By the mid-1980s, South Korea's GNP per person was three times that of Pakistan's.[42] A survey of 14 statistical studies that looked at the relationship between a country's investment in education and its subsequent growth rates concluded investment in education did have a positive and statistically significant impact on a country's rate of economic growth.[43] Similarly, the work by Sachs discussed above suggests that investments in education help explain why some countries in Southeast

Asia, such as Indonesia, Malaysia, and Singapore, have been able to overcome the disadvantages associated with their tropical geography and grow far more rapidly than tropical nations in Africa and Latin America.

States in Transition

LEARNING OBJECTIVE 5
Discuss the macro-political and economic changes taking place worldwide.

The political economy of many of the world's nation-states has changed radically since the late 1980s. Two trends have been evident. First, during the late 1980s and early 1990s, a wave of democratic revolutions swept the world. Totalitarian governments collapsed and were replaced by democratically elected governments that were typically more committed to free market capitalism than their predecessors had been. Second, there has been a strong move away from centrally planned and mixed economies and toward a more free market economic model. We shall look first at the spread of democracy and then turn our attention to the spread of free market economics.

THE SPREAD OF DEMOCRACY One notable development of the past 15 years has been the spread of democracy (and, by extension, the decline of totalitarianism). Map 2.5 reports on the extent of totalitarianism in the world as determined by Freedom House.[44] This map charts political freedom in 2005, grouping countries into three broad groupings, free, partly free, and not free. In "free" countries, citizens enjoy a high degree of political and civil freedoms. "Partly free" countries are characterized by some restrictions on political rights and civil liberties, often in the context of corruption, weak rule of law, ethnic strife, or civil war. In "not free" countries, the political process is tightly controlled and basic freedoms are denied.

Freedom House classified some 89 countries as free in 2005, accounting for some 46 percent of the world's population. These countries respect a broad range of political rights. Another 58 countries accounting for 30 percent of the world's population were classified as partly free, while 45 countries representing some 24 percent of the world's population were classified as not free. The number of democracies in the world has increased from 69 nations in 1987 to 122 in 2005, the highest number in history. But not all democracies are free, according to Freedom House, because some democracies still restrict certain political and civil liberties. For example, Russia was rated "not free." According to Freedom House,

> Russia's step backwards into the Not Free category is the culmination of a growing trend under President Vladimir Putin to concentrate political authority, harass and intimidate the media, and politicize the country's law-enforcement system.[45]

Many of these newer democracies are to be found in Eastern Europe and Latin America, although there also have been notable gains in Africa during this time, such as in South Africa. Entrants into the ranks of the world's democracies include Mexico, which held its first fully free and fair presidential election in 2000 after free and fair parliamentary and state elections in 1997 and 1998; Senegal, where free and fair presidential elections led to a peaceful transfer of power; Yugoslavia, where a democratic election took place despite attempted fraud by the incumbent; and Ukraine, where popular unrest following widespread ballot fraud in the 2004 presidential election resulted in a second election, the victory of a reform candidate, and a marked improvement in civil liberties.

Three main reasons account for the spread of democracy.[46] First, many totalitarian regimes failed to deliver economic progress to the vast bulk of their populations. The collapse of communism in Eastern Europe, for example, was precipitated by the growing gulf between the vibrant and wealthy economies of the West and the stagnant

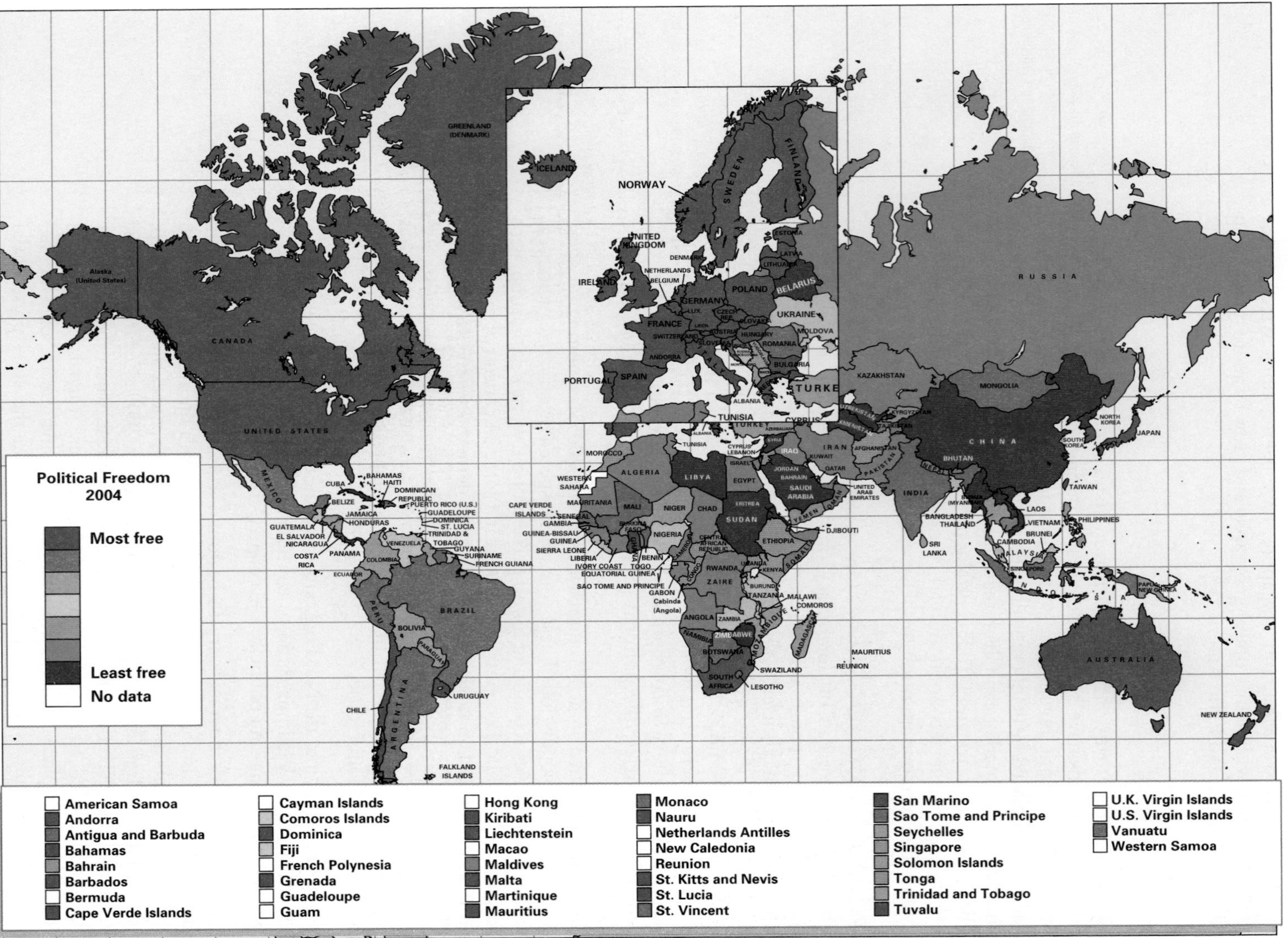

map 2.5 Political Freedom, 2005

Source: Map data from Freedom House, *Freedom in the World 2005: The Annual Survey of Political Rights and Civil Liberties*, www.freedomhouse.org. Reprinted with permission.

economies of the Communist East. In looking for alternatives to the socialist model, the populations of these countries could not have failed to notice that most of the world's strongest economies were governed by representative democracies. Today, the economic success of many of the newer democracies, such as Poland and the Czech Republic in the former Communist bloc, the Philippines and Taiwan in Asia, and Chile in Latin America, has strengthened the case for democracy as a key component of successful economic advancement.

Second, new information and communication technologies, including shortwave radio, satellite television, fax machines, desktop publishing, and, most important, the Internet, have reduced the state's ability to control access to uncensored information. These technologies have created new conduits for the spread of democratic ideals and information from free societies. Today, the Internet is allowing democratic ideals to penetrate closed societies as never before.[47]

Third, in many countries the economic advances of the past quarter century have led to the emergence of increasingly prosperous middle and working classes who have pushed for democratic reforms. This was certainly a factor in the democratic transformation of South Korea. Entrepreneurs and other business leaders, eager to protect their property rights and ensure the dispassionate enforcement of contracts, are another force pressing for more accountable and open government.

Despite this, it would be naive to conclude that the global spread of democracy will continue unchallenged. Democracy is still rare in large parts of the world. In sub-Saharan Africa in 2005, only 11 countries are considered free, 23 are partly free, and 14 are not free. Among the 27 post-Communist countries in Eastern and Central Europe, 7 are still not electoral democracies and Freedom House classifies only 13 of these states as free (primarily in Eastern Europe). And there are no free states among the 16 Arab nations of the Middle East and North Africa.

THE NEW WORLD ORDER AND GLOBAL TERRORISM The end of the Cold War and the "new world order" that followed the collapse of communism in Eastern Europe and the former Soviet Union, taken together with the demise of many authoritarian regimes in Latin America, have given rise to intense speculation about the future shape of global geopolitics. Author Francis Fukuyama has argued, "We may be witnessing . . . the end of history as such: that is, the end point of mankind's ideological evolution and the universalization of Western liberal democracy as the final form of human government."[48] Fukuyama goes on to say that the war of ideas may be at an end and that liberal democracy has triumphed.

Others question Fukuyama's vision of a more harmonious world dominated by a universal civilization characterized by democratic regimes and free market capitalism. In a controversial book, the influential political scientist Samuel Huntington argues that there is no "universal" civilization based on widespread acceptance of Western liberal democratic ideals.[49] Huntington maintains that while many societies may be modernizing—they are adopting the material paraphernalia of the modern world, from automobiles to Coca-Cola and MTV—they are not becoming more Western. On the contrary, Huntington theorizes that modernization in non-Western societies can result in a retreat toward the traditional, such as the resurgence of Islam in many traditionally Muslim societies. He writes,

> The Islamic resurgence is both a product of and an effort to come to grips with modernization. Its underlying causes are those generally responsible for indigenization trends in non-Western societies: urbanization, social mobilization, higher levels of literacy and education, intensified communication and media consumption, and expanded interaction with Western and other cultures. These

developments undermine traditional village and clan ties and create alienation and an identity crisis. Islamist symbols, commitments, and beliefs meet these psychological needs, and Islamist welfare organizations, the social, cultural, and economic needs of Muslims caught in the process of modernization. Muslims feel a need to return to Islamic ideas, practices, and institutions to provide the compass and the motor of modernization.[50]

Thus, the rise of Islamic fundamentalism is portrayed as a response to the alienation produced by modernization.

In contrast to Fukuyama, Huntington sees a world that is split into different civilizations, each of which has its own value systems and ideology. In addition to Western civilization, Huntington predicts the emergence of strong Islamic and Sinic (Chinese) civilizations, as well as civilizations based on Japan, Africa, Latin America, Eastern Orthodox Christianity (Russian), and Hinduism (Indian). Huntington also sees the civilizations as headed for conflict, particularly along the "fault lines" that separate them, such as Bosnia (where Muslims and Orthodox Christians have clashed), Kashmir (where Muslims and Hindus clash), and the Sudan (where a bloody war between Christians and Muslims has persisted for decades). Huntington predicts conflict between the West and Islam and between the West and China. He bases his predictions on an analysis of the different value systems and ideology of these civilizations, which in his view tend to bring them into conflict with each other. While some commentators originally dismissed Huntington's thesis, in the aftermath of the terrorist attacks on the United States on September 11, 2001, Huntington's views received new attention.

If Huntington's views are even partly correct—and there is little doubt that the events surrounding September 11 added more weight to his thesis—they have important implications for international business. They suggest many countries may be increasingly difficult places in which to do business, either because they are shot through with violent conflicts or because they are part of a civilization that is in conflict with an enterprise's home country. Huntington's views are speculative and controversial. It is not clear that his predictions will come to pass. More likely is the evolution of a global political system that is positioned somewhere between Fukuyama's universal global civilization based on liberal democratic ideals and Huntington's vision of a fractured world. That would still be a world, however, in which geopolitical forces periodically limit the ability of business enterprises to operate in certain foreign countries.

In Huntington's thesis, global terrorism is a product of the tension between civilizations and the clash of value systems and ideology. Others point to terrorism's roots in long-standing conflicts that seem to defy political resolution, the Palestinian, Kashmir, and Northern Ireland conflicts being obvious examples. It should also be noted that a substantial amount of terrorist activity in some parts of the world, such as Colombia, has been interwoven with the illegal drug trade. The attacks of September 11, 2001, created the impression that global terror is on the rise, although accurate statistics on this are hard to come by. What we do know is that according to data from the U.S. Department of State, in 2005 there were some 11,111 terrorist attacks worldwide that resulted in 14,602 fatalities. Iraq alone accounted for 30 percent of the attacks and some 8,300 fatalities. As former U.S. secretary of state Colin Powell has maintained, terrorism represents one of the major threats to world peace and economic progress in the twenty-first century.[51]

THE SPREAD OF MARKET-BASED SYSTEMS Paralleling the spread of democracy since the 1980s has been the transformation from centrally planned command economies to market-based economies. More than 30 countries that were in the former Soviet Union or the Eastern European Communist bloc have changed their economic systems. A complete list of countries where change is now occurring also would include Asian states such as China and Vietnam, as well as African countries such as Angola, Ethiopia, and Mozambique.[52] There has been a similar shift away from a mixed economy. Many states in Asia, Latin America, and Western Europe have sold state-owned businesses to private investors (privatization) and deregulated their economies to promote greater competition.

The rationale for economic transformation has been the same the world over (see Another Perspective box at right). In general, command and mixed economies failed to deliver the kind of sustained economic performance that was achieved by countries adopting market-based systems, such as the United States, Switzerland, Hong Kong, and Taiwan. As a consequence, even more states have gravitated toward the market-based model. Map 2.6, based on data from the Heritage Foundation, a politically conservative U.S. research foundation, gives some idea of the degree to which the world has shifted toward market-based economic systems. The Heritage Foundation's index of economic freedom is based on 10 indicators, such as the extent to which the government intervenes in the economy, trade policy, the degree to which property rights are protected, foreign investment regulations, and taxation rules. A country can score between 1 (most free) and 5 (least free) on each of these indicators. The lower a country's average score across all 10 indicators, the more closely its economy represents the pure market model. According to the 2006 index, which is summarized in Map 2.6, the world's freest economies are (in rank order) Hong Kong, Singapore, Ireland, Luxembourg, United Kingdom, Iceland, Estonia, Denmark, and the United States. Japan came in at 27; France at 44; Mexico, 60; Brazil, 81; China, 111; India, 121; and Russia, 122. The economies of Cuba, Laos, Iran, Venezuela and North Korea are to be found at the bottom of the rankings.[53]

Another Perspective

Call to Business Students: Visualize World Peace through Commerce

The Association to Advance Collegiate Business Schools of Business (AACSB), which accredits business schools worldwide, has a new mission. Its Peace Through Commerce program aims to raise awareness about what business schools can do to promote peace. Task force representatives to the program hail from around the globe, including Italy and South Korea. Some representatives believe MBA programs should teach students about the role of business in achieving and stabilizing world peace.

As odd as it may sound to us today, the concept of promoting peace through commerce was espoused by philosophers as early as the 1700s, and the idea was in the air after WWII, when the United Nations was founded. It is also a basic tenet of the European Union: countries that trade together don't go to war. AACSB's notion is: "If we educate students that it's their responsibility to advance society, over a generation, we may be able to have more impact than governments have had." Visit www.AACSB.edu to learn more. (Rhea Wessel, "Business Schools' New Mission: Promoting Peace," *The Wall Street Journal*, June 2, 2006, http://online.wsj.com/article/SB114918067881868806.html)

Economic freedom does not necessarily equate with political freedom, as detailed in Map 2.6. For example, the two top states in the Heritage Foundation index, Hong Kong and Singapore, cannot be classified as politically free. Hong Kong was reabsorbed into Communist China in 1997, and the first thing Beijing did was shut down Hong Kong's freely elected legislature. Singapore is ranked as only partly free on Freedom House's index of political freedom due to practices such as widespread press censorship.

LEARNING OBJECTIVE 6
Describe how transition economies are moving toward market-based systems.

THE NATURE OF ECONOMIC TRANSFORMATION

The shift toward a market-based economic system often entails a number of steps: deregulation, privatization, and creation of a legal system to safeguard property rights.[54]

Deregulation

Deregulation involves removing legal restrictions to the free play of markets, the establishment of private enterprises, and the manner in which private enterprises operate. Before the collapse of communism, the governments in most command economies exercised tight control over prices and output, setting both through detailed state planning. They also prohibited private enterprises from operating in most sectors of the economy, severely restricted direct investment by foreign enterprises, and limited international trade. Deregulation in these cases involved removing price controls, thereby

Deregulation
The process of removing legal restrictions to the free play of markets, the establishment of private enterprises, and the manner in which private enterprises operate.

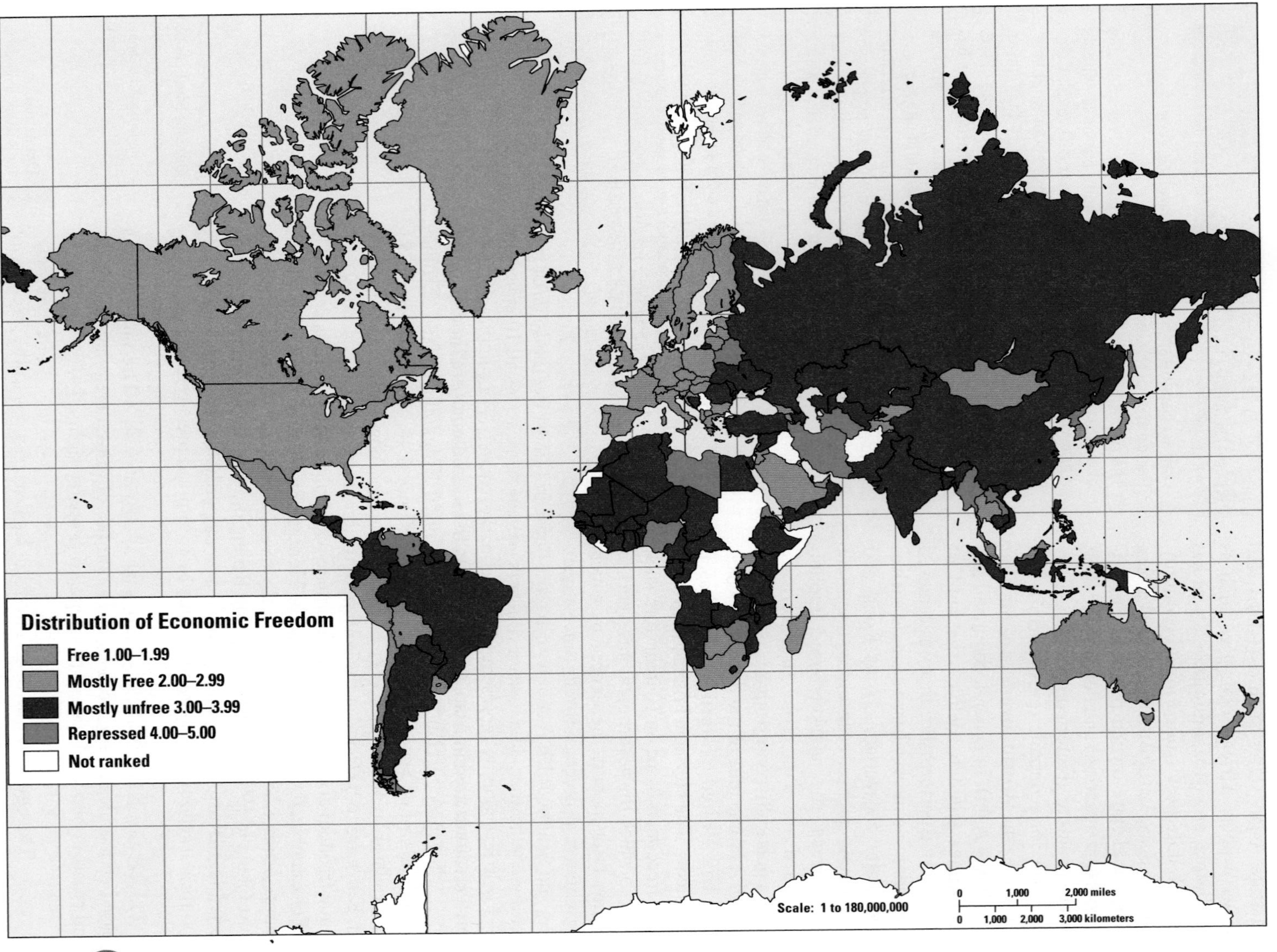

map 2.6 Distribution of Economic Freedom, 2006

Source: Heritage Foundation, www.heritage.org/research/features/index/downloads/Index2006_EconFreedomMAP.jpg.

allowing prices to be set by the interplay between demand and supply; abolishing laws regulating the establishment and operation of private enterprises; and relaxing or removing restrictions on direct investment by foreign enterprises and international trade.

In mixed economies, the role of the state was more limited; but here too, in certain sectors the state set prices, owned businesses, limited private enterprise, restricted investment by foreigners, and restricted international trade (for an example, see the Country Focus on India). For these countries, deregulation has involved the same kind of initiatives that we have seen in former command economies, although the transformation has been easier because these countries often had a vibrant private sector.

Privatization Hand in hand with deregulation has come a sharp increase in privatization. Privatization, as we discussed earlier in this chapter, transfers the ownership of state property into the hands of private individuals, frequently by the sale of state assets through an auction.[55] Privatization is seen as a way to stimulate gains in economic efficiency by giving new private owners a powerful incentive—the reward of greater profits—to search for increases in productivity, to enter new markets, and to exit losing ones.[56]

The privatization movement started in Great Britain in the early 1980s when then prime minister Margaret Thatcher started to sell state-owned assets such as the British telephone company, British Telecom (BT). In a pattern that has been repeated around the world, this sale was linked with the deregulation of the British telecommunications industry. By allowing other firms to compete head-to-head with BT, deregulation ensured that privatization did not simply replace a state-owned monopoly with a private monopoly. Since the 1980s, privatization has become a worldwide phenomenon. More than 8,000 acts of privatization were completed around the world between 1995 and 1999.[57] In total, these sales were valued at more than $1 trillion (in 1985 dollars). In the United Kingdom alone, some 139 state-owned enterprises were sold for a total of $130 billion. Some of the most dramatic privatization programs occurred in the economies of the former Soviet Union and its Eastern European satellite states. In the Czech Republic, for example, three-quarters of all state-owned enterprises were privatized between 1989 and 1996, helping to push the share of gross domestic product accounted for by the private sector up from 11 percent in 1989 to 60 percent in 1995.[58]

As privatization has proceeded around the world, it has become clear that simply selling state-owned assets to private investors is not enough to guarantee economic growth. Studies of privatization in central Europe have shown that the process often fails to deliver predicted benefits if the newly privatized firms continue to receive subsidies from the state and if they are protected from foreign competition by barriers to international trade and foreign direct investment.[59] In such cases, the newly privatized firms are sheltered from competition and continue acting like state monopolies. When these circumstances prevail, the newly privatized entities often have little incentive to restructure their operations to become more efficient. For privatization to work, it must also be accompanied by a more general deregulation and opening of the economy. Thus, when Brazil decided to privatize the state-owned telephone monopoly, Telebras Brazil, the government also split the company into four independent units that were to compete with each other and removed barriers to foreign direct investment in telecommunications services. This action ensured that the newly privatized entities would face significant competition and thus would have to improve their operating efficiency to survive.

The ownership structure of newly privatized firms also is important.[60] Many former command economies, for example, lack the legal regulations regarding corporate governance that are found in advanced Western economies. In advanced market economies, boards of directors are appointed by shareholders to make sure managers consider the interests of shareholders when making decisions and try to manage the firm in a manner that is consistent with maximizing the wealth of shareholders. However, some

Country FOCUS

Building a Market Economy in India

After gaining independence from Britain in 1947, India adopted a democratic system of government. The economic system that developed in India was a mixed economy characterized by a large number of state-owned enterprises, centralized planning, and subsidies. Private companies could expand only with government permission. It could take years to get permission to diversify into a new product. Much of heavy industry, such as auto, chemical, and steel production, was reserved for state-owned enterprises. Production quotas and high tariffs on imports also stunted the development of a healthy private sector, as did labor laws that made it difficult to fire employees.

By the early 1990s, it was clear that this system was incapable of delivering the kind of economic progress that many Southeastern Asian nations had started to enjoy. In 1994, India's economy was still smaller than Belgium's, despite having a population of 950 million. Its GDP per capita was a paltry $310; less than half the population could read; only 6 million had access to telephones; only 14 percent had access to clean sanitation; the World Bank estimated that some 40 percent of the world's desperately poor lived in India; and only 2.3 percent of the population had a household income in excess of $2,484.

In 1991, the lack of progress led the government to embark on an ambitious economic reform program. Much of the industrial licensing system was dismantled, and several areas once closed to the private sector were opened, including electricity generation, parts of the oil industry, steelmaking, air transport, and some areas of the telecommunications industry. Investment by foreign enterprises, formerly allowed only grudgingly and subject to arbitrary ceilings, was suddenly welcomed. Approval was made automatic for foreign equity stakes of up to 51 percent in an Indian enterprise, and 100 percent foreign ownership was allowed under certain circumstances. Raw materials and many industrial goods could be freely imported and the maximum tariff that could be levied on imports was reduced from 400 percent to 65 percent. The top income tax rate was also reduced, and corporate tax fell from 57.5 percent to 46 percent in 1994, and then to 35 percent in 1997. The government also announced plans to start privatizing India's state-owned businesses, some 40 percent of which were losing money in the early 1990s.

Judged by some measures, the response to these economic reforms has been impressive. The economy expanded at an annual rate of about 6.3 percent from 1994 to 2004. Foreign investment, a key indicator of how attractive foreign companies thought the Indian economy was, jumped from $150 million in 1991 to $6 billion in 2005. Some economic sectors have done particularly well, such as the information technology sector, where India has emerged as a vibrant global center for software development with sales of $21 billion in 2005, up from just $150 million in 1990. In pharmaceuticals too, Indian companies are emerging as credible players on the global marketplace, primarily by selling low-cost, generic versions of drugs that have come off patent in the developed world.

However, the country still has a long way to go. Attempts to further reduce import tariffs have been stalled by political opposition from employers, employees, and politicians, who fear that if barriers come down, a flood of inexpensive Chinese products will enter India. The privatization program continues to hit speed bumps—the latest in September 2003 when the Indian Supreme Court ruled that the government could not privatize two state-owned oil companies without explicit approval from the parliament. There has also been strong resistance to reforming many of India's laws that make it difficult for private business to operate efficiently. For example, labor laws make it almost impossible for firms with more than 100 employees to fire workers. Other laws mandate that certain products can be manufactured only by small companies, effectively making it impossible for companies in these industries to attain the scale required to compete internationally.

Sources: "India's Breakthrough Budget?" *The Economist,* March 3, 2001; Shankar Aiyar, "Reforms: Time to Just Do It," *India Today,* January 24, 2000, p. 47; "America's Pain, India's Gain," *The Economist,* January 11, 2003, p. 57; Joanna Slater, "In Once Socialist India, Privatizations Are Becoming More Like Routine Matters," *The Wall Street Journal,* July 5, 2002, p. A8; "India's Economy: Ready to Roll Again?" *The Economist,* September 20, 2003, pp. 39–40; Joanna Slater, "Indian Pirates Turned Partners," *The Wall Street Journal,* November 13, 2003, p. A14; "The Next Wave: India," *The Economist,* December 17, 2005, p. 67; and M. Dell, "The Digital Sector Can Make Poor Nations Prosper," *Financial Times,* May 4, 2006, p. 17.

former Communist states still lack laws requiring corporations to establish effective boards. In such cases, managers with a small ownership stake can often gain control over the newly privatized entity and run it for their own benefit, while ignoring the interests of other shareholders. Sometimes these managers are the same Communist bureaucrats who ran the enterprise before privatization. Because they have been schooled in the old ways of doing things, they often hesitate to take drastic action to increase the efficiency of the enterprise. Instead, they continue to run the firm as a private fiefdom, seeking to extract whatever economic value they can for their own betterment (in the form of perks that are not reported) while doing little to increase the economic efficiency of the enterprise so that shareholders benefit. Such developments seem less likely to occur, however, if a foreign investor takes a stake in the newly privatized entity. The foreign investor, who usually is a major provider of capital, is often able to use control over a critical resource (money) to push through needed change.

Legal Systems As noted earlier in this chapter, a well-functioning market economy requires laws protecting private property rights and providing mechanisms for contract enforcement. Without a legal system that protects property rights, and without the machinery to enforce that system, the incentive to engage in economic activity can be reduced substantially by private and public entities, including organized crime, that expropriate the profits generated by the efforts of private-sector entrepreneurs. When communism collapsed, many of these countries lacked the legal structure required to protect property rights, all property having been held by the state. Although many nations have made big strides toward instituting the required system, it will be many more years before the legal system is functioning as smoothly as it does in the West. For example, in most Eastern European nations, the title to urban and agricultural property is often uncertain because of incomplete and inaccurate records, multiple pledges on the same property, and unsettled claims resulting from demands for restitution from owners in the pre-Communist era. Also, although most countries have improved their commercial codes, institutional weaknesses still undermine contract enforcement. Court capacity is often inadequate, and procedures for resolving contract disputes out of court are often lacking or poorly developed.[61]

LEARNING OBJECTIVE 7
Articulate the implications for management practice of national differences in political economy.

IMPLICATIONS OF CHANGING POLITICAL ECONOMY

The global changes in political and economic systems discussed above have several implications for international business. The long-standing ideological conflict between collectivism and individualism that defined the twentieth century is less in evidence today. The West won the Cold War, and Western ideology has never been more widespread than it is now. Although command economies remain and totalitarian dictatorships can still be found around the world, the tide has been running in favor of free markets and democracy.

The implications for business are enormous. For nearly 50 years, half of the world was off-limits to Western businesses. Now all that is changing. Many of the national markets of Eastern Europe, Latin America, Africa, and Asia may still be undeveloped and impoverished, but they are potentially enormous. With a population of more than 1.2 billion, the Chinese market alone is potentially bigger than that of the United States, the European Union, and Japan combined. Similarly India, with its nearly 1 billion people, is a potentially huge future market. Latin America has another 400 million potential consumers. It is unlikely that China, Russia, Vietnam, or any of the other states now moving toward a free market system will attain the living standards of the West soon. Nevertheless, the upside potential is so large that companies need to consider making inroads now.

However, just as the potential gains are large, so are the risks. There is no guarantee that democracy will thrive in many of the world's newer democratic states, particularly if these states have to grapple with severe economic setbacks. Totalitarian dictatorships could return, although they are unlikely to be of the communist variety. Although the bipolar world of the Cold War era has vanished, it may be replaced by a multipolar world dominated by a number of civilizations. In such a world, much of the economic promise inherent in the global shift toward market-based economic systems may stall in the face of conflicts between civilizations. While the long-term potential for economic gain from investment in the world's new market economies is large, the risks associated with any such investment are also substantial. It would be foolish to ignore these.

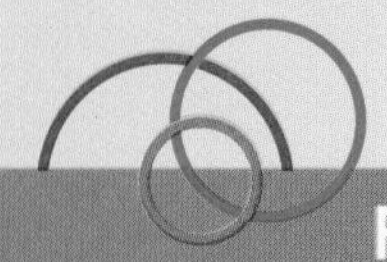

Focus on Managerial Implications

The material discussed in this chapter has two broad implications for international business. First, the political, economic, and legal systems of a country raise important ethical issues that have implications for the practice of international business. For example, what ethical implications are associated with doing business in totalitarian countries where citizens are denied basic human rights, corruption is rampant, and bribes are necessary to gain permission to do business? Is it right to operate in such a setting? A full discussion of the ethical implications of country differences in political economy is reserved for Chapter 4, where we explore ethics in international business in much greater depth.

Second, the political, economic, and legal environments of a country clearly influence the attractiveness of that country as a market or investment site. The benefits, costs, and risks associated with doing business in a country are a function of that country's political, economic, and legal systems. The overall attractiveness of a country as a market or investment site depends on balancing the likely long-term benefits of doing business in that country against the likely costs and risks. Below we consider the determinants of benefits, costs, and risks.

Benefits

In the most general sense, the long-run monetary benefits of doing business in a country are a function of the size of the market, the present wealth (purchasing power) of consumers in that market, and the likely future wealth of consumers. While some markets are very large when measured by number of consumers (e.g., China and India), low living standards may imply limited purchasing power and therefore a relatively small market when measured in economic terms. International businesses need to be aware of this distinction, but they also need to keep in mind the likely future prospects of a country. In 1960, South Korea was viewed as just another impoverished Third World nation. By 2004 it was the world's eleventh-largest economy, measured in terms of GDP. International firms that recognized South Korea's potential in 1960 and began to do business in that country may have reaped greater benefits than those that wrote off South Korea.

By identifying and investing early in a potential future economic star, international firms may build brand loyalty and gain experience in that country's business practices. These will pay back substantial dividends if that country achieves sustained high economic growth rates. In contrast, late entrants may find that they lack the brand loyalty and experience necessary to achieve a significant presence in the market. In the language of business strategy, early entrants into potential future economic stars may be able to reap substantial first-mover advantages, while late entrants may fall victim to late-mover disadvantages.[62] (**First-mover advantages** are the advantages that accrue to early entrants into a market. **Late-mover disadvantages** are the handicaps that late entrants might suffer.) This kind of reasoning has been driving significant inward investment into China, which may become the world's largest economy by 2020 if it continues growing at current rates (China is already the world's sixth-largest economy). For more than a decade, China has been the largest recipient of foreign direct investment in the developing world as international businesses ranging from General Motors and Volkswagen to Coca-Cola and Unilever try to establish a sustainable advantage in this nation.

First-Mover Advantages
Advantages accruing to the first to enter a market.

Late-Mover Disadvantages
Handicaps experienced by being a late entrant to a market.

A country's economic system and property rights regime are reasonably good predictors of economic prospects. Countries with free market economies in which property rights are protected tend to achieve greater economic growth rates than command economies or economies where property rights are poorly protected.

It follows that a country's economic system, property rights regime, and market size (in terms of population) probably constitute reasonably good indicators of the potential long-run benefits of doing business in a country. In contrast, countries where property rights are not well respected and where corruption is rampant tend to have lower levels of economic growth.

Costs

A number of political, economic, and legal factors determine the costs of doing business in a country. With regard to political factors, a company may have to pay off politically powerful entities in a country before the government allows it to do business there. The need to pay what are essentially bribes is greater in closed totalitarian states than in open democratic societies where politicians are held accountable by the electorate (although this is not a hard-and-fast distinction). Whether a company should actually pay bribes in return for market access should be determined on the basis of the legal and ethical implications of such action. We discuss this consideration in Chapter 4, when we look closely at the issue of business ethics.

With regard to economic factors, one of the most important variables is the sophistication of a country's economy. It may be more costly to do business in relatively primitive or undeveloped economies because of the lack of infrastructure and supporting businesses. At the extreme, an international firm may have to provide its own infrastructure and supporting business, which obviously raises costs. When McDonald's decided to open its first restaurant in Moscow, it found that to serve food and drink indistinguishable from that served in McDonald's restaurants elsewhere, it had to vertically integrate backward to supply its own needs. The quality of Russian-grown potatoes and meat was too poor. Thus, to protect the quality of its product, McDonald's set up its own dairy farms, cattle ranches, vegetable plots, and food processing plants within Russia. This raised the cost of doing business in Russia, relative to the cost in more sophisticated economies where high-quality inputs could be purchased on the open market.

As for legal factors, it can be more costly to do business in a country where local laws and regulations set strict standards with regard to product safety, safety in the workplace, environmental pollution, and the like (since adhering to such regulations is costly). It can also be more costly to do business in a country like the United States, where the absence of a cap on damage awards has meant spiraling liability insurance rates. It can be more costly to do business in a country that lacks well-established laws for regulating business practice (as is the case in many of the former Communist nations). In the absence of a well-developed body of business contract law, international firms may find no satisfactory way to resolve contract disputes and, consequently, routinely face large losses from contract violations. Similarly, local laws that fail to adequately protect intellectual property can lead to the theft of an international business's intellectual property and lost income.

Risks

As with costs, the risks of doing business in a country are determined by a number of political, economic, and legal factors. **Political risk** has been defined as the likelihood that political forces will cause drastic changes in a country's business environment that adversely affect the profit and other goals of a business enterprise.[63] So defined, political risk tends to be greater in countries experiencing social unrest and disorder or in countries where the underlying nature of a society increases the likelihood of social unrest. Social unrest typically finds expression in strikes, demonstrations, terrorism, and violent conflict. Such unrest is more likely to be found in countries that contain more than one ethnic nationality, in countries where competing ideologies are battling for political control, in countries where economic mismanagement has created high inflation and falling living standards, or in countries that straddle the "fault lines" between civilizations.

Political Risk
The likelihood that political forces will cause drastic changes in a country's business environment that will adversely affect the profit and other goals of a particular business enterprise.

Social unrest can result in abrupt changes in government and government policy or, in some cases, in protracted civil strife. Such strife tends to have negative economic implications for the profit goals of business enterprises. For example, in the aftermath of the 1979 Islamic revolution in Iran, the Iranian assets of numerous U.S. companies were seized by the new Iranian government without compensation. Similarly, the violent disintegration of the Yugoslavian federation into warring states, including Bosnia, Croatia, and Serbia, precipitated a collapse in the local economies and in the profitability of investments in those countries.

More generally, a change in political regime can result in the enactment of laws that are less favorable to international business. In Venezuela, for example, the populist socialist politician Hugo Chavez won power in 1998, was reelected as president in 2000, and was reaffirmed in a 2004 referendum called after the failure of an attempted coup to remove him. Chavez has declared himself to be a "Fidelista," a follower of Cuba's Fidel Castro. He has pledged to improve the lot of the poor in Venezuela through government intervention in private business and has frequently railed against American imperialism, all of which is of concern to Western enterprises doing business in the country. Among other actions, he increased the royalties foreign oil companies operating in Venezuela have to pay the government from 1 to 30 percent of sales (see the opening case).

Economic Risk
The likelihood that events, including economic mismanagement, will cause drastic changes in a country's business environment that adversely affect the profit and other goals of a particular business enterprise.

Other risks may arise from a country's mismanagement of its economy. An **economic risk** can be defined as the likelihood that economic mismanagement will cause drastic changes in a country's business environment that hurt the profit and other goals of a particular business enterprise. Economic risks are not independent of political risk. Economic mismanagement may give rise to significant social unrest and hence political risk. Nevertheless, economic risks are worth emphasizing as a separate category because there is not always a one-to-one relationship between economic mismanagement and social unrest. One visible indicator of economic mismanagement tends to be a country's inflation rate. Another is the level of business and government debt in the country.

In Asian states such as Indonesia, Thailand, and South Korea, businesses increased their debt rapidly during the 1990s, often at the bequest of the government, which was encouraging them to invest in industries deemed to be of "strategic importance" to the country. The result was overinvestment, with more industrial (factories) and commercial capacity (office space) being built than could be justified by demand conditions. Many of these investments turned out to be uneconomic. The borrowers failed to generate the profits necessary to service their debt payment obligations. In turn, the banks that had lent money to these businesses suddenly found that they had rapid increases in nonperforming loans on their books. Foreign investors, believing that many local companies and banks might go bankrupt, pulled their money out of these countries, selling local stock, bonds, and currency. This action precipitated the 1997–98 financial crises in Southeast Asia. The crisis included a precipitous decline in the value of Asian stock markets, which in some cases exceeded 70 percent; a similar collapse in the value of many Asian currencies against the U.S. dollar; an implosion of local demand; and a severe economic recession that will affect many Asian countries for years to come. In short, economic risks were rising throughout Southeast Asia during the 1990s. Astute foreign businesses and investors limited their exposure in this part of the world. More naive businesses and investors lost their shirts.

Legal Risk
The likelihood that a trading partner will opportunistically break a contract or expropriate intellectual property rights.

On the legal front, risks arise when a country's legal system fails to provide adequate safeguards in the case of contract violations or to protect property rights. When legal safeguards are weak, firms are more likely to break contracts or steal intellectual property if they perceive it as being in their interests to do so. Thus, a **legal risk** can be defined as the likelihood that a trading partner will opportunistically break a contract or expropriate property rights. When legal risks in a country are high, an international business might hesitate before entering into a long-term contract or joint-venture agreement with a firm in that country. For example, in the 1970s when the Indian government passed a law requiring all foreign investors to enter into joint ventures with Indian companies, U.S. companies such as IBM and Coca-Cola closed their investments in India. They believed that the Indian legal system did not provide for adequate protection of intellectual property rights, creating the very real danger that their Indian partners might expropriate the intellectual property of the American companies—which for IBM and Coca-Cola amounted to the core of their competitive advantage.

Overall Attractiveness

The overall attractiveness of a country as a potential market or investment site for an international business depends on balancing the benefits, costs, and risks associated with doing business in that country (see Figure 2.3). Generally, the costs and risks associated with doing business in a foreign country are typically lower in economically advanced and politically stable democratic nations and greater in less developed and politically unstable nations. The calculus is complicated, however, because the potential long-run benefits are dependent not only upon a nation's current stage of economic development or political stability but also on likely future economic growth rates. Economic growth appears to be a function of a free market system and a country's capacity for growth (which may be greater in less developed nations). This leads one to conclude that, other things being equal, the benefit–cost–risk trade-off is likely to be most favorable in politically stable developed and developing nations that have free market systems and no dramatic upsurge in either inflation rates or private-sector debt. It is likely to be least favorable in politically unstable developing nations that operate with a mixed or command economy or in developing nations where speculative financial bubbles have led to excess borrowing.

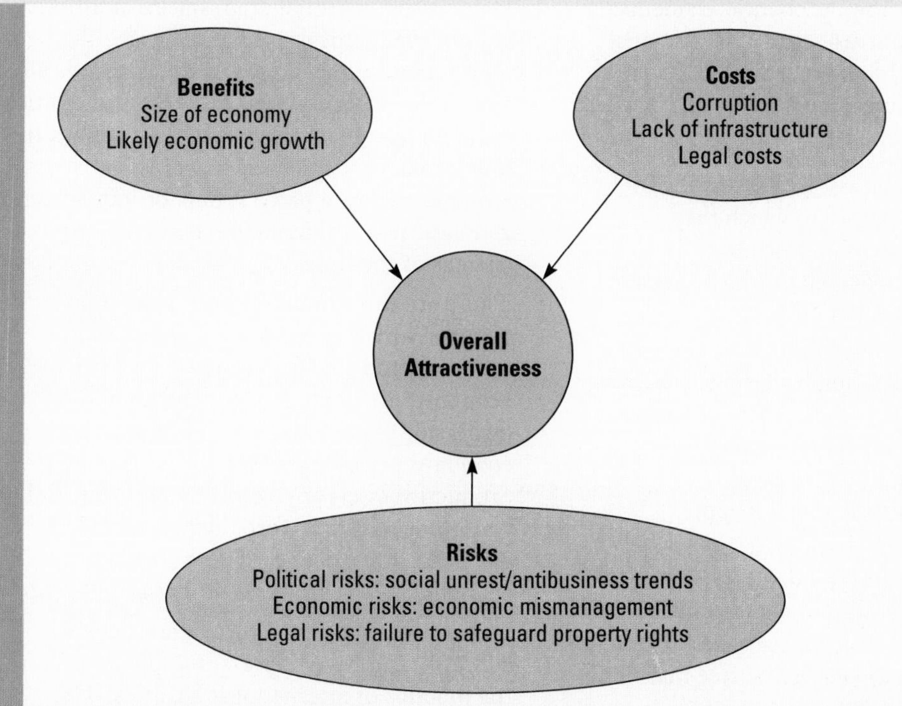

figure 2.3
Country Attractiveness

Key Terms

political economy, p. 43
political system, p. 43
collectivism, p. 43
socialism, p. 44
communists, p. 44
social democrats, p. 44
privatization, p. 45
individualism, p. 45
democracy, p. 46
totalitarianism, p. 46
representative democracy, p. 47
communist totalitarianism, p. 47
theocratic totalitarianism, p. 47
tribal totalitarianism, p. 47
right-wing totalitarianism, p. 47
market economy, p. 48
command economy, p. 49
mixed economy, p. 50
legal system, p. 50
common law, p. 50
civil law system, p. 51
theocratic law system, p. 51
contract, p. 52
contract law, p. 52
United Nations Convention on Contracts for the International Sale of Goods (CIGS), p. 52
property rights, p. 52
private action, p. 53
public action, p. 53
Foreign Corrupt Practices Act, p. 54
intellectual property, p. 56
patent, p. 56
copyrights, p. 56
trademark, p. 56
World Intellectual Property Organization, p. 56
Paris Convention for the Protection of Industrial Property, p. 56
product safety laws, p. 58
product liability, p. 58
gross national income (GNI), p. 59
purchasing power parity (PPP), p. 59
Human Development Index (HDI), p. 64
innovation, p. 64
entrepreneurs, p. 64
deregulation, p. 73
first-mover advantages, p. 78
late-mover disadvantages, p. 78
political risk, p. 79
economic risk, p. 80
legal risk, p. 80

Summary

This chapter has reviewed how the political, economic, and legal systems of countries vary. The potential benefits, costs, and risks of doing business in a country are a function of its political, economic, and legal systems. The chapter made the following points:

1. Political systems can be assessed according to two dimensions: the degree to which they emphasize collectivism as opposed to individualism, and the degree to which they are democratic or totalitarian.
2. Collectivism is an ideology that views the needs of society as being more important than the needs of the individual. Collectivism translates into an advocacy for state intervention in economic activity and, in the case of communism, a totalitarian dictatorship.
3. Individualism is an ideology that is built on an emphasis of the primacy of individual's freedoms in the political, economic, and cultural realms. Individualism translates into an advocacy for democratic ideals and free market economics.
4. Democracy and totalitarianism are at different ends of the political spectrum. In a representative democracy, citizens periodically elect individuals to represent them and political freedoms are guaranteed by a constitution. In a totalitarian state, political power is monopolized by a party, group, or individual, and basic political freedoms are denied to citizens of the state.
5. There are three broad types of economic systems: a market economy, a command economy, and a mixed economy. In a market economy, prices are free of controls and private ownership is predominant. In a command economy, prices are set by central planners, productive assets are owned by the state, and private ownership is forbidden. A mixed economy has elements of both a market economy and a command economy.
6. Differences in the structure of law between countries can have important implications for the practice of international business. The

degree to which property rights are protected can vary dramatically from country to country, as can product safety and product liability legislation and the nature of contract law.

7. The rate of economic progress in a country seems to depend on the extent to which that country has a well-functioning market economy in which property rights are protected.
8. Many countries are now in a state of transition. There is a marked shift away from totalitarian governments and command or mixed economic systems and toward democratic political institutions and free market economic systems.
9. The attractiveness of a country as a market and/or investment site depends on balancing the likely long-run benefits of doing business in that country against the likely costs and risks.
10. The benefits of doing business in a country are a function of the size of the market (population), its present wealth (purchasing power), and its future growth prospects. By investing early in countries that are currently poor but are nevertheless growing rapidly, firms can gain first-mover advantages that will pay back substantial dividends in the future.
11. The costs of doing business in a country tend to be greater where political payoffs are required to gain market access, where supporting infrastructure is lacking or underdeveloped, and where adhering to local laws and regulations is costly.
12. The risks of doing business in a country tend to be greater in countries that are politically unstable, subject to economic mismanagement, and lacking a legal system to provide adequate safeguards in the case of contract or property rights violations.

Critical Thinking and Discussion Questions

1. Free market economies stimulate greater economic growth, whereas state-directed economies stifle growth. Discuss.
2. A democratic political system is an essential condition for sustained economic progress. Discuss.
3. What is the relationship between corruption in a country (i.e., bribe taking by government officials) and economic growth? Is corruption always bad?
4. The Nobel Prize–winning economist Amartya Sen argues that the concept of development should be broadened to include more than just economic development. What other factors does Sen think should be included in an assessment of development? How might adoption of Sen's views influence government policy? Do you think Sen is correct that development is about more than just economic development? Explain.
5. You are the CEO of a company that has to choose between making a $100 million investment in Russia or the Czech Republic. Both investments promise the same long-run return, so your choice is driven by risk considerations. Assess the various risks of doing business in each of these nations. Which investment would you favor and why?
6. Read the Country Focus on India in this chapter and answer the following questions:
   a. What kind of economic system did India operate under during 1947 to 1990? What kind of system is it moving toward today? What are the impediments to completing this transformation?
   b. How might widespread public ownership of businesses and extensive government regulations have impacted (*i*) the efficiency of state and private businesses, and (*ii*) the rate of new business formation in India during the 1947–90 time frame? How do you think these factors affected the rate of economic growth in India during this time frame?
   c. How would privatization, deregulation, and the removal of barriers to foreign direct investment affect the efficiency of business, new business formation, and the rate of economic growth in India during the post-1990 time period?
   d. India now has pockets of strengths in key high-technology industries such as software and pharmaceuticals. Why do you think India is developing strength in these areas? How might success in these industries help

to generate growth in the other sectors of the Indian economy?

e. Given what is now occurring in the Indian economy, do you think the country represents an attractive target for inward investment by foreign multinationals selling consumer products? Why?

Research Task

http://globalEDGE.msu.edu

Use the globalEDGE site (http://globalEDGE.msu.edu/) to complete the following exercises:

1. The *Freedom in the World* survey evaluates the state of political rights and civil liberties around the world. Provide a description of this survey and a ranking, in terms of "freedom", of the leaders and laggards. What factors are considered in this survey when forming the rankings?
2. *Market Potential Indicators* (MPI) is an indexing study conducted by the Michigan State University Center for International Business Education and Research (MSU-CIBER) to compare emerging markets on a variety of dimensions. Provide a description of the indicators used in the indexing procedure. Which of the indicators would have greater importance for a company that markets laptop computers? Considering the MPI rankings, which developing countries would you advise such a company to enter first?

closing case

Indonesia—The Troubled Giant

Indonesia is a vast country. Its 220 million people are spread out over some 17,000 islands that span an arc 3,200 miles long from Sumatra in the west to Irian Jaya in the east. It is the world's most populous Muslim nation—some 85 percent of the population count themselves as Muslims—but also one of the most ethnically diverse. More than 500 languages are spoken in the country, and separatists are active in a number of provinces. For 30 years, this sprawling nation was held together by the strong arm of President Suharto. Suharto was a virtual dictator who was backed by the military establishment. Under his rule, the Indonesian economy grew steadily, but there was a cost. Suharto brutally repressed internal dissent. He was also famous for "crony capitalism," using his command of the political system to favor the business enterprises of his supporters and family.

In the end, Suharto was overtaken by massive debts that Indonesia had accumulated during the 1990s. In 1997, the Indonesian economy went into a tailspin. The International Monetary Fund stepped in with a $43 billion rescue package. When it was revealed that much of this money found its way into the personal coffers of Suharto and his cronies, people took to the streets in protest and he was forced to resign.

After Suharto, Indonesia moved rapidly toward a vigorous democracy, culminating in October 2004 with the inauguration of Susilo Bambang Yudhoyono, the country's first directly elected president. The economic front has also seen progress. Public debt as a percentage of GDP fell from close to 100 percent in 2000 to less than 60 percent by 2004. Inflation declined from 12 percent annually in 2001 to 6 percent in 2004, and the economy grew by around 4 percent per annum during 2001–05.

But Indonesia lags behind its Southeast Asian neighbors. Its economic growth trails that of China, Malaysia, and Thailand. Unemployment is still high at around 10 percent of the working population. Inflation started to reaccelerate in 2005, hitting 14 percent by year end. Growth in labor productivity has been nonexistent for a decade. Worse still, foreign capital is fleeing the country. Sony made headlines by shutting down an audio equipment factory in 2003, and a number of apparel enterprises have left Indonesia for China and Vietnam. In total, the stock of foreign direct investment in Indonesia fell from $24.8 billion in 2001 to $11.4 billion in 2004 as foreign firms left the nation.

Some observers feel that Indonesian is hobbled by its poor infrastructure. Public infrastructure investment has been declining for years. It was about $3 billion in 2003, down from $16 billion in 1996. The road system is a mess, half of the country's population has no access to electricity, the number of brownouts is on the rise as the electricity grid ages, and nearly 99 percent of the population lacks access to modern sewerage facilities. The tsunami that ravaged the coast of Sumatra in late 2004 only made matters worse. Mirroring the decline in public investment has been a slump in private investment. Investment in the country's all-important oil industry fell from $3.8 billion in 1996 to just $187 million in 2002. Oil production has declined even though oil prices are at record highs. Investment in mining has also fallen from $2.6 billion in 1997 to $177 million in 2003.

According to a World Bank study, business activity in Indonesia is hurt by excessive red tape. It takes 151 days on average to complete the paperwork necessary to start a business, compared to 30 days in Malaysia and just 8 days in Singapore. Another problem is the endemically high level of corruption. Transparency International, which studies corruption around the world, ranks Indonesia among the most corrupt, listing it 137 out of the 158 countries it tracked in 2005. Government bureaucrats, whose salaries are very low, inevitably demand bribes from any company that crosses their path—and Indonesia's penchant for bureaucratic red tape means a long line of officials might require bribes. Abdul Rahman Saleh, the attorney general in Indonesia, has stated that the entire legal system, including the police and the prosecutors, is mired in corruption. The police have been known to throw the executives of foreign enterprises into jail on the flimsiest of pretexts, although some well-placed bribes can secure their release. Even though Indonesia has recently launched an anticorruption drive, critics claim it lacks any teeth. The political elite are reportedly so corrupt that it is not in their interests to do anything meaningful to fix the system.

Sources: "A Survey of Indonesia: Time to Deliver," *The Economist,* December 11, 2004; "A Survey of Indonesia: Enemies of Promise," *The Economist,* December 11, 2004, pp. 4–5; "A Survey of Indonesia: The Importance of Going Straight," *The Economist,* December 11, 2004, pp. 6–7; World Bank, *World Development Indicators Online,* 2006; Transparency International, *Global Corruption Report,* 2006; and S. Donnan. "Indonesian Workers Mark May Day with Protests at Planned Changes to Labor Laws," *Financial Times,* May 2, 2006, p. 4.

Case Discussion Questions

1. What political factors explain Indonesia's poor economic performance? What economic factors? Are these two related?
2. Why do you think foreign firms have been exiting Indonesia in recent years? What are the implications for the country? What is required to reverse this trend?
3. Why is corruption so endemic in Indonesia? What are its consequences?
4. What are the risks facing foreign firms that do business in Indonesia? What is required to reduce these risks?

Royalty Free/Corbis/DIL

part 2 Country Differences

LEARNING OBJECTIVES

1. Know what is meant by the culture of a society.
2. Identify the forces that lead to differences in social culture.
3. Identify the business and economic implications of differences in culture.
4. Understand how differences in social culture influence values in the workplace.
5. Develop an appreciation for the economic and business implications of cultural change.

chapter 3

Differences in Culture

DMG-Shanghai

opening Case

Back in 1993, New Yorker Dan Mintz moved to China as a freelance film director with no contacts, no advertising experience, and no Mandarin. By 2006, the company he subsequently founded in China, DMG, had emerged as one of China's fastest-growing advertising agencies with a client list that includes Budweiser, Unilever, Sony, Nabisco, Audi, Volkswagen, China Mobile, and dozens of other Chinese brands. Mintz attributes his success in part to what the Chinese call *guanxi.*

Guanxi literally means relationships, although in business settings it can be better understood as connections. *Guanxi* has its roots in the Confucian philosophy of valuing social hierarchy and reciprocal obligations. Confucian ideology has a 2,000-year-old history in China. Confucianism stresses the importance of relationships, both within the family and between master and servant. Confucian ideology teaches that people are not created equal. In Confucian thought, loyalty and obligations to one's superiors (or to family) is regarded as a sacred duty, but at the same time, this loyalty has its price. Social superiors are obligated to reward the loyalty of their social inferiors by bestowing "blessings" upon them; thus, the obligations are reciprocal.

Today, Chinese will often cultivate a *guanxiwang,* or "relationship network," for help. Reciprocal obligations are the glue that holds such networks together. If those obligations are not met—if favors done are not paid back or reciprocated—the reputation of the transgressor is tarnished, and he or she will be less able to draw on his or her *guanxiwang* for help in the future. Thus, the implicit threat of social sanctions is often sufficient to ensure that favors are repaid, obligations are met, and relationships are honored. In a society that lacks a strong rule-based legal tradition, and thus legal ways of redressing wrongs such as violations of business agreements, *guanxi* is an important mechanism for building long-term business relationships and getting business done in China. There is a tacit acknowledgment that if you have the right *guanxi,* legal rules can be broken, or at least bent.

Mintz, who is now fluent in Mandarin, cultivated his *guanxiwang* by going into business with two young Chinese who had connections, Bing Wu and Peter Xiao. Bing Wu, who works on the production side of the business, was a former national gymnastics champion, which translates into prestige and access to business and government officials. Peter Xiao comes from a military family with major political connections. Together, these three have been able to open doors that long-established Western advertising agencies have not. They have done it in large part by leveraging the contacts of Wu and Xiao, and by backing up their connections with what the Chinese call *Shi li,* the ability to do good work.

A case in point was DMG's campaign for Volkswagen, which helped the German company to become ubiquitous in China. The ads used traditional Chinese characters, which had been banned by Chairman Mao during the cultural revolution in favor of simplified versions. To get permission to use the characters in film and print ads--a first in modern China--the trio had to draw on high-level government contacts in Beijing. They won over officials by arguing that the old characters should be thought of not as "characters" but as art. Later, they shot TV spots for the ad on Shanghai's famous Bund, a congested boulevard that runs along the waterfront of the old city. Drawing again on government contacts, they were able to shut down the Bund to make the shoot. Steven Spielberg had been able to close down only a portion of the street when he filmed *Empire of the Sun* there in 1986. DMG has also filmed inside Beijing's Forbidden City, even though it is against the law to do so. Using his contacts, Mintz persuaded the government to lift the law for 24 hours. As Mintz has noted, "We don't stop when we come across regulations. There are restrictions everywhere you go. You have to know how get around them and get things done."

Sources: J. Bryan, "The Mintz Dynasty," *Fast Company,* April 2006, pp. 56–62; and M. Graser, "Featured Player," *Variety,* October 18, 2004, p. 6.

Introduction

International business is different from domestic business because countries are different. In Chapter 2, we saw how national differences in political, economic, and legal systems influence the benefits, costs, and risks associated with doing business in different countries. In this chapter, we will explore how differences in culture across and within countries can affect international business. Several themes run through this chapter.

Cross-Cultural Literacy
An understanding of how cultural differences across and within nations can affect the way business is practiced.

The first theme is that business success in a variety of countries requires cross-cultural literacy. By **cross-cultural literacy,** we mean an understanding of how cultural differences across and within nations can affect the way business is practiced. In these days of global communications, rapid transportation, and worldwide markets, when the era of the global village seems just around the corner, it is easy to forget just how different various cultures really are. Underneath the veneer of modernism, deep cultural differences often remain. Westerners in general, and Americans in particular, are quick to conclude that because people from other parts of the world also wear blue jeans, listen to Western popular music, eat at McDonald's, and drink Coca-Cola, they also accept the basic tenets of Western (or American) culture. However, this is not true. For example, increasingly, the Chinese are embracing the material products of modern society. Anyone who has visited Shanghai cannot fail to be struck by how modern the city seems, with its skyscrapers, department stores, and freeways. Yet as the opening case demonstrates, beneath the veneer of Western modernism, long-standing cultural traditions rooted in a 2,000-year-old ideology continue to have an important influence on the way business is transacted in China. In China, *guanxi*, or relationships backed by reciprocal obligations, are central to getting business done. Firms that lack sufficient *guanxi* may find themselves at a disadvantage when doing business in China. In this chapter, we shall argue that it is important for foreign businesses to gain an understanding of the culture that prevails in those countries where they do business. Dan Mintz has been successful at doing business in China because he has developed a deep understanding of Chinese culture.

Another theme developed in this chapter is that a relationship may exist between culture and the cost of doing business in a country or region. Different cultures are more or less supportive of the capitalist mode of production and may increase or lower the costs of doing business. For example, some observers have argued that cultural factors lowered the costs of doing business in Japan and helped to explain Japan's rapid economic ascent during the 1960s, 70s, and 80s.[1] Similarly, cultural factors can sometimes raise the costs of doing business. Historically, class divisions were an important aspect of British culture, and for a long time, firms operating in Great Britain found it difficult to achieve cooperation between management and labor. Class divisions led to a high level of industrial disputes in that country during the 1960s and 1970s and raised the costs of doing business relative to the costs in countries such as Switzerland, Norway, Germany, or Japan, where class conflict was historically less prevalent.

The British example, however, brings us to another theme we will explore in this chapter. Culture is not static. It can and does evolve, although the rate at which culture can change is the subject of some dispute. Important aspects of British culture have changed significantly over the past 20 years, and this is reflected in weaker class distinctions and a lower level of industrial disputes. Between 1994 and 2003, the number of days lost per 1,000 workers due to strikes in the United Kingdom was on average 23 each year, significantly less than in the United States (44 each year), Ireland (71), and Canada (185).[2]

What is Culture?

LEARNING OBJECTIVE 1
Know what is meant by the culture of a society.

Scholars have never been able to agree on a simple definition of *culture*. In the 1870s, the anthropologist Edward Tylor defined culture as "that complex whole which includes knowledge, belief, art, morals, law, custom, and other capabilities acquired by man as a member of society."[3] Since then hundreds of other definitions have been offered. Geert Hofstede, an expert on cross-cultural differences and management, defined culture as "the collective programming of the mind which distinguishes the members of one human group from another. . . . Culture, in this sense, includes systems of values; and values are among the building blocks of culture."[4] Another definition of culture comes from sociologists Zvi Namenwirth and Robert Weber, who see culture as a system of ideas and argue that these ideas constitute a design for living.[5]

Culture
A system of values and norms that are shared among a group of people and that when taken together constitute a design for living.

Here we follow both Hofstede and Namenwirth and Weber by viewing **culture** as a system of values and norms that are shared among a group of people and that when

Values
Abstract ideas about what a group believes to be good, right, and desirable.

Norms
The social rules and guidelines that prescribe appropriate behavior in particular situations.

Society
A group of people who share a common set of values and norms.

taken together constitute a design for living. By **values** we mean abstract ideas about what a group believes to be good, right, and desirable. Put differently, values are shared assumptions about how things ought to be.[6] By **norms** we mean the social rules and guidelines that prescribe appropriate behavior in particular situations. We shall use the term **society** to refer to a group of people who share a common set of values and norms. While a society may be equivalent to a country, some countries harbor several societies (i.e., they support multiple cultures), and some societies embrace more than one country. See the Another Perspective box below for an example of cultural power in Chengdu, China.

VALUES AND NORMS Values form the bedrock of a culture. They provide the context within which a society's norms are established and justified. They may include a society's attitudes toward such concepts as individual freedom, democracy, truth, justice, honesty, loyalty, social obligations, collective responsibility, the role of women, love, sex, marriage, and so on. Values are not just abstract concepts; they are invested with considerable emotional significance. People argue, fight, and even die over values such as freedom. Values also often are reflected in the political and economic systems of a society. As we saw in Chapter 2, democratic free market capitalism is a reflection of a philosophical value system that emphasizes individual freedom.

Norms are the social rules that govern people's actions toward one another. Norms can be subdivided further into two major categories: folkways and mores. **Folkways** are the routine conventions of everyday life. Generally, folkways are actions of little moral significance. Rather, they are social conventions concerning things such as the appropriate dress code in a particular situation, good social manners, eating with the correct utensils, neighborly behavior, and the like. Although folkways define the way people are expected to behave, violation of them is not normally a serious matter. People who violate folkways may be thought of as eccentric or ill-mannered, but they are not usually considered to be evil or bad. In many countries, foreigners may initially be excused for violating folkways.

A good example of folkways concerns attitudes toward time in different countries. People are keenly aware of the passage of time in the United States and in Northern European cultures such as Germany and Britain. Businesspeople are very conscious about scheduling their time and are quickly irritated when their time is wasted because a business associate is late for a meeting or if they are kept waiting. They talk about time as though it were money, as something that can be spent, saved, wasted, and lost.[7] Alternatively, in Arab, Latin, and Mediterranean cultures, time has a more elastic character. Keeping to a schedule is viewed as less important than finishing an interaction with people. For example, an American businesswoman might feel slighted if she is kept waiting for 30 minutes outside the office of a Latin

Another Perspective

The Power of Culture: Chengdu Resists

The "party" culture of Chengdu, a southwestern city in Sichuan Province, China, is proving to be an obstacle to China's "Go West Campaign," which was designed to spur economic development by convincing corporations such as Intel and Motorola to set up shop and invest hundreds of millions of dollars in the city. Chengdu moves to its own beat and knows how to live it up. With about 3,000 pubs and karaoke bars and 4,000 teahouses, Chengdu beats out Shanghai in entertainment establishments, though its population of 10.5 million is half Shanghai's size.

For foreign companies used to operating 24-7, Chengdu's laid-back culture presents challenges. Many people in Chengdu are used to working 9 to 5, and often taking long lunch breaks. Many refuse to work overtime or on weekends, extra pay or not. A recent Chinese survey found Chengdu ranked last in income among Chinese cities, about $190 a month, almost half of Shanghai's figure. But Chengdu rated higher than any other city (except Hangzhou) in "happiness." No matter rich or poor, everyone in Chengdu enjoys life and entertainment. Some scholars believe the key to this cultural trait lies in its irrigation system, built in 256 BC, which solved all the city's agricultural problems and made the area free from any natural disasters for 2,000 years.

The question becomes: What was China and international business thinking its success rate would be in promoting an almost "counterculture" in Chengdu? Even cheap labor, free land and tax breaks can't make a company. It takes the culture. (Don Lee, "In China's Party Capital, Residents Put Play before Work," *Boston Sunday Globe,* February 12, 2006; originally in *Los Angeles Times*)

American executive before a meeting; but the Latin American may simply be completing an interaction with an associate and view the information gathered from this as more important than sticking to a rigid schedule. The Latin American executive intends no disrespect, but due to a mutual misunderstanding about the importance of time, the American may see things differently. Similarly, Saudi attitudes to time have been shaped by their nomadic Bedouin heritage, in which precise time played no real role and arriving somewhere tomorrow might mean next week. Like Latin Americans, many Saudis are unlikely to understand the American obsession with precise time and schedules, and Americans need to adjust their expectations accordingly.

Folkways
The routine conventions of everyday life.

Folkways include rituals and symbolic behavior. Rituals and symbols are the most visible manifestations of a culture and constitute the outward expression of deeper values. For example, upon meeting a foreign business executive, a Japanese executive will hold his business card in both hands and bow while presenting the card to the foreigner.[8] This ritual behavior is loaded with deep cultural symbolism. The card specifies the rank of the Japanese executive, which is a very important piece of information in a hierarchical society such as Japan (Japanese often have business cards with Japanese printed on one side, and English printed on the other). The bow is a sign of respect, and the deeper the angle of the bow, the greater the reverence one person shows for the other. The person receiving the card is expected to examine it carefully, which is a way of returning respect and acknowledging the card giver's position in the hierarchy. The foreigner is also expected to bow when taking the card, and to return the greeting by presenting the Japanese executive with his own card, similarly bowing in the process. To not do so, and to fail to read the card that he has been given, instead casually placing it in his jacket, violates this important folkway and is considered rude.

Mores are norms that are seen as central to the functioning of a society and to its social life. They have much greater significance than folkways. Accordingly, violating mores can bring serious retribution. Mores include such factors as indictments against theft, adultery, incest, and cannibalism. In many societies, certain mores have been enacted into law. Thus, all advanced societies have laws against theft, incest, and cannibalism. However, there are also many differences between cultures. In America, for example, drinking alcohol is widely accepted, whereas in Saudi Arabia the consumption of alcohol is viewed as violating important social mores and is punishable by imprisonment (as some Western citizens working in Saudi Arabia have discovered).

Mores
Norms that are seen as central to the functioning of a society and to its social life.

CULTURE, SOCIETY, AND THE NATION-STATE We have defined a society as a group of people that share a common set of values and norms; that is, people who are bound together by a common culture. There is not a strict one-to-one correspondence between a society and a nation-state. Nation-states are political creations. They may contain a single culture or several cultures. While the French nation can be thought of as the political embodiment of French culture, the nation of Canada has at least three cultures—an Anglo culture, a French-speaking "Quebecois" culture, and a Native American culture. Similarly, many African nations have important cultural differences between tribal groups, as exhibited in the early 1990s when Rwanda dissolved into a bloody civil war between two tribes, the Tutsis and Hutus. Africa is not alone in this regard. India is composed of many distinct cultural groups. During the first Gulf War, the prevailing view presented to Western audiences was that Iraq was a homogenous Arab nation. However, over the past 15 years, we have learned several different societies exist within Iraq, each with its own culture. The Kurds in the north do not view themselves as Arabs and have their own distinct history and traditions. There are two Arab societies: the Shiites in the South and the Sunnis

Another Perspective

Online View of Other Cultures

Visit the online versions of some English language foreign newspapers in major international cities to get a sense of their cultural values, social structure, and markets. Look at the ads and business names. Check out the classifieds. A good list link is at www.newhopepa.com/News/Intl_News/default.htm.

who populate the middle of the country and who ruled Iraq under the regime of Saddam Hussein (the terms *Shiites* and *Sunnis* refer to different sects within the religion of Islam). Among the southern Sunnis is another distinct society of 500,000 Marsh Arabs who live at the confluence of the Tigris and Euphrates rivers, pursuing a way of life that dates back 5,000 years.[9]

At the other end of the scale are cultures that embrace several nations. Several scholars argue that we can speak of an Islamic society or culture that is shared by the citizens of many different nations in the Middle East, Asia, and Africa. As you will recall from the last chapter, this view of expansive cultures that embrace several nations underpins Samuel Huntington's view of a world that is fragmented into different civilizations, including Western, Islamic, and Sinic (Chinese).[10]

To complicate things further, it is also possible to talk about culture at different levels. It is reasonable to talk about "American society" and "American culture," but there are several societies within America, each with its own culture. One can talk about African American culture, Cajun culture, Chinese American culture, Hispanic culture, Indian culture, Irish American culture, and Southern culture. The relationship between culture and country is often ambiguous. One cannot always characterize a country as having a single homogenous culture, and even when one can, one must also often recognize that the national culture is a mosaic of subcultures (see the Another Perspective box above for tips on researching culture).

LEARNING OBJECTIVE 2
Identify the forces that lead to differences in social culture.

THE DETERMINANTS OF CULTURE

The values and norms of a culture do not emerge fully formed. They are the evolutionary product of a number of factors, including the prevailing political and economic philosophies, the social structure of a society, and the dominant religion, language, and education (see Figure 3.1). We discussed political and economic philosophies at length in Chapter 2. Such philosophies

figure 3.1

The Determinants of Culture

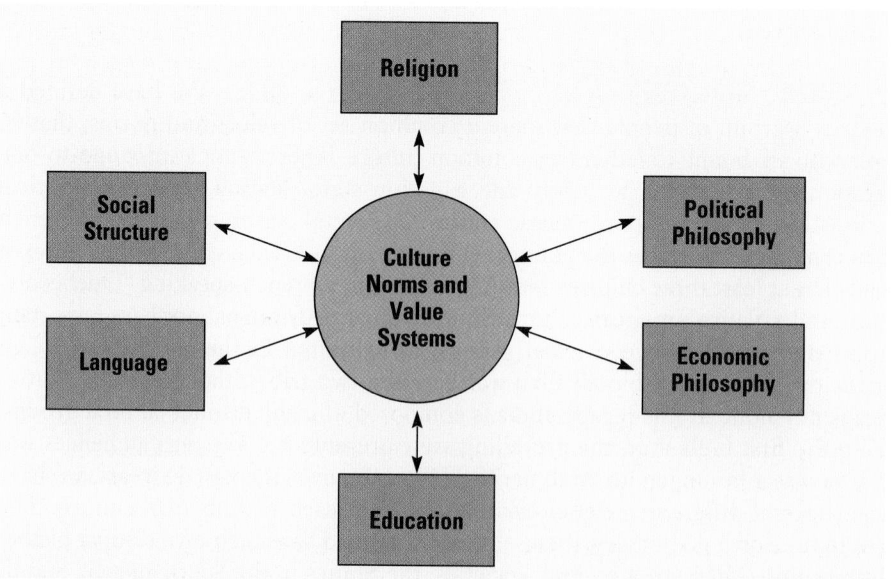

clearly influence the value systems of a society. For example, the values found in Communist North Korea toward freedom, justice, and individual achievement are clearly different from the values found in the United States, precisely because each society operates according to different political and economic philosophies. Below we will discuss the influence of social structure, religion, language, and education. The chain of causation runs both ways. While factors such as social structure and religion clearly influence the values and norms of a society, the values and norms of a society can influence social structure and religion.

Social Structure

A society's **social structure** refers to its basic social organization. Although social structure consists of many different aspects, two dimensions are particularly important when explaining differences between cultures. The first is the degree to which the basic unit of social organization is the individual, as opposed to the group. In general, Western societies tend to emphasize the primacy of the individual, whereas groups tend to figure much larger in many other societies. The second dimension is the degree to which a society is stratified into classes or castes. Some societies are characterized by a relatively high degree of social stratification and relatively low mobility between strata (e.g., Indian); other societies are characterized by a low degree of social stratification and high mobility between strata (e.g., American).

Social Structure
The basic social organization of a society.

INDIVIDUALS AND GROUPS

A **group** is an association of two or more individuals who have a shared sense of identity and who interact with each other in structured ways on the basis of a common set of expectations about each other's behavior.[11] Human social life is group life. Individuals are involved in families, work groups, social groups, recreational groups, and so on. However, while groups are found in all societies, societies differ according to the degree to which the group is viewed as the primary means of social organization.[12] In some societies, individual attributes and achievements are viewed as being more important than group membership; in others the reverse is true.

Group
An association of two or more individuals who have a shared sense of identity and who interact with each other in structured ways on the basis of a common set of expectations about each other's behavior.

The Individual

In Chapter 2, we discussed individualism as a political philosophy. However, individualism is more than just an abstract political philosophy. In many Western societies, the individual is the basic building block of social organization. This is reflected not just in the political and economic organization of society but also in the way people perceive themselves and relate to each other in social and business settings. The value systems of many Western societies, for example, emphasize individual achievement. The social standing of individuals is not so much a function of whom they work for as of their individual performance in whatever work setting they choose.

The emphasis on individual performance in many Western societies has both beneficial and harmful aspects. In the United States, the emphasis on individual performance finds expression in an admiration of rugged individualism and entrepreneurship. One benefit of this is the high level of entrepreneurial activity in the United States and other Western societies. New products and new ways of doing business (e.g., personal computers, photocopiers, computer software, biotechnology, supermarkets, and discount retail stores) have repeatedly been created in the United States by entrepreneurial individuals. One can argue that the dynamism of the U.S. economy owes much to the philosophy of individualism.

LEARNING OBJECTIVE 3
Identify the business and economic implications of differences in culture.

Individualism also finds expression in a high degree of managerial mobility between companies, and this is not always a good thing. Although moving from company to company may be good for individual managers who are trying to build impressive résumés, it is not necessarily a good thing for American companies. The lack of loyalty and commitment to an individual company, and the tendency to move on for a better offer, can result in managers who have good general skills but lack the knowledge, experience, and network of interpersonal contacts that come from years of working within the same company. An effective manager draws on company-specific experience, knowledge, and a network of contacts to find solutions to current problems, and American companies may suffer if their managers lack these attributes. One positive aspect of high managerial mobility is that executives are exposed to different ways of doing business. The ability to compare business practices helps U.S. executives identify how good practices and techniques developed in one firm might be profitably applied to other firms.

The emphasis on individualism may also make it difficult to build teams within an organization to perform collective tasks. If individuals are always competing with each other on the basis of individual performance, it may be difficult for them to cooperate. A study of U.S. competitiveness by the Massachusetts Institute of Technology concluded that U.S. firms are being hurt in the global economy by a failure to achieve cooperation both within a company (e.g., between functions; between management and labor) and between companies (e.g., between a firm and its suppliers). Given the emphasis on individualism in the American value system, this failure is not surprising.[13] The emphasis on individualism in the United States, while helping to create a dynamic entrepreneurial economy, may raise the costs of doing business due to its adverse impact on managerial stability and cooperation.

The Group In contrast to the Western emphasis on the individual, the group is the primary unit of social organization in many other societies. For example, in Japan, the social status of an individual is determined as much by the standing of the group to which he or she belongs as by his or her individual performance.[14] In traditional Japanese society, the group was the family or village to which an individual belonged. Today, the group has frequently come to be associated with the work team or business organization to which an individual belongs. In a now-classic study of Japanese society, Nakane noted how this expresses itself in everyday life:

> When a Japanese faces the outside (confronts another person) and affixes some position to himself socially he is inclined to give precedence to institution over kind of occupation. Rather than saying, "I am a typesetter" or "I am a filing clerk," he is likely to say, "I am from B Publishing Group" or "I belong to S company."[15]

LEARNING OBJECTIVE 3
Identify the business and economic implications of differences in culture.

Nakane goes on to observe that the primacy of the group to which an individual belongs often evolves into a deeply emotional attachment in which identification with the group becomes all-important in one's life. One central value of Japanese culture is the importance attached to group membership. This may have beneficial implications for business firms. Strong identification with the group is argued to create pressures for mutual self-help and collective action. If the worth of an individual is closely linked to the achievements of the group (e.g., firm), as Nakane maintains is the case in Japan, this creates a strong incentive for individual members of the group to work together for the common good. Some argue that the success of Japanese enterprises in the global economy has been based partly on their ability to achieve close cooperation between individuals within a company and between companies. This has found expression in the widespread diffusion of self-managing work teams within Japanese organizations, the close cooperation among different functions within Japanese companies (e.g., among manufacturing, marketing, and R&D), and the cooperation between a company and its suppliers on issues such as design, quality control, and inventory reduction.[16] In all of these cases, cooperation is driven by the need to improve the performance of the group (i.e., the business firm).

The primacy of the value of group identification also discourages managers and workers from moving from company to company. Lifetime employment in a particular company was long the norm in certain sectors of the Japanese economy (estimates suggest that between 20 and 40 percent of all Japanese employees have formal or informal lifetime employment guarantees). Over the years, managers and workers build up knowledge, experience, and a network of interpersonal business contacts. All these things can help managers perform their jobs more effectively and achieve cooperation with others.

However, the primacy of the group is not always beneficial. Just as U.S. society is characterized by a great deal of dynamism and entrepreneurship, reflecting the primacy of values associated with individualism, some argue that Japanese society is characterized by a corresponding lack of dynamism and entrepreneurship. Although the long-run consequences are unclear, the United States could continue to create more new industries than Japan and continue to be more successful at pioneering radically new products and new ways of doing business.

Social Stratification

All societies are stratified on a hierarchical basis into social categories—that is, into **social strata.** These strata are typically defined on the basis of characteristics such as family background, occupation, and income. Individuals are born into a particular stratum. They become a member of the social category to which their parents belong. Individuals born into a stratum toward the top of the social hierarchy tend to have better life chances than those born into a stratum toward the bottom of the hierarchy. They are likely to have better education, health, standard of living, and work opportunities. Although all societies are stratified to some degree, they differ in two related ways. First, they differ from each other with regard to the degree of mobility between social strata; second, they differ with regard to the significance attached to social strata in business contexts.

Social Strata
The hierarchical categories within a society, defined on the basis of such elements as family background, income, and occupation.

Social Mobility
The extent to which individuals can move out of the strata into which they are born.

Social Mobility

The term **social mobility** refers to the extent to which individuals can move out of the strata into which they are born. Social mobility varies significantly from society to society. The most rigid system of stratification is a caste system. A **caste system** is a closed system of stratification in which social position is determined by the family into which a person is born, and change in that position is usually not possible during an individual's lifetime. Often a caste position carries with it a specific occupation. Members of one caste might be shoemakers, members of another might be butchers, and so on. These occupations are embedded in the caste and passed down through the family to succeeding generations. Although the number of societies with caste systems diminished rapidly during the twentieth century, one partial example still remains. India has four main castes and several thousand subcastes. Even though the caste system was officially abolished in 1949, two years after India became independent, it is still a force in rural Indian society where occupation and marital opportunities are still partly related to caste.

Caste System
A closed system of stratification in which social position is determined by the family into which a person is born, and change out of that strata is usually not possible during a person's lifetime.

A **class system** is a less rigid form of social stratification in which social mobility is possible. It is a form of open stratification in which the position a person has by birth can be changed through his or her own achievements or luck. Individuals born into a class at the bottom of the hierarchy can work their way up; conversely, individuals born into a class at the top of the hierarchy can slip down.

Class System
A less rigid social stratification system, in which mobility is possible depending on a person's achievements or even just luck.

While many societies have class systems, social mobility within a class system varies from society to society. For example, some sociologists have argued that Britain has a more rigid class structure than certain other Western societies, such as the United States.[17] Historically, British society was divided into three main classes: the upper class, which was made up of individuals whose families for generations had wealth, prestige, and occasionally power; the middle class, whose members were involved in professional, managerial, and clerical occupations; and the working class, whose members earned their living from manual occupations. The middle class was further subdivided into the upper-middle class, whose members were involved in important managerial occupations and the prestigious professions (e.g., lawyers, accountants, doctors), and the lower-middle class, whose members were involved in clerical work (e.g., bank tellers) and the less prestigious professions (e.g., schoolteachers).

Historically, the British class system exhibited significant divergence between the life chances of members of different classes. The upper and upper-middle classes typically sent their children to a select group of private schools, where they wouldn't mix with lower-class children, and where they picked up many of the speech accents and social norms that marked them as being from the higher strata of society. These same private schools also had close ties with the most prestigious universities, such as Oxford and Cambridge. Until fairly recently, Oxford and Cambridge guaranteed a certain number of places for the graduates of these private schools. Having been to a prestigious university, the offspring of the upper and upper-middle classes then had an excellent chance of being offered a prestigious job in companies, banks, brokerage firms, and law firms run by members of the upper and upper-middle classes.

In contrast, the members of the British working and lower-middle classes typically went to state schools. The majority left at 16, and those who went on to higher education found it more difficult to get accepted at the best universities. When they did, they found that their lower-class accent and lack of social skills marked them as being from a lower social stratum, which made it more difficult for them to get access to the most prestigious jobs.

Because of this, the class system in Britain perpetuated itself from generation to generation, and mobility was limited. Although upward mobility was possible, it could not normally be achieved in one generation. While an individual from a working-class background may have established an income level that was consistent with membership in the upper-middle class, he or she may not have been accepted as such by others of that class due to accent and background. However, by sending his or her offspring to the "right kind of school," the individual could ensure that his or her children were accepted.

According to many commentators, modern British society is now rapidly leaving this class structure behind and moving toward a classless society. However, sociologists continue to dispute this finding and present evidence that this is not the case. For example, a study reported that in the mid-1990s, state schools in the London suburb of Islington, which has a population of 175,000, had only 79 candidates for university, while one prestigious private school alone, Eton, sent more than that number to Oxford and Cambridge.[18] This, according to the study's authors, implies that "money still begets money." They argue that a good school means a good university, a good university means a good job, and merit has only a limited chance of elbowing its way into this tight little circle.

The class system in the United States is less extreme than in Britain and mobility is greater. Like Britain, the United States has its own upper, middle, and working classes. However, class membership is determined to a much greater degree by individual economic achievements, as opposed to background and schooling. Thus, an individual can, by his or her own economic achievement, move smoothly from the working class to the upper class in a lifetime. Successful individuals from humble origins are highly respected in American society.

Until the late 1970s, social mobility in China was very limited, but now sociologists believe a new class system is emerging in China based less on the rural-urban divide and more on urban occupation. *D. Normark/PhotoLink/Getty Images/DIL*

Another society where class divisions have historically been of some importance has been China, where there has been a long-standing difference between the life chances of the rural peasantry and urban dwellers. Ironically, this historic division was strengthened during the high point of Communist rule because of a rigid system of household registration that restricted most Chinese to the place of their birth for their lifetime. Bound to collective farming, peasants were cut off from many urban privileges—compulsory education, quality schools, health care, public housing, varieties of foodstuffs, to name only a few—and they largely lived in poverty. Social mobility was thus very limited. This system crumbled following reforms of the late 1970s and early 1980s, and as a consequence, migrant peasant laborers have flooded into China's cities looking for work. Sociologists now hypothesize that a new class system is emerging in China based less on the rural-urban divide and more on urban occupation.[19]

LEARNING OBJECTIVE 3
Identify the business and economic implications of differences in culture.

Significance From a business perspective, the stratification of a society is significant if it affects the operation of business organizations. In American society, the high degree of social mobility and the extreme emphasis on individualism limit the impact of class back ground on business operations. The same is true in Japan, where most of the population perceives itself to be middle class. In a country such as Great Britain, however, the relative lack of class mobility and the differences between classes have resulted in the emergence of class consciousness. **Class consciousness** refers to a condition where people tend to perceive themselves in terms of their class background, and this shapes their relationships with members of other classes.

Class Consciousness
A condition where people tend to perceive themselves in terms of their class background, shaping how they relate with members of other classes.

This has been played out in British society in the traditional hostility between upper-middle-class managers and their working-class employees. Mutual antagonism and lack of respect historically made it difficult to achieve cooperation between management and labor in many British companies and resulted in a relatively high level of industrial disputes. However, as noted earlier, the last two decades have seen a dramatic reduction in industrial disputes, which bolsters the arguments of those who claim that the country is moving toward a classless society (the level of industrial disputes in the United Kingdom is now lower than in the United States). Alternatively, as noted above, class consciousness may be reemerging in urban China, and it may ultimately prove to be significant there.

An antagonistic relationship between management and labor classes, and the resulting lack of cooperation and high level of industrial disruption, tends to raise the costs of production in countries characterized by significant class divisions. In turn, this can make it more difficult for companies based in such countries to establish a competitive advantage in the global economy.

Religious and Ethical Systems

Religion
A system of shared beliefs and rituals that are concerned with the realm of the sacred.

Ethical System
A set of moral principles, or values, that are used to guide and shape behavior.

Religion may be defined as a system of shared beliefs and rituals that are concerned with the realm of the sacred.[20] **Ethical systems** refer to a set of moral principles, or values, that are used to guide and shape behavior. Most of the world's ethical systems are the product of religions. Thus, we can talk about Christian ethics and Islamic ethics. However, there is a major exception to the principle that ethical systems are grounded in religion. Confucianism and Confucian ethics influence behavior and shape culture in parts of Asia, yet it is incorrect to characterize Confucianism as a religion.

The relationship among religion, ethics, and society is subtle and complex. Among the thousands of religions in the world today, four dominate in terms of numbers of adherents: Christianity with 1.7 billion adherents, Islam with around 1 billion adherents, Hinduism with 750 million adherents (primarily in India), and Buddhism with 350 million adherents (see Map 3.1). Although many other religions have an important influence in certain parts of the modern world (for example, Judaism, which has 18 million adherents), their numbers pale in comparison with these dominant religions (however, as the precursor of both Christianity and Islam, Judaism has an indirect influence that goes beyond its numbers). We will review these four religions, along with Confucianism, focusing on their business implications. Some scholars have argued that the most important business implications of religion center on the extent to which different religions shape attitudes toward work and entrepreneurship and the degree to which the religious ethics affect the costs of doing business in a country.

It is hazardous to make sweeping generalizations about the nature of the relationship between religion and ethical systems and business practice. While some scholars argue that there is a relationship between religious and ethical systems and business practice in a society, in a world where nations with Catholic, Protestant, Muslim, Hindu, and Buddhist majorities all show evidence of entrepreneurial activity and sustainable economic growth, it is important to view such proposed relationships with a degree of skepticism. The proposed relationships may exist, but their impact is probably small compared to the impact of economic policy. Alternatively, recent research by economists Robert Barro and Rachel McCleary does suggest that strong religious beliefs, and particularly beliefs in heaven, hell, and an afterlife, have a positive impact on economic growth rates, irrespective of the particular religion in question.[21] Barro and McCleary looked at religious beliefs and economic growth rates in 59 countries during the 1980s and 1990s. Their conjecture was that higher religious beliefs stimulate economic growth because they help to sustain aspects of individual behavior that lead to higher productivity.

CHRISTIANITY Christianity is the most widely practiced religion in the world. Approximately 20 percent of the world's people identify themselves as Christians. The vast majority of Christians live in Europe and the Americas, although their numbers are growing rapidly in Africa. Christianity grew out of Judaism. Like Judaism, it is a monotheistic religion (monotheism is the belief in one god). A religious division in the eleventh century led to the establishment of two major Christian organizations—the Roman Catholic Church and the Orthodox Church.

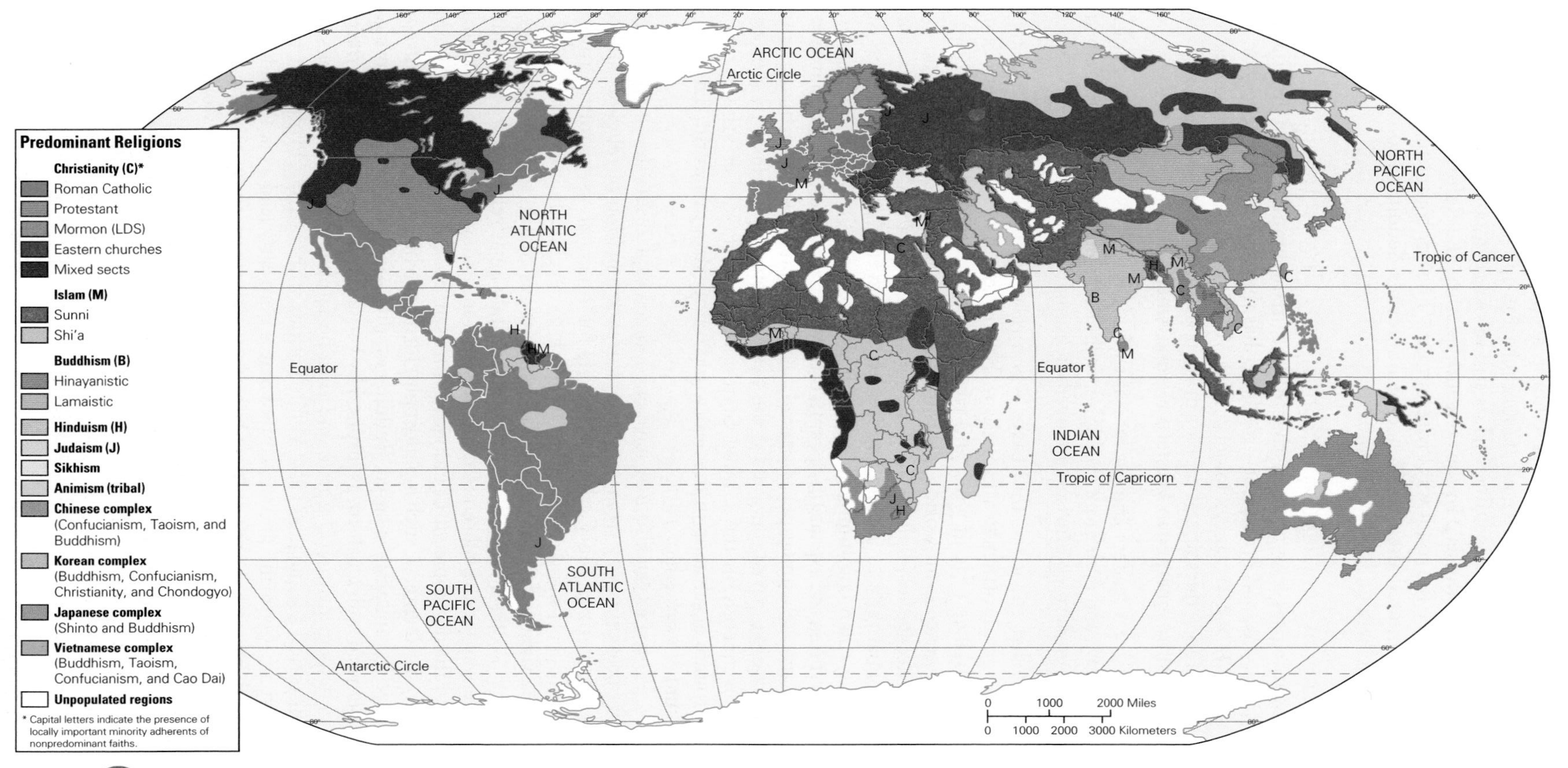

map 3.1 World Religions

Source: John L. Allen, *Student Atlas of World Politics*, 7e. map 8, Copyright © 2006 by the McGraw-Hill Companies, Inc. All rights reserved. Reprinted by permission of McGraw-Hill Contemporary Learning Series.

Today, the Roman Catholic Church accounts for more than half of all Christians, most of whom are found in southern Europe and Latin America. The Orthodox Church, while less influential, is still of major importance in several countries (e.g., Greece and Russia). In the sixteenth century, the Reformation led to a further split with Rome; the result was Protestantism. The nonconformist nature of Protestantism has facilitated the emergence of numerous denominations under the Protestant umbrella (e.g., Baptist, Methodist, Calvinist).

LEARNING OBJECTIVE 3
Identify the business and economic implications of differences in culture.

Economic Implications of Christianity: The Protestant Work Ethic Several sociologists have argued that of the main branches of Christianity—Catholic, Orthodox, and Protestant—the latter has the most important economic implications. In 1904, a German sociologist, Max Weber, made a connection between Protestant ethics and "the spirit of capitalism" that has since become famous.[22] Weber noted that capitalism emerged in Western Europe, where

> business leaders and owners of capital, as well as the higher grades of skilled labor, and even more the higher technically and commercially trained personnel of modern enterprises, are overwhelmingly Protestant.[23]

Weber theorized that there was a relationship between Protestantism and the emergence of modern capitalism. He argued that Protestant ethics emphasize the importance of hard work and wealth creation (for the glory of God) and frugality (abstinence from worldly pleasures). According to Weber, this kind of value system was needed to facilitate the development of capitalism. Protestants worked hard and systematically to accumulate wealth. However, their ascetic beliefs suggested that rather than consuming this wealth by indulging in worldly pleasures, they should invest it in the expansion of capitalist enterprises. Thus, the combination of hard work and the accumulation of capital, which could be used to finance investment and expansion, paved the way for the development of capitalism in Western Europe and subsequently in the United States. In contrast, Weber argued that the Catholic promise of salvation in the next world, rather than this world, did not foster the same kind of work ethic.

Protestantism also may have encouraged capitalism's development in another way. By breaking away from the hierarchical domination of religious and social life that characterized the Catholic Church for much of its history, Protestantism gave individuals significantly more freedom to develop their own relationship with God. The right to freedom of form of worship was central to the nonconformist nature of early Protestantism. This emphasis on individual religious freedom may have paved the way for the subsequent emphasis on individual economic and political freedoms and the development of individualism as an economic and political philosophy. As we saw in Chapter 2, such a philosophy forms the bedrock on which entrepreneurial free market capitalism is based. Building on this, some scholars claim there is a connection between individualism, as inspired by Protestantism, and the extent of entrepreneurial activity in a nation.[24] Again, one must be careful not to generalize too much from this historical sociological view. While nations with a strong Protestant tradition such as Britain, Germany, and the United States were early leaders in the industrial revolution, nations with Catholic or Orthodox majorities show significant and sustained entrepreneurial activity and economic growth in the modern world.

ISLAM With around 1 billion adherents, Islam is the second largest of the world's major religions. Islam dates back to AD 610 when the prophet Muhammad began spreading the word, although the Muslim calendar begins in AD 622 when, to escape growing opposition, Muhammad left Mecca for the oasis settlement of Yathrib, later known as Madina. Adherents of Islam are referred to as Muslims. Muslims constitute a majority in more than 35 countries and inhabit a nearly contiguous stretch of land from the northwest coast of Africa, through the Middle East, to China and Malaysia in the Far East.

Islam has roots in both Judaism and Christianity (Islam views Jesus Christ as one of God's prophets). Like Christianity and Judaism, Islam is a monotheistic religion. The central principle of Islam is that there is but the one true omnipotent God. Islam requires unconditional acceptance of the uniqueness, power, and authority of God and the understanding that the objective of life is to fulfill the dictates of his will in the hope of admission to paradise. According to Islam, worldly gain and temporal power are an illusion. Those who pursue riches on earth may gain them, but those who forgo worldly ambitions to seek the favor of Allah may gain the greater treasure—entry into paradise. Other major principles of Islam include (1) honoring and respecting parents, (2) respecting the rights of others, (3) being generous but not a squanderer, (4) avoiding killing except for justifiable causes, (5) not committing adultery, (6) dealing justly and equitably with others, (7) being of pure heart and mind, (8) safeguarding the possessions of orphans, and (9) being humble and unpretentious.[25] Obvious parallels exist with many of the central principles of both Judaism and Christianity.

Islam is an all-embracing way of life governing the totality of a Muslim's being.[26] As God's surrogate in this world, a Muslim is not a totally free agent but is circumscribed by religious principles—by a code of conduct for interpersonal relations—in social and economic activities. Religion is paramount in all areas of life. The Muslim lives in a social structure that is shaped by Islamic values and norms of moral conduct. The ritual nature of everyday life in a Muslim country is striking to a Western visitor. Among other things, orthodox Muslim ritual requires prayer five times a day (business meetings may be put on hold while the Muslim participants engage in their daily prayer ritual), requires that women should be dressed in a certain manner, and forbids the consumption of pork and alcohol.

Islamic Fundamentalism The past three decades have witnessed the growth of a social movement often referred to as Islamic fundamentalism.[27] In the West, Islamic fundamentalism is associated in the media with militants, terrorists, and violent upheavals, such as the bloody conflict occurring in Algeria, the killing of foreign tourists in Egypt, and the September 11, 2001, attacks on the World Trade Center and Pentagon in the United States. This characterization is misleading. Just as Christian fundamentalists are motivated by sincere and deeply held religious values firmly rooted in their faith, so are Islamic fundamentalists. The violence that the Western media associates with Islamic fundamentalism is perpetrated by a small minority of radical "fundamentalists" who have hijacked the religion to further their own political and violent ends. (Some Christian "fundamentalists" have done exactly the same, including Jim Jones and David Koresh.) The vast majority of Muslims point out that Islam teaches peace, justice, and tolerance, not violence and intolerance, and that Islam explicitly repudiates the violence that a radical minority practices.

The rise of fundamentalism has no one cause. In part, it is a response to the social pressures created in traditional Islamic societies by the move toward modernization and by the influence of Western ideas, such as liberal democracy, materialism, equal rights for women, and attitudes toward sex, marriage, and alcohol. In many Muslim countries, modernization has been accompanied by a growing gap between a rich urban minority and an impoverished urban and rural majority. For the impoverished majority, modernization has offered little in the way of tangible economic progress, while threatening the traditional value system. Thus, for a Muslim who cherishes his

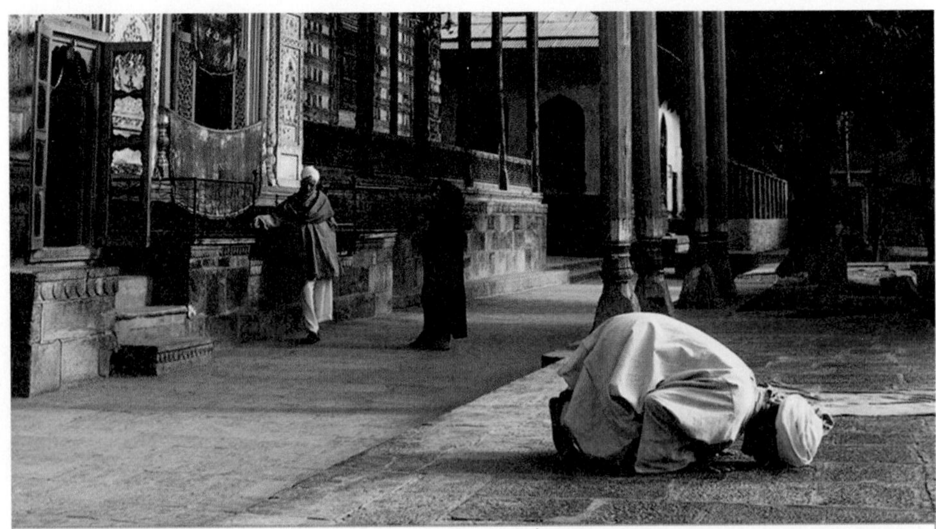

The rise of Islamic fundamentalism as a reaction against globalization and the prevalence of Western cultural ideas has sent many scrambling to try to understand Muslim culture and promote greater dialogue. *Royalty Free/Corbis/DIL*

or her traditions and feels that his or her identity is jeopardized by the encroachment of alien Western values, Islamic fundamentalism has become a cultural anchor.

Fundamentalists demand a rigid commitment to traditional religious beliefs and rituals. The result has been a marked increase in the use of symbolic gestures that confirm Islamic values. In areas where fundamentalism is strong, women have resumed wearing floor-length, long-sleeved dresses and covering their hair; religious studies have increased in universities; the publication of religious tracts has increased; and public religious orations have risen.[28] Also, the sentiments of some fundamentalist groups are increasingly anti-Western. Rightly or wrongly, Western influence is blamed for a range of social ills, and many fundamentalists' actions are directed against Western governments, cultural symbols, businesses, and even individuals.

In several Muslim countries, fundamentalists have gained political power and have used this to try to make Islamic law (as set down in the Koran, the bible of Islam) the law of the land. There are good grounds for this in Islam. Islam makes no distinction between church and state. It is not just a religion; Islam is also the source of law, a guide to statecraft, and an arbiter of social behavior. Muslims believe that every human endeavor is within the purview of the faith—and this includes political activity—because the only purpose of any activity is to do God's will.[29] (Some Christian fundamentalists also share this view.) Muslim fundamentalists have been most successful in Iran, where a fundamentalist party has held power since 1979, but they also have had an influence in many other countries, such as Algeria, Afghanistan (where the Taliban established an extreme fundamentalist state until removed by the U.S.-led coalition in 2002), Egypt, Pakistan, the Sudan, and Saudi Arabia.

LEARNING OBJECTIVE 3
Identify the business and economic implications of differences in culture.

Economic Implications of Islam

The Koran establishes some explicit economic principles, many of which are pro-free enterprise.[30] The Koran speaks approvingly of free enterprise and of earning legitimate profit through trade and commerce (the prophet Mohammed was once a trader). The protection of the right to private property is also embedded within Islam, although Islam asserts that all property is a favor from Allah (God), who created and so owns everything. Those who hold property are

Country FOCUS

The Rise of Islamic Banking in Pakistan

The Koran clearly condemns interest, which is called *riba* in Arabic, as exploitative and unjust. For many years, banks operating in Islamic countries conveniently ignored this condemnation, but starting about 30 years ago with the establishment of an Islamic bank in Egypt, Islamic banks started to open in predominantly Muslim countries. By 2005, some 176 Islamic financial institutions worldwide managed more than $240 billion in assets, making an average return on capital of more than 16 percent. Even conventional banks are entering the market—both Citigroup and HSBC, two of the world's largest financial institutions, now offer Islamic financial services. While only Iran and the Sudan enforce Islamic banking conventions, in an increasing number of countries customers can choose between conventional banks and Islamic banks. Recently, Pakistan has become one of those countries.

Conventional banks make a profit on the spread between the interest rate they have to pay to depositors and the higher interest rate they charge borrowers. Because Islamic banks cannot pay or charge interest, they must find a different way of making money. Islamic banks have experimented with two different banking methods—the *mudarabah* and the *murabaha.*

A *mudarabah* contract is similar to a profit-sharing scheme. Under *mudarabah,* when an Islamic bank lends money to a business, rather than charging that business interest on the loan, it takes a share in the profits that are derived from the investment. Similarly, when a business (or individual) deposits money at an Islamic bank in a savings account, the deposit is treated as an equity investment in whatever activity the bank uses the capital for. Thus, the depositor receives a share in the profit from the bank's investment (as opposed to interest payments) according to an agreed-on ratio. Some Muslims claim this is a more efficient system than the Western banking system, since it encourages both long-term savings and long-term investment. However, there is no hard evidence of this, and many believe that a *mudarabah* system is less efficient than a conventional Western banking system.

The second Islamic banking method, the *murabaha* contract, is the most widely used among the world's Islamic banks, primarily because it is the easiest to implement. In a *murabaha* contract, when a firm wishes to purchase something using a loan—let's say a piece of equipment that costs $1,000—the firm tells the bank after having negotiated the price with the equipment manufacturer. The bank then buys the equipment for $1,000, and the borrower buys it back from the bank at some later date for, say, $1,100, a price that includes a $100 markup for the bank. A cynic might point out that such a markup is functionally equivalent to an interest payment, and it is the similarity between this method and conventional banking that makes it so much easier to adopt.

With regard to Pakistan, the development of Islamic banking dates to 1992 when Pakistan's Federal Shariat Court, the highest Islamic law court in the country, pronounced interest to be un-Islamic and therefore illegal. The court demanded that the government amend all financial laws accordingly. In 1999, Pakistan's Supreme Court affirmed that Islamic banking methods should be used in the country, and set a date of July 1, 2001, for their introduction, but in a concession to practical considerations, the higher court agreed that Western banking methods could still be used alongside Islamic banking methods.

Three fears underlay the decision to establish a dual banking system in Pakistan, with Islamic banks operating alongside conventional banks, and some banks offering both Islamic and conventional banking services. One fear was that if there was a mandated shift to Islamic banking methods, it might trigger large-scale withdrawals by depositors worried that they could suffer in the absence of fixed interest rates. Another concern was that the country needed to have a tight regulatory regime to ensure that unscrupulous borrowers using a *mudarabah* contract did not declare themselves bankrupt, even when their businesses were making a profit. That regime did not exist in 1999. A third concern was that the uncertainty created by the transition would scare off foreign investors, leaving Pakistan starved of capital.

After a slow start, by early 2005 Islamic banks were starting to gain traction in Pakistan. Two full-fledged Islamic banks were operating 25 branches in Pakistan, and a third was scheduled to start operating in early 2005. In addition, nine conventional banks, including Standard Charter and AG Zurich, had opened some 23 branches offering Islamic banking services, and several other major conventional banks, including Citibank and ABN Amro, were negotiating for licensees with the Pakistani banking authorities to start offering Islamic banking services in the country. Estimates now suggest that by 2010, some 20 percent of all assets in the Pakistani banking system will be held by Islamic banks.

Their growth seems assured. As one customer stated, "I never went for conventional banking as it is based on interest, which is prohibited in Islam and amounts to waging war against Allah. Now I have my bank account in an Islamic bank and it satisfies my faith."

Sources: "Forced Devotion," *The Economist,* February 17, 2001, pp. 76–77; "Islamic Banking Marches On," *The Banker,* February 1, 2000; F. Bokhari, "Bankers Fear Introduction of Islamic System Will Prompt Big Withdrawals," *Financial Times,* March 6, 2001, p. 4; and *Agence France Presse,* "Islamic Banking Booms in Pakistan," January 2005 (source of quote).

regarded as trustees rather than owners in the Western sense of the word. As trustees they are entitled to receive profits from the property but are admonished to use it in a righteous, socially beneficial, and prudent manner. This reflects Islam's concern with social justice. Islam is critical of those who earn profit through the exploitation of others. In the Islamic view of the world, humans are part of a collective in which the wealthy and successful have obligations to help the disadvantaged. Put simply, in Muslim countries, it is fine to earn a profit, so long as that profit is justly earned and not based on the exploitation of others for one's own advantage. It also helps if those making profits undertake charitable acts to help the poor. Furthermore, Islam stresses the importance of living up to contractual obligations, of keeping one's word, and of abstaining from deception.

Given the Islamic proclivity to favor market-based systems, Muslim countries are likely to be receptive to international businesses as long as those businesses behave in a manner that is consistent with Islamic ethics. Businesses that are perceived as making an unjust profit through the exploitation of others, by deception, or by breaking contractual obligations are unlikely to be welcomed in an Islamic country. In addition, in Islamic countries where fundamentalism is on the rise, hostility toward Western-owned businesses is likely to increase.

In the previous chapter, we noted that one economic principle of Islam prohibits the payment or receipt of interest, which is considered usury. This is not just a matter of theology; in several Islamic states, it is also becoming a matter of law. In 1992, for example, Pakistan's Federal Shariat Court, the highest Islamic law court in the country, pronounced interest to be un-Islamic and therefore illegal and demanded that the government amend all financial laws accordingly. In 1999, Pakistan's Supreme Court ruled that Islamic banking methods should be used in the country after July 1, 2001, but also ruled that Western banking methods could still be used.[31] The accompanying Country Focus takes a closer look at how Islamic banking is being introduced in Pakistan.

HINDUISM Hinduism has approximately 750 million adherents, most of them on the Indian subcontinent. Hinduism began in the Indus Valley in India more than 4,000 years ago, making it the world's oldest major religion. Unlike Christianity and Islam, its founding is not linked to a particular person. Nor does it have an officially sanctioned sacred book such as the Bible or the Koran. Hindus believe that a moral force in society requires the acceptance of certain responsibilities, called *dharma*. Hindus believe in reincarnation, or rebirth into a different body, after death. Hindus also believe in *karma* the spiritual progression of each person's soul. A person's karma is affected by the way he or she lives. The moral state of an individual's karma determines the challenges he or she will face in the next life. By perfecting the soul in each new life, Hindus believe that an individual can eventually achieve *nirvana*, a state of complete spiritual perfection that renders reincarnation no longer necessary. Many Hindus believe that the way to achieve nirvana is to lead a severe ascetic lifestyle of material and physical self-denial, devoting life to a spiritual rather than material quest.

One of the interesting aspects of Hindu culture is the reverence for the cow, which Hindus see as a gift of the gods to the human race. The sacred status of the cow created some unique problems for McDonald's when it entered India in the 1990s, since devout Hindus do not eat beef (and many are also vegetarians). The accompanying Management Focus looks at how McDonald's dealt with that challenge.

LEARNING OBJECTIVE 3
Identify the business and economic implications of differences in culture.

Economic Implications of Hinduism Max Weber, famous for expounding on the Protestant work ethic, also argued that the ascetic principles embedded in Hinduism do not encourage the kind of entrepreneurial activity in pursuit of wealth creation that we find in Protestantism.[32] According to Weber, traditional Hindu values

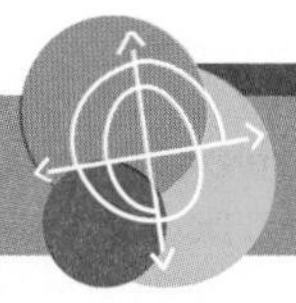

Management FOCUS

McDonald's and Hindu Culture

In many ways, McDonald's Corporation has written the book on global expansion. Every day, on average, somewhere around the world 4.2 new McDonald's restaurants are opened. By 2004, the company had 30,000 restaurants in more than 120 countries that collectively served close to 50 million customers each day.

One of the latest additions to McDonald's list of countries hosting the famous golden arches is India, where McDonald's started to establish restaurants in the late 1990s. Although India is a poor nation, the large and relatively prosperous middle class, estimated to number between 150 million and 200 million, attracted McDonald's. India, however, offered McDonald's unique challenges. For thousands of years, India's Hindu culture has revered the cow. Hindu scriptures state that the cow is a gift of the gods to the human race. The cow represents the Divine Mother that sustains all human beings. Cows give birth to bulls that are harnessed to pull plows, cow milk is highly valued and used to produce yogurt and ghee (a form of butter), cow urine has a unique place in traditional Hindu medicine, and cow dung is used as fuel. Some 300 million of these animals roam India, untethered, revered as sacred providers. They are everywhere, ambling down roads, grazing in rubbish dumps, and resting in temples—everywhere, that is, except on your plate, for Hindus do not eat the meat of the sacred cow.

McDonald's is the world's largest user of beef. Since its founding in 1955, countless animals have died to produce Big Macs. How can a company whose fortunes are built upon beef enter a country where the consumption of beef is a grave sin? Use pork instead? However, there are some 140 million Muslims in India, and Muslims don't eat pork. This leaves chicken and mutton. McDonald's responded to this cultural food dilemma by creating an Indian version of its Big Mac—the "Maharaja Mac"—which is made from mutton. Other additions to the menu conform to local sensibilities such as the "McAloo Tikki Burger," which is made from chicken. All foods are strictly segregated into vegetarian and nonvegetarian lines to conform with preferences in a country where many Hindus are vegetarian. According to the head of McDonald's Indian operations, "We had to reinvent ourselves for the Indian palate."

For a while, this seemed to work. Then in 2001 McDonald's was blindsided by a class-action lawsuit brought against it in the United States by three Indian businessmen living in Seattle. The businessmen, all vegetarians and two of whom were Hindus, sued McDonald's for "fraudulently concealing" the existence of beef in McDonald's French fries! McDonald's had said it used only 100 percent vegetable oil to make French fries, but the company soon admitted that it used a "minuscule" amount of beef extract in the oil. McDonald's settled the suit for $10 million and issued an apology, which read, "McDonald's sincerely apologizes to Hindus, vegetarians, and others for failing to provide the kind of information they needed to make informed dietary decisions at our U.S. restaurants." Going forward, the company pledged to do a better job of labeling the ingredients of its food and to find a substitute for the beef extract used in its oil.

However, news travels fast in the global society of the twenty-first century, and the revelation that McDonald's used beef extract in its oil was enough to bring Hindu nationalists onto the streets in Delhi, where they vandalized one McDonald's restaurant, causing $45,000 in damage; shouted slogans outside of another; picketed the company's headquarters; and called on India's prime minister to close McDonald's stores in the country. McDonald's Indian franchise holders quickly issued denials that they used oil that contained beef extract, and Hindu extremists responded by stating they would submit McDonald's oil to laboratory tests to see if they could detect beef extract.

The negative publicity seemed to have little impact on McDonald's long-term plans in India, however. The company continued to open restaurants, and by 2005 had 65 restaurants in the country with plans to open another 30 or so. When asked why they frequented McDonald's restaurants, Indian customers noted that their children enjoyed the "American" experience, the food was of a consistent quality, and the toilets were always clean!

Sources: Luke Harding, "Give Me a Big Mac—But Hold the Beef," *The Guardian,* December 28, 2000, p. 24; Luke Harding, "Indian McAnger," *The Guardian,* May 7, 2001, p. 1; A. Dhillon, "India Has No Beef with Fast Food Chains," *Financial Times,* March 23, 2002, p. 3; and "McDonald's Plans More Outlets in India," *Associated Press Worldstream,* December 24, 2004.

emphasize that individuals should be judged not by their material achievements but by their spiritual achievements. Hindus perceive the pursuit of material well-being as making the attainment of nirvana more difficult. Given the emphasis on an ascetic lifestyle, Weber thought that devout Hindus would be less likely to engage in entrepreneurial activity than devout Protestants would.

Mahatma Gandhi, the famous Indian nationalist and spiritual leader, was certainly the embodiment of Hindu asceticism. It has been argued that the values of Hindu asceticism and self-reliance that Gandhi advocated had a negative impact on the economic development of postindependence India.[33] But one must be careful not to read too much into Weber's arguments. Modern India is a very dynamic entrepreneurial society, and millions of hardworking entrepreneurs form the economic backbone of the country's rapidly growing economy.

Historically, Hinduism also supported India's caste system. The concept of mobility between castes within an individual's lifetime makes no sense to traditional Hindus. Hindus see mobility between castes as something that is achieved through spiritual progression and reincarnation. An individual can be reborn into a higher caste in his or her next life if he or she achieves spiritual development in this life. In so far as the caste system limits individuals' opportunities to adopt positions of responsibility and influence in society, the economic consequences of this religious belief are somewhat negative. For example, within a business organization, the most able individuals may find their route to the higher levels of the organization blocked simply because they come from a lower caste. By the same token, individuals may get promoted to higher positions within a firm as much because of their caste background as because of their ability. However, the caste system has been abolished in India and its influence is now fading.

BUDDHISM Buddhism was founded in India in the sixth century BC by Siddhartha Gautama, an Indian prince who renounced his wealth to pursue an ascetic lifestyle and spiritual perfection. Siddhartha achieved nirvana but decided to remain on earth to teach his followers how they too could achieve this state of spiritual enlightenment. Siddhartha became known as the Buddha (which means "the awakened one"). Today, Buddhism has 350 million followers, most of whom are found in Central and Southeast Asia, China, Korea, and Japan. According to Buddhism, suffering originates in people's desires for pleasure. Cessation of suffering can be achieved by following a path for transformation. Siddhartha offered the Noble Eightfold Path as a route for transformation. This emphasizes right seeing, thinking, speech, action, living, effort, mindfulness, and meditation. Unlike Hinduism, Buddhism does not support the caste system. Nor does Buddhism advocate the kind of extreme ascetic behavior that is encouraged by Hinduism. Nevertheless, like Hindus, Buddhists stress the afterlife and spiritual achievement rather than involvement in this world.

LEARNING OBJECTIVE 3
Identify the business and economic implications of differences in culture.

Economic Implications of Buddhism Because of this, the emphasis on wealth creation that is embedded in Protestantism is not found in Buddhism. Thus, in Buddhist societies, we do not see the same kind of historical cultural stress on entrepreneurial behavior that Weber claimed could be found in the Protestant West. But unlike Hinduism, the lack of support for the caste system and extreme ascetic behavior suggests that a Buddhist society may represent a more fertile ground for entrepreneurial activity than a Hindu culture.

LEARNING OBJECTIVE 3
Identify the business and economic implications of differences in culture.

CONFUCIANISM Confucianism was founded in the fifth century BC by K'ung-Fu-tzu, more generally known as Confucius. For more than 2,000 years until the 1949 Communist revolution, Confucianism was the official ethical system of China. While observance of Confucian ethics has been weakened in China since 1949, more than 200 million people still follow the teachings of Confucius, principally in China, Korea, and Japan. Confucianism teaches the importance of attaining personal salvation through right action. Although not a religion, Confucian ideology has become deeply embedded in the culture of these countries over the centuries, and through that, has an impact on the lives of many millions more. Confucianism is built around a comprehensive ethical code that sets down guidelines for relationships with others. High moral and ethical conduct and loyalty to others are central to Confucianism. Unlike religions, Confucianism is not concerned with the supernatural and has little to say about the concept of a supreme being or an afterlife.

LEARNING OBJECTIVE 3
Identify the business and economic implications of differences in culture.

Economic Implications of Confucianism

Some scholars maintain that Confucianism may have economic implications as profound as those Weber argued were to be found in Protestantism, although they are of a different nature.[34] Their basic thesis is that the influence of Confucian ethics on the culture of China, Japan, South Korea, and Taiwan, by lowering the costs of doing business in those countries, may help explain their economic success. In this regard, three values central to the Confucian system of ethics are of particular interest: loyalty, reciprocal obligations, and honesty in dealings with others.

In Confucian thought, loyalty to one's superiors is regarded as a sacred duty—an absolute obligation. In modern organizations based in Confucian cultures, the loyalty that binds employees to the heads of their organization can reduce the conflict between management and labor that we find in more class-conscious societies. Cooperation between management and labor can be achieved at a lower cost in a culture where the virtue of loyalty is emphasized in the value systems.

However, in a Confucian culture, loyalty to one's superiors, such as a worker's loyalty to management, is not blind loyalty. The concept of reciprocal obligations is important. Confucian ethics stress that superiors are obliged to reward the loyalty of their subordinates by bestowing blessings on them. If these "blessings" are not forthcoming, then neither will be the loyalty. This Confucian ethic is central to the Chinese concept of *guanxi*, which refers to relationship networks supported by reciprocal obligations (which we discussed in the opening case).[35] *Guanxi* means relationships, although in business settings it can be better understood as connections. Today, Chinese will often cultivate a *guanxiwang*, or "relationship network," for help. Reciprocal obligations are the glue that holds such networks together. If those obligations are not met—if favors done are not paid back or reciprocated—the reputation of the transgressor is tarnished and the person will be less able to draw on his or her *guanxiwang* for help in the future. Thus, the implicit threat of social sanctions is often sufficient to ensure that favors are repaid, obligations are met, and relationships are honored. In a society that lacks a rule-based legal tradition, and thus legal ways of redressing wrongs such as violations of business agreements, *guanxi* is an important mechanism for building long-term business relationships and getting business done in China.

A third concept found in Confucian ethics is the importance attached to honesty. Confucian thinkers emphasize that, although dishonest behavior may yield short-term benefits for the transgressor, dishonesty does not pay in the long run. The importance attached to honesty has major economic implications. When companies can trust each other not to break contractual obligations, the costs of doing business are lowered. Expensive lawyers are not needed to resolve contract disputes.

Another Perspective

Ecology: A Force That Crosses Religions

Concern for the environment brings a sense of shared purpose and urgency and cuts across religious traditions. Ecumenical Patriarch Bartholomew I, leader of the world's Orthodox Christians and nicknamed the "green patriarch," suggested more than a decade ago that pollution and other attacks on the environment could be considered sins.

Today, this is no longer such a radical view. Eco-friendly attitudes have moved into mainstream faiths, from Muslim clerics urging water conservation in the fast-growing Persian Gulf States to evangelistic preachers in the United States calling for attention to global warming. Many *fatwas*, or religious edicts, across the Muslim world echo Quranic readings that God entrusted humans to protect the earth. Muslim imams in Kenya are encouraging their followers to denounce the widespread use of dynamite to catch fish and push for a return to traditional nets, which trap larger fish and allow smaller, breeding-age fish to escape. Biblical commands and Judaic traditions have also been linked to environmental stewardship. (Brian Murphy, *Associated Press*, July 7, 2006).

In a Confucian society, people may be less hesitant to commit substantial resources to cooperative ventures than in a society where honesty is less pervasive. When companies adhere to Confucian ethics, they can trust each other not to violate the terms of cooperative agreements. Thus, the costs of achieving cooperation between companies may be lower in societies such as Japan relative to societies where trust is less pervasive.

For example, it has been argued that the close ties between the automobile companies and their component parts suppliers in Japan are facilitated by a combination of trust and reciprocal obligations. These close ties allow the auto companies and their suppliers to work together on a range of issues, including inventory reduction, quality control, and design. The competitive advantage of Japanese auto companies such as Toyota may in part be explained by such factors.[36] Similarly, as seen in the opening case, the combination of trust and reciprocal obligations is central to the workings and persistence of *guanxi* networks in China. Someone seeking and receiving help through a *guanxi* network is then obligated to return the favor and faces social sanctions if that obligation is not reciprocated when it is called upon. If the person does not return the favor, his or her reputation will be tarnished and he or she will be unable to draw on the resources of the network in the future. It is claimed that these relationship-based networks can be more important in helping to enforce agreements between businesses than the Chinese legal system. Some claim that *guanxi* networks are a substitute for the legal system.[37]

Language

One obvious way in which countries differ is language. By language, we mean both the spoken and the unspoken means of communication. Language is one of the defining characteristics of a culture.

SPOKEN LANGUAGE Language does far more than just enable people to communicate with each other. The nature of a language also structures the way we perceive the world. The language of a society can direct the attention of its members to certain features of the world rather than others. The classic illustration of this phenomenon is that whereas the English language has but one word for snow, the language of the Inuit (Eskimos) lacks a general term for it. Instead, because distinguishing different forms of snow is so important in the lives of the Inuit, they have 24 words that describe different types of snow (e.g., powder snow, falling snow, wet snow, drifting snow).[38]

Because language shapes the way people perceive the world, it also helps define culture. Countries with more than one language often have more than one culture. Canada has an English-speaking culture and a French-speaking culture. Tensions between the two can run quite high, with a substantial proportion of the French-speaking minority demanding independence from a Canada "dominated by English speakers." The same phenomenon can be observed in many other countries. Belgium is divided into Flemish and French speakers, and tensions between the two groups exist; in Spain, a Basque-speaking minority with its own distinctive culture has been agitating for independence from the Spanish-speaking majority for decades; on the Mediterranean island of Cyprus, the culturally diverse Greek- and Turkish-speaking populations of the island engaged in open conflict in the 1970s, and the island is now partitioned into two parts. While it does not necessarily follow that language differences create differences in culture and, therefore, separatist pressures (e.g., witness the harmony in Switzerland, where four languages are spoken), there certainly seems to be a tendency in this direction.[39]

LEARNING OBJECTIVE 3
Identify the business and economic implications of differences in culture.

Chinese is the mother tongue of the largest number of people, followed by English and Hindi, which is spoken in India. However, the most widely spoken language in the world is English, followed by French, Spanish, and Chinese (i.e., many people speak

English as a second language). English is increasingly becoming the language of international business. When a Japanese and a German businessperson get together to do business, it is almost certain that they will communicate in English. However, although English is widely used, learning the local language yields considerable advantages. Most people prefer to converse in their own language, and being able to speak the local language can build rapport, which may be very important for a business deal. International businesses that do not understand the local language can make major blunders through improper translation. For example, the Sunbeam Corporation used the English words for its "Mist-Stick" mist-producing hair curling iron when it entered the German market, only to discover after an expensive advertising campaign that *mist* means excrement in German. General Motors was troubled by the lack of enthusiasm among Puerto Rican dealers for its new Chevrolet Nova. When literally translated into Spanish, *nova* means star. However, when spoken it sounds like "no va," which in Spanish means "it doesn't go." General Motors changed the name of the car to Caribe.[40] See the Another Perspective box above for more on cultural differences.

Another Perspective

Sticky Problems in Culture Research

Conducting research across cultural borders is difficult for many reasons. First there are the more obvious issues connected to travel and building collaborative relationships in other countries, both of which are time-consuming and always full of surprises. One of the most difficult issues, though, is how to be certain that the concept about which you want to communicate has a similar meaning when it crosses a cultural border. This challenge is more than one of *word* translation; it is *concept* translation, which researchers term *concept equivalence*. Take the concept of bribery. Does it have the same meaning in the middle of Manhattan as it does in an underdeveloped, centralized economy such as North Korea? What do you think?

UNSPOKEN LANGUAGE Unspoken language refers to nonverbal communication. We all communicate with each other by a host of nonverbal cues. The raising of eyebrows, for example, is a sign of recognition in most cultures, while a smile is a sign of joy. Many nonverbal cues, however, are culturally bound. A failure to understand the nonverbal cues of another culture can lead to a communication failure. For example, making a circle with the thumb and the forefinger is a friendly gesture in the United States, but it is a vulgar sexual invitation in Greece and Turkey. Similarly, while most Americans and Europeans use the thumbs-up gesture to indicate that "it's all right," in Greece the gesture is obscene.

Another aspect of nonverbal communication is personal space, which is the comfortable amount of distance between you and someone you are talking with. In the United States, the customary distance apart adopted by parties in a business discussion is five to eight feet. In Latin America, it is three to five feet. Consequently, many North Americans unconsciously feel that Latin Americans are invading their personal space and can be seen backing away from them during a conversation. Indeed, the American may feel that the Latin is being aggressive and pushy. In turn, the Latin American may interpret such backing away as aloofness. The result can be a regrettable lack of rapport between two businesspeople from different cultures.

Education

Formal education plays a key role in a society. Formal education is the medium through which individuals learn many of the language, conceptual, and mathematical skills that are indispensable in a modern society. Formal education also supplements the family's role in socializing the young into the values and norms of a society. Values and norms are taught both directly and indirectly. Schools generally teach basic facts about the social and political nature of a society. They also focus on the fundamental obligations of citizenship. Cultural norms are also taught indirectly at school. Respect for others, obedience to authority, honesty, neatness, being on time, and so on, are all part of the "hidden curriculum" of schools. The use of a grading system also teaches children the value of personal achievement and competition.[41]

LEARNING OBJECTIVE 3
Identify the business and economic implications of differences in culture.

From an international business perspective, one important aspect of education is its role as a determinant of national competitive advantage.[42] The availability of a pool of skilled and educated workers seems to be a major determinant of the likely economic success of a country. In analyzing the competitive success of Japan since 1945, for example, Michael Porter notes that after the war, Japan had almost nothing except for a pool of skilled and educated human resources.

> With a long tradition of respect for education that borders on reverence, Japan possessed a large pool of literate, educated, and increasingly skilled human resources. . . . Japan has benefited from a large pool of trained engineers. Japanese universities graduate many more engineers per capita than in the United States. . . . A first-rate primary and secondary education system in Japan operates based on high standards and emphasizes math and science. Primary and secondary education is highly competitive. . . . Japanese education provides most students all over Japan with a sound education for later education and training. A Japanese high school graduate knows as much about math as most American college graduates.[43]

Porter's point is that Japan's excellent education system is an important factor explaining the country's postwar economic success. Not only is a good education system a determinant of national competitive advantage, but it is also an important factor guiding the location choices of international businesses. The recent trend to outsource information technology jobs to India, for example, is partly due to the presence of significant numbers of trained engineers in India, which in turn is a result of the Indian education system. By the same token, it would make little sense to base production facilities that require highly skilled labor in a country where the education system was so poor that a skilled labor pool wasn't available, no matter how attractive the country might seem on other dimensions. It might make sense to base production operations that require only unskilled labor in such a country.

The general education level of a country is also a good index of the kind of products that might sell in a country and of the type of promotional material that should be used. For example, a country where more than 70 percent of the population is illiterate is unlikely to be a good market for popular books. Promotional material containing written descriptions of mass-marketed products is unlikely to have an effect in a country where almost three-quarters of the population cannot read. It is far better to use pictorial promotions in such circumstances.

Culture and the Workplace

LEARNING OBJECTIVE 4
Understand how differences in social culture influence values in the workplace.

Of considerable importance for an international business with operations in different countries is how a society's culture affects the values found in the workplace. Management process and practices may need to vary according to culturally determined work-related values. For example, if the cultures of the United States and France result in different work-related values, an international business with operations in both countries should vary its management process and practices to account for these differences.

Probably the most famous study of how culture relates to values in the workplace was undertaken by Geert Hofstede.[44] As part of his job as a psychologist working for IBM, Hofstede collected data on employee attitudes and values for more than 100,000 individuals from 1967 to 1973. These data enabled him to compare dimensions of culture across 40 countries. Hofstede isolated four dimensions that he claimed summarized different cultures—power distance, uncertainty avoidance, individualism versus collectivism, and masculinity versus femininity.

Hofstede's **power distance** dimension focused on how a society deals with the fact that people are unequal in physical and intellectual capabilities. According to Hofstede, high power distance cultures were found in countries that let inequalities grow over time into inequalities of power and wealth. Low power distance cultures were found in societies that tried to play down such inequalities as much as possible.

Power Distance
Extent to which a society allows inequalities of physical and intellectual capabilities between people to grow into inequalities of power and wealth.

The **individualism versus collectivism** dimension focused on the relationship between the individual and his or her fellows. In individualistic societies, the ties between individuals were loose and individual achievement and freedom were highly valued. In societies where collectivism was emphasized, the ties between individuals were tight. In such societies, people were born into collectives, such as extended families, and everyone was supposed to look after the interest of his or her collective.

Individualism versus Collectivism
Extent to which a society teaches individuals either to prize personal achievement or to conversely look after the interests of their collective first and foremost.

Hofstede's **uncertainty avoidance** dimension measured the extent to which different cultures socialized their members into accepting ambiguous situations and tolerating uncertainty. Members of high uncertainty avoidance cultures placed a premium on job security, career patterns, retirement benefits, and so on. They also had a strong need for rules and regulations; the manager was expected to issue clear instructions, and subordinates' initiatives were tightly controlled. Lower uncertainty avoidance cultures were characterized by a greater readiness to take risks and less emotional resistance to change.

Uncertainty Avoidance
Extent to which cultures socialize members to accept ambiguous situations and to tolerate uncertainty.

Hofstede's **masculinity versus femininity** dimension looked at the relationship between gender and work roles. In masculine cultures, sex roles were sharply differentiated and traditional "masculine values," such as achievement and the effective exercise of power, determined cultural ideals. In feminine cultures, sex roles were less sharply distinguished, and little differentiation was made between men and women in the same job.

Masculinity versus Femininity
Extent to which a society differentiates and emphasizes traditional gender and work roles; a masculine characterization means there is more differentiation, whereas a feminine level means there is less.

Hofstede created an index score for each of these four dimensions that ranged from 0 to 100 and scored high for high individualism, high power distance, high uncertainty avoidance, and high masculinity. He averaged the score for all employees from a given country. Table 3.1 summarizes these data for 20 selected countries. Western nations such as the United States, Canada, and Britain score high on the individualism scale and low on the power distance scale. At the other extreme are a group of Latin American and Asian countries that emphasize collectivism over individualism and score high on the power distance scale. Table 3.1 also reveals that Japan's culture has strong uncertainty avoidance and high masculinity. This characterization fits the standard stereotype of Japan as a country that is male dominant and where uncertainty avoidance exhibits itself in the institution of lifetime employment. Sweden and Denmark stand out as countries that have both low uncertainty avoidance and low masculinity (high emphasis on "feminine" values).

Hofstede's results are interesting for what they tell us in a very general way about differences between cultures. Many of Hofstede's findings are consistent with standard Western stereotypes about cultural differences. For example, many people believe Americans are more individualistic and egalitarian than the Japanese (they have a lower power distance), who in turn are more individualistic and egalitarian than Mexicans. Similarly, many might agree that Latin countries such as Mexico place a higher emphasis on masculine value—they are machismo cultures—than the Nordic countries of Denmark and Sweden.

However, one should be careful about reading too much into Hofstede's research. It has been criticized on a number of points.[45] First, Hofstede assumes there is a one-to-one correspondence between culture and the nation-state, but as we saw earlier, many countries have more than one culture. Hofstede's results do not capture this distinction. Second, the research may have been culturally bound. The research team was composed of Europeans and Americans. The questions they asked of IBM employees and their analysis of the answers may have been shaped by their own cultural

table 3.1

Work-Related Values for 20 Selected Countries

Source: G. Hofstede, *Culture's Consequences.* © 1988, Sage Publications. Cited in G. Hofstede, "The Cultural Relativity of Organizational Practices and Theories," *Journal of International Business Studies* 14 (Fall 1983), pp. 75–89. Reprinted by permission of Geert Hofstede.

	Power Distance	Uncertainty Avoidance	Individualism	Masculinity
Argentina	49	86	46	56
Australia	36	51	90	61
Brazil	69	76	38	49
Canada	39	48	80	52
Denmark	18	23	74	16
France	68	86	71	43
Germany (F.R.)	35	65	67	66
Great Britain	35	35	89	66
Indonesia	78	48	14	46
India	77	40	48	56
Israel	13	81	54	47
Japan	54	92	46	95
Mexico	81	82	30	69
Netherlands	38	53	80	14
Panama	95	86	11	44
Spain	57	86	51	42
Sweden	31	29	71	5
Thailand	64	64	20	34
Turkey	66	85	37	45
United States	40	46	91	62

biases and concerns. So it is not surprising that Hofstede's results confirm Western stereotypes, because it was Westerners who undertook the research.

Third, Hofstede's informants worked not only within a single industry, the computer industry, but also within one company, IBM. At the time, IBM was renowned for its own strong corporate culture and employee selection procedures, making it possible that the employees' values were different in important respects from the values of the cultures from which those employees came. Also, certain social classes (such as unskilled manual workers) were excluded from Hofstede's sample. A final caution is that Hofstede's work is now beginning to look dated. Cultures do not stand still; they evolve, albeit slowly. What was a reasonable characterization in the 1960s and 1970s may not be so today.

Still, just as it should not be accepted without question, Hofstede's work should not be dismissed either. It represents a starting point for managers trying to figure out how cultures differ and what that might mean for management practices. Also, several other scholars have found strong evidence that differences in culture affect values and practices in the workplace, and Hofstede's basic results have been replicated using more diverse samples of individuals in different settings.[46] Still, managers should use the results with caution, for they are not necessarily accurate.

Hofstede subsequently expanded his original research to include a fifth dimension that he argued captured additional cultural differences not brought out in his earlier work.[47] He referred to this dimension as "Confucian dynamism" (sometimes called *long-term orientation*). According to Hofstede, **Confucian dynamism** captures attitudes toward time, persistence, ordering by status, protection of face, respect for tradition, and reciprocation of gifts and favors. The label refers to these "values" being derived from Confucian teachings. As might be expected, East Asian countries such as Japan, Hong Kong, and Thailand scored high on Confucian dynamism, while nations such as the United States and Canada scored low. Hofstede and his associates went on to argue that their evidence suggested that nations with higher economic growth rates scored high on Confucian dynamism and low on individualism—the implication being Confucianism is good for growth. However, subsequent studies have shown that this finding does not hold up under more sophisticated statistical analysis.[48] During the past decade, countries with high individualism and low Confucian dynamics such as the United States have attained high growth rates, while some Confucian cultures such as Japan have had stagnant economic growth. In reality, while culture might influence the economic success of a nation, it is just one of many factors, and while its importance should not be ignored, it should not be overstated either. The factors discussed in Chapter 2—economic, political, and legal systems—are probably more important than culture in explaining differential economic growth rates over time.

Confucian Dynamism
Extent to which a society adheres to Confucian values about time, persistence, ordering by status, protection of face, respect for tradition, and reciprocation of gifts.

Cultural Change

LEARNING OBJECTIVE 5
Develop an appreciation for the economic and business implications of cultural change.

Culture is not a constant; it evolves over time.[49] Changes in value systems can be slow and painful for a society. In the 1960s, for example, American values toward the role of women, love, sex, and marriage underwent significant changes. Much of the social turmoil of that time reflected these changes. Change, however, does occur and can often be quite profound. For example, at the beginning of the 1960s, the idea that women might hold senior management positions in major corporations was not widely accepted. Many scoffed at the idea. Today, it is a reality, and few in the mainstream of American society question the development or the capability of women in the business world. American culture has changed (although it is still more difficult for women to gain senior management positions than men). Similarly, the value systems of many ex-communist states, such as Russia, are undergoing significant changes as those countries move away from values that emphasize collectivism and toward those that emphasize individualism. While social turmoil is an inevitable outcome of such a shift, the shift will still probably occur. See Another Perspective box at right for another example.

Similarly, some claim that a major cultural shift is occurring in Japan, with a move toward greater individualism.[50] The model Japanese office worker, or "salaryman," is characterized as being loyal to his boss and the organization to the point of giving up evenings, weekends, and vacations to serve the organization, which is the collective of which the employee is a member. However, a new generation of office workers does not seem to fit this model. An individual from the new generation is likely to be more direct than the traditional Japanese. He acts more like a Westerner, a *gaijin*. He does not live for the company and will move on if he gets the offer of a better job. He is not

Another Perspective

The Train Designed to Bring Cultural Change

The Beijing-Lhasa Express boomed its maiden voyage from Beijing to Tibet on the world's highest railway in July 2006. Praised as a magnificent technological and engineering feat by the Chinese government, the $4.6 billion railway crosses mountain passes up to 16,500 feet high and forbidding terrain on the treeless Tibetan plateau.

The opening of the railroad coincided with the eighty-fifth anniversary of the ruling Communist Party as part of its efforts to develop China's poor west and bind those traditional cultures to the booming east. Tibetans and other critics warn that the train will bring a flood of Chinese immigrants, dilute the Tibetan culture, and threaten its fragile environment. Much of the Tibetan culture has been preserved through its geographical isolation. Let's keep an eye on what happens. (Alexa Olson, *Associated Press*, July 2, 2006).

keen on overtime, especially if he has a date. He has his own plans for his free time, and they may not include drinking or playing golf with the boss.[51]

Several studies have suggested that economic advancement and globalization may be important factors in societal change.[52] For example, there is evidence that economic progress is accompanied by a shift in values away from collectivism and toward individualism.[53] Thus, as Japan has become richer, the cultural emphasis on collectivism has declined and greater individualism is being witnessed. One reason for this shift may be that richer societies exhibit less need for social and material support structures built on collectives, whether the collective is the extended family or the paternalistic company. People are better able to take care of their own needs. As a result, the importance attached to collectivism declines, while greater economic freedoms lead to an increase in opportunities for expressing individualism.

The culture of societies may also change as they become richer because economic progress affects a number of other factors, which in turn influence culture. For example, increased urbanization and improvements in the quality and availability of education are both a function of economic progress, and both can lead to declining emphasis on the traditional values associated with poor rural societies. A 25-year study of values in 78 countries, known as the World Values Survey, coordinated by the University of Michigan's Institute for Social Research, has documented how values change. The study linked these changes in values to changes in a country's level of economic development.[54] According to this research, as countries get richer, a shift occurs away from "traditional values" linked to religion, family, and country, and toward "secular rational" values. Traditionalists say religion is important in their lives. They have a strong sense of national pride; they also think that children should be taught to obey and that the first duty of a child is to make his or her parents proud. They say abortion, euthanasia, divorce, and suicide are never justified. At the other end of this spectrum are secular rational values.

Another category in the World Values Survey is quality of life attributes. At one end of this spectrum are "survival values," the values people hold when the struggle for survival is of paramount importance. These values tend to stress that economic and physical security are more important than self-expression. People who cannot take

The 2006 MTV awards show in India demonstrates the globalization of what was originally American pop culture. Do you think traditional Indian values are at risk from the importation of MTV? *Rajesh Nirgude/AP Wide World*

food or safety for granted tend to be xenophobic, are wary of political activity, have authoritarian tendencies, and believe that men make better political leaders than women. "Self-expression" or "well-being" values stress the importance of diversity, belonging, and participation in political processes.

As countries get richer, there seems to be a shift from "traditional" to "secular rational" values, and from "survival values" to "well-being" values. The shift, however, takes time, primarily because individuals are socialized into a set of values when they are young and find it difficult to change as they grow older. Substantial changes in values are linked to generations, with younger people typically being in the vanguard of a significant change in values.

With regard to globalization, some have argued that advances in transportation and communication technologies, the dramatic increase in trade that we have witnessed since World War II, and the rise of global corporations such as Hitachi, Disney, Microsoft, and Levi Strauss, whose products and operations can be found around the globe, are creating conditions for the merging of cultures.[55] With McDonald's hamburgers in China, The Gap in India, iPods in South Africa, and MTV everywhere helping to foster a ubiquitous youth culture, some argue that the conditions for less cultural variation have been created. At the same time, one must not ignore important countertrends, such as the shift toward Islamic fundamentalism in several countries; the separatist movement in Quebec, Canada; or the continuing ethnic strains and separatist movements in Russia. Such countertrends in many ways are a reaction to the pressures for cultural convergence. In an increasingly modern and materialistic world, some societies are trying to reemphasize their cultural roots and uniqueness. Cultural change is not unidirectional, with national cultures converging toward some homogenous global entity. Also, while some elements of culture change quite rapidly—particularly the use of material symbols—other elements change slowly if at all. Thus, just because people the world over wear blue jeans and eat at McDonald's, one should not assume that they have also adopted American values—for more often than not, they have not.

Focus on Managerial Implications

LEARNING OBJECTIVE 3
Identify the business and economic implications of differences in culture.

International business is different from national business because countries and societies are different. In this chapter, we have seen just how different societies can be. Societies differ because their cultures vary. Their cultures vary because of profound differences in social structure, religion, language, education, economic philosophy, and political philosophy. Three important implications for international business flow from these differences. The first is the need to develop cross-cultural literacy. There is a need not only to appreciate that cultural differences exist but also to appreciate what such differences mean for international business. A second implication centers on the connection between culture and national competitive advantage. A third implication looks at the connection between culture and ethics in decision making. In this section, we will explore the first two of these issues in depth. The connection between culture and ethics is explored in the next chapter.

Cross-Cultural Literacy

One of the biggest dangers confronting a company that goes abroad for the first time is the danger of being ill-informed. International businesses that are ill-informed about the practices of another culture are likely to fail. Doing business in different cultures requires adaptation to conform with the value systems and norms of that culture. Adaptation can embrace all aspects of an international firm's operations in a foreign country. The way in which deals are negotiated, the appropriate incentive pay systems for salespeople, the structure of the organization, the name of a product, the tenor of relations between management and labor, the manner in which the product is promoted, and so on, are all sensitive to cultural differences. What works in one culture might not work in another.

To combat the danger of being ill-informed, international businesses should consider employing local citizens to help them do business in a particular culture. They must also ensure that home-country executives are cosmopolitan enough to understand how differences in culture affect the practice of international business. Transferring executives overseas at regular intervals to expose them to different cultures will help build a cadre of cosmopolitan executives. An international business must also be constantly on guard against the dangers of *ethnocentric behavior*. **Ethnocentrism** is a belief in the superiority of one's own ethnic group or culture. Hand in hand with ethnocentrism goes a disregard or contempt for the culture of other countries. Unfortunately, ethnocentrism is all too prevalent; many Americans are guilty of it, as are many French people, Japanese people, British people, and so on. Ugly as it is, ethnocentrism is a fact of life, one that international businesses must be on guard against.

Ethnocentrism
A belief in the superiority of one's own ethnic group or culture.

Simple examples illustrate how important cross-cultural literacy can be. Anthropologist Edward T. Hall has described how Americans, who tend to be informal in nature, react strongly to being corrected or reprimanded in public.[56] This can cause problems in Germany, where a cultural tendency toward correcting strangers can shock and offend most Americans. For their part, Germans can be a bit taken aback by the tendency of Americans to call everyone by their first name. This is uncomfortable enough among executives of the same rank, but it can be seen as insulting when a young and junior American executive addresses an older and more senior German manager by his first name without having been invited to do so. Hall concludes it can take a long time to get on a first-name basis with a German; if you rush the process you will be perceived as overfriendly and rude, and that may not be good for business.

Hall also notes that cultural differences in attitude to time can cause a myriad of problems. He notes that in the United States, giving a person a deadline is a way of increasing the urgency or relative importance of a task. However, in the Middle East, giving a deadline can have exactly the opposite effect. The American who insists an Arab business associate make his mind up in a hurry is likely to be perceived as overly demanding and exerting undue pressure. The result may be exactly the opposite of what the American intended, with the Arab going slow as a reaction to the American's arrogance and rudeness. For his part, the American may believe that an Arab associate is being rude if he shows up late to a meeting because he met a friend in the street and stopped to talk. The American, of course, is very concerned about time and scheduling. But for the Arab, who lives in a society where social networks are a major source of information, and maintaining relationships is important, finishing the discussion with a friend is more important than adhering to a strict schedule. Indeed, the Arab may be puzzled as to why the American attaches so much importance to time and schedule.

Social networking and the importance of communal eating are some of the collectivist values Arabs bring to business. *Adrian Wilson/Corbis*

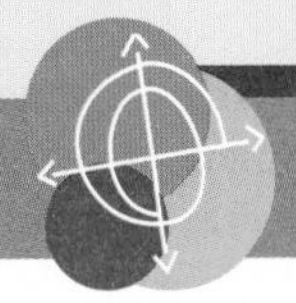

Management FOCUS

Cross-Cultural Illiteracy

An advertisement for a revolutionary new plane—the Osprey, which can fly like a plane and hover like a helicopter—recently landed the aircraft's makers, Boeing and Bell Helicopter, in a lot of trouble. The ad, which depicted the Osprey hovering above a mosque with soldiers being lowered down on ropes onto the roof, contained the tag lines "It descends from the heavens, ironically it unleashes hell. . . . Consider it a gift from above."

The offending picture initially appeared in the *Armed Forces Journal.* When senior managers at Boeing and Bell saw what had been put together by their Texas advertising agency, they immediately withdrew it from circulation. For some reasons, however, the ad was subsequently published in the *National Journal*, causing an outcry from the Council on American Islamic Relations, which feared that the ad conveyed the impression that the war on terror was in fact a war on Islam. Embarrassed by the slip up, Boeing and Bell issued a press release stating that the ad was ill-conceived, offensive, and should never have been published. Apparently, the Bell executive who cleared the ad for publication was not authorized to do so.

Source: "A Hellish Controversy," *The Economist,* October 8, 2005, p. 73.

For another example of the consequences of a lack of cultural sensitivity, see the Management Focus feature on cross-cultural illiteracy.

Culture and Competitive Advantage

One theme that continually surfaces in this chapter is the relationship between culture and national competitive advantage. Put simply, the value systems and norms of a country influence the costs of doing business in that country. The costs of doing business in a country influence the ability of firms to establish a competitive advantage in the global marketplace. We have seen how attitudes toward cooperation between management and labor, toward work, and toward the payment of interest are influenced by social structure and religion. It can be argued that the class-based conflict between workers and management in class-conscious societies, when it leads to industrial disruption, raises the costs of doing business in that society. Similarly, we have seen how some sociologists have argued that the ascetic "other-worldly" ethics of Hinduism may not be as supportive of capitalism as the ethics embedded in Protestantism and Confucianism. Also, Islamic laws banning interest payments may raise the costs of doing business by constraining a country's banking system.

Japan presents an interesting example of how culture can influence competitive advantage. Some scholars have argued that the culture of modern Japan lowers the costs of doing business relative to the costs in most Western nations. Japan's emphasis on group affiliation, loyalty, reciprocal obligations, honesty, and education all boost the competitiveness of Japanese companies. The emphasis on group affiliation and loyalty encourages individuals to identify strongly with the companies in which they work. This tends to foster an ethic of hard work and cooperation between management and labor "for the good of the company." Similarly, reciprocal obligations and honesty help foster an atmosphere of trust between companies and their suppliers. This encourages them to enter into long-term relationships with each other to work on inventory reduction, quality control, and design—all of which have been shown to improve an organization's competitiveness. This level of cooperation has often been lacking in the West, where the relationship between a company and its suppliers tends to be a short-term one structured around competitive bidding rather than one based on long-term mutual commitments. In addition, the availability of a pool of highly skilled labor, particularly engineers, has helped Japanese enterprises develop cost-reducing process innovations that have boosted their productivity.[57] Thus, cultural factors may help explain the competitive advantage enjoyed by many Japanese businesses in the global marketplace. The rise of Japan as an economic power during the second half of the twentieth century may be in part attributed to the economic consequences of its culture.

It also has been argued that the Japanese culture is less supportive of entrepreneurial activity than, say, American society. In many ways, entrepreneurial activity is a product of an individualistic mind-set, not a classic characteristic of the Japanese. This may explain why American enterprises, rather than Japanese corporations, dominate industries where entrepreneurship and innovation are highly valued, such as computer software and biotechnology. Of course, obvious and significant exceptions to this generalization exist. Masayoshi Son recognized the potential of software far faster than any of Japan's corporate giants; set up his company, Softbank, in 1981; and has since built it into Japan's top software distributor. Similarly, dynamic entrepreneurial individuals established major Japanese companies such as Sony and Matsushita. But these examples may be the exceptions that prove the rule, for as yet there has been no surge in entrepreneurial high-technology enterprises in Japan equivalent to what has occurred in the United States.

For the international business, the connection between culture and competitive advantage is important for two reasons. First, the connection suggests which countries are likely to produce the most viable competitors. For example, one might argue that U.S. enterprises are likely to see continued growth in aggressive, cost-efficient competitors from those Pacific Rim nations where a combination of free market economics, Confucian ideology, group-oriented social structures, and advanced education systems can all be found (e.g., South Korea, Taiwan, Japan, and, increasingly, China).

Second, the connection between culture and competitive advantage has important implications for the choice of countries in which to locate production facilities and do business. Consider a hypothetical case when a company has to choose between two countries, A and B, for locating a production facility. Both countries are characterized by low labor costs and good access to world markets. Both countries are of roughly the same size (in terms of population) and both are at a similar stage of economic development. In country A, the education system is undeveloped, the society is characterized by a marked stratification between the upper and lower classes, and there are six major linguistic groups. In country B, the education system is well developed, social stratification is lacking, group identification is valued by the culture, and there is only one linguistic group. Which country makes the best investment site?

Country B probably does. In country A, conflict between management and labor, and between different language groups, can be expected to lead to social and industrial disruption, thereby raising the costs of doing business.[58] The lack of a good education system also can be expected to work against the attainment of business goals.

The same kind of comparison could be made for an international business trying to decide where to push its products, country A or B. Again, country B would be the logical choice because cultural factors suggest that in the long run, country B is the nation most likely to achieve the greatest level of economic growth.

But as important as culture is, it is probably less important than economic, political, and legal systems in explaining differential economic growth between nations. Cultural differences are significant, but we should not overemphasize their importance in the economic sphere. For example, earlier we noted that Max Weber argued that the ascetic principles embedded in Hinduism do not encourage entrepreneurial activity. While this is an interesting academic thesis, recent years have seen an increase in entrepreneurial activity in India, particularly in the information technology sector where India is rapidly becoming an important global player. The ascetic principles of Hinduism and caste-based social stratification have apparently not held back entrepreneurial activity in this sector.

Key Terms

cross-cultural literacy, p. 88
culture, p. 89
values, p. 90
norms, p. 90
society, p. 90
folkways, p. 91
mores, p. 91
social structure, p. 93
group, p. 93
social strata, p. 95
social mobility, p. 95
caste system, p. 95
class system, p. 95
class consciousness, p. 97
religion, p. 98
ethical system, p. 98
power distance, p. 111
individualism versus collectivism, p. 111
uncertainty avoidance, p. 111
masculinity versus femininity, p. 111
Confucian dynamism, p. 113
ethnocentrism, p. 116

Summary

We have looked at the nature of social culture and studied some implications for business practice. The chapter made the following points:

1. Culture is a complex whole that includes knowledge, beliefs, art, morals, law, customs, and other capabilities acquired by people as members of society.
2. Values and norms are the central components of a culture. Values are abstract ideals about what a society believes to be good, right, and desirable. Norms are social rules and guidelines that prescribe appropriate behavior in particular situations.
3. Values and norms are influenced by political and economic philosophy, social structure, religion, language, and education.
4. The social structure of a society refers to its basic social organization. Two main dimensions along which social structures differ are the individual–group dimension and the stratification dimension.
5. In some societies, the individual is the basic building block of social organization. These societies emphasize individual achievements above all else. In other societies, the group is the basic building block of social organization. These societies emphasize group membership and group achievements above all else.
6. All societies are stratified into different classes. Class-conscious societies are characterized by low social mobility and a high degree of stratification. Less class-conscious societies are characterized by high social mobility and a low degree of stratification.
7. Religion may be defined as a system of shared beliefs and rituals that is concerned with the realm of the sacred. Ethical systems refer to a set of moral principles, or values, that are used to guide and shape behavior. The world's major religions are Christianity, Islam, Hinduism, and Buddhism. Although not a religion, Confucianism has an impact on behavior that is as profound as that of many religions. The value systems of different religious and ethical systems have different implications for business practice.
8. Language is one defining characteristic of a culture. It has both spoken and unspoken dimensions. In countries with more than one spoken language, we tend to find more than one culture.
9. Formal education is the medium through which individuals learn skills and are socialized into the values and norms of a society. Education plays an important role in the determination of national competitive advantage.
10. Geert Hofstede studied how culture relates to values in the workplace. He isolated four dimensions that he claimed summarized different cultures: power distance, uncertainty avoidance, individualism versus collectivism, and masculinity versus femininity.
11. Culture is not a constant; it evolves. Economic progress and globalization seem to be two important engines of cultural change.

12. One danger confronting a company that goes abroad for the first time is being ill-informed. To develop cross-cultural literacy, international businesses need to employ host-country nationals, build a cadre of cosmopolitan executives, and guard against the dangers of ethnocentric behavior.
13. The value systems and norms of a country can affect the costs of doing business in that country.

Critical Thinking and Discussion Questions

1. Outline why the culture of a country might influence the costs of doing business in that country. Illustrate your answer with examples.
2. Do you think that business practices in an Islamic country are likely to differ from business practices in the United States? If so, how?
3. What are the implications for international business of differences in the dominant religion or ethical system of a country?
4. Choose two countries that appear to be culturally diverse. Compare the cultures of those countries and then indicate how cultural differences influence (*a*) the costs of doing business in each country, (*b*) the likely future economic development of that country, and (*c*) business practices.

Research Task 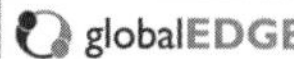 http://globalEDGE.msu.edu

Use the globalEDGE site (http://globalEDGE.msu.edu/) to complete the following exercises:

1. You are preparing for a business trip to Venezuela where you will need to interact extensively with local professionals. Therefore, you consider collecting information regarding local culture and business habits before your departure. Prepare a short description of the most striking cultural characteristics involved in *meeting and greeting new people* that may effect business interactions in this country.
2. Asian cultures exhibit significant differences in *business etiquette* when compared to Western cultures. For example, in China, it is considered offensive to point while speaking. Find five additional tips regarding the business etiquette of an Asian country of your choice.

closing case

Matsushita's Culture Changes with Japan

Established in 1920, the consumer electronics giant Matsushita was at the forefront of the rise of Japan to the status of major economic power during the 1970s and 1980s. Like many other long-standing Japanese businesses, Matsushita was regarded as a bastion of traditional Japanese values based on strong group identification, reciprocal obligations, and loyalty to the company. Several commentators attributed Matsushita's success, and that of the Japanese economy, to the existence of Confucian values in the workplace. At Matsushita, employees were taken care of by the company from "cradle to the grave." Matsushita provided them with a wide range of benefits including cheap housing, guaranteed lifetime employment, seniority-based pay systems, and generous retirement bonuses. In return, Matsushita expected, and got, loyalty and hard work from its employees. To Japan's postwar generation, struggling to recover from the humiliation of defeat, it seemed like a fair bargain. The employees worked hard for the greater good of Matsushita, and Matsushita reciprocated by bestowing "blessings" on employees.

However, culture does not stay constant. According to some observers, the generation born after 1964 lacked the same commitment to traditional Japanese values as their parents. They grew up in a world that was richer, where Western ideas were beginning to make themselves felt, and where the possibilities seemed greater. They did not want to be tied to a company for life, to be a "salaryman." These trends came to the fore in the 1990s, when the Japanese economy entered a prolonged economic slump. As the decade progressed, one

Japanese firm after another was forced to change its traditional ways of doing business. Slowly at first, troubled companies started to lay off older workers, effectively abandoning lifetime employment guarantees. As younger people saw this happening, they concluded that loyalty to a company might not be reciprocated, effectively undermining one of the central bargains made in postwar Japan.

Matsushita was one of the last companies to turn its back on Japanese traditions, but in 1998, after years of poor performance, it began to modify traditional practices. The principle agents of change were a group of managers who had extensive experience in Matsushita's overseas operations, and included Kunio Nakamura, who became the chief executive of Matsushita in 2000.

First, Matsushita changed the pay scheme for its 11,000 managers. In the past, the traditional twice-a-year bonuses had been based almost entirely on seniority, but now Matsushita said they would be based on performance. In 1999, Matsushita announced this process would be made transparent; managers would be shown what their performance rankings were and how these fed into pay bonuses. As elementary as this might sound in the West, for Matsushita it represented the beginning of a revolution in human resource practices.

About the same time, Matsushita took aim at the lifetime employment system and the associated perks. Under the new system, recruits were given the choice of three employment options. First, they could sign on to the traditional option. Under this, they were eligible to live in subsidized company housing, go free to company-organized social events, and buy subsidized services such as banking from group companies. They also still would receive a retirement bonus equal to two years' salary. Under a second scheme, employees could forgo the guaranteed retirement bonus in exchange for higher starting salaries and keep perks such as cheap company housing. Under a third scheme, they would lose both the retirement bonus and the subsidized services, but they would start at a still higher salary. In its first two years of operation, only 3 percent of recruits chose the third option—suggesting there is still a hankering for the traditional paternalistic relationship—but 41 percent took the second option.

In other ways Matsushita's designs are grander still. As the company has moved into new industries such as software engineering and network communications technology, it has begun to sing the praises of democratization of employees, and it has sought to encourage individuality, initiative taking, and risk seeking among its younger employees. But while such changes may be easy to articulate, they are hard to implement. For all of its talk, Matsushita has been slow to dismantle its lifetime employment commitment to those hired under the traditional system. This was underlined in early 2001 when, in response to continued poor performance, Matsushita announced it would close 30 factories in Japan, cut 13,000 jobs including 1,000 management jobs, and sell a "huge amount of assets" over the next three years. While this seemed to indicate a final break with the lifetime employment system—it represented the first layoffs in the company's history—the company also said unneeded management staff would not be fired but instead transferred to higher growth areas such as health care.

With so many of its managers a product of the old way of doing things, a skeptic might question the ability of the company to turn its intentions into a reality. As growth has slowed, Matsushita has had to cut back on its hiring, but its continued commitment to long-standing employees means that the average age of its workforce is rising. In the 1960s it was around 25; by the early 2000s it was 35, a trend that might counteract Matsushita's attempts to revolutionize the workplace, for surely those who benefited from the old system will not give way easily to the new. Still, by 2004 it was clear that Matsushita was making progress. After significant losses in 2002, the company broke even in 2003 and started to make profits again in 2004 and in 2005 recorded record profits of $1.3 billion. New growth drivers, such as sales of DVD equipment, certainly helped, but so did the cultural and organizational changes that enabled the company to better exploit these new growth opportunities.

Sources: "Putting the Bounce Back into Matsushita," *The Economist,* May 22, 1999, pp. 67–68; "In Search of the New Japanese Dream," *The Economist,* February 19, 2000, pp. 59–60; P. Landers, "Matsushita to Restructure in Bid to Boost Thin Profits," *The Wall Street Journal,* December 1, 2000, p. A13; M. Tanikawa, "A Pillar of Japan Inc. Finally Turns Around; Work in Progress," *International Herald Tribune,* August 28, 2004, pp. 17–18; and M. Nakamoto, "Shift to Digital Drives Growth for Matsushita," *Financial Times,* May 1, 2006, p. 17.

Case Discussion Questions

1. What were the triggers of cultural change in Japan during the 1990s? How is cultural change starting to affect traditional values in Japan?
2. How might Japan's changing culture influence the way Japanese businesses operate in the future? What are the potential implications of such changes for the Japanese economy?
3. How did traditional Japanese culture benefit Matsushita during the period from the 1950s to the 1980s? Did traditional values become more of a liability during the 1990s and early 2000s? How so?
4. What is Matsushita trying to achieve with human resource changes it has announced? What are the impediments to successfully implementing these changes? What are the implications for Matsushita if (*a*) the changes are made quickly or (*b*) it takes years or even decades to fully implement the changes?
5. What does the Matsushita case teach you about the relationship between societal culture and business success?

Courtesy United Nations Oil for Food Parogram

part 2 Country Differences

LEARNING OBJECTIVES

1. Be familiar with the ethical issues faced by international businesses.
2. Recognize an ethical dilemma.
3. Discuss the causes of unethical behavior by managers.
4. Be familiar with the different philosophical approaches to ethics.
5. Know what managers can do to incorporate ethical considerations into their decision making.

chapter 4

Ethics in International Business

Oil for Bribes

opening case

Between 1997 and 2003, the United Nations administered an "oil for food" program with Iraq. During this period, Iraq was under UN sanctions because Saddam Hussein's regime failed to comply with UN resolutions. The UN designed the oil for food program to alleviate the suffering of the Iraq people by allowing Iraq to sell limited amounts of oil in international markets and to use that money to purchase food and other essential humanitarian goods. By 2003, however, it became clear that Saddam's regime had manipulated the program to extract significant funds from international oil traders and foreign enterprises. In 2004, the UN charged a committee, headed by Paul Volcker, former chairman of the U.S. Federal Reserve, to investigate allegations of widespread corruption under the oil for food program. The final report, issued in late 2005, represented a damming indictment of the ethics of many international businesses that had traded with Iraq under the program.

The Volcker committee concluded that companies handed some $1.8 billion in illegal payments to the Iraqi regime. About $229 million was raised from an illicit surcharge that the Iraqi government placed on every barrel of oil; some international oil traders were apparently willing to pay the surcharge in order to get access to cheap Iraqi oil that they could then resell at a good profit. The traders paid the surcharge, which amounted to between $0.10 and $0.30 a barrel, into bank accounts controlled directly by the Iraqi government. Far worse, however, was the revelation that some 2,200 of the 4,000 companies that sold goods to Iraq under the oil for food program agreed to pay nearly $1.6 billion in kickbacks to the Iraqi regime. These kickbacks were disguised as "after-sale service fees" and "inland transportation fees" that were significantly higher than market rates. Among the companies named for participating in the kickback scheme were DaimlerChrysler and Siemens of Germany, Swedish automaker Volvo, and the Weir Group of the UK.

Typical of the transactions was that of Wolfgang Denk, an area manager at Daimler. In 2001, Denk agreed to pay a €6,950 kickback, representing a 10 percent addition to the initial price, on a contract to sell an armored van to Iraq. Denk submitted the inflated price to the UN personnel administering the program, who approved the contract and many others like it. The €6,950 kickback was deposited in a Jordanian bank account controlled by the Iraqi government. The source account for the money was a Swiss bank account controlled by the attorney of Hussam Rassam, a former sales agent for Mercedes-Benz in Iraq who during the oil for food program ran service centers for Mercedes vehicles in Iraq. According to the Volker report, Denk subsequently signed two more side agreements to pay another €80,000 in kickbacks on the sale of additional vehicles. In early 2006, following an internal investigation, DaimlerChrysler reportedly suspended at least six of its high-ranking managers, most of whom worked in the international division of the company.

Sources: Paul A. Volcker et al., *Manipulation of the Oil for Food Program by the Iraqi Regime*, Independent Inquiry Committee into the United Nations Oil for Food Program, October 27, 2005; and R. Milne and M. Turner, "Daimler Suspends Managers over Iraq Truck Deal," *Financial Times*, January 17, 2006, p. 1.

Introduction

This chapter focuses on the ethical issues that arise when companies do business in different nations. Many of these ethical issues arise because of the differences in economic development, politics, legal systems, and culture that we reviewed in the last two chapters. The term *ethics* refers to accepted principles of right or wrong that govern the conduct of a person, the members of a profession, or the actions of an organization. **Business ethics** are the accepted principles of right or wrong governing the conduct of businesspeople, and an **ethical strategy** is a strategy, or course of action, that does not violate these accepted principles.

Business Ethics
The accepted principles of right or wrong governing the conduct of businesspeople.

Ethical Strategy
A course of action, that does not violate ethical principles.

The opening case illustrates some of the issues that we will discuss in this chapter. It is clearly unethical to give bribes to government officials in return for business. Yet the Volcker report on the administration of the oil for food program in Iraq between 1997 and 2003 suggests that is exactly what the representatives of some 2,200 companies did, including those who worked for large, well-respected organizations such as DaimlerChrysler and Volvo. As we saw in Chapter 2, unfortunately corruption is still widespread in much of the world. There is always temptation for managers in an international firm to adopt the "when in Rome" principle when dealing with corrupt regimes and to give kickbacks in return for business. As we shall argue in this chapter, however, such behavior is clearly unethical. It corrupts both the bribe giver and the taker. If disclosed, bribery can seriously damage the reputation of the company giving the bribe and end the career of the participating managers. To limit such behavior, many companies are now adopting a zero-tolerance policy toward ethical violations and are pushing hard to educate their employees about the importance of behaving in an ethical manner.

This chapter examines ethical issues in decision making in international business. We start by looking at the source and nature of ethical issues in an international business. Next, we review the reasons for poor ethical decision making. Then we discuss different philosophical approaches to business ethics. We close the chapter by reviewing the different processes that managers can adopt to make sure that ethical considerations are incorporated into decision making in an international business firm.

Ethical Issues in International Business

LEARNING OBJECTIVE 1
Be familiar with the ethical issues faced by international businesses.

Many of the ethical issues in international business are rooted in the fact that political systems, law, economic development, and culture vary significantly from nation to nation. What is considered normal practice in one nation may be considered unethical in another. Because they work for an institution that transcends national borders and cultures, managers in a multinational firm need to be particularly sensitive to these differences. In the international business setting, the most common ethical issues involve employment practices, human rights, environmental regulations, corruption, and the moral obligation of multinational corporations.

EMPLOYMENT PRACTICES When work conditions in a host nation are clearly inferior to those in a multinational's home nation, what standards should be applied? Those of the home nation, those of the host nation, or something in between? While few would suggest that pay and work conditions should be the same across nations, how much divergence is acceptable? For example, while 12-hour workdays, extremely low pay, and a failure to protect workers against toxic chemicals may be common in some developing nations, does this mean that it is okay for a multinational to tolerate such working conditions in its subsidiaries there, or to condone it by using local subcontractors?

In the 1990s, Nike found itself at the center of a storm of protests when news reports revealed that working conditions at many of its subcontractors were very poor. Typical of the allegations were those detailed in a *48 Hours* program that aired in 1996. The report described young women employees of a Vietnamese subcontractor who worked with toxic materials six days a week in poor conditions for only 20 cents an hour. The report also stated that a living wage in Vietnam was at least $3 a day, an income that an employee of the subcontractor could not achieve without working substantial overtime. Nike and its subcontractors were not breaking any laws, but this report, and others like it, raised questions about the ethics of using sweatshop labor to make what were essentially fashion accessories. It may have been legal, but was it ethical to use subcontractors who by Western standards clearly exploited their workforce? Nike's critics thought not, and the company found itself the focus of a wave of demonstrations and consumer boycotts. These exposés surrounding Nike's use of subcontractors forced the company to reexamine its policies. Realizing that even though it was breaking no law its subcontracting policies were perceived as unethical, Nike's management established a code of conduct for the company's subcontractors and instituted annual monitoring by independent auditors of all subcontractors.[1]

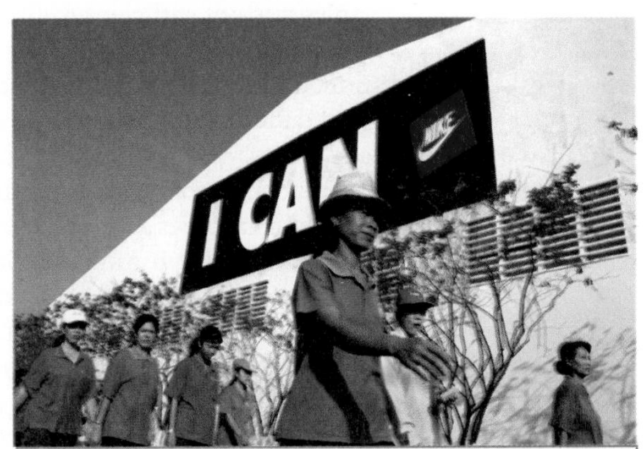

It may have been legal for a Vietnamese contractor to allow employees to work with toxic materials six days a week in poor conditions for 20 cents an hour at a Nike factory. But was it ethical for Nike to use subcontractors who by western standards clearly exploited their workers? *AP/Wide World*

As the Nike case demonstrates, a strong argument can be made that it is not okay for a multinational firm to tolerate poor working conditions in its foreign operations, or those of subcontractors. However, this still leaves unanswered the question about the standards that should be applied. We shall return to and consider this issue in more detail later in the chapter. For now, note that good safeguards against ethical abuses include establishing minimal acceptable standards that protect the basic rights and dignity of employees, auditing foreign subsidiaries and subcontractors on a regular basis to make sure those standards are met, and taking corrective action if they are not. Another apparel company, Levi Strauss, has long taken such an approach. The company terminated a long-term contract with one of its large suppliers, the Tan family, after it discovered that the Tans were allegedly forcing 1,200 Chinese and Filipino women to work 74 hours per week in guarded compounds on the Mariana Islands.[2]

HUMAN RIGHTS Questions of human rights can arise in international business. Basic human rights still are not respected in many nations. Rights that we take for granted in developed nations, such as freedom of association, freedom of speech, freedom of assembly, freedom of movement, freedom from political repression, and so on, are by no means universally accepted (see Chapter 2 for details). One of the most obvious examples was South Africa during the days of white rule and apartheid, which did not end until 1994. The apartheid system denied basic political rights to the majority nonwhite population of South Africa, mandated segregation between whites and nonwhites, reserved certain occupations exclusively for whites, and prohibited blacks from holding positions in which they would manage whites. Despite the odious nature of this system, Western businesses operated in South Africa. By the 1980s, however, many questioned the ethics of doing so. They argued that inward investment by foreign multinationals boosted the South African economy and thus supported the repressive apartheid regime.

Sullivan Principles
A twofold approach to doing business in apartheid South Africa, comprising passive resistance to apartheid laws and attempts to influence the abolition of apartheid laws.

Several Western businesses started to change their policies in the late 1970s and early 1980s.[3] General Motors, which had significant activities in South Africa, was at the forefront of this trend. GM adopted what came to be called the **Sullivan principles,** named after Leon Sullivan, a black Baptist minister and a member of GM's board of directors. Sullivan argued that it was ethically justified for GM to operate in South Africa so long as two conditions were fulfilled. First, the company should not obey the apartheid laws in its own South African operations (a form of passive resistance). Second, that the company should do everything within its power to promote the abolition of apartheid laws. Sullivan's principles were widely adopted by U.S. firms operating in South Africa. Further, the South Africa government, which clearly did not want to antagonize important foreign investors, ignored the firms' violation of apartheid laws.

However, after 10 years, Leon Sullivan concluded that simply following the principles was not sufficient to break down the apartheid regime and that any American company, even those adhering to his principles, could not ethically justify their continued presence in South Africa. Over the next few years, numerous companies divested their South African operations, including Exxon, General Motors, Kodak, IBM, and Xerox. At the same time, many state pension funds signaled they would no longer hold stock in companies that did business in South Africa, which helped to persuade several companies to divest their South African operations. These divestments, coupled with the imposition of economic sanctions from the U.S. and other governments, contributed to the abandonment of white minority rule and apartheid in South Africa and the introduction of democratic elections in 1994. Thus, adopting an ethical stance appears to have helped improve human rights in South Africa.[4]

Although change has come in South Africa, many repressive regimes still exist in the world. Western countries also have histories of exploiting workers, as described in the Another Perspective box on the next page. Is it ethical for multinationals to do business in those countries? Many argue that inward investment by a multinational can be a force for economic, political, and social progress that ultimately improves the rights of people in repressive regimes. We discussed this position in Chapter 2, noting that economic progress in a nation could create pressure for democratization. In general, this belief suggests it is ethical for a multinational to do business in nations that lack the democratic structures and human rights records of developed nations. However, although human rights groups often question China's human rights record, and although the country is not a democracy, many justify investment in China on the grounds that continuing inward investment will help boost economic growth and raise living standards. These developments will ultimately create pressures from the Chinese people for more participative government, political pluralism, and freedom of expression and speech.

However, there is a limit to this argument. As in the case of South Africa, some regimes are so repressive that investment cannot be justified on ethical grounds. A current example is Myanmar (formally known as Burma). Ruled by a military dictatorship for more than 40 years, Myanmar has one of the worst human rights records in the world. Beginning in the mid-1990s, many Western companies exited Myanmar, judging the human rights violations to be so extreme that doing business there could not be justified on ethical grounds. (In contrast, the accompanying Management Focus looks at the controversy surrounding one company, Unocal, that chose to stay in Myanmar.) However, a cynic might note that Myanmar has a small economy and that divestment carries no great economic penalty for Western firms, unlike, for example, divestment from China.

Another Perspective

Immigration and Human Rights

More than a century ago, some 15,000 Chinese immigrants were brought into Canada to help build the Canadian Pacific Railway. Thousands of workers lost their lives in this massive effort. In addition, the Canadian government collected a "head tax" from the Chinese laborers, which was a fee for a residency permit and the right to bring in their families from China. Some 81,000 Chinese immigrants paid the head tax. When introduced 1885, the tax was $50; it grew to $500 in 1903, which at that time was two years' wages for these workers. Collections ended in 1923, when Canadian immigration from China was banned. Canada began admitting Chinese again in 1947. Many countries have had similar policies targeted at immigrant labor in their pasts, the United States and Japan among them. What must have seemed normal, ethical, and justifiable then shocks us today. Do you think we're becoming better, more capable of ethical decision making?

In an atonement ceremony in 2006, Canada apologized and announced that compensation packages were being given to the survivors, widows, and children of those who paid the head tax. A granddaughter of a survivor said, "The impact is still felt today. I can't even put it into words." She explained that her 106-year-old grandfather could not afford to have his family join him in Canada for more than 20 years. (*Associated Press,* June 24, 2006)

Nigeria is another country where serious questions have arisen over the extent to which foreign multinationals doing business in the country have contributed to human rights violations. Most notably, the largest foreign oil producer in the country, Royal Dutch Shell, has been repeatedly criticized.[5] In the early 1990s, several ethnic groups in Nigeria, which was ruled by a military dictatorship, protested against foreign oil companies for causing widespread pollution and failing to invest in the communities from which they extracted oil. Shell reportedly requested the assistance of Nigeria's Mobile Police Force (MPF) to quell the demonstrations. According to the human rights group Amnesty International, the results were bloody. In 1990, the MPF put down protests against Shell in the village of Umuechem, killing 80 people and destroying 495 homes. In 1993, following protests in the Ogoni region of Nigeria that were designed to stop contractors from laying a new pipeline for Shell, the MPF raided the area to quell the unrest. In the chaos that followed, it has been alleged that 27 villages were razed, 80,000 Ogoni people displaced, and 2,000 people killed.

Critics argued that Shell shouldered some of the blame for the massacres. The company never acknowledged this, and the MPF probably used the demonstrations as a pretext for punishing an ethnic group that had been agitating against the central government for some time. Nevertheless, these events did prompt Shell to look at its own ethics and to set up internal mechanisms to ensure that its subsidiaries acted in a manner that was consistent with basic human rights.[6]

More generally, the question remains, What is the responsibility of a foreign multinational operating in a country whose government tramples on basic human rights?

Should the company be there at all, and if it is there, what actions should it take to avoid a situation similar to the one in which Shell found itself?

ENVIRONMENTAL POLLUTION Ethical issues arise when environmental regulations in host nations are inferior to those in the home nation. Many developed nations have substantial regulations governing the emission of pollutants, the dumping of toxic chemicals, the use of toxic materials in the workplace, and so on. Such regulations are often lacking in developing nations, and according to critics, the result can be higher levels of pollution from the operations of multinationals than would be allowed at home. For example, consider again the case of foreign oil companies in Nigeria. According to a 1992 report prepared by environmental activists in Nigeria, in the Niger Delta region,

> Apart from air pollution from the oil industry's emissions and flares day and night, producing poisonous gases that are silently and systematically wiping out vulnerable airborne biota and endangering the life of plants, game, and man himself, we have widespread water pollution and soil/land pollution that results in the death of most aquatic eggs and juvenile stages of the life of fin fish and shell fish on the one hand, whilst, on the other hand, agricultural land contaminated with oil spills becomes dangerous for farming, even where they continue to produce significant yields.[7]

The implication in this description is that pollution controls applied by foreign companies in Nigeria were much laxer than those in developed nations were.

Should a multinational feel free to pollute in a developing nation? (To do so hardly seems ethical.) Is there a danger that amoral management might move production to a developing nation precisely because costly pollution controls are not required, and the company is therefore free to despoil the environment and perhaps endanger local people in its quest to lower production costs and gain a competitive advantage? What is the right and moral thing to do in such circumstances: pollute to gain an economic advantage, or make sure that foreign subsidiaries adhere to common standards regarding pollution controls?

These questions take on added importance because some parts of the environment are a public good that no one owns but anyone can despoil. No one owns the atmosphere or the oceans, but polluting both, no matter where the pollution originates, harms all.[8] The atmosphere and oceans can be viewed as a global commons from which everyone benefits but for which no one is specifically responsible. In such cases, a phenomenon known as the *tragedy of the commons* becomes applicable. The tragedy of the commons occurs when individuals overuse a resource held in common by all, but owned by no one, resulting in its degradation. The phenomenon was first named by Garrett Hardin when describing a particular problem in sixteenth century England. Large open areas, called commons, were free for all to use as pasture. The poor put out livestock on these commons and supplemented their meager incomes. It was advantageous for each person to put out more and more livestock, but the social consequence was far more livestock than the commons could handle. The result was overgrazing, degradation of the commons, and the loss of this much-needed supplement.[9]

In the modern world, corporations can contribute to the global tragedy of the commons by moving production to locations where they are free to pump pollutants into the atmosphere or dump them in oceans or rivers, thereby harming these valuable global commons. While such action may be legal, is it ethical? Again, such actions seem to violate basic societal notions of ethics and social responsibility.

Management FOCUS

Unocal in Myanmar

In 1995, Unocal, an oil and gas enterprise based in California, took a 29 percent stake in a partnership with the French oil company Total and state-owned companies from both Myanmar and Thailand to build a gas pipeline from Myanmar to Thailand. At the time, the $1 billion project was expected to bring Myanmar about $200 million in annual export earnings, a quarter of the country's total. The gas used domestically would increase Myanmar's generating capacity by 30 percent. Unocal made this investment when a number of other American companies were exiting Myanmar. Myanmar's government, a military dictatorship, had a reputation for brutally suppressing internal dissent. Citing the political climate, the apparel companies Levi Strauss and Eddie Bauer had both withdrawn from the country. However, as far as Unocal's management was concerned, the giant infrastructure project would generate healthy returns for the company and, by boosting economic growth, a better life for Myanmar's 43 million people. Moreover, while Levi Strauss and Eddie Bauer could easily shift production of clothes to another low-cost location, Unocal argued it had to go where the oil and gas were located.

However, Unocal's investment quickly became highly controversial. Under the terms of the contract, the government of Myanmar was contractually obliged to clear a corridor for the pipeline through Myanmar's tropical forests and to protect the pipeline from attacks by the government's enemies. According to human rights groups, the Myanmar army forcibly moved villages and ordered hundreds of local peasants to work on the pipeline in conditions that were no better than slave labor. Those who refused suffered retaliation. News reports cite the case of one woman who was thrown into a fire, along with her baby, after her husband tried to escape from troops forcing him to work on the project. The baby died and she suffered burns. Other villagers report being beaten, tortured, raped, and otherwise mistreated when the alleged slave labor conditions were occurring.

In 1996, human rights activists brought a lawsuit against Unocal in the United States on behalf of 15 Myanmar villagers who had fled to refugee camps in Thailand. The suit claimed that Unocal was aware of what was going on, even if it did not participate or condone it, and that awareness was enough to make Unocal in part responsible for the alleged crimes. The presiding judge dismissed the case, arguing that Unocal could not be held liable for the actions of a foreign government against its own people—although the judge did note that Unocal was indeed aware of what was going on in Myanmar. The plaintiffs appealed, and in late 2003 the case wound up at a superior court. In 2005, the case was settled out of court for an undisclosed amount.

Irrespective of the legal rulings, one can question the ethical validity of Unocal's decision to enter into partnership with a brutal military dictatorship for financial gain.

Sources: Jim Carlton, "Unocal Trial for Slave Labor Claims Is Set to Start Today," *The Wall Street Journal,* December 9, 2003, p. A19; Seth Stern, "Big Business Targeted for Rights Abuse," *Christian Science Monitor,* September 4, 2003, p. 2; "Trouble in the Pipeline," *The Economist,* January 18, 1997, p. 39; Irtani Evelyn, "Feeling the Heat: Unocal Defends Myanmar Gas Pipeline Deal," *Los Angeles Times,* February 20, 1995, p. D1; and "Unocal Settles Myanmar Human Rights Cases," *Business and Environment* 16 (February 2005), pp. 14–16.

CORRUPTION As noted in Chapter 2, corruption has been a problem in almost every society in history, and it continues to be one today. There always have been and always will be corrupt government officials. International businesses can and have gained economic advantages by making payments to those officials. A classic example concerns a well-publicized incident in the 1970s. Carl Kotchian, the president of Lockheed, made a $12.5 million payment to Japanese agents and government officials to secure a large order for Lockheed's TriStar jet from Nippon Air. When the payments were discovered, U.S. officials charged Lockheed with falsification of its records and tax violations. Although such payments were supposed to be an accepted business practice in Japan (they might be viewed as an exceptionally lavish form of gift giving), the revelations created a scandal there too. The government ministers in question were criminally charged, one committed suicide, the government fell in disgrace, and the Japanese people were outraged. Apparently, such a payment was not an accepted way of doing business in Japan! The payment was nothing more than a bribe, paid to corrupt officials, to secure a large order that might otherwise have gone to another

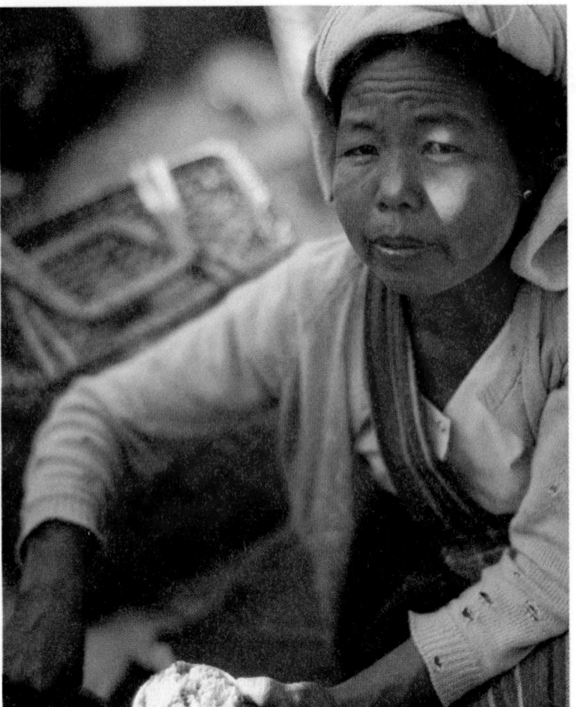

A Burmese woman at market. Many activists question Unocal's continued involvement in Myanmar/Burma because the state's dictatorship harshly punishes proponents of democracy. *Royalty Free/Corbis/DIL*

manufacturer, such as Boeing. Kotchian clearly engaged in unethical behavior, and to argue that the payment was an "acceptable form of doing business in Japan" was self-serving and incorrect.

The Lockheed case was the impetus for the 1977 passage of the **Foreign Corrupt Practices Act** in the United States, which we first discussed in Chapter 2. The act outlawed the paying of bribes to foreign government officials to gain business. Some U.S. businesses immediately objected that the act would put U.S. firms at a competitive disadvantage (there is no evidence that subsequently occurred).[10] Congress subsequently amended the act to allow for "facilitating payments," sometimes known as speed money or grease payments. Facilitating payments are distinguished from bribes in that they are *not* payments businesses make to secure contracts they would not otherwise get or to obtain exclusive preferential treatment. Rather, they are payments made to foreign officials to ensure that there is no obstruction to the transaction—they are meant to ensure that the officials expedite the performance of the duties that they are already obligated to perform.

In 1997, the trade and finance ministers from the member states of the Organization for Economic Cooperation and Development (OECD) followed the U.S. lead and adopted the **Convention on Combating Bribery of Foreign Public Officials in International Business Transactions.**[11] The convention, which went into force in 1999, obliges member states and other signatories to make the bribery of foreign public officials a criminal offense. The convention excludes facilitating payments made to expedite routine government action from the convention. To date, some 36 countries have signed the convention, six of which are not OECD members.

Foreign Corrupt Practices Act
A U.S. act outlawing the payment of bribes to foreign government officials in order to gain business.

Convention on Combating Bribery of Foreign Public Officials in International Business Transactions
A convention obliging member states to make the bribery of foreign public officials a criminal offense.

While facilitating payments, or speed money, are excluded from both the Foreign Corrupt Practices Act and the OECD convention on bribery, the ethical implications of making such payments are unclear. In many countries, payoffs to government officials in the form of speed money are a part of life. One can argue that not investing because government officials demand speed money ignores the fact that such investment can bring substantial benefits to the local populace in terms of income and jobs. From a pragmatic standpoint, giving bribes, although a little evil, might be the price that must be paid to do a greater good (assuming that the investment creates jobs where none existed and that the practice is not illegal). Several economists advocate this reasoning, suggesting that in the context of pervasive and cumbersome regulations in developing countries, corruption may improve efficiency and help growth. These economists theorize that in a country where preexisting political structures distort or limit the workings of the market mechanism, corruption in the form of black-marketeering, smuggling, and side payments to government bureaucrats to "speed up" approval for business investments may enhance welfare.[12] Arguments such as this persuaded the U.S. Congress to exempt facilitating payments from the Foreign Corrupt Practices Act.

In contrast, other economists have argued that corruption reduces the returns on business investment and leads to low economic growth.[13] In a country where corruption is common, unproductive bureaucrats who demand side payments for granting the enterprise permission to operate may siphon off the profits from a business activity. This reduces businesses' incentive to invest and may retard a country's economic growth rate. One study of the connection between corruption and economic growth in 70 countries found that corruption had a significant negative impact on a country's growth rate.[14]

Given the debate and the complexity of this issue, one again might conclude that generalization is difficult and the demand for speed money creates a genuine ethical dilemma. Yes, corruption is bad, and yes, it may harm a country's economic development, but yes, there are also cases where side payments to government officials can remove the bureaucratic barriers to investments that create jobs. However, this pragmatic stance ignores the fact that corruption tends to corrupt both the bribe giver and the bribe taker. Corruption feeds on itself, and once an individual starts down the road of corruption, pulling back may be difficult if not impossible. This argument strengthens the ethical case for never engaging in corruption, no matter how compelling the benefits might seem.

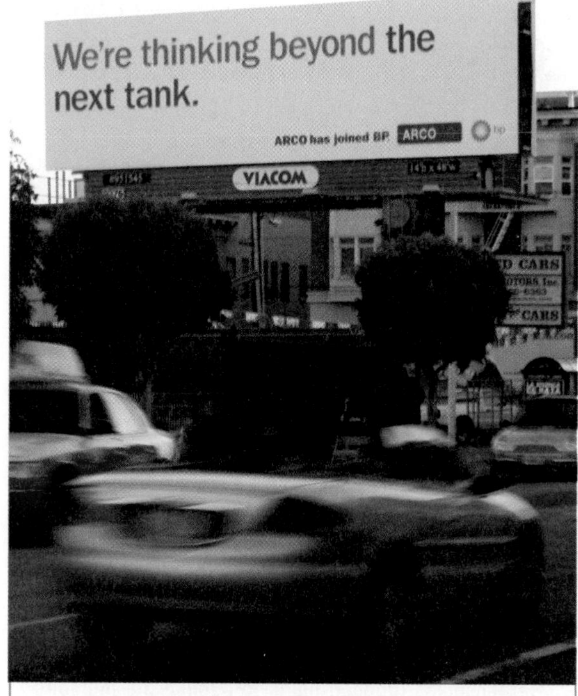

In addition to a commitment to introduce cleaner fuels and renewable energy, BP also supports urban renewal programs, art sponsorships, literacy drives, and conservation programs. *The McGraw-Hill Companies/John Flournoy, photographer/DIL*

Many multinationals have accepted this argument. The large oil multinational BP, for example, has a zero-tolerance approach toward facilitating payments. Other corporations have a more nuanced approach. For example, consider the following from the code of ethics at Dow Corning:

> Dow Corning employees will not authorize or give payments or gifts to government employees or their beneficiaries or anyone else in order to obtain or retain business. Facilitating payments to expedite the performance of routine services are strongly discouraged. In countries where local business practice dictates such payments and there is no alternative, facilitating payments are to be for the minimum amount necessary and must be accurately documented and recorded.[15]

This statement allows for facilitating payments when "there is no alternative," although they are strongly discouraged.

MORAL OBLIGATIONS Multinational corporations have power that comes from their control over resources and their ability to move production from country to country. Although that power is constrained not only by laws and regulations but also by the discipline of the market and the competitive process, it is nevertheless substantial. Some moral philosophers argue that with power comes the social responsibility for multinationals to give something back to the societies that enable them to prosper and grow. The concept of **social responsibility** refers to the idea that businesspeople should consider the social consequences of economic actions when making business decisions, and that there should be a presumption in favor of decisions that have both good economic and social consequences.[16] In its purest form, social responsibility can be supported for its own sake simply because it is the right way for a

Social Responsibility
The idea that businesspeople should consider the social consequences of economic actions and give preference to outcomes with positive social and economic consequences when making business decisions.

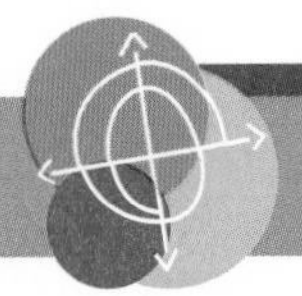

Management FOCUS

News Corporation in China

Rupert Murdoch built News Corporation into one of the largest media conglomerates in the world with interests that include newspapers, publishing, and television broadcasting. According to critics, however, Murdoch abused his power to gain preferential access to the Chinese media market by systematically suppressing media content that was critical of China and publishing material designed to ingratiate the company with the Chinese leadership.

In 1994, News Corporation excluded BBC news broadcasts from Star TV coverage in the region after it had become clear that Chinese politicians were unhappy with the BBC's continual reference to repression in China and, most notably, the 1989 massacre of student protesters for democracy in Beijing's Tiananmen Square. In 1995, News Corporation's book publishing subsidiary, HarperCollins, published a flattering biography of Deng Xiaoping, the former leader of China, written by his daughter. Then in 1998, HarperCollins dropped plans to publish the memoirs of Chris Patten, the last governor of Hong Kong before its transfer to the Chinese. Patten, a critic of Chinese leaders, had aroused their wrath by attempting to introduce a degree of democracy into the administration of the old British territory before its transfer back to China in 1997.

In a 1998 interview in *Vanity Fair,* Murdoch took another opportunity to ingratiate himself with the Chinese leadership when he described the Dalai Lama, the exiled leader of Chinese-occupied Tibet, as "a very political old monk shuffling around in Gucci shoes." On the heels of this, in 2001 Murdoch's son James, who was in charge of running Star TV, made disparaging remarks about Falun Gong, a spiritual movement involving breathing exercises and meditation that had become so popular in China that the Communist regime regarded it as a political threat and suppressed its activities. According to James Murdoch, Falun Gong was a "dangerous," "apocalyptic cult" that "clearly does not have the success of China at heart."

Critics argued that these events were all part of a deliberate and unethical effort on the part of News Corporation to curry favor with the Chinese. The company received its reward in 2001 when Star TV struck an agreement with the Chinese government to launch a Mandarin-language entertainment channel for the affluent southern coastal province of Guangdong. Earlier that year, China's leader, Jiang Zemin, had publicly praised Murdoch and Star TV for their efforts to "to present China objectively and to cooperate with the Chinese press."

Source: Daniel Litvin, *Empires of Profit* (New York: Texere, 2003).

Noblesse Oblige
A French term referring to the honorable and benevolent behavior required of persons of noble birth.

business to behave. Advocates of this approach argue that businesses, particularly large successful businesses, need to recognize their **noblesse oblige** and give something back to the societies that have made their success possible. *Noblesse oblige* is a French term that refers to honorable and benevolent behavior considered the responsibility of people of high (noble) birth. In a business setting, it is taken to mean benevolent behavior that is the responsibility of *successful* enterprises. This has long been recognized by many businesspeople, resulting in a substantial and venerable history of corporate giving to society and in businesses making social investments designed to enhance the welfare of the communities in which they operate.

However, there are examples of multinationals that have abused their power for private gain. The most famous historic example relates to one of the earliest multinationals, the British East India Company. Established in 1600, the East India Company grew to dominate the entire Indian subcontinent in the nineteenth century. At the height of its power, the company deployed more than 40 warships, possessed the largest standing army in the world, was the de facto ruler of India's 240 million people, and even hired its own church bishops, extending its dominance into the spiritual realm.[17]

Power itself is morally neutral; how power is used is what matters. It can be used in a positive way to increase social welfare, which is ethical, or it can be used in a manner that is ethically and morally suspect. Consider the case of News Corporation, one of the largest media conglomerates in the world, which is profiled in the accompanying Management Focus. The power of media companies derives from their ability to shape public perceptions by the material they choose to publish. News Corporation founder and CEO Rupert Murdoch has long considered China to be one of the most promising media markets in the world and has sought permission to expand News Corporation's operations in China, particularly the satellite broadcasting operations of Star TV. Some critics believe that Murdoch used the power of News Corporation in an unethical way to attain this objective.

Some multinationals have acknowledged a moral obligation to use their power to enhance social welfare in the communities where they do business. BP, one of the world's largest oil companies, has made it part of the company policy to undertake "social investments" in the countries where it does business.[18] In Algeria, BP has been investing in a major project to develop gas fields near the desert town of Salah. When the company noticed the lack of clean water in Salah, it built two desalination plants to provide drinking water for the local community and distributed containers to residents so they could take water from the plants to their homes. There was no economic reason for BP to make this social investment, but the company believes it is morally obligated to use its power in constructive ways. The action, while a small thing for BP, is a very important thing for the local community.

Ethical Dilemmas

LEARNING OBJECTIVE 2
Recognize an ethical dilemma.

The ethical obligations of a multinational corporation toward employment conditions, human rights, corruption, environmental pollution, and the use of power are not always clear-cut. There may be no agreement about accepted ethical principles. From an international business perspective, some argue that what is ethical depends upon one's cultural perspective.[19] In the United States, it is considered acceptable to execute murderers; but in many other cultures execution is viewed as an affront to human dignity and the death penalty is outlawed. Many Americans find this attitude strange, but many Europeans find the American approach barbaric. For a more business-oriented example, consider the practice of "gift giving" between the parties to a business negotiation. While this is considered right and proper behavior in many Asian cultures, some Westerners view the practice as a form of bribery, and therefore unethical, particularly if the gifts are substantial.

Managers often confront very real ethical dilemmas where the appropriate course of action is not clear. For example, imagine that a visiting American executive finds that a foreign subsidiary in a poor nation has hired a 12-year-old girl to work on a factory floor. Appalled to find that the subsidiary is using child labor in direct violation of the company's own ethical code, the American instructs the local manager to replace the child with an adult. The local manager dutifully complies. The girl, an orphan, who is the only breadwinner for herself and her six-year-old brother, is unable to find another job, so in desperation she turns to prostitution. Two years later she dies of AIDS. Meanwhile, her brother takes up begging. He encounters the American while begging outside the local McDonald's. Oblivious that this was the man responsible for his fate, the boy begs him for money. The American quickens his pace and walks rapidly past the outstretched hand into the McDonald's, where he orders a quarter-pound cheeseburger with fries and cold milk shake. A year later, the boy contracts tuberculosis and dies.

Had the visiting American understood the gravity of the girl's situation, would he still have requested her replacement? Perhaps not! Would it have been better, therefore, to stick with the status quo and allow the girl to continue working? Probably not, because that would have violated the reasonable prohibition against child labor found in the company's own ethical code. What then would have been the right thing to do? What was the obligation of the executive given this ethical dilemma?

Ethical Dilemma A situation in which none of the available alternatives seems ethically acceptable.

There is no easy answer to these questions. That is the nature of **ethical dilemmas**—they are situations in which none of the available alternatives seems ethically acceptable.[20] In this case, employing child labor was not acceptable, but given that she was employed, neither was denying the child her only source of income. What the American executive needed, what all managers need, was a moral compass, or perhaps an ethical algorithm, that would guide him through such an ethical dilemma to find an acceptable solution. Later we will outline what such a moral compass, or ethical algorithm, might look like. For now, it is enough to note that ethical dilemmas exist because many real-world decisions are complex, difficult to frame, and involve first-, second-, and third-order consequences that are hard to quantify. Doing the right thing, or even knowing what the right thing might be, is often far from easy.

The Roots of Unethical Behavior

LEARNING OBJECTIVE 3 Discuss the causes of unethical behavior by managers.

As we have seen, examples abound of managers behaving in a manner that some might judge to be unethical in an international business setting. Why do managers behave unethically? There is no simple answer; the causes are complex, but we can make some generalizations (see Figure 4.1).[21]

Personal Ethics The generally accepted principles of right and wrong governing the conduct of individuals.

PERSONAL ETHICS Business ethics are not divorced from **personal ethics,** which are the generally accepted principles of right and wrong governing the conduct of individuals. As individuals, we are typically taught that it is wrong to lie and cheat—it is unethical—and that it is right to behave with integrity and honor and to stand up for what we believe to be right and true. This is generally true across societies. The personal ethical code that guides our behavior comes from a number of sources, including our parents, our schools, our religion, and the media. Our personal ethical code exerts a profound influence on the way we behave as businesspeople. An individual with a strong sense of personal ethics is less likely to behave in an unethical manner in a business setting. It follows that the first step to establishing a strong sense of business ethics is for a society to emphasize strong personal ethics.

Home-country managers working abroad in multinational firms (expatriate managers) may experience more than the usual degree of pressure to violate their

figure 4.1 Determinants of Ethical Behavior

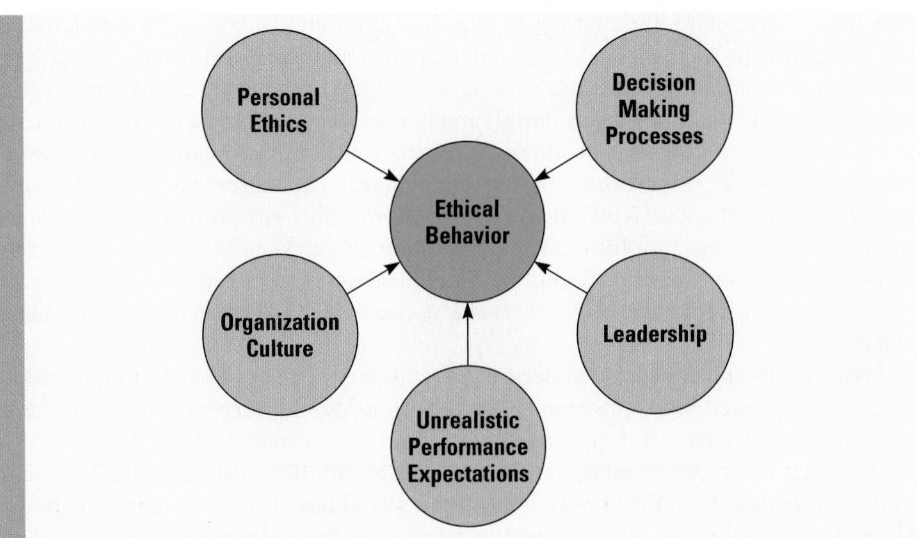

personal ethics. They are away from their ordinary social context and supporting culture, and they are psychologically and geographically distant from the parent company. They may be based in a culture that does not place the same value on ethical norms important in the manager's home country, and they may be surrounded by local employees who have less rigorous ethical standards. The parent company may pressure expatriate managers to meet unrealistic goals that they can fulfill only by cutting corners or acting unethically. For example, to meet centrally mandated performance goals, expatriate managers might give bribes to win contracts or might implement working conditions and environmental controls that are below minimal acceptable standards. Local managers might encourage the expatriate to adopt such behavior. Because of its geographical distance, the parent company may be unable to see how expatriate managers are meeting goals, or it may choose not to see how they are doing so, allowing such behavior to flourish and persist.

DECISION-MAKING PROCESSES Several studies of unethical behavior in a business setting have concluded that businesspeople sometimes do not realize they are behaving unethically, primarily because they simply fail to ask, Is this decision or action ethical?[22] Instead, they apply a straightforward business calculus to what they perceive to be a business decision, forgetting that the decision may also have an important ethical dimension. The fault lies in processes that do not incorporate ethical considerations into business decision making. This may have been the case at Nike when managers originally made subcontracting decisions (see the earlier discussion). Perhaps using what they considered to be good economic logic, the key managers likely chose the subcontractors on the basis of business variables such as cost, delivery, and product quality. They simply failed to ask, How does this subcontractor treat its workforce? If they thought about the question at all, they probably reasoned that it was the subcontractor's concern, not theirs. (For another example of a business decision that may have been unethical, see the Management Focus describing Pfizer's decision to test an experimental drug on children suffering from meningitis in Nigeria.)

ORGANIZATION CULTURE The climate in some businesses does not encourage people to think through the ethical consequences of business decisions. This brings us to the third cause of unethical behavior in businesses: an organizational culture that deemphasizes business ethics, reducing all decisions to the purely economic. The term **organization culture** refers to the values and norms shared among employees of an organization. You will recall from Chapter 3 that *values* are abstract ideas about what a group believes to be good, right, and desirable, and *norms* are the social rules and guidelines that prescribe appropriate behavior in particular situations. Just as societies have cultures, so do business organizations. Together, values and norms shape the culture of a business organization, and that culture has an important influence on the ethics of business decision making.

Organization Culture
The values and norms that are shared among employees of an organization.

Author Robert Bryce has explained how the organization culture at now-bankrupt multinational energy company Enron was built on values that emphasized greed and deception.[23] According to Bryce, the tone was set by top managers who engaged in self-dealing to enrich themselves and their own families. Bryce tells how former Enron CEO Kenneth Lay made sure his own family benefited handsomely from Enron. Much of Enron's corporate travel business was handled by a travel agency part-owned by Lay's sister. When an internal auditor recommended that the company could do better by using another travel agency, he soon found himself out of a job. In 1997, Enron acquired a company owned by Kenneth Lay's son, Mark Lay, which was trying to establish a business trading paper and pulp products. At the time, Mark Lay and another company he controlled were targets of a federal criminal investigation of bankruptcy fraud and embezzlement. As part of the deal, Enron hired Mark Lay as an executive with a three-year contract that guaranteed him at least $1 million in pay over that period, plus options to purchase about 20,000 shares of Enron. Bryce also details how Lay's grown daughter used an Enron jet to transport her king-sized bed to France. With Kenneth Lay as an example, it is perhaps not surprising that self-dealing soon became endemic at Enron. The most notable example was chief financial officer Andrew Fastow, who set up "off-balance sheet" partnerships that not only hid Enron's true financial condition from investors but also paid tens of millions of dollars directly to Fastow. (The federal government subsequently indicted Fastow for criminal fraud, and he went to jail.)

UNREALISTIC PERFORMANCE EXPECTATIONS We have already hinted at a fourth cause of unethical behavior: pressure from the parent company to meet unrealistic performance goals that managers can attain only by cutting corners or acting in an unethical manner. Again, Bryce discusses how this may have occurred at Enron. Lay's successor as CEO, Jeff Skilling, put a performance evaluation system in place that weeded out 15 percent of underperformers every six months. This created a pressure-cooker culture with a myopic focus on short-run performance, and some executives and energy traders responded to that pressure by falsifying their performance—inflating the value of trades, for example—to make it look as if they were performing better than was actually the case.

The lesson from the Enron debacle is that an organizational culture can legitimize behavior that society would judge as unethical, particularly when combined with a focus on unrealistic performance goals, such as maximizing short-term economic performance, no matter what the costs. In such circumstances, there is a greater than average probability that managers will violate their own personal ethics and engage in unethical behavior. Conversely, an organization culture can do just the opposite and reinforce the need for ethical behavior. At Hewlett-Packard, for example, Bill Hewlett and David Packard, the company's founders, propagated a set of values known as The HP Way. These values, which shape the way business is conducted both within and by the corporation, have an important ethical component. Among other things, they stress the need for confidence in and respect for people, open communication, and concern for the individual employee.

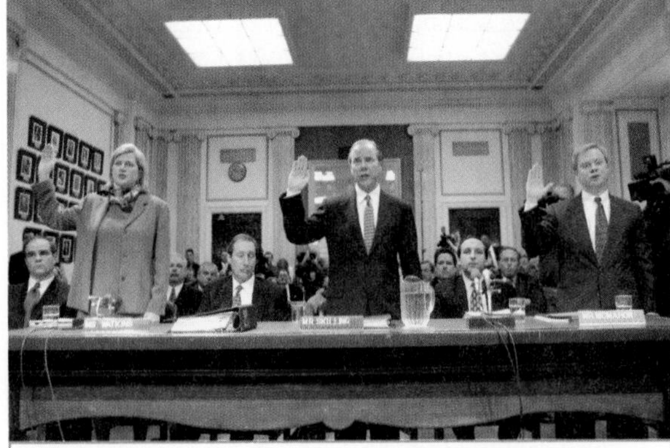

Enron executive Jeff Skilling has become a well-known example of corporate greed and deception. *Mark Wilson/Getty Images*

LEADERSHIP The Enron and HP examples suggest a fifth root cause of unethical behavior: leadership. Leaders help to establish the culture of an organization, and they set the example that others follow. Other employees in a business often take their cue from business leaders, and if those leaders do not behave in an ethical manner, they might not either. It is not what leaders say that matters, but what they do. Enron, for example, had a code of ethics that Kenneth Lay himself often referred to, but Lay's own actions to enrich family members spoke louder than any words.

Management FOCUS

Pfizer's Drug Testing Strategy in Nigeria

The drug development process is long, risky, and expensive. It can take 10 years and cost in excess of $500 million to develop a new drug. Moreover, between 80 and 90 percent of drug candidates fail in clinical trials. Pharmaceutical companies rely upon a handful of successes to pay for their failures. Among the most successful of the world's pharmaceutical companies is New York–based Pfizer. Given the risks and costs of developing a new drug, pharmaceutical companies will jump at opportunities to reduce them, and in 1996 Pfizer thought it saw one.

Pfizer had been developing a novel antibiotic, Trovan, that was proving to be useful in treating a wide range of bacterial infections. Wall Street analysts were predicting that Trovan could be a blockbuster, one of a handful of drugs capable of generating sales of more than $1 billion a year. In 1996, Pfizer was pushing to submit data on Trovan's efficacy to the Food and Drug Administration (FDA) for review. A favorable review would allow Pfizer to sell the drug in the United States, the world's largest market. Pfizer wanted the FDA to approve the drug for both adults and children, but it was having trouble finding sufficient numbers of sick children in the United States on whom to test the drug. Then in early 1996, a researcher at Pfizer read about an emerging epidemic of bacterial meningitis in Kano, Nigeria. This seemed like a quick way to test the drug on a large number of sick children.

Within weeks, a team of six doctors had flown to Kano and they were administering the drug, in oral form, to children with meningitis. Desperate for help, Nigerian authorities gave the go-ahead for Pfizer to give the drug to children (the epidemic would ultimately kill nearly 16,000 people). Over the next few weeks, Pfizer treated 198 children. The protocol called for half the patients to get Trovan and half to get a comparison antibiotic already approved for the treatment of children. After a few weeks, the Pfizer team left, the experiment complete. Trovan seemed to be about as effective and safe as the already-approved antibiotic. The company put the data from the trial into a package with data from other trials of Trovan and delivered the results to the FDA.

Questions were soon raised about the nature of Pfizer's experiment. Allegations charged that the Pfizer team kept children on Trovan, even after they failed to show a response to the drug, instead of switching them quickly to another drug. The result, according to critics, was that some children died who might have been saved had they been taken off Trovan sooner. Questions were also raised about the safety of the oral formulation of Trovan, which some doctors feared might lead to arthritis in children. Fifteen children who took Trovan showed signs of joint pain during the experiment, three times the rate of children taking the other antibiotic. Then there were questions about consent. The FDA requires that patient (or parent) consent be given before patients are enrolled in clinical trials, no matter where in the world the trials are conducted. Critics argue that in the rush to get the trial established in Nigeria, Pfizer did not follow proper procedures, and that many parents of the infected children did not know their children were participating in a trial for an experimental drug. Many of the parents were illiterate, could not read the consent forms, and had to rely upon the questionable translation of the Nigerian nursing staff. Pfizer rejected these charges and contends that it did nothing wrong.

The FDA approved Trovan for use by adults in 1997, but it never approved the drug for use by children. Launched in 1998, by 1999 there were reports that up to 140 patients in Europe had suffered liver damage after taking Trovan. The FDA subsequently restricted the use of Trovan to those cases where the benefits of treatment outweighed the risk of liver damage. European regulators banned sales of the drug.

Did Pfizer behave unethically by rushing to take advantage of an epidemic in Nigeria to test an experimental drug on children? Should it have been less opportunistic and proceeded more carefully? Did it cut corners with regard to patient consent in the rush to establish a trial? Did doctors keep patients on Trovan too long, when they should have switched them to another medication? Is it ethical to test an experimental drug on children in a crisis setting in the developing world, where the overall standard of health care is so much lower than in the developed world and proper protocols might not be followed? These questions are all raised by the Pfizer case, and they remain unanswered, by the company at least.

Sources: Joe Stephens, "Where Profits and Lives Hang in the Balance," *Washington Post,* December 17, 2000, p. A1; Andra Brichacek, "What Price Corruption?" *Pharmaceutical Executive* 21, no. 11 (November 2001), p. 94; and Scott Hensley, "Court Revives Suit against Pfizer on Nigeria Study," *The Wall Street Journal,* October 13, 2004, p. B4.

Philosophical Approaches to Ethics

LEARNING OBJECTIVE 4
Be familiar with the different philosophical approaches to ethics.

We shall look at several different approaches to business ethics here, beginning with some that can best be described as straw men, which either deny the value of business ethics or apply the concept in a very unsatisfactory way. Having discussed, and dismissed, the straw men, we then move on to consider approaches that are favored by most moral philosophers and form the basis for current models of ethical behavior in international businesses.

STRAW MEN Straw men approaches to business ethics are raised by business ethics scholars primarily to demonstrate that they offer inappropriate guidelines for ethical decision making in a multinational enterprise. Four such approaches to business ethics are commonly discussed in the literature. These approaches can be characterized as the Friedman doctrine, cultural relativism, righteous moralism, and naive immoralism. All of these approaches have some inherent value, but all are unsatisfactory in important ways. Nevertheless, sometimes companies adopt these approaches.

The Friedman Doctrine Nobel Prize–winning economist Milton Friedman wrote an article in 1970 that has since become a classic straw man that business ethics scholars outline only to then tear down.[24] Friedman's basic position is that the only social responsibility of business is to increase profits, so long as the company stays within the rules of law. He explicitly rejects the idea that businesses should undertake social expenditures beyond those mandated by the law and required for the efficient running of a business. For example, his arguments suggest that improving working conditions beyond the level required by the law and necessary to maximize employee productivity will reduce profits and are therefore not appropriate. His belief is that a firm should maximize its profits because that is the way to maximize the returns that accrue to the owners of the firm, its stockholders. If stockholders then wish to use the proceeds to make social investments, that is their right, according to Friedman, but managers of the firm should not make that decision for them.

Although Friedman is talking about social responsibility rather than business ethics per se, many business ethics scholars equate social responsibility with ethical behavior and thus believe Friedman is also arguing against business ethics. However, the assumption that Friedman is arguing against ethics is not quite true, for he does state,

> There is one and only one social responsibility of business—to use its resources and engage in activities designed to increase its profits so long as it stays within the rules of the game, which is to say that it engages in open and free competition without deception or fraud.[25]

In other words, Friedman states that businesses should behave in an ethical manner and not engage in deception and fraud.

Nevertheless, Friedman's arguments do break down under examination. This is particularly true in international business where the "rules of the game" are not well established and differ from country to county. Consider again the case of sweatshop labor. Child labor may not be against the law in a developing nation, and maximizing productivity may not require that a multinational firm stop using child labor in that country; but it is still immoral to use child labor because the practice conflicts with widely held views about what is the right and proper thing to do. Similarly, there may be no rules against pollution in a developed nation and spending money on pollution control may reduce the profit rate of the firm; but generalized notions of morality would hold that it is still unethical to dump toxic pollutants into rivers or foul the air with gas releases. In addition to the local consequences of such pollution, which may have serious health effects for the surrounding population, there is also a global consequence as pollutants degrade those two global commons so important to us all—the atmosphere and the oceans.

Cultural Relativism The belief that ethics are nothing more than a reflection of a culture and that firms should simply adopt the ethics of the cultures in which they operate.

Cultural Relativism

Another straw man often raised by business ethics scholars is **cultural relativism,** which is the belief that ethics are nothing more than the reflection of a culture—all ethics are culturally determined—and that accordingly, a firm should adopt the ethics of the culture in which it is operating.[26] This approach is often summarized by the maxim "when in Rome do as the Romans." As with Friedman's approach, cultural relativism does not stand up to a closer look. At its extreme, cultural relativism suggests that if a culture supports slavery, it is okay to use slave labor in a country. Clearly, it is not! Cultural relativism implicitly rejects the idea that universal notions of morality transcend different cultures, but as we shall argue later in the chapter, some universal notions of morality are found across cultures.

While dismissing cultural relativism in its most sweeping form, some ethicists argue there is residual value in this approach.[27] As we noted in Chapter 3, societal values and norms do vary from culture to culture, customs do differ; so it might follow that certain business practices are ethical in one country but not another. Indeed, the facilitating payments allowed in the Foreign Corrupt Practices Act can be seen as an acknowledgment that in some countries the payment of speed money to government officials is necessary to get business done, and if not ethically desirable, it is at least ethically acceptable.

However, not all ethicists or companies agree with this pragmatic view. As noted earlier, oil company BP explicitly states it will not make facilitating payments, no matter what the prevailing cultural norms are. In 2002, BP enacted a zero-tolerance policy for facilitation payments, primarily on the basis that such payments are a low-level form of corruption and thus cannot be justified because corruption corrupts both the bribe giver and the bribe taker and perpetuates the corrupt system. As BP notes on its Web site, because of its zero-tolerance policy,

> Some oil product sales in Vietnam involved inappropriate commission payments to the managers of customers in return for placing orders with BP. These were stopped during 2002 with the result that BP failed to win certain tenders with potential profit totaling $300k. In addition, two sales managers resigned over the issue. The business, however, has recovered using more traditional sales methods and has exceeded its targets at year-end.[28]

BP's experience suggests that companies should not use cultural relativism as an argument for justifying behavior that is clearly based upon suspect ethical grounds, even if that behavior is both legal and routinely accepted in the country where the company is doing business.

Another Perspective

Cooking the Books: Cultural Relativism Here at Home

We often think of cultural relativism as occurring in the international business domain when companies, in order to compete, adopt the ethics of the country in which they are operating. The concept of cultural relativism suggests that their perception of those ethics may be a case of seeing what they want to see. However, the force of cultural relativism may also be at work here at home. Many observers argue that the greed, booming economy, and stock market bubble of the 1990s in the United States produced a culture that was responsible for the Enron, Tyco, and WorldCom breakdowns of business ethics and their corporate scandals. One explanation is that the underlying profit motive of capitalism became exaggerated in parts of those organizations to the point that a new business model emerged in which anything goes.

The executives of those corporations misjudged their home culture, and their actions sparked outrage. This outrage led Congress to enact the most sweeping revision of corporate securities law since the Great Depression of the 1930s. The Sarbanes-Oxley Act of 2002 greatly increased the financial reporting requirements and established liability on the part of the CEO and CFO for their certification of the financial reports. So much for cooking the books! (John R. Emshwiller, Rebecca Smith and Alan Murray, "Lay's Legacy: Corporate Culture--But Not the Kind He Expected," *The Wall Street Journal*, July 6, 2006)

Righteous Moralism The belief that a multinational's home-country standards of ethics are the appropriate ones for companies to follow in foreign countries.

Righteous Moralism **Righteous moralism** is the belief that a multinational's home-country standards of ethics are the appropriate ones for companies to follow in foreign countries. This approach is typically associated with managers from developed nations. While this seems reasonable at first blush, the approach can create problems. Consider the following example: An American bank manager was sent to Italy and was appalled to learn that the local branch's accounting department recommended grossly underreporting the bank's profits for income tax purposes.[29] The manager insisted that the bank report its earnings accurately, American style. When he was called by the Italian tax department to the firm's tax hearing, he was told the firm owed three times as much tax as it had paid, reflecting the department's standard assumption that each firm underreports its earnings by two-thirds. Despite his protests, the new assessment stood. In this case, the righteous moralist has run into a problem caused by the prevailing cultural norms in the country where he is doing business. How should he respond? The righteous moralist would argue for maintaining the position, but a more pragmatic view might be that in this case, the right thing to do is to follow the prevailing cultural norms, since there is a big penalty for not doing so.

The main criticism of the righteous moralism approach is that its proponents go too far. While there are some universal moral principles that should not be violated, it does not always follow that the appropriate thing to do is adopt home-country standards. For example, U.S. laws set down strict guidelines with regard to minimum wage and working conditions. Does this mean it is ethical to apply the same guidelines in a foreign country, paying people the same as they are paid in the United States, providing the same benefits and working conditions? Probably not, because doing so might nullify the reason for investing in that country and therefore deny locals the benefits of inward investment by the multinational. Clearly, a more nuanced approach is needed.

Naive Immoralism The belief that if a manager of a multinational sees that firms from other nations are not following ethical norms in a host nation, that manager should not either.

Naive Immoralism **Naive immoralism** is the belief that if a manager of a multinational sees that firms from other nations are not following ethical norms in a host nation, that manager should not either. The classic example to illustrate the approach is known as the drug lord problem. In one variant of this problem, an American manager in Colombia routinely pays off the local drug lord to guarantee that his plant will not be bombed and that none of his employees will be kidnapped. The manager argues that such payments are ethically defensible because everyone is doing it.

The objection is twofold. First, to say that an action is ethically justified if everyone is doing it is not sufficient. If firms in a country routinely employ 12-year-olds and makes them work 10-hour days, is it therefore ethically defensible to do the same? Obviously not, and the company does have a clear choice. It does not have to abide by local practices, and it can decide not to invest in a country where the practices are particularly odious. Second, the multinational must recognize that it does have the ability to change the prevailing practice in a country. It can use its power for a positive moral purpose. This is what BP is doing by adopting a zero-tolerance policy with regard to facilitating payments. BP is stating that the prevailing practice of making facilitating payments is ethically wrong, and it is incumbent upon the company to use its power to try to change the standard. Some might argue that such an approach smells of moral imperialism and a lack of cultural sensitivity; however, if it is consistent with widely accepted moral standards in the global community, it may be ethically justified.

To return to the drug lord problem, an argument can be made that it is ethically defensible to make such payments, not because everyone else is doing so but because not doing so would cause greater harm (i.e., the drug lord might seek retribution and engage in killings and kidnappings). Another solution to the problem is to refuse to invest in a country where the rule of law is so weak that drug lords can demand protection money. This solution, however, is also imperfect, for it might mean denying the law-abiding citizens of that country the benefits associated with inward investment by the multinational (i.e., jobs, income, greater economic growth and welfare). Clearly, the drug lord problem constitutes one of those intractable ethical dilemmas where there is no obvious right solution, and managers need a moral compass to help them find an acceptable solution to the dilemma.

UTILITARIAN AND KANTIAN ETHICS In contrast to the straw men just discussed, most moral philosophers see value in utilitarian and Kantian approaches to business ethics. These approaches were developed in the eighteenth and nineteenth centuries, and although they have been largely superseded by more modern approaches, they form part of the tradition upon which newer approaches have been constructed.

The utilitarian approach to business ethics dates to philosophers such as David Hume (1711–76), Jeremy Bentham (1784–1832), and John Stuart Mill (1806–73). **Utilitarian approaches to ethics** hold that the moral worth of actions or practices is determined by their consequences.[30] An action is judged desirable if it leads to the best possible balance of good consequences over bad consequences. Utilitarianism is committed to the maximization of good and the minimization of harm. Utilitarianism recognizes that actions have multiple consequences, some of which are good in a social sense and some of which are harmful. As a philosophy for business ethics, it focuses attention on the need to weigh carefully all of the social benefits and costs of a business action and to pursue only those actions where the benefits outweigh the costs. The best decisions, from a utilitarian perspective, are those that produce the greatest good for the greatest number of people.

Utilitarian Approaches to Ethics
These hold that the moral worth of actions or practices is determined by their consequences.

Many businesses have adopted specific tools such as cost–benefit analysis and risk assessment that are firmly rooted in a utilitarian philosophy. Managers often weigh the benefits and costs of an action before deciding whether to pursue it. An oil company considering drilling in the Alaskan wildlife preserve must weigh the economic benefits of increased oil production and the creation of jobs against the costs of environmental degradation in a fragile ecosystem. An agricultural biotechnology company such as Monsanto must decide whether the benefits of genetically modified crops that produce natural pesticides outweigh the risks. The benefits include increased crop yields and reduced need for chemical fertilizers. The risks include the possibility that Monsanto's insect-resistant crops might make matters worse over time if insects evolve a resistance to the natural pesticides engineered into Monsanto's plants, rendering the plants vulnerable to a new generation of superbugs.

For all of its appeal, utilitarian philosophy does have some serious drawbacks as an approach to business ethics. One problem is measuring the benefits, costs, and risks of a course of action. In the case of an oil company considering drilling in Alaska, how does one measure the potential harm done to the region's ecosystem? In the Monsanto example, how can one quantify the risk that genetically engineered crops might ultimately result in the evolution of superbugs that are resistant to the natural pesticide engineered into the crops? In general, utilitarian philosophers recognize that the measurement of benefits, costs, and risks is often not possible due to limited knowledge.

The second problem with utilitarianism is that the philosophy omits the consideration of justice. The action that produces the greatest good for the greatest number of people may result in the unjustified treatment of a minority. Such action cannot be ethical, precisely because it is unjust. For example, suppose that in the interests of keeping down health insurance costs, the government decides to screen people for the HIV virus and deny insurance coverage to those who are HIV positive. By reducing health costs, such action might produce significant benefits for a large number of people, but the action is unjust because it discriminates unfairly against a minority.

Kantian Ethics
The belief that people should be treated as ends and never as means to the ends of others.

Kantian ethics are based on the philosophy of Immanuel Kant (1724–1804). **Kantian ethics** hold that people should be treated as ends and never purely as *means* to the ends of others. People are not instruments, like a machine. People have dignity and need to be respected as such. Employing people in sweatshops, making them work long hours for low pay in poor working conditions, is a violation of ethics, according to Kantian philosophy, because it treats people as mere cogs in a machine and not as conscious moral beings who have dignity. Although contemporary moral philosophers tend to view Kant's ethical philosophy as incomplete—for example, his system has no place for moral emotions or sentiments such as sympathy or caring— the notion that people should be respected and treated with dignity still resonates in the modern world.

Rights Theories
A twentieth century ethical approach based on the belief that human beings have fundamental rights and privileges that transcend national boundaries and cultures.

RIGHTS THEORIES Developed in the twentieth century, **rights theories** recognize that human beings have fundamental rights and privileges that transcend national boundaries and cultures. Rights establish a minimum level of morally acceptable behavior. One well-known definition of a fundamental right construes it as something that takes precedence over, or "trumps," a collective good. Thus, we might say that free speech is a fundamental right that trumps all but the most compelling collective goals and overrides, for example, the interest of the state in civil harmony or moral consensus.[31] Moral theorists argue that fundamental human rights form the basis for the *moral compass* that managers should navigate by when making decisions that have an ethical component. More precisely, they should not pursue actions that violate these rights.

Universal Declaration of Human Rights
A UN document inspired by Kantian and rights theories and ratified by almost every country on the planet; it lays down basic principles that should always be adhered to, irrespective of the culture in which one is doing business.

The notion that there are fundamental rights that transcend national borders and cultures was the underlying motivation for the UN **Universal Declaration of Human Rights**, which has been ratified by almost every country on the planet and lays down basic principles that should always be adhered to, irrespective of the culture in which one is doing business.[32] Echoing Kantian ethics, Article 1 of this declaration states the following:

> All human beings are born free and equal in dignity and rights. They are endowed with reason and conscience and should act towards one another in a spirit of brotherhood.

Article 23 of this declaration, which relates directly to employment, states,

> Everyone has the right to work, to free choice of employment, to just and favorable conditions of work, and to protection against unemployment.
>
> Everyone, without any discrimination, has the right to equal pay for equal work.
>
> Everyone who works has the right to just and favorable remuneration ensuring for himself and his family an existence worthy of human dignity, and supplemented, if necessary, by other means of social protection.
>
> Everyone has the right to form and to join trade unions for the protection of his interests.

Clearly, the rights to "just and favorable work conditions," "equal pay for equal work," and remuneration that ensures an "existence worthy of human dignity" embodied in Article 23 imply that it is unethical to employ child labor in sweatshop settings and pay less than subsistence wages, even if that happens to be common practice in some countries. These are fundamental human rights that transcend national borders.

It is important to note that along with *rights* come *obligations*. Because we have the right to free speech, we are also obligated to make sure that we respect the free speech of others. The notion that people have obligations is stated in Article 29 of the Universal Declaration of Human Rights:

> Everyone has duties to the community in which alone the free and full development of his personality is possible.

Within the framework of a theory of rights, certain people or institutions are obligated to provide benefits or services that secure the rights of others. Such obligations also fall upon more than one class of moral agent (a moral agent is any person or institution that is capable of moral action such as a government or corporation).

For example, to escape the high costs of toxic waste disposal in the West, in the late 1980s several firms shipped their waste in bulk to African nations, where it was disposed of at a much lower cost. In 1987, five European ships unloaded toxic waste containing dangerous poisons in Nigeria. Workers wearing sandals and shorts unloaded the barrels for $2.50 a day and placed them in a dirt lot in a residential area. They were not told about the contents of the barrels.[33] Who bears the obligation for protecting the rights of workers and residents to safety in a case like this? According to rights theorists, the obligation rests not with one moral agent but on the shoulders of all moral agents whose actions might harm or contribute to the harm of the workers and residents. Thus, it was the obligation not just of the Nigerian government but also of the multinational firms that shipped the toxic waste to make sure it did no harm to residents and workers. In this case, both the government and the multinationals apparently failed to recognize their basic obligation to protect the fundamental human rights of others.

Justice Theories
Ethical approaches that focus on the attainment of a just distribution of economic goods and services

Just Distribution
A distribution that is considered fair and equitable.

JUSTICE THEORIES **Justice theories** focus on the attainment of a just distribution of economic goods and services. A **just distribution** is one that is considered fair and equitable. There is no one theory of justice, and several theories of justice conflict with each other in important ways.[34] Here we shall focus on one particular theory of justice that is both very influential and has important ethical implications. The theory is attributed to philosopher John Rawls.[35] Rawls argues that all economic goods and services should be distributed equally except when an unequal distribution would work to everyone's advantage.

According to Rawls, valid principles of justice are those with which all persons would agree if they could freely and impartially consider the situation. Impartiality is guaranteed by a conceptual device that Rawls calls the *veil of ignorance.* Under the veil of ignorance, everyone is imagined to be ignorant of all of his or her particular characteristics, for example, race, sex, intelligence, nationality, family background, and special talents. Rawls then asks what system people would design under a veil of ignorance. Under these conditions, people would unanimously agree on two fundamental principles of justice.

The first principle is that each person be permitted the maximum amount of basic liberty compatible with a similar liberty for others. Rawls takes these to be political liberty (e.g., the right to vote), freedom of speech and assembly, liberty of conscience and freedom of thought, the freedom and right to hold personal property, and freedom from arbitrary arrest and seizure.

Another Perspective

Ethical Analysis: *In a Different Voice*
In addition to utilitarian, Kantian, rights, and justice approaches to business ethics, Carol Gilligan offers another way to think about our moral actions: as a series of caring relationships that evolve over time, focused first on the self, then on dependent others, and finally, on establishing equality of needs between self and others so that dynamic relationships can replace dependent ones. Such an approach (self, dependent other, dynamic equality) may be a helpful way of thinking about a multinational's evolving corporate involvement in a developing country. (Carol Gilligan, *In a Different Voice*, 1982.)

The second principle is that once equal basic liberty is assured, inequality in basic social goods—such as income and wealth distribution, and opportunities—is to be allowed *only* if such inequalities benefit everyone. Rawls accepts that inequalities can be just if the system that produces inequalities is to the advantage of everyone. More precisely, he formulates what he calls the *difference principle*, which is that inequalities are justified if they benefit the position of the least-advantaged person. So, for example, wide variations in income and wealth can be considered just if the market-based system that produces this unequal distribution also benefits the least-advantaged members of society. One can argue that a well-regulated, market-based economy and free trade, by promoting economic growth, benefit the least-advantaged members of society. In principle at least, the inequalities inherent in such systems are therefore just (in other words, the rising tide of wealth created by a market-based economy and free trade lifts all boats, even those of the most disadvantaged).

LEARNING OBJECTIVE 5
Know what managers can do to incorporate ethical considerations into their decision making.

In the context of international business ethics, Rawls's theory creates an interesting perspective. Managers could ask themselves whether the policies they adopt in foreign operations would be considered just under Rawls's veil of ignorance. Is it just, for example, to pay foreign workers less than workers in the firm's home country? Rawls's theory would suggest it is, so long as the inequality benefits the least-advantaged members of the global society (which is what economic theory suggests). Alternatively, it is difficult to imagine that managers operating under a veil of ignorance would design a system where foreign employees were paid subsistence wages to work long hours in sweatshop conditions in which they were exposed to toxic materials. Such working conditions are clearly unjust in Rawls's framework, and therefore, it is unethical to adopt them. Similarly, operating under a veil of ignorance, most people would probably design a system that imparts some protection from environmental degradation to important global commons, such as the oceans, atmosphere, and tropical rain forests. To the extent that this is the case, it follows that it is unjust, and by extension unethical, for companies to pursue actions that contribute toward extensive degradation of these commons. Thus, Rawls's veil of ignorance is a conceptual tool that contributes to the moral compass that managers can use to help them navigate through difficult ethical dilemmas.

Focus on Managerial Implications

What then is the best way for managers in a multinational firm to make sure that ethical considerations figure into international business decisions? How do managers decide upon an ethical course of action when confronted with decisions pertaining to working conditions, human rights, corruption, and environmental pollution? From an ethical perspective, how do managers determine the moral obligations that flow from the power of a multinational? In many cases, there are no easy answers to these questions; many of the most vexing ethical problems arise because there are very real dilemmas inherent in them and no obvious correct action. Nevertheless, managers can and should do many things to make sure that basic ethical principles are adhered to and that ethical issues are routinely inserted into international business decisions.

Here we focus on five things that an international business and its managers can do to make sure ethical issues are considered in business decisions. These are (1) favor hiring and promoting people with a well-grounded sense of personal ethics; (2) build an organizational culture that places a high value on ethical behavior, and make sure that leaders within the business not only articulate the rhetoric of ethical behavior but also act in a manner that is consistent with that rhetoric; (3) put decision-making processes in place that require people to consider the ethical dimension of business decisions; (4) hire ethics officers; and (5) develop moral courage.

Hiring and Promotion

It seems obvious that businesses should strive to hire people who have a strong sense of personal ethics and would not engage in unethical or illegal behavior. Similarly, you would expect a business to avoid promoting people, perhaps even to fire people, whose behavior does not match generally accepted ethical standards. However, actually doing so is difficult. How do you know that someone has a poor sense of personal ethics? In our society, we have an incentive to hide a lack of personal ethics from public view. Once people realize you are unethical, they will no longer trust you.

Is there anything that businesses can do to make sure they do not hire people who subsequently turn out to have poor personal ethics, particularly given that people have an incentive to hide this from public view (indeed, the unethical person may lie about his or her nature)? Businesses can give potential employees psychological tests to try to discern their ethical predisposition, and they can check with prior employees regarding someone's reputation (e.g., by asking for letters of reference and talking to people who have worked with the prospective employee). The latter is common and does influence the hiring process. Promoting people who have displayed poor ethics should not occur in a company where the organization culture values the need for ethical behavior and where leaders act accordingly.

Not only should businesses strive to identify and hire people with a strong sense of personal ethics, but it also is in the interests of prospective employees to find out as much as they can about the ethical climate in an organization. Who wants to work at a multinational such as Enron, which ultimately entered bankruptcy because unethical executives had established risky partnerships that were hidden from public view and that existed in part to enrich those same executives? Table 4.1 lists some questions job seekers might want to ask a prospective employer.

table 4.1

A Job Seeker's Ethics Audit

Some probing questions to ask about a prospective employer:

1. Is there a formal code of ethics? How widely is it distributed? Is it reinforced in other formal ways such as through decision-making systems?
2. Are workers at all levels trained in ethical decision making? Are they also encouraged to take responsibility for their behavior or to question authority when asked to do something they consider wrong?
3. Do employees have formal channels available to make their concerns known confidentially? Is there a formal committee high in the organization that considers ethical issues?
4. Is misconduct disciplined swiftly and justly within the organization?
5. Is integrity emphasized to new employees?
6. How are senior managers perceived by subordinates in terms of their integrity? How do such leaders model ethical behavior?

Source: Linda K. Trevino, professor, Organizational Behavior and Cook Fellow in Business Ethics, Pennsylvania State University, adapted from Trevino, L. K. and Nelson, K. A. *Managing Business Ethics*, 2nd Ed. (New York: John Wiley & Sons, Inc., 1999). Copyright © 1999 John Wiley & Sons, Inc. Used by permission.

Organization Culture and Leadership

To foster ethical behavior, businesses need to build an organization culture that values ethical behavior. Three things are particularly important in building an organization culture that emphasizes ethical behavior. First, the businesses must explicitly articulate values that emphasize ethical behavior. Many companies now do this by drafting a **code of ethics,** a formal statement of the ethical priorities to which a business adheres. Often, the code of ethics draws heavily upon documents such as the UN Universal Declaration of Human Rights, which itself is grounded in Kantian and rights-based theories of moral philosophy. Others have incorporated ethical statements into documents that articulate the values or mission of the business. For example, the food and consumer products multinational Unilever has a code of ethics that includes points on their commitment to hire diverse employees, provide safe working conditions, and refuse to employ any sort of forced or child labor, based on their commitment to respect each individual's dignity. Unilever also refuses to give or receive indirect, as well as, direct bribes, including gifts to employees that could possibly be construed as bribes. In addition, Unilever commits to making sure that all transactions are discussed and recorded.

Code of Ethics
A formal statement of the ethical priorities to which a business adheres.

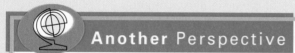

It is clear from these principles, that among other things, Unilever will not tolerate substandard working conditions, use child labor, or give bribes under any circumstances. Their reference to clearly respecting the dignity of employees is a statement grounded in Kantian ethics. Unilever's principles send a clear message about appropriate ethics to managers and employees.

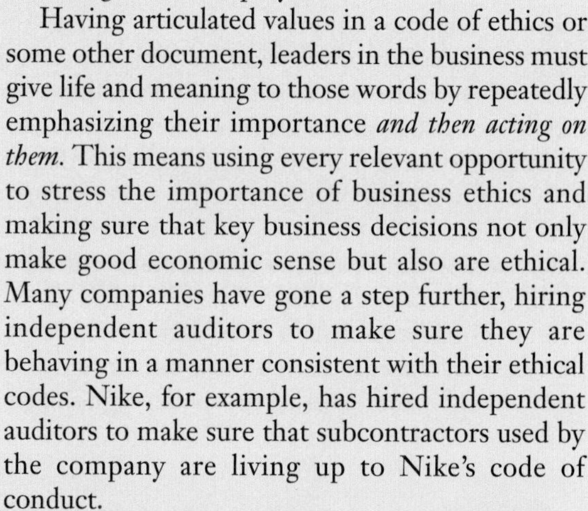

Having articulated values in a code of ethics or some other document, leaders in the business must give life and meaning to those words by repeatedly emphasizing their importance *and then acting on them.* This means using every relevant opportunity to stress the importance of business ethics and making sure that key business decisions not only make good economic sense but also are ethical. Many companies have gone a step further, hiring independent auditors to make sure they are behaving in a manner consistent with their ethical codes. Nike, for example, has hired independent auditors to make sure that subcontractors used by the company are living up to Nike's code of conduct.

Finally, building an organization culture that places a high value on ethical behavior requires incentive and reward systems, including promotions that reward people who engage in ethical behavior and sanction those who do not. At General Electric, for example, the former CEO Jack Welch has described how he reviewed the performance of managers, dividing them into several different groups. These included overperformers who displayed the right values and were singled out for advancement and bonuses and overperformers who displayed the wrong values and were let go. Welch was not willing to tolerate leaders within the company who did not

Another Perspective

Starbucks Sets the Ethics Bar High

At its strategic planning level, top management at Starbucks is making socially responsible decisions, including in the ethical minefield of international sourcing. The company's "good coffee, doing good" program develops mutually beneficial relationships with coffee farmers in Central America to make their businesses successful. As stated by a company spokesperson, "The success of the farmers with whom we do business is a critical component of our own success."

Starbucks' approach includes paying farmers premium prices; providing them access to affordable credit so they can invest in their farms and grow their businesses; purchasing conservation and certified coffees; including the Fair Trade certification; buying from farmers who follow sustainable business practices and practice social responsibility in their own businesses; investing in social development programs for the communities from which it buys; and providing farmers technical support and training from its center in Costa Rica.

Starbucks seems to be a model company for conducting business responsibly for all its stakeholders. Check out its Web site at www.starbucks.com to view its list of stakeholders, to learn how it serves each, and to see how it is reducing its "environmental footprint." (www.starbucks.com/aboutus/origins.asp)

act in accordance with the central values of the company, even if they were in all other respects skilled managers.[36]

Decision-Making Processes

In addition to establishing the right kind of ethical culture in an organization, businesspeople must be able to think through the ethical implications of decisions in a systematic way. To do this, they need a moral compass, and both rights theories and Rawls's theory of justice help to provide such a compass. Beyond these theories, some experts on ethics have proposed a straightforward practical guide—or ethical algorithm—to determine whether a decision is ethical.[37] According to these experts, a decision is acceptable on ethical grounds if a businessperson can answer yes to each of these questions:

- Does my decision fall within the accepted values or standards that typically apply in the organizational environment (as articulated in a code of ethics or some other corporate statement)?
- Am I willing to see the decision communicated to all stakeholders affected by it—for example, by having it reported in newspapers or on television?
- Would the people with whom I have a significant personal relationship, such as family members, friends, or even managers in other businesses, approve of the decision?

Others have recommended a five-step process to think through ethical problems (this is another example of an ethical algorithm).[38] In step 1, businesspeople should identify which stakeholders a decision would affect and in what ways. A firm's **stakeholders** are individuals or groups that have an interest, claim, or stake in the company, in what it does, and in how well it performs.[39] They can be divided into internal stakeholders and external stakeholders. **Internal stakeholders** are individuals or groups that work for or own the business. They include all employees, the board of directors, and stockholders. **External stakeholders** are all other individuals and groups that have some claim on the firm. Typically, this group comprises customers, suppliers, lenders, governments, unions, local communities, and the general public.

All stakeholders are in an exchange relationship with the company. Each stakeholder group supplies the organization with important resources (or contributions), and in exchange, each expects its interests to be satisfied (by inducements).[40] For example, employees provide labor, skills, knowledge, and time and in exchange expect commensurate income, job satisfaction, job security, and good working conditions. Customers provide a company with its revenues and in exchange they want quality products that represent value for money. Communities provide businesses with local infrastructure; in exchange, they want businesses that are responsible citizens, and they seek some assurance that the quality of life will be improved as a result of the business firm's existence.

Stakeholder analysis involves a certain amount of what has been called **moral imagination.**[41] This means standing in the shoes of a stakeholder and asking how a proposed decision might affect that stakeholder. For example, when considering outsourcing to subcontractors, managers might need to ask themselves how it might feel to be working under substandard health conditions for long hours.

Step 2 involves judging the ethics of the proposed strategic decision, given the information gained in step 1. Managers need to determine whether a proposed decision would violate the **fundamental rights of** any **stakeholders.** For example, we might argue that the right to information about health risks in the workplace is a

Stakeholders
Individuals or groups that have an interest, claim, or stake in a company, what it does, and how well it performs.

Internal Stakeholders
Individuals or groups that work for or own the business.

External Stakeholders
All other individuals and groups that have some claim on a firm, such as the government, suppliers, and the general public.

Moral Imagination
Standing in the shoes of a stakeholder and asking how a proposed decision will affect that stakeholder.

Fundamental Rights of Stakeholders
Basic rights of stakeholders, such as the right to information about products and working conditions, that should be considered when business decisions are made.

fundamental entitlement of employees. Similarly, the right to know about potentially dangerous features of a product is a fundamental entitlement of customers (something tobacco companies violated when they did not reveal to their customers what they knew about the health risks of smoking). Managers might also want to ask themselves whether they would allow the proposed strategic decision if they were designing a system under Rawls's veil of ignorance. For example, if the issue under consideration was whether to outsource work to a subcontractor with low pay and poor working conditions, managers might want to ask themselves whether they would allow for such action if they were considering it under a veil of ignorance, where they themselves might ultimately be the ones to work for the subcontractor.

The judgment at this stage should be guided by various moral principles that should not be violated. The principles might be those articulated in a corporate code of ethics or other company documents. In addition, certain moral principles that we have adopted as members of society—for instance, the prohibition on stealing—should not be violated. The judgment at this stage will also be guided by the decision rule that is chosen to assess the proposed strategic decision. Although maximizing long-run profitability is the decision rule that most businesses stress, it should be applied subject to the constraint that no moral principles are violated—that the business behaves in an ethical manner.

Ethics Officer
An individual hired by a company to be responsible for making sure that all employees are trained to be ethically aware, that ethical considerations enter the decision-making process, and that employees follow the company's code of ethics.

Step 3 requires managers to establish moral intent. This means the business must resolve to place moral concerns ahead of other concerns in cases where either the fundamental rights of stakeholders or key moral principles have been violated. At this stage, input from top management might be particularly valuable. Without the proactive encouragement of top managers, middle-level managers might tend to place the narrow economic interests of the company before the interests of stakeholders. They might do so in the (usually erroneous) belief that top managers favor such an approach.

Step 4 requires the company to engage in ethical behavior. Step 5 requires the business to audit its decisions, reviewing them to make sure they were consistent with ethical principles, such as those stated in the company's code of ethics. This final step is critical and often overlooked. Without auditing past decisions, businesspeople may not know if their decision process is working and if changes should be made to ensure greater compliance with a code of ethics.

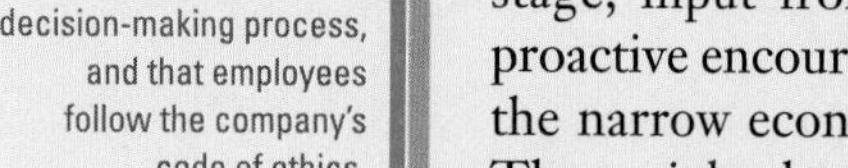

Another Perspective

How Do You Know What Is Really Happening? Giving Meaning across Cultures

One of the difficulties in making ethical decisions across cultural borders is that expatriate managers may tend to interpret a local cultural practice in the ways such behavior would be understood in their home culture. If the manager's process of meaning-giving stops there, rather than continue in an attempt to understand the practice's meaning *in the local culture*, the manager may miss a huge step in ethical analysis. For example, if women's covering their heads and faces in conservative Muslim cultures is given meaning in a Western context, it would lead to different conclusions than were it given meaning with knowledge of the specific, local, Muslim context. Remember to consider context when conducting an ethical analysis. In such a process, a local informant can be helpful. At the same time, be aware of the ethical trap of cultural relativism. (Example from H. Lane, M. Maznevski, M. Mendenhall, and J. McNett, *The Blackwell Handbook of Global Management: A Guide to Managing Complexity* (2004).)

Ethics Officers

To make sure that a business behaves in an ethical manner, a number of firms now have **ethics officers.** These individuals are responsible for making sure that all employees are trained to be ethically aware, that ethical considerations enter the business decision-making process, and that employees follow the company's code of ethics. Ethics officers may also be responsible for auditing decisions to make sure they are consistent with this code. In many businesses, ethics officers act as an internal ombudsperson with responsibility for handling confidential inquiries from employees, investigating complaints from employees or others, reporting findings, and making recommendations for change.

For example, United Technologies, a multinational aerospace company with worldwide revenues of more than $28 billion, has had a formal code of ethics since 1990.[42] There are some 160 business practice officers within United Technologies (this is the company's name for ethics officers). They are responsible for making sure the code is followed. United Technologies also established an ombudsperson program in 1986 that lets employees inquire anonymously about ethics issues. The program has received some 56,000 inquiries since 1986, and 8,000 cases have been handled by an ombudsperson.

United Technologies, the maker of Sikorsky helicopters such as the one pictured here, demonstrates its commitment to ethical behavior by employing over 160 business practices officers. *Business Wire/Getty Images*

Moral Courage

Finally, it is important to recognize that employees in an international business may need significant *moral courage*. Moral courage enables managers to walk away from a decision that is profitable but unethical. Moral courage gives an employee the strength to say no to a superior who instructs him or her to pursue unethical actions. Moral courage gives employees the integrity to go public to the media and blow the whistle on persistent unethical behavior in a company. Moral courage does not come easily; there are well-known cases where individuals have lost their jobs because they blew the whistle on corporate behaviors they thought unethical, telling the media about what was occurring.[43]

However, companies can strengthen the moral courage of employees by committing themselves not to retaliate against employees who exercise moral courage, say no to superiors, or otherwise complain about unethical actions. For example, consider the following extract from Unilever's code of ethics. For example, Unilever's code of ethics expressly states that the Board will not criticize management for any loss of business that results from adherence to the ethical code. It also promises that no employees will suffer as a consequence of reporting ethical breaches.

This approach gives permission to employees to exercise moral courage. Companies can also set up ethics hotlines, which allow employees to anonymously register a complaint with a corporate ethics officer.

Summary of Managerial Actions

All of the steps discussed here—hiring and promoting people based upon ethical considerations as well as more traditional metrics of performance, establishing an ethical culture in the organization, instituting ethical decision-making processes, appointing ethics officers, and creating an environment that facilitates moral courage—can help to make sure that when making business decisions, managers are cognizant of the ethical implications and do not violate basic ethical prescripts. At the same time, it must be recognized that not all ethical dilemmas have a clean and obvious solution—that is why they are dilemmas. There are clearly things international businesses should not do and things they should do, but there are also actions that present managers with true dilemmas. In these cases, company's should place a premium on managers' ability to make sense out of complex situations and make balanced decisions that are as just as possible.

Key Terms

business ethics, p. 124
ethical strategy, p. 124
Sullivan principles, p. 126
Foreign Corrupt Practices Act, p. 130
Convention on Combating Bribery of Foreign Public Officials in International Business Transactions, p. 130
social responsibility, p. 131
noblesse oblige, p. 132
ethical dilemma, p. 134
personal ethics, p. 134
organization culture, p. 135
cultural relativism, p. 139
righteous moralism, p. 140
naive immoralism, p. 140
utilitarian approaches to ethics, p. 141
Kantian ethics, p. 142
rights theories, p. 142
Universal Declaration of Human Rights, p. 142
justice theories, p. 143
just distribution, p. 143
code of ethics, p. 146
stakeholders, p. 147
internal stakeholders, p. 147
external stakeholders, p. 147
moral imagination, p. 147
fundamental rights of stakeholders, p. 147
ethics officer, p. 148

Summary

This chapter has discussed the source and nature of ethical issues in international businesses, the different philosophical approaches to business ethics, and the steps managers can take to ensure that ethical issues are respected in international business decisions. The chapter made these points:

1. The term *ethics* refers to accepted principles of right or wrong that govern the conduct of a person, the members of a profession, or the actions of an organization. Business ethics are the accepted principles of right or wrong governing the conduct of businesspeople, and an ethical strategy is one that does not violate these accepted principles.
2. Ethical issues and dilemmas in international business are rooted in the variations among political systems, law, economic development, and culture from nation to nation.
3. The most common ethical issues in international business involve employment practices, human rights, environmental regulations, corruption, and the moral obligation of multinational corporations.
4. Ethical dilemmas are situations in which none of the available alternatives seems ethically acceptable.
5. Unethical behavior is rooted in poor personal ethics, the psychological and geographical distances of a foreign subsidiary from the home office, a failure to incorporate ethical issues into strategic and operational decision making, a dysfunctional culture, and failure of leaders to act in an ethical manner.
6. Moral philosophers contend that approaches to business ethics such as the Friedman doctrine, cultural relativism, righteous moralism, and naive immoralism are unsatisfactory in important ways.
7. The Friedman doctrine states that the only social responsibility of business is to increase profits, as long as the company stays within the rules of law. Cultural relativism contends that one should adopt the ethics of the culture in which one is doing business. Righteous moralism monolithically applies home-country ethics to a foreign situation, whereas naive immoralism holds that if a manager of a multinational sees that firms from other nations are not following ethical norms in a host nation, that manager should not either.
8. Utilitarian approaches to ethics hold that the moral worth of actions or practices is determined by their consequences, and the best decisions are those that produce the greatest good for the greatest number of people.
9. Kantian ethics state that people should be treated as ends and never purely as *means* to the ends of others. People are not instruments, like a machine. People have dignity and need to be respected as such.

10. Rights theories recognize that human beings have fundamental rights and privileges that transcend national boundaries and cultures. These rights establish a minimum level of morally acceptable behavior.
11. The concept of justice developed by John Rawls suggests that a decision is just and ethical if people would allow for it when designing a social system under a veil of ignorance.
12. To make sure that ethical issues are considered in international business decisions, managers should (*a*) favor hiring and promoting people with a well-grounded sense of personal ethics; (*b*) build an organization culture that places a high value on ethical behavior, and make sure that leaders within the business not only articulate the rhetoric of ethical behavior but also act in a manner that is consistent with that rhetoric; (*c*) put decision-making processes in place that require people to consider the ethical dimension of business decisions; (*d*) hire ethics officers; and (*e*) be morally courageous and encourage others to do the same.

Critical Thinking and Discussion Questions

1. Review the Management Focus on testing drugs in the developing world, and discuss the following questions:
   a. Did Pfizer behave unethically by rushing to take advantage of a Nigerian epidemic to test an experimental drug on sick children? Should the company have proceeded more carefully?
   b. Is it ethical to test an experimental drug on children in emergency settings in the developing world where the overall standard of health care is much lower than in the developed world and where proper protocols might not be followed?
2. A visiting American executive finds that a foreign subsidiary in a poor nation has hired a 12-year-old girl to work on a factory floor, in violation of the company's prohibition on child labor. He tells the local manager to replace the child and tell her to go back to school. The local manager tells the American executive that the child is an orphan with no other means of support, and she will probably become a street child if she is denied work. What should the American executive do?
3. Drawing upon John Rawls's concept of the veil of ignorance, develop an ethical code that will (*a*) guide the decisions of a large oil multinational toward environmental protection, and (*b*) influence the policies of a clothing company on outsourcing of manufacturing process.
4. Under what conditions is it ethically defensible to outsource production to the developing world where labor costs are lower when such actions also involve laying off long-term employees in the firm's home country?
5. Are facilitating payments ethical?

http://globalEDGE.msu.edu globalEDGE Research Task

Use the globalEDGE site (http://globalEDGE.msu.edu/) to complete the following exercises:

1. Promoting respect for universal human rights is a dimension of many countries' foreign policy. Begun in 1977, the annual *Country Reports on Human Rights Practices* are designed to assess the state of democracy and human rights around the world, call attention to violations, and—where needed—prompt changes in U.S. governmental policies toward particular countries. Find the annual Country Reports on Human Rights Practices and provide information on how these reports are prepared.
2. The *Corruption Perceptions Index (CPI)* is a comparative assessment of integrity performance in a variety of countries. Provide a description of this index and its ranking. Identify the five countries with the lowest and highest CPI scores. Do you notice any trends or similarities among the countries listed?

Mired in Corruption: Kellogg, Brown and Root in Nigeria

In 1998, the large Texas-based oil and gas service firm Halliburton acquired Dresser Industries. Among other businesses, Dresser owned M.W. Kellogg, one of the world's largest general contractors for construction projects in distant parts of the globe. After the acquisition, Kellogg was combined with an existing Halliburton business and renamed Kellogg, Brown & Root, or KBR for short. At the time it looked like a good deal for Halliburton. Among other things, Kellogg was involved in a four-firm consortium that was building a series of liquefied natural gas (LNG) plants in Nigeria. By early 2004, the total value of the contracts associated with these plants had exceeded $8 billion.

In early 2005, however, Halliburton put KBR up for sale. The sale was seen as an attempt by Halliburton to distance itself from several scandals that had engulfed KBR. One of these concerned allegations that KBR had systematically overcharged the Pentagon for services it provided to the U.S. military in Iraq. Another scandal centered on the Nigerian LNG plants and involved KBR employees, several former officials of the Nigeria government, and a mysterious British lawyer named Jeffrey Tesler.

The roots of the Nigerian scandal date back to 1994 when Kellogg and its consortium partners were trying to win an initial contract from the Nigerian government to build two LNG plants. The contract was valued at around $2 billion. Each of the four firms held a 25 percent stake in the consortium, and each had veto power over its decisions. Kellogg employees held many of the top positions at the consortium, and two of the other members, Technip of France and JGC of Japan, have claimed that Kellogg managed the consortium (the fourth member, ENI of Italy, has not made any statement regarding management).

The KBR consortium was one of two to submit a bid on the initial contract, and its bid was the lower of the two. By early 1995, the KBR consortium was deep in final negotiations on the contract. It was at this point that Nigeria's oil minister had a falling out with the country's military dictator, General Abacha, and was replaced by Dan Etete. Etete proved to be far less accommodating to the KBR consortium, and suddenly the entire deal looked to be in jeopardy. According to some observers, Etete was a tough customer who immediately began to use his influence over the LNG project for personal gain. Whether this is true or not, what is known is that the KBR consortium quickly entered into a contract with Jeffrey Tesler, the British lawyer. The contract, signed by a Kellogg executive, called on Tesler to obtain government permits for the LNG project, maintain good relations with government officials, and provide advice on sales strategy. Tesler's fee for these services was $60 million.

Tesler, it turned out, had long-standing relations with some 20 to 30 senior Nigeria government and military officials. In his capacity as a lawyer, for years he had handled the London affairs of those officials, helping them to purchase real estate and set up financial accounts. Kellogg had a relationship with Tesler that dated back to the mid-1980s, when they had employed him to broker the sale of Kellogg's minority interest in a Nigerian fertilizer plant to the Nigerian government.

What happened next is currently the subject of government investigations in France, Nigeria, and the United States. The suspicion is that Tesler promised to funnel big sums to Nigerian government officials if the deal was done. Investigators base these suspicions on a number of factors, including the known corruption of General Abacha's government, the size of the payment to Tesler, which seemed out of all proportion to the services he was contracted to provide, and a series of notes turned up by internal investigators at Halliburton. The handwritten notes, taken by Wojciech Chodan, a Kellogg executive, document a meeting between Chodan and Tesler in which they discussed the possibility of channeling $40 million of Tesler's $60 million payment to General Abacha.

It is not known whether a bribe was actually paid. What is known is that in December 1995, Nigeria awarded the $2 billion contract to the KBR consortium. The LNG plant soon became a success. Nigeria contracted to build a second plant in 1999, two more in 2002, and a sixth in July 2004. KBR rehired Jeffrey Tesler in 1999 and again in 2001 to help secure the new contracts, all of which it won. In total, Tesler was paid some $132.3 million from 1994 through to early 2004 by the KBR consortium.

Tesler's involvement in the project might have remained unknown were it not for an unrelated event. Georges Krammer, an employee of the French company Technip, which along with KBR was a member of the consortium, was charged by the French government for embezzlement. When Technip refused to defend Krammer, he turned around and aired what he perceived to be Technip's dirty linen. This included the payments to Tesler to secure the Nigeria LNG contracts.

This turn of events led French and Swiss officials to investigate Tesler's Swiss bank accounts. They discovered that Tesler was kicking back some of the funds he received to executives in the consortium and at subcontractors. One of the alleged kickbacks was a transfer of $5 million from Tesler's account to that of Albert J. "Jack" Stanley, who was head of M.W. Kellogg and then Halliburton's KBR unit. Tesler also transferred some $2.5 million into Swiss bank accounts held under a false name by the Nigerian oil minister Dan Etete. Other payments included a $1 million transfer into an account controlled by Wojciech Chodan, the former Kellogg executive whose extensive handwritten notes suggest the payment of a bribe to General Abacha, and $5 million to a German subcontractor on the LNG project in exchange for "information and advice."

After this all came out in June 2004, Halliburton promptly fired Jack Stanley and severed its long-standing relationship with Jeffrey Tesler, asking its three partners in the Nigeria consortium to do the same. The U.S. Justice Department took things further, establishing a grand jury investigation to determine if Halliburton, through its KBR subsidiary, had been in violation of the Foreign Corrupt Practices Act. In November 2004, the Justice Department widened its investigation to include payments in connection with the Nigeria fertilizer plant that Kellogg had been involved with during the 1980s under the leadership of Jack Stanley. In March 2005, the Justice Department also stated that it was looking at whether Stanley had tried to coordinate bidding with rivals and fix prices on certain foreign construction projects.

Sources: R. Gold and C. Flemming, "Out of Africa: In Halliburton Nigeria Inquiry, a Search for Bribes to a Dictator," *The Wall Street Journal*, September 29, 2004, p. A1; R. Gold, "Halliburton to Put KBR Unit on Auction Block," *The New York Times*, January 31, 2005, p. A2; T. Sawyer, "Citing Violations, Halliburton Cuts off Former KBR Chairman," *ENR*, June 28, 2004, p. 16; and D. Ivanovich, "Halliburton: Contracts Investigated," *Houston Chronicle*, March 2, 2005, p. 1.

Case Discussion Questions

1. Could the alleged payment of bribes to Nigerian government officials by Jeffrey Tesler be considered facilitating payments or speed money under the terms of the Foreign Corrupt Practices Act?
2. Irrespective of the legality of any payments Tesler may have made, do you think it was reasonable for KBR to hire him as an intermediary?
3. Given the known corruption of the Abacha government in Nigeria, should Kellogg and its successor, KBR, have had a policy in place to deal with bribery and corruption? What might that policy have looked like?
4. Should Kellogg have walked away from the Nigerian LNG project once it became clear that the payment of bribes might be required to secure the contract?
5. There is evidence that Jack Stanley, the former head of M.W. Kellogg and KBR, may have taken kickback payments from Tesler. At least one other former Kellogg employee, Wojciech Chodan, may have taken kickback payments. What does this tell you about the possible nature of the ethical climate at Kellogg and then KBR?
6. Should Halliburton be called to account if it is shown that its KBR unit used bribery to gain business in Nigeria? To what extent should a corporation and its officers be held accountable for ethically suspect activities by the managers in one of its subsidiaries, particularly given that many of those activities were initiated before the subsidiary was owned by Halliburton?

C. Borland/Photo Link/Getty Images/DIL

part 3 Cross-Border Trade and Investment

LEARNING OBJECTIVES

1 Understand why nations trade with each other.

2 Be familiar with the different theories explaining trade flows between nations.

3 Understand why many economists believe that unrestricted free trade between nations will raise the economic welfare of countries that participate in a free trade system.

4 Be familiar with the arguments of those who maintain that government can play a proactive role in promoting national competitive advantage in certain industries.

5 Understand the important implications that international trade theory holds for business practice.

chapter 5

International Trade Theory

International Trade in Information Technology and U.S. Economic Growth

opening case

Entrepreneurial enterprises in the United States invented most of the information technology that we use today, including computer and communications hardware, software, and services. In the 1960s and 1970s, the information technology sector was led by companies like IBM and DEC, which developed first mainframe and then midrange computers. In the 1980s, the locus of growth in the sector shifted to personal computers, and the innovations of companies like Intel, Apple, IBM, Dell, and Compaq helped to develop the mass market for the product. Along the way, however, something happened to this uniquely American industry: It started to move the production of hardware offshore.

In the early 1980s, production of "commodity components" for computers such as DRAMs (memory chips) migrated to low-cost producers in Japan, and then later to Taiwan and Korea. Soon hard disk drives, display screens, keyboards, computer mice, and a host of other components were outsourced to foreign manufacturers. By the early 2000s, American factories were specializing in making only the highest-value components, such as the microprocessors made by Intel, and in final assembly. (Dell for example, assembles PCs in two North American facilities.) Just about every other component was made overseas–because it cost less to do so. There was a lot of hand-wringing among politicians and journalists about the possible negative implication for the U.S. economy of this trend. According to the critics, high-paying manufacturing jobs in the information technology sector were being exported to foreign producers.

Was this trend bad for the U.S. economy, as the critics claimed? The evidence suggests not. According to recent research, the globalization of production made information technology hardware about 20 percent less expensive than it would otherwise have been. The price declines supported additional investments in information technology by businesses and households. Because they were getting cheaper, computers diffused throughout the United States faster. In turn, the rapid diffusion of information technology translated into faster productivity growth as businesses used computers to streamline processes. Between 1995 and 2002, productivity grew by 2.8 percent annually in the United States, well above the historic norm. According to recent calculations, some 0.3 percent of this annual growth could be attributed directly to the reduced prices of information technology hardware made possible by the move to offshore production. In turn, the 0.3 percent annual gain in productivity over 1995 to 2002 resulted in an additional $230 billion in accumulated gross domestic product in the United States. In short, the American economy grew at a faster rate precisely because production of information technology hardware was shifted to foreigners.

Moreover, there is ample evidence that the reduced price for hardware made possible by international trade created a boom in jobs in two related industries: computer software and services. During the 1990s, the number of information technology jobs in the United States grew by 22 percent, twice the rate of job creation in the economy as a whole, and this at a time when manufacturing information technology jobs were moving offshore. The growth could be attributed partly to robust demand for computer software and services within the United States and partly to demand for software and services from foreigners, including those same foreigners who were now making much of the hardware. In sum, buying computer hardware from foreigners, as opposed to making it in the United States, had a significant *positive* impact upon the U.S. economy that outweighed any adverse effects from job losses in the manufacturing sector.

Sources: C.L.Mann, "Globalization of IT Services and White-Collar Jobs," *International Economic Policy Briefs,* Institute of International Economics, December 2003; A. Bernstein, "Shaking up Trade Theory," *BusinessWeek,* December 6, 2004, pp. 116–20; "Semiconductor Trade: A Wafer Thin Case," *The Economist,* July 27, 1996, pp. 53–54; and K.J. Stiroh, "Information Technology and the U.S. Productivity Revival," Federal Reserve Bank of New York, January 2001.

Introduction

The opening case goes to the heart of a debate that has been played out many times over the past half century. Some argue that free trade leads to a migration of jobs overseas and will ultimately create higher unemployment and lower living standards. These people see the trend for U.S. information technology companies to shift manufacturing jobs to other nations where goods can be produced more cheaply as a disturbing development that represents nothing less than the "hollowing out" of America. However, economists schooled in international trade theory argue that free trade ultimately benefits *all* countries that participate in a free trade system. Those who take this position concede that some individuals lose because of a shift to free trade, but, they argue, the gains outweigh the losses.

The opening case provides evidence in support of this position. As noted, the shift to offshore production of information technology hardware had tangible benefits for the U.S. economy. As a result of globalization, costs of information technology hardware in the United States fell by 20 percent more than would have been the case had the transfer of production to other countries not occurred. Lower prices for hardware speeded up the diffusion of information technology in the United States, boosted productivity, and added some $230 billion to the nation's GDP between 1995 and 2002. Moreover, the availability of cheap information technology helped to create additional jobs in the computer software and service sectors, where employment grew at twice the national average during the 1995–2002 period.

The arguments surrounding the benefits and costs of free trade are not abstract academic ones. International trade theory has shaped the economic policy of many nations for the past 50 years and is the driver behind the formation of the World Trade Organization and regional trade blocs such as the European Union and the North American Free Trade Agreement. The 1990s, in particular, saw a global move toward greater free trade. It is crucially important to understand, therefore, what these theories are and why they have been successful in shaping the economic policy of so many nations and the competitive environment in which international businesses compete.

This chapter has two goals that go to the heart of this debate. The first is to review a number of theories that explain why it is beneficial for a country to engage in international trade. The second is to explain the pattern of international trade that we observe in the world economy. With regard to the pattern of trade, we will be primarily concerned with explaining the pattern of exports and imports of goods and services between countries. In Chapter 7, we will discuss the pattern of foreign direct investment between countries.

An Overview of Trade Theory

We open this chapter with a discussion of mercantilism. Propagated in the sixteenth and seventeenth centuries, mercantilism advocated that countries should simultaneously encourage exports and discourage imports. Although mercantilism is an old and largely discredited doctrine, its echoes remain in modern political debate and in the trade policies of many countries. Next we will look at Adam Smith's theory of absolute advantage. Proposed in 1776, Smith's theory was the first to explain why unrestricted free trade is beneficial to a country. **Free trade** refers to a situation in which a government does not attempt to influence through quotas or duties on what its citizens can buy from another country, or what they can produce and sell to another country. Smith argued that the invisible hand of the market mechanism, rather than government policy, should determine what a country imports and what it exports. His arguments imply that such a laissez-faire stance toward trade was in the best interests of a country. Building on Smith's work are two additional theories. One is the theory of comparative advantage, advanced by the nineteenth-century English economist David Ricardo. This theory is the intellectual basis of the modern argument for unrestricted free trade. In the twentieth century, two Swedish economists, Eli Heckscher and Bertil Ohlin, refined Ricardo's work with what is known as the Heckscher-Ohlin theory.

Free Trade
The absence of government-imposed barriers, such as quotas or duties, that impede the free flow of goods and services between countries.

THE BENEFITS OF TRADE The great strength of the theories of Smith, Ricardo, and Heckscher-Ohlin is that they identify with precision the specific benefits of international trade. Common sense suggests that some international trade is beneficial. For example, nobody would suggest that Iceland should grow its own oranges. Iceland can benefit from trade by exchanging some of the products that it can produce at a low cost (fish) for some products that it cannot produce at all (oranges). Thus, by engaging in international trade, Icelanders are able to add oranges to their diets.

LEARNING OBJECTIVE 1
Understand why nations trade with each other.

The theories of Smith, Ricardo, and Heckscher-Ohlin go beyond this commonsense notion, however, to show why it is beneficial for a country to engage in international

Another Perspective

Outsourcing: Putting Jobs into Growing Markets
Another way of looking at the hollowing out of the American knowledge-based economy through outsourcing is to see the process from the perspective of developing nations. To them, outsourcing brings with it the benefits of trade. It is one of the positive outcomes of globalization. Multinational corporations doing some business in their markets can locate their production in the very markets into which they are selling. As India, the Philippines, and China develop a knowledge-based labor supply, companies like Intel and EMC that are selling into these markets may want to locate some of their research and development and other knowledge-based activities in these markets as a commitment to a local presence, as a way to learn more about the customer, and as a way to establish sustained and sustaining relationships. Yes, there are cost savings, especially on labor, but long term, such cost savings may be secondary.

trade *even for products it is able to produce for itself.* This is a difficult concept for people to grasp. For example, many people in the United States believe that American consumers should buy products made in the United States by American companies whenever possible to help save American jobs from foreign competition. Moreover, people in many other countries hold similar nationalistic sentiments.

However, the theories of Smith, Ricardo, and Heckscher-Ohlin tell us that a country's economy may gain if its citizens buy certain products from other nations that could be produced at home. The gains arise because international trade allows a country to specialize in the manufacture and export of products that can be produced most efficiently in that country, while importing products that can be produced more efficiently in other countries. For example, it makes sense for the United States to specialize in the production and export of commercial jet aircraft, because the efficient production of such aircraft requires resources that are abundant in the country, such as a highly skilled labor force and cutting-edge technological know-how. On the other hand, it may make sense for the United States to import textiles from China since the efficient production of textiles requires a relatively cheap labor force—and cheap labor is not abundant in the United States.

Of course, segments of a country's population may find this economic argument difficult to accept. With their future threatened by imports, U.S. textile companies and their employees have tried hard to persuade the government to limit the importation of textiles by demanding quotas and tariffs. Although such import controls may benefit particular groups, such as textile businesses and their employees, the theories of Smith, Ricardo, and Heckscher-Ohlin suggest that such action would hurt the economy as a whole. Limits on imports are often in the interests of domestic producers but not domestic consumers. See the Another Perspective box at left for more on how outsourcing affects all of a product's life cycle.

THE PATTERN OF INTERNATIONAL TRADE The theories of Smith, Ricardo, and Heckscher-Ohlin help to explain the pattern of international trade that we observe in the world economy. Some aspects of the pattern are easy to understand. Climate and natural resource endowments explain why Ghana exports cocoa, Brazil exports coffee, Saudi Arabia exports oil, and China exports crawfish. But much of the observed pattern of international trade is more difficult to explain. For example, why does Japan export automobiles, consumer electronics, and machine tools? Why does Switzerland export chemicals, pharmaceuticals, watches, and jewelry? Ricardo's theory of comparative advantage offers an explanation in terms of international differences in labor productivity. The more sophisticated Heckscher-Ohlin theory emphasizes the interplay between the proportions in which the factors of production (such as land, labor, and capital) are available in different countries and the proportions in which they are needed for producing particular goods. This explanation rests on the assumption that countries have varying endowments of the various factors of production. Tests of this theory, however, suggest that it is a less powerful explanation of real-world trade patterns than once thought.

One early response to the failure of the Heckscher-Ohlin theory to explain the observed pattern of international trade was the product life-cycle theory. Proposed by

Raymond Vernon, this theory suggests that early in their life cycle, most new products are produced in and exported from the country in which they were developed. As a new product becomes widely accepted internationally, however, production starts in other countries. As a result, the theory suggests, the product may ultimately be exported back to the country of its original innovation.

In a similar vein, during the 1980s economists such as Paul Krugman developed what has come to be known as the *new trade theory*. New trade theory stresses that in some cases countries specialize in the production and export of particular products not because of underlying differences in factor endowments, but because in certain industries the world market can support only a limited number of firms. (This is argued to be the case for the commercial aircraft industry.) In such industries, firms that enter the market first are able to build a competitive advantage that is subsequently difficult to challenge. Thus, the observed pattern of trade between nations may be due in part to the ability of firms within a given nation to capture first-mover advantages. The United States is a major exporter of commercial jet aircraft because American firms such as Boeing were first movers in the world market. Boeing built a competitive advantage that has subsequently been difficult for firms from countries with equally favorable factor endowments to challenge (although Europe's Airbus Industries has succeeded in doing that).

In a work related to the new trade theory, Michael Porter developed what is referred to as the theory of national competitive advantage. It attempts to explain why particular nations achieve international success in particular industries. In addition to factor endowments, Porter points out the importance of country factors such as domestic demand and domestic rivalry in explaining a nation's dominance in the production and export of particular products.

TRADE THEORY AND GOVERNMENT POLICY Although all these theories agree that international trade is beneficial to a country, they lack agreement in their recommendations for government policy. Mercantilism makes a crude case for government involvement in promoting exports and limiting imports. The theories of Smith, Ricardo, and Heckscher-Ohlin form part of the case for unrestricted free trade. The argument for unrestricted free trade is that both import controls and export incentives (such as subsidies) are self-defeating and result in wasted resources. Both the new trade theory and Porter's theory of national competitive advantage can be interpreted as justifying some limited government intervention to support the development of certain export-oriented industries. We will discuss the pros and cons of this argument, known as strategic trade policy, as well as the pros and cons of the argument for unrestricted free trade, in Chapter 6.

Mercantilism

LEARNING OBJECTIVE 2
Be familiar with the different theories explaining trade flows between nations.

The first theory of international trade, **mercantilism**, emerged in England in the mid-sixteenth century. The principle assertion of mercantilism was that gold and silver were the mainstays of national wealth and essential to vigorous commerce. At that time, gold and silver were the currency of trade between countries; a country could earn gold and silver by exporting goods. Conversely, importing goods from other countries would result in an outflow of gold and silver to those countries. The main tenet of mercantilism was that it was in a country's best interests to maintain a trade surplus, to export more than it imported. By doing so, a country would accumulate gold and silver and, consequently, increase its national wealth, prestige, and power. As the English mercantilist writer Thomas Mun put it in 1630,

Mercantilism
The economic philosophy advocating that countries should simultaneously encourage exports and discourage imports.

> The ordinary means therefore to increase our wealth and treasure is by foreign trade, wherein we must ever observe this rule: to sell more to strangers yearly than we consume of theirs in value.[1]

Country **FOCUS**

Is China a Neo-Mercantilist Nation?

China's rapid rise in economic power has been built upon export-led growth. The country has taken raw material imports from other countries, and using its cheap labor, converted them into products that it sells to developed nations like the United States. For years, the country's exports have been growing faster than its imports, leading some critics to claim that China is pursuing a neo-mercantilist policy, trying to amass record trade surpluses and foreign currency that will give it economic power over developed nations. This rhetoric reached new heights in 2005 when China's trade surplus hit a record $121 billion and its foreign exchange reserves topped $800 billion, some 70 percent of which are held in U.S. dollars. Observers worry that if China ever decides to sell its holdings of U.S. currency, this could depress the value of the dollar against other currencies and increase the price of imports into America.

Throughout 2005, China's exports grew at twice the rate of imports, leading some to argue that China was limiting imports by pursuing an import substitution policy, encouraging domestic investment in the production of products like steel, aluminum, and paper, which it had historically imported from other nations. At the same time, China has resisted attempts to let its currency float freely against the U.S. dollar. Many claim that China's currency is too cheap, which keeps the prices of China's goods artificially low and fuels the country's exports.

So is China a neo-mercantilist nation that is deliberately discouraging imports and encouraging exports in order to grow its trade surplus and accumulate foreign exchange reserves, which might give it economic power? The jury is out on this issue. Skeptics suggest that the slowdown in imports to China is temporary and that the country will have no choice but to increase its imports of commodities that it lacks, such as oil. They also note that China did start allowing the value of the *renminbi* (China's currency) to appreciate against the dollar in July 2005, although the initial appreciation was limited to just 2.1 percent—hardly enough say critics. In a sign that pressure on China to change its ways is growing, in early 2006 the U.S. treasury secretary renewed calls for the Chinese to allow the renminbi to continue rising against the U.S. dollar.

Sources: A. Browne, "China's Wild Swings Can Roil the Global Economy," *The Wall Street Journal,* October 24, 2005, p. A2; S.H. Hanke, "Stop the Mercantilists," *Forbes,* June 20, 2005, p. 164; and G. Dyer and A. Balls, "Dollar Threat as China Signals Shift," *Financial Times,* January 6, 2006, p. 1.

Consistent with this belief, the mercantilist doctrine advocated government intervention to achieve a surplus in the balance of trade. The mercantilists saw no virtue in a large volume of trade. Rather, they recommended policies to maximize exports and minimize imports. To achieve this, they advocated that the government limit imports by tariffs and quotas while subsidizing exports.

The classical economist David Hume pointed out an inherent inconsistency in the mercantilist doctrine in 1752. According to Hume, if England had a balance-of-trade surplus with France (it exported more than it imported), the resulting inflow of gold and silver would swell the domestic money supply and generate inflation in England. In France, however, the outflow of gold and silver would have the opposite effect. France's money supply would contract, and its prices would fall. This change in relative prices between France and England would encourage the French to buy fewer English goods (because they were becoming more expensive) and the English to buy more French goods (because they were becoming cheaper). The result would be a deterioration in the English balance of trade and an improvement in France's trade balance, until the English surplus was eliminated. Hence, according to Hume, in the long run no country could sustain a surplus in the balance of trade and so accumulate gold and silver as the mercantilists had envisaged.

Zero-Sum Game
A situation in which a gain by one country results in a loss by another.

The flaw with mercantilism was that it viewed trade as a zero-sum game. (A **zero-sum game** is one in which a gain by one country results in a loss by another.) It was left to Adam Smith and David Ricardo to show the shortsightedness of this approach and to demonstrate that trade is a positive-sum game, or a situation in which all countries can benefit. Unfortunately, the mercantilist doctrine is by no means dead. Neo-mercantilists equate political power with economic power and economic power with a balance-of-trade surplus. Critics argue that many nations have adopted a neo-mercantilist strategy that is designed to simultaneously boost exports and limit imports.[2] For example, critics charge that China is pursuing a neo-mercantilist policy, deliberately keeping the value of its currency low against the U.S. dollar in order to sell more goods to the United States and thus amass a trade surplus and foreign exchange reserves (see the Country Focus on the previous page).

Absolute Advantage

LEARNING OBJECTIVE 2
Be familiar with the different theories explaining trade flows between nations.

In his 1776 landmark book *The Wealth of Nations*, Adam Smith attacked the mercantilist assumption that trade is a zero-sum game. Smith argued that countries differ in their ability to produce goods efficiently. In his time, the English, by virtue of their superior manufacturing processes, were the world's most efficient textile manufacturers. Due to the combination of favorable climate, good soils, and accumulated expertise, the French had the world's most efficient wine industry. The English had an *absolute advantage* in the production of textiles, whereas the French had an *absolute advantage* in the production of wine. Thus, a country has an **absolute advantage** in the production of a product when it is more efficient than any other country in producing it.

Absolute Advantage
When one country is more efficient than any other country in producing a particular product.

According to Smith, countries should specialize in the production of goods for which they have an absolute advantage and then trade these for goods produced by other countries. In Smith's time, this suggested that the English should specialize in the production of textiles while the French should specialize in the production of wine. England could get all the wine it needed by selling its textiles to France and buying wine in exchange. Similarly, France could get all the textiles it needed by selling wine to England and buying textiles in exchange. Smith's basic argument, therefore, is that a country should never produce goods at home that it can buy at a lower cost from other countries. Smith demonstrates that, by specializing in the production of goods in which each has an absolute advantage, both countries benefit by engaging in trade.

Consider the effects of trade between two countries, Ghana and South Korea. The production of any good (output) requires resources (inputs) such as land, labor, and capital. Assume that Ghana and South Korea both have the same amount of resources and that these resources can be used to produce either rice or cocoa. Assume further that 200 units of resources are available in each country. Imagine that in Ghana it takes 10 resources to produce one ton of cocoa and 20 resources to produce one ton of rice. Thus, Ghana could produce 20 tons of cocoa and no rice, 10 tons of rice and no cocoa, or some combination of rice and cocoa between these two extremes. The different combinations that Ghana could produce are represented by the line GG' in Figure 5.1. This is referred to as Ghana's **production possibility frontier (PPF).** Similarly, imagine that in South Korea it takes 40 resources to produce one ton of cocoa and 10 resources to produce one ton of rice. Thus, South Korea could produce 5 tons of cocoa and no rice, 20 tons of rice and no cocoa, or some combination between these two extremes. The different combinations available to South Korea are represented by the line KK' in Figure 5.1, which is South Korea's PPF. Clearly, Ghana has an absolute advantage in the production of cocoa. (More resources are needed to produce a ton of cocoa in South Korea than in Ghana.) By the same token, South Korea has an absolute advantage in the production of rice.

Production Possibility Frontier (PPF)
The various output possibilities a country can produce from its resource pool.

Now consider a situation in which neither country trades with any other. Each country devotes half of its resources to the production of rice and half to the production of cocoa. Each country must also consume what it produces. Ghana would be able to produce 10 tons of cocoa and 5 tons of rice (point A in Figure 5.1), while South Korea would be able to produce 10 tons of rice and 2.5 tons of cocoa. Without trade, the

The Theory of Absolute Advantage

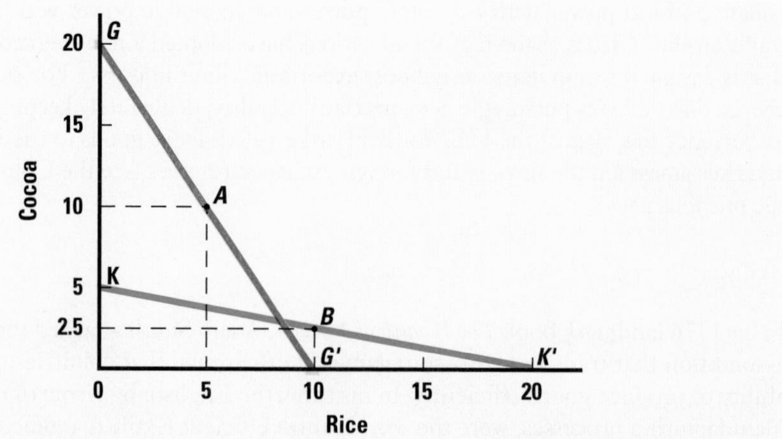

combined production of both countries would be 12.5 tons of cocoa (10 tons in Ghana plus 2.5 tons in South Korea) and 15 tons of rice (5 tons in Ghana and 10 tons in South Korea). If each country were to specialize in producing the good for which it had an absolute advantage and then trade with the other for the good it lacks, Ghana could produce 20 tons of cocoa, and South Korea could produce 20 tons of rice. Thus, by specializing, the production of both goods could be increased. Production of cocoa would increase from 12.5 tons to 20 tons, while production of rice would increase from 15 tons to 20 tons. The increase in production that would result from specialization is therefore 7.5 tons of cocoa and 5 tons of rice. Table 5.1 summarizes these figures.

By engaging in trade and swapping one ton of cocoa for one ton of rice, producers in both countries could consume more of both cocoa and rice. Imagine that Ghana and South Korea swap cocoa and rice on a one-to-one basis; that is, the price of one ton of cocoa is equal to the price of one ton of rice. If Ghana decided to export 6 tons of cocoa to South Korea and import 6 tons of rice in return, its final consumption after trade would be 14 tons of cocoa and 6 tons of rice. This is 4 tons more cocoa than it could have consumed before specialization and trade and 1 ton more rice. Similarly, South Korea's final consumption after trade would be 6 tons of cocoa and 14 tons of rice. This is 3.5 tons more cocoa than it could have consumed before specialization and trade and 4 tons more rice. Thus, as a result of specialization and trade, output of both cocoa and rice would be increased, and consumers in both nations would be able to consume more. Thus, we can see that trade is a positive-sum game; it produces net gains for all involved.

Comparative Advantage

LEARNING OBJECTIVE 2
Be familiar with the different theories explaining trade flows between nations.

David Ricardo took Adam Smith's theory one step further by exploring what might happen when one country has an absolute advantage in the production of all goods.[3] Smith's theory of absolute advantage suggests that such a country might derive no benefits from international trade. In his 1817 book *Principles of Political Economy*, Ricardo showed that this was not the case. According to Ricardo's theory of comparative advantage, it makes sense for a country to specialize in the production of those goods that it produces most efficiently and to buy the goods that it produces less efficiently from other countries, even if this means buying goods from other countries that it could produce more efficiently itself.[4] While this may seem counterintuitive, the logic can be explained with a simple example.

Assume that Ghana is more efficient in the production of both cocoa and rice; that is, Ghana has an absolute advantage in the production of both products. In Ghana it

table 5.1

Absolute Advantage and the Gains from Trade

Resources Required to Produce 1 Ton of Cocoa and Rice		
	Cocoa	**Rice**
Ghana	10	20
South Korea	40	10
Production and Consumption without Trade		
	Cocoa	**Rice**
Ghana	10.0	5.0
South Korea	2.5	10.0
Total production	12.5	15.0
Production with Specialization		
	Cocoa	**Rice**
Ghana	20.0	0.0
South Korea	0.0	20.0
Total production	20.0	20.0
Consumption after Ghana Trades 6 Tons of Cocoa for 6 Tons of South Korean Rice		
	Cocoa	**Rice**
Ghana	14.0	6.0
South Korea	6.0	14.0
Increase in Consumption as a Result of Specialization and Trade		
	Cocoa	**Rice**
Ghana	4.0	1.0
South Korea	3.5	4.0

takes 10 resources to produce one ton of cocoa and $13\frac{1}{3}$ resources to produce one ton of rice. Thus, given its 200 units of resources, Ghana can produce 20 tons of cocoa and no rice, 15 tons of rice and no cocoa, or any combination in between on its PPF (the line GG' in Figure 5.2). In South Korea it takes 40 resources to produce one ton of cocoa and 20 resources to produce one ton of rice. Thus, South Korea can produce 5 tons of cocoa and no rice, 10 tons of rice and no cocoa, or any combination on its PPF (the line KK' in Figure 5.2). Again assume that without trade, each country uses half of its resources to produce rice and half to produce cocoa. Thus, without trade, Ghana will produce 10 tons of cocoa and 7.5 tons of rice (point A in Figure 5.2), while South Korea will produce 2.5 tons of cocoa and 5 tons of rice (point B in Figure 5.2).

In light of Ghana's absolute advantage in the production of both goods, why should it trade with South Korea? Although Ghana has an absolute advantage in the production of both cocoa and rice, it has a comparative advantage only in

figure 5.2

The Theory of Comparative Advantage

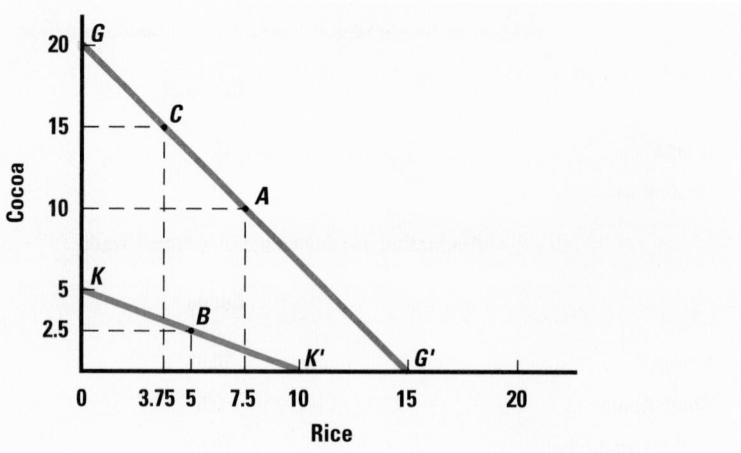

the production of cocoa: Ghana can produce 4 times as much cocoa as South Korea, but only 1.5 times as much rice. Ghana is *comparatively* more efficient at producing cocoa than it is at producing rice.

Without trade the combined production of cocoa will be 12.5 tons (10 tons in Ghana and 2.5 in South Korea), and the combined production of rice will also be 12.5 tons (7.5 tons in Ghana and 5 tons in South Korea). Without trade, each country must consume what it produces. By engaging in trade, the two countries can increase their combined production of rice and cocoa, and consumers in both nations can consume more of both goods.

THE GAINS FROM TRADE Imagine that Ghana exploits its comparative advantage in the production of cocoa to increase its output from 10 tons to 15 tons. This uses up 150 units of resources, leaving the remaining 50 units of resources to use in producing 3.75 tons of rice (point C in Figure 5.2). Meanwhile, South Korea specializes in the production of rice, producing 10 tons. The combined output of both cocoa and rice has now increased. Before specialization, the combined output was 12.5 tons of cocoa and 12.5 tons of rice. Now it is 15 tons of cocoa and 13.75 tons of rice (3.75 tons in Ghana and 10 tons in South Korea). The source of the increase in production is summarized in Table 5.2.

Not only is output higher, but both countries also can now benefit from trade. If Ghana and South Korea swap cocoa and rice on a one-to-one basis, with both countries choosing to exchange 4 tons of their export for 4 tons of the import, both countries are able to consume more cocoa and rice than they could before specialization and trade (see Table 5.2). Thus, if Ghana exchanges 4 tons of cocoa with South Korea for 4 tons of rice, it is still left with 11 tons of cocoa, which is 1 ton more than it had before trade. The 4 tons of rice it gets from South Korea in exchange for its 4 tons of cocoa, when added to the 3.75 tons it now produces domestically, leaves it with a total of 7.75 tons of rice, which is .25 of a ton more than it had before specialization. Similarly, after swapping 4 tons of rice with Ghana, South Korea still ends up with 6 tons of rice, which is more than it had before specialization. In addition, the 4 tons of cocoa it receives in exchange is 1.5 tons more than it produced before trade. Thus, consumption of cocoa and rice can increase in both countries as a result of specialization and trade.

LEARNING OBJECTIVE 3
Understand why many economists believe that unrestricted free trade between nations will raise the economic welfare of countries that participate in a free trade system.

The basic message of the theory of comparative advantage is that *potential world production is greater with unrestricted free trade than it is with restricted trade.* Ricardo's theory suggests that consumers in all nations can consume more if there are no restrictions on trade. This occurs even in countries that lack an absolute advantage

table 5.2

Comparative Advantage and the Gains from Trade

Resources Required to Produce 1 Ton of Cocoa and Rice		
	Cocoa	**Rice**
Ghana	10	13.33
South Korea	40	20
Production and Consumption without Trade		
	Cocoa	**Rice**
Ghana	10.0	7.5
South Korea	2.5	5.0
Total production	12.5	12.5
Production with Specialization		
	Cocoa	**Rice**
Ghana	15.0	3.75
South Korea	0.0	10.0
Total production	15.0	13.75
Consumption after Ghana Trades 4 Tons of Cocoa for 4 Tons of South Korean Rice		
	Cocoa	**Rice**
Ghana	11.0	7.75
South Korea	4.0	6.0
Increase in Consumption as a Result of Specialization and Trade		
	Cocoa	**Rice**
Ghana	1.0	0.25
South Korea	1.5	1.0

in the production of any good. In other words, to an even greater degree than the theory of absolute advantage, *the theory of comparative advantage suggests that trade is a positive-sum game in which all countries that participate realize economic gains.* As such, this theory provides a strong rationale for encouraging free trade. So powerful is Ricardo's theory that it remains a major intellectual weapon for those who argue for free trade.

QUALIFICATIONS AND ASSUMPTIONS The conclusion that free trade is universally beneficial is a rather bold one to draw from such a simple model. Our simple model includes many unrealistic assumptions:

1. We have assumed a simple world in which there are only two countries and two goods. In the real world, there are many countries and many goods.

2. We have assumed away transportation costs between countries.
3. We have assumed away differences in the prices of resources in different countries. We have said nothing about exchange rates, simply assuming that cocoa and rice could be swapped on a one-to-one basis.
4. We have assumed that resources can move freely from the production of one good to another within a country. In reality, this is not always the case.
5. We have assumed constant returns to scale; that is, that specialization by Ghana or South Korea has no effect on the amount of resources required to produce one ton of cocoa or rice. In reality, both diminishing and increasing returns to specialization exist. The amount of resources required to produce a good might decrease or increase as a nation specializes in production of that good.
6. We have assumed that each country has a fixed stock of resources and that free trade does not change the efficiency with which a country uses its resources. This static assumption makes no allowances for the dynamic changes in a country's stock of resources and in the efficiency with which the country uses its resources that might result from free trade.
7. We have assumed away the effects of trade on income distribution within a country.

Given these assumptions, can the conclusion that free trade is mutually beneficial be extended to the real world of many countries, many goods, positive transportation costs, volatile exchange rates, immobile domestic resources, nonconstant returns to specialization, and dynamic changes? Although a detailed extension of the theory of comparative advantage is beyond the scope of this book, economists have shown that the basic result derived from our simple model can be generalized to a world composed of many countries producing many different goods.[5] Despite the shortcomings of the Ricardian model, research suggests that the basic proposition that countries will export the goods that they are most efficient at producing is borne out by the data.[6]

However, once all the assumptions are dropped, some economists associated with the "new trade theory" have argued that the case for unrestricted free trade, while still positive, loses some of its strength.[7] We return to this issue later in this chapter and in the next when we discuss the new trade theory. In a recent and widely discussed analysis, the Nobel Prize–winning economist Paul Samuelson argued that contrary to the standard interpretation, in certain circumstances the theory of comparative advantage predicts that a rich country might actually be *worse* off by switching to a free trade regime with a poor nation.[8] We will consider Samuelson's critique in the next section.

EXTENSIONS OF THE RICARDIAN MODEL Let us explore the effect of relaxing two of the assumptions identified above in the simple comparative advantage model. Below we relax the assumption that resources move freely from the production of one good to another within a country and the assumption that trade does not change a country's stock of resources or the efficiency with which those resources are utilized.

Immobile Resources In our simple comparative model of Ghana and South Korea, we assumed that producers (farmers) could easily convert land from the production of cocoa to rice and vice versa. Although this assumption may hold for some agricultural products, resources do not always shift quite so easily from producing one good to another. A certain amount of friction is involved. For example, embracing a free trade regime for an advanced economy such as the United States often implies that the country will produce less of some labor-intensive goods, such as textiles, and more of some knowledge-intensive goods, such as computer software or biotechnology products. Although the country as a whole will gain from such a shift, textile producers will lose. A textile worker in South Carolina is probably not qualified to write software for Microsoft. Thus, the shift to free trade may mean that the person becomes unemployed or has to accept another less attractive job, such as working at a fast-food restaurant.

Resources do not always move easily from one economic activity to another. The process creates friction and human suffering too. While the theory predicts that the benefits of free trade outweigh the costs by a significant margin, this is of cold comfort to those who bear the costs. Accordingly, political opposition to the adoption of a free trade regime typically comes from those whose jobs are most at risk. In the United States, for example, textile workers and their unions have long opposed the move toward free trade precisely because this group has much to lose from free trade. Governments often ease the transition toward free trade by helping to retrain those who lose their jobs as a result. The pain caused by the movement toward a free trade regime is a short-term phenomenon, whereas the gains from trade once the transition has been made are both significant and enduring.

LEARNING OBJECTIVE 3
Understand why many economists believe that unrestricted free trade between nations will raise the economic welfare of countries that participate in a free trade system.

Dynamic Effects and Economic Growth The simple comparative advantage model assumed that trade does not change a country's stock of resources or the efficiency with which it utilizes those resources. This static assumption makes no allowances for the dynamic changes that might result from trade. If we relax this assumption, it becomes apparent that opening an economy to trade is likely to generate dynamic gains of two sorts.[9] First, free trade might increase a country's stock of resources as increased supplies of labor and capital from abroad become available for use within the country. For example, this has been occurring in Eastern Europe since the early 1990s, with many Western businesses investing significant capital in the former Communist countries.

Second, free trade might also increase the efficiency with which a country uses its resources. Gains in the efficiency of resource utilization could arise from a number of factors. For example, economies of large-scale production might become available as trade expands the size of the total market available to domestic firms. Trade might make better technology from abroad available to domestic firms; better technology can increase labor productivity or the productivity of land. (The so-called green revolution had this effect on agricultural outputs in developing countries.) Also, opening an economy to foreign competition might stimulate domestic producers to look for ways to increase their efficiency. Again, this phenomenon has arguably been occurring in the once-protected markets of Eastern Europe, where many former state monopolies are increasing the efficiency of their operations to survive in the competitive world market.

Dynamic gains in both the stock of a country's resources and the efficiency with which resources are utilized will cause a country's PPF to shift outward. This is illustrated in Figure 5.3, where the shift from PPF_1 to PPF_2 results from the dynamic gains that arise from free trade. As a consequence of this outward shift, the country in Figure 5.3 can produce more of both goods than it did before introduction of free trade. The theory suggests that opening an economy to free trade not only results in static gains of the type discussed earlier, but it also results in dynamic gains that stimulate economic growth. If this is so, then one might think that the case for free trade becomes stronger still, and in general it does. However, as noted above, in a recent article one of the leading economic theorists of the twentieth century, Paul Samuelson, argued that in some circumstances, dynamic gains can lead to an outcome that is not so beneficial.

The Influence of Free Trade on the PPF

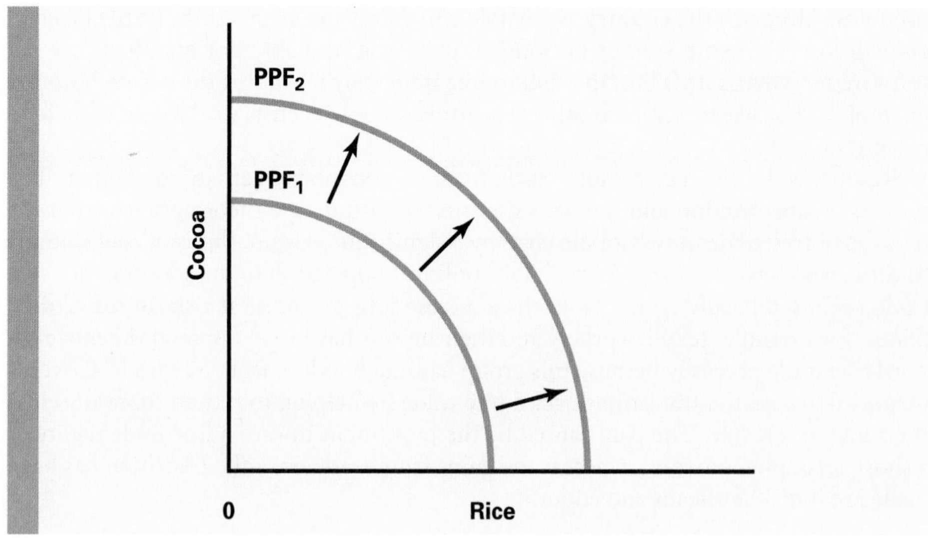

The Samuelson Critique Samuelson's critique looks at what happens when a rich country—the United States—enters into a free trade agreement with a poor country—China—that rapidly improves its productivity after the introduction of a free trade regime (i.e. there is a dynamic gain in the efficiency with which resources are used in the poor country). The Samuelson model suggests that in such cases, the lower prices that U.S. consumers pay for goods imported from China following the introduction of a free trade regime *may* not be enough to produce a net gain to for the U.S. economy if the dynamic effect of free trade is to lower real wage rates in the United States. As Samuelson stated in a *New York Times* interview, "being able to purchase groceries 20 percent cheaper at Wal-Mart (due to international trade) does not necessarily make up for the wage losses (in America)."[10]

Samuelson goes on to note that he is particularly concerned about the ability to send service jobs offshore that traditionally were not internationally mobile, such as software debugging, call center jobs, accounting jobs, and even medical diagnosis of MRI scans (see the Country Focus on the next page for details). Recent advances in communications technology have made this possible, effectively expanding the labor market for these jobs to include educated people in places like India, the Philippines, and China. When coupled with rapid advances in the productivity of foreign labor that result from better education, the effect on middle-class wages in the United States, according to Samuelson, may be similar to mass inward migration into the Unites States: It will lower the market clearing wage rate, *perhaps* by enough to outweigh the positive benefits of international trade.

Having said this, it should be noted that Samuelson concedes that free trade has historically benefited rich counties (as data discussed below seem to confirm). Moreover, he notes that introducing protectionist measures (e.g., trade barriers) to guard against the theoretical possibility that free trade may harm the United States in the future may produce a situation that is worse than the disease they are trying to prevent. As Samuelson put it, "Free trade may turn out pragmatically to be still best for each region in comparison to lobbyist-induced tariffs and quotas which involve both a perversion of democracy and nonsubtle deadweight distortion losses."[11]

Some economists have been quick to dismiss Samuelson's fears.[12] While not questioning his analysis, they note that as a practical matter developing nations are

Country FOCUS

Moving U.S. White-Collar Jobs Offshore

Economists have long argued that free trade produces gains for all countries that participate in a free trading system, but as the next wave of globalization sweeps through the U.S. economy, many people are wondering if this is true, particularly those who stand to lose their jobs because of this wave of globalization. In the popular imagination for much of the past quarter century, free trade was associated with the movement of low-skill, blue-collar manufacturing jobs out of rich countries such as the United States and toward low-wage countries—textiles to Costa Rica, athletic shoes to the Philippines, steel to Brazil, electronic products to Malaysia, and so on. While many observers bemoaned the "hollowing out" of U.S. manufacturing, economists stated that high-skilled and high-wage, white-collar jobs associated with the knowledge-based economy would stay in the United States. Computers might be assembled in Malaysia, so the argument went, but they would continue to be designed in Silicon Valley by high-skilled U.S. engineers.

Recent developments have some people questioning this assumption. As the global economy slowed after 2000 and corporate profits slumped, many American companies responded by moving white collar "knowledge-based" jobs to developing nations where they could be performed for a fraction of the cost. During the long economic boom of the 1990s, Bank of America had to compete with other organizations for the scarce talents of information technology specialists, driving annual salaries to more than $100,000. However, with business under pressure, between 2002 and early 2003 the bank cut nearly 5,000 jobs from its 25,000-strong, U.S.-based information technology workforce. Some of these jobs are being transferred to India, where work that costs $100 an hour in the United States can be done for $20 an hour.

One beneficiary of Bank of America's downsizing is Infosys Technologies Ltd., a Bangalore, India, information technology firm where 250 engineers now develop information technology applications for the bank. Other Infosys employees are busy processing home loan applications for Greenpoint Mortgage of Novato, California. Nearby in the offices of another Indian firm, Wipro Ltd., five radiologists interpret 30 CT scans a day for Massachusetts General Hospital that are sent over the Internet. At yet another Bangalore business, engineers earn $10,000 a year designing leading-edge semiconductor chips for Texas Instruments. Nor is India the only beneficiary of these changes. Accenture, a large U.S. management consulting and information technology firm, moved 5,000 jobs in software development and accounting to the Philippines. Also in the Philippines, Procter & Gamble employs 650 professionals who prepare the company's global tax returns. The work used to be done in the United States, but now it is done in Manila, with just final submission to local tax authorities in the United States and other countries handled locally.

Some architectural work also is being outsourced to lower-cost locations. Flour Corp., a California-based construction company, employs some 1,200 engineers and draftsmen in the Philippines, Poland, and India to turn layouts of industrial facilities into detailed specifications. For a Saudi Arabian chemical plant Flour is designing, 200 young engineers based in the Philippines earning less than $3,000 a year collaborate in real time over the Internet with elite U.S. and British engineers who make up to $90,000 a year. Why does Flour do this? According to the company, the answer is simple. Doing so reduces the prices of a project by 15 percent, giving the company a cost-based competitive advantage in the global market for construction design.

The companies that outsource such skilled jobs clearly benefit from lower costs, enhanced competitiveness in the global economy, and greater profits. American consumers benefit from the lower prices made possible by global outsourcing. Developing nations such as India and the Philippines with a good supply of well-educated, skilled, and (by global standards) low-cost labor also benefit. However, some wonder whether the United States will suffer from the loss of high-skilled and high-paying jobs? Will the trend to global outsourcing ultimately depress the salaries of white-color employees nationwide? If that does happen, might it not have negative implications for the entire U.S. economy?

Sources: P. Engardio, A. Bernstein, and M. Kripalani, "Is Your Job Next?" *BusinessWeek,* February 3, 2003, pp. 50–60; "America's Pain, India's Gain," *The Economist,* January 11, 2003, p. 57; and M. Schroeder and T. Aeppel, "Skilled Workers Mount Opposition to Free Trade, Swaying Politicians," *The Wall Street Journal,* October 10, 2003, pp. A1, A11.

unlikely to be able to upgrade the skill level of their workforce rapidly enough to give rise to the situation in Samuelson's model. In other words, they will quickly run into diminishing returns. To quote one such rebuttal: "The notion that India and China will quickly educate 300 million of their citizens to acquire sophisticated and complex skills at stake borders on the ludicrous. The educational sectors in these countries face enormous difficulties."[13] As such rebuttals indicate, Samuelson's stature is such that his work will undoubtedly be debated for some time to come.

Evidence for the Link between Trade and Growth

Many economic studies have looked at the relationship between trade and economic growth.[14] In general, these studies suggest that, as predicted by the standard theory of comparative advantage, countries that adopt a more open stance toward international trade enjoy higher growth rates than those that close their economies to trade (the opening case provides evidence of the link between trade and growth). Jeffrey Sachs and Andrew Warner created a measure of how "open" to international trade an economy was and then looked at the relationship between "openness" and economic growth for a sample of more than 100 countries from 1970 to 1990.[15] Among other findings, they reported,

> We find a strong association between openness and growth, both within the group of developing and the group of developed countries. Within the group of developing countries, the open economies grew at 4.49 percent per year, and the closed economies grew at 0.69 percent per year. Within the group of developed economies, the open economies grew at 2.29 percent per year, and the closed economies grew at 0.74 percent per year.[16]

A study by Wacziarg and Welch updated the Sachs and Warner data through the late 1990s. They found that over the 1950–98 period, countries that liberalized their trade regimes experienced, on average, increases in their annual growth rates of 1.5 percent compared to preliberalization times.[17]

The message of these studies seems clear: Adopt an open economy and embrace free trade, and your nation will be rewarded with higher economic growth rates. Higher growth will raise income levels and living standards. This last point has been confirmed by a study that looked at the relationship between trade and growth in incomes. The study, undertaken by Jeffrey Frankel and David Romer, found that on average, a 1 percent increase in the ratio of a country's trade to its gross domestic product increases income per person by at least 0.5 percent.[18] For every 10 percent increase in the importance of international trade in an economy, average income levels will rise by at least 5 percent. Despite the short-term adjustment costs associated with adopting a free trade regime, trade would seem to produce greater economic growth and higher living standards in the long run, just as the theory of Ricardo would lead us to expect.[19]

LEARNING OBJECTIVE 2
Be familiar with the different theories explaining trade flows between nations.

Heckscher-Ohlin Theory

Factor Endowments
The extent to which a country is endowed with such resources as land, labor, and capital.

Ricardo's theory contends that comparative advantage arises from differences in productivity. Thus, whether Ghana is more efficient than South Korea in the production of cocoa depends on how productively it uses its resources. Ricardo argued that differences in labor productivity between nations underlie the notion of comparative advantage. Swedish economists Eli Heckscher (in 1919) and Bertil Ohlin (in 1933) put forward a different explanation of comparative advantage. They argued that comparative advantage arises from differences in national factor endowments.[20] The term **factor endowments** refers to the extent to which a country is endowed with such resources as land, labor, and capital. Nations have varying factor endowments, and those differences explain differences in factor costs;

specifically, the more abundant a factor, the lower its cost. The Heckscher-Ohlin theory predicts that countries will export those goods that make intensive use of factors that are locally abundant, while importing goods that make intensive use of factors that are locally scarce. Thus, the Heckscher-Ohlin theory attempts to explain the pattern of international trade that we observe in the world economy. Like Ricardo's theory, the Heckscher-Ohlin theory argues that free trade is beneficial. Unlike Ricardo's theory, however, the Heckscher-Ohlin theory argues that the pattern of international trade is determined by differences in factor endowments rather than differences in productivity.

The Heckscher-Ohlin theory has commonsense appeal. For example, the United States has long been a substantial exporter of agricultural goods, reflecting in part its unusual abundance of arable land. In contrast, China excels in the exportation of goods produced in labor-intensive manufacturing industries, such as textiles and footwear. This reflects China's relative abundance of low-cost labor. The United States, which lacks abundant low-cost labor, has been a primary importer of these goods. Note that it is relative, not absolute, endowments that are important; a country may have larger absolute amounts of land and labor than another country but be relatively abundant in only one of them.

THE LEONTIEF PARADOX The Heckscher-Ohlin theory has been one of the most influential theoretical ideas in international economics. Most economists prefer the Heckscher-Ohlin theory to Ricardo's theory because it makes fewer simplifying assumptions. Because of its influence, the theory has been subjected to many empirical tests. Beginning with a famous study published in 1953 by Wassily Leontief (winner of the Nobel Prize in economics in 1973), many of these tests have raised questions about the validity of the Heckscher-Ohlin theory.[21] Using the Heckscher-Ohlin theory, Leontief postulated that since the United States was relatively abundant in capital compared with other nations, the United States would be an exporter of capital-intensive goods and an importer of labor-intensive goods. To his surprise, however, he found that U.S. exports were less capital intensive than U.S. imports. Since this result was at variance with the predictions of the theory, it has become known as the Leontief paradox.

No one is quite sure why we observe the Leontief paradox. One possible explanation is that the United States has a special advantage in producing new products or goods made with innovative technologies. Such products may be less capital intensive than products whose technology has had time to mature and become suitable for mass production. Thus, the United States may be exporting goods that heavily use skilled labor and innovative entrepreneurship, such as computer software, while importing heavy manufacturing products that use large amounts of capital. Some empirical studies tend to confirm this.[22] Still, tests of the Heckscher-Ohlin theory using data for a large number of countries tend to confirm the existence of the Leontief paradox.[23]

This leaves economists with a difficult dilemma. They prefer the Heckscher-Ohlin theory on theoretical grounds, but it is a relatively poor predictor of real-world international trade patterns. On the other hand, the theory they regard as being too limited, Ricardo's theory of comparative advantage, actually predicts trade patterns with greater accuracy. The best solution to this dilemma may be to return to the Ricardian idea that trade patterns are largely driven by international differences in productivity. Thus, one might argue that the United States exports commercial aircraft and imports textiles not because its factor endowments are especially suited to aircraft manufacture and not suited to textile manufacture, but because the United States is relatively more efficient at producing aircraft than textiles. A key assumption in the Heckscher-Ohlin theory is that technologies are the same across countries. This may not be the case. Differences in technology may lead to differences in productivity, which in turn drives international trade patterns.[24] Thus, Japan's success in exporting automobiles in the 1970s and 1980s resulted not just from the relative abundance of capital but also from its development of innovative manufacturing technology that enabled it to achieve higher productivity levels in automobile production than other countries that also had abundant capital. More recent empirical work suggests that this theoretical explanation may be correct.[25] Controlling for differences in technology across countries, the new research shows that countries do indeed export those goods that make intensive use of factors that are locally abundant and import goods that make intensive use of factors that are locally scarce. In other words, once the impact of differences of technology on productivity is controlled for, the Heckscher-Ohlin theory seems to gain predictive power.

The Product Life-Cycle Theory

LEARNING OBJECTIVE 2
Be familiar with the different theories explaining trade flows between nations.

Raymond Vernon initially proposed the product life-cycle theory in the mid-1960s.[26] Vernon's theory was based on the observation that for most of the twentieth century a large proportion of the world's new products had been developed by U.S. firms and sold first in the U.S. market (e.g., mass-produced automobiles, televisions, instant cameras, photocopiers, personal computers, and semiconductor chips). To explain this, Vernon argued that the wealth and size of the U.S. market gave U.S. firms a strong incentive to develop new consumer products. In addition, the high cost of U.S. labor gave U.S. firms an incentive to develop cost-saving process innovations.

Just because a new product is developed by a U.S. firm and first sold in the U.S. market, it does not follow that the product must be produced in the United States. It could be produced abroad at some low-cost location and then exported back into the United States. However, Vernon argued that most new products were initially produced in America. Apparently, the pioneering firms believed it was better to keep production facilities close to the market and to the firm's center of decision making, given the uncertainty and risks inherent in introducing new products. Also, the demand for most new products tends to be based on nonprice factors. Consequently, firms can charge relatively high prices for new products, which obviates the need to look for low-cost production sites in other countries.

Vernon went on to argue that early in the life cycle of a typical new product, while demand is starting to grow rapidly in the United States, demand in other advanced countries is limited to high-income groups. The limited initial demand in other advanced countries does not make it worthwhile for firms in those countries to start producing the new product, but it does necessitate some exports from the United States to those countries.

Over time, demand for the new product starts to grow in other advanced countries (e.g., Great Britain, France, Germany, and Japan). As it does, it becomes worthwhile for foreign producers to begin producing for their home markets. In addition, U.S. firms might set up production facilities in those advanced countries where demand is growing. Consequently, production within other advanced countries begins to limit the potential for exports from the United States.

As the market in the United States and other advanced nations matures, the product becomes more standardized, and price becomes the main competitive weapon. As this occurs, cost considerations start to play a greater role in the competitive process. Producers based in advanced countries where labor costs are lower than in the United States (e.g., Italy or Spain) might now be able to export to the United States. If cost pressures become intense, the process might not stop there. The cycle by which the United States lost its advantage to other advanced countries might be repeated once more, as developing countries (e.g., Thailand) begin to acquire a production advantage over advanced countries. Thus, the locus of global production initially switches from the United States to other advanced nations and then from those nations to developing countries.

The consequence of these trends for the pattern of world trade is that over time the United States switches from being an exporter of the product to an importer of the product as production becomes concentrated in lower-cost foreign locations. Figure 5.4 shows the growth of production and consumption over time in the United States, other advanced countries, and developing countries.

EVALUATING THE PRODUCT LIFE-CYCLE THEORY Historically, the product life-cycle theory seems to be an accurate explanation of international trade patterns. Consider photocopiers: the product was first developed in the early 1960s by Xerox in the United States and sold initially to U.S. users. Originally, Xerox exported photocopiers from the United States, primarily to Japan and the advanced countries of Western Europe. As demand began to grow in those countries, Xerox entered into joint ventures to set up production in Japan (Fuji–Xerox) and Great Britain (Rank–Xerox). In addition, once Xerox's patents on the photocopier process expired, other foreign competitors began to enter the market (e.g., Canon in Japan, Olivetti in Italy). As a consequence, exports from the United States declined, and U.S. users began to buy some of their photocopiers from lower-cost foreign sources, particularly Japan. More recently, Japanese companies have found that manufacturing costs are too high in their own country, so they have begun to switch production to developing countries such as Singapore and Thailand. Thus, initially the United States and now other advanced countries (e.g., Japan and Great Britain) have switched from being exporters of photocopiers to importers. This evolution in the pattern of international trade in photocopiers is consistent with the predictions of the product life-cycle theory that mature industries tend to go out of the United States and into low-cost assembly locations.

However, the product life-cycle theory is not without weaknesses. Viewed from an Asian or European perspective, Vernon's argument that most new products are developed and introduced in the United States seems ethnocentric. Although it may have been true that most new products were introduced in the United States during the country's dominance of the global economy (from 1945 to 1975), there were important exceptions; and exceptions have become more common in recent years. Many new products are now first introduced in Japan (e.g., videogame consoles) or Europe (new wireless phones). Moreover, with the increased globalization and integration of the world economy, discussed in Chapter 1, a growing number of new products (e.g., laptop computers, compact disks, and digital cameras) are now introduced simultaneously in the United States, Japan, and the advanced European nations. This may be accompanied by globally dispersed production, with particular components of a new product being produced in those locations around the globe where the mix of factor costs and skills is most favorable (as predicted by the theory of comparative advantage). In sum, although Vernon's theory may be useful for explaining the pattern of international trade during the brief period of American global dominance, recently it appears to be less relevant.

figure 

The Product Life-Cycle Theory

Source: Adapted from R. Vernon and L. T. Wells, *The Economic Environment of International Business*, 4th ed., (Upper Saddle River, NJ: Prentice Hall, 1986).

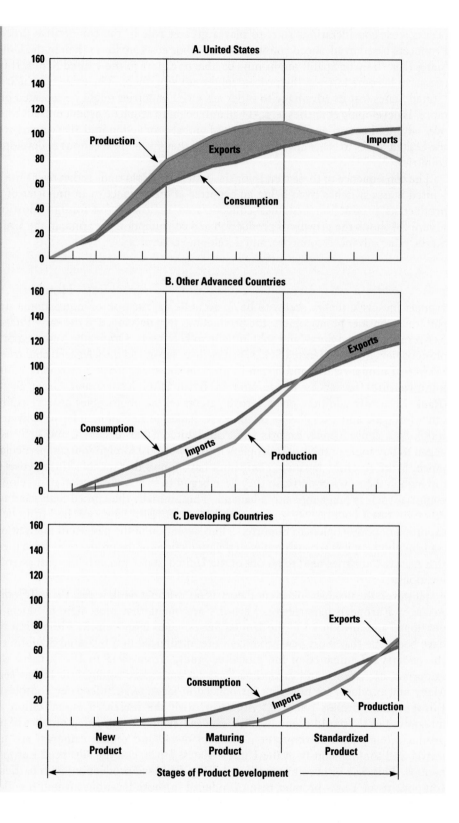

New Trade Theory

LEARNING OBJECTIVE 2
Be familiar with the different theories explaining trade flows between nations.

The new trade theory began to emerge in the 1970s when a number of economists pointed out that the ability of firms to attain economies of scale might have important implications for international trade. **Economies of scale** are unit cost reductions associated with a large scale of output. Economies of scale have a number of sources, including the ability to spread fixed costs over a large volume and the ability of large volume producers to utilize specialized employees and equipment that are more productive than less specialized employees and equipment. Economies of scale are a major source of cost reductions in many industries, including computer software, automobiles, pharmaceuticals, aerospace, and many more. For example, Microsoft realizes economies of scale by spreading the fixed costs of developing new versions of its Windows operating system, which run to about $1 billion, over the 100 million or so personal computers upon which each new system is ultimately installed. Similarly, automobile companies realize economies of scale by producing a high volume of automobiles from an assembly line on which each employee has a specialized task.

Economies of Scale
Unit cost reductions associated with a large scale of output.

New trade theory makes two important points: First, through its impact on economies of scale, trade can increase the variety of goods available to consumers and decrease the average costs of those goods. Second, for those industries in which the output required to attain economies of scale represents a significant proportion of total world demand, the global market may be able to support only a small number of enterprises. Thus, world trade in certain products may be dominated by countries whose firms were first movers in their production.

LEARNING OBJECTIVE 3
Understand why many economists believe that unrestricted free trade between nations will raise the economic welfare of countries that participate in a free trade system.

INCREASING PRODUCT VARIETY AND REDUCING COSTS Imagine first a world without trade. For industries in which economies of scale are important, both the variety of goods that a country can produce and the scale of production are limited by the size of the market. If a national market is small, there may not be enough demand to enable producers to realize economies of scale for certain products. Accordingly, those products may not be produced, thereby limiting the variety of products available to consumers. Alternatively, they may be produced, but at such low volumes that unit costs and prices are considerably higher than they might be if economies of scale could be realized.

Now consider what happens when nations trade with each other. Individual national markets are combined into a larger world market. As the size of the market expands as a result of trade, individual firms may be better able to attain economies of scale. The implication, according to new trade theory, is that each nation may be able to specialize in producing a narrower range of products than it would in the absence of trade, yet by buying goods that it does not make from other countries, each nation can simultaneously increase the *variety* of goods available to its consumers and *lower the costs* of those goods—thus, trade offers an opportunity for mutual gain even when countries do not differ in their resource endowments or technology.

Suppose there are two countries, each with an annual market for 1 million automobiles. By trading with each other, these countries can create a combined market for 2 million cars. Because they are better able to realize economies of scale in this combined market than in either market alone, firms can produce more varieties (models) of cars and at a lower average cost. For example, demand for a sports car may be 55,000 units in each national market, but a total output of at least 100,000 per year may be required to realize significant scale economies. Similarly, demand for a minivan may be 80,000 units in each national market, and again a total output of at least 100,000 per year may be required to realize significant scale economies. Faced with limited domestic market demand, firms in each nation may decide not to produce a sports car, since the costs of doing so at such low volume are too great. Although they may produce minivans, the cost of doing so will be higher, as will prices, than if significant economies of scale had been attained. Once the two countries decide to trade however, a firm in one nation may specialize in producing sports cars, while a firm in the other nation may produce minivans. The combined demand for 110,000 sports cars and 160,000 minivans allows each firm to realize scale economies. Consumers in this case benefit from having access to a product (sports cars) that was not available before international trade, and from the lower price for another product (minivans) that could not be produced at the most efficient scale before international trade. Trade is thus mutually beneficial because it allows for the specialization of production, the realization of economies of scale, the production of a greater variety of products, and lower prices.

ECONOMIES OF SCALE, FIRST-MOVER ADVANTAGES, AND THE PATTERN OF TRADE A second theme in new trade theory is that the pattern of trade we observe in the world economy may be the result of economies of scale and first-mover advantages. **First-mover advantages** are the economic and strategic advantages that accrue to early entrants into an industry.[27] The ability to capture economies of scale ahead of later entrants, and thus benefit from a lower cost structure, is an important first-mover advantage. New trade theory argues that for those products for which economies of scale are significant and represent a substantial proportion of world demand, the first movers in an industry can gain a scale-based cost advantage that later entrants find almost impossible to match. Thus, the pattern of trade that we observe for such products may reflect first-mover advantages. Countries may dominate in the export of certain goods because economies of scale are important in their production, and because firms located in those countries were the first to capture economies of scale, giving them a first-mover advantage.

First-Mover Advantages
The economic and strategic advantages that accrue to early entrants into an industry.

For example, consider the commercial aerospace industry. In aerospace there are substantial economies of scale that come from the ability to spread the fixed costs of developing a new jet aircraft over a large number of sales. It is costing Airbus some $14 billion to develop its new super-jumbo jet, the 550 seat A380. To recoup those

The European Union might come to dominate in the export of super-jumbo jets primarily because Airbus, a European-based firm, was the first to produce a 550-seat aircraft and realize economies of scale. *Courtesy Airbus*

costs and break even, Airbus will have to sell at least 250 A380 planes. If Airbus can sell more than 350 A380 planes, it will apparently be a profitable venture. However, total demand over the next 20 years for this class of aircraft is estimated to be somewhere between 400 and 600 units. Thus, the global market can probably profitably support only one producer of jet aircraft in the super-jumbo category. It follows that the European Union might come to dominate in the export of very large jet aircraft, primarily because a European-based firm, Airbus, was the first to produce a 550-seat jet aircraft and realize economies of scale. Other potential producers, such as Boeing, might be shut out of the market because they will lack the economies of scale that Airbus will enjoy. By pioneering this market category, Airbus may have captured a first-mover advantage based on economies of scale that will be difficult for rivals to match, and that will result in the European Union becoming the leading exporter of very large jet aircraft.

IMPLICATIONS OF NEW TRADE THEORY New trade theory has important implications. The theory suggests that nations may benefit from trade even when they do not differ in resource endowments or technology. Trade allows a nation to specialize in the production of certain products, attaining economies of scale and lowering the costs of producing those products, while buying products that it does not produce from other nations that specialize in the production of those products. By this mechanism, the variety of products available to consumers in each nation is increased, and the average costs of those products should fall, as should their price, freeing resources to produce other goods and services.

The theory also suggests that a country may predominate in the export of a good simply because it was lucky enough to have one or more firms among the first to produce that good. Because they are able to gain economies of scale, the first movers in an industry may get a lock on the world market that discourages subsequent entry. First movers' ability to benefit from increasing returns creates a barrier to entry. In the commercial aircraft industry, the fact that Boeing and Airbus are already in the industry and have the benefits of economies of scale discourages new entries and reinforces the dominance of America and Europe in the trade of midsized and large jet aircraft. This dominance is further reinforced because global demand may not be sufficient to profitably support another producer of midsized and large jet aircraft in the industry. So although Japanese firms might be able to compete in the market, they have decided not to enter the industry but to ally themselves as major subcontractors with primary producers (e.g., Mitsubishi Heavy Industries is a major subcontractor for Boeing on the 777 and 787 programs).

New trade theory is at variance with the Heckscher-Ohlin theory, which suggests that a country will predominate in the export of a product when it is particularly well endowed with those factors used intensively in its manufacture. New trade theorists argue that the United States is a major exporter of commercial jet aircraft not because it is better endowed with the factors of production required to manufacture aircraft, but because one of the first movers in the industry, Boeing, was a U.S. firm. The new trade theory is not at variance with the theory of comparative advantage. Economies of scale increase productivity. Thus, the new trade theory identifies an important source of comparative advantage.

This theory is quite useful in explaining trade patterns. Empirical studies seem to support the predictions of the theory that trade increases the specialization of production within an industry, increases the variety of products available to consumers, and results in lower average prices.[28] With regard to international trade, a study by Harvard business historian Alfred Chandler suggests the existence of first-mover advantages is an important factor in explaining the dominance of firms from certain nations in specific industries.[29] The number of firms is limited in many global industries, including the chemical industry, the heavy construction-equipment industry, the heavy truck industry, the tire industry, the consumer electronics industry, the jet engine industry, and the computer software industry.

LEARNING OBJECTIVE 4
Be familiar with the arguments of those who maintain that government can play a proactive role in promoting national competitive advantage in certain industries.

Perhaps the most contentious implication of the new trade theory is the argument that it generates for government intervention and strategic trade policy.[30] New trade theorists stress the role of luck, entrepreneurship, and innovation in giving a firm first-mover advantages. According to this argument, the reason Boeing was the first mover in commercial jet aircraft manufacture—rather than firms like Great Britain's DeHavilland and Hawker Siddley, or Holland's Fokker, all of which could have been—was that Boeing was both lucky and innovative. One way Boeing was lucky is that DeHavilland shot itself in the foot when its Comet jet airliner, introduced two years earlier than Boeing's first jet airliner, the 707, was found to be full of serious technological flaws. Had DeHavilland not made some serious technological mistakes, Great Britain might have become the world's leading exporter of commercial jet aircraft. Boeing's innovativeness was demonstrated by its independent development of the technological know-how required to build a commercial jet airliner. Several new trade theorists have pointed out, however, that Boeing's R&D was largely paid for by the U.S. government; the 707 was a spin-off from a government-funded military program (the entry of Airbus into the industry was also supported by significant government subsidies). By the sophisticated and judicious use of subsidies, could a government increase the chances of its domestic firms becoming first movers in newly emerging industries, as the U.S. government apparently did with Boeing (and the European Union did with Airbus)? If this is possible, and the new trade theory suggests it might be, we have an economic rationale for a proactive governmental trade policy that is at variance with the free trade prescriptions of the trade theories we have reviewed so far. We will consider the policy implications of this issue in Chapter 6.

National Competitive Advantage: Porter's Diamond

LEARNING OBJECTIVE 2
Be familiar with the different theories explaining trade flows between nations.

In 1990, Michael Porter of the Harvard Business School published the results of an intensive research effort that attempted to determine why some nations succeed and others fail in international competition.[31] Porter and his team looked at 100 industries in 10 nations. Like the work of the new trade theorists, Porter's work was driven by a belief that existing theories of international trade told only part of the story. For Porter, the essential task was to explain why a nation achieves international success in a particular industry. Why does Japan do so well in the automobile industry? Why does Switzerland excel in the production and export of precision instruments and pharmaceuticals? Why do Germany and the United States do so well in the chemical industry? These questions cannot be answered easily by the Heckscher-Ohlin theory, and the theory of comparative advantage offers only a partial explanation. The theory of comparative advantage would say that Switzerland excels in the production and export of precision instruments because it uses its resources very productively in these industries. Although this may be correct, this does not explain why Switzerland is more productive in this industry than Great Britain, Germany, or Spain. Porter tries to solve this puzzle.

Porter theorizes that four broad attributes of a nation shape the environment in which local firms compete, and these attributes promote or impede the creation of competitive advantage (see Figure 5.5). These attributes are:

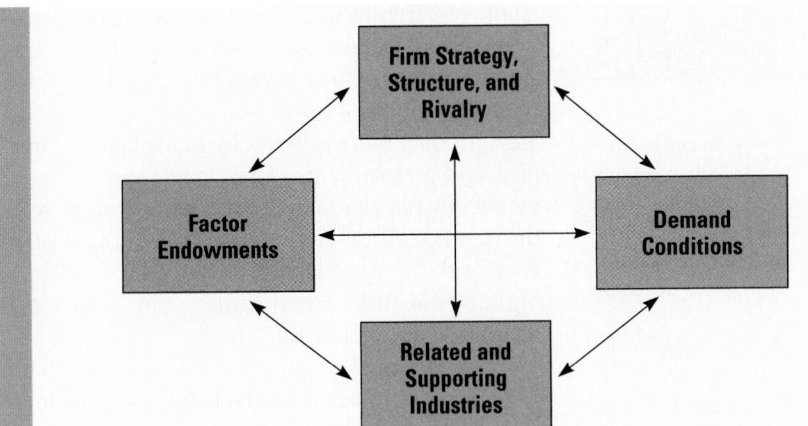

figure 5.5

Determinants of National Competitive Advantage: Porter's Diamond

Source: Reprinted by permission of the *Harvard Business Review.* Exhibit from "The Competitive Advantage of Nations" by Michael E. Porter, March–April 1990, p. 77. Copyright © 1990 by the Harvard Business School Publishing Corporation; all rights reserved.

- *Factor endowments*—a nation's position in factors of production such as skilled labor or the infrastructure necessary to compete in a given industry.
- *Demand conditions*—the nature of home demand for the industry's product or service.
- *Relating and supporting industries*—the presence or absence of supplier industries and related industries that are internationally competitive.
- *Firm strategy, structure, and rivalry*—the conditions governing how companies are created, organized, and managed and the nature of domestic rivalry.

Porter speaks of these four attributes as constituting the *diamond.* He argues that firms are most likely to succeed in industries or industry segments where the diamond is most favorable. He also argues that the diamond is a mutually reinforcing system. The effect of one attribute is contingent on the state of others. For example, Porter argues favorable demand conditions will not result in competitive advantage unless the state of rivalry is sufficient to cause firms to respond to them.

Porter maintains that two additional variables can influence the national diamond in important ways: chance and government. Chance events, such as major innovations, can reshape industry structure and provide the opportunity for one nation's firms to supplant another's. Government, by its choice of policies, can detract from or improve national advantage. For example, regulation can alter home demand conditions, antitrust policies can influence the intensity of rivalry within an industry, and government investments in education can change factor endowments.

Another Perspective

Flower Power in Ethiopia

In a nation where five million people need food aid to survive, the horticultural sector in Ethiopia is beginning to show impressive signs of success, especially with flowers. The government is building its factor endowments in the area, augmenting fertile land, good climate, and a decent transportation system with greenhouses and irrigation systems. Flower farmers can import goods duty-free, they have a five-year income tax exemption, and they lease land from the government at good rates. Such conditions tempt foreign agriculturalists to join in with locals. The result is Ethiopia's comparative advantage in horticultural exports.

Progress has been slow, due to its war with Eritrea and a fragmented domestic political scene. The flower export initiative is the beginning, a success for a government that faces many development issues. (Andrew England, "Ethiopia Sows the Seeds of Growth with Flower Power," *Financial Times,* June 15, 2005, p. 16)

FACTOR ENDOWMENTS Factor endowments lie at the center of the Heckscher-Ohlin theory. While Porter does not propose anything radically new, he does analyze the characteristics of factors of production. He recognizes hierarchies among factors, distinguishing between *basic factors* (e.g., natural resources, climate, location, and demographics) and *advanced factors* (e.g., communication infrastructure, sophisticated and skilled

Another Perspective

Factor Endowments: A Quiz

One of the most significant factor endowments is the education level. Important measures of education level are the literacy rate and the literacy rate gap between men and women. Which of the following countries or regions has the largest gap between adult male and female literacy rates? *(a)* the Middle East; *(b)* Sub-Saharan Africa, *(c)* Latin America, *(d)* India

The correct answer is not the Middle East, although men there are more likely to be literate than are women. There is a 13-point gap in the Middle East. Nor is it Sub-Saharan Africa, with an 18-point gap and a 59 percent overall rate. Nor is it Latin America, with a 2-point percent gap and an 89 percent overall literacy rate. It is India, with an overall adult literacy rate of 61 percent, yet a 26-point gap between the overall rate and the female rate.

labor, research facilities, and technological know-how). He argues that advanced factors are the most significant for competitive advantage. Unlike the naturally endowed basic factors, advanced factors are a product of investment by individuals, companies, and governments. Thus, government investments in basic and higher education, by improving the general skill and knowledge level of the population and by stimulating advanced research at higher-education institutions, can upgrade a nation's advanced factors.

The relationship between advanced and basic factors is complex. Basic factors can provide an initial advantage that is subsequently reinforced and extended by investment in advanced factors. Conversely, disadvantages in basic factors can create pressures to invest in advanced factors. An obvious example of this phenomenon is Japan, a country that lacks arable land and mineral deposits and yet through investment has built a substantial endowment of advanced factors. Porter notes that Japan's large pool of engineers (reflecting a much higher number of engineering graduates per capita than almost any other nation) has been vital to Japan's success in many manufacturing industries.

DEMAND CONDITIONS Porter emphasizes the role home demand plays in upgrading competitive advantage. Firms are typically most sensitive to the needs of their closest customers. Thus, the characteristics of home demand are particularly important in shaping the attributes of domestically made products and in creating pressures for innovation and quality. Porter argues that a nation's firms gain competitive advantage if their domestic consumers are sophisticated and demanding. Such consumers pressure local firms to meet high standards of product quality and to produce innovative products. Porter notes that Japan's sophisticated and knowledgeable buyers of cameras helped stimulate the Japanese camera industry to improve product quality and to introduce innovative models. A similar example can be found in the wireless telephone equipment industry, in which sophisticated and demanding local customers in Scandinavia helped push Nokia of Finland and Ericsson of Sweden to invest in cellular phone technology long before demand for cellular phones took off in other developed nations. The case of Nokia is reviewed in more depth in the accompanying Management Focus.

RELATED AND SUPPORTING INDUSTRIES The third broad attribute of national advantage in an industry is the presence of suppliers or related industries that are internationally competitive. The benefits of investments in advanced factors of production by related and supporting industries can spill over into an industry, thereby helping it achieve a strong competitive position internationally. Swedish strength in fabricated steel products (e.g., ball bearings and cutting tools) has drawn on strengths in Sweden's specialty steel industry. Technological leadership in the U.S. semiconductor industry provided the basis for U.S. success in personal computers and several other technically advanced electronic products. Similarly, Switzerland's success in pharmaceuticals is closely related to its previous international success in the technologically related dye industry.

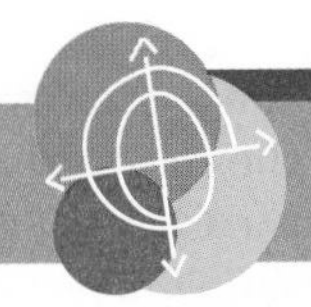

Management FOCUS

The Rise of Finland's Nokia

The wireless phone market is one of the great growth stories of the last decade. Starting from a very low base in 1990, annual global sales of wireless phones surged to reach 780 million units in 2005. By the end of 2005, there were more than 2 billion wireless subscribers worldwide, up from less than 10 million in 1990. Nokia is a dominant player in the market for mobile telephone sales. Nokia's roots are in Finland, not normally a country that comes to mind when one talks about leading-edge technology companies. In the 1980s, Nokia was a rambling Finnish conglomerate with activities that embraced tire manufacturing, paper production, consumer electronics, and telecommunication equipment. By 2005, it had transformed itself into a focused telecommunications equipment manufacturer with a global reach, sales of more than $40 billion, earnings of more than $6 billion, and a 33 percent share of the global market for wireless phones. How has this former conglomerate emerged to take a global leadership position in wireless telecommunication equipment? Much of the answer lies in the history, geography, and political economy of Finland and its Nordic neighbors.

The story starts in 1981 when the Nordic nations got together to create the world's first international wireless telephone network. Sparsely populated and inhospitably cold, they had good reason to become pioneers: It cost far too much to lay down a traditional wire-line telephone service. Yet the same features that made it difficult make telecommunications all the more valuable there: People driving through the Arctic winter and owners of remote northern houses needed a telephone to summon help if things go wrong. As a result, Sweden, Norway, and Finland became the first nations in the world to take wireless telecommunications seriously. They found, for example, that although it cost up to $800 per subscriber to bring a traditional wireline service to remote locations, the same locations could be linked by wireless cellular for only $500 per person. As a consequence, 12 percent of people in Scandinavia owned cellular phones by 1994, compared with less than 6 percent in the United States, the world's second most developed market. This lead continued over the next decade. By the end of 2003, 85 percent of the population in Finland owned a wireless phone, compared with 55 percent in the United States.

Nokia, a longtime telecommunications equipment supplier, was well positioned to take advantage of this development from the start, but there were also other forces at work that helped the company develop its competitive edge. Unlike virtually every other developed nation, Finland has never had a national telephone monopoly. Instead, the country's telephone services have long been provided by about 50 or so autonomous local telephone companies whose elected boards set prices by referendum (which naturally means low prices). This army of independent and cost-conscious telephone service providers prevented Nokia from taking anything for granted in its home country. With typical Finnish pragmatism, its customers were willing to buy from the lowest-cost supplier, whether that was Nokia, Ericsson, Motorola, or some other company. This situation contrasted sharply with that prevailing in most developed nations until the late 1980s and early 1990s, where domestic telephone monopolies typically purchased equipment from a dominant local supplier or made it themselves. Nokia responded to this competitive pressure by doing everything possible to drive down its manufacturing costs while staying at the leading edge of wireless technology.

The consequences of these forces are clear. Nokia is now the leader in digital wireless technology, which is the wave of the future. Many now regard Finland as the lead market for wireless telephone services. If you want to see the future of wireless, you don't go to New York or San Francisco, you go to Helsinki. The Finns were the first to use their wireless handsets not just to talk to each other, but also to browse the Web, execute e-commerce transactions, control household heating and lighting systems, or purchase Coke from wireless-enabled vending machines. Nokia has gained this lead because Scandinavia started switching to digital technology five years before the rest of the world. Spurred on by its cost-conscious Finnish customers, Nokia now has the lowest cost structure of any cellular phone equipment manufacturer in the world.

Source: "Lessons from the Frozen North," *The Economist*, October 8, 1994, pp. 76–77; "A Finnish Fable," *The Economist*, October 14, 2000; M. Newman, "The U.S. Starts to Catch Up," *The Wall Street Journal*, September 23, 2002, p. R6; D. Pringle, "How Nokia Thrives by Breaking the Rules," *The Wall Street Journal*, January 3, 2003, p. A7; M. Hansson, "Nokia Boosts Net, Phone Forecast, but Margins Slip," *The Wall Street Journal*, October 21, 2005, p. B3; and the Nokia Web site, www.nokia.com.

One consequence of this process is that successful industries within a country tend to be grouped into clusters of related industries. This was one of the most pervasive findings of Porter's study. One such cluster Porter identified was in the German textile and apparel sector, which included high-quality cotton, wool, synthetic fibers, sewing machine needles, and a wide range of textile machinery. Such clusters are important, because valuable knowledge can flow between the firms within a geographic cluster, benefiting all within that cluster. Knowledge flows occur when employees move between firms within a region and when national industry associations bring employees from different companies together for regular conferences or workshops.[32]

FIRM STRATEGY, STRUCTURE, AND RIVALRY The fourth broad attribute of national competitive advantage in Porter's model is the strategy, structure, and rivalry of firms within a nation. Porter makes two important points here. First, different nations are characterized by different management ideologies, which either help them or do not help them to build national competitive advantage. For example, Porter noted the predominance of engineers in top management at German and Japanese firms. He attributed this to these firms' emphasis on improving manufacturing processes and product design. In contrast, Porter noted a predominance of people with finance backgrounds leading many U.S. firms. He linked this to U.S. firms' lack of attention to improving manufacturing processes and product design. He argued that the dominance of finance led to an overemphasis on maximizing short-term financial returns. According to Porter, one consequence of these different management ideologies was a relative loss of U.S. competitiveness in those engineering-based industries for which manufacturing processes and product design issues are all-important (e.g., the automobile industry).

Porter's second point is that there is a strong association between vigorous domestic rivalry and the creation and persistence of competitive advantage in an industry. Vigorous domestic rivalry induces firms to look for ways to improve efficiency, which makes them better international competitors. Domestic rivalry creates pressures to innovate, to improve quality, to reduce costs, and to invest in upgrading advanced factors. All this helps to create world-class competitors. Porter cites the case of Japan:

> Nowhere is the role of domestic rivalry more evident than in Japan, where it is all-out warfare in which many companies fail to achieve profitability. With goals that stress market share, Japanese companies engage in a continuing struggle to outdo each other. Shares fluctuate markedly. The process is prominently covered in the business press. Elaborate rankings measure which companies are most popular with university graduates. The rate of new product and process development is breathtaking.[33]

A similar point about the stimulating effects of strong domestic competition can be made with regard to the rise of Nokia of Finland to global preeminence in the market for cellular telephone equipment. For details, see the Management Focus.

LEARNING OBJECTIVE 4
Be familiar with the arguments of those who maintain that government can play a proactive role in promoting national competitive advantage in certain industries.

EVALUATING PORTER'S THEORY Porter contends that the degree to which a nation is likely to achieve international success in a certain industry is a function of the combined impact of factor endowments, domestic demand conditions, related and supporting industries, and domestic rivalry. He argues that the presence of all four components is usually required for this diamond to boost competitive performance (although there are exceptions). Porter also contends that government can influence each of the four components of the diamond, either positively or negatively. Factor endowments can be affected by subsidies, policies toward capital markets, policies toward education, and so on. Government can shape domestic demand through local product standards or with regulations that mandate or influence buyer needs. Government policy can influence supporting and related industries through regulation and influence firm rivalry through such devices as capital market regulation, tax policy, and antitrust laws.

If Porter is correct, we would expect his model to predict the pattern of international trade that we observe in the real world. Countries should be exporting products from those industries where all four components of the diamond are favorable, while importing in those areas where the components are not favorable. Is he correct? We simply do not know. Porter's theory has not been subjected to detailed empirical testing. Much about the theory rings true, but the same can be said for the new trade theory, the theory of comparative advantage, and the Heckscher-Ohlin theory. It may be that each of these theories, which complement each other, explains something about the pattern of international trade.

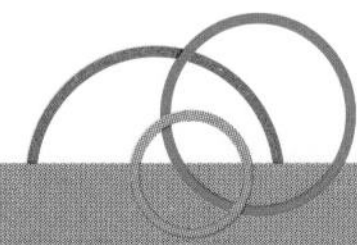

Focus on Managerial Implications

LEARNING OBJECTIVE 5
Understand the important implications that international trade theory holds for business practice.

Why does all this matter for business? There are at least three main implications for international businesses of the material discussed in this chapter: location implications, first-mover implications, and policy implications.

Location

Underlying most of the theories we have discussed is the notion that different countries have particular advantages in different productive activities. Thus, from a profit perspective, it makes sense for a firm to disperse its productive activities to those countries where, according to the theory of international trade, they can be performed most efficiently. If design can be performed most efficiently in France, that is where design facilities should be located; if the manufacture of basic components can be performed most efficiently in Singapore, that is where they should be manufactured; and if final assembly can be performed most efficiently in China, that is where final assembly should be performed. The result is a global web of productive activities, with different activities being performed in different locations around the globe depending on considerations of comparative advantage, factor endowments, and the like. If the firm does not do this, it may find itself at a competitive disadvantage relative to firms that do.

Consider the production of a laptop computer, a process with four major stages: (1) basic research and development of the product design, (2) manufacture of standard electronic components (e.g., memory chips), (3) manufacture of advanced components (e.g., flat-top color display screens and microprocessors), and (4) final assembly. Basic R&D requires a pool of highly skilled and educated workers with good backgrounds in microelectronics. The two countries with a comparative advantage in basic microelectronics R&D and design are Japan and the United States, so most producers of laptop computers locate their R&D facilities in one, or both, of these countries. (Apple, IBM, Motorola, Texas Instruments, Toshiba, and Sony all have major R&D facilities in both Japan and the United States.)

The manufacture of standard electronic components is a capital-intensive process requiring semiskilled labor, and cost pressures are intense. The best locations for such activities today are places such as Taiwan, Malaysia, and South Korea. These countries have pools of relatively skilled, moderate-cost labor. Thus, many producers of laptop computers have standard components, such as memory chips, produced at these locations.

The manufacture of advanced components such as microprocessors is a capital-intensive process requiring skilled labor. Because cost pressures are not so intense at this stage, these components can be, and are, manufactured in countries with high labor costs that also have pools of highly skilled labor (e.g., Japan and the United States).

Finally, assembly is a relatively labor-intensive process requiring only low-skilled labor, and cost pressures are intense. As a result, final assembly may be carried out in a country such as Mexico, which has an abundance of low-cost, low-skilled labor. A laptop computer produced by a U.S. manufacturer may be designed in California, have its standard components produced in Taiwan and Singapore, its advanced components produced in Japan and the United States, its final assembly in Mexico, and be sold in the United States or elsewhere in the world. By dispersing production activities to different locations around the globe, the U.S. manufacturer is taking advantage of the differences between countries identified by the various theories of international trade.

First-Mover Advantages

According to the new trade theory, firms that establish a first-mover advantage with regard to the production of a particular new product may subsequently dominate global trade in that product. This is particularly true in industries for which the global market can profitably support only a limited number of firms, such as the aerospace market; but early commitments also seem to be important in less concentrated industries such as the market for cellular telephone equipment (refer back to the Management Focus on Nokia). For the individual firm, the clear message is that it pays to invest substantial financial resources in trying to build a first-mover, or early-mover, advantage, even if that means several years of losses before a new venture becomes profitable. The idea is to preempt the available demand, gain cost advantages related to volume, build an enduring brand ahead of later competitors, and, consequently, establish a long-term sustainable competitive advantage. Although the details of how to achieve this are beyond the scope of this book, many publications offer strategies for exploiting first-mover advantages and for avoiding the traps associated with pioneering a market (first-mover disadvantages).[34]

Government Policy

The theories of international trade also matter to international businesses because firms are major players on the international trade scene. Business firms produce exports, and business firms import the products of other countries. Because of their pivotal role in international trade, businesses can exert a strong influence on government trade policy, lobbying to promote free trade or trade restrictions. The theories of international trade claim that promoting free trade is generally in the best interests of a country, although it may not always be in the best interest of an individual firm. Many firms recognize this and lobby for open markets.

For example, when the U.S. government announced in 1991 its intention to place a tariff on Japanese imports of liquid crystal display (LCD) screens, IBM and Apple Computer protested strongly. Both IBM and Apple pointed out that (1) Japan was the lowest-cost source of LCD screens, (2) they used these screens in their own laptop computers, and (3) the proposed tariff, by increasing the cost of LCD screens, would increase the cost of laptop computers produced by IBM and Apple, thus making them less competitive in the world market. In other words, the tariff, designed to protect U.S. firms, would be self-defeating. In response to these pressures, the U.S. government reversed its posture.

Unlike IBM and Apple, however, businesses do not always lobby for free trade. In the United States, for example, restrictions on imports of steel are the result of direct pressure by U.S. firms on the government. In some cases, the government has responded to pressure by getting foreign companies to agree to "voluntary" restrictions on their imports, using the implicit threat of more comprehensive formal trade barriers to get them to adhere to these agreements (historically, this has occurred in the automobile industry). In other cases, the government has used what are called "antidumping" actions to justify tariffs on imports from other nations (these mechanisms will be discussed in detail in the next chapter).

As predicted by international trade theory, many of these agreements have been self-defeating, such as the voluntary restriction on machine tool imports agreed to in 1985. As a result of limited import competition from more efficient foreign suppliers, the prices of machine tools in the United States rose to higher levels than would have prevailed under free trade. Because machine tools are used throughout the manufacturing industry, the result was to increase the costs of U.S. manufacturing in general, creating a corresponding loss in world market competitiveness. Shielded from international competition by import barriers, the U.S. machine tool industry had no incentive to increase its efficiency. Consequently, it lost many of its export markets to more efficient foreign competitors. Because of this misguided action, the U.S. machine tool industry shrunk during the period when the agreement was in force. For anyone schooled in international trade theory, this was not surprising.[35] A similar scenario unfolded in the U.S. steel industry, in which tariff barriers erected by the government in 2001 raised the cost of steel to important U.S. users, such as automobile companies and appliance makers, making their products more uncompetitive.

Finally, Porter's theory of national competitive advantage also contains policy implications. Porter's theory suggests that it is in the best interest of business for a firm to invest in upgrading advanced factors of production; for example, to invest in better training for its employees and to increase its commitment to research and development. It is also in the best interests of business to lobby the government to adopt policies that have a favorable impact on each component of the national diamond. Thus, according to Porter, businesses should urge government to increase investment in education, infrastructure, and basic research (since all these enhance advanced factors) and to adopt policies that promote strong competition within domestic markets (since this makes firms stronger international competitors, according to Porter's findings).

Key Terms

free trade, p. 157
mercantilism, p. 159
zero-sum game, p. 160
absolute advantage, p. 161
production possibility frontier (PPF), p. 161
factor endowments, p. 170
economies of scale, p. 175
first-mover advantages, p. 176

Summary

This chapter has reviewed a number of theories that explain why it is beneficial for a country to engage in international trade and has explained the pattern of international trade observed in the world economy. We have seen how the theories of Smith, Ricardo, and Heckscher-Ohlin all make strong cases for unrestricted free trade. In contrast, the mercantilist doctrine and, to a lesser extent, the new trade theory can be interpreted to support government intervention to promote exports through subsidies and to limit imports through tariffs and quotas.

In explaining the pattern of international trade, the second objective of this chapter, we have seen that with the exception of mercantilism, which is silent on this issue, the different theories offer largely complementary explanations. Although no one theory may explain the apparent pattern of international trade, taken together, the theory of comparative advantage, the Heckscher-Ohlin theory, the product life-cycle theory, the new trade theory, and Porter's theory of national competitive advantage do suggest which factors are important. Comparative advantage tells us that productivity differences are important; Heckscher-Ohlin tells us that factor endowments matter; the product life-cycle theory tells us that where a new product is introduced is important; the new trade theory tells us that increasing returns to specialization and first-mover advantages matter; and Porter tells us that all these factors may be important insofar as they impact the four components of the national diamond. The chapter made these major points:

1. Mercantilists argued that it was in a country's best interests to run a balance-of-trade surplus. They viewed trade as a zero-sum game, in which one country's gains cause losses for other countries.
2. The theory of absolute advantage suggests that countries differ in their ability to produce goods efficiently. The theory suggests that a country should specialize in producing goods in areas where it has an absolute advantage and import goods in areas where other countries have absolute advantages.
3. The theory of comparative advantage suggests that it makes sense for a country to specialize in producing those goods that it can produce most efficiently, while buying goods that it can produce relatively less efficiently from other countries—even if that means buying goods from other countries that it could produce more efficiently itself.
4. The theory of comparative advantage suggests that unrestricted free trade brings about increased world production; that is, that trade is a positive-sum game.
5. The theory of comparative advantage also suggests that opening a country to free trade stimulates economic growth, which creates dynamic gains from trade. The empirical evidence seems to be consistent with this claim.
6. The Heckscher-Ohlin theory argues that the pattern of international trade is determined by differences in factor endowments. It predicts that countries will export those goods that make intensive use of locally abundant factors and will import goods that make intensive use of factors that are locally scarce.
7. The product life-cycle theory suggests that trade patterns are influenced by where a new product is introduced. In an increasingly integrated global economy, the product life-cycle theory seems to be less predictive than it once was.
8. New trade theory states that trade allows a nation to specialize in the production of certain goods, attaining scale economies and lowering the costs of producing those goods, while buying goods that it does not produce from other nations that are similarly specialized. By this mechanism, the variety of goods available to consumers in each nation is increased, while the average costs of those goods should fall.
9. New trade theory also states that in those industries where substantial economies of scale imply that the world market will profitably support only a few firms, countries may predominate in the export of certain products simply because they had a firm that was a first mover in that industry.
10. Some new trade theorists have promoted the idea of strategic trade policy. The argument is that government, by the sophisticated and judicious use of subsidies, might be able to increase the chances of domestic firms

becoming first movers in newly emerging industries.

11. Porter's theory of national competitive advantage suggests that the pattern of trade is influenced by four attributes of a nation: (*a*) factor endowments, (*b*) domestic demand conditions, (*c*) relating and supporting industries, and (*d*) firm strategy, structure, and rivalry.
12. Theories of international trade are important to an individual business firm primarily because they can help the firm decide where to locate its various production activities.
13. Firms involved in international trade can and do exert a strong influence on government policy toward trade. By lobbying government, business firms can promote free trade or trade restrictions.

Critical Thinking and Discussion Questions

1. Mercantilism is a bankrupt theory that has no place in the modern world. Discuss.
2. Is free trade fair? Discuss.
3. Unions in developed nations often oppose imports from low-wage countries and advocate trade barriers to protect jobs from what they often characterize as "unfair" import competition. Is such competition unfair? Do you think that this argument is in the best interests of (*a*) the unions, (*b*) the people they represent, or (*c*) the country as a whole?
4. What are the potential costs of adopting a free trade regime? Do you think governments should do anything to reduce these costs? What?
5. Reread the Country Focus feature on outsourcing service jobs. Is there a difference between the transference of high-paying white-collar jobs, such as computer programming and accounting, to developing nations, and low-paying blue-collar jobs? If so, what is the difference, and should government do anything to stop the flow of white-collar jobs out of the country to countries like India?
6. Drawing upon the new trade theory and Porter's theory of national competitive advantage, outline the case for government policies that would build national competitive advantage in biotechnology. What kinds of policies would you recommend that the government adopt? Are these policies at variance with the basic free trade philosophy?
7. The world's poorest countries are at a competitive disadvantage in every sector of their economies. They have little to export. They have no capital; their land is of poor quality; they often have too many people given available work opportunities; and they are poorly educated. Free trade cannot possibly be in the interests of such nations. Discuss.

http://globalEDGE.msu.edu globalEDGE Research Task

Use the globalEDGE site (http://globalEDGE.msu.edu/) to complete the following exercises:

1. Since you work for a rice production company, your current project is to determine the ten countries which—in your estimation—should have an advantage in producing rice. Using a resource that tracks *statistics on economic factors* like worldwide rice production, develop a list and brief report about the top 10 rice producing countries with data from the most recent year. Were you surprised by any countries listed? Why (or, why not)?
2. Your firm is looking to find new sources of coffee to sustain growth as it internationalizes. Currently, your company only purchases green coffee beans from South America and is hoping to begin purchasing coffee from the Central American countries of Costa Rica, El Salvador, Guatemala, Honduras, and Panama. Applying the most current information from *FAOSTAT*, a United Nations agency website that gathers data on food and agricultural trade flows, determine which three countries have the highest export value of green coffee. Prepare a brief report outlining your reason(s) for choosing these three countries.

Logitech

Best known as one of the world's largest producers of computer mice, Logitech is in many ways the epitome of the modern global corporation. Founded in 1981 in Apples, Switzerland, by two Italians and a Swiss, the company now generates annual sales of more than $1.5 billion, most from products such as mice, keyboards, and low-cost videocams that cost under $100. Logitech made its name as a technological innovator in the highly competitive business of personal computer peripherals. It was the first company to introduce a mouse that used infrared tracking, rather than a tracking ball, and the first to introduce wireless mice and keyboards. Logitech is differentiated from competitors by its continuing innovation, high brand recognition, and strong retail presence. Less obvious to consumers, but equally important, has been the way the company has configured its global value chain to lower production costs while maintaining the value of those assets that lead to differentiation.

Nowadays, Logitech still undertakes basic R&D work (primarily software programming) in Switzerland, where it has 200 employees. Indeed, the company is still legally Swiss, but the corporate headquarters are in Fremont, California, close to many of America's high-technology enterprises, where it has 450 employees. Some R&D work (again, primarily software programming) is also carried out in Fremont. Most significant though, Fremont is the headquarters for the company's global marketing, finance, and logistics operations. The ergonomic design of Logitech's products–their look and feel–is done in Ireland by an outside design firm. Most of Logitech's products are manufactured in Asia.

Logitech's expansion into Asian manufacturing began in the late 1980s when it opened a factory in Taiwan. At the time, most of its mice were produced in the United States. Logitech was trying to win two of the most prestigious OEM customers, Apple Computer and IBM. Both bought their mice from Alps, a large Japanese firm that supplied Microsoft. To attract discerning customers like Apple, Logitech not only needed the capacity to produce at high volume and low cost, it also had to offer a better-designed product. The solution: manufacture in Taiwan. Cost was a factor in the decision, but it was not as significant as might be expected, since direct labor accounted for only 7 percent of the cost of Logitech's mouse. Taiwan offered a well-developed supply base for parts, qualified people, and a rapidly expanding local computer industry. As an inducement to fledgling innovators, Taiwan provided space in its science-based industrial park in Hsinchu for the modest fee of $200,000. Sizing this up as a deal that was too good to pass up, Logitech signed the lease. Shortly afterward, Logitech won the OEM contract with Apple. The Taiwanese factory was soon outproducing Logitech's U.S. facility. After the Apple contract, Logitech began serving its other OEM business from Taiwan; the plant's total capacity increased to 10 million mice per year.

By the late 1990s, Logitech needed more production capacity. This time it turned to China. A wide variety of the company's retail products are now made there. Take one of Logitech's biggest sellers, a wireless infrared mouse called Wanda. The mouse itself is assembled in Suzhou, China, in a factory that Logitech owns. The factory employs 4,000 people, mostly young women such as Wang Yan, an 18-year-old employee from the impoverished rural province of Anhui. She is paid $75 a month to sit all day at a conveyer belt plugging three tiny bits of metal into circuit boards. She does this about 2,000 times each day. The mouse Wang Yan helps assemble sells to American consumers for about $40. Of this, Logitech takes about $8, which is used to fund R&D, marketing, and corporate overhead; what remains of that $8 after the corporate expenses is the profit due to Logitech's shareholders. Distributors and retailers around the world take a further $15. Another $14 goes to the suppliers who make Wanda's parts. For example, a Motorola plant in Malaysia makes the mouse's chips, and another American company, Agilent Technologies, supplies the optical sensors from a plant in the Philippines. That leaves just $3 for the Chinese factory, which is used to cover wages, power, transportation, and other overhead costs.

Logitech is not alone in exploiting China to manufacture products. According to China's ministry of commerce, foreign companies account for three-quarters of China's high-tech exports. China's top 10 exporters include American companies with Chinese operations, such as Motorola and Seagate technologies, a maker of disk drives for computers. Intel now produces some 50 million chips a year in China, the majority of which end up in computers and other goods that are exported to other parts of Asia or back to the United States. Yet Intel's plant in Shanghai doesn't really make chips, it tests and assembles chips from silicon wafers made in Intel plants abroad, mostly in the United States. China adds less than 5 percent of the value. The U.S. operations of Intel generate the bulk of the value and profits.

Sources: V.K. Jolly and K.A. Bechler, "Logitech: The Mouse That Roared," *Planning Review* 20, no. 6 (1992), pp. 20–34; K. Guerrino, "Lord of the Mice," *Chief Executive* 190 (July 2003), pp. 42–44; A. Higgins. "As China Surges, It Also Proves a Buttress to American Strength," *The Wall Street Journal,* January 30, 2004, pp. A1, A8; and J. Fox, "Where Is Your Job Going," *Fortune,* November 24, 2003, pp. 84–88.

Case Discussion Questions

1. In a world without trade, what would happen to the costs that American consumers would have to pay for Logitech's products?
2. Explain how trade lowers the costs of making computer peripherals such as mice and keyboards?
3. Use the theory of comparative advantage to explain the way in which Logitech has configured its global operations. Why does the company manufacture in China and Taiwan, undertake basic R&D in California and Switzerland, design products in Ireland, and coordinate marketing and operations from California?
4. Who creates more value for Logitech, the 650 people it employs in Fremont and Switzerland, or the 4,000 employees at its Chinese factory? What are the implications of this observation for the argument that free trade is beneficial?
5. Why do you think the company decided to shift its corporate headquarters from Switzerland to Fremont?
6. To what extent can Porter's diamond help explain the choice of Taiwan as a major manufacturing site for Logitech?
7. Why do you think China is now a favored location for so much high-technology manufacturing activity? How will China's increasing involvement in global trade help that country? How will it help the world's developed economies? What potential problems are associated with moving work to China?

Jack Dabaghian/Reuters/Corbis

part 3 Cross-Border Trade and Investment

LEARNING OBJECTIVES

1. Describe the policy instruments used by governments to influence international trade flows.
2. Understand why governments sometimes intervene in international trade.
3. Articulate the arguments against strategic trade policy.
4. Describe the development of the world trading system and the current trade issues.
5. Explain the implications for managers of developments in the world trading system.

chapter

The Political Economy of International Trade

Boeing, Airbus, and the World Trade Organization

opening case

In December 2003, Boeing announced it would go ahead with the development of its latest commercial jetliner, the 787, which will be positioned against Airbus's popular A330. Built out of new ultralight composite materials and using new engine technology, Boeing hopes to reduce the 787's operating costs by as much as 20 percent compared to a traditional design. If it is successful, this will make the plane a potent competitor against the best-selling A330.

The 787 is a risky project for Boeing. The aircraft will cost about $7 billion to develop, according to industry estimates, and demand is uncertain. To share the costs and risks of development, Boeing has taken on several partners. Most important among these are a trio of three Japanese companies—Mitsubishi Heavy Industries, Kawasaki Heavy Industries, and Fuji Heavy Industries—which will build as much as 35 percent of the 787 by value, including parts of the fuselage, wings, and landing gear. They will ship the finished components to Everett, Washington, for final assembly. The three companies are longtime Boeing partners. They contributed about 21 percent by value to the Boeing's 777.

Although there has been a long history of development subsidies in the commercial aerospace industry, a 1992 agreement between Boeing and Airbus limits the state aid either company can get from their respective governments. Airbus, now a private company, is limited to repayable launch aid that must not exceed one-third of the development costs of a new aircraft. The launch aid has to be repaid only if aircraft sales are high enough for Airbus to turn a profit on the investment in a new plane. As for Boeing, indirect aid from U.S. government agencies such as R&D contracts from the Pentagon and NASA are capped at 4 percent of its total revenues.

It is unclear if the 1992 agreement extends to other parties in the projects. The Japanese Aircraft Development Corporation, an association of Japanese aircraft makers, has asked the Japanese government for help with the 787 project. The country's Ministry of Economy, Trade, and Industry has submitted a budget request that would make the 787 a "national project." Newspaper reports put the request at about $1.6 billion.

Upon hearing this, Airbus officials were quick to claim that the arrangement could violate several international agreements, including a 1994 WTO prohibition against subsidies that can harm competitors. Behind the scenes, Airbus executives started to urge the European Union to look at the issue and possibly file a case on their behalf. They also noted that Boeing received aid from the states of Washington and Kansas, where its factories are located, an action that constituted an unfair subsidy that was outside the scope of the 1992 agreement.

In mid-2004, the issue became even more contentious when the U.S. government demanded an end to Airbus's launch aid. Airbus had already been granted loans of $3.7 billion to develop its latest aircraft, the A380 super-jumbo, but what really got attention in America were signs from Airbus that it would also build a direct competitor to the 787, the A350, and ask for launch aid to help cover the development costs of that plane. Estimates suggested the launch aid for the A350 could total $1.75 billion. Furthermore, in 2004 Airbus surpassed Boeing in global market share. American officials felt that given the strength of the company, subsidies were no longer appropriate. In late 2004, the EU and U.S. government entered into negotiations to try to resolve the dispute, but talks ended with no agreement, and in July 2005 the dispute went to the World Trade Organization, which must rule on the legality of the various subsidies. A ruling is not expected until 2007. Meanwhile, Boeing is starting to pile up orders for the 787, which by May 2006 totaled 349 aircraft.

Sources: D. Michaels and J. L. Lunsford, "Airbus Contends That Boeing's Plan to Fund Plane Breaks Trade Rules," *The Wall Street Journal,* December 11, 2003, p. A3; M. Mecham, "Overseas Shipments Alenia and the Japanese Heavies Will Play Major Roles in the Design and Manufacture of the 7E7's Structure," *Aviation Week,* November 24, 2003, p. 36–37; M. Lander, "A Dogfight between Jetliners," *The New York Times,* April 13, 2005, pp. C1, 18; and E. Alden and F. Williams, "U.S. and EU Ramp up Dispute over Aircraft Subsidies," *Financial Times,* February 3, 2006, p. 8.

Introduction

Free Trade
The absence of barriers to the free flow of goods and services between countries.

Our review of the classical trade theories of Smith, Ricardo, and Heckscher-Ohlin in Chapter 5 showed us that in a world without trade barriers, trade patterns are determined by the relative productivity of different factors of production in different countries. Countries will specialize in products that they can make most efficiently, while importing products that they can produce less efficiently. Chapter 5 also laid out the intellectual case for free trade. Remember, **free trade** refers to a situation in which a government does not attempt to restrict what its citizens can buy from or sell to another country. As we saw in Chapter 5, the theories of Smith, Ricardo, and

Heckscher-Ohlin predict that the consequences of free trade include both static economic gains (because free trade supports a higher level of domestic consumption and more efficient utilization of resources) and dynamic economic gains (because free trade stimulates economic growth and the creation of wealth).

Another Perspective

Rankings of the World Economic Forum (WEF)
The WEF is an independent economic organization whose mission is to improve the state of the world. It holds an annual meeting and regional meetings as well, which serve international leaders as a forum for collaboration. The WEF annual report contains country competitiveness rankings. In the latest report (2005–06), the top countries in competitiveness were Finland, the United States, and Sweden, followed by Denmark, Taiwan, and Singapore. If you visit the report site (www.weforum.org) and look at the complete list of rankings, you'll note a strong correlation between a country's ranking and its political system.

In this chapter, we look at the political reality of international trade. Although many nations are nominally committed to free trade, they tend to intervene in international trade to protect the interests of politically important groups or promote the interests of key domestic producers. The opening case illustrates the nature of such political realities. To try and establish Airbus as a global competitor against Boeing, the four original government backers of Airbus (France, Germany, the United Kingdom, and Spain) have invested some $15 billion in subsidies since the aircraft maker was first established in 1970. For years, Boeing complained that this gave Airbus an unfair advantage. In 1992, both sides agreed to limit future subsidies, but the issue will not go away. Airbus now claims that Boeing is receiving subsidies to build its 787 jetliners, and Boeing has countered that Airbus is counting on subsidies to reduce the launch costs of its latest offering, the A350. Having failed to negotiate an agreement to limit subsidies, in 2005 both the United States and the European Union referred their complaints to the World Trade Organization, which must now rule on the issue.

In this chapter, we explore the political and economic reasons that governments have for intervening in international trade. When governments intervene, they often do so by restricting imports of goods and services into their nation, while adopting policies that promote exports (the subsidies given to Airbus can be seen as an export promotion strategy). Normally their motives are to protect domestic producers and jobs from foreign competition while increasing the foreign market for products of domestic producers. However, in recent years, social issues have intruded into the decision-making calculus. In the United States, for example, a movement is growing to ban imports of goods from countries that do not abide by the same labor, health, and environmental regulations as the United States.

We start this chapter by describing the range of policy instruments that governments use to intervene in international trade. This is followed by a detailed review of the various political and economic motives that governments have for intervention. In the third section of this chapter, we consider how the case for free trade stands up in view of the various justifications given for government intervention in international trade. Then we look at the emergence of the modern international trading system, which is based on the General Agreement on Tariffs and Trade and its successor, the WTO. The GATT and WTO are the creations of a series of multinational treaties. The most recent was completed in 1995, involved more than 120 countries, and resulted in the creation of the WTO. The purpose of these treaties has been to lower barriers to the free flow of goods and services between nations. Like the GATT before it, the WTO promotes free trade by limiting the ability of national governments to adopt policies that restrict imports into their nations. In the final section of this chapter, we discuss the implications of this material for management practice.

Instruments of Trade Policy

LEARNING OBJECTIVE 1
Describe the policy instruments used by governments to influence international trade flows.

Trade policy uses seven main instruments: tariffs, subsidies, import quotas, voluntary export restraints, local content requirements, administrative policies, and antidumping duties. Tariffs are the oldest and simplest instrument of trade policy. As we shall see later in this chapter, they are also the instrument that the GATT and WTO have been most successful in limiting. A fall in tariff barriers in recent decades has been accompanied by a rise in nontariff barriers, such as subsidies, quotas, voluntary export restraints, and antidumping duties.

Tariff
A tax levied by governments on imports or exports.

Specific Tariff
Levied as a fixed charge for each unit of good imported.

Ad Valorem Tariff
Levied as a proportion of the value of the imported good.

TARIFFS A **tariff** is a tax levied on imports (or exports). Tariffs fall into two categories. **Specific tariffs** are levied as a fixed charge for each unit of a good imported (for example, $3 per barrel of oil). **Ad valorem tariffs** are levied as a proportion of the value of the imported good. In most cases, tariffs are placed on imports to protect domestic producers from foreign competition by raising the price of imported goods. However, tariffs also produce revenue for the government. Until the income tax was introduced, for example, the U.S. government received most of its revenues from tariffs.

The important thing to understand about an import tariff is who suffers and who gains. The government gains, because the tariff increases government revenues. Domestic producers gain, because the tariff affords them some protection against foreign competitors by increasing the cost of imported foreign goods. Consumers lose because they must pay more for certain imports. For example, in March 2002 the U.S. government placed an ad valorem tariff of 8 percent to 30 percent on imports of foreign steel. The idea was to protect domestic steel producers from cheap imports of foreign steel. The effect, however, was to raise the price of steel products in the United States by between 30 and 50 percent. A number of U.S. steel consumers, ranging from appliance makers to automobile companies, objected that the steel tariffs would raise their costs of production and make it more difficult for them to compete in the global marketplace. Whether the gains to the government and domestic producers exceed the loss to consumers depends on various factors such as the amount of the tariff, the importance of the imported good to domestic consumers, the number of jobs saved in the protected industry, and so on. In the steel case, many argued that the losses to steel consumers apparently outweighed the gains to steel producers. In November 2003, the World Trade Organization declared that the tariffs represented a violation of the WTO treaty, and the United States removed them in December of that year.

In general, two conclusions can be derived from economic analysis of the effect of import tariffs.[1] First, tariffs are unambiguously pro-producer and anti-consumer. While they protect producers from foreign competitors, this restriction of supply also raises domestic prices. For example, a study by Japanese economists calculated that tariffs on imports of foodstuffs, cosmetics, and chemicals into Japan in 1989 cost the average Japanese consumer about $890 per year in the form of higher prices.[2] Almost all studies find that import tariffs impose significant costs on domestic consumers in the form of higher prices.[3]

Second, import tariffs reduce the overall efficiency of the world economy. They reduce efficiency because a protective tariff encourages domestic firms to produce products at home that, in theory, could be produced more efficiently abroad. The consequence is an inefficient utilization of resources. For example, tariffs on the importation of rice into South Korea have led to an increase in rice production in that country; however, rice farming is an unproductive use of land in South Korea. It would make more sense for the South Koreans to purchase their rice from lower-cost foreign producers and to utilize the land now employed in rice production in some other way, such as growing foodstuffs that cannot be produced more efficiently elsewhere or for residential and industrial purposes.

Sometimes tariffs are levied on exports of a product from a country. Export tariffs are far less common than import tariffs. In general, export tariffs have two objectives: first, to raise revenue for the government, and second, to reduce exports from a sector, often for political reasons. For example, in 2004 China imposed a tariff on textile exports. The primary objective was to moderate the growth in exports of textiles from China, thereby alleviating tensions with other trading partners.

Another Perspective

U.S. Tariff Rates

Because the U.S. takes a free trade public position, many people assume that the U.S. government has few tariffs. Information about U.S. trade is readily available online. For example, you can review the U.S. government's current tariffs at the U.S. Office of Tariff Affairs and Trade Agreements (www.usitc.gov/tata/index.htm). However, with many schedules and fine distinctions among similar items made, this is not good browsing territory for most people. Check out the Center for Trade Policy Studies for interesting summaries at www.freetrade.org. The U.S. footwear tariff is around 10 percent. Clothing is around 11 percent, while the truck tariff (called the chicken tax in reference to a trade dispute over U.S. chicken exports) is 25 percent. The average applied tariff rate in 2005 was only 1.4 percent, but some tariffs on necessities are quite high.

SUBSIDIES A **subsidy** is a government payment to a domestic producer. Subsidies take many forms, including cash grants, low-interest loans, tax breaks, and government equity participation in domestic firms. By lowering production costs, subsidies help domestic producers in two ways: (1) competing against foreign imports and (2) gaining export markets.

Subsidy
Government financial assistance to a domestic producer.

Agriculture tends to be one of the largest beneficiaries of subsidies in most countries. In 2002, the European Union was paying $43 billion annually in farm subsidies. Not to be outdone, in May 2002 President George W. Bush signed into law a bill that contained subsidies of more than $180 billion for U.S. farmers spread out over 10 years. The Japanese have a long history of supporting inefficient domestic producers with farm subsidies. See the accompanying Country Focus on the next page for a look at subsidies to wheat producers in Japan.

Nonagricultural subsidies are much lower, but they are still significant. As noted in the opening case, subsidies historically were given to Boeing and Airbus to help them lower the cost of developing new commercial jet aircraft. In Boeing's case, subsides came in the form of tax credits for R&D spending or Pentagon money that was used to develop military technology, which then was transferred to civil aviation projects. In the case of Airbus, subsidies took the form of government loans at below-market interest rates.

The main gains from subsidies accrue to domestic producers, whose international competitiveness is increased as a result. Advocates of strategic trade policy (which, as you will recall from Chapter 5, is an outgrowth of the new trade theory) favor subsidies to help domestic firms achieve a dominant position in those industries in which economies of scale are important and the world market is not large enough to profitably support more than a few firms (e.g., aerospace, semiconductors). According to this argument, subsidies can help a firm achieve a first-mover advantage in an emerging industry (just as U.S. government subsidies, in the form of substantial R&D grants, allegedly helped Boeing). If this is achieved, further gains to the domestic economy arise from the employment and tax revenues that a major global company can generate. However, government subsidies must be paid for, typically by taxing individuals.

Whether subsidies generate national benefits that exceed their national costs is debatable. In practice, many subsidies are not that successful at increasing the international competitiveness of domestic producers. Rather, they tend to protect the inefficient and promote excess production. For example, agricultural subsidies (1) allow inefficient farmers to stay in business, (2) encourage countries

Country FOCUS

Subsidized Wheat Production in Japan

Japan is not a particularly good environment for growing wheat. Wheat produced on large fields in the dry climates of North America, Australia, and Argentina is far cheaper and of much higher quality than anything produced in Japan. Indeed, Japan imports some 80 percent of its wheat from foreign producers. Yet tens of thousands of farmers in Japan still grow wheat, usually on small fields where yields are low and costs high, and production is rising. The reason is government subsidies designed to keep inefficient Japanese wheat producers in business. In 2004, Japanese farmers were selling their output at market prices, which were running at $9 per bushel, but they received an average of at least $35 per bushel for their 2004 production! The difference—$26 a bushel—was government subsidies paid to producers. The estimated costs of these subsidies were more than $700 million in 2004.

To finance its production subsidy, Japan operates a tariff rate quota on wheat imports in which a higher tariff rate is imposed once wheat imports exceed the quota level. The in-quota rate tariff is zero, while the over-quota tariff rate for wheat is $500 a ton. The tariff raises the cost so much that it deters over-quota imports, essentially restricting supply and raising the price for wheat inside Japan. The Japanese Ministry of Agriculture, Forestry and Fisheries (MAFF) has the sole right to purchase wheat imports within the quota (and since there are very few over-quota imports, the MAFF is a monopoly buyer on wheat imports into Japan). The MAFF buys wheat at world prices then resells it to millers in Japan at the artificially high prices that arise due to the restriction on supply engineered by the tariff rate quota. Estimates suggest that in 2003, the world market price for wheat was $5.96 per bushel, but within Japan the average price for imported wheat was $10.23 a bushel. The markup of $4.27 a bushel yielded the MAFF in excess of $450 million in profit. This "profit" was then used to help cover the $700 million cost of subsidies to inefficient wheat farmers, with the rest of the funds coming from general government tax revenues.

Thanks to these policies, the price of wheat in Japan can be anything from 80 to 120 percent higher than the world price, and Japanese wheat production, which exceeded 850,000 tons in 2004, is significantly greater than it would be if a free market was allowed to operate. Indeed, under free market conditions, there would be virtually no wheat production in Japan since the costs of production are simply too high. The beneficiaries of this policy are the thousands of small farmers in Japan who grow wheat. The losers include Japanese consumers, who must pay more for products containing wheat and who must finance wheat subsidies through taxes, and foreign producers, who are denied access to a chunk of the Japanese market by the over-quota tariff rate. Why then does the Japanese government continue to pursue this policy? It continues because small farmers are an important constituency and Japanese politicians want their votes.

Sources: J. Dyck and H. Fukuda, "Taxes on Imports Subsidize Wheat Production in Japan," *Amber Waves*, February 2005, p. 2; and H. Fukuda, J. Dyck, and J. Stout, "Wheat and Barley Policies in Japan," U.S. Department of Agriculture research report, WHS-04i-01, November 2004.

to overproduce heavily subsidized agricultural products, (3) encourage countries to produce products that could be grown more cheaply elsewhere and imported, and therefore (4) reduce international trade in agricultural products. One study estimated that if advanced countries abandoned subsidies to farmers, global trade in agricultural products would be 50 percent higher and the world as a whole would be better off by $160 billion.[4] This increase in wealth arises from the more efficient use of agricultural land. For a specific example, see the Country Focus on wheat subsidies in Japan.

Import Quota
A direct restriction on the quantity of some good that can be imported into a country.

IMPORT QUOTAS AND VOLUNTARY EXPORT RESTRAINTS An **import quota** is a direct restriction on the quantity of some good that may be imported into a country. The restriction is usually enforced by issuing import licenses to a group of individuals or firms. For example, the United States has a quota on cheese imports. The only firms allowed to import cheese are certain trading companies, each

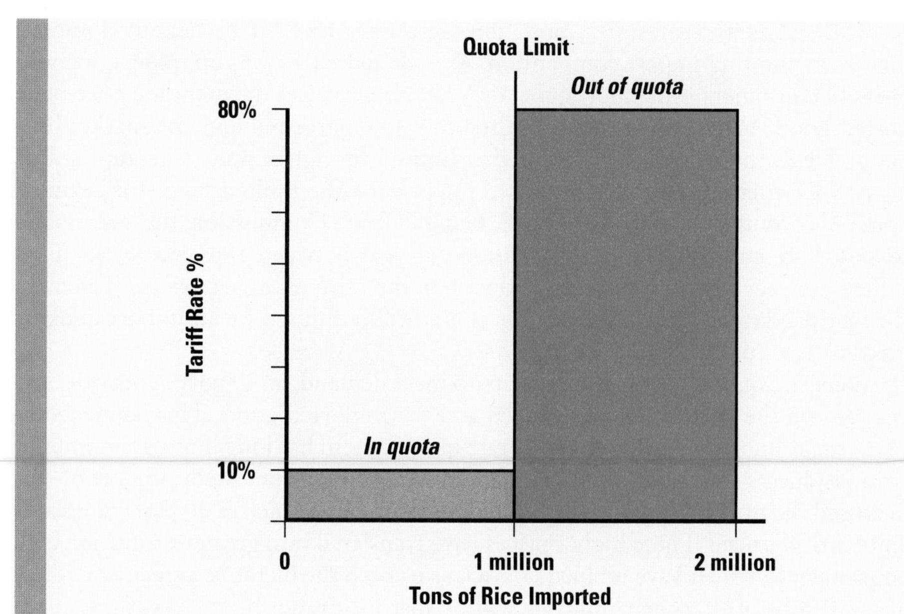

figure 6.1

Hypothetical Tariff Rate Quota

of which is allocated the right to import a maximum number of pounds of cheese each year. In some cases, the right to sell is given directly to the governments of exporting countries. Historically this is the case for sugar and textile imports in the United States. As discussed in the closing case, however, the international agreement governing the imposition of import quotas on textiles, the Multi-Fiber Agreement, expired in December 2004.

A common hybrid of a quota and a tariff is known as a tariff rate quota. Under a **tariff rate quota,** a lower tariff rate is applied to imports within the quota than those over the quota. For example, as illustrated in Figure 6.1, an ad valorem tariff rate of 10 percent might be levied on rice imports into South Korea of 1 million tons, after which an out-of-quota rate of 80 percent might be applied. Thus, South Korea might import 2 million tons of rice, 1 million at a 10 percent tariff rate and another 1 million at an 80 percent tariff. Tariff rate quotas are common in agriculture, where their goal is to limit imports over quota. An example is given in the Country Focus that looks at how Japan uses the combination of a tariff rate quota and subsidies to protect inefficient Japanese wheat farmers from foreign competition.

Tariff Rate Quota
The process of applying a lower tariff rate to imports within the import quota than those over the quota.

A variant on the import quota is the voluntary export restraint. A **voluntary export restraint (VER)** is a quota on trade imposed by the exporting country, typically at the request of the importing country's government. One of the most famous examples is the limitation on auto exports to the United States enforced by Japanese automobile producers in 1981. A response to direct pressure from the U.S. government, this VER limited Japanese imports to no more than 1.68 million vehicles per year. The agreement was revised in 1984 to allow 1.85 million Japanese vehicles per year. The agreement was allowed to lapse in 1985, but the Japanese government indicated its intentions at that time to continue to restrict exports to the United States to 1.85 million vehicles per year.[5] Foreign producers agree to VERs because they fear more damaging punitive tariffs or import quotas might follow if they do not. Agreeing to a VER is seen as a way to make the best of a bad situation by appeasing protectionist pressures in a country.

Voluntary Export Restraint (VER)
A quota on trade imposed by the exporting country, typically at the request of the importing country's government.

As with tariffs and subsidies, both import quotas and VERs benefit domestic producers by limiting import competition. As with all restrictions on trade, quotas do not benefit consumers. An import quota or VER always raises the domestic price of an imported good. When imports are limited to a low percentage of the market by a quota or VER, the price is bid up for that limited foreign supply. The automobile industry VER mentioned above increased the price of the limited supply of Japanese imports. According to a study by the U.S. Federal Trade Commission, the automobile VER cost U.S. consumers about $1 billion per year between 1981 and 1985. That $1 billion per year went to Japanese producers in the form of higher prices.[6] The extra profit that producers make when supply is artificially limited by an import quota is referred to as a **quota rent.**

Quota Rent
The extra profit producers make when supply is artificially limited by an import quota.

If a domestic industry lacks the capacity to meet demand, an import quota can raise prices for *both* the domestically produced and the imported good. This happened in the U.S. sugar industry, in which a tariff rate quota system has long limited the amount foreign producers can sell in the U.S. market. According to one study, import quotas have caused the price of sugar in the United States to be as much as 40 percent greater than the world price.[7] These higher prices have translated into greater profits for U.S. sugar producers, which have lobbied politicians to keep the lucrative agreement. They argue U.S. jobs in the sugar industry will be lost to foreign producers if the quota system is scrapped.

Local Content Requirement
A requirement that some specific fraction of a good be produced domestically.

LOCAL CONTENT REQUIREMENTS A **local content requirement** is a requirement that some specific fraction of a good be produced domestically. The requirement can be expressed either in physical terms (e.g., 75 percent of component parts for this product must be produced locally) or in value terms (e.g., 75 percent of the value of this product must be produced locally). Local content regulations have been widely used by developing countries to shift their manufacturing base from the simple assembly of products whose parts are manufactured elsewhere into the local manufacture of component parts. They have also been used in developed countries to try to protect local jobs and industry from foreign competition. For example, a little-known law in the United States, the Buy America Act, specifies that government agencies must give preference to American products when putting contracts for equipment out to bid unless the foreign products have a significant price advantage. The law specifies a product as "American" if 51 percent of the materials by value are produced domestically. This amounts to a local content requirement. If a foreign company, or an American one for that matter, wishes to win a contract from a U.S. government agency to provide some equipment, it must ensure that at least 51 percent of the product by value is manufactured in the United States.

Local content regulations provide protection for a domestic producer of parts in the same way an import quota does: by limiting foreign competition. The aggregate economic effects are also the same; domestic producers benefit, but the restrictions on imports raise the prices of imported components. In turn, higher prices for imported components are passed on to consumers of the final product in the form of higher final prices. So as with all trade policies, local content regulations tend to benefit producers and not consumers.

Administrative Trade Policies
Rules adopted by governments that can be used to restrict imports or boost exports.

ADMINISTRATIVE POLICIES In addition to the formal instruments of trade policy, governments of all types sometimes use informal or administrative policies to restrict imports and boost exports. **Administrative trade policies** are bureaucratic rules designed to make it difficult for imports to enter a country. Some would argue that the Japanese are the masters of this trade barrier. In recent years, Japan's formal tariff and nontariff barriers have been among the lowest in the world. However, critics charge that the country's informal administrative barriers to imports more than compensate for this. For example, the Netherlands exports tulip bulbs to almost every country in the world except Japan. In Japan, customs inspectors insist on checking every tulip bulb by cutting it vertically down the middle, and even Japanese ingenuity cannot put them back together. Federal Express has had a tough time expanding its global express shipping services into Japan because Japanese customs inspectors insist on opening a large proportion of express packages to check for pornography, a process that can delay an "express" package for days. Japan is not the only country that engages in such policies. France once required that all imported videotape recorders arrive through a small customs entry point that was both remote and poorly staffed. The resulting delays kept Japanese VCRs out of the French market until a VER agreement was negotiated.[8] As with all instruments of trade policy, administrative instruments benefit producers and hurt consumers, who are denied access to possibly superior foreign products.

ANTIDUMPING POLICIES In the context of international trade, **dumping** is variously defined as selling goods in a foreign market at below their costs of production or as selling goods in a foreign market at below their "fair" market value. There is a difference between these two definitions; the fair market value of a good is normally judged to be greater than the costs of producing that good because the former includes a "fair" profit margin. Dumping is viewed as a method by which firms unload excess production in foreign markets. Some dumping may be the result of predatory behavior, with producers using substantial profits from their home markets to subsidize prices in a foreign market with a view to driving indigenous competitors out of that market. Once this has been achieved, so the argument goes, the predatory firm can raise prices and earn substantial profits.

Dumping
Selling goods in a foreign market for less than their cost of production or below their fair market value.

An alleged example of dumping occurred in 1997, when two South Korean manufacturers of semiconductors, LG Semicon and Hyundai Electronics, were accused of selling dynamic random access memory chips (DRAMs) in the U.S. market at below their costs of production. This action occurred in the middle of a worldwide glut of chip-making capacity. It was alleged that the firms were trying to unload their excess production in the United States.

Antidumping policies are designed to punish foreign firms that engage in dumping. The ultimate objective is to protect domestic producers from unfair foreign competition. Although antidumping policies vary somewhat from country to country, the majority are similar to those used in the United States. If a domestic producer believes that a foreign firm is dumping production in the U.S. market, it can file a petition with two government agencies, the Commerce Department and the International Trade Commission. In the Korean DRAM case, Micron Technology, a U.S. manufacturer of DRAMs, filed the petition. The government agencies then investigate the complaint. If a complaint has merit, the Commerce Department may impose an antidumping duty on the offending foreign imports (antidumping duties are often called **countervailing duties**). These duties, which represent a special tariff, can be fairly substantial and stay in place for up to five years. For example, after reviewing Micron's complaint, the Commerce Department imposed 9 percent and 4 percent countervailing duties on LG Semicon and Hyundai DRAM chips, respectively. The Management Focus box, next page, discusses another example of how a firm, U.S. Magnesium, used antidumping legislation to gain protection from unfair foreign competitors.

Antidumping Policies
Rules designed to punish foreign firms that engage in dumping and thus protect domestic producers from unfair foreign competition.

Countervailing Duties
Antidumping duties.

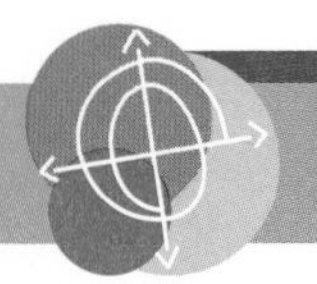

Management FOCUS

U.S. Magnesium Seeks Protection

In February 2004, U.S. Magnesium, the sole surviving U.S. producer of magnesium, a metal that is primarily used in the manufacture of certain automobile parts and aluminum cans, filed a petition with the U.S. International Trade Commission (ITC) contending that a surge in imports had caused material damage to the U.S. industry's employment, sales, market share, and profitability. According to U.S. Magnesium, Russian and Chinese producers had been selling the metal at prices significantly below market value. During 2002 and 2003, imports of magnesium into the United States rose 70 percent, while prices fell by 40 percent and the market share accounted for by imports jumped to 50 percent from 25 percent.

"The United States used to be the largest producer of magnesium in the world," a U.S. Magnesium spokesman said at the time of the filing. "What's really sad is that you can be state of the art and have modern technology, and if the Chinese, who pay people less than 90 cents an hour, want to run you out of business, they can do it. And that's why we are seeking relief."

During a yearlong investigation, the ITC solicited input from various sides in the dispute. Foreign producers and consumers of magnesium in the United States argued that falling prices for magnesium during 2002 and 2003 simply reflected an imbalance between supply and demand due to additional capacity coming on stream not from Russia or China but from a new Canadian plant that opened in 2001 and from a planned Australian plant. The Canadian plant shut down in 2003, the Australian plant never came on stream, and prices for magnesium rose again in 2004.

Magnesium consumers in the United States also argued to the ITC that imposing antidumping duties on foreign imports of magnesium would raise prices in the United States significantly above world levels. A spokesman for Alcoa, which mixes magnesium with aluminum to make alloys for cans, predicted that if antidumping duties were imposed, high magnesium prices in the United States would force Alcoa to move some production out of the United States. Alcoa also noted that in 2003, U.S. Magnesium was unable to supply all of Alcoa's needs, forcing the company to turn to imports. Consumers of magnesium in the automobile industry asserted that high prices in the United States would drive engineers to design magnesium out of automobiles, or force manufacturing elsewhere, which would ultimately hurt everyone.

The six members of the ITC were not convinced by these arguments. In March 2005, the ITC ruled that both China and Russia had been dumping magnesium in the United States. The government decided to impose duties ranging from 50 percent to more than 140 percent on imports of magnesium from China. Russian producers face duties ranging from 19 percent to 22 percent. The duties will be levied for five years, after which the ITC will revisit the situation.

According to U.S. Magnesium, the favorable ruling will now allow the company to reap the benefits of nearly $50 million in investments made in its manufacturing plant during the last few years and enable the company to boost its capacity by 28 percent by the end of 2005. Commenting on the favorable ruling, a U.S. Magnesium spokesman noted, "Once unfair trade is removed from the marketplace we'll be able to compete with anyone." U.S. Magnesium's customers and competitors, however, did not view the situation in the 2002–03 period as one of unfair trade. While the imposition of antidumping duties no doubt will help to protect U.S. Magnesium and the 400 people it employs from foreign competition, magnesium consumers in the United States are left wondering if they will be the ultimate losers.

Sources: D. Anderton, "U.S. Magnesium Lands Ruling on Unfair Imports," *Desert News,* October 1, 2004, p. D10; "U.S. Magnesium and Its Largest Consumers Debate before U.S. ITC," *Platt's Metals Week,* February 28, 2005, p. 2; and S. Oberbeck, "U.S. Magnesium Plans Big Utah Production Expansion," *Salt Lake Tribune,* March 30, 2005.

The Case For Government Intervention

LEARNING OBJECTIVE 2
Understand why governments sometimes intervene in international trade.

Now that we have reviewed the various instruments of trade policy that governments can use, it is time to look at the case for government intervention in international trade. Arguments for government intervention take two paths: political and economic. Political arguments for intervention are concerned with protecting the interests of certain groups within a nation (normally producers), often at the expense of other groups (normally consumers). Economic arguments for intervention are typically concerned with boosting the overall wealth of a nation (to the benefit of all, both producers and consumers).

POLITICAL ARGUMENTS FOR INTERVENTION Political arguments for government intervention cover a range of issues, including preserving jobs, protecting industries deemed important for national security, retaliating against unfair foreign competition, protecting consumers from "dangerous" products, furthering the goals of foreign policy, and advancing the human rights of individuals in exporting countries.

Protecting Jobs and Industries Perhaps the most common political argument for government intervention is that it is necessary for protecting jobs and industries from unfair foreign competition. The tariffs placed on imports of foreign steel by President George W. Bush in March 2002 were designed to do this. (Many steel producers were located in states that Bush needed to win reelection in 2004.) A political motive also underlay establishment of the Common Agricultural Policy (CAP) by the European Union. The CAP was designed to protect the jobs of Europe's politically powerful farmers by restricting imports and guaranteeing prices. However, the higher prices that resulted from the CAP have cost Europe's consumers dearly. This is true of most attempts to protect jobs and industries through government intervention. For example, the imposition of steel tariffs in 2002 raised steel prices for American consumers, such as automobile companies, making them less competitive in the global marketplace.

National Security Countries sometimes argue that it is necessary to protect certain industries because they are important for national security. Defense-related industries often get this kind of attention (e.g., aerospace, advanced electronics, semiconductors, etc.). Although not as common as it used to be, this argument is still made. Those in favor of protecting the U.S. semiconductor industry from foreign competition, for example, argue that semiconductors are now such important components of defense products that it would be dangerous to rely primarily on foreign producers for them. In 1986, this argument helped persuade the federal government to support Sematech, a consortium of 14 U.S. semiconductor companies that accounted for 90 percent of the U.S. industry's revenues. Sematech's mission was to conduct joint research into manufacturing techniques that can be parceled out to members. The government saw the venture as so critical that Sematech was specially protected from antitrust laws. Initially, the U.S. government provided Sematech with $100 million per year in subsidies. By the mid-1990s, however, the U.S. semiconductor industry had regained its leading market position, largely through the personal computer boom and demand for microprocessor chips made by Intel. In 1994, the consortium's board voted to seek an end to federal funding, and since 1996 the consortium has been funded entirely by private money.[9]

Retaliation Some argue that governments should use the threat to intervene in trade policy as a bargaining tool to help open foreign markets and force trading partners to "play by the rules of the game." The U.S. government has used the threat of punitive trade sanctions to try to get the Chinese government to enforce its intellectual property laws. Lax enforcement of these laws had given rise to massive copyright infringements in China that had been costing U.S. companies such as Microsoft hundreds of millions of dollars per year in lost sales revenues. After the United States threatened to impose 100 percent tariffs on a range of Chinese imports, and after harsh words between officials from the two countries, the Chinese agreed to tighter enforcement of intellectual property regulations.[10]

If it works, such a politically motivated rationale for government intervention may liberalize trade and bring with it resulting economic gains. It is a risky strategy, however. A country that is being pressured may not back down and instead may respond to the imposition of punitive tariffs by raising trade barriers of its own. This is exactly what the Chinese government threatened to do when pressured by the United States, although it ultimately did back down. If a government does not back down, however, the results could be higher trade barriers all around and an economic loss to all involved.

Protecting Consumers Many governments have long had regulations to protect consumers from unsafe products. The indirect effect of such regulations often is to limit or ban the importation of such products. In 1998, the U.S. government decided to permanently ban imports of 58 types of military-style assault weapons. (The United States already prohibited the sale of such weapons in the United States by U.S.-based firms.) The ban was motivated by a desire to increase public safety. It followed on the heels of a rash of random and deadly shootings by deranged individuals using such weapons, including one in President Clinton's home state of Arkansas that left four children and a schoolteacher dead.[11]

The accompanying Country Focus describes how the European Union banned the sale and importation of hormone-treated beef. The ban was motivated by a desire to protect European consumers from the possible health consequences of eating meat from animals treated with growth hormones. The conflict over the importation of hormone-treated beef into the EU may prove to be a taste of things to come. In addition to the use of hormones to promote animal growth and meat production, biotechnology has made it possible to genetically alter many crops so that they resist common herbicides, produce proteins that are natural insecticides, grow dramatically improved yields, or withstand inclement weather conditions. A new breed of genetically modified tomatoes has an antifreeze gene inserted into its genome and can thus be grown in colder climates than hitherto possible. Another example is a genetically engineered cotton seed produced by Monsanto. The seed has been engineered to express a protein that protects against three common insect pests: the cotton bollworm, tobacco budworm, and pink bollworm. Use of this seed reduces or eliminates the need for traditional pesticide applications for these pests.

A genetically engineered cotton seed that protects against three common insects has been met with resistance in Europe due to a fear that these genetically altered seeds could potentially be harmful to humans. *Kent Knudson/Photo Link/Getty Images/DIL*

Country FOCUS

Trade in Hormone-Treated Beef

In the 1970s, scientists discovered how to synthesize certain hormones and use them to accelerate the growth rate of livestock animals, reduce the fat content of meat, and increase milk production. Bovine somatotropin (BST), a growth hormone produced by cattle, was first synthesized by the biotechnology firm Genentech. Injections of BST could be used to supplement an animal's own hormone production and increase its growth rate. These hormones soon became popular among farmers, who found that they could cut costs and help satisfy consumer demands for leaner meat. Although these hormones occurred naturally in animals, consumer groups in several countries soon raised concerns about the practice. They argued that the use of hormone supplements was unnatural and that the health consequences of consuming hormone-treated meat were unknown but might include hormonal irregularities and cancer.

The European Union responded to these concerns in 1989 by banning the use of growth-promoting hormones in the production of livestock and the importation of hormone-treated meat. The ban was controversial because a reasonable consensus existed among scientists that the hormones posed no health risk. Although the EU banned hormone-treated meat, many other countries did not, including big meat-producing countries such as Australia, Canada, New Zealand, and the United States. The use of hormones soon became widespread in these countries. According to trade officials outside the EU, the European ban constituted an unfair restraint on trade. As a result of this ban, exports of meat to the EU fell. For example, U.S. red meat exports to the EU declined from $231 million in 1988 to $98 million in 1994. The complaints of meat exporters were bolstered in 1995 when Codex Alimentarius, the international food standards body of the UN's Food and Agriculture Organization and the World Health Organization, approved the use of growth hormones. In making this decision, Codex reviewed the scientific literature and found no evidence of a link between the consumption of hormone-treated meat and human health problems, such as cancer.

Fortified by such decisions, in 1995 the United States pressed the EU to drop the import ban on hormone-treated beef. The EU refused, citing "consumer concerns about food safety." In response, both Canada and the United States independently filed formal complaints with the World Trade Organization. The United States was joined in its complaint by a number of other countries, including Australia and New Zealand. The WTO created a trade panel of three independent experts. After reviewing evidence and hearing from a range of experts and representatives of both parties, the panel in May 1997 ruled that the EU ban on hormone-treated beef was illegal because it had no scientific justification. The EU immediately indicated it would appeal the finding to the WTO court of appeals. The WTO court heard the appeal in November 1997 and in February 1998 agreed with the findings of the trade panel that the EU had not presented any scientific evidence to justify the hormone ban.

This ruling left the EU in a difficult position. Legally, the EU had to lift the ban or face punitive sanctions, but the ban had wide public support in Europe. The EU feared that lifting the ban could produce a consumer backlash. Instead the EU did nothing, so in February 1999 the United States asked the WTO for permission to impose punitive sanctions on the EU. The WTO responded by allowing the United States to impose punitive tariffs valued at $120 million on EU exports to the United States. The EU decided to accept these tariffs rather than lift the ban on hormone-treated beef, and as of 2006, the ban and punitive tariffs were still in place.

Sources: C. Southey, "Hormones Fuel a Meaty EU Row," *Financial Times*, September 7, 1995, p. 2; E. L. Andrews, "In Victory for U.S., European Ban on Treated Beef Is Ruled Illegal," *The New York Times*, May 9, 1997, p. A1; F. Williams and G. de Jonquieres, "WTO's Beef Rulings Give Europe Food for Thought," *Financial Times*, February 13, 1998, p. 5; R. Baily, "Food and Trade: EU Fear Mongers' Lethal Harvest," *Los Angeles Times*, August 18, 2002, p. M3; "The US-EU Dispute over Hormone Treated Beef," *The Kiplinger Agricultural Letter*, January 10, 2003; and Scott Miller, "EU Trade Sanctions Have Dual Edge," *The Wall Street Journal*, February 26, 2004, p. A3.

As enticing as such innovations sound, they have met with intense resistance from consumer groups, particularly in Europe. The fear is that the widespread use of genetically altered seed corn could have unanticipated and harmful effects on human health and may result in "genetic pollution." (An example of genetic pollution would be when the widespread use of crops that produce natural pesticides stimulates the evolution of "superbugs" that are resistant to those pesticides.) Such concerns have led Austria and Luxembourg to outlaw the importation, sale, or use of genetically

Beijing's Tiananmen Square, a tangible reminder of China's history of human rights abuses. *Royalty Free/Corbis/DIL*

altered organisms. Sentiment against genetically altered organisms also runs strong in several other European countries, most notably Germany and Switzerland. It seems likely, therefore, that the World Trade Organization will be drawn into the conflict between those that want to expand the global market for genetically altered organisms, such as Monsanto, and those that want to limit it, such as Austria and Luxembourg.[12]

Furthering Foreign Policy Objectives

Governments sometimes use trade policy to support their foreign policy objectives.[13] A government may grant preferential trade terms to a country with which it wants to build strong relations. Trade policy has also been used several times to pressure or punish "rogue states" that do not abide by international law or norms. Iraq labored under extensive trade sanctions after the UN coalition defeated the country in the 1991 Gulf War until the 2003 invasion of Iraq by U.S.-led forces. The theory is that such pressure might persuade the rogue state to mend its ways, or it might hasten a change of government. In the case of Iraq, the sanctions were seen as a way of forcing that country to comply with several UN resolutions. The United States has maintained long-running trade sanctions against Cuba. Their principal function is to impoverish Cuba in the hope that the resulting economic hardship will lead to the downfall of Cuba's Communist government and its replacement with a more democratically inclined (and pro-U.S.) regime. The United States also has had trade sanctions in place against Libya and Iran, both of which it accuses of supporting terrorist action against U.S. interests and building weapons of mass destruction. In late 2003, the sanctions against Libya seemed to yield some returns when that country announced it would terminate a program to build nuclear weapons, and the U.S. government responded by relaxing those sanctions.

Other countries can undermine unilateral trade sanctions. The U.S. sanctions against Cuba, for example, have not stopped other Western countries from trading with Cuba. The U.S. sanctions have done little more than help create a vacuum into which other trading nations, such as Canada and Germany, have stepped. In an attempt to halt this and further tighten the screws on Cuba, in 1996 the U.S. Congress passed the **Helms-Burton Act.** This act allows Americans to sue foreign firms that use property in Cuba confiscated from them after the 1959 revolution. Later in 1996, Congress passed a similar law, the **D'Amato Act,** aimed at Libya and Iran.

Helms-Burton Act
Passed in 1996, this law allows Americans to sue foreign firms that use Cuban property confiscated from them during Cuba's 1959 revolution.

The passage of Helms-Burton elicited protests from America's trading partners, including the European Union, Canada, and Mexico, all of which claim the law violates their sovereignty and is illegal under World Trade Organization rules. For example, Canadian companies that have been doing business in Cuba for years see no reason they should suddenly be sued in U.S. courts when Canada does not restrict trade with Cuba. They are not violating Canadian law, and they are not U.S. companies, so why should they be subject to U.S. law? Despite such protests, the law is still on the books in the United States, although the U.S. government has not enforced this act—probably because it is unenforceable.

D'Amato Act
Passed in 1996, this law allows Americans to sue foreign firms that use property in Libya or Iran confiscated from Americans.

Protecting Human Rights

Protecting and promoting human rights in other countries is an important element of foreign policy for many democracies. Governments sometimes use trade policy to try to improve the human rights policies of trading partners. For years, the most obvious example of this was the annual debate in the United States over whether to grant most favored nation (MFN) status to China. MFN status allows countries to export goods to the United States under favorable terms. Under MFN rules, the average tariff on Chinese goods imported into the United States was 8 percent. If China's MFN status were rescinded, tariffs could have risen to about 40 percent. Trading partners who are signatories of the World Trade Organization, as most are, automatically receive MFN status. However, China did not join the WTO until 2001, so historically the decision of whether to grant MFN status to China was a real one. The decision was made more difficult by the perception that China had a poor human rights record. As indications of the country's disregard for human rights, critics of China often point to the 1989 Tiananmen Square massacre, China's continuing subjugation of Tibet (which China occupied in the 1950s), and the squashing of political dissent in China.[14] These critics argue that it was wrong for the United States to grant MFN status to China, and that instead, the United States should withhold MFN status until China showed measurable improvement in its human rights record. The critics argue that trade policy should be used as a political weapon to force China to change its internal policies toward human rights.

Others contend that limiting trade with such countries would make matters worse, not better. They argue that the best way to change the internal human rights stance of a country is to engage it through international trade. At its core, the argument is simple: Growing bilateral trade raises the income levels of both countries, and as a state becomes richer, its people begin to demand, and generally receive, better treatment with regard to their human rights. This is a variant of the argument in Chapter 2 that economic progress begets political progress (if political progress is measured by the adoption of a democratic government that respects human rights). This argument ultimately won the day in 1999 when the Clinton administration blessed China's application to join the WTO and announced that trade and human rights issues should be decoupled.

ECONOMIC ARGUMENTS FOR INTERVENTION

With the development of the new trade theory and strategic trade policy (see Chapter 5), the economic arguments for government intervention have undergone a renaissance in recent years. Until the early 1980s, most economists saw little benefit in government intervention and strongly advocated a free trade policy. This position has changed at the margins with the development of strategic trade policy, although as we will see in the next section, there are still strong economic arguments for sticking to a free trade stance.

The Infant Industry Argument

The **infant industry argument** is by far the oldest economic argument for government intervention. Alexander Hamilton proposed it in 1792. According to this argument, many developing countries have a potential comparative advantage in manufacturing, but new manufacturing industries cannot initially compete with established industries in developed countries. To allow manufacturing to get a toehold, the argument is that governments should temporarily support new industries (with tariffs, import quotas, and subsidies) until they have grown strong enough to meet international competition.

Infant Industry Argument
Proposed by Alexander Hamilton in 1792, this oldest economic argument for government intervention states that developing countries have a comparative advantage in manufacturing.

This argument has had substantial appeal for the governments of developing nations during the past 50 years, and the GATT has recognized the infant industry argument as a legitimate reason for protectionism. Nevertheless, many economists remain critical of this argument for two main reasons. First, protection of manufacturing from foreign competition does no good unless the protection helps make the industry efficient. In case after case, however, protection seems to have done little more than foster the development of inefficient industries that have little hope of ever competing in the world market. Brazil, for example, built the world's tenth-largest auto industry behind tariff barriers and quotas. Once those barriers were removed in the late 1980s, however, foreign imports soared, and the industry was forced to face up to the fact that after 30 years of protection, the Brazilian industry was one of the world's most inefficient.[15]

Second, the infant industry argument relies on an assumption that firms are unable to make efficient long-term investments by borrowing money from the domestic or international capital market. Consequently, governments have been required to subsidize long-term investments. Given the development of global capital markets over the past 20 years, this assumption no longer looks as valid as it once did. Today, if a developing country has a potential comparative advantage in a manufacturing industry, firms in that country should be able to borrow money from the capital markets to finance the required investments. Given financial support, firms based in countries with a potential comparative advantage have an incentive to endure the necessary initial losses in order to make long-run gains without requiring government protection. Many Taiwanese and South Korean firms did this in industries such as textiles, semiconductors, machine tools, steel, and shipping. Thus, given efficient global capital markets, the only industries that would require government protection would be those that are not worthwhile.

Strategic Trade Policy

Some new trade theorists have proposed the strategic trade policy argument.[16] We reviewed the basic argument in Chapter 5 when we considered the new trade theory. The new trade theory argues that in industries in which the existence of substantial economies of scale implies that the world market will profitably support only a few firms, countries may predominate in the export of certain products simply because they had firms that were able to capture first-mover advantages. The long-term dominance of Boeing in the commercial aircraft industry has been attributed to such factors.

Strategic Trade Policy
Government policy aimed at either helping the country's domestic firms retain first-mover gains or helping domestic firms find entry into a market; applied when the world market will profitably support only a few firms and certain countries may predominate in the export of certain products simply because they had first-mover firms.

The **strategic trade policy** argument has two components. First, it is argued that by appropriate actions, a government can help raise national income if it can somehow ensure that the firm or firms that gain first-mover advantages in an industry are domestic rather than foreign enterprises. Thus, according to the strategic trade policy argument, a government should use subsidies to support promising firms that are active in newly emerging industries. Advocates of this argument point out that the substantial R&D grants that the U.S. government gave Boeing in the 1950s and 1960s probably helped tilt the field of competition in the newly emerging market for passenger jets in Boeing's favor. (Boeing's 707 jet airliner was derived from a military plane.) Similar arguments are now made with regard to Japan's dominance in the production of liquid crystal display screens (used in laptop computers). Although these screens were invented in the United States, the Japanese government, in cooperation with major electronics companies, targeted this industry for research support in the late 1970s and early 1980s. The result was that Japanese firms, not U.S. firms, subsequently captured first-mover advantages in this market.

The second component of the strategic trade policy argument is that it might pay a government to intervene in an industry by helping domestic firms overcome the barriers to entry created by foreign firms that have already reaped first-mover advantages. This argument underlies government support of Airbus Industrie, Boeing's major competitor. Formed in 1966 as a consortium of four companies from Great Britain, France, Germany, and Spain, Airbus had less than 5 percent of the world commercial aircraft market when it began production in the mid-1970s. By 2004, it had increased its share to more than 50 percent, threatening Boeing's long-term dominance of the market. How did Airbus achieve this? According to the U.S. government, the answer is a $15 billion subsidy from the governments of Great Britain, France, Germany, and Spain.[17] Without this subsidy, Airbus would never have been able to break into the world market.

If these arguments are correct, they support a rationale for government intervention in international trade. Governments should target technologies that may be important in the future and use subsidies to support development work aimed at commercializing those technologies. Furthermore, government should provide export subsidies until the domestic firms have established first-mover advantages in the world market. Government support may also be justified if it can help domestic firms overcome the first-mover advantages enjoyed by foreign competitors and emerge as viable competitors in the world market (as in the Airbus and semiconductor examples). In this case, a combination of home-market protection and export-promoting subsidies may be needed.

The Revised Case for Free Trade

LEARNING OBJECTIVE 3
Articulate the arguments against strategic trade policy.

The strategic trade policy arguments of the new trade theorists suggest an economic justification for government intervention in international trade. This justification challenges the rationale for unrestricted free trade found in the work of classic trade theorists such as Adam Smith and David Ricardo. In response to this challenge to economic orthodoxy, a number of economists—including some of those responsible for the development of the new trade theory, such as Paul Krugman—point out that although strategic trade policy looks appealing in theory, in practice it may be unworkable. This response to the strategic trade policy argument constitutes the revised case for free trade.[18]

RETALIATION AND TRADE WAR Krugman argues that a strategic trade policy aimed at establishing domestic firms in a dominant position in a global industry is a beggar-thy-neighbor policy that boosts national income at the expense of other countries. A country that attempts to use such policies will probably provoke retaliation. In many cases, the resulting trade war between two or more interventionist governments will leave all countries involved worse off than if a hands-off approach had been adopted in the first place. If the U.S. government were to respond to the Airbus subsidy by increasing its own subsidies to Boeing, for example, the result might be that the subsidies would cancel each other out. In the process, both European and U.S. taxpayers would end up supporting an expensive and pointless trade war, and both Europe and the United States would be worse off.

Krugman may be right about the danger of a strategic trade policy leading to a trade war. The problem, however, is how to respond when one's competitors are already being supported by government subsidies; that is, how should Boeing and the United States respond to the subsidization of Airbus? According to Krugman, the answer is probably not to engage in retaliatory action but to help establish rules of the game that minimize the use of trade-distorting subsidies. This is what the World Trade Organization seeks to do.

DOMESTIC POLICIES Governments do not always act in the national interest when they intervene in the economy; politically important interest groups often influence them. The European Union's support for the Common Agricultural Policy (CAP), which arose because of the political power of French and German farmers, is an example. The CAP benefited inefficient farmers and the politicians who relied on the farm vote, but not consumers in the EU, who end up paying more for their foodstuffs. Thus, a further reason for not embracing strategic trade policy, according to Krugman, is that such a policy is almost certain to be captured by special-interest groups within the economy, who will distort it to their own ends. Krugman concludes that in the United States,

> To ask the Commerce Department to ignore special-interest politics while formulating detailed policy for many industries is not realistic: To establish a blanket policy of free trade, with exceptions granted only under extreme pressure, may not be the optimal policy according to the theory but may be the best policy that the country is likely to get.[19]

Development of the World Trading System

LEARNING OBJECTIVE 4
Describe the development of the world trading system and the current trade issues.

Strong economic arguments support unrestricted free trade. While many governments have recognized the value of these arguments, they have been unwilling to unilaterally lower their trade barriers for fear that other nations might not follow suit. Consider the problem that two neighboring countries, say, Brazil and Argentina, face when deciding whether to lower trade barriers between them. In principle, the government of Brazil might favor lowering trade barriers, but it might be unwilling to do so for fear that Argentina will not do the same. Instead, the government might fear that the Argentineans will take advantage of Brazil's low barriers to enter the Brazilian market, while at the same time continuing to shut Brazilian products out of their market through high trade barriers. The Argentinean government might believe that it faces the same dilemma. The essence of the problem is a lack of trust. Both governments recognize that their respective nations will benefit from lower trade barriers between them, but neither government is willing to lower barriers for fear that the other might not follow.[20]

Such a deadlock can be resolved if both countries negotiate a set of rules to govern cross-border trade and lower trade barriers. But who is to monitor the governments to make sure they are playing by the trade rules? And who is to impose sanctions on a government that cheats? Both governments could set up an independent body to act as a referee. This referee could monitor trade between the countries, make sure that no side cheats, and impose sanctions on a country if it does cheat in the trade game.

While it might sound unlikely that any government would compromise its national sovereignty by submitting to such an arrangement, since World War II an international trading framework has evolved that has exactly these features. For its first 50 years, this framework was known as the General Agreement on Tariffs and Trade. Since 1995, it has been known as the World Trade Organization. Here we look at the evolution and workings of the GATT and WTO.

FROM SMITH TO THE GREAT DEPRESSION As noted in Chapter 5, the theoretical case for free trade dates to the late eighteenth century and the work of Adam Smith and David Ricardo. Free trade as a government policy was first officially embraced by Great Britain in 1846, when the British Parliament repealed the Corn Laws. The Corn Laws placed a high tariff on imports of foreign corn. The objectives of the Corn Laws tariff were to raise government revenues and to protect British corn producers. There had been annual motions in Parliament in favor of free trade since the 1820s when David Ricardo was a member. However, agricultural protection was withdrawn only as a result of a protracted debate when the effects of a harvest failure in Great Britain were compounded by the imminent threat of famine in Ireland. Faced with considerable hardship and suffering among the populace, Parliament narrowly reversed its long-held position.

During the next 80 years or so, Great Britain, as one of the world's dominant trading powers, pushed the case for trade liberalization; but the British government was a voice in the wilderness. Its major trading partners did not reciprocate the British policy of unilateral free trade. The only reason Britain kept this policy for so long was that as the world's largest exporting nation, it had far more to lose from a trade war than did any other country.

By the 1930s, the British attempt to stimulate free trade was buried under the economic rubble of the Great Depression. The Great Depression had roots in the failure of the world economy to mount a sustained economic recovery after the end of World War I in 1918. Things got worse in 1929 with the U.S. stock market collapse and the subsequent run on the U.S. banking system. Economic problems were compounded in 1930 when the U.S. Congress passed the Smoot-Hawley tariff. Aimed at avoiding rising unemployment by protecting domestic industries and diverting consumer demand away from foreign products, the **Smoot-Hawley Act** erected an enormous wall of tariff barriers. Almost every industry was rewarded with its "made-to-order" tariff. A particularly odd aspect of the Smoot-Hawley tariff-raising binge was that the United States was running a balance-of-payment surplus at the time and it was the world's largest creditor nation. The Smoot-Hawley Act had a damaging effect on employment abroad. Other countries reacted to the U.S. action by raising their own tariff barriers. U.S. exports tumbled in response, and the world slid further into the Great Depression.[21]

Smoot-Hawley Act
Passed in 1930, this U. S. law erected a wall of tariff barriers against imports.

1947–1979: GATT, TRADE LIBERALIZATION, AND ECONOMIC GROWTH Economic damage caused by the beggar-thy-neighbor trade policies that the Smoot-Hawley Act ushered in exerted a profound influence on the economic institutions and ideology of the post-World War II world. The United States emerged from the war both victorious and economically dominant. After the debacle of the Great Depression, opinion in the U.S. Congress had swung strongly in favor of free trade. Under U.S. leadership, the GATT was established in 1947.

The GATT was a multilateral agreement whose objective was to liberalize trade by eliminating tariffs, subsidies, import quotas, and the like. From its foundation in 1947 until it was superseded by the WTO, the GATT's membership grew from 19 to more than 120 nations. The GATT did not attempt to liberalize trade restrictions in one fell swoop; that would have been impossible. Rather, tariff reduction was spread over eight rounds. The last, the Uruguay Round, was launched in 1986 and completed in December 1993. In these rounds, mutual tariff reductions were negotiated among all members, who then committed themselves not to raise import tariffs above negotiated rates. GATT regulations were enforced by a mutual monitoring mechanism. If a country believed that one of its trading partners was violating a GATT regulation, it could ask the Geneva-based bureaucracy that administered the GATT to investigate. If GATT investigators found the complaints to be valid, member countries could be asked to pressure the offending party to change its policies. In general, such pressure was sufficient to get an offending country to change its policies. If it were not, the offending country could be expelled from the GATT.

In its early years, the GATT was by most measures very successful. For example, the average tariff declined by nearly 92 percent in the United States between the Geneva Round of 1947 and the Tokyo Round of 1973–79. Consistent with the theoretical arguments first advanced by Ricardo and reviewed in Chapter 5, the move toward free trade under the GATT appeared to stimulate economic growth. From 1953 to 1963, world trade grew at an annual rate of 6.1 percent, and world income grew at an annual rate of 4.3 percent. Performance from 1963 to 1973 was even better; world trade grew at 8.9 percent annually, and world income grew at 5.1 percent annually.[22]

1980–1993: PROTECTIONIST TRENDS During the 1980s and early 1990s, the world trading system erected by the GATT came under strain as pressures for greater protectionism increased around the world. Three reasons caused the rise in such pressures during the 1980s. First, the economic success of Japan strained the world trading system. Japan was in ruins when the GATT was created. By the early 1980s, however, it had become the world's second-largest economy and its largest exporter. Japan's success in such industries as automobiles and semiconductors might have been enough to strain the world trading system. Things were made worse by the widespread perception in the West that despite low tariff rates and subsidies, Japanese markets were closed to imports and foreign investment by administrative trade barriers.

Second, the world trading system was strained by the persistent trade deficit in the world's largest economy, the United States. Although the deficit peaked in 1987 at more than $170 billion, by the end of 1992 the annual rate was still running about $80 billion. From a political perspective, the matter was worsened in 1992 by the $45 billion U.S. trade deficit with Japan, a country perceived as not playing by the rules. The consequences of the U.S. deficit included painful adjustments in industries such as automobiles, machine tools, semiconductors, steel, and textiles, where domestic producers steadily lost market share to foreign competitors. The resulting unemployment gave rise to renewed demands in the U.S. Congress for protection against imports.

A third reason for the trend toward greater protectionism was that many countries found ways to get around GATT regulations. Bilateral voluntary export restraints, or VERs, circumvent GATT agreements, because neither the importing country nor the exporting country complain to the GATT bureaucracy in Geneva—and without a complaint, the GATT bureaucracy can do nothing. Exporting countries agreed to VERs to avoid more damaging punitive tariffs. One of the best-known examples is the automobile VER between Japan and the United States, under which Japanese producers promised to limit their auto imports into the United States as a way of defusing growing trade tensions. According to a World Bank study, 13 percent of the imports of industrialized countries in 1981 were subjected to nontariff trade barriers such as VERs. By 1986, this figure had increased to 16 percent. The most rapid rise was in the United States, where the value of imports affected by nontariff barriers (primarily VERs) increased by 23 percent between 1981 and 1986.[23]

THE URUGUAY ROUND AND THE WORLD TRADE ORGANIZATION Against the background of rising pressures for protectionism, in 1986 GATT members embarked on their eighth round of negotiations to reduce tariffs, the Uruguay Round (so named because it occurred in Uruguay). This was the most difficult round of negotiations yet, primarily because it was also the most ambitious. Until then, GATT rules had applied only to trade in manufactured goods and commodities. In the Uruguay Round, member countries sought to extend GATT rules to cover trade in services. They also sought to write rules governing the protection of intellectual property, to reduce agricultural subsidies, and to strengthen the GATT's monitoring and enforcement mechanisms.

The Uruguay Round dragged on for seven years before an agreement was reached December 15, 1993. It went into effect July 1, 1995. The Uruguay Round contained the following provisions:

1. Tariffs on industrial goods were to be reduced by more than one-third, and tariffs were to be scrapped on more than 40 percent of manufactured goods.
2. Average tariff rates imposed by developed nations on manufactured goods were to be reduced to less than 4 percent of value, the lowest level in modern history.
3. Agricultural subsidies were to be substantially reduced.
4. GATT fair trade and market access rules were to be extended to cover a wide range of services.
5. GATT rules also were to be extended to provide enhanced protection for patents, copyrights, and trademarks (intellectual property).
6. Barriers on trade in textiles were to be significantly reduced over 10 years.
7. The World Trade Organization was to be created to implement the GATT agreement.

Services and Intellectual Property In the long run, the extension of GATT rules to cover services and intellectual property may be particularly significant. Until 1995, GATT rules applied only to industrial goods (i.e., manufactured goods and commodities). In 2005, world trade in services amounted to \$2,415 billion (compared to world trade in goods of \$10,120 billion).[24] Ultimately, extension of GATT rules to this important trading arena could significantly increase both the total share of world trade accounted for by services and the overall volume of world trade. The extension of GATT rules to cover intellectual property will make it much easier for high-technology companies to do business in developing nations where intellectual property rules historically have been poorly enforced (see Chapter 2 for details).

The World Trade Organization The clarification and strengthening of GATT rules and the creation of the World Trade Organization also hold out the promise of more effective policing and enforcement of GATT rules. The WTO acts as an umbrella organization that encompasses the GATT along with two new sister bodies, one on services and the other on intellectual property. The WTO's General Agreement on Trade in Services (GATS) has taken the lead in extending free trade agreements to services. The WTO's Agreement on Trade-Related Aspects of Intellectual Property Rights (TRIPS) is an attempt to narrow the gaps in the way intellectual property rights are protected around the world and to bring them under common international rules. WTO has taken over responsibility for arbitrating trade disputes and monitoring the trade policies of member countries. While the WTO operates on the basis of consensus as the GATT did, in the area of dispute settlement, member countries are no longer able to block adoption of arbitration reports. Arbitration panel reports on trade disputes between member countries are automatically adopted by the WTO unless there is a consensus to reject them. Countries that have been found by the arbitration panel to violate GATT rules may appeal to a permanent appellate body, but its verdict is binding. If offenders fail to comply with the recommendations of the arbitration panel, trading partners have the right to compensation or, in the last resort, to impose (commensurate) trade sanctions. Every stage of the procedure is subject to strict time limits. Thus, the WTO has something that the GATT never had—teeth.[25]

WTO: EXPERIENCE TO DATE By 2006, the WTO had 149 members, including China, which joined at the end of 2001. Another 25 countries, including the Russian Federation and Saudi Arabia, were negotiating for membership into the organization. Since its formation, the WTO has remained at the forefront of efforts to promote global free trade. Its creators expressed the hope that the enforcement mechanisms granted to the WTO would make it more effective at policing global trade rules than the GATT had been. The great hope was that the WTO might emerge as an effective advocate and facilitator of future trade deals, particularly in areas such as services. The experience so far has been encouraging, although the collapse of WTO talks in Seattle in late 1999 raised a number of questions about the future direction of the WTO.

WTO as Global Police The first decade in the life of the WTO suggests that its policing and enforcement mechanisms are having a positive effect.[26] Between 1995 and early 2006, more than 340 trade disputes between member countries were brought to the WTO.[27] This record compares with a total of 196 cases handled by the GATT over almost half a century. Of the cases brought to the WTO, three-fourths had been resolved by late 2005 following informal consultations between the disputing countries. Resolving the remainder has involved more formal procedures, but these have been largely successful. In general, countries involved have adopted the WTO's recommendations. The fact that countries are using the WTO represents an important vote of confidence in the organization's dispute resolution procedures.

Expanding Trade Agreements As explained above, the Uruguay Round of GATT negotiations extended global trading rules to cover trade in services. The WTO was given the role of brokering future agreements to open up global trade in services. The WTO was also encouraged to extend its reach to encompass regulations governing foreign direct investment, something the GATT had never done. Two of the first industries targeted for reform were the global telecommunication and financial services industries.

In February 1997, the WTO brokered a deal to get countries to agree to open their telecommunication markets to competition, allowing foreign operators to purchase ownership stakes in domestic telecommunication providers and establishing a set of common rules for fair competition. Under the pact, 68 countries accounting for more than 90 percent of world telecommunication revenues pledged to start opening their markets to foreign competition and to abide by common rules for fair competition in telecommunications. Most of the world's biggest markets, including the United States, European Union, and Japan, were fully liberalized by January 1, 1998, when the pact went into effect. All forms of basic telecommunication service are covered, including voice telephony, data and fax transmissions, and satellite and radio communications. Many telecommunication companies responded positively to the deal, pointing out that it would give them much greater ability to offer their business customers one-stop shopping—a global, seamless service for all their corporate needs and a single bill.[28]

This was followed in December 1997 with an agreement to liberalize cross-border trade in financial services.[29] The deal covers more than 95 percent of the world's financial services market. Under the agreement, which took effect at the beginning of March 1999, 102 countries pledged to open to varying degrees their banking, securities, and insurance sectors to foreign competition. In common with the telecommunication deal, the accord covers not just cross-border trade but also foreign direct investment. Seventy countries agreed to dramatically lower or eradicate barriers to foreign direct investment in their financial services sectors. The United States and the European Union, with minor exceptions, are fully open to inward investment by foreign banks, insurance, and securities companies. As part of the deal, many Asian countries made important concessions that allow significant foreign participation in their financial services sectors for the first time.

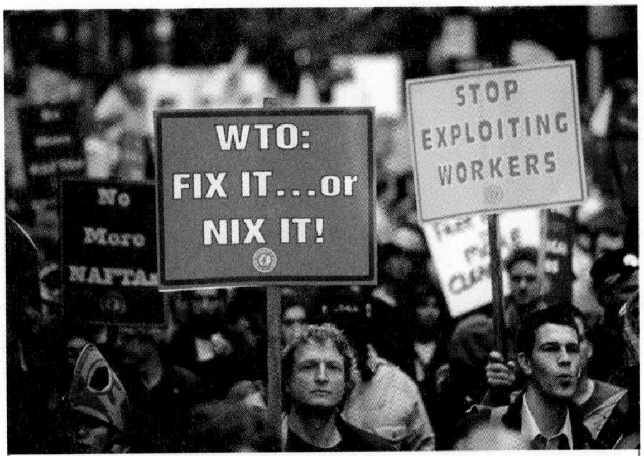

WTO protesters gather in front of the Niketown store at Fifth Avenue and Pike Street in downtown Seattle before the opening of the WTO sessions in Seattle. *Daniel Sheehan/Getty Images*

The WTO in Seattle: A Watershed? At the end of November 1999, representatives from the WTO's member states met in Seattle, Washington. The goal of the meeting was to launch a new round of talks—dubbed "the millennium round"—aimed at further reducing barriers to cross-border trade and investment. Prominent on the agenda was an attempt to get the assembled countries to agree to work toward the reduction of barriers to cross-border trade in agricultural products and trade and investment in services.

These expectations were dashed on the rocks of a hard and unexpected reality. The talks ended December 3, 1999, without any agreement being reached. Inside the meeting rooms, the problem was an inability to reach consensus on the primary goals for the next round of talks. A major stumbling block was friction between the United States and the European Union over whether to endorse the aim of ultimately eliminating subsidies to agricultural exporters. The United States wanted the elimination of such subsidies to be a priority. The EU, with its politically powerful farm lobby and long history of farm subsidies, was unwilling to take this step. Another stumbling block was related to efforts by the United States to write "basic labor rights" into the law of the world trading system. The United States wanted the WTO to allow governments to impose tariffs on goods imported from countries that did not abide by what the United States saw as fair labor practices. Representatives from developing nations reacted angrily to this proposal, suggesting it was simply an attempt by the United States to find a legal way of restricting imports from poorer nations.

While the disputes inside the meeting rooms were acrimonious, it was events outside that captured the attention of the world press. The WTO talks proved to be a lightning rod for a diverse collection of organizations from environmentalists and human rights groups to labor unions. For various reasons, these groups oppose free trade. All these organizations argued that the WTO is an undemocratic institution that was usurping the national sovereignty of member states and making decisions of great importance behind closed doors. They took advantage of the Seattle meetings to voice their opposition, which the world press recorded. Environmentalists expressed concern about the impact that free trade in agricultural products might have on the rate of global deforestation. They argued that lower tariffs on imports of lumber from developing nations will stimulate demand and accelerate the rate at which virgin forests are logged, particularly in nations such as Malaysia and Indonesia. They also pointed to the adverse impact that some WTO rulings have had on environmental policies. For example, the WTO had recently blocked a U.S. rule that ordered shrimp nets be equipped with a device that allows endangered sea turtles to escape. The WTO found the rule discriminated against foreign importers who lacked such nets.[30] Environmentalists argued that the rule was necessary to protect the turtles from extinction.

Human rights activists see WTO rules as outlawing the ability of nations to stop imports from countries where child labor is used or working conditions are hazardous. Similarly, labor unions oppose trade laws that allow imports from low-wage countries and result in a loss of jobs in high-wage countries. They buttress their position by arguing that American workers are losing their jobs to imports from developing nations that do not have adequate labor standards.

Supporters of the WTO and free trade dismiss these concerns. They have repeatedly pointed out that the WTO exists to serve the interests of its member states, not subvert them. The WTO lacks the ability to force any member nation to take an action to which it is opposed. The WTO can allow member nations to impose retaliatory tariffs on countries that do not abide by WTO rules, but that is the limit of its power. Furthermore, supporters argue, it is rich countries that pass strict environmental laws and laws governing labor standards, not poor ones. In their view, free trade, by raising living standards in developing nations, will be followed by the passage of such laws in these nations. Using trade regulations to try to impose such practices on developing nations, they believe, will produce a self-defeating backlash.

Many representatives from developing nations, which make up about 110 of the WTO's 149 members, also reject the position taken by environmentalists and advocates of human and labor rights. Poor countries, which depend on exports to boost their economic growth rates and work their way out of poverty, fear that rich countries will use environmental concerns, human rights, and labor-related issues to erect barriers to the products of the developing world. They believe that attempts to incorporate language about the environment or labor standards in future trade agreements will amount to little more than trade barriers by another name.[31] If this were to occur, they argue that the effect would be to trap the developing nations of the world in a grinding cycle of poverty and debt.

These pro-trade arguments fell on deaf ears. As the WTO representatives gathered in Seattle, environmentalists, human rights activists, and labor unions marched in the streets. Some of the more radical elements in these organizations, together with groups of anarchists who were philosophically opposed to "global capitalism" and "the rape of the world by multinationals," succeeded not only in shutting down the opening ceremonies of the WTO but also in sparking violence in the normally peaceful streets of Seattle. A number of demonstrators damaged property and looted; and the police responded with tear gas, rubber bullets, pepper spray, and baton charges. When it was over, 600 demonstrators had been arrested, millions of dollars in property had been damaged in downtown Seattle, and the global news media had their headline: "WTO Talks Collapse amid Violent Demonstrations."

What happened in Seattle is notable because it may have been a watershed of sorts. In the past, previous trade talks were pursued in relative obscurity with only interested economists, politicians, and businesspeople paying much attention. Seattle demonstrated that the issues surrounding the global trend toward free trade have moved to center stage in the popular consciousness. The debate on the merits of free trade and globalization has become mainstream. Whether further liberalization occurs, therefore, may depend on the importance that popular opinion in countries such as the United States attaches to issues such as human rights and labor standards, job security, environmental policies, and national sovereignty. It will also depend on the ability of advocates of free trade to articulate in a clear and compelling manner the argument that, in the long run, free trade is the best way of promoting adequate labor standards, of providing more jobs, and of protecting the environment.

THE FUTURE OF THE WTO: UNRESOLVED ISSUES AND THE DOHA ROUND Much remains to be done on the international trade front. Four issues at the forefront of the current agenda of the WTO are the increase in antidumping policies, the high level of protectionism in agriculture, the lack of strong protection for intellectual property rights in many nations, and continued high tariff rates on nonagricultural goods and services in many nations. We shall look at each in turn before discussing the latest round of talks between WTO members aimed at reducing trade barriers, the Doha Round, which began in 2001 but stalled in 2006.

Antidumping Actions Antidumping actions proliferated during the 1990s. WTO rules allow countries to impose antidumping duties on foreign goods that are being sold cheaper than at home, or below their cost of production, when domestic producers can show that they are being harmed. Unfortunately, the rather vague definition of what constitutes "dumping" has proved to be a loophole that many countries are exploiting to pursue protectionism.

Between January 1995 and December 2005, WTO members had reported implementation of some 2,840 antidumping actions to the WTO. India initiated the largest number of antidumping actions, some 425; the EU initiated 327 over the same period, and the United States 366 (see Figure 6.2). Antidumping actions seem to be concentrated in certain sectors of the economy such as basic metal industries (e.g., aluminum and steel), chemicals, plastics, and machinery and electrical equipment.[32] These sectors account for some 70 percent of all antidumping actions reported to the WTO. These four sectors since 1995 have been characterized by periods of intense competition and excess productive capacity, which have led to low prices and profits (or losses) for firms in those industries. It is not unreasonable, therefore, to hypothesize that the high level of antidumping actions in these industries represents an attempt by beleaguered manufacturers to use the political process in their nations to seek protection from foreign competitors, who they claim are

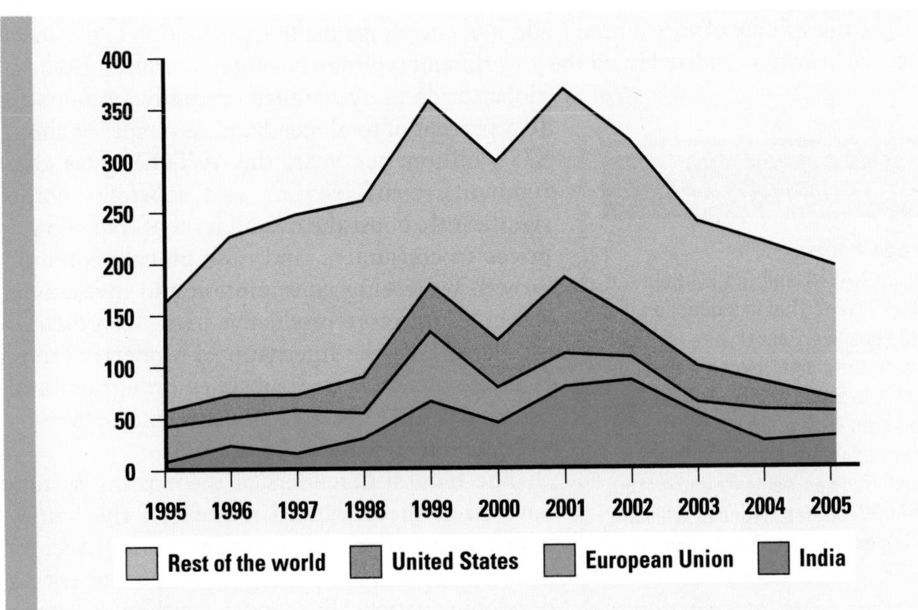

figure 6.2

Antidumping Actions, 1995–2005

engaging in unfair competition. While some of these claims may have merit, the process can become very politicized as representatives of businesses and their employees lobby government officials to "protect domestic jobs from unfair foreign competition," and government officials, mindful of the need to get votes in future elections, oblige by pushing for antidumping actions. The WTO is clearly worried by this trend, suggesting that it reflects persistent protectionist tendencies and pushing members to strengthen the regulations governing the imposition of antidumping duties. On the other hand, since the WTO signaled that antidumping would be a focus of the Doha Round, the number of antidumping actions has declined somewhat (see Figure 6.2).

Protectionism in Agriculture Another recent focus of the WTO has been the high level of tariffs and subsidies in the agricultural sector of many economies. Tariff rates on agricultural products are generally much higher than tariff rates on manufactured products or services. For example, in 2003 the average tariff rates on nonagricultural products were 4.2 percent for Canada, 3.8 percent for the European Union, 3.9 percent for Japan, and 4.4 percent for the United States. On agricultural products, however, the average tariff rates were 21.2 percent for Canada, 15.9 percent for the European Union, 18.6 percent for Japan, and 10.3 percent for the United States.[33] The implication is that consumers in these countries are paying significantly higher prices than necessary for agricultural products imported from abroad, which leaves them with less money to spend on other goods and services.

The historically high tariff rates on agricultural products reflect a desire to protect domestic agriculture and traditional farming communities from foreign competition. In addition to high tariffs, agricultural producers also benefit from substantial subsidies. According to estimates from the OECD, government subsidies on average account for some 17 percent of the cost of agricultural production in Canada, 21 percent in the United States, 35 percent in the European Union, and 59 percent in Japan.[34] In total, OECD countries spend more than $300 billion a year in subsidies to agricultural producers.

Not surprising, the combination of high tariff barriers and significant subsidies introduces significant distortions into the production of agricultural products and international trade of those products. The net effect is to raise prices to consumers, reduce the volume of agricultural trade, and encourage the overproduction of products that are heavily subsidized (with the government typically buying the surplus). Because global trade in agriculture currently amounts to 10.5 percent of total merchandized trade, or about $750 billion per year, the WTO argues that removing tariff barriers and subsidies could significantly boost the overall level of trade, lower prices to consumers, and raise global economic growth by freeing consumption and investment resources for more productive uses. According to estimates from the International Monetary Fund, removal of tariffs and subsidies on agricultural products would raise global economic welfare by $128 billion annually.[35]

The biggest defenders of the existing system have been the advanced nations of the world, which want to protect their agricultural sectors from competition by low-cost producers in developing nations. In contrast, developing nations

Another Perspective

WTO and Regional Trade Pacts

Do regional groups such as NAFTA and the EU help the WTO and the growth of free trade? That is a question the WTO wants to answer in the positive. Pascal Lamy, director general of the WTO, is sure they can "become building blocks, not stumbling blocks, to world trade." The number of regional trade agreements has doubled in the last decade. The WTO has recently approved a process for assessing the impact of such trade agreements and making sure they are consistent with WTO rules. (Frances Williams, "Accord on Unblocking Regional Trade Pacts," *Financial Times,* July 12, 2006, p. 6)

have been pushing hard for reforms that would allow their producers greater access to the protected markets of the developed nations. Estimates suggest that removing all subsidies on agricultural production alone in OECD countries could return to the developing nations of the world three times more than all the foreign aid they currently receive from the OECD nations.[36] In other words, free trade in agriculture could help to jump-start economic growth among the world's poorer nations and alleviate global poverty.

Protecting Intellectual Property Another issue that has become increasingly important to the WTO has been protecting intellectual property. The 1995 Uruguay agreement that established the WTO also contained an agreement to protect intellectual property (the Trade-Related Aspects of Intellectual Property Rights, or TRIPS, agreement). The TRIPS regulations oblige WTO members to grant and enforce patents lasting at least 20 years and copyrights lasting 50 years. Rich countries had to comply with the rules within a year. Poor countries, in which such protection generally was much weaker, had five years' grace, and the very poorest had 10 years. The basis for this agreement was a strong belief among signatory nations that the protection of intellectual property through patents, trademarks, and copyrights must be an essential element of the international trading system. Inadequate protections for intellectual property reduce the incentive for innovation. Because innovation is a central engine of economic growth and rising living standards, the argument has been that a multilateral agreement is needed to protect intellectual property.

Without such an agreement it is feared that producers in a country, let's say India, might market imitations of patented innovations pioneered in a different country, say the United States. This can affect international trade in two ways. First, it reduces the export opportunities in India for the original innovator in the United States. Second, to the extent that the Indian producer is able to export its pirated imitation to additional countries, it also reduces the export opportunities in those countries for the U.S. inventor. Also, one can argue that because the size of the total world market for the innovator is reduced, its incentive to pursue risky and expensive innovations is also reduced. The net effect would be less innovation in the world economy and less economic growth.

Something very similar to this has been occurring in the pharmaceutical industry, with Indian drug companies making copies of patented drugs discovered elsewhere. In 1970, the Indian government stopped recognizing product patents on drugs, but it elected to continue respecting process patents. This permitted Indian companies to reverse-engineer Western pharmaceuticals without paying licensing fees. As a result, foreigners' share of the Indian drug market fell from 75 percent in 1970 to 30 percent in 2000. For example, an Indian company sells a version of Bayer's patented antibiotic Cipro for $0.12 a pill, versus the $5.50 it costs in the United States. Under the WTO TRIPS agreement, India agreed to adopt and enforce the international drug patent regime by 2005.[37]

As noted in Chapter 2, intellectual property rights violation is also an endemic problem in several other industries, most notably computer software and music. The WTO believes that reducing piracy rates in areas such as drugs, software, and music recordings would have a significant impact on the volume of world trade and increase the incentive for producers to invest in the creation of intellectual property. A world without piracy would have more new drugs, computer software, and music recordings produced every year. In turn, this would boost economic and social welfare, and global economic growth rates. It is thus in the interests of WTO members to make sure that intellectual property rights are respected and enforced. While the 1995 Uruguay agreement that created the WTO did make headway with the TRIPS agreement, some believe these requirements do not go far enough and further commitments are necessary.

Market Access for Nonagricultural Goods and Services Although the WTO and the GATT have made big strides in reducing the tariff rates on nonagricultural products, much work remains. Although most developed nations have brought their tariff rates on industrial products down to an *average* of 3.8 percent of value, exceptions still remain. In particular, while average tariffs are low, high tariff rates persist on certain imports into developed nations, which limit market access and economic growth. For example, Australia and South Korea, both OECD countries, still have bound tariff rates of 15.1 percent and 24.6 percent, respectively, on imports of transportation equipment (*bound tariff rates* are the highest rate that can be charged, which is often, but not always, the rate that is charged). In contrast, the bound tariff rates on imports of transportation equipment into the United States, EU, and Japan are 2.7 percent, 4.8 percent, and 0 percent, respectively (see Table 6.1). A particular area for concern is high tariff rates on imports of selected goods from developing nations into developed nations.

In addition, tariffs on services remain higher than on industrial goods. The average tariff on business and financial services imported into the United States, for example, is 8.2 percent, into the EU it is 8.5 percent, and into Japan it is 19.7 percent.[38] Given the rising value of cross-border trade in services, reducing these figures can be expected to yield substantial gains.

The WTO would like to bring down tariff rates still further and reduce the scope for the selective use of high tariff rates. The ultimate aim is to reduce tariff rates to zero. Although this might sound ambitious, 40 nations have already moved to zero tariffs on information technology goods, so a precedent exists. Empirical work suggests that further reductions in average tariff rates toward zero would yield substantial gains. One estimate by economists at the World Bank suggests that a broad global trade agreement coming out of the current Doha negotiations could increase world income by $263 billion annually by 2015, of which $109 billion would go to poor countries.[39] See the accompanying Country Focus box, next page, for estimates of the benefits to the American economy from free trade.

Looking further out, the WTO would like to bring down tariff rates on imports of nonagricultural goods into developing nations. Many of these nations use the infant industry argument to justify the continued imposition of high tariff rates; however, ultimately these rates need to come down for these nations to reap the full benefits of international trade. For example, the bound tariff rates of 53.9 percent on imports of transportation equipment into India and 33.6 percent on imports into Brazil, by raising domestic prices, help to protect inefficient domestic producers and limit

table 6.1

Bound Tariffs on Select Industrial Products—Simple Averages

Source: WTO.

Country	Metals	Transportation Equipment	Electric Machinery
Canada	2.8%	6.8%	5.2%
United States	1.8	2.7	2.1
Brazil	33.4	33.6	31.9
Mexico	34.7	35.8	34.1
European Union	1.6	4.7	3.3
Australia	4.5	15.1	13.3
Japan	0.9	0.0	0.2
South Korea	7.7	24.6	16.1

Country FOCUS

Estimating the Gains from Trade for America

A study published by the Institute for International Economics has tried to estimate the gains to the American economy from free trade. According to the study, due to reductions in tariff barriers under the GATT and WTO since 1947, by 2003 the GDP of the United States was 7.3 percent higher than would otherwise be the case. The benefits of that amount to roughly $1 trillion a year, or $9,000 extra income for each American household per year.

The same study tried to estimate what would happen if America concluded free trade deals with all its trading partners, reducing tariff barriers on all goods and services to zero. Using several methods to estimate the impact, the study concluded that additional annual gains of between $450 billion and $1.3 trillion could be realized. This final march to free trade, according to the authors of the study, could safely be expected to raise incomes of the average American household by an additional $4,500 per year.

The authors also tried to estimate the scale and cost of employment disruption that would be caused by a move to universal free trade. Jobs would be lost in certain sectors and gained in others if the country abolished all tariff barriers. Using historical data as a guide, they estimated that 226,000 jobs would be lost every year due to expanded trade, although some two-thirds of those losing jobs would find reemployment after a year. Reemployment, however, would be at a wage that was 13 to 14 percent lower. The study concluded that the disruption costs would total some $54 billion annually, primarily in the form of lower lifetime wages to those whose jobs were disrupted as a result of free trade. Offset against this, however, must be the higher economic growth resulting from free trade, which creates many new jobs and raises household incomes, creating another $450 billion to $1.3 trillion annually in *net* gains to the economy. In other words, the estimated annual gains from trade are far greater than the estimated annual costs associated with job disruption, and more people benefit than lose as result of shift to a universal free trade regime.

Source: S. C. Bradford, P. L. E. Grieco, and G. C. Hufbauer, "The Payoff to America from Global Integration," in *The United States and the World Economy: Foreign Policy for the Next Decade,* C. F. Bergsten, ed. (Washington, DC: Institute for International Economics, 2005).

economic growth by reducing the real income of consumers who must pay more for transportation equipment and related services.

A New Round of Talks: Doha Antidumping actions, trade in agricultural products, better enforcement of intellectual property laws, and expanded market access were four of the issues the WTO wanted to tackle at the 1999 meetings in Seattle, but those meetings were derailed. In late 2001, the WTO tried again to launch a new round of talks between member states aimed at further liberalizing the global trade and investment framework. For this meeting, it picked the remote location of Doha in the Persian Gulf state of Qatar, no doubt with an eye on the difficulties that antiglobalization protesters would have in getting there. Unlike the Seattle meetings, at Doha, the member states of the WTO agreed to launch a new round of talks and staked out an agenda. The talks were originally scheduled to last three years, although they have already gone on longer and may not be concluded for a while.

The agenda agreed upon at Doha was a game plan for negotiations. The agenda included cutting tariffs on industrial goods and services, phasing out subsidies to agricultural producers, reducing barriers to cross-border investment, and limiting the use of antidumping laws. Some difficult compromises were made to reach agreement on this agenda. The EU and Japan had to give significant ground on the issue of agricultural subsidies, which are used extensively by both entities to support politically powerful farmers. The United States bowed to pressure from virtually every other nation to negotiate revisions of antidumping rules, which the United States has used extensively to protect its steel producers from foreign competition. Europe had to scale back its efforts to include environmental policy in the trade talks, primarily because of pressure from developing nations that see environmental protection policies as trade barriers by another name. Excluded from the agenda was any language pertaining to attempts to tie trade to labor standards in a country.

Countries with big pharmaceutical sectors acquiesced to demands from African, Asian, and Latin American nations on the issue of drug patents. Specifically, the language in the agreement declares that WTO regulation on intellectual property "does not and should not prevent members from taking measures to protect public health." This language was meant to assure the world's poorer nations that they can make or buy generic equivalents to fight such killers as AIDS and malaria.

However, it is one thing to agree to an agenda and quite another to reach a consensus on a new treaty. If Doha is ever concluded, the agreement will yield some potential winners. These include low-cost agricultural producers in the developing world and developed nations such as Australia and the United States. If the talks are successful, agricultural producers in these nations will ultimately see the global markets for their goods expand. Developing nations also gain from the lack of language on labor standards, which many saw as an attempt by rich nations to erect trade barriers. The sick and poor of the world also benefit from guaranteed access to cheaper medicines. There are also clear losers here, including EU and Japanese farmers, U.S. steelmakers, environmental activists, and pharmaceutical firms in the developed world. These losers can be expected to lobby their governments hard during the ensuing years to make sure that the final agreement is more in their favor.[40] In general, though, if successful, the Doha Round of negotiations could significantly raise global economic welfare. The World Bank has estimated that a successful Doha Round would raise global incomes by more than $500 billion a year by 2015, with 60 percent of the gain going to the world's poorer nations, which would help to pull 144 million people out of poverty.[41]

LEARNING OBJECTIVE 5
Explain the implications for managers of developments in the world trading system.

The talks are currently stalled. As is normal in these cases, they have been characterized by halting progress punctuated by significant setbacks and missed deadlines. A September 2003 meeting in Cancun, Mexico, broke down, primarily because there was no agreement on how to proceed with reducing agricultural subsidies and tariffs; the EU, United States, and India, among others, proved less than willing to reduce tariffs and subsidies to their politically important farmers, while countries such as Brazil and certain West African nations wanted free trade as quickly as possible. However, in early 2004, both the United States and the EU made a determined push to start the talks again, and in mid-2004 both seemed to commit themselves to sweeping reductions in agricultural tariffs and subsidies. However, in June 2006 the talks stalled again. The basic problem: nobody seems willing to make the concessions that are necessary to strike a deal. Although all parties have committed to restarting talks, it remains to be seen if and when the Doha Round of talks will be completed.

Focus on Managerial Implications

What are the implications of all this for business practice? Why should the international manager care about the political economy of free trade or about the relative merits of arguments for free trade and protectionism? There are two answers to this question. The first concerns the impact of trade barriers on a firm's strategy. The second concerns the role that business firms can play in promoting free trade or trade barriers.

Trade Barriers and Firm Strategy

To understand how trade barriers affect a firm's strategy, consider first the material in Chapter 5. Drawing on the theories of international trade, we discussed how it makes sense for the firm to disperse its various production activities to those countries around the globe where they can be performed most efficiently. Thus, it may make sense for a firm to design and engineer its product in one country, to manufacture components in another, to perform final assembly operations in yet another country, and then export the finished product to the rest of the world.

Clearly, trade barriers constrain a firm's ability to disperse its productive activities in such a manner. First and most obvious, tariff barriers raise the costs of exporting products to a country (or of exporting partly finished products between countries). This may put the firm at a competitive disadvantage to indigenous competitors in that country. In response, the firm may then find it economical to locate production facilities in that country so that it can compete on an even footing. Second, quotas may limit a firm's ability to serve a country from locations outside of that country. Again, the response by the firm might be to set up production facilities in that country—even though it may result in higher production costs. Such reasoning was one of the factors behind the rapid expansion of Japanese automaking capacity in the United States during the 1980s and 1990s. This followed the establishment of a VER agreement between the United States and Japan that limited U.S. imports of Japanese automobiles.

Third, to conform to local content regulations, a firm may have to locate more production activities in a given market than it would otherwise. Again, from the firm's perspective, the consequence might be to raise costs above the level that could be achieved if each production activity was dispersed to the optimal location for that activity. And finally, even when trade barriers do not exist, the firm may still want to locate some production activities in a given country to reduce the threat of trade barriers being imposed in the future.

All these effects are likely to raise the firm's costs above the level that could be achieved in a world without trade barriers. The higher costs that result need not translate into a significant competitive disadvantage relative to other foreign firms, however, if the countries imposing trade barriers do so to the imported products of all foreign firms, irrespective of their national origin. But when trade barriers are targeted at exports from a particular nation, firms based in that nation are at a competitive disadvantage to firms of other nations. The firm may deal with such targeted trade barriers by moving production into the country imposing barriers. Another strategy may be to move production to countries whose exports are not targeted by the specific trade barrier.

Finally, the threat of antidumping action limits the ability of a firm to use aggressive pricing to gain market share in a country. Firms in a country also can make strategic use of antidumping measures to limit aggressive competition from low-cost foreign producers. For example, the U.S. steel industry has been very aggressive in bringing antidumping actions against foreign steelmakers, particularly in times of weak global demand for steel and excess capacity. In 1998 and 1999, the United States faced a surge in low-cost steel imports as a severe recession in Asia left producers there with excess capacity. The U.S. producers filed several complaints with the International Trade Commission. One argued that Japanese producers of hot rolled steel were selling it at below cost in the United States. The ITC agreed and levied tariffs ranging from 18 percent to 67 percent on imports of certain steel products from Japan (these tariffs are separate from the steel tariffs discussed earlier).[42]

Policy Implications

As noted in Chapter 5, business firms are major players on the international trade scene. Because of their pivotal role in international trade, firms can and do exert a strong influence on government policy toward trade. This influence can encourage protectionism or it can encourage the government to support the WTO and push for open markets and freer trade among all nations. Government policies with regard to international trade can have a direct impact on business.

Consistent with strategic trade policy, examples can be found of government intervention in the form of tariffs, quotas, antidumping actions, and subsidies helping firms and industries establish a competitive advantage in the world economy. In general, however, the arguments contained in this chapter and in Chapter 5 suggest that government intervention has three drawbacks. Intervention can be self-defeating because it tends to protect the inefficient rather than help firms become efficient global competitors. Intervention is dangerous; it may invite retaliation and trigger a trade war. Finally, intervention is unlikely to be well executed, given the opportunity for such a policy to be captured by special-interest groups. Does this mean that business should simply encourage government to adopt a laissez-faire free trade policy?

Most economists would probably argue that the best interests of international business are served by a free trade stance, but not a laissez-faire stance. It is probably in the best long-run interests of the business community to encourage the government to aggressively promote greater free trade by, for example, strengthening the WTO. Business probably has much more to gain from government efforts to open protected markets to imports and foreign direct investment than from government efforts to support certain domestic industries in a manner consistent with the recommendations of strategic trade policy.

This conclusion is reinforced by a phenomenon we touched on in Chapter 1—the increasing integration of the world economy and internationalization of production that has occurred over the past two decades. We live in a world where many firms of all national origins increasingly depend for their competitive advantage on globally dispersed production systems. Such systems are the result of freer trade. Freer trade has brought great advantages to firms that have exploited it and to consumers who benefit from the resulting lower prices. Given the danger of retaliatory action, business firms that lobby their governments to engage in protectionism must realize that by doing so they may be denying themselves the opportunity to build a competitive advantage by constructing a globally dispersed production system. By encouraging their governments to engage in protectionism, their own activities and sales overseas may be jeopardized if other governments retaliate. This does not mean a firm should never seek protection in the form of antidumping actions and the like, but it should review its options carefully and think through the larger consequences.

Key Terms

free trade, p. 192
tariff, p. 194
specific tariff, p. 194
ad valorem tariff, p. 194
subsidy, p. 195
import quota, p. 196
tariff rate quota, p. 197
voluntary export restraint (VER), p. 197
quota rent, p. 198
local content requirement, p. 198
administrative trade policies, p. 198
dumping, p. 199
antidumping policies, p. 199
countervailing duties, p. 199
Helms-Burton Act, p. 204
D'Amato Act, p. 204
infant industry argument, p. 205
strategic trade policy argument, p. 206
Smoot-Hawley Act, p. 209

Summary

The goal of this chapter was to describe how the reality of international trade deviates from the theoretical ideal of unrestricted free trade reviewed in Chapter 5. In this chapter, we have reported the various instruments of trade policy, reviewed the political and economic arguments for government intervention in international trade, reexamined the economic case for free trade in light of the strategic trade policy argument, and looked at the evolution of the world trading framework. While a policy of free trade may not always be the theoretically optimal policy (given the arguments of the new trade theorists), in practice it is probably the best policy for a government to pursue. In particular, the long-run interests of business and consumers may be best served by strengthening international institutions such as the WTO. Given the danger that isolated protectionism might escalate into a trade war, business probably has far more to gain from government efforts to open protected markets to imports and foreign direct investment (through the WTO) than from government efforts to protect domestic industries from foreign competition. The chapter made the following points:

1. Trade policies, such as tariffs, subsidies, antidumping regulations, and local content requirements tend to be pro-producer and anti-consumer. Gains accrue to producers (who are protected from foreign competitors), but consumers lose because they must pay more for imports.
2. There are two types of arguments for government intervention in international trade: political and economic. Political arguments for intervention are concerned with protecting the interests of certain groups, often at the expense of other groups, or with promoting goals with regard to foreign policy, human rights, consumer protection, and the like. Economic arguments for intervention are about boosting the overall wealth of a nation.
3. A common political argument for intervention is that it is necessary to protect jobs. However, political intervention often hurts consumers and it can be self-defeating. Countries sometimes argue that it is important to protect certain industries for reasons of national security. Some argue that government should use the threat to intervene in trade policy as a bargaining tool to open foreign markets. This can be a risky policy; if it fails, the result can be higher trade barriers.
4. The infant industry argument for government intervention contends that to let manufacturing get a toehold, governments should temporarily support new industries. In practice, however, governments often end up protecting the inefficient.
5. Strategic trade policy suggests that with subsidies, government can help domestic firms gain first-mover advantages in global industries where economies of scale are important. Government subsidies may also help domestic firms overcome barriers to entry into such industries.
6. The problems with strategic trade policy are twofold: (*a*) such a policy may invite retaliation, in which case all will lose, and (*b*) strategic trade policy may be captured by special-interest groups, which will distort it to their own ends.
7. The GATT was a product of the postwar free trade movement. The GATT was successful in lowering trade barriers on manufactured goods and commodities. The move toward greater free trade under the GATT appeared to stimulate economic growth.
8. The completion of the Uruguay Round of GATT talks and the establishment of the World Trade Organization have strengthened the world trading system by extending GATT rules to services, increasing protection for intellectual property, reducing agricultural subsidies, and enhancing monitoring and enforcement mechanisms.
9. Trade barriers act as a constraint on a firm's ability to disperse its various production activities to optimal locations around the globe. One response to trade barriers is to establish more production activities in the protected country.
10. Business may have more to gain from government efforts to open protected markets to imports and foreign direct investment than from government efforts to protect domestic industries from foreign competition.

Critical Thinking and Discussion Questions

1. Do you think governments should consider human rights when granting preferential trading rights to countries? What are the arguments for and against taking such a position?
2. Whose interests should be the paramount concern of government trade policy—the interests of producers (businesses and their employees) or those of consumers?
3. Given the arguments relating to the new trade theory and strategic trade policy, what kind of trade policy should business be pressuring government to adopt?
4. You are an employee of a U.S. firm that produces personal computers in Thailand and then exports them to the United States and other countries for sale. The personal computers were originally produced in Thailand to take advantage of relatively low labor costs and a skilled workforce. Other possible locations considered at the time were Malaysia and Hong Kong. The U.S. government decides to impose punitive 100 percent ad valorem tariffs on imports of computers from Thailand to punish the country for administrative trade barriers that restrict U.S. exports to Thailand. How should your firm respond? What does this tell you about the use of targeted trade barriers?

Research Task 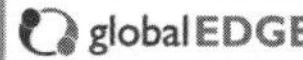 http://globalEDGE.msu.edu

Use the globalEDGE site (http://globalEDGE.msu.edu/) to complete the following exercises:

1. Your company is considering exporting its agriculture and fishery products to Egypt, but management's current knowledge of the country's trade policies and barriers for this sector is limited. Conduct the appropriate level of research in a trade barriers database to identify any information on Egypt's current certification requirements for agriculture and fishery products. Prepare an executive summary of your findings.
2. You work for a raw materials provider that sells leather to a large baseball glove manufacturer. Due to a recent disruption in your leather supply from Asia, you are seeking to find new partners in Africa through a well-known *trade contact database*. Which five African countries have the most contacts for possible leather suppliers? Of these five countries, choose three to focus on and develop relationships. Sometimes, managers make choices related to suppliers based on volume and uniformity of the product to be supplied. What were your criteria for selecting your three countries?

closing case

TRADE IN TEXTILES—HOLDING THE CHINESE JUGGERNAUT IN CHECK

Since 1974, international trade in textiles has been governed by a system of quotas known as the Multi-Fiber Agreement (MFA). Designed to protect textile producers in developed nations from foreign competition, the MFA assigned countries quotas that specified the amount of textiles they could export. The quotas restrained textile exports from some countries, such as China, but in other cases created a textile industry that might not have existed. Countries such as Bangladesh, Sri Lanka, and Cambodia were able to take advantage of favorable quota allocations to build significant textile industries that generated substantial exports. In 2003, textiles accounted for more than 70 percent of exports from Bangladesh and Cambodia and 50 percent of those from Sri Lanka.

This is now changing. When the World Trade Organization was created in 1995, member countries agreed to let the MFA expire on December 31, 2004. At the time, many textile exporters in the developing world expected to gain from the elimination of the quota system. What they did not anticipate, however, was that China would join the WTO in 2001 and that Chinese textile exports would surge. By 2003, China was making 17 percent of the world's textiles, but this may only be a start. The WTO forecasts that China's share may rise to 50 percent by 2007 as the country's producers take advantage of the removal of quotas to expand their exports to the United States and European Union, displacing exports from many other developing nations. China's gains are due to its comparative advantage in the manufacture of textiles. Not only does the country benefit from low wages and a productive labor force, but China's huge factories also enable its producers to attain economies of scale unimaginable in most developing nations. Also, the country's good infrastructure ensures quick transport of products and a timely turnaround of ships at ports, a critical asset in the clothing industry where fashion trends can result in rapid changes in demand. Chinese producers have been able to reduce the order-to-shipment cycle to as low as 60 days, far below the 90 to 120 days achieved by many other producers in the developing world. In addition, Chinese textile producers have garnered a reputation for reliably delivering on commitments, unlike those in some other countries. Producers in Bangladesh, for example, have a reputation for low quality and poor delivery that offsets their low prices.

Fearful that they will lose market share to China, trade associations from more than 50 other textile-producing nations, many of them low- and middle-income nations, signed the "Istanbul declaration" in 2004 asking the WTO to delay the removal of quotas, but to no avail. Many developing nations now fear that they will lose substantial market share to China. This could conceivably cripple the economies of countries such as Bangladesh, where some 2 million people, most of them women, are employed in the textile industry. Other developing nations, however, think that they might benefit from the removal of the MFA. They believe that buyers in developed nations will need to diversify their supply base as a hedge against disruption in China. Among this second group are Vietnam, India, and Pakistan, all of which expect rising textile exports after 2004. The Indian textile manufacturers group expects Indian textile exports to grow by 18 percent a year after 2004, reaching $40 billion in 2010, or one-third of the country's exports.

In developing nations, too, the prospect of surging imports from China causes unease. In the United States, textile producers lobbied the government to impose quotas on Chinese imports after the MFA expired. Under the terms of China's entry into the WTO, the United States and other major trading nations reserved the right until 2008 to impose annual quotas on Chinese textile imports if they are deemed to be "disruptive."

China tried to head off protectionist pressures in December 2004 by announcing it would impose a tariff on textile exports. By raising the costs of Chinese textiles, the tariff was designed to reduce overseas demand. However, the tariffs are modest, ranging from 2.4 to 6 cents per item, with most at the low end of the range. Many observers see them as little more than a token gesture.

The first eight months of 2005 provided a glimpse of what may be to come. Imports of Chinese textiles into the United States surged 64 percent compared with the same period in 2004 to $15.4 billion. Chinese textile imports into the EU also rose. However, others noted that total textile imports into the U.S. remained flat, and that the surge represented a shift from other producers to China, rather than an absolute increase in the volume of imports. Notwithstanding this, the increase in imports resulted in renewed calls in the United States for quotas on Chinese textile imports. Recognizing reality, in mid-2005 the Chinese entered into bilateral negotiations with the United States to limit imports of Chinese textiles. In November 2005, they reached an agreement that capped the growth in Chinese imports into the United States to around 15 percent per annum through until 2008, after which restrictions will be lifted. The EU struck a similar deal with China some months earlier.

Sources: "The Looming Revolution—The Textile Industry," *The Economist,* November 13, 2004, pp. 92–96; "A New Knot in Textile Trade," *The Economist,* December 18, 2004, p. 138; "Textile Disruption," *The Wall Street Journal,* April 11, 2005, p. A21; M. Fong and W. Echikson, "China Bristles at U.S. Inquiry on Textiles Trade," *The Wall Street Journal,* April 6, 2005, p. A9; and M. Fong, "China, U.S. Sign Three-Year Pact on Textile Trade," *The Wall Street Journal,* November 9, 2005, p. A14.

Case Discussion Questions

1. Was the removal of the Multi-Fiber Agreement a positive thing for the world economy? Why?
2. As a producer in a developing nation such as Bangladesh that benefited from the MFA agreement, how should you respond to the expiration of the agreement?
3. Do you think China was right to place a tariff on exports of textiles from China? Why? Does such action help or harm the world economy?
4. Whose interests were served by the November 2005 agreement between the United States and China to limit the growth of Chinese textile imports into the United States? Do you think the agreement was a good one for the United States?
5. What kind of trade barrier was erected by the November 2005 agreement between China and the United States?

Shizuo Kambayashi/AP Wide World

part 3 Cross-Border Trade and Investment

LEARNING OBJECTIVES

1. Be familiar with current trends regarding FDI in the world economy.
2. Understand the different theories of foreign direct investment.
3. Appreciate how political ideology shapes a government's attitudes toward FDI.
4. Understand the benefits and costs of FDI to home and host countries.
5. Be able to discuss the range of policy instruments that governments use to influence FDI.
6. Articulate the implications for management practice of the theory and government policies associated with FDI.

chapter 7

Foreign Direct Investment

Starbucks' Foreign Direct Investment

opening case

Thirty years ago, Starbucks was a single store in Seattle's Pike Place Market selling premium roasted coffee. Today it is a global roaster and retailer of coffee with over 11,300 stores, more than 3,300 of which are to be found in 37 foreign countries. Starbucks Corporation set out on its current course in the 1980s when the company's director of marketing, Howard Schultz, came back from a trip to Italy enchanted with the Italian coffeehouse experience. Schultz, who later became CEO, persuaded the company's owners to experiment with the coffeehouse format—and the Starbucks experience was born. The strategy was to sell the company's own premium roasted coffee and freshly brewed espresso-style coffee beverages, along with a variety of pastries, coffee accessories, teas, and other products, in a tastefully designed coffeehouse setting. The company also focused on providing superior customer service. Reasoning that motivated employees provide the best customer service, Starbucks' executives devoted a lot of attention to employee hiring and training programs and progressive compensation policies that gave even part-time employees stock option grants and medical benefits. The formula led to spectacular success in the United States, where Starbucks went from obscurity to one of the best-known brands in the country in a decade.

In 1995, with 700 stores across the United States, Starbucks began exploring foreign opportunities. Its first target market was Japan. Although Starbucks had resisted a franchising strategy in North America, where its stores are company owned, Starbucks initially decided to license its format in Japan. However, the company also realized that a pure licensing agreement would not give it the control needed to ensure that the Japanese licensees closely followed Starbucks' successful formula. So the company established a joint venture with a local retailer, Sazaby Inc. Each company held a 50 percent stake in the venture, Starbucks Coffee of Japan. Starbucks initially invested $10 million in this venture, its first foreign direct investment. The Starbucks format was then licensed to the venture, which was charged with taking over responsibility for growing Starbucks' presence in Japan.

To make sure the Japanese operations replicated the "Starbucks experience" in North America, Starbucks transferred some employees to the Japanese operation. The licensing agreement required all Japanese store managers and employees to attend training classes similar to those given to U.S. employees. The agreement also required that stores adhere to the design parameters established in the United States. In 2001, the company introduced a stock option plan for all Japanese employees, making it the first company in Japan to do so. Skeptics doubted that Starbucks would be able to replicate its North American success overseas, but by 2005 Starbucks' had some 575 stores in Japan and plans to continue opening them at a brisk pace.

After Japan, the company embarked on an aggressive foreign investment program. In 1998, it purchased Seattle Coffee, a British coffee chain with 60 retail stores, for $84 million. An American couple, originally from Seattle, had started Seattle Coffee with the intention of establishing a Starbucks-like chain in Britain. In the late 1990s, Starbucks opened stores in Taiwan, China, Singapore, Thailand, New Zealand, South Korea, and Malaysia.

In Asia, Starbucks' most common strategy was to license its format to a local operator in return for initial licensing fees and royalties on store revenues. As in Japan, Starbucks insisted on an intensive employee training program and strict specifications regarding the format and layout of the store. However, Starbucks became disenchanted with some of the straight licensing arrangements and converted several into joint-venture arrangements or wholly owned subsidiaries. In Thailand, for example, Starbucks initially entered into a licensing agreement with Coffee Partners, a local Thai company. Under the terms of the licensing agreement, Coffee Partners was required to open at least 20 Starbucks coffee stores in Thailand within five years. However, Coffee Partners found it difficult to raise funds from Thai banks to finance this expansion. In July 2000, Starbucks acquired Coffee Partners for about $12 million. Its goal was to gain tighter control over the expansion strategy in Thailand.

By 2002, Starbucks was pursuing an aggressive expansion in mainland Europe. As its first entry point, Starbucks chose Switzerland. Drawing on its experience in Asia, the company entered into a joint venture with a Swiss company, Bon Appetit Group, Switzerland's largest food service company. Bon Appetit was to hold a majority stake in the venture, and Starbucks would license its format to the Swiss company using a similar agreement to those it had used successfully in Asia. This was followed by a joint venture in other countries. In early 2006, Starbucks announced that it believed there was the potential for up to 15,000 stores outside of the United States, with major opportunities in China which the company now views as the largest single market opportunity outside of the United States.

Sources: Starbucks 10K, various years; C. McLean, "Starbucks Set to Invade Coffee-Loving Continent," *Seattle Times,* October 4, 2000, p. E1; J. Ordonez, "Starbucks to Start Major Expansion in Overseas Market," *The Wall Street Journal,* October 27, 2000, p. B10; S. Homes and D. Bennett, "Planet Starbucks," *Business Week,* September 9, 2002, pp. 99–110; "Starbucks Outlines International Growth Strategy," *Business Wire,* October 14, 2004; and A. Yeh, "Starbucks Aims for New Tier in China," *Financial Times,* February 14, 2006, p. 17.

Introduction

Foreign direct investment (FDI) occurs when a firm invests directly in facilities to produce or market a product in a foreign country. According to the U.S. Department of Commerce, FDI occurs whenever a U.S. citizen, organization, or affiliated group takes an interest of 10 percent or more in a foreign business entity. Once a firm undertakes FDI, it becomes a *multinational enterprise*. An example of FDI is given in the opening case. Starting in 1995, Starbucks began to move into other nations. By 2006, this FDI had transformed Starbucks into a global brand with operations in 37 countries.

FDI takes on two main forms. The first is a **greenfield investment,** which involves the establishment of a new operation in a foreign country. The second involves acquiring or merging with an existing firm in the foreign country (most of Starbucks' expansion has been in the form of greenfield investments, although it did acquire Britain's Seattle Coffee). Acquisitions can be a minority (where the foreign firm takes a 10 percent to 49 percent interest in the firm's voting stock), majority (foreign interest of 50 percent to 99 percent), or full outright stake (foreign interest of 100 percent).[1]

Greenfield Investment
Establishing a new operation in a foreign country.

We begin this chapter by looking at the importance of foreign direct investment in the world economy. Next, we review the theories that have been used to explain foreign direct investment. The chapter then moves on to look at government policy toward foreign direct investment and closes with a section on implications for business.

Foreign Direct Investment in the World Economy

LEARNING OBJECTIVE 1
Be familiar with current trends regarding FDI in the world economy.

When discussing foreign direct investment, it is important to distinguish between the flow of FDI and the stock of FDI. The **flow of FDI** refers to the amount of FDI undertaken over a given time period (normally a year). The **stock of FDI** refers to the total accumulated value of foreign-owned assets at a given time. We also talk of **outflows of FDI,** meaning the flow of FDI out of a country, and **inflows of FDI,** the flow of FDI into a country.

Flow of FDI
The amount of FDI undertaken over a given time.

Stock of FDI
The total accumulated value of foreign-owned assets at a given time.

Outflows of FDI
The flow of FDI out of a country.

Inflows of FDI
The flow of FDI into a country.

TRENDS IN FDI The past 30 years have seen a marked increase in both the flow and stock of FDI in the world economy. The average yearly outflow of FDI increased from $25 billion in 1975 to a record $1.2 trillion in 2000, before falling back to an estimated $897 billion in 2005 (see Figure 7.1).[2] Over this period, the flow of FDI accelerated faster than the growth in world trade and world output. For example, between 1992 and 2005, the total flow of FDI from all countries increased more than fivefold while world trade by value grew by some 140 percent and world output by around 40 percent.[3] As a result of the strong FDI flow, by 2004 the global stock of FDI exceeded $9 trillion. At least 70,000 parent companies had 690,000 affiliates in foreign markets that collectively employed more than 50 million people abroad and generated value accounting for about one-tenth of global GDP. The foreign affiliates of multinationals had an estimated $19 trillion in global sales, much higher than the value of global exports, which stood at close to $11 trillion.[4]

FDI has grown more rapidly than world trade and world output for several reasons. First, despite the general decline in trade barriers over the past 30 years, business firms still fear protectionist pressures. Executives see FDI as a way of circumventing future trade barriers. Second, much of the recent increase in FDI is being driven by the political and economic changes that have been occurring in many of the world's developing nations. The general shift toward democratic political institutions and free market economies that we discussed in Chapter 2 has encouraged FDI. Across much of Asia, Eastern Europe, and Latin America, economic growth, economic deregulation, privatization

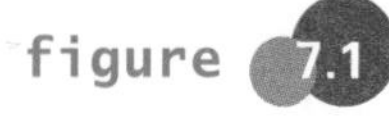

FDI Outflows 1982–2005 ($ billions)

Source: Raw data from United Nations, *World Investment Report*, various editions.

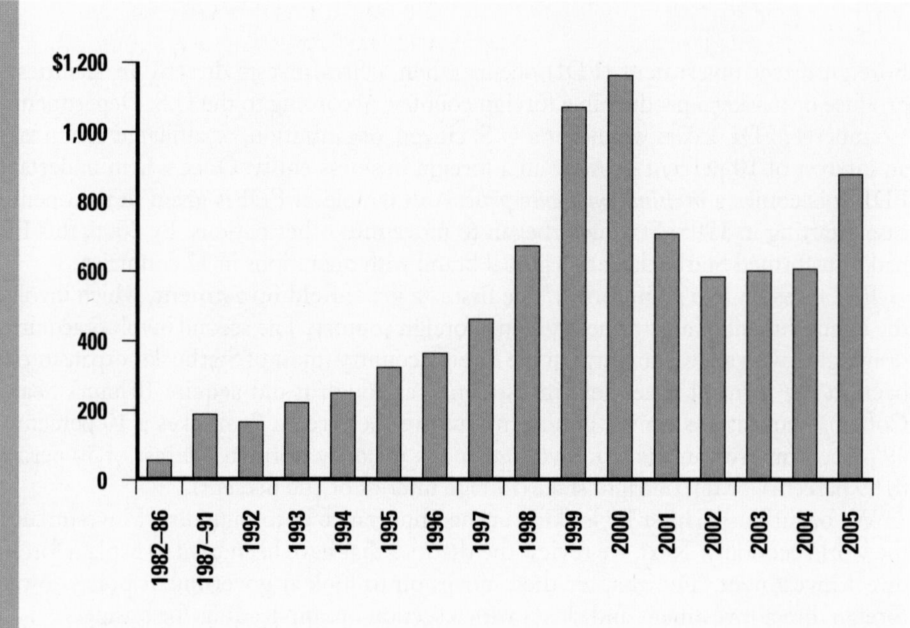

programs that are open to foreign investors, and removal of many restrictions on FDI have made these countries more attractive to foreign multinationals. According to the United Nations, some 93 percent of the 2,156 changes made worldwide between 1991 and 2004 in the laws governing foreign direct investment created a more favorable environment for FDI.[5] The desire of governments to facilitate FDI also has been reflected in a dramatic increase in the number of bilateral investment treaties designed to protect and promote investment between two countries. As of 2004, 2,392 such treaties involved more than 160 countries, a 12-fold increase from the 181 treaties that existed in 1980.[6] Third, the globalization of the world economy is also having a positive impact on the volume of FDI. Firms such as Starbucks now see the whole world as their market, and they are undertaking FDI in an attempt to make sure they have a significant presence in many regions of the world. For reasons that we shall explore later in this book, many firms now believe it is important to have production facilities based close to their major customers. This, too, creates pressure for greater FDI.

THE DIRECTION OF FDI Historically, most FDI has been directed at the developed nations of the world as firms based in advanced countries invested in the others' markets (see Figure 7.2). During the 1980s and 1990s, the United States was often the favorite target for FDI inflows. The United States has been an attractive target for FDI because of its large and wealthy domestic markets, its dynamic and stable economy, a favorable political environment, and the openness of the country to FDI. Investors include firms based in Great Britain, Japan, Germany, Holland, and France. Inward investment into the United States remained high during the early 2000s, totaling $106 billion in 2005. The developed nations of the European Union have also been recipients of significant FDI inflows, principally from U.S. and Japanese enterprises and from other member states of the EU. In 2005, inward investment into the EU reached a record $445 billion, or roughly half of all FDI in that year. France was the largest national recipient, with inward investments of some $49 billion.[7]

Even though developed nations still account for the largest share of FDI inflows, FDI into developing nations has increased (see Figure 7.2). From 1985 to 1990, the annual

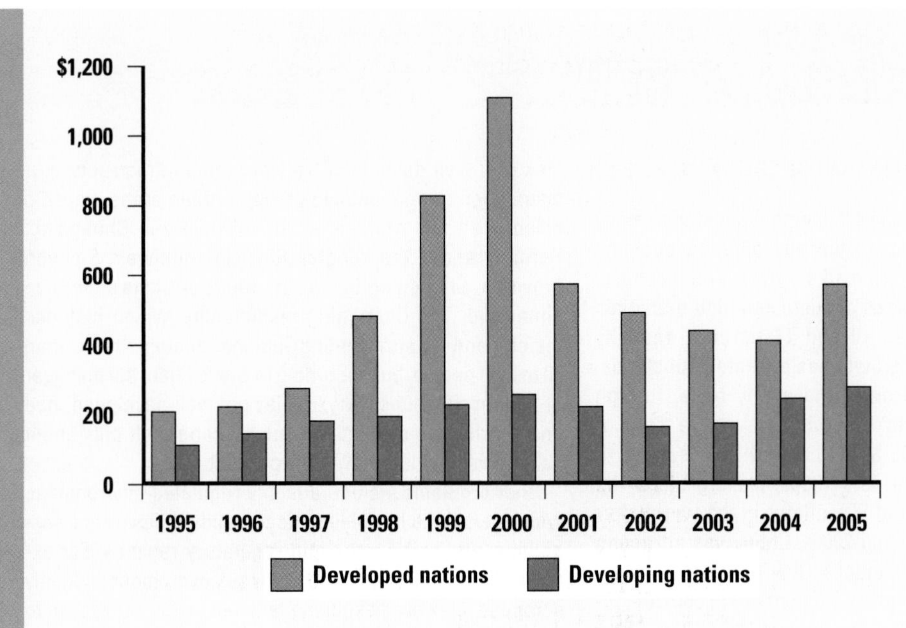

figure 7.2

FDI Flows by Region ($ billions), 1995–2005

Source: Raw data from United Nations, *World Investment Report*, various editions.

inflow of FDI into developing nations averaged $27.4 billion, or 17.4 percent of the total global flow. In the mid- to late 1990s, the inflow into developing nations was generally between 35 and 40 percent of the total, before falling back to account for about 25 percent of the total in the 2000–02 period and then rising to around 33 to 36 percent in 2004 and 2005. Most recent inflows into developing nations have been targeted at the emerging economies of South, East, and Southeast Asia. Driving much of the increase has been the growing importance of China as a recipient of FDI, which attracted around $60 billion of FDI in 2004 and again in 2005.[8] The reasons for the strong flow of investment into China are discussed in the accompanying Country Focus on page 232.

Latin America emerged as the next most important region in the developing world for FDI inflows. In 2005, total inward investments into this region reached about $72 billion. Mexico and Brazil have historically been the two top recipients of inward FDI in Latin America, a trend that continued in 2005. At the other end of the scale, Africa has long received the smallest amount of inward investment, about $28 billion in 2005. The inability of Africa to attract greater investment is in part a reflection of the political unrest, armed conflict, and frequent changes in economic policy in the region.[9]

Another way of looking at the importance of FDI inflows is to express them as a percentage of gross fixed capital formation. **Gross fixed capital formation** summarizes the total amount of capital invested in factories, stores, office buildings, and the like. Other things being equal, the greater the capital investment in an economy, the more favorable its future growth prospects are likely to be. Viewed this way, FDI can be seen as an important source of capital investment and a determinant of the future growth rate of an economy. Figure 7.3 (page 233) summarizes inward flows of FDI as a percentage of gross fixed capital formation for developed and developing economies for the 1992–2004 period. During the 1992–97 period, FDI accounted for about 4 percent of gross fixed capital formation in developed nations and 8 percent in developing nations. By the 1998–2004 period, the figure was 12.2 percent worldwide, suggesting that FDI had become an increasingly important source of investment in the world's economies.

Gross Fixed Capital Formation
The summary of the total amount of capital invested in factories, stores, office buildings, and the like.

These gross figures hide important individual country differences. For example, in 2004, inward FDI accounted for some 22 percent of gross fixed capital formation in

Country FOCUS

Foreign Direct Investment in China

Beginning in late 1978, China's leadership decided to move the economy away from a centrally planned socialist system to one that was more market driven. The result has been close to three decades of sustained high economic growth rates of between 10 and 11 percent annually compounded. This rapid growth has attracted substantial foreign investment. Starting from a tiny base, foreign investment increased to an annual average rate of $2.7 billion between 1985 and 1990 and then surged to $40 billion annually in the late 1990s, making China the second-biggest recipient of FDI inflows in the world after the United States. By the mid-2000s, China was attracting around $60 billion of FDI annually. Over the past 20 years, this inflow has resulted in establishment of 215,000 foreign-funded enterprises in China. The total stock of FDI in China grew from effectively zero in 1978 to $245 billion in 2004 ($457 billion if Hong Kong is added to this figure). FDI amounted to about 15 percent of China's total GDP in 2004 and some 10 percent of annualized gross fixed capital formation between 1998 and 2004.

The reasons for the investment are fairly obvious. With a population of more than 1 billion people, China represents the largest market in the world. Import tariffs have made it difficult to serve this market via exports, so FDI was required if a company wanted to tap into the country's huge potential. Although China joined the World Trade Organization in 2001, which will ultimately mean a reduction in import tariffs, this will occur slowly, so this motive for investing in China will persist. Also, many foreign firms believe that doing business in China requires a substantial presence in the country to build *guanxi,* the crucial relationship networks (see Chapter 3 for details). Furthermore, a combination of cheap labor and tax incentives, particularly for enterprises that establish themselves in special economic zones, makes China an attractive base from which to serve Asian or world markets with exports.

Less obvious, at least to begin with, was how difficult it would be for foreign firms to do business in China. Blinded by the size and potential of China's market, many firms have paid scant attention to the complexities of operating a business in this country until after the investment has been made. China may have a huge population, but despite two decades of rapid growth, it is still a poor country. The lack of purchasing power translates into a weak market for many Western consumer goods. Another problem is the lack of a well-developed transportation infrastructure or distribution system outside of major urban areas. PepsiCo discovered this problem at its subsidiary in Chongqing. Perched above the Yangtze River in southwest Sichuan province, Chongqing lies at the heart of China's massive hinterland. The Chongqing municipality, which includes the city and its surrounding regions, contains more than 30 million people, but according to Steve Chen, the manager of the PepsiCo subsidiary, the lack of well-developed road and distribution systems means he can reach only about half of this population with his product.

Other problems include a highly regulated environment, which can make it problematic to conduct business transactions, and shifting tax and regulatory regimes. For example, a few years ago, the Chinese government suddenly scrapped a tax credit scheme that had made it attractive to import capital equipment into China. This immediately made it more expensive to set up operations in the country. Then there are problems with local joint-venture partners that are inexperienced, opportunistic, or simply operate according to different goals. One U.S. manager explained that when he laid off 200 people to reduce costs, his Chinese partner hired them all back the next day. When he inquired why they had been hired back, the executive of the Chinese partner, which was government owned, explained that as an agency of the government, it had an "obligation" to reduce unemployment.

To continue to attract foreign investment, the Chinese government has committed itself to invest more than $800 billion in infrastructure projects over the next 10 years. This should improve the nation's poor highway system. By giving preferential tax breaks to companies that invest in special regions, such as that around Chongqing, the Chinese have created incentives for foreign companies to invest in China's vast interior where markets are underserved. They have been pursuing a macroeconomic policy that includes an emphasis on maintaining steady economic growth, low inflation, and a stable currency, all of which are attractive to foreign investors. Given these developments, it seems likely that the country will continue to be an important magnet for foreign investors well into the future.

Sources: Interviews by the author while in China; United Nations, *World Investment Report, 2005* (New York and Geneva: United Nations, 2005); Linda Ng and C. Tuan, "Building a Favorable Investment Environment: Evidence for the Facilitation of FDI in China," *The World Economy,* 2002, pp. 1095–114; and S. Chan and G. Qingyang, "Investment in China Migrates Inland," *Far Eastern Economic Review,* May 2006, pp 52–57.

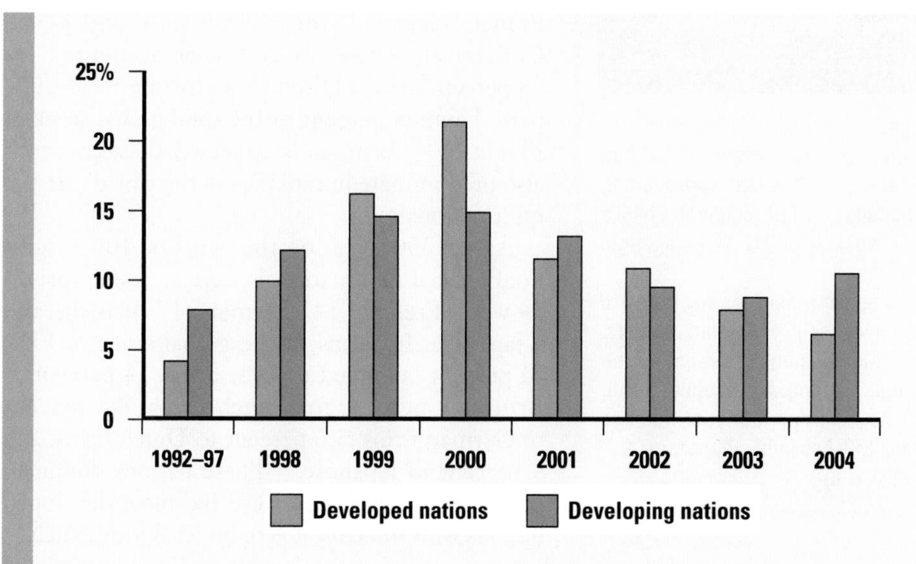

figure 7.3

Inward FDI as a Percentage of Gross Fixed Capital Formation, 1992–2004

Source: Raw data from United Nations, *World Investment Report*, various editions.

Britain and 53 in Belgium, but only 3.4 percent in India and 0.7 percent in Japan—suggesting that FDI is an important source of investment capital, and thus economic growth, in the first two countries but not the latter two. These differences can be explained by several factors, including the perceived ease and attractiveness of investing in a nation. To the extent that burdensome regulations limit the opportunities for foreign investment in countries such as Japan and India, these nations may be hurting themselves by limiting their access to needed capital investments.

THE SOURCE OF FDI Since World War II, the United States has been the largest source country for FDI, a position it retained during the late 1990s and early 2000s (see Figure 7.4). Other important source countries include the United Kingdom,

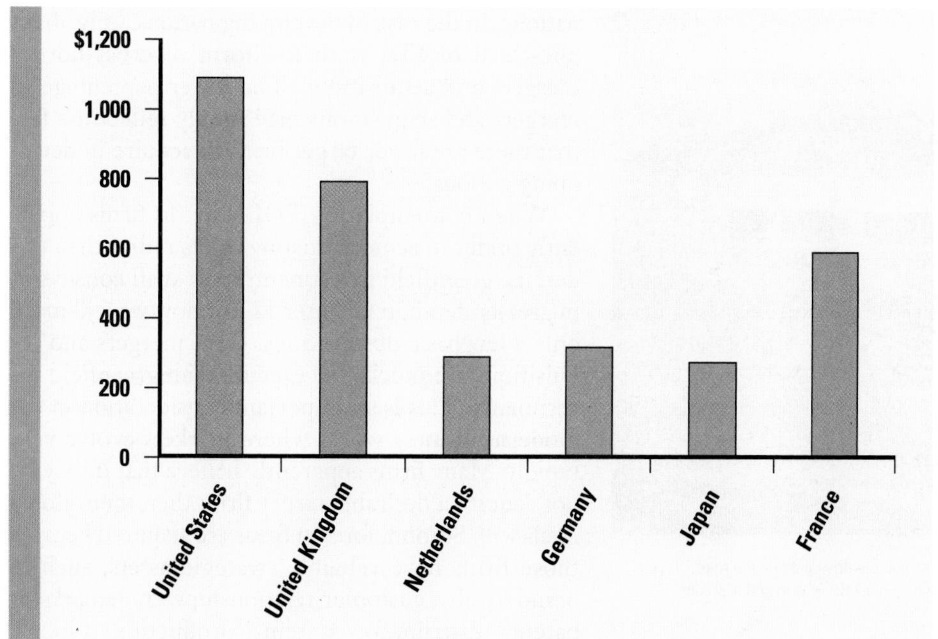

figure 7.4

Cumulative FDI Outflows ($ billions), 1998–2004

Source: Raw data from United Nations, *World Investment Report*, various editions.

Another Perspective

China's FDI: Both Ways!

As the Country Focus indicates, China's inward FDI has been growing at record rates, and it is fast approaching the United States as the number one FDI recipient. China's neighbors find that China is soaking up FDI like a sponge, and away from them.

China is also using its domestic resources for *outward* FDI to establish its influence, especially in Asian markets. China just announced that it is bringing production of the MG sportscar to Oklahoma. Nanjing Automobile Group bought the bankrupt MG Rover group last year. (James Mackintosh, "Nanjing Plans MG Assembly Plant for U.S.," *Financial Times,* July 13, 2006, p. 6)

France, Germany, the Netherlands, and Japan. Collectively, these six countries accounted for 58 percent of all FDI outflows for the 1998–2004 period and 64 percent of the total global stock of FDI in 2004. As might be expected, these countries also predominate in rankings of the world's largest multinationals.

As of 2004, 25 of the world's 100 largest nonfinancial multinationals were U.S. enterprises; 14 were French; 14 German; 12 British; and 9 Japanese. In terms of the global stock of FDI, 21 percent belonged to U.S. firms, 14 percent to British, 8 percent to French firms, 8.5 percent to German firms, 5.6 percent to Dutch firms, and 4 percent to Japanese.[10] These nations dominate primarily because they were the most developed nations with the largest economies during much of the postwar period and therefore home to many of the largest and best-capitalized enterprises. Many of these countries also had a long history as trading nations and naturally looked to foreign markets to fuel their economic expansion. Thus, it is no surprise that enterprises based there have been at the forefront of foreign investment trends.

THE FORM OF FDI: ACQUISITIONS VERSUS GREENFIELD INVESTMENTS FDI can take the form of a greenfield investment in a new facility or an acquisition of or a merger with an existing local firm. The data suggest the majority of cross-border investment is in the form of mergers and acquisitions rather than greenfield investments. UN estimates indicate that some 40 to 80 percent of all FDI inflows were in the form of mergers and acquisitions between 1998 and 2003. In 2001, for example, mergers and acquisitions accounted for some 78 percent of all FDI inflows. In 2004, the figure was 59 percent.[11] However, FDI flows into developed nations differ markedly from those into developing nations. In the case of developing nations, only about one-third of FDI is in the form of cross-border mergers and acquisitions. The lower percentage of mergers and acquisitions may simply reflect the fact that there are fewer target firms to acquire in developing nations.

When you see a BP gas station as you are driving down the road, do you realize that the company is British owned? BP = British Petroleum.
Courtesy BP plc

When contemplating FDI, why do firms apparently prefer to acquire existing assets rather than undertake greenfield investments? We shall consider it in greater depth in Chapter 12; for now we will make only a few basic observations. First, mergers and acquisitions are quicker to execute than greenfield investments. This is an important consideration in the modern business world where markets evolve very rapidly. Many firms apparently believe that if they do not acquire a desirable target firm, then their global rivals will. Second, foreign firms are acquired because those firms have valuable strategic assets, such as brand loyalty, customer relationships, trademarks or patents, distribution systems, production systems, and the like. It is easier and perhaps less risky for a firm to acquire those assets than to build them from the ground up through a greenfield investment. Third, firms make acquisitions because they believe they can increase the efficiency of the acquired unit by transferring capital, technology, or management skills. However, there is evidence that many mergers and acquisitions fail to realize their anticipated gains.[12] Chapter 12 further studies this issue.

THE SHIFT TO SERVICES In the past two decades, the sector composition of FDI has shifted sharply away from extractive industries and manufacturing and toward services. In 1990, some 47 percent of outward FDI stock was in service industries; by 2004, this figure had increased to 66 percent. Similar trends can be seen in the composition of cross-border mergers and acquisitions, in which services are playing a much larger role. The composition of FDI in services has also changed. Until recently it was concentrated in trade and financial services. However, industries such as electricity, water, telecommunications, and business services (such as information technology consulting services) are becoming more prominent.

The shift to services is being driven by four factors that will probably stay in place for some time. First, the shift reflects the general move in many developed economies away from manufacturing and toward service industries. By the early 2000s, services accounted for 72 percent of the GDP in developed economies and 52 percent in developing economies. Second, many services cannot be traded internationally. They need to be produced where they are consumed. Starbucks, which is a service business, cannot sell hot lattes to Japanese consumers from its Seattle stores—it has to set up shops in Japan. FDI is the principal way to bring services to foreign markets. Third, many countries have liberalized their regimes governing FDI in services (Chapter 6 revealed that the WTO engineered global deals to remove barriers to cross-border investment in telecommunications and financial services during the late 1990s). This liberalization has made large inflows possible. After Brazil privatized its telecommunications company in the late 1990s and removed restrictions on investment by foreigners in this sector, FDI surged into the Brazilian telecommunications sector.

Finally, the rise of Internet-based global telecommunications networks has allowed some service enterprises to relocate some of their value-creation activities to different nations to take advantage of favorable factor costs. Procter & Gamble, for example, has shifted some of its back-office accounting functions to the Philippines where accountants trained in U.S. accounting rules can be hired at a much lower salary. Dell has call answering centers in India for the same reason. Similarly, both Microsoft and IBM now have some software development and testing facilities located in India. Software code written at Microsoft during the day can now be transmitted instantly to India and then tested while the code writers at Microsoft sleep. By the time the U.S. code writers arrive for work the next morning, the code has been tested, bugs have been identified, and they can start working on corrections. By locating testing facilities in India, Microsoft can work on its code 24 hours a day, reducing the time it takes to develop new software products.

Theories of Foreign Direct Investment

LEARNING OBJECTIVE 2
Understand the different theories of foreign direct investment.

In this section, we review several theories of foreign direct investment. These theories approach the various phenomena of foreign direct investment from three complementary perspectives. One set of theories seeks to explain why a firm will favor direct investment as a means of entering a foreign market when two other alternatives, exporting and licensing, are open to it. Another set of theories seeks to explain why firms in the same industry often undertake foreign direct investment at the same time, and why they favor certain locations over others as targets for foreign direct investment. Put differently, these theories attempt to explain the observed *pattern* of foreign direct investment flows. A third theoretical perspective, known as the **eclectic paradigm,** attempts to combine the two other perspectives into a single holistic explanation of foreign direct investment (this theoretical perspective is *eclectic* because the best aspects of other theories are taken and combined into a single explanation).

Eclectic Paradigm
The theory that combining location-specific assets or resource endowments and the firm's own unique assets often requires FDI; it requires the firm to establish production facilities where those foreign assets or resource endowments are located.

WHY FOREIGN DIRECT INVESTMENT? Why do firms go to all of the trouble of establishing operations abroad through foreign direct investment when two alternatives, exporting and licensing, are available to them for exploiting the profit opportunities in a foreign market? **Exporting** involves producing goods at home and then shipping them to the receiving country for sale. **Licensing** involves granting a foreign entity (the licensee) the right to produce and sell the firm's product in return for a royalty fee on every unit sold. The question is important, given that a cursory examination of the topic suggests that foreign direct investment may be both expensive and risky compared with exporting and licensing. FDI is expensive because a firm must bear the costs of establishing production facilities in a foreign country or of acquiring a foreign enterprise. FDI is risky because of the problems associated with doing business in a different culture where the "rules of the game" may be very different. Relative to indigenous firms, there is a greater probability that a foreign firm undertaking FDI in a country for the first time will make costly mistakes due to its ignorance. When a firm exports, it need not bear the costs associated with FDI, and it can reduce the risks associated with selling abroad by using a native sales agent. Similarly, when a firm allows another enterprise to produce its products under license, the licensee bears the costs or risks. So why do so many firms apparently prefer FDI over either exporting or licensing? The answer can be found by examining the limitations of exporting and licensing as means for capitalizing on foreign market opportunities.

Exporting
Sale of products produced in one country to residents of another country.

Licensing
Occurs when a firm (the licensor) grants a foreign entity (the licensee) the right to produce its product, use its production processes, or use its brand name or trademark in return for a royalty fee on every unit sold.

Limitations of Exporting

The viability of an exporting strategy is often constrained by transportation costs and trade barriers. When transportation costs are added to production costs, it becomes unprofitable to ship some products over a large distance. This is particularly true of products that have a low value-to-weight ratio and that can be produced in almost any location (e.g., cement, soft drinks, etc.). For such products, the attractiveness of exporting decreases, relative to either FDI or licensing. For products with a high value-to-weight ratio, however, transportation costs are normally a minor component of total landed cost (e.g., electronic components, personal computers, medical equipment, computer software, etc.) and have little impact on the relative attractiveness of exporting, licensing, and FDI.

Transportation costs aside, some firms undertake foreign direct investment as a response to actual or threatened trade barriers such as import tariffs or quotas. By placing tariffs on imported goods, governments can increase the cost of exporting relative to foreign direct investment and licensing. Similarly, by limiting imports through quotas, governments increase the attractiveness of FDI and licensing. For example, the wave of FDI by Japanese auto companies in the United States during the 1980s and 1990s was partly driven by protectionist threats from Congress and by quotas on the importation of Japanese cars. For Japanese auto companies, these factors decreased the profitability of exporting and increased that of foreign direct investment. In this context, it is important to understand that trade barriers do not have to be physically in place for FDI to be favored over exporting. Often, the desire to reduce the threat that trade barriers might be imposed is enough to justify foreign direct investment as an alternative to exporting.

Internalization Theory The argument that firms prefer FDI over licensing in order to retain control over know-how, manufacturing, marketing, and strategy or because some firm capabilities are not amenable to licensing.

Limitations of Licensing

There is a branch of economic theory known as **internalization theory** that seeks to explain why firms often prefer foreign direct investment over licensing as a strategy for entering foreign markets.[13] According to internalization theory, licensing has three major drawbacks as a strategy for exploiting foreign market opportunities. First, *licensing may result in a firm's giving away valuable technological know-how to a potential foreign competitor*. For example, back in the 1960s, RCA licensed its leading-edge color television technology to a number of Japanese companies, including Matsushita and Sony. At the time, RCA saw licensing as a way to earn a good return from its technological know-how in the Japanese market without the costs and risks associated with foreign direct investment. However, Matsushita and Sony quickly assimilated RCA's technology and used it to enter the U.S. market to compete directly against RCA. As a result, RCA is now a minor player in its home market, while Matsushita and Sony have a much bigger market share.

A second problem is that *licensing does not give a firm the tight control over manufacturing, marketing, and strategy in a foreign country that may be required to maximize its profitability*. With licensing, control over manufacturing, marketing, and strategy is granted to a licensee in return for a royalty fee. However, for both strategic and operational reasons, a firm may want to retain control over these functions. The rationale for wanting control over the strategy of a foreign entity is that a firm might want its foreign subsidiary to price and market very aggressively as a way of keeping a foreign competitor in check. Unlike a wholly owned subsidiary, a licensee would probably not accept such an imposition, because it would likely reduce the licensee's profit, or it might even cause the licensee to take a loss.

The rationale for wanting control over the operations of a foreign entity is that the firm might wish to take advantage of differences in factor costs across countries, producing only part of its final product in a given country, while importing other parts from elsewhere where they can be produced at lower cost. Again, a licensee would be unlikely to accept such an arrangement, since it would limit the licensee's autonomy. Thus, for these reasons, when tight control over a foreign entity is desirable, foreign direct investment is preferable to licensing.

A third problem with licensing arises when the firm's competitive advantage is based not as much on its products as on the management, marketing, and manufacturing capabilities that produce those products. The problem here is that *such capabilities are often not amenable to licensing*. While a foreign licensee may be able to physically reproduce the firm's product under license, it often may not be able to do so as efficiently as the firm could itself. As a result, the licensee may not be able to fully exploit the profit potential inherent in a foreign market.

For example, consider Toyota, a company whose competitive advantage in the global auto industry is acknowledged to come from its superior ability to manage the overall process of designing, engineering, manufacturing, and selling automobiles; that is, from its management and organizational capabilities. Indeed, Toyota is credited with pioneering the development of a new production process, known as *lean production*, that enables it to produce higher-quality automobiles at a lower cost than its global rivals.[14] Although Toyota could license certain products, its real competitive advantage comes from its management and process capabilities. These kinds of skills are difficult to articulate or codify; they certainly cannot be written down in a simple licensing contract. They are organizationwide and have been developed over the years. They are not embodied in any one individual but instead are widely dispersed throughout the company. Put another way, Toyota's skills are embedded in its organizational culture, and culture is something that cannot be licensed. Thus, if Toyota were to allow a foreign entity to produce its cars under license, the chances are that the entity could not do so anywhere as near as efficiently as could Toyota. In turn, this would limit the ability of the foreign entity to fully develop the market potential of that product. Such reasoning underlies Toyota's preference for direct investment in foreign markets, as opposed to allowing foreign automobile companies to produce its cars under license.

All of this suggests that when one or more of the following conditions holds, markets fail as a mechanism for selling know-how and FDI is more profitable than licensing: (1) when the firm has valuable know-how that cannot be adequately protected by a licensing contract; (2) when the firm needs tight control over a foreign entity to maximize its market share and earnings in that country; and (3) when a firm's skills and know-how are not amenable to licensing.

Advantages of Foreign Direct Investment It follows that a firm will favor foreign direct investment over exporting as an entry strategy when transportation costs or trade barriers make exporting unattractive. Furthermore, the firm will favor foreign direct investment over licensing (or franchising) when it wishes to maintain control over its technological know-how, or over its operations and business strategy, or when the firm's capabilities are simply not amenable to licensing, as may often be the case.

THE PATTERN OF FOREIGN DIRECT INVESTMENT

Observation suggests that firms in the same industry often undertake foreign direct investment at around the same time. Moreover, there is a clear tendency for firms to direct their investment activities toward certain locations. The two theories we consider in this section attempt to explain the patterns that we observe in FDI flows.

Strategic Behavior One theory is based on the idea that FDI flows are a reflection of strategic rivalry between firms in the global marketplace. An early variant of this argument was expounded by F. T. Knickerbocker, who looked at the relationship between FDI and rivalry in oligopolistic industries.[15] An **oligopoly** is an industry composed of a limited number of large firms (e.g., an industry in which four firms control 80 percent of a domestic market would be defined as an oligopoly). A critical competitive feature of such industries is interdependence of the major players: What one firm does can have an immediate impact on the major competitors, forcing a response in kind. By cutting prices, one firm in an oligopoly can take market share away from its competitors, forcing them to respond with similar price cuts to retain their market share. Thus, the interdependence between firms in an oligopoly leads to imitative behavior; rivals often quickly imitate what a firm does in an oligopoly.

Oligopoly
An industry composed of a limited number of large firms.

Imitative behavior can take many forms in an oligopoly. One firm raises prices, the others follow; one expands capacity, and the rivals imitate lest they be left at a disadvantage in the future. Knickerbocker argued that the same kind of imitative behavior characterizes FDI. Consider an oligopoly in the United States in which three firms—A, B, and C—dominate the market. Firm A establishes a subsidiary in France. Firms B and C decide that if successful, this new subsidiary may knock out their export business to France and give firm A a first-mover advantage. Furthermore, firm A might discover some competitive asset in France that it could repatriate to the United States to torment firms B and C on their native soil. Given these possibilities, firms B and C decide to follow firm A and establish operations in France.

Studies that looked at FDI by U.S. firms during the 1950s and 60s show that firms based in oligopolistic industries tended to imitate each other's FDI.[16] The same phenomenon has been observed with regard to FDI undertaken by Japanese firms during the 1980s.[17] For example, Toyota and Nissan responded to investments by Honda in the United States and Europe by undertaking their own FDI in the United States and Europe. More recently, research has shown that models of strategic behavior in a global oligopoly can explain the pattern of FDI in the global tire industry.[18]

Knickerbocker's theory can be extended to embrace the concept of multipoint competition. **Multipoint competition** arises when two or more enterprises encounter each other in different regional markets, national markets, or industries.[19] Economic theory suggests that rather like chess players jockeying for advantage, firms will try to match each other's moves in different markets to try to hold each other in check. The idea is to ensure that a rival does not gain a commanding position in one market and then use the profits generated there to subsidize competitive attacks in other markets. Kodak and Fuji Photo Film Co., for example, compete against each other around the world. If Kodak enters a particular foreign market, Fuji will not be far behind. Fuji feels compelled to follow Kodak to ensure that Kodak does not gain a dominant position in the foreign market that it could then leverage to gain a competitive advantage elsewhere. The converse also holds, with Kodak following Fuji when the Japanese firm is the first to enter a foreign market.

Multipoint Competition
When two or more enterprises encounter each other in different regional markets, national markets, or industries.

Although Knickerbocker's theory and its extensions can help to explain imitative FDI behavior by firms in oligopolistic industries, it does not explain why the first firm in an oligopoly decides to undertake FDI rather than to export or license. Internalization theory addresses this phenomenon. The imitative theory also does not address the issue of whether FDI is more efficient than exporting or licensing for expanding abroad. Again, internalization theory addresses the efficiency issue. For these reasons, many economists favor the internalization theory explanation for FDI, although most would agree that the imitative explanation tells an important part of the story.

The Product Life Cycle

Raymond Vernon's product life-cycle theory, described in Chapter 5, also is used to explain FDI. Vernon argued that often the same firms that pioneer a product in their home markets undertake FDI to produce a product for consumption in foreign markets. Thus, Xerox introduced the photocopier in the United States, and it was Xerox that set up production facilities in Japan (Fuji–Xerox) and Great Britain (Rank–Xerox) to serve those markets. Vernon's view is that firms undertake FDI at particular stages in the life cycle of a product they have pioneered. They invest in other advanced countries when local demand in those countries grows large enough to support local production (as Xerox did). They subsequently shift production to developing countries when product standardization and market saturation give rise to price competition and cost pressures. Investment in developing countries, where labor costs are lower, is seen as the best way to reduce costs.

Vernon's theory has merit. Firms do invest in a foreign country when demand in that country will support local production, and they do invest in low-cost locations (e.g., developing countries) when cost pressures become intense.[20] However, Vernon's theory fails to explain why it is profitable for a firm to undertake FDI at such times, rather than continuing to export from its home base or licensing a foreign firm to produce its product. Just because demand in a foreign country is large enough to support local production, it does not necessarily follow that local production is the most profitable option. It may still be more profitable to produce at home and export to that country (to realize the economies of scale that arise from serving the global market from one location). Alternatively, it may be more profitable for the firm to license a foreign company to produce its product for sale in that country. The product life-cycle theory ignores these options and, instead, simply argues that once a foreign market is large enough to support local production, FDI will occur. This limits its explanatory power and its usefulness to business in that it fails to identify when it is profitable to invest abroad.

THE ECLECTIC PARADIGM

The eclectic paradigm has been championed by the British economist John Dunning.[21] Dunning argues that in addition to the various factors discussed above, location-specific advantages are also of considerable

Location-Specific Advantages Advantages that arise from utilizing resource endowments or assets that are tied to a particular foreign location and that a firm finds valuable to combine with its own unique assets, such as technological, marketing, or management capabilities.

importance in explaining both the rationale for and the direction of foreign direct investment. By **location-specific advantages,** Dunning means the advantages that arise from utilizing resource endowments or assets that are tied to a particular foreign location and that a firm finds valuable to combine with its own unique assets (such as the firm's technological, marketing, or management capabilities). Dunning accepts the argument of internalization theory that it is difficult for a firm to license its own unique capabilities and know-how. Therefore, he argues that combining location-specific assets or resource endowments with the firm's own unique capabilities often requires foreign direct investment. That is, it requires the firm to establish production facilities where those foreign assets or resource endowments are located.

An obvious example of Dunning's arguments are natural resources, such as oil and other minerals, which are by their character specific to certain locations. Dunning suggests that to exploit such foreign resources, a firm must undertake FDI. Clearly, this explains the FDI undertaken by many of the world's oil companies, which have to invest where oil is located in order to combine their technological and managerial capabilities with this valuable location-specific resource. Another obvious example is valuable human resources, such as low-cost, highly skilled labor. The cost and skill of labor varies from country to country. Since labor is not internationally mobile, according to Dunning it makes sense for a firm to locate production facilities in those countries where the cost and skills of local labor is most suited to its particular production processes.

Externalities Knowledge spillovers.

However, Dunning's theory has implications that go beyond basic resources such as minerals and labor. Consider Silicon Valley, which is the world center for the computer and semiconductor industry. Many of the world's major computer and semiconductor companies, such as Apple Computer, Hewlett-Packard, and Intel, are located close to each other in the Silicon Valley region of California. As a result, much of the cutting-edge research and product development in computers and semiconductors takes place there. According to Dunning's arguments, there is knowledge being generated in Silicon Valley with regard to the design and manufacture of computers and semiconductors that is available nowhere else in the world. To be sure, as it is commercialized that knowledge diffuses throughout the world, but the leading edge of knowledge generation in the computer and semiconductor industries is to be found in Silicon Valley. In Dunning's language, this means that Silicon Valley has a *location-specific advantage* in the generation of knowledge related to the computer and semiconductor industries. In part, this advantage comes from the sheer concentration of intellectual talent in this area, and in part it arises from a network of informal contacts that allows firms to benefit from each others' knowledge generation. Economists refer to such knowledge "spillovers" as **externalities,** and there is a well-established theory suggesting that firms can benefit from such externalities by locating close to their source.[22]

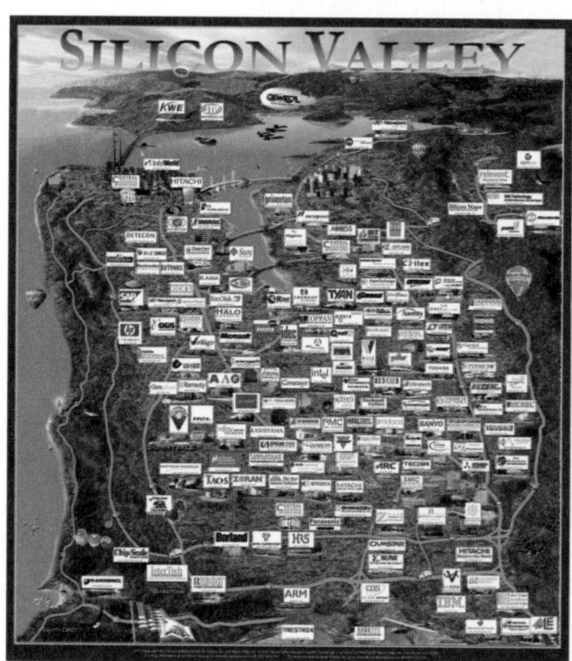

Silicon Valley has long been known as the epicenter of the computer and semiconductor industry.

In so far as this is the case, it makes sense for foreign computer and semiconductor firms to invest in research and, perhaps, production facilities so they too can learn about and utilize valuable new knowledge before those based elsewhere, thereby giving them a competitive advantage in the global marketplace.[23] Evidence suggests that European, Japanese, South Korean, and Taiwanese computer and semiconductor firms are investing in the Silicon Valley region, precisely because they wish to benefit from the externalities that arise there.[24] Others have argued that direct investment by foreign firms in the U.S. biotechnology industry has been motivated by desires to gain access to the unique location-specific technological knowledge of U.S. biotechnology firms.[25] Dunning's theory, therefore, seems to be a useful addition to those outlined above, for it helps explain how location factors affect the direction of FDI.[26]

Political Ideology and Foreign Direct Investment

LEARNING OBJECTIVE 3
Appreciate how political ideology shapes a government's attitudes toward FDI.

Historically, political ideology toward FDI within a nation has ranged from a dogmatic radical stance that is hostile to all inward FDI at one extreme to an adherence to the noninterventionist principle of free market economics at the other. Between these two extremes is an approach that might be called *pragmatic nationalism*.

THE RADICAL VIEW The radical view traces its roots to Marxist political and economic theory. Radical writers argue that the multinational enterprise (MNE) is an instrument of imperialist domination. They see the MNE as a tool for exploiting host countries to the exclusive benefit of their capitalist-imperialist home countries. They argue that MNEs extract profits from the host country and take them to their home country, giving nothing of value to the host country in exchange. They note, for example, that key technology is tightly controlled by the MNE, and that important jobs in the foreign subsidiaries of MNEs go to home-country nationals rather than to citizens of the host country. Because of this, according to the radical view, FDI by the MNEs of advanced capitalist nations keeps the less developed countries of the world relatively backward and dependent on advanced capitalist nations for investment, jobs, and technology. Thus, according to the extreme version of this view, no country should ever permit foreign corporations to undertake FDI, since they can never be instruments of economic development, only of economic domination. Where MNEs already exist in a country, they should be immediately nationalized.[27]

From 1945 until the 1980s, the radical view was very influential in the world economy. Until the collapse of communism between 1989 and 1991, the countries of Eastern Europe were opposed to FDI. Similarly, communist countries elsewhere, such as China, Cambodia, and Cuba, were all opposed in principle to FDI (although in practice the Chinese started to allow FDI in mainland China in the 1970s). Many socialist countries, particularly in Africa where one of the first actions of many newly independent states was to nationalize foreign-owned enterprises, also embraced the radical position. Countries whose political ideology was more nationalistic than socialistic further embraced the radical position. This was true in Iran and India, for example, both of which adopted tough policies restricting FDI and nationalized many foreign-owned enterprises. Iran is a particularly interesting case because its Islamic government, while rejecting Marxist theory, has essentially embraced the radical view that FDI by MNEs is an instrument of imperialism.

By the end of the 1980s, the radical position was in retreat almost everywhere. There seem to be three reasons for this: (1) the collapse of communism in Eastern Europe; (2) the generally abysmal economic performance of those countries that embraced the radical position, and a growing belief by many of these countries that FDI can be an important source of technology and jobs and can stimulate economic growth; and (3) the strong economic performance of those developing countries that embraced capitalism rather than radical ideology (e.g., Singapore, Hong Kong, and Taiwan).

THE FREE MARKET VIEW The free market view traces its roots to classical economics and the international trade theories of Adam Smith and David Ricardo (see Chapter 5). The free market view argues that international production should be distributed among countries according to the theory of comparative advantage. Countries should specialize in the production of those goods and services that they can produce most efficiently. Within this framework, the MNE is an instrument for dispersing the production of goods and services to the most efficient locations around the globe. Viewed this way, FDI by MNEs increases the overall efficiency of the world economy.

Imagine that Dell Computers decided to move assembly operations for many of its personal computers from the United States to Mexico to take advantage of lower labor costs in Mexico. According to the free market view, moves such as this can be seen as increasing the overall efficiency of resource utilization in the world economy. Mexico, due to its lower labor costs, has a comparative advantage in the assembly of PCs. By moving the production of PCs from the United States to Mexico, Dell frees U.S. resources for use in activities in which the United States has a comparative advantage (e.g., the design of computer software, the manufacture of high-value-added components such as microprocessors, or basic R&D). Also, consumers benefit because the PCs cost less than they would if they were produced domestically. In addition, Mexico gains from the technology, skills, and capital that the PC company transfers with its FDI. Contrary to the radical view, the free market view stresses that such resource transfers benefit the host country and stimulate its economic growth. Thus, the free market view argues that FDI is a benefit to both the source country and the host country.

For reasons explored earlier in this book (see Chapter 2), the free market view has been ascendant worldwide in recent years, spurring a global move toward the removal of restrictions on inward and outward foreign direct investment. However, in practice no country has adopted the free market view in its pure form (just as no country has adopted the radical view in its pure form). Countries such as Great Britain and the United States are among the most open to FDI, but the governments of these countries both have still reserved the right to intervene. Britain does so by reserving the right to block foreign takeovers of domestic firms if the takeovers are seen as "contrary to national security interests" or if they have the potential for "reducing competition." (In practice, the UK government has rarely exercised this right.) U.S. controls on FDI are more limited and largely informal. For political reasons, the United States will occasionally restrict U.S. firms from undertaking FDI in certain countries (e.g., Cuba and Iran). In addition, inward FDI meets some limited restrictions. For example, foreigners are prohibited from purchasing more than 25 percent of any U.S. airline or from acquiring a controlling interest in a U.S. television broadcast network. Since 1988, the government has had the right to review the acquisition of a U.S. enterprise by a foreign firm on the grounds of national security. However, of the 1,500 bids reviewed by the Committee on Foreign Investment in the United States under this law by 2005, only one has been nullified: the sale of a Seattle-based aircraft parts manufacturer to a Chinese enterprise in the early 1990s.[28]

PRAGMATIC NATIONALISM In practice, many countries have adopted neither a radical policy nor a free market policy toward FDI, but instead a policy that can best be described as pragmatic nationalism.[29] The pragmatic nationalist view is that FDI has both benefits and costs. FDI can benefit a host country by bringing capital, skills, technology, and jobs, but those benefits come at a cost. When a foreign company rather than a domestic company produces products, the profits from that investment go abroad. Many countries are also concerned that a foreign-owned manufacturing plant may import many components from its home country, which has negative implications for the host country's balance-of-payments position.

Recognizing this, countries adopting a pragmatic stance pursue policies designed to maximize the national benefits and minimize the national costs. According to this view, FDI should be allowed so long as the benefits outweigh the costs. Japan offers an example of pragmatic nationalism. Until the 1980s, Japan's policy was probably one of the most restrictive among countries adopting a pragmatic nationalist stance. This was due to Japan's perception that direct entry of foreign (especially U.S.) firms with ample managerial resources into the Japanese markets could hamper the development and growth of their own industry and technology.[30] This belief led Japan to block the majority of applications to invest in Japan. However, there were always exceptions to this policy. Firms that had important technology were often permitted to undertake FDI if they insisted that they would neither license their technology to a Japanese firm nor enter into a joint venture with a Japanese enterprise. IBM and Texas Instruments were able to set up wholly owned subsidiaries in Japan by adopting this negotiating position. From the perspective of the Japanese government, the benefits of FDI in such cases—the stimulus that these firms might impart to the Japanese economy—outweighed the perceived costs.

Another aspect of pragmatic nationalism is the tendency to aggressively court FDI believed to be in the national interest by, for example, offering subsidies to foreign MNEs in the form of tax breaks or grants. The countries of the European Union often seem to be competing with each other to attract U.S. and Japanese FDI by offering large tax breaks and subsidies. Britain has been the most successful at attracting Japanese investment in the automobile industry. Nissan, Toyota, and Honda now have major assembly plants in Britain and use the country as their base for serving the rest of Europe—with obvious employment and balance-of-payments benefits for Britain.

SHIFTING IDEOLOGY Recent years have seen a marked decline in the number of countries that adhere to a radical ideology. Although few countries have adopted a pure free market policy stance, an increasing number of countries are gravitating toward the free market end of the spectrum and have liberalized their foreign investment regime. This includes many countries that less than two decades ago were firmly in the radical camp (e.g., the former communist countries of Eastern Europe and many of the socialist countries of Africa) and several countries that until recently could best be described as pragmatic nationalists with regard to FDI (e.g., Japan, South Korea, Italy, Spain, and most Latin American countries). One result has been the surge in the volume of FDI worldwide, which, as we noted earlier, has been growing twice as fast as the growth in world trade. Another result has been an increase in the volume of FDI directed at countries that have recently liberalized their FDI regimes, such as China, India, and Vietnam.

As a counterpoint, there is recent evidence of the beginnings of what might become a shift to a more hostile approach to foreign direct investment. Venezuela and Bolivia have become increasingly hostile to foreign direct investment. In 2005 and 2006, the governments of both nations unilaterally rewrote contracts for oil and gas exploration, raising the royalty rate that foreign enterprises had to pay the government for oil and gas extracted in their territories. Moreover, following his election victory, in 2006 Bolivian president Evo Morales nationalized the nation's gas fields and stated that he would evict foreign firms unless they agreed to pay about 80 percent of their revenues to the state and relinquish production oversight. In some developed nations too, there is increasing evidence of hostile reactions to inward FDI. In Europe in 2006, there was a hostile political reaction to

Management FOCUS

DP World and the United States

In February 2006, DP World, a ports operator with global reach owned by the government of Dubai, a member of the United Arab Emirates and a staunch U.S. ally, paid $6.8 billion to acquire P&O, a British firm that runs a global network of marine terminals. With P&O came the management operations of six U.S. ports: Miami, Philadelphia, Baltimore, New Orleans, New Jersey, and New York. The acquisition had already been approved by U.S. regulators when it suddenly became front-page news. Upon hearing about the deal, several prominent U.S. senators raised concerns about the acquisition. Their objections were twofold. First, they raised questions about the security risks associated with management operations in key U.S. ports being owned by a foreign enterprise that was based in the Middle East. The implication was that terrorists could somehow take advantage of the ownership arrangement to infiltrate U.S. ports. Second, they were concerned that DP World was a state-owned enterprise and argued that foreign governments should not be in a position of owning key "U.S. strategic assets."

The Bush administration was quick to defend the takeover, stating that it posed no threat to national security. Others noted that DP World was a respected global firm with an American chief operating officer and an American educated chairman; the head of the global ports management operation would also be an American. DP World would not own the U.S. ports in question, just manage them, while security issues would remain in the hands of American customs officials and the U.S. Coast Guard. Dubai was also a member of America's Container Security Initiative, which allows American customs officials to inspect cargo in foreign ports before it leaves for the United States. Most of the DP World employees at American ports would be U.S. citizens, and any UAE citizen transferred to DP World would be subject to American visa approval.

These arguments fell on deaf ears. With several U.S. senators threatening to pass legislation to prohibit foreign ownership of U.S. port operations, DP World bowed to the inevitable and announced that it would sell off the right to manage the six U.S. ports for about $750 million. Looking forward however, DP World stated that it would seek an initial public offering in 2007, and that the then-private firm would in all probability continue to look for ways to enter the United States. In the words of the firm's CEO, "this is the world's largest economy. How can you just ignore it?"

Sources: "Trouble at the Waterfront," *The Economist,* February 25, 2006, p. 48; "Paranoia about Dubai Ports Deals Is Needless," *Financial Times,* February 21, 2006, p. 16; and "DP World: We'll Be Back," *Traffic World,* May 29, 2006, p. 1.

the attempted takeover of Europe's largest steel company, Arcelor, by Mittal Steel, a global company controlled by the Indian entrepreneur, Lakshmi Mittal. In mid-2005 China National Offshore Oil Company withdrew a takeover bid for Unocal of the United States after highly negative reaction in Congress about the proposed takeover of a "strategic asset" by a Chinese company. Similarly, as detailed in the above Management Focus feature, in 2006 a Dubai-owned company withdrew its planned takeover of some operations at six U.S. ports after negative political reactions. So far, these countertrends are nothing more than isolated incidents, but if they become more widespread, the 30-year-long movement toward lower barriers to cross-boarder investment could be in jeopardy.

Benefits and Costs of FDI

LEARNING OBJECTIVE 4
Understand the benefits and costs of FDI to home and host countries.

To a greater or lesser degree, many governments can be considered pragmatic nationalists when it comes to FDI. Accordingly, their policy is shaped by a consideration of the costs and benefits of FDI. Here we explore the benefits and costs of FDI, first from the perspective of a host (receiving) country, and then from the perspective of the home (source) country. In the next section, we look at the policy instruments governments use to manage FDI.

HOST-COUNTRY BENEFITS The main benefits of inward FDI for a host country arise from resource-transfer effects, employment effects, balance-of-payments effects, and effects on competition and economic growth.

Resource-Transfer Effects Foreign direct investment can make a positive contribution to a host economy by supplying capital, technology, and management resources that would otherwise not be available and thus boost that country's economic growth rate.[31]

With regard to capital, many MNEs, by virtue of their large size and financial strength, have access to financial resources not available to host-country firms. These funds may be available from internal company sources, or, because of their reputation, large MNEs may find it easier to borrow money from capital markets than host-country firms would.

As for technology, you will recall from Chapter 2 that technology can stimulate economic development and industrialization. Technology can take two forms, both of which are valuable. Technology can be incorporated in a production process (e.g., the technology for discovering, extracting, and refining oil) or it can be incorporated in a product (e.g., personal computers). However, many countries lack the research and development resources and skills required to develop their own indigenous product and process technology. This is particularly true in less developed nations. Such countries must rely on advanced industrialized nations for much of the technology required to stimulate economic growth, and FDI can provide it.

Research supports the view that multinational firms often transfer significant technology when they invest in a foreign country.[32] For example, a study of FDI in Sweden found that foreign firms increased both the labor and total factor productivity of Swedish firms that they acquired, suggesting that significant technology transfers had occurred (technology typically boosts productivity).[33] Also, a study of FDI by the Organization for Economic Cooperation and Development (OECD) found that foreign investors invested significant amounts of capital in R&D in the countries in which they had invested, suggesting that not only were they transferring technology to those countries, but they may also have been upgrading existing technology or creating new technology in those countries.[34]

Foreign management skills acquired through FDI may also produce important benefits for the host country. Foreign managers trained in the latest management techniques can often help to improve the efficiency of operations in the host country, whether those operations are acquired or greenfield developments. Beneficial spin-off effects may also arise when local personnel who are trained to occupy managerial, financial, and technical posts in the subsidiary of a foreign MNE leave the firm and help to establish indigenous firms. Similar benefits may arise if the superior management skills of a foreign MNE stimulate local suppliers, distributors, and competitors to improve their own management skills.

Employment Effects Another beneficial employment effect claimed for FDI is that it brings jobs to a host country that would otherwise not be created there. The effects of FDI on employment are both direct and indirect. Direct effects arise when a foreign MNE employs a number of host-country citizens. Indirect effects arise when jobs are created in local suppliers as a result of the investment and when jobs are created because of increased local spending by employees of the MNE. The indirect employment effects are often as large as, if not larger than, the direct effects. For example, when Toyota decided to open a new auto plant in France in 1997, estimates suggested that the plant would create 2,000 direct jobs and perhaps another 2,000 jobs in support industries.[35]

Another Perspective

Alabama Courts FDI from Korea

In 2002, the South Korean auto company Hyundai decided to invest in an auto plant in the United States. They used the accounting firm KPMG to narrow their choices to four states: Alabama, Kentucky, Ohio, and Mississippi. Alabama began a full-court press on the Koreans and ended up offering them $76.7 million in tax breaks, $61.8 million in training grants, and $34 million in land purchase assistance. The total package was worth $252.8 million. Hyundi built a $1.1 billion plant and created 2,700 jobs in Montgomery (www.fdimagazine.com).

The competition among U.S. states can get fierce for FDI flows. The stiffest competition tends to come from the southern states Kentucky, Louisiana, Mississippi, South Carolina, Georgia, and Alabama.

Cynics argue that not all the "new jobs" created by FDI represent net additions in employment. In the case of FDI by Japanese auto companies in the United States, some argue that the jobs created by this investment have been more than offset by the jobs lost in U.S.-owned auto companies, which have lost market share to their Japanese competitors. As a consequence of such substitution effects, the net number of new jobs created by FDI may not be as great as initially claimed by an MNE. The issue of the likely net gain in employment may be a major negotiating point between an MNE wishing to undertake FDI and the host government.

When FDI takes the form of an acquisition of an established enterprise in the host economy as opposed to a greenfield investment, the immediate effect may be to reduce employment as the multinational tries to restructure the operations of the acquired unit to improve its operating efficiency. However, even in such cases, research suggests that once the initial period of restructuring is over, enterprises acquired by foreign firms tend to grow their employment base at a faster rate than domestic rivals. For example, an OECD study found that between 1989 and 1996 foreign firms created new jobs at a faster rate than their domestic counterparts.[36] In America, the workforce of foreign firms grew by 1.4 percent per year, compared with 0.8 percent per year for domestic firms. In Britain and France, the workforce of foreign firms grew at 1.7 percent per year, while employment at domestic firms fell by 2.7 percent. The same study found that foreign firms tended to pay higher wage rates than domestic firms, suggesting that the quality of employment was better. Another study looking at FDI in Eastern European transition economies found that although employment fell following the acquisition of an enterprise by a foreign firm, often those enterprises were in competitive difficulties and would not have survived if they had not been acquired. Also, after an initial period of adjustment and retrenchment, employment downsizing was often followed by new investments, and employment either remained stable or increased.[37]

Balance-of-Payments Accounts
National accounts that track both payments to and receipts from foreigners.

Current Account
In the balance of payments, this records transactions involving the export or import of goods and services.

Balance-of-Payments Effects

FDI's effect on a country's balance-of-payments accounts is an important policy issue for most host governments. A country's **balance-of-payments accounts** track both its payments to and its receipts from other countries. Governments normally are concerned when their country is running a deficit on the current account of their balance of payments. The **current account** tracks the export and import of goods and services. A current account deficit, or trade deficit as it is often called, arises when a country is importing more goods and services than it is exporting. Governments typically prefer to see a current account surplus than a deficit. The only way in which a current account deficit can be supported in the long run is buy selling off assets to foreigners (for a detailed explanation of why this is the case, see Krugman and Obstfeld's *International Economics*).[38] For example, the persistent U.S. current account deficit since the 1980s has been financed by a steady sale of U.S. assets (stocks, bonds, real estate, and whole corporations) to foreigners. Since national governments invariably dislike seeing the assets of their country fall into foreign hands, they prefer their nation to run a current account surplus. There are two ways in which FDI can help a country to achieve this goal.

First, if the FDI is a substitute for imports of goods or services, the effect can be to improve the current account of the host country's balance of payments. Much of the FDI by Japanese automobile companies in the United States and United Kingdom, for example, can be seen as substituting for imports from Japan. Thus, the current account of the U.S. balance of payments has improved somewhat, because many Japanese companies are now supplying the U.S. market from production facilities in the United States, as opposed to facilities in Japan. Insofar as this has reduced the need to finance a current account deficit by asset sales to foreigners, the United States has clearly benefited. A second potential benefit arises when the MNE uses a foreign subsidiary to export goods and services to other countries.

According to a UN report, inward FDI by foreign multinationals has been a major driver of export-led economic growth in a number of developing and developed nations over the last decade.[39] For example, in China exports increased from $26 billion in 1985 to more than $250 billion by 2001. Much of this export growth was due to the presence of foreign multinationals that invested heavily in China during the 1990s. The subsidiaries of foreign multinationals accounted for 50 percent of all exports from that country in 2001, up from 17 percent in 1991. In mobile phones, for example, the Chinese subsidiaries of foreign multinationals—primarily Nokia, Motorola, Ericsson, and Siemens—accounted for 95 percent of China's exports.

Effect on Competition and Economic Growth Economic theory tells us that the efficient functioning of markets depends on an adequate level of competition between producers. When FDI takes the form of a greenfield investment, the result is to establish a new enterprise, increasing the number of players in a market and thus consumer choice. In turn, this can increase the level of competition in a national market, thereby driving down prices and increasing the economic welfare of consumers. Increased competition tends to stimulate capital investments by firms in plant, equipment, and R&D as they struggle to gain an edge over their rivals. The long-term results may include increased productivity growth, product and process innovations, and greater economic growth.[40] Such beneficial effects seem to have occurred in the South Korean retail sector following the liberalization of FDI regulations in 1996. FDI by large Western discount stores, including Wal-Mart, Costco, Carrefour, and Tesco, seems to have encouraged indigenous discounters such as E-Mart to improve the efficiency of their own operations. The results have included more competition and lower prices, which benefit South Korean consumers.

FDI's impact on competition in domestic markets may be particularly important in the case of services, such as telecommunications, retailing, and many financial services, where exporting is often not an option because the service has to be produced where it is delivered.[41] For example, under a 1997 agreement sponsored by the World Trade Organization, 68 countries accounting for more than 90 percent of world telecommunications revenues pledged to start opening their markets to foreign investment and competition and to abide by common rules for fair competition in telecommunications. Before this agreement, most of the world's telecommunications markets were closed to foreign competitors, and in most countries the market was monopolized by a single carrier, which was often a state-owned enterprise. The agreement has dramatically increased the level of competition in many national telecommunications markets producing two major benefits. First, inward investment has increased competition and stimulated investment in the modernization of telephone networks around the world, leading to better service. Second, the increased competition has resulted in lower prices.

HOST-COUNTRY COSTS Three costs of FDI concern host countries. They arise from possible adverse effects on competition within the host nation, adverse effects on the balance of payments, and the perceived loss of national sovereignty and autonomy.

Adverse Effects on Competition Host governments sometimes worry that the subsidiaries of foreign MNEs may have greater economic power than indigenous competitors. If it is part of a larger international organization, the foreign MNE may be able to draw on funds generated elsewhere to subsidize its costs in the host market, which could drive indigenous companies out of business and allow the firm to monopolize the market. Once the market is monopolized, the foreign MNE could raise prices above those that would prevail in competitive markets, with harmful effects on the economic welfare of the host nation. This concern tends to be greater in countries that have few large firms of their own (generally less developed countries). It tends to be a relatively minor concern in most advanced industrialized nations.

In general, while FDI in the form of greenfield investments should increase competition, it is less clear that this is the case when the FDI takes the form of acquisition of an established enterprise in the host nation, as was the case when Volvo acquired Samsung's excavation division (see the Management Focus). Because an acquisition does not result in a net increase in the number of players in a market, the effect on competition may be neutral. When a foreign investor acquires two or more firms in a host country, and subsequently merges them, the effect may be to reduce the level of competition in that market, create monopoly power for the foreign firm, reduce consumer choice, and raise prices. For example, in India, Hindustan Lever Ltd., the Indian subsidiary of Unilever, acquired its main local rival, Tata Oil Mills, to assume a dominant position in the bath soap (75 percent) and detergents (30 percent) markets. Hindustan Lever also acquired several local companies in other markets, such as the ice cream makers Dollops, Kwality, and Milkfood. By combining these companies, Hindustan Lever's share of the Indian ice cream market went from zero in 1992 to 74 percent in 1997.[42] However, although such cases are of obvious concern, there is little evidence that such developments are widespread. In many nations, domestic competition authorities have the right to review and block any mergers or acquisitions that they view as having a detrimental impact on competition. If such institutions are operating effectively, this should be sufficient to make sure that foreign entities do not monopolize a country's markets.

Adverse Effects on the Balance of Payments The possible adverse effects of FDI on a host country's balance-of-payments position are twofold. First, set against the initial capital inflow that comes with FDI must be the subsequent outflow of earnings from the foreign subsidiary to its parent company. Such outflows show up as capital outflow on balance of payments accounts. Some governments have responded to such outflows by restricting the amount of earnings that can be repatriated to a foreign subsidiary's home country. A second concern arises when a foreign subsidiary imports a substantial number of its inputs from abroad, which results in a debit on the current account of the host country's balance of payments. One criticism leveled against Japanese-owned auto assembly operations in the United States, for example, is that they tend to import many component parts from Japan. Because of this, the favorable impact of this FDI on the current account of the U.S. balance-of-payments position may not be as great as initially supposed. The Japanese auto companies have responded to these criticisms by pledging to purchase 75 percent of their component parts from U.S.-based manufacturers (but not necessarily U.S.-owned manufacturers). When the Japanese auto company Nissan invested in the United Kingdom, Nissan responded to concerns about local content by pledging to increase the proportion of local content to 60 percent and subsequently raising it to more than 80 percent.

National Sovereignty and Autonomy Some host governments worry that FDI is accompanied by some loss of economic independence. The concern is that key decisions that can affect the host country's economy will be made by a foreign parent that has no real commitment to the host country, and over which the host country's government has no real control. Most economists dismiss such concerns as groundless and irrational. Political scientist Robert Reich has noted that such concerns are the product of outmoded thinking because they fail to account for the growing interdependence of the world economy.[43] In a world in which firms from all advanced nations are increasingly investing in each other's markets, it is not possible for one country to hold another to "economic ransom" without hurting itself. See the Another Perspective box at right.

Another Perspective

FDI Effects: Look at the Whole Picture

Some critics of globalization suggest that FDI is an advanced form of colonialism that destroys local cultures in developing countries. What these critics say may have some limited validity, but it isn't the whole picture. Take Freeport McMoRan, a U.S.-based mining company with operations in West Papua, the former Irian Jaya, Indonesia, where the world's largest gold, mineral, and copper reserves have been found. Freeport formed a joint-venture with the Indonesian government to mine a concession, an isolated tract of land the size of Massachusetts on a remote island, half of which is the country of Papua New Guinea.

Freeport has brought education, Internet-connections, world-class health care, and the modern world to the isolated local tribes in West Papua, nomadic peoples who wear loincloths and hunt in the forest. Their traditional, subsistence way of life is threatened, while at the same time, they gain from their share of the operation's profits, from their increased health care and education, and from local employment opportunities with FCX. Is this colonialism or a kind of ethical investing? See more on this issue at www.FCX.com and www.corpwatch.org.

HOME-COUNTRY BENEFITS The benefits of FDI to the home (source) country arise from three sources. First, the home country's balance of payments benefits from the inward flow of foreign earnings. FDI can also benefit the home country's balance of payments if the foreign subsidiary creates demands for home-country exports of capital equipment, intermediate goods, complementary products, and the like.

Second, benefits to the home country from outward FDI arise from employment effects. As with the balance of payments, positive employment effects arise when the foreign subsidiary creates demand for home-country exports. Thus, Toyota's investment in auto assembly operations in Europe has benefited both the Japanese balance-of-payments position and employment in Japan, because Toyota imports some component parts for its European-based auto assembly operations directly from Japan.

Third, benefits arise when the home-country MNE learns valuable skills from its exposure to foreign markets that can subsequently be transferred back to the home country. This amounts to a reverse resource-transfer effect. Through its exposure to a foreign market, an MNE can learn about superior management techniques and superior product and process technologies. These resources can then be transferred back to the home country, contributing to the home country's economic growth rate.[44] For example, one reason General Motors and Ford invested in Japanese automobile companies (GM owns part of Isuzu, and Ford owns part of Mazda) was to learn about their production processes. If GM and Ford are successful in transferring this know-how back to their U.S. operations, the result may be a net gain for the U.S. economy.

HOME-COUNTRY COSTS Against these benefits must be set the apparent costs of FDI for the home (source) country. The most important concerns center on the balance-of-payments and employment effects of outward FDI. The home country's balance of payments may suffer in three ways. First, the balance of payments suffers from the initial capital outflow required to finance the FDI. This effect, however, is usually more than offset by the subsequent inflow of foreign earnings. Second, the current account of the balance of payments suffers if the purpose of the foreign investment is to serve the home market from a low-cost production location. Third, the current account of the balance of payments suffers if the FDI is a substitute for direct exports. Thus, insofar as Toyota's assembly operations in the United States are intended to substitute for direct exports from Japan, the current account position of Japan will deteriorate.

With regard to employment effects, the most serious concerns arise when FDI is seen as a substitute for domestic production. This was the case with Toyota's investments in the United States and Europe. One obvious result of such FDI is reduced home-country employment. If the labor market in the home country is already tight, with little unemployment, this concern may not be that great. However, if the home country is suffering from unemployment, concern about the export of jobs may arise. For example, one objection frequently raised by U.S. labor leaders to the free trade pact between the United States, Mexico, and Canada (see the next chapter) is that the United States will lose hundreds of thousands of jobs as U.S. firms invest in Mexico to take advantage of cheaper labor and then export back to the United States.[45]

INTERNATIONAL TRADE THEORY AND FDI When assessing the costs and benefits of FDI to the home country, keep in mind the lessons of international trade theory (see Chapter 5). International trade theory tells us that home-country concerns about the negative economic effects of offshore production may be misplaced. The term **offshore production** refers to FDI undertaken to serve the home market. Far from reducing home-country employment, such FDI may actually stimulate economic growth (and hence employment) in the home country by freeing home-country resources to concentrate on activities where the home country has a comparative advantage. In addition, home-country consumers benefit if the price of the particular product falls as a result of the FDI. Also, if a company were prohibited from making such investments on the grounds of negative employment effects while its international competitors reaped the benefits of low-cost production locations, it would undoubtedly lose market share to its international competitors. Under such a scenario, the adverse long-run economic effects for a country would probably outweigh the relatively minor balance-of-payments and employment effects associated with offshore production

Offshore Production
FDI undertaken to serve the home market.

Government Policy Instruments and FDI

LEARNING OBJECTIVE 5
Be able to discuss the range of policy instruments that governments use to influence FDI.

We have now reviewed the costs and benefits of FDI from the perspective of both home country and host country. We now turn our attention to the policy instruments that home (source) countries and host countries can use to regulate FDI.

HOME-COUNTRY POLICIES Through their choice of policies, home countries can both encourage and restrict FDI by local firms. We look at policies designed to encourage outward FDI first. These include foreign risk insurance, capital assistance, tax incentives, and political pressure. Then we will look at policies designed to restrict outward FDI.

Encouraging Outward FDI Many investor nations now have government-backed insurance programs to cover major types of foreign investment risk. The types of risks insurable through these programs include the risks of expropriation (nationalization), war losses, and the inability to transfer profits back home. Such programs are particularly useful in encouraging firms to undertake investments in politically unstable countries.[46] In addition, several advanced countries also have special funds or banks that make government loans to firms wishing to invest in developing countries. As a further incentive to encourage domestic firms to undertake FDI, many countries have eliminated double taxation of foreign income (i.e., taxation of income in both the host country and the home country). Last, and perhaps most significant, a number of investor countries (including the United States) have used their political influence to persuade host countries to relax their restrictions on inbound FDI. For example, in response to direct U.S. pressure, Japan relaxed many of its formal restrictions on inward FDI in the 1980s. Now, in response to further U.S. pressure, Japan moved toward relaxing its informal barriers to inward FDI. One beneficiary of this trend has been Toys "R" Us, which, after five years of intensive lobbying by company and U.S. government officials, opened its first retail stores in Japan in December 1991. By 2006, Toys "R" Us had 148 more stores in Japan, and its Japanese operation, in which Toys "R" Us retained a controlling stake, had a listing on the Japanese stock market.

Restricting Outward FDI

Virtually all investor countries, including the United States, have exercised some control over outward FDI from time to time. One policy has been to limit capital outflows out of concern for the country's balance of payments. From the early 1960s until 1979, for example, Britain had exchange-control regulations that limited the amount of capital a firm could take out of the country. Although the main intent of such policies was to improve the British balance of payments, an important secondary intent was to make it more difficult for British firms to undertake FDI.

In addition, countries have occasionally manipulated tax rules to try to encourage their firms to invest at home. The objective behind such policies is to create jobs at home rather than in other nations. At one time, Britain adopted such policies. The British advanced corporation tax system taxed British companies' foreign earnings at a higher rate than their domestic earnings. This tax code created an incentive for British companies to invest at home.

Finally, countries sometimes prohibit national firms from investing in certain countries for political reasons. Such restrictions can be formal or informal. For example, formal U.S. rules prohibited U.S. firms from investing in countries such as Cuba and Iran, whose political ideology and actions are judged to be contrary to U.S. interests. Similarly, during the 1980s, informal pressure was applied to dissuade U.S. firms from investing in South Africa. In this case, the objective was to pressure South Africa to change its apartheid laws, which happened during the early 1990s.

HOST-COUNTRY POLICIES

Host countries adopt policies designed both to restrict and to encourage inward FDI. As noted earlier in this chapter, political ideology has determined the type and scope of these policies in the past. In the last decade of the twentieth century, many countries moved quickly away from a situation where many countries adhered to some version of the radical stance and prohibited much FDI, and toward a situation where a combination of free market objectives and pragmatic nationalism took hold.

Encouraging Inward FDI

It is common for governments to offer incentives to foreign firms to invest in their countries. Such incentives take many forms, but the most common are tax concessions, low-interest loans, and grants or subsidies.

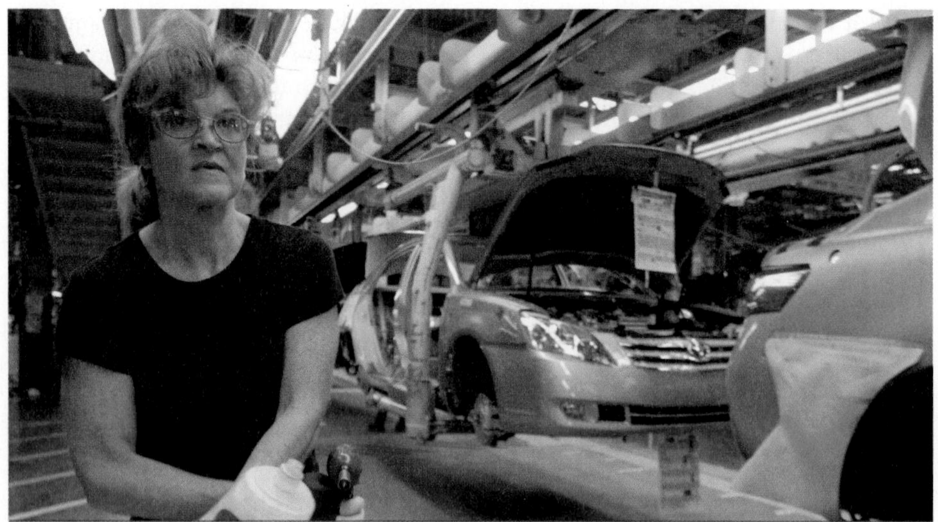

Often, governments provide incentives to attract foreign firms. For example, Kentucky offered Toyota an incentive package worth $112 million to build its assembly plant there. *Al Behrman/AP Wide World*

Incentives are motivated by a desire to gain from the resource-transfer and employment effects of FDI. They are also motivated by a desire to capture FDI away from other potential host countries. For example, in the mid-1990s, the governments of Britain and France competed with each other on the incentives they offered Toyota to invest in their respective countries. In the United States, state governments often compete with each other to attract FDI. For example, Kentucky offered Toyota an incentive package worth $112 million to persuade it to build its U.S. automobile assembly plants there. The package included tax breaks, new state spending on infrastructure, and low-interest loans.[47]

Restricting Inward FDI Host governments use a wide range of controls to restrict FDI in one way or another. The two most common are ownership restraints and performance requirements. Ownership restraints can take several forms. In some countries, foreign companies are excluded from specific fields. They are excluded from tobacco and mining in Sweden and from the development of certain natural resources in Brazil, Finland, and Morocco. In other industries, foreign ownership may be permitted although a significant proportion of the equity of the subsidiary must be owned by local investors. Foreign ownership is restricted to 25 percent or less of an airline in the United States. In India, foreign firms were prohibited from owning media businesses until 2001, when the rules were relaxed, allowing foreign firms to purchase up to 26 percent of a foreign newspaper.[48]

The rationale underlying ownership restraints seems to be twofold. First, foreign firms are often excluded from certain sectors on the grounds of national security or competition. Particularly in less developed countries, the feeling seems to be that local firms might not be able to develop unless foreign competition is restricted by a combination of import tariffs and controls on FDI. This is a variant of the infant industry argument discussed in Chapter 6.

Second, ownership restraints seem to be based on a belief that local owners can help to maximize the resource-transfer and employment benefits of FDI for the host country. Until the early 1980s, the Japanese government prohibited most FDI but allowed joint ventures between Japanese firms and foreign MNEs if the MNE had a valuable technology. The Japanese government clearly believed such an arrangement would speed up the subsequent diffusion of the MNE's valuable technology throughout the Japanese economy.

Performance requirements can also take several forms. Performance requirements are controls over the behavior of the MNE's local subsidiary. The most common performance requirements are related to local content, exports, technology transfer, and local participation in top management. As with certain ownership restrictions, the logic underlying performance requirements is that such rules help to maximize the benefits and minimize the costs of FDI for the host country. Many countries employ some form of performance requirements when it suits their objectives. However, performance requirements tend to be more common in less developed countries than in advanced industrialized nations.[49]

INTERNATIONAL INSTITUTIONS AND THE LIBERALIZATION OF FDI Until the 1990s, there was no consistent involvement by multinational institutions in the governing of FDI. This changed with the formation of the World Trade Organization in 1995. The WTO embraces the promotion of international trade in services. Since many services have to be produced where they are sold, exporting is not an option (for example, one cannot export McDonald's hamburgers or consumer banking services). Given this, the WTO has become involved in regulations governing FDI. As might be expected for an institution created to promote free trade, the thrust of the WTO's efforts has been to push for the liberalization of regulations governing FDI, particularly in services. Under the auspices of the WTO, two extensive multinational agreements were reached in 1997 to liberalize trade in telecommunications and financial services. Both these agreements contained detailed clauses that require signatories to liberalize their regulations governing inward FDI, essentially opening their markets to foreign telecommunications and financial services companies.

The WTO has had less success trying to initiate talks aimed at establishing a universal set of rules designed to promote the liberalization of FDI. Led by Malaysia and India, developing nations have so far rejected efforts by the WTO to start such discussions. In an attempt to make some progress on this issue, the Organization for Economic Cooperation and Development (OECD) in 1995 initiated talks between its members. (The OECD is a Paris-based intergovernmental organization of "wealthy" nations whose purpose is to provide its 29 member states with a forum in which governments can compare their experiences, discuss the problems they share, and seek solutions that can then be applied within their own national contexts. The members include most EU countries, the United States, Canada, Japan, and South Korea). The aim of the talks was to draft a multilateral agreement on investment (MAI) that would make it illegal for signatory states to discriminate against foreign investors. This would liberalize rules governing FDI between OECD states.

LEARNING OBJECTIVE 6
Articulate the implications for management practice of the theory and government policies associated with FDI.

These talks broke down in early 1998, primarily because the United States refused to sign the agreement. According to the United States, the proposed agreement contained too many exceptions that would weaken its powers. For example, the proposed agreement would not have barred discriminatory taxation of foreign-owned companies, and it would have allowed countries to restrict foreign television programs and music in the name of preserving culture. Environmental and labor groups also campaigned against the MAI, criticizing the proposed agreement because it contained no binding environmental or labor agreements. Despite such setbacks, negotiations on a revised MAI treaty might restart in the future. Moreover, as noted earlier, many individual nations have continued to liberalize their policies governing FDI to encourage foreign firms to invest in their economies.[50]

Focus on Managerial Implications

Several implications for business are inherent in the material discussed in this chapter. In this section, we deal first with the implications of the theory and then turn our attention to the implications of government policy.

The Theory of FDI

The implications of the theories of FDI for business practice are straightforward. First, it is worth noting that the location-specific advantages argument associated with John Dunning does help explain the *direction* of FDI. However, the location-specific advantages argument does not explain *why* firms prefer FDI to licensing or to exporting. In this regard, from both an explanatory and a business perspective perhaps the most useful theories are those that focus on the limitations of exporting and licensing. These theories are useful because they identify with some precision how the relative profitability of foreign direct investment, exporting, and licensing vary with circumstances. The theories suggest that exporting is preferable to licensing and FDI so long as transportation costs are minor and trade barriers are trivial. As transportation costs or trade barriers increase, exporting becomes unprofitable, and the choice is between FDI and licensing. Since FDI is more costly and more risky than licensing, other things being equal, the theories argue that licensing is preferable to FDI. Other things are seldom equal, however. Although licensing may work, it is not an attractive option when one or more of the following conditions exist: (*a*) the firm has valuable know-how that cannot be adequately protected by a licensing contract, (*b*) the firm needs tight control over a foreign entity in order to maximize its market share and earnings in that country, and (*c*) a firm's skills and capabilities are not amenable to licensing. Figure 7.5 presents these considerations as a decision tree.

Firms for which licensing is not a good option tend to be clustered in three types of industries:

1. High-technology industries in which protecting firm-specific expertise is of paramount importance and licensing is hazardous.
2. Global oligopolies, in which competitive interdependence requires that multinational firms maintain tight control over foreign operations so that they have the ability to launch coordinated attacks against their global competitors (as Kodak has done with Fuji.)
3. Industries in which intense cost pressures require that multinational firms maintain tight control over foreign operations (so that they can disperse manufacturing to locations around the globe where factor costs are most favorable in order to minimize costs).

Although empirical evidence is limited, the majority of the evidence seems to support these conjectures.[51] In addition, licensing is not a good option if the competitive advantage of a firm is based upon managerial or marketing knowledge that is embedded in the routines of the firm or the skills of its managers, and that is difficult to codify in a "book of blueprints." This would seem to be the case for firms based in a fairly wide range of industries.

Firms for which licensing is a good option tend to be in industries whose conditions are opposite to those specified above. That is, licensing tends to be more common, and more profitable, in fragmented, low-technology industries in which globally dispersed manufacturing is not an option. A good example is the fast-food

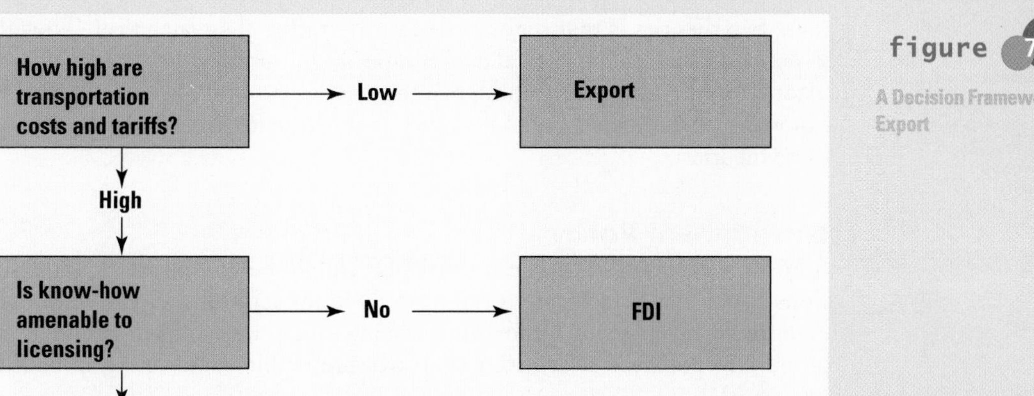

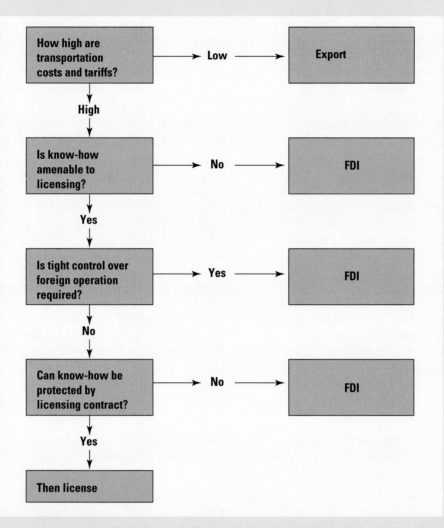

figure 7.5

A Decision Framework

Export

industry. McDonald's has expanded globally by using a franchising strategy. Franchising is essentially the service-industry version of licensing, although it normally involves much longer term commitments than licensing. With franchising, the firm licenses its brand name to a foreign firm in return for a percentage of the franchisee's profits. The franchising contract specifies the conditions that the franchisee must fulfill if it is to use the franchisor's brand name. Thus McDonald's allows foreign firms to use its brand name so long as they agree to run their restaurants on exactly the same lines as McDonald's restaurants elsewhere in the world. This strategy makes sense for McDonald's because (*a*) like many services, fast food cannot be exported, (*b*) franchising economizes the costs and risks associated with opening up foreign markets, (*c*) unlike technological know-how, brand names are relatively easy to protect using a contract, (*d*) there is no compelling reason for McDonald's to have tight control over franchisees, and (*e*) McDonald's know-how, in terms of how to run a fast-food restaurant, is amenable to being specified in a written contract (e.g., the contract specifies the details of how to run a McDonald's restaurant).

Finally, it should be noted that the product life-cycle theory and Knickerbocker's theory of FDI tend to be less useful from a business perspective. The problem with these two theories is that they are descriptive rather than analytical. They do a good job of describing the historical evolution of FDI, but they do a relatively poor job of identifying the factors that influence the relative profitability of FDI, licensing, and exporting. Indeed, the issue of licensing as an alternative to FDI is ignored by both of these theories.

Government Policy

A host government's attitude toward FDI should be an important variable in decisions about where to locate foreign production facilities and where to make a foreign direct investment. Other things being equal, investing in countries that have permissive policies toward FDI is clearly preferable to investing in countries that restrict FDI.

However, often the issue is not this straightforward. Despite the move toward a free market stance in recent years, many countries still have a rather pragmatic stance toward FDI. In such cases, a firm considering FDI usually must often negotiate the specific terms of the investment with the country's government. Such negotiations center on two broad issues. If the host government is trying to attract FDI, the central issue is likely to be the kind of incentives the host government is prepared to offer to the MNE and what the firm will commit in exchange. If the host government is uncertain about the benefits of FDI and might choose to restrict access, the central issue is likely to be the concessions that the firm must make in order to be allowed to go forward with a proposed investment.

To a large degree, the outcome of any negotiated agreement depends on the relative bargaining power of both parties. Each side's bargaining power depends on three factors:

- The value each side places on what the other has to offer.
- The number of comparable alternatives available to each side.
- Each party's time horizon.

From the perspective of a firm negotiating the terms of an investment with a host government, the firm's bargaining power is high when the host government places a high value on what the firm has to offer, the number of comparable alternatives open to the firm is greater, and the firm has a long time in which to complete the negotiations. The converse also holds. The firm's bargaining power is low when the host government places a low value on what the firm has to offer, the number of comparable alternatives open to the firm is fewer, and the firm has a short time in which to complete the negotiations.[52]

Key Terms

greenfield investment, p. 229
flow of FDI, p. 229
stock of FDI, p. 229
outflows of FDI, p. 229
inflows of FDI, p. 229
gross fixed capital formation, p. 231
eclectic paradigm, p. 236
exporting, p. 236
licensing, p. 236
internalization theory, p. 237
oligopoly, p. 238
multipoint competition, p. 239
location-specific advantages, p. 240
externalities, p. 240
balance-of-payments accounts, p. 246
current account, p. 246
offshore production, p. 250

Summary

The objectives of this chapter were to review theories that attempt to explain the pattern of FDI between countries and to examine the influence of governments on firms' decisions to invest in foreign countries. The following points were made:

1. Any theory seeking to explain FDI must explain why firms go to the trouble of acquiring or establishing operations abroad, when the alternatives of exporting and licensing are available to them.
2. High transportation costs or tariffs imposed on imports help explain why many firms prefer FDI or licensing over exporting.
3. Firms often prefer FDI to licensing when: (*a*) a firm has valuable know-how that cannot be adequately protected by a licensing contract, (*b*) a firm needs tight control over a foreign entity in order to maximize its market share and earnings in that country, and (*c*) a firm's skills and capabilities are not amenable to licensing.
4. Knickerbocker's theory suggests that much FDI is explained by imitative behavior by rival firms in an oligopolistic industry.
5. Vernon's product life-cycle theory suggests that firms undertake FDI at particular stages in the life cycle of products they have pioneered. However, Vernon's theory does not address the issue of whether FDI is more efficient than exporting or licensing for expanding abroad.
6. Dunning has argued that location-specific advantages are of considerable importance in explaining the nature and direction of FDI. According to Dunning, firms undertake FDI to exploit resource endowments or assets that are location specific.
7. Political ideology is an important determinant of government policy toward FDI. Ideology ranges from a radical stance that is hostile to FDI to a noninterventionist, free market stance. Between the two extremes is an approach best described as pragmatic nationalism.
8. Benefits of FDI to a host country arise from resource transfer effects, employment effects, and balance-of-payments effects.
9. The costs of FDI to a host country include adverse effects on competition and balance of payments and a perceived loss of national sovereignty.
10. The benefits of FDI to the home (source) country include improvement in the balance of payments as a result of the inward flow of foreign earnings, positive employment effects when the foreign subsidiary creates demand for home-country exports, and benefits from a reverse resource-transfer effect. A reverse resource-transfer effect arises when the foreign subsidiary learns valuable skills abroad that can be transferred back to the home country.
11. The costs of FDI to the home country include adverse balance-of-payments effects that arise from the initial capital outflow and from the export substitution effects of FDI. Costs also arise when FDI exports jobs abroad.
12. Home countries can adopt policies designed to both encourage and restrict FDI. Host countries try to attract FDI by offering incentives and try to restrict FDI by dictating ownership restraints and requiring that foreign MNEs meet specific performance requirements.

Critical Thinking and Discussion Questions

1. In 2004, inward FDI accounted for some 24 percent of gross fixed capital formation in Ireland, but only 0.6 percent in Japan. What do you think explains this difference in FDI inflows into the two countries?
2. Compare and contrast these explanations of horizontal FDI: the market imperfections approach, Vernon's product life-cycle theory, and Knickerbocker's theory of FDI. Which theory do you think offers the best

explanation of the historical pattern of FDI? Why?

3. Read the opening case on Starbucks and then answer the following questions:
   a. Initially Starbucks expanded internationally by licensing its format to foreign operators. It soon became disenchanted with this strategy. Why?
   b. Why do you think Starbucks has now elected to expand internationally primarily through local joint ventures, to whom it licenses its format, as opposed to using a pure licensing strategy?
   c. What are the advantages of a joint-venture entry mode for Starbucks over entering through wholly owned subsidiaries? On occasion, Starbucks has chosen a wholly owned subsidiary to control its foreign expansion (e.g., in Britain and Thailand). Why?
   d. Which theory of FDI best explains the international expansion strategy adopted by Starbucks?
4. You are the international manager of a U.S. business that has just developed a revolutionary new personal computer that can perform the same functions as existing PCs but costs only half as much to manufacture. Several patents protect the unique design of this computer. Your CEO has asked you to formulate a recommendation for how to expand into Western Europe. Your options are (*a*) to export from the United States, (*b*) to license a European firm to manufacture and market the computer in Europe, or (*c*) to set up a wholly owned subsidiary in Europe. Evaluate the pros and cons of each alternative and suggest a course of action to your CEO.

Research Task 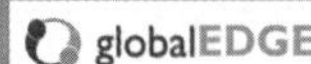 http://globalEDGE.msu.edu

Use the globalEDGE site (http://globalEDGE.msu.edu/) to complete the following exercises:

1. You are working for a company that is considering investing in a foreign country. Management has requested a report regarding the attractiveness of alternative countries based on the potential return of FDI. Accordingly, the ranking of the top 25 countries in terms of FDI attractiveness is a crucial ingredient for your report. A colleague mentioned a potentially useful tool called the "*FDI Confidence Index*" which is updated periodically. Find this index and provide additional information regarding how the index is constructed.
2. Your company is considering opening a new factory in Latin America and management is evaluating the specific country locations for this direct investment. The pool of candidate countries has been narrowed to Argentina, Brazil, and Mexico. Prepare a short report comparing the foreign direct investment (*FDI*) environment and regulations of these three countries.

closing case

Cemex's Foreign Direct Investment

In little more than a decade, Mexico's largest cement manufacturer, Cemex, has transformed itself from a primarily Mexican operation into the third-largest cement company in the world behind Holcim of Switzerland and Lafarge Group of France with 2005 sales of $15 billion and more than $2 billion in net profits. Cemex has long been a powerhouse in Mexico and currently controls more than 60 percent of the market for cement in that country. Cemex's domestic success has been based in large part on an obsession with efficient manufacturing and a focus on customer service that is tops in the industry.

Cemex is a leader in using information technology to match production with consumer demand. The company sells ready-mixed cement that can survive for only about 90 minutes before solidifying, so precise delivery is important. But Cemex can never predict with total certainty what demand will be on any given day, week, or month. To better manage unpredictable demand patterns, Cemex developed a system of seamless information technology, including truck-mounted global positioning systems, radio transmitters, satellites, and computer hardware, that allows it to control the production and distribution of cement like no other company can, responding quickly to unanticipated changes in demand and reducing waste. The results are lower costs and superior customer service, both differentiating factors for Cemex.

The company also pays lavish attention to its distributors—some 5,000 in Mexico alone—who can earn points toward rewards for hitting sales targets. The distributors can then convert those points into Cemex stock. High-volume distributors can purchase trucks and other supplies through Cemex at significant discounts. Cemex also is known for its marketing drives that focus on end users, the builders themselves. For example, Cemex trucks drive around Mexican building sites, and if Cemex cement is being used, the construction crews win soccer balls, caps, and T-shirts.

Cemex's international expansion strategy was driven by a number of factors. First, the company wished to reduce its reliance on the Mexican construction market, which was characterized by very volatile demand. Second, the company realized there was tremendous demand for cement in many developing countries, where significant construction was being undertaken or needed. Third, the company believed that it understood the needs of construction businesses in developing nations better than the established multinational cement companies, all of which were from developed nations. Fourth, Cemex believed that it could create significant value by acquiring inefficient cement companies in other markets and transferring its skills in customer service, marketing, information technology, and production management to those units.

The company embarked in earnest on its international expansion strategy in the early 1990s. Initially, Cemex targeted other developing nations, acquiring established cement makers in Venezuela, Colombia, Indonesia, the Philippines, Egypt, and several other countries. It also purchased two stagnant companies in Spain and turned them around. Bolstered by the success of its Spanish ventures, Cemex began to look for expansion opportunities in developed nations. In 2000, Cemex purchased Houston-based Southland, one of the largest cement companies in the United States, for $2.5 billion. Following the Southland acquisition, Cemex had 56 cement plants in 30 countries, most of which were gained through acquisitions. In all cases, Cemex devoted great attention to transferring its technological, management, and marketing know-how to acquired units, thereby improving their performance.

In 2004, Cemex made another major foreign investment move, purchasing RMC of Great Britain for $5.8 billion. RMC was a huge multinational cement firm with sales of $8.0 billion, only 22 percent of which were in the United Kingdom, and operations in more than 20 other nations, including many European nations where Cemex had no presence. Finalized in March 2005, the RMC acquisition has transformed Cemex into a global powerhouse in the cement industry with more than $15 billion in annual sales and operations in 50 countries. Only about 15 percent of the company's sales are now generated in Mexico. Following the acquisition of RMC, Cemex found that the RMC plant in Rugby, England was only running at 70 percent of capacity, partly because repeated production problems kept causing a kiln shutdown. Cemex brought in an international team of specialists to fix the problem, and quickly increased production to 90 percent of capacity.

Going forward, Cemex has made it clear that it will continue to expand and is eyeing opportunities in the fast-growing economies of China and India where currently it lacks a presence, and where its global rivals are already expanding. Still, not all of Cemex's expansions have worked out as planned. In 2006, Cemex announced that it would exit Indonesia after a long-running dispute with the government there. Cemex entered Indonesia in 1998 as part of an IMF-sponsored privatization program by purchasing a 25 percent stake in a government-owned Indonesian cement maker, Semen Gresik. At the time, Indonesia promised to allow Cemex to acquire a majority stake in Semen Gresik in 2001. However, the country never granted that permission, as local vested interests, including politicians and unions, voiced worries about "Indonesian assets falling into foreign hands" and lobbied the central government to block the deal. A frustrated Cemex eventually reached an agreement to sell its 25 percent stake to another Indonesian enterprise.

Sources: C. Piggott, "Cemex's Stratospheric Rise," *Latin Finance,* March 2001, p. 76; J. F. Smith, "Making Cement a Household Word," *Los Angeles Times,* January 16, 2000, p. C1; D. Helft, "Cemex Attempts to Cement Its Future," *The Industry Standard,* November 6, 2000; Diane Lindquist, "From Cement to Services," *Chief Executive,* November 2002, pp. 48–50; "Cementing Global Success," *Strategic Direct Investor,* March 2003, p. 1; M. T. Derham, "The Cemex Surprise," *Latin Finance,* November 2004, pp. 1–2; "Holcim Seeks to Acquire Aggregate," *The Wall Street Journal,* January 13, 2005, p. 1; J. Lyons, "Cemex Prowls for Deals in Both China and India," *The Wall Street Journal,* January 27, 2006, p. C4; and S. Donnan, "Cemex Sells 25 Percent Stake in Semen Gresik," *FT.com,* May 4, 2006, p. 1.

Case Discussion Questions

1. Which theoretical explanation, or explanations, of FDI best explains Cemex's FDI?
2. What is the value that Cemex brings to a host economy? Can you see any potential drawbacks of inward investment by Cemex in an economy?
3. Cemex has a strong preference for acquisitions over greenfield ventures as an entry mode. Why?
4. Why do you think Cemex decided to exit Indonesia after failing to gain majority control of Semen Gresik? Why is majority control so important to Cemex?
5. Why do you think politicians in Indonesia tried to block Cemex's attempt to gain majority control over Semen Gresik? Do you think Indonesia's best interests were served by limiting Cemex's FDI in the country?

Bob Daemmrich/Corbis

part 3 Cross-Border Trade and Investment

LEARNING OBJECTIVES

1. Be able to explain the different levels of regional economic integration.
2. Understand the economic and political arguments for regional economic integration.
3. Understand the economic and political arguments against regional economic integration.
4. Be familiar with the history, current scope, and future prospects of the world's most important regional economic agreements.
5. Understand the implications for business that are inherent in regional economic integration agreements.

chapter 8

Regional Economic Integration

NAFTA and the U.S. Textile Industry

opening case

When the North American Free Trade Agreement (NAFTA) went into effect in 1994, many expressed fears that large job losses in the U.S. textile industry would occur as companies moved production from the United States to Mexico. NAFTA opponents argued passionately, but unsuccessfully, that the treaty should not be adopted because of the negative impact it would have on U.S. employment.

A quick glance at the data available 10 years after the passage of NAFTA suggests the critics had a point. Between 1994 and 2004, overall U.S. demand for apparel grew by almost 60 percent; however, production of apparel in the United States fell by 40 percent and production of textiles by 20 percent. During the same period, employment in textile mills in the United Stated dropped from 478,000 to 239,000, employment in apparel plummeted from 858,000 to 296,000, while exports of apparel from Mexico to the United States surged from $1.26 billion to $3.84 billion. Such data seem to indicate that the job losses have been due to apparel production migrating from the United States to Mexico.

There is anecdotal evidence to support this assertion. For example, in 1995, Fruit of the Loom Inc., the largest manufacturer of underwear in the United States, said it would close six of its domestic plants and cut back operations at two others, laying off about 3,200 workers, or 12 percent of its U.S. workforce. The company announced the closures were part of its drive to move its operations to cheaper plants abroad, particularly in Mexico. Before the closures, less than 30 percent of its sewing was done outside the United States, but Fruit of the Loom planned to move the majority of that work to Mexico. For textile manufacturers, the advantages of locating in Mexico include cheap labor and inputs. Labor rates in Mexico average between $10 and $20 a day, compared with $10 to $12 an hour for U.S. textile workers.

However, job losses in the U.S. textile industry do not mean that the overall effects of NAFTA have been negative. Clothing prices in the United States have also fallen since 1994 as textile production shifted from high-cost U.S. producers to lower-cost Mexican producers. This benefits consumers, who now have more money to spend on other items. The cost of a typical pair of designer jeans, for example, fell from $55 in 1994 to about $48 today. In 1994, blank T-shirts wholesaled for $24 a dozen. Now they sell for $14 a dozen.

In addition to lower prices, the shift in textile production to Mexico also benefited the U.S. economy in other ways. Despite the move of fabric and apparel production to Mexico, exports have surged for U.S. yarn makers, many of which are in the chemical industry. Before the passage of NAFTA, U.S. yarn producers, such as E. I. du Pont, supplied only small amounts of product to Mexico. However, as apparel production moved to Mexico, exports of fabric and yarn to that country have surged. U.S. producers supply 70 percent of the raw material going to Mexican sewing shops. Between 1994 and 2004, U.S. cotton and yarn exports to Mexico grew from $293 million to $1.21 billion. Moreover, although the U.S. textile industry has lost jobs, advocates of NAFTA argue that the U.S. economy has benefited in the form of lower clothing prices and an increase in exports from fabric and yarn producers. NAFTA supporters argue that trade has been created because of NAFTA. The gains from trade are being captured by U.S. consumers and by producers in certain sectors. As always, the establishment of a free trade area creates winners and losers—and the losers have been employees in the textile industry—but advocates of free trade argue that the gains outweigh the losses.

Sources: C. Burritt, "Seven Years into NAFTA, Textile Makers Seek a Payoff in Mexico," *Atlanta Journal-Constitution,* December 17, 2000, p. Q1; I. McAllister, "Trade Agreements: How They Affect U.S. Textile," *Textile World,* March 2000, pp. 50–54; J. Millman, "Mexico Weaves More Ties," *The Wall Street Journal,* August 21, 2000, p. A12; J. R. Giermanski, "A Fresh Look at NAFTA: What Really Happened?" *Logistics,* September 2002, pp. 43–46; G.C. Hufbauer and J.C. Schott, *NAFTA Revisited: Achievements and Challenges,* Institute for International Economics, 2005; American Textile Manufactures Institute, www.atmi.org/index.asp; and U.S. Department of Commerce Trade Stat Express, http://tse.export.gov.

Introduction

Regional Economic Integration Agreements among countries in a geographic region to reduce, and ultimately remove, tariff and nontariff barriers to the free flow of goods, services, and factors of production between each other.

One notable trend in the global economy in recent years has been the accelerated movement toward regional economic integration. **Regional economic integration** refers to agreements among countries in a geographic region to reduce, and ultimately remove, tariff and nontariff barriers to the free flow of goods, services, and factors of production between each other. The North American Free Trade Agreement is an example of regional economic integration. The last two decades have witnessed an unprecedented proliferation of regional trade arrangements. World Trade Organization members are required to notify the WTO of any regional trade agreements in which they participate. By 2006, nearly all of the WTO members had notified the organization of participation in one or more regional trade agreements. The total number of regional trade agreements currently in force is around 300.[1]

Consistent with the predictions of international trade theory and particularly the theory of comparative advantage (see Chapter 5), agreements designed to promote freer trade within regions are believed to produce gains from trade for all member countries. As we saw in Chapter 6, the General Agreement on Tariffs and Trade and its successor, the World Trade Organization, also seek to reduce trade barriers. With 149 member states, the WTO has a worldwide perspective. By entering into regional agreements, groups of countries aim to reduce trade barriers more rapidly than can be achieved under the auspices of the WTO.

Nowhere has the movement toward regional economic integration been more successful than in Europe. On January 1, 1993, the European Union (EU) formally removed many barriers to doing business across borders within the EU in an attempt to create a single market with 340 million consumers. However, the EU did not stop there. The member states of the EU have launched a single currency, the euro; they are moving toward a closer political union; and on May 1, 2004, the EU expanded from 15 to 25 countries with a population of 450 million consumers and a gross domestic product approaching that of the United States.

Similar moves toward regional integration are being pursued elsewhere in the world. Canada, Mexico, and the United States have implemented the North American Free Trade Agreement. Ultimately, this promises to remove all barriers to the free flow of goods and services between the three countries. As detailed in the opening case, the implementation of NAFTA has resulted in job losses in some sectors of the American economy (e.g., among textile producers); but in aggregate and consistent with the predications of international trade theory, the benefits of greater regional trade are argued to outweigh any costs. South American, too, is moving toward regional integration. In 1991, Argentina, Brazil, Paraguay, and Uruguay implemented an agreement known as MERCOSUR to start reducing barriers to trade between each other, and although progress within MERCOSUR has been halting, the institution is still in place. There are also active attempts at regional economic integration in Central America, the Andean region of South America, Southeast Asia, and parts of Africa.

While the move toward regional economic integration is generally seen as a good thing, some observers worry that it will lead to a world in which regional trade blocs compete against each other. In this possible future scenario, free trade will exist within each bloc, but each bloc will protect its market from outside competition with high tariffs. The specter of the EU and NAFTA turning into economic fortresses that shut out foreign producers with high tariff barriers is worrisome to those who believe in unrestricted free trade. If such a situation were to materialize, the resulting decline in trade between blocs could more than offset the gains from free trade within blocs.

With these issues in mind, this chapter will explore the economic and political debate surrounding regional economic integration, paying particular attention to the economic and political benefits and costs of integration; review progress toward regional economic integration around the world; and map the important implications of regional economic integration for the practice of international business. Before tackling these objectives, we first need to examine the levels of integration that are theoretically possible.

Another Perspective

Economic Integration in the Classical World

Traditionally, the success of the Roman Empire has been explained by economic historians as an example of centralized, forced reallocation of goods. Recent scholarship, though, suggests that there was not a single empirewide, centralized market for all goods, but that local markets were connected and that most exchanges were voluntary, based on reciprocity and exchange. Ancient Rome had an economic system that was an enormous, integrated conglomeration of interdependent markets. Transportation and communication took time, and the discipline of the market was loose. But there were many voluntary economic connections between even far-flung parts of the early Roman Empire. (Karl Polanyi, *The Livelihood of Man;* and Peter Temin, "Market Economy in the Early Roman Empire," University of Oxford, Discussion Papers in Economic and Social History)

Levels of Economic Integration

LEARNING OBJECTIVE 1
Be able to explain the different levels of regional economic integration.

Several levels of economic integration are possible in theory (see Figure 8.1). From least integrated to most integrated, they are a free trade area, a customs union, a common market, an economic union, and, finally, a full political union.

Free Trade Area An area in which all barriers to the trade of goods and services among member countries are removed.

In a **free trade area,** all barriers to the trade of goods and services among member countries are removed. In the theoretically ideal free trade area, no discriminatory tariffs, quotas, subsidies, or administrative impediments are allowed to distort trade between members. Each country, however, is allowed to determine its own trade policies with regard to nonmembers. Thus, for example, the tariffs placed on the products of nonmember countries may vary from member to member. Free trade agreements are the most popular form of regional economic integration, accounting for almost 90 percent of regional agreements.[2]

European Free Trade Association (EFTA) The most enduring free trade area in the world, which focuses on free trade in industrial goods and currently includes Norway, Iceland, Liechtenstein, and Switzerland.

The most enduring free trade area in the world is the **European Free Trade Association (EFTA).** Established in January 1960, EFTA currently joins four countries—Norway, Iceland, Liechtenstein, and Switzerland—down from seven in 1995 (three EFTA members, Austria, Finland, and Sweden, joined the EU on January 1, 1996). The EFTA was founded by those Western European countries that initially decided not to be part of the European Community (the forerunner of the EU). Its original members included Austria, Great Britain, Denmark, Finland, and Sweden, all of which are now members of the EU. The emphasis of the EFTA has been on free trade in industrial goods. Agriculture was left out of the arrangement, each member being allowed to determine its own level of support. Members are also free to determine the level of protection applied to goods coming from outside the EFTA. Other free trade areas include the North American Free Trade Agreement, which we shall discuss in depth later in the chapter.

Customs Union A group of countries committed to eliminating trade barriers and adopting a common external trade policy.

The customs union is one step farther along the road to full economic and political integration. A **customs union** eliminates trade barriers between member countries and adopts a common external trade policy. Establishment of a common external trade

figure 8.1 Levels of Economic Integration

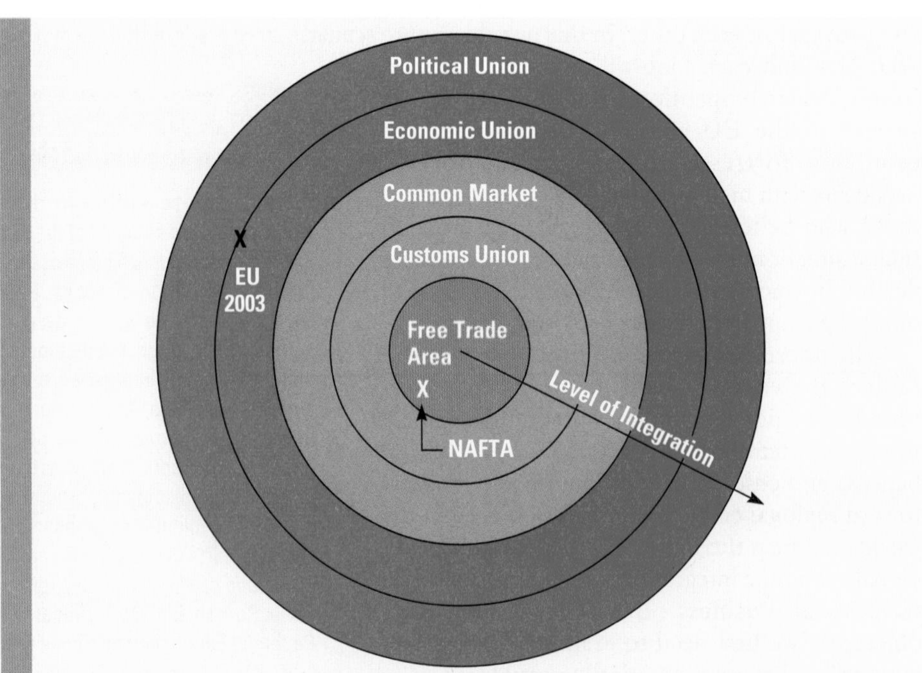

policy necessitates significant administrative machinery to oversee trade relations with nonmembers. Most countries that enter into a customs union desire even greater economic integration down the road. The EU began as a customs union, but it has now moved beyond this stage. Other customs unions around the world include the current version of the Andean Community (formally known as the Andean Pact) between Bolivia, Colombia, Ecuador, Peru, and Venezuela. The Andean Community established free trade between member countries and imposes a common tariff, of 5 to 20 percent, on products imported from outside.[3]

The next level of economic integration, a **common market** has no barriers to trade between member countries, includes a common external trade policy, and allows factors of production to move freely between members. Labor and capital are free to move because there are no restrictions on immigration, emigration, or cross-border flows of capital between member countries. Establishing a common market demands a significant degree of harmony and cooperation on fiscal, monetary, and employment policies. Achieving this degree of cooperation has proven very difficult. For years, the European Union functioned as a common market, although it has now moved beyond this stage. MERCOSUR, the South American grouping of Argentina, Brazil, Paraguay, Uruguay, and (as of 2006) Venezuela, hopes to eventually establish itself as a common market.

Common Market
A group of countries committed to eliminating trade barriers, adopting a common external trade policy, and allowing factors of production to move freely between members.

An economic union entails even closer economic integration and cooperation than a common market. Like the common market, an **economic union** involves the free flow of products and factors of production between member countries and the adoption of a common external trade policy, but it also requires a common currency, harmonization of members' tax rates, and a common monetary and fiscal policy. Such a high degree of integration demands a coordinating bureaucracy and the sacrifice of significant amounts of national sovereignty to that bureaucracy. The EU is an economic union, although an imperfect one since not all members of the EU have adopted the euro, the currency of the EU, and differences in tax rates and regulations across countries still remain.

Economic Union
A group of countries committed to removing trade barriers, adopting a common currency, harmonizing tax rates, and pursuing a common external trade policy.

The move toward economic union raises the issue of how to make a coordinating bureaucracy accountable to the citizens of member nations. The answer is through **political union** in which a central political apparatus coordinates the economic, social, and foreign policy of the member states. The EU is on the road toward at least partial political union. The European Parliament, which is playing an ever more important role in the EU, has been directly elected by citizens of the EU countries since the late 1970s. In addition, the Council of Ministers (the controlling, decision-making body of the EU) is composed of government ministers from each EU member. The United States provides an example of even closer political union; in the United States, independent states are effectively combined into a single nation. Ultimately, the EU may move toward a similar federal structure.

Political Union
A central political apparatus coordinating the economic, social, and foreign policy of its member states.

The Case for Regional Integration

LEARNING OBJECTIVE 2
Understand the economic and political arguments for regional economic integration.

The case for regional integration is both economic and political. Typically, however, there are many groups within a country that argue against regional economic integration, which explains why most attempts to achieve it have been contentious and halting. In this section, we examine the economic and political cases for integration and two impediments to achieving it. In the next section, we look at the case against integration.

THE ECONOMIC CASE FOR INTEGRATION The economic case for regional integration is straightforward. We saw in Chapter 5 how economic theories of international trade predict that unrestricted free trade will allow countries to

Another Perspective

Economic Integration and the EU Worker

Being a citizen of a country that is regionally integrated, such as the countries of the EU, may have benefits related to career development. From an employer's perspective, workers are more mobile. They can move from Spain to Finland, Latvia to France, and never have to think about work permits and, depending on the countries, currencies. In addition, labor and commercial law is becoming integrated across the EU. The mobility and flexibility of such employees may be attractive to a U.S. MNE as well, because it could use them in many markets.

specialize in the production of goods and services that they can produce most efficiently. The result is greater world production than would be possible with trade restrictions. That chapter also revealed how opening a country to free trade stimulates economic growth, which creates dynamic gains from trade. Chapter 7 detailed how foreign direct investment can transfer technological, marketing, and managerial know-how to host nations. Given the central role of knowledge in stimulating economic growth, opening a country to FDI also is likely to stimulate economic growth. In sum, economic theories suggest that free trade and investment is a positive-sum game, in which all participating countries stand to gain.

Given this, the theoretical ideal is an absence of barriers to the free flow of goods, services, and factors of production among nations. However, as we saw in Chapters 6 and 7, a case can be made for government intervention in international trade and FDI. Because many governments have accepted part or all of the case for intervention, unrestricted free trade and FDI have proved to be only an ideal. Although international institutions such as the WTO have been moving the world toward a free trade regime, success has been less than total. In a world of many nations and many political ideologies, it is very difficult to get all countries to agree to a common set of rules.

Against this background, regional economic integration can be seen as an attempt to achieve additional gains from the free flow of trade and investment between countries beyond those attainable under international agreements such as the WTO. It is easier to establish a free trade and investment regime among a limited number of adjacent countries than among the world community. Coordination and policy harmonization problems are largely a function of the number of countries that seek agreement. The greater the number of countries involved, the more perspectives that must be reconciled, and the harder it will be to reach agreement. Thus, attempts at regional economic integration are motivated by a desire to exploit the gains from free trade and investment.

THE POLITICAL CASE FOR INTEGRATION The political case for regional economic integration also has loomed large in most attempts to establish free trade areas, customs unions, and the like. Linking neighboring economies and making them increasingly dependent on each other creates incentives for political cooperation between the neighboring states and reduces the potential for violent conflict. In addition, by grouping their economies, the countries can enhance their political weight in the world.

These considerations underlay the 1957 establishment of the European Community (EC), the forerunner of the EU. Europe had suffered two devastating wars in the first half of the twentieth century, both arising out of the unbridled ambitions of nation-states. Those who have sought a united Europe have always had a desire to make another war in Europe unthinkable. Many Europeans also believed that after World War II, the European nation-states were no longer large enough to hold their own in world markets and politics. The need for a united Europe to deal with the United States and the politically alien Soviet Union loomed large in the minds of many of the EC's founders.[4] A long-standing joke in Europe is that the European Commission should erect a statue to Joseph Stalin, for without the aggressive policies of the former dictator of the old Soviet Union, the countries of Western Europe might have lacked the incentive to cooperate and form the EC.

IMPEDIMENTS TO INTEGRATION Despite the strong economic and political arguments in support, integration has never been easy to achieve or sustain for two main reasons. First, although economic integration aids the majority, it has its costs. While a nation as a whole may benefit significantly from a regional free trade agreement, certain groups may lose. Moving to a free trade regime involves painful adjustments. For example, as a result of the 1994 establishment of NAFTA, some Canadian and U.S. workers in such industries as textiles, which employ low-cost, low-skilled labor, lost their jobs as Canadian and U.S. firms moved production to Mexico (see the opening case). The promise of significant net benefits to the Canadian and U.S. economies as a whole is little comfort to those who lose as a result of NAFTA. Such groups have been at the forefront of opposition to NAFTA and will continue to oppose any widening of the agreement.

A second impediment to integration arises from concerns over national sovereignty. For example, Mexico's concerns about maintaining control of its oil interests resulted in an agreement with Canada and the United States to exempt the Mexican oil industry from any liberalization of foreign investment regulations achieved under NAFTA. Concerns about national sovereignty arise because close economic integration demands that countries give up some degree of control over such key issues as monetary policy, fiscal policy (e.g., tax policy), and trade policy. This has been a major stumbling block in the EU. To achieve full economic union, the EU introduced a common currency, the euro, controlled by a central EU bank. Although most member states have signed on, Great Britain remains an important holdout. A politically important segment of public opinion in that country opposes a common currency on the grounds that it would require relinquishing control of the country's monetary policy to the EU, which many British perceive as a bureaucracy run by foreigners. In 1992, the British won the right to opt out of any single currency agreement, and as of 2006, the British government had yet to reverse its decision.

The Case against Regional Integration

LEARNING OBJECTIVE 2
Understand the economic and political arguments against regional economic integration.

Although the tide has been running strongly in favor of regional free trade agreements in recent years, some economists have expressed concern that the benefits of regional integration have been oversold, while the costs have often been ignored.[5] They point out that the benefits of regional integration are determined by the extent of trade creation, as opposed to trade diversion. **Trade creation** occurs when high-cost domestic producers are replaced by low-cost producers within the free trade area. It may also occur when higher-cost external producers are replaced by lower-cost external producers within the free trade area. **Trade diversion** occurs when lower-cost external suppliers are replaced by higher-cost suppliers within the free trade area. A regional free trade agreement will benefit the world only if the amount of trade it creates exceeds the amount it diverts.

Trade Creation
Trade created within a free trade area due to the replacement of high-cost domestic or external producers by low-cost external producers.

Trade Diversion
Trade diverted within a free trade area when lower-cost external suppliers are replaced by higher-cost external suppliers.

Suppose the United States and Mexico imposed tariffs on imports from all countries, and then they set up a free trade area, scrapping all trade barriers between themselves but maintaining tariffs on imports from the rest of the world. If the United States began to import textiles from Mexico, would this change be for the better? If the United States previously produced all its own textiles at a higher cost than Mexico, then the free trade agreement has shifted production to the cheaper source. According to the theory of comparative advantage, trade has been created within the regional grouping, and there would be no decrease in trade with the rest of the world. Clearly, the change would be for the better. If, however, the United States previously imported textiles from Costa Rica, which produced them more cheaply than either Mexico or the United States, then trade has been diverted from a low-cost source, a change for the worse.

In theory, WTO rules should ensure that a free trade agreement does not result in trade diversion. These rules allow free trade areas to be formed only if the members set tariffs that are not higher or more restrictive to outsiders than the ones previously in effect. However, as we saw in Chapter 6, GATT and the WTO do not cover some nontariff barriers. As a result, regional trade blocs could emerge whose markets are protected from outside competition by high nontariff barriers. In such cases, the trade diversion effects might outweigh the trade creation effects. The only way to guard against this possibility, according to those concerned about this potential, is to increase the scope of the WTO so it covers nontariff barriers to trade. There is no sign that this is going to occur anytime soon, however; so the risk remains that regional economic integration will result in trade diversion.

Regional Economic Integration in Europe

LEARNING OBJECTIVE 3
Be familiar with the history, current scope, and future prospects of the world's most important regional economic agreements.

Europe has two trade blocs: the European Union and the European Free Trade Association. Of the two, the EU is by far the more significant, not just in terms of membership (the EU currently has 25 members; the EFTA has 4), but also in terms of economic and political influence in the world economy. Many now see the EU as an emerging economic and political superpower of the same order as the United States and Japan. Accordingly, we will concentrate our attention on the EU.[6]

European Union (EU)
The regional economical union of most European countries, formed as a result of the two world wars and the European nations' desire to hold their own in the world's political and economic stage.

EVOLUTION OF THE EUROPEAN UNION The **European Union** (EU) is the product of two political factors: (1) the devastation of Western Europe during two world wars and the desire for a lasting peace, and (2) the European nations' desire to hold their own on the world's political and economic stage. In addition, many Europeans were aware of the potential economic benefits of closer economic integration of the countries.

The forerunner of the EU, the European Coal and Steel Community, was formed in 1951 by Belgium, France, West Germany, Italy, Luxembourg, and the Netherlands. Its objective was to remove barriers to intragroup shipments of coal, iron, steel, and scrap metal. With the signing of the **Treaty of Rome** in 1957, the European Community was established. The name changed again in 1994, when the European Community became the European Union following the ratification of the Maastricht Treaty (discussed later).

Treaty of Rome
Signed in 1957, this established the European Community, a forerunner to the European Union, and created the common European market.

The Treaty of Rome provided for the creation of a common market. Article 3 of the treaty laid down the key objectives of the new community, calling for the elimination of internal trade barriers and the creation of a common external tariff and requiring member states to abolish obstacles to the free movement of factors of production among the members. To facilitate the free movement of goods, services, and factors of production, the treaty provided for any necessary harmonization of the member states' laws. Furthermore, the treaty committed the EC to establish common policies in agriculture and transportation.

The community grew in 1973, when Great Britain, Ireland, and Denmark joined. These three were followed in 1981 by Greece, in 1986 by Spain and Portugal, and in 1996 by Austria, Finland, and Sweden, bringing the total membership to 15 (East Germany became part of the EC after the reunification of Germany in 1990). Another 10 countries joined the EU on May 1, 2004, 8 of them from Eastern Europe plus the small Mediterranean nations of Malta and Cyprus (see Map 8.1). With a population of 450 million and a GDP of $11 trillion, similar to that of the United States, the EU through these enlargements has become a global superpower.[7] Three more countries are currently considered candidates for entry into the EU—Romania, Bulgaria, and Turkey—with Romania and Bulgaria set to join in 2007.

map 8.1

European Union Members in 2005

Source: www.europarl.org.uk.

POLITICAL STRUCTURE OF THE EUROPEAN UNION The economic policies of the EU are formulated and implemented by a complex and still-evolving political structure. The four main institutions in this structure are the European Commission, the Council of the European Union, the European Parliament, and the Court of Justice.[8]

The **European Commission** is responsible for proposing EU legislation, implementing it, and monitoring compliance with EU laws by member states. Headquartered in Brussels, Belgium, the commission has more than 24,000 employees. It is run by a group of commissioners appointed by each member country for five-year renewable terms. There are 25 commissioners, one from each member state. A president of the commission is chosen by member states, and the president then chooses other members in consultation with the states. The entire commission has to be approved by

European Commission
Responsible for proposing, implementing, and monitoring compliance with EU legislation; run by a group of commissioners appointed by each member country.

In 2000, a proposed merger between Time Warner of the United States and EMI of the United Kingdom failed after the Federal Trade Comission expressed the concern that the merger would monopolize the record industry. *Alastair Grant/AP Wide World*

the European Parliament before it can begin work. The commission has a monopoly in proposing European Union legislation. The commission makes a proposal, which goes to the Council of the European Union and then to the European Parliament. The council cannot legislate without a commission proposal in front of it. The commission is also responsible for implementing aspects of EU law, although in practice much of this must be delegated to member states. Another responsibility of the commission is to monitor member states to make sure they are complying with EU laws. In this policing role, the commission will normally ask a state to comply with any EU laws that are being broken. If this persuasion is not sufficient, the commission can refer a case to the Court of Justice.

The European Commission's role in competition policy has become increasingly important to business in recent years. Since 1990 when the office was formally assigned a role in competition policy, the EU's competition commissioner has been steadily gaining influence as the chief regulator of competition policy in the member nations of the EU. As with antitrust authorities in the United States, which include the Federal Trade Commission and the Department of Justice, the role of the competition commissioner is to ensure that no one enterprise uses its market power to drive out competitors and monopolize markets. The commissioner also reviews proposed mergers and acquisitions to make sure they do not create a dominant enterprise with substantial market power.[9] For example, in 2000 a proposed merger between Time Warner of the United States and EMI of the United Kingdom, both music recording companies, was withdrawn after the commission expressed concerns that the merger would reduce the number of major record companies from five to four and create a dominant player in the $40 billion global music industry. Similarly, the commission blocked a proposed merger between two U.S. telecommunication companies, WorldCom and Sprint, because their combined holdings of Internet infrastructure in Europe would give the merged companies so much market power that the commission argued the combined company would dominate that market. Another example of the commission's influence over business combinations is given in the Management Focus box, next page, which looks at the commission's role in shaping mergers and joint ventures in the media industry.

Council of the European Union The ultimate decision-making body of the EU, it passes legislation from the commission into law and is comprised of one representative from each member state's government.

The **Council of the European Union** represents the interests of member states. It is clearly the ultimate controlling authority within the EU since draft legislation from the commission can become EU law only if the council agrees. The council is composed of one representative from the government of each member state. The membership, however, varies depending on the topic being discussed. When agricultural issues are being discussed, the agriculture ministers from each state attend council meetings; when transportation is being discussed, transportation ministers attend; and so on. Before 1993, all council issues had to be decided by unanimous agreement between member states. This often led to marathon council sessions and a failure to make progress or reach agreement on commission proposals. In an attempt to clear the resulting logjams, the Single European Act formalized the use of majority voting rules on issues "which have as their object the establishment and functioning of a single market." Most other issues, however, such as tax regulations and immigration policy, still require unanimity among council members if they are to become law. The votes that a

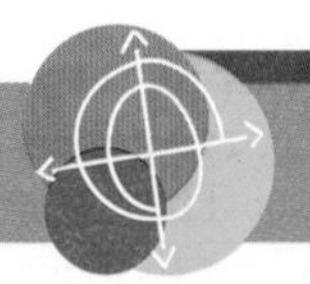

Management FOCUS

The European Commission and Media Industry Mergers

In late 1999, U.S. Internet giant AOL announced it would merge with the music and publishing conglomerate Time Warner. Both the U.S. companies had substantial operations in Europe. The European commissioner for competition, Mario Monti, announced the commission would investigate the impact of the merger on competition in Europe.

The investigation took on a new twist when Time Warner subsequently announced it would form a joint venture with British-based EMI. Time Warner and EMI are two of the top five music publishing companies in the world. The proposed joint venture would have been three times as large as its nearest global competitor. The European Commission now had two concerns. The first was that the joint venture between EMI and Time Warner would reduce the level of competition in the music publishing industry. The second was that a combined AOL–Time Warner would dominate the emerging market for downloading music over the Internet, particularly given the fact that AOL would be able to gain preferential access to the music libraries of both Warner and EMI. This would potentially put other online service providers at a disadvantage. The commission was also concerned that AOL Europe was a joint venture between AOL and Bertelsmann, a German media company that also had considerable music publishing interests. Accordingly, the commission announced it would undertake a separate investigation of the proposed deal between Time Warner and EMI.

These investigations continued into late 2000 and were resolved by a series of concessions extracted by the European Commission. First, under pressure from the commission, Time Warner and EMI agreed to drop their proposed joint venture, thereby maintaining the level of competition in the music publishing business. Second, AOL and Time Warner agreed to allow rival Internet service providers access to online music on the same terms as AOL would receive from Warner Music Group for the next five years. Third, AOL agreed to sever all ties with Bertelsmann, and the German company agreed to withdraw from AOL Europe. These developments alleviated the commission's concern that the AOL–Time Warner combination would dominate the emerging market for the digital downloading of music. With these concessions in hand, the commission approved the AOL–Time Warner merger in early October 2000.

By late 2000, the AOL-Timer Warner merger had been completed. The shape of the media business, both in Europe and worldwide, now looked very different, and the European Commission had played a pivotal role in determining the outcome. Its demand for concessions altered the strategy of several companies, led to somewhat different combinations from those originally planned and, the Commission believed, preserved competition in the global media business.

Sources: W. Drozdiak, "EU Allows Vivendi Media Deal," *Washington Post,* October 14, 2000, p. E2; D. Hargreaves, "Business as Usual in the New Economy," *Financial Times,* October 6, 2000, p. 1; and D. Hargreaves, "Brussels Clears AOL–Time Warner Deal," *Financial Times,* October 12, 2000, p. 12.

country gets in the council are related to the size of the country. For example, Britain, a large country, has 29 votes, whereas Denmark, a much smaller state, has 7 votes.

The **European Parliament,** which now has 732 members, is directly elected by the populations of the member states. The parliament, which meets in Strasbourg, France, is primarily a consultative rather than legislative body. It debates legislation proposed by the commission and forwarded to it by the council. It can propose amendments to that legislation, which the commission and ultimately the council are not obliged to take up but often will. The power of the parliament recently has been increasing, although not by as much as parliamentarians would like. The European Parliament now has the right to vote on the appointment of commissioners as well as veto some laws (such as the EU budget and single-market legislation). One major debate now being waged in Europe is whether the council or the parliament should ultimately be the most powerful body in the EU. Some in Europe express concern over the democratic accountability of the EU bureaucracy. One side thinks the answer to this apparent democratic deficit lies in increasing the power of the parliament, while others think that true democratic legitimacy lies with elected governments, acting through the Council of the European Union.[10]

European Parliament
Made up of 732 members directly elected by member states' populations, it serves as a consultative body to debate and propose amendments to the legislation forwarded from the council.

Court of Justice Comprised of one judge from each member state, this is the supreme appeals court for EU law.

The **Court of Justice,** which is comprised of one judge from each country, is the supreme appeals court for EU law. Like commissioners, the judges are required to act as independent officials rather than as representatives of national interests. The commission or a member country can bring other members to the court for failing to meet treaty obligations. Similarly, member countries, companies, or institutions can bring the commission or council to the court for failure to act according to an EU treaty.

THE SINGLE EUROPEAN ACT Two revolutions occurred in Europe in the late 1980s. The first was the collapse of communism in Eastern Europe. The second revolution was much quieter, but its impact on Europe and the world may have been just as profound as the first. It was the adoption of the **Single European Act** by the member nations of the European Community in 1987. This act committed member countries to work toward establishment of a single market by December 31, 1992.

Single European Act Adopted by members of the European Community in 1987, this act committed member countries to establish a single market by the end of 1992.

The Single European Act was born of a frustration among members that the community was not living up to its promise. By the early 1980s, it was clear that the EC had fallen short of its objectives to remove barriers to the free flow of trade and investment between member countries and to harmonize the wide range of technical and legal standards for doing business. Against this background, many of the EC's prominent businesspeople mounted an energetic campaign in the early 1980s to end the EC's economic divisions. The EC responded by creating the Delors Commission. Under the chairmanship of Jacques Delors, the commission proposed that all impediments to the formation of a single market be eliminated by December 31, 1992. The result was the Single European Act, which was independently ratified by the parliaments of each member country and became EC law in 1987.

The Objectives of the Act The purpose of the Single European Act was to have one market in place by December 31, 1992. The act proposed the following changes:[11]

- Remove all frontier controls between EC countries, thereby abolishing delays and reducing the resources required for complying with trade bureaucracy.
- Apply the principle of "mutual recognition" to product standards. A standard developed in one EC country should be accepted in another, provided it meets basic requirements in such matters as health and safety.
- Open public procurement to nonnational suppliers, reducing costs directly by allowing lower-cost suppliers into national economies and indirectly by forcing national suppliers to compete.
- Lift barriers to competition in the retail banking and insurance businesses, which should drive down the costs of financial services, including borrowing, throughout the EC.
- Remove all restrictions on foreign exchange transactions between member countries by the end of 1992.
- Abolish restrictions on cabotage—the right of foreign truckers to pick up and deliver goods within another member state's borders—by the end of 1992. Estimates suggested this would reduce the cost of haulage within the EC by 10 to 15 percent.

All those changes were predicted to lower the costs of doing business in the EC, but the single-market program was also expected to have more complicated supply-side effects. For example, the expanded market was predicted to give EC firms greater opportunities to exploit economies of scale. In addition, it was thought that the increase in competitive intensity brought about by removing internal barriers to trade and investment would force EC firms to become more efficient. To signify the

Country FOCUS

Creating a Single European Market in Financial Services

The European Union in 1999 embarked upon an ambitious action plan to create a single market in financial services by January 1, 2005. Launched a few months after the euro, the EU's single currency, the goal was to dismantle barriers to cross-border activity in financial services, creating a continent-wide market for banking services, insurance services, and investment products. In this vision of a single Europe, a citizen of France might use a German firm for basic banking services, borrow a home mortgage from an Italian institution, buy auto insurance from a Dutch enterprise, and keep her savings in mutual funds managed by a British company. Similarly, an Italian firm might raise capital from investors across Europe, using a German firm as its lead underwriter to issue stock for sale through stock exchanges in London and Frankfurt.

One main benefit of a single market, according to its advocates, would be greater competition for financial services, which would give consumers more choices, lower prices, and require financial service firms in the EU to become more efficient, thereby increasing their global competitiveness. Another major benefit would be the creation of a single European capital market. The increased liquidity of a larger capital market would make it easier for firms to borrow funds, lowering their cost of capital (the price of money) and stimulating business investment in Europe, which would create more jobs. A European Commission study suggested that the creation of a single market in financial services would increase the EU's gross domestic product by 1.1 percent a year, creating an additional 130 billion euros (€) in wealth over a decade. Total business investment would increase by 6 percent annually in the long run, private consumption by 0.8 percent, and total employment by 0.5 percent a year.

Creating a single market, however, has been anything but easy. The financial markets of different EU member states have historically been segmented from each other, and each has its own regulatory framework. In the past, EU financial services firms rarely did business across national borders because of a host of different national regulations with regard to taxation, oversight, accounting information, cross-border takeovers, and the like, all of which had to be harmonized. To complicate matters, long-standing cultural and linguistic barriers complicated the move toward a single market. While in theory an Italian might benefit by being able to purchase homeowners' insurance from a British company, in practice he might be predisposed to purchase it from a local enterprise, even if the price were higher.

By 2006, the EU had made significant progress. Some 41 measures designed to create a single market in financial services had become EU law. The new rules embraced issues as diverse as the conduct of business by investment firms, stock exchanges, and banks; disclosure standards for listing companies on public exchanges; and the harmonization of accounting standards across nations. However, there had also been some significant setbacks. Most notably, legislation designed to make it easier for firms to make hostile cross-border acquisitions was defeated, primarily due to opposition from German members of the European Parliament, making it more difficult for financial service firms to build pan-European operations. In addition, national governments have still reserved the right to block even friendly cross-border mergers between financial service firms. For example, Italian banking law still requires the governor of the Bank of Italy to give permission to any foreign enterprise that wishes to purchase more than 5 percent of an Italian bank—and no foreigners have yet to acquire a majority position in an Italian bank, primarily, say critics, due to nationalistic concerns on the part of the Italians.

The critical issue now is enforcement of the rules that have been put in place. Some believe that it will be at least another decade before the benefits of the new regulations become apparent. In the meantime, the changes may impose significant costs on financial institutions as they attempt to deal with the new raft of regulations.

Sources: C. Randzio-Plath, "Europe Prepares for a Single Financial Market," *Intereconomic,* May–June 2004, pp. 142–46; T. Buck, D. Hargreaves, and P. Norman, "Europe's Single Financial Market," *Financial Times,* January 18, 2005, p. 17; "The Gatekeeper," *The Economist,* February 19, 2005, p. 79; P. Hofheinz, "A Capital Idea: The European Union Has a Grand Plan to Make Its Financial Markets More Efficient," *The Wall Street Journal,* October 14, 2002, p. R4; and "Banking on McCreevy: Europe's Single Market," *The Economist,* November 26, 2005, p. 91.

importance of the Single European Act, the European Community also decided to change its name to the European Union once the act took effect.

Impact The Single European Act has had a significant impact on the EU economy.[12] The act provided the impetus for the restructuring of substantial sections of European industry. Many firms have shifted from national to pan-European production

The creation of a single financial services market in the EU has taken longer than expected due to member states differing regulations and the significant amount of inertia involved in getting people to accept this change. *Getty Images/DIL*

and distribution systems in an attempt to realize scale economies and better compete in a single market. The results have included faster economic growth than would otherwise have been the case.

However, 15 years after the formation of a single market, the reality still falls short of the ideal. For example, as described in the accompanying Country Focus, as of 2006 there was still not a fully functioning single market for financial services in the EU (although much of the groundwork is now in place for one to emerge). Thus, although the EU is undoubtedly moving toward a single marketplace, established legal, cultural, and language differences between nations have caused implementation to be uneven.

Maastricht Treaty
A 1991 treaty committing members of the EC to adopt a common currency by 1999.

THE ESTABLISHMENT OF THE EURO In December 1991, EC members signed the **Maastricht Treaty,** which committed them to adopting a common currency by January 1, 1999.[13] The euro is now used by 12 of the 25 member states of the European Union; these 12 states are members of what is often referred to as the euro zone. The 10 countries that joined the EU on May 1, 2004, will adopt the euro when they fulfill certain economic criteria: a high degree of price stability, a sound fiscal situation, stable exchange rates, and converged long-term interest rates. The current members had to meet the same criteria.

Establishment of the euro has rightly been described as an amazing political feat with few historical precedents. Establishing the euro required participating national governments not only to give up their own currencies, but also to give up control over monetary policy. Governments do not routinely sacrifice national sovereignty for the greater good, indicating the importance that the Europeans attach to the euro. By adopting the euro, the EU has created the second-largest currency zone in the world after that of the U.S. dollar. Some believe that ultimately the euro could come to rival the dollar as the most important currency in the world.

Three long-term EU members, Great Britain, Denmark, and Sweden, are still sitting on the sidelines. The 12 countries agreeing to the euro locked their exchange rates against each other January 1, 1999. Euro notes and coins were not actually issued until January 1, 2002. In the interim, national currencies circulated in each of the 12 countries. However, in each participating state, the national currency stood for a defined amount of euros. After January 1, 2002, euro notes and coins were issued and the national currencies were taken out of circulation. By mid-2002, all prices and routine economic transactions within the euro zone were in euros.

Benefits of the Euro Europeans decided to establish a single currency in the EU for a number of reasons. First, they believe that businesses and individuals will realize significant savings from having to handle one currency, rather than many. These savings come from lower foreign exchange and hedging costs. For example, people going from Germany to France will no longer have to pay a commission to a bank to change German deutsche marks into French francs. Instead, they will be able to use euros. According to the European Commission, such savings should amount to 0.5 percent of the European Union's GDP, or about $45 billion a year.

Second, and perhaps more important, the adoption of a common currency will make it easier to compare prices across Europe. This should increase competition because it will be much easier for consumers to shop around. For example, if a German finds that cars sell for less in France than Germany, he may be tempted to purchase from a French car dealer rather than his local car dealer. Alternatively, traders may engage in arbitrage to exploit such price differentials, buying cars in France and reselling them in Germany. The only way that German car dealers will be able to hold on to business in the face of such competitive pressures will be to reduce the prices they charge for cars. As a consequence of such pressures, the introduction of a common currency should lead to lower prices. This should translate into substantial gains for European consumers.

Third, faced with lower prices, European producers will be forced to look for ways to reduce their production costs to maintain their profit margins. The introduction of a common currency, by increasing competition, should ultimately produce long-run gains in the economic efficiency of European companies.

Fourth, the introduction of a common currency should give a strong boost to the development of a highly liquid pan-European capital market. The development of such a capital market should lower the cost of capital and lead to an increase in both the level of investment and the efficiency with which investment funds are allocated. This could be especially helpful to smaller companies that have historically had difficulty borrowing money from domestic banks. For example, the capital market of Portugal is very small and illiquid, which makes it extremely difficult for bright Portuguese entrepreneurs with a good idea to borrow money at a reasonable price. However, in theory, such companies should soon be able to tap a much more liquid pan-European capital market. Currently, Europe has no continentwide capital market, such as the NASDAQ market in the United States, that funnels investment capital to dynamic young growth companies. The euro's introduction could facilitate establishment of such a market, particularly when coupled with regulations designed to create a single market in financial services. The long-run benefits of such a development should not be underestimated.

Finally, the development of a pan-European, euro-denominated capital market will increase the range of investment options open to both individuals and institutions. For example, it will now be much easier for individuals and institutions based in, say, Holland to invest in Italian or French companies. This will enable European investors to better diversify their risk, which again lowers the cost of capital, and should also increase the efficiency with which capital resources are allocated.[14]

Costs of the Euro

The drawback, for some, of a single currency is that national authorities have lost control over monetary policy. Thus, it is crucial to ensure that the EU's monetary policy is well managed. The Maastricht Treaty called for establishment of the independent European Central Bank (ECB), similar in some respects to the U.S. Federal Reserve, with a clear mandate to manage monetary policy so as to ensure price stability. The ECB, based in Frankfurt, is meant to be independent from political pressure, although critics question this. Among other things, the ECB sets interest rates and determines monetary policy across the euro zone.

The implied loss of national sovereignty to the ECB underlies the decision by Great Britain, Denmark, and Sweden to stay out of the euro zone for now. Many in these countries are suspicious of the ECB's ability to remain free from political pressure and to keep inflation under tight control.

In theory, the design of the ECB should ensure that it remains free of political pressure. The ECB is modeled on the German Bundesbank, which historically has been the most independent and successful central bank in Europe. The Maastricht Treaty prohibits the ECB from taking orders from politicians. The executive board of the bank, which consists of a president, vice president, and four other members, carries out policy by issuing instructions to national central banks. The policy itself is determined by the governing council, which consists of the executive board plus the central bank governors from the 12 euro zone countries. The governing council votes on interest rate changes. Members of the executive board are appointed for eight-year nonrenewable terms, insulating them from political pressures to get reappointed.

Optimal Currency Area
An area of countries where similarities in the underlying economic activity structure make it feasible to adopt a single currency and use a single exchange rate.

Nevertheless, the jury is still out on the issue of the ECB's independence, and it will take some time for the bank to establish its credentials.

According to critics, another drawback of the euro is that the EU is not what economists would call an optimal currency area. In an **optimal currency area,** similarities in the underlying structure of economic activity make it feasible to adopt a single currency and use a single exchange rate as an instrument of macroeconomic policy. Many of the European economies in the euro zone, however, are very dissimilar. For example, Finland and Portugal have different wage rates, tax regimes, and business cycles, and they may react very differently to external economic shocks. A change in the euro exchange rate that helps Finland may hurt Portugal. Obviously, such differences complicate macroeconomic policy. For example, when euro economies are not growing in unison, a common monetary policy may mean that interest rates are too high for depressed regions and too low for booming regions. It will be interesting to see how the EU copes with the strains caused by such divergent economic performance.

One way of dealing with such divergent effects within the euro zone might be for the EU to engage in fiscal transfers, taking money from prosperous regions and pumping it into depressed regions. Such a move, however, would open a political can of worms. Would the citizens of Germany forgo their "fair share" of EU funds to create jobs for underemployed Portuguese workers?

Several critics believe that the euro puts the economic cart before the political horse. In their view, a single currency should follow, not precede, political union. They argue that the euro will unleash enormous pressures for tax harmonization and fiscal transfers from the center, both policies that cannot be pursued without the appropriate political structure. The most apocalyptic vision that flows from these negative views is that far from stimulating economic growth, as its advocates claim, the euro will lead to lower economic growth and higher inflation within Europe. As one critic put it,

> Imposing a single exchange rate and an inflexible exchange rate on countries that are characterized by different economic shocks, inflexible wages, low labor mobility, and separate national fiscal systems without significant cross-border fiscal transfers will raise the overall level of cyclical unemployment among EMU members. The shift from national monetary policies dominated by the (German) Bundesbank within the European Monetary System to a European Central Bank governed by majority voting with a politically determined exchange rate policy will almost certainly raise the average future rate of inflation.[15]

The Early Experience Since its establishment January 1, 1999, the euro has had a volatile trading history against the world's major currency, the U.S. dollar. After starting life in 1999 at €1 = \$1.17, the euro steadily fell until it reached a low of €1 = \$0.83 in October 2000, leading critics to claim the euro was a failure. A major reason for the fall in the euro's value was that international investors were investing money in booming U.S. stocks and bonds and taking money out of Europe to finance this investment. In other words, they were selling euros to buy dollars so that they could invest in dollar-denominated assets. This increased the demand for dollars and decreased the demand for the euro, driving the value of the euro down against the dollar.

The fortunes of the euro began improving in late 2001 when the dollar weakened, and the currency stood at a robust five-year high of €1 = \$1.33 in early March 2005. One reason for the rise in the value of the euro was that the flow of capital into the United States had stalled as the U.S. financial markets fell.[16] Many investors were now taking money out of the United States, selling dollar-denominated assets such as U.S. stocks and bonds, and purchasing euro-denominated assets. Falling demand for U.S. dollars and rising demand for euros translated into a fall in the value of the dollar against the euro. Furthermore, in a vote of confidence in both the euro and the ability of the ECB to manage monetary policy within the euro zone, many foreign central banks added more euros to their supply of foreign currencies during the 2002–04 period. In the first three years of its life, the euro never reached the 13 percent of global reserves made up by the deutsche mark and other former euro zone currencies. The euro didn't jump that hurdle until early 2002, but by 2003 it made up 15 percent of global reserves. Currency specialists expected the growing U.S. current account deficit, which reached 7 percent of GDP in 2005, to drive the dollar down further, and the euro still higher over the next two to four years.[17] So far this has not occurred (in March 2006 the exchange rate was €1 = $1.21). If the euro does appreciate against the dollar, it will be a mixed blessing for the EU. A strengthening euro, while a source of pride, will make it harder for euro zone exporters to sell their goods abroad.

Another Perspective

The EU and Free Movement of Labor

The 15 older EU members are worried about cheap labor flooding their markets. In France in the summer of 2006, there was a scare that Polish plumbers moving to Paris would destroy the French plumbing industry. Poland responded with a good humored "Come Visit Poland and Meet our Plumbers" campaign, but other new members have voiced a fear of being second-class citizens in the EU. Western Europeans may be concerned about the migration of low-cost labor, especially that of the Roma from the Czech Republic, Hungary, and Slovakia. (We may know these people by the disparaging name "gypsy.") Spain and Finland have decided to open their labor markets to the new EU members, along with Britain, Ireland, and Sweden. Economic integration isn't always easy, especially at an emotional level.

ENLARGEMENT OF THE EUROPEAN UNION A major issue facing the EU over the past few years has been that of enlargement. Enlargement of the EU into Eastern Europe has been a possibility since the collapse of communism at the end of the 1980s, and by the end of the 1990s, 13 countries had applied to become EU members. To qualify for EU membership, the applicants had to privatize state assets, deregulate markets, restructure industries, and tame inflation. They also had to incorporate complex EU laws into their own systems, establish stable democratic governments, and respect human rights.[18] In December 2002, the EU formally agreed to accept the applications of 10 countries, and they joined on May 1, 2004. The new members include the Baltic countries, the Czech Republic, and the larger nations of Hungary and Poland. The only new members not in Eastern Europe are the Mediterranean island nations of Malta and Cyprus. Their inclusion in the EU expanded the union to 25 states, stretching from the Atlantic to the borders of Russia; added 23 percent to the landmass of the EU; brought 75 million new citizens into the EU, building an EU with a population of 450 million people; and created a single continental economy with a GDP of close to €11 trillion.

The new members will not be able to adopt the euro until 2007, and free movement of labor between the new and existing members will not be allowed until then. Consistent with theories of free trade, the enlargement should create added benefits for all members. However, given the small size of the Eastern European economies (together they amount to only 5 percent of the GDP of current EU members), the initial impact will probably be small. The biggest notable change might be in the EU bureaucracy and decision-making processes, where budget negotiations among 25 nations are bound to prove more problematic than negotiations among 15 nations.

Left standing at the door were Turkey, Romania, and Bulgaria. Turkey, which has long lobbied to join the union, presents the EU with some difficult issues. The country has had a customs union with the EU since 1995, and about half of its international trade is already with the EU. However, full membership has been denied because of concerns over human rights issues (particularly Turkish policies toward its Kurdish minority). In addition, some on the Turk side suspect the EU is not eager to let a primarily Muslim nation of 66 million people, which has one foot in Asia, join the EU. The EU formally indicated in December 2002 that it would allow the Turkish application to proceed with no further delay in December 2004 if the country improved its human rights record to the satisfaction of the EU. In December, the EU agreed to allow Turkey to start accession talks in October 2005. It now looks as if Romania and Bulgaria could join the EU by 2007, and Turkey by 2009, bringing the total number of nations to 28.

Regional Economic Integration in the Americas

LEARNING OBJECTIVE 4
Be familiar with the history, current scope, and future prospects of the world's most important regional economic agreements.

No other attempt at regional economic integration comes close to the EU in its boldness or its potential implications for the world economy, but regional economic integration is on the rise in the Americas. The most significant attempt is the North American Free Trade Agreement. In addition to NAFTA, several other trade blocs are in the offing in the Americas (see Map 8.2), the most significant of which appear to be the Andean Community and MERCOSUR. Also, negotiations are under way to

map 

Economic Integration in the Americas

Source: *The Economist,* April 21, 2001, p. 20. Copyright © 2001 The Economist Newspaper Ltd. All rights reserved. Reprinted with permission. Further reproduction prohibited. www.economist.com.

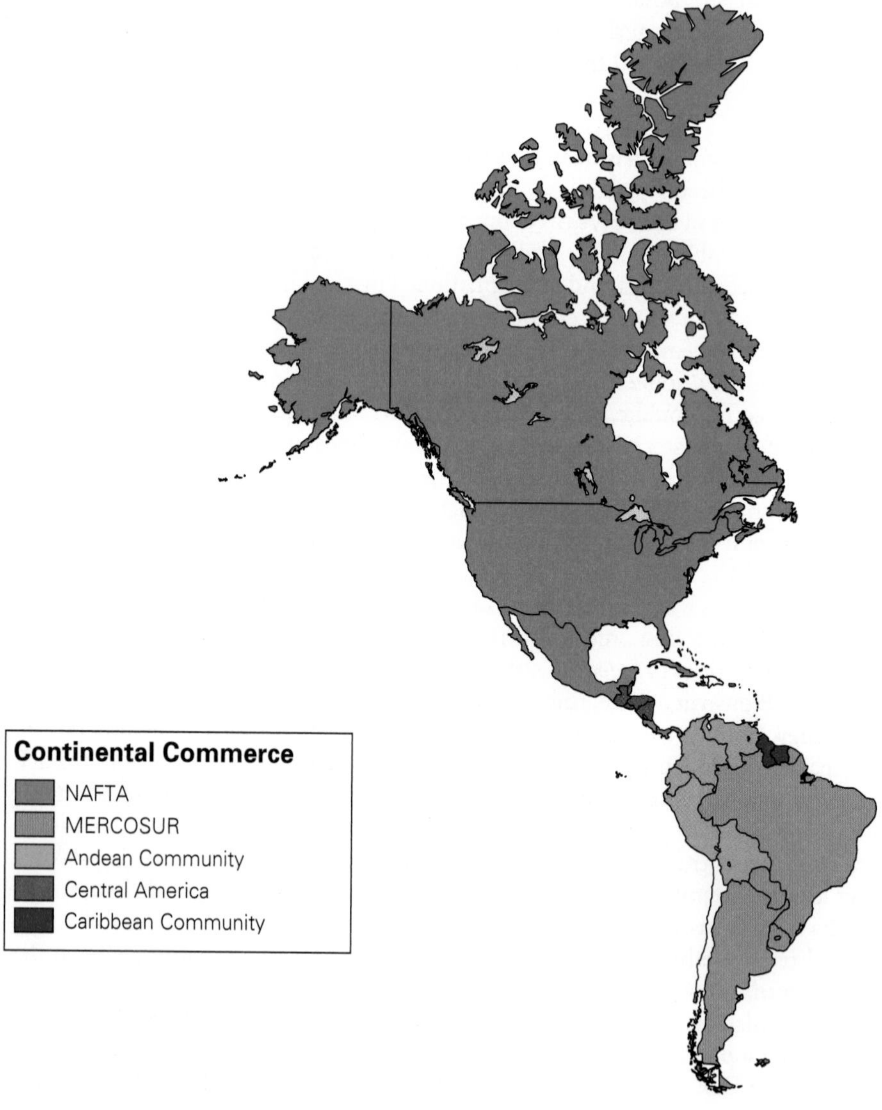

Continental Commerce
NAFTA
MERCOSUR
Andean Community
Central America
Caribbean Community

establish a hemisphere wide Free Trade Area of the Americas (FTAA), although currently they seem to be stalled.

THE NORTH AMERICAN FREE TRADE AGREEMENT

The governments of the United States and Canada in 1988 agreed to enter into a free trade agreement, which took effect January 1, 1989. The goal of the agreement was to eliminate all tariffs on bilateral trade between Canada and the United States by 1998. This was followed in 1991 by talks among the United States, Canada, and Mexico aimed at establishing a **North American Free Trade Agreement (NAFTA)** for the three countries. The talks concluded in August 1992 with an agreement in principle, and the following year the agreement was ratified by the governments of all three countries. The agreement became law January 1, 1994.[19]

North American Free Trade Agreement (NAFTA) The free trade agreement between Canada, Mexico, and the United States, officially implemented in 1994.

NAFTA's Contents

The contents of NAFTA include the following:

- Abolition by 2004 of tariffs on 99 percent of the goods traded between Mexico, Canada, and the United States.
- Removal of most barriers on the cross-border flow of services, allowing financial institutions, for example, unrestricted access to the Mexican market by 2000.
- Protection of intellectual property rights.
- Removal of most restrictions on foreign direct investment between the three member countries, although special treatment (protection) will be given to Mexican energy and railway industries, American airline and radio communications industries, and Canadian culture.
- Application of national environmental standards, provided such standards have a scientific basis; lowering of standards to lure investment is described as being inappropriate.
- Establishment of two commissions with the power to impose fines and remove trade privileges when environmental standards or legislation involving health and safety, minimum wages, or child labor are ignored.

The Case for NAFTA

Proponents of NAFTA have argued that the free trade area should be viewed as an opportunity to create an enlarged and more efficient productive base for the entire region. Advocates acknowledge that one effect of NAFTA would be that some U.S. and Canadian firms would move production to Mexico to take advantage of lower labor costs. (In 2004, the average hourly labor cost in Mexico was still one-tenth of that in the United States and Canada.) Movement of production to Mexico, they argued, was most likely to occur in low-skilled, labor-intensive manufacturing industries where Mexico might have a comparative advantage (e.g., textiles; see the Opening Case). Advocates of NAFTA argued that many would benefit from such a trend. Mexico would benefit from much-needed inward investment and employment. The United States and Canada would benefit because the increased incomes of the Mexicans would allow them to import more U.S. and Canadian goods, thereby increasing demand and making up for the jobs lost in industries that moved production to Mexico. U.S. and Canadian consumers would benefit from the lower prices of products made in Mexico. In addition, the international competitiveness of U.S. and Canadian firms that move production to Mexico to take advantage of lower labor costs would be enhanced, enabling them to better compete with Asian and European rivals.

The Case against NAFTA

Those who opposed NAFTA claimed that ratification would be followed by a mass exodus of jobs from the United States and Canada into Mexico as employers sought to profit from Mexico's lower wages and less strict environmental and labor laws. According to one extreme opponent, Ross Perot, up to

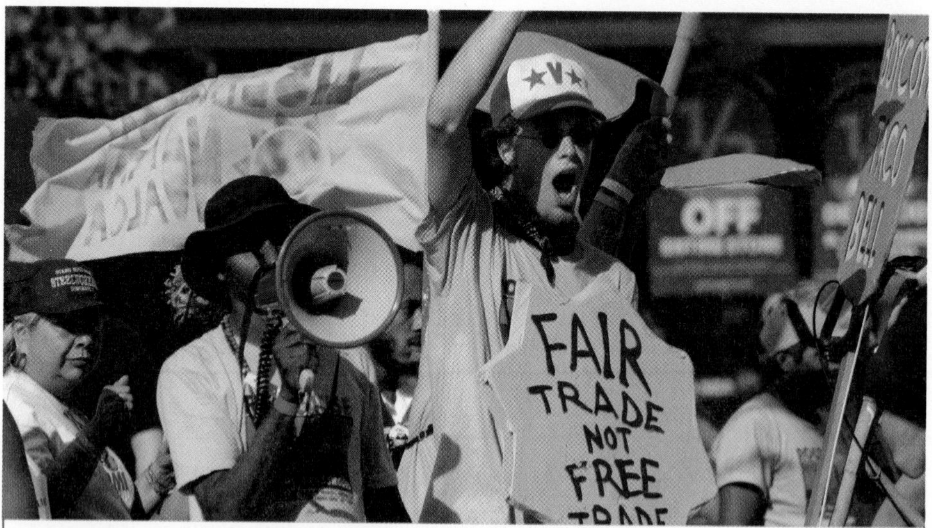

Many workers in the United States initially felt that NAFTA would take away their jobs as employers looked for cheaper labor in Mexico. However, a 1996 study by researchers at the University of California–Los Angeles concluded the impact on jobs was a net gain of 3,000 for the United States in the first two years of the NAFTA regime. *Spencer Platt/Getty Images*

5.9 million U.S. jobs would be lost to Mexico after NAFTA in what he famously characterized as a "giant sucking sound." Most economists, however, dismissed these numbers as being absurd and alarmist. They argued that Mexico would have to run a bilateral trade surplus with the United States of close to $300 billion for job loss on such a scale to occur—and $300 billion was the size of Mexico's GDP. In other words, such a scenario seemed implausible.

More sober estimates of the impact of NAFTA ranged from a net creation of 170,000 jobs in the United States (due to increased Mexican demand for U.S. goods and services) and an increase of $15 billion per year to the joint U.S. and Mexican GDP, to a net loss of 490,000 U.S. jobs. To put these numbers in perspective, employment in the U.S. economy was predicted to grow by 18 million from 1993 to 2003. As most economists repeatedly stressed, NAFTA would have a small impact on both Canada and the United States. It could hardly be any other way, since the Mexican economy was only 5 percent of the size of the U.S. economy. Signing NAFTA required the largest leap of economic faith from Mexico rather than Canada or the United States. Falling trade barriers would expose Mexican firms to highly efficient U.S. and Canadian competitors that, when compared to the average Mexican firm, had far greater capital resources, access to highly educated and skilled workforces, and much greater technological sophistication. The short-run outcome was likely to be painful economic restructuring and unemployment in Mexico. But advocates of NAFTA claimed there would be long-run dynamic gains in the efficiency of Mexican firms as they adjusted to the rigors of a more competitive marketplace. To the extent that this occurred, they argued, Mexico's economic growth rate would accelerate, and Mexico might become a major market for Canadian and U.S. firms.[20]

Environmentalists also voiced concerns about NAFTA. They pointed to the sludge in the Rio Grande River and the smog in the air over Mexico City and warned that Mexico could degrade clean air and toxic waste standards across the continent. They pointed out that the lower Rio Grande was the most polluted river in the United States, and that with NAFTA, chemical waste and sewage would increase along its course from El Paso, Texas, to the Gulf of Mexico.

There was also opposition in Mexico to NAFTA from those who feared a loss of national sovereignty. Mexican critics argued that their country would be dominated by U.S. firms that would not really contribute to Mexico's economic growth, but instead would use Mexico as a low-cost assembly site, while keeping their high-paying, high-skilled jobs north of the border.

NAFTA: The Results so Far Studies of NAFTA's impact to date suggest its initial effects were at best muted, and both advocates and detractors may have been guilty of exaggeration.[21] The most comprehensive early study was undertaken by researchers at the University of California–Los Angeles and funded by various departments of the U.S. government.[22] This study focused on the effects of NAFTA in its first three and a half years. The authors concluded that the growth in trade between Mexico and the United States began to change nearly a decade before the implementation of NAFTA when Mexico unilaterally started to liberalize its own trade regime to conform to GATT standards. The initial period since NAFTA took effect had little impact on trends already in place. The study found that trade growth in those sectors that underwent tariff liberalization in the first two and a half years of NAFTA was only marginally higher than trade growth in sectors not yet liberalized. For example, between 1993 and 1996, U.S. exports to Mexico in sectors liberalized under NAFTA grew by 5.83 percent annually, while exports in sectors not liberalized under NAFTA grew by 5.35 percent. In short, the authors argued that NAFTA had only a marginal impact on the level of trade between the United States and Mexico.

As for NAFTA's much-debated impact on jobs in the United States, the study concluded the impact was positive but very small. The study found that while NAFTA created 31,158 new jobs in the United States, 28,168 jobs were lost due to imports from Mexico, for a net job gain of about 3,000 in the first two years of the NAFTA regime. However, as the report's authors point out, trade flows and employment in 1995 and 1996 were significantly affected by an economic crisis that gripped Mexico in early 1995. Given this, it may have been too early to draw conclusions about the true impact of NAFTA on trade flows and employment.

More recent surveys indicate that NAFTA's overall impact has been small but positive.[23] From 1993 to 2005, trade between NAFTA's partners grew by 250 percent.[24] Canada and Mexico are now the number one and two trade partners of the United States, suggesting the economies of the three NAFTA nations have become more closely integrated. In 1990, U.S. trade with Canada and Mexico accounted for about a quarter of total U.S. trade. By 2005, the figure was close to one-third. Canada's trade with its NAFTA partners increased from about 70 percent to more than 80 percent of all Canadian foreign trade between 1993 and 2005, while Mexico's trade with NAFTA increased from 66 percent to 80 percent over the same period. All three countries also experienced strong productivity growth over this period. In Mexico, labor productivity has increased by 50 percent since 1993, and the passage of NAFTA may have contributed to this. However, estimates suggest that employment effects of NAFTA have been small. The most pessimistic estimates suggest the United States lost 110,000 jobs per year due to NAFTA between 1994 and 2000—and many economists dispute this figure—which is tiny compared to the more than 2 million jobs a year created in the United States during the same period. Perhaps the most significant impact of NAFTA has not been economic but political. Many observers credit NAFTA with helping to create the background for increased political stability in

Mexico. Mexico is now viewed as a stable democratic nation with a steadily growing economy, something that is beneficial to the United States, which shares a 2,000-mile border with the country.[25]

Enlargement One issue confronting NAFTA is that of enlargement. A number of other Latin American countries have indicated their desire to eventually join NAFTA. The governments of both Canada and the United States are adopting a wait-and-see attitude with regard to most countries. Getting NAFTA approved was a bruising political experience, and neither government is eager to repeat the process soon. Nevertheless, the Canadian, Mexican, and U.S. governments began talks in 1995 regarding Chile's possible entry into NAFTA. As of 2006, however, these talks had yielded little progress, partly because of political opposition in the U.S. Congress to expanding NAFTA. In December 2002, however, the United States and Chile did sign a bilateral free trade pact.

Andean Pact
Based on the EU model and begun in 1969, this agreement unites Bolivia, Chile, Ecuador, Colombia, and Peru in free trade, but it has been unsuccessful at achieving its stated goals; renamed the Andean Community in 1997.

THE ANDEAN COMMUNITY Bolivia, Chile, Ecuador, Colombia, and Peru signed an agreement in 1969 to create the Andean Pact. The **Andean Pact** was largely based on the EU model, but it was far less successful at achieving its stated goals. The integration steps begun in 1969 included an internal tariff reduction program, a common external tariff, a transportation policy, a common industrial policy, and special concessions for the smallest members, Bolivia and Ecuador.

By the mid-1980s, the Andean Pact had all but collapsed and had failed to achieve any of its stated objectives. There was no tariff-free trade between member countries, no common external tariff, and no harmonization of economic policies. Political and economic problems seem to have hindered cooperation between member countries. The countries of the Andean Pact have had to deal with low economic growth, hyperinflation, high unemployment, political unrest, and crushing debt burdens. In addition, the dominant political ideology in many of the Andean countries during this period tended toward the radical/socialist end of the political spectrum. Since such an ideology is hostile to the free market economic principles on which the Andean Pact was based, progress toward closer integration could not be expected.

The tide began to turn in the late 1980s when, after years of economic decline, the governments of Latin America began to adopt free market economic policies. In 1990, the heads of the five current members of the Andean Community—Bolivia, Ecuador, Peru, Colombia, and Venezuela—met in the Galápagos Islands. The resulting Galápagos Declaration effectively relaunched the Andean Pact, which was renamed the Andean Community in 1997. The declaration's objectives included the establishment of a free trade area by 1992, a customs union by 1994, and a common market by 1995. This last milestone has not been reached. A customs union was implemented in 1995, although until 2003 Peru opted out and Bolivia received preferential treatment. The Andean Community now operates as a customs union. In December 2003, it signed an agreement with MERCOSUR to restart stalled negotiations on the creation of a free trade area between the two trading blocs. Those negotiations are currently proceeding at a slow pace.

MERCOSUR
The free trade pact between Brazil, Argentina, Paraguay, Uruguay, and Venezuela, originating in 1988.

MERCOSUR **MERCOSUR** originated in 1988 as a free trade pact between Brazil and Argentina. The modest reductions in tariffs and quotas accompanying this pact reportedly helped bring about an 80 percent increase in trade between the two countries in the late 1980s.[26] This success encouraged the expansion of the pact in

March 1990 to include Paraguay and Uruguay. In 2005, the pact was further expanded when Venezuela, which is also a member of the Andean Community, joined MERCOSUR, although it may take years for Venezuela to become fully integrated into the pact.

The initial aim of MERCOSUR was to establish a full free trade area by the end of 1994 and a common market sometime thereafter. In December 1995, MERCOSUR's members agreed to a five-year program under which they hoped to perfect their free trade area and move toward a full customs union—something that has yet to be achieved.[27] For its first eight years or so, MERCOSUR seemed to be making a positive contribution to the economic growth rates of its member states. Trade between MERCOSUR's four core members quadrupled between 1990 and 1998. The combined GDP of the four member states grew at an annual average rate of 3.5 percent between 1990 and 1996, a performance that is significantly better than the four attained during the 1980s.[28]

However, MERCOSUR had its critics, including Alexander Yeats, a senior economist at the World Bank, who wrote a stinging critique of the pact.[29] According to Yeats, the trade diversion effects of MERCOSUR outweigh its trade creation effects. Yeats pointed out that the fastest-growing items in intra-MERCOSUR trade were cars, buses, agricultural equipment, and other capital-intensive goods that are produced relatively inefficiently in the four member countries. In other words, MERCOSUR countries, insulated from outside competition by tariffs that run as high as 70 percent of value on motor vehicles, are investing in factories that build products that are too expensive to sell to anyone but themselves. The result, according to Yeats, is that MERCOSUR countries might not be able to compete globally once the group's external trade barriers come down. In the meantime, capital is being drawn away from more efficient enterprises. In the near term, countries with more efficient manufacturing enterprises lose because MERCOSUR's external trade barriers keep them out of the market.

MERCOSUR hit a significant roadblock in 1998, when its member states slipped into recession and intrabloc trade slumped. Trade fell further in 1999 following a financial crisis in Brazil that led to the devaluation of the Brazilian real, which immediately made the goods of other MERCOSUR members 40 percent more expensive in Brazil, their largest export market. At this point, progress toward establishing a full customs union all but stopped. Things deteriorated further in 2001 when Argentina, beset by economic stresses, suggested the customs union be temporarily suspended. Argentina wanted to suspend MERCOSUR's tariff so that it could abolish duties on imports of capital equipment, while raising those on consumer goods to 35 percent (MERCOSUR had established a 14 percent import tariff on both sets of goods). Brazil agreed to this request, effectively halting MERCOSUR's quest to become a fully functioning customs union.[30] Hope for a revival arose in 2003 when new Brazilian president Lula da Silva announced his support for a revitalized and expanded MERCOSUR modeled after the EU with a larger membership, a common currency, and a democratically elected MERCOSUR parliament.[31] As of 2006, however, little progress had been made in moving MERCOSUR down that road, and critics felt that the customs union was if anything becoming more imperfect over time.[32]

Central American Common Market
A trade pact between Costa Rica, El Salvador, Guatemala, Honduras, and Nicaragua, which began in the early 1960s but collapsed in 1969 due to war.

CENTRAL AMERICAN COMMON MARKET, CAFTA, AND CARICOM Two other trade pacts in the Americas have not made much progress. In the early 1960s, Costa Rica, El Salvador, Guatemala, Honduras, and Nicaragua attempted to set up a **Central American Common Market.** It collapsed in 1969 when war broke out between Honduras and El Salvador after a riot at a soccer

Central America Free Trade Agreement (CAFTA)
The agreement of the member states of the Central American Common Market joined by the Dominican Republic to trade freely with the United States.

CARICOM
Established in 1973 to promote a customs union between the English-speaking Caribbean countries by 1991, but it failed.

Caribbean Single Market and Economy (CSME)
Unites six CARICOM members in agreeing to lower trade barriers and harmonize macroeconomic and monetary policies.

match between teams from the two countries. Since then the six member countries have made some progress toward reviving their agreement (the five founding members were joined by the Dominican Republic). The proposed common market was given a boost in 2003 when the United States signaled its intention to enter into bilateral free trade negotiations with the group. These negotiations cumulated in a 2005 agreement to establish a free trade agreement between the six countries and the United States. Known as the **Central America Free Trade Agreement,** or CAFTA, the aim is to lower trade barriers between the U.S. and the six countries for most goods and services.

A customs union was to have been created in 1991 between the English-speaking Caribbean countries under the auspices of the Caribbean Community. Referred to as **CARICOM,** it was established in 1973. However, it repeatedly failed to progress toward economic integration. A formal commitment to economic and monetary union was adopted by CARICOM's member states in 1984, but since then little progress has been made. In October 1991, the CARICOM governments failed, for the third consecutive time, to meet a deadline for establishing a common external tariff. Despite this, CARICOM expanded to 15 members by 2005. In early 2006, six CARICOM members established the **Caribbean Single Market and Economy (CSME)**. Modeled on the EU's single market, the goal of CSME is to lower trade barriers and harmonize macroeconomic and monetary policy between member states.[33]

FREE TRADE AREA OF THE AMERICAS

At a hemisphere-wide Summit of the Americas in December 1994, a Free Trade Area of the Americas was proposed. It took more than three years for the talks to start, but in April 1998, 34 heads of state traveled to Santiago, Chile, for the second Summit of the Americas where they formally inaugurated talks to establish an FTAA by January 1, 2005—something that didn't occur. The continuing talks have addressed a wide range of economic, political, and environmental issues related to cross-border trade and investment. Although both the United States and Brazil were early advocates of the FTAA, support from both countries seems to be mixed at this point. Because the United States and Brazil have the largest economies in North and South America, respectively, strong U.S. and Brazilian support is a precondition for establishment of the free trade area.

The major stumbling blocks so far have been twofold. First, the United States wants its southern neighbors to agree to tougher enforcement of intellectual property rights and lower manufacturing tariffs, which they do not seem to be eager to embrace. Second, Brazil and Argentina want the United States to reduce its subsidies to U.S. agricultural producers and scrap tariffs on agricultural imports, which the U.S. government does not seem inclined to do. For progress to be made, most observers agree that the United States and Brazil have to first reach an agreement on these crucial issues.[34] If the FTAA is eventually established, it will have major implications for cross-border trade and investment flows within the hemisphere. The FTAA would provide a free trade umbrella over 850 million people who accounted for some $14 trillion in GDP in 2005.

Currently, however, the FTAA is very much a work in progress, and the progress has been slow. The most recent attempt to get talks going again, in November 2005 at the summit of 34 heads of state from North and South America, failed when opponents, led by Venezuela's populist president, Hugo Chavez, blocked efforts by the Bush administration to set an agenda for further talks on FTAA. In voicing his opposition, Chavez condemned the U.S. free trade model as a "perversion" that would unduly benefit the United States to the detriment of poor people in Latin America whom Chavez claims have not benefited from free trade details.[35] Such views make it unlikely that there will be much progress on establishing a FTAA in the near term.

Regional Economic Integration Elsewhere

Numerous attempts at regional economic integration have been tried throughout Asia and Africa. However, few exist in anything other than name. Perhaps the most significant is the Association of Southeast Asian Nations. In addition, the Asia-Pacific Economic Cooperation forum has recently emerged as the seed of a potential free trade region.

LEARNING OBJECTIVE 4
Be familiar with the history, current scope, and future prospects of the world's most important regional economic agreements.

ASSOCIATION OF SOUTHEAST ASIAN NATIONS Formed in 1967, the **Association of Southeast Asian Nations (ASEAN)** includes Brunei, Cambodia, Indonesia, Laos, Malaysia, Myanmar, Philippines, Singapore, Thailand, and Vietnam. Laos, Myanmar, Vietnam, and Cambodia have all joined recently, creating a regional grouping of 500 million people with a combined GDP of some $740 billion (see Map 8.3). The basic objective of ASEAN is to foster freer trade between member countries and to achieve cooperation in their industrial policies. Progress so far has been limited, however.

Association of Southeast Asian Nations (ASEAN)
An attempt at regional economic integration between Brunei, Cambodia, Indonesia, Laos, Malaysia, Myanmar, the Philippines, Singapore, Thailand, and Vietnam.

Until recently, only 5 percent of intra-ASEAN trade consisted of goods whose tariffs had been reduced through an ASEAN preferential trade arrangement. This may be changing. In 2003, an ASEAN Free Trade Area (AFTA) between the six original members of ASEAN came into full effect. The AFTA has cut tariffs on manufacturing and agricultural products to less than 5 percent. However, there are some significant exceptions to this tariff reduction. Malaysia, for example, refused to bring down tariffs on imported cars until 2005, and then agreed to lower the tariff to 20 percent, not the 5 percent called for under the AFTA. Malaysia wants to protect Proton, and other inefficient local carmakers, from foreign competition. Similarly, the Philippines has refused to lower tariff rates on petrochemicals, and rice, the largest agricultural product in the region, will remain subject to higher tariff rates until at least 2020.[36]

Notwithstanding such issues, ASEAN and AFTA are at least progressing toward establishing a free trade zone. Vietnam will join the AFTA in 2006, Laos and Myanmar in 2008, and Cambodia in 2010. The goal is to reduce import tariffs among the six original members to zero by 2010, and to do so by 2015 for the newer members (although important exceptions to that goal, such as tariffs on rice, will no doubt persist). ASEAN is also pushing for free trade agreements with China, Japan, and South Korea.

ASIA-PACIFIC ECONOMIC COOPERATION The **Asia-Pacific Economic Cooperation (APEC)** was founded in 1990 at the suggestion of Australia. APEC currently has 21 member states, including such economic powerhouses as the United States, Japan, and China. Collectively, the member states account for about 57 percent of the world's GNP, 46 percent of world trade, and much of the growth in the world economy. The stated aim of APEC is to increase multilateral cooperation in view of the economic rise of the Pacific nations and the growing interdependence within the region. U.S. support for APEC was also based on the belief that it might prove a

Asia-Pacific Economic Cooperation (APEC)
Made up of 21 member states whose goal is to increase multilateral cooperation in view of the economic rise of the Pacific nations.

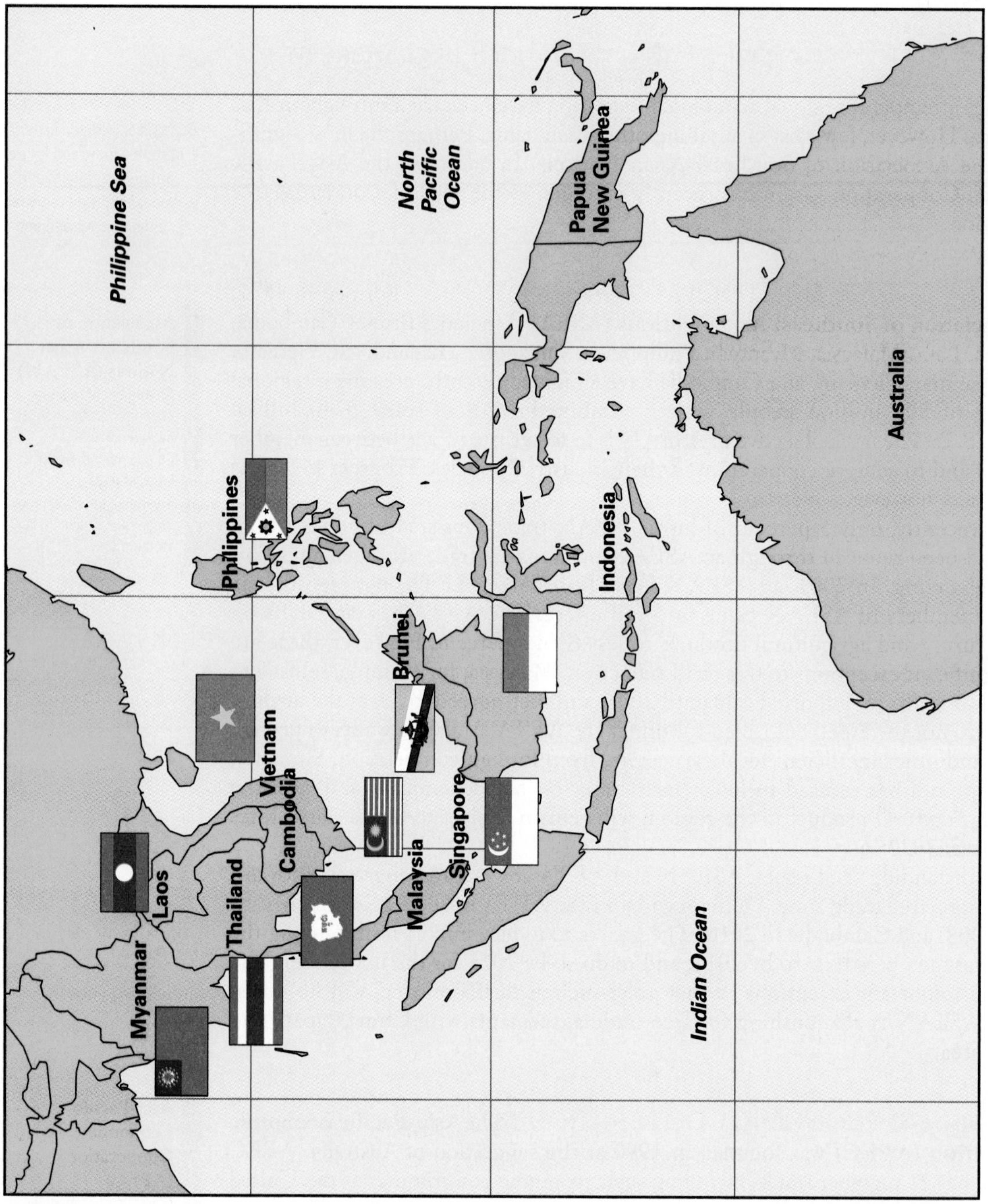

Philippine Sea
North Pacific Ocean
Papua New Guinea
Australia
Indonesia
Philippines
Brunei
Vietnam
Cambodia
Laos
Thailand
Malaysia
Singapore
Myanmar
Indian Ocean

map 8.3 ASEAN Countries

Source: www.aseansec.org/69.htm.

viable strategy for heading off any moves to create Asian groupings from which it would be excluded.

Interest in APEC was heightened considerably in November 1993 when the heads of APEC member states met for the first time at a two-day conference in Seattle. Debate before the meeting speculated on the likely future role of APEC. One view was that APEC should commit itself to the ultimate formation of a free trade area. Such a move would transform the Pacific Rim from a geographical expression into the world's largest free trade area. Another view was that APEC would produce no more than hot air and lots of photo opportunities for the leaders involved. As it turned out, the APEC meeting produced little more than some vague commitments from member states to work together for greater economic integration and a general lowering of trade barriers. However, significantly, member states did not rule out the possibility of closer economic cooperation in the future.[37]

The heads of state have met again on a number of occasions, most recently in late 2005. At a 1997 meeting, member states formally endorsed proposals designed to remove trade barriers in 15 sectors, ranging from fish to toys. However, the vague plan committed APEC to doing no more than holding further talks, which is all that they have done to date. Commenting on the vagueness of APEC pronouncements, the influential Brookings Institution, a U.S.-based economic policy institution, noted that APEC "is in grave danger of shrinking into irrelevance as a serious forum." Despite the slow progress, APEC is worth watching. If it eventually does transform itself into a free trade area, it will probably be the world's largest.[38]

REGIONAL TRADE BLOCS IN AFRICA African countries have been experimenting with regional trade blocs for half a century. There are now nine trade blocs on the African continent. Many countries are members of more than one group. Although the number of trade groups is impressive, progress toward the establishment of meaningful trade blocs has been slow.

Many of these groups have been dormant for years. Significant political turmoil in several African nations has persistently impeded any meaningful progress. Also, deep suspicion of free trade exists in several African countries. The argument most frequently heard is that because these countries have less developed and less diversified economies, they need to be protected by tariff barriers from unfair foreign competition. Given the prevalence of this argument, it has been hard to establish free trade areas or customs unions. The most recent attempt to reenergize the free trade movement in Africa occurred in early 2001, when Kenya, Uganda, and Tanzania, member states of the East African Community (EAC), committed themselves to relaunching their bloc, 24 years after it collapsed. The three countries, with 80 million inhabitants, intend to establish a customs union, regional court, legislative assembly, and, eventually, a political federation.

Their program includes cooperation on immigration, road and telecommunication networks, investment, and capital markets. However, while local business leaders welcomed the relaunch as a positive step, they were critical of the EAC's failure in practice to make progress on free trade. At the EAC treaty's signing in November 1999, members gave themselves four years to negotiate a customs union, with a draft slated for the end of 2001. But that fell far short of earlier plans for an immediate free trade zone, shelved after Tanzania and Uganda, fearful of Kenyan competition, expressed concerns that the zone could create imbalances similar to those that contributed to the breakup of the first community.[39] It remains to be seen if these countries can succeed this time, but if history is any guide, it will be an uphill road.

Focus on Managerial Implications

LEARNING OBJECTIVE 5
Understand the implications for business that are inherent in regional economic integration agreements.

Currently, the most significant developments in regional economic integration are occurring in the EU and NAFTA. Although some of the Latin American trade blocs, ASEAN, and the proposed FTAA may have economic significance in the future, the EU and NAFTA currently have more profound and immediate implications for business practice. Accordingly, in this section we will concentrate on the business implications of those two groups. Similar conclusions, however, could be drawn with regard to the creation of a single market anywhere in the world.

Opportunities

The creation of a single market through regional economic integration offers significant opportunities because markets that were formerly protected from foreign competition are opened. For example, in Europe before 1992 the large French and Italian markets were among the most protected. These markets are now much more open to foreign competition in the form of both exports and direct investment. Nonetheless, to fully exploit such opportunities, it may pay non-EU firms to set up EU subsidiaries.

Many major U.S. firms have long had subsidiaries in Europe. Those that do not would be advised to consider establishing them now, lest they run the risk of being shut out of the EU by nontariff barriers. Non-EU firms have rapidly increased their direct investment in the EU in anticipation of the creation of a single market. Between 1985 and 1989, for example, approximately 37 percent of the FDI inflows into industrialized countries was directed at the EC. By 1991, this figure had risen to 66 percent, and FDI inflows into the EU have been substantial ever since (see Chapter 7).[40]

Additional opportunities arise from the inherent lower costs of doing business in a single market—as opposed to 25 national markets in the case of the EU or 3 national markets in the case of NAFTA. Free movement of goods across borders, harmonized product standards, and simplified tax regimes make it possible for firms based in the EU and the NAFTA countries to realize potentially significant cost economies by centralizing production in those EU and NAFTA locations where the mix of factor costs and skills is optimal. Rather than producing a product in each of the 25 EU countries or the three NAFTA countries, a firm may be able to serve the whole EU or North American market from a single location. This location must be chosen carefully, of course, with an eye on local factor costs and skills.

For example, in response to the changes created by EU after 1992, the St. Paul–based 3M Company consolidated its European manufacturing and distribution facilities to take advantage of economies of scale. Thus, a plant in Great Britain now produces 3M's printing products and a German factory its reflective traffic control materials for all of the EU. In each case, 3M chose a location for centralized production after carefully considering the likely production costs in alternative locations within the EU. The ultimate goal of 3M is to dispense with all national distinctions, directing R&D, manufacturing, distribution, and marketing for each product group from an EU headquarters.[41] Similarly, Unilever, one of Europe's largest companies, began rationalizing its production in advance of 1992 to attain scale economies. Unilever concentrated its production of dishwashing powder for the EU in one plant, bath soap in another, and so on.[42]

Even after the removal of barriers to trade and investment, enduring differences in culture and competitive practices often limit the ability of companies to realize cost economies by centralizing production in key locations and producing a standardized product for a single multicountry market. Consider the case of Atag Holdings NV, a Dutch maker of kitchen appliances.[43] Atag thought it was well placed to benefit from the single market, but found it tough going. Atag's plant is just one mile from the German border and near the center of the EU's population. The company thought it could cater to both the "potato" and "spaghetti" belts—marketers' terms for consumers in northern and southern Europe—by producing two main product lines and selling these standardized "euro-products" to "euro-consumers." The main benefit of doing so is the economy of scale derived from mass production of a standardized range of products. Atag quickly discovered that the "euro-consumer" was a myth. Consumer preferences vary much more across nations than Atag had thought. Consider ceramic cooktops; Atag planned to market just 2 varieties throughout the EU but has found it needs 11. Belgians, who cook in huge pots, require extra-large burners. Germans like oval pots and burners to fit. The French need small burners and very low temperatures for simmering sauces and broths. Germans like oven knobs on the top; the French want them on the front. Most Germans and French prefer black and white ranges; the British demand a range of colors including peach, pigeon blue, and mint green.

Threats

Just as the emergence of single markets creates opportunities for business, it also presents a number of threats. For one thing, the business environment within each grouping will become more competitive. The lowering of barriers to trade and investment between countries is likely to lead to increased price competition throughout the EU and NAFTA. For example, before 1992 a Volkswagen Golf cost 55 percent more in Great Britain than in Denmark and 29 percent more in Ireland than in Greece.[44] Over time, such price differentials will vanish in a single market. This is a direct threat to any firm doing business in EU or NAFTA countries. To survive in the tougher single-market environment, firms must take advantage of the opportunities offered by the creation of a single market to rationalize their production and reduce their costs. Otherwise, they will be at a severe disadvantage.

A further threat to firms outside these trading blocs arises from the likely long-term improvement in the competitive position of many firms within the areas. This is particularly relevant in the EU, where many firms have historically been limited by a high cost structure in their ability to compete globally with North American and Asian firms. The creation of a single market and the resulting increased competition in the EU is beginning to produce serious attempts by many EU firms to reduce their cost structure by rationalizing production. This is transforming many EU companies into efficient global competitors. The message for non-EU businesses is that they need to prepare for the emergence of more capable European competitors by reducing their own cost structures.

Another threat to firms outside of trading areas is the threat of being shut out of the single market by the creation of a "trade fortress." The charge that regional economic integration might lead to a fortress mentality is most often leveled at the EU. Although the free trade philosophy underpinning the EU theoretically argues against the creation of any fortress in Europe, occasional signs indicate the EU may raise barriers to imports and investment in certain "politically sensitive" areas, such as autos. Non-EU firms might be well advised, therefore, to set up their own EU operations. This could also occur in the NAFTA countries, but it seems less likely.

Finally, the emerging role of the European Commission in competition policy suggests the EU is increasingly willing and able to intervene and impose conditions on companies proposing mergers and acquisitions. This is a threat insofar as it limits the ability of firms to pursue the corporate strategy of their choice. As we saw in the Management Focus on the media industry mergers, the commission may require significant concessions from businesses as a precondition for allowing proposed mergers and acquisitions to proceed. While this constrains the strategic options for firms, it should be remembered that in taking such action, the commission is trying to maintain the level of competition in Europe's single market, which should benefit consumers.

Key Terms

regional economic integration, p. 262
free trade area, p. 264
European Free Trade Association (EFTA), p. 264
customs union p. 264
common market, p. 265
economic union, p. 265
political union, p. 265
trade creation, p. 267
trade diversion, p. 267
European Union (EU), p. 268
Treaty of Rome, p. 268
European Commission, p. 269
Council of the European Union, p. 270
European Parliament, p. 271
Court of Justice, p. 272
Single European Act, p. 272
Maastricht Treaty, p. 274
optimal currency area, p. 276
North American Free Trade Agreement (NAFTA), p. 279
Andean Pact, p. 282
MERCOSUR, p. 282
Central American Common Market, p. 283
Central America Free Trade Agreement (CAFTA), p. 284
CARICOM, p. 284
Caribbean Single Market and Economy (CSME), p. 284
Association of Southeast Asian Nations (ASEAN), p. 285
Asia-Pacific Economic Cooperation (APEC), p. 285

Summary

This chapter pursued three main objectives: to examine the economic and political debate surrounding regional economic integration; to review the progress toward regional economic integration in Europe, the Americas, and elsewhere; and to distinguish the important implications of regional economic integration for the practice of international business. The chapter made the following points:

1. A number of levels of economic integration are possible in theory. In order of increasing integration, they include a free trade area, a customs union, a common market, an economic union, and full political union.
2. In a free trade area, barriers to trade between member countries are removed, but each country determines its own external trade policy. In a customs union, internal barriers to trade are removed and a common external trade policy is adopted. A common market is similar to a customs union, except that a common market also allows factors of production to move freely between countries. An economic union involves even closer integration, including the establishment of a common currency and the harmonization of tax rates. A political union is the logical culmination of attempts to achieve ever closer economic integration.
3. Regional economic integration is an attempt to achieve economic gains from the free flow of trade and investment between neighboring countries.
4. Integration is not easily achieved or sustained. Although integration brings benefits to the majority, it is never without costs for the minority. Concerns over national sovereignty often slow or stop integration attempts.

5. Regional integration will not increase economic welfare if the trade creation effects in the free trade area are outweighed by the trade diversion effects.
6. The Single European Act sought to create a true single market by abolishing administrative barriers to the free flow of trade and investment between EU countries.
7. Twelve EU members now use a common currency, the euro. The economic gains from a common currency come from reduced exchange costs, reduced risk associated with currency fluctuations, and increased price competition within the EU.
8. Increasingly, the European Commission is taking an activist stance with regard to competition policy, intervening to restrict mergers and acquisitions that it believes will reduce competition in the EU.
9. Although no other attempt at regional economic integration comes close to the EU in terms of potential economic and political significance, various other attempts are being made in the world. The most notable include NAFTA in North America, the Andean Community and MERCOSUR in Latin America, ASEAN in Southeast Asia, and perhaps APEC.
10. The creation of single markets in the EU and North America means that many markets that were formerly protected from foreign competition are now more open. This creates major investment and export opportunities for firms within and outside these regions.
11. The free movement of goods across borders, the harmonization of product standards, and the simplification of tax regimes make it possible for firms based in a free trade area to realize potentially enormous cost economies by centralizing production in those locations within the area where the mix of factor costs and skills is optimal.
12. The lowering of barriers to trade and investment between countries within a trade group will probably be followed by increased price competition.

Critical Thinking and Discussion Questions

1. NAFTA has produced significant net benefits for the Canadian, Mexican, and U.S. economies. Discuss.
2. What are the economic and political arguments for regional economic integration? Given these arguments, why don't we see more substantial examples of integration in the world economy?
3. What effect is creation of a single market and a single currency within the EU likely to have on competition within the EU? Why?
4. Do you think it is correct for the European Commission to restrict mergers between American companies that do business in Europe? (For example, the European Commission vetoed the proposed merger between WorldCom and Sprint, both U.S. companies, and it carefully reviewed the merger between AOL and Time Warner, again both U.S. companies.)
5. How should a U.S. firm that currently exports only to ASEAN countries respond to the creation of a single market in this regional grouping?
6. How should a firm with self-sufficient production facilities in several ASEAN countries respond to the creation of a single market? What are the constraints on its ability to respond in a manner that minimizes production costs?
7. After a promising start, MERCOSUR, the major Latin American trade agreement, has faltered and made little progress since 2000. What problems are hurting MERCOSUR? What can be done to solve these problems?
8. Would establishment of a Free Trade Area of the Americas (FTAA) be good for the two most advanced economies in the hemisphere, the United States and Canada? How might the establishment of the FTAA impact the strategy of North American firms?

Research Task globalEDGE http://globalEDGE.msu.edu

Use the globalEDGE site (http://globalEDGE.msu.edu/) to complete the following exercises:

1. Your company is considering expanding its market by placing new representatives in the European Union. The size of the investment is significant and top management wishes to have a clear picture of the current economic status of the EU prior to entry. By analyzing short-term business indicators of different European communities and nations, available from *Eurostat*, a more detailed view can be attained for management. Prepare an executive summary describing the features you consider as crucial in making an entry decision.
2. The establishment of the Free Trade Area of the Americas can be a threat as well as an opportunity for your company. Identify the countries participating in the negotiations for the *FTAA*. What are the main themes of the negotiation process?

closing case

Car Price Differentials in the European Union

The Single European Act became law among the member states of the European Union on January 1, 1993. The goal of the act was to remove barriers to cross-border trade and investment within the confines of the EU, thereby creating a single market instead of a collection of distinct national markets. Among the benefits claimed for this act were an increase in competition and a corresponding reduction in prices. The move toward a single market received another boost January 1, 1999, when the majority of the EU's member states formally adopted the euro as a common currency. As of 2005, 12 of the 25 member states of the EU used the euro as their currency (these 12 countries are referred to as members of the euro zone). Proponents claimed that the euro would benefit European consumers by making it easier to compare prices across nations, which should in theory lead to the harmonization of prices within the euro zone. For example, as a result of the adoption of a common currency within a single market, a car sold in Germany should in theory be priced the same as a car sold in France.

In the automobile market, the reality has been somewhat different. By the end of 2005, significant variations remained between the prices of the same automobiles in different countries. According to the European Commission, in November 2005 there was a 26.7 percent differential between the price of a Volkswagen Golf in the cheapest and the most expensive national markets in the euro zone. There was also a 22.7 percent differential in the price of a Ford Focus, a 17 percent differential in the price of a Peugeot 206, and a 13.2 percent differential in the price of an Audi A4 Opel Vectra. However, these differentials with regard to certain models hid the fact that on average, prices have been converging on EU-wide norms. As of late 2005, the average price differential of cars across countries in the euro zone was just 4.4 percent, a marked improvement from November 1999, when the average price differential was 17.5 percent. The average price differential of cars across all EU member states was 6.4 percent in November 2005.

Within the euro zone, Germany was the most expensive car market. In Germany, 38 car models were sold to consumers at the highest prices in the euro zone in November 2005, and 16 of these were 20 percent more expensive than the cheapest national market within the euro zone. Within the euro zone countries, cars are cheapest in Finland. A VW Passat, for example, cost €3,200 less in Finland than in Germany. The United Kingdom is perennially among the most expensive car markets within the EU, with the average new car costing British consumers €800 more than comparable models sold in cheaper EU markets.

One reason for the persistence of price differentials within the EU is that since 1985, regulations have allowed automobile manufacturers to restrict competition between dealers. The "block exemption" clause in EU competition policy allowed automakers to dictate where a dealership could be located, to limit the number of brands that a dealer could sell, and to prohibit a dealer from selling vehicles outside of its home country. For example, Volkswagen might tell a dealer in Belgium that if it wanted to become, or remain, a Volkswagen dealer, it (*a*) could not sell models made by other car companies and (*b*) could not sell Volkswagen cars on its lot to consumers in Germany. This practice effectively allowed automobile companies to restrict competition, segment the

European market, and price cars differently in various countries to reflect underlying demand conditions.

In response to persistent complaints from consumers, the European Commission in late 2002 scrapped the block exemption clause and issued a new set of regulations designed to encourage competition within the EU car market. Under the new rules, dealers are allowed to sell anywhere they want to, open new locations where they choose, and sell more than one brand of car. Thus, a Belgian car dealer is now able to sell Volkswagens to German consumers. In a concession to automobile companies, which lobbied against the proposed revisions, the new rules were phased in over three years and took full effect in September 2005.

Sources: K. Kelly, "Global Politics Shift Auto Industry Focus," *Ward's Auto World,* November 2002, pp. 39–40; S. Miller, "Benefits of EU Car Sales Rules Are Questionable," *The Wall Street Journal,* July 17, 2002, p. A14; and "Competition: Car Prices Differentials across Europe Remain Unchanged," European Commission press release, December 11, 2005.

Case Discussion Questions

1. What are the sources of significant price differentials in the EU automobile market?
2. In a pure single market would these price differentials exist? By what process might price differentials be eradicated?
3. Why do you think the United Kingdom is one of the most expensive car markets in Europe?
4. What do you think will happen to price differentials in the EU automobile market under the new regulations that took effect in September 2005?
5. What will the impact of these new regulations be on (*a*) competitive intensity in the EU automobile market and (*b*) the profitability of automobile operations in the EU?
6. Which automobile companies will do best in the post-2005 environment?

part 4 Global Money System

LEARNING OBJECTIVES

1. Be conversant with the functions of the foreign exchange market.
2. Understand what is meant by spot exchange rates.
3. Appreciate the role that forward exchange rates play in insuring against foreign exchange risk.
4. Understand the different theories explaining how currency exchange rates are determined and their relative merits.
5. Be familiar with the merits of different approaches toward exchange rate forecasting.
6. Understand the differences between translation, transaction, and economic exposure, and what managers can do to manage each type of exposure.

chapter 9

The Foreign Exchange Market

The Curse of the Strong Dollar at STMicro

opening case

Europe's STMicro is the world's sixth-largest manufacturer of semiconductor chips, with 2005 sales of nearly $9 billion. The company makes chips for mobile phones, printers, and cars, among other things. It counts Nokia, the world's largest maker of wireless handsets, among its customers. STMicro was formed in 1987 from a merger between an Italian and a French firm, so the majority of its operations have long been in Western Europe. During the early 2000s, when the dollar was strong against the euro, the currency adopted by 12 member states of the European Union, this worked in STMicro's favor. Some 70 percent of the company's costs were denominated in euros, whereas semiconductors, like oil, were priced in U.S. dollars. The combination of a weak euro and a strong dollar translated into robust profits for STMicro.

However, in 2003 the euro began to rise against the dollar, rapidly shifting the profit calculus against STMicro. The euro, which traded as low as €1 = $0.83 in October 2000, had reached parity of €1 = $1.00 in late 2002. Few analysts predicted a rapid rise in the value of the euro against the dollar during 2003. As so often happens in the foreign exchange markets, the experts were wrong; by late 2003, the exchange rate stood at €1 = $1.20. The rise continued through 2004, with the exchange rate peaking at €1 = $1.32 in early 2005, before falling back to €1 = $1.20 in early 2006.

One cause of the rise in the value of the euro against the dollar were record U.S. foreign trade deficits in the 2002–05 period. The U.S. economy grew rapidly from 2003 to 2005, sucking in imports from foreign nations while generating anemic export growth. The result was a flow of dollars out of the United States into the hands of foreigners. Historically, foreigners had reinvested those dollars in the United States, and the return flow had kept the dollar strong despite persistent trade deficits. This didn't happen to the same extent in the 2003–05 period. Instead, many foreigners sold the dollars they received for other currencies, such as the euro, Japanese yen, or British pound. They did this because they had become increasingly pessimistic about the future value of the dollar and were reducing their dollar holdings accordingly. Their pessimism was itself a function of two factors. First, U.S. government officials stated that they would prefer a weaker dollar in order to increase the competitiveness of U.S. companies in the global marketplace (the theory being that a falling dollar would make U.S. exports more competitive). With the government talking the dollar down, many foreigners decided to reduce their dollar holdings. Second, the U.S. government ran record budget deficits in the 2003–05 period, and these were projected to remain high for some time. Looking at this, some foreigners concluded that the U.S. government might be forced to finance its spending by expanding the supply of dollars (i.e., by printing money), which would lead to inflation and reduce the value of the dollar even further. Thus, they sold dollars and purchased currencies thought to be less prone to inflation.

For STMicro, the results of these macroeconomic events were serious. The company does very little currency hedging, so as the dollar fell, the euro value of STMicro's sales compressed, while costs, being largely dominated in euros, stayed high. Although strong global chip sales helped to offset the fall in the value of the dollar, STMicro's profits still slumped in 2004 and 2005. In response, STMicro's CEO, Carlo Bozotti, pledged to take some $500 million out of the company's cost structure, primarily by shutting down some high-cost European operations, cutting 3,000 jobs, and moving production to Asia where it planned to add 1,500 jobs. Bozotti described the strategy as one of "real hedging" that would allow STMicro to move production from Europe to Asia, and back if necessary, in order to deal with the consequences of shifts in exchange rates against the dollar.

Sources: M. Pesola, "STMicro Unveils More Job Cuts in Chip Making," *Financial Times,* May 17, 2005, p. 22; B. Lagrotteria and C. Bryan-Low, "Dealing with the Dollar: Strong Euro Bedevils EU Firms," *The Wall Street Journal,* June 21, 2005, p. A14; and H. Schoemaker, "STMicro Profit Slips, but First Quarter Looks Upbeat," *The Wall Street Journal,* January 26, 2006, p. B5.

Introduction

This chapter has three main objectives. The first is to explain how the foreign exchange market works. The second is to examine the forces that determine exchange rates and to discuss the degree to which it is possible to predict future exchange rate movements. The third is to map the implications for international business of exchange rate movements and the foreign exchange market. This chapter is the first of two that deal with the international monetary system and its relationship to international business. In the next chapter, we will explore the institutional structure of the international monetary system. The institutional structure is the context within which the foreign exchange market functions. As we shall see, changes in the institutional structure of the international monetary system can exert a profound influence on the development of foreign exchange markets.

The **foreign exchange market** is a market for converting the currency of one country into that of another country. An **exchange rate** is simply the rate at which one currency is converted into another. For example, STMicro uses the foreign exchange market to convert the dollars it earns from selling semiconductor chips (which are priced in dollars) into euros. Without the foreign exchange market, international trade and international investment on the scale that we see today would be impossible; companies would have to resort to barter. The foreign exchange market is the lubricant that enables companies based in countries that use different currencies to trade with each other.

Foreign Exchange Market
A market for converting the currency of one country into that of another country.

Exchange Rate
The rate at which one currency is converted into another.

We know from earlier chapters that international trade and investment have their risks. As the opening case illustrates, some of these risks exist because future exchange rates cannot be perfectly predicted. The rate at which one currency is converted into another can change over time. In January 1999, for example, the U.S. dollar/European euro exchange rate stood at €1 = $1.17, by October 2000 it stood at €1 = $0.82, by December 2002 it was up to €1 = $1.00, and in early 2005 it stood at €1 = $1.30. One function of the foreign exchange market is to provide some insurance against the risks that arise from such volatile changes in exchange rates, commonly referred to as *foreign exchange risk*. Although the foreign exchange market offers some insurance against foreign exchange risk, it cannot provide complete insurance. It is not unusual for international businesses to suffer losses because of unpredicted changes in exchange rates. Currency fluctuations can make seemingly profitable trade and investment deals unprofitable, and vice versa. The opening case on STMicro contains an example.

We begin this chapter by looking at the functions and the form of the foreign exchange market. This includes distinguishing among spot exchanges, forward exchanges, and currency swaps. Then we will consider the factors that determine exchange rates. We will also look at how foreign trade is conducted when a country's currency cannot be exchanged for other currencies; that is, when its currency is not convertible. The chapter closes with a discussion of these things in terms of their implications for business.

The Functions of the Foreign Exchange Market

LEARNING OBJECTIVE 1
Be conversant with the functions of the foreign exchange market.

The foreign exchange market serves two main functions. The first is to convert the currency of one country into the currency of another. The second is to provide some insurance against **foreign exchange risk,** by which we mean the adverse consequences of unpredictable changes in exchange rates.[1]

Foreign Exchange Risk
The risk that changes in exchange rates will hurt the profitability of a business deal.

CURRENCY CONVERSION Each country has a currency in which the prices of goods and services are quoted. In the United States, it is the dollar ($); in Great Britain, the pound (£); in France, Germany, and other members of the euro zone it is the euro (€); in Japan, the yen (¥); and so on. In general, within the borders of a particular country, one must use the national currency. A U.S. tourist cannot walk into a store in Edinburgh, Scotland, and use U.S. dollars to buy a bottle of Scotch whisky. Dollars are not recognized as legal tender in Scotland; the tourist must use British pounds. Fortunately, the tourist can go to a bank and exchange her dollars for pounds. Then she can buy the whisky.

When changing one currency into another, the tourist is participating in the foreign exchange market. The exchange rate is the rate at which the market converts one currency into another. For example, an exchange rate of €1 = $1.30 specifies that one euro buys $1.30 U.S. dollars. The exchange rate allows us to compare the relative prices of goods

Another Perspective

The Business Traveler's Ethics Challenged by Foreign Exchange

In preparation for a trip to Japan, you exchange U.S. dollars for yen in late April, just before you leave. For $1,000 your bank gives you ¥120,000. During your time in Tokyo, the dollar weakens against the yen, to ¥110 to the dollar. Meanwhile, you enjoyed Japanese hospitality and spent only ¥10,000. Back in LA, you take your remaining ¥100,000 to the bank to convert back to dollars. How much have you spent on your trip? Will you list these expenses on your expense report?

and services in different countries. Our U.S. tourist wishing to buy a bottle of Scotch whisky in Edinburgh may find that she must pay £30 for the bottle, knowing that the same bottle costs $45 in the United States. Is this a good deal? Imagine the current pound/dollar exchange rate is £1.00 = $1.80 (i.e., one British pound buys $1.80). Our intrepid tourist takes out her calculator and converts £30 into dollars. (The calculation is 30 × 1.8). She finds that the bottle of Scotch costs the equivalent of $54. She is surprised that a bottle of Scotch whisky could cost less in the United States than in Scotland (alcohol is taxed heavily in Great Britain). See the Another Perspective at left for another example.

Tourists are minor participants in the foreign exchange market; companies engaged in international trade and investment are major ones. International businesses have four main uses of foreign exchange markets. First, the payments a company receives for its exports, the income it receives from foreign investments, or the income it receives from licensing agreements with foreign firms may be in foreign currencies. To use those funds in its home country, the company must convert them to its home country's currency. Consider the Scotch distillery that exports its whisky to the United States. The distillery is paid in dollars, but since those dollars cannot be spent in Great Britain, they must be converted into British pounds. Similarly, when Volkswagen sells cars in the United States for dollars, it must convert those dollars into euros to use them in Germany.

Second, international businesses use foreign exchange markets when they must pay a foreign company for its products or services in its country's currency. For example, Dell buys many of the components for its computers from Malaysian firms. The Malaysian companies must be paid in Malaysia's currency, the ringgit, so Dell must convert money from dollars into ringgit to pay them.

Third, international businesses use foreign exchange markets when they have spare cash that they wish to invest for short terms in money markets. For example, consider a U.S. company that has $10 million it wants to invest for three months. The best interest rate it can earn on these funds in the United States may be 4 percent. Investing in a South Korean money market account, however, may earn 12 percent. Thus, the company may change its $10 million into Korean won and invest it in South Korea. Note, however, that the rate of return it earns on this investment depends not only on the Korean interest rate, but also on the changes in the value of the Korean won against the dollar in the intervening period.

Currency Speculation
Moving funds from one currency to another over the short-term in hopes of profiting from shifts in exchange rates.

Finally, currency speculation is another use of foreign exchange markets. **Currency speculation** typically involves the short-term movement of funds from one currency to another in the hopes of profiting from shifts in exchange rates. Consider again a U.S. company with $10 million to invest for three months. Suppose the company suspects that the U.S. dollar is overvalued against the Japanese yen. That is, the company expects the value of the dollar to depreciate (fall) against that of the yen. Imagine the current dollar/yen exchange rate is $1 = ¥120. The company exchanges its $10 million into yen, receiving ¥1.2 billion ($10 million × 120 = ¥1.2 billion). Over the next three months, the value of the dollar depreciates against the yen until $1 = ¥100. Now the company exchanges its ¥1.2 billion back into dollars and finds that it has $12 million. The company has made a $2 million profit on currency speculation in three months on an initial investment of $10 million. In general, however, companies should beware, for speculation by definition is a very risky business. The company cannot know for sure what will happen to exchange rates. Although a speculator may profit handsomely if his speculation about future currency movements turns out to be correct, he can also lose vast amounts of money if it turns out to be wrong.

Using insurance to protect against forward exchange rates helps companies hedge against financial risk. *Daisuke Morita/Getty Images/DIL*

INSURING AGAINST FOREIGN EXCHANGE RISK The second function of the foreign exchange market is to provide insurance against foreign exchange risk, which is the possibility that unpredicted changes in future exchange rates will have adverse consequences for the firm. When a firm insures itself against foreign exchange risk, we say that is it engaging in **hedging.** To explain how the market performs this function, we must first distinguish among spot exchange rates, forward exchange rates, and currency swaps.

Hedging
The process of insuring one's business against foreign exchange risk by using forward exchanges or currency swaps.

Spot Exchange Rates When two parties agree to exchange currency and execute the deal immediately, the transaction is referred to as a *spot exchange*. Exchange rates governing such "on the spot" trades are referred to as spot exchange rates. The **spot exchange rate** is the rate at which a foreign exchange dealer converts one currency into another currency on a particular day. Thus, when our U.S. tourist in Edinburgh goes to a bank to convert her dollars into pounds, the exchange rate is the spot rate for that day.

LEARNING OBJECTIVE 2
Understand what is meant by spot exchange rates.

Spot exchange rates are reported on a real-time basis on many financial web sites. Table 9.1 shows the exchange rates for a selection of currencies traded in the New York foreign exchange market as of 2:25 p.m., on March 27, 2006. An exchange rate can be quoted in two ways: as the amount of foreign currency one U.S. dollar will buy, or as the value in dollars of one unit of foreign currency. Thus, one U.S. dollar bought €0.8327 on March 27, 2006, and one euro bought $1.2009 US dollars.

Spot Exchange Rate
The rate at which a foreign exchange dealer converts currency on any particular day.

Spot rates change continually, often on a minute-by-minute basis (although the magnitude of changes over such short periods is usually small). The value of a currency is determined by the interaction between the demand and supply of that currency relative to the demand and supply of other currencies. For example, if lots of people want U.S.

Currency		U.S. $	¥en	Euro	Can $	UK £	AU $	Swiss Franc
1 U.S. $	=	1	116.6800	0.8327	1.1694	0.5723	1.4180	1.3092
1 ¥en	=	0.008570	1	0.007137	0.010022	0.004905	0.012153	0.011221
1 euro	=	1.2009	140.1210	1	1.4043	0.6873	1.7029	1.5723
1 Can $	=	0.8551	99.7777	0.7121	1	0.4894	1.2126	1.1196
1 UK £	=	1.7474	203.8809	1.4550	2.0434	1	2.4778	2.2877
1 AU $	=	0.7052	82.2827	0.5872	0.8247	0.4036	1	0.9233
1 Swiss franc	=	0.7638	89.1197	0.6360	0.8932	0.4371	1.0831	1

table 9.1

Spot Exchange Rates at 2:25 p.m., March 27, 2006

Source: *Yahoo! Finance.*

dollars and dollars are in short supply, and few people want British pounds and pounds are in plentiful supply, the spot exchange rate for converting dollars into pounds will change. The dollar is likely to appreciate against the pound (or the pound will depreciate against the dollar). Imagine the spot exchange rate is £1 = $1.50 when the market opens. As the day progresses, dealers demand more dollars and fewer pounds. By the end of the day, the spot exchange rate might be £1 = $1.48. Each pound now buys fewer dollars than at the start of the day. The dollar has appreciated, and the pound has depreciated.

LEARNING OBJECTIVE 3
Appreciate the role that forward exchange rates play in insuring against foreign exchange risk.

Forward Exchange Rates As we saw in the opening case, changes in spot exchange rates can be problematic for an international business. For example, a U.S. company that imports laptop computers from Japan knows that in 30 days it must pay yen to a Japanese supplier when a shipment arrives. The company will pay the Japanese supplier ¥200,000 for each laptop computer, and the current dollar/yen spot exchange rate is $1 = ¥120. At this rate, each computer costs the importer $1,667 (i.e., 1,667 = 200,000/120). The importer knows she can sell the computers the day they arrive for $2,000 each, which yields a gross profit of $333 on each computer ($2,000 − $1,667). However, the importer will not have the funds to pay the Japanese supplier until the computers have been sold. If over the next 30 days the dollar unexpectedly depreciates against the yen, say, to $1 = ¥95, the importer will still have to pay the Japanese company ¥200,000 per computer, but in dollar terms that would be equivalent to $2,105 per computer, which is more than she can sell the computers for. A depreciation in the value of the dollar against the yen from $1 = ¥120 to $1 = ¥95 would transform a profitable deal into an unprofitable one.

Forward Exchange
When two parties agree to exchange currency and execute a deal at some specific date in the future.

Forward Exchange Rate
The exchange rate governing forward exchange transactions, calculated at the time of the exchange but based on future expectations.

To *insure* or *hedge* against this risk, the U.S. importer might want to engage in a forward exchange. A **forward exchange** occurs when two parties agree to exchange currency and execute the deal at some specific date in the future. Exchange rates governing such future transactions are referred to as **forward exchange rates.** For most major currencies, forward exchange rates are quoted for 30 days, 90 days, and 180 days into the future. In some cases, it is possible to get forward exchange rates for several years into the future. Returning to our computer importer example, let us assume the 30-day forward exchange rate for converting dollars into yen is $1 = ¥110. The importer enters into a 30-day forward exchange transaction with a foreign exchange dealer at this rate and is guaranteed that she will have to pay no more than $1,818 for each computer (1,818 = 200,000/110). This guarantees her a profit of $182 per computer ($2,000 − $1,818). She also insures herself against the possibility that an unanticipated change in the dollar/yen exchange rate will turn a profitable deal into an unprofitable one.

In this example, the spot exchange rate ($1 = ¥120) and the 30-day forward rate ($1 = ¥110) differ. Such differences are normal; they reflect the expectations of the foreign exchange market about future currency movements. In our example, the fact that $1 bought more yen with a spot exchange than with a 30-day forward exchange indicates foreign exchange dealers expected the dollar to depreciate against the yen in the next 30 days. When this occurs, we say the dollar is selling at a discount on the 30-day forward market (i.e., it is worth less than on the spot market). Of course, the opposite can also occur. If the 30-day forward exchange rate were $1 = ¥130, for example, $1 would buy more yen with a forward exchange than with a spot exchange. In such a case, we say the dollar is selling at a premium on the 30-day forward market. This reflects the foreign exchange dealers' expectations that the dollar will appreciate against the yen over the next 30 days.

In sum, when a firm enters into a forward exchange contract, it is taking out insurance against the possibility that future exchange rate movements will make a transaction unprofitable by the time that transaction has been executed. Although many firms routinely enter into forward exchange contracts to hedge their foreign exchange risk, there are some spectacular examples of what happens when firms don't take out this insurance.

Management FOCUS

South African Airlines' Disastrous Currency Hedge

The management of South African Airlines in 2002 decided to enter into forward exchange contracts valued at $1.3 billion to protect against a possible drop in the value of South Africa's currency, the rand, against the U.S. dollar. The contracts were designed to ensure that South African Airlines could lock in the price that it would have to pay for future purchases of jet fuel and 41 new aircraft from Airbus Industrie, both of which are priced in U.S. dollars. For several years the rand had been weak against the dollar, and management felt that further declines were likely. The contracts, which extended out over 10 years, assumed that the rand would average 10.80 to one U.S. dollar.

This hedge seemed logical. It was certainly a conservative thing to do. However, management declined to hedge against the possibility that the rand might appreciate against the dollar. Apparently, such a possibility seemed so remote that they decided to forgo the costs of entering into additional forward exchange contracts to guard against a possible rise in the value of the rand against the dollar. They were wrong. In 2002 and early 2003, the South African rand appreciated against the U.S. dollar by almost 30 percent, to 6.09 rand to the dollar. For South African Airlines, this was an unmitigated disaster. In March 2003, the company announced it had recorded $1.05 billion in unrealized foreign exchange losses. This wiped out the airline's profit and pushed its loss for the year to $808 million. In the aftermath, the CFO resigned, followed later by the CEO. The company also announced that its financial difficulties meant it had to cancel orders for 15 Airbus planes.

Sources: D. Robertson, "SAA Up against Rand Hedge," *Business Day,* August 27, 2003, p. 3; J. Flottau, "SAA under Duress," *Aviation Week,* July 12, 2004, p. 40; and J. Wallace, "Order Cancellations a Hard Hit to Airbus," *Seattle Post Intelligencer,* August 28, 2004, p. E6.

One such example was given in the opening case, which looked at STMicro. Another is given in the Management Focus box above, which explains how a failure to fully insure against foreign exchange risk cost South African Airlines $1.05 billion.

Currency Swaps The above discussion of spot and forward exchange rates might lead you to conclude that the option to buy forward is very important to companies engaged in international trade—and you would be right. By April 2004, the latest date for which information is available, forward instruments accounted for some 65 percent of all foreign exchange transactions, while spot exchanges accounted for 35 percent.[2] However, the vast majority of these forward exchanges were not forward exchanges of the type we have been discussing; rather, they involved more sophisticated instruments known as *currency swaps.*

Currency Swap The simultaneous purchase and sale of a given amount of foreign exchange for two different value dates.

A **currency swap** is the simultaneous purchase and sale of a given amount of foreign exchange for two different value dates. Swaps are transacted between international businesses and their banks, between banks, and between governments when it is desirable to move out of one currency into another for a limited period without incurring foreign exchange risk. A common kind of swap is *spot against forward.* Consider a company such as Apple Computer. Apple assembles laptop computers in the United States, but the screens are made in Japan. Apple also sells some of the finished laptops in Japan. So, like many companies, Apple both buys from and sells to Japan. Imagine Apple needs to change $1 million into yen to pay its supplier of laptop screens today. Apple knows that in 90 days it will be paid ¥120 million by the Japanese importer that buys its finished laptops. It will want to convert these yen into dollars for use in the United States. Let us say today's spot exchange rate is $1 = ¥120 and the 90-day forward exchange rate is $1 = ¥110. Apple sells $1 million to its bank in return for ¥120 million. Now Apple can pay its Japanese supplier. At the same time, Apple enters into a 90-day forward exchange deal with its bank for converting ¥120 million into dollars. Thus, in 90 days Apple will receive $1.09 million (¥120 million/110 = $1.09 million). Because the yen is trading at a premium

Another Perspective

Key into Exchange Rate Language

The language used to describe exchange rates can be confusing, even though the ideas themselves are simple. Here's why: Any given observation describes a changing relationship (the movement in the currencies) that itself describes two relationships (the exchange rates for both currencies). The important thing to remember is that an exchange rate is described in terms of other exchange rates.

The language we use to describe these moving phenomena works in a similar, dual way: The euro gains against the dollar, so the euro is strengthening, or becoming dearer, from a dollar perspective. Meanwhile, the same observation indicates its mirror image, that the dollar is weakening, becoming cheaper against the euro, from a euro perspective.

on the 90-day forward market, Apple ends up with more dollars than it started with (although the opposite could also occur). The swap deal is just like a conventional forward deal in one important respect: It enables Apple to insure itself against foreign exchange risk. By engaging in a swap, Apple knows today that the ¥120 million payment it will receive in 90 days will yield $1.09 million.

The Nature of the Foreign Exchange Market

The foreign exchange market is not located in any one place. It is a global network of banks, brokers, and foreign exchange dealers connected by electronic communications systems. When companies wish to convert currencies, they typically go through their own banks rather than entering the market directly. The foreign exchange market has been growing at a rapid pace, reflecting a general growth in the volume of cross-border trade and investment (see Chapter 1). In March 1986, the average total value of global foreign exchange trading was about $200 billion per day. By April 1995, it was more than $1,200 billion per day, and by April 2004 it reached $1.8 trillion per day.[3] The most important trading centers are London (31 percent of activity), New York (19 percent), Tokyo (8 percent), and Singapore (5 percent).[4] Major secondary trading centers include Zurich, Frankfurt, Paris, Hong Kong, and Sydney.

London's dominance in the foreign exchange market is due to both history and geography. As the capital of the world's first major industrial trading nation, London had become the world's largest center for international banking by the end of the nineteenth century, a position it has retained. Today, London's central position between Tokyo and Singapore to the east and New York to the west has made it the critical link between the East Asian and New York markets. Due to the particular differences in time zones, London opens soon after Tokyo closes for the night and is still open for the first few hours of trading in New York.[5]

Two features of the foreign exchange market are of particular note. The first is that the market never sleeps. Tokyo, London, and New York are all shut for only 3 hours out of every 24. During these three hours, trading continues in a number of minor centers, particularly San Francisco and Sydney, Australia. The second feature of the market is the integration of the various trading centers. High-speed computer linkages between trading centers around the globe have effectively created a single market. The integration of financial centers implies there can be no significant difference in exchange rates quoted in the trading centers. For example, if the yen/dollar exchange rate quoted in London at 3 p.m. is ¥120 = $1, the yen/dollar exchange rate quoted in New York at the same time (10 a.m. New York time) will be identical. If the New York yen/dollar exchange rate were ¥125 = $1, a dealer could make a profit through **arbitrage,** buying a currency low and selling it high. For example, if the prices differed in London and New York as given, a dealer in New York could take $1 million and use that to purchase ¥125 million. The dealer could then immediately sell the ¥125 million for dollars in London, where the transaction would yield $1.046666 million, resulting in a profit of $46,666 on the transaction. If all dealers tried to cash in on the opportunity, however, the demand for yen in New York would rise, resulting in an

Arbitrage
The purchase of securities in one market for immediate resale in another market to profit from a price discrepancy.

appreciation of the yen against the dollar such that the price differential between New York and London would quickly disappear. Because foreign exchange dealers are always watching their computer screens for arbitrage opportunities, the few that arise tend to be small, and they disappear in minutes.

Another feature of the foreign exchange market is the important role played by the U.S. dollar. Although a foreign exchange transaction can involve any two currencies, most transactions involve dollars on one side. This is true even when a dealer wants to sell a nondollar currency and buy another. A dealer wishing to sell Korean won for Brazilian real, for example, will usually sell the won for dollars and then use the dollars to buy real. Although this may seem a roundabout way of doing things, it is actually cheaper than trying to find a holder of real who wants to buy won. Because the volume of international transactions involving dollars is so great, it is not hard to find dealers who wish to trade dollars for won or real.

Even though the British pound has declined in its importance as a vehicle currency, London remains the key location for global foreign exchange.
Kim Steele/Getty Images/DIL

Due to its central role in so many foreign exchange deals, the dollar is a vehicle currency. In 2004, 89 percent of all foreign exchange transactions involved dollars on one side of the transaction. After the dollar, the most important vehicle currencies were the euro, the Japanese yen, and the British pound—reflecting the importance of these trading entities in the world economy. The euro has replaced the Germany mark as the world's second most important vehicle currency. The British pound used to be second in importance to the dollar as a vehicle currency, but its importance has diminished in recent years. Despite this, London has retained its leading position in the global foreign exchange market.

Economic Theories of Exchange Rate Determination

LEARNING OBJECTIVE 4
Understand the different theories explaining how currency exchange rates are determined and their relative merits.

At the most basic level, exchange rates are determined by the demand and supply of one currency relative to the demand and supply of another. For example, if the demand for dollars outstrips the supply of them and if the supply of Japanese yen is greater than the demand for them, the dollar/yen exchange rate will change. The dollar will appreciate against the yen (or the yen will depreciate against the dollar). However, while differences in relative demand and supply explain the determination of exchange rates, they do so only in a superficial sense. This simple explanation does not tell us what factors underlie the demand for and supply of a currency. Nor does it tell us when the demand for dollars will exceed the supply (and vice versa) or when the supply of Japanese yen will exceed demand for them (and vice versa). Neither does it tell us under what conditions a currency is in demand or under what conditions it is not demanded. In this section, we will review economic theory's answers to these questions. This will give us a deeper understanding of how exchange rates are determined.

If we understand how exchange rates are determined, we may be able to forecast exchange rate movements. Because future exchange rate movements influence export opportunities, the profitability of international trade and investment deals, and the price competitiveness of foreign imports, this is valuable information for an international business. Unfortunately, there is no simple explanation. The forces that determine exchange rates are complex, and no theoretical consensus exists, even among academic economists who study the phenomenon every day. Nonetheless, most economic theories of exchange rate movements seem to agree that three factors have an important impact on future exchange rate movements in a country's currency: the country's price inflation, its interest rate, and market psychology.[6]

PRICES AND EXCHANGE RATES To understand how prices are related to exchange rate movements, we first need to discuss an economic proposition known as the *law of one price*. Then we will discuss the theory of purchasing power parity (PPP), which links changes in the exchange rate between two countries' currencies to changes in the countries' price levels.

Law of One Price
The principle that in competitive markets free of transportation costs and barriers to trade, identical products sold in different countries must sell of the same price when their price is expressed in the same currency.

The Law of One Price The **law of one price** states that in competitive markets free of transportation costs and barriers to trade (such as tariffs), identical products sold in different countries must sell for the same price when their price is expressed in terms of the same currency.[7] For example, if the exchange rate between the British pound and the dollar is £1 = \$1.50, a jacket that retails for \$75 in New York should sell for £50 in London (since \$75/1.50 = £50). Consider what would happen if the jacket cost £40 in London (\$60 in U.S. currency). At this price, it would pay a trader to buy jackets in London and sell them in New York (an example of arbitrage). The company initially could make a profit of \$15 on each jacket by purchasing it for £40 (\$60) in London and selling it for \$75 in New York (we are assuming away transportation costs and trade barriers). However, the increased demand for jackets in London would raise their price in London, and the increased supply of jackets in New York would lower their price there. This would continue until prices were equalized. Thus, prices might equalize when the jacket cost £44 (\$66) in London and \$66 in New York (assuming no change in the exchange rate of £1 = \$1.50).

Efficient Market
A market in which prices reflect all available information and trade is not restricted.

Purchasing Power Parity If the law of one price were true for all goods and services, the purchasing power parity exchange rate could be found from any individual set of prices. By comparing the prices of identical products in different currencies, it would be possible to determine the "real" or PPP exchange rate that would exist if markets were efficient. (An **efficient market** has no impediments to the free flow of goods and services, such as trade barriers.)

Relatively Efficient Market
A market in which few impediments to international trade and investment exist.

A less extreme version of the PPP theory states that given **relatively efficient markets**—that is, markets in which few impediments to international trade exist—the price of a basket of goods should be roughly equivalent in each country. To express the PPP theory in symbols, let P\$ be the U.S. dollar price of a basket of particular goods and P¥ be the price of the same basket of goods in Japanese yen. The PPP theory predicts that the dollar/yen exchange rate, E\$/¥, should be equivalent to

$$E_{\$/¥} = P_{\$}/P_{¥}$$

Thus, if a basket of goods costs \$200 in the United States and ¥20,000 in Japan, PPP theory predicts that the dollar/yen exchange rate should be \$200/¥20,000, or \$0.01 per Japanese yen (i.e., \$1 = ¥100).

Every year, the newsmagazine *The Economist* publishes its own version of the PPP theorem, which it refers to as the "Big Mac Index." *The*

Another Perspective

The Law of One Price and the Internet
Presently, the law of one price applies to Internet buying that crosses national borders. Internet research provides accurate pricing information across markets. Many American consumers are trying to invoke the law of one price in the U.S. pharmaceutical market. They see that prices for prescription drugs are lower in Canada, and despite U.S. law prohibiting the importation of foreign drugs, they are having their prescriptions filled in Canada. If this trend continues, the law of one price suggests that U.S. drug prices will fall.

Economist has selected McDonald's Big Mac as a proxy for a basket of goods because it is produced according to more or less the same recipe in about 120 countries. The Big Mac PPP is the exchange rate that would have hamburgers costing the same in each country. According to *The Economist*, comparing a country's actual exchange rate with the one predicted by the PPP theorem based on relative prices of Big Macs is a test on whether a currency is undervalued or not. This is not a totally serious exercise, as *The Economist* admits, but it does provide us with a useful illustration of the PPP theorem.

The Big Mac index for June 2005 is reproduced in Table 9.2. To calculate the index, *The Economist* converts the price of a Big Mac in a country into dollars at current exchange rates and divides that by the average price of a Big Mac in America (which is $3.06). According to the PPP theorem, the prices should be the same. If they are not, it implies that the currency is either overvalued against the dollar or undervalued. For example, the average price of a Big Mac in the euro area was $3.58 at the euro/dollar exchange rate prevailing in June 2005. Dividing this by the average price of a Big Mac in the United States gives 1.17 (i.e., 3.58/3.06), which suggests that the euro was overvalued by 17 percent against the U.S. dollar in June 2005.

Another Perspective

The Starbucks Index

To test the Big Mac index, which applies the PPP theory using the price of a Big Mac in various markets to determine the equilibrium value of the foreign currency, *The Economist* established a Starbucks index in 2004. After all, like the Big Mac, a cup of Starbucks coffeecan be found in many foreign markets and can be seen as a proxy for a basket of goods. The results of the Starbucks index followed the Big Mac index in most markets, except in Asia, where the former indicated that the dollar was at parity with the Chinese yuan; the Big Mac index suggested that the yuan was 56 percent undervalued. Neither of these consumer items is a good proxy for a basket of goods, but comparing their relative prices with exchange rates is an interesting and playful approach to quickly grasping how under- or overvalued the foreign currency is against the dollar.

The next step in the PPP theory is to argue that the exchange rate will change if relative prices change. For example, imagine there is no price inflation in the United States, while prices in Japan are increasing by 10 percent a year. At the beginning of the year, a basket of goods costs $200 in the United States and ¥20,000 in Japan, so the dollar/yen exchange rate, according to PPP theory, should be $1 = ¥100. At the end of the year, the basket of goods still costs $200 in the United States, but it costs ¥22,000 in Japan. PPP theory predicts that the exchange rate should change as a result. More precisely, by the end of the year

$$E_{\$/¥} = \$200/¥22{,}000$$

Thus, ¥1 = $0.0091 (or $1 = ¥110). Because of 10 percent price inflation, the Japanese yen has depreciated by 10 percent against the dollar. One dollar will buy 10 percent more yen at the end of the year than at the beginning.

Money Supply and Price Inflation In essence, PPP theory predicts that changes in relative prices will result in a change in exchange rates. Theoretically, a country in which price inflation is running wild should expect to see its currency depreciate against that of countries in which inflation rates are lower. If we can predict what a country's future inflation rate is likely to be, we can also predict how the value of its currency relative to other currencies—its exchange rate—is likely to change. The growth rate of a country's money supply determines its likely future inflation rate.[8] Thus, in theory at least, we can use information about the growth in money supply to forecast exchange rate movements.

Inflation is a monetary phenomenon. It occurs when the quantity of money in circulation rises faster than the stock of goods and services; that is, when the money supply increases faster than output increases. Imagine what would happen if everyone in the country was suddenly given $10,000 by the government. Many people would rush out

	Big Mac price in dollars*	Implied PPP[†] of the dollar	Under (−)/ over (+) valuation against the dollar, %		Big Mac price in dollars*	Implied PPP[†] of the dollar	Under (−)/ over (+) valuation against the dollar, %
United States[‡]	3.06	—	—	Aruba	2.77	1.62	−10
Argentina	1.64	1.55	−46	Bulgaria	1.88	0.98	−39
Australia	2.50	1.06	−18	Colombia	2.79	2124	−9
Brazil	2.39	1.93	−22	Croatia	2.50	4.87	−18
Britain	3.44	1.63[§]	+12	Dominican Rep	2.12	19.6	−31
Canada	2.63	1.07	−14	Estonia	2.31	9.64	−24
Chile	2.53	490	−17	Fiji	2.50	1.39	−18
China	1.27	3.43	−59	Georgia	2.00	1.19	−34
Czech Republic	2.30	18.4	−25	Guatemala	2.20	5.47	−28
Denmark	4.58	9.07	+50	Honduras	1.91	11.7	−38
Egypt	1.55	2.94	−49	Iceland	6.67	143	+118
Euro area	3.58**	1.05[††]	+17	Jamaica	2.70	53.9	−12
Hong Kong	1.54	3.92	−50	Jordan	3.66	0.85	+19
Hungary	2.60	173	−15	Latvia	1.92	0.36	−37
Indonesia	153	4.771	−50	Lebanon	2.85	1405	−7
Japan	2.34	81.7	−23	Lithuania	2.31	2.12	−24
Malaysia	1.38	1.72	−55	Macau	1.40	3.66	−54
Mexico	2.58	9.15	−16	Macedonia	1.90	31.0	−38
New Zealand	3.17	1.45	+4	Moldova	1.84	7.52	−40
Peru	2.76	2.94	−10	Morocco	2.73	8.02	−11
Philippines	1.47	26.1	−52	Nicaragua	2.11	11.3	−31
Poland	1.96	2.12	−36	Norway	6.06	12.7	+98
Russia	1.48	13.7	−52	Pakistan	2.18	42.5	−29
Singapore	2.17	1.18	−29	Paraguay	1.44	2941	−53
South Africa	2.10	4.56	−31	Qatar	0.68	0.81	−78
South Korea	2.49	817	−19	Saudi Arabia	2.40	2.94	−22
Sweden	4.17	10.1	+36	Serbia & Montenegro	2.08	45.8	−32
Switzerland	5.05	2.06	+65	Slovakia	2.09	21.6	−32
Taiwan	2.41	24.5	−21	Slovenia	2.56	163	−16
Thailand	1.48	19.6	−52	Sri Lanka	1.75	57.2	−43
Turkey	2.92	1.31	−5	Ukraine	1.43	2.37	−53
Venezuela	2.13	1.830	−30	UAE	2.45	2.94	−20
				Uruguay	1.82	14.4	−40*

table 9.2 The Big Mac Index, June 2005

*At current exchange rates.
[†]Purchasing-power parity.
[‡]Average of New York, Chicago, San Francisco, and Atlanta.
[§]Dollars per pound.
**Weighted average of member countries.
[††]Dollars per euro.

Source: *The Economist*, June 9, 2005.

to spend their extra money on those things they had always wanted—new cars, new furniture, better clothes, and so on. There would be a surge in demand for goods and services. Car dealers, department stores, and other providers of goods and services would respond to this upsurge in demand by raising prices. The result would be price inflation.

A government increasing the money supply is analogous to giving people more money. An increase in the money supply makes it easier for banks to borrow from the government and for individuals and companies to borrow from banks. The resulting increase in credit causes increases in demand for goods and services. Unless the output of goods and services is growing at a rate similar to that of the money supply, the result will be inflation. This relationship has been observed time after time in country after country.

So now we have a connection between the growth in a country's money supply, price inflation, and exchange rate movements. Put simply, *when the growth in a country's money supply is faster than the growth in its output, price inflation is fueled.* The PPP theory tells us that a country with a high inflation rate will see depreciation in its currency exchange rate. In one of the clearest historical examples, in the mid-1980s, Bolivia experienced hyperinflation—an explosive and seemingly uncontrollable price inflation in which money loses value very rapidly. Table 9.3 presents data on Bolivia's money

table 

Macroeconomic Data for Bolivia, April 1984–October 1985

Month	Money Supply (billions of pesos)	Price Level Relative to 1982 (average = 1)	Exchange Rate (pesos per dollar)
1984			
April	270	21.1	3,576
May	330	31.1	3,512
June	440	32.3	3,342
July	599	34.0	3,570
August	718	39.1	7,038
September	889	53.7	13,685
October	1,194	85.5	15,205
November	1,495	112.4	18,469
December	3,296	180,9	24,515
1985			
January	4,630	305.3	73,016
February	6,455	863.3	141,101
March	9,089	1,078.6	128,137
April	12,885	1,205.7	167,428
May	21,309	1,635.7	272,375
June	27,778	2,919.1	481,756
July	47,341	4,854.6	885,476
August	74,306	8,081.1	1,182,300
September	103,272	12,647.6	1,087,440
October	132,550	12,411.8	1,120,210

Source: Juan-Antino Morales, "Inflation Stabilization in Bolivia," in *Inflation Stabilization: The Experience of Israel, Argentina, Brazil, Bolivia, and Mexico*, ed. Michael Bruno et al. (Cambridge, MA: MIT Press, 1988).

supply, inflation rate, and its peso's exchange rate with the U.S. dollar during the period of hyperinflation. The exchange rate is actually the "black market" exchange rate, as the Bolivian government prohibited converting the peso to other currencies during the period. The data show that the growth in money supply, the rate of price inflation, and the depreciation of the peso against the dollar all moved in step with each other. This is just what PPP theory and monetary economics predict. Between April 1984 and July 1985, Bolivia's money supply increased by 17,433 percent, prices increased by 22,908 percent, and the value of the peso against the dollar fell by 24,662 percent! In October 1985, the Bolivian government instituted a dramatic stabilization plan—which included the introduction of a new currency and tight control of the money supply—and by 1987 the country's annual inflation rate was down to 16 percent.[9]

Another way of looking at the same phenomenon is that an increase in a country's money supply, which increases the amount of currency available, changes the relative demand and supply conditions in the foreign exchange market. If the U.S. money supply is growing more rapidly than U.S. output, dollars will be relatively more plentiful than the currencies of countries where monetary growth is closer to output growth. As a result of this relative increase in the supply of dollars, the dollar will depreciate on the foreign exchange market against the currencies of countries with slower monetary growth.

Government policy determines whether the rate of growth in a country's money supply is greater than the rate of growth in output. A government can increase the money supply simply by telling the country's central bank to issue more money. Governments tend to do this to finance public expenditure (building roads, paying government workers, paying for defense, etc.). Governments could finance public expenditure by raising taxes; but since nobody likes paying more taxes, politicians, in an effort to retain the support of voters, have a natural preference for expanding the money supply. Unfortunately, there is no magic money tree. The inevitable result of excessive growth in money supply is price inflation. However, this has not stopped governments around the world from expanding the money supply, with predictable results. If an international business is attempting to predict future movements in the value of a country's currency on the foreign exchange market, it should examine that country's policy toward monetary growth. If the government seems committed to controlling the rate of growth in money supply, the country's future inflation rate may be low (even if the current rate is high) and its currency should not depreciate too much on the foreign exchange market. If the government seems to lack the political will to control the rate of growth in money supply, the future inflation rate may be high, which is likely to cause its currency to depreciate. Historically, many Latin American governments have fallen into this latter category, including Argentina, Bolivia, and Brazil. More recently, many of the newly democratic states of Eastern Europe made the same mistake.

Empirical Tests of PPP Theory

PPP theory predicts that exchange rates are determined by relative prices, and that changes in relative prices will result in a change in exchange rates. A country in which price inflation is running wild should expect to see its currency depreciate against that of countries with lower inflation rates. This is intuitively appealing, but is it true in practice? There are several good examples of the connection between a country's price inflation and exchange rate position (such as Bolivia). However, extensive empirical testing of PPP theory has yielded mixed results.[10] Although PPP theory seems to yield relatively accurate predictions in the long run, it does not appear to be a strong predictor of short-run movements in exchange rates covering time spans of five years or less.[11] In addition, the theory seems to best predict exchange rate changes for countries with high rates of inflation and underdeveloped capital markets. The theory is less useful for predicting short-term exchange rate movements between the currencies of advanced industrialized nations that have relatively small differentials in inflation rates.

The failure to find a strong link between relative inflation rates and exchange rate movements has been referred to as the purchasing power parity puzzle. Several factors may explain the failure of PPP theory to predict exchange rates more accurately.[12] PPP theory assumes away transportation costs and barriers to trade. In practice, these factors are significant and they tend to create significant price differentials between countries. Transportation costs are certainly not trivial for many goods. Moreover, as we saw in Chapter 6, governments routinely intervene in international trade, creating tariff and nontariff barriers to cross-border trade. Barriers to trade limit the ability of traders to use arbitrage to equalize prices for the same product in different countries, which is required for the law of one price to hold. Government intervention in cross-border trade, by violating the assumption of efficient markets, weakens the link between relative price changes and changes in exchange rates predicted by PPP theory.

In addition, the PPP theory may not hold if many national markets are dominated by a handful of multinational enterprises that have sufficient market power to be able to exercise some influence over prices, control distribution channels, and differentiate their product offerings between nations.[13] In fact, this situation seems to prevail in a number of industries. In the detergent industry, two companies, Unilever and Procter & Gamble, dominate the market in nation after nation. In heavy earthmoving equipment, Caterpillar and Komatsu are global market leaders. In the market for semiconductor equipment, Applied Materials has a commanding market share lead in almost every important national market. Microsoft dominates the market for personal computer operating systems and applications systems around the world, and so on. In such cases, dominant enterprises may be able to exercise a degree of pricing power, setting different prices in different markets to reflect varying demand conditions. This is referred to as *price discrimination*. For price discrimination to work, arbitrage must be limited. According to this argument, enterprises with some market power may be able to control distribution channels and therefore limit the unauthorized resale (arbitrage) of products purchased in another national market. They may also be able to limit resale (arbitrage) by differentiating otherwise identical products among nations along some line, such as design or packaging.

For example, even though the version of Microsoft Office sold in China may be less expensive than the version sold in the United States, the use of arbitrage to equalize prices may be limited because few Americans would want a version that was based on Chinese characters. The design differentiation between Microsoft Office for China and for the United States means that the law of one price would not work for Microsoft Office, even if transportation costs were trivial and tariff barriers between the United States and China did not exist. If the inability to practice arbitrage were widespread enough, it would break the connection between changes in relative prices and exchange rates predicted by the PPP theorem and help explain the limited empirical support for this theory.

Another factor of some importance is that governments also intervene in the foreign exchange market in attempting to influence the value of their currencies. We will look at why and how they do this in Chapter 10. For now, the important thing to note is that governments regularly intervene in the foreign exchange market, and this further weakens the link between price changes and changes in exchange rates. One more factor explaining the failure of PPP theory to predict short-term movements in foreign exchange rates is the impact of investor psychology and other factors on currency purchasing decisions and exchange rate movements. We will discuss this issue in more detail later in this chapter.

INTEREST RATES AND EXCHANGE RATES Economic theory tells us that interest rates reflect expectations about likely future inflation rates. In countries where inflation is expected to be high, interest rates also will be high, because investors want compensation for the decline in the value of their money. This relationship was first formalized by economist Irvin Fisher and is referred to as the Fisher effect. The **Fisher effect** states that a country's nominal interest rate (i) is the sum of the required real rate of interest (r) and the expected rate of inflation over the period for which the funds are to be lent (I). More formally,

Fisher Effect
The theory that nominal interest rates (i) in each country equal the required real rate of interest (r) and expected rate of inflation (I) over the time period for which the funds are to be lent. That is, $i = r + I$.

$$i = r + I$$

For example, if the real rate of interest in a country is 5 percent and annual inflation is expected to be 10 percent, the nominal interest rate will be 15 percent. As predicted by the Fisher effect, a strong relationship seems to exist between inflation rates and interest rates.[14]

We can take this one step further and consider how it applies in a world of many countries and unrestricted capital flows. When investors are free to transfer capital between countries, real interest rates will be the same in every country. If differences in real interest rates did emerge between countries, arbitrage would soon equalize them. For example, if the real interest rate in Japan was 10 percent and only 6 percent in the United States, it would pay investors to borrow money in the United States and invest it in Japan. The resulting increase in the demand for money in the United States would raise the real interest rate there, while the increase in the supply of foreign money in Japan would lower the real interest rate there. This would continue until the two sets of real interest rates were equalized.

It follows from the Fisher effect that if the real interest rate is the same worldwide, any difference in interest rates between countries reflects differing expectations about inflation rates. Thus, if the expected rate of inflation in the United States is greater than that in Japan, U.S. nominal interest rates will be greater than Japanese nominal interest rates.

Since we know from PPP theory that there is a link (in theory at least) between inflation and exchange rates, and since interest rates reflect expectations about inflation, it follows that there must also be a link between interest rates and exchange rates. This link is known as the international Fisher effect (IFE). The **international Fisher effect** states that for any two countries, the spot exchange rate should change in an equal amount but in the opposite direction to the difference in nominal interest rates between the two countries. Stated more formally, the change in the spot exchange rate between the United States and Japan, for example, can be modeled as follows:

International Fisher Effect
The theory that for any two countries, the spot exchange rate should change in an equal amount but in the opposite direction to the difference in normal interest rates between countries.

$$[(S_1 - S_2)/S_2] \times 100 = i_\$ - i_¥$$

where $i_\$$ and $i_¥$ are the respective nominal interest rates in the United States and Japan, S_1 is the spot exchange rate at the beginning of the period, and S_2 is the spot exchange rate at the end of the period. If the U.S. nominal interest rate is higher than Japan's, reflecting greater expected inflation rates, the value of the dollar against the yen should fall by that interest rate differential in the future. So if the interest rate in the United States is 10 percent and in Japan it is 6 percent, we would expect the value of the dollar to depreciate by 4 percent against the Japanese yen.

Do interest rate differentials help predict future currency movements? The evidence is mixed; as in the case of PPP theory, in the long run, there seems to be a relationship between interest rate differentials and subsequent changes in spot exchange rates. However, considerable short-run deviations occur. Like PPP, the international Fisher effect is not a good predictor of short-run changes in spot exchange rates.[15]

INVESTOR PSYCHOLOGY AND BANDWAGON EFFECTS Empirical evidence suggests that neither PPP theory nor the international Fisher effect are particularly good at explaining short-term movements in exchange rates. One reason may be the impact of investor psychology on short-run exchange rate movements. Evidence accumulated over the last decade reveals that various psychological factors play an important role in determining the expectations of market traders as to likely future exchange rates.[16] In turn, expectations have a tendency to become self-fulfilling prophecies.

George Soros, whose Quantum Fund has been fantastically successful in managing hedge funds, has been criticized by world leaders for being able to cause huge changes in currency markets by his actions.
Najlah Feanny/Corbis

A good example of this mechanism occurred in September 1992 when the famous international financier George Soros made a huge bet against the British pound. Soros borrowed billions of pounds, using the assets of his investment funds as collateral, and immediately sold those pounds for German deutsche marks (this was before the advent of the euro). This technique, known as *short selling*, can earn the speculator enormous profits if he can subsequently buy back the pounds he sold at a much better exchange rate, and then use those pounds, purchased cheaply, to repay his loan. By selling pounds and buying deutsche marks, Soros helped to start pushing down the value of the pound on the foreign exchange markets. More important, when Soros started shorting the British pound, many foreign exchange traders, knowing Soros's reputation, jumped on the bandwagon and did likewise. This triggered a classic **bandwagon effect,** with traders moving as a herd in the same direction at the same time. As the bandwagon effect gained momentum, with more traders selling British pounds and purchasing deutsche marks in expectation of a decline in the pound, their expectations became a self-fulfilling prophecy. Massive selling forced down the value of the pound against the deutsche mark. In other words, the pound declined in value not so much because of any major shift in macroeconomic fundamentals, but because investors followed a bet placed by a major speculator, George Soros.

Bandwagon Effect
When traders move like a herd, all in the same direction and at the same time, in response to each others' perceived actions.

According to a number of studies, investor psychology and bandwagon effects play a major role in determining short-run movements of exchange rates.[17] However, these effects can be hard to predict. Investor psychology can be influenced by political factors and by microeconomic events, such as the investment decisions of individual firms, many of which are only loosely linked to macroeconomic fundamentals, such as relative inflation rates. Also, idiosyncratic behavior of politicians can both trigger and exacerbate bandwagon effects. Something like this seems to have occurred in Southeast Asia during 1997 when, one after another, the currencies of Thailand, Malaysia, South Korea, and Indonesia lost between 50 percent and 70 percent of their value against the U.S. dollar in a few months. For a detailed look at what occurred in South Korea, see the accompanying Country Focus box, next page. The collapse in the value of the Korean currency did not occur because South Korea had a higher inflation rate than the United States. It occurred because of an excessive buildup of dollar-denominated debt among South Korean firms. By mid-1997, it was clear that these companies were having trouble servicing this debt. Foreign investors, fearing a wave of corporate bankruptcies, took their money out of the country, exchanging won for U.S. dollars. As this began to depress the exchange rate, currency traders jumped on the bandwagon and speculated against the won (selling it short), and it was this that produced a collapse in the value of the won.

SUMMARY Relative monetary growth, relative inflation rates, and nominal interest rate differentials are all moderately good predictors of long-run changes in

Country **FOCUS**

Why Did the Korean Won Collapse?

In early 1997, South Korea could look back with pride on a 30-year "economic miracle" that had raised the country from the ranks of the poor and given it the world's eleventh-largest economy. By the end of 1997, the Korean currency, the won, had lost a staggering 67 percent of its value against the U.S. dollar, the South Korean economy lay in tatters, and the International Monetary Fund was overseeing a $55 billion rescue package. This sudden turn of events had its roots in investments made by South Korea's large industrial conglomerates, or *chaebol,* during the 1990s, often at the behest of politicians. In 1993, Kim Young-Sam, a populist politician, became president of South Korea. Kim took office during a mild recession and promised to boost economic growth by encouraging investment in export-oriented industries. He urged the *chaebol* to invest in new factories. South Korea enjoyed an investment-led economic boom in the 1994–95 period, but at a cost. The *chaebol,* always reliant on heavy borrowing, built up massive debts that were equivalent, on average, to four times their equity.

As the volume of investments ballooned during the 1990s, the quality of many of these investments declined significantly. The investments often were made on the basis of unrealistic projections about future demand conditions. This resulted in significant excess capacity and falling prices. An example is investments made by South Korean *chaebol* in semiconductor factories. Investments in such facilities surged in 1994 and 1995 when a temporary global shortage of dynamic random access memory chips (DRAMs) led to sharp price increases for this product. However, supply shortages had disappeared by 1996 and excess capacity was beginning to make itself felt, just as the South Koreans started to bring new DRAM factories on stream. The results were predictable; prices for DRAMs plunged and the earnings of South Korean DRAM manufacturers fell by 90 percent, which meant it was difficult for them to make scheduled payments on the debt they had acquired to build the extra capacity. The risk of corporate bankruptcy increased significantly, and not just in the semiconductor industry. South Korean companies were also investing heavily in a wide range of other industries, including automobiles and steel.

Matters were complicated further because much of the borrowing had been in U.S. dollars, as opposed to Korean won. This had seemed like a smart move at the time. The dollar/won exchange rate had been stable at around $1 = won 850. Interest rates on dollar borrowings were two to three percentage points lower than rates on borrowings in Korean won. Much of this borrowing was in the form of short-term, dollar-denominated debt that had to be paid back to the lending institution within one year. Although the borrowing strategy seemed to make sense, it involved risk. If the won were to depreciate against the dollar, the size of the debt burden that South Korean companies would have to service would increase when measured in the local currency. Currency depreciation would raise borrowing costs, depress corporate earnings, and increase the risk of bankruptcy. This is exactly what happened.

By mid-1997, foreign investors had become alarmed at the rising debt levels of South Korean companies, particularly given the emergence of excess capacity and plunging prices in several areas where the companies had made huge investments, including semiconductors, automobiles, and steel. Given increasing speculation that many South Korean companies would not be able to service their debt payments, foreign investors began to withdraw their money from the Korean stock and bond markets. In the process, they sold Korean won and purchased U.S. dollars. The selling of won accelerated in mid-1997 when two of the smaller chaebol filed for bankruptcy, citing their inability to meet scheduled debt payments. The increased supply of won and the increased demand for U.S. dollars pushed down the price of won in dollar terms from around won 840 = $1 to won 900 = $1.

At this point, the South Korean central bank stepped into the foreign exchange market to try to keep the exchange rate above won 1,000 = $1. It used dollars that it held in reserve to purchase won. The idea was to try to push up the price of the won in dollar terms and restore investor confidence in the stability of the exchange rate. This action, however, did not address the underlying debt problem faced by South Korean companies. Against a backdrop of more corporate bankruptcies in South Korea, and the government's stated intentions to take some troubled companies into state ownership, Standard & Poor's, the U.S. credit rating agency, downgraded South Korea's sovereign debt. This caused the Korean stock market to plunge 5.5 percent, and the Korean won to fall to won 930 = $1. According to S&P, "The downgrade of . . . ratings reflects the escalating cost to the government of supporting the country's ailing corporate and financial sectors."

The S&P downgrade triggered a sharp sale of the Korean won. In an attempt to protect the won against what was fast becoming a classic bandwagon effect, the South Korean central bank raised short-term interest rates to over 12 percent, more than double the inflation rate. The bank also stepped up its intervention in the currency exchange markets, selling dollars and purchasing won in an attempt to keep the exchange rate above won 1,000 = $1. The main effect of this action, however, was to rapidly deplete South Korea's foreign exchange reserves. These stood at $30 billion on November 1, but fell to only $15 billion two weeks later. With its foreign exchange reserves almost exhausted, the South Korean central bank gave up its defense of the won November 17. Immediately, the price of won in dollars plunged to around won 1,500 = $1, effectively increasing by 60 to 70 percent the amount of won heavily indebted Korean companies had to pay to meet scheduled payments on their dollar-denominated debt. These losses, due to adverse changes in foreign exchange rates, depressed the profits of many firms. South Korean firms suffered foreign exchange losses of more than $15 billion in 1997.

Sources: J. Burton and G. Baker, "The Country That Invested Its Way into Trouble," *Financial Times,* January 15, 1998, p. 8; J. Burton, "South Korea's Credit Rating Is Lowered," *Financial Times,* October 25, 1997, p. 3; J. Burton, "Currency Losses Hit Samsung Electronics," *Financial Times,* March 20, 1998, p. 24; and "Korean Firms' Foreign Exchange Losses Exceed US $15 Billion," *Business Korea,* February 1998, p. 55.

exchange rates. They are poor predictors of short-run changes in exchange rates, however, perhaps because of the impact of psychological factors, investor expectations, and bandwagon effects on short-term currency movements. This information is useful for an international business. Insofar as the long-term profitability of foreign investments, export opportunities, and the price competitiveness of foreign imports are all influenced by long-term movements in exchange rates, international businesses would be advised to pay attention to countries' differing monetary growth, inflation, and interest rates. International businesses that engage in foreign exchange transactions on a day-to-day basis could benefit by knowing some predictors of short-term foreign exchange rate movements. Unfortunately, short-term exchange rate movements are difficult to predict.

Exchange Rate Forecasting

LEARNING OBJECTIVE 5
Be familiar with the merits of different approaches toward exchange rate forecasting.

A company's need to predict future exchange rate variations raises the issue of whether it is worthwhile for the company to invest in exchange rate forecasting services to aid decision making. Two schools of thought address this issue. The efficient market school argues that forward exchange rates do the best possible job of forecasting future spot exchange rates, and, therefore, investing in forecasting services would be a waste of money. The other school of thought, the inefficient market school, argues that companies can improve the foreign exchange market's estimate of future exchange rates (as contained in the forward rate) by investing in forecasting services. In other words, this school of thought does not believe the forward exchange rates are the best possible predictors of future spot exchange rates.

THE EFFICIENT MARKET SCHOOL Forward exchange rates represent market participants' collective predictions of likely spot exchange rates at specified future dates. If forward exchange rates are the best possible predictor of future spot rates, it would make no sense for companies to spend additional money trying to forecast short-run exchange rate movements. Many economists believe the foreign exchange market is efficient at setting forward rates.[18] Remember that an efficient market is one in which prices reflect all available public information. (If forward rates reflect all available information about likely future changes in exchange rates, a company cannot beat the market by investing in forecasting services.)

If the foreign exchange market is efficient, forward exchange rates should be unbiased predictors of future spot rates. This does not mean the predictions will be accurate in any specific situation. It means inaccuracies will not be consistently above or below future spot rates; they will be random. Many empirical tests have addressed the efficient market hypothesis. Although most of the early work seems to confirm the hypothesis (suggesting that companies should not waste their money on forecasting services) some recent studies have challenged it.[19] There is some evidence that forward rates are not unbiased predictors of future spot rates and that more accurate predictions of future spot rates can be calculated from publicly available information.[20]

Inefficient Market A market in which prices do not reflect all available information.

THE INEFFICIENT MARKET SCHOOL

Citing evidence against the efficient market hypothesis, some economists believe the foreign exchange market is inefficient. An **inefficient market** is one in which prices do not reflect all available information. In an inefficient market, forward exchange rates will not be the best possible predictors of future spot exchange rates.

If this is true, it may be worthwhile for international businesses to invest in forecasting services (as many do). The belief is that professional exchange rate forecasts might provide better predictions of future spot rates than forward exchange rates do. However, the track record of professional forecasting services is not that good.[21] For example, forecasting services did not predict the 1997 currency crisis that swept through Southeast Asia.

APPROACHES TO FORECASTING

Assuming the inefficient market school is correct that the foreign exchange market's estimate of future spot rates can be improved, on what basis should forecasts be prepared? Here again, there are two schools of thought. One adheres to fundamental analysis, while the other uses technical analysis.

Fundamental Analysis Draws on economic theory to construct econometric models for predicting exchange rate movements.

Fundamental Analysis

Fundamental analysis draws on economic theory to construct sophisticated econometric models for predicting exchange rate movements. The variables contained in these models typically include those we have discussed, such as relative money supply growth rates, inflation rates, and interest rates. In addition, they may include variables related to balance-of-payments positions.

Running a deficit on a balance-of-payments current account (a country is importing more goods and services than it is exporting) creates pressures that may result in the depreciation of the country's currency on the foreign exchange market.[22] Consider what might happen if the United States was running a persistent current account balance-of-payments deficit (as in fact, it has been). Since the United States would be importing more than it was exporting, people in other countries would be increasing their holdings of U.S. dollars. If these people were willing to hold their dollars, the dollar's exchange rate would not be influenced. However, if these people converted their dollars into other currencies, the supply of dollars in the foreign exchange market would increase (as would demand for the other currencies). This shift in demand and supply would create pressures that could lead to the depreciation of the dollar against other currencies.

This argument hinges on whether people in other countries are willing to hold dollars. This depends on such factors as U.S. interest rates, the return on holding other dollar-denominated assets such as stocks in U.S. companies, and, most important, inflation rates. So, in a sense, the balance-of-payments situation is not a fundamental predictor of future exchange rate movements. For example, between 1998 and 2001, the U.S. dollar appreciated against most major currencies despite a growing balance-of-payments deficit. Relatively high real interest rates in the United States, coupled with low inflation and a booming U.S. stock market that attracted inward investment from foreign capital, made the dollar very attractive to foreigners, so they did not convert their dollars into other currencies. On the contrary, they converted other currencies into dollars to invest in U.S. financial assets, such as bonds and stocks, because they believed they could earn a high return by doing so. Capital flows into the United States fueled by foreigners who wanted to buy U.S. stocks and bonds kept the dollar strong despite the current account deficit. But what makes financial assets such as stocks and bonds attractive? The answer is prevailing interest rates and inflation rates, both of which affect underlying economic growth and the real return to holding U.S. financial assets. Given this, we are back to the argument that the fundamental determinants of exchange rates are monetary growth, inflation rates, and interest rates.

Technical Analysis **Technical analysis** uses price and volume data to determine past trends, which are expected to continue into the future. This approach does not rely on a consideration of economic fundamentals. Technical analysis is based on the premise that there are analyzable market trends and waves and that previous trends and waves can be used to predict future trends and waves. Since there is no theoretical rationale for this assumption of predictability, many economists compare technical analysis to fortune-telling. Despite this skepticism, technical analysis has gained favor in recent years.[23]

Technical Analysis
Uses price and volume data to determine past trends, which are expected to continue into the future.

Currency Convertibility

Until this point we have invalidly assumed that the currencies of various countries are freely convertible into other currencies. Due to government restrictions, a significant number of currencies are not freely convertible into other currencies. A country's currency is said to be **freely convertible** when the country's government allows both residents and nonresidents to purchase unlimited amounts of a foreign currency with it. A currency is said to be **externally convertible** when only nonresidents may convert it into a foreign currency without any limitations. A currency is **nonconvertible** when neither residents nor nonresidents are allowed to convert it into a foreign currency.

Freely Convertible Currency
When a country's government allows both residents and nonresidents to convert its currency into foreign currency.

Free convertibility is not universal. Many countries place some restrictions on their residents' ability to convert the domestic currency into a foreign currency (a policy of external convertibility). Restrictions range from the relatively minor (such as restricting the amount of foreign currency they may take with them out of the country on trips) to the major (such as restricting domestic businesses' ability to take foreign currency out of the country). External convertibility restrictions can limit domestic companies' ability to invest abroad, but they present few problems for foreign companies wishing to do business in that country. For example, even if the Japanese government tightly controlled the ability of its residents to convert the yen into U.S. dollars, all U.S. businesses with deposits in Japanese banks may at any time convert all their yen into dollars and take them out of the country. Thus, a U.S. company with a subsidiary in Japan is assured that it will be able to convert the profits from its Japanese operation into dollars and take them out of the country.

Externally Convertible Currency
When a country's government allows only nonresidents to convert the currency into foreign currency.

Serious problems arise, however, under a policy of nonconvertibility. This was the practice of the former Soviet Union, and it continued to be the practice in Russia until recently. When strictly applied, nonconvertibility means that although a U.S. company doing business in a country such as Russia may be able to generate significant ruble profits, it may not convert those rubles into dollars and take them out of the country. Obviously, this is not desirable for international business.

Nonconvertible Currency
When a country's government allows neither residents nor nonresidents to convert its currency into a foreign currency.

Governments limit convertibility to preserve their foreign exchange reserves. A country needs an adequate supply of these reserves to service its international debt commitments and to purchase imports. Governments typically impose convertibility restrictions on their currency when they fear that free convertibility will lead to a run on their foreign exchange reserves. This occurs when residents and nonresidents rush to convert their holdings of domestic currency into a foreign currency—a phenomenon

Capital Flight
When residents and nonresidents rush to convert their holdings of domestic currency into a foreign currency, usually taking place when domestic currency is depreciating rapidly or a country is facing dim economic prospects.

generally referred to as **capital flight.** Capital flight is most likely to occur when the value of the domestic currency is depreciating rapidly because of hyperinflation, or when a country's economic prospects are shaky in other respects. Under such circumstances, both residents and nonresidents tend to believe that their money is more likely to hold its value if it is converted into a foreign currency and invested abroad. Not only will a run on foreign exchange reserves limit the country's ability to service its international debt and pay for imports, but it will also lead to a precipitous depreciation in the exchange rate as residents and nonresidents unload their holdings of domestic currency on the foreign exchange markets (thereby increasing the market supply of the country's currency). Governments fear that the rise in import prices resulting from currency depreciation will lead to further increases in inflation. This fear provides another rationale for limiting convertibility.

Countertrade
The trade of goods and services produced in one country for the goods and services of another country.

Companies can deal with the nonconvertibility problem by engaging in countertrade. **Countertrade** refers to a range of barterlike agreements by which goods and services can be traded for other goods and services. Countertrade can make sense when a country's currency is nonconvertible. For example, consider the deal that General Electric struck with the Romanian government in 1984, when that country's currency was nonconvertible. When General Electric won a contract for a \$150 million generator project in Romania, it agreed to take payment in the form of Romanian goods that could be sold for \$150 million on international markets. In a similar case, the Venezuelan government negotiated a contract with Caterpillar in 1986 under which Venezuela would trade 350,000 tons of iron ore for Caterpillar heavy construction equipment. Caterpillar subsequently traded the iron ore to Romania in exchange for Romanian farm products, which it then sold on international markets for dollars.[24] More recently, in a 2003 deal the government of Indonesia entered into a countertrade with Libya under which Libya agreed to purchase \$540 million in Indonesian goods, including textiles, tea, coffee, electronics, plastics, and auto parts, in exchange for 50,000 barrels per day of Libyan crude oil.[25]

LEARNING OBJECTIVE 6
Understand the differences between translation, transaction, and economic exposure, and what managers can do to manage each type of exposure.

How important is countertrade? Twenty years ago, a large number of nonconvertible currencies existed in the world, and countertrade was quite significant. However, in recent years many governments have made their currencies freely convertible, and the percentage of world trade that involves countertrade is probably below 10 percent.[26]

To deal with nonconvertibility problems, companies will barter instead. Venezuela traded iron ore for Caterpillar construction equipment. Caterpillar in turn sold the iron ore to Romania for farm products, which it then sold on international markets for dollars. *Reprinted courtesy of Caterpillar, Inc.*

Focus on Managerial Implications

This chapter contains a number of clear implications for business. First, it is critical that international businesses understand the influence of exchange rates on the profitability of trade and investment deals. Adverse changes in exchange rates can make apparently profitable deals unprofitable. As noted, the risk introduced into international business transactions by changes in exchange rates is referred to as foreign exchange risk. Foreign exchange risk is usually divided into three main categories: transaction exposure, translation exposure, and economic exposure.

Transaction Exposure

Transaction exposure is the extent to which the income from individual transactions is affected by fluctuations in foreign exchange values. Such exposure includes obligations for the purchase or sale of goods and services at previously agreed prices and the borrowing or lending of funds in foreign currencies. For example, suppose in 2001 an American airline agrees to purchase 10 Airbus 330 aircraft for €120 million each for a total price of €1.20 billion, with delivery scheduled for 2005 and payment due then. When the contract was signed in 2001 the dollar/euro exchange rate stood at $1 = €1.10, so the American airline anticipates paying $1.09 billion for the 10 aircraft when they are delivered (€1.2 billion/1.1 = $1.09 billion). However, imagine that the value of the dollar depreciates against the euro over the intervening period, so that one dollar only buys €0.80 in 2005 when payment is due ($1 = €0.80). Now the total cost in U.S. dollars is $1.5 billion (€1.2 billion/0.80 = $1.5 billion), an increase of $0.41 billion! The transaction exposure here is $0.41 billion, which is the money lost due to an adverse movement in exchange rates between the time when the deal was signed and when the aircraft were paid for.

Transaction Exposure
The extent to which the income from individual transactions is affected by fluctuations in foreign exchange values.

Translation Exposure

Translation exposure is the impact of currency exchange rate changes on the reported financial statements of a company. Translation exposure is concerned with the present measurement of past events. The resulting accounting gains or losses are said to be unrealized—they are "paper" gains and losses—but they are still important. Consider a U.S. firm with a subsidiary in Mexico. If the value of the Mexican peso depreciates significantly against the dollar this would substantially reduce the dollar value of the Mexican subsidiary's equity. In turn, this would reduce the total dollar value of the firm's equity reported in its consolidated balance sheet. This would raise the apparent leverage of the firm (its debt ratio), which could increase the firm's cost of borrowing and potentially limit its access to the capital market. Similarly, if an American firm has a subsidiary in the European Union, and if the value of the euro depreciates rapidly against that of the dollar over a year, this will reduce the dollar value of the euro profit made by the European subsidiary, resulting in negative translation exposure. In fact, many U.S. firms suffered from significant negative translation exposure in Europe during 2000, precisely because the euro did depreciate rapidly against the dollar. The accompanying Management Focus box, next page, describes the experience of one such firm, Baxter International. In the 2002–04 period, the euro rose in value against the dollar. This positive translation exposure boosted the dollar profits of American multinationals with significant operations in Europe.

Translation Exposure
The extent to which the reported consolidated results and balance sheets of a corporation are affected by fluctuations in foreign exchange values.

Economic Exposure

Economic exposure is the extent to which a firm's future international earning power is affected by changes in exchange rates. Economic exposure is concerned with the long-run effect of changes in exchange rates on future prices, sales, and costs.

Economic Exposure
The extent to which a firm's future international earning power is affected by changes in exchange rates.

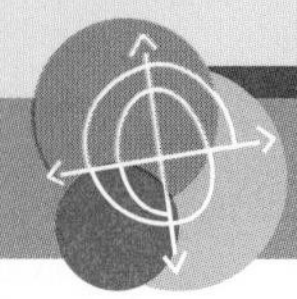

Management FOCUS

Translation Exposure at Baxter International

On July 20, 2000, the CEO of Baxter International, a U.S. producer of medical products, announced that the company's second-quarter results were better than expected due to strong global sales. The CEO confidently predicted that the company would hit its earnings and sales targets for all of 2000 and, due to continuing strong global sales, would grow revenues and earnings by a figure in the mid-teens for 2001.

Three months later when the company released its third-quarter results, the CEO had a less optimistic story to tell. Year 2000 earnings and revenues were still on track, but the company now expected much slower growth in 2001, which would reduce the projected increase in operating income by some $100 million. The main culprit, according to the CEO, was the continuing weakness of the euro against the U.S. dollar. At €1 = $0.83 the euro had depreciated by 10 percent since July, and 30 percent since the beginning of 1999. The continued weakness meant that the dollar value of Baxter's European revenues and earnings, which accounted for about 27 percent of the company's 2000 revenues, would decline significantly. Baxter was not alone; a host of other U.S. companies also announced that due to negative translation exposure to the euro, their financial results for late 2000 and probably much of 2001 would be lower than previously thought. According to one estimate, the decline in the value of the euro between June and September 2000 reduced the value of earnings for the Standard & Poor's index of 500 large U.S. companies by 3 percent.

In the aftermath, many wondered why companies such as Baxter hadn't hedged their European earnings against a fall in the value of the euro by entering the foreign exchange market and buying forward, locking in a more favorable dollar/euro exchange rate. The answer was that the costs of hedging had risen dramatically during 2000 due to the high volatility of the euro against the dollar. The high volatility meant that foreign exchange dealers were worried about the risk associated with selling forward contracts. It was very difficult for them to predict where the dollar/euro exchange rate might be in a few months, so they demanded a high premium from companies in return for selling a forward contract or writing a currency option. The costs of hedging an exchange rate are related to the volatility of that exchange rate (i.e., how much the value of currencies fluctuate against each other), with a doubling in volatility often tripling the cost of hedging as foreign exchange dealers demand a higher premium for writing increasingly risky forward contracts or other derivative contracts such as currency options. The average annual volatility between two currencies over a year is about 8 to 10 percent, but the volatility of the dollar/euro exchange rate had risen to 18 to 20 percent, tripling the cost of hedging. For Baxter, that volatility meant the costs of hedging the euro against the dollar would run into tens of millions of dollars. So in mid-2000, Baxter decided to take a risk and not hedge, effectively betting that the euro would stabilize against the dollar. It didn't, and Baxter lost the gamble.

Source: S. McMurray, "The Lost Art of Hedging," *Institutional Investor*, December 2000, pp. 63–69.

This is distinct from transaction exposure, which is concerned with the effect of exchange rate changes on individual transactions, most of which are short-term affairs that will be executed within a few weeks or months. Consider the effect of wide swings in the value of the dollar on many U.S. firms' international competitiveness. The rapid rise in the value of the dollar on the foreign exchange market in the 1990s hurt the price competitiveness of many U.S. producers in world markets. U.S. manufacturers that relied heavily on exports, such as Caterpillar, saw their export volume and world market share decline. The reverse phenomenon occurred in the 2000–04 period, when the dollar declined against most major currencies. The fall in the value of the dollar helped increase the price competitiveness of U.S. manufacturers in world markets.

Reducing Translation and Transaction Exposure

A number of tactics can help firms minimize their transaction and translation exposure. These tactics primarily protect short-term cash flows from adverse changes in exchange rates. We have already discussed two of these tactics at length in the chapter, entering into forward exchange rate contracts and buying swaps. In addition to buying forward and using swaps, firms can minimize their foreign exchange exposure through leading and lagging payables and receivables—that is, paying suppliers and collecting payment from customers early or late depending on expected exchange rate movements. A **lead strategy** involves attempting to collect foreign currency receivables (payments from customers) early when a foreign currency is expected to depreciate and paying foreign currency payables (to suppliers) before they are due when a currency is expected to appreciate. A **lag strategy** involves delaying collection of foreign currency receivables if that currency is expected to appreciate and delaying payables if the currency is expected to depreciate. Leading and lagging involves accelerating payments from weak-currency to strong-currency countries and delaying inflows from strong-currency to weak-currency countries.

Lead Strategy
Attempting to collect foreign currency receivables early when a foreign currency is expected to depreciate and paying foreign currency payables before they are due when a currency is expected to appreciate.

Lead and lag strategies can be difficult to implement, however. The firm must be in a position to exercise some control over payment terms. Firms do not always have this kind of bargaining power, particularly when they are dealing with important customers who are in a position to dictate payment terms. Also, because lead and lag strategies can put pressure on a weak currency, many governments limit leads and lags. For example, some countries set 180 days as a limit for receiving payments for exports or making payments for imports.

Lag Strategy
Delaying collection of foreign currency receivables if that currency is expected to appreciate and delaying payables if that currency is expected to depreciate.

Reducing Economic Exposure

Reducing economic exposure requires strategic choices that go beyond the realm of financial management. The key to reducing economic exposure is to distribute the firm's productive assets to various locations so the firm's long-term financial well-being is not severely affected by adverse changes in exchange rates. As discussed in the opening case, STMicro is now pursuing this strategy. It is moving some of its production from Europe to Asia as a *real hedge* against the possibility that the euro may continue to gain strength against the U.S. dollar in the future. In theory, by locating production in different regions that use different currencies, the company can adjust capacity utilization so that it produces more in the region where currency values are most favorable. Thus, having factories in France (part of the euro zone) and China gives STMicro the ability to adjust capacity if, say, the euro weakens significantly against the dollar and the Chinese currency appreciates against the dollar; the company can then work three shifts in France and just one shift in China.

Other Steps for Managing Foreign Exchange Risk

The firm needs to develop a mechanism for ensuring it maintains an appropriate mix of tactics and strategies for minimizing its foreign exchange exposure. Although there is no universal agreement as to the components of this mechanism, a number of common themes stand out.[27] First, central control of exposure is needed to protect resources efficiently and ensure that each subunit adopts the correct mix of tactics and strategies. Many companies have set up in-house foreign exchange centers. Although such centers may not be able to execute all foreign exchange deals—particularly in large, complex multinationals where myriad transactions may be pursued simultaneously—they should at least set guidelines for the firm's subsidiaries to follow.

Second, firms should distinguish between, on one hand, transaction and translation exposure and, on the other, economic exposure. Many companies seem to focus on reducing their transaction and translation exposure and pay scant attention to economic exposure, which may have more profound long-term implications.[28] Firms need to develop strategies for dealing with economic exposure. For example, Black & Decker, the maker of power tools, has a strategy for actively managing its economic risk. The key to Black & Decker's strategy is flexible sourcing. In response to foreign exchange movements, Black & Decker can move production from one location to another to offer the most competitive pricing. The company manufactures in more than a dozen locations around the world—in Europe, Australia, Brazil, Mexico, and Japan. More than 50 percent of the company's productive assets are based outside North America. Although each of Black & Decker's factories focuses on one or two products to achieve economies of scale, there is considerable overlap. On average, the company runs its factories at no more than 80 percent capacity, so most are able to switch rapidly from producing one product to producing another or to add a product. This allows a factory's production to be changed in response to foreign exchange movements. For example, if the dollar depreciates against other currencies, the amount of imports into the United States from overseas subsidiaries can be reduced and the amount of exports from U.S. subsidiaries to other locations can be increased.[29]

Third, the need to forecast future exchange rate movements cannot be overstated, though, as we saw earlier in the chapter, this is a tricky business. No model comes close to perfectly predicting future movements in foreign exchange rates. The best that can be said is that in the short run, forward exchange rates provide the best predictors of exchange rate movements, and in the long run, fundamental economic factors—particularly relative inflation rates—should be watched because they influence exchange rate movements. Some firms attempt to forecast exchange rate movements in-house; others rely on outside forecasters. However, all such forecasts are imperfect attempts to predict the future.

Fourth, firms need to establish good reporting systems so the central finance function (or in-house foreign exchange center) can regularly monitor the firm's exposure positions. Such reporting systems should enable the firm to identify any exposed accounts, the exposed position by currency of each account, and the time periods covered.

Finally, on the basis of the information it receives from exchange rate forecasts and its own regular reporting systems, the firm should produce monthly foreign exchange exposure reports. These reports should identify how cash flows and balance sheet elements might be affected by forecasted changes in exchange rates. The reports can then be used by management as a basis for adopting tactics and strategies to hedge against undue foreign exchange risks.

Surprisingly, some of the largest and most sophisticated firms don't take such precautionary steps, exposing themselves to very large foreign exchange risks. Thus as we have seen in this chapter, STMicro, South African Airlines, and Baxter International all suffered significant losses during the early 2000s due to a failure to hedge their foreign exchange exposure.

Key Terms

foreign exchange market, p. 297
exchange rate p. 297
foreign exchange risk p. 297
currency speculation p. 298
hedging p. 299
spot exchange rates p. 299
forward exchange p. 300
forward exchange rates p. 300
currency swap p. 301
arbitrage p. 302
law of one price p. 304
efficient market p. 304
relatively efficient markets p. 304
Fisher effect p. 310
international Fisher effect p. 310
bandwagon effect p. 311
inefficient market p. 314
fundamental analysis p. 314
technical analysis p. 315
freely convertible currency p. 315
externally convertible currency p. 315
nonconvertible currency p. 315
capital flight p. 316
countertrade p. 316
transaction exposure p. 317
translation exposure p. 317
economic exposure p. 317
lead strategy p. 319
lag strategy p. 319

Summary

This chapter explained how the foreign exchange market works, examined the forces that determine exchange rates, and then discussed the implications of these factors for international business. Given that changes in exchange rates can dramatically alter the profitability of foreign trade and investment deals, this is an area of major interest to international business. The chapter made the following points:

1. One function of the foreign exchange market is to convert the currency of one country into the currency of another. A second function of the foreign exchange market is to provide insurance against foreign exchange risk.
2. The spot exchange rate is the exchange rate at which a dealer converts one currency into another currency on a particular day.
3. Foreign exchange risk can be reduced by using forward exchange rates. A forward exchange rate is an exchange rate governing future transactions. Foreign exchange risk can also be reduced by engaging in currency swaps. A swap is the simultaneous purchase and sale of a given amount of foreign exchange for two different value dates.
4. The law of one price holds that in competitive markets that are free of transportation costs and barriers to trade, identical products sold in different countries must sell for the same price when their price is expressed in the same currency.
5. Purchasing power parity theory states the price of a basket of particular goods should be roughly equivalent in each country. It predicts that the exchange rate will change if relative prices change.
6. The rate of change in countries' relative prices depends on their relative inflation rates. A country's inflation rate seems to be a function of the growth in its money supply.
7. The PPP theory of exchange rate changes yields relatively accurate predictions of long-term trends in exchange rates, but not of short-term movements. The failure of PPP theory to predict exchange rate changes more accurately may be due to transportation costs, barriers to trade and investment, and the impact of psychological factors such as bandwagon effects on market movements and short-run exchange rates.
8. Interest rates reflect expectations about inflation. In countries where inflation is expected to be high, interest rates also will be high.
9. The international Fisher effect states that for any two countries, the spot exchange rate should change in an equal amount but in the opposite direction to the difference in nominal interest rates.
10. The most common approach to exchange rate forecasting is fundamental analysis. This relies on variables such as money supply growth, inflation rates, nominal interest rates, and balance-of-payments positions to predict future changes in exchange rates.
11. In many countries, the ability of residents and nonresidents to convert local currency into a foreign currency is restricted by government policy. A government restricts the convertibility of its currency to protect the country's foreign exchange reserves and to halt any capital flight.
12. Problematic for international business is a policy of nonconvertibility, which prohibits residents and nonresidents from exchanging local currency for foreign currency. Nonconvertibility makes it very difficult to engage in international trade and investment in the country. One way of coping with the nonconvertibility problem is to engage in countertrade—to trade goods and services for other goods and services.
13. The three types of exposure to foreign exchange risk are transaction exposure, translation exposure, and economic exposure.
14. Tactics that insure against transaction and translation exposure include buying forward, using currency swaps, leading and lagging payables and receivables, manipulating transfer prices, using local debt financing, accelerating dividend payments, and adjusting capital budgeting to reflect foreign exchange exposure.
15. Reducing a firm's economic exposure requires strategic choices about how the firm's productive assets are distributed around the globe.

16. To manage foreign exchange exposure effectively, the firm must exercise centralized oversight over its foreign exchange hedging activities, recognize the difference between transaction exposure and economic exposure, forecast future exchange rate movements, establish good reporting systems within the firm to monitor exposure positions, and produce regular foreign exchange exposure reports that can be used as a basis for action.

Critical Thinking and Discussion Questions

1. The interest rate on South Korean government securities with one-year maturity is 4 percent, and the expected inflation rate for the coming year is 2 percent. The interest rate on U.S. government securities with one-year maturity is 7 percent, and the expected rate of inflation is 5 percent. The current spot exchange rate for Korean won is \$1 = W1,200. Forecast the spot exchange rate one year from today. Explain the logic of your answer.
2. Two countries, Great Britain and the United States, produce just one good: beef. Suppose the price of beef in the United States is \$2.80 per pound and in Britain it is £3.70 per pound.
   a. According to PPP theory, what should the dollar/pound spot exchange rate be?
   b. Suppose the price of beef is expected to rise to \$3.10 in the United States and to £4.65 in Britain. What should the one-year forward dollar/pound exchange rate be?
   c. Given your answers to parts a and b, and given that the current interest rate in the United States is 10 percent, what would you expect the current interest rate to be in Britain?
3. You manufacture wine goblets. In mid-June you receive an order for 10,000 goblets from Japan. Payment of ¥400,000 is due in mid-December. You expect the yen to rise from its present rate of \$1 = ¥130 to \$1 = ¥100 by December. You can borrow yen at 6 percent a year. What should you do?
4. You are the CFO of a U.S. firm whose wholly owned subsidiary in Mexico manufactures component parts for your U.S. assembly operations. The subsidiary has been financed by bank borrowings in the United States. One of your analysts told you that the Mexican peso is expected to depreciate by 30 percent against the dollar on the foreign exchange markets over the next year. What actions, if any, should you take?

Research Task  http://globalEDGE.msu.edu

Use the globalEDGE site (http://globalEDGE.msu.edu/) to complete the following exercises:

1. You are assigned the duty of ensuring the availability of 100 million Japanese Yen for a payment scheduled for tomorrow. Your company possesses only US Dollars, so identify a website that provides *real-time exchange rates*, and find the spot exchange rate for Japanese Yen. How many dollars do you have to spend to acquire the amount of Yen required?
2. As an entrepreneur, you are interested in expanding your energy business to Kuwait. As part of your initial analysis, you would like a general analysis performed on the current state of the Kuwaiti power and energy industry. Using a resource that allows you to conduct *country analysis*, develop a short report of the current status of Kuwait's energy industry. Convert all relevant financial estimates to Kuwaiti Dinar, using the resource from the previous exercise. Is the exchange rate listed in the report similar to the current rate of exchange? How much has the exchange rate changed since the publication of this report?

The Rising Euro Hammers Auto Parts Manufacturers

Udo Pfeiffer, the CEO of SMS Elotherm, a German manufacturer of machine tools to engineer crankshafts for cars, signed a deal in late November 2004, to supply the U.S. operations of DaimlerChrysler with $1.5 million worth of machines. The machines would be manufactured in Germany and exported to the United States. When the deal was signed, Pfeiffer calculated that at the agreed price, the machines would yield a profit of €30,000 each. Within three days that profit had declined by €8,000! The dollar had slid precipitously against the euro. SMS would be paid in dollars by DaimlerChrysler, but when translated back into euros, the price had declined. Since the company's costs were in euros, the declining revenues when expressed in euros were squeezing profit margins.

With the exchange rate standing at €1 = $1.33 in early December 2004, Pfeiffer was deeply worried. He knew that if the dollar declined further to around €1 = $1.50, SMS would be losing money on its sales to America. He could try to raise the dollar price of his products to compensate for the fall in the value of the dollar, but he knew that was unlikely to work. The market for machine tools was very competitive, and manufacturers were constantly pressuring machine tool companies to lower prices, not raise them.

Another small German supplier to U.S. automobile companies, Keiper, was faring somewhat better. In 2001 Keiper, which manufactures metal frames for automobile seats, opened a plant in London, Ontario, to supply the U.S. operations of DaimlerChrysler. At the time the investment was made, the exchange rate was €1 = $1. Management at Keiper had agonized over whether the investment made sense. Some in the company felt that it was better to continue exporting from Germany. Others argued that Keiper would benefit from being close to a major customer. Now with the euro appreciating every day, it looked like a smart move. Keiper had a real hedge against the rising value of the euro. But the advantages of being based in Canada were tempered by two things; first, the U.S. dollar had also depreciated against the Canadian dollar, although not by as much as its depreciation against the euro. Second, Keiper was still importing parts from Germany, and the euro had also appreciated against the Canadian dollar, raising the costs at Keiper's Ontario plant.

Source: Adapted from M. Landler, "Dollar's Fall Drains Profit of European Small Business," *The New York Times,* December 2, 2004, p. C1.

Case Discussion Questions

1. Could SMS Elotherm have taken steps to avoid the position in which it eventually found itself? What are those steps? Why do you think the company did not take these steps?
2. Why was Keiper weathering the rise of the euro better than SMS?
3. In retrospect, what might Keiper have done differently to improve the value of its real hedge against a rise in the value of the euro?
4. If the U.S. dollar had appreciated against the euro and Canadian dollar, instead of depreciating, which company would have done better? Why?

part 4 Global Money System

LEARNING OBJECTIVES:

1. Be familiar with the historical development of the modern global monetary system.
2. Discuss the role played by the world bank and the IMF in the international monetary system.
3. Be familiar with the differences between a fixed and floating exchange rate system.
4. Know what exchange rate regimes are used in the world today and why countries adopt different exchange rate regimes.
5. Understand the debate surrounding the role of the IMF in the management of financial crises.
6. Understand the implications of the global monetary system for currency management and business strategy.

chapter 10

The International Monetary System

China's Managed Float

opening case

In 1994, China pegged the value of its currency, the yuan, to the U.S. dollar at an exchange rate of $1 = 8.28 yuan. For the next 11 years, the value of the yuan moved in lockstep with the value of the U.S. dollar against other currencies. By early 2005, however, pressure was building for China to alter its exchange rate policy and let the yuan float freely against the dollar.

Underlying this pressure were claims that after years of rapid economic growth and foreign capital inflows, the pegged exchange rate undervalued the yuan by as much as 40 percent. In turn, the cheap yuan was helping to fuel a boom in Chinese exports to the West, particularly to the United States, whose trade deficit with China expanded to a record $160 billion in 2004. Job losses among American manufacturing companies created political pressures in the United States for the government to push the Chinese to let the yuan float freely against the dollar. American manufacturers complained that they could not compete against "artificially cheap" Chinese imports. In early 2005, senators Charles Schumer and Lindsay Graham tried to get the Senate to impose a 27.5 percent tariff on imports from China unless the Chinese agreed to revalue its currency against the U.S. dollar. Although the move was defeated, Schumer and Graham vowed to revisit the issue. For its part, the Bush administration pressured China from 2003 onward, urging the government to adopt a more flexible exchange rate policy.

Keeping the yuan pegged to the dollar was also becoming increasingly problematic for the Chinese. The trade surplus with the United States, coupled with strong inflows of foreign investment, led to a surge of dollars into China. To maintain the exchange rate, the Chinese central bank regularly purchased dollars from commercial banks, issuing them yuan at the official exchange rate. As a result, by mid-2005 China's foreign exchange reserves had risen to more than $700 billion. They were forecast to hit $1 trillion by the end of

2006. The Chinese were reportedly buying some $15 billion each month in an attempt to maintain the dollar/yuan exchange rate. When the Chinese central bank issues yuan to mop up excess dollars, the authorities are in effect expanding the domestic money supply. The Chinese banking system is now awash with money, and there is growing concern that excessive lending could create a financial bubble and a surge in price inflation, which might destabilize the economy.

On July 25, 2005, the Chinese finally bowed to the pressure. The government announced that it would abandon the peg against the dollar in favor of a "link" to a basket of currencies, which included the euro, yen, and U.S. dollar. Simultaneously, the government would revalue the yuan against the U.S. dollar by 2.1 percent and allow that value to move by 0.3 percent a day. The yuan was allowed to move by 1.5 percent a day against other currencies.

Many American observers and politicians thought that the Chinese move was too limited. They called for the Chinese to relax further their control over the dollar/yuan exchange rate. The Chinese resisted, but by early 2006, pressure was increasing on the Chinese to take action. With the U.S. trade deficit with China hitting a new record of $202 billion in 2005, senators Schumer and Graham once more crafted a bill that would place a 27.5 percent tariff on Chinese imports unless the Chinese allowed the yuan to depreciate further against the dollar. The Chinese responded by inviting the senators to China, where they convinced them, for now at least, that the country will move progressively toward a more flexible exchange rate policy.

Sources: B. Bremner et al., "The Yuan Grows Up," *BusinessWeek*, August 8, 2005, p. 44; "Patching the Basket: The Yuan," *The Economist*, October 1, 2005, p. 83; R. McGregor, "Renminbi Revaluation Will Slow Rise in Foreign Exchange Reserves," *Financial Times*, January 1, 2006, p. 3; and "Senators Back off Showdown with China over Yuan," *China Daily*, March 29, 2006, **www.chinadaily.com.**

Introduction

International Monetary System The institutional arrangements countries adopt that govern exchange rates.

Floating Exchange Rate A system under which the exchange rate for converting one currency into another is continuously adjusted depending on the law of supply and demand.

The **international monetary system** refers to the institutional arrangements that govern exchange rates. In Chapter 9, we assumed the foreign exchange market was the primary institution for determining exchange rates, and the impersonal market forces of demand and supply determined the relative value of any two currencies (i.e., their exchange rate). Furthermore, we explained that the demand and supply of currencies is influenced by their respective countries' relative inflation rates and interest rates. When the foreign exchange market determines the relative value of a currency, we say that the country is adhering to a **floating exchange rate** regime. The world's four major trading currencies—the U.S. dollar, the EU euro, the Japanese yen, and the British pound—are all free to float against each other. Thus, their exchange rates are determined by market forces and fluctuate against each other day to day, if not minute to minute. However, the exchange rates of many currencies are not determined by the free play of market forces; other institutional arrangements are adopted.

Many of the world's developing nations peg their currencies, primarily to the dollar or the euro. A **pegged exchange rate** means the value of the currency is fixed relative to a reference currency, such as the U.S. dollar, and then the exchange rate between that currency and other currencies is determined by the reference currency exchange rate. For example, as discussed in the opening case, until July 2005 China pegged its currency to the dollar, and the exchange rate between the Chinese yuan and the euro was determined by the U.S. dollar/euro exchange rate.

Pegged Exchange Rate
A system under which the value of a country's currency is fixed relative to a reference currency, and then the exchange rate between that currency and other currencies is determined by the reference currency exchange rate.

Other countries, while not adopting a formal pegged rate, try to hold the value of their currency within some range against an important reference currency such as the U.S. dollar, or a "basket" of currencies. This is often referred to as a **dirty float**. It is a float because in theory, the value of the currency is determined by market forces, but it is a *dirty float* (as opposed to a clean float) because the central bank of a country will intervene in the foreign exchange market to try to maintain the value of its currency if it depreciates too rapidly against an important reference currency. This has been the policy adopted by the Chinese since July 2005 (see the opening case). The value of the Chinese currency, the yuan, has been linked to a basket of other currencies, including the dollar, yen, and euro, and it is allowed to vary in value against individual currencies, but only within tight limits.

Dirty Float
A system under which a country's currency is nominally allowed to float freely against other currencies, but in which the government will intervene if it believes the currency has deviated too far from its fair value.

Still other countries have operated with a **fixed exchange rate**; that is, the values of a set of currencies are fixed against each other at some mutually agreed on exchange rate. Before the introduction of the euro in 2000, several member states of the European Union operated with fixed exchange rates within the context of the European Monetary System (EMS). For a quarter of a century after World War II, the world's major industrial nations participated in a fixed exchange rate system. Although this system collapsed in 1973, some still argue that the world should attempt to reestablish it.

Fixed Exchange Rate
A system under which the exchange rate for converting one currency into another is set at a constant rate.

In this chapter, we will explain how the international monetary system works and point out its implications for international business. To understand how the system works, we must review its evolution. We will begin with a discussion of the gold standard and its breakup during the 1930s. Then we will discuss the 1944 Bretton Woods conference. This established the basic framework for the post–World War II international monetary system. The Bretton Woods system called for fixed exchange rates against the U.S. dollar. Under this fixed exchange rate system, the value of most currencies in terms of U.S. dollars was fixed for long periods and allowed to change only under a specific set of circumstances. The Bretton Woods conference also created two major international institutions that play a role in the international monetary system—the International Monetary Fund and the World Bank. The IMF was given the task of maintaining order in the international monetary system; the World Bank's role was to promote development.

Today, both these institutions continue to play major roles in the world economy and in the international monetary system. In 1997 and 1998, for example, the IMF helped several Asian countries deal with the dramatic decline in the value of their currencies that occurred during the Asian financial crisis that started in 1997. By 2005, the IMF had programs in 59 countries, the majority in the developing world, and had some $71 billion in loans to nations.[1] However, there has been a vigorous debate about the role of the IMF and to a lesser extent the World Bank and the appropriateness of their policies for many developing nations. Several prominent critics claim that in some cases, IMF policies make things worse, not better. The debate over the role of the IMF took on new urgency given the institution's extensive involvement in the economies of developing countries during the late 1990s and early 2000s. Accordingly, we shall discuss the issue in some depth.

The Bretton Woods system of fixed exchange rates collapsed in 1973. Since then, the world has operated with a mixed system in which some currencies are allowed to float freely, but many are either managed by government intervention or pegged to another currency. We will explain the reasons for the failure of the Bretton Woods system as well as the nature of the present system. We will also discuss how pegged exchange rate systems work. More than three decades after the breakdown of the Bretton Woods system, the debate continues over what kind of exchange rate regime is best for the world. Some economists advocate a system in which major currencies are allowed to float against each other. Others argue for a return to a fixed exchange rate regime similar to the one established at Bretton Woods. This debate is intense and important, and we will examine the arguments of both sides.

Finally, we will discuss the implications of all this material for international business. We will see how the exchange rate policy adopted by a government can have an important impact on the outlook for business operations in a given country. If government exchange rate policies result in a currency devaluation, for example, exporters based in that country may benefit as their products become more price competitive in foreign markets. Alternatively, importers will suffer from an increase in the price of their products. We will also look at how the policies adopted by the IMF can have an impact on the economic outlook for a country and, accordingly, on the costs and benefits of doing business in that country.

The Gold Standard

LEARNING OBJECTIVE 1
Be familiar with the historical development of the modern global monetary system.

The gold standard had its origin in the use of gold coins as a medium of exchange, unit of account, and store of value—a practice that dates to ancient times. When international trade was limited in volume, payment for goods purchased from another country was typically made in gold or silver. However, as the volume of international trade expanded in the wake of the Industrial Revolution, a more convenient means of financing international trade was needed. Shipping large quantities of gold and silver around the world to finance international trade seemed impractical. The solution adopted was to arrange for payment in paper currency and for governments to agree to convert the paper currency into gold on demand at a fixed rate.

Gold Standard
The practice of pegging currencies to gold and guaranteeing convertibility.

MECHANICS OF THE GOLD STANDARD A country that follows the **gold standard** pegs its currency to gold and guarantees convertibility. By 1880, most of the world's major trading nations, including Great Britain, Germany, Japan, and the United States, had adopted the gold standard. Given a common gold standard, the value of any currency in units of any other currency (the exchange rate) was easy to determine.

For example, under the gold standard, one U.S. dollar was defined as equivalent to 23.22 grains of "fine" (pure) gold. Thus, one could, in theory, demand that the U.S. government convert that one dollar into 23.22 grains of gold. Since there are 480 grains in an ounce, one ounce of gold cost \$20.67 (480/23.22). The amount of a currency needed to purchase one ounce of gold was referred to as the **gold par value**. The British pound was valued at 113 grains of fine gold. In other words, one ounce of gold cost £4.25 (480/113). From the gold par values of pounds and dollars, we can calculate what the exchange rate was for converting pounds into dollars; it was £1 = \$4.87 (i.e., \$20.67/£4.25).

Gold Par Value
The amount of currency needed to purchase one ounce of gold.

STRENGTH OF THE GOLD STANDARD The great strength claimed for the gold standard was that it contained a powerful mechanism for achieving balance-of-trade equilibrium by all countries.[2] A country is said to be in **balance-of-trade equilibrium** when the income its residents earn from exports is equal to the money its residents pay to other countries for imports (the current account of its balance of payments is in balance). Suppose there are only two countries in the world, Japan and the United States. Imagine Japan's trade balance is in surplus because it exports more to the United States than it imports from the United States. Japanese

Balance-of-Trade Equilibrium
Reached when the income a country's residents earned from exports equals the money they pay for imports.

exporters are paid in U.S. dollars, which they exchange for Japanese yen at a Japanese bank. The Japanese bank submits the dollars to the U.S. government and demands payment of gold in return. (This is a simplification of what would occur, but it will make our point.)

Under the gold standard, when Japan has a trade surplus, there will be a net flow of gold from the United States to Japan. These gold flows automatically reduce the U.S. money supply and swell Japan's money supply. As we saw in Chapter 9, there is a close connection between money supply growth and price inflation. An increase in money supply will raise prices in Japan, while a decrease in the U.S. money supply will push U.S. prices downward. The rise in the price of Japanese goods will decrease demand for these goods, while the fall in the price of U.S. goods will increase demand for these goods. Thus, Japan will start to buy more from the United States, and the United States will buy less from Japan, until a balance-of-trade equilibrium is achieved.

This adjustment mechanism seems so simple and attractive that even today, almost 70 years after the final collapse of the gold standard, some people believe the world should return to a gold standard.

THE PERIOD BETWEEN THE WARS: 1918–1939 The gold standard worked reasonably well from the 1870s until the start of World War I in 1914, when it was abandoned. During the war, several governments financed part of their massive military expenditures by printing money. This resulted in inflation, and by the war's end in 1918, price levels were higher everywhere. The United States returned to the gold standard in 1919, Great Britain in 1925, and France in 1928.

Great Britain returned to the gold standard by pegging the pound to gold at the prewar gold parity level of £4.25 per ounce, despite substantial inflation between 1914 and 1925. This priced British goods out of foreign markets, which pushed the country into a deep depression. When foreign holders of pounds lost confidence in Great Britain's commitment to maintaining its currency's value, they began converting their holdings of pounds into gold. The British government saw that it could not satisfy the demand for gold without seriously depleting its gold reserves, so it suspended convertibility in 1931.

The United States followed suit and left the gold standard in 1933 but returned to it in 1934, raising the dollar price of gold from $20.67 per ounce to $35 per ounce. Since more dollars were needed to buy an ounce of gold than before, the implication was that the dollar was worth less. This effectively amounted to a devaluation of the dollar relative to other currencies. Thus, before the devaluation, the pound/dollar exchange rate was £1 = $4.87, but after the devaluation it was £1 = $8.24. By reducing the price of U.S. exports and increasing the price of imports, the government was trying to create employment in the United States by boosting output (the U.S. government was basically using the exchange rate as an instrument of trade policy—something it now accuses China of doing). However, a number of other countries adopted a similar tactic, and in the cycle of competitive devaluations that soon emerged, no country could win.

The net result was the shattering of any remaining confidence in the system. With countries devaluing their currencies at will, one could no longer be certain how much gold a currency could buy. Instead of holding onto another country's currency, people often tried to change it into gold immediately, lest the country devalue its currency in the intervening period. This put pressure on the gold reserves of various countries, forcing them to suspend gold convertibility. By the start of World War II in 1939, the gold standard was dead.

The Bretton Woods System

LEARNING OBJECTIVE 2
Discuss the role played by the world bank and the IMF in the international monetary system.

In 1944, at the height of World War II, representatives from 44 countries met at Bretton Woods, New Hampshire, to design a new international monetary system. With the collapse of the gold standard and the Great Depression of the 1930s fresh in their minds, these statesmen were determined to build an enduring economic order that would facilitate postwar economic growth. There was consensus that fixed exchange rates were desirable. In addition, the conference participants wanted to avoid the senseless competitive devaluations of the 1930s, and they recognized that the gold standard would not assure this. The major problem with the gold standard as previously constituted was that no multinational institution could stop countries from engaging in competitive devaluations.

The agreement reached at Bretton Woods established two multinational institutions: the International Monetary Fund and the World Bank. The task of the IMF would be to maintain order in the international monetary system and that of the World Bank would be to promote general economic development. The Bretton Woods agreement also called for a system of fixed exchange rates that would be policed by the IMF. Under the agreement, all countries were to fix the value of their currency in terms of gold but were not required to exchange their currencies for gold. Only the dollar remained convertible into gold—at a price of $35 per ounce. Each country decided what it wanted its exchange rate to be vis-à-vis the dollar and then calculated the gold par value of the currency based on that selected dollar exchange rate. All participating countries agreed to try to maintain the value of their currencies within 1 percent of the par value by buying or selling currencies (or gold) as needed. For example, if foreign exchange dealers were selling more of a country's currency than demanded, that country's government would intervene in the foreign exchange markets, buying its currency in an attempt to increase demand and maintain its gold par value.

Another aspect of the Bretton Woods agreement was a commitment not to use devaluation as a weapon of competitive trade policy. However, if a currency became too weak to defend, a devaluation of up to 10 percent would be allowed without any formal approval by the IMF. Larger devaluations required IMF approval.

In 1944, at the height of World War II, representatives from 44 countries met at Bretton Woods, New Hampshire, to design a new international monetary system. Pictured here is Henry Morgenthau, then secretary of the Treasury, addressing the opening meeting of the conference where the IMF and the World Bank were established. *© Bettmann/Corbis*

THE ROLE OF THE IMF The IMF Articles of Agreement were heavily influenced by the worldwide financial collapse, competitive devaluations, trade wars, high unemployment, hyperinflation in Germany and elsewhere, and general economic disintegration that occurred between the two world wars. The aim of the Bretton Woods agreement, of which the IMF was the main custodian, was to try to avoid a repetition of that chaos through a combination of discipline and flexibility.

Discipline A fixed exchange rate regime imposes discipline in two ways. First, the need to maintain a fixed exchange rate puts a brake on competitive devaluations and brings stability to the world trade environment. Second, a fixed exchange rate regime imposes monetary discipline on countries, thereby curtailing price inflation. For example, consider what would happen under a fixed exchange rate regime if Great Britain rapidly increased its money supply by printing pounds. As explained in Chapter 9, the increase in money supply would lead to price inflation. Given fixed exchange rates, inflation would make British goods uncompetitive in world markets, while the prices of imports would become more attractive in Great Britain. The result would be a widening trade deficit in Great Britain, with the country importing more than it exports. To correct this trade imbalance under a fixed exchange rate regime, Great Britain would be required to restrict the rate of growth in its money supply to bring price inflation back under control. Thus, fixed exchange rates are seen as a mechanism for controlling inflation and imposing economic discipline on countries.

Flexibility Although monetary discipline was a central objective of the Bretton Woods agreement, it was recognized that a rigid policy of fixed exchange rates would be too inflexible. It would probably break down just as the gold standard had. In some cases, a country's attempts to reduce its money supply growth and correct a persistent balance-of-payments deficit could force the country into recession and create high unemployment. The architects of the Bretton Woods agreement wanted to avoid high unemployment, so they built limited flexibility into the system. Two major features of the IMF Articles of Agreement fostered this flexibility: IMF lending facilities and adjustable parities.

The IMF stood ready to lend foreign currencies to members to tide them over during short periods of balance-of-payments deficits, when a rapid tightening of monetary or fiscal policy would hurt domestic employment. A pool of gold and currencies contributed by IMF members provided the resources for these lending operations. A persistent balance-of-payments deficit can lead to a depletion of a country's reserves of foreign currency, forcing it to devalue its currency. By providing deficit-laden countries with short-term foreign currency loans, IMF funds would buy time for countries to bring down their inflation rates and reduce their balance-of-payments deficits. The belief was that such loans would reduce pressures for devaluation and allow for a more orderly and less painful adjustment.

Countries were to be allowed to borrow a limited amount from the IMF without adhering to any specific agreements. However, extensive drawings from IMF funds would require a country to agree to increasingly stringent IMF supervision of its macroeconomic policies. Heavy borrowers from the IMF must agree to monetary and fiscal conditions set down by the IMF, which typically include IMF-mandated targets on domestic money supply growth, exchange rate policy, tax policy, government spending, and so on.

The system of adjustable parities allowed for the devaluation of a country's currency by more than 10 percent if the IMF agreed that a country's balance of payments was in "fundamental disequilibrium." The term *fundamental disequilibrium* was not defined in the IMF's Articles of Agreement, but it was intended to apply to countries that had suffered permanent adverse shifts in the demand for their products. Without devaluation, such a country would experience high unemployment and a persistent trade deficit until the domestic price level had fallen far enough to restore a balance-of-payments equilibrium. The belief was that devaluation could help sidestep a painful adjustment process in such circumstances.

THE ROLE OF THE WORLD BANK The official name for the World Bank is the International Bank for Reconstruction and Development (IBRD). When the Bretton Woods participants established the World Bank, the need to reconstruct the war-torn economies of Europe was foremost in their minds. The bank's initial mission was to help finance the building of Europe's economy by providing low-interest loans. As it turned out, the World Bank was overshadowed in this role by the Marshall Plan, under which the United States lent money directly to European nations to help them rebuild. So the bank turned its attention to "development" and began lending money to Third World nations. In the 1950s, the bank concentrated on public-sector projects. Power stations, road building, and other transportation investments were much in favor. During the 1960s, the bank also began to lend heavily in support of agriculture, education, population control, and urban development.

The bank lends money under two schemes. Under the IBRD scheme, money is raised through bond sales in the international capital market. Borrowers pay what the bank calls a *market rate of interest*—the bank's cost of funds plus a margin for expenses. This "market" rate is lower than commercial banks' market rate. Under the IBRD scheme, the bank offers low-interest loans to risky customers whose credit rating is often poor, such as the governments of underdeveloped nations.

A second scheme is overseen by the International Development Association (IDA), an arm of the bank created in 1960. Resources to fund IDA loans are raised through subscriptions from wealthy members such as the United States, Japan, and Germany. IDA loans go only to the poorest countries. Borrowers have 50 years to repay at an interest rate of 1 percent a year. The world's poorest nations receive grants and noninterest loans.

The Collapse of the Fixed Exchange Rate System

LEARNING OBJECTIVE 1
Be familiar with the historical development of the modern global monetary system.

The system of fixed exchange rates established at Bretton Woods worked well until the late 1960s, when it began to show signs of strain. The system finally collapsed in 1973, and since then we have had a managed-float system. To understand why the system collapsed, one must appreciate the special role of the U.S. dollar in the system. As the only currency that could be converted into gold, and as the currency that served as the reference point for all others, the dollar occupied a central place in the system. Any pressure on the dollar to devalue could wreak havoc with the system, and that is what occurred.

Most economists trace the breakup of the fixed exchange rate system to the U.S. macroeconomic policy package of the 1965–68 period.[3] To finance both the Vietnam conflict and his welfare programs, President Lyndon Johnson backed an increase in U.S. government spending that was not financed by an increase in taxes. Instead, it was financed by an increase in the money supply, which led to a rise in price inflation from less than 4 percent in 1966 to close to 9 percent by 1968. At the same time, the rise in government spending had stimulated the economy. With more money in their pockets, people spent more—particularly on imports—and the U.S. trade balance began to deteriorate. (The perceptive reader will note that there are parallels here with the situation prevailing in America in the 2002–06 period, where once again a government expanded spending to pay for a foreign war and financed that spending through monetary expansion—in essence, more government borrowing—that stimulated the economy and led to a surge in imports. Some observers worry that the implied expansion in the U.S. money supply may ultimately lead to acceleration in the inflation rate in the United States.)

The increase in inflation and the worsening of the U.S. foreign trade position gave rise to speculation in the foreign exchange market that the dollar would be devalued. Things came to a head in the spring of 1971 when U.S. trade figures showed that for the first time since 1945, the United States was importing more than it was exporting. This set off massive purchases of German deutsche marks in the foreign exchange market by speculators who guessed that the mark would be revalued against the dollar. On a single day, May 4, 1971, the Bundesbank (Germany's central bank) had to buy $1 billion to hold the dollar/deutsche mark exchange rate at its fixed exchange rate given the great demand for deutsche marks. On the morning of May 5, the Bundesbank purchased another $1 billion during the first hour of foreign exchange trading! At that point, the Bundesbank faced the inevitable and allowed its currency to float.

In the weeks following the decision to float the deutsche mark, the foreign exchange market became increasingly convinced that the dollar would have to be devalued. However, devaluation of the dollar was no easy matter. Under the Bretton Woods provisions, any other country could change its exchange rates against all currencies simply by fixing its dollar rate at a new level. But as the key currency in the system, the dollar could be devalued only if all countries agreed to simultaneously revalue against the dollar. Many countries did not want this, because it would make their products more expensive relative to U.S. products.

To force the issue, President Nixon announced in August 1971 that the dollar was no longer convertible into gold. He also announced that a new 10 percent tax on imports would remain in effect until U.S. trading partners agreed to revalue their currencies against the dollar. This brought the trading partners to the bargaining table, and in December 1971 an agreement was reached to devalue the dollar by about 8 percent against foreign currencies. The import tax was then removed.

The problem was not solved, however. The U.S. balance-of-payments position continued to deteriorate throughout 1972, while the nation's money supply continued to expand at an inflationary rate. Speculation continued to grow that the dollar was still overvalued and that a second devaluation would be necessary. In anticipation, foreign exchange dealers began converting dollars to deutsche marks and other currencies. After a massive wave of speculation in February 1972, which culminated with European central banks spending $3.6 billion on March 1 to try to prevent their currencies from appreciating against the dollar, the foreign exchange market was closed. When the foreign exchange market reopened March 19, the currencies of Japan and most European countries were floating against the dollar, although many developing countries continued to peg their currency to the dollar, and many do to this day. At that time, the switch to a floating system was viewed as a temporary response to unmanageable speculation in the foreign exchange market. But it is now more than 30 years since the Bretton Woods system of fixed exchange rates collapsed, and the temporary solution looks permanent.

Another Perspective

United States off the Gold Standard

When Nixon took the United States off the gold standard in 1971, his decision established the dollar as the standard against which other currencies would be measured. The U.S. gold reserves, which in 1945 had held 80 percent of all gold reserves worldwide, had been under serious pressure since France, under the leadership of Charles De Gaulle, had demanded to convert the French dollar reserves to gold in 1965, the first of many central bank requests. Nixon's decision set up the dollar to be the de facto standard of the new floating system, and it continues that way today.

The Bretton Woods system had an Achilles' heel: The system could not work if its key currency, the U.S. dollar, was under speculative attack. The Bretton Woods system could work only as long as the U.S. inflation rate remained low and the United States did not run a balance-of-payments deficit. Once these things occurred, the system soon became strained to the breaking point.

The Floating Exchange Rate Regime

LEARNING OBJECTIVE 1
Be familiar with the historical development of the modern global monetary system.

The floating exchange rate regime that followed the collapse of the fixed exchange rate system was formalized in January 1976 when IMF members met in Jamaica and agreed to the rules for the international monetary system that are in place today.

THE JAMAICA AGREEMENT The Jamaica meeting revised the IMF's Articles of Agreement to reflect the new reality of floating exchange rates. The main elements of the Jamaica agreement include the following:

- Floating rates were declared acceptable. IMF members were permitted to enter the foreign exchange market to even out "unwarranted" speculative fluctuations.
- Gold was abandoned as a reserve asset. The IMF returned its gold reserves to members at the current market price, placing the proceeds in a trust fund to help poor nations. IMF members were permitted to sell their own gold reserves at the market price.
- Total annual IMF quotas—the amount member countries contribute to the IMF—were increased to $41 billion. (Since then they have been increased to $311 billion while the membership of the IMF has been expanded to include 184 countries.) Non-oil-exporting, less developed countries were given greater access to IMF funds.

After Jamaica, the IMF continued its role of helping countries cope with macroeconomic and exchange rate problems, albeit within the context of a radically different exchange rate regime.

EXCHANGE RATES SINCE 1973 Since March 1973, exchange rates have become much more volatile and less predictable than they were between 1945 and 1973.[4] This volatility has been partly due to a number of unexpected shocks to the world monetary system, including

- The oil crisis in 1971, when the Organization of Petroleum Exporting Countries (OPEC) quadrupled the price of oil. The harmful effect of this on the U.S. inflation rate and trade position resulted in a further decline in the value of the dollar.
- The loss of confidence in the dollar that followed a sharp rise in the U.S. inflation rate during the 1977–78 period.
- The oil crisis of 1979, when OPEC once again increased the price of oil dramatically—this time it was doubled.
- The unexpected rise in the dollar between 1980 and 1985, despite a deteriorating balance-of-payments picture.
- The rapid fall of the U.S. dollar against the Japanese yen and German deutsche mark between 1985 and 1987, and against the yen between 1993 and 1995.
- The partial collapse of the European Monetary System in 1992.
- The 1997 Asian currency crisis, when the Asian currencies of several countries, including South Korea, Indonesia, Malaysia, and Thailand, lost between 50 and 80 percent of their value against the U.S. dollar in a few months.

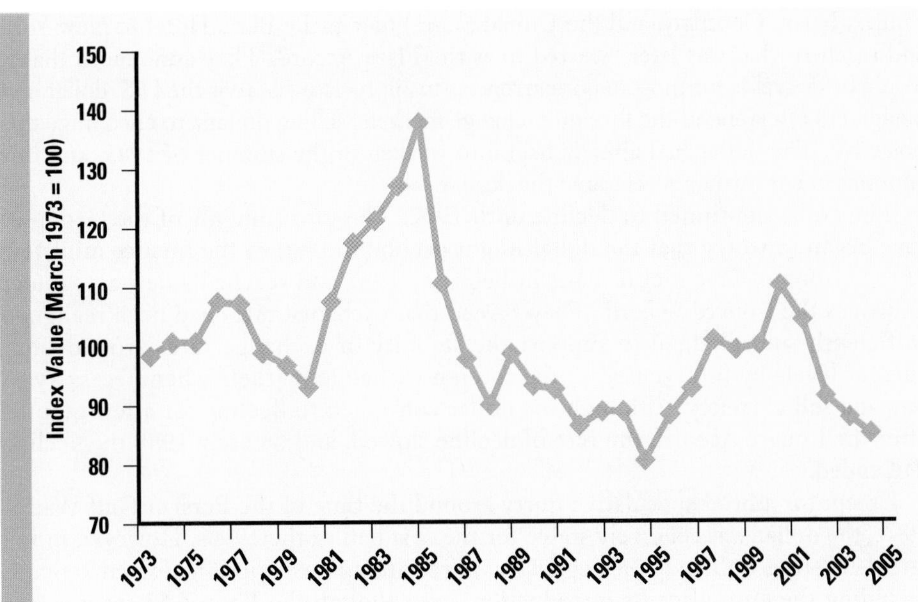

figure 10.1

Major Currencies Dollar Index, 1973–2005

Source: Constructed by the author from Federal Reserve Board statistics at *www.federalreserve.gov/releases/H10/summary*.

Figure 10.1 summarizes how the value of the U.S. dollar has fluctuated against an index of major trading currencies between 1973 and 2005. (The index, which was set equal to 100 in March 1973, is a weighted average of the foreign exchange values of the U.S. dollar against currencies that circulate widely outside the country of issue). An interesting phenomenon in Figure 10.1 is the rapid rise in the value of the dollar between 1980 and 1985 and its subsequent fall between 1985 and 1988. A similar, though less pronounced, rise and fall in the value of the dollar occurred between 1995 and 2005. We will briefly discuss the rise and fall of the dollar during these periods, which will tell us something about how the international monetary system has operated in recent years.[5]

The rise in the value of the dollar between 1980 and 1985 occurred when the United States was running a large and growing trade deficit, importing substantially more than it exported. Conventional wisdom would suggest that the increased supply of dollars in the foreign exchange market as a result of the trade deficit should lead to a reduction in the value of the dollar, but as shown in Figure 10.1 it increased in value. Why?

A number of favorable factors overcame the unfavorable effect of a trade deficit. Strong economic growth in the United States attracted heavy inflows of capital from foreign investors seeking high returns on capital assets. High real interest rates attracted foreign investors seeking high returns on financial assets. At the same time, political turmoil in other parts of the world, along with relatively slow economic growth in the developed countries of Europe, helped create the view that the United States was a good place to invest. These inflows of capital increased the demand for dollars in the foreign exchange market, which pushed the value of the dollar upward against other currencies.

The fall in the value of the dollar between 1985 and 1988 was caused by a combination of government intervention and market forces. The rise in the dollar, which priced U.S. goods out of foreign markets and made imports relatively cheap, had contributed to a dismal trade picture. In 1985, the United States posted a record-high trade deficit of more than $160 billion. This led to growth in demands for protectionism in the United States. In September 1985, the finance ministers and central bank governors of the so-called Group of Five major industrial countries (Great Britain,

France, Japan, Germany, and the United States) met at the Plaza Hotel in New York and reached what was later referred to as the Plaza Accord. They announced that it would be desirable for most major currencies to appreciate vis-à-vis the U.S. dollar and pledged to intervene in the foreign exchange markets, selling dollars, to encourage this objective. The dollar had already begun to weaken in the summer of 1985, and this announcement further accelerated the decline.

The dollar continued to decline until 1987. The governments of the Group of Five began to worry that the dollar might decline too far, so the finance ministers of the Group of Five met in Paris in February 1987 and reached a new agreement known as the Louvre Accord. They agreed that exchange rates had been realigned sufficiently and pledged to support the stability of exchange rates around their current levels by intervening in the foreign exchange markets when necessary to buy and sell currency. Although the dollar continued to decline for a few months after the Louvre Accord, the rate of decline slowed, and by early 1988 the decline had ended.

Except for a brief speculative flurry around the time of the Persian Gulf War in 1991, the dollar was relatively stable for the first half of the 1990s. However, in the late 1990s the dollar again began to appreciate against most major currencies, including the euro after its introduction, even though the United States was still running a significant balance-of-payments deficit. Once again, the driving force for the appreciation in the value of the dollar was that foreigners continued to invest in U.S. financial assets, primarily stocks and bonds, and the inflow of money drove up the value of the dollar on foreign exchange markets. The inward investment was due to a belief that U.S. financial assets offered a favorable rate of return.

By 2002, however, foreigners had started to lose their appetite for U.S. stocks and bonds, and the inflow of money into the United States slowed. Instead of reinvesting dollars earned from exports to the United States in U.S. financial assets, they exchanged those dollars for other currencies, particularly euros, to invest them in nondollar-denominated assets. One reason for this was the continued growth in the U.S. trade deficit, which hit a record $767 billion in 2005. Although the U.S. trade deficits had been hitting records for decades, this deficit was the largest ever when measured as a percentage of the country's GDP (7 percent of GDP in 2005).

The record deficit meant that ever more dollars were flowing out of the United States into foreign hands, and those foreigners were less inclined to reinvest those dollars in the United States at a rate required to keep the dollar stable. This growing reluctance of foreigners to invest in the United States was in turn due to several factors. First, there was a slowdown in U.S. economic activity during the 2001–02 period, and a somewhat slow recovery thereafter, which made U.S. assets less attractive. Second, the U.S. government's budget deficit expanded rapidly after 2001 hitting a record $318 billion in 2005. This led to fears that ultimately the budget deficit would be financed by an expansionary monetary policy that could lead to higher price inflation. Because inflation would reduce the value of the dollar, foreigners decided to hedge against this risk by holding fewer dollar assets in their investment portfolios. Third, from

Another Perspective

Floating Dollars and OPEC

In the early 1970s, dollars became the currency for oil trades through an agreement between the United States and OPEC. This commitment of OPEC to dollar oil sales was made secretly by the United States and Saudi Arabia, first, and then the United States and other OPEC countries. The impact of petrodollars, as they are known, is huge. Petrodollars lead oil-producing countries to be likely to invest their dollar surpluses in the United States. In fact, OPEC dollar surpluses help to fund the U.S. trade deficit. Iraq, Iran, and Venezuela have at times initiated a push to move trading in oil to the euro, but so far OPEC has stayed with the dollar. (Peter Dale Scott, *Drugs, Oil, and War: The United States in Afghanistan, Colombia, and Indochina* (Lanham, MD: Rowman & Littlefield, 2003), pp. 41–42)

2003 onward U.S. government officials began to "talk down" the value of the dollar, in part because the administration believed that a cheaper dollar would increase exports and reduce imports, thereby improving the U.S. balance of trade position.[6] Foreigners saw this as a signal that the U.S. government would not intervene in the foreign exchange markets to prop up the value of the dollar, which increased their reluctance to reinvest dollars earned from export sales in U.S. financial assets. As a result of these factors, demand for dollars weakened and the value of the dollar slid on the foreign exchange markets, hitting an index value of 80.19 in December 2004, its lowest value since the index began in 1973. Although the dollar strengthened a little in 2005, many commentators believe that it could resume its fall in coming years.

Thus, we see that in recent history the value of the dollar has been determined by both market forces and government intervention. Under a floating exchange rate regime, market forces have produced a volatile dollar exchange rate. Governments have sometimes responded by intervening in the market—buying and selling dollars—in an attempt to limit the market's volatility and to correct what they see as overvaluation (in 1985) or potential undervaluation (in 1987) of the dollar. In addition to direct intervention, the value of the dollar has frequently been influenced by statements from government officials. The dollar may not have declined by as much as it did in 2004, for example, had not U.S. government officials publicly ruled out any action to stop the decline. Paradoxically, a signal not to intervene can affect the market. The frequency of government intervention in the foreign exchange market explains why the current system is sometimes thought of as a **managed-float system,** or a dirty-float system.

Managed-Float System
System under which some currencies are allowed to float freely, but the majority are either managed by government intervention or pegged to another currency.

Fixed versus Floating Exchange Rates

LEARNING OBJECTIVE 3
Be familiar with the differences between a fixed and floating exchange rate system.

The breakdown of the Bretton Woods system has not stopped the debate about the relative merits of fixed versus floating exchange rate regimes. Disappointment with the system of floating rates in recent years has led to renewed debate about the merits of fixed exchange rates. In this section, we review the arguments for fixed and floating exchange rate regimes.[7] We will discuss the case for floating rates before discussing why many commentators are disappointed with the experience under floating exchange rates and yearn for a system of fixed rates.

THE CASE FOR FLOATING EXCHANGE RATES

The case in support of floating exchange rates has two main elements: monetary policy autonomy and automatic trade balance adjustments.

Monetary Policy Autonomy

It is argued that under a fixed system, a country's ability to expand or contract its money supply as it sees fit is limited by the need to maintain exchange rate parity. Monetary expansion can lead to inflation, which puts downward pressure on a fixed exchange rate (as predicted by the PPP theory; see Chapter 9). Similarly, monetary contraction requires high interest rates (to reduce the demand for money). Higher interest rates lead to an inflow of money from abroad, which puts upward pressure on a fixed exchange rate. Thus, to maintain exchange rate parity under a fixed system, countries were limited in their ability to use monetary policy to expand or contract their economies.

Advocates of a floating exchange rate regime argue that removal of the obligation to maintain exchange rate parity would restore monetary control to a government. If a government faced with unemployment wanted to increase its money supply to stimulate domestic demand and reduce unemployment, it could do so unencumbered by the need to maintain its exchange rate. However, monetary expansion might lead to inflation, which would lead to a depreciation in the country's currency. If PPP theory is correct, the resulting currency depreciation on the foreign exchange markets should offset the effects of inflation. Although under a floating exchange rate regime domestic inflation would have an impact on the exchange rate, it should have no impact on businesses' international cost competitiveness due to exchange rate depreciation. The rise in domestic costs should be exactly offset by the fall in the value of the country's currency on the foreign exchange markets. Similarly, a government could use monetary policy to contract the economy without worrying about the need to maintain parity.

Trade Balance Adjustments Under the Bretton Woods system, if a country developed a permanent deficit in its balance of trade (importing more than it exported) that could not be corrected by domestic policy, this would require the IMF to agree to a currency devaluation. Critics of this system argue that the adjustment mechanism works much more smoothly under a floating exchange rate regime. They argue that if a country is running a trade deficit, the imbalance between the supply and demand of that country's currency in the foreign exchange markets (supply exceeding demand) will lead to depreciation in its exchange rate. In turn, by making its exports cheaper and its imports more expensive, an exchange rate depreciation should correct the trade deficit.

THE CASE FOR FIXED EXCHANGE RATES The case for fixed exchange rates rests on arguments about monetary discipline, speculation, uncertainty, and the lack of connection between the trade balance and exchange rates.

Monetary Discipline We have already discussed the nature of monetary discipline inherent in a fixed exchange rate system when we discussed the Bretton Woods system. The need to maintain a fixed exchange rate parity ensures that governments do not expand their money supplies at inflationary rates. While advocates of floating rates argue that each country should be allowed to choose its own inflation rate (the monetary autonomy argument), advocates of fixed rates argue that governments all too often give in to political pressures and expand the monetary supply far too rapidly, causing unacceptably high price inflation. A fixed exchange rate regime would ensure that this does not occur.

Speculation Critics of a floating exchange rate regime also argue that speculation can cause fluctuations in exchange rates. They point to the dollar's rapid rise and fall during the 1980s, which they claim had nothing to do with comparative inflation rates and the U.S. trade deficit, but everything to do with speculation. They argue that when foreign exchange dealers see a currency depreciating, they tend to sell the currency in the expectation of future depreciation regardless of the currency's longer-term prospects. As more traders jump on the bandwagon, the expectations of depreciation are realized. Such destabilizing speculation tends to accentuate the fluctuations around the exchange rate's long-run value. It can damage a country's economy by distorting export and import prices. Thus, advocates of a fixed exchange rate regime argue that such a system will limit the destabilizing effects of speculation.

Uncertainty Speculation also adds to the uncertainty surrounding future currency movements that characterizes floating exchange rate regimes. The unpredictability of exchange rate movements in the post–Bretton Woods era has made business planning difficult, and it adds risk to exporting, importing, and foreign investment activities. Given a volatile exchange rate, international businesses do not know how to react to the changes—and often they do not react. Why change plans for exporting, importing, or foreign investment after a 6 percent fall in the dollar this month, when the dollar may rise 6 percent next month? This uncertainty, according to the critics, dampens the growth of international trade and investment. They argue that a fixed exchange rate, by eliminating such uncertainty, promotes the growth of international trade and investment. Advocates of a floating system reply that the forward exchange market insures against the risks associated with exchange rate fluctuations (see Chapter 9), so the adverse impact of uncertainty on the growth of international trade and investment has been overstated.

Trade Balance Adjustments Those in favor of floating exchange rates argue that floating rates help adjust trade imbalances. Critics question the closeness of the link between the exchange rate and the trade balance. They claim trade deficits are determined by the balance between savings and investment in a country, not by the external value of its currency.[8] They argue that depreciation in a currency will lead to inflation (due to the resulting increase in import prices). This inflation will wipe out any apparent gains in cost competitiveness that arise from currency depreciation. In other words, a depreciating exchange rate will not boost exports and reduce imports, as advocates of floating rates claim; it will simply boost price inflation. In support of this argument, those who favor floating rates point out that the 40 percent drop in the value of the dollar between 1985 and 1988 did not correct the U.S. trade deficit. In reply, advocates of a floating exchange rate regime argue that between 1985 and 1992, the U.S. trade deficit fell from more than $160 billion to about $70 billion, and they attribute this in part to the decline in the value of the dollar.

WHO IS RIGHT? Which side is right in the vigorous debate between those who favor a fixed exchange rate and those who favor a floating exchange rate? Economists cannot agree. Business, as a major player on the international trade and investment scene, has a large stake in the resolution of the debate. Would international business be better off under a fixed regime, or are flexible rates better? The evidence is not clear.

We do, however, know that a fixed exchange rate regime modeled along the lines of the Bretton Woods system will not work. Speculation ultimately broke the system, a phenomenon that advocates of fixed rate regimes claim is associated with floating exchange rates. Nevertheless, a different kind of fixed exchange rate system might be more enduring and might foster the stability that would facilitate more rapid growth in international trade and investment. In the next section, we look at potential models for such a system and the problems with such systems.

Exchange Rate Regimes in Practice

LEARNING OBJECTIVE 4
Know what exchange rate regimes are used in the world today and why countries adopt different exchange rate regimes.

Governments around the world pursue a number of different exchange rate policies. These range from a pure "free float," where the exchange rate is determined by market forces, to a pegged system that has some aspects of the pre-1973 Bretton Woods system of fixed exchange rates. Figure 10.2 summarizes the exchange rate policies adopted by member states of the IMF in 2005. Some 19 percent of the IMF's members allow their currency to float freely. Another 26 percent intervene in only a limited way (the so-called managed float). A further 22 percent of IMF members now have no separate legal tender of their own. These include the 12 EU countries that have adopted the euro, effectively giving up their own currencies, along with 29 smaller states mostly in Africa or the Caribbean that have no domestic currency and have adopted a foreign currency as legal tender within their borders, typically the U.S. dollar or the euro. The remaining countries use more inflexible systems, including a fixed peg

Exchange Rate Policies, IMF Members, 2005

Source: Constructed by the author from IMF data.

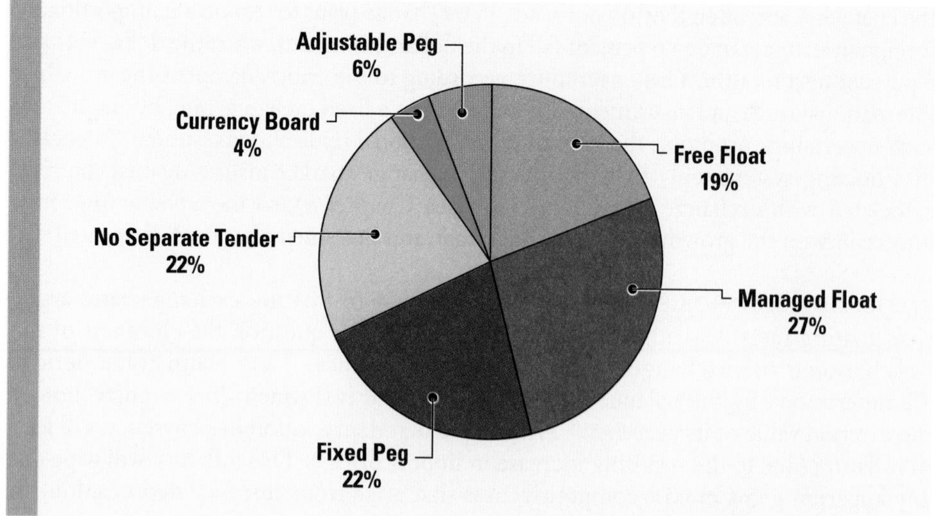

arrangement (22 percent) under which they peg their currencies to other currencies, such as the U.S. dollar or the euro, or to a basket of currencies. Other countries have adopted a system under which their exchange rate is allowed to fluctuate against other currencies within a target zone (an adjustable peg system). In this section, we will look more closely at the mechanics and implications of exchange rate regimes that rely on a currency peg or target zone.

PEGGED EXCHANGE RATES Under a pegged exchange rate regime, a country will peg the value of its currency to that of a major currency so that, for example, as the U.S. dollar rises in value, its own currency rises too. For example, as noted in the opening case, China pegged the value of its currency, the yuan, to that of the U.S. dollar between 1993 and 2005. Pegged exchange rates are popular among many of the world's smaller nations (China is obviously an exception to this). As with a full fixed exchange rate regime, the great virtue claimed for a pegged exchange rate is that it imposes monetary discipline on a country and leads to low inflation. For example, if Belize pegs the value of the Belizean dollar to that of the U.S. dollar so that US$1 = B$1.97 (the peg as of 2006), then the Belizean government must make sure the inflation rate in Belize is similar to that in the United States. If the Belizean inflation rate is greater than the U.S. inflation rate, this will lead to pressure to devalue the Belizean dollar (i.e., to alter the peg). To maintain the peg, the Belizean government would be required to rein in inflation. Of course, for a pegged exchange rate to impose monetary discipline on a country, the country whose currency is chosen for the peg must also pursue sound monetary policy.

Evidence shows that adopting a pegged exchange rate regime moderates inflationary pressures in a country. An IMF study concluded that countries with pegged exchange rates had an average annual inflation rate of 8 percent, compared with 14 percent for intermediate regimes and 16 percent for floating regimes.[9] However, many countries operate with only a nominal peg and in practice are willing to devalue their currency rather than pursue a tight monetary policy. It can be very difficult for a smaller country to maintain a peg against another currency if capital is flowing out of the country and foreign exchange traders are speculating against the currency. Something like this occurred in 1997 when a combination of adverse capital flows and currency speculation forced several Asian countries, including Thailand and Malaysia, to abandon pegs against the U.S. dollar and let their currencies float freely. Malaysia and Thailand would not have been in this position had they dealt with a number of problems that began to arise in their economies during the 1990s, including excessive private-sector debt and expanding current account trade deficits.

CURRENCY BOARDS Hong Kong's experience during the 1997 Asian currency crisis added a new dimension to the debate over how to manage a pegged exchange rate. During late 1997 when other Asian currencies were collapsing, Hong Kong maintained the value of its currency against the U.S. dollar at about HK$15 = $7.8 despite several concerted speculative attacks. Hong Kong's currency board has been given credit for this success. A country that introduces a **currency board** commits itself to converting its domestic currency on demand into another currency at a fixed exchange rate. To make this commitment credible, the currency board holds reserves of foreign currency equal at the fixed exchange rate to at least 100 percent of the domestic currency issued. The system used in Hong Kong means its currency must be fully backed by the U.S. dollar at the specified exchange rate. This is still not a true fixed exchange rate regime, because the U.S. dollar, and by extension the Hong Kong dollar, floats against other currencies, but it has some features of a fixed exchange rate regime.

Currency Board
A country's currency authority that holds reserves of foreign currency equal at the fixed exchange rate to at least 100 percent of the domestic currency issued in order to keep inflation down.

Under this arrangement, the currency board can issue additional domestic notes and coins only when there are foreign exchange reserves to back it. This limits the ability of the government to print money and, thereby, create inflationary pressures. Under a strict currency board system, interest rates adjust automatically. If investors want to switch out of domestic currency into, for example, U.S. dollars, the supply of domestic currency will shrink. This will cause interest rates to rise until it eventually becomes attractive for investors to hold the local currency again. In the case of Hong Kong, the interest rate on three-month deposits climbed as high as 20 percent in late 1997, as investors switched out of Hong Kong dollars and into U.S. dollars. The dollar peg held, however, and interest rates declined again.

Since its establishment in 1983, the Hong Kong currency board has weathered several storms, including the latest. This success persuaded several other countries in the developing world to consider a similar system. Argentina introduced a currency board in 1991 (but abandoned it in 2002) and Bulgaria, Estonia, and Lithuania have all gone down this road in recent years (seven IMF members had currency boards in 2005). Despite growing interest in the arrangement, however, critics are quick to point out that currency boards have their drawbacks.[10] If local inflation rates remain higher than the inflation rate in the country to which the currency is pegged, the currencies of countries with currency boards can become uncompetitive and overvalued. Also, under a currency board system, government lacks the ability to set interest rates. Interest rates in Hong Kong, for example, are effectively set by the U.S. Federal Reserve. In addition, economic collapse in Argentina in 2001 and the subsequent decision to abandon its currency board dampened much of the enthusiasm for this mechanism of managing exchange rates.

Crisis Management by the IMF

LEARNING OBJECTIVE 5
Understand the debate surrounding the role of the IMF in the management of financial crises.

Many observers initially believed that the collapse of the Bretton Woods system in 1973 would diminish the role of the IMF within the international monetary system. The IMF's original function was to provide a pool of money from which members could borrow, short term, to adjust their balance-of-payments position and maintain their exchange rate. Some believed the demand for short-term loans would be considerably diminished under a floating exchange rate regime. A trade deficit would presumably lead to a decline in a country's exchange rate, which would help reduce imports and boost exports. No temporary IMF adjustment loan would be needed. Consistent with this,

Another Perspective

IMF: All That Independent?

The IMF was begun in 1944, at Bretton Woods, just before the United Nations took shape in October of 1945. When the UN was formed, the IMF was brought into relationship with it. This relationship preserved the IMF's independence, which was justified at the time by the need for independent control of monetary management. Today, this independence is a source of criticism. Technically speaking, though, the IMF reports to its 189-member countries through its board of governors. John W. Snow, U.S. secretary of the treasury, is the U.S. member of the board, and Ben Bernanke, chairman of the U.S. Federal Reserve Board is the alternate member. They control the U.S. share of the votes on the board of governors, which is 17.08 percent.

after 1973, most industrialized countries tended to let the foreign exchange market determine exchange rates in response to demand and supply. No major industrial country has borrowed funds from the IMF since the mid-1970s, when Great Britain and Italy did. Since the early 1970s, the rapid development of global capital markets has allowed developed countries such as Great Britain and the United States to finance their deficits by borrowing private money, as opposed to drawing on IMF funds. Despite these developments, the activities of the IMF have expanded over the past 30 years. By 2006, the IMF had 189 members, 59 of which had some kind of IMF program in place. In 1997, the institution implemented its largest rescue packages, committing more than $110 billion in short-term loans to three troubled Asian countries: South Korea, Indonesia, and Thailand. This was followed by additional IMF rescue packages in Turkey, Russia, Argentina, and Brazil.

The IMF's activities have expanded because periodic financial crises have continued to hit many economies in the post–Bretton Woods era, particularly among the world's developing nations. The IMF has repeatedly lent money to nations experiencing financial crises, requesting in return that the governments enact certain macroeconomic policies. Critics of the IMF claim these policies have not always been as beneficial as the IMF might have hoped and in some cases may have made things worse. Following the IMF loans to several Asian economies, these criticisms reached new levels and a vigorous debate was waged as to the appropriate role of the IMF. In this section, we shall discuss some of the main challenges the IMF has had to deal with over the past quarter of a century and review the ongoing debate over the role of the IMF.

Currency Crisis
When a speculative attack on the exchange value of a currency results in a sharp depreciation of the currency or forces authorities to expend large volumes of international currency reserves and sharply increase interest rates to defend the prevailing exchange rate.

FINANCIAL CRISES IN THE POST–BRETTON WOODS ERA A number of broad types of financial crises have occurred over the past 30 years, many of which have required IMF involvement. A **currency crisis** occurs when a speculative attack on the exchange value of a currency results in a sharp depreciation in the value of the currency or forces authorities to expend large volumes of international currency reserves and sharply increase interest rates to defend the prevailing exchange rate. This is what happened in Brazil in 2002, and the IMF stepped in to help stabilize the value of the Brazilian currency on foreign exchange markets. A **banking crisis** refers to a loss of confidence in the banking system that leads to a run on banks, as individuals and companies withdraw their deposits. A **foreign debt crisis** is a situation in which a country cannot service its foreign debt obligations, whether private-sector or government debt.

Banking Crisis
When individuals and companies lose confidence in the banking system and withdraw their deposits in what is called a *run on banks.*

These crises tend to have common underlying macroeconomic causes: high relative price inflation rates, a widening current account deficit, excessive expansion of domestic borrowing, and asset price inflation (such as sharp increases in stock and property prices).[11] At times, elements of currency, banking, and debt crises may be present simultaneously, as in the 1997 Asian crisis and the 2000–02 Argentinean crisis.

Foreign Debt Crisis
A situation in which a country cannot service its foreign debt obligations, whether private-sector or government debt.

To assess the frequency of financial crises, the IMF looked at the macroeconomic performance of a group of 53 countries from 1975 to 1997 (22 of these countries were developed nations, and 31 were developing countries).[12] The IMF found there had been 158 currency crises, including 55 episodes in which a country's currency declined by more than 25 percent. There were also 54 banking crises. The IMF's data suggest that developing nations were more than twice as likely to experience currency and banking crises as developed nations. It is not surprising, therefore, that most of the IMF's loan activities since the mid-1970s have been targeted toward developing nations.

Here we look at two crises that have been of particular significance in terms of IMF involvement since the early 1990s: the 1995 Mexican currency crisis and the 1997 Asian financial crisis. These crises were the result of excessive foreign borrowings, a weak or poorly regulated banking system, and high inflation rates. These factors came together to trigger simultaneous debt and currency crises. Checking the resulting crises required IMF involvement.

MEXICAN CURRENCY CRISIS OF 1995 The Mexican peso had been pegged to the dollar since the early 1980s when the International Monetary Fund made it a condition for lending money to the Mexican government to help bail the country out of a 1982 financial crisis. Under the IMF-brokered arrangement, the peso had been allowed to trade within a tolerance band of plus or minus 3 percent against the dollar. The band was also permitted to "crawl" down daily, allowing for an annual peso depreciation of about 4 percent against the dollar. The IMF believed that the need to maintain the exchange rate within a fairly narrow trading band would force the Mexican government to adopt stringent financial policies to limit the growth in the money supply and contain inflation.

Until the early 1990s, it looked as if the IMF policy had worked. However, the strains were beginning to show by 1994. Since the mid-1980s, Mexican producer prices had risen 45 percent more than prices in the United States, and yet there had not been a corresponding adjustment in the exchange rate. By late 1994, Mexico was running a $17 billion trade deficit, which amounted to some 6 percent of the country's gross domestic product, and there had been an uncomfortably rapid expansion in public- and private-sector debt. Despite these strains, Mexican government officials had been stating publicly that they would support the peso's dollar peg at around $1 = 3.5 pesos by adopting appropriate monetary policies and by intervening in the currency markets if necessary. Encouraged by such statements, $64 billion of foreign investment money poured into Mexico between 1990 and 1994 as corporations and money managers sought to take advantage of the booming economy.

However, many currency traders concluded the peso would have to be devalued, and they began to dump pesos on the foreign exchange market. The government tried to hold the line by buying pesos and selling dollars, but it lacked the foreign currency reserves required to halt the speculative tide (Mexico's foreign exchange reserves fell from $6 billion at the beginning of 1994 to less than $3.5 billion at the end of the year). In mid-December 1994, the Mexican government abruptly announced a devaluation. Immediately, much of the short-term investment money that had flowed into Mexican stocks and bonds over the previous year reversed its course, as foreign investors bailed out of peso-denominated financial assets. This exacerbated the sale of the peso and contributed to the rapid 40 percent drop in its value.

The IMF stepped in again, this time arm in arm with the U.S. government and the Bank for International Settlements. Together, the three institutions pledged close to $50 billion to help Mexico stabilize the peso and to redeem $47 billion of public- and private-sector debt that was set to mature in 1995. Of this amount, $20 billion came from the U.S. government and another $18 billion came from the

IMF (which made Mexico the largest recipient of IMF aid up to that point). Without the aid package, Mexico would probably have defaulted on its debt obligations, and the peso would have gone into free fall. As is normal in such cases, the IMF insisted on tight monetary policies and further cuts in public spending, both of which helped push the country into a deep recession. However, the recession was relatively short-lived, and by 1997 the country was once more on a growth path, had pared down its debt, and had paid back the $20 billion borrowed from the U.S. government ahead of schedule.[13]

THE ASIAN CRISIS The financial crisis that erupted across Southeast Asia during the fall of 1997 emerged as the biggest challenge to date for the IMF. Holding the crisis in check required IMF loans to help the shattered economies of Indonesia, Thailand, and South Korea stabilize their currencies. In addition, although they did not request IMF loans, the economies of Japan, Malaysia, Singapore, and the Philippines were also hurt by the crisis.

The seeds of this crisis were sown during the previous decade when these countries were experiencing unprecedented economic growth. Although there were and remain important differences between the individual countries, a number of elements were common to most. Exports had long been the engine of economic growth in these countries. From 1990 to 1996, the value of exports from Malaysia had grown by 18 percent annually, Thai exports had grown by 16 percent per year, Singapore's by 15 percent, Hong Kong's by 14 percent, and those of South Korea and Indonesia by 12 percent annually.[14]

The nature of these exports had also shifted in recent years from basic materials and products such as textiles to complex, high-technology products such as automobiles, semiconductors, and consumer electronics.

The Investment Boom The wealth created by export-led growth helped fuel an investment boom in commercial and residential property, industrial assets, and infrastructure. The value of commercial and residential real estate in cities such as Hong Kong and Bangkok started to soar. This fed a building boom the likes of which had never been seen in Asia. Heavy borrowing from banks financed much of this construction. As for industrial assets, the success of Asian exporters encouraged them to make bolder investments in industrial capacity. This was exemplified most clearly by South Korea's giant diversified conglomerates, or *chaebol*, many of which had ambitions to build a major position in the global automobile and semiconductor industries.

An added factor behind the investment boom in most Southeast Asian economies was the government. In many cases, the governments had embarked on huge infrastructure projects. In Malaysia, for example, a new government administrative center was being constructed in Putrajaya for M$20 billion (US$8 billion at the pre-July 1997 exchange rate), and the government was funding the development of a massive high-technology communications corridor and the huge Bakun dam, which at a cost of M$13.6 billion was to be the most expensive power-generation plant in the country.[15] Throughout the region, governments also encouraged private businesses to invest in certain sectors of the economy in accordance with "national goals" and "industrialization strategy." In South Korea, long a country in which the government played a proactive role in private-sector investments, President Kim Young-Sam urged the *chaebol* to invest in new factories as a way of boosting economic growth. South Korea enjoyed an investment-led economic boom during the 1994–95 period, but at a cost. The *chaebol*, always reliant on heavy borrowings, built up massive debts that were equivalent, on average, to four times their equity.[16]

In Indonesia, President Suharto had long supported investments in a network of an estimated 300 businesses owned by his family and friends in a system known as "crony capitalism." Many of these businesses were granted lucrative monopolies by the president. For example, Suharto announced in 1995 that he had decided to manufacture a national car, built by a company owned by one of his sons, Hutomo Mandala Putra, in association with Kia Motors of South Korea. To support the venture, a consortium of Indonesian banks was "ordered" by the government to offer almost $700 million in start-up loans to the company.[17]

By the mid-1990s, Southeast Asia was in the grips of an unprecedented investment boom, much of it financed with borrowed money. Between 1990 and 1995, gross domestic investment grew by 16.3 percent annually in Indonesia, 16 percent in Malaysia, 15.3 percent in Thailand, and 7.2 percent in South Korea. By comparison, investment grew by 4.1 percent annually over the same period in the United States and 0.8 percent in all high-income economies.[18] And the rate of investment accelerated in 1996. In Malaysia, for example, spending on investment accounted for a remarkable 43 percent of GDP in 1996.[19]

Excess Capacity As the volume of investments ballooned during the 1990s, often at the bequest of national governments, the quality of many of these investments declined significantly. The investments often were made on the basis of unrealistic projections about future demand conditions. The result was significant excess capacity. For example, South Korean *chaebol* investments in semiconductor factories surged in 1994 and 1995 when a temporary global shortage of dynamic random access memory chips (DRAMs) led to sharp price increases for this product. However, supply shortages had disappeared by 1996 and excess capacity was beginning to make itself felt, just as the South Koreans started to bring new DRAM factories on stream. The results were predictable; prices for DRAMs plunged, and the earnings of South Korean DRAM manufacturers fell by 90 percent, which meant it was difficult for them to make scheduled payments on the debt they had taken on to build the extra capacity.[20]

In another example, a building boom in Thailand resulted in excess capacity in residential and commercial property. By early 1997, an estimated 365,000 apartment units were unoccupied in Bangkok. With another 100,000 units scheduled to be completed in 1997, years of excess demand in the Thai property market had been replaced by excess supply. By one estimate, Bangkok's building boom had produced enough excess space by 1997 to meet its residential and commercial needs for five years.[21]

The Debt Bomb By early 1997, what was happening in the South Korean semiconductor industry and the Bangkok property market was being played out elsewhere in the region. Massive investments in industrial assets and property had created excess capacity and plunging prices, leaving the companies that had made the investments groaning under huge debt burdens that they were now finding it difficult to service.

To make matters worse, much of the borrowing had been in U.S. dollars, as opposed to local currencies. This had originally seemed like a smart move. Throughout the region, local currencies were pegged to the dollar, and interest rates on dollar borrowings

By 1997, years of excess demand in the Thai property market resulted in enough excess space to meet its residential and commercial needs for five years. *Udo Weitz/Bloomberg News/Landov*

were generally lower than rates on borrowings in domestic currency. Thus, it often made economic sense to borrow in dollars if the option was available. However, if the governments could not maintain the dollar peg and their currencies started to depreciate against the dollar, the size of the debt burden would increase when measured in the local currency. Currency depreciation would raise borrowing costs and could result in companies defaulting on their debt obligations.

Expanding Imports A final complicating factor was that by the mid-1990s, although exports were still expanding across the region, imports were too. The investments in infrastructure, industrial capacity, and commercial real estate were sucking in foreign goods at unprecedented rates. To build infrastructure, factories, and office buildings, Southeast Asian countries were purchasing capital equipment and materials from America, Europe, and Japan. Many Southeast Asian states saw the current accounts of their balance of payments shift strongly into the red during the mid-1990s. By 1995, Indonesia was running a current account deficit that was equivalent to 3.5 percent of its GDP, Malaysia's was 5.9 percent, and Thailand's was 8.1 percent.[22] With deficits like these, it was increasingly difficult for the governments of these countries to maintain their currencies against the U.S. dollar. If that peg could not be held, the local currency value of dollar-denominated debt would increase, raising the specter of large-scale default on debt service payments. The scene was now set for a potentially rapid economic meltdown.

The Crisis The Asian meltdown began in mid-1997 in Thailand when it became clear that several key Thai financial institutions were on the verge of default. These institutions had been borrowing dollars from international banks at low interest rates and lending Thai baht at higher interest rates to local property developers. However, due to speculative overbuilding, these developers could not sell their commercial and residential property, forcing them to default on their debt obligations. In turn, the Thai financial institutions seemed increasingly likely to default on their dollar-denominated debt obligations to international banks. Sensing the beginning of the crisis, foreign investors fled the Thai stock market, selling their positions and converting them into U.S. dollars. The increased demand for dollars and increased supply of Thai baht pushed down the dollar/Thai baht exchange rate, while the stock market plunged.

Seeing these developments, foreign exchange dealers and hedge funds started speculating against the baht, selling it short. For the previous 13 years, the Thai baht had been pegged to the U.S. dollar at an exchange rate of about \$1 = Bt25. The Thai government tried to defend the peg, but it only succeeded in depleting its foreign exchange reserves. On July 2, 1997, the Thai government abandoned its defense and announced it would allow the baht to float freely against the dollar. The baht started a slide that would bring the exchange rate down to \$1 = Bt55 by January 1998. As the baht declined, the Thai debt bomb exploded. The 55 percent decline in the value of the baht against the dollar doubled the amount of baht required to serve the dollar-denominated debt commitments taken on by Thai financial institutions and businesses. This increased the probability of corporate bankruptcies and further pushed down the battered Thai stock market. The Thailand Set stock market index ultimately declined from 787 in January 1997 to a low of 337 in December of that year, on top of a 45 percent decline in 1996.

On July 28, the Thai government called in the International Monetary Fund. With its foreign exchange reserves depleted, Thailand lacked the foreign currency needed to finance its international trade and service debt commitments and desperately needed the capital the IMF could provide. It also needed to restore international confidence in its currency and needed the credibility associated with gaining access to IMF funds. Without IMF loans, the baht likely would increase its free fall against the U.S. dollar and the whole country might go into default. The IMF agreed to provide the Thai government with $17.2 billion in loans, but the conditions were restrictive.[23] The IMF required the Thai government to increase taxes, cut public spending, privatize several state-owned businesses, and raise interest rates—all steps designed to cool Thailand's overheated economy. The IMF also required Thailand to close illiquid financial institutions. In December 1997, the government shut 56 financial institutions, laying off 16,000 people and further deepening the recession that now gripped the country.

Following the devaluation of the Thai baht, wave after wave of speculation hit other Asian currencies. One after another in a period of weeks, the Malaysian ringgit, Indonesian rupiah, and the Singaporean dollar were all marked sharply lower. With its foreign exchange reserves down to $28 billion, Malaysia let the ringgit float on July 14, 1997. Before the devaluation, the ringgit was trading at $1 = 2.525 ringgit; six months later it had declined to $1 = 4.15 ringgit. Singapore followed on July 17, and the Singaporean dollar quickly dropped in value from $1 = S$1.495 before the devaluation to $1 = S$2.68 a few days later. Next up was Indonesia, whose rupiah was allowed to float August 14. For Indonesia, this was the beginning of a precipitous decline in the value of its currency, which was to fall from $1 = 2,400 rupiah in August 1997 to $1 = 10,000 rupiah on January 6, 1998, a loss of 76 percent.

With the exception of Singapore, whose economy is probably the most stable in the region, these devaluations were driven by factors similar to those behind the earlier devaluation of the Thai baht: a combination of excess investment; high borrowings, much of it in dollar-denominated debt; and a deteriorating balance-of-payments position. Although both Malaysia and Singapore were able to halt the slide in their currencies and stock markets without the help of the IMF, Indonesia was not. Indonesia was struggling with a private-sector, dollar-denominated debt of close to $80 billion. With the rupiah sliding precipitously almost every day, the cost of servicing this debt was exploding, pushing more Indonesian companies into technical default.

On October 31, 1997, the IMF announced it had assembled a $37 billion rescue deal for Indonesia in conjunction with the World Bank and the Asian Development Bank. In return, the Indonesian government agreed to close a number of troubled banks, reduce public spending, remove government subsidies on basic foodstuffs and energy, balance the budget, and unravel the crony capitalism that was so widespread in Indonesia. But the government of President Suharto appeared to backtrack several times on commitments made to the IMF. This precipitated further declines in the Indonesian currency and stock markets. Ultimately, Suharto removed costly government subsidies, only to see the country dissolve into chaos as the populace took to the streets to protest the resulting price increases. This unleashed a chain of events that led to Suharto's removal from power in May 1998.

The final domino to fall was South Korea. During the 1990s, South Korean companies had built up huge debt loads as they invested heavily in new industrial capacity. Now they found they had too much industrial capacity and could not generate the income required to service their debt. South Korean banks and companies had also made the mistake of borrowing in dollars, much of it in the form of short-term loans that would come due within a year. Thus, when the Korean won started to decline in the fall of 1997 in sympathy with the problems elsewhere in Asia, South Korean companies saw their debt obligations balloon. Several large companies were forced to file for bankruptcy. This triggered a decline in the South Korean currency and stock market that was difficult to halt. The South Korean central bank tried to keep the dollar/won exchange rate above $1 = W1,000 but found that this only depleted its foreign exchange reserves. On November 17, the South Korean central bank gave up the defense of the won, which quickly fell to $1 = W1,500.

With its economy on the verge of collapse, the South Korean government on November 21 requested $20 billion in standby loans from the IMF. As the negotiations progressed, it became apparent that South Korea was going to need far more than $20 billion. Among other problems, the country's short-term foreign debt was found to be twice as large as previously thought at close to $100 billion, while the country's foreign exchange reserves were down to less than $6 billion. On December 3, 1997, the IMF and South Korean government reached a deal to lend $55 billion to the country. The agreement with the IMF called for the South Koreans to open their economy and banking system to foreign investors. South Korea also pledged to restrain the *chaebol* by reducing their share of bank financing and requiring them to publish consolidated financial statements and undergo annual independent external audits. On trade liberalization, the IMF said South Korea would comply with its commitments to the World Trade Organization to eliminate trade-related subsidies and restrictive import licensing and would streamline its import certification procedures, all of which should open the South Korean economy to greater foreign competition.[24]

EVALUATING THE IMF's POLICY PRESCRIPTIONS By 2005, the IMF was committing loans to some 59 countries that were struggling with economic and currency crises. A detailed example of one such program is given in the Country Focus, which looks at IMF loans to Turkey. All IMF loan packages come with conditions attached. In general, the IMF insists on a combination of tight macroeconomic policies, including cuts in public spending, higher interest rates, and tight monetary policy. It also often pushes for the deregulation of sectors formerly protected from domestic and foreign competition, privatization of state-owned assets, and better financial reporting from the banking sector. These policies are designed to cool overheated economies by reining in inflation and reducing government spending and debt. Recently, this set of policy prescriptions has come in for tough criticisms from many observers.[25]

Inappropriate Policies One criticism is that the IMF's one-size-fits-all approach to macroeconomic policy is inappropriate for many countries. In the case of the Asian crisis, critics argue that the tight macroeconomic policies imposed by the IMF are not well suited to countries that are suffering not from excessive government spending and inflation, but from a private-sector debt crisis with deflationary undertones.[26] In South Korea, for example, the government had been running a budget surplus for years (it was 4 percent of South Korea's GDP in the 1994–96 period) and inflation was low at about 5 percent. South Korea had the second strongest financial position of any country in the Organization for Economic Cooperation and Development. Despite this, critics say, the IMF insisted on applying the same policies that it applies to countries suffering from high inflation. The IMF required South Korea to maintain an inflation rate of 5 percent. However, given the collapse in the value of its currency and the subsequent rise in price for imports such as oil, critics claimed inflationary pressures would inevitably increase in South Korea. So to hit a 5 percent inflation rate, the South Koreans would be forced to apply an unnecessarily tight monetary policy. Short-term interest rates in South Korea did jump from 12.5 percent to 21 percent immediately after the country signed its initial deal with the IMF. Increasing interest rates made it even more difficult for companies to service their already excessive short-term debt obligations, and critics used this as evidence to argue that the cure prescribed by the IMF may actually increase the probability of widespread corporate defaults, not reduce them.

The IMF rejected this criticism. According to the IMF, the central task was to rebuild confidence in the won. Once this was achieved, the won would recover from its oversold levels, reducing the size of South Korea's dollar-denominated debt burden when expressed in won, making it easier for companies to service their debt. The IMF also argued that by requiring South Korea to remove restrictions on foreign direct investment, foreign capital would flow into the country to take advantage of cheap assets. This, too, would increase demand for the Korean currency and help to improve the dollar/won exchange rate.

Korea did recover fairly quickly from the crisis, supporting the position of the IMF. While the economy contracted by 7 percent in 1998, by 2000 it had rebounded and grew at a 9 percent rate (measured by growth in GDP). Inflation, which peaked at 8 percent in 1998, fell to 2 percent by 2000, and unemployment fell from 7 percent to 4 percent over the same period. The won hit a low of \$1 = W1,812 in early 1998, but by 2000 it was back to an exchange rate of around \$1 = W1,200, at which it seems to have stabilized.

Moral Hazard
When people behave recklessly because they know they will be saved if things go wrong.

Moral Hazard

A second criticism of the IMF is that its rescue efforts are exacerbating a problem known to economists as moral hazard. **Moral hazard** arises when people behave recklessly because they know they will be saved if things go wrong. Critics point out that many Japanese and Western banks were far too willing to lend large amounts of capital to overleveraged Asian companies during the boom years of the 1990s. These critics argue that the banks should now be forced to pay the price for their rash lending policies, even if that means some banks must close.[27] Only by taking such drastic action, the argument goes, will banks learn the error of their ways and not engage in rash lending in the future. By providing support to these countries, the IMF is reducing the probability of debt default and in effect bailing out the banks whose loans gave rise to this situation.

This argument ignores two critical points. First, if some Japanese or Western banks with heavy exposure to the troubled Asian economies were forced to write off their loans due to widespread debt default, the impact would have been difficult to contain. The failure of large Japanese banks, for example, could have triggered a meltdown in the Japanese financial markets. That would almost inevitably lead to a serious decline in stock markets around the world, which was the very risk the IMF was trying to avoid by stepping in with financial support. Second, it is incorrect to imply that some banks have not had to pay the price for rash lending policies. The IMF has insisted on the closure of banks in South Korea, Thailand, and Indonesia. Foreign banks with short-term loans outstanding to South Korean enterprises have been forced by circumstances to reschedule those loans at interest rates that do not compensate for the extension of the loan maturity.

Lack of Accountability

The final criticism of the IMF is that it has become too powerful for an institution that lacks any real mechanism for accountability.[28] The IMF has determined macroeconomic policies in those countries, yet according to critics such as noted economist Jeffrey Sachs, the IMF, with a staff of less than 1,000, lacks the expertise required to do a good job. Evidence of this, according to Sachs, can be found in the fact that the IMF was singing the praises of the Thai and South Korean governments only months before both countries lurched into crisis.

Country FOCUS

Turkey and the IMF

In May 2001, the International Monetary Fund agreed to lend $8 billion to Turkey to help the country stabilize its economy and halt a sharp slide in the value of its currency. This was the third time in two years that the international lending institution had put together a loan program for Turkey, and it was the eighteenth program since Turkey became a member of the IMF in 1958.

Many of Turkey's problems stemmed from a large and inefficient state sector and heavy subsidies to various private sectors of the economy such as agriculture. Although the Turkish government started to privatize state-owned companies in the late 1980s, the programs proceeded at a glacial pace, hamstrung by political opposition within Turkey. Instead of selling state-owned assets to private investors, successive governments increased support to unprofitable state-owned industries and raised the wage rates of state employees. Nor did the government cut subsidies to politically powerful private sectors of the economy, such as agriculture. To support state industries and finance subsidies, Turkey issued significant amounts of government debt. To limit the amount of debt, the government expanded the money supply to finance spending. The result was rampant inflation and high inte-rest rates. During the 1990s, inflation averaged more than 80 percent a year while real interest rates rose to more than 50 percent on a number of occasions. Despite this, the Turkish economy continued to grow at a healthy pace of 6 percent annually in real terms, a remarkable achievement given the high inflation rates and interest rates.

By the late 1990s the "Turkish miracle" of sustained growth in the face of high inflation and interest rates was running out of steam. Government debt had risen to 60 percent of gross domestic product, government borrowing was leaving little capital for private enterprises, and the cost of financing government debt was spiraling out of control. Rampant inflation was putting pressure on the Turkish currency, the lira. Realizing that it needed to reform its economy, the Turkish government sat down with the IMF in late 1999 to work out a recovery program, adopted in January 2000.

As with most IMF programs, the focus was on bringing down the inflation rate, stabilizing the value of the Turkish currency, and restructuring the economy to reduce government debt. The Turkish government committed itself to reducing government debt by taking a number of steps. These included an accelerated privatization program, using the proceeds to pay down debt; the reduction of agricultural subsidies; reform to make it more difficult for people to qualify for public pension programs; and tax increases. The government also agreed to rein in the growth in the money supply to better control inflation. To limit the possibility of speculative attacks on the Turkish currency in the foreign exchange markets, the Turkish government and IMF announced that Turkey would peg the value of the lira against a basket of currencies and devalue the lira by a predetermined amount each month throughout 2000, bringing the total devaluation for the year to 25 percent. To ease the pain, the IMF agreed to provide the Turkish government with $5 billion in loans that could be used to support the value of the lira.

Initially the program seemed to be working. Inflation fell to 35 percent in 2000, while the economy grew by 6 percent. By the end of 2000, however, the program was in trouble. Burdened with nonperforming loans, a number of Turkish banks faced default and had been taken into public ownership by the government. When a criminal fraud investigation uncovered evidence that several of these banks had been pressured by politicians into providing loans at below-market interest rates, foreign investors, worried that more banks might be involved, started to pull their money out of Turkey. This sent the Turkish stock market into a tailspin and put enormous pressure on the Turkish lira. The government raised Turkish overnight interbank lending rates to as high as 1,950 percent to try to stem the outflow of capital, but it was clear that Turkey alone could not halt the flow.

The IMF stepped once more into the breach, December 6, 2000, announcing a quickly arranged $7.5 billion loan program for the country. In return for the loan, the IMF required the Turkish government to close 10 insolvent banks, speed up its privatization plans (which had once more stalled), and cap any pay increases for government workers. The IMF also reportedly urged the Turkish government to let its currency float freely in the foreign exchange markets, but the government refused, arguing that the result would be a rapid devaluation in the lira, which would raise import prices and fuel price inflation. The government insisted that reducing inflation should be its first priority.

This plan started to come apart in February 2001. A surge in inflation and a rapid slowdown in economic growth once more spooked foreign investors. Into this explosive mix waded Turkey's prime minister and president, who engaged in a highly public argument about economic policy and political corruption. This triggered a rapid outflow of capital. The government raised the overnight interbank lending rate to 7,500 percent to try to persuade foreigners to leave their money in the country, but to no avail. Realizing that it would be unable to keep the lira within its planned monthly devaluation range without raising interest rates to absurd levels or seriously depleting the country's foreign exchange reserves, on February 23, 2001, the Turkish government decided to let the lira float freely. The lira immediately dropped 50 percent in value against the U.S. dollar, but ended the day down some 28 percent.

Over the next two months, the Turkish economy continued to weaken as a global economic slowdown affected the nation. Inflation stayed high, and progress at reforming the country's economy remained bogged down by political considerations. By early April, the lira had fallen 40 percent against the dollar since February 23, and the country was teetering on the brink of an economic meltdown. For the third time in 18 months, the IMF stepped in, arranging for another $8 billion in loans. Once more, the IMF insisted that the Turkish government accelerate privatization, close insolvent banks, deregulate its market, and cut government spending. Critics of the IMF, however, claimed this "austerity program" would only slow the Turkish economy and make matters worse, not better. These critics advocated a mix of sound monetary policy and tax cuts to boost Turkey's economic growth.

By late 2005, significant progress had been made. Initially the Turkish government failed to fully comply with IMF mandates on economic policy, causing the institution to hold back a scheduled $1.6 billion in IMF loans until the government passed an "austerity budget," which it did reluctantly in March 2003 after months of public hand-wringing. Since then, things have improved. Inflation fell from a peak of 65 percent in December 2000 to about 8.2 percent for 2005. Economic growth increased to a robust 9 percent in 2004, followed by 5.9 percent in 2005. The pace of the privatization program has increased. The government also generated budget surpluses in the 2003–05 period. Can Turkey finally be counted as an IMF success?

Sources: P. Blustein, "Turkish Crisis Weakens the Case for Intervention," *Washington Post,* March 2, 2001, p. E1; H. Pope, "Can Turkey Finally Mend Its Economy?" *The Wall Street Journal,* May 22, 2001, p. A18; "Turkish Bath," *The Wall Street Journal,* February 23, 2001, p. A14; E. McBride, "Turkey—Fingers Crossed," *The Economist,* June 10, 2000, p. SS16–17; "Turkey and the IMF," *The Economist,* December 9, 2000, pp. 81–82; G. Chazan, "Turkey's Decision on Aid Is Sinking In," *The Wall Street Journal,* March 6, 2003, p. A11; S. Fittipaldi, "Markets Keep a Wary Eye on Ankara," *Global Finance,* October 2003, p. 88; "Plumper: Turkey," *The Economist,* December 18, 2004, p. 141; and "Turkey: Country Forecast Summary," *The Economist Intelligence Unit,* January 26, 2006.

Then the IMF put together a draconian program for South Korea without having deep knowledge of the country. Sachs's solution to this problem is to reform the IMF so it makes greater use of outside experts and its operations are open to greater outside scrutiny.

Observations As with many debates about international economics, it is not clear which side has the winning hand about the appropriateness of IMF policies. There are cases in which one can argue that IMF policies have been counterproductive, or only had limited success. For example, one might question the success of the IMF's involvement in Turkey given that the country has had to implement some 18 IMF programs since 1958 (see the accompanying Country Focus)! But the IMF can also point to some notable accomplishments, including its success in containing the Asian crisis, which could have rocked the global international monetary system to its core. Similarly, many observers give the IMF credit for its deft handling of politically difficult situations, such as the Mexican peso crisis, and for successfully promoting a free market philosophy.

LEARNING OBJECTIVE 6
Understand the implications of the global monetary system for currency management and business strategy.

Several years after the IMF's intervention, the economies of Asia and Mexico recovered. Certainly they all averted the kind of catastrophic implosion that might have occurred had the IMF not stepped in, and although some countries still faced considerable problems, it is not clear that the IMF should take much blame for this. The IMF cannot force countries to adopt the policies required to correct economic mismanagement. While a government may commit to taking corrective action in return for an IMF loan, internal political problems may make it difficult for a government to act on that commitment. In such cases, the IMF is caught between a rock and a hard place, for if it decided to withhold money, it might trigger financial collapse and the kind of contagion that it seeks to avoid.

Focus on Managerial Implications

The implications for international businesses of the material discussed in this chapter fall into three main areas: currency management, business strategy, and corporate–government relations.

Currency Management

An obvious implication with regard to currency management is that companies must recognize that the foreign exchange market does not work quite as depicted in Chapter 9. The current system is a mixed system in which a combination of government intervention and speculative activity can drive the foreign exchange market. Companies engaged in significant foreign exchange activities need to be aware of this and to adjust their foreign exchange transactions accordingly. For example, the currency management unit of Caterpillar claims it made millions of dollars in the hours following the announcement of the Plaza Accord by selling dollars and buying currencies that it expected to appreciate on the foreign exchange market following government intervention.

Under the present system, speculative buying and selling of currencies can create very volatile movements in exchange rates (as exhibited by the rise and fall of the dollar during the 1980s and the Asian currency crisis of the late 1990s). Contrary to the predictions of the purchasing power parity theory (see Chapter 9), exchange rate movements during the 1980s and 1990s often did not seem to be strongly influenced by relative inflation rates. Insofar as volatile exchange rates increase foreign exchange risk, this is not good news for business. On the other hand, as we saw in Chapter 9, the foreign exchange market has developed a number of instruments, such as the forward market and swaps, that can help to insure against foreign exchange risk. Not surprisingly, use of these instruments has increased markedly since the breakdown of the Bretton Woods system in 1973.

Business Strategy

The volatility of the present global exchange rate regime presents a conundrum for international businesses. Exchange rate movements are difficult to predict, and yet their movement can have a major impact on a business's competitive position. For a detailed example, see the accompanying Management Focus box, next page, on Airbus. Faced with uncertainty about the future value of currencies, firms can utilize the forward exchange market, which Airbus has done. However, the forward exchange market is far from perfect as a predictor of future exchange rates (see Chapter 9). It is also difficult, if not impossible, to get adequate insurance coverage for exchange rate changes that might occur several years in the future. The forward market tends to offer coverage for exchange rate changes a few months, not years, ahead. Given this, it makes sense to pursue strategies that will increase the company's strategic flexibility in the face of unpredictable exchange rate movements—that is, to pursue strategies that reduce the economic exposure of the firm (which we first discussed in Chapter 9).

Maintaining strategic flexibility can take the form of dispersing production to different locations around the globe as a real hedge against currency fluctuations (this seems to be what Airbus is now considering). Consider the case of Daimler-Benz (now DaimlerChrysler), Germany's export-oriented automobile and aerospace company. In June 1995, the company stunned the German business community when it announced it expected to post a severe loss in 1995 of about $720 million. The cause was Germany's strong currency, which had appreciated by 4 percent against a basket of major currencies since the beginning of 1995 and had risen by more than 30 percent

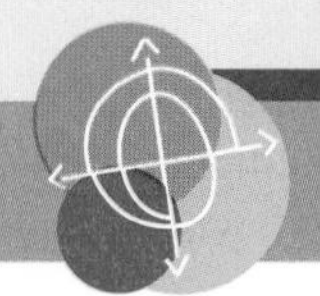

Management FOCUS

Airbus and the Euro

Airbus had reason to celebrate in 2003; for the first time in the company's history it delivered more commercial jet aircraft than longtime rival Boeing. Airbus delivered 305 planes in 2003, compared to Boeing's 281. The celebration, however, was muted, for the strength of the euro against the U.S. dollar was casting a cloud over the company's future. Airbus, which is based in Toulouse, France, prices planes in dollars, just as Boeing has always done. But more than half of Airbus's costs are in euros. So as the dollar drops in value against the euro, and it dropped by more than 50 percent between 2002 and the end of 2004, Airbus's costs rise in proportion to its revenue, squeezing profits in the process.

In the short run, the fall in the value of the dollar against the euro will not hurt Airbus. The company fully hedged its dollar exposure until 2005 and was mostly hedged for 2006. However, anticipating that the dollar will stay weak against the euro, Airbus is taking other steps to reduce its economic exposure to a strong European currency. Recognizing that raising prices is not an option given the strong competition from Boeing, Airbus has decided to focus on reducing its costs by some 15 percent by 2006. As a step toward doing this, Airbus is giving U.S. suppliers a greater share of work on new aircraft models, such as the A380 super-jumbo. It is also shifting supply work on some of its older models from European to American-based suppliers. This will increase the proportion of its costs that are in dollars, making profits less vulnerable to a rise in the value of the euro and reducing the costs of building an aircraft when they are converted back into euros.

In addition, Airbus is pushing its European-based suppliers to start pricing in U.S. dollars. Because the costs of many of these suppliers are in euros, the suppliers are finding that to comply with Airbus's wishes, they too have to move more work to the United States, or to countries whose currency is pegged to the U.S. dollar. Thus, one large French-based supplier, Zodiac, has announced that it was considering acquisitions in the United States. Not only is Airbus pushing suppliers to price components for commercial jet aircraft in dollars, but the company is also requiring suppliers to its A400M program, a military aircraft that will be sold to European governments and priced in euros, to price components in U.S. dollars. Beyond these steps, the CEO of EADS, Airbus's parent company, has publicly stated that it might be prepared to assemble aircraft in the United States if that helps to win important U.S. contracts.

Sources: D. Michaels, "Airbus Deliveries Top Boeing's; but Several Obstacles Remain," *The Wall Street Journal,* January 16, 2004, p. A9; J. L. Gerondeau, "Airbus Eyes U.S. Suppliers as Euro Gains," *Seattle Times,* February 21, 2004, p. C4; and "Euro's Gains Create Worries in Europe," *Houston Chronicle.com,* January 13, 2004, p. 3.

against the U.S. dollar since late 1994. By mid-1995, the exchange rate against the dollar stood at $1 = DM1.38. Daimler's management believed it could not make money with an exchange rate under $1 = DM1.60. Daimler's senior managers concluded that the appreciation of the mark against the dollar was probably permanent, so they decided to move substantial production outside of Germany and increase purchasing of foreign components. The idea was to reduce the vulnerability of the company to future exchange rate movements. The Mercedes-Benz division has begun to implement this move. Even before its acquisition of Chrysler Corporation in 1998, Mercedes planned to produce 10 percent of its cars outside of Germany by 2000, mostly in the United States.[29] Similarly, the move by Japanese automobile companies to expand their productive capacity in the United States and Europe can be seen in the context of the increase in the value of the yen between 1985 and 1995, which raised the price of Japanese exports. For the Japanese companies, building production capacity overseas is a hedge against continued appreciation of the yen (as well as against trade barriers).

Another way of building strategic flexibility and reducing economic exposure involves contracting out manufacturing. This allows a company to shift suppliers from country to country in response to changes in relative costs brought about by exchange rate movements. However, this kind of strategy may work only for low-value-added manufacturing (e.g., textiles), in which the individual manufacturers have few if any firm-specific skills that contribute to the value of the product. It may be less appropriate for high-value-added manufacturing, in which firm-specific technology and skills add significant value to the product (e.g., the heavy equipment industry) and in which switching costs are correspondingly high. For high-value-added manufacturing, switching suppliers will lead to a reduction in the value that is added, which may offset any cost gains arising from exchange rate fluctuations.

The roles of the IMF and the World Bank in the present international monetary system also have implications for business strategy. Increasingly, the IMF has been acting as the macroeconomic police of the world economy, insisting that countries seeking significant borrowings adopt IMF-mandated macroeconomic policies. These policies typically include anti-inflationary monetary policies and reductions in government spending. In the short run, such policies usually result in a sharp contraction of demand. International businesses selling or producing in such countries need to be aware of this and plan accordingly. In the long run, the kind of policies imposed by the IMF can promote economic growth and an expansion of demand, which create opportunities for international business.

Corporate–Government Relations

As major players in the international trade and investment environment, businesses can influence government policy toward the international monetary system. For example, intense government lobbying by U.S. exporters helped convince the U.S. government that intervention in the foreign exchange market was necessary. With this in mind, business can and should use its influence to promote an international monetary system that facilitates the growth of international trade and investment. Whether a fixed or floating regime is optimal is a subject for debate. However, exchange rate volatility such as the world experienced during the 1980s and 1990s creates an environment less conducive to international trade and investment than one with more stable exchange rates. Therefore, it would seem to be in the interests of international business to promote an international monetary system that minimizes volatile exchange rate movements, particularly when those movements are unrelated to long-run economic fundamentals.

Key Terms

international monetary system, p. 326
floating exchange rate, p. 326
pegged exchange rate, p. 327
dirty float, p. 327
fixed exchange rate, p. 327
gold standard, p. 328
gold par value, p. 328
balance-of-trade equilibrium, p. 328
managed-float system, p. 337
currency board, p. 341
currency crisis, p. 342
banking crisis, p. 342
foreign debt crisis, p. 342
moral hazard, p. 349

Summary

This chapter explained the workings of the international monetary system and pointed out its implications for international business. The chapter made the following points:

1. The gold standard is a monetary standard that pegs currencies to gold and guarantees convertibility to gold. It was thought that the gold standard contained an automatic mechanism that contributed to the simultaneous achievement of a balance-of-payments equilibrium by all countries. The gold standard broke down during the 1930s as countries engaged in competitive devaluations.

2. The Bretton Woods system of fixed exchange rates was established in 1944. The U.S. dollar was the central currency of this system; the value of every other currency was pegged to its value. Significant exchange rate devaluations were allowed only with the permission of the IMF. The role of the IMF was to maintain order in the international monetary system (*a*) to avoid a repetition of the competitive devaluations of the 1930s and (*b*) to control price inflation by imposing monetary discipline on countries.
3. The fixed exchange rate system collapsed in 1973, primarily due to speculative pressure on the dollar following a rise in U.S. inflation and a growing U.S. balance-of-trade deficit.
4. Since 1973, the world has operated with a floating exchange rate regime, and exchange rates have become more volatile and far less predictable. Volatile exchange rate movements have helped reopen the debate over the merits of fixed and floating systems.
5. The case for a floating exchange rate regime claims (*a*) such a system gives countries autonomy regarding their monetary policy and (*b*) floating exchange rates facilitate smooth adjustment of trade imbalances.
6. The case for a fixed exchange rate regime claims (*a*) the need to maintain a fixed exchange rate imposes monetary discipline on a country, (*b*) floating exchange rate regimes are vulnerable to speculative pressure, (*c*) the uncertainty that accompanies floating exchange rates dampens the growth of international trade and investment, and (*d*) far from correcting trade imbalances, depreciating a currency on the foreign exchange market tends to cause price inflation.
7. In today's international monetary system, some countries have adopted floating exchange rates, some have pegged their currency to another currency such as the U.S. dollar, and some have pegged their currency to a basket of other currencies, allowing their currency to fluctuate within a zone around the basket.
8. In the post–Bretton Woods era, the IMF has continued to play an important role in helping countries navigate their way through financial crises by lending significant capital to embattled governments and by requiring them to adopt certain macroeconomic policies.
9. An important debate is occurring over the appropriateness of IMF-mandated macroeconomic policies. Critics charge that the IMF often imposes inappropriate conditions on developing nations that are the recipients of its loans.
10. The present managed-float system of exchange rate determination has increased the importance of currency management in international businesses.
11. The volatility of exchange rates under the present managed-float system creates both opportunities and threats. One way of responding to this volatility is for companies to build strategic flexibility and limit their economic exposure by dispersing production to different locations around the globe by contracting out manufacturing (in the case of low-value-added manufacturing) and other means.

Critical Thinking and Discussion Questions

1. Why did the gold standard collapse? Is there a case for returning to some type of gold standard? What is it?
2. What opportunities might current IMF lending policies to developing nations create for international businesses? What threats might they create?
3. Do you think the standard IMF policy prescriptions of tight monetary policy and reduced government spending are always appropriate for developing nations experiencing a currency crisis? How might the IMF change its approach? What would the implications be for international businesses?
4. Debate the relative merits of fixed and floating exchange rate regimes. From the perspective of an international business, what are the most important criteria in a choice between the

systems? Which system is the more desirable for an international business?

5. Imagine that Canada, the United States, and Mexico decide to adopt a fixed exchange rate system. What would be the likely consequences of such a system for (*a*) international businesses and (*b*) the flow of trade and investment among the three countries?
6. Reread the opening case, then answer the following questions:
   a. Why do you think the Chinese government originally pegged the value of the yuan against the U.S. dollar? What were the benefits of doing this for China? What were the costs?
   b. Over the last decade, many foreign firms have invested in China and used their Chinese factories to produce goods for export. If the yuan is allowed to float freely against the U.S. dollar on the foreign exchange markets and appreciates in value, how might this affect the fortunes of those enterprises?
   c. How might a decision to let the yuan float freely affect future foreign direct investment flows into China?
   d. Under what circumstances might a decision to let the yuan float freely destabilize the Chinese economy? What might the global implications of this be?
   e. Do you think the U.S. government should push the Chinese to let the yuan float freely? Why?
   f. What do you think the Chinese government should do? Let the yuan float, maintain the peg, or change the peg in some way?

Research Task 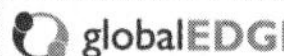 http://globalEDGE.msu.edu

Use the globalEDGE site (http://globalEDGE.msu.edu/) to complete the following exercises:

1. Until recently, the U.S. Department of State has provided annual *country reports on economic policy and trade practices*. Locate the archives of these reports and prepare a description of the exchange rate and debt management policies of an emerging market of your choice based on the latest report available.
2. The Biz/ed Web site presents a "Trade Balance and Exchange Rate Simulation" that explains how a change in exchange rate influences the trade balance. Locate the online simulator (check under the Academy section of globalEDGE) and identify what the trade balance is assumed to be a function of. Run the simulation to identify how exchange rate changes impact exports, imports and trade balance.

closing case

Recycling Petrodollars

In 2004, 2005, and 2006, global oil prices surged, reaching more than $60 a barrel, a 170 percent increase in real terms since 2001. The rise in oil prices was due to a combination of greater than expected demand for oil, particularly from rapidly developing giants such as China and India, tight supplies, and perceived geopolitical risks in the Middle East, the world's largest oil-producing region. With these conditions predicted to persist for some time, oil prices could remain high for the foreseeable future.

The surge in oil prices has been a windfall for oil-producing countries. Collectively, they earned around $700 billion in oil revenues in 2005, some $450 billion of which went to members of OPEC, with Saudi Arabia, the world's largest oil producer, reaping a major share of that. Since oil is priced in U.S. dollars, the rise in oil prices has translated into a substantial increase in the dollar holdings of oil producers (the dollars earned from the sale of oil are often referred to as *petrodollars*). In essence, rising oil prices represent a net transfer of dollars from oil consumers in countries like the United States, to oil producers in Russia, Saudi Arabia, and Venezuela. Now many people are asking, What will they do with those dollars?

One possibility is that the producing countries will spend their petrodollars on public sector infrastructure, such as health services, education, roads, and telecommunications systems. Among other things, this could boost economic growth in those countries and pull in foreign imports, which would help to counterbalance the trade surpluses enjoyed by oil producers and support global economic growth. There is some evidence that spending has picked up in many oil-producing countries. However, according to the IMF, OPEC members only spent around 40 percent of their windfall profits from higher oil prices in the 2002–05 period. The last time oil prices increased sharply in 1979, oil producers significantly ramped up spending on infrastructure, only to find themselves saddled with excessive debt when oil prices collapsed a few years later. This time they are being more cautious.

Another possibility is that the oil producers will invest a good chunk of the dollars they earn from oil sales in dollar-denominated assets, such as U.S. bonds, stocks, and real estate. So far, this seems to have been happening, with OPEC members in particular funneling dollars back into U.S. assets, mostly bonds and stocks. The implication is that by recycling their petrodollars, oil producers are helping to finance the large and growing current account deficit of the United States, enabling it to pay its growing oil import bills. Indeed, the 13.5 percent appreciation in the value of the dollar against the euro during 2005 has been attributed in part to the flow of petrodollars back into U.S. assets.

A third possibility is that oil producers will invest in nondollar-denominated assets, for example, euro- and yen-denominated assets, including European and Japanese bonds and stocks. This too has been happening. Moreover, there has been a trend for some OPEC investors to purchase not just small equity positions but entire companies. In 2005, for example, Dubai International Capital purchased the Tussauds Group, a British theme-park firm, and DP World of Dubai purchased P&O, Britain's biggest port and ferries group. (As it turns out, P&O held the contract to manage operations at six U.S. ports, and the takeover bid led to a storm of protest in the United States from those who feared that an Arab takeover of P&O might create a security risk.) Despite examples such as these, in 2005 at least, the bulk of petrodollars appear to have been recycled into dollar-denominated assets, in large part because U.S. interest rates increased throughout 2004 and 2005. The big question, however, is whether this will continue, and if it does not, how it will affect the value of the dollar.

Sources: "Recycling the Petrodollars; Oil Producers' Surpluses," *The Economist*, November 12, 2005, pp. 101–2; and S. Johnson, "Dollar's Rise Aided by OPEC Holdings," *Financial Times*, December 5, 2005, p. 17.

Case Discussion Questions

1. What will happen to the value of the U.S. dollar if oil producers decide to invest most of their earnings from oil sales in domestic infrastructure projects?
2. What factors determine the relative attractiveness of dollar-, euro-, and yen-denominated assets to oil producers flush with petrodollars? What might lead them to direct more funds toward nondollar-denominated assets?
3. What will happen to the value of the U.S. dollar if OPEC members decide to invest more of their petrodollars towards nondollar assets, such as euro-denominated stocks and bonds?
4. In addition to oil producers, China is also accumulating a large stock of dollars, currently estimated to total $1,000 billion by the end of 2006 (see opening case for details). What would happen to the value of the dollar if China and oil-producing nations all shifted out of dollar-denominated assets at the same time? What would be the consequence for the United States economy?

Nacho Doce/Corbis

part 5 Competing in the Global Marketplace

LEARNING OBJECTIVES

1. Explain the concept of strategy.
2. Understand how firms can profit by expanding globally.
3. Understand how pressures for cost reductions and pressures for local responsiveness influence strategic choice.
4. Be familiar with different strategies for competing globally and their pros and cons.
5. Explain the pros and cons of using strategic alliances to support global strategies.

chapter 11

The Strategy of International Business

MTV's Global Strategy

opening case

MTV Networks has become a symbol of globalization. Established in 1981, the U.S.-based music TV network has been expanding outside of its North American base since 1987 when it opened MTV Europe. Now owned by media conglomerate Viacom, MTV Networks, which includes siblings Nickelodeon and VH1, the music station for the aging baby boomers, generates more than $2 billion in revenues outside the United States. Since 1987, MTV has become the most ubiquitous cable programmer in the world. By 2005 the network reached a combined total of 443 million households in 140 countries outside of the United States.

While the United States still leads in number of households, with more than 85 million, the most rapid growth is elsewhere, particularly in Asia, where nearly two-thirds of the region's 3 billion people are under 35, the middle class is expanding quickly, and TV ownership is spreading rapidly. MTV Networks figures that every second of every day more than 2 million people are watching MTV around the world, the majority outside the United States.

Despite its international success, MTV's global expansion got off to a weak start. In 1987, it piped a single feed across Europe almost entirely composed of American programming with English-speaking veejays. Naively, the network's U.S. managers thought Europeans would flock to the American programming. But while viewers in Europe shared a common interest in a handful of global superstars, who at the time included Madonna and Michael Jackson, their tastes turned out to be surprisingly local. What was popular in Germany might not be popular in Great Britain. Many staples of the American music scene left Europeans cold. MTV suffered as a result. Soon local copycat stations were springing up in Europe that focused on the music scene in individual countries. They took viewers and advertisers away from MTV. As Tom Freston, chairman of MTV Networks, explained, "We were going for the most shallow layer of what united viewers and brought them together. It didn't go over too well."

In 1995, MTV changed its strategy and broke Europe into regional feeds, of which there are now more than a dozen, including feeds for the United Kingdom and Ireland; another for Germany, Austria, and Switzerland; one for Scandinavia; one for Italy; one for France; one for Spain; one for Holland; and a feed for other European nations including Belgium and Greece. The network adopted the same localization strategy elsewhere in the world. For example, in Asia it has an English-Hindi channel for India, separate Mandarin feeds for China and Taiwan, a Korean feed for South Korea, a Bahasa-language feed for Indonesia, Japanese feed for Japan, and so on. Digital and satellite technology have made the localization of programming cheaper and easier. MTV Networks can now beam half a dozen feeds off one satellite transponder.

While MTV Networks exercises creative control over these different feeds, and all the channels have the same familiar frenetic look and feel of MTV in the United States, a significant share of the programming and content is now local. When MTV opens a local station now, it begins with expatriates from elsewhere in the world to do a "gene transfer" of company culture and operating principles. Once these are established, however, the network switches to local employees and the expatriates move on. The idea is to "get inside the heads" of the local population and produce programming that matches their tastes. Although as much as 60 percent of programming ideas still originates in the United States, with staples such as *The Real World* having equivalents in different countries, an increasing share of programming is local in conception. In Italy, *MTV Kitchen* combines cooking with a music countdown. *Erotica* airs in Brazil and features a panel of youngsters discussing sex. The Indian channel produces 21 homegrown shows hosted by local veejays who speak "Hinglish," a city-bred mix of Hindi and English. Hit shows include *MTV Cricket in Control*, appropriate for a land where cricket is a national obsession, *MTV Housefull*, which hones in on Hindi film stars (India has the biggest film industry outside of Hollywood), and *MTV Bakra*, which is modeled after *Candid Camera*.

This localization push reaped big benefits for MTV, allowing the network to capture viewers back from local imitators. In India, for example, ratings increased by more than 700 percent between 1996, when the localization push began, and 2000. In turn, localization helps MTV to capture more of those all-important advertising revenues, even from other multinationals such as Coca-Cola, whose own advertising budgets are often locally determined.

Sources: M. Gunther, "MTV's Passage to India," *Fortune,* August 9, 2004, pp. 117–22; B. Pulley and A. Tanzer, "Sumner's Gemstone," *Forbes,* February 21, 2000, pp. 107–11; K. Hoffman, "Youth TV's Old Hand Prepares for the Digital Challenge," *Financial Times,* February 18, 2000, p. 8; presentation by Sumner M. Redstone, chairman and CEO, Viacom Inc., delivered to Salomon Smith Barney 11th Annual Global Entertainment Media, Telecommunications Conference, Scottsdale, AZ, January 8, 2001, archived at www.viacom.com; and Viacom 10K statement, 2005.

Introduction

Our primary concern thus far in this book has been with aspects of the larger environment in which international businesses compete. As we have described it in the preceding chapters, this environment has included the different political, economic, and cultural institutions found in nations, the international trade and investment framework, and the international monetary system. Now our focus shifts from the environment to the firm itself and, in particular, to the actions managers can take to compete more effectively as an international business. In this chapter, we look at how firms can increase their profitability by expanding their operations in foreign markets. We discuss the different strategies that firms pursue when competing internationally. We consider the pros and cons of these strategies. We discuss the various factors that affect a firm's choice of strategy. We also look at why firms often enter into strategic alliances with their global competitors, and we discuss the benefits, costs, and risks of strategic alliances.

MTV Networks, profiled in the opening case, gives us a preview of some issues that we will explore in this chapter. Like many other companies, MTV moved into other countries because it saw huge growth opportunities there, and it thought it could create value by transferring its business model and American-style music programming to foreign markets. MTV initially treated foreign markets much like the United States, right down to airing the same music videos worldwide, but it soon found that this was not the correct approach. Many American music stars drew big yawns in Europe and Asia, where most stars were local. These national differences in customer tastes and preferences required MTV to change its approach to programming. It moved away from its one-size-fits-all strategy of global standardization and became more local in its orientation, adapting its programming to different markets, with different music videos and programs being aired in different markets. At the same time, MTV's foreign affiliates still have the same look, feel, and overall programming philosophy of the U.S. parent. Striking the right balance between global standardization and local responsiveness let MTV reap big dividends, enabling the network to gain viewers and advertisers at the expense of competitors. As we shall see, many other enterprises have sought to do the same thing.

Strategy and the Firm

LEARNING OBJECTIVE 1
Explain the concept of strategy.

Before we discuss the strategies that managers in the multinational enterprise can pursue, we need to review some basic principles of strategy. A firm's **strategy** can be defined as the actions that managers take to attain the goals of the firm. For most firms, the preeminent goal is to maximize the value of the firm for its owners, its shareholders (subject to the very important constraint that this is done in a legal, ethical, and socially responsible manner—see Chapter 5 for details). To maximize the value of a firm, managers must pursue strategies that increase the *profitability* of the enterprise and its rate of *profit growth* over time (see Figure 11.1). **Profitability** can be measured in a number of ways, but for consistency, we shall define it as the rate of return that the firm makes on its invested capital (ROIC), which is calculated by dividing the net profits of the firm by total invested capital.[1] **Profit growth** is measured by the percentage increase in net profits over time. In general, higher profitability and a higher rate of profit growth will increase the value of an enterprise and thus the returns garnered by its owners, the shareholders.[2]

Strategy
The actions that managers take to attain company goals.

Profitability
The rate of return concept.

Profit Growth
The percentage increase in net profits over time.

Managers can increase the profitability of the firm by pursuing strategies that lower costs or by pursuing strategies that add value to the firm's products, which enables the firm to raise prices. Managers can increase the rate at which the firm's profits grow

figure 11.1

Determinates of Enterprise Value

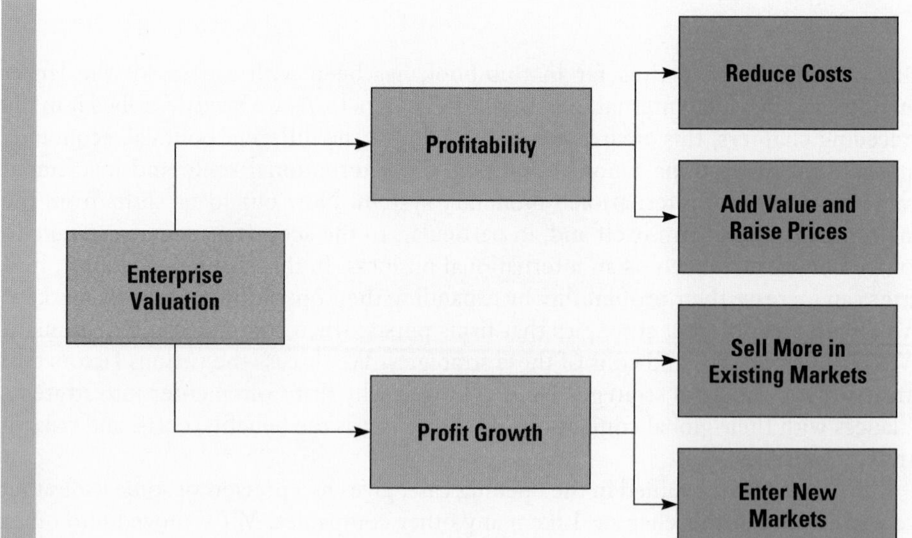

over time by pursuing strategies to sell more products in existing markets or by pursuing strategies to enter new markets. As we shall see, as with MTV, expanding internationally can help managers boost the firm's profitability *and* increase the rate of profit growth over time.

VALUE CREATION The way to increase the profitability of a firm is to create more value. The amount of value a firm creates is measured by the difference between its costs of production and the value that consumers perceive in its products. See the Another Perspective box below. In general, the more value customers place on a firm's products, the higher the price the firm can charge for those products. However, the price a firm charges for a good or service is typically less than the value placed on that good or service by the customer. This is because the customer captures some of that value in the form of what economists call a *consumer surplus*.[3] The customer is able to do this because the firm is competing with other firms for the customer's business, so the firm must charge a lower price than it could were it a monopoly supplier. Also, it is normally impossible to segment the market to such a degree that the firm can charge each customer a price that reflects that individual's assessment of the value of a product, which economists refer to as a *customer's reservation price*. For these reasons, the price that gets charged tends to be less than the value placed on the product by many customers.

Figure 11.2 illustrates these concepts. The value of a product to an *average* consumer is V; the average price that the firm can charge a consumer for that product given competitive pressures and its ability to segment the market is P; and the average unit cost of producing that product is C (C comprises all relevant costs, including the firm's cost of capital). The firm's profit per unit sold (π) is equal to $P - C$, while

Another Perspective

Education as a Part of Your Value Chain

The concept of value chain can be used to examine the role your undergraduate education plays in your life plans. If you look closely at your personal development plans (education, internship, physical and emotional/spiritual fitness, extracurricular activities) and think about them in terms of primary and support activities, how does your choice of major fit into your personal development strategy? How do your choices of how you spend your time fit into your value chain? Do you ever spend time doing things that don't support the strategic goals of your personal value chain?

Value Creation

V - P
P - C
V - C
C
V P C

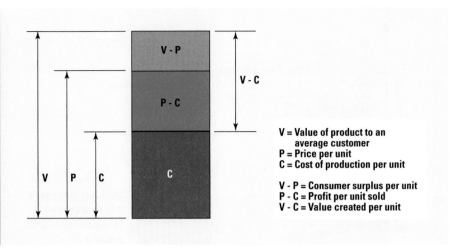

V = Value of product to an average customer
P = Price per unit
C = Cost of production per unit

V - P = Consumer surplus per unit
P - C = Profit per unit sold
V - C = Value created per unit

the consumer surplus per unit is equal to V − P (another way of thinking of the consumer surplus is as "value for the money"; the greater the consumer surplus, the greater the value for the money the consumer gets). The firm makes a profit so long as P is greater than C, and its profit will be greater the lower C is *relative* to P. The difference between V and P is in part determined by the intensity of competitive pressure in the marketplace; the lower the intensity of competitive pressure, the higher the price charged relative to V.[4] In general, the higher the firm's profit per unit sold is, the greater its profitability will be, all else being equal.

The firm's **value creation** is measured by the difference between V and C (V − C); a company creates value by converting inputs that cost C into a product on which consumers place a value of V. A company can create more value (V − C) either by lowering production costs, C, or by making the product more attractive through superior design, styling, functionality, features, reliability, after-sales service, and the like, so that consumers place a greater value on it (V increases) and, consequently, are willing to pay a higher price (P increases). This discussion suggests that *a firm has high profits when it creates more value for its customers and does so at a lower cost.* We refer to a strategy that focuses primarily on lowering production costs as a *low-cost strategy.* We refer to a strategy that focuses primarily on increasing the attractiveness of a product as a *differentiation strategy.*[5] MTV primarily focuses on the differentiation side of this equation; it tried to differentiate itself from rivals through more compelling programming.

Value Creation
Performing activities that increase the value of goods or services to consumers.

Michael Porter has argued that *low cost* and *differentiation* are two basic strategies for creating value and attaining a competitive advantage in an industry.[6] According to Porter, superior profitability goes to those firms that can create superior value, and the way to create superior value is to drive down the cost structure of the business or differentiate the product in some way so that consumers value it more and are prepared to pay a premium price. Superior value creation relative to rivals does not necessarily require a firm to have the lowest cost structure in an industry, or to create the most valuable product in the eyes of consumers. However, it does require that the gap between value (V) and cost of production (C) be greater than the gap attained by competitors.

STRATEGIC POSITIONING Porter notes that it is important for a firm to be explicit about its choice of strategic emphasis with regard to value creation (differentiation) and low cost, and to configure its internal operations to support that strategic

figure 11.3

Strategic Choice in the International Hotel Industry

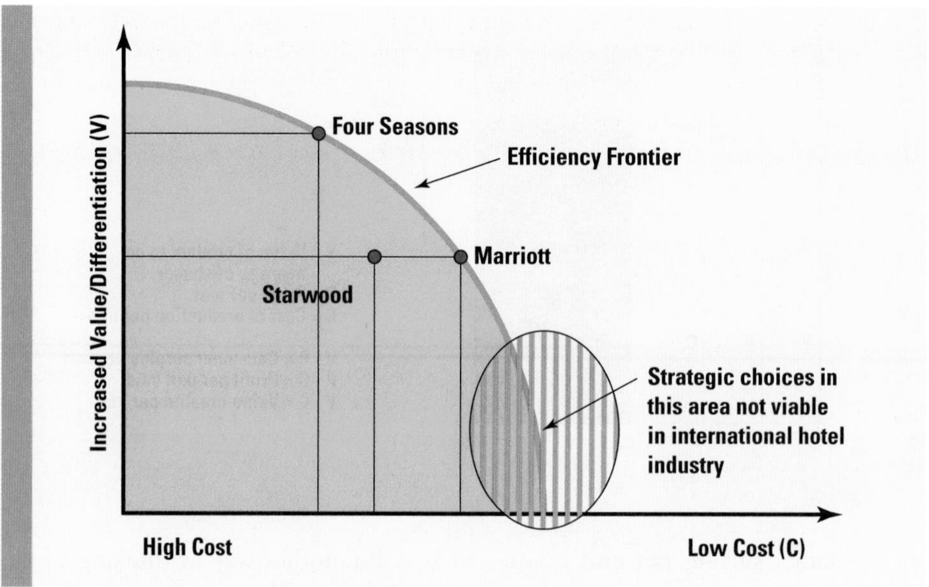

emphasis.[7] Figure 11.3 illustrates his point. The convex curve in Figure 11.3 is what economists refer to as an *efficiency frontier*. The efficiency frontier shows all of the different positions that a firm can adopt with regard to adding value to the product (V) and low cost (C), assuming that its internal operations are configured efficiently to support a particular position (note that the horizontal axis in Figure 11.3 is reverse scaled—moving along the axis to the right implies lower costs). The efficiency frontier has a convex shape because of diminishing returns. Diminishing returns imply that when a firm already has significant value built into its product offerings, increasing value by a relatively small amount requires significant additional costs. The converse also holds, when a firm already has a low-cost structure, it has to give up a lot of value in its product offerings to get additional cost reductions.

Three hotel firms with a global presence that cater to international travelers are plotted on Figure 11.3: Four Seasons, Marriott International, and Starwood (Starwood owns the Sheraton and Westin chains). Four Seasons positions itself as a luxury chain and emphasizes the value of its product offerings, which drives up its costs of operations. Marriott and Starwood are positioned more in the middle of the market. Both emphasize sufficient value to attract international business travelers, but they are not luxury chains like Four Seasons. In Figure 11.3, Four Seasons and Marriott are shown to be on the efficiency frontier, indicating that their internal operations are well configured to their strategy and run efficiently. Starwood is inside the frontier, indicating that its operations are not running as efficiently as they might be, and that its costs are too high. This implies that Starwood is less profitable than Four Seasons and Marriott and that its managers must take steps to improve the company's performance.

Porter emphasizes that it is very important for management to decide where the company wants to be positioned with regard to value (V) and cost (C), to configure operations accordingly, and to manage them efficiently to make sure the firm is operating on the efficiency frontier. However, not all positions on the efficiency frontier are viable. In the international hotel industry, for example, there might not be enough demand to support a chain that emphasizes low cost and strips all the value out of its product offerings (see Figure 11.3). International travelers are relatively affluent and expect a degree of comfort (value) when they travel away from home.

A central tenet of the basic strategy paradigm is that to maximize its profitability, a firm must do three things: (*a*) pick a position on the efficiency frontier that is viable in the sense that there is enough demand to support that choice; (*b*) configure its internal operations, such as manufacturing, marketing, logistics, information systems, human resources, and so on, so that they support that position; and (*c*) make sure that the firm has the right organization structure in place to execute its strategy. *The strategy, operations, and organization of the firm must all be consistent with each other if it is to attain a competitive advantage and garner superior profitability.* By **operations** we mean the different value-creation activities a firm undertakes, which we shall review next.

Operations The various value-creation activities a firm undertakes.

OPERATIONS: THE FIRM AS A VALUE CHAIN

The operations of a firm can be thought of as a value chain composed of a series of distinct value-creation activities, including production, marketing and sales, materials management, R&D, human resources, information systems, and the firm infrastructure. We can categorize these value-creation activities, or operations, as primary activities and support activities (see Figure 11.4).[8] As noted above, if a firm is to implement its strategy efficiently, and position itself on the efficiency frontier shown in Figure 11.3, it must manage these activities effectively and in a manner that is consistent with its strategy.

Primary Activities

Primary activities have to do with the design, creation, and delivery of the product; its marketing; and its support and after-sale service. Following normal practice, in the value chain illustrated in Figure 11.4, the primary activities are divided into four functions: research and development, production, marketing and sales, and customer service.

Research and development (R&D) is concerned with the design of products and production processes. Although we think of R&D as being associated with the design of physical products and production processes in manufacturing enterprises, many service companies also undertake R&D. For example, banks compete with each other by developing new financial products and new ways of delivering those products to customers. Online banking and smart debit cards are two examples of product development in the banking industry. Earlier examples of innovation in the banking industry included automated teller machines, credit cards, and debit cards. Through superior product design, R&D can increase the functionality of products, which makes them more attractive to consumers (raising V). Alternatively, R&D may result in more

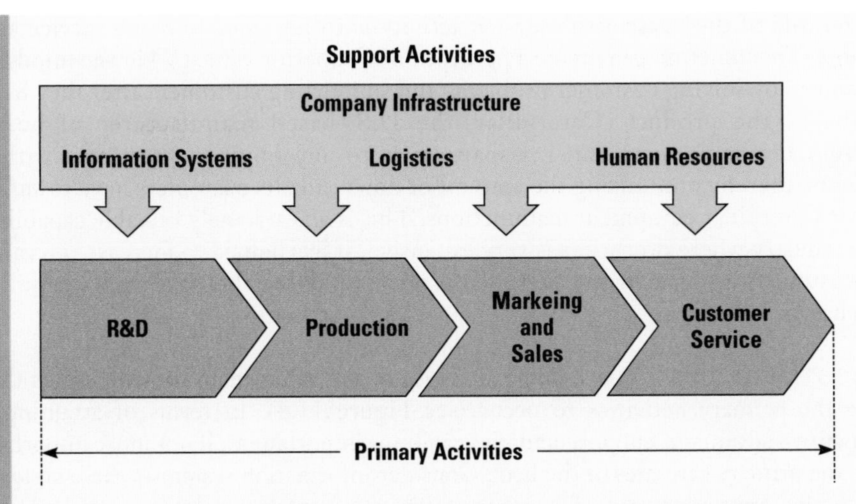

figure 11.4
The Value Chain

efficient production processes, thereby cutting production costs (lowering C). Either way, the R&D function can create value.

Production is concerned with the creation of a good or service. For physical products, when we talk about production we generally mean manufacturing. Thus, we can talk about the production of an automobile. For services such as banking or health care, production typically occurs when the service is delivered to the customer (e.g., when a bank originates a loan for a customer it is engaged in "production" of the loan). For a retailer such as Wal-Mart, production is concerned with selecting the merchandise, stocking the store, and ringing up the sale at the cash register. For MTV, production is concerned with the creation, programming, and broadcasting of content, such as music videos and thematic shows. The production activity of a firm creates value by performing its activities efficiently so lower costs result (lower C) or by performing them in such a way that a higher-quality product is produced (which results in higher V).

The marketing and sales functions of a firm can help to create value in several ways. Through brand positioning and advertising, the marketing function can increase the value (V) that consumers perceive to be contained in a firm's product. If these create a favorable impression of the firm's product in the minds of consumers, they increase the price that can be charged for the firm's product. For example, Ford has produced a high-value version of its Ford Expedition SUV. Sold as the Lincoln Navigator and priced around $10,000 higher, the Navigator has the same body, engine, chassis, and design as the Expedition, but through skilled advertising and marketing, supported by some fairly minor features changes (e.g., more accessories and the addition of a Lincoln-style engine grille and nameplate), Ford has fostered the perception that the Navigator is a "luxury SUV." This marketing strategy has increased the perceived value (V) of the Navigator relative to the Expedition, which enables Ford to charge a higher price for the car (P).

Marketing and sales can also create value by discovering consumer needs and communicating them back to the R&D function of the company, which can then design products that better match those needs. For example, the allocation of research budgets at Pfizer, the world's largest pharmaceutical company, is determined by the marketing function's assessment of the potential market size associated with solving unmet medical needs. Thus, Pfizer is currently directing significant monies to R&D efforts aimed at finding treatments for Alzheimer's disease, principally because marketing has identified the treatment of Alzheimer's as a major unmet medical need in nations around the world where the population is aging.

The role of the enterprise's service activity is to provide after-sale service and support. This function can create a perception of superior value (V) in the minds of consumers by solving customer problems and supporting customers after they have purchased the product. Caterpillar, the U.S.-based manufacturer of heavy earthmoving equipment, can get spare parts to any point in the world within 24 hours, thereby minimizing the amount of downtime its customers have to suffer if their Caterpillar equipment malfunctions. This is an extremely valuable capability in an industry where downtime is very expensive. It has helped to increase the value that customers associate with Caterpillar products and thus the price that Caterpillar can charge.

Support Activities

The support activities of the value chain provide inputs that allow the primary activities to occur (see Figure 11.4). In terms of attaining a competitive advantage, support activities can be as important as, if not more important than, the primary activities of the firm. Consider information systems—these systems refer to the electronic systems for managing inventory, tracking sales, pricing products, selling products, dealing with customer service inquiries, and so on. Information systems, when coupled with the communications features of the Internet, can alter the efficiency and effectiveness with which a firm manages its other value-creation activities. Dell Computer, for example, has used its information systems to attain a competitive advantage over rivals. When customers place an order for a Dell product over the firm's Web site, that information is immediately transmitted, via the Internet, to suppliers, who then configure their production schedules to produce and ship that product so that it arrives at the right assembly plant at the right time. These systems have reduced the amount of inventory that Dell holds at its factories to under two days, which is a major source of cost savings.

The logistics function controls the transmission of physical materials through the value chain, from procurement through production and into distribution. The efficiency with which this is carried out can significantly reduce cost (lower C), thereby creating more value. The combination of logistics systems and information systems is a particularly potent source of cost savings in many enterprises. For example, using its information systems, Dell can locate parts in its global logistics network on a real-time basis, determine when they will arrive at an assembly plant, and thus efficiently schedule production.

The human resource function can help create more value in a number of ways. It ensures that the company has the right mix of skilled people to perform its value-creation activities effectively. The human resource function also ensures that people are adequately trained, motivated, and compensated to perform their value-creation tasks. In a multinational enterprise, one of the things human resources can do to boost the competitive position of the firm is to advantage of its transnational reach to identify, recruit, and develop a cadre of skilled managers, regardless of their nationality, who can be groomed to take on senior management positions. They can find the very best, wherever they are in the world. Indeed, the senior management ranks of many multinationals are becoming increasingly diverse, as managers from a variety of national backgrounds have ascended to senior leadership positions. Japan's Sony, for example, is now headed not by a Japanese national, but by Howard Stringer, a Welshman.

The final support activity is the company infrastructure, or the context within which all the other value-creation activities occur. The infrastructure includes the organizational structure, control systems, and culture of the firm. Because top management can exert considerable influence in shaping these aspects of a firm, top management should also be viewed as part of the firm's infrastructure. Through strong leadership, top management can consciously shape the infrastructure of a firm and through that the performance of all its value-creation activities.

Organization Architecture
The totality of a firm's organization, including formal organizational structure, control systems and incentives, organizational culture, processes, and people.

ORGANIZATION: THE IMPLEMENTATION OF STRATEGY The strategy of a firm is implemented through its organization. For a firm to have superior ROIC, its organization must support its strategy and operations. The term **organization architecture** refers to the totality of a firm's organization, including formal organizational structure, control systems and incentives, organizational culture, processes, and people.[9] Figure 11.5 illustrates these different elements. By **organizational structure,** we mean three things: first, the formal division of the organization into subunits such as product divisions, national operations, and functions (most organizational charts display this aspect of structure); second, the location of decision-making responsibilities within that structure (e.g., centralized or decentralized); and third, the establishment of integrating mechanisms to coordinate the activities of subunits, including cross-functional teams and or panregional committees.

Organizational Structure
The three-part structure of an organization, including its formal division into subunits such as product divisions, its location of decision-making responsibilities within that structure, and the establishment of integrating mechanisms to coordinate the activities of all subunits.

figure 11.5

Organization Architecture

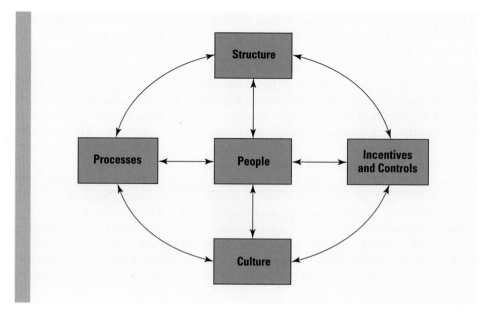

Controls
The metrics used to measure the performance of subunits and make judgments about how well managers are running those subunits.

Incentives
The devices used to reward appropriate managerial behavior.

Processes
The manner in which decisions are made and work is performed within any organization.

Organizational Culture
The norms and value systems that are shared among the employees of an organization.

People
The employees of an organization, its recruiting, compensation, and retention strategies, and the type of people who work at the organization.

Controls are the metrics used to measure the performance of subunits and make judgments about how well managers are running those subunits. **Incentives** are the devices used to reward appropriate managerial behavior. Incentives are closely tied to performance metrics. For example, the incentives of a manager in charge of a national operating subsidiary might be linked to the performance of that company. Specifically, she might receive a bonus if her subsidiary exceeds its performance targets.

Processes are the manner in which decisions are made and work is performed within the organization. Examples are the processes for formulating strategy, for deciding how to allocate resources within a firm, or for evaluating the performance of managers and giving feedback. Processes are conceptually distinct from the location of decision-making responsibilities within an organization, although both involve decisions. While the CEO might have ultimate responsibility for deciding what the strategy of the firm should be (i.e., the decision-making responsibility is centralized), the process he or she uses to make that decision might include the solicitation of ideas and criticism from lower-level managers.

Organizational culture is the norms and value systems that are shared among the employees of an organization. Just as societies have cultures (see Chapter 3 for details), so do organizations. Organizations are societies of individuals who come together to perform collective tasks. They have their own distinctive patterns of culture and subculture.[10] As we shall see, organizational culture can have a profound impact on how a firm performs. Finally, by **people** we mean not just the employees of the organization, but also the strategy used to recruit, compensate, and retain those individuals and the type of people that they are in terms of their skills, values, and orientation (discussed in depth in Chapter 16).

As illustrated by the arrows in Figure 11.5, the various components of an organization's architecture are not independent of each other: Each component shapes, and is shaped by, other components of architecture. An obvious example is the strategy regarding people. This can be used proactively to hire individuals whose internal values are consistent with those that the firm wishes to emphasize in its organizational culture. Thus, the people component of architecture can be used to reinforce (or not) the prevailing culture of the organization.

If a firm to going to maximize its profitability, it must pay close attention to achieving internal consistency between the various components of its architecture, and the architecture must support the strategy and operations of the firm. For illustration, again consider MTV. To attain the right balance between global standardization and local responsiveness, MTV had to decide what activities to centralize in the United States and what to decentralize. Initially MTV centralized most of the decisions regarding program content in the United States. However, it soon realized that this was the wrong approach, so it decentralized responsibility for programming to local subsidiaries, who were free to take content developed in the United States and customize it for their own markets, or to develop unique content that matched local requirements. In other words, when MTV decided to emphasize local responsiveness, it also had to make changes to its organizational architecture, decentralizing key decision-making responsibilities to local subsidiaries so that its structure matched its strategy.

IN SUM: STRATEGIC FIT In sum, as we have repeatedly stressed, for a firm to attain superior performance and earn a high return on capital, its strategy (as captured by its desired strategic position on the efficiency frontier), must make sense given market conditions (there must be sufficient demand to support that strategic choice). The operations of the firm must be configured in a way that supports the strategy of the firm, and the organization architecture of the firm must match the operations and strategy of the firm. In other words, as illustrated in Figure 11.6, market conditions, strategy, operations and organization must all be consistent with each other, or fit each other, for superior performance to be attained.

Of course, the issue is more complex than as illustrated in Figure 11.6. For example, the firm can influence market conditions through its choice of strategy: It can create demand by leveraging core skills to create new market opportunities. In addition, because of shifts in market conditions caused by new technologies, government action such as deregulation, demographics, or social trends, the strategy of the firm may no longer fit the market. In such circumstances, the firm must change its strategy, operations, and organization to fit the new reality, which can be an extraordinarily difficult challenge. And last but by no means least, international expansion adds an additional layer of complexity to the strategic challenges facing the firm. We shall now consider this.

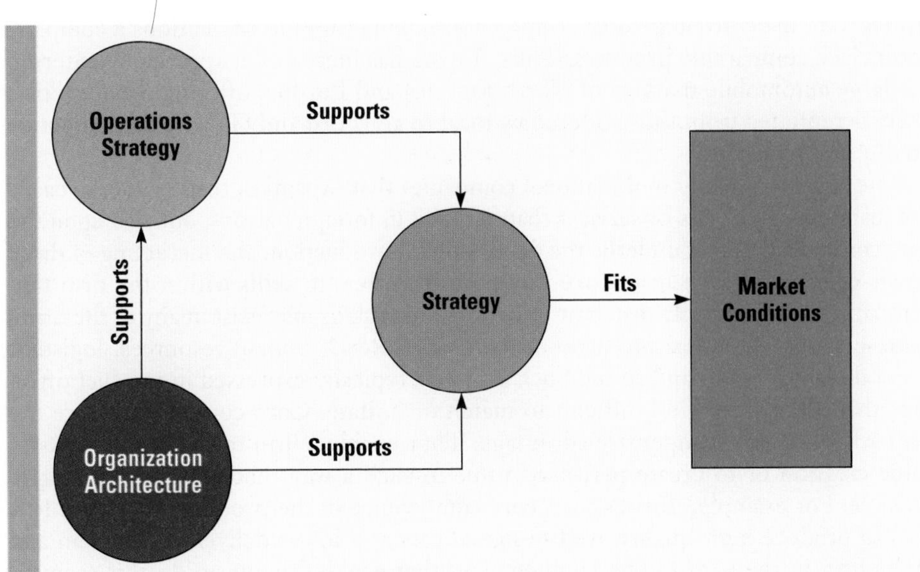

figure 11.6

Strategic Fit

Global Expansion, Profitability, and Profit Growth

LEARNING OBJECTIVE 2
Understand how firms can profit by expanding globally.

Expanding globally allows firms to increase their profitability and rate of profit growth in ways not available to purely domestic enterprises.[11] Firms that operate internationally are able to

1. Expand the market for their domestic product offerings by selling those products in international markets.
2. Realize location economies by dispersing individual value-creation activities to those locations around the globe where they can be performed most efficiently and effectively.
3. Realize greater cost economies from experience effects by serving an expanded global market from a central location, thereby reducing the costs of value creation.
4. Earn a greater return by leveraging any valuable skills developed in foreign operations and transferring them to other entities within the firm's global network of operations.

As we will see, however, a firm's ability to increase its profitability and profit growth by pursuing these strategies is constrained by the need to customize its product offerings, marketing strategy, and business strategy to differing national conditions; that is, by the imperative of localization.

EXPANDING THE MARKET: LEVERAGING PRODUCTS AND COMPETENCIES A company can increase its growth rate by taking goods or services developed at home and selling them internationally. Almost all multinationals started out doing just this. Procter & Gamble, for example, developed most of its best-selling products such as Pampers disposable diapers and Ivory soap in the United States and subsequently sold them around the world. Similarly, although Microsoft developed its software in the United States, from its earliest days the company has always focused on selling that software in international markets. Automobile companies such as Volkswagen and Toyota also grew by developing products at home and then selling them in international markets. The returns from such a strategy are likely to be greater if indigenous competitors in the nations a company enters lack comparable products. Thus, Toyota has increased its profits by entering the large automobile markets of North America and Europe, offering products that are differentiated from those offered by local rivals (Ford and GM) by their superior quality and reliability.

The success of many multinational companies that expand in this manner is based not just upon the goods or services that they sell in foreign nations, but also upon the core competencies that underlie the development, production, and marketing of those goods or services. The term **core competence** refers to skills within the firm that competitors cannot easily match or imitate.[12] These skills may exist in any of the firm's value-creation activities: production, marketing, R&D, human resources, logistics, general management, and so on. Such skills are typically expressed in product offerings that other firms find difficult to match or imitate. Core competencies are the bedrock of a firm's competitive advantage. They enable a firm to reduce the costs of value creation or to create perceived value in such a way that premium pricing is possible. For example, Toyota has a core competence in the production of cars. It is able to produce high-quality, well-designed cars at a lower delivered cost than any other firm in the world. The competencies that enable Toyota to do this seem to

Core Competence
The skills within a firm that competitors cannot easily match or imitate.

reside primarily in the firm's production and logistics functions.[13] McDonald's has a core competence in managing fast-food operations (it seems to be one of the most skilled firms in the world in this industry); Procter & Gamble has a core competence in developing and marketing name-brand consumer products (it is one of the most skilled firms in the world in this business); Starbucks has a core competence in the management of retail outlets selling high volumes of freshly brewed coffee-based drinks.

Since core competencies are by definition the source of a firm's competitive advantage, the successful global expansion by manufacturing companies such as Toyota and P&G was based not just on leveraging products and selling them in foreign markets, but also on the transfer of core competencies to foreign markets where indigenous competitors lacked them. The same can be said of companies engaged in the service sectors of an economy, such as financial institutions, retailers, restaurant chains, and hotels. Expanding the market for their services often means replicating their business model in foreign nations (albeit with some changes to account for local differences, which we will discuss in more detail shortly). Starbucks, for example, is expanding rapidly outside of the United States by using its basic U.S. business model as a blueprint for establishing international operations. As explained in the opening case, MTV has done the same thing, and it now serves 140 nations. Similarly, McDonald's is famous for its international expansion strategy, which has taken the company into more than 120 nations that collectively generate over half of the company's revenues.

LOCATION ECONOMIES We know from earlier chapters that countries differ along a range of dimensions, including the economic, political, legal, and cultural, and that these differences can either raise or lower the costs of doing business in a country. The theory of international trade also teaches us that due to differences in factor costs, certain countries have a comparative advantage in the production of certain products. Japan might excel in the production of automobiles and consumer electronics; the United States in the production of computer software, pharmaceuticals, biotechnology products, and financial services; Switzerland in the production of precision instruments and pharmaceuticals; South Korea in the production of semiconductors; and China in the production of apparel.[14]

For a firm that is trying to survive in a competitive global market, this implies that *trade barriers and transportation costs* permitting, the firm will benefit by basing each value-creation activity it performs at that location where economic, political, and cultural conditions, including relative factor costs, are most conducive to the performance of that activity. Thus, if the best designers for a product live in France, a firm should base its design operations in France. If the most productive labor force for assembly operations is in Mexico, assembly operations should be based in Mexico. If the best marketers are in the United States, the marketing strategy should be formulated in the United States. And so on.

Firms that pursue such a strategy can realize what we refer to as **location economies,** which are the economies that arise from performing a value-creation activity in the optimal location for that activity, wherever in the world that might be (transportation costs and trade barriers permitting). Locating a value-creation activity in the optimal location for that activity can have one of two effects. *It can lower the costs of value creation and help the firm to achieve a low-cost position, or it can enable a firm to differentiate its product offerings from those of competitors.* In terms of Figure 11.2, it can lower C or increase V (which in general supports higher pricing), both of which boost the profitability of the enterprise.

Location Economies
The economies that arise from performing a value-creation activity in the optimal location for that activity, wherever in the world that may be found, at a cost advantage to the firm.

For an example of how this works in an international business, consider Clear Vision, a manufacturer and distributor of eyewear. Started in the 1980s by David Glassman, the firm now generates annual gross revenues of more than $100 million. Not exactly small, but no corporate giant either, Clear Vision is a multinational firm with production facilities on three continents and customers around the world. Clear Vision began its move toward becoming a multinational in the 1980s. The strong dollar at that time made U.S.-based manufacturing very expensive. Low-priced imports were taking an ever-larger share of the U.S. eyewear market, and Clear Vision realized it could not survive unless it also began to import. Initially, the firm bought from independent overseas manufacturers, primarily in Hong Kong. However, it became dissatisfied with these suppliers' product quality and delivery. As Clear Vision's volume of imports increased, Glassman decided the best way to guarantee quality and delivery was to set up Clear Vision's own manufacturing operation overseas. Accordingly, Clear Vision found a Chinese partner, and together they opened a manufacturing facility in Hong Kong, with Clear Vision being the majority shareholder.

The choice of the Hong Kong location was influenced by its combination of low labor costs, a skilled workforce, and tax breaks given by the Hong Kong government. The firm's objective at this point was to lower production costs by locating value-creation activities at an appropriate location. After a few years, however, the increasing industrialization of Hong Kong and a growing labor shortage had pushed up wage rates to the extent that it was no longer a low-cost location. In response, Glassman and his Chinese partner moved part of their manufacturing to a plant in mainland China to take advantage of the lower wage rates there. Again, the goal was to lower production costs. The parts for eyewear frames manufactured at this plant are shipped to the Hong Kong factory for final assembly and then distributed to markets in North and South America. The Hong Kong factory now employs 80 people and the China plant between 300 and 400.

At the same time, Clear Vision was looking for opportunities to invest in foreign eyewear firms with reputations for fashionable design and high quality. Its objective was not to reduce production costs but to launch a line of high-quality differentiated, "designer" eyewear. Clear Vision did not have the design capability in-house to support such a line, but Glassman knew that certain foreign manufacturers did. As a result, Clear Vision invested in factories in Japan, France, and Italy, holding a minority shareholding in each case. These factories now supply eyewear for Clear Vision's Status Eye division, which markets high-priced designer eyewear.[15]

Thus, to deal with a threat from foreign competition, Clear Vision adopted a strategy intended to lower its cost structure (lower C): shifting its production from a high-cost location, the United States, to a low-cost location, first Hong Kong and later China. Then Clear Vision adopted a strategy intended to increase the perceived value of its product (increase V) so it could charge a premium price (P). Reasoning that premium pricing in eyewear depended on superior design, its strategy involved investing capital in French, Italian, and Japanese factories that had reputations for superior design. In sum, Clear Vision's strategies included some actions intended to reduce its costs of creating value and other actions intended to add perceived value to its product through differentiation. The overall goal was to increase the value created by Clear Vision and thus the profitability of the enterprise. To the extent that these strategies were successful, the firm should have attained a higher profit margin and greater profitability than if it had remained a U.S.-based manufacturer of eyewear.

Global Web
When different stages of a value chain are dispersed to those locations around the globe where value added is maximized or where costs of value creation are minimized.

Creating a Global Web Generalizing from the Clear Vision example, one result of this kind of thinking is the creation of a **global web** of value-creation activities, with different stages of the value chain being dispersed to those locations around the globe where perceived value is maximized or where the costs of value creation are minimized.[16] Consider Lenova's ThinkPad laptop computers (Lenova is the Chinese computer company that purchased IBM's personal computer operations in 2005).[17] This product is designed in the United States by engineers because Lenova believes that the United States is the best location in the world to do the basic design work. The case, keyboard, and hard drive are made in Thailand; the display screen and memory in South Korea; the built-in wireless card in Malaysia; and the microprocessor in the United States. In each case, these components are manufactured and sourced from the optimal location given current factor costs. These components are then shipped to an assembly operation in Mexico, where the product is assembled before being shipped to the United States for final sale. Lenova assembles the ThinkPad in Mexico because of the low labor costs there. The marketing and sales strategy for North America is developed by Lenova personnel in the United States, primarily because managers believe that due to their knowledge of the local marketplace, U.S. personnel add more value to the product through their marketing efforts than personnel based elsewhere.

In theory, a firm that realizes location economies by dispersing each of its value-creation activities to its optimal location should have a competitive advantage vis-à-vis a firm that bases all of its value-creation activities at a single location. It should be able to better differentiate its product offering (thereby raising perceived value, V) and lower its cost structure (C) than its single-location competitor. In a world in which competitive pressures are increasing, such a strategy may become an imperative for survival.

Some Caveats

Introducing transportation costs and trade barriers complicates this picture. Due to favorable factor endowments, New Zealand may have a comparative advantage for automobile assembly operations, but high transportation costs would make it an uneconomical location from which to serve global markets. Another caveat concerns the importance of assessing political and economic risks when making location decisions. Even if a country looks attractive as a production location when measured against all the standard criteria, if its government is unstable or totalitarian, the firm might be advised not to base production there. (Political risk is discussed in Chapter 2.) Similarly, if the government appears to be pursuing inappropriate economic policies that could lead to foreign exchange risk, that might be another reason for not basing production in that location, even if other factors look favorable.

EXPERIENCE EFFECTS

The **experience curve** refers to systematic reductions in production costs that have been observed to occur over the life of a product.[18] A number of studies have observed that a product's production costs decline by some quantity about each time *cumulative* output doubles. The relationship was first observed in the aircraft industry, where each time cumulative output of airframes was doubled, unit costs typically declined to 80 percent of their previous level.[19] Thus, production cost for the fourth airframe would be 80 percent of production cost for the second airframe, the eighth airframe's production costs 80 percent of the fourth's, the sixteenth's 80 percent of the eighth's, and so on. Figure 11.7 illustrates this experience curve relationship between unit production costs and cumulative output (the relationship is for cumulative output over time, and *not* output in any one period, such as a year). Two things explain this: learning effects and economies of scale.

Experience Curve
Systematic reductions in production costs that have been observed to occur over the life of a product.

Learning Effects

Learning effects refer to cost savings that come from learning by doing. Labor, for example, learns by repetition how to carry out a task, such as assembling airframes, most efficiently. Labor productivity increases over time as

Learning Effects
Cost savings that come from learning by doing.

figure 11.7

The Experience Curve

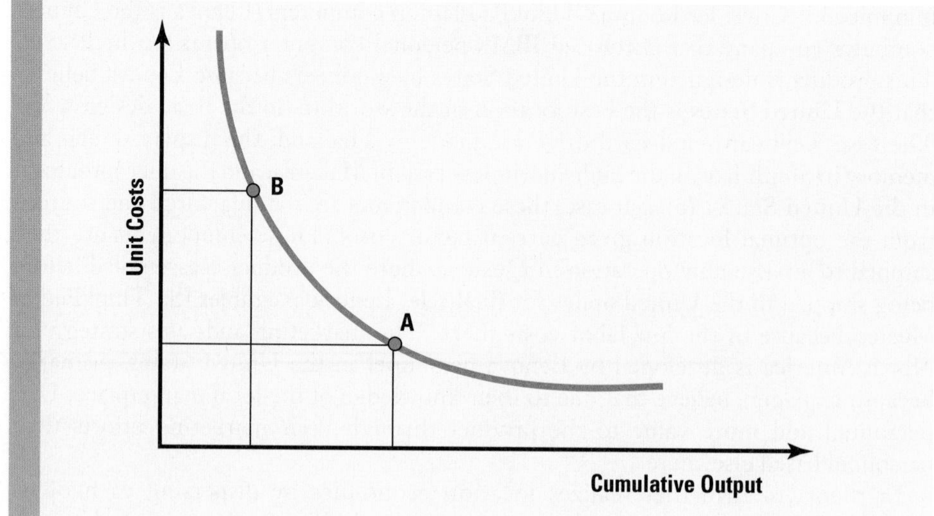

individuals learn the most efficient ways to perform particular tasks. Equally important, in new production facilities management typically learns how to manage the new operation more efficiently over time. Hence, production costs decline due to increasing labor productivity and management efficiency, which increases the firm's profitability.

Learning effects tend to be more significant when a technologically complex task is repeated, because there is more that can be learned about the task. Thus, learning effects will be more significant in an assembly process involving 1,000 complex steps than in one of only 100 simple steps. No matter how complex the task, however, learning effects typically disappear after a while. It has been suggested that they are important only during the start-up period of a new process and that they cease after two or three years.[20] Any decline in the experience curve after such a point is due to economies of scale.

Economies of Scale
The reductions in unit cost achieved by producing a large volume of a product.

Economies of Scale **Economies of scale** refer to the reductions in unit cost achieved by producing a large volume of a product. Attaining economies of scale lowers a firm's unit costs and increases its profitability. Economies of scale have a number of sources. One is the ability to spread fixed costs over a large volume.[21] Fixed costs are the costs required to set up a production facility, develop a new product, and the like. They can be substantial. For example, the fixed cost of establishing a new production line to manufacture semiconductor chips now exceeds $1 billion. Similarly, according to one estimate, developing a new drug and bringing it to market costs about $800 million and takes about 12 years.[22] The only way to recoup such high fixed costs may be to sell the product worldwide, which reduces average unit costs by spreading fixed costs over a larger volume. The more rapidly that cumulative sales volume is built up, the more rapidly fixed costs can be amortized over a large production volume, and the more rapidly unit costs will fall.

Second, a firm may not be able to attain an efficient scale of production unless it serves global markets. In the automobile industry, for example, an efficiently scaled factory is one designed to produce about 200,000 units a year. Automobile firms would prefer to produce a single model from each factory since this eliminates the costs associated with switching production from one model to another. If domestic demand for a particular model is only 100,000 units a year, the inability to attain a 200,000-unit output will drive up average unit costs. By serving international markets as well, however, the firm may be able to push production volume up to 200,000 units a year, thereby reaping greater economies of scale, lowering unit costs, and boosting profitability. By serving domestic and international markets from its production facilities a firm may be able to utilize those facilities more intensively. For example, if Intel sold microprocessors only in the United States, it may only be able to keep its factories open for one shift, five days a week. By serving international markets from the same factories, Intel can utilize its productive assets more intensively, which translates into higher capital productivity and greater profitability.

Finally, as global sales increase the size of the enterprise, so its bargaining power with suppliers increases, which may allow it to attain economies of scale in purchasing, bargaining down the cost of key inputs and boosting profitability that way. For example, Wal-Mart has been able to use its enormous sales volume as a lever to bargain down the price it pays suppliers for merchandise sold through its stores.

The only way to recoup the high fixed cost of a high-priced product, such as microprocessors, is to sell the product worldwide, which reduces average unit costs by spreading fixed costs over a larger volume.
Steve Dunwell/Getty Images

Strategic Significance The strategic significance of the experience curve is clear. Moving down the experience curve allows a firm to reduce its cost of creating value (to lower C in Figure 11.2) and increase its profitability. The firm that moves down the experience curve most rapidly will have a cost advantage vis-à-vis its competitors. Firm A in Figure 11.7, because it is farther down the experience curve, has a clear cost advantage over firm B.

Many of the underlying sources of experience-based cost economies are plant based. This is true for most learning effects as well as for the economies of scale derived by spreading the fixed costs of building productive capacity over a large output, attaining an efficient scale of output, and utilizing a plant more intensively. Thus, one key to progressing downward on the experience curve as rapidly as possible is to increase the volume produced by a single plant as rapidly as possible. Because global markets are larger than domestic markets, a firm that serves a global market from a single location is likely to build accumulated volume more quickly than a firm that serves only its home market or that serves multiple markets from multiple production locations. Thus, serving a global market from a single location is consistent with moving down the experience curve and establishing a low-cost position. In addition, to get down the experience curve rapidly, a firm may need to price and market aggressively so demand will expand rapidly. It will also need to build sufficient production capacity for serving a global market. Also, the cost advantages of serving the world market from a single location will be even more significant if that location is the optimal one for performing the particular value-creation activity.

Once a firm has established a low-cost position, it can act as a barrier to new competition. Specifically, an established firm that is well down the experience curve, such as firm A in Figure 11.7, can price so that it is still making a profit while new entrants, which are farther up the curve, are suffering losses.

The classic example of the successful pursuit of such a strategy concerns the Japanese consumer electronics company Matsushita. Along with Sony and Philips, Matsushita was in the race to develop a commercially viable videocassette recorder in the 1970s. Although

Matsushita initially lagged behind Philips and Sony, it was able to get its VHS format accepted as the world standard and to reap enormous experience curve–based cost economies in the process. This cost advantage subsequently constituted a formidable barrier to new competition. Matsushita's strategy was to build global volume as rapidly as possible. To ensure it could accommodate worldwide demand, the firm increased its production capacity 33-fold from 205,000 units in 1977 to 6.8 million units by 1984. By serving the world market from a single location in Japan, Matsushita was able to realize significant learning effects and economies of scale. These allowed Matsushita to drop its prices 50 percent within five years of selling its first VHS-format VCR. As a result, Matsushita was the world's major VCR producer by 1983, accounting for about 45 percent of world production and enjoying a significant cost advantage over its competitors. The next largest firm, Hitachi, accounted for only 11.1 percent of world production in 1983.[23] Today, firms such as Intel are the masters of this kind of strategy. The costs of building a state-of-the-art facility to manufacture microprocessors are so large (now in excess of $2 billion) that to make this investment pay Intel *must* pursue experience curve effects, serving world markets from a limited number of plants to maximize the cost economies that derive from scale and learning effects.

LEVERAGING SUBSIDIARY SKILLS Implicit in our earlier discussion of core competencies is the idea that valuable skills are developed first at home and then transferred to foreign operations. Thus, MTV developed its programming skills in the United States before transferring them to foreign locations. However, for more mature multinationals that have already established a network of subsidiary operations in foreign markets, the development of valuable skills can just as well occur in foreign subsidiaries.[24] Skills can be created anywhere within a multinational's global network of operations, wherever people have the opportunity and incentive to try new ways of doing things. The creation of skills that help to lower the costs of production, or to enhance perceived value and support higher product pricing, is not the monopoly of the corporate center.

Leveraging the skills created within subsidiaries and applying them to other operations within the firm's global network may create value. For example, McDonald's increasingly is finding that its foreign franchisees are a source of valuable new ideas. Faced with slow growth in France, its local franchisees have begun to experiment not only with the menu, but also with the layout and theme of restaurants. Gone are the ubiquitous golden arches, gone too are many of the utilitarian chairs and tables and other plastic features of the fast-food giant. Many McDonald's restaurants in France now have hardwood floors, exposed brick walls, and even armchairs. Half of the 930 or so outlets in France have been upgraded to a level that would make them unrecognizable to an American. The menu, too, has been changed to include premier sandwiches, such as chicken on focaccia bread, priced some 30 percent higher than the average hamburger. In France at least, the strategy seems to be working. Following the change, increases in same-store sales rose from 1 percent annually to 3.4 percent. Impressed with the impact, McDonald's executives are now considering adopting similar changes at other McDonald's restaurants in markets where same-store sales growth is sluggish, including the United States.[25]

For the managers of the multinational enterprise, this phenomenon creates important new challenges. First, they must have the humility to recognize that valuable skills that lead to competencies can arise anywhere within the firm's global network, not just at the corporate center. Second, they must establish an incentive system that encourages local employees to acquire new skills. This is not as easy as it sounds. Creating new skills involves a degree of risk. Not all new skills add value. For every valuable idea created by a McDonald's subsidiary in a foreign country, there may be several failures. The management of the multinational must install incentives that encourage employees to take the necessary risks. The company must reward people for successes and not sanction them unnecessarily for taking risks that did not pan out. Third, managers must have a process for identifying when valuable new skills have been created in a subsidiary. And finally, they need to act as facilitators, helping to transfer valuable skills within the firm.

SUMMARY We have seen how firms that expand globally can increase their profitability and profit growth by entering new markets where indigenous competitors lack similar competencies, by lowering costs and adding value to their product offering through the attainment of location economies, by exploiting experience curve effects, and by transferring valuable skills between their global network of subsidiaries. For completeness it should be noted that strategies that increase profitability may also expand a firm's business, and thus enable it to attain a higher rate of profit growth. For example, by simultaneously realizing location economies and experience effects a firm may be able to produce a more highly valued product at a lower unit cost, thereby boosting profitability. The increase in the perceived value of the product may also attract more customers, thereby growing revenues and profits as well. Furthermore, rather than raising prices to reflect the higher perceived value of the product, the firm's managers may elect to hold prices low in order to increase global market share and attain greater scale economies (in other words, they may elect to offer consumers better "value for money"). Such a strategy could increase the firm's rate of profit growth even further, since consumers will be attracted by prices that are low relative to value. The strategy might also increase profitability if the economies of scale that result from market share gains are substantial. In sum, managers need to keep in mind the complex relationship between profitability and profit growth when making strategic decisions about pricing.

Cost Pressures and Pressures for Local Responsiveness

LEARNING OBJECTIVE 3
Understand how pressures for cost reductions and pressures for local responsiveness influence strategic choice.

Firms that compete in the global marketplace typically face two types of competitive pressure that affect their ability to realize location economies and experience effects, to leverage products and transfer competencies and skills within the enterprise. They face *pressures for cost reductions* and *pressures to be locally responsive* (see Figure 11.8).[26]

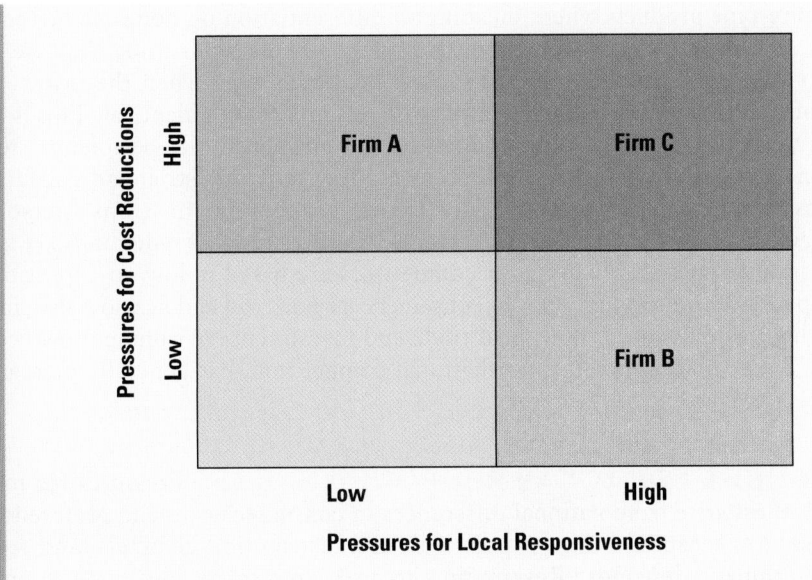

figure 11.8
Pressures for Cost Reductions and Local Responsiveness

These competitive pressures place conflicting demands on a firm. Responding to pressures for cost reductions requires that a firm try to minimize its unit costs. But responding to pressures to be locally responsive requires that a firm differentiate its product offerings and marketing strategy from country to country in an effort to accommodate the diverse demands arising from national differences in consumer tastes and preferences, business practices, distribution channels, competitive conditions, and government policies. Because differentiation across countries can involve significant duplication and a lack of product standardization, it may raise costs.

While some enterprises, such as firm A in Figure 11.8, face high pressures for cost reductions and low pressures for local responsiveness, and others, such as firm B, face low pressures for cost reductions and high pressures for local responsiveness, many companies are in the position of firm C. They face high pressures for *both* cost reductions and local responsiveness. Dealing with these conflicting and contradictory pressures is a difficult strategic challenge, primarily because being locally responsive tends to raise costs.

PRESSURES FOR COST REDUCTIONS

In competitive global markets, international businesses often face pressures for cost reductions. Responding to pressures for cost reduction requires a firm to try to lower the costs of value creation. A manufacturer, for example, might mass-produce a standardized product at the optimal location in the world, wherever that might be, to realize economies of scale, learning effects, and location economies. Alternatively, a firm might outsource certain functions to low-cost foreign suppliers in an attempt to reduce costs. Thus, many computer companies have outsourced their telephone-based customer service functions to India, where qualified technicians who speak English can be hired for a lower wage rate than in the United States. In the same manner, a retailer such as Wal-Mart might push its suppliers (manufacturers) to do the same. (The pressure that Wal-Mart has placed on its suppliers to reduce prices has been cited as a major cause of the trend among North American manufacturers to shift production to China.)[27] A service business such as a bank might respond to cost pressures by moving some back-office functions, such as information processing, to developing nations where wage rates are lower.

Universal Needs
Arise when the tastes and preferences of consumers in different nations are similar if not identical.

Pressures for cost reduction can be particularly intense in industries producing commodity-type products where meaningful differentiation on nonprice factors is difficult and price is the main competitive weapon. This tends to be the case for products that serve universal needs. **Universal needs** exist when the tastes and preferences of consumers in different nations are similar if not identical. This is the case for conventional commodity products such as bulk chemicals, petroleum, steel, sugar, and the like. It also tends to be the case for many industrial and consumer products, for example, handheld calculators, semiconductor chips, personal computers, and liquid crystal display screens. Pressures for cost reductions are also intense in industries in which major competitors are based in low-cost locations, there is persistent excess capacity, and consumers are powerful and face low switching costs. The liberalization of the world trade and investment environment in recent decades, by facilitating greater international competition, has generally increased cost pressures.[28]

PRESSURES FOR LOCAL RESPONSIVENESS

Pressures for local responsiveness arise from national differences in consumer tastes and preferences, infrastructure, accepted business practices, and distribution channels, and from host-government demands. Responding to pressures to be locally responsive requires a firm to differentiate its products and marketing strategy from country to country to accommodate these factors, all of which tends to raise the firm's cost structure.

Differences in Customer Tastes and Preferences

Strong pressures for local responsiveness emerge when customer tastes and preferences differ significantly between countries, as they often do for deeply embedded historic or cultural reasons. In such cases, a multinational's products and marketing message have to be customized to appeal to the tastes and preferences of local customers. This typically creates pressure to delegate production and marketing responsibilities and functions to a firm's overseas subsidiaries.

For example, the automobile industry in the 1980s and early 1990s moved toward the creation of "world cars." The idea was that global companies such as General Motors, Ford, and Toyota would be able to sell the same basic vehicle the world over, sourcing it from centralized production locations. If successful, the strategy would have enabled automobile companies to reap significant gains from global economies of scale. However, this strategy frequently ran aground upon the hard rocks of consumer reality. Consumers in different automobile markets seem to have different tastes and preferences, thus they demand different types of vehicles. North American consumers show a strong demand for pickup trucks. This is particularly true in the South and West, where many families have a pickup truck as a second or third car. But in European countries, pickup trucks are seen purely as utility vehicles and are purchased primarily by firms rather than individuals. As a consequence, the product mix and marketing message need to be tailored according to the different nature of demand in North America and Europe. Another example that illustrates the need to respond to national differences in tastes and preferences is that of MTV networks, which we looked at in the opening case.

Some commentators have argued that customer demands for local customization are on the decline worldwide.[29] According to this argument, modern communications and transport technologies have created the conditions for a convergence of the tastes and preferences of consumers from different nations. The result is the emergence of enormous global markets for standardized consumer products. The worldwide acceptance of McDonald's hamburgers, Coca-Cola, Gap clothes, Nokia cell phones, and Sony PlayStations, all of which are sold globally as standardized products, are often cited as evidence of the increasing homogeneity of the global marketplace.

However, as illustrated by the MTV example, this argument seems somewhat naive. Significant differences in consumer tastes and preferences still exist across nations and cultures. Managers in international businesses do not yet have the luxury of being able to ignore these differences, and they may not for a long time to come. Even in a modern industry such as the cell phone business, important national differences in consumer usage patterns can be observed. Americans, for example, tend to think of cell phones primarily as devices for talking, and not as devices that can also send e-mails and browse the Web. Consequently, when selling to U.S. consumers, cell phone manufacturers focus more on slim, good looks and less on advanced functions and features. This is in direct contrast to Asia and Europe, where text messaging and Web browsing functions have been much more widely embraced.

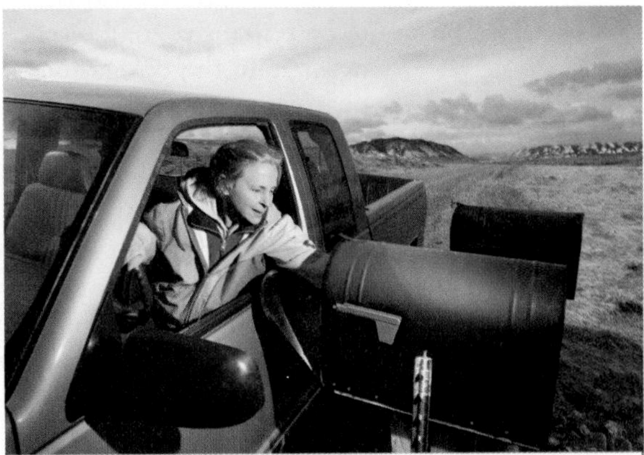

Pickup trucks may be used in the South and West of the United States as a second or third car; but in Europe, they're seen purely as utility vehicles, which affects the marketing message being sent. *Royalty Free/Corbis*

Another Perspective

The International Love Affair with Pizza = Domino's Global Strategy

The success of Domino's global strategy offers evidence that global markets are indeed on the rise, as explained by the company's chairman and CEO, David Brandon: "As countries develop and embrace busier lifestyles, Domino's has seen sales spikes. As these countries get more two-wage earning households and as they get more fixated on technology and start living life at a faster pace, you see the corresponding impact on our sales."

As a result, Domino's is aggressively expanding its international presence in 55 countries. Of the 322 stores it opened last year, 238 were outside the United States. Domino's has more than 500 stores in Mexico, 300 in Britain and Australia, and 200 in South Korea and Canada. It wants to open its 10,000th Domino's store in the next few years. It boasts $5 billion in global sales, proof there really is an international love affair with pizza! (Brian Charlton, *Associated Press,* July 5, 2006)

A cultural issue seems to be at work here. People in Europe and Asia often have more time to browse the Web on their phones because they spend more time commuting on trains, whereas Americans tend to spend more time in cars, where their hands are occupied.[30] See the Another Perspective at left. What changes do you think Domino's will need to make as it pursues markets in Britain?

Differences in Infrastructure and Traditional Practices Pressures for local responsiveness arise from differences in infrastructure or traditional practices among countries, creating a need to customize products accordingly. Fulfilling this need may require the delegation of manufacturing and production functions to foreign subsidiaries. For example, in North America, consumer electrical systems are based on 110 volts, whereas in some European countries, 240-volt systems are standard. Thus, domestic electrical appliances have to be customized for this difference in infrastructure. Traditional practices also often vary across nations. For example, in Britain, people drive on the left-hand side of the road, creating a demand for right-hand-drive cars, whereas in France (and the rest of Europe), people drive on the right-hand side of the road and therefore want left-hand-drive cars. Obviously, automobiles have to be customized to accommodate this difference in traditional practice.

Although many national differences in infrastructure are rooted in history, some are quite recent. For example, in the wireless telecommunications industry different technical standards exist in different parts of the world. A technical standard known as GSM is common in Europe, and an alternative standard, CDMA, is more common in the United States and parts of Asia. Equipment designed for GSM will not work on a CDMA network, and vice versa. Thus, companies such as Nokia, Motorola, and Ericsson, which manufacture wireless handsets and infrastructure such as switches, need to customize their product offering according to the technical standard prevailing in a given country.

Differences in Distribution Channels A firm's marketing strategies may have to be responsive to differences in distribution channels among countries, which may necessitate the delegation of marketing functions to national subsidiaries. In the pharmaceutical industry, for example, the British and Japanese distribution systems are radically different from the U.S. system. British and Japanese doctors will not accept or respond favorably to a U.S.-style high-pressure sales force. Thus, pharmaceutical companies have to adopt different marketing practices in Britain and Japan compared with the United States—soft sell versus hard sell. Similarly, Poland, Brazil, and Russia all have similar per capita income on a purchasing power parity basis, but there are big differences in distribution systems across the three countries. In Brazil, supermarkets account for 36 percent of food retailing, in Poland for 18 percent, and in Russia, less than 1 percent.[31] These differences in channels require that companies adapt their own distribution and sales strategy.

Host Government Demands Economic and political demands imposed by host-country governments may require local responsiveness. For example, pharmaceutical companies are subject to local clinical testing, registration procedures, and pricing restrictions, all of which make it necessary that the manufacturing and marketing of a drug should meet local requirements. Because governments and government agencies control a significant proportion of the health care budget in most countries, they are in a powerful position to demand a high level of local responsiveness.

More generally, threats of protectionism, economic nationalism, and local content rules (which require that a certain percentage of a product should be manufactured locally) dictate that international businesses manufacture locally. For example, consider Bombardier, the Canadian-based manufacturer of railcars, aircraft, jet boats, and snowmobiles. Bombardier has 12 railcar factories across Europe. Critics of the company argue that the resulting duplication of manufacturing facilities leads to high costs and helps explain why Bombardier makes lower profit margins on its railcar operations than on its other business lines. In reply, managers at Bombardier argue that in Europe, informal rules with regard to local content favor companies that use local workers. To sell railcars in Germany, they claim, you must manufacture in Germany. The same goes for Belgium, Austria, and France. To try to address its cost structure in Europe, Bombardier has centralized its engineering and purchasing functions, but it has no plans to centralize manufacturing.[32]

Choosing a Strategy

LEARNING OBJECTIVE 4
Be familiar with different strategies for competing globally and their pros and cons.

Pressures for local responsiveness imply that it may not be possible for a firm to realize the full benefits from economies of scale, learning effects, and location economies. It may not be possible to serve the global marketplace from a single low-cost location, producing a globally standardized product, and marketing it worldwide to attain the cost reductions associated with experience effects. The need to customize the product offering to local conditions may work against the implementation of such a strategy. For example, automobile firms have found that Japanese, American, and European consumers demand different kinds of cars, which necessitates producing products that are customized for local markets. In response, firms such as Honda, Ford, and Toyota are pursuing a strategy of establishing top-to-bottom design and production facilities in each of these regions so that they can better serve local demands. Although such customization brings benefits, it also limits the ability of a firm to realize significant scale and location economies.

In addition, pressures for local responsiveness imply that it may not be possible to leverage skills and products associated with a firm's core competencies wholesale from one nation to another. Concessions often have to be made to local conditions. Despite being depicted as poster boy for the proliferation of standardized global products, even McDonald's has found that it has to customize its product offerings (i.e., its menu) to account for national differences in tastes and preferences.

How do differences in the strength of pressures for cost reductions versus those for local responsiveness affect the firm's choice of strategy? Firms typically choose among four main strategic postures when competing internationally. These can be characterized as a global standardization strategy, a localization strategy, a transnational strategy, and an international strategy.[33] The appropriateness of each strategy varies given the extent of pressures for cost reductions and local responsiveness. Figure 11.9 illustrates the conditions under which each of these strategies is most appropriate.

Global Standardization Strategy
Pursuing a low-cost strategy on a global scale and increasing profitability and profit growth by reaping the cost reductions that come from economies of scale, learning effects, and location economies.

GLOBAL STANDARDIZATION STRATEGY

Firms that pursue a **global standardization strategy** focus on increasing profitability and profit growth by reaping the cost reductions that come from economies of scale, learning effects, and location economies; that is, their strategic goal is to pursue a low-cost strategy on a

Four Basic Strategies

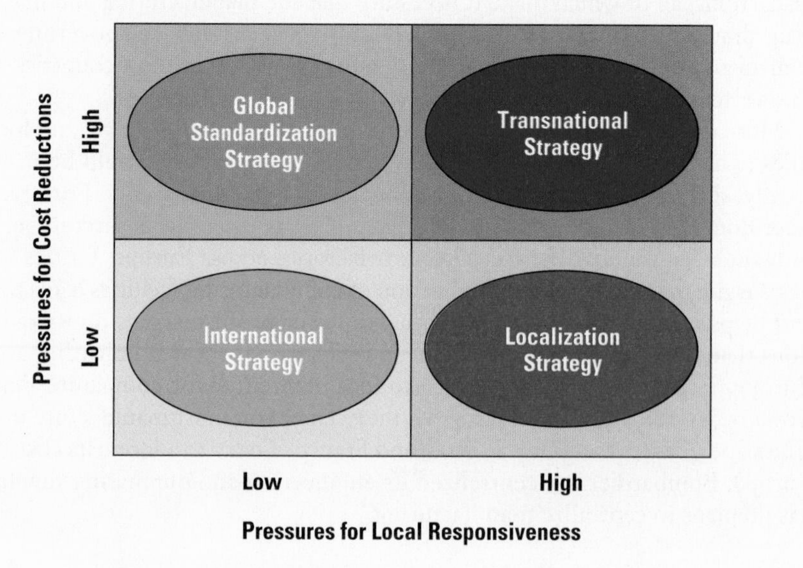

global scale. The production, marketing, and R&D activities of firms pursuing a global standardization strategy are concentrated in a few favorable locations. Firms pursuing a global standardization strategy try not to customize their product offering and marketing strategy to local conditions because customization involves shorter production runs and the duplication of functions, which tends to raise costs. Instead, they prefer to market a standardized product worldwide so that they can reap the maximum benefits from economies of scale and learning effects. They also tend to use their cost advantage to support aggressive pricing in world markets.

This strategy makes most sense when there are strong pressures for cost reductions and demands for local responsiveness are minimal. Increasingly, these conditions prevail in many industrial goods industries, whose products often serve universal needs. In the semiconductor industry, for example, global standards have emerged, creating enormous demands for standardized global products. Accordingly, companies such as Intel, Texas Instruments, and Motorola all pursue a global standardization strategy. However, these conditions are not yet found in many consumer goods markets, where demands for local responsiveness remain high. The strategy is inappropriate when demands for local responsiveness are high.

Localization Strategy
Increasing profitability by customizing the firm's goods and services so that they provide a good match to tastes and preferences in different national markets.

LOCALIZATION STRATEGY A **localization strategy** focuses on increasing profitability by customizing the firm's goods or services so that they provide a good match to tastes and preferences in different national markets. Localization is most appropriate when there are substantial differences across nations with regard to consumer tastes and preferences, and where cost pressures are not too intense. By customizing the product offering to local demands, the firm increases the value of that product in the local market. On the downside, because it involves some duplication of functions and smaller production runs, customization limits the ability of the firm to capture the cost reductions associated with mass-producing a standardized product for global consumption. The strategy may make sense, however, if the added value associated with local customization supports higher pricing, which enables the firm to recoup its higher costs, or if it leads to substantially greater local demand, enabling the firm to reduce costs through the attainment of some scale economies in the local market.

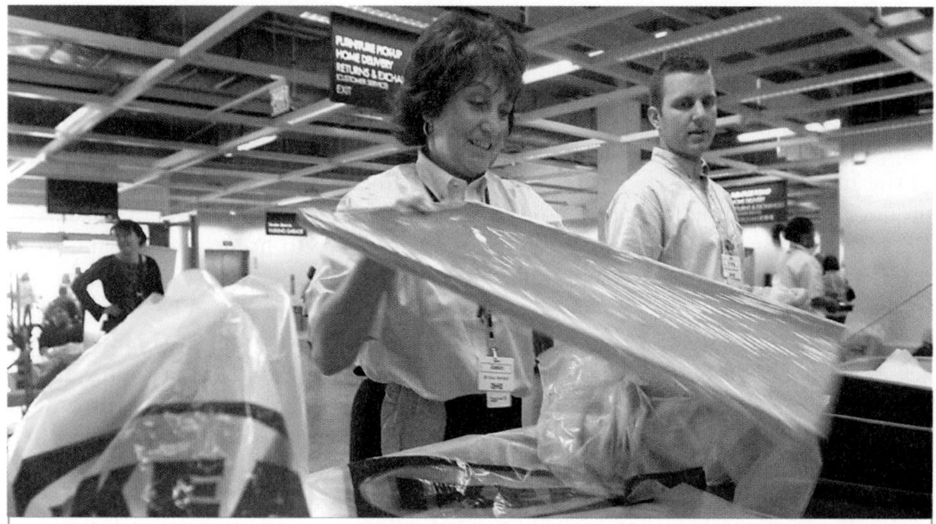

IKEA, realizing that it could not sell a "typically Swedish" product line in North America, redesigned and customized its products to fit North American consumers' tastes as part of its transnational strategy. *AP/Wide World*

MTV is a good example of a company that has had to pursue a localization strategy (see the opening case). If MTV had not localized its programming to match the demands of viewers in different nations, it would have lost market share to local competitors, its advertising revenues would have fallen, and its profitability would have declined. Thus, even though it raised costs, localization was a strategic imperative at MTV.

At the same time, firms such as MTV still have to keep an eye on costs. Firms pursuing a localization strategy still need to be efficient and, whenever possible, to capture some scale economies from their global reach. As noted earlier, many automobile companies have found that they have to customize some of their product offerings to local market demands—for example, producing large pickup trucks for U.S. consumers and small fuel-efficient cars for Europeans and Japanese. At the same time, these multinationals try to get some scale economies from their global volume by using common vehicle platforms and components across many different models, and manufacturing those platforms and components at efficiently scaled factories that are optimally located. By designing their products in this way, these companies have been able to localize their product offerings, yet simultaneously capture some scale economies, learning effects, and location economies.

TRANSNATIONAL STRATEGY We have argued that a global standardization strategy makes most sense when cost pressures are intense, and demands for local responsiveness limited. Conversely, a localization strategy makes most sense when demands for local responsiveness are high but cost pressures are moderate or low. What happens, however, when the firm simultaneously faces both strong cost pressures and strong pressures for local responsiveness? How can managers balance the competing and inconsistent demands such divergent pressures place on the firm? According to some researchers, the answer is to pursue what has been called a *transnational strategy*.

Two of these researchers, Christopher Bartlett and Sumantra Ghoshal, argue that in today's global environment, competitive conditions are so intense that to survive, firms must do all they can to respond to pressures for cost reductions and local responsiveness. They must try to realize location economies and experience effects, to leverage products internationally, to transfer core competencies and skills within the company, and to simultaneously pay attention to pressures for local responsiveness.[34] Bartlett and Ghoshal note that in the modern multinational enterprise, core competencies and skills do not reside just in the home country but can develop in any of the firm's worldwide operations. Thus, they maintain that the flow of skills and product offerings should not be all one way, from home country to foreign subsidiary. Rather, the flow should also be from foreign subsidiary to home country and from foreign subsidiary to foreign subsidiary. Transnational enterprises, in other words, must also focus on leveraging subsidiary skills.

Transnational Strategy Attempting to simultaneously achieve low costs through location economies, economies of scale, and learning effects while also differentiating product offerings across geographic markets to account for local differences and fostering multidirectional flows of skills between different subsidiaries in the firm's global network of operations.

In essence, firms that pursue a **transnational strategy** are trying to simultaneously achieve low costs through location economies, economies of scale, and learning effects; differentiate their product offerings across geographic markets to account for local differences; and foster a multidirectional flow of skills between different subsidiaries in the firm's global network of operations. As attractive as this may sound in theory, the strategy is not an easy one to pursue since it places conflicting demands on the company. Differentiating the product to respond to local demands in different geographic markets raises costs, which runs counter to the goal of reducing costs. Companies such as Ford and ABB (one of the world's largest engineering conglomerates) have tried to embrace a transnational strategy and found it difficult to implement.

How best to implement a transnational strategy is one of the most complex questions that large multinationals are grappling with today. Few if any enterprises have perfected this strategic posture. But some clues as to the right approach can be derived from a number of companies. For example, consider the case of Caterpillar. The need to compete with low-cost competitors such as Komatsu of Japan forced Caterpillar to look for greater cost economies. However, variations in construction practices and government regulations across countries mean that Caterpillar also has to be responsive to local demands. Therefore, Caterpillar confronted significant pressures for cost reductions *and* for local responsiveness.

To deal with cost pressures, Caterpillar redesigned its products to use many identical components and invested in a few large-scale component manufacturing facilities, sited at favorable locations, to fill global demand and realize economies of scale. At the same time, the company augments the centralized manufacturing of components with assembly plants in each of its major global markets. At these plants, Caterpillar adds local product features, tailoring the finished product to local needs. Thus, Caterpillar is able to realize many of the benefits of global manufacturing while reacting to pressures for local responsiveness by differentiating its product among national markets.[35] Caterpillar started to pursue this strategy in 1979, and by 1997 it had succeeded in doubling output per employee, significantly reducing its overall cost structure in the process. Meanwhile, Komatsu and Hitachi, which are still wedded to a Japan-centric global strategy, have seen their cost advantages evaporate and have been steadily losing market share to Caterpillar.

Changing a firm's strategic posture to build an organization capable of supporting a transnational strategy is a complex and challenging task. Some would say it is too complex, because the strategy implementation problems of creating a viable organizational structure and control systems to manage this strategy are immense.

INTERNATIONAL STRATEGY Sometimes it is possible to identify multinational firms that find themselves in the fortunate position of being confronted with low cost pressures and low pressures for local responsiveness. Many of these enterprises have pursued an **international strategy,** taking products first produced for their domestic market and selling them internationally with only minimal local customization. The distinguishing feature of many such firms is that they are selling a product that serves universal needs, but they do not face significant competitors, and thus unlike firms pursuing a global standardization strategy, they are not confronted with pressures to reduce their cost structure. Xerox found itself in this position in the 1960s after its invention and commercialization of the photocopier. The technology underlying the photocopier was protected by strong patents, so for several years Xerox did not face competitors—it had a monopoly. The product serves universal needs, and it was highly valued in most developed nations. Thus, Xerox was able to sell the same basic product the world over, charging a relatively high price for that product. Because Xerox did not face direct competitors, it did not have to deal with strong pressures to minimize its cost structure.

International Strategy
When a firm takes products first produced for its domestic market and sells them internationally with only minimal local customization.

Enterprises pursuing an international strategy have followed a similar developmental pattern as they expanded into foreign markets. They tend to centralize product development functions such as R&D at home. However, they also tend to establish manufacturing and marketing functions in each major country or geographic region in which they do business. The resulting duplication can raise costs, but this is less of an issue if the firm does not face strong pressures for cost reductions. Although they may undertake some local customization of product offerings and marketing strategy, this tends to be rather limited in scope. Ultimately, in most firms that pursue an international strategy, the head office retains fairly tight control over marketing and product strategy.

Other firms that have pursued this strategy include Procter & Gamble and Microsoft. Historically, Procter & Gamble developed innovative new products in Cincinnati and then transferred them wholesale to local markets (see the Management Focus box on page 386). Similarly, the bulk of Microsoft's product development work takes place in Redmond, Washington, where the company is headquartered. Although some localization work is undertaken elsewhere, this is limited to producing foreign-language versions of popular Microsoft programs.

THE EVOLUTION OF STRATEGY The Achilles' heel of the international strategy is that over time, competitors inevitably emerge, and if managers do not take proactive steps to reduce their firm's cost structure, it will be rapidly outflanked by efficient global competitors. This is exactly what happened to Xerox. Japanese companies such as Canon ultimately invented their way around Xerox's patents, produced their own photocopiers in very efficient manufacturing plants, priced them below Xerox's products, and rapidly took global market share from Xerox. In the final analysis, Xerox's demise was not due to the emergence of competitors, for ultimately that was bound to occur, but due to its failure to proactively reduce its cost structure in advance of the emergence of efficient global competitors. The message in this story is that an international strategy may not be viable in the long term, and to survive, firms need to shift toward a global standardization strategy or a transnational strategy in advance of competitors (see Figure 11.10).

The same can be said about a localization strategy. Localization may give a firm a competitive edge, but if it is simultaneously facing aggressive competitors, the company will also have to reduce its cost structure, and the only way to do that may be to shift toward a transnational strategy. This is what Procter & Gamble has been doing (see the Management Focus box on page 386). Thus, as competition intensifies, international and localization strategies tend to become less viable, and managers need to orient their companies toward either a global standardization strategy or a transnational strategy.

Management FOCUS

The Evolution of Strategy at Procter & Gamble

Founded in 1837, Cincinnati-based Procter & Gamble has long been one of the world's most international of companies. Today, P&G is a global colossus in the consumer products business, with annual sales in excess of $50 billion, some 54 percent of which are generated outside of the United States. P&G sells more than 300 brands—including Ivory soap, Tide, Pampers, IAMS pet food, Crisco, and Folgers—to consumers in 160 countries. It has operations in 80 countries and employs close to 100,000 people globally. P&G established its first foreign factory in 1915 when it opened a plant in Canada to produce Ivory soap and Crisco. This was followed in 1930 by the establishment of the company's first foreign subsidiary in Britain. The pace of international expansion quickened in the 1950s and 1960s as P&G expanded rapidly in Western Europe, and then again in the 1970s when the company entered Japan and other Asian nations. Sometimes P&G entered a nation by acquiring an established competitor and its brands, as occurred in the case of Great Britain and Japan, but more typically the company set up operations from the ground floor.

By the late 1970s, the strategy at P&G was well established. The company developed new products in Cincinnati and then relied on semiautonomous foreign subsidiaries to manufacture, market, and distribute those products in different nations. In many cases, foreign subsidiaries had their own production facilities and tailored the packaging, brand name, and marketing message to local tastes and preferences. For years this strategy delivered a steady stream of new products and reliable growth in sales and profits. By the 1990s, however, profit growth at P&G was slowing.

The essence of the problem was simple: P&G's costs were too high because of extensive duplication of manufacturing, marketing, and administrative facilities in different national subsidiaries. The duplication of assets made sense in the world of the 1960s, when national markets were segmented from each other by barriers to cross-border trade. Products produced in Great Britain, for example, could not be sold economically in Germany due to high tariff duties levied on imports into Germany. By the 1980s, however, barriers to cross-border trade were falling rapidly worldwide and fragmented national markets were merging into larger regional or global markets. Also, the retailers through which P&G distributed its products were growing larger and more global, such as Wal-Mart, Tesco from the United Kingdom, and Carrefour from France. These emerging global retailers were demanding price discounts from P&G.

In 1993, P&G embarked on a major reorganization in an attempt to control its cost structure and recognize the new reality of emerging global markets. The company shut down some 30 manufacturing plants around the globe, laid off 13,000 employees, and concentrated production in fewer plants that could better realize economies of scale and serve regional markets. These actions cut some $600 million a year out of P&G's cost structure. It wasn't enough! Profit growth remained sluggish.

In 1998, P&G launched its second reorganization of the decade. Named "Organization 2005," the goal was to transform P&G into a truly global company. The company tore up its old organization, which was based on countries and regions, and replaced it with one based on seven self-contained global business units, ranging from baby care to food products. Each business unit was given complete responsibility for generating profits from its products and for manufacturing, marketing, and product development. Each business unit was told to rationalize production, concentrating it in fewer larger facilities; to try to build global brands wherever possible, thereby eliminating marketing difference between countries; and to accelerate the development and launch of new products. In 1999, P&G announced that as a result of this initiative, it would close another 10 factories and lay off 15,000 employees, mostly in Europe, where there was still extensive duplication of assets. The annual cost savings were estimated to be about $800 million. P&G planned to use the savings to cut prices and increase marketing spending in an effort to gain market share and thus further lower costs through the attainment of economies of scale. This time the strategy seemed to be working. Between 2003 and 2005, P&G reported strong growth in both sales and profits. Significantly, P&G's global competitors, such as Unilever, Kimberly-Clark, and Colgate-Palmolive, were struggling in 2003 to 2005.

Source: J. Neff, "P&G Outpacing Unilever in Five-Year Battle," *Advertising Age,* November 3, 2003, pp. 1–3; G. Strauss, "Firm Restructuring into Truly Global Company," *USA Today,* September 10, 1999, p. B2; Procter & Gamble 10K report, 2005; and M. Kolbasuk McGee, "P&G Jump-Starts Corporate Change," *Information Week,* November 1, 1999, pp. 30–34.

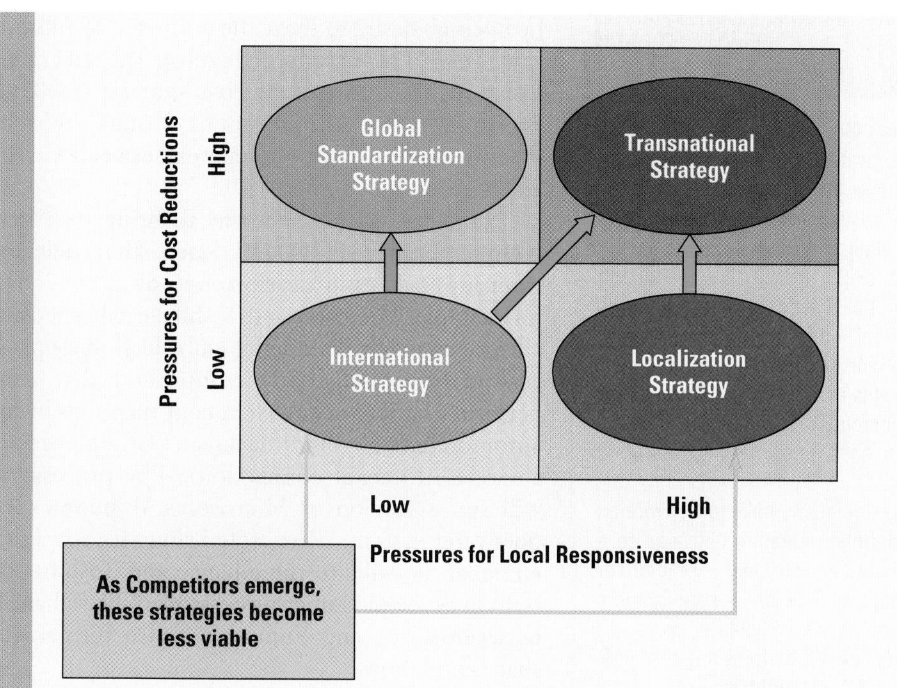

figure 11.10

Changes in Strategy over Time

Strategic Alliances

LEARNING OBJECTIVE 5
Explain the pros and cons of using strategic alliances to support global strategies.

Strategic alliances refer to cooperative agreements between potential or actual competitors. In this section, we are concerned specifically with strategic alliances between firms from different countries. Strategic alliances run the range from formal joint ventures, in which two or more firms have equity stakes (e.g., Fuji–Xerox), to short-term contractual agreements, in which two companies agree to cooperate on a particular task (such as developing a new product). Collaboration between competitors is fashionable; recent decades have seen an explosion in the number of strategic alliances.

Strategic Alliances
Cooperative agreements between potential or actual competitors for the benefit of all companies concerned.

THE ADVANTAGES OF STRATEGIC ALLIANCES Firms ally themselves with actual or potential competitors for various strategic purposes.[36] First, strategic alliances may facilitate entry into a foreign market. For example, many firms feel that if they are to successfully enter the Chinese market, they need a local partner who understands business conditions and who has good connections (or *guanxi*—see Chapter 3). Thus, in 2004 Warner Brothers entered into a joint venture with two Chinese partners to produce and distribute films in China. As a foreign film company, Warner found that if it wanted to produce films on its own for the Chinese market it had to go through a complex approval process for every film, and it had to farm out distribution to a local company, which made doing business in China very difficult. Due to the participation of Chinese firms, however, the joint-venture films will go through a streamlined approval process, and the venture will be able to distribute any films it produces. Moreover, the joint venture will be able to produce films for Chinese TV, something that foreign firms are not allowed to do.[37]

Second, strategic alliances allow firms to share the fixed costs (and associated risks) of developing new products or processes. An alliance between Boeing and a number of Japanese companies to build Boeing's latest commercial jetliner, the 787, was motivated by Boeing's desire to share the estimated $8 billion investment required to develop the aircraft. For another example of cost sharing, see the accompanying Management Focus, which discusses the strategic alliances between Cisco and Fujitsu.

Third, an alliance is a way to bring together complementary skills and assets that neither company could easily develop on its own.[38] In 2003, for example, Microsoft and Toshiba established an alliance aimed at developing embedded microprocessors (essentially tiny computers) that can perform a variety of entertainment functions in an automobile (e.g., run a backseat DVD player or a wireless Internet connection). The processors will run a version of Microsoft's Windows CE operating system. Microsoft brings its software engineering skills to the alliance and Toshiba its skills in developing microprocessors.[39] The alliance between Cisco and Fujitsu was also formed to share know-how.

Fourth, it can make sense to form an alliance that will help the firm establish technological standards for the industry that will benefit the firm. For example, in 1999 Palm Computer, the leading maker of personal digital assistants (PDAs), entered into an alliance with Sony under which Sony agreed to license and use Palm's operating system in Sony PDAs. The motivation for the alliance was in part to help establish Palm's operating system as the industry standard for PDAs, as opposed to a rival Windows-based operating system from Microsoft.[40] See the Another Perspective at left for GM's take on foreign strategic alliances.

Another Perspective

The Big Question Facing General Motors

The American company General Motors is the world's largest automaker by sales volume, but for nearly two decades it has been unable to come up with a viable plan to keep its position in the global marketplace. It is considering an alliance with French automaker Renault SA and Japanese automaker Nissan Motor Co. These three companies combined produce more than 14 million vehicles annually, or about 24 percent of the world's total vehicle consumption. The major reason for this alliance of the three major companies is to obtain substantial savings in purchasing supplies and parts and in developing new models and technology.

But should GM give up its significant stake to two foreign rivals in hopes that the resulting alliance will lead to a restructuring of the global auto industry and a windfall for its shareholders? GM's board of directors is conducting a review of the pros and cons of this possible alliance. It's considering questions such as, What form might a GM-Renault-Nissan alliance take? Who would win or lose from such a deal? Would any major rivals take steps to derail the alliance or seek out their own alliances?

These questions will prove to be good points of study in global alliances. Whatever the outcome, the fact that GM, once synonymous with American economic preeminence, is now considering an alliance shows that all business is now global. (Neal Boudette, Stephen Power, and Norihiko Shirouzu, "GM Approaches a Crossroad as It Considers Renault-Nissan Alliance," *The Wall Street Journal,* July 17, 2006)

THE DISADVANTAGES OF STRATEGIC ALLIANCES The advantages we have discussed can be significant. Despite this, some commentators have criticized strategic alliances on the grounds that they give competitors a low-cost route to new technology and markets.[41] For example, a few years ago some commentators argued that many strategic alliances between U.S. and Japanese firms were part of an implicit Japanese strategy to keep high-paying, high-value-added jobs in Japan while gaining the project engineering and production process skills that underlie the competitive success of many U.S. companies.[42] They argued that Japanese success in the machine tool and semiconductor industries was built on U.S. technology acquired through strategic alliances. And they argued that U.S. managers were aiding the Japanese by entering alliances that channel new inventions to Japan and provide a U.S. sales and distribution network for the resulting products. Although such deals may generate short-term profits, so the argument goes, in the long run the result is to "hollow out" U.S. firms, leaving them with no competitive advantage in the global marketplace.

These critics have a point; alliances have risks. Unless a firm is careful, it can give away more than it receives. But there are so many examples of apparently successful alliances between firms—including alliances between U.S. and Japanese firms—that

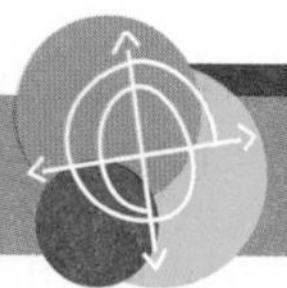

Management FOCUS

Cisco and Fujitsu

In late 2004, Cisco Systems, the world's largest manufacturer of Internet routers, entered into an alliance with Fujitsu, the Japanese computer, electronics, and telecommunications equipment firm. The stated purpose of the alliance was to jointly develop next-generation high-end routers for sales in Japan. Routers are the digital switches that sit at the heart of the Internet and direct traffic; they are in effect, the traffic cops of the Internet. Although Cisco has long held the leading share in the market for routers—indeed, it pioneered the original router technology—it faces increasing competition from other firms such as Juniper Technologies and China's fast-growing Huawei Technologies. At the same time, demand in the market is shifting as more and more telecommunications companies adopt Internet-based telecommunications services. Although Cisco has long had a strong global presence, management felt that the company needed to have better presence in Japan, which is shifting rapidly to second-generation high-speed Internet-based telecommunications networks.

By entering into an alliance with Fujitsu, Cisco feels it can achieve a number of goals. First, both firms can pool their R&D efforts, which will enable them to share complementary technology and develop products quicker, thereby gaining an advantage over competitors. Second, by combining Cisco's proprietary leading-edge router technology with Fujitsu's production expertise, the companies believe that they can produce products that are more reliable than those currently on offer. Third, Fujitsu will give Cisco a stronger sales presence in Japan. Fujitsu has good links with Japan's telecommunications companies and a well-earned reputation for reliability. It will leverage these assets to sell the routers produced by the alliance, which will be co-branded as Fujitsu–Cisco products. Fourth, sales may be further enhanced by bundling the co-branded routers together with other telecommunications equipment that Fujitsu sells and marketing an entire solution to customers. Fujitsu sells many telecommunications products, but it lacks a strong presence in routers. Cisco is strong in routers, but it lacks strong offerings elsewhere. The combination of the two companies' products will enable Fujitsu to offer Japan's telecommunications companies end-to-end communications solutions. Since many companies prefer to purchase their equipment from a single provider, this should drive sales.

The alliance introduced its first products in May 2006. If it is successful, both firms should benefit. Development costs will be lower than if they did not cooperate. Cisco will grow its sales in Japan, and Fujitsu can use the co-branded routers to fill out its product line and sell more bundles of products to Japan's telecommunications companies.

Sources: "Fujitsu, Cisco Systems to Develop High-End Routers for Web Traffic," *Knight Ridder Tribune Business News,* December 6, 2004, p. 1; and "Fujitsu and Cisco Introduce New High-Performance Routers for IP Next Generation Networks," *JCN Newswire,* May 25, 2006.

their position seems extreme. It is difficult to see how the Microsoft–Toshiba alliance, the Boeing–Mitsubishi alliance for the 787, or the Fuji–Xerox alliance fit the critics' thesis. In these cases, both partners seem to have gained from the alliance. Why do some alliances benefit both firms while others benefit one firm and hurt the other? The next section provides an answer to this question.

MAKING ALLIANCES WORK The failure rate for international strategic alliances seems to be high. One study of 49 international strategic alliances found that two-thirds run into serious managerial and financial troubles within two years of their formation, and that although many of these problems are solved, 33 percent are ultimately rated as failures by the parties involved.[43] The success of an alliance seems to be a function of three main factors: partner selection, alliance structure, and the manner in which the alliance is managed.

Partner Selection One key to making a strategic alliance work is to select the right ally. A good ally, or partner, has three characteristics. First, a good partner helps the firm achieve its strategic goals, whether they are market access, sharing the costs and risks of product development, or gaining access to critical core competencies. The partner must have capabilities that the firm lacks and that it values. Second, a good partner shares the firm's vision for the purpose of the alliance. If two firms approach an alliance with radically different agendas, the chances are great that the relationship will not be harmonious, will not flourish, and will end in divorce. Third, a good partner is unlikely to try to opportunistically exploit the alliance for its own ends; that is, to expropriate the firm's technological know-how while giving away little in return. In this respect, firms with reputations for fair play to maintain probably make the best allies. For example, IBM is involved in so many strategic alliances that it would not pay the company to trample over individual alliance partners (in early 2003, IBM reportedly had more than 150 major strategic alliances).[44] This would tarnish IBM's reputation of being a good ally and would make it more difficult for the company to attract alliance partners. Because IBM attaches great importance to its alliances, it is unlikely to engage in the kind of opportunistic behavior that critics highlight. Similarly, their reputations make it less likely (but by no means impossible) that such Japanese firms as Sony, Toshiba, and Fuji, which have histories of alliances with non-Japanese firms, would opportunistically exploit an alliance partner.

To select a partner with these three characteristics, a firm needs to conduct comprehensive research on potential alliance candidates. To increase the probability of selecting a good partner, the firm should

1. Collect as much pertinent, publicly available information on potential allies as possible.
2. Gather data from informed third parties. These include firms that have had alliances with the potential partners, investment bankers who have had dealings with them, and former employees.
3. Get to know the potential partner as well as possible before committing to an alliance. This should include face-to-face meetings between senior managers (and perhaps middle-level managers) to ensure that the chemistry is right.

Alliance Structure A partner having been selected, the alliance should be structured so that the firm's risks of giving too much away to the partner are reduced to an acceptable level. First, alliances can be designed to make it difficult, if not impossible, to transfer technology not meant to be transferred. The design, development, manufacture, and service of a product manufactured by an alliance can be structured so as to wall off sensitive technologies to prevent their leakage to the other participant. In an alliance between General Electric and Snecma to build commercial aircraft engines, for example, GE reduced the risk of excess transfer by walling off certain sections of the production process. The modularization effectively cut off the transfer of what GE regarded as key competitive technology, while permitting Snecma access to final assembly. Similarly, in the alliance between Boeing and the Japanese to build the 767, Boeing walled off research, design, and marketing functions considered central to its competitive position, while allowing the Japanese to share in production technology. Boeing also walled off new technologies not required for 767 production.[45]

Second, contractual safeguards can be written into an alliance agreement to guard against the risk of opportunism by a partner. (Opportunism includes the theft of technology or markets.) For example, TRW, Inc., has three strategic alliances with large Japanese auto component suppliers to produce seat belts, engine valves, and steering gears for sale to Japanese-owned auto assembly plants in the United States. TRW has clauses in each of its alliance contracts that bar the Japanese firms from competing with TRW to supply U.S.-owned auto companies with component parts. By doing this, TRW protects itself against the possibility that the Japanese companies are entering into the alliances merely to gain access to the North American market to compete with TRW in its home market.

Third, both parties to an alliance can agree in advance to swap skills and technologies that the other covets, thereby ensuring a chance for equitable gain. Cross-licensing agreements are one way to achieve this goal. Fourth, the risk of opportunism by an alliance partner can be reduced if the firm extracts a significant credible commitment from its partner in advance. The long-term alliance between Xerox and Fuji to build photocopiers for the Asian market perhaps best illustrates this. Rather than enter into an informal agreement or a licensing arrangement (which Fuji Photo initially wanted), Xerox insisted that Fuji invest in a 50/50 joint venture to serve Japan and East Asia. This venture constituted such a significant investment in people, equipment, and facilities that Fuji was committed from the outset to making the alliance work in order to earn a return on its investment. By agreeing to the joint venture, Fuji essentially made a credible commitment to the alliance. Given this, Xerox felt secure in transferring its photocopier technology to Fuji.[46]

Managing the Alliance

Once a firm has selected a partner and the parties have agreed on an appropriate alliance structure, the task facing each is to maximize the benefits it gains from the alliance. As in all international business deals, an important factor is sensitivity to cultural differences (see Chapter 3). Many differences in management style are attributable to cultural differences, and managers need to make allowances for these in dealing with their partner. Beyond this, maximizing the benefits from an alliance seems to involve building trust between partners and learning from partners.[47]

Managing an alliance successfully requires building interpersonal relationships between the firms' managers, or what is sometimes referred to as *relational capital*.[48] This is one lesson that can be drawn from a successful strategic alliance between Ford and Mazda. The two companies set up a framework of meetings within which their managers not only discuss matters pertaining to the alliance but also have time to get to know each other better. The belief is that the resulting friendships help build trust and facilitate harmonious relations between the two firms. Personal relationships also foster an informal management network between the firms. This network can then be used to help solve problems arising in more formal contexts (such as in joint committee meetings between personnel from the two firms).

Academics have argued that a major determinant of how much knowledge a company gains from an alliance is its ability to learn from its alliance partner.[49] For example, in a five-year study of 15 strategic alliances between major multinationals, Gary Hamel, Yves Doz, and C. K. Prahalad focused on a number of alliances between Japanese companies and Western (European or American) partners.[50] In every case in which a Japanese company emerged from an alliance stronger than its Western partner, the Japanese company had made a greater effort to learn. Few Western companies studied seemed to want to learn from their Japanese partners. They tended to regard the alliance purely as a cost-sharing or risk-sharing device, rather than as an opportunity to learn how a potential competitor does business.

Consider the alliance between General Motors and Toyota constituted in 1985 to build the Chevrolet Nova. This alliance was structured as a formal joint venture, called New United Motor Manufacturing, Inc., and each party had a 50 percent equity stake. The venture owned an auto plant in Fremont, California. According to one Japanese manager, Toyota quickly achieved most of its objectives from the alliance: "We learned about U.S. supply and transportation. And we got the confidence to manage U.S. workers."[51] All that knowledge was then transferred to Georgetown, Kentucky, where

Toyota opened its own plant in 1988. Possibly all GM got was a new product, the Chevrolet Nova. Some GM managers complained that the knowledge they gained through the alliance with Toyota has never been put to good use inside GM. They believe they should have been kept together as a team to educate GM's engineers and workers about the Japanese system. Instead, they were dispersed to various GM subsidiaries.

To maximize the learning benefits of an alliance, a firm must try to learn from its partner and then apply the knowledge within its own organization. It has been suggested that all operating employees should be well briefed on the partner's strengths and weaknesses and should understand how acquiring particular skills will bolster their firm's competitive position. Hamel, Doz, and Prahalad note that this is already standard practice among Japanese companies. They made this observation:

> We accompanied a Japanese development engineer on a tour through a partner's factory. This engineer dutifully took notes on plant layout, the number of production stages, the rate at which the line was running, and the number of employees. He recorded all this despite the fact that he had no manufacturing responsibility in his own company, and that the alliance did not encompass joint manufacturing. Such dedication greatly enhances learning.[52]

For such learning to be of value, it must be diffused throughout the organization (as was seemingly not the case at GM after the GM–Toyota joint venture). To achieve this, the managers involved in the alliance should educate their colleagues about the skills of the alliance partner.

Key Terms

strategy, p. 361
profitability, p. 361
profit growth, p. 361
value creation, p. 363
operations, p. 365
organization architecture, p. 367
organizational structure, p. 367
controls, p. 368
incentives, p. 368
processes, p. 368
organizational culture, p. 368
people, p. 368
core competence, p. 370
location economies, p. 371
global web, p. 372
experience curve, p. 373
learning effects, p. 373
economies of scale, p. 374
universal needs, p. 378
global standardization strategy, p. 381
localization strategy, p. 382
transnational strategy, p. 384
international strategy, p. 385
strategic alliances, p. 387

Summary

In this chapter, we reviewed basic principles of strategy and the various ways in which firms can profit from global expansion, and we looked at the strategies that firms that compete globally can adopt. The chapter made these major points:

1. A strategy can be defined as the actions that managers take to attain the goals of the firm. For most firms, the preeminent goal is to maximize shareholder value. Maximizing shareholder value requires firms to focus on increasing their profitability and the growth rate of profits over time.
2. International expansion may enable a firm to earn greater returns by transferring the product offerings derived from its core competencies to markets where indigenous

competitors lack those product offerings and competencies.

3. It may pay a firm to base each value-creation activity it performs at that location where factor conditions are most conducive to the performance of that activity. We refer to this strategy as focusing on the attainment of location economies.
4. By rapidly building sales volume for a standardized product, international expansion can assist a firm in moving down the experience curve by realizing learning effects and economies of scale.
5. A multinational firm can create additional value by identifying valuable skills created within its foreign subsidiaries and leveraging those skills within its global network of operations.
6. The best strategy for a firm to pursue often depends on a consideration of the pressures for cost reductions and for local responsiveness.
7. Firms pursuing an international strategy transfer the products derived from core competencies to foreign markets, while undertaking some limited local customization.
8. Firms pursuing a localization strategy customize their product offerings, marketing strategy, and business strategy to national conditions.
9. Firms pursuing a global standardization strategy focus on reaping the cost reductions that come from experience curve effects and location economies.
10. Many industries are now so competitive that firms must adopt a transnational strategy. This involves a simultaneous focus on reducing costs, transferring skills and products, and boosting local responsiveness. Implementing such a strategy may not be easy.
11. Strategic alliances are cooperative agreements between actual or potential competitors.
12. The advantage of alliances are that they facilitate entry into foreign markets, enable partners to share the fixed costs and risks associated with new products and processes, facilitate the transfer of complementary skills between companies, and help firms establish technical standards.
13. A disadvantage of a strategic alliance is that the firm risks giving away technological know-how and market access to its alliance partner in return for very little.
14. The disadvantages associated with alliances can be reduced if the firm selects partners carefully, paying close attention to the firm's reputation and the structure of the alliance so as to avoid unintended transfers of know-how.
15. Two keys to making alliances work seem to be building trust and informal communications networks between partners and taking proactive steps to learn from alliance partners.

Critical Thinking and Discussion Questions

1. In a world of zero transportation costs, no trade barriers, and nontrivial differences between nations with regard to factor conditions, firms must expand internationally if they are to survive. Discuss.
2. Plot the position of the following firms on Figure 11.8: Procter & Gamble, IBM, Nokia, Coca-Cola, Dow Chemicals, US Steel, and McDonald's. In each case justify your answer.
3. Reread the Management Focus box on Procter & Gamble and then answer the following questions:
   a. What strategy was Procter & Gamble pursuing when it first entered foreign markets in the period up until the 1980s?
   b. Why do you think this strategy became less viable in the 1990s?
   c. What strategy does P&G appear to be moving toward? What are the benefits of this strategy? What are the potential risks associated with it?
4. What do you see as the main organizational problems that are likely to be associated with implementation of a transnational strategy?
5. Reread the Management Focus box on the alliance between Cisco and Fujitsu. What are the benefits to Cisco and Fujitsu respectively of the alliances? What are the risks to Cisco? How can Cisco mitigate those risks?

Research Task 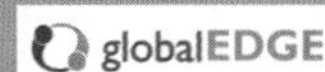 http://globalEDGE.msu.edu

Use the globalEDGE site (http://globalEDGE.msu.edu/) to complete the following exercises:

1. Several classifications and rankings of the *world's largest companies* are prepared by a variety of sources. Find one such ranking system and identify the criteria that are used in ranking the top global companies. Extract the list of the highest ranked 25 companies, paying particular attention to the home countries of the companies.
2. The top management of your company, a manufacturer and marketer of laptop computers, has decided to pursue international expansion opportunities in Eastern Europe. To achieve economies of scale, management is aiming toward a strategy of minimum local adaptation. Focusing on an eastern European country of your choice, and using the Country Insights section of globalEDGE, prepare an executive summary that features those aspects of the product where standardization will simply not work and adaptation to local conditions will be essential.

closing case

Wal-Mart's Global Expansion

Established in Arkansas in 1962 by Sam Walton, over the last four decades Wal-Mart has grown rapidly to become the largest retailer in the world, with 2005 sales of $315 billion, 1.8 million associates (Wal-Mart's term for employees), and almost 7,000 stores. Until 1991, Wal-Mart's operations were confined to the United States. There it established a competitive advantage based upon a combination of efficient merchandising, buying power, and human relations policies. Among other things, Wal-Mart was a leader in the implementation of information systems to track product sales and inventory, developed one of the most efficient distribution systems in the world, and was one of the first companies to promote widespread stock ownership among employees. These practices led to high productivity that enabled Wal-Mart to drive down its operating costs, which it passed on to consumers in the form of everyday low prices, a strategy that enabled the company to gain market share first in general merchandising, where it now dominates, and later in food retailing, where it is taking market share from established supermarkets.

By 1990, however, Wal-Mart realized that its opportunities for growth in the United States were becoming more limited. Management calculated that by the early 2000s, domestic growth opportunities would be constrained due to market saturation. So the company decided to expand globally. Initially, the critics scoffed. Wal-Mart, they said, was too American a company. While its retailing practices were well suited to America, they would not work in other countries where infrastructure was different, consumer tastes and preferences vary, and where established retailers already dominated.

Unperturbed, in 1991 Wal-Mart started to expand internationally with the opening of its first stores in Mexico. The Mexican operation was established as a joint venture with Cifera, the largest local retailer. Initially, Wal-Mart made a number of missteps that seemed to prove the critics right. Wal-Mart had problems replicating its efficient distribution system in Mexico. Poor infrastructure, crowded roads, and a lack of leverage with local suppliers, many of which could not or would not deliver directly to Wal-Mart's stores or distribution centers, resulted in stocking problems and raised costs and prices. Initially, prices at Wal-Mart in Mexico were some 20 percent above prices for comparable products in the company's U.S. stores, which limited Wal-Mart's ability to gain market share. There were also problems with merchandise selection. Many of the stores in Mexico carried items that were popular in the United States. These included ice skates, riding lawn mowers, leaf blowers, and fishing tackle. Not surprisingly, these items did not sell well in Mexico, so managers would slash prices to move inventory, only to find that the company's automated information systems would immediately order more inventory to replenish the depleted stock.

By the mid-1990s, however, Wal-Mart had learned from its early mistakes and adapted its Mexican operations to match the local environment. A partnership with a Mexican trucking company dramatically improved the distribution system, while more careful stocking practices meant that the Mexican stores sold merchandise that appealed more to local tastes and preferences. As Wal-Mart's presence grew, many of Wal-Mart's suppliers built factories near its Mexican distribution centers so that they could better serve the company, which helped to further drive down inventory and logistics costs. Today, Mexico is a leading light in Wal-Mart's international operations. In 1998, Wal-Mart acquired a controlling interest in Cifera. By 2005, Wal-Mart was more than twice the size of its nearest rival in Mexico, with some 700 stores and revenues of $12.5 billion.

The Mexican experience proved to Wal-Mart that it could compete outside of the United States. It has subsequently expanded into 13 other countries. Wal-Mart entered Canada, Great Britain, Germany, Japan, and South Korea, by acquiring existing retailers and then transferring its information systems, logistics, and management expertise. In other nations Wal-Mart established its own stores. As a result of these moves, by mid-2006 the company had more than 2,700 stores outside the United States, employed some 500,000 associates, and generated international revenues of more than $62 billion.

In addition to greater growth, expanding internationally has bought Wal-Mart two other major benefits. First, Wal-Mart has also been able to reap significant economies of scale from its global buying power. Many of Wal-Mart's key suppliers have long been international companies; for example, GE (appliances), Unilever (food products), and Procter & Gamble (personal care products) are all major Wal-Mart suppliers that have long had their own global operations. By building international reach, Wal-Mart has used its enhanced size to demand deeper discounts from the local operations of its global suppliers, increasing the company's ability to lower prices to consumers, gain market share, and ultimately earn greater profits. Second, Wal-Mart has found that it is benefiting from the flow of ideas across the 14 countries in which it now competes. For example, a two-level store in New York State came about because of the success of multilevel stores in South Korea. Other ideas, such as wine departments in its stores in Argentina, have now been integrated into layouts worldwide.

Wal-Mart realized that if it didn't expand internationally, other global retailers would beat it to the punch. Wal-Mart faces significant global competition from Carrefour of France, Ahold of Holland, and Tesco from the United Kingdom. Carrefour, the world's second-largest retailer, is perhaps the most global of the lot. The pioneer of the hypermarket concept now operates in 26 countries and generates more than 50 percent of its sales outside France. In comparison, Wal-Mart is a laggard with less than 20 percent of its sales in 2005 generated from international operations. However, there is room for significant global expansion. The global retailing market is still very fragmented. The top 25 retailers controlled less than 20 percent of worldwide retail sales in 2005, although forecasts suggest the figure could reach 40 percent by 2010, with Latin America, Southeast Asia, and Eastern Europe being the main battlegrounds.

Sources: A. Lillo, "Wal-Mart Says Global Going Good," *Home Textiles Today,* September 15, 2003, p. 12–13; A. de Rocha and L. A. Dib, "The Entry of Wal-Mart into Brazil," *International Journal of Retail and Distribution Management,* 30 (2002), pp. 61–73; "Wal-Mart: Mexico's Biggest Retailer," *Chain Store Age,* June 2001, pp. 52–54; M. N. Hamilton, "Global Food Fight," *Washington Post,* November 19, 2000, p. H1; "Global Strategy—Why Tesco Will Beat Carrefour," *Retail Week,* April 6, 2001, p. 14; "Shopping All over the World," *The Economist,* June 19, 1999, pp. 59–61; G. Samor and C. Rohwedder and A. Zimmerman, "Innocents Abroad?" *The Wall Street Journal,* May 16, 2006, p. B1; and Wal-Mart Web site, accessed June 2006.

Case Discussion Questions

1. How does expanding internationally benefit Wal-Mart?
2. What are the risks that Wal-Mart faces when entering other retail markets? How can these risks be mitigated?
3. Why do you think that Wal-Mart first entered Mexico via a joint venture? Why did it purchase its Mexican joint venture partner in 1998?
4. What strategy is Wal-Mart pursuing: a global strategy, localization strategy, international strategy, or transnational strategy? Does this strategic choice make sense? Why?

Daniel Acker/Bloomberg News/Landov

part 5 Competing in the Global Marketplace

LEARNING OBJECTIVES

1. Explain the three basic decisions that firms contemplating foreign expansion must make: which markets to enter, when to enter those markets, and on what scale.
2. Outline the advantages and disadvantages of the different modes that firms use to enter foreign markets.
3. Identify the factors that influence a firm's choice of entry mode.
4. Evaluate the pros and cons of acquisitions versus greenfield ventures as an entry strategy.

chapter 12

Entering Foreign Markets

JCB in India

opening case

In 1979, JCB, the large British manufacturer of construction equipment, entered into a joint venture with Escorts, an Indian engineering conglomerate, to manufacture backhoe loaders for sale in India. Escorts held a majority 60 percent stake in the venture, and JCB 40 percent. The joint venture was a first for JCB, which historically had exported as much as two-thirds of its production from Britain to a wide range of nations. The decision to enter into a joint venture in India was driven by a number of factors. First, high tariff barriers made direct exports to India difficult. Second, although JCB would have preferred to go it alone in India, government regulations at the time required foreign investors to create joint ventures with local companies. Third, JCB felt that the Indian construction market was ripe for growth, which could become very large indeed. The company's managers believed that it was better to get a foothold in the nation, thereby gaining an advantage over global competitors, rather than wait until the growth potential was realized.

Twenty years later, some of JCB's foresight had been rewarded. The joint venture was selling some 2,000 backhoes in India, and it had an 80 percent share of the Indian market. Moreover, after years of deregulation, the Indian economy was booming. However, JCB felt that the joint venture limited its ability to expand. For one thing, much of JCB's global success was based upon its utilization of leading-edge manufacturing technologies and relentless product innovation, but the company was hesitant about transferring this know-how to a venture in which it did not have a majority stake and therefore lacked control. The last thing JCB wanted was for these valuable technologies to leak out of the joint venture into Escorts, which was one of the largest manufacturers of tractors in India and might conceivably become a direct competitor in the future. Moreover, JCB was unwilling to make the investment in India required to take the joint venture to the next level unless it could capture more of the long-run returns. Accordingly, in 1999 JCB took advantage of changes in government regulations to renegotiate the terms of the venture with Escorts, purchasing 20 percent of its partner's equity to give JCB majority control. In 2002, JCB took this to its logical end when it responded to further relaxation of government regulations on foreign investment to purchase all of Escorts' remaining equity, transforming the joint venture into a wholly owned subsidiary. Around the same time, JCB also invested in wholly owned factories in the United States and Brazil.

Having gained full control, in early 2005 JCB increased its investment in India, announcing that it would build a second factory that it would use to serve the fast-growing Indian market. At the same time, JCB also announced that it would set up another wholly owned factory in China to serve that market. The strategy was clear; India and China, the two most populous nations in the world, were growing rapidly, construction was booming, and JCB, then the world's fifth-largest manufacturer of construction equipment, was eager to expand its presence in order to match its global rivals, particularly Caterpillar, Komatsu, and Volvo, which were also expanding aggressively in these markets. By mid-2006 there were signs that JCB's foreign investment was starting to bear fruit. The product line had been expanded from 120 machines in 2001 to some 257 in 2006. JCB's sales approached £1.5 billion, earnings were a record £110 million, and the company had moved up to number four in the industry, with almost 10 percent of global market share.

Sources: P. Marsh, "Partnerships Feel the Indian Heat," *Financial Times,* June 22, 2006, p. 11; P. Marsh, "JCB Targets Asia to Spread Production," *Financial Times,* March 16, 2005, p. 26; D. Jones, "Profits Jump at JCB," *Daily Post,* June 20, 2006, p. 21; and R. Bentley, "Still Optimistic about Asia," *Asian Business Review,* October 1, 1999, p. 1.

Introduction

This chapter is concerned with two closely related topics: (1) the decisions of which foreign markets to enter, when to enter them, and on what scale; and (2) the choice of entry mode. Any firm contemplating foreign expansion must first struggle with the issue of which foreign markets to enter and the timing and scale of entry. The choice of which markets to enter should be driven by an assessment of relative long-run growth and profit potential. In the opening case, for example, we saw that JCB's original decision to enter the Indian market through a joint venture was based upon a favorable outlook for growth in demand.

The choice of mode for entering a foreign market is another major issue with which international businesses must wrestle. The various modes for serving foreign markets are exporting, licensing or franchising to host-country firms, establishing joint ventures with a host-country firm, setting up a new wholly owned subsidiary in a host country to serve its market, or acquiring an established enterprise in the host nation to serve that market. Each of these options has advantages and disadvantages. The magnitude of the advantages and disadvantages associated with each entry mode is determined by a number of factors, including transportation costs, trade barriers, political risks, economic risks, business risks, costs, and firm strategy. The optimal entry mode varies by situation, depending on these factors. Thus, whereas some firms may best serve a given market by exporting, other firms may better serve the market by setting up a new wholly owned subsidiary or by acquiring an established enterprise.

As discussed in the opening case, JCB originally entered the India market through a joint venture, primarily because tariff barriers made exporting difficult and government regulations required foreign investors to enter joint ventures with local partners. However, JCB was never entirely happy with this arrangement, and when regulations permitted, the company acquired a majority stake in the venture; then in 2005, it purchased all of the remaining equity. Its quest for full control of the Indian venture was a strategic decision, based upon an assessment of the business risks of transferring technology to a venture that was part owned by a potential competitor. As we shall see, many firms prefer a wholly owned subsidiary for precisely this reason.

Basic Entry Decisions

LEARNING OBJECTIVE 1
Explain the three basic decisions that firms contemplating foreign expansion must make.

There are three basic decisions that a firm contemplating foreign expansion must make: which markets to enter, when to enter those markets, and on what scale.[1]

WHICH FOREIGN MARKETS? There are more than 200 nation-states in the world. They do not all hold the same profit potential for a firm contemplating foreign expansion. Ultimately, the choice must be based on an assessment of a nation's long-run profit potential. This potential is a function of several factors, many of which we have studied in earlier chapters. In Chapter 2, we looked in detail at the economic and political factors that influence the potential attractiveness of a foreign market. There we noted that the attractiveness of a country as a potential market for an international business depends on balancing the benefits, costs, and risks associated with doing business in that country.

Chapter 2 also noted that the long-run economic benefits of doing business in a country are a function of factors such as the size of the market (in terms of demographics), the present wealth (purchasing power) of consumers in that market, and the likely future wealth of consumers, which depends upon economic growth rates. Although some markets are very large when measured by number of consumers (e.g., China, India, and Indonesia), businesses must also consider living standards and economic growth. On this basis, China and, to a lesser extent, India, while relatively poor, are growing so rapidly that they are attractive targets for inward investment (see the Another Perspective at right). Alternatively, weak growth in Indonesia implies that this populous nation is a far less attractive target for inward investment. As we saw in Chapter 2, likely future economic growth rates appear to be a function of a free market system and a country's capacity for growth (which may be greater in less-developed nations). We also argued in Chapter 2 that the costs and risks associated with doing

Another Perspective

Microsoft in China: Where Does Freedom of Information Fit into Modes of Entry?

The almost meteoric rise of information on the Internet presents decisions and challenges that extend to human rights issues.

Microsoft says it was simply "facing reality" when it agreed to shut down the MSN Spaces Web site, a demand made by the Chinese government, in order to gain access to the 103 million Chinese Internet users—and that figure is growing wildly. China added almost 10 million new Internet users in the first six months of 2005. Microsoft's official statement about the site shutdown in China was:

> Microsoft does business in many countries around the world. While different countries have different standards, Microsoft and other multinational companies have to ensure that our products and services comply with local laws, norms and industry standards.

Reporters Without Borders, a group in Paris that tracks censorship around the world, vehemently protested Microsoft's actions. They call on all corporations to uphold the free flow of information and even recommend that Western governments take action against corporations that restrict the flow of information. They see it as a loss of freedom for Chinese Web users and a fundamental human rights issue.

How do you see it? Give your answer some serious thought. (Tom Zeller Jr., "China, Still Winning against the Web," *The New York Times,* January 15, 2006)

business in a foreign country are typically lower in economically advanced and politically stable democratic nations, and they are greater in less developed and politically unstable nations.

The discussion in Chapter 2 suggests that, other things being equal, the benefit–cost–risk trade-off is likely to be most favorable in politically stable developed and developing nations that have free market systems, and where there is not a dramatic upsurge in either inflation rates or private-sector debt. The trade-off is likely to be least favorable in politically unstable developing nations that operate with a mixed or command economy or in developing nations where speculative financial bubbles have led to excess borrowing (see Chapter 2 for further details).

Another important factor is the value an international business can create in a foreign market. This depends on the suitability of its product offerings to that market and the nature of indigenous competition.[2] If the international business can offer a product that has not been widely available in that market and that satisfies an unmet need, the value of that product to consumers is likely to be much greater than if the international business simply offers the same type of product that indigenous competitors and other foreign entrants are already offering. Greater value translates into an ability to charge higher prices or to build sales volume more rapidly.

By considering such factors, a firm can rank countries in terms of their attractiveness and long-run profit potential. Preference is then given to entering markets that rank highly. For example, in the case of JCB, entering emerging markets in India and China made sense given the lack of strong local competitors in these markets, the strong underlying growth trends, and the move by JCB's global rivals into these same markets (see the opening case).

Timing of Entry
When a business enters a foreign market; said to be early when it does so before other firms, and late when it does so after other businesses have already established themselves.

First-Mover Advantages
Advantages accruing to firms that enter markets early.

First-Mover Disadvantages
Disadvantages affecting early entrants to a foreign market.

Pioneering Costs
Costs an early entrant has to bear that a later entrant can avoid.

TIMING OF ENTRY Once the firm has identified attractive markets, it must consider the **timing of entry.** We say that entry is early when an international business enters a foreign market before other foreign firms and late when it enters after other international businesses have already established themselves. The advantages frequently associated with entering a market early are commonly known as **first-mover advantages.**[3] One first-mover advantage is the ability to preempt rivals and capture demand by establishing a strong brand name. A second advantage is the ability to build sales volume in that country and ride down the experience curve ahead of rivals, giving the early entrant a cost advantage over later entrants. This cost advantage may enable the early entrant to cut prices below that of later entrants, thereby driving them out of the market. A third advantage is the ability of early entrants to create switching costs that tie customers into their products or services. Such switching costs make it difficult for later entrants to win business. By entering the Indian market for backhoes in 1979, JCB was able to gain significant first-mover advantages, cumulating in an 80 percent share of the market for backhoes by the early 2000s (see opening case).

There can also be disadvantages associated with entering a foreign market before other international businesses. These are often referred to as **first-mover disadvantages.**[4] A primary disadvantage is that an early entry may entail **pioneering costs,** costs that the firm has to bear that a later entrant can avoid. Pioneering costs arise when the business system in a foreign country is so different from that in a firm's home market that the enterprise has to devote considerable effort, time, and expense to learning the rules of the game. Pioneering costs include the costs of business failure if the firm, due to its ignorance of the foreign environment, makes some major mistakes. A certain liability is associated with being a foreigner, and this liability is greater for foreign firms that enter a national market early.[5] Research seems to confirm that the probability of survival increases if an international business enters a national market after several other foreign firms have already done so.[6] The late entrant may benefit by observing and learning from the mistakes made by early entrants.

Pioneering costs also include the costs of promoting and establishing a product offering, including the costs of educating customers. These can be significant when the product being promoted is unfamiliar to local consumers. In contrast, later entrants may be able to ride on an early entrant's investments in learning and customer education by watching how the early entrant proceeded in the market, by avoiding costly mistakes made by the early entrant, and by exploiting the market potential created by the early entrant's investments in customer education. For example, KFC introduced the Chinese to American-style fast food, but a later entrant, McDonald's, has capitalized on the market in China.

An early entrant may be put at a severe disadvantage, relative to a later entrant, if regulations change in a way that diminishes the value of an early entrant's investments. This is a serious risk in many developing nations where the rules that govern business practices are still evolving. Early entrants can find themselves at a disadvantage if a subsequent change in regulations invalidates prior assumptions about the best business model for operating in that country.

SCALE OF ENTRY AND STRATEGIC COMMITMENTS Another issue that an international business needs to consider when contemplating market entry is the scale of entry. Entering a market on a large scale involves the commitment of significant resources; it also implies rapid entry. Consider the entry of the Dutch insurance company ING into the U.S. insurance market in 1999 (described in detail in the Management Focus on page 402). ING had to spend several billion dollars to acquire its U.S. operations. Not all firms have the resources necessary to enter on a large scale, and even some large firms prefer to enter foreign markets on a small scale and then build slowly as they become more familiar with the market.

The consequences of entering on a significant scale—entering rapidly—are associated with the value of the resulting **strategic commitments.**[7] A strategic commitment has a long-term impact and is difficult to reverse. Deciding to enter a foreign market on a significant scale is a major strategic commitment. Strategic commitments, such as rapid large-scale market entry, can have an important influence on the nature of competition in a market. For example, by entering the U.S. financial services market on a significant scale, ING has signaled its commitment to the market (see the Management Focus box, next page). This will have several effects. On the positive side, it will make it easier for the company to attract customers and distributors (such as insurance agents). The scale of entry gives both customers and distributors reasons for believing that ING will remain in the market for the long run. The scale of entry may also give other foreign institutions considering entry into the United States pause; now they will have to compete against not only indigenous institutions in the United States but also an aggressive and successful European institution. On the negative side, by committing itself heavily to the United States, ING may have fewer resources available to support expansion in other desirable markets, such as Japan. The commitment to the United States limits the company's strategic flexibility.

Strategic Commitment
A decision that has a long-term impact and is difficult to reverse.

As suggested by the ING example, significant strategic commitments are neither unambiguously good nor bad. Rather, they tend to change the competitive playing field and unleash a number of changes, some of which may be desirable and some of which will not be. It is important for a firm to think through the implications of large-scale entry into a market and act accordingly. Of particular relevance is trying to identify how actual and potential competitors might react to large-scale entry into a market. Also, the large-scale entrant is more likely than the small-scale entrant to be able to capture first-mover advantages associated with demand preemption, economies of scale, and switching costs.

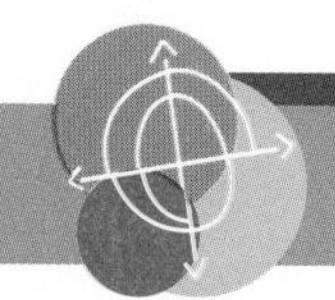

Management FOCUS

International Expansion at ING Group

ING Group was formed in 1991 from the merger between the third-largest bank in the Netherlands and the country's largest insurance company. Since then, the company has grown rapidly to become one of the top 10 financial services firms in the world, with operations in 65 countries and a wide range of products in banking, insurance, and asset management. ING's strategy has been to expand rapidly across national borders, primarily through a series of careful acquisitions. Its formula has been to pick a target that has good managers and a strong local presence, take a small stake in the company, win the trust of managers, and then propose a takeover. After the deal, the management and products of the acquired companies have been left largely intact, but ING has required them to sell ING products alongside their own. ING's big push has been the selling of insurance, banking, and investment products, something it has been doing in Holland since the original 1991 merger (in Holland, some 20 percent of ING's insurance products are sold through banks).

Two changes in the regulatory environment have helped ING pursue this strategy. One has been a trend to remove regulatory barriers that traditionally kept different parts of the financial services industry separate. In the United States, for example, a Depression-era law known as the Glass-Steagall Act disallowed insurance companies, banks, and asset managers such as mutual fund companies from selling each other's products. The U.S. Congress repealed this act in 1999, opening the way for the consolidation of the U.S. financial services industry. Many other countries that had similar regulations removed them in the 1990s. ING's native Holland was one of the first countries to remove barriers between different areas of the financial services industry. ING took advantage of this to become a pioneer of banking and insurance combinations in Europe. Another significant regulatory development occurred in 1997 when the World Trade Organization struck a deal between its member nations that effectively removed barriers to cross-border investment in financial services. This made it much easier for a company such as ING to build a global financial services business.

ING's expansion was initially centered on Europe where its largest acquisitions have included banks in Germany and Belgium. However, in recent years the centerpiece of ING's strategy has been its aggressive moves into the United States. While ING's Dutch insurance predecessor, Nationale-Nederlanden, had owned several small, regional U.S. insurance companies since the 1970s, the big push into the United States began with the 1997 acquisition of Equitable Life Insurance Company of Lowa. This was followed by the acquisition of Furman Selz, a New York investment bank, whose activities complement those of Barings, a British-based investment bank with significant U.S. activities that ING acquired in 1995. In 2000, ING acquired ReliaStar Financial Services and the nonhealth insurance units of Aetna Financial Services. These acquisitions combined to make ING one of the top 10 financial services companies in the United States.

ING was attracted to the United States by several factors. The United States is by far the world's largest financial services market, so any company aspiring to be a global player must have a significant presence there. Deregulation made ING's strategy of cross-selling financial service products feasible in the United States. Despite some state-by-state regulation of insurance, ING says it is easier to do business in the United States than in the European Union, where the patchwork of languages and cultures makes it difficult to build a pan-European business with a single identity. Another lure is that with more and more Americans responsible for managing their own retirement with 401(k) plans and the like rather than traditional pensions, the personal investment business in the United States is booming, which has increased ING's appetite for U.S. financial services firms. In contrast, pensions are still primarily taken care of by national governments in Europe. Furthermore, in recent years U.S. insurance companies have traded at relatively low price–earnings ratios, making them seem like bargains compared to their European counterparts, which trade at higher valuations. Building a substantial U.S. presence also brings with it the benefits of geographic diversification, allowing ING to offset any revenue or profit shortfalls in one region with earnings elsewhere in the world.

Finally, ING has found it somewhat easier to make acquisitions in the United States than in Europe, where national pride has made it difficult for ING to acquire local companies. ING's initial attempt to acquire a Belgian bank in 1992 was rebuffed, primarily due to nationalistic concerns, and it took ING until 1997 to make the acquisition. Similarly, a 1999 attempt to acquire a major French bank, Credit Commercial de France, in which it already held a 19 percent stake, was turned down. According to news reports, French regulators had expressed concerns over what would have been the first foreign acquisition of a French bank, and the board of CCF believed the acquisition should not proceed without the regulators' blessing.

Sources: J. Carreyrou, "Dutch Financial Giant Maps Its U.S. Invasion," *The Wall Street Journal,* June 22, 2000, p. A17; J. B. Treaster, "ING Group Makes Its Move in Virtual Banking and Insurance," *The New York Times,* August 26, 2000, p. C1; "The Lion's Friendly Approach," *The Economist,* December 18, 2000; S. Kirsner, "Would You Like a Mortgage with Your Mocha?" *Fast Company,* March 2003, pp. 110–14; O. O'Sullivan, "Tough Love Bank Thrives," *ABA Banking Journal,* December 2003, p. 12; L. Bielski, "Bucking the Back to Bricks Trend," *ABA Banking Journal,* November 2004, pp. 25–32; and I. Bickerton, "ING Permanently Watching for Deals," *Financial Times,* May 3, 2006, p. 27.

The value of the commitments that flow from rapid large-scale entry into a foreign market must be balanced against the resulting risks and lack of flexibility associated with significant commitments. But strategic inflexibility can also have value. A famous example from military history illustrates the value of inflexibility. When Hernán Cortés landed in Mexico, he ordered his men to burn all but one of his ships. Cortés reasoned that by eliminating their only method of retreat, his men had no choice but to fight hard to win against the Aztecs—and ultimately they did.[8]

Balanced against the value and risks of the commitments associated with large-scale entry are the benefits of a small-scale entry. Small-scale entry allows a firm to learn about a foreign market while limiting the firm's exposure to that market. Small-scale entry is a way to gather information about a foreign market before deciding whether to enter on a significant scale and how best to enter. By giving the firm time to collect information, small-scale entry reduces the risks associated with a subsequent large-scale entry. But the lack of commitment associated with small-scale entry may make it more difficult for the small-scale entrant to build market share and to capture first-mover or early-mover advantages. The risk-averse firm that enters a foreign market on a small scale may limit its potential losses, but it may also miss the chance to capture first-mover advantages.

SUMMARY There are no "right" decisions here, just decisions that are associated with different levels of risk and reward. Entering a large developing nation such as China or India before most other international businesses in the firm's industry, and entering on a large scale, will be associated with high levels of risk. In such cases, the liability of being foreign is increased by the absence of prior foreign entrants whose experience can be a useful guide. At the same time, the potential long-term rewards associated with such a strategy are great. The early large-scale entrant into a major developing nation may be able to capture significant first-mover advantages that will bolster its long-run position in that market.[9] In contrast, entering developed nations such as Australia or Canada after other international businesses in the firm's industry, and entering on a small scale to first learn more about those markets, will be associated with much lower levels of risk. However, the potential long-term rewards are also likely to be lower because the firm is essentially forgoing the opportunity to capture

Jollibee may be heading your way! Unlike many fast-food chains that have their roots within the United States, the Jollibee chain originated in the Philippines using McDonald's as a role model. *AP/Wide World Photos*

first-mover advantages and because the lack of commitment signaled by small-scale entry may limit its future growth potential.

This section has been written largely from the perspective of a business based in a developed country considering entry into foreign markets. Christopher Bartlett and Sumantra Ghoshal have pointed out the ability that businesses based in developing nations have to enter foreign markets and become global players.[10] Although such firms tend to be late entrants into foreign markets, and although their resources may be limited, Bartlett and Ghoshal argue that such late movers can still succeed against well-established global competitors by pursuing appropriate strategies. In particular, they argue that companies based in developing nations should use the entry of foreign multinationals as an opportunity to learn from these competitors by benchmarking their operations and performance against them. Furthermore, they suggest that the local company may be able to find ways to differentiate itself from a foreign multinational, for example, by focusing on market niches that the multinational

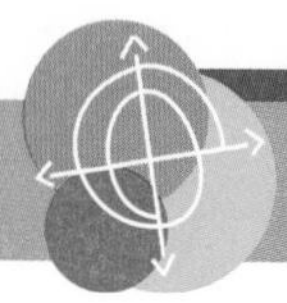

Management FOCUS

The Jollibee Phenomenon—A Philippine Multinational

Jollibee is one of the Philippines' phenomenal business success stories. Jollibee, which stands for "Jolly Bee," began operations in 1975 as a two-branch ice cream parlor. It later expanded its menu to include hot sandwiches and other meals. Encouraged by early success, Jollibee Foods Corporation was incorporated in 1978, with a network that had grown to seven outlets. In 1981, when Jollibee had 11 stores, McDonald's began to open stores in Manila. Many observers thought Jollibee would have difficulty competing against McDonald's. However, Jollibee saw this as an opportunity to learn from a very successful global competitor. Jollibee benchmarked its performance against that of McDonald's and started to adopt operational systems similar to those used at McDonald's to control its quality, cost, and service at the store level. This helped Jollibee to improve its performance.

As it came to better understand McDonald's business model, Jollibee began to look for a weakness in Mc Donald's global strategy. Jollibee executives concluded that McDonald's fare was too standardized for many locals, and that the local firm could gain share by tailoring its menu to local tastes. Jollibee's hamburgers were set apart by a secret mix of spices blended into the ground beef to make the burgers sweeter than those produced by McDonald's, appealing more to Philippine tastes. It also offered local fare including various rice dishes, pineapple burgers, and banana *langka* and peach mango pies for desserts. By pursuing this strategy, Jollibee maintained a leadership position over the global giant. By 2006, Jollibee had over 540 stores in the Philippines, a market share of more than 60 percent, and revenues in excess of $600 million. McDonald's, in contrast, had around 250 stores.

In the mid-1980s, Jollibee had gained enough confidence to expand internationally.

Its initial ventures were into neighboring Asian countries such as Indonesia, where it pursued the strategy of localizing the menu to better match local tastes, thereby differentiating itself from McDonald's. In 1987, Jollibee entered the Middle East, where a large contingent of expatriate Filipino workers provided a ready-made market for the company. The strategy of focusing on expatriates worked so well that in the late 1990s Jollibee decided to enter another foreign market where there was a large Filipino population—the United States. Between 1999 and 2004, Jollibee opened eight stores in the United States, all in California. Even though many believe the U.S. fast-food market is saturated, the stores have performed well. While the initial clientele was strongly biased toward the expatriate Filipino community, where Jollibee's brand awareness is high, non-Filipinos increasingly are coming to the restaurant. In the San Francisco store, which has been open the longest, more than half the customers are now non-Filipino. Today, Jollibee has 37 international stores and a potentially bright future as a niche player in a market that has historically been dominated by U.S. multinationals.

Sources: Christopher Bartlett and Sumantra Ghoshal, "Going Global: Lessons from Late Movers," *Harvard Business Review*, March–April 2000, pp. 132–45; "Jollibee Battles Burger Giants in US Market," *Philippine Daily Inquirer*, July 13, 2000; M. Ballon, "Jollibee Struggling to Expand in U.S.," *Los Angeles Times*, September 16, 2002, p. C1; J. Hookway, "Burgers and Beer," *Far Eastern Economic Review*, December 2003, pp. 72–74; S.E. Lockyer, "Coming to America," *Nation's Restaurant News*, February 14, 2005, pp. 33–35; and www.jollibee.com.ph.

ignores or is unable to serve effectively if it has a standardized global product offering. Having improved its performance through learning and differentiated its product offering, the firm from a developing nation may then be able to pursue its own international expansion strategy. Even though the firm may be a late entrant into many countries, by benchmarking and then differentiating itself from early movers in global markets, the firm from the developing nation may still be able to build a strong international business presence. A good example of how this can work is given in the accompanying Management Focus at left, which looks at how Jollibee, a Philippines-based fast-food chain, has started to build a global presence in a market dominated by U.S. multinationals such as McDonald's and KFC.

Entry Modes

LEARNING OBJECTIVE 2
Outline the advantages and disadvantages of the different modes that firms use to enter foreign markets.

Once a firm decides to enter a foreign market, the question arises as to the best mode of entry. Firms can use six different modes to enter foreign markets: exporting, turnkey projects, licensing, franchising, establishing joint ventures with a host-country firm, or setting up a new wholly owned subsidiary in the host country. Each entry mode has advantages and disadvantages. Managers need to consider these carefully when deciding which to use.[11]

EXPORTING

Many manufacturing firms begin their global expansion as exporters and only later switch to another mode for serving a foreign market. We take a close look at the mechanics of exporting in the next chapter. Here we focus on the advantages and disadvantages of exporting as an entry mode.

Advantages

Exporting has two distinct advantages. First, it avoids the often substantial costs of establishing manufacturing operations in the host country. Second, exporting may help a firm achieve experience curve and location economies (see Chapter 11). By manufacturing the product in a centralized location and exporting it to other national markets, the firm may realize substantial scale economies from its global sales volume. This is how Sony came to dominate the global TV market, how Matsushita came to dominate the VCR market, how many Japanese automakers made inroads into the U.S. market, and how South Korean firms such as Samsung gained market share in computer memory chips.

Disadvantages

Exporting has a number of drawbacks. First, exporting from the firm's home base may not be appropriate if lower-cost locations for manufacturing the product can be found abroad (i.e., if the firm can realize location economies by moving production elsewhere). Thus, particularly for firms pursuing global or transnational strategies, it may be preferable to manufacture where the mix of factor conditions is most favorable from a value-creation perspective and to export to the rest of the world from that location. This is not so much an argument against exporting as an argument against exporting from the firm's home country. Many U.S. electronics firms have moved some of their manufacturing to the Far East because of the availability of low-cost, highly skilled labor there. They then export from that location to the rest of the world, including the United States.

A second drawback to exporting is that high transportation costs can make exporting uneconomical, particularly for bulk products. One way of getting around this is to manufacture bulk products regionally. This strategy enables the firm to realize some economies from large-scale production and at the same time to limit its transportation costs. For example, many multinational chemical firms manufacture their products regionally, serving several countries from one facility.

Another drawback is that tariff barriers can make exporting uneconomical. It was high tariff barriers that persuaded JCB to initially invest in the Indian market for construction equipment (see the opening case). Similarly, the threat of tariff barriers by the host-country government can make it very risky. A fourth drawback to exporting arises when a firm delegates its marketing, sales, and service in each country where it does business to another company. This is a common approach for manufacturing firms that are just beginning to expand internationally. The other company may be a local agent, or it may be another multinational with extensive international distribution operations. Local agents often carry the products of competing firms and so have divided loyalties. In such cases, the local agent may not do as good a job as the firm would if it managed its marketing itself. Similar problems can occur when another multinational takes on distribution.

The way around such problems is to set up wholly owned subsidiaries in foreign nations to handle local marketing, sales, and service. By doing this, the firm can exercise tight control over marketing and sales in the country while reaping the cost advantages of manufacturing the product in a single location, or a few choice locations.

Turnkey Project
A project in which a firm agrees to set up an operating plant for a foreign client and hand over the "key" when the plant is fully operational.

TURNKEY PROJECTS

Firms that specialize in the design, construction, and start-up of turnkey plants are common in some industries. In a **turnkey project,** the contractor agrees to handle every detail of the project for a foreign client, including the training of operating personnel. At completion of the contract, the foreign client is handed the "key" to a plant that is ready for full operation—hence, the term *turnkey.* This is a means of exporting process technology to other countries. Turnkey projects are most common in the chemical, pharmaceutical, petroleum refining, and metal refining industries, all of which use complex, expensive production technologies.

Advantages

The know-how required to assemble and run a technologically complex process, such as refining petroleum or steel, is a valuable asset. Turnkey projects are a way of earning great economic returns from that asset. The strategy is particularly useful where FDI is limited by host-government regulations. For example, the governments of many oil-rich countries have set out to build their own petroleum refining industries, so they restrict FDI in their oil and refining sectors. But because many of these countries lack petroleum-refining technology, they gain it by entering into turnkey projects with foreign firms that have the technology. Such deals are often attractive to the selling firm because without them, they would have no way to earn a return on their valuable know-how in that country. A turnkey strategy can also be less risky than conventional FDI. In a country with unstable political and economic environments, a longer-term investment might expose the firm to unacceptable political or economic risks (e.g., the risk of nationalization or of economic collapse).

Disadvantages

Three main drawbacks are associated with a turnkey strategy. First, the firm that enters into a turnkey deal will have no long-term interest in the foreign country. This can be a disadvantage if that country subsequently proves to be a major market for the output of the process that has been exported. One way around this is to take a minority equity interest in the operation. Second, the firm that enters into a turnkey project with a foreign enterprise may inadvertently create a competitor. For example, many of the Western firms that sold oil-refining technology to firms in Saudi Arabia, Kuwait, and other Gulf states now find themselves competing with these firms in the world oil market. Third, if the firm's process technology is a source of competitive advantage, then selling this technology through a turnkey project is also selling competitive advantage to potential or actual competitors.

LICENSING A **licensing agreement** is an arrangement whereby a licensor grants the rights to intangible property to another entity (the licensee) for a specified period, and in return, the licensor receives a royalty fee from the licensee.[12] Intangible property includes patents, inventions, formulas, processes, designs, copyrights, and trademarks. For example, to enter the Japanese market, Xerox, inventor of the photocopier, established a joint venture with Fuji Photo that is known as Fuji–Xerox. Xerox then licensed its xerographic know-how to Fuji–Xerox. In return, Fuji–Xerox paid Xerox a royalty fee equal to 5 percent of the net sales revenue that Fuji–Xerox earned from the sales of photocopiers based on Xerox's patented know-how. In the Fuji–Xerox case, the license was originally granted for 10 years, and it has been renegotiated and extended several times since. The licensing agreement between Xerox and Fuji–Xerox also limited Fuji–Xerox's direct sales to the Asian Pacific region (although Fuji–Xerox does supply Xerox with photocopiers that are sold in North America under the Xerox label).[13]

Licensing Agreement
Arrangement in which a licensor grants the rights to intangible property to the licensee for a specified period and receives a royalty fee in return.

Advantages In the typical international licensing deal, the licensee puts up most of the capital necessary to get the overseas operation going. Thus, a primary advantage of licensing is that the firm does not have to bear the development costs and risks associated with opening a foreign market. Licensing is attractive for firms lacking the capital to develop operations overseas. In addition, licensing can be attractive when a firm is unwilling to commit substantial financial resources to an unfamiliar or politically volatile foreign market. A firm may use licensing when it wishes to participate in a foreign market but is prohibited from doing so by barriers to investment. This was one of the original reasons for the formation of the Fuji–Xerox joint venture in 1962. Xerox wanted to participate in the Japanese market but was prohibited from setting up a wholly owned subsidiary by the Japanese government. So Xerox set up the joint venture with Fuji and then licensed its know-how to the joint venture.

Finally, licensing is frequently used when a firm possesses some intangible property that might have business applications, but it does not want to develop those applications itself. For example, Bell Laboratories at AT&T originally invented the transistor circuit in the 1950s, but AT&T decided it did not want to produce transistors, so it licensed the technology to a number of other companies, such as Texas Instruments. Similarly, Coca-Cola has licensed its famous trademark to clothing manufacturers, which have incorporated the design into clothing.

Disadvantages Licensing has three serious drawbacks. First, it does not give a firm the tight control over manufacturing, marketing, and strategy that is required for realizing experience curve and location economies. Licensing typically involves each licensee setting up its own production operations. This severely limits the firm's ability to realize experience curve and location economies by producing its product in a centralized location. When these economies are important, licensing may not be the best way to expand overseas.

Second, competing in a global market may require a firm to coordinate strategic moves across countries by using profits earned in one country to support competitive attacks in another. By its very nature, licensing limits a firm's ability to do this. A licensee is unlikely to allow a multinational firm to use its profits (beyond those due in the form of royalty payments) to support a different licensee operating in another country.

A third problem with licensing is one that we encountered in Chapter 7 when we reviewed the economic theory of FDI. This is the risk associated with licensing technological know-how to foreign companies. Technological know-how constitutes the basis of many multinational firms' competitive advantage. Most firms wish to maintain

RCA found one disadvantage to licensing: when it licensed its color TV technology to Japanese firms, these firms quickly assimilated the technology, improved it, and entered the U.S. market, taking market share away from RCA. *Christopher Kerrigan*

control over how their know-how is used, and a firm can quickly lose control over its technology by licensing it. Many firms have made the mistake of thinking they could maintain control over their know-how within the framework of a licensing agreement. RCA Corporation, for example, once licensed its color TV technology to Japanese firms including Matsushita and Sony. The Japanese firms quickly assimilated the technology, improved on it, and used it to enter the U.S. market, taking substantial market share away from RCA.

There are ways of reducing this risk. One way is by entering into a **cross-licensing agreement** with a foreign firm. Under a cross-licensing agreement, a firm might license some valuable intangible property to a foreign partner, but in addition to a royalty payment, the firm might also request that the foreign partner license some of its valuable know-how to the firm. Such agreements may reduce the risks associated with licensing technological know-how, because the licensee realizes that if it violates the licensing contract (by using the knowledge obtained to compete directly with the licensor), the licensor can do the same to it. Cross-licensing agreements enable firms to hold each other hostage, which reduces the probability that they will behave opportunistically toward each other.[14] Such cross-licensing agreements are increasingly common in high-technology industries. For example, the U.S. biotechnology firm Amgen licensed one of its key drugs, Nuprogene, to Kirin, the Japanese pharmaceutical company. The license gives Kirin the right to sell Nuprogene in Japan. In return, Amgen receives a royalty payment and, through a licensing agreement, gained the right to sell some of Kirin's products in the United States.

Cross-Licensing Agreement
An arrangement in which a company licenses valuable intangible property to a foreign partner and receives a license for the partner's valuable knowledge.

Another way of reducing the risk associated with licensing is to follow the Fuji–Xerox model and link an agreement to license know-how with the formation of a joint venture in which the licensor and licensee take important equity stakes. Such an approach aligns the interests of licensor and licensee, because both have a stake in ensuring that the venture is successful. Thus, the risk that Fuji Photo might appropriate Xerox's technological know-how, and then compete directly against Xerox in the global photocopier market, was reduced by the establishment of a joint venture in which both Xerox and Fuji Photo had an important stake.

FRANCHISING Franchising is similar to licensing, although franchising tends to involve longer-term commitments than licensing. **Franchising** is basically a specialized form of licensing in which the franchiser not only sells intangible property (normally a trademark) to the franchisee, but it also insists that the franchisee agree to abide by strict rules as to how it does business. The franchiser will also often assist the franchisee to run the business on an ongoing basis. As with licensing, the franchiser typically receives a royalty payment, which amounts to some percentage of the franchisee's revenues. Whereas licensing is pursued primarily by manufacturing firms, franchising is employed primarily by service firms.[15] McDonald's is a good example of a firm that has grown by using a franchising strategy. McDonald's strict rules as to how franchisees should operate a restaurant extend to control over the menu, cooking methods, staffing policies, and design and location. McDonald's also organizes the supply chain for its franchisees and provides management training and financial assistance.[16]

Franchising
A specialized form of licensing in which the franchiser not only sells intangible property (normally a trademark) to the franchisee, but it also insists that the franchisee agree to abide by strict rules as to how it does business.

Advantages The advantages of franchising as an entry mode are similar to those of licensing. The firm is relieved of many of the costs and risks of opening a foreign market on its own. Instead, the franchisee typically assumes those costs and risks. This creates a good incentive for the franchisee to build a profitable operation as quickly as possible. Thus, using a franchising strategy, a service firm can build a global presence quickly and at a relatively low cost and risk, as McDonald's has.

Disadvantages The disadvantages of franchising can be less pronounced than in the case of licensing. Many service companies, such as hotels, use franchising; in such instances, the firm has no reason to consider the need for coordination of manufacturing to achieve experience curve and location economies. But franchising may inhibit the firm's ability to take profits out of one country to support competitive attacks in another. A more significant disadvantage of franchising is quality control. The foundation of franchising arrangements is that the firm's brand name conveys a message to consumers about the quality of the firm's product. Thus, a business traveler checking in at a Four Seasons hotel in Hong Kong can reasonably expect the same quality of room, food, and service that she would receive in New York. The Four Seasons name is supposed to guarantee consistent product quality. This presents a problem in that foreign franchisees may not be as concerned about quality as they are supposed to be, and the result of poor quality can extend beyond lost sales in a particular foreign market to a decline in the firm's worldwide reputation. For example, if the business traveler has a bad experience at the Four Seasons in Hong Kong, she may never go to another Four Seasons hotel and may urge her colleagues to do likewise. The geographical distance of the firm from its foreign franchisees can make poor quality difficult to detect. In addition, the sheer numbers of franchisees—in the case of McDonald's, tens of thousands—can make quality control difficult. Due to these factors, quality problems may persist.

One way around this disadvantage is to set up a subsidiary in each country in which the firm expands. The subsidiary might be wholly owned by the company or a joint venture with a foreign company. The subsidiary assumes the rights and obligations to establish franchises throughout the particular country or region. McDonald's, for example, establishes a master franchisee in many countries. Typically, this master franchisee is a joint venture between McDonald's and a local firm. The proximity and the smaller number of franchises to oversee reduce the quality-control challenge. In addition, because the subsidiary (or master franchisee) is at least partly owned by the firm, the firm can place its own managers in the subsidiary to help ensure that it is doing a good job of monitoring the franchises. This organizational arrangement has proven very satisfactory for McDonald's, KFC, and others.

JOINT VENTURES A **joint venture** entails establishing a firm that is jointly owned by two or more otherwise independent firms. Fuji–Xerox, for example, was set up as a joint venture between Xerox and Fuji Photo. Establishing a joint venture with a foreign firm has long been a popular mode for entering a new market. As we saw in the opening case, JCB used a joint venture to enter the Indian markets. The most typical joint venture is a 50/50 venture, in which there are two parties, each of which holds a 50 percent ownership stake and contributes a team of managers to share operating control (this was the case with the Fuji–Xerox joint venture until 2001; it is now a 25/75 venture, with Xerox holding 25 percent). Some firms, however, have sought joint ventures in which they have a majority share and thus tighter control.[17]

Joint Venture
Establishing a firm that is jointly owned by two or more otherwise independent firms.

Advantages Joint ventures have a number of advantages. First, a firm benefits from a local partner's knowledge of the host country's competitive conditions, culture, language, political systems, and business systems. Thus, for many U.S. firms, joint ventures have involved the U.S. company providing technological know-how and products and the local partner providing the marketing expertise and the local knowledge necessary for competing in that country. Second, when the development costs or risks of opening a foreign market are high, a firm might gain by sharing these costs and or risks with a local partner. Third, in many countries, political considerations make joint ventures the only feasible entry mode (again, that was why JCB entered into a joint venture with Escorts). Research suggests joint ventures with local partners face a low risk of being subject to nationalization or other forms of adverse government interference.[18] This appears to be because local equity partners, who may have some influence on host-government policy, have a vested interest in speaking out against nationalization or government interference.

Disadvantages Despite these advantages, there are major disadvantages with joint ventures. First, as with licensing, a firm that enters into a joint venture risks giving control of its technology to its partner. Thus, a proposed joint venture in 2002 between Boeing and Mitsubishi Heavy Industries to build a new wide-body jet raised fears that Boeing might unwittingly give away its commercial airline technology to the Japanese. However, joint-venture agreements can be constructed to minimize this risk. One option is to hold majority ownership in the venture. This allows the dominant partner to exercise greater control over its technology. But it can be difficult to find a foreign partner who is willing to settle for minority ownership. Another option is to "wall off" from a partner technology that is central to the core competence of the firm, while sharing other technology.

A second disadvantage is that a joint venture does not give a firm the tight control over subsidiaries that it might need to realize experience curve or location economies. Nor does it give a firm the tight control over a foreign subsidiary that it might need for engaging in coordinated global attacks against its rivals. Consider the entry of Texas Instruments (TI) into the Japanese semiconductor market. When TI established semiconductor facilities in Japan, it did so for the dual purpose of checking Japanese manufacturers' market share and limiting their cash available for invading TI's global market. In other words, TI was engaging in global strategic coordination. To implement this strategy, TI's subsidiary in Japan had to be prepared to take instructions from corporate headquarters regarding competitive strategy. The strategy also required the Japanese subsidiary to run at a loss if necessary. Few if any potential joint-venture partners would have been willing to accept such conditions, since it would have necessitated a willingness to accept a negative return on investment. Indeed, many joint ventures establish a degree of autonomy that would make such direct control over strategic decisions all but impossible to establish.[19] Thus, to implement this strategy, TI set up a wholly owned subsidiary in Japan.

A third disadvantage with joint ventures is that the shared ownership arrangement can lead to conflicts and battles for control between the investing firms if their goals and objectives change or if they take different views as to what the strategy should be. This was apparently not a problem with the Fuji–Xerox joint venture. According to Yotaro Kobayashi, currently the chairman of Fuji–Xerox, a primary reason is that both Xerox and Fuji Photo adopted an arm's-length relationship with Fuji–Xerox, giving the venture's management considerable freedom to determine its own strategy.[20] However, much research indicates that conflicts of interest over strategy and goals often arise in joint ventures. These conflicts tend to be greater when the venture is between firms of different nationalities, and they often end in the dissolution of the venture.[21] Such conflicts tend to be triggered by shifts in the relative bargaining power of venture partners. For example, in the case of ventures between a foreign firm and a local firm, as a foreign partner's knowledge about local market conditions increases, it depends less on the expertise of a local partner. This increases the bargaining power of the foreign partner and ultimately leads to conflicts over control of the venture's strategy and goals.[22] Some firms have sought to limit such problems by entering into joint ventures in which one partner has a controlling interest.

Wholly Owned Subsidiary
A subsidiary in which the firm owns 100 percent of the stock.

WHOLLY OWNED SUBSIDIARIES

In a **wholly owned subsidiary,** the firm owns 100 percent of the stock. Establishing a wholly owned subsidiary in a foreign market can be done two ways. The firm either can set up a new operation in that country, often referred to as a *greenfield venture,* or it can acquire an established firm in that host nation and use that firm to promote its products.[23] For example, as we saw in the Management Focus, ING's strategy for entering the U.S. market was to acquire established U.S. enterprises rather than try to build an operation from the ground floor.

Advantages

There are several clear advantages of wholly owned subsidiaries. First, when a firm's competitive advantage is based on technological competence, a wholly owned subsidiary will often be the preferred entry mode because it reduces the risk of losing control over that competence. (See Chapter 7 for more details.) Many high-tech firms prefer this entry mode for overseas expansion (e.g., firms in the semiconductor, electronics, and pharmaceutical industries). It is notable that JCB was unwilling to transfer key technology to its Indian joint venture with Escorts, and only did so once it had purchased its venture partner (see the opening case). Second, a wholly owned subsidiary gives a firm tight control over operations in different countries. This is necessary for engaging in global strategic coordination (i.e., using profits from one country to support competitive attacks in another).

Third, a wholly owned subsidiary may be required if a firm is trying to realize location and experience curve economies (as firms pursuing global and transnational strategies try to do). As we saw in Chapter 11, when cost pressures are intense, it may pay a firm to configure its value chain in such a way that the value added at each stage is maximized. Thus, a national subsidiary may specialize in manufacturing only part of the product line or certain components of the end product, exchanging parts and products with other subsidiaries in the firm's global system. Establishing such a global production system requires a high degree of control over the operations of each affiliate. The various operations must be prepared to accept centrally determined decisions as to how they will produce, how much they will produce, and how their output will be priced for transfer to the next operation. Because licensees or joint-venture partners are unlikely to accept such a subservient role, establishing wholly owned subsidiaries may be necessary. Finally, establishing a wholly owed subsidiary gives the firm a 100 percent share in the profits generated in a foreign market.

Disadvantages

Establishing a wholly owned subsidiary is generally the most costly method of serving a foreign market from a capital investment standpoint. Firms doing this must bear the full capital costs and risks of setting up overseas operations. The risks associated with learning to do business in a new culture are less if the firm acquires an established host-country enterprise. However, acquisitions raise additional problems, including those associated with trying to marry divergent corporate cultures. These problems may more than offset any benefits derived by acquiring an established operation. Because the choice between greenfield ventures and acquisitions is such an important one, we shall discuss it in more detail later in the chapter.

Selecting an Entry Mode

LEARNING OBJECTIVE 3
Identify the factors that influence a firm's choice of entry mode.

As the preceding discussion demonstrated, all the entry modes have advantages and disadvantages, as summarized in Table 12.1. See the Another Perspective on page 413 for another look at entry challenges. Thus, trade-offs are inevitable when selecting an entry mode. For example, when considering entry into an unfamiliar country with a track record for discriminating against foreign-owned enterprises when awarding government contracts, a firm might favor a joint venture with a local enterprise. Its rationale might be that the local partner will help it establish operations in an unfamiliar environment and will help the company win government contracts. However, if the firm's core competence is based on proprietary technology, entering a joint venture might risk losing control of that technology to the joint-venture partner, in which case the strategy may seem unattractive. Despite the existence of such trade-offs, it is possible to make some generalizations about the optimal choice of entry mode.[24]

CORE COMPETENCIES AND ENTRY MODE As we saw in Chapter 11, often firms expand internationally to earn greater returns from their core competencies, transferring the skills and products derived from their core competencies to foreign markets where indigenous competitors lack those skills. The optimal entry mode for these firms depends to some degree on the nature of their core competencies. A distinction can be drawn between firms whose core competency is in technological know-how and those whose core competency is in management know-how.

table 12.1
Advantages and Disadvantages of Entry Modes

Entry Mode	Advantages	Disadvantages
Exporting	Ability to realize location and experience curve economies	High Transport costs Trade barriers Problems with local marketing agents
Turnkey contracts	Ability to earn returns from process technology skills in countries where FDI is restricted	Creating efficient competitors Lack of long-term market presence
Licensing	Low development costs and risks	Lack of control over technology Inability to realize location and experience curve economies Inability to engage in global strategic coordination
Franchising	Low development costs and risks	Lack of control over quality Inability to engage in global strategic coordination
Joint ventures	Access to local partner's knowledge Sharing development costs and risks Politically acceptable	Lack of control over technology Inability to engage in global strategic coordination Inabilty to realize location and experience economies
Wholly owned subsidiaries	Protection of technology Ability to engage in global strategic coordination Abiltity to realize location and experience economies	High costs and risks

Technological Know-How

As was observed in Chapter 7, if a firm's competitive advantage (its core competence) is based on control over proprietary technological know-how, it should avoid licensing and joint-venture arrangements if possible to minimize the risk of losing control over that technology. Thus, if a high-tech firm sets up operations in a foreign country to profit from a core competency in technological know-how, it will probably do so through a wholly owned subsidiary. This rule should not be viewed as hard and fast, however. Sometimes a licensing or joint-venture arrangement can be structured to reduce the risk of the licensee's or joint-venture partner's expropriation of technological know-how. Another exception exists when a firm perceives its technological advantage to be only transitory, when it expects rapid imitation of its core technology by competitors. In such cases, the firm might want to license its technology as rapidly as possible to foreign firms to gain global acceptance for its technology before the imitation occurs.[25] Such a strategy has some advantages. By licensing its technology to competitors, the firm may deter them from developing their own, possibly superior, technology. Further, by licensing its technology, the firm may establish its technology as the dominant design in the industry (as Matsushita did with its VHS format for VCRs). This may ensure a steady stream of royalty payments. However, the attractions of licensing are frequently outweighed by the risks of losing control over technology, and if this is a risk, the firm should avoid licensing.

Another Perspective

Take Another Look: Factors Outside the Advantages/Disadvantages Entry Mode Grid

Citigroup Inc. is literally branching out its banking system big time in Russia in 2006. It plans to add as many as 40 additional branches, doubling the number it has in Moscow and St. Petersburg. This makes perfect business sense, because the consumer borrowing market there is almost untapped: 87 percent of Russians have never taken out a bank loan! However, this expansion comes with major challenges, including high rent costs for these branches, a sometimes poor communications system, and a labor market that has made it difficult to find qualified workers. So it is important to also consider country-specific economic and cultural conditions in entry modes. (Carrick Mollenkamp, "Citigroup Plans Rapid Expansion of Russia Branches," *The Wall Street Journal*, June 7, 2006)

Management Know-How

The competitive advantage of many service firms is based on management know-how (e.g., McDonald's). For such firms, the risk of losing control over the management skills to franchisees or joint-venture partners is not that great. These firms' valuable asset is their brand name, and brand names are generally well protected by international laws pertaining to trademarks. Given this, many of the issues arising in the case of technological know-how are of less concern here. As a result, many service firms favor a combination of franchising and subsidiaries to control the franchises within particular countries or regions. The subsidiaries may be wholly owned or joint ventures, but most service firms have found that joint ventures with local partners work best for the controlling subsidiaries. A joint venture is often politically more acceptable and brings a degree of local knowledge to the subsidiary.

PRESSURES FOR COST REDUCTIONS AND ENTRY MODE

The greater the pressures for cost reductions are, the more likely a firm will want to pursue some combination of exporting and wholly owned subsidiaries. By manufacturing in those locations where factor conditions are optimal and then exporting to the rest of the world, a firm may be able to realize substantial location and experience curve economies. The firm might then want to export the finished product to marketing subsidiaries based in various countries. These subsidiaries will typically be wholly owned and have the responsibility for overseeing distribution in their particular countries. Setting up wholly owned marketing subsidiaries is preferable to joint-venture arrangements and to using foreign marketing agents because it gives the firm tight control that might be required for coordinating a globally dispersed value chain. It also gives the firm the ability to use the profits generated in one market to improve its competitive position in another market. In other words, firms pursuing global standardization or transnational strategies tend to prefer establishing wholly owned subsidiaries. See the Another Perspective on page 413 for Citibank's approach to entering Russia.

Greenfield Venture versus Acquisition

LEARNING OBJECTIVE 4
Evaluate the pros and cons of acquisitions versus greenfield ventures as an entry strategy.

A firm can establish a wholly owned subsidiary in a country by building a subsidiary from the ground up, the so-called greenfield strategy, or by acquiring an enterprise in the target market.[26] The volume of cross-border acquisitions has been growing at a rapid rate for two decades. Over the last decade, between 50 and 80 percent of all FDI inflows have been in the form of mergers and acquisitions. In 2001, for example, mergers and acquisitions accounted for 80 percent of all FDI inflows. In 2004 the figure was 51 percent, or some $381 billion.[27]

PROS AND CONS OF ACQUISITIONS Acquisitions have three major points in their favor. First, they are quick to execute. By acquiring an established enterprise, a firm can rapidly build its presence in the target foreign market. When the German automobile company Daimler-Benz decided it needed a bigger presence in the U.S. automobile market, it did not increase that presence by building new factories to serve the United States, a process that would have taken years. Instead, it acquired the number-three U.S. automobile company, Chrysler, and merged the two operations to form DaimlerChrysler. When the Spanish telecommunications service provider Telefonica wanted to build a service presence in Latin America, it did so through a series of acquisitions, purchasing telecommunications companies in Brazil and Argentina. In these cases, the firms made acquisitions because they knew that was the quickest way to establish a sizable presence in the target market.

Three pros to acquisitions, such as Vodafone's purchase of AirTouch, include a quick execution, preemption of the competition, and less risk than greenfield ventures. *Dave Caulkin/AP Wide World*

Second, in many cases firms make acquisitions to preempt their competitors. The need for preemption is particularly great in markets that are rapidly globalizing, such as telecommunications, where a combination of deregulation within nations and liberalization of regulations governing cross-border foreign direct investment has made it much easier for enterprises to enter foreign markets through acquisitions. Such markets may see concentrated waves of acquisitions as firms race each other to attain global scale. In the telecommunications industry, for example, regulatory changes triggered what can be called a feeding frenzy, with firms entering each other's markets via acquisitions to establish a global presence. These included the $60 billion acquisition of AirTouch Communications in the United States by the British company Vodafone, which was the largest acquisition ever; the $13 billion acquisition of One 2 One in Britain by the German company Deutsche Telekom; and the $6.4 billion acquisition of Excel Communications in the United States by Teleglobe of Canada, all of which occurred in 1998 and 1999.[28] A similar wave of cross-border acquisitions occurred in the global automobile industry over the same time period, with Daimler acquiring Chrysler, Ford acquiring Volvo, and Renault acquiring Nissan.

Third, managers may believe acquisitions to be less risky than greenfield ventures. When a firm makes an acquisition, it buys a set of assets that are producing a known revenue and profit stream. In contrast, the revenue and profit stream that a greenfield venture might generate is uncertain because it does not yet exist. When a firm makes an acquisition in a foreign market, it not only acquires a set of tangible assets, such as factories, logistics systems, customer service systems, and so on, but it also acquires valuable intangible assets including a local brand name and managers' knowledge of the business environment in that nation. Such knowledge can reduce the risk of mistakes caused by ignorance of the national culture.

Despite the arguments for making acquisitions, acquisitions often produce disappointing results.[29] For example, a study by Mercer Management Consulting looked at 150 acquisitions worth more than $500 million each that were undertaken between January 1990 and July 1995.[30] The Mercer study concluded that 50 percent of these acquisitions eroded shareholder value, while another 33 percent created only marginal returns. Only 17 percent were judged to be successful. Similarly, a study by KPMG, an accounting and management consulting company, looked at 700 large acquisitions between 1996 and 1998. The study found that while some 30 percent of these actually created value for the acquiring company, 31 percent destroyed value, and the remainder had little impact.[31] A similar study by McKenzie & Co. estimated that some 70 percent of mergers and acquisitions failed to achieve expected revenue synergies.[32] In a seminal study of the postacquisition performance of acquired companies, David Ravenscraft and Mike Scherer concluded that on average the profits and market shares of acquired companies declined following acquisition.[33] They also noted that a smaller but substantial subset of those companies experienced traumatic difficulties, which ultimately led to their being sold by the acquiring company. Ravenscraft and Scherer's evidence suggests that many acquisitions destroy rather than create value. Most of this research has looked at domestic acquisitions; however, the findings probably also apply to cross-border acquisitions.[34]

Why Do Acquisitions Fail?

Acquisitions fail for several reasons. First, the acquiring firms often overpay for the assets of the acquired firm. The price of the target firm can get bid up if more than one firm is interested in its purchase, as is often the case. In addition, the management of the acquiring firm is often too optimistic about the value that can be created via an acquisition and is thus willing to pay a significant premium over a target firm's market capitalization. This is called the ***hubris hypothesis*** of why acquisitions fail. The hubris hypothesis postulates that top managers typically overestimate their ability to create value from an acquisition, primarily because rising to the top of a corporation has given them an exaggerated sense of their own capabilities.[35] For example, Daimler acquired Chrysler in 1998 for $40 billion, a premium of 40 percent over the market value of Chrysler before the takeover bid. Daimler paid this much because it thought it could use Chrysler to help it grow market share in the United States. At the time, Daimler's management issued bold announcements about the "synergies" that would be created from combining the operations of the two companies. Executives believed they could attain greater economies of scale from the global presence, take costs out of the German and U.S. operations, and boost the profitability of the combined entity. However, within a year of the acquisition, Daimler's German management was faced with a crisis at Chrysler, which was suddenly losing money because of weak sales in the United States. In retrospect, Daimler's management had been far too optimistic about the potential for future demand in the U.S. auto market and about the opportunities for creating value from synergies. Daimler acquired Chrysler at the end of a multiyear boom in U.S. auto sales and paid a large premium over Chrysler's market value just before demand slumped.[36]

Second, many acquisitions fail because there is a clash between the cultures of the acquiring and acquired firm. After an acquisition, many acquired companies experience high management turnover, possibly because their employees do not like the acquiring company's way of doing things.[37] This happened at DaimlerChrysler; many senior managers left Chrysler in the first year after the merger. Apparently, Chrysler executives disliked the dominance in decision making by Daimler's German managers, while the Germans resented that Chrysler's American managers were paid two to three times as much as their German counterparts. These cultural differences created tensions, which ultimately exhibited themselves in high management turnover at Chrysler.[38] The loss of management talent and expertise can materially harm the performance of the acquired unit.[39] This may be particularly problematic in an international business, where management of the acquired unit may have valuable local knowledge that can be difficult to replace.

Third, many acquisitions fail because attempts to realize synergies by integrating the operations of the acquired and acquiring entities often run into roadblocks and take much longer than forecast. Differences in management philosophy and company culture can slow the integration of operations. Differences in national culture may exacerbate these problems. Bureaucratic haggling between managers also complicates the process. Again, this reportedly occurred at DaimlerChrysler, where grand plans to integrate the operations of the two companies were bogged down by endless committee meetings and by simple logistical considerations such as the six-hour time difference between Detroit and Germany. By the time an integration plan had been worked out, Chrysler was losing money, and Daimler's German managers suddenly had a crisis on their hands.

Finally, many acquisitions fail due to inadequate preacquisition screening.[40] Many firms decide to acquire other firms without thoroughly analyzing the potential benefits and costs. They often move with undue haste to execute the acquisition, perhaps because they fear another competitor may preempt them. After the acquisition, however, many acquiring firms discover that instead of buying a well-run business, they have purchased a troubled organization. This may be a particular problem in cross-border acquisitions because the acquiring firm may not fully understand the target firm's national culture and business system.

Reducing the Risks of Failure A firm can overcome all these problems if it is careful about its acquisition strategy.[41] Screening of the foreign enterprise to be acquired, including a detailed auditing of operations, financial position, and management culture, can help to make sure the firm (1) does not pay too much for the acquired unit, (2) does not uncover any nasty surprises after the acquisition, and (3) acquires a firm whose organization culture is not antagonistic to that of the acquiring enterprise. It is also important for the acquirer to allay any concerns that management in the acquired enterprise might have. The objective should be to reduce unwanted management attrition after the acquisition. Finally, managers must move rapidly after an acquisition to put an integration plan in place and to act on that plan. Some people in both the acquiring and acquired units will try to slow or stop any integration efforts, particularly when losses of employment or management power are involved, and managers should have a plan for dealing with such impediments before they arise.

PROS AND CONS OF GREENFIELD VENTURES The big advantage of establishing a greenfield venture in a foreign country is that it gives the firm a much greater ability to build the kind of subsidiary company that it wants. For example, it is much easier to build an organization culture from scratch than it is to change the culture of an acquired unit. Similarly, it is much easier to establish a set of operating routines in a new subsidiary than it is to convert the operating routines of an acquired unit. This is a very important advantage for many international businesses, where transferring products, competencies, skills, and know-how from the established operations of the firm to the new subsidiary are principal ways of creating value. For example, when Lincoln Electric, the U.S. manufacturer of arc welding equipment, first ventured overseas in the mid-1980s, it did so by acquisitions, purchasing arc welding equipment companies in Europe. However, Lincoln's competitive advantage in the United States was based on a strong organizational culture and a unique set of incentives that encouraged its employees to do everything possible to increase productivity. Lincoln found through bitter experience that it was almost impossible to transfer its organizational culture and incentives to acquired firms, which had their own distinct organizational cultures and incentives. As a result, the firm switched its entry strategy in the mid-1990s and began to enter foreign countries by establishing greenfield ventures, building operations from the ground up. While this strategy takes more time to execute, Lincoln has found that it yields greater long-run returns than the acquisition strategy.

Set against this significant advantage are the disadvantages of establishing a greenfield venture. Greenfield ventures are slower to establish. They are also risky. As with any new venture, a degree of uncertainty is associated with future revenue and profit prospects. However, if the firm has already been successful in other foreign markets and understands what it takes to do business in other countries, these risks may not be that great. For example, having already gained great knowledge about operating internationally, the risk to McDonald's of entering yet another country is probably not that great. Also, greenfield ventures are less risky than acquisitions in the sense that there is less potential for unpleasant surprises. A final disadvantage is the possibility of being preempted by more aggressive global competitors that enter via acquisitions and build a big market presence that limits the market potential for the greenfield venture. See the Another Perspective at right for more on risk taking.

GREENFIELD OR ACQUISITION? The choice between making an acquisition or establishing a greenfield venture is not an easy one. Both modes have their advantages and disadvantages. In general, the choice will depend on the circumstances confronting the firm. If the firm is seeking to enter a market in which there are already well-established incumbent enterprises, and in which global competitors are also interested in establishing a presence, acquisition may be the better mode of entry. In such circumstances, a greenfield venture may be too slow to establish a sizable presence. However, if the firm is going to make an acquisition, its management should be

Another Perspective

Risks and Entering Foreign Markets

Business is all about risk, the right risks. Choosing which risks to accept and which to avoid is at the heart of management. These risks increase and become more interesting with entry into foreign markets. Scholar David Conklin discusses the idea of managing risk through planned uncertainty. By planned uncertainty he means an awareness of contingencies, with possible what-if scenarios developed in advance. The key idea here is that through an ongoing monitoring of the various risk areas, decision makers can have much of the data they may need to address a number of possible outcomes. Of course, we have to know what uncertainty to plan for, and we don't know what we don't know. Planning for everything is impossible, but what Conklin suggests is that planned uncertainty is a way of thinking. Given that we don't know the future, this way of thinking may be helpful in career development and other parts of our lives. Who ever said business wasn't like surfing?

cognizant of the risks discussed earlier and consider these when determining which firms to purchase. It may be better to enter by the slower route of a greenfield venture than to make a bad acquisition.

If the firm is considering entering a country in which there are no incumbent competitors to be acquired, then a greenfield venture may be the only mode. Even when incumbents exist, if the competitive advantage of the firm is based on the transfer of organizationally embedded competencies, skills, routines, and culture, it may still be preferable to enter via a greenfield venture. Things such as skills and organizational culture, which are based on significant knowledge that is difficult to articulate and codify, are much easier to embed in a new venture than they are in an acquired entity, where the firm may have to overcome the established routines and culture of the acquired firm. Thus, as our earlier examples suggest, firms such as McDonald's and Lincoln Electric prefer to enter foreign markets by establishing greenfield ventures.

Key Terms

timing of entry, p. 400
first-mover advantages, p. 400
first-mover disadvantages, p. 400
pioneering costs, p. 400
strategic commitment, p. 401
turnkey project, p. 406
licensing agreement, p. 407
cross-licensing agreement, p. 408
franchising, p. 408
joint venture, p. 409
wholly owned subsidiary, p. 411

Summary

The chapter made the following points:

1. Basic entry decisions include identifying which markets to enter, when to enter those markets, and on what scale.
2. The most attractive foreign markets tend to be found in politically stable developed and developing nations that have free market systems and where there is not a dramatic upsurge in either inflation rates or private-sector debt.
3. There are several advantages associated with entering a national market early, before other international businesses have established themselves. These advantages must be balanced against the pioneering costs that early entrants often have to bear, including the greater risk of business failure.
4. Large-scale entry into a national market constitutes a major strategic commitment that is likely to change the nature of competition in that market and limit the entrant's future strategic flexibility. Although making major strategic commitments can yield many benefits, there are also risks associated with such a strategy.
5. There are six modes of entering a foreign market: exporting, creating turnkey projects, licensing, franchising, establishing joint ventures, and setting up a wholly owned subsidiary.
6. Exporting has the advantages of facilitating the realization of experience curve economies and of avoiding the costs of setting up manufacturing operations in another country. Disadvantages include high transportation costs, trade barriers, and problems with local marketing agents.
7. Turnkey projects allow firms to export their process know-how to countries where FDI might be prohibited, thereby enabling the firm to earn a greater return from this asset. The

disadvantage is that the firm may inadvertently create efficient global competitors in the process.

8. The main advantage of licensing is that the licensee bears the costs and risks of opening a foreign market. Disadvantages include the risk of losing technological know-how to the licensee and a lack of tight control over licensees.
9. The main advantage of franchising is that the franchisee bears the costs and risks of opening a foreign market. Disadvantages center on problems of quality control of distant franchisees.
10. Joint ventures have the advantages of sharing the costs and risks of opening a foreign market and of gaining local knowledge and political influence. Disadvantages include the risk of losing control over technology and a lack of tight control.
11. The advantages of wholly owned subsidiaries include tight control over technological know-how. The main disadvantage is that the firm must bear all the costs and risks of opening a foreign market.
12. The optimal choice of entry mode depends on the firm's strategy. When technological know-how constitutes a firm's core competence, wholly owned subsidiaries are preferred, since they best control technology. When management know-how constitutes a firm's core competence, foreign franchises controlled by joint ventures seem to be optimal. When the firm is pursuing a global standardization or transnational strategy, the need for tight control over operations to realize location and experience curve economies suggests wholly owned subsidiaries are the best entry mode.
13. When establishing a wholly owned subsidiary in a country, a firm must decide whether to do so by a greenfield venture strategy or by acquiring an established enterprise in the target market.
14. Acquisitions are quick to execute, may enable a firm to preempt its global competitors, and involve buying a known revenue and profit stream. Acquisitions may fail when the acquiring firm overpays for the target, when the culture of the acquiring and acquired firms clash, when there is a high level of management attrition after the acquisition, and when there is a failure to integrate the operations of the acquiring and acquired firm.
15. The advantage of a greenfield venture in a foreign country is that it gives the firm a much greater ability to build the kind of subsidiary company that it wants. For example, it is much easier to build an organization culture from scratch than it is to change the culture of an acquired unit.

Critical Thinking and Discussion Questions

1. Review the Management Focus on ING. ING chose to enter the U.S. financial services market via acquisitions rather than greenfield ventures. What do you think are the advantages to ING of doing this? What might the drawbacks be? Does this strategy make sense? Why?
2. Licensing proprietary technology to foreign competitors is the best way to give up a firm's competitive advantage. Discuss.
3. Discuss how the need for control over foreign operations varies with firms' strategies and core competencies. What are the implications for the choice of entry mode?
4. A small Canadian firm that has developed some valuable new medical products using its unique biotechnology know-how is trying to decide how best to serve the European Community market. Its choices are given below. The cost of investment in manufacturing facilities will be a major one for the Canadian firm, but it is not outside its reach. If these are the firm's only options, which one would you advise it to choose? Why?
   a. Manufacture the product at home and let foreign sales agents handle marketing.
   b. Manufacture the products at home and set up a wholly owned subsidiary in Europe to handle marketing.
   c. Enter into an alliance with a large European pharmaceutical firm. The product would be manufactured in Europe by the 50/50 joint venture and marketed by the European firm.

Research Task globalEDGE globalEDGE.msu.edu

Use the globalEDGE site (http://globalEDGE.msu.edu/) to complete the following exercises:

1. *Entrepreneur Magazine* annually publishes a ranking of America's top 200 franchisers seeking international franchisees. Provide a list of the top 10 companies that pursue franchising as a mode of international expansion. Study one of these companies in detail and provide a description of its business model, its international expansion pattern, the qualifications it looks for in its franchisees, and the type of support and training it provides.
2. The U.S. Commercial Service prepares a series of reports titled the *Country Commercial Guide* for each country of interest to U.S. investors. Utilize this guide to gather information on Brazil. Imagine that your company is producing laptop computers and is considering entering this country. Select the most appropriate entry method, supporting your decision with the information collected from the commercial guide.

closing case

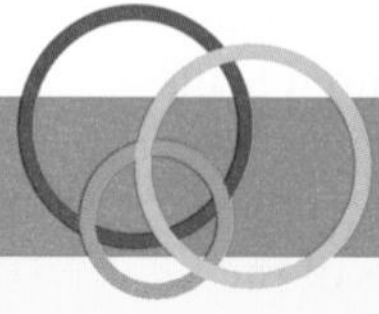

Tesco Goes Global

Tesco is the largest grocery retailer in the United Kingdom, with a 25 percent share of the local market. In its home market, the company's strengths are reputed to come from strong competencies in marketing and store site selection, logistics and inventory management, and its own-label product offerings. By the early 1990s, these competencies had already given the company a leading position in the United Kingdom. The company was generating strong free cash flows, and senior management had to decide how to use that cash. One strategy they settled on was overseas expansion. As they looked at international markets, they soon concluded that the best opportunities were not in established markets, such as those in North America and Western Europe, where strong local competitors already existed, but in the emerging markets of Eastern Europe and Asia where there were few capable competitors but strong underlying growth trends.

Tesco's first international foray was into Hungary in 1994, when it acquired an initial 51 percent stake in Global, a 43-store, state-owned grocery chain. By 2004, Tesco was the market leader in Hungary, with some 60 stores and a 14 percent market share. In 1995, Tesco acquired 31 stores in Poland from Stavia; a year later it added 13 stores purchased from Kmart in the Czech Republic and Slovakia; and the following year it entered the Republic of Ireland.

Tesco's Asian expansion began in 1998 in Thailand when it purchased 75 percent of Lotus, a local food retailer with 13 stores. Building on that base, Tesco had 64 stores in Thailand by 2004. In 1999, the company entered South Korea when it partnered with Samsung to develop a chain of hypermarkets. This was followed by entry into Taiwan in 2000, Malaysia in 2002, and China in 2004. The move into China came after three years of careful research and discussions with potential partners. Like many other Western companies, Tesco was attracted to the Chinese market by its large size and rapid growth. In the end, Tesco settled on a 50/50 joint venture with Hymall, a hypermarket chain that is controlled by Ting Hsin, a Taiwanese group, which had been operating in China for six years. Currently, Hymall has 25 stores in China, and it plans to open another 10 each year. Ting Hsin is a well-capitalized enterprise in its own right, and it will match Tesco's investments, reducing the risks Tesco faces in China.

As a result of these moves, by early 2005 Tesco had 814 stores outside the United Kingdom, which generated £9.2 billion in annual revenues. In the United Kingdom, Tesco had some 1,900 stores, generating £32 billion. The addition of international stores has helped to make Tesco the fourth-largest company in the global grocery market behind Wal-Mart, Carrefour of France, and Ahold of Holland. Of the four, however, Tesco may be the most successful internationally. By 2005, all of its foreign ventures were making money.

In explaining the company's success, Tesco's managers have detailed a number of important factors. First, the company devotes considerable attention to transferring its core capabilities in retailing to its new ventures. At the same time, it does not send in an army of expatriate managers to run local operations, preferring to hire local managers and support them with a few operational experts from the United Kingdom. Second, the company believes that its partnering strategy in Asia has been a great asset. Tesco has teamed up with good companies that have a deep understanding of the markets in which they are participating but that lack Tesco's financial strength and retailing capabilities. Consequently, both Tesco and its partners have brought useful assets to the venture, which have increased the probability of success. As the venture becomes established, Tesco has typically increased its ownership stake in its partner. Thus, under current plans, by 2011 Tesco will own 99 percent of Homeplus, its South Korean hypermarket chain. When the venture was established, Tesco owned 51 percent. Third, the company has focused on markets with good growth potential but that lack strong indigenous competitors, which provides Tesco with ripe ground for expansion.

In March 2006, Tesco took its international expansion strategy to the next level when it announced it would enter the crowded United States grocery market with its Tesco Express concept. Currently running in five countries, Tesco Express stores are smaller, high-quality neighborhood grocery outlets that feature a large selection of prepared and healthy foods. Tesco will initially enter on the West Coast, investing some £250 million per year, with breakeven expected in the second year of operation. Although some question the wisdom of this move, others point out that in the United Kingdom Tesco has consistently outperformed the ASDA chain which is owned by Wal-Mart. Moreover, the Tesco Express format is not something found in the United States.

Sources: P. N. Child, "Taking Tesco Global," *The McKenzie Quarterly,* no. 3 (2002); H. Keers, "Global Tesco Sets Out Its Stall in China," *Daily Telegraph,* July 15, 2004, p. 31; K. Burgess, "Tesco Spends Pounds 140m on Chinese Partnership," *Financial Times,* July 15, 2004, p. 22; J. McTaggart, "Industry Awaits Tesco Invasion," *Progressive Grocer,* March 1, 2006, pp. 8–10; and Tesco's annual reports, archived at www.tesco.com.

Case Discussion Questions

1. Why did Tesco's initial international expansion strategy focus on developing nations?
2. How does Tesco create value in its international operations?
3. In Asia, Tesco has a long history of entering into joint venture agreements with local partners. What are the benefits of doing this for Tesco? What are the risks? How are those risks mitigated?
4. In March 2006, Tesco announced that it would enter the United States. This represents a departure from its historic strategy of focusing on developing nations. Why do you think Tesco made this decision? How is the U.S. market different from others Tesco has entered? What are the risks here? How do you think Tesco will do?

Courtesy FCX Systems, Inc.

part 5 Competing in the Global Marketplace

LEARNING OBJECTIVES

1. Explain the promises and risks associated with exporting.
2. Outline the steps managers can take to improve their firm's export performance.
3. Identify information sources and government programs that exist to help exporters.
4. Grasp the basic steps involved in export financing.
5. Define countertrade and its three major types.
6. Articulate how countertrade can be used to facilitate exporting.

chapter 13

Exporting, Importing, and Countertrade

FCX Systems

opening case

Founded in 1987 with the help of a $20,000 loan from the Small Business Administration, FCX Systems is an American exporting success story. FCX makes power converters for the aerospace industry. These devices convert common electric utility frequencies into the higher frequencies used in aircraft systems and are primarily used to provide power to aircraft while they are on the ground. In 2004, the West Virginia enterprise generated some 60 percent of its $20 million in annual sales from exports to more than 50 countries. FCX's prowess in opening up foreign markets has earned the company several awards for export excellence, including a 1999 presidential award for achieving extraordinary growth in export sales.

FCX initially got into exporting because it found that foreigners were often more receptive to the company's products than potential American customers. According to Don Gallion, president of FCX, "In the overseas market, they were looking for a good technical product, preferably made in the U.S., but they weren't asking questions about 'How long have you been in business? Are you still going to be here tomorrow?' They were just anxious to get the product."

In 1989, FCX signed on with an international distribution company to help with exporting, but Gallion became disillusioned with that company, and in 1994 FCX started to handle the exporting process on its own. At the time, exports represented 12 percent of sales, but by 1997 they had jumped to more than 50 percent of the total, where they have stayed since.

In explaining the company's export success, Gallion cites a number of factors. One was the extensive assistance that FCX has received over the years from a number of federal and state agencies, including the U.S. Department of Commerce and the Development Office of West Virginia. These agencies demystified the process of exporting and provided good contacts for FCX. Finding a good local representative to help work through local regulations and customs is another critical factor, according to Gallion: "A good rep will keep you out of trouble when it comes to customs and what you should and shouldn't do." Persistence is also very important, says Gallion, particularly when trying to break into markets where personal relationships are crucial, such as China.

China has been an interesting story for FCX. In 2004, the company booked $2 million in sales to China, but it took years to get to this point. China had been on Gallion's radar screen since the early 1990s, primarily because of the country's rapid modernization and its plans to build or remodel some 179 airports between 1998 and 2008. This constituted a potentially large market opportunity for FCX, particularly compared with the United States, where perhaps only three new airports would be built during the same period. Despite the scale of the opportunity, progress was slow. The company had to identify airports and airline projects, government agencies, customers, and decision makers, as well as work through different languages—and make friends. According to Gallion, "Only after they consider you a friend will they buy a product. They believe a friend would never cheat you." To make friends in China, Gallion estimates he had to make more than 100 trips to the country since 1990, but now that the network has been established, it is starting to pay dividends.

Sources: J. Sparshott, "Businesses Must Export to Compete," *The Washington Times,* September 1, 2004, p. C8; "Entrepreneur of the Year 2001: Donald Gallion, FCX Systems," *The State Journal,* June 18, 2001, p. S10; and T. Pierro, "Exporting Powers Growth of FCX Systems," *The State Journal,* April 6, 1998, p. 1.

Introduction

In the previous chapter, we reviewed exporting from a strategic perspective. We considered exporting as just one of a range of strategic options for profiting from international expansion. This chapter is more concerned with the nuts and bolts of exporting (and importing). Here we look at how to export. As the opening case makes clear, exporting is not just for large enterprises; many small firms such as FCX Systems have benefited significantly from the moneymaking opportunities of exporting.

The volume of export activity in the world economy is increasing as exporting has become easier. The gradual decline in trade barriers under the umbrella of GATT and now the WTO (see Chapter 6) along with regional economic agreements such as the European Union and the North American Free Trade Agreement (see Chapter 8) have significantly increased export opportunities. At the same time, modern communication and transportation technologies have alleviated the logistical problems associated with exporting. Firms are increasingly using fax machines, the World Wide Web, toll-free 800 phone numbers, and international air express services to reduce the costs of exporting. Consequently, it is no longer unusual to find small companies that are thriving as exporters.

Nevertheless, exporting remains a challenge for many firms. Smaller enterprises can find the process intimidating. The firm wishing to export must identify foreign market opportunities, avoid a host of unanticipated problems that are often associated with doing business in a foreign market, familiarize itself with the mechanics of export and import financing, learn where it can get financing and export credit insurance, and learn how it should deal with foreign exchange risk. The process can be made more problematic by currencies that are not freely convertible. Arranging payment for exports to countries with weak currencies can be a problem. This brings us to the topic of countertrade, by which payment for exports is received in goods and services rather than money. In this chapter, we will discuss all these issues with the exception of foreign exchange risk, which was covered in Chapter 9. We open the chapter by considering the promise and pitfalls of exporting.

Another Perspective

Autarky: Not in the Vocabulary of Globalization!

The vocabulary word is *autarky:* the idea that a country should be self-sufficient and not take part in international trade. The experience of countries that have pursued this utopian ideal by substituting domestic production for imports is an unhappy one. No country has been able to produce the full range of goods demanded by its population at competitive prices. Indeed, those that have tried to do so have condemned themselves to inefficiency and comparative poverty, compared with countries that engage in international trade. ("Economics A–Z," www.economist.com)

The Promise and Pitfalls of Exporting

LEARNING OBJECTIVE 1
Explain the promises and risks associated with exporting.

The great promise of exporting is that large revenue and profit opportunities are to be found in foreign markets for most firms in most industries. This was true for FCX Systems, the company profiled in the opening case. The international market is normally so much larger than the firm's domestic market that exporting is nearly always a way to increase the revenue and profit base of a company. By expanding the size of the market, exporting can enable a firm to achieve economies of scale, thereby lowering its unit costs. Firms that do not export often lose out on significant opportunities for growth and cost reduction.[1]

Studies have shown that while many large firms tend to be proactive about seeking opportunities for profitable exporting, systematically scanning foreign markets to see where the opportunities lie for leveraging their technology, products, and marketing skills in foreign countries, many medium-sized and small firms are very reactive.[2] Typically, such reactive firms do not even consider exporting until their domestic market is saturated and the emergence of excess productive capacity at home forces them to look for growth opportunities in foreign markets. Also, many small and medium-sized firms tend to wait for the world to come to them, rather than going out into the world to seek opportunities. Even when the world does come to them, they may not respond. An example is MMO Music Group, which makes sing-along tapes for karaoke machines. Foreign sales accounted for about 15 percent of MMO's revenues of $8 million in the mid-1990s, but the firm's CEO admits that this figure would probably have been much higher had he paid attention to building international sales during the 1980s and early 1990s. At that time, unanswered faxes and phone messages from Asia and Europe piled up while he was trying to manage the burgeoning domestic side of the business. By the time MMO did turn its attention to foreign markets, other competitors had stepped into the breach and MMO found it tough going to build export volume.[3]

MMO's experience is common, which suggests that firms need to become more proactive about seeking export opportunities. One reason more firms are not proactive is that they are unfamiliar with foreign market opportunities; they simply do not know how big the opportunities actually are or where they might lie. Simple ignorance of the potential opportunities is a huge barrier to exporting.[4] Also, many would-be exporters, particularly smaller firms, are often intimidated by the complexities and mechanics of exporting to countries where business practices, language, culture, legal systems, and currency are very different from the home market.[5] This combination of unfamiliarity and intimidation probably explains why exporters still account for only a tiny percentage of U.S. firms, less than 5 percent of firms with fewer than 500 employees, according to the Small Business Administration.[6]

To make matters worse, many neophyte exporters run into significant problems when first trying to do business abroad, which sours them on future exporting ventures. Common pitfalls include poor market analysis, a poor understanding of competitive conditions in the foreign market, a failure to customize the product offering to the needs of foreign customers, lack of an effective distribution program, a poorly executed promotional campaign, and problems securing financing.[7] Novice exporters tend to underestimate the time and expertise needed to cultivate business in foreign countries.[8] Few realize the amount of management resources that have to be dedicated to this activity. Many foreign customers require face-to-face negotiations on their home turf. An exporter may have to spend months learning about a country's trade regulations, business practices, and more before a deal can be closed. The opening case, which documents the experience of FCX Systems in China, suggests that it may take years before foreigners are comfortable enough to purchase in significant quantities.

Exporters often face voluminous paperwork, complex formalities, and many potential delays and errors. According to a UN report on trade and development, a typical international trade transaction may involve 30 parties, 60 original documents, and 360 document copies, all of which have to be checked, transmitted, reentered into various information systems, processed, and filed. The UN has calculated that the time involved in preparing documentation, along with the costs of common errors in paperwork, often amounts to 10 percent of the final value of goods exported.[9]

Improving Export Performance

LEARNING OBJECTIVE 2
Outline the steps managers can take to improve their firm's export performance.

Inexperienced exporters have a number of ways to gain information about foreign market opportunities and avoid common pitfalls that tend to discourage and frustrate novice exporters.[10] In this section, we look at information sources exporters can use to increase their knowledge of foreign market opportunities, we consider the pros and cons of using export management companies (EMCs) to assist in the export process, and we review various exporting strategies that can increase the probability of successful exporting. We begin, however, with a look at how several nations try to help domestic firms export.

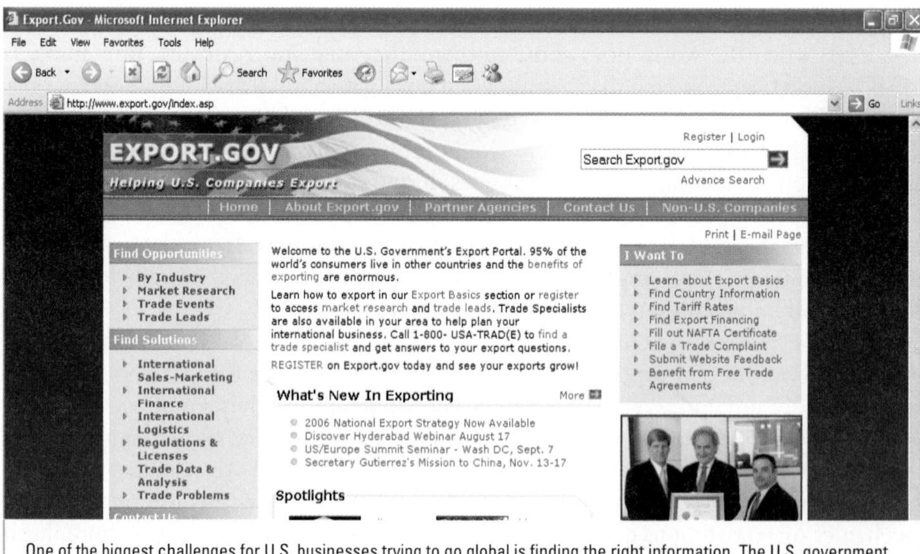

One of the biggest challenges for U.S. businesses trying to go global is finding the right information. The U.S. government provides assistance and links to other helpful sources on its www.export.gov Web site. *Courtesy of Export.gov*

AN INTERNATIONAL COMPARISON

One big impediment to exporting is the simple lack of knowledge of the opportunities available. Often there are many markets for a firm's product, but because they are in countries separated from the firm's home base by culture, language, distance, and time, the firm does not know of them. Identifying export opportunities is made even more complex because more than 200 countries with widely differing cultures compose the world of potential opportunities. Faced with such complexity and diversity, firms sometimes hesitate to seek export opportunities.

The way to overcome ignorance is to collect information. In Germany, one of the world's most successful exporting nations, trade associations, government agencies, and commercial banks gather information, helping small firms identify export opportunities. A similar function is provided by the Japanese Ministry of International Trade and Industry (MITI), which is always on the lookout for export opportunities. In addition, many Japanese firms are affiliated in some way with the *sogo shosha*, Japan's great trading houses. The *sogo shosha* have offices all over the world, and they proactively, continuously seek export opportunities for their affiliated companies, large and small.[11]

Another Perspective

A Purely Biological View of Export–Import Business Activity: Yes, Biological!

Ready for a new way of thinking? Here goes. . . Think of FedEx, the global air and ground delivery service, as a biological system—specifically an export–import circulatory system. This is how it sees itself: "Air transportation now serves as the circulatory system of the global economy, carrying people and products and services to marketplaces around the world."

And FedEx has the figures to back up its view. While its own revenue exceeded $18 billion in FY2000, the combined direct and indirect revenues generated by FedEx transportation activities totaled nearly $53 billion.

FedEx's global circulatory system is carrying an increasing amount of world trade in merchandise—but more important, it is becoming more than just a global trade facilitator; it is a trade center. Where is this FedEx trade center? Not in any geographical location—the trade center is its "circulatory system." Fascinated? Learn more at www.fedex.com/us/about/overview/economy/economicimpact.html.

German and Japanese firms can draw on the large reservoirs of experience, skills, information, and other resources of their respective export-oriented institutions. Unlike their German and Japanese competitors, many U.S. firms are relatively blind when they seek export opportunities; they are information disadvantaged. In part, this reflects historical differences. Both Germany and Japan have long made their living as trading nations, whereas until recently the United States has been a relatively self-contained continental economy in which international trade played a minor role. This is changing; both imports and exports now play a greater role in the U.S. economy than they did 20 years ago. However, the United States has not yet evolved an institutional structure for promoting exports similar to that of either Germany or Japan. See the Another Perspective above for the ways that Fed Ex has worked to position itself in promoting its exporting capabilities.

LEARNING OBJECTIVE 3
Identify information sources and government programs that exist to help exporters.

INFORMATION SOURCES

Despite institutional disadvantages, U.S. firms can increase their awareness of export opportunities. The most comprehensive source of information is the U.S. Department of Commerce and its district offices all over the country. Within that department are two organizations dedicated to providing businesses with intelligence and assistance for attacking foreign markets: the International Trade Administration and the United States and Foreign Commercial Service Agency.

These agencies provide the potential exporter with a "best prospects" list, which gives the names and addresses of potential distributors in foreign markets along with businesses they are in, the products they handle, and their contact person. In addition, the Department of Commerce has assembled a "comparison shopping service" for 14 countries that are major markets for U.S. exports. For a small fee, a firm can receive a customized market research survey on a product of its choice. This survey provides information on marketability, the competition, comparative prices, distribution channels, and names of potential sales representatives. Each study is conducted on-site by an officer of the Department of Commerce.

The Department of Commerce also organizes trade events that help potential exporters make foreign contacts and explore export opportunities. The department organizes exhibitions at international trade fairs, which are held regularly in major cities worldwide. It also has a matchmaker program, in which department representatives accompany groups of U.S. businesspeople abroad to meet with qualified agents, distributors, and customers.

Another government organization, the Small Business Administration (SBA), can help potential exporters (see the Management Focus below for examples of the SBA's work). The SBA employs 76 district international trade officers and 10 regional international trade officers throughout the United States as well as a 10-person international trade staff in Washington, D.C. Through its Service Corps of Retired

Management FOCUS

Exporting with a Little Government Help

Exporting can seem like a daunting prospect, but the reality is that in the United States, as in many other countries, many small enterprises have built profitable export businesses. For example, Landmark Systems of Virginia had virtually no domestic sales before it entered the European market. Landmark had developed a software program for IBM mainframe computers and located an independent distributor in Europe to represent its product. In the first year, 80 percent of sales were attributed to exporting. In the second year, sales jumped from $100,000 to $1.4 million, with 70 percent attributable to exports. Landmark is not alone; government data suggest that in the United States nearly 89 percent of firms that export are small businesses that employ fewer than 100 people. Their share of total U.S. exports has grown steadily over the last decade and reached 21 percent by the early 2000s. Firms with less than 500 employees account for 97 percent of all U.S. exporters and almost 30 percent of all exports by value.

To help jump-start the exporting process, many small companies have drawn on the expertise of government agencies, financial institutions, and export management companies. Consider the case of Novi, Inc., a California-based business. Company president Michael Stoff tells how he utilized the services of the U.S. Small Business Administration Office of International Trade to start exporting: "In November of 1986, when I began my business venture, Novi, Inc., I knew that my Tune-Tote (a stereo system for bicycles) had the potential to be successful in international markets. Although I had no prior experience in this area, I began researching and collecting information on international markets. I was willing to learn, and by targeting key sources for information and guidance, I was able to penetrate international markets in a short period of time. One vital source I used from the beginning was the SBA. Through the SBA I was directed to a program that dealt specifically with business development—the Service Corps of Retired Executives (SCORE). I was assigned an adviser who had run his own import–export business for 30 years. The services of SCORE are provided on a continual basis and are free.

"As I began to pursue exporting, my first step was a thorough marketing evaluation. I targeted trade shows with a good presence of international buyers. I also went to DOC (Department of Commerce) for counseling and information about the rules and regulations of exporting. I advertised my product in "Commercial News USA," distributed through U.S. embassies to buyers worldwide. I utilized DOC's World Traders Data Reports to get background information on potential foreign buyers. As a result, I received 60 to 70 inquiries about Tune-Tote from around the world. Once I completed my research and evaluation of potential buyers, I decided which ones would be most suitable to market my product internationally. Then I decided to grant exclusive distributorship. In order to effectively communicate with my international customers, I invested in a fax. I chose a U.S. bank to handle international transactions. The bank also provided guidance on methods of payment and how best to receive and transmit money. This is essential know-how for anyone wanting to be successful in foreign markets."

In just one year of exporting, export sales at Novi topped $1 million and increased 40 percent in the second year of operations. Today, Novi, Inc., is a large distributor of wireless intercom systems that exports to more than 10 countries.

Sources: Small Business Administration Office of International Trade, "Guide to Exporting," www.sba.gov/oit/info/Guide-To-Exporting/index.html; and U.S. Department of Commerce, "A Profile of U.S. Exporting Companies, 2000–2001," February 2003, available at www.census.gov/foreign-trade/aip/index.html#profile.

Executives (SCORE) program, the SBA also oversees some 850 volunteers with international trade experience to provide one-on-one counseling to active and new-to-export businesses. The SBA also coordinates the Export Legal Assistance Network (ELAN), a nationwide group of international trade attorneys who provide free initial consultations to small businesses on export-related matters.

In addition to the Department of Commerce and SBA, nearly every state and many large cities maintain active trade commissions whose purpose is to promote exports. Most of these provide business counseling, information gathering, technical assistance, and financing. Unfortunately, many have fallen victim to budget cuts or to turf battles for political and financial support with other export agencies.

A number of private organizations are also beginning to provide more assistance to would-be exporters. Commercial banks and major accounting firms are more willing to assist small firms in starting export operations than they were a decade ago. In addition, large multinationals that have been successful in the global arena are typically willing to discuss opportunities overseas with the owners or managers of small firms.[12]

UTILIZING EXPORT MANAGEMENT COMPANIES One way for first-time exporters to identify the opportunities associated with exporting and to avoid many of the associated pitfalls is to hire an **export management company** (EMC). EMCs are export specialists that act as the export marketing department or international department for their client firms. EMCs normally accept two types of export assignments. They start exporting operations for a firm with the understanding that the firm will take over operations after they are well established. In another type, start-up services are performed with the understanding that the EMC will have continuing responsibility for selling the firm's products. Many EMCs specialize in serving firms in particular industries and in particular areas of the world. Thus, one EMC may specialize in selling agricultural products in the Asian market, whereas another may focus on exporting electronics products to Eastern Europe.

Export Management Company
Export specialists that act as an export marketing or international department for their client firms.

In theory, the advantage of EMCs is that they are experienced specialists that can help the neophyte exporter identify opportunities and avoid common pitfalls. A good EMC will have a network of contacts in potential markets, have multilingual employees, have a good knowledge of different business mores, and be fully conversant with the ins and outs of the exporting process and with local business regulations. However, the quality of EMCs varies.[13] Some perform their functions very well, but others appear to add little value to the exporting company. Therefore, an exporter should review carefully a number of EMCs and check references. One drawback of relying on EMCs is that the company can fail to develop its own exporting capabilities.

EXPORT STRATEGY In addition to using EMCs, a firm can reduce the risks associated with exporting if it is careful about its choice of export strategy.[14] A few guidelines can help firms improve their odds of success. For example, one of the most successful exporting firms in the world, the Minnesota Mining and Manufacturing Co. (3M), has built its export success on three main principles: enter on a small scale to reduce risks, add additional product lines once the exporting operations start to become successful, and hire locals to promote the firm's products (3M's export strategy is profiled in the Management Focus on page 430). Another successful exporter, Red Spot Paint & Varnish, emphasizes the importance of cultivating personal relationships when trying to build an export business (see the Management Focus at the end of this section).

The probability of exporting successfully can be increased dramatically by taking a handful of simple strategic steps. First, particularly for the novice exporter, it helps to hire an EMC or at least an experienced export consultant to help identify opportunities and navigate the paperwork and regulations so often involved in exporting. Second, it often makes sense to initially focus on one market or a handful of markets. Learn what is required to succeed in those markets before moving on to other markets. The firm that enters many markets at once runs the risk of spreading its limited management resources too thin. The result of such a shotgun approach to exporting may be a failure to become established in any one market. Third, as with 3M, it often makes sense to enter a foreign market on a small scale to reduce the costs of any subsequent failure. Most important, entering on a small scale provides the time and opportunity to learn about the foreign country before making significant capital commitments to that market. Fourth, the exporter needs to recognize the time and managerial commitment involved in building export sales and should hire additional personnel to oversee this activity. Fifth, in many countries, the exporter must devote a lot of attention to building strong and enduring relationships with local distributors or customers (see the Management Focus on Red Spot Paint, next page, for an example). Sixth, as 3M often does, the firm should hire local personnel to help establish itself in a foreign market. Local people are likely to have a much greater sense of how to do business in a given country than a manager from an exporting firm who has previously never set foot in that country. Seventh, several studies have suggested the firm needs to be proactive

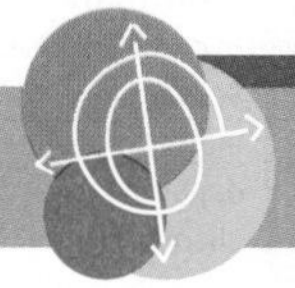

Management FOCUS

Export Strategy at 3M

The Minnesota Mining and Manufacturing Co. (3M), which makes more than 40,000 products, including tape, sandpaper, medical products, and the ever-present Post-it notes, is one of the world's great multinational operations. In 2005, 61 percent of the firm's $21 billion in revenues was generated outside the United States. Although the bulk of these revenues came from foreign-based operations, 3M remains a major exporter, with more than $2 billion in exports. The company often uses its exports to establish an initial presence in a foreign market, building foreign production facilities only after sales volume rises to a level that justifies local production.

The export strategy is built around simple principles. One is known as FIDO, which stands for First In (to a new market) Defeats Others. The essence of FIDO is to gain an advantage over other exporters by getting into a market first and learning about that country and how to sell there before others do. A second principle is "make a little, sell a little," which is the idea of entering on a small scale with a modest investment and pushing one basic product, such as reflective sheeting for traffic signs in Russia or scouring pads in Hungary. Once 3M believes it has learned enough about the market to reduce the risk of failure to reasonable levels, it adds additional products.

A third principle at 3M is to hire local employees to sell the firm's products. The company normally sets up a local sales subsidiary to handle its export activities in a country. It then staffs this subsidiary with local hires because it believes they are likely to have a much better idea of how to sell in their own country than American expatriates. Because of the implementation of this principle, just 160 of 3M's 39,500 foreign employees are U.S. expatriates.

Another common practice at 3M is to formulate global strategic plans for the export and eventual overseas production of its products. Within the context of these plans, 3M gives local managers considerable autonomy to find the best way to sell the product within their country. Thus, when 3M first exported its Post-it notes, it planned to "sample the daylights" out of the product, but it also told local managers to find the best way of doing this. Local managers hired office cleaning crews to pass out samples in Great Britain and Germany; in Italy, office products distributors were used to pass out free samples; and in Malaysia, local managers employed young women to go from office to office handing out samples of the product. In typical 3M fashion, when the sales volume of Post-it notes was sufficient to justify it, exports from the United States were replaced by local production. Thus, after several years 3M found it worthwhile to set up production facilities in France to produce Post-it notes for the European market.

Sources: R. L. Rose, "Success Abroad," *The Wall Street Journal,* March 29, 1991, p. A1; T. Eiben, "US Exporters Keep on Rolling," *Fortune,* June 14, 1994, pp. 128–31; 3M Company, *A Century of Innovation,* 3M, 2002; and 2005 10K form archived at 3M's Web site, www.mmm.com.

Management FOCUS

Red Spot Paint & Varnish

Established in 1903 and based in Evansville, Indiana, Red Spot Paint & Varnish Company is in many ways typical of the companies that can be found in the small towns of America's heartland. The closely held company, whose CEO, Charles Storms, is the great-grandson of the founder, has 500 employees and annual sales of close to $90 million. The company's main product is paint for plastic components used in the automobile industry. Red Spot products are seen on automobile bumpers, wheel covers, grilles, headlights, instrument panels, door inserts, radio buttons, and other components. Unlike many other companies of a similar size and location, however, Red Spot has a thriving international business. International sales (which include exports and local production by licensees) now account for between 15 and 25 percent of revenue in any one year, and Red Spot does business in about 15 countries.

Red Spot has long had some international sales and won an export award in the early 1960s. To further its international business in the late 1980s, Red Spot hired a Central Michigan University professor, Bryan Williams. Williams, who was hired because of his foreign-language skills (he speaks German, Japanese, and some Chinese), was the first employee at Red Spot whose exclusive focus was international marketing and sales. His first challenge was the lack of staff skilled in the business of exporting. He found that it was difficult to build an international business without in-house expertise in the basic mechanics of exporting. According to Williams, Red Spot needed people who understood the nuts and bolts of exporting—letters of credit, payment terms, bills of lading, and so on. As might be expected for a business based in the heartland of America, no ready supply of such individuals was in the vicinity. It took Williams several years to solve this problem. Now Red Spot has a full-time staff of two who have been trained in the principles of exporting and international operations.

A second problem that Williams encountered was the clash between the quarter-to-quarter mentality that frequently pervades management practice in the United States and the long-term perspective that is often necessary to build a successful international business. Williams has found that building long-term personal relationships with potential foreign customers is often the key to getting business. When foreign customers visit Evansville, Williams often invites them home for dinner. His young children even started calling one visitor from Hong Kong "Uncle." Even with such efforts, however, the business may not come quickly. Meeting with potential foreign customers yields no direct business 90 percent of the time, although Williams points out that it often yields benefits in terms of competitive information and relationship building. He has found that perseverance pays. For example, Williams and Storms called on a major German automobile parts manufacturer for seven years before finally landing some business from the company.

Sources: R. L. Rose and C. Quintanilla, "More Small U.S. Firms Take up Exporting with Much Success," *The Wall Street Journal,* December 20, 1996, p. A1, A10; and interview with Bryan Williams of Red Spot Paint.

about seeking export opportunities.[15] Armchair exporting does not work! The world will not normally beat a pathway to your door. Finally, it is important for the exporter to retain the option of local production. Once exports reach a sufficient volume to justify cost-efficient local production, the exporting firm should consider establishing production facilities in the foreign market. Such localization helps foster good relations with the foreign country and can lead to greater market acceptance. Exporting is often not an end in itself; it is merely a step on the road toward establishment of foreign production (again, 3M provides an example of this philosophy).

Export and Import Financing

LEARNING OBJECTIVE 4 Grasp the basic steps involved in export financing.

Mechanisms for financing exports and imports have evolved over the centuries in response to a problem that can be particularly acute in international trade: the lack of trust that exists when one must put faith in a stranger. In this section, we examine the financial devices that have evolved to cope with this problem in the context of international trade: the letter of credit, the draft (or bill of exchange), and the bill of lading. Then we will trace the 14 steps of a typical export–import transaction.

LACK OF TRUST Firms engaged in international trade have to trust someone they may have never seen, who lives in a different country, who speaks a different language, who abides by (or does not abide by) a different legal system, and who could be very difficult to track down if he or she defaults on an obligation. Consider a U.S. firm exporting to a distributor in France. The U.S. businessman might be concerned that if he ships the products to France before he receives payment from the French businesswoman, she might take delivery of the products and not pay him. Conversely, the French importer might worry that if she pays for the products before they are shipped, the U.S. firm might keep the money and never ship the products or might ship defective products. Neither party to the exchange completely trusts the other. This lack of trust is exacerbated by the distance between the two parties—in space, language, and culture—and by the problems of using an underdeveloped international legal system to enforce contractual obligations.

Due to the (quite reasonable) lack of trust between the two parties, each has his or her own preferences as to how the transaction should be configured. To make sure he is paid, the manager of the U.S. firm would prefer the French distributor to pay for the products before he ships them (see Figure 13.1 below). Alternatively, to ensure she receives the products, the French distributor would prefer not to pay for them until they arrive (see Figure 13.2, page 433). Thus, each party has a different set of preferences. Unless there is some way of establishing trust between the parties, the transaction might never occur.

The problem is solved by using a third party trusted by both—normally a reputable bank—to act as an intermediary. What happens can be summarized as follows (see Figure 13.3, page 433). First, the French importer obtains the bank's promise to pay on her behalf, knowing the U.S. exporter will trust the bank. This promise is known as a *letter of credit*. Having seen the letter of credit, the U.S. exporter now ships the products to France. Title to the products is given to the bank in the form of a document called a *bill of lading*. In return, the U.S. exporter tells the bank to pay for the products, which the bank does. The document for requesting this payment is referred to as a *draft*. The bank, having paid for the products, now passes the title on to the French importer, whom the bank trusts. At that time or later, depending on

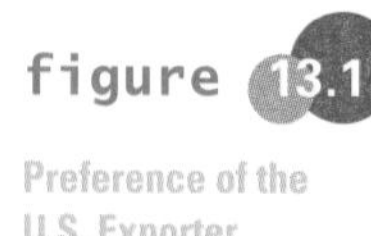

figure 13.1

Preference of the U.S. Exporter

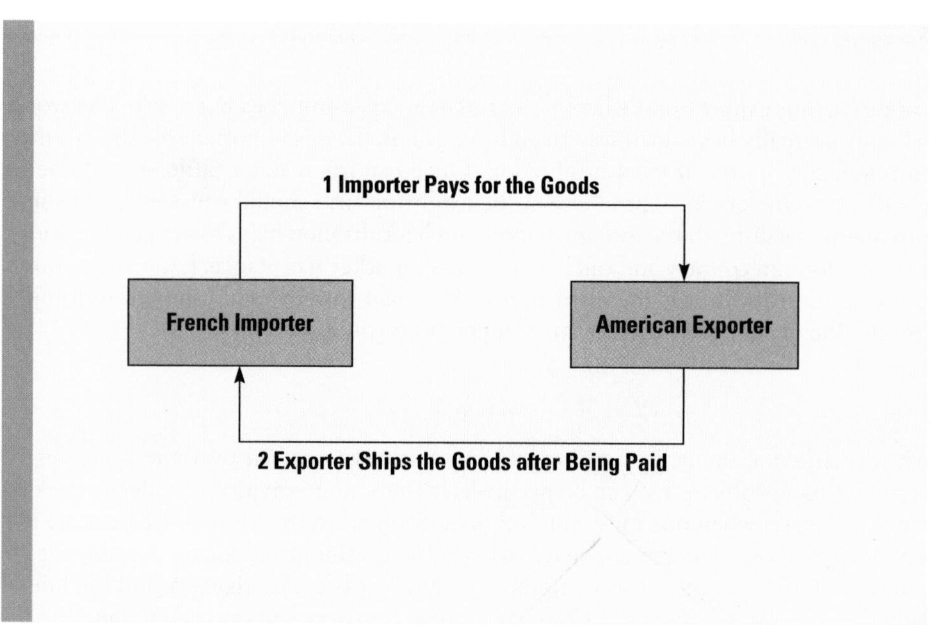

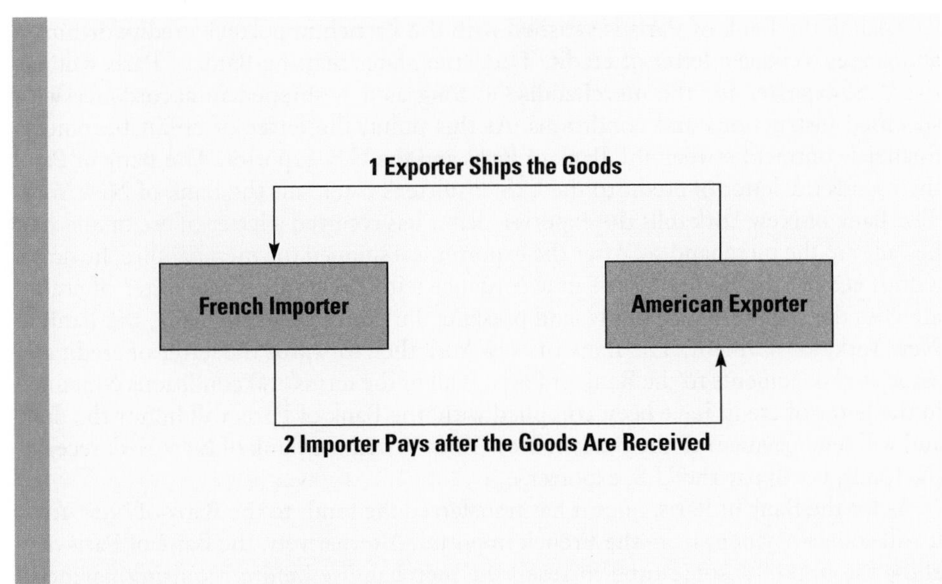

figure 13.2
Preference of the French Importer

their agreement, the importer reimburses the bank. In the remainder of this section, we examine how this system works in more detail.

LETTER OF CREDIT A letter of credit, abbreviated as L/C, stands at the center of international commercial transactions. Issued by a bank at the request of an importer, the **letter of credit** states that the bank will pay a specified sum of money to a beneficiary, normally the exporter, on presentation of particular, specified documents.

Letter of Credit
Document issued by a bank indicating that it will make payments to a beneficiary upon presentation of particular documents.

Consider again the example of the U.S. exporter and the French importer. The French importer applies to her local bank, say, the Bank of Paris, for the issuance of a letter of credit. The Bank of Paris then undertakes a credit check of the importer. If the Bank of Paris is satisfied with her creditworthiness, it will issue a letter of credit. However, the Bank of Paris might require a cash deposit or some other form of collateral from her first. In addition, the Bank of Paris will charge the importer a fee for this service. Typically, this amounts to between 0.5 and 2 percent of the value of the letter of credit, depending on the importer's creditworthiness and the size of the transaction. (As a rule, the larger the transaction, the lower the percentage.)

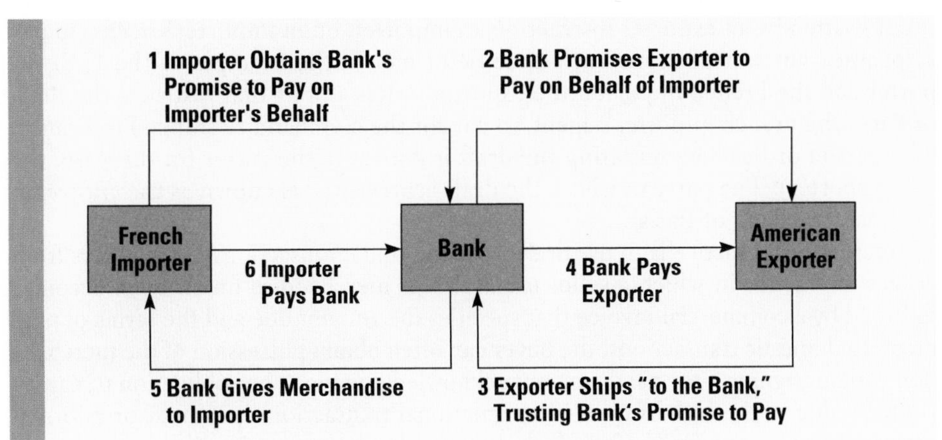

figure 13.3
The Use of a Third Party

Assume the Bank of Paris is satisfied with the French importer's creditworthiness and agrees to issue a letter of credit. The letter states that the Bank of Paris will pay the U.S. exporter for the merchandise as long as it is shipped in accordance with specified instructions and conditions. At this point, the letter of credit becomes a financial contract between the Bank of Paris and the U.S. exporter. The Bank of Paris then sends the letter of credit to the U.S. exporter's bank, say, the Bank of New York. The Bank of New York tells the exporter that it has received a letter of credit and that he can ship the merchandise. After the exporter has shipped the merchandise, he draws a draft against the Bank of Paris in accordance with the terms of the letter of credit, attaches the required documents, and presents the draft to his own bank, the Bank of New York, for payment. The Bank of New York then forwards the letter of credit and associated documents to the Bank of Paris. If all of the terms and conditions contained in the letter of credit have been complied with, the Bank of Paris will honor the draft and will send payment to the Bank of New York. When the Bank of New York receives the funds, it will pay the U.S. exporter.

As for the Bank of Paris, once it has transferred the funds to the Bank of New York, it will collect payment from the French importer. Alternatively, the Bank of Paris may allow the importer some time to resell the merchandise before requiring payment. This is not unusual, particularly when the importer is a distributor and not the final consumer of the merchandise, since it helps the importer's cash flow. The Bank of Paris will treat such an extension of the payment period as a loan to the importer and will charge an appropriate rate of interest.

The great advantage of this system is that both the French importer and the U.S. exporter are likely to trust reputable banks, even if they do not trust each other. Once the U.S. exporter has seen a letter of credit, he knows that he is guaranteed payment and will ship the merchandise. Also, an exporter may find that having a letter of credit will facilitate obtaining preexport financing. For example, having seen the letter of credit, the Bank of New York might be willing to lend the exporter funds to process and prepare the merchandise for shipping to France. This loan may not have to be repaid until the exporter has received his payment for the merchandise. As for the French importer, she does not have to pay for the merchandise until the documents have arrived and unless all conditions stated in the letter of credit have been satisfied. The drawback for the importer is the fee she must pay the Bank of Paris for the letter of credit. In addition, since the letter of credit is a financial liability against her, it may reduce her ability to borrow funds for other purposes.

Bill of Exchange
Otherwise called a *draft*, the instrument normally used in international commerce to effect payment.

Draft
An order written by an exporter instructing an importer, or an importer's agent, to pay a specified amount of money at a specified time.

DRAFT A draft, sometimes referred to as a **bill of exchange,** is the instrument normally used in international commerce to effect payment. A **draft** is simply an order written by an exporter instructing an importer, or an importer's agent, to pay a specified amount of money at a specified time. In the example of the U.S. exporter and the French importer, the exporter writes a draft that instructs the Bank of Paris, the French importer's agent, to pay for the merchandise shipped to France. The person or business initiating the draft is known as the *maker* (in this case, the U.S. exporter). The party to whom the draft is presented is known as the *drawee* (in this case, the Bank of Paris).

International practice is to use drafts to settle trade transactions. This differs from domestic practice in which a seller usually ships merchandise on an open account, followed by a commercial invoice that specifies the amount due and the terms of payment. In domestic transactions, the buyer can often obtain possession of the merchandise without signing a formal document acknowledging his or her obligation to pay. In contrast, due to the lack of trust in international transactions, payment or a formal promise to pay is required before the buyer can obtain the merchandise.

Drafts fall into two categories, sight drafts and time drafts. A **sight draft** is payable on presentation to the drawee. A **time draft** allows for a delay in payment, normally 30, 60, 90, or 120 days. It is presented to the drawee, who signifies acceptance of it by writing or stamping a notice of acceptance on its face. Once accepted, the time draft becomes a promise to pay by the accepting party. When a time draft is drawn on and accepted by a bank, it is called a *banker's acceptance*. When it is drawn on and accepted by a business firm, it is called a *trade acceptance*.

Sight Draft
Payable upon presentation to the drawee.

Time Draft
Allows for a delay in payment to set future date.

Time drafts are negotiable instruments; that is, once the draft is stamped with an acceptance, the maker can sell the draft to an investor at a discount from its face value. Imagine the agreement between the U.S. exporter and the French importer calls for the exporter to present the Bank of Paris (through the Bank of New York) with a time draft requiring payment 120 days after presentation. The Bank of Paris stamps the time draft with an acceptance. Imagine further that the draft is for $100,000.

The exporter can either hold onto the accepted time draft and receive $100,000 in 120 days or he can sell it to an investor, say, the Bank of New York, for a discount from the face value. If the prevailing discount rate is 7 percent, the exporter could receive $97,700 by selling it immediately (7 percent per year discount rate for 120 days for $100,000 equals $2,300, and $100,000 − $2,300 = $97,700). The Bank of New York would then collect the full $100,000 from the Bank of Paris in 120 days. The exporter might sell the accepted time draft immediately if he needed the funds to finance merchandise in transit or to cover cash flow shortfalls.

BILL OF LADING The third key document for financing international trade is the bill of lading. The **bill of lading** is issued to the exporter by the common carrier transporting the merchandise. It serves three purposes: it is a receipt, a contract, and a document of title. As a receipt, the bill of lading indicates that the carrier has received the merchandise described on the face of the document. As a contract, it specifies that the carrier is obligated to provide a transportation service in return for a certain charge. As a document of title, it can be used to obtain payment or a written promise of payment before the merchandise is released to the importer. The bill of lading can also function as collateral against which funds may be advanced to the exporter by its local bank before or during shipment and before final payment by the importer.

Bill of Lading
A document issued to an exporter by the common carrier transporting the merchandise; serves as a receipt, a contract, and a document of title.

A TYPICAL INTERNATIONAL TRADE TRANSACTION Now that we have reviewed the elements of an international trade transaction, let us see how the process works in a typical case, sticking with the example of the U.S. exporter and the French importer. The typical transaction involves 14 steps (see Figure 13.4 on page 436 for the complete process).

1. The French importer places an order with the U.S. exporter and asks the American if he would be willing to ship under a letter of credit.
2. The U.S. exporter agrees to ship under a letter of credit and specifies relevant information such as prices and delivery terms.
3. The French importer applies to the Bank of Paris for a letter of credit to be issued in favor of the U.S. exporter for the merchandise the importer wishes to buy.
4. The Bank of Paris issues a letter of credit in the French importer's favor and sends it to the U.S. exporter's bank, the Bank of New York.
5. The Bank of New York advises the exporter of the opening of a letter of credit in his favor.
6. The U.S. exporter ships the goods to the French importer on a common carrier. An official of the carrier gives the exporter a bill of lading.
7. The U.S. exporter presents a 90-day time draft drawn on the Bank of Paris in accordance with its letter of credit and the bill of lading to the Bank of

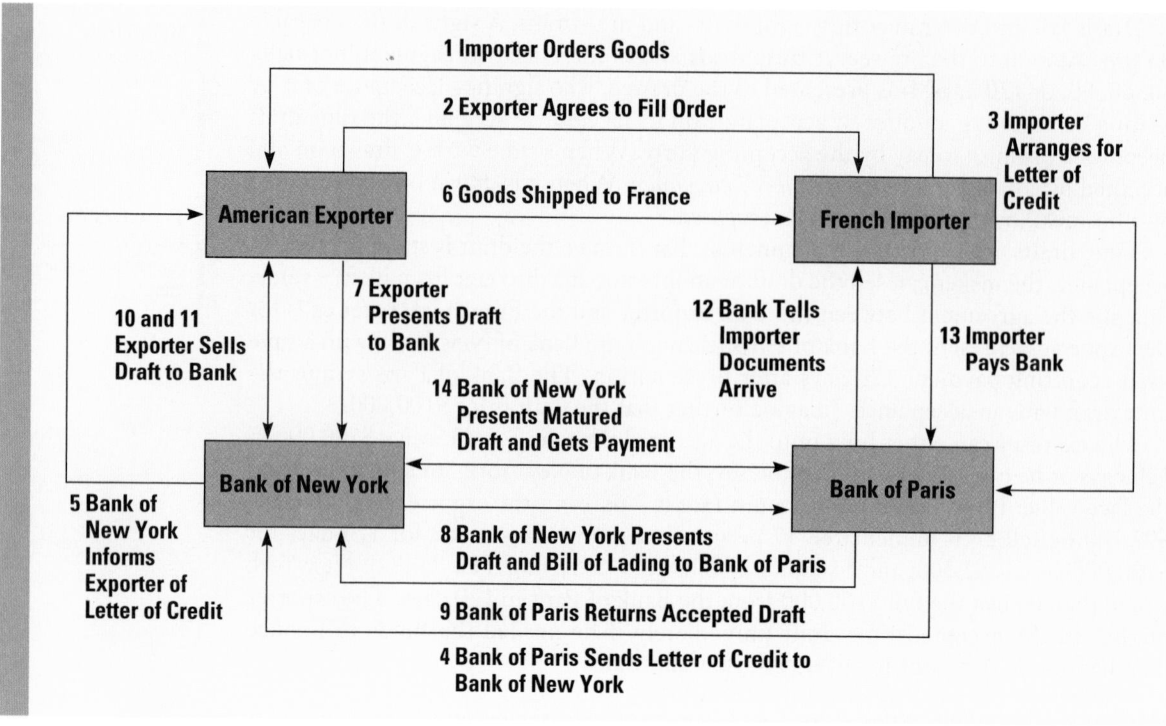

figure 13.4

A Typical International Trade Transaction

New York. The exporter endorses the bill of lading so title to the goods is transferred to the Bank of New York.

8. The Bank of New York sends the draft and bill of lading to the Bank of Paris. The Bank of Paris accepts the draft, taking possession of the documents and promising to pay the now-accepted draft in 90 days.
9. The Bank of Paris returns the accepted draft to the Bank of New York.
10. The Bank of New York tells the U.S. exporter that it has received the accepted bank draft, which is payable in 90 days.
11. The exporter sells the draft to the Bank of New York at a discount from its face value and receives the discounted cash value of the draft in return.
12. The Bank of Paris notifies the French importer of the arrival of the documents. She agrees to pay the Bank of Paris in 90 days. The Bank of Paris releases the documents so the importer can take possession of the shipment.
13. In 90 days, the Bank of Paris receives the importer's payment, so it has funds to pay the maturing draft.
14. In 90 days, the holder of the matured acceptance (in this case, the Bank of New York) presents it to the Bank of Paris for payment. The Bank of Paris pays.

Export Assistance

LEARNING OBJECTIVE 3
Identify information sources and government programs that exist to help exporters.

Prospective U.S. exporters can draw on two forms of government-backed assistance to help finance their export programs. They can get financing aid from the Export–Import Bank and export credit insurance from the Foreign Credit Insurance Association.

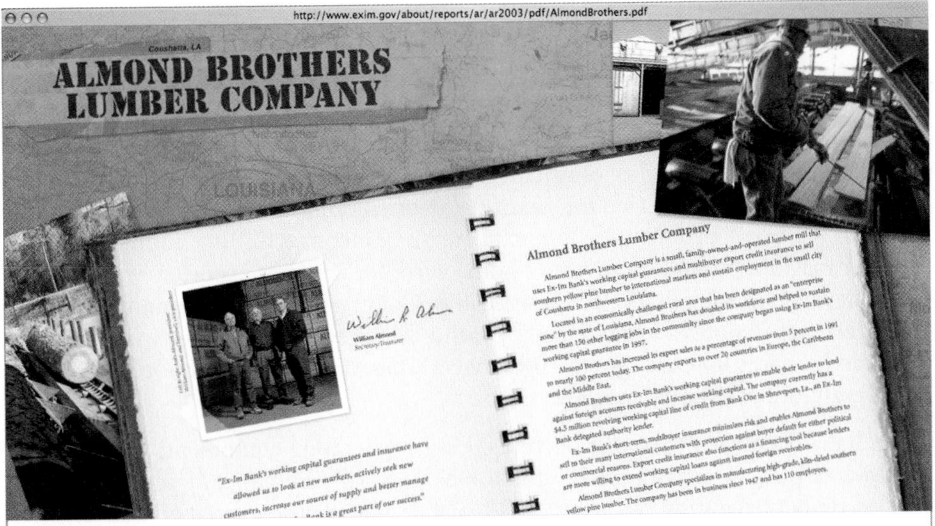

Ex–Im Bank provides financing aid to companies, such as the example above, that require assistance with imports, exports, and the exchange of commodities. *Courtesy Export–Import Bank of the United States*

EXPORT–IMPORT BANK The **Export–Import Bank,** often referred to as the Ex–Im Bank, is an independent agency of the U.S. government. Its mission is to provide financing aid that will facilitate exports, imports, and the exchange of commodities between the United States and other countries. The Ex–Im Bank pursues this mission with various loan and loan-guarantee programs. The agency guarantees repayment of medium and long-term loans U.S. commercial banks make to foreign borrowers for purchasing U.S. exports. The guarantee makes the commercial banks more willing to lend cash to foreign enterprises.

Export–Import Bank
An independent agency of the U.S. government whose mission is to provide financing aid that will facilitate exports, imports, and commodities exchanges between the United States and other countries; also referred to as the Ex–Im Bank.

The Ex–Im Bank also has a direct lending operation under which it lends dollars to foreign borrowers for use in purchasing U.S. exports. In some cases, it grants loans that commercial banks would not if it sees a potential benefit to the United States in doing so. The foreign borrowers use the loans to pay U.S. suppliers and repay the loans to the Ex–Im Bank with interest.

EXPORT CREDIT INSURANCE For reasons outlined earlier, exporters clearly prefer to get letters of credit from importers. However, sometimes an exporter who insists on a letter of credit will lose an order to one who does not require a letter of credit. Thus, when the importer is in a strong bargaining position and able to play competing suppliers against each other, an exporter may have to forgo a letter of credit.[16] The lack of a letter of credit exposes the exporter to the risk that the foreign importer will default on payment. The exporter can insure against this possibility by buying export credit insurance. If the customer defaults, the insurance firm will cover a major portion of the loss.

In the United States, export credit insurance is provided by the Foreign Credit Insurance Association (FCIA), an association of private commercial institutions operating under the guidance of the Export–Import Bank. The FCIA provides coverage against commercial risks and political risks. Losses due to commercial risk result from the buyer's insolvency or payment default. Political losses arise from actions of governments that are beyond the control of either buyer or seller.

Countertrade

LEARNING OBJECTIVE 5
Define countertrade and its three major types.

Countertrade is an alternative means of structuring an international sale when conventional means of payment are difficult, costly, or nonexistent. We first encountered countertrade in Chapter 9 in our discussion of currency convertibility. A government may restrict the convertibility of its currency to preserve its foreign exchange reserves so they can be used to service international debt commitments and purchase crucial imports.[17] This is problematic for exporters. Nonconvertibility implies that the exporter may not be paid in his or her home currency; and few exporters would desire payment in a currency that is not convertible. Countertrade is a common solution.[18] **Countertrade** denotes a whole range of barterlike agreements; its principle is to trade goods and services for other goods and services when they cannot be traded for money. Some examples of countertrade are

Countertrade
The trade of goods and services for other goods and services via a whole range of barterlike agreements.

- An Italian company that manufactures power-generating equipment, ABB SAE Sadelmi SpA, was awarded a 720 million baht ($17.7 million) contract by the Electricity Generating Authority of Thailand. The contract specified that the company had to accept 218 million baht ($5.4 million) of Thai farm products as part of the payment.
- Saudi Arabia agreed to buy 10 747 jets from Boeing with payment in crude oil, discounted at 10 percent below posted world oil prices.
- General Electric won a contract for a $150 million electric generator project in Romania by agreeing to market $150 million of Romanian products in markets to which Romania did not have access.
- The Venezuelan government negotiated a contract with Caterpillar under which Venezuela would trade 350,000 tons of iron ore for Caterpillar earthmoving equipment.
- Albania offered such items as spring water, tomato juice, and chrome ore in exchange for a $60 million fertilizer and methanol complex.
- Philip Morris ships cigarettes to Russia, for which it receives chemicals that can be used to make fertilizer. Philip Morris ships the chemicals to China, and in return, China ships glassware to North America for retail sale by Philip Morris.[19]

THE INCIDENCE OF COUNTERTRADE In the modern era, countertrade arose in the 1960s as a way for the Soviet Union and the Communist states of Eastern Europe, whose currencies were generally nonconvertible, to purchase imports. During the 1980s, the technique grew in popularity among many developing nations that lacked the foreign exchange reserves required to purchase necessary imports. Today, reflecting their own shortages of foreign exchange reserves, some successor states to the former Soviet Union and the Eastern European Communist nations periodically engage in countertrade to purchase their imports. Estimates of the percentage of world trade covered by some sort of countertrade agreement range from highs of 8 and 10 percent by value to lows of around 2 percent.[20] The precise figure is unknown, but it may well be at the low end of these estimates given the increasing liquidity of international financial markets and wider currency convertibility. However, periodic financial crises can be followed by short-term spikes in the volume of countertrade. For example, countertrade activity increased notably after the Asian financial crisis of 1997. That crisis left many Asian nations with little hard currency to finance international trade. In the tight monetary regime that followed the crisis in 1997, many Asian firms found it difficult to get access to export credits to finance their own international trade. Thus, they turned to the only option available to them: countertrade.

Given that countertrade is a means of financing international trade, albeit a relatively minor one, prospective exporters may have to engage in this technique from time to time to gain access to certain international markets. The governments of developing nations sometimes insist on a certain amount of countertrade.[21] For example, all foreign companies contracted by Thai state agencies for work costing more than 500 million baht ($12.3 million) are required to accept at least 30 percent of their payment in Thai agricultural products. Between 1994 and mid-1998, foreign firms purchased 21 billion baht ($517 million) in Thai goods under countertrade deals.[22]

Another Perspective

Corporate America Takes to Barter in Making Charitable Contributions

We all know and hear about corporations giving away their products to communities, nonprofit organizations, schools, colleges, charities, and religious groups, and we see it as them fulfilling their corporate social responsibility or perhaps as a way to enhance and promote their corporate image. According to a recent survey by the Conference Board, a New York business research think tank, for the first time ever, a bit more than half of all charitable contributions—54.2 percent—were in merchandise, not cash. Why merchandise and not cash? Answer: Congress passed a tax provision in 1976 that allows major corporations to deduct up to double their manufacturing costs when their products go to organizations that serve the ill, needy, or minor children. Also, it is a method to reduce inventories of unwanted goods. Thus, "product philanthropy" was born. (www.barternews.com/archive/12_13_05.htm)

TYPES OF COUNTERTRADE With its roots in the simple trading of goods and services for other goods and services, countertrade has evolved into a diverse set of activities that can be categorized as five distinct types of trading arrangements: barter, counterpurchase, offset, switch trading, and compensation or buyback.[23] Many countertrade deals involve not just one arrangement, but elements of two or more.

Barter **Barter** is the direct exchange of goods or services between two parties without a cash transaction. Although barter is the simplest arrangement, it is not common. Its problems are twofold. First, if goods are not exchanged simultaneously, one party ends up financing the other for a period. Second, firms engaged in barter run the risk of having to accept goods they do not want, cannot use, or have difficulty reselling at a reasonable price. For these reasons, barter is viewed as the most restrictive countertrade arrangement. It is primarily used for one-time-only deals in transactions with trading partners who are not creditworthy or trustworthy. See the Another Perspective above for bartering in charitable giving.

Barter
The direct exchange of goods or services between two parties without a cash transaction.

Counterpurchase **Counterpurchase** is a reciprocal buying agreement. It occurs when a firm agrees to purchase a certain amount of materials back from a country to which it made a sale. Suppose a U.S. firm sells some products to China. China pays the U.S. firm in dollars, but in exchange, the U.S. firm agrees to spend some of its proceeds from the sale on textiles produced by China. Thus, although China must draw on its foreign exchange reserves to pay the U.S. firm, it knows it will receive some of those dollars back because of the counterpurchase agreement. In one counterpurchase agreement, Rolls-Royce sold jet parts to Finland. As part of the deal, Rolls-Royce agreed to use some of the proceeds from the sale to purchase Finnish-manufactured TV sets that it would then sell in Great Britain.

Counterpurchase
When a firm agrees to purchase a certain amount of materials back from a country to which it made a sale.

Offset An **offset** is similar to a counterpurchase insofar as one party agrees to purchase goods or services with a specified percentage of the proceeds from the original sale. The difference is that this party can fulfill the obligation with any firm in the country to which it made the sale. From an exporter's perspective, this is more attractive than a straight counterpurchase agreement because it gives the exporter greater flexibility to choose the goods that it wishes to purchase.

Offset
When a firm agrees to purchase goods or services from any firm within the country to which it made a sale.

Switch Trading The term **switch trading** refers to the use of a specialized third-party trading house in a countertrade arrangement. When a firm enters a

Switch Trading
Using a specialized third-party trading house in a countertrade agreement.

counterpurchase or offset agreement with a country, it often ends up with what are called *counterpurchase credits*, which can be used to purchase goods from that country. Switch trading occurs when a third-party trading house buys the firm's counterpurchase credits and sells them to another firm that can better use them. For example, a U.S. firm concludes a counterpurchase agreement with Poland for which it receives some number of counterpurchase credits for purchasing Polish goods. The U.S. firm cannot use and does not want any Polish goods, however, so it sells the credits to a third-party trading house at a discount. The trading house finds a firm that can use the credits and sells them at a profit.

In one example of switch trading, Poland and Greece had a counterpurchase agreement that called for Poland to buy the same U.S.-dollar value of goods from Greece that it sold to Greece. However, Poland could not find enough Greek goods that it required, so it ended up with a dollar-denominated counterpurchase balance in Greece that it was unwilling to use. A switch trader bought the right to 250,000 counterpurchase dollars from Poland for $225,000 and sold them to a European sultana (grape) merchant for $235,000, who used them to purchase sultanas from Greece.

Buyback
When a firm builds a plant in a country and agrees to take a certain percentage of the plant's output as partial payment of the contract.

Compensation or Buybacks A **buyback** occurs when a firm builds a plant in a country—or supplies technology, equipment, training, or other services to the country—and agrees to take a certain percentage of the plant's output as partial payment for the contract. For example, Occidental Petroleum negotiated a deal with Russia under which Occidental would build several ammonia plants in Russia and as partial payment receive ammonia over a 20-year period.

LEARNING OBJECTIVE 6
Articulate how countertrade can be used to facilitate exporting.

THE PROS AND CONS OF COUNTERTRADE Countertrade's main attraction is that it can give a firm a way to finance an export deal when other means are not available. Given the problems that many developing nations have in raising the foreign exchange necessary to pay for imports, countertrade may be the only option available when doing business in these countries. Even when countertrade is not the only option for structuring an export transaction, many countries prefer it to cash deals. Thus, if a firm is unwilling to enter a countertrade agreement, it may lose an export opportunity to a competitor that is willing to make a countertrade agreement.

In addition, a countertrade agreement may be required by the government of a country to which a firm is exporting goods or services. Boeing often has to agree to counterpurchase agreements to capture orders for its commercial jet aircraft. For example, in exchange for gaining an order from Air India, Boeing may be required to purchase certain component parts, such as aircraft doors, from an Indian company. Taking this one step further, Boeing can use its willingness to enter into a counterpurchase agreement as a way of winning orders in the face of intense competition from its global rival Airbus Industrie. Thus, countertrade can become a strategic marketing weapon.

However, the drawbacks of countertrade agreements are substantial. Other things being equal, firms would normally prefer to be paid in hard currency. Countertrade contracts may involve the exchange of unusable or poor-quality goods that the firm cannot dispose of profitably. For example, a few years ago, one U.S. firm got burned when 50 percent of the television sets it received in a countertrade agreement with Hungary were defective and could not be sold. In addition, even if the goods it receives are of high quality, the firm still needs to dispose of them profitably. To do this, countertrade requires the firm to invest in an in-house trading department dedicated to arranging and managing countertrade deals. This can be expensive and time-consuming.

Given these drawbacks, countertrade is most attractive to large, diverse multinational enterprises that can use their worldwide network of contacts to dispose of goods acquired in countertrading. The masters of countertrade are Japan's giant trading firms, the *sogo shosha*, which use their vast networks of affiliated companies to profitably dispose of goods acquired through countertrade agreements. The trading firm of Mitsui & Company, for example, has about 120 affiliated companies in almost every sector of the manufacturing and service industries. If one of Mitsui's affiliates receives goods in a countertrade agreement that it cannot consume, Mitsui & Company will normally be able to find another affiliate that can profitably use them. Firms affiliated with one of Japan's *sogo shosha* often have a competitive advantage in countries where countertrade agreements are preferred.

Large, diverse Western firms that have a global reach (e.g., General Electric, Philip Morris, and 3M) have similar profit advantages from countertrade agreements. Indeed, 3M has established its own trading company—3M Global Trading, Inc.—to develop and manage the company's international countertrade programs. Unless there is no alternative, small and medium-sized exporters should probably try to avoid countertrade deals because they lack the worldwide network of operations that may be required to profitably utilize or dispose of goods acquired through them.[24]

Key Terms

export management company, p. 429
letter of credit, p. 433
bill of exchange, p. 434
draft, p. 434
sight draft, p. 435
time draft, p. 435
bill of lading, p. 435
Export–Import Bank, p. 437
countertrade, p. 438
barter, p. 439
counterpurchase, p. 439
offset, p. 439
switch trading, p. 439
buyback, p. 440

Summary

In this chapter, we examined the steps that firms must take to establish themselves as exporters. The chapter made the following points:

1. One big impediment to exporting is ignorance of foreign market opportunities.
2. Neophyte exporters often become discouraged or frustrated with the exporting process because they encounter many problems, delays, and pitfalls.
3. The way to overcome ignorance is to gather information. In the United States, a number of institutions, most important of which is the Department of Commerce, can help firms gather information in the matchmaking process. Export management companies can also help identify export opportunities.
4. Many of the pitfalls associated with exporting can be avoided if a company hires an experienced export management company, or export consultant, and if it adopts the appropriate export strategy.
5. Firms engaged in international trade must do business with people they cannot trust and people who may be difficult to track down if they default on an obligation. Due to the lack of trust, each party to an international transaction has a different set of preferences regarding the configuration of the transaction.
6. The problems arising from lack of trust between exporters and importers can be solved by using a third party that is trusted by both, normally a reputable bank.
7. A letter of credit is issued by a bank at the request of an importer. It states that the bank promises to pay a beneficiary, normally the exporter, on presentation of documents specified in the letter.
8. A draft is the instrument normally used in international commerce to effect payment. It is

an order written by an exporter instructing an importer, or an importer's agent, to pay a specified amount of money at a specified time.

9. Drafts are either sight drafts or time drafts. Time drafts are negotiable instruments.
10. A bill of lading is issued to the exporter by the common carrier transporting the merchandise. It serves as a receipt, a contract, and a document of title.
11. U.S. exporters can draw on two types of government-backed assistance to help finance their exports: loans from the Export–Import Bank and export credit insurance from the FCIA.
12. Countertrade includes a range of barterlike agreements. It is primarily used when a firm exports to a country whose currency is not freely convertible and may lack the foreign exchange reserves required to purchase the imports.
13. The main attraction of countertrade is that it gives a firm a way to finance an export deal when other means are not available. A firm that insists on being paid in hard currency may be at a competitive disadvantage vis-à-vis one that is willing to engage in countertrade.
14. The main disadvantage of countertrade is that the firm may receive unusable or poor-quality goods that cannot be disposed of profitably.

Critical Thinking and Discussion Questions

1. A firm based in Washington State wants to export a shipload of finished lumber to the Philippines. The would-be importer cannot get sufficient credit from domestic sources to pay for the shipment but insists that the finished lumber can quickly be resold in the Philippines for a profit. Outline the steps the exporter should take to effect this export to the Philippines.
2. You are the assistant to the CEO of a small textile firm that manufactures quality, premium-priced, stylish clothing. The CEO has decided to see what the opportunities are for exporting and has asked you for advice as to the steps the company should take. What advice would you give the CEO?
3. An alternative to using a letter of credit is export credit insurance. What are the advantages and disadvantages of using export credit insurance rather than a letter of credit for exporting (*a*) a luxury yacht from California to Canada and (*b*) machine tools from New York to Ukraine?
4. How do you explain the popularity of countertrade? Under what scenarios might its popularity increase still further by 2010? Under what scenarios might its popularity decline?
5. How might a company make strategic use of countertrade schemes as a marketing weapon to generate export revenues? What are the risks associated with pursuing such a strategy?

Research Task 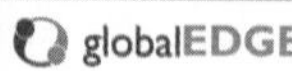 http://globalEDGE.msu.edu

Use the globalEDGE site (http://globalEDGE.msu.edu/) to complete the following exercises:

1. The Internet is rich with resources that provide guidance for companies that wish to expand their markets through exporting. globalEDGE provides links to these "Trade Tutorials." Identify three of these sources and provide a description of the services available for new exporters through each of these sources.
2. You work for a banking company that hopes to provide financial services in India. After searching a resource that enumerates the *import and export regulations* for a variety of countries, outline the most important foreign trade barriers your firm's managers must keep in mind while developing a strategy for entry into the Indian banking market.

closing case

Megahertz Communications

Established in 1982, U.K.-based Megahertz Communications quickly became one of Great Britain's leading independent broadcasting system builders. The company's core skill is in the design, manufacture, and installation of TV and radio broadcast systems, including broadcast and news-gathering vehicles with satellite links. In 1998, Megahertz's managing director, Ashley Coles, set up a subsidiary company, Megahertz International, to sell products to the Middle East, Africa, and Eastern Europe.

While the EU market for media and broadcasting is both mature and well served by large established companies, the Middle East, Africa, and Eastern Europe are growth markets with significant long-term potential for media and broadcasting. They also were not well served by other companies, and all three regions lacked an adequate supply of local broadcast engineers.

Megahertz International's export strategy was simple. The company aimed to provide a turnkey solution to emerging broadcast and media entities in Africa, the Middle East, and Eastern Europe, offering to custom-design, manufacture, install, and test broadcasting systems. To gain access to customers, Megahertz hired salespeople with significant experience in these regions and opened a foreign sales office in Italy. Megahertz also exhibited at a number of exhibitions that focused on the targeted regions, sent mailings and e-mail messages to local broadcasters, and set up a Web page, which drew a number of international inquiries.

The response was swift. By early 2000, Megahertz had already been involved in projects in Namibia, Oman, Romania, Russia, Nigeria, Poland, South Africa, Iceland, and Ethiopia. The international operations had expanded to a staff of 75 and were generating £10 million annually. The average order size was about £250,000, and the largest, £500,000. In recognition of the company's success, in January 2000 the British government picked Megahertz to receive a Small Business Export Award.

Despite the company's early success, it was not all smooth sailing. According to Coles, preshipment financing became a major headache. Coles described his working life as a juggling act, with as much as 20 percent of his time spent chasing money. Due to financing problems, one week Megahertz could have next to nothing in the bank; the next it might have £300,000. The main problem was getting money to finance an order. Megahertz needed additional working capital to finance the purchase of component parts that go into the systems it builds for customers. The company found that banks were very cautious, particularly when they heard that the customers for the order were in Africa or Eastern Europe. The banks worried that Megahertz would not get paid on time, or at all, or that currency fluctuations would reduce the value of payments to Megahertz. Even when Megahertz had a letter of credit from the customer's bank and export insurance documentation, many lenders still saw the risks as too great and declined to lend bridging funds to Megahertz. As a partial solution, Megahertz turned to lending companies that specialize in financing international trade, but many of these companies charged interest rates significantly greater than those charged by banks, thereby squeezing Megahertz's profit margins.

Coles hoped these financing problems were temporary. Once Megahertz established a more sustained cash flow from its international operations, and once banks better appreciated the ability of Coles and his team to secure payment from foreign customers, he hoped that they would become more amenable to lending capital to Megahertz at rates that would help to protect the company's profit margins. By 2002, however, it was clear that the company's growth was too slow to achieve these goals anytime soon. As an alternative solution, in 2003 Coles agreed to sell Megahertz Communications to AZCAR of Canada. AZCAR acquired Megahertz to gain access to the expanding EU market and Megahertz's contacts in the Middle East. For Megahertz, the acquisition gave the company additional working capital that enabled it to take full advantage of export opportunities.

Sources: www.megahertz.co.uk; W. Smith, "Today Batley, Tomorrow the World?" *Director,* January 2000, pp. 42–49; and "AZCAR Acquires 80% of Megahertz Broadcast Systems," *Canadian Corporate Newswire*, March 31, 2003.

Case Discussion Questions

1. What was the motivation for Megahertz's shift toward a strategy of export-led growth? Why do you think the opportunities for growth might be greater in foreign markets? Do you think that developing countries are likely to be a major market opportunity for Megahertz? Why?
2. Does Megahertz's strategy for building exports make sense given the nature of the broadcast industry? Why?
3. Why do you think Megahertz found it difficult to raise the working capital required to finance its international trade activities? What does the experience of Megahertz tell you about the problems facing small firms that wish to export?
4. Megahertz solved its financing problem by selling the company to AZCAR of Canada. What other solutions might the company have adopted?

Paul Hilton/Bloomberg News/Landov

part 5 Competing in the Global Marketplace

1. Explain why production and logistics decisions are of central importance to many multinational businesses.
2. Explain how country differences, production technology, and product features all affect the choice of where to locate production activities.
3. Discuss how the role of foreign subsidiaries in production can be enhanced over time as they accumulate knowledge.
4. Identify the factors that influence a firm's decision of whether to source supplies from within the company or from foreign suppliers.
5. Articulate what is required to efficiently coordinate a globally dispersed production system.

chapter 14

Global Production, Outsourcing, and Logistics

Li & Fung

opening case

Established in 1906, Hong Kong–based Li & Fung is now one of the largest multinational trading companies in the developing world, with annual sales of more than $7 billion in 2005, up from just $1.2 billion in 2000. The company, which is still run by the grandsons of the founder, Victor and William Fung, does not see itself as a traditional trading enterprise. Rather, it sees itself as an expert in supply chain management for its 500 or so customers. These customers are a diverse group and include clothing retailers and consumer electronics companies. Li & Fung takes orders from customers and then sifts through its network of 7,500 independent suppliers located in 40 countries to find the right manufacturing enterprises to produce the product for customers at the most attractive combination of cost and quality. Attaining this goal frequently requires Li & Fung to break up the value chain and disperse different productive activities to manufacturers located in different countries depending on an assessment of factors such as labor costs, trade barriers, transportation costs, and so on. Li & Fung then coordinates the whole process, managing the logistics and arranging for the shipment of the finished product to the customer.

Typical of its customers is The Limited, Inc., a large U.S.-based chain of retail clothing stores. The Limited outsources much of its manufacturing and logistics functions to Li & Fung. The process starts when The Limited comes to Li & Fung with designer sketches of clothes for the next fashion season. Li & Fung takes the basic product concepts and researches the market to find the right kind of yarn, dye, buttons, and so on; it then assembles these into prototypes that The Limited can inspect. Once The Limited has settled on a prototype, it will give Li & Fung an order and ask for delivery within five weeks. The short time between an order and requested delivery is necessitated by the rapid rate of product obsolescence in the fashion clothing industry. With order in hand, Li & Fung distributes the various aspects of the overall manufacturing process to different producers depending on their capabilities and costs. For example, Li & Fung might decide to purchase yarn from a Korean company but have it woven and dyed in Taiwan. So Li & Fung will arrange for the yarn to be picked up from Korea and shipped to Taiwan. The Japanese might have the best zippers and buttons, but they manufacture them mostly in China. So Li & Fung will go to YKK, a big Japanese zipper manufacturer, and order the right zippers from its Chinese plants. Then Li & Fung might decide that due to constraints imposed by export quotas and labor costs, the best place to make the final garments might be in Thailand. So everything will be shipped to Thailand. In addition, because The Limited, like many retail customers, needs quick delivery, Li & Fung might divide the order across five factories in Thailand. Five weeks after the order has been received, the garments will arrive on the shelves of The Limited, all looking like they came from one factory, with colors perfectly matched. The result is a product that may have a label that says "Made in Thailand," but it is a global product.

To better serve the needs of its customers, Li & Fung is divided into numerous small, customer-focused divisions. There is a theme store division that serves a handful of customers such as Warner Brothers; there is a division for The Limited, and another for Gymboree, a U.S.-based children's clothing store. Walk into one of these divisions, such as the one for Gymboree, and you will see that every one of the 40 or so people there is focused solely on meeting Gymboree's needs. On every desk is a computer with a direct software link to Gymboree. The staff is organized into specialized teams in areas such as design, technical support, merchandising, raw material purchasing, quality assurance, and shipping. These teams also have direct electronic links to dedicated staff in Li & Fung's branch offices in various countries where Gymboree buys in volume, such as China, Indonesia, and the Philippines. Thus, Li & Fung uses information systems to manage, coordinate, and control the globally dispersed design, production, and shipping process to ensure that the time between receipt of an order and delivery is minimized, as are overall costs.

Sources: J. Magretta, "Fast, Global, and Entrepreneurial: Supply Chain Management Hong Kong Style," *Harvard Business Review,* September–October 1998, pp. 102–14; J. Ridding, "A Multinational Trading Group with Chinese Characteristics," *Financial Times,* November 7, 1997, p. 16; J. Ridding, "The Family in the Frame," *Financial Times,* October 28, 1996, p. 12; J. Lo, "Second Half Doubts Shadow Li & Fung Strength in Interims," *South China Morning Post,* August 27, 1998, p. 3; and R. Meredith, "At the Crossroads," *Forbes,* April 17, 2006, pp. 31–32.

Introduction

As trade barriers fall and global markets develop, more and more firms are confronting a set of interrelated issues. First, where in the world should production activities be located? Should they be concentrated in a single country, or should they be dispersed around the globe, matching the type of activity with country differences in factor costs, tariff barriers, political risks, and the like to minimize costs and maximize value added?

Second, what should be the long-term strategic role of foreign production sites? Should the firm abandon a foreign site if factor costs change, moving production to another more favorable location, or is there value to maintaining an operation at a given location even if underlying economic conditions change? Third, should the firm own foreign production activities, or is it better to outsource those activities to independent vendors? Fourth, how should a globally dispersed supply chain be managed, and what is the role of Internet-based information technology in the management of global logistics? Fifth, should the firm manage global logistics itself, or should it outsource the management to enterprises that specialize in this activity?

Li & Fung, which we reviewed in the opening case, is an excellent example of an enterprise that has grown rapidly by taking over the global logistics activities of other companies, such as Warner Brothers, The Limited, and Toys "R" Us. As a logistics specialist, Li & Fung deals with a number of issues that many other firms competing in today's global economy also have had to confront. To serve the needs of its customers, Li & Fung has to decide how best to distribute manufacturing activities among operations based in various countries so as to minimize costs, produce products that have an acceptable level of quality, and do so in a timely manner. Li & Fung scans its global network of some 7,500 suppliers located in 40 countries to make these decisions, weighing factors such as labor costs, trade barriers, transportation costs, and product quality, and only then deciding what should be produced where and in what quantities. Li & Fung often unbundles the value chain associated with producing a product, dispersing various parts of the chain to different locations depending on an assessment of the value that can be created by performing an activity in a particular location. Li & Fung must then coordinate and control the globally dispersed value chain so that it minimizes the time between receipt of an order and delivery of the finished product.

Strategy, Production, and Logistics

In Chapter 11, we introduced the concept of the value chain and discussed a number of value-creation activities, including production, marketing, logistics, R&D, human resources, and information systems. In this chapter, we will focus on two of these activities—production and logistics—and attempt to clarify how they might be performed internationally to (1) lower the costs of value creation and (2) add value by better serving customer needs. We will discuss the contributions of information technology to these activities, which has become particularly important in the era of the Internet. In later chapters, we will look at other value-creation activities in this international context (marketing, R&D, and human resource management).

LEARNING OBJECTIVE 1
Explain why production and logistics decisions are of central importance to many multinational businesses.

Production refers to the activities involved in creating a product. In Chapter 11, we used the term *production* to denote both service and manufacturing activities, because a business can produce a service or produce a physical product. Although in this chapter we focus more on the production of physical goods, do not forget that the term can also be applied to services. This has become more evident in recent years with the trend among U.S. firms to outsource the "production" of certain service activities to developing nations where labor costs are lower (for example, the trend among many U.S. companies to outsource customer care services to places such as India, where English is widely spoken and labor costs are much lower). **Logistics** is the activity that controls the transmission of physical materials through the value chain, from procurement through production and into distribution. Production and logistics are closely linked since a firm's ability to perform its production activities efficiently depends on a timely supply of high-quality material inputs, for which logistics is responsible.

Production
The activities involved in creating a product.

Logistics
The procurement and transmission of material through the supply chain, from suppliers to customers.

Another Perspective

Logistics and Supply Chain Management: The Place to Be

With increased outsourcing, foreign production sites, and foreign customers, logistics has become a growing field. The weekly professional publication *IndustryWeek* (www.industryweek.com) reports that value chain and supply chain management positions are projected to grow at least 8.6 percent annually over the next five years. In addition to growth in the U.S. market, *IndustryWeek* forecasts strong growth in developing markets where manufacturers want to take full advantage of their new capital investment in factories in order to be competitive in the global market. See www.arcweb.com/res/scm for more information about career development in this sector.

The production and logistics functions of an international firm have a number of important strategic objectives.[1] One is to lower costs. Dispersing production activities to various locations around the globe where each activity can be performed most efficiently can lower costs. See the Another Perspective at left. Costs can also be cut by managing the global supply chain efficiently so as to better match supply and demand. Efficient supply chain management reduces the amount of inventory in the system and increases inventory turnover, which means the firm has to invest less working capital in inventory and is less likely to find excess inventory on hand that cannot be sold and has to be written off.

A second strategic objective shared by production and logistics is to increase product quality by eliminating defective products from both the supply chain and the manufacturing process.[2] (In this context, *quality* means *reliability*, implying that the product has no defects and performs well.) The objectives of reducing costs and increasing quality are not independent of each other. As illustrated in Figure 14.1, a firm that improves its quality control will also reduce its costs of value creation. Improved quality control reduces costs by

- Increasing productivity because time is not wasted producing poor-quality products that cannot be sold, leading to a direct reduction in unit costs.
- Lowering rework and scrap costs associated with defective products.
- Reducing the warranty costs and time associated with fixing defective products.

The effect is to lower the costs of value creation by reducing both production and after-sales service costs.

figure 14.1

The Relationship between Quality and Costs

Source: Reprinted from "What Does Product Quality Really Mean?" by David A. Garvin, *Sloan Management Review* 26 (Fall 1984), fig. 1, p. 37, by permission of the publisher. Copyright © 1984 by Massachusetts Institute of Technology. All rights reserved.

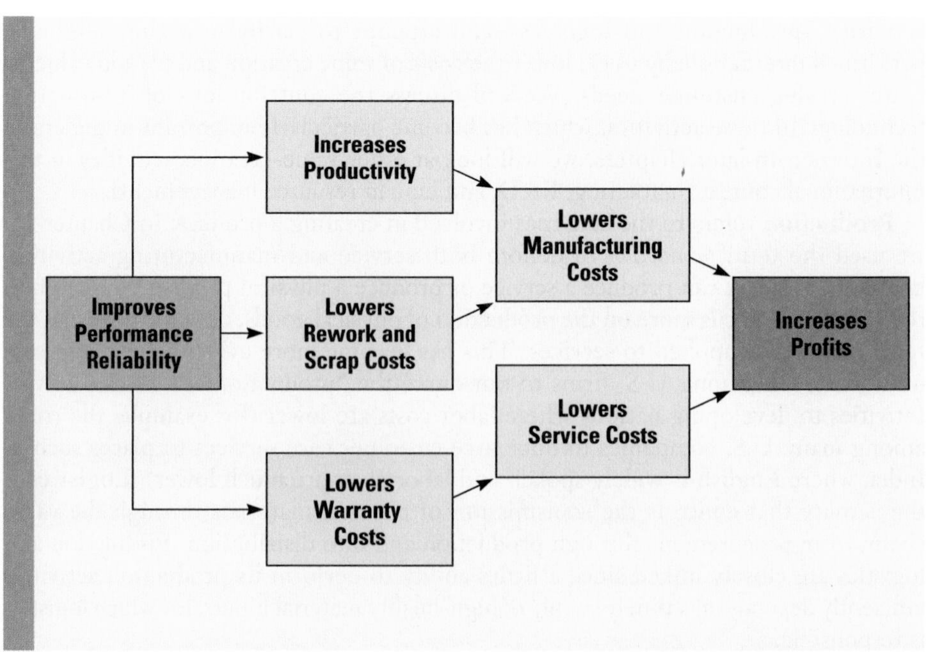

The principal tool that most managers now use to increase the reliability of their product offering is the Six Sigma quality improvement methodology. The Six Sigma methodology is a direct descendant of the **total quality management (TQM)** philosophy that was widely adopted, first by Japanese companies and then American companies, during the 1980s and early 1990s.[3] The TQM philosophy was developed by a number of American consultants such as W. Edward Deming, Joseph Juran, and A. V. Feigenbaum.[4] Deming identified a number of steps that should be part of any TQM program. He argued that management should embrace the philosophy that mistakes, defects, and poor-quality materials are not acceptable and should be eliminated. He suggested that the quality of supervision should be improved by allowing more time for supervisors to work with employees and by providing them with the tools they need to do the job. Deming recommended that management should create an environment in which employees will not fear reporting problems or recommending improvements. He believed that work standards should not only be defined as numbers or quotas, but they should also include some notion of quality to promote the production of defect-free output. He argued that management has the responsibility to train employees in new skills to keep pace with changes in the workplace. In addition, he believed that achieving better quality requires the commitment of everyone in the company.

Total Quality Management (TQM)
Philosophy of management that focuses on improving the quality of a company's products and services.

Six Sigma, the modern successor to TQM, is a statistically based philosophy that aims to reduce defects, boost productivity, eliminate waste, and cut costs throughout a company. Six Sigma programs have been adopted by several major corporations, such as Motorola, General Electric, and Allied Signal. Sigma comes from the Greek letter that statisticians use to represent a standard deviation from a mean—the higher the number of sigmas, the smaller the number of errors. At six sigma, a production process would be 99.99966 percent accurate, creating just 3.4 defects per million units. Although it is almost impossible for a company to achieve such perfection, Six Sigma quality is a goal toward which several strive. Increasingly, companies are adopting Six Sigma programs to try to boost their product quality and productivity.[5]

Six Sigma
The modern successor to TQM, a statistically based management philosophy that aims to reduce defects, boost productivity, eliminate waste, and cut costs throughout a company.

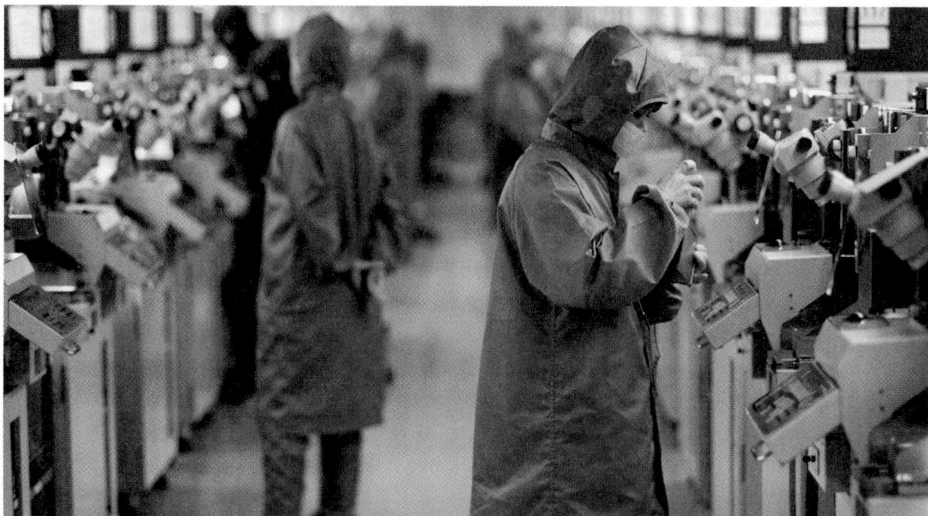

Motorola is one company that uses the Six Sigma philosophy, which aims to reduce defects, boost productivity, eliminate waste, and cut costs throughout a company. *George Steinmetz/Corbis*

The growth of international standards has also focused greater attention on the importance of product quality. For example, the European Union requires that the quality of a firm's manufacturing processes and products be certified under a quality standard known as **ISO 9000** before the firm is allowed access to the EU marketplace. Although the ISO 9000 certification process has proved to be somewhat bureaucratic and costly for many firms, it does focus management attention on the need to improve the quality of products and processes.[6]

ISO 9000
Certification process that requires certain quality standards to be met.

In addition to the lowering of costs and the improvement of quality, two other objectives have particular importance in international businesses. First, production and logistics functions must be able to accommodate demands for local responsiveness. As we saw in Chapter 11, demands for local responsiveness arise from national differences in consumer tastes and preferences, infrastructure, distribution channels, and host-government demands. Demands for local responsiveness create pressures to decentralize production activities to the major national or regional markets in which the firm does business or to implement flexible manufacturing processes that enable the firm to customize the product coming out of a factory according to the market in which it is to be sold.

Second, production and logistics must be able to respond quickly to shifts in customer demand. In recent years, time-based competition has grown more important.[7] When consumer demand is prone to large and unpredictable shifts, the firm that can adapt most quickly to these shifts will gain an advantage. As we shall see, both production and logistics play critical roles here. Part of the competitive advantage of Li & Fung, for example, is based on its ability to use real-time information about ordering patterns and inventory to bring demand and supply into alignment, thereby quickly satisfying customer needs and taking excess inventory out of the supply chain (see the opening case).

Where to Produce

LEARNING OBJECTIVE 2
Explain how country differences, production technology, and product features all affect the choice of where to locate production activities.

An essential decision facing an international firm is where to locate its production activities to best minimize costs and improve product quality. A firm contemplating international production must consider a number of factors. These can be grouped under three broad headings: country factors, technological factors, and product factors.[8]

COUNTRY FACTORS We reviewed country-specific factors in some detail earlier in the book. Political economy, culture, and relative factor costs differ from country to country. In Chapter 5, we saw that due to differences in factor costs, some countries have a comparative advantage for producing certain products. In Chapters 2 and 3, we saw how differences in political economy and national culture influence the benefits, costs, and risks of doing business in a country. Other things being equal, a firm should locate its various manufacturing activities where the economic, political, and cultural conditions, including relative factor costs, are conducive to the performance of those activities (for an example, see the accompanying Management Focus, which looks at the Philips NV investment in China). In Chapter 11, we referred to the benefits derived from such a strategy as location economies. We argued that one result of the strategy is the creation of a global web of value-creation activities.

Also important in some industries is the presence of global concentrations of activities at certain locations. In Chapter 7, we discussed the role of location externalities in influencing foreign direct investment decisions. Externalities include the presence of an appropriately skilled labor pool and supporting industries.[9] Such externalities can play an important role in deciding where to locate manufacturing activities. For example, because

Management FOCUS

Philips in China

The Dutch consumer electronics, lighting, semiconductor, and medical equipment conglomerate Philips NV has been operating factories in China since 1985 when the country first opened its markets to foreign investors. Then China was seen as the land of unlimited demand, and Philips, like many other Western companies, dreamed of Chinese consumers snapping up its products by the millions. But the company soon found out that one of the big reasons it liked China—the low wage rates—also meant that few Chinese workers could afford to buy the products it was producing. Chinese wage rates are currently one-third of those in Mexico and Hungary, and 5 percent of those in the United States or Japan. So Philips hit on a new strategy: keep the factories in China but export most of the goods to the United States and elsewhere.

By 2003, Philips had invested some $2.5 billion in China. The company now operates 25 wholly owned subsidiaries and joint ventures in China. Together they employ some 30,000 people. Philips exports nearly two-thirds of the $7 billion in products that the factories produce every year. Philips accelerated its Chinese investment in anticipation of China's entry into the World Trade Organization. The company plans to move even more production to China over the next few years. In 2003, Philips announced it would phase out production of electronic razors in the Netherlands, lay off 2,000 Dutch employees, and move production to China by 2005. A week earlier, Philips had stated that it would expand capacity at its semiconductor factories in China, while phasing out production in higher-cost locations elsewhere.

The attractions of China to Philips include continuing low wage rates, an educated workforce, a robust Chinese economy, a stable exchange rate that is pegged to the U.S. dollar, a rapidly expanding industrial base that includes many other Western and Chinese companies that Philips uses as suppliers, and easier access to world markets given China's entry into the WTO. Philips has stated that ultimately its goal is to turn China into a global supply base from which the company's products will be exported around the world. In 2003, more than 20 percent of everything Philips made worldwide came from China, and executives say the figure is rising rapidly. Several products, such as CD and DVD players, are now made only in China. Philips is also starting to give its Chinese factories a greater role in product development. In the TV business, for example, basic development used to occur in Holland but was moved to Singapore in the early 1990s. Now Philips is transferring TV development work to Suzhou near Shanghai. Similarly, basic product development work on LCD screens for cell phones was recently shifted to Shanghai.

Philips is hardly alone in this process. By 2003, more than half of all exports from China came from foreign manufacturers or their joint ventures in China. China was the source of more than 80 percent of the DVD players sold worldwide, 50 percent of the cameras, 40 percent of all microwave ovens, 30 percent of the air conditioners, 25 percent of the washing machines, and 20 percent of all refrigerators.

Some observers worry that Philips and companies pursuing a similar strategy might be overdoing it. Too much dependence on China could be dangerous if political, economic, or other problems disrupt production and the company's ability to supply global markets. Some observers believe that it might be better if the manufacturing facilities of companies were more geographically diverse as a hedge against problems in China. The fears of the critics were given some substance in early 2003 when an outbreak of the pneumonia-like SARS (severe acute respiratory syndrome) virus in China resulted in the temporary shutdown of several plants operated by foreign companies and disrupted their global supply chains. Although Philips was not directly affected, it did restrict travel by its managers and engineers to its Chinese plants.

Sources: B. Einhorn. "Philips' Expanding Asia Connections," *BusinessWeek Online,* November 27, 2003; K. Leggett and P. Wonacott, "The World's Factory: A Surge in Exports from China Jolts the Global Industry," *The Wall Street Journal,* October 10, 2002, p. A1; "Philips NV: China Will Be Production Site for Electronic Razors," *The Wall Street Journal,* April 8, 2003, p. B12; "Philips Plans China Expansion," *The Wall Street Journal,* September 25, 2003, p. B13; and M. Saunderson, "Eight out of 10 DVD Players Will Be Made in China," *Dealerscope,* July 2004, p. 28.

of a cluster of semiconductor manufacturing plants in Taiwan, a pool of labor with experience in the semiconductor business has developed there. In addition, the plants have attracted a number of supporting industries, such as the manufacturers of semiconductor capital equipment and silicon, which have established facilities in Taiwan to be near their customers. This implies that there are real benefits to locating in Taiwan, as opposed to another location that lacks such externalities. Other things being equal, the externalities make Taiwan an attractive location for semiconductor manufacturing facilities.

Of course, other things are not equal. Differences in relative factor costs, political economy, culture, and location externalities are important, but other factors also loom large. Formal and informal trade barriers obviously influence location decisions (see Chapter 6), as do transportation costs and rules and regulations regarding foreign direct investment (see Chapter 7). For example, although relative factor costs may make a country look attractive as a location for performing a manufacturing activity, regulations prohibiting foreign direct investment may eliminate this option. Similarly, a consideration of factor costs might suggest that a firm should source production of a certain component from a particular country, but trade barriers could make this uneconomical.

Another country factor is expected future movements in its exchange rate (see Chapters 9 and 10). Adverse changes in exchange rates can quickly alter a country's attractiveness as a manufacturing base. Currency appreciation can transform a low-cost location into a high-cost location. Many Japanese corporations had to grapple with this problem during the 1990s and early 2000s. The relatively low value of the yen on foreign exchange markets between 1950 and 1980 helped strengthen Japan's position as a low-cost location for manufacturing. Between 1980 and the mid-1990s, however, the yen's steady appreciation against the dollar increased the dollar cost of products exported from Japan, making Japan less attractive as a manufacturing location. In response, many Japanese firms moved their manufacturing offshore to lower-cost locations in East Asia.

TECHNOLOGICAL FACTORS The type of technology a firm uses to perform specific manufacturing activities can be pivotal in location decisions. For example, because of technological constraints, in some cases it is necessary to perform certain manufacturing activities in only one location and serve the world market from there. In other cases, the technology may make it feasible to perform an activity in multiple locations. Three characteristics of a manufacturing technology are of interest here: the level of fixed costs, the minimum efficient scale, and the flexibility of the technology.

Fixed Costs As noted in Chapter 11, in some cases the fixed costs of setting up a production plant are so high that a firm must serve the world market from a single location or from a very few locations. For example, it now costs more than $1 billion to set up a state-of-the-art plant to manufacture semiconductor chips. Given this, other things being equal, serving the world market from a single plant sited at a single (optimal) location can make sense.

Conversely, a relatively low level of fixed costs can make it economical to perform a particular activity in several locations at once. This allows the firm to better accommodate demands for local responsiveness. Manufacturing in multiple locations may also help the firm avoid becoming too dependent on one location. Being too dependent on one location is particularly risky in a world of floating exchange rates. Many firms disperse their manufacturing plants to different locations as a real hedge against potentially adverse moves in currencies.

Minimum Efficient Scale The concept of economies of scale tells us that as plant output expands, unit costs decrease. The reasons include the greater utilization of capital equipment and the productivity gains that come with specialization of employees within the plant.[10] However, beyond a certain level of output, few additional economies of scale are available. Thus, the unit-cost curve declines with output until a certain output level is reached, at which point further increases in output realize little reduction

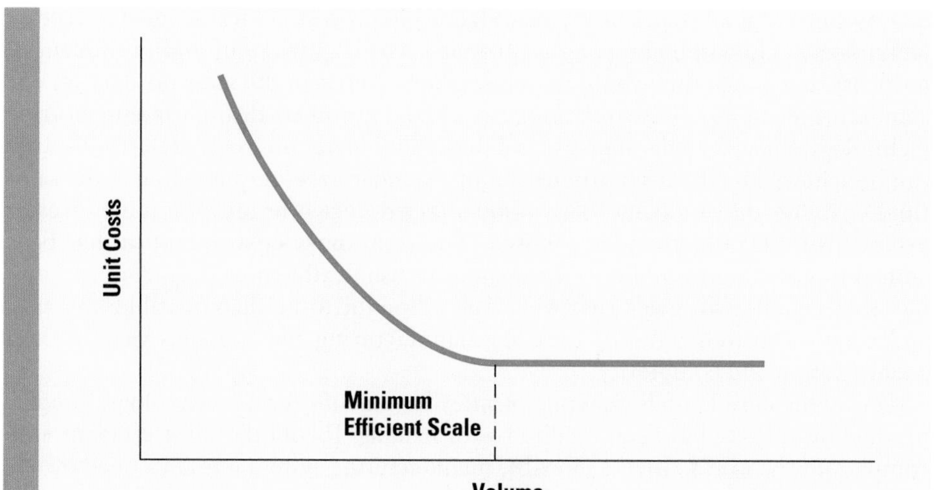

figure 14.2
A Typical Unit-Cost Curve

in unit costs. The level of output at which most plant-level economies of scale are exhausted is referred to as the **minimum efficient scale** of output. This is the scale of output at which a plant must operate to realize all major plant-level economies of scale (see Figure 14.2).

Minimum Efficient Scale
The level of output at which most plant-level scale economies are exhausted.

The implications of this concept are as follows: The larger the minimum efficient scale of a plant relative to total global demand, the greater the argument for centralizing production in a single location or a limited number of locations. Alternatively, when the minimum efficient scale of production is low relative to global demand, it may be economical to manufacture a product at several locations. For example, the minimum efficient scale for a plant to manufacture personal computers is about 250,000 units a year, while the total global demand exceeds 35 million units a year. The low level of minimum efficient scale in relation to total global demand makes it economically feasible for a company such as Dell to manufacture PCs in six locations.

As in the case of low fixed costs, the advantages of a low minimum efficient scale include allowing the firm to accommodate demands for local responsiveness or to hedge against currency risk by manufacturing the same product in several locations.

Flexible Manufacturing and Mass Customization

Central to the concept of economies of scale is the idea that the best way to achieve high efficiency, and hence low unit costs, is through the mass production of a standardized output. The trade-off implicit in this idea is between unit costs and product variety. Producing greater product variety from a factory implies shorter production runs, which in turn implies an inability to realize economies of scale. That is, wide product variety makes it difficult for a company to increase its production efficiency and thus reduce its unit costs. According to this logic, the way to increase efficiency and drive down unit costs is to limit product variety and produce a standardized product in large volumes.

Flexible Manufacturing Technology (lean production)
Manufacturing technology designed to reduce setup time, improve job scheduling, and improve quality control.

This view of production efficiency has been challenged by the rise of flexible manufacturing technologies. The term **flexible manufacturing technology**—or **lean production,** as it is often called—covers a range of manufacturing technologies designed to (1) reduce setup times for complex equipment, (2) increase the utilization of individual machines through better scheduling, and (3) improve quality control at all stages of the manufacturing process.[11] Flexible manufacturing technologies allow the company to produce a wider variety of end products at a unit cost that at one time could be achieved only through the mass production of a standardized output. Research suggests the adoption of flexible manufacturing technologies may actually increase efficiency and lower unit costs relative to what can be achieved by the mass production of a standardized output, while at the same time enabling the company to customize its product offering to a much greater extent than was once thought possible. The term **mass customization** has been coined to describe the ability of companies to use flexible manufacturing technology to reconcile two goals that were once thought to be incompatible: low cost and product customization.[12] Flexible manufacturing technologies vary in their sophistication and complexity.

Mass Customization
The ability of companies to use flexible manufacturing technology to achieve product customization at low cost.

One of the most famous examples of a flexible manufacturing technology, Toyota's production system, has been credited with making Toyota the most efficient auto company in the world. Toyota's flexible manufacturing system was developed by one of the company's engineers, Ohno Taiichi. After working at Toyota for five years and visiting Ford's U.S. plants, Ohno became convinced that the mass production philosophy for making cars was flawed. He saw numerous problems with mass production.

First, long production runs created massive inventories that had to be stored in large warehouses. This was expensive, both because of the cost of warehousing and because inventories tied up capital in unproductive uses. Second, if the initial machine settings were wrong, long production runs resulted in the production of a large number of defects (i.e., waste). Third, the mass production system was unable to accommodate consumer preferences for product diversity.

In response, Ohno looked for ways to make shorter production runs economical. He developed a number of techniques designed to reduce setup times for production equipment (a major source of fixed costs). By using a system of levers and pulleys, he reduced the time required to change dies on stamping equipment from a full day in 1950 to three minutes by 1971. This made small production runs economical, which allowed Toyota to respond better to consumer demands for product diversity. Small production runs also eliminated the need to hold large inventories, thereby reducing warehousing costs. Plus, small product runs and the lack of inventory meant that defective parts were produced only in small numbers and entered the assembly process immediately. This reduced waste and helped trace defects back to their source to fix the problem. In sum, these innovations enabled Toyota to produce a more diverse product range at a lower unit cost than was possible with conventional mass production.[13]

Flexible Machine Cells
A grouping of various types of machinery, a common materials handler, and a centralized cell controller computer that produces a family of products.

Flexible machine cells are another common flexible manufacturing technology. A flexible machine cell is a grouping of various types of machinery, a common materials handler, and a centralized cell controller (computer). Each cell normally contains four to six machines capable of performing a variety of operations. The typical cell is dedicated to the production of a family of parts or products. The settings on machines are computer controlled, which allows each cell to switch quickly between the production of different parts or products.

Improved capacity utilization and reductions in work in progress (that is, stockpiles of partly finished products) and in waste are major efficiency benefits of flexible machine cells. Improved capacity utilization arises from the reduction in setup times and from the computer-controlled coordination of production flow between machines, which eliminates bottlenecks. The tight coordination between machines also reduces work-in-progress inventory. Reductions in waste are due to the ability of computer-controlled machinery to identify ways to transform inputs into outputs while producing a minimum of unusable waste material. While freestanding machines might be in use 50 percent of the time, the same machines when grouped into a cell can be used more than 80 percent of the time and produce the same end product with half the waste. This increases efficiency and results in lower costs.

The installation of flexible manufacturing technologies can have a dramatic effect on a company's cost structure. The Ford Motor Company is currently introducing flexible manufacturing technologies into its automotive plants around the world. These new technologies should allow Ford to produce multiple models from the same line and to switch production from one model to another much more quickly than in the past. In total, Ford hopes to take \$2 billion out of its cost structure by 2010.[14]

Besides improving efficiency and lowering costs, flexible manufacturing technologies also enable companies to customize products to the demands of small consumer groups—at a cost that at one time could be achieved only by mass-producing a standardized output. Thus, the technologies help a company achieve mass customization, which increases its customer responsiveness. Most important for international business, flexible manufacturing technologies can help a firm customize products for different national markets. The importance of this advantage cannot be overstated. When flexible manufacturing technologies are available, a firm can manufacture products customized to various national markets at a single factory sited at the optimal location. And it can do this without absorbing a significant cost penalty. Thus, firms no longer need to establish manufacturing facilities in each major national market to provide products that satisfy specific consumer tastes and preferences, part of the rationale for a localization strategy (Chapter 11).

Summary A number of technological factors support the economic arguments for concentrating production facilities in a few choice locations or even in a single location. Other things being equal, when fixed costs are substantial, the minimum efficient scale of production is high, and flexible manufacturing technologies are available, the arguments for concentrating production at a few choice locations are strong. This is true even when substantial differences in consumer tastes and preferences exist between national markets, because flexible manufacturing technologies allow the firm to customize products to national differences at a single facility. Alternatively, when fixed costs are low, the minimum efficient scale of production is low, and flexible manufacturing technologies are not available, the arguments for concentrating production at one or a few locations are not as compelling. In such cases, it may make more sense to manufacture in each major market in which the firm is active if this helps the firm better respond to local demands. This holds only if the increased local responsiveness more than offsets the cost disadvantages of not concentrating manufacturing. With the advent of flexible manufacturing technologies and mass customization, such a strategy is becoming less attractive. In sum, technological factors are making it feasible, and necessary, for firms to concentrate manufacturing facilities at optimal locations. Trade barriers and transportation costs are major brakes on this trend.

PRODUCT FACTORS Two product features affect location decisions. The first is the product's *value-to-weight* ratio because of its influence on transportation costs. Many electronic components and pharmaceuticals have high value-to-weight ratios; they are expensive and they do not weigh very much. Thus, even if they are shipped halfway around the world, their transportation costs account for a small percentage of total costs. Given this, other things being equal, there is great pressure to produce these products in the optimal location and to serve the world market from there. The opposite holds for products with low value-to-weight ratios. Refined sugar, certain bulk chemicals, paint, and petroleum products all have low value-to-weight ratios; they are relatively inexpensive products that weigh a lot. Accordingly, when they are shipped long distances, transportation costs account for a large percentage of total costs. Thus, other things being equal, there is great pressure to make these products in multiple locations close to major markets to reduce transportation costs.

The other product feature that can influence location decisions is whether the product serves universal needs, needs that are the same all over the world. Examples include many industrial products (e.g., industrial electronics, steel, bulk chemicals) and modern consumer products (e.g., handheld calculators, personal computers, video game consoles). Because there are few national differences in consumer taste and preference for such products, the need for local responsiveness is reduced. This increases the attractiveness of concentrating production at an optimal location.

LOCATING PRODUCTION FACILITIES There are two basic strategies for locating production facilities: concentrating them in a centralized location and serving the world market from there, or decentralizing them in various regional or national locations that are close to major markets. The appropriate strategic choice is determined by the various country-specific, technological, and product factors we have discussed in this section, summarized in Table 14.1.

As can be seen, concentration of production makes most sense when

- Differences between countries in factor costs, political economy, and culture have a substantial impact on the costs of manufacturing in various countries.
- Trade barriers are low.

table 14.1

Location Strategy and Production

	Concentrated Production Favored	Decentralized Production Favored
Country factors		
Difference in political economy	Substantial	Few
Difference in culture	Substantial	Few
Difference in factor costs	Substantial	Few
Trade barriers	Substantial	Few
Location externalities	Important in industry	Not important in industry
Exchange rates	Stable	Volatile
Technological factors		
Fixed costs	High	Low
Minimum efficient scale	High	Low
Flexible manufacturing technology	Available	Not Available
Product factors		
Value-to-weight ratio	High	Low
Serves universal needs	Yes	No

- Externalities arising from the concentration of like enterprises favor certain locations.
- Important exchange rates are expected to remain relatively stable.
- The production technology has high fixed costs and high minimum efficient scale relative to global demand, or flexible manufacturing technology exists.
- The product's value-to-weight ratio is high.
- The product serves universal needs.

Alternatively, decentralization of production is appropriate when

- Differences between countries in factor costs, political economy, and culture do not have a substantial impact on the costs of manufacturing in various countries.
- Trade barriers are high.
- Location externalities are not important.
- Volatility in important exchange rates is expected.
- The production technology has low fixed costs and low minimum efficient scale, and flexible manufacturing technology is not available.
- The product's value-to-weight ratio is low.
- The product does not serve universal needs (that is, significant differences in consumer tastes and preferences exist between nations).

In practice, location decisions are seldom clear cut. For example, it is not unusual for differences in factor costs, technological factors, and product factors to point toward concentrated production while a combination of trade barriers and volatile exchange rates points toward decentralized production. This seems to be the case in the world automobile industry. Although the availability of flexible manufacturing and cars' relatively high value-to-weight ratios suggest concentrated manufacturing, the combination of formal and informal trade barriers and the uncertainties of the world's current floating exchange rate regime (see Chapter 10) have inhibited firms' ability to pursue this strategy. For these reasons, several automobile companies have established top-to-bottom manufacturing operations in three major regional markets: Asia, North America, and Western Europe.

The Strategic Role of Foreign Factories

LEARNING OBJECTIVE 3
Discuss how the role of foreign subsidiaries in production can be enhanced over time as they accumulate knowledge.

Whatever the rationale behind establishing a foreign production facility, the strategic role of foreign factories can evolve over time.[15] Initially, many foreign factories are established where labor costs are low. Their strategic role typically is to produce labor-intensive products at as low a cost as possible. For example, beginning in the 1970s, many U.S. firms in the computer and telecommunication equipment businesses established factories across Southeast Asia to manufacture electronic components, such as circuit boards and semiconductors, at the lowest possible cost. They located their factories in countries such as Malaysia, Thailand, and Singapore precisely because each of these countries offered an attractive combination of low labor costs, adequate infrastructure, and favorable tax and trade regime. Initially, the components produced by these factories were designed elsewhere and the final product was assembled elsewhere. Over time, however, the strategic role of some of these factories has expanded; they have become important centers for the design and final assembly of products for the global marketplace. For example, Hewlett-Packard's operation in Singapore was established as a low-cost location for the production of circuit boards, but the facility has become the center for the design and final assembly of portable ink-jet printers for the global marketplace (see the

Management Focus on page 459 for details). A similar process seems to be occurring at some of the factories that Philips has established in China (see the previovs Management Focus on Philips).

Such upward migration in the strategic role of foreign factories arises because many foreign factories upgrade their own capabilities.[16] This improvement comes from two sources. First, corporate pressure to improve a factory's cost structure or customize a product to the demands of consumers in a particular nation can start a chain of events that ultimately leads to development of additional capabilities at that factory. For example, to meet corporate-mandated directions to drive down costs, engineers at HP's Singapore factory argued that they needed to redesign products so they could be manufactured at a lower cost. This led to the establishment of a design center in Singapore. As this design center proved its worth, HP executives realized the importance of co-locating design and manufacturing operations. They increasingly transferred more design responsibilities to the Singapore factory. In addition, the Singapore factory ultimately became the center for the design of products tailored to the needs of the Asian market. This made good strategic sense because it meant products were being designed by engineers who were close to the Asian market and probably had a good understanding of the needs of that market, as opposed to engineers located in the United States.

A second source of improvement in the capabilities of a foreign factory can be the increasing abundance of advanced factors of production in the nation in which the factory is located. Many nations that were considered economic backwaters a generation ago have been experiencing rapid economic development during the past 20 years. Their communication and transportation infrastructures and the education level of the population have improved. Although they once lacked the advanced infrastructure required to support sophisticated design, development, and manufacturing operations, this is no longer the case for many of these countries. This has made it much easier for factories based in these nations to take on a greater strategic role.

Because of such developments, many international businesses are moving away from thinking of their foreign factories as nothing more than low-cost manufacturing facilities and toward viewing them as globally dispersed centers of excellence.[17] In this new model, foreign factories take the lead role for the design and manufacture of products to serve important national or regional markets or even the global market. The development of such dispersed centers of excellence is consistent with the concept of a transnational strategy, introduced in Chapter 11. A major aspect of a transnational strategy is a belief in **global learning,** the idea that valuable knowledge does not reside just in a firm's domestic operations; it may also be found in its foreign subsidiaries. Foreign factories that upgrade their capabilities over time are creating valuable knowledge that might benefit the whole corporation.

Global Learning
The idea that valuable knowledge resides not only in a firm's domestic operations but in its foreign subsidiaries as well.

Managers of international businesses need to remember that foreign factories can improve their capabilities over time, and this can be of immense strategic benefit to the firm. Rather than viewing foreign factories simply as sweatshops where unskilled labor churns out low-cost goods, managers need to see them as potential centers of excellence and to encourage and foster attempts by local managers to upgrade the capabilities of their factories and, thereby, enhance their strategic standing within the corporation.

Such a process implies that once a foreign factory has been established and valuable skills have been accumulated, it may not be wise to switch production to another location simply because some underlying variable, such as wage rates, has changed.[18] HP has kept its facility in Singapore, rather than switching production to a location where

Management FOCUS

Hewlett-Packard in Singapore

In the late 1960s, Hewlett-Packard was looking around Asia for a low-cost location to produce electronic components that were to be manufactured using labor-intensive processes. The company looked at several Asian locations and eventually settled on Singapore, opening its first factory there in 1970. Although Singapore did not have the lowest labor costs in the region, costs were low relative to North America. Plus, the Singapore location had several important benefits that could not be found at many other locations in Asia. The education level of the local workforce was high. English was widely spoken. The government of Singapore seemed stable and committed to economic development, and the city-state had one of the better infrastructures in the region, including good communication and transportation networks and a rapidly developing industrial and commercial base. HP also extracted favorable terms from the Singapore government with regard to taxes, tariffs, and subsidies.

At its start, the plant manufactured only basic components. The combination of low labor costs and a favorable tax regime helped to make this plant profitable early. In 1973, HP transferred the manufacture of one of its basic handheld calculators from the United States to Singapore. The objective was to reduce manufacturing costs, which the Singapore factory was quickly able to do. Increasingly confident in the capability of the Singapore factory to handle entire products, as opposed to just components, HP's management transferred other products to Singapore over the next few years including keyboards, solid-state displays, and integrated circuits. However, all these products were still designed, developed, and initially produced in the United States.

The plant's status shifted in the early 1980s when HP embarked on a worldwide campaign to boost product quality and reduce costs. HP transferred the production of its HP41C handheld calculator to Singapore. The managers at the Singapore plant were given the goal of substantially reducing manufacturing costs. They argued that this could be achieved only if they were allowed to redesign the product so it could be manufactured at a lower overall cost. HP's central management agreed, and 20 engineers from the Singapore facility were transferred to the United States for one year to learn how to design application-specific integrated circuits. They then brought this expertise back to Singapore and set about redesigning the HP41C.

The results were a huge success. By redesigning the product, the Singapore engineers reduced manufacturing costs for the HP41C by 50 percent. Using this newly acquired capability for product design, the Singapore facility then set about redesigning other products it produced. HP's corporate managers were so impressed with the progress made at the factory that they transferred production of the entire calculator line to Singapore in 1983. This was followed by the partial transfer of ink-jet production to Singapore in 1984 and keyboard production in 1986. In all cases, the facility redesigned the products and often reduced unit manufacturing costs by more than 30 percent. The initial development and design of all these products, however, still occurred in the United States.

In the late 1980s and early 1990s, the Singapore plant assumed added responsibilities, particularly in the ink-jet printer business. In 1990, the factory was given the job of redesigning an HP ink-jet printer for the Japanese market. Although the initial product redesign was a market failure, the managers at Singapore pushed to be allowed to try again, and in 1991 they were given the job of redesigning HP's DeskJet 505 printer for the Japanese market. This time the redesigned product was a success, garnering significant sales in Japan. Emboldened by this success, the plant has continued to take on additional design responsibilities. Today, it is viewed as a "lead plant" within HP's global network, with primary responsibility not just for manufacturing, but also for the development and design of a family of small ink-jet printers targeted at the Asian market.

Sources: K. Ferdows, "Making the Most of Foreign Factories," *Harvard Business Review,* March–April 1997, pp. 73–88; and "Hewlett-Packard: Singapore," Harvard Business School case no. 694–035.

wage rates are now much lower, such as Vietnam, because it recognizes that the Singapore factory has accumulated valuable skills that more than make up for the higher wage rates. Thus, when reviewing the location of production facilities, the international manager must consider the valuable skills that may have been accumulated at various locations and the impact of those skills on factors such as productivity and product design.

Outsourcing Production: Make-or-Buy Decisions

LEARNING OBJECTIVE 4
Identify the factors that influence a firm's decision of whether to source supplies from within the company or from foreign suppliers.

Make-or-Buy Decisions
Whether a firm should make or outsource the making of component parts.

International businesses frequently face **make-or-buy decisions,** decisions about whether they should perform a certain value-creation activity themselves or outsource it to another entity. Historically, most outsourcing decisions have involved the manufacture of physical products. Most manufacturing firms have done their own final assembly, but they have had to decide whether to vertically integrate and manufacture their own component parts or outsource the production of such parts, purchasing them from independent suppliers. Such make-or-buy decisions are an important aspect of the strategy of many firms. In the automobile industry, for example, the typical car contains more than 10,000 components, so automobile firms constantly face make-or-buy decisions. Toyota produces less than 30 percent of the value of cars that roll off its assembly lines. The remaining 70 percent, mainly accounted for by component parts and complex subassemblies, comes from independent suppliers. In the athletic shoe industry, the make-or-buy issue has been taken to an extreme with companies such as Nike and Reebok having no involvement in manufacturing; all production has been outsourced, primarily to manufacturers based in low-wage countries.

In recent years, the outsourcing decision has gone beyond the manufacture of physical products to embrace the production of service activities. For example, many U.S.-based companies, from credit card issuers to computer companies, have outsourced their customer call centers to India. They are "buying" the customer call center function, while "making" other parts of the product in house. Similarly, many information technology companies have been outsourcing some parts of the software development process, such as testing computer code written in the United States, to independent providers based in India. Such companies are "making" (writing) most of the code in-house but "buying," or outsourcing, part of the production process (testing) to independent companies. India is often the focus of such outsourcing because English is widely spoken there; the nation has a well-educated workforce, particularly in engineering fields; and the pay is much lower than in the United States (a call center worker in India earns about $200 to $300 a month, about one-tenth of the comparable U.S. wage).[19]

Nike relies on outsourcing to manufacture its products; however, the company has received worldwide criticism for turning its back on social responsibility for the sake of profit. *AP/Wide World Photos*

Outsourcing decisions pose plenty of problems for purely domestic businesses but even more problems for international businesses. These decisions in the international arena are complicated by the volatility of countries' political economies, exchange rate movements, changes in relative factor costs, and the like. In this section, we examine the arguments for making products in-house and for buying them, and we consider the trade-offs involved in such a decision. See the Another Perspective, next page, for details. Then we discuss strategic alliances as an alternative to producing all or part of a product within the company.

THE ADVANTAGES OF MAKE The arguments that support making all or part of a product in-house—vertical integration—are fourfold. Vertical integration may be associated with lower costs, facilitate investments in highly specialized assets, protect proprietary product technology, and ease the scheduling of adjacent processes.

Another Perspective

Outsourcing as a Strategy for the Future

In addition to seeing outsourcing decisions as a way to increase quality and lower price, some other perspectives add to outsourcing's strategic role. Outsourcing is one of the benefits of globalization, from the developing country's perspective. Outsourcing is also a way for a global business to get into its future markets while they are still developing. Such early presence can build a kind of first-mover advantage—product loyalty from the consumer and more market knowledge for the producer. The example of HP in Singapore illustrates these motivations, as does Intel's in India.

Lowering Costs

It may pay a firm to continue manufacturing a product or component part in-house if the firm is more efficient at that production activity than any other enterprise. Boeing, for example, has looked closely at its make-or-buy decisions with regard to commercial jet aircraft (see the Management Focus on page 463). It decided to outsource the production of some component parts but keep the design and final integration of aircraft. Boeing's rationale was that it has a core competence in large systems integration, and it is more efficient at this activity than any other comparable enterprise in the world. Therefore, it makes little sense for Boeing to outsource this particular activity.

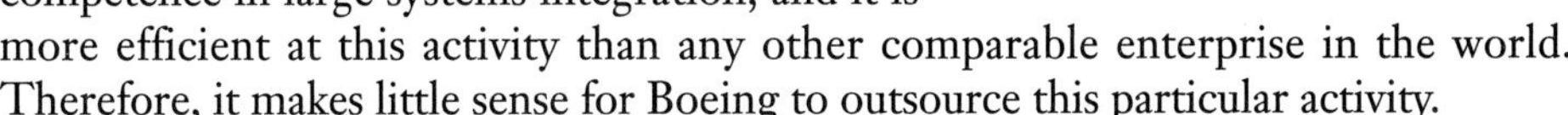

Facilitating Specialized Investments

Sometimes firms have to invest in specialized assets in order to do business with another enterprise.[20] A **specialized asset** is an asset whose value is contingent upon a particular persisting relationship. For example, imagine Ford of Europe has developed a new, high-performance, high-quality, and uniquely designed fuel injection system. The increased fuel efficiency will help sell Ford cars. Ford must decide whether to make the system in-house or to contract out the manufacturing to an independent supplier. Manufacturing these uniquely designed systems requires investments in equipment that can be used only for this purpose; it cannot be used to make fuel injection systems for any other auto firm. Thus, investment in this equipment constitutes an investment in specialized assets. When, as in this situation, one firm must invest in specialized assets to supply another, mutual dependency is created. In such circumstances, each party might fear the other will abuse the relationship by seeking more favorable terms.

Specialized Asset
An asset whose value is contingent upon a particular persisting relationship.

To appreciate this, let us first examine this situation from the perspective of an independent supplier that has been asked by Ford to make this investment. The supplier might reason that once it has made the investment, it will become dependent on Ford for business since Ford is the only possible customer for the output of this equipment. The supplier perceives this as putting Ford in a strong bargaining position and worries that once the specialized investment has been made, Ford might use this to squeeze down prices for the systems. Given this risk, the supplier declines to make the investment in specialized equipment.

Now take the position of Ford. Ford might reason that if it contracts out production of these systems to an independent supplier, it might become too dependent on that supplier for a vital input. Because specialized equipment is required to produce the fuel injection systems, Ford cannot easily switch its orders to other suppliers that lack that equipment. (It would face high switching costs.) Ford perceives this as increasing the bargaining power of the supplier and worries that the supplier might use its bargaining strength to demand higher prices.

Thus, the mutual dependency that outsourcing would create makes Ford nervous and scares away potential suppliers. The problem here is lack of trust. Neither party completely trusts the other to play fair. Consequently, Ford might reason that the only safe way to get the new fuel injection systems is to manufacture them itself. It may be unable to persuade any independent supplier to manufacture them. Thus, Ford decides to make rather than buy.

In general, we can predict that when substantial investments in specialized assets are required to manufacture a component, the firm will prefer to make the component internally rather than contract it out to a supplier. Substantial empirical evidence supports this prediction.[21]

Protecting Proprietary Product Technology

Proprietary product technology is unique to a firm. If it enables the firm to produce a product containing superior features, proprietary technology can give the firm a competitive advantage. The firm would not want competitors to get this technology. If the firm outsources the production of entire products or components containing proprietary technology, it runs the risk that those suppliers will expropriate the technology for their own use or that they will sell it to the firm's competitors. Thus, to maintain control over its technology, the firm might prefer to make such products or component parts in-house. An example of a firm that has made such decisions is given in the Management Focus, next page, which looks at make-or-buy decisions at Boeing. While Boeing has decided to outsource a number of important components that go toward the production of an aircraft, it has explicitly decided not to outsource the manufacture of cockpits because it believes that doing so would give away key technology to potential competitors.

Improving Scheduling

Another argument for producing all or part of a product in-house is that production cost savings result because it makes planning, coordination, and scheduling of adjacent processes easier.[22] This is particularly important in firms with just-in-time inventory systems (discussed later in the chapter). In the 1920s, for example, Ford profited from tight coordination and scheduling made possible by backward vertical integration into steel foundries, iron ore shipping, and mining. Deliveries at Ford's foundries on the Great Lakes were coordinated so well that ore was turned into engine blocks within 24 hours. This substantially reduced Ford's production costs by eliminating the need to hold excessive ore inventories.

For international businesses that source worldwide, scheduling problems can be exacerbated by the time and distance between the firm and its suppliers. This is true whether the firms use their own subunits as suppliers or use independent suppliers. However, ownership of upstream production facilities is not the issue here. By using information technology, firms can attain tight coordination between different stages in the production process.

THE ADVANTAGES OF BUY

Buying component parts, or an entire product, from independent suppliers can give the firm greater flexibility, can help drive down the firm's cost structure, and may help the firm capture orders from international customers.

Strategic Flexibility

The great advantage of buying component parts, or even an entire product, from independent suppliers is that the firm can maintain its flexibility, switching orders between suppliers as circumstances dictate. This is particularly important internationally, where changes in exchange rates and trade barriers can alter the attractiveness of supply sources. One year Hong Kong might offer the lowest cost for a particular component, and the next year, Mexico may. Many firms source the same products from suppliers based in two countries, primarily as a hedge against adverse movements in factor costs, exchange rates, and the like. Li & Fung, which we discussed in the opening case, specializes in sourcing products from producers based in different countries, switching orders from nation to nation in order to get the best deal.

Management FOCUS

Outsourcing at the Boeing Company

The Boeing Company is one of the two premier manufacturers of commercial jet aircraft in the world, holding around half of the global market for large commercial jet aircraft. Despite its market share, over the last decade Boeing found it tough going. The company's problems are twofold. First, Boeing faces an aggressive competitor in Europe's Airbus Industrie. The dogfight between Boeing and Airbus for market share has enabled major airlines to play the two companies off against each other in an attempt to bargain down the prices for commercial jet aircraft. Second, the airline business is quite cyclical, and airlines sharply reduce orders for new aircraft when their own business is in a downturn. This occurred in the early 1990s and again after the events of September 11, 2001, hit the airline industry hard, resulting in slumping orders for Boeing and Airbus.

During downturns, some of which can be lengthy, intense price competition often occurs between Airbus and Boeing as they struggle to maintain market share and order volume in the face of falling demand. Given these pricing pressures, the only way that Boeing can maintain its profitability is to reduce its own manufacturing costs. With this in mind, Boeing is constantly studying make-or-buy decisions. The objective is to identify activities that can be outsourced to subcontractors, both in the United States and abroad, to reduce production costs.

When making outsourcing decisions, Boeing applies a number of criteria. First, it looks at the basic economics. The central issue is whether an activity could be performed more cost-effectively by an outside manufacturer or by Boeing. Second, Boeing considers the strategic risk associated with outsourcing an activity. Boeing has decided it will not outsource any activity deemed to be part of its long-term competitive advantage, particularly design work and final integration and assembly. Third, Boeing looks at the operational risk associated with outsourcing an activity. The basic objective is to make sure Boeing does not become too dependent on a single outside supplier for critical components. Boeing's philosophy is to hedge operational risk by purchasing from two or more suppliers. Finally, Boeing considers whether it makes sense to outsource certain activities to a supplier in a given country to help secure orders for commercial jet aircraft from that country. This practice is known as *offsetting,* and it is common in many industries. For example, Boeing decided to outsource the production of certain components to China. This decision was influenced by forecasts suggesting that the Chinese will purchase more than $100 billion worth of commercial jets over the next 20 years. Boeing's hope is that pushing some subcontracting work China's way will help Boeing gain a larger share of this market than its global competitor, Airbus.

By 2005, Boeing was outsourcing around two-thirds of the work involved in building a commercial jet aircraft, up from one-half a decade earlier, with companies in Japan, Italy, and elsewhere shipping fuselage sections or even entire wings to Boeing. For its part, Boeing has decided to focus its efforts on design, final manufacturing integration and assembly, and marketing and sales. Every other activity can be potentially outsourced. Boeing will outsource substantially more work than ever when making its latest jet, the 787, a "super-efficient" wide-body jet scheduled for market introduction in 2008. Subcontractors in Japan, Australia, and Canada will supply much of the wing and fuselage, the passenger doors and landing gear will come from France, the cargo doors from Sweden, the horizontal stabilizer from Italy, and the wing tips from South Korea.

Sources: D. Gates, "Boeing Buzzes about 'Source' of Work," *Seattle Times,* March 9, 2003, p. A1; S. Wilhelm, "Tough Contest Ahead over 787," *Puget Sound Business Journal,* April 11, 2002, p. 50; M. Tatge, "Global Gamble," *Forbes,* April 17, 2006, pp. 78(79; and interviews between Charles Hill and senior management personnel at Boeing.

Sourcing products from independent suppliers can also be advantageous when the optimal location for manufacturing a product is beset by political risks. Under such circumstances, foreign direct investment to establish a component manufacturing operation in that country would expose the firm to political risks. The firm can avoid many of these risks by buying from an independent supplier in that country, thereby maintaining the flexibility to switch sourcing to another country if a war, revolution, or other political change alters that country's attractiveness as a supply source.

However, maintaining strategic flexibility has its downside. If a supplier perceives the firm will change suppliers in response to changes in exchange rates, trade barriers, or general political circumstances, that supplier might not be willing to make investments in specialized plants and equipment that would ultimately benefit the firm.

Lower Costs Although making a product or component part in-house—vertical integration—is often undertaken to lower costs, it may have the opposite effect. When this is the case, outsourcing may lower the firm's cost structure. Making all or part of a product in-house increases an organization's scope, and the resulting increase in organizational complexity can raise a firm's cost structure. There are three reasons for this.

First, the greater the number of subunits in an organization, the more problems coordinating and controlling those units. Coordinating and controlling subunits require top management to process large amounts of information about subunit activities. The greater the number of subunits, the more information top management must process and the harder it is to do well. Theoretically, when the firm becomes involved in too many activities, management at headquarters will be unable to effectively control all of them, and the resulting inefficiencies will more than offset any advantages derived from vertical integration.[23] This can be particularly serious in an international business, where the problem of controlling subunits is exacerbated by distance and differences in time, language, and culture.

Second, the firm that vertically integrates into component part manufacture may find that because its internal suppliers have a captive customer in the firm, they lack an incentive to reduce costs. The fact that they do not have to compete for orders with other suppliers may result in high operating costs. The managers of the supply operation may be tempted to pass on cost increases to other parts of the firm in the form of higher transfer prices rather than looking for ways to reduce those costs.

Third, vertically integrated firms have to determine appropriate prices for goods transferred to subunits within the firm. This is a challenge in any firm, but it is even more complex in international businesses. Different tax regimes, exchange rate movements, and headquarters' ignorance about local conditions all increase the complexity of transfer pricing decisions. This complexity enhances internal suppliers' ability to manipulate transfer prices to their advantage, passing cost increases downstream rather than looking for ways to reduce costs.

The firm that buys its components from independent suppliers can avoid all these problems and the associated costs. The firm that sources from independent suppliers has fewer subunits to control. The incentive problems that occur with internal suppliers do not arise when the firm uses independent suppliers. Independent suppliers know they must continue to be efficient if they are to win business from the firm. Also, because independent suppliers' prices are set by market forces, the transfer pricing problem does not exist. In sum, the bureaucratic inefficiencies and resulting costs that can arise when firms vertically integrate backward and produce their own components are avoided by buying component parts from independent suppliers.

Offsets Another reason for outsourcing some manufacturing to independent suppliers based in other countries is that it may help the firm capture more orders from that country. As noted in the Management Focus on Boeing, offsets are common in the commercial aerospace industry. For example, before Air India places a large order with Boeing, the Indian government might ask Boeing to push some subcontracting work toward Indian manufacturers. This is not unusual in international business. Representatives of the U.S. government have repeatedly urged Japanese automobile companies to purchase more component parts from U.S. suppliers to partially offset the large volume of automobile exports from Japan to the United States.

TRADE-OFFS Clearly, there are trade-offs in make-or-buy decisions. The benefits of making all or part of a product in-house seem to be greatest when highly specialized assets are involved, when vertical integration is necessary for protecting proprietary technology, or when the firm is simply more efficient than external suppliers at performing a particular activity. When these conditions are not present, the risk of strategic inflexibility and organizational problems suggest it may be better to contract out some or all production to independent suppliers. Because issues of strategic flexibility and organizational control loom even larger for international businesses than purely domestic ones, an international business should be particularly wary of vertical integration into component part manufacture. In addition, some outsourcing in the form of offsets may help a firm gain larger orders in the future.

STRATEGIC ALLIANCES WITH SUPPLIERS Several international businesses have tried to reap some benefits of vertical integration without the associated organizational problems by entering into strategic alliances with essential suppliers. For example, there is an alliance between Kodak and Canon, under which Canon builds photocopiers for sale by Kodak; an alliance between Apple and Sony, under which Sony builds laptop computers for Apple; and an alliance between Microsoft and Flextronics, under which Flextronics builds the Xbox for Microsoft. By these alliances, Kodak, Apple, and Microsoft have committed themselves to long-term relationships with these suppliers, which have encouraged the suppliers to undertake specialized investments. Strategic alliances build trust between the firm and its suppliers. Trust is built when a firm makes a credible commitment to continue purchasing from a supplier on reasonable terms. For example, the firm may invest money in a supplier—perhaps by taking a minority shareholding—to signal its intention to build a productive, mutually beneficial long-term relationship.

This kind of arrangement between the firm and its parts suppliers was pioneered in Japan by large auto companies such as Toyota. Many Japanese automakers have cooperative relationships with their suppliers that go back decades. In these relationships, the auto companies and their suppliers collaborate on ways to increase value added by, for example, implementing just-in-time inventory systems or cooperating in the design of component parts to improve quality and reduce assembly costs. These relationships have been formalized when the auto firms acquired minority shareholdings in many of their essential suppliers to symbolize their desire for long-term cooperative relationships with them. At the same time, the relationship between the firm and each essential supplier remains market mediated and terminable if the supplier fails to perform. By pursuing such a strategy, the Japanese automakers capture many of the benefits of vertical integration, particularly those arising from investments in specialized assets, without suffering the organizational problems that come with formal vertical integration. The parts suppliers also benefit from these relationships because they grow with the firm they supply and share in its success.[24]

In general, the trends toward just-in-time inventory systems (JIT), computer-aided design (CAD), and computer-aided manufacturing (CAM) seem to have increased pressures for firms to establish long-term relationships with their suppliers. JIT, CAD, and CAM systems all rely on close links between firms and their suppliers supported by substantial specialized investment in equipment and information systems hardware. To get a supplier to agree to adopt such systems, a firm must make a credible commitment to an enduring relationship with the supplier—it must build trust with the supplier. It can do this within the framework of a strategic alliance.

Alliances are not all good. Like formal vertical integration, a firm that enters long-term alliances may limit its strategic flexibility by the commitments it makes to its alliance partners. As we saw in Chapter 11 when we considered alliances between competitors, a firm that allies itself with another firm risks giving away key technological know-how to a potential competitor.

Managing a Global Supply Chain

LEARNING OBJECTIVE 4
Identify the factors that influence a firm's decision of whether to source supplies from within the company or from foreign suppliers.

Logistics encompasses the activities necessary to get materials from suppliers to a manufacturing facility, through the manufacturing process, and out through a distribution system to the end user.[25] In the international business, the logistics function manages the global supply chain. The twin objectives of logistics are to manage a firm's global supply chain at the lowest possible cost and in a way that best serves customer needs, thereby lowering the costs of value creation and helping the firm establish a competitive advantage through superior customer service.

The potential for reducing costs through more efficient logistics is enormous. For the typical manufacturing enterprise, material costs account for between 50 and 70 percent of revenues, depending on the industry. Even a small reduction in these costs can have a substantial impact on profitability. According to one estimate, for a firm with revenues of $1 million, a return on investment rate of 5 percent, and materials costs that are 50 percent of sales revenues, a $15,000 increase in total profits could be achieved either by increasing sales revenues 30 percent or by reducing materials costs by 3 percent.[26] In a saturated market, it would be much easier to reduce materials costs by 3 percent than to increase sales revenues by 30 percent. See the Another Perspective below for more details.

THE ROLE OF JUST-IN-TIME INVENTORY Pioneered by Japanese firms during the 1950s and 60s, just-in-time inventory systems now play a major role in most manufacturing firms. The basic philosophy behind **just-in-time (JIT) systems** is to economize on inventory holding costs by having materials arrive at a manufacturing plant just in time to enter the production process and not before. The major cost saving comes from speeding up inventory turnover. This reduces inventory holding costs, such as warehousing and storage costs. It means the company can reduce the amount of working capital it needs to finance inventory, freeing capital for other uses or lowering the total capital requirements of the enterprise. Other things being equal, this will boost the company's profitability as measured by return on capital invested. It also means the company is less likely to have excess unsold inventory that it has to write off against earnings or price low to sell.

Just-in-Time (JIT) System
Logistics systems designed to deliver parts to a production process as they are needed, not before.

In addition to the cost benefits, JIT systems can also help firms improve product quality. Under a JIT system, parts enter the manufacturing process immediately; they are not warehoused. This allows defective inputs to be spotted right away. The problem can then be traced to the supply source and fixed before more defective parts are produced. Under a more traditional system, warehousing parts for weeks before they are used allows many defective parts to be produced before a problem is recognized.

The drawback of a JIT system is that it leaves a firm without a buffer stock of inventory. Although buffer stocks are expensive to store, they can help

Another Perspective

Logistics in the Service Industry: Global Account Management (GAM)

Firms have been learning how to better manage services on a global basis, too. Increasingly, multinational accounting firms are dealing with other multinational firms in a new way, using one supplier for all their accounting-related needs around the world. The traditional approach involved the development of market-specific relationships, so the same multinational client would have 5 to 20 individual accounting relationships, one in each major market for each company division. In the case of PepsiCo, for example, that would be five relationships in every market: five negotiations, five contracts, and so on. With GAM, there is one relationship that has a global span and one contract. Such logistics allow for more effective relationship management, a better sense of what the client needs, more product extension opportunities, and better pricing and economies.

a firm respond quickly to increases in demand and tide a firm over shortages brought about by disruption among suppliers. Such a disruption occurred after the September 11, 2001, attacks on the World Trade Center, when the subsequent shutdown of international air travel and shipping left many firms that relied upon globally dispersed suppliers and tightly managed JIT supply chains without a buffer stock of inventory. A less pronounced but similar situation occurred again in April 2003 when the outbreak of the pneumonia-like SARS virus in China resulted in the temporary shutdown of several plants operated by foreign companies and disrupted their global supply chains. Similarly, in late 2004, record imports into the United States left several major West Coast shipping ports clogged with too many ships from Asia that could not be unloaded fast enough, disrupting the finely tuned supply chains of several major U.S. enterprises.[27]

There are ways of reducing the risks associated with a global supply chain that operates on just-in-time principles. To reduce the risks associated with depending on one supplier for an important input, some firms source these inputs from several suppliers located in different countries. Although this does not help in the case of an event with global ramifications, such as September 11, 2001, it does help manage country-specific supply disruptions, which are more common.

THE ROLE OF INFORMATION TECHNOLOGY AND THE INTERNET Web-based information systems play a crucial role in modern materials management. By tracking component parts as they make their way across the globe toward an assembly plant, information systems enable a firm to optimize its production scheduling according to when components are expected to arrive. By locating component parts in the supply chain precisely, good information systems allow the firm to accelerate production when needed by pulling key components out of the regular supply chain and having them flown to the manufacturing plant.

Firms increasingly use electronic data interchange (EDI) to coordinate the flow of materials into manufacturing, through manufacturing, and out to customers. EDI systems require computer links between a firm, its suppliers, and its shippers. Sometimes customers also are integrated into the system. These electronic links are then used to place orders with suppliers, to register parts leaving a supplier, to track them as they travel toward a manufacturing plant, and to register their arrival. Suppliers typically use an EDI link to send invoices to the purchasing firm. One consequence of an EDI system is that suppliers, shippers, and the purchasing firm can communicate with each other with no time delay, which increases the flexibility and responsiveness of the whole global supply system. A second consequence is that much of the paperwork between suppliers, shippers, and the purchasing firm is eliminated. Good EDI systems can help a firm decentralize materials management decisions to the plant level by giving corporate-level managers the information they need for coordinating and controlling decentralized materials management groups.

Before the emergence of the Internet as a major communication medium, firms and their suppliers normally had to purchase expensive proprietary software solutions to implement EDI systems. The ubiquity of the Internet and the availability of Web-based applications have made most of these proprietary solutions obsolete. Less expensive Web-based systems that are much easier to install and manage now dominate the market for global supply chain management software. These systems are rapidly transforming the management of globally dispersed supply chains, allowing even small firms to achieve a much better balance between supply and demand, thereby reducing the inventory in their systems and reaping the associated economic benefits. With increasing numbers of firms adopting these systems, those that don't may find themselves at a significant competitive disadvantage.

Key Terms

production, p. 447
logistics, p. 447
total quality management (TQM), p. 449
Six Sigma, p. 449
ISO 9000, p. 450
minimum efficient scale, p. 453
flexible manufacturing technology (lean production), p. 453
mass customization, p. 454
flexible machine cells, p. 454
global learning, p. 458
make-or-buy decisions, p. 460
specialized asset, p. 461
just-in-time (JIT) systems, p. 466

Summary

This chapter explained how efficient production and logistics functions can improve an international business's competitive position by lowering the costs of value creation and by performing value-creation activities in such ways that customer service is enhanced and value added is maximized. We looked closely at three issues central to international production and logistics: where to produce, what to make and what to buy, and how to coordinate a globally dispersed manufacturing and supply system. The chapter made the following points:

1. The choice of an optimal production location must consider country factors, technological factors, and product factors.
2. Country factors include the influence of factor costs, political economy, and national culture on production costs, along with the presence of location externalities.
3. Technological factors include the fixed costs of setting up production facilities, the minimum efficient scale of production, and the availability of flexible manufacturing technologies that allow for mass customization.
4. Product factors include the value-to-weight ratio of the product and whether the product serves universal needs.
5. Location strategies either concentrate or decentralize manufacturing. The choice should be made in light of country, technological, and product factors. All location decisions involve trade-offs.
6. Foreign factories can improve their capabilities over time, and this can be of immense strategic benefit to the firm. Managers need to view foreign factories as potential centers of excellence and to encourage and foster attempts by local managers to upgrade factory capabilities.
7. An essential issue in many international businesses is determining which component parts should be manufactured in-house and which should be outsourced to independent suppliers.
8. Making components in-house facilitates investments in specialized assets and helps the firm protect its proprietary technology. It may also improve scheduling between adjacent stages in the value chain. In-house production also makes sense if the firm is an efficient, low-cost producer of a technology.
9. Buying components from independent suppliers facilitates strategic flexibility and helps the firm avoid the organizational problems associated with extensive vertical integration. Outsourcing might also be employed as part of an offset policy, which is designed to win more orders for the firm from a country by pushing some subcontracting work to that country.
10. Several firms have tried to attain the benefits of vertical integration and avoid its associated organizational problems by entering long-term strategic alliances with essential suppliers.
11. Although alliances with suppliers can give a firm the benefits of vertical integration without dispensing entirely with the benefits of a market relationship, alliances have drawbacks. The firm that enters a strategic alliance may find its strategic flexibility limited by commitments to alliance partners.
12. Logistics encompasses all the activities that move materials to a production facility,

through the production process, and out through a distribution system to the end user. The logistics function is complicated in an international business by distance, time, exchange rates, custom barriers, and other things.

13. Just-in-time systems generate major cost savings from reducing warehousing and inventory holding costs and from reducing the need to write off excess inventory. In addition, JIT systems help the firm spot defective parts and remove them from the manufacturing process quickly, thereby improving product quality.
14. Information technology, particularly Internet-based electronic data interchange, plays a major role in materials management. EDI facilitates the tracking of inputs, allows the firm to optimize its production schedule, lets the firm and its suppliers communicate in real time, and eliminates the flow of paperwork between a firm and its suppliers.

Critical Thinking and Discussion Questions

1. An electronics firm is considering how best to supply the world market for microprocessors used in consumer and industrial electronic products. A manufacturing plant costs about $500 million to construct and requires a highly skilled workforce. The total value of the world market for this product over the next 10 years is estimated to be between $10 billion and $15 billion. The tariffs prevailing in this industry are currently low. Should the firm adopt a concentrated or decentralized manufacturing strategy? What kind of location(s) should the firm favor for its plant(s)?
2. A chemical firm is considering how best to supply the world market for sulfuric acid. A manufacturing plant costs about $20 million to construct and requires a moderately skilled workforce. The total value of the world market for this product over the next 10 years is estimated to be between $20 billion and $30 billion. The tariffs prevailing in this industry are moderate. Should the firm favor concentrated manufacturing or decentralized manufacturing? What kind of location(s) should the firm seek for its plant(s)?
3. A firm must decide whether to make a component part in-house or to contract it out to an independent supplier. Manufacturing the part requires a nonrecoverable investment in specialized assets. The most efficient suppliers are located in countries with currencies that many foreign exchange analysts expect to appreciate substantially over the next decade. What are the pros and cons of (*a*) manufacturing the component in-house and (*b*) outsourcing manufacturing to an independent supplier? Which option would you recommend? Why?
4. Explain how an efficient logistics function can help an international business compete more effectively in the global marketplace.

http://globalEDGE.msu.edu globalEDGE Research Task

Use the globalEDGE site (http://globalEDGE.msu.edu/) to complete the following exercises:

1. The size of a country's seaports can be considered an informal measure of the level of production and logistics needed to direct goods and services to market. Using *Geohive*, a resource that provides global statistics, analyze charts supplying data on the world's largest seaports. Which countries are the most represented on this list? Which regions of the world are most represented? From your own knowledge and experience as well as your findings here, what can you infer about global trade?
2. *IndustryWeek* magazine ranks the world's largest manufacturing companies by sales revenue. Identify the largest Chinese manufacturing companies as provided in the most recent ranking. Which industries are represented by the Chinese companies in the ranking? How does this compare with the companies representing India and Malaysia?

Microsoft–Outsourcing Xbox Production

When Microsoft decided to enter the video game market with its Xbox gaming console it faced a crucial strategic decision: Should it manufacture the Xbox, or outsource manufacturing to a third party, and if so, whom? Although Microsoft is primarily known as a software company, it has long had a small but important hardware business selling computer mice, keyboards, and joysticks under the Microsoft brand name. However, Xbox was different. This was not a simple computer peripheral; it was a fully functional specialized computer, with multiple components, including microprocessors, memory chips, graphics chips, and an internal hard drive.

Microsoft quickly decided that it lacked the manufacturing and logistics capabilities to make the Xbox itself and manage a global supply chain. After reviewing potential suppliers, it decided to outsource assembly and significant logistics functions to Flextronics, a Singapore-based contract manufacturer. Flextronics has global sales in excess of $13 billion and more than 100,000 employees. In addition to Microsoft, customers include Dell, Ericsson Telecom AB, Hewlett-Packard, Siemens AG, Sony-Ericsson, and Xerox. The company manufactures products for these companies in 28 countries. Its largest concentration of activities is in China, where it has 35,000 employees.

Microsoft had already contracted out the manufacture of computer mice to Flextronics, so it knew something about how the company operated and was happy with the cost and quality of Flextronics products. In looking for a supplier, Microsoft wanted a partner that could manufacture the Xbox at a low cost, maintain very high product quality, respond quickly to shifts in demand, and share detailed information on production schedules, product quality, and inventory with Microsoft on a real-time basis. Flextronics seemed to fit the bill for a number of reasons.

First, Flextronics had been pursuing an "industrial park" strategy that enabled the company to tightly manage its own supply chain, reduce the chances of supply disruptions, and lower costs, which could then be passed on to Microsoft in the form of lower prices for the Xbox. Flextronics' industrial park strategy requires key suppliers to site their factories next to a Flextronics assembly plant at low-cost locations near customers' end markets. Flextronics has large industrial parks in Brazil, China, Hungary, Mexico, and Poland. In addition to a Flextronics factory, each park contains the manufacturers of printed circuit boards, components, cables, plastics, and metal parts needed for assembly of a product such as Xbox. The co-location of Flextronics and its suppliers at an industrial park minimizes logistics costs by facilitating just-in-time inventory systems and reducing transportation costs. Supply problems that might arise from a breakdown in globally dispersed supply chains—as occurred after September 11, 2001, and again in 2003 due to the SARS epidemic—are also minimized by the co-location.

Second, Flextronics' global presence enables the company to shift production from location to location as cost and demand conditions warrant, something that Microsoft wanted. Initially, the Xbox was produced in Hungary (for sale in Europe) and Mexico (for sale in North America and Asia). Within a year, however, Flextronics shifted production from Hungary to China, where labor costs were a fraction of those in Hungary. In 2003, it also moved Xbox production from Mexico to China, for the same reason. Today, all Xbox production is in China. Flextronics can execute production shifts very quickly—the company says within three weeks—since all of the relevant manufacturing data are stored in centralized information systems. Thus, if China proves to be a suboptimal location for Xbox production in the future, Flextronics can shift production elsewhere.

Third, using Web-based information systems, Flextronics and Microsoft have the ability to share information in real time with each other. Microsoft feeds information on demand conditions to Flextronics, which enables Flextronics to configure its own production schedules to minimize inventory and closely match supply with demand. In addition, Microsoft has access to real-time information from Flextronics regarding production schedules, inventory, and product quality. This is crucially important, because Microsoft handles the overall management of about 40 strategic suppliers for Xbox, including the manufacturers of microprocessors, graphics chips, hard drives, and flash memory (Flextronics handles the supply of commodity-like inputs, such as circuit boards and plastic molding). The information exchange between Microsoft and Flextronics ensures that production schedules between all of the players in the supply chain are tightly coordinated so that inventory is minimized, shortages are avoided, and demand and supply are balanced.

Finally, Microsoft trusted Flextronics. Microsoft had worked with the company for years, and there were strong personal relationships between employees of the two companies. This helped to cement the business transaction. To facilitate joint design, which is important for reducing manufacturing costs, some Microsoft people are located at the Flextronics U.S. operations center in San Jose, California, and some Flextronics people are located at Microsoft's headquarters in Redmond, Washington. The two companies had worked together on product design before, and Microsoft knew that could be replicated with the Xbox. Microsoft also believed that Flextronics could deliver production of Xbox on time, even though assembly of the product was far more complex than the assembly of a computer mouse.

Sources: J. Carborne, "Outsourcing the Xbox," *Purchasing,* August 15, 2002, pp. 22–25; H. B. Hayes, "Outsourcing Xbox Manufacturing," *Pharmaceutical Technology North America,* November 2002, pp. 88–91; "Weathering the Tech Storm," *BusinessWeek,* May 2, 2003, pp. 24–25; and Flextronics 10K Report 2003.

Case Discussion Questions

1. What is the strategic advantage to Microsoft of outsourcing Xbox production to Flextronics?
2. What are the risks associated with outsourcing to Flextronics? Has Microsoft mitigated these risks? Do you think Microsoft would be better off making the Xbox itself?
3. How does Flextronics' industrial park strategy enable the company to respond to national changes in relative factor costs?
4. How important are Web-based information systems to the relationship between Microsoft and Flextronics? What are the economic advantages of real-time information flows between Microsoft, Flextronics, and Flextronics' own subcontractors?

The McGraw-Hill Companies, Inc./John Flournoy, photographer/DIL

part 5 Competing in the Global Marketplace

LEARNING OBJECTIVES

1. Explain why it might make sense to vary the attributes of a product from country to country.
2. Articulate why and how a firm's distribution strategy might vary among countries.
3. Identify why and how advertising and promotional strategies might vary among countries.
4. Explain why and how a firm's pricing strategy might vary among countries.
5. Discuss how the globalization of the world economy is affecting new-product development within the international business firm.

chapter 15

Global Marketing and R&D

Levi Strauss Goes Local

opening case

It's been a tough few years for Levi Strauss, the iconic manufacturer of blue jeans. The company, whose 501 jeans became the global symbol of the baby boom generation and were sold in more than 100 countries, saw its sales drop from a peak of $7.1 billion in 1996 to just $4.0 billion in 2004. Fashion trends had moved on, its critics charged, and Levi Strauss, hamstrung by high costs and a stagnant product line, was looking more faded than a well-worn pair of 501s. Perhaps so, but 2005 and early 2006 bought signs that a turnaround was in progress. Sales increased for the first time in eight years, and after a string of losses the company started to register profits again in 2006.

There were three parts to this turnaround. First, there were cost reductions at home. Levi's closed its last remaining American factories and moved production offshore where jeans could be produced more cheaply. Second, the company broadened its product line, introducing the Levi's Signature brand that could be sold through lower-priced outlets in markets that were more competitive, including the core American market where Wal-Mart had driven down prices. Third, there was a decision in the late 1990s to give more responsibility to national managers, allowing them to better tailor the product offering and marketing mix to local conditions. Prior to this, Levi's had basically sold the same product worldwide, often using the same advertising message. The old strategy was designed to enable Levi's to realize economies of scale in production and advertising, but it wasn't working.

Under the new strategy, variations between national markets have become more pronounced. Jeans have been tailored to different body types. In Asian, shorter leg lengths are common, whereas in South Africa, more room is needed for the backside of women's jeans, so Levi's has customized the product offering to account for these physical differences. Then there are sociocultural differences: In Japan, tight-fitting black jeans are popular; in Islamic countries, women are discouraged from wearing tight-fitting jeans, so Levi's offerings in countries like Turkey are roomier. Climate also has an effect on product design. In northern Europe, standard weight jeans are sold, whereas in hotter countries lighter denim in used, along with brighter colors that are not washed out by the tropical sun.

Levi's ads, which used to be global, have also been tailored to regional differences. In Europe, the ads now talk about the cool fit. In Asia, they talk about the rebirth of an original. In the United States, the ads show real people who are themselves originals: ranchers, surfers, great musicians.

There are also differences in distribution channels and pricing strategy. In the fiercely competitive American market, prices are as low as $25 and Levi's are sold through mass-market discount retailers, such as Wal-Mart. In India, strong sales growth is being driven by Levi's low-priced Signature brand. In Spain, jeans are seen as higher fashion items and are being sold for $50 in higher-quality outlets. In the United Kingdom too, prices for 501s are much higher than in the United States, reflecting a more benign competitive environment.

This variation in marketing mix seems to be reaping dividends; although demand in the United States and Europe remains sluggish, growth in many other countries is strong. Turkey, South Korea, and South Africa all recorded growth rates in excess of 20 percent in the 2004–05 period. Looking forward, Levi's expects 60 percent of its growth to come from emerging markets.

Sources: "How Levi Strauss Rekindled the Allure of Brand America," *World Trade,* March 2005, p. 28; "Levi Strauss Walks with a Swagger into New Markets," *Africa News,* March 17, 2005; "Levi's Adaptable Standards," *Strategic Direction,* June 2005, pp. 14–16; and A. Benady, "Levi's Looks to the Bottom Line," *Financial Times,* February 15, 2005, p. 14.

Introduction

In the previous chapter, we looked at the roles of global production and logistics in an international business. In this chapter, we continue our focus on specific business functions by examining the roles of marketing and research and development (R&D) in an international business. We focus on how marketing and R&D can be performed so they will reduce the costs of value creation and add value by better serving customer needs.

In Chapter 11, we spoke of the tension existing in most international businesses between the needs to reduce costs and at the same time to respond to local conditions, which tends to raise costs. This tension continues to be a persistent theme in this chapter. A global marketing strategy that views the world's consumers as similar in their tastes and preferences is consistent with the mass production of a standardized output. By mass-producing a standardized output, the firm can realize substantial unit cost reductions from experience curve and other economies of scale. This is basically the strategy that Levi Strauss adopted through the late 1990s, but as the opening case makes clear, by then it was no longer working. Ignoring country differences in consumer tastes and preferences can lead to failure. Thus, an international business's marketing function needs to determine when product standardization is appropriate and when it is not, and to adjust the marketing strategy accordingly. Moreover, even if product standardization is appropriate, the way in which a product is positioned in a market, and the promotions and messages used to sell that product, may still have to be customized so that they resonate with local consumers. Similarly, the firm's R&D function needs to be able to develop globally standardized products when appropriate as well as products customized to local requirements when that makes most sense.[1]

We consider marketing and R&D within the same chapter because of their close relationship. A critical aspect of the marketing function is identifying gaps in the market so that the firm can develop new products to fill those gaps. Developing new products requires R&D—thus, the linkage between marketing and R&D. A firm should develop new products with market needs in mind, and only marketing can define those needs for R&D personnel. Also, only marketing can tell R&D whether to produce globally standardized or locally customized products. Research has long maintained that a major contributor to the success of new-product introductions is a close relationship between marketing and R&D.[2]

In this chapter, we begin by reviewing the debate on the globalization of markets. Then we discuss the issue of market segmentation. Next we look at four elements that constitute a firm's marketing mix: product attributes, distribution strategy, communication strategy, and pricing strategy. The **marketing mix** is the set of choices the firm offers to its targeted markets. Many firms vary their marketing mix from country to country, depending on differences in national culture, economic development, product standards, distribution channels, and so on. In the opening case, for example, we saw how Levi Strauss has adjusted its marketing mix from country to country, changing product design, distribution strategy, pricing, and promotion strategy to better match local conditions. In the case of Levi Strauss, varying the marketing mix to take local differences into account has been a good thing: The firm has stopped the erosion of its sales and has started to gain market share again.

Marketing Mix
Choices about product attributes, distribution strategies, communication strategies, and pricing strategies that a firm offers its targeted markets.

The chapter closes with a look at new-product development in an international business and at the implications of this for the organization of the firm's R&D function.

The Globalization of Markets and Brands

In a now-classic *Harvard Business Review* article, Theodore Levitt wrote lyrically about the globalization of world markets. Levitt's arguments have become something of a lightning rod in the debate about the extent of globalization. According to Levitt,

> A powerful force drives the world toward a converging commonalty, and that force is technology. It has proletarianized communication, transport, and travel. The result is a new commercial reality—the emergence of global markets for standardized consumer products on a previously unimagined scale of magnitude.
>
> Gone are accustomed differences in national or regional preferences. The globalization of markets is at hand. With that, the multinational commercial world nears its end, and so does the multinational corporation. The multinational corporation operates in a number of countries and adjusts its products and practices to each—at high relative costs. The global corporation operates with resolute consistency—at low relative cost—as if the entire world were a single entity; it sells the same thing in the same way everywhere.
>
> Commercially, nothing confirms this as much as the success of McDonald's from the Champs Élysées to the Ginza, of Coca-Cola in Bahrain and Pepsi-Cola in Moscow, and of rock music, Greek salad, Hollywood movies, Revlon cosmetics, Sony television, and Levi's jeans everywhere.

Ancient differences in national tastes or modes of doing business disappear. The commonalty of preference leads inescapably to the standardization of products, manufacturing, and the institutions of trade and commerce.[3]

This is eloquent and evocative writing, but is Levitt correct? The rise of global media phenomena from CNN to MTV, and the ability of such media to help shape a global culture, would seem to lend weight to Levitt's argument. If Levitt is correct, his argument has major implications for the marketing strategies pursued by international business. However, the consensus among academics is that Levitt overstates his case.[4] Although Levitt may have a point when it comes to many basic industrial products, such as steel, bulk chemicals, and semiconductor chips, globalization in the sense used by Levitt seems to be the exception rather than the rule in many consumer goods markets and industrial markets. Even a firm such as McDonald's, which Levitt holds up as the archetypal example of a consumer products firm that sells a standardized product worldwide, modifies its menu from country to country in light of local consumer preferences. In the Middle East, for example, McDonald's sells the McArabia, a chicken sandwich on Arabian style bread, and in France, the Croque McDo, a hot ham and cheese sandwich.[5] In addition, as we saw in the opening case, despite have a strong global brand, Levi's has had to adapt its marketing mix in order to succeed in foreign nations.

On the other hand, Levitt is probably correct to assert that modern transportation and zons technologies are facilitating a convergence of certain tastes and preferences among consumers in the more advanced countries of the world. The popularity of sushi in Los Angeles, hamburgers in Tokyo, hip-hop music, and global media phenomena such as MTV all support this. In the long run, such technological forces may lead to the evolution of a global culture. At present, however, the continuing persistence of cultural and economic differences between nations acts as a brake on any trend toward the standardization of consumer tastes and preferences across nations. Indeed, that may never occur. Some writers have argued that the rise of global culture doesn't mean that consumers share the same tastes and preferences.[6] See the Another Perspective at left. Rather, people in different nations, often with conflicting viewpoints, are increasingly participating in a shared "global" conversation, drawing upon shared symbols that include global brands from Nike and Kodak to Coca-Cola and Sony. But the way in which these brands are perceived, promoted, and used still varies from country to country, depending upon local differences in tastes and preferences. Furthermore, trade barriers and differences in product and technical standards also constrain a firm's ability to sell a standardized product to a global market using a standardized marketing strategy. We discuss the sources of these differences in subsequent sections when we look at how products must be altered from country to country. In short, Levitt's globally standardized markets seem a long way off in many industries.

Another Perspective

The British Tradition of Chocolate KitKat Bars and Afternoon Tea

The classic chocolate KitKat bar was invented back in 1935 by a York-based chocolate maker, Rowntree, and has been going very strong every since. It has become a British candy mainstay as the Brits typically enjoy a KitKat along with their daily afternoon tea. The candy's slogan, "Have a break today, have a KitKat," has almost become a British institution since it was introduced in 1957. Marketers estimate that one of the chocolate-covered wafers is eaten every 47 seconds in the United Kingdom!

No wonder the Brits took exception when Nestlé decided to extend its KitKat brand by introducing what many considered to be almost ridiculous new flavors and styles. The Brits didn't even take to the "Christmas pudding" or tiramisu flavors introduced during the winter holiday time. Consumers said the new wafer flavors were too strange and too sweet. Distributors began to discount the wafers and demand that Nestlé pay them for the difference. Candy competitors tried to get shopkeepers to take KitKats off the main candy counter and move them into discount bins. Sales of wafers in the United Kingdom plunged by 18 percent, or $253 million, in just two years (2004–06).

Nestlé's brand extension failed. It just proves international marketers shouldn't attempt to change some consumer preferences, especially when it comes to the British, who seem to love tradition and chocolates. Brits consume 19.4 pounds of chocolate per capita per year, compared with 11.6 for Americans, according to Caobisco, a European candy trade group. (Deborah Ball, "Flavor Experiment for KitKat Leaves Nestlé with a Bad Taste," *The Wall Street Journal*, July 6, 2006)

Market Segmentation

Market segmentation refers to identifying distinct groups of consumers whose purchasing behavior differs from others in important ways. Markets can be segmented in numerous ways: by geography, demography (sex, age, income, race, education level, etc.), sociocultural factors (social class, values, religion, lifestyle choices), and psychological factors (personality). Because different segments exhibit different patterns of purchasing behavior, firms often adjust their marketing mix from segment to segment. Thus, the precise design of a product, the pricing strategy, the distribution channels used, and the choice of communication strategy may all be varied from segment to segment. The goal is to optimize the fit between the purchasing behavior of consumers in a given segment and the marketing mix, thereby maximizing sales to that segment. Automobile companies, for example, use a different marketing mix to sell cars to different socioeconomic segments. Thus, Toyota uses its Lexus division to sell high-priced luxury cars to high-income consumers, while selling its entry-level models, such as the Toyota Corolla, to lower-income consumers. Similarly, personal computer manufacturers will offer different computer models, embodying different combinations of product attributes and price points, precisely to appeal to consumers from different market segments (e.g., business users and home users).

Market Segmentation
Identifying distinct groups of consumers whose purchasing behavior differs from others in important ways, based on criteria such as geography, demographics, sociocultural factors, and psychological factors.

When managers in an international business consider market segmentation in foreign countries, they need to be cognizant of two main issues: the differences between countries in the structure of market segments and the existence of segments that transcend national borders. The structure of market segments may differ significantly from country to country. An important market segment in a foreign country may have no parallel in the firm's home country, and vice versa. The firm may have to develop a unique marketing mix to appeal to the purchasing behavior of a certain segment in a given country. An example of such a market segment is given in the accompanying Management Focus on page 478, which looks at the African Brazilian market segment in Brazil, which as you will see is very different from the African American segment in the United States. In another example, a research project identified a segment of consumers in China in the 45-to-55 age range that has few parallels in other countries.[7] This group came of age

Youth around the world have responded to Quiksilver, a company whose products range from clothing to wet suits. Quiksilver uses similar marketing tactics regardless of where stores are located because the popularity of surfing and winter sports transcends international boundaries. *AP/Wide World Photos*

Management FOCUS

Marketing to Black Brazil

Brazil is home to the largest black population outside of Nigeria. Nearly half of the 160 million people in Brazil are of African or mixed race origin. Despite this, until recently businesses have made little effort to target this numerically large segment. Part of the reason is rooted in economics. Black Brazilians have historically been poorer than Brazilians of European origin and thus have not received the same attention as whites. But after a decade of relatively strong economic performance in Brazil, an emerging black middle class is beginning to command the attention of consumer product companies. To take advantage of this, companies such as Unilever have introduced a range of skin care products and cosmetics aimed at black Brazilians, and Brazil's largest toy company recently introduced a black Barbie-like doll, Susi Olodum, sales of which quickly caught up with sales of a similar white doll.

But there is more to the issue than simple economics. Unlike the United States, where a protracted history of racial discrimination gave birth to the civil rights movement, fostered black awareness, and produced an identifiable subculture in U.S. society, the history of blacks in Brazil has been very different. Although Brazil did not abolish slavery until 1888, racism in Brazil has historically been much subtler than in the United States. Brazil has never excluded blacks from voting or had a tradition of segregating the races. Historically, too, the government encouraged intermarriage between whites and blacks in order to "bleach" society. Partly due to this more benign history, Brazil has not had a black rights movement similar to that in the United States, and racial self-identification is much weaker. Surveys routinely find that African Brazilian consumers decline to categorize themselves as either black or white; instead they choose one of dozens of skin tones and see themselves as being part of a culture that transcends race.

This subtler racial dynamic has important implications for market segmentation and tailoring the marketing mix in Brazil. Unilever had to face this issue when launching a Vaseline Intensive Care lotion for black consumers in Brazil. The company learned in focus groups that for the product to resonate with nonwhite women, its promotions had to feature women of different skin tones, excluding neither whites nor blacks. The campaign Unilever devised features three women with different skin shades at a fitness center. The bottle says the lotion is for "tan and black skin," a description that could include many white women considering that much of the population lives near the beach. Unilever learned that the segment exists, but it is more difficult to define and requires more subtle marketing messages than the African American segment in the United States or middle-class segments in Africa.

Source: M. Jordan, "Marketers Discover Black Brazil," *The Wall Street Journal,* November 24, 2000, pp. A11, A14.

during China's Cultural Revolution in the late 1960s and early 1970s. This group's values have been shaped by their experiences during the Cultural Revolution. They tend to be highly sensitive to price and respond negatively to new products and most forms of marketing. Thus, firms doing business in China may need to customize their marketing mix to address the unique values and purchasing behavior of the group. The existence of such a segment constrains the ability of firms to standardize their global marketing strategy.

In contrast, the existence of market segments that transcend national borders clearly enhances the ability of an international business to view the global marketplace as a single entity and pursue a global strategy, selling a standardized product worldwide and using the same basic marketing mix to help position and sell that product in a variety of national markets. For a segment to transcend national borders, consumers in that segment must have some compelling similarities along important dimensions—such as age, values, lifestyle choices—and those similarities must translate into similar purchasing behavior. Although such segments clearly exist in certain industrial markets, they are somewhat rarer in consumer markets. One emerging global segment that is attracting the attention of international marketers of consumer goods is the so-called global youth segment. Global media are paving the way for a global youth segment. Evidence that such a segment exists comes from a study of the cultural attitudes and purchasing behavior of more than 6,500 teenagers in 26 countries.[8] The findings suggest that teens around the world are increasingly living parallel lives that share many common values. It follows that they are likely to purchase the same kind of consumer goods and for the same reasons.

Product Attributes

LEARNING OBJECTIVE 1
Explain why it might make sense to vary the attributes of a product from country to country.

A product can be viewed as a bundle of attributes.[9] For example, the attributes that make up a car include power, design, quality, performance, fuel consumption, and comfort; the attributes of a hamburger include taste, texture, and size; a hotel's attributes include atmosphere, quality, comfort, and service. Products sell well when their attributes match consumer needs (and when their prices are appropriate). BMW cars sell well to people who have high needs for luxury, quality, and performance, precisely because BMW builds those attributes into its cars. If consumer needs were the same the world over, a firm could simply sell the same product worldwide. However, consumer needs vary from country to country, depending on culture and the level of economic development. A firm's ability to sell the same product worldwide is further constrained by countries' differing product standards. In this section, we review each of these issues and discuss how they influence product attributes.

CULTURAL DIFFERENCES We discussed countries' cultural differences in Chapter 3. Countries differ along a whole range of dimensions, including social structure, language, religion, and education. These differences have important implications for marketing strategy. For example, hamburgers do not sell well in Islamic countries, where the consumption of ham is forbidden by Islamic law. The most important aspect of cultural differences is probably the impact of tradition. Tradition is particularly important in foodstuffs and beverages. For example, reflecting differences in traditional eating habits, the Findus frozen food division of Nestlé, the Swiss food giant, markets fish cakes and fish fingers in Great Britain, but beef bourguignon and coq au vin in France and vitéllo con funghi and braviola in Italy. In addition to its normal range of products, Coca-Cola in Japan markets Georgia, a cold coffee in a can, and Aquarius, a tonic drink, both of which appeal to traditional Japanese tastes.

For historical and idiosyncratic reasons, a range of other cultural differences exist between countries. For example, scent preferences differ from one country to another. SC Johnson, a manufacturer of waxes and polishes, encountered resistance to its lemon-scented Pledge furniture polish among older consumers in Japan. Careful market research revealed that the polish smelled similar to a latrine disinfectant used widely in Japan in the 1950s. Sales rose sharply after the scent was adjusted.[10] In another example, Cheetos, the bright orange and cheesy-tasting snack from PepsiCo's Frito-Lay unit, do not have a cheese taste in China. Chinese consumers generally do not like the taste of cheese because it has never been part of traditional cuisine and because many Chinese are lactose-intolerant.[11]

There is some evidence of the trends Levitt talked about. Tastes and preferences are becoming more cosmopolitan. Coffee is gaining ground against tea in Japan and Great Britain, while American-style frozen dinners have become popular in Europe (with some fine-tuning to local tastes). Taking advantage of these trends, Nestlé has found that it can market its instant coffee, spaghetti bolognese, and Lean Cuisine frozen dinners in essentially the same manner in both North America and Western Europe. However, there is no market for Lean Cuisine dinners in most of the rest of the world, and there may not be for years or decades. Although some cultural convergence has occurred, particularly among the advanced industrial nations of North America and Western Europe, Levitt's global culture characterized by standardized tastes and preferences is still a long way off.

ECONOMIC DEVELOPMENT Just as important as differences in culture are differences in the level of economic development. We discussed the extent of country differences in economic development in Chapter 2. Consumer behavior is influenced by the level of economic development of a country. Firms based in highly developed countries such as the United States tend to build a lot of extra performance attributes into their products. These extra attributes are not usually demanded by consumers in less developed nations, where the preference is for more basic products. Thus, cars sold in less developed nations typically lack many of the features found in developed nations, such as air-conditioning, power steering, power windows, radios, and cassette players. For most consumer durables, product reliability may be a more important attribute in less developed nations, where such a purchase may account for a major proportion of a consumer's income, than it is in advanced nations.

Contrary to Levitt's suggestions, consumers in the most developed countries are often not willing to sacrifice their preferred attributes for lower prices. Consumers in the most advanced countries often shun globally standardized products that have been developed with the lowest common denominator in mind. They are willing to pay more for products that have additional features and attributes customized to their tastes and preferences. For example, demand for top-of-the-line four-wheel-drive sport utility vehicles, such as Chrysler's Jeep, Ford's Explorer, and Toyota's Land Cruiser, is almost totally restricted to the United States. This is due to a combination of factors, including the high-income level of U.S. consumers, the country's vast distances, the relatively low cost of gasoline, and the culturally grounded "outdoor" theme of American life.

PRODUCT AND TECHNICAL STANDARDS Even with the forces that are creating some convergence of consumer tastes and preferences among advanced, industrialized nations, Levitt's vision of global markets may still be a long way off because of national differences in product and technological standards.

Differing government-mandated product standards can rule out mass production and marketing of a standardized product. Differences in technical standards also constrain the globalization of markets. Some of these differences result from idiosyncratic decisions made long ago, rather than from government actions, but their long-term effects are profound. For example, DVD equipment manufactured for sale in the United States will not play DVDs recorded on equipment manufactured for sale in Great Britain, Germany, and France (and vice versa). Different technical standards for television signal frequency emerged in the 1950s that require television and video equipment to be customized to prevailing standards. RCA stumbled in the 1970s when it failed to account for this in its marketing of TVs in Asia. Although several Asian countries adopted the U.S. standard, Singapore, Hong Kong, and Malaysia adopted the British standard. People who bought RCA TVs in those countries could receive a picture but no sound![12]

Distribution Strategy

LEARNING OBJECTIVE 2
Articulate why and how a firm's distribution strategy might vary among countries.

A critical element of a firm's marketing mix is its distribution strategy: the means it chooses for delivering the product to the consumer. The way the product is delivered is determined by the firm's entry strategy, discussed in Chapter 12. In this section, we examine a typical distribution system, discuss how its structure varies between countries, and look at how appropriate distribution strategies vary from country to country.

Figure 15.1 illustrates a typical distribution system consisting of a channel that includes a wholesale distributor and a retailer. If the firm manufactures its product in the particular country, it can sell directly to the consumer, to the retailer, or to the wholesaler. The same options are available to a firm that manufactures outside the country.

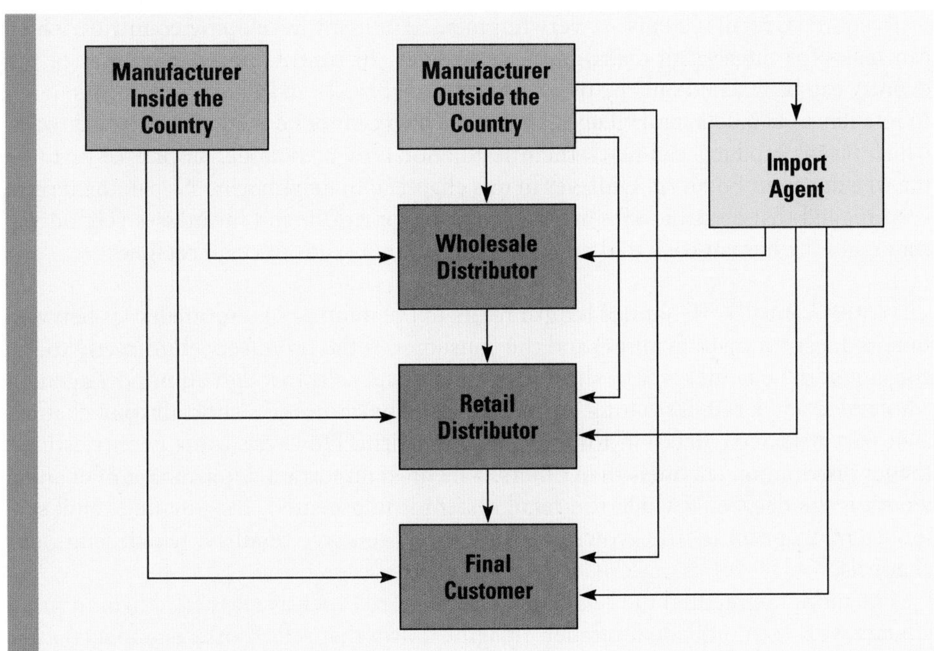

figure 15.1

A Typical Distribution System

Plus, this firm may decide to sell to an import agent, which then deals with the wholesale distributor, the retailer, or the consumer. Later in the chapter we will consider the factors that determine the firm's choice of channel.

DIFFERENCES BETWEEN COUNTRIES

The four main differences between distribution systems are retail concentration, channel length, channel exclusivity, and channel quality.

Retail Concentration

In some countries, the retail system is very concentrated, but it is fragmented in others. In a **concentrated retail system**, a few retailers supply most of the market. A **fragmented retail system** is one in which there are many retailers, no one of which has a major share of the market. Many of the differences in concentration are rooted in history and tradition. In the United States, the importance of the automobile and the relative youth of many urban areas have resulted in a retail system centered on large stores or shopping malls to which people can drive. This has facilitated system concentration. Japan, with a much greater population density and a large number of urban centers that grew up before the automobile, has a more fragmented retail system, with many small stores serving local neighborhoods and to which people frequently walk. In addition, the Japanese legal system protects small retailers. Small retailers can try to block the establishment of a large retail outlet by petitioning their local government.

Concentrated Retail System
One in which a few retailers supply most of the market.

Fragmented Retail System
One in which many retailers supply a market, with no one having a major share.

There is a tendency for greater retail concentration in developed countries. Three factors that contribute to this are the increases in car ownership, number of households with refrigerators and freezers, and number of two-income households. All these factors have changed shopping habits and facilitated the growth of large retail establishments sited away from traditional shopping areas. The last decade has seen consolidation in the global retail industry, with companies such as Wal-Mart and Carrefour attempting to become global retailers by acquiring retailers in different countries. This has increased retail concentration.

In contrast, retail systems are very fragmented in many developing countries, which can make for interesting distribution challenges. In rural China, large areas of the country can be reached only by traveling rutted dirt roads. In India, Unilever has to sell to retailers in 600,000 rural villages, many of which cannot be accessed via paved roads, which means products can reach their destination only by bullock, bicycle, or cart (see the Management Focus on Unilever in this chapter). In neighboring Nepal, the terrain is so rugged that even bicycles and carts are not practical, and businesses rely on yak trains and the human back to deliver products to thousands of small retailers.

Channel Length
The number of intermediaries between the producer (or manufacturer) and the consumer.

Channel Length

Channel length refers to the number of intermediaries between the producer (or manufacturer) and the consumer. If the producer sells directly to the consumer, the channel is very short. If the producer sells through an import agent, a wholesaler, and a retailer, a long channel exists. The choice of a short or long channel is in part a strategic decision for the producing firm. However, some countries have longer distribution channels than others. The most important determinant of channel length is the degree to which the retail system is fragmented. Fragmented retail systems tend to promote the growth of wholesalers to serve retailers, which lengthens channels.

The more fragmented the retail system, the more expensive it is for a firm to make contact with each individual retailer. Imagine a firm that sells toothpaste in a country where there are more than a million small retailers, as in rural India and China. To sell directly to the retailers, the firm would have to build a huge sales force. This would be very expensive, particularly since each sales call would yield a very small order. But suppose a few hundred wholesalers in the country supply retailers not only with toothpaste but also with all other personal care and household products. Because these wholesalers carry a wide range of products, they get bigger orders with each sales call, making it worthwhile for them to deal directly with the retailers. Accordingly, it makes economic sense for the firm to sell to the wholesalers and the wholesalers to deal with the retailers.

Because of such factors, countries with fragmented retail systems also tend to have long channels of distribution, sometimes with multiple layers. The classic example is Japan, where there are often two or three layers of wholesalers between the firm and retail outlets. In countries such as Great Britain, Germany, and the United States where the retail system is far more concentrated, channels are much shorter. When the retail sector is very concentrated, it makes sense for the firm to deal directly with retailers, cutting out wholesalers. A relatively small sales force is required to deal with a concentrated retail sector, and the orders generated from each sales call can be large. Such circumstances tend to prevail in the United States, where large food companies may sell directly to supermarkets rather than going through wholesale distributors.

The rapid development of the Internet in recent years has helped to shorten channel length. For example, the Seattle-based outdoor equipment retailer REI sells its products in Japan via a Japanese-language Web site, thereby eliminating the need for a retail presence on the ground in Japan, which obviously shortens the channel length between REI and its customers. However, there are definite drawbacks with such a strategy. In the case of REI, consumers cannot receive the same level of advice over the Web as in physical retail stores, where salespeople can help customers choose the right gear for their needs. So although REI benefits from a short channel in Japan, it may lose significant sales due to the lack of point-of-sale service.

Another factor that is shortening channel length in some counties is the entry of large discount superstores, such as Carrefour, Wal-Mart, and Tesco. The business model of these retailers is in part based upon the idea that in an attempt to lower prices, they cut out wholesalers and instead deal directly with manufacturers. Thus, when Wal-Mart entered Mexico, its policy of dealing directly with manufacturers, instead of buying merchandise through wholesalers, helped to shorten distribution channels in that nation. Similarly, Japan's historically long distribution channels are now being shortened by the rise of large retailers, some of them foreign owned, such as Toys "R" Us, and some of them indigenous enterprises that are imitating the American model, all of which are progressively cutting out wholesalers and dealing directly with manufacturers.

Exclusive Distribution Channel
A channel that outsiders find difficult to access.

Channel Exclusivity An **exclusive distribution channel** is one that is difficult for outsiders to access. For example, it is often difficult for a new firm to get access to shelf space in supermarkets. This occurs because retailers tend to prefer to carry the products of established manufacturers of foodstuffs with national reputations rather than gamble on the products of unknown firms. The exclusivity of a distribution system varies between countries. Japan's system is often held up as an example of a very exclusive system. In Japan, relationships between manufacturers, wholesalers, and retailers often go back decades. Many of these relationships are based on the understanding that distributors will not carry the products of competing firms. In return, the distributors are guaranteed an attractive markup by the manufacturer. As many U.S. and European manufacturers have learned, the close ties that result from this arrangement can make access to the Japanese market difficult. However, it is possible to break into the Japanese market with a new consumer product. Procter & Gamble did during the 1990s with its Joy brand of dish soap. P&G was able to overcome a tradition of exclusivity for two reasons. First, after a decade of lackluster economic performance, Japan is changing. In their search for profits, retailers are far more willing than they have been historically to violate the old norms of exclusivity. Second, P&G has been in Japan long enough and has a broad enough portfolio of consumer products to give it considerable leverage with distributors, enabling it to push new products out through the distribution channel.

Channel Quality
The expertise, competencies, and skills of established retailers in a nation, and their ability to sell and support the products of international businesses.

Channel Quality **Channel quality** refers to the expertise, competencies, and skills of established retailers in a nation, and their ability to sell and support the products of international businesses. Although the quality of retailers is good in most developed nations, in emerging markets and less developed nations from Russia to Indonesia, channel quality is variable at best. The lack of a high quality channel may impede market entry, particularly in the case of new or sophisticated products that require significant point of sale assistance and after-sales services and support. When channel quality is poor, an international business may have to devote considerable attention to upgrading the channel, for example, by providing extensive education and support to existing retailers, and in extreme cases, by establishing its own channel. Thus, after pioneering its Apple retail store concept in the United States, Apple is now opening up retail stores in several nations, such as the United Kingdom, in order to provide point-of-sales education, service, and support for its popular iPod and computer products. Apple believes that this strategy will help it to gain market share in these nations.

CHOOSING A DISTRIBUTION STRATEGY A choice of distribution strategy determines which channel the firm will use to reach potential consumers. Should the firm try to sell directly to the consumer or should it go through retailers; should it go through a wholesaler; should it use an import agent; or should it invest in establishing its own channel? The optimal strategy is determined by the relative costs and benefits of each alternative, which vary from country to country, depending on the four factors we have just discussed: retail concentration, channel length, channel exclusivity, and channel quality.

Because each intermediary in a channel adds its own markup to the products, there is generally a critical link between channel length, the final selling price, and the firm's profit margin. The longer a channel, the greater is the aggregate markup, and the higher the price that consumers are charged for the final product. To ensure that prices do not get too high as a result of markups by multiple intermediaries, a firm might be forced to operate with lower profit margins. Thus, if price is an important competitive weapon, and if the firm does not want to see its profit margins squeezed, other things being equal, the firm would prefer to use a shorter channel.

However, the benefits of using a longer channel may outweigh these drawbacks. As we have seen, one benefit of a longer channel is that it cuts selling costs when the retail sector is very fragmented. Thus, it makes sense for an international business to use longer channels in countries where the retail sector is fragmented and shorter channels in countries where the retail sector is concentrated. Another benefit of using a longer channel is market access—the ability to enter an exclusive channel. Import agents may have long-term relationships with wholesalers, retailers, or important consumers and thus be better able to win orders and get access to a distribution system. Similarly, wholesalers may have long-standing relationships with retailers and be better able to persuade them to carry the firm's product than the firm itself would.

Import agents are not limited to independent trading houses; any firm with a strong local reputation could serve as well. For example, to break down channel exclusivity and gain greater access to the Japanese market, Apple Computer signed distribution agreements with five large Japanese firms, including business equipment giant Brother Industries, stationery leader Kokuyo, Mitsubishi, Sharp, and Minolta. These firms use their own long-established distribution relationships with consumers, retailers, and wholesalers to push Apple computers through the Japanese distribution system. As a result, Apple's share of the Japanese market increased from less than 1 percent to 13 percent in the four years following the signing of the agreements.[13]

If such an arrangement is not possible, the firm might want to consider other, less traditional alternatives to gaining market access. Frustrated by channel exclusivity in Japan, some foreign manufacturers of consumer goods have attempted to sell directly to Japanese consumers using direct mail and catalogs. REI had trouble persuading Japanese wholesalers and retailers to carry its products, so it began a direct-mail campaign and then a Web-based strategy to enter Japan that is proving successful.

Finally, if channel quality is poor, a firm should consider what steps it could take to upgrade the quality of the channel, including establishing its own distribution channel.

Communication Strategy

LEARNING OBJECTIVE 3
Identify why and how advertising and promotional strategies might vary among countries.

Another critical element in the marketing mix is communicating the attributes of the product to prospective customers. A number of communication channels are available to a firm, including direct selling, sales promotion, direct marketing, and advertising. A firm's communication strategy is partly defined by its choice of channel. Some firms rely primarily on direct selling, others on point-of-sale promotions or direct marketing, and others on mass advertising; still others use several channels simultaneously to communicate their message to prospective customers. In this section, we will look first at the barriers to international communication. Then we will survey the various factors that determine which communication strategy is most appropriate in a particular country. After that we discuss global advertising.

BARRIERS TO INTERNATIONAL COMMUNICATION International communication occurs whenever a firm uses a marketing message to sell its products in another country. The effectiveness of a firm's international communication can be jeopardized by three potentially critical variables: cultural barriers, source effects, and noise levels.

Cultural Barriers Cultural barriers can make it difficult to communicate messages across cultures. We discussed some sources and consequences of cultural differences between nations in Chapter 3 and in the previous section of this chapter. Because of cultural differences, a message that means one thing in one country may mean something quite different in another. For example, when Procter & Gamble promoted its Camay soap in Japan in the 1980s it ran into unexpected trouble. In a TV commercial, a Japanese man walked into the bathroom while his wife was bathing. The woman began telling her husband all about her new soap, but the husband, stroking her shoulder, hinted that suds were not on his mind. This ad had been popular in Europe, but it flopped in Japan because it is considered bad manners there for a man to intrude on his wife.[14]

Benetton, the Italian clothing manufacturer and retailer, is another firm that has run into cultural problems with its advertising. The company launched a worldwide advertising campaign with the theme "United Colors of Benetton" that had won awards in France. One of its ads featured a black woman breast-feeding a white baby, and another one showed a black man and a white man handcuffed together. Benetton was surprised when the ads were attacked by U.S. civil rights groups for promoting white racial domination. Benetton withdrew its ads and fired its advertising agency, Eldorado of France.

The best way for a firm to overcome cultural barriers is to develop cross-cultural literacy (see Chapter 3). In addition, it should use local input, such as a local advertising agency, in developing its marketing message. If the firm uses direct selling rather than advertising to communicate its message, it should develop a local sales force whenever possible. Cultural differences limit a firm's ability to use the same marketing message and selling approach worldwide. What works well in one country may be offensive in another. The Management Focus on page 487, which profiles Procter & Gamble's strategy for selling Tampax tampons internationally, demonstrates how cultural factors can influence the choice of communication strategy.

You may not be able to recognize its products on the street, but Benetton has become famous for controversial advertising, which countries frequently refuse to run because it is deemed offensive or inappropriate. *The McGraw-Hill Companies, Inc./Andrew Resek, photographer/DIL*

Another Perspective

Language and Symbol Complexity

Consider this international complexity in interpretation of colors, numbers, and symbols:

White: Symbol for mourning or death in Far East; happiness, purity in the United States.

Purple: Associated with death in many Latin American countries.

Blue: Femininity in Holland; masculinity in Sweden and the United States.

Red: Unlucky or negative in Chad, Nigeria, and Germany; positive in Denmark, Romania, and Argentina. Brides wear red in China, but it is a masculine color in the United Kingdom and France.

Yellow flowers: Sign of death in Mexico; infidelity in France.

7: Unlucky number in Singapore, Kenya, and Ghana; lucky in India, Morocco, Czechoslovakia, Nicaragua, and the United States.

Owl: Wisdom in the United States; bad luck in India.

Deer: Speed, grace in the United States; homosexuality in Brazil.

(J. Cohen, "The Search for Universal Symbols," *Journal of International Consumer Marketing* 3–4 (1996), pp. 187–210)

Source and Country of Origin Effects

Source effects occur when the receiver of the message (the potential consumer in this case) evaluates the message on the basis of status or image of the sender. Source effects can be damaging for an international business when potential consumers in a target country have a bias against foreign firms. For example, a wave of "Japan bashing" swept the United States in the early 1990s. Worried that U.S. consumers might view its products negatively, Honda responded by creating ads that emphasized the U.S. content of its cars to show how "American" the company had become.

Many international businesses try to counter negative source effects by deemphasizing their foreign origins. When the French antiglobalization protestor Jose Bove was hailed as a hero by some in France for razing a partly built McDonald's in 1999, the French franchisee of McDonald's responded with an ad depicting a fat, ignorant Americans who could not understand why McDonald's France used locally produced food that wasn't genetically modified. The edgy ad worked, and McDonald's French operations are now among the most robust in the company's global network.[15] Similarly, when British Petroleum acquired Mobil Oil's extensive network of U.S. gas stations, it changed its name to BP, diverting attention away from the fact that one of the biggest operators of gas stations in the United States is a British firm.

Source Effects When the receiver of the message evaluates the message on the basis of status or image of the sender.

A subset of source effects is referred to as **country of origin effects,** or the extent to which the place of manufacturing influences product evaluations. Research suggests that the consumer may use country of origin as a cue when evaluating a product, particularly if he or she lacks more detailed knowledge of the product. For example, one study found that Japanese consumers tended to rate Japanese products more favorably than U.S. products across multiple dimensions, even when independent analysis showed that they were actually inferior.[16] When a negative country of origin effect exists, an international business may have to work hard to counteract this effect by, for example, using promotional messages that stress the positive performance attributes of its product. Thus, the South Korean automobile company Hyundai tried to overcome negative perceptions about the quality of its vehicle in the United States by running advertisements that favorably compare the company's cars to more prestigious brands.

Country of Origin Effects The extent to which the place of a product's manufacturing influences its evaluations in the market.

Source effects and country of origin effects are not always negative. French wine, Italian clothes, and German luxury cars benefit from nearly universal positive source effects. In such cases, it may pay a firm to emphasize its foreign origins. In Japan, for example, there is strong demand for high-quality foreign goods, particularly those from Europe. It has become chic to carry a Gucci handbag, sport a Rolex watch, drink expensive French wine, and drive a BMW.

Noise The amount of other messages competing for a potential consumer's attention.

Noise Levels

Noise tends to reduce the probability of effective communication. **Noise** refers to the amount of other messages competing for a potential consumer's attention, and this too varies across countries. In highly developed countries such as

Management FOCUS

Overcoming Cultural Barriers to Selling Tampons

In 1997, Procter & Gamble purchased Tambrands, the manufacturer of Tampax tampons, for $1.87 billion. P&G's goal was to make Tampax a global brand. At the time of the acquisition, tampons were used by some 70 percent of women in North America and a significant majority in northwestern Europe. However, usage elsewhere was very low, ranging from single digits in countries such as Spain and Japan, to less than 2 percent throughout Latin America. P&G believed that it could use its global marketing skills and distribution networks to grow the product, particularly in underserved markets such as Latin America and southern Europe. But P&G has found it tough going.

A big part of the problem has been religious and cultural taboos. A persistent myth in many countries holds that if a girl uses a tampon, she might lose her virginity. This concern seems to crop up most often in countries that are predominantly Catholic. Although the Roman Catholic Church states it has no official position on tampons, some priests have spoken out against the product, associating it with birth control and sexual activities that are prohibited by the church! Women must also understand their bodies to use a tampon. P&G is finding that in countries where school health education is limited, that understanding is difficult to foster.

After failed attempts to market the product in India and Brazil using conventional marketing strategies, such as print media advertising and retail distribution, P&G has decided to change to an approach based on direct selling and relationship marketing. It tested this model in Monterrey, Mexico. A centerpiece of the strategy has been the hiring of a sales force of counselors. The counselors are young women. They must first promise to become regular tampon users. Most have never tried a tampon. P&G trains each woman and observes her early classes. After passing a written test, the women are equipped with anatomy charts, a blue foam model of a woman's reproductive system, and a box of samples. In navy pantsuits or a doctor's white coat embroidered with the Tampax logo, the counselors are dispatched to speak in stores, schools, gyms, and anywhere women gather. The counselors talk to about 60 women a day, explaining how the product works with the aid of flip charts. About one-third of those women end up buying a product.

The counselors also use these meetings as an opportunity to recruit young women to host gatherings in their homes. Modeled on Tupperware parties, about 20 women typically attend these "bonding sessions" where the counselor explains the product and how it is used, answers questions, and dispenses free samples. About 40 percent of women who attend these gatherings go on to host one.

P&G also found that about half of all doctors in Monterrey thought that tampons were bad for women. The company believes that this is based on ignorance; most of the doctors are men and they simply do not understand how the product works. To combat this, P&G used its sales force, which already called on doctors to sell products such as Pepto-Bismol and Metamucil, to give away tampons and explain how the product works. As a result, P&G believes it has reduced resistance among doctors to less than 10 percent.

Will this selling strategy work? The early signs were encouraging. In just a few months, sales of tampons grew from 2 percent to 4 percent of the total feminine hygiene market in Monterrey, and sales of the Tampax brand tripled. On the basis of these results, P&G decided to launch its first full campaign in Venezuela in early 2001, with several other Latin American countries following soon after.

Sources: E. Nelson and M. Jordan, "Seeking New Markets for Tampons, P&G Faces Cultural Barriers," *The Wall Street Journal*, December 8, 2000, pp. A1, A8.

the United States, noise is extremely high. Fewer firms vie for the attention of prospective customers in developing countries, thus the noise level is lower.

Push Strategy
Emphasizes personal selling to potential customers rather than mass media advertising.

PUSH VERSUS PULL STRATEGIES The main decision with regard to communications strategy is the choice between a push strategy and a pull strategy. A **push strategy** emphasizes personal selling rather than mass media advertising in the promotional mix. Although effective as a promotional tool, personal selling requires intensive use of a sales force and is relatively costly. A **pull strategy** depends more on mass media advertising to communicate the marketing message to potential consumers.

Pull Strategy
Depends more on mass media advertising to communicate the marketing message to potential customers.

Although some firms employ only a pull strategy and others only a push strategy, still other firms combine direct selling with mass advertising to maximize communication effectiveness. Factors that determine the relative attractiveness of push and pull strategies include product type relative to consumer sophistication, channel length, and media availability.

Product Type and Consumer Sophistication Firms in consumer goods industries that are trying to sell to a large segment of the market generally favor a pull strategy. Mass communication has cost advantages for such firms, thus they rarely use direct selling. Exceptions can be found in poorer nations with low literacy levels, where direct selling may be the only way to reach consumers (see the Management Focus on Unilever on the next page). Firms that sell industrial products or other complex products favor a push strategy. Direct selling allows the firm to educate potential consumers about the features of the product. This may not be necessary in advanced nations where a complex product has been in use for some time, where the product's attributes are well understood, where consumers are sophisticated, and where high-quality channels exist that can provide point-of-sale assistance. However, customer education may be important when consumers have less sophistication toward the product, which can be the case in developing nations or in advanced nations when a new complex product is being introduced, or where high-quality channels are absent or scarce.

Channel Length The longer the distribution channel, the more intermediaries there are that must be persuaded to carry the product for it to reach the consumer. This can lead to inertia in the channel, which can make entry difficult. Using direct selling to push a product through many layers of a distribution channel can be expensive. In such circumstances, a firm may try to pull its product through the channels by using mass advertising to create consumer demand—once demand is created, intermediaries will feel obliged to carry the product.

In Japan, products often pass through two, three, or even four wholesalers before they reach the final retail outlet. This can make it difficult for foreign firms to break into the Japanese market. Not only must the foreign firm persuade a Japanese retailer to carry its product, but it may also have to persuade every intermediary in the chain to carry the product. Mass advertising may be one way to break down channel resistance in such circumstances. However, in countries such as India, which has a very long distribution channel to serve its massive rural population, mass advertising may not work because of low literacy levels, in which case, the firm may need to fall back on direct selling or rely on the good will of distributors (see the Management Focus on Unilever).

Media Availability A pull strategy relies on access to advertising media. In the United States, a large number of media are available, including print media (newspapers and magazines), broadcasting media (television and radio), and the Internet. The rise of cable television in the United States has facilitated extremely focused advertising (e.g., MTV for teens and young adults, Lifetime for women, ESPN for sports enthusiasts). The same is true of the Internet, with different Web sites attracting different kinds of users. While this level of media sophistication is found in some other developed countries, it is not universal. Even many advanced nations have far fewer electronic media available for advertising than the United States. In Scandinavia, for example, no commercial television or radio stations existed until recently; all electronic media were state owned and carried no commercials, although this has now changed with the advent of satellite television deregulation.

Management FOCUS

Unilever—Selling to India's Poor

One of the world's largest and oldest consumer products companies, Unilever has long had a substantial presence in many of the world's poorer nations, such as India. Outside of major urban areas, low income, unsophisticated consumers, illiteracy, fragmented retail distribution systems, and the lack of paved roads have made for difficult marketing challenges. Despite this, Unilever has built a significant presence among impoverished rural populations by adopting innovative selling strategies.

Take India as an example. The country's large rural population is dispersed among some 600,000 villages, more than 500,000 of which cannot be reached by a motor vehicle. Some 91 percent of the rural population lives in villages of fewer than 2,000 people, and of necessity, rural retail stores are very small and carry limited stock. The population is desperately poor, making perhaps a dollar a day, and two-thirds of that income is spent on food, leaving about 30 cents a day for other items. Literacy levels are low, and TVs are rare, making traditional media ineffective. Despite these drawbacks, Hindustan Lever, Unilever's Indian subsidiary, has made a concerted effort to reach the rural poor. Although the revenues generated from rural sales are small, Unilever hopes that as the country develops and income levels rise, the population will continue to purchase the Unilever brands that they are familiar with, giving the company a long-term competitive advantage.

To contact rural consumers, Hindustan Lever tries to establish a physical presence wherever people frequently gather in numbers. This means ensuring that advertisements are seen in places where people congregate and make purchases, such as at village wells and weekly rural markets, and where they consume products, such as at riverbanks where people gather to wash their clothes using (the company hopes) Unilever soap. It is not uncommon to see the villages well plastered with advertisements for Unilever products. The company also takes part in weekly rural events, such as market day, at which farm produce is sold and family provisions purchased. Hindustan Lever salesmen will visit these gatherings, display their products, explain how they work, give away some free samples, make a few sales, and seed the market for future demand.

The backbone of Hindustan Lever's selling effort, however, is a rural distribution network that encompasses 100 factories, 7,500 distributors, and an estimated 3 million retail stores, many of which are little more than a hole in a wall or a stall at a market. The total stock of Unilever products in these stores may be no more than a few sachets of shampoo and half a dozen bars of soap. A depot in each of India's states feeds products to major wholesalers, which then sell directly to retailers in thousands of small towns and villages that can be reached by motor vehicles. If access via motor vehicles is not possible, the major wholesalers sell to smaller second-tier wholesalers, which then handle distribution to India's 500,000 inaccessible rural villages, reaching them by bicycle, bullock, cart, or baskets carried on a human back.

Sources: K. Merchant, "Striving for Success—One Sachet at a Time," *Financial Times*, December 11, 2000, p. 14; M. Turner, "Bicycle Brigade Takes Unilever to the People," *Financial Times*, August 17, 2000, p. 8; and "Brands Thinking Positively," *Brand Strategy*, December 2003, pp. 28–29.

In many developing nations, the situation is even more restrictive because mass media of all types are typically more limited. A firm's ability to use a pull strategy is limited in some countries by media availability. In such circumstances, a push strategy is more attractive. For example, Unilever uses a push strategy to sell consumer products in rural India, where few mass media are available (see the Management Focus above).

Media availability is limited by law in some cases. Few countries allow advertisements for tobacco and alcohol products on television and radio, though they are usually permitted in print media. When the leading Japanese whiskey distiller, Suntory, entered the U.S. market, it had to do so without television, its preferred medium. The firm spends about $50 million annually on television advertising in Japan. Similarly, while advertising pharmaceutical products directly to consumers is allowed in the United States, it is prohibited in many other advanced nations. In such cases, pharmaceutical firms must rely heavily upon advertising and direct-sales efforts focused explicitly at doctors in order to get their products prescribed.

The Push–Pull Mix

The optimal mix between push and pull strategies depends on product type and consumer sophistication, channel length, and media sophistication. Push strategies tend to be emphasized

- For industrial products or complex new products.
- When distribution channels are short.
- When few print or electronic media are available.

Pull strategies tend to be emphasized

- For consumer goods.
- When distribution channels are long.
- When sufficient print and electronic media are available to carry the marketing message.

GLOBAL ADVERTISING

In recent years, largely inspired by the work of visionaries such as Theodore Levitt, there has been much discussion about the pros and cons of standardizing advertising worldwide.[17] One of the most successful standardized campaigns in history was Philip Morris's promotion of Marlboro cigarettes. The campaign was instituted in the 1950s, when the brand was repositioned, to assure smokers that the flavor would be unchanged by the addition of a filter. The campaign theme of "Come to where the flavor is: Come to Marlboro country" was a worldwide success. Marlboro built on this when it introduced "the Marlboro man," a rugged cowboy smoking his Marlboro while riding his horse through the great outdoors. This ad proved successful in almost every major market around the world, and it helped propel Marlboro to the top of the world market.

For Standardized Advertising

The support for global advertising is threefold. First, it has significant economic advantages. Standardized advertising lowers the costs of value creation by spreading the fixed costs of developing the advertisements over many countries. For example, Levi Strauss paid an advertising agency $550,000 to produce a series of TV commercials. By reusing this series in many countries, rather than developing a series for each country, the company enjoyed significant cost savings. Similarly, Coca-Cola's advertising agency, McCann-Erickson, claims to have saved Coca-Cola $90 million over 20 years by using certain elements of its campaigns globally.

Second, there is the concern that creative talent is scarce and so one large effort to develop a campaign will produce better results than 40 or 50 smaller efforts. A third justification for a standardized approach is that many brand names are global. With the substantial amount of international travel today and the considerable overlap in media across national borders, many international firms want to project a single brand image to avoid confusion caused by local campaigns. This is particularly important in regions such as Western Europe, where travel across borders is almost as common as travel across state lines in the United States.

Many global companies do not use standardized advertising because one message may have different meanings in different countries. For example, Kellogg's tag line "Kellogg's makes their cornflakes the best they have ever been," could not be used in Germany because of a prohibition against competitive claims. *Peter Yates/Corbis*

Against Standardized Advertising

There are two main arguments against globally standardized advertising. First, as we have seen repeatedly in this chapter and in Chapter 3, cultural differences between nations are such that a message that works in one nation can fail miserably in another. Cultural diversity makes it extremely difficult to develop a single advertising theme that is effective worldwide. Messages directed at the culture of a given country may be more effective than global messages.

Second, advertising regulations may block implementation of standardized advertising. For example, Kellogg could not use a television commercial it produced in Great Britain to promote its cornflakes in many other European countries. A reference to the iron and vitamin content of its cornflakes was not permissible in the Netherlands, where claims relating to health and medical benefits are outlawed. A child wearing a Kellogg T-shirt had to be edited out of the commercial before it could be used in France, because French law forbids the use of children in product endorsements. The key line "Kellogg's makes their cornflakes the best they have ever been" was disallowed in Germany because of a prohibition against competitive claims.[18] Similarly, American Express ran afoul of regulatory authorities in Germany when it launched a promotional scheme that had proved successful in other countries. The scheme advertised the offer of "bonus points" every time American Express cardholders used their cards. According to the advertisements, these bonus points could be used toward air travel with three airlines and hotel accommodations. American Express was charged with breaking Germany's competition law, which prevents an offer of free gifts in connection with the sale of goods, and the firm had to withdraw the advertisements at considerable cost.[19]

Dealing with Country Differences Some firms are experimenting with capturing some benefits of global standardization while recognizing differences in countries' cultural and legal environments. A firm may select some features to include in all its advertising campaigns and localize other features. By doing so, it may be able to save on some costs and build international brand recognition and yet customize its advertisements to different cultures.

Nokia, the Finish cell phone manufacture, has recently been trying to do this. Historically, Nokia had used a different advertising campaign in different markets. In 2004, however, the company launched a global advertising campaign that used the slogan "1001 reasons to have a Nokia imaging phone." Nokia did this to reduce advertising costs and capture some economies of scale. In addition, in an increasingly integrated world the company believes that there is value in trying to establish a consistent global brand image. At the same time, Nokia is tweaking the advertisements for different cultures. The campaign uses actors from the region where the ad runs to reflect the local population, though they will say the same lines. Local settings are also modified when showcasing the phones by, for example, using a marketplace when advertising in Italy or a bazaar when advertising in the Middle East.[20]

Pricing Strategy

International pricing strategy is an important component of the overall international marketing mix.[21] In this section, we look at three aspects of international pricing strategy. First, we examine the case for pursuing price discrimination, charging different prices for the same product in different countries. Second, we look at what might be called strategic pricing. Third, we review some regulatory factors, such as government-mandated price controls and antidumping regulations, which limit a firm's ability to charge the prices it would prefer in a country.

LEARNING OBJECTIVE 4
Explain why and how a firm's pricing strategy might vary among countries.

PRICE DISCRIMINATION Price discrimination exists whenever consumers in different countries are charged different prices for the same product.[22] Price discrimination involves charging whatever the market will bear; in a competitive market, prices may have to be lower than in a market where the firm has a monopoly. Price discrimination can help a company maximize its profits. It makes economic sense to charge different prices in different countries.

Two conditions are necessary for profitable price discrimination. First, the firm must be able to keep its national markets separate. If it cannot do this, individuals or businesses may undercut its attempt at price discrimination by engaging in arbitrage. Arbitrage occurs when an individual or business capitalizes on a price differential for a firm's product between two countries by purchasing the product in the country where prices are lower and reselling it in the country where prices are higher. For example, many automobile firms have long practiced price discrimination in Europe. A Ford Escort once cost $2,000 more in Germany than it did in Belgium. This policy broke down when car dealers bought Escorts in Belgium and drove them to Germany, where they sold them at a profit for slightly less than Ford was selling Escorts in Germany. To protect the market share of its German auto dealers, Ford had to bring its German prices into line with those being charged in Belgium. Ford could not keep these markets separate.

However, Ford still practices price discrimination between Great Britain and Belgium. A Ford car can cost up to $3,000 more in Great Britain than in Belgium. In this case, arbitrage has not been able to equalize the price, because right-hand-drive cars are sold in Great Britain and left-hand-drive cars in the rest of Europe. Because there is no market for left-hand-drive cars in Great Britain, Ford has been able to keep the markets separate.

Price Elasticity of Demand
A measure of how responsive demand for a product is to changes in its price.

Elastic
When a small change in price produces a large change in demand.

Inelastic
When a large change in price produces only a small change in demand.

The second necessary condition for profitable price discrimination is different price elasticities of demand in different countries. The **price elasticity of demand** is a measure of the responsiveness of demand for a product to change in price. Demand is said to be **elastic** when a small change in price produces a large change in demand; it is said to be **inelastic** when a large change in price produces only a small change in demand. Figure 15.2 illustrates elastic and inelastic demand curves. Generally, a firm can charge a higher price in a country where demand is inelastic.

The elasticity of demand for a product in a given country is determined by a number of factors, of which income level and competitive conditions are the two most important. Price elasticity tends to be greater in countries with low income levels. Consumers with limited incomes tend to be very price conscious; they have less to spend, so they look much more closely at price. Thus, price elasticities for products such as television sets are greater in countries such as India, where a television set is still a luxury item, than in the United States, where it is considered a necessity.

Elastic and Inelastic Demand Curves

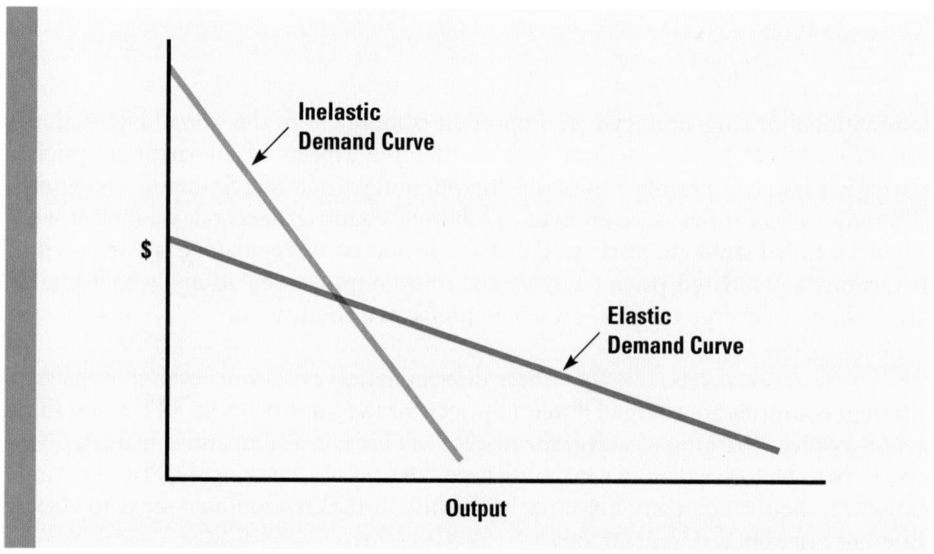

In general, the more competitors there are, the greater consumers' bargaining power will be and the more likely consumers will be to buy from the firm that charges the lowest price. Thus, many competitors cause high elasticity of demand. In such circumstances, if a firm raises its prices above those of its competitors, consumers will switch to the competitors' products. The opposite is true when a firm faces few competitors. When competitors are limited, consumers' bargaining power is weaker and price is less important as a competitive weapon. Thus, a firm may charge a higher price for its product in a country where competition is limited than in one where competition is intense.

STRATEGIC PRICING The concept of **strategic pricing** has three aspects, which we will refer to as predatory pricing, multipoint pricing, and experience curve pricing. Both predatory pricing and experience curve pricing may violate antidumping regulations. After we review predatory and experience curve pricing, we will look at antidumping rules and other regulatory policies.

Strategic Pricing
Pricing aimed at giving a company a competitive advantage over its rivals.

Predatory Pricing **Predatory pricing** is the use of price as a competitive weapon to drive weaker competitors out of a national market. Once the competitors have left the market, the firm can raise prices and enjoy high profits. For such a pricing strategy to work, the firm must normally have a profitable position in another national market, which it can use to subsidize aggressive pricing in the market it is trying to monopolize. Historically, many Japanese firms were accused of pursuing such a policy. The argument ran like this: Because the Japanese market was protected from foreign competition by high informal trade barriers, Japanese firms could charge high prices and earn high profits at home. They then used these profits to subsidize aggressive pricing overseas, with the goal of driving competitors out of those markets. Once this had occurred, so it is claimed, the Japanese firms then raised prices. Matsushita was accused of using this strategy to enter the U.S. TV market. As one of the major TV producers in Japan, Matsushita earned high profits at home. It then used these profits to subsidize the losses it made in the United States during its early years there, when it priced low to increase its market penetration. Ultimately, Matsushita became the world's largest manufacturer of TVs.[23]

Predatory Pricing
Pricing products below fair market values as a competitive weapon to drive weaker competitors out of the market.

Multipoint Pricing Strategy Multipoint pricing becomes an issue when two or more international businesses compete against each other in two or more national markets. For example, multipoint pricing was been an issue for Kodak and Fuji Photo because the companies have long competed against each other around the world.[24] **Multipoint pricing** refers to the fact a firm's pricing strategy in one market may have an impact on its rivals' pricing strategy in another market. Aggressive pricing in one market may elicit a competitive response from a rival in another market. For example, Fuji launched an aggressive competitive attack against Kodak in the U.S. company's home market in January 1997, cutting prices on multiple-roll packs of 35mm film by as much as 50 percent.[25] This price cutting resulted in a 28 percent increase in shipments of Fuji color film during the first six months of 1997, while Kodak's shipments dropped by 11 percent. This attack created a dilemma for Kodak; the company did not want to start price discounting in its largest and most profitable market. Kodak's response was to aggressively cut prices in Fuji's largest market, Japan. This strategic response recognized the interdependence between Kodak and Fuji and the fact that they compete against each other in many different nations. Fuji responded to Kodak's counterattack by pulling back from its aggressive stance in the United States.

Multipoint Pricing
Occurs when a pricing strategy in one market may have an impact on a rival's pricing strategy in another market.

The Kodak story illustrates an important aspect of multipoint pricing: Aggressive pricing in one market may elicit a response from rivals in another market. The firm needs to consider how its global rivals will respond to changes in its pricing strategy before making those changes. A second aspect of multipoint pricing arises when two or more global companies focus on particular national markets and launch vigorous price wars in those markets in an attempt to gain market dominance. In the Brazil market for disposable diapers, two U.S. companies, Kimberly-Clark Corp. and Procter & Gamble, entered a price war as each struggled to establish dominance in the market.[26] As a result, over three years the cost of disposable diapers fell from $1 per diaper to 33 cents per diaper, while several other competitors, including indigenous Brazilian firms, were driven out of the market. Kimberly-Clark and Procter & Gamble are engaged in a global struggle for market share and dominance, and Brazil is one of their battlegrounds. Both companies can afford to engage in this behavior, even though it reduces their profits in Brazil, because they have profitable operations elsewhere in the world that can subsidize these losses.

Pricing decisions around the world need to be centrally monitored. It is tempting to delegate full responsibility for pricing decisions to the managers of various national subsidiaries, thereby reaping the benefits of decentralization. However, because pricing strategy in one part of the world can elicit a competitive response in another, central management needs to at least monitor and approve pricing decisions in a given national market, and local managers need to recognize that their actions can affect competitive conditions in other countries.

Experience Curve Pricing

We first encountered the experience curve in Chapter 11. As a firm builds its accumulated production volume over time, unit costs fall due to experience effects. Learning effects and economies of scale underlie the experience curve. Price comes into the picture because aggressive pricing (along with aggressive promotion and advertising) can build accumulated sales volume rapidly and thus move production down the experience curve. Firms further down the experience curve have a cost advantage vis-à-vis those further up the curve.

Experience Curve Pricing
Aggressive pricing designed to increase volume and help the firm realize experience curve economies.

Many firms pursuing an **experience curve pricing** strategy on an international scale will price low worldwide in attempting to build global sales volume as rapidly as possible, even if this means taking large losses initially. Such a firm believes that in several years, when it has moved down the experience curve, it will be making substantial profits and have a cost advantage over its less-aggressive competitors.

REGULATORY INFLUENCES ON PRICES

The ability to engage in either price discrimination or strategic pricing may be limited by national or international regulations. Most important, a firm's freedom to set its own prices is constrained by antidumping regulations and competition policy.

Antidumping Regulations

Both predatory pricing and experience curve pricing can run afoul of antidumping regulations. Dumping occurs whenever a firm sells a product for a price that is less than the cost of producing it. Most regulations, however, define dumping more vaguely. For example, a country is allowed to bring antidumping actions against an importer under Article 6 of GATT as long as two criteria are met: sales at "less than fair value" and "material injury to a domestic industry." The problem with this terminology is that it does not indicate what is a fair value? The ambiguity has led some to argue that selling abroad at prices below those in the country of origin, as opposed to below cost, is dumping.

Such logic led the Bush administration to place a 20 percent duty on imports of foreign steel in 2001. Foreign manufacturers protested that they were not selling below cost. Admitting that their prices were lower in the United States than some other countries, they argued that this simply reflected the intensely competitive nature of the U.S. market (i.e., different price elasticities).

Antidumping rules set a floor under export prices and limit firms' ability to pursue strategic pricing. The rather vague terminology used in most antidumping actions suggests that a firm's ability to engage in price discrimination also may be challenged under antidumping legislation.

Competition Policy

Most developed nations have regulations designed to promote competition and to restrict monopoly practices. These regulations can be used to limit the prices a firm can charge in a given country. For example, at one time the Swiss pharmaceutical manufacturer Hoffmann-LaRoche had a monopoly on the supply of Valium and Librium tranquilizers. The company was investigated by the British Monopolies and Mergers Commission, which is responsible for promoting fair competition in Great Britain. The commission found that Hoffmann-LaRoche was overcharging for its tranquilizers and ordered the company to reduce its prices 35 to 40 percent. Hoffmann-LaRoche maintained unsuccessfully that it was merely engaging in price discrimination. Similar actions were later brought against Hoffmann-LaRoche by the German cartel office and by the Dutch and Danish governments.[27]

Configuring the Marketing Mix

A firm might vary aspects of its marketing mix from country to country to take into account local differences in culture, economic conditions, competitive conditions, product and technical standards, distribution systems, government regulations, and the like. Such differences may require variation in product attributes, distribution strategy, communications strategy, and pricing strategy. The cumulative effect of these factors makes it rare for a firm to adopt the same marketing mix worldwide.

For example, the financial service industry is often thought of as one in which global standardization of the marketing mix is the norm. However, while a financial services company such as American Express may sell the same basic charge card service worldwide, utilize the same basic fee structure for that product, and adopt the same basic global advertising message ("don't leave home without it"), differences in national regulations still mean that it has to vary aspects of its communications strategy from country to country (as pointed out earlier, the promotional strategy it had developed in the United States was illegal in Germany). Similarly, while McDonald's is often thought of as the quintessential example of a firm that sells the same basic standardized product worldwide, in reality it varies one important aspect of its marketing mix—its menu—from country to country. McDonald's also varies its distribution strategy. In Canada and the United States, most McDonald's are located in areas that are easily accessible by car, whereas in more densely populated and less automobile-reliant societies of the world, such as Japan and Great Britain, location decisions are driven by the accessibility of a restaurant to pedestrian traffic. Because countries typically still differ along one or more of the dimensions discussed above, some customization of the marketing mix is normal.

However, there are often significant opportunities for standardization along one or more elements of the marketing mix.[28] Firms may find that it is possible and desirable to standardize their global advertising message or core product attributes to realize substantial cost economies. They may find it desirable to customize their distribution and pricing strategy to take advantage of local differences. In reality, the "customization versus standardization" debate is not an all or nothing issue; it frequently makes sense to standardize some aspects of the marketing mix and customize others, depending on conditions in various national marketplaces. An explicit example, that of Castrol Oil, is given in the Management Focus on the next page. Castrol sells a standardized

Management FOCUS

Castrol Oil in Vietnam

Castrol is the lubricants division of the British chemical, oil, and gas company Burmah Castrol. In Europe and in the United States, where Castrol has a 15 percent share of the do-it-yourself lubricants market, Castrol targets motorists who want to cosset their engine by paying a bit more for Castrol's high-margin GTX brand rather than a standard lubricant. This differentiated positioning strategy is supported by sponsoring Formula 1 racing and the Indy car series in the United States and by heavy spending on television and in automobile magazines in both Europe and the United States.

Some of Castrol's most notable successes in recent years, however, have been in the developing nations of Asia, where Castrol reaps only one-sixth of its sales but more than one-quarter of its operating profits. In Vietnam, automobiles are still relatively rare, so Castrol has targeted motorcycle owners. Castrol's strategy is to target people who want to take care of their new motorcycles. The long-term goal is to build brand loyalty, so that when automobile ownership becomes common in Vietnam, as Castrol believes it will, former motorcycle owners will stick with Castrol when they trade up to cars. This strategy has already worked in Thailand. Castrol has held the leading share of the motorcycle market in Thailand since the early 1980s, and it now holds the leading share in that country's rapidly growing automobile market.

Unlike its practice in more developed countries, Castrol's communications strategy in Vietnam does not focus on television and glossy print media (there is relatively little of either in Vietnam). Rather, Castrol focuses on building consumer awareness through extensive use of billboards, car stickers, and some 4,000 signs at Vietnam's ubiquitous roadside garages and motorcycle cleaning shops. Castrol also developed a unique slogan that has a rhythmic quality in Vietnamese—*Dau nhot tot nhat,* or "best-quality lubricants"—and sticks in consumers' minds. Castrol's researchers say the slogan is now recognized by a remarkable 99 percent of people in Ho Chi Minh City.

At the same time, Castrol is starting to leverage some of its international promotional strategies and use them in Vietnam. In 2003, the company developed a global advertising campaign that featured English soccer star David Beckham, who is probably the most recognizable athlete in the world outside of the United States. As part of the campaign, Beckham visited several Asian nations, including Vietnam, where he attended a soccer tournament sponsored by Castrol.

As elsewhere, Castrol has adopted a premium pricing strategy in Vietnam, which is consistent with the company's attempt to build a global brand image of high quality. Castrol oil costs about $1.5 per liter in Vietnam, about three times as much as the price of cheaper oil imported from Taiwan and Thailand. Despite the high price of its product, Castrol claims it is gaining share in Vietnam as its branding strategy wins converts.

Castrol has had to tailor its distribution strategy to Vietnam's unique conditions. In most countries where it operates, Castrol divides the country into regions and has a single distributor in each region. In Vietnam, however, Castrol will often have two distinct distributors in a region—one to deal with state-owned customers, of which there are still many in this nominally Communist country, and one to deal with private customers. Castrol acknowledges the system is costly but says it is the only way to operate in a country where there is still some tension between state and private entities.

Sources: V. Mallet, "Climbing the Slippery Slope," *Financial Times,* July 28, 1994, p. 7; A. Bolger, "Growth by Successful Targeting," *Financial Times,* June 21, 1994, p. 27; "A Decade in Lubricants," *Vietnam Investment Review,* August 27, 2001; and V. Bao, "England's Beckham to Visit Vietnam Despite Broken Wrist," *Saigon Times,* May 26, 2003.

product worldwide—lubricating oil—yet it varies other aspects of its marketing mix from country to country, depending on economic conditions, competitive conditions, and distribution systems. Decisions about what to customize and what to standardize should be driven by a detailed examination of the costs and benefits of doing so for each element in the marketing mix.

LEARNING OBJECTIVE 5
Discuss how the globalization of the world economy is affecting new-product development within the international business firm.

New-Product Development

Firms that successfully develop and market new products can earn enormous returns. Examples include Du Pont, which has produced a steady stream of successful innovations such as cellophane, nylon, Freon, and Teflon (nonstick pans); Sony, whose successes include the Walkman, the compact disk, and the PlayStation; Pfizer, the drug company that during the 1990s produced several major new drugs, including Viagra; 3M, which has applied its core competency in tapes and adhesives to developing a wide range of new products; Intel, which has consistently managed to lead in the development of innovative microprocessors to run personal computers; and Cisco Systems, which developed the routers that sit at the hubs of Internet connections, directing the flow of digital traffic.

In today's world, competition is as much about technological innovation as anything else. The pace of technological change has accelerated since the Industrial Revolution in the eighteenth century, and it continues to do so today. The result has been a dramatic shortening of product life cycles. Technological innovation is both creative and destructive.[29] An innovation can make established products obsolete overnight. But an innovation can also make a host of new products possible. Witness recent changes in the electronics industry. For 40 years before the early 1950s, vacuum tubes were a major component in radios and then in record players and early computers. The advent of transistors destroyed the market for vacuum tubes, but at the same time it created new opportunities connected with transistors. Transistors took up far less space than vacuum tubes, creating a trend toward miniaturization that continues today. The transistor held its position as the major component in the electronics industry for just a decade. Microprocessors were developed in the 1970s, and the market for transistors declined rapidly. The microprocessor created yet another set of new-product opportunities: handheld calculators (which destroyed the market for slide rules), compact disk players (which destroyed the market for analog record players), personal computers (which destroyed the market for typewriters), cell phones (which may ultimately replace land line phones), to name a few.

This "creative destruction" unleashed by technological change makes it critical that a firm stay on the leading edge of technology, lest it lose out to a competitor's innovations. As we explain in the next subsection, this not only creates a need for the firm to invest in R&D, but it also requires the firm to establish R&D activities at those locations where expertise is concentrated. As we shall see, leading-edge technology on its own is not enough to guarantee a firm's survival. The firm must also apply that technology to developing products that satisfy consumer needs, and it must design the product so that it can be manufactured in a cost-effective manner. To do that, the firm needs to build close links between R&D, marketing, and manufacturing. This is difficult enough for the domestic firm, but it is even more problematic for the international business competing in an industry where consumer tastes and preferences differ from country to country.[30] See the Another Perspective at right for ways Staples, Inc. works to beat these issues. With all of this in mind, we move on to examine locating R&D activities and building links between R&D, marketing, and manufacturing.

Another Perspective

New-Product Development Takes to the Streets

Makes sense! Staples' R&D starts with new ideas and innovations from its consumers. How? Through a yearly contest called InventionQuest, Staples solicits ideas and innovations from its consumers for products it can brand and sell exclusively. Winners of the contest receive $25,000 and up to 8 percent royalty. The annual contest—now in its third year—continues to attract innovators, up to 10,000 of them last year. It's a unique organizational structure, if you will, designed to contribute toward Staples' corporate strategy to the make its own products the top national office products brand.

In addition, Staples has launched in-house product and packaging design departments. Unusual for a retailer, Staples filed for 50 patents in the past two years. This "intrapreneur" concept is another creative approach to R&D. (William M. Bulkeley, "Got a Better Letter Opener?" *The Wall Street Journal*, July 13, 2006)

THE LOCATION OF R&D Ideas for new products are stimulated by the interactions of scientific research, demand conditions, and competitive conditions. Other things being equal, the rate of new-product development seems to be greater in countries where

- More money is spent on basic and applied research and development.
- Underlying demand is strong.
- Consumers are affluent.
- Competition is intense.[31]

Basic and applied research and development discovers new technologies and then commercializes them. Strong demand and affluent consumers create a potential market for new products. Intense competition between firms stimulates innovation as the firms try to beat their competitors and reap potentially enormous first-mover advantages that result from successful innovation.

For most of the post–World War II period, the country that ranked highest on these criteria was the United States. The United States devoted a greater proportion of its gross domestic product to R&D than any other country did. Its scientific establishment was the largest and most active in the world. U.S. consumers were the most affluent, the market was large, and competition among U.S. firms was brisk. Due to these factors, the United States was the market where most new products were developed and introduced. Accordingly, it was the best location for R&D activities; it was where the action was.

Over the past 20 years, things have been changing quickly. The U.S. monopoly on new-product development has weakened considerably. Although U.S. firms are still at the leading edge of many new technologies, Asian and European firms are also strong players, with companies such as Sony, Sharp, Samsung, Ericsson, Nokia, and Philips NV driving product innovation in their respective industries. In addition, both Japan and the European Union are large, affluent markets, and the wealth gap between them and the United States is closing.

As a result, it is often no longer appropriate to consider the United States as the lead market. In video games, for example, Japan is often the lead market, with companies like Sony and Nintendo introducing their latest video game players in Japan some six months before they introduce them in the United States. In wireless telecommunications, Europe is generally reckoned to be ahead of the United States. Some of the most advanced applications of wireless telecommunications services are being pioneered not in the United States but in Finland, where more than 80 percent of the population has wireless telephones, compared with 40 percent of the U.S. population. However, it often is questionable whether any developed nation can be considered the lead market. To succeed in today's high-technology industries, it is often necessary to simultaneously introduce new products in all major industrialized markets. When Intel introduces a new microprocessor, for example, it does not first introduce it in the United States and then roll it out in Europe a year later. It introduces it simultaneously around the world.

Because leading-edge research is now carried out in many locations around the world, the argument for centralizing R&D activity in the United States is now much weaker than it was two decades ago. (It used to be argued that centralized R&D eliminated duplication.) Much leading-edge research is now occurring in Japan and Europe. Dispersing R&D activities to those locations allows a firm to stay close to the center of leading-edge activity to gather scientific and competitive information and to draw on local scientific resources.[32] This may result in some duplication of R&D activities, but the cost disadvantages of duplication are outweighed by the advantages of dispersion.

For example, to expose themselves to the research and new-product development work being done in Japan, many U.S. firms have set up satellite R&D centers in Japan.

Kodak's R&D center in Japan employs about 200 people. The company hired about 100 Japanese researchers and directed the lab to concentrate on electronic imaging technology. U.S. firms that have established R&D facilities in Japan include Corning, Texas Instruments, IBM, Digital Equipment, Procter & Gamble, Upjohn, Pfizer, Du Pont, Monsanto, and Microsoft.[33] The National Science Foundation (NSF) has documented a sharp increase in the proportion of total R&D spending by U.S. firms that is now done abroad.[34] For example, Motorola now has 14 dedicated R&D facilities located in seven countries, and Bristol-Myers Squibb has 12 facilities in six countries. At the same time, to internationalize their own research and gain access to U.S. talent, many European and Japanese firms are investing in U.S.-based research facilities, according to the NSF.

INTEGRATING R&D, MARKETING, AND PRODUCTION Although a firm that is successful at developing new products may earn enormous returns, new-product development has a high failure rate. One study of product development in 16 companies in the chemical, drug, petroleum, and electronics industries suggested that only about 20 percent of R&D projects result in commercially successful products or processes.[35] Another in-depth case study of product development in three companies (one in chemicals and two in drugs) reported that about 60 percent of R&D projects reached technical completion, 30 percent were commercialized, and only 12 percent earned an economic profit that exceeded the company's cost of capital.[36] Along the same lines, another study concluded that one in nine major R&D projects, or about 11 percent, produced commercially successful products.[37] In sum, the evidence suggests that only 10 to 20 percent of major R&D projects give rise to commercially successful products. Well-publicized product failures include Apple Computer's Newton personal digital assistant, Sony's Betamax format in the video player and recorder market, and Sega's Dreamcast videogame console.

The reasons for such high failure rates are various and include development of a technology for which demand is limited, failure to adequately commercialize promising technology, and inability to manufacture a new product cost effectively. Firms can reduce the probability of making such mistakes by insisting on tight cross-functional coordination and integration between three core functions involved in the development of new products: R&D, marketing, and production.[38] Tight cross-functional integration between R&D, production, and marketing can help a company to ensure that

1. Product development projects are driven by customer needs.
2. New products are designed for ease of manufacture.
3. Development costs are kept in check.
4. Time to market is minimized.

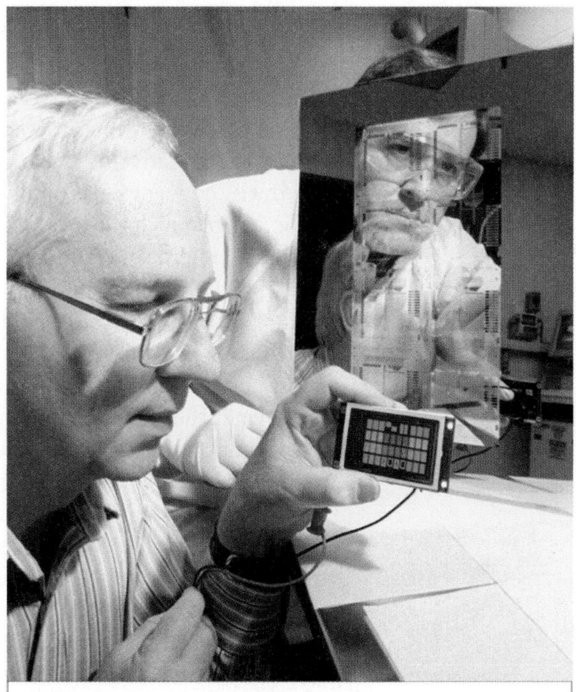

Companies such as Kodak have R&D centers in both the United States and Japan in order to stay on the cutting edge of the trends in their industries. Here, in a joint research venture with Sanyo Electronics of Japan, Eastman Kodak Co. research scientists inspect a glass substrate used in the development of next-generation flat-panel displays that enable brighter, thinner, more power-efficient displays for cellular phones, personal data assistants, and computer terminals. *Feature Photo Service/Kodak/AP/Wide World Photos*

Close integration between R&D and marketing is required to ensure that product development projects are driven by the needs of customers. A company's customers can be a primary source of new-product ideas. Identification of customer needs, particularly unmet needs, can set the context within which successful product innovation occurs. As the point of contact with customers, the marketing function of a company can provide valuable information in this regard. Integration of R&D and marketing is crucial if a new product is to be properly commercialized. Without integration of R&D and marketing, a company runs the risk of developing products for which there is little or no demand.

Integration between R&D and production can help a company design products with manufacturing requirements in mind. Designing for manufacturing can lower costs and increase product quality. Integrating R&D and production can also help lower development costs and speed products to market. If a new product is not designed with manufacturing capabilities in mind, it may prove too difficult to build. Then the product will have to be redesigned, and both overall development costs and the time it takes to bring the product to market may increase significantly. Making design changes during product planning could increase overall development costs by 50 percent and add 25 percent to the time it takes to bring the product to market.[39] Many quantum product innovations require new processes to manufacture them, which makes it all the more important to achieve close integration between R&D and production. Minimizing time to market and development costs may require the simultaneous development of new products and new processes.[40]

CROSS-FUNCTIONAL TEAMS One way to achieve cross-functional integration is to establish cross-functional product development teams composed of representatives from R&D, marketing, and production. Because these functions may be located in different countries, the team will sometimes have a multinational membership. The objective of a team should be to take a product development project from the initial concept development to market introduction. A number of attributes seem to be important for a product development team to function effectively and meet all its development milestones.[41]

First, the team should be led by a "heavyweight" project manager who has high status within the organization and who has the power and authority required to get the financial and human resources the team needs to succeed. The leader should be dedicated primarily, if not entirely, to the project. He or she should be someone who believes in the project (a champion) and who is skilled at integrating the perspectives of different functions and at helping personnel from different functions and countries work together for a common goal. The leader should also be able to act as an advocate of the team to senior management.

Second, the team should be composed of at least one member from each key function. The team members should have a number of attributes, including an ability to contribute functional expertise, high standing within their function, a willingness to share responsibility for team results, and an ability to put functional and national advocacy aside. It is generally preferable if core team members are 100 percent dedicated to the project for its duration. This assures their focus on the project, not on the ongoing work of their function.

Third, the team members should physically be in one location if possible to create a sense of camaraderie and to facilitate communication. This presents problems if the team members are drawn from facilities in different nations. One solution is to transfer key individuals to one location for the duration of a product development project. Fourth, the team should have a clear plan and clear goals, particularly with regard to critical development milestones and development budgets. The team should have incentives to attain those goals, such as receiving pay bonuses when major development milestones are hit. Fifth, each team needs to develop its own processes for communication and conflict resolution. For example, one product development team at Quantum Corporation, a California-based manufacturer of disk drives for personal computers, instituted a rule that all major decisions would be made and conflicts resolved at meetings that were held every Monday afternoon. This simple rule helped the team meet its development goals. In this case, it was also common for team members to fly in from Japan, where the product was to be manufactured, to the U.S. development center for the Monday morning meetings.[42]

BUILDING GLOBAL R&D CAPABILITIES The need to integrate R&D and marketing to adequately commercialize new technologies poses special problems in the international business because commercialization may require different versions of a new product to be produced for various countries.[43] To do this, the firm must build close links between its R&D centers and its various country operations. A similar argument applies to the need to integrate R&D and production, particularly in those international businesses that have dispersed production activities to different locations around the globe in consideration of relative factor costs and the like.

Integrating R&D, marketing, and production in an international business may require R&D centers in North America, Asia, and Europe that are linked by formal and informal integrating mechanisms with marketing operations in each country in their regions and with the various manufacturing facilities. In addition, the international business may have to establish cross-functional teams whose members are dispersed around the globe. This complex endeavor requires the company to utilize formal and informal integrating mechanisms to knit its far-flung operations together so they can produce new products in an effective and timely manner.

While there is no one best model for allocating product development responsibilities to various centers, one solution adopted by many international businesses involves establishing a global network of R&D centers. Within this model, fundamental research is undertaken at basic research centers around the globe. These centers are normally located in regions or cities where valuable scientific knowledge is being created and where there is a pool of skilled research talent (e.g., Silicon Valley in the United States, Cambridge in England, Kobe in Japan, Singapore). These centers are the innovation engines of the firm. Their job is to develop the basic technologies that become new products.

These technologies are picked up by R&D units attached to global product divisions and are used to generate new products to serve the global marketplace. At this level, commercialization of the technology and design for manufacturing are emphasized. If further customization is needed so the product appeals to the tastes and preferences of consumers in individual markets, such redesign work will be done by an R&D group based in a subsidiary in that country or at a regional center that customizes products for several countries in the region.

Hewlett-Packard has four basic research centers located in Palo Alto, California; Bristol, England; Haifa, Israel; and Tokyo, Japan.[44] These labs are the seedbed for technologies that ultimately become new products and businesses. They are the company's innovation engines. The Palo Alto center, for example, pioneered HP's thermal ink-jet technology. The products are developed by R&D centers associated with HP's global product divisions. Thus, the Consumer Products Group, which has its worldwide headquarters in San Diego, California, designs, develops, and manufactures a range of imaging products using HP-pioneered thermal ink-jet technology. Subsidiaries might then customize the product so that it best matches the needs of important national markets. HP's subsidiary in Singapore, for example, is responsible for the design and production of thermal ink-jet printers for Japan and other Asian markets. This subsidiary takes products originally developed in San Diego and redesigns them for the Asian market. In addition, the Singapore subsidiary has taken the lead from San Diego in the design and development of certain portable thermal ink-jet printers. HP delegated this responsibility to Singapore because this subsidiary has acquired important competencies in the design and production of thermal ink-jet products, so it has become the best place in the world to undertake this activity.

Microsoft offers a similar example. The company has basic research sites in Redmond, Washington (its headquarters); Cambridge, England; Tokyo, Japan; and Silicon Valley, California. Staff at these research sites work on the fundamental problems that underlie the design of future products. For example, a group at Redmond is working on natural language recognition software, while another works on artificial intelligence. These research centers don't produce new products; rather, they produce the technology that is used to enhance existing products or help produce new products. The products are produced by dedicated product groups (e.g., desktop operating systems, applications). Customization of the products to match the needs of local markets is sometimes carried out at local subsidiaries. Thus, the Chinese subsidiary in Singapore will do some basic customization of programs such as Microsoft Office, adding Chinese characters and customizing the interface.

Key Terms

marketing mix, p. 475
market segmentation, p. 477
concentrated retail system, p. 481
fragmented retail system, p. 481
channel length, p. 482
exclusive distribution channel, p. 483
channel quality, p. 483
source effects, p. 486
country of origin effects, p. 486
noise p. 486
push strategy, p. 487
pull strategy, p. 487
price elasticity of demand, p. 492
elastic, p. 492
inelastic, p. 492
strategic pricing, p. 493
predatory pricing, p. 493
multipoint pricing, p. 493
experience curve pricing, p. 494

Summary

This chapter discussed the marketing and R&D functions in international business. A persistent theme of the chapter is the tension that exists between the need to reduce costs and the need to be responsive to local conditions, which raises costs. The chapter made these major points:

1. Theodore Levitt argued that due to the advent of modern communications and transport technologies, consumer tastes and preferences are becoming global, which is creating global markets for standardized consumer products. However, this position is regarded as extreme by many commentators, who argue that substantial differences still exist between countries.
2. Market segmentation refers to the process of identifying distinct groups of consumers whose purchasing behavior differs from each other in important ways. Managers in an international business need to be aware of two main issues relating to segmentation: the extent to which there are differences between countries in the structure of market segments, and the existence of segments that transcend national borders.
3. A product can be viewed as a bundle of attributes. Product attributes need to be varied from country to country to satisfy different consumer tastes and preferences.
4. Country differences in consumer tastes and preferences are due to differences in culture

and economic development. In addition, differences in product and technical standards may require the firm to customize product attributes from country to country.

5. A distribution strategy decision is an attempt to define the optimal channel for delivering a product to the consumer.
6. Significant country differences exist in distribution systems. In some countries, the retail system is concentrated; in others, it is fragmented. In some countries, channel length is short; in others, it is long. Access to distribution channels is difficult to achieve in some countries, and the quality of the channel may be poor.
7. A critical element in the marketing mix is communication strategy, which defines the process the firm will use in communicating the attributes of its product to prospective customers.
8. Barriers to international communication include cultural differences, source effects, and noise levels.
9. A communication strategy is either a push strategy or a pull strategy. A push strategy emphasizes personal selling, and a pull strategy emphasizes mass media advertising. Whether a push strategy or a pull strategy is optimal depends on the type of product, consumer sophistication, channel length, and media availability.
10. A globally standardized advertising campaign, which uses the same marketing message all over the world, has economic advantages, but it fails to account for differences in culture and advertising regulations.
11. Price discrimination exists when consumers in different countries are charged different prices for the same product. Price discrimination can help a firm maximize its profits. For price discrimination to be effective, the national markets must be separate and their price elasticities of demand must differ.
12. Predatory pricing is the use of profit gained in one market to support aggressive pricing in another market to drive competitors out of that market.
13. Multipoint pricing refers to the fact that a firm's pricing strategy in one market may affect rivals' pricing strategies in another market. Aggressive pricing in one market may elicit a competitive response from a rival in another market that is important to the firm.
14. Experience curve pricing is the use of aggressive pricing to build accumulated volume as rapidly as possible to quickly move the firm down the experience curve.
15. New-product development is a high-risk, potentially high-return activity. To build a competency in new-product development, an international business must do two things: disperse R&D activities to those countries where new products are being pioneered, and integrate R&D with marketing and manufacturing.
16. Achieving tight integration among R&D, marketing, and manufacturing requires the use of cross-functional teams.

Critical Thinking and Discussion Questions

1. Imagine you are the marketing manager for a U.S. manufacturer of disposable diapers. Your firm is considering entering the Brazilian market. Your CEO believes the advertising message that has been effective in the United States will suffice in Brazil. Outline some possible objections to this. Your CEO also believes that the pricing decisions in Brazil can be delegated to local managers. Why might she be wrong?
2. Within 20 years, we will have seen the emergence of enormous global markets for standardized consumer products. Do you agree with this statement? Justify your answer.
3. You are the marketing manager of a food products company that is considering entering the Indian market. The retail system in India tends to be very fragmented. Also, retailers and wholesalers tend to have long-term ties with Indian food companies, which makes access to distribution channels difficult. What distribution strategy would you advise the company to pursue? Why?
4. Price discrimination is indistinguishable from dumping. Discuss the accuracy of this statement.
5. You work for a company that designs and manufactures personal computers. Your company's R&D center is in North Dakota. The

computers are manufactured under contract in Taiwan. Marketing strategy is delegated to the heads of three regional groups: a North American group (based in Chicago), a European group (based in Paris), and an Asian group (based in Singapore). Each regional group develops the marketing approach within its region. In order of importance, the largest markets for your products are North America, Germany, Great Britain, China, and Australia. Your company is experiencing problems in its product development and commercialization process. Products are late to market, the manufacturing quality is poor, costs are higher than projected, and market acceptance of new products is less than hoped for. What might be the source of these problems? How would you fix them?

Research Task globalEDGE http://globalEDGE.msu.edu

Use the globalEDGE site (http://globalEDGE.msu.edu/) to complete the following exercises:

1. Locate and retrieve the most current ranking of *global brands*. Identify the criteria that are utilized in the ranking. Which country dominates the top 100 global brands list? Prepare a short report identifying the countries that possess global brands and the potential reasons for success.
2. The *globalization of research and development* (R&D) in developing countries has received considerable attention. As such, a recent report by the United Nations Conference on Trade and Development (UNCTAD) published a report that captures the different types of R&D units that can exist in developing countries. Develop a brief summary and description of each R&D unit type. Which type(s) of R&D unit would you establish if your firm aimed to implement a product standardization strategy?

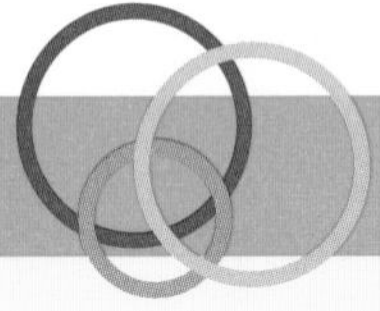

closing case

Kodak in Russia

In the early 1990s, Kodak entered Russia. At the time, the country was deep in the middle of a turbulent transition from a Communist-run command economy to a fledgling democracy that was committed to pushing through the privatization of state-owned enterprises and economic reforms designed to establish competitive markets. Kodak's entry into this market posed a number of challenges. Russian consumers had little knowledge of Kodak's products, and the consumer market for photography was very underdeveloped. Moreover, apart from state-run stores that were generally poorly run, there was little or no infrastructure in place for distributing photographic equipment and films and for processing film. To compound matters, Russian consumers were poor and unlikely to be able to afford all but the most inexpensive cameras and films.

A decade later, Kodak's entry into Russia is widely regarded as a major success. Russia accounts for a significant proportion of the $2.59 billion in international sales in emerging markets that Kodak registered in 2004; and with a growth rate of 26 percent over the prior year, Russia is the fastest-growing emerging market for Kodak, outstripping even China. How did Kodak do it?

First, Kodak had a clear and consistent marketing message that it communicated to Russian consumers through a number of media, including radio, television, and print advertising. The marketing message was based upon the idea of "saving memories" by taking pictures in a quick and easy way. "You press the button and we will do the rest" the ads stated. As it turned out, this was the perfect message for a consumer market that was not used to photography. To complement the core marketing message, Kodak spent heavily on promotional campaigns, exhibitions, conventions, sponsored events, and the like, in an attempt to educate consumers and raise awareness of the Kodak brand name. For example, in addition to standard media advertising, Kodak owns a traveling photo park with a fleet of hot air balloons that have become very popular in Russia.

Kodak has also invested heavily in promoting a corporate image as a firm that takes a stand against corruption and black market practices. The company has been very clear about its business practices and about its refusal to engage in shady dealings. In a country where such practices were once commonplace, and still persist to a degree, this stance has been well received by consumers and has helped to build the company's brand image as an enterprise that can be trusted—which as it turns out, has been good for business. Kodak also boosted its corporate image by opening a factory in Russia to produce cameras, film, and chemicals for film processing. In addition to the public relations benefit, this move also helped Kodak to lower its costs by utilizing cheap Russian labor and by avoiding tariffs on imports of photographic products into Russia.

Recognizing the limited income of Russian consumers, Kodak's product strategy has been to sell lower-end film and cameras in Russia. Kodak offers simple cameras for around $20 to Russian consumers, something that the company can afford to do because the cameras are made locally. It does not sell disposable cameras in Russia, since at $10 each the cost would be too much. Instead of trying to sell top-quality Kodak Gold film, which is popular in the West, the cheaper brand, Kodak Color Plus, is heavily marketed in Russia.

Another of Kodak's marketing tactics has been to try and build demand for its products by encouraging major enterprises to give cameras to valued employees, rather than the traditional bottle of Vodka. Kodak has also worked closely with travel agents, giving them cameras to give away to their customers. Kodak's hope of course, has been that consumers will purchase Kodak film to use in these cameras, and to a large degree, that seems to have occurred.

Finally, Kodak realized that it needed to build a distribution channel for its products. Rather than invest directly in its own stores, the company set up a franchising program to open Kodak Express stores throughout Russia to sell its products and develop film. These owner-operated stores adhere to strict business guidelines set down by Kodak in its master franchise agreement. The stores are clean, attractively designed, have a consistent appearance that helps to promote the Kodak brand, and are staffed by friendly and polite employees. These stores rapidly set a new standard for retailing in Russia. Within three years, more than 350 Kodak Express outlets had opened up in Russia, and today there are several thousand.

Sources: G.C. Anders and D.A. Usachev, "Strategic Elements of Eastman Kodak's Successful Market Entry in Russia," *Thunderbird International Business Review* 45, no. 2 (March–April 2003), pp. 171–83; S. McNamara, "Kodak Stores Set U.S. Standards in Russia," *USA Today,* December 21, 1998, p. 12B; and "Making Foreign Policy Work with Kodak and Norske Skog," *Strategic Direction* 19, no. 11 (November–December 2003), pp. 27–30.

Case Discussion Questions

1. How did the Russian market differ from markets in developed Western nations? How were these differences likely to impact upon demand for photographic products?
2. How did Kodak adjust its marketing mix in Russia to match local requirements? Do you think this was the right thing to do?
3. Kodak's traditional film business is now under attack from digital photography (in which Kodak is also a leader). Should Kodak adjust its marketing mix for digital products to the Russian market? Why?

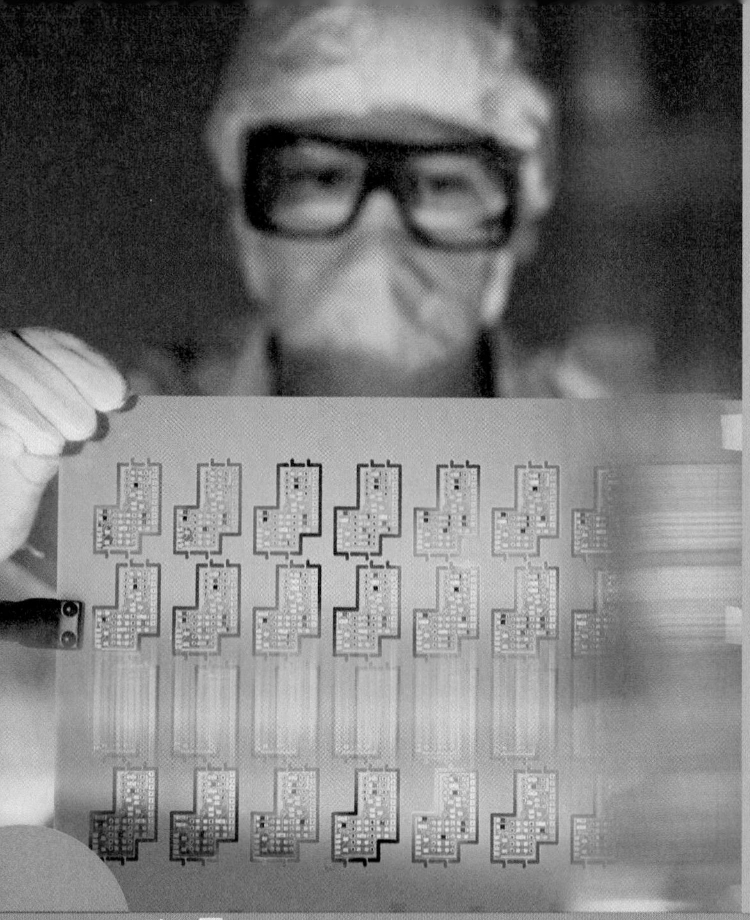

Digital Vision/DIL

part 5 Competing in the Global Marketplace

LEARNING OBJECTIVES

1. Articulate the strategic role of human resource management in an international business.
2. Discuss the pros and cons of different approaches to staffing policy in an international business.
3. Explain why managers may fail to thrive in foreign postings.
4. Articulate how management development and training programs can increase the value of human capital in an international business firm.
5. Explain how and why performance appraisal systems might vary across nations.
6. Explain how and why compensation systems might vary across nations.

chapter 16

Global Human Resource Management

XCO China

opening case

It had been a bad morning for John Ross, the general manager of XCO's Chinese joint venture. He had just got off the phone with his boss in St Louis, Phil Smith, who was demanding to know why the joint venture's return on investment was still in the low single digits four years after Ross had taken over the top post in the operation. "We had expected much better performance by now," said Smith, "particularly given your record of achievement; you need to fix this Phil. Our patience is not infinite. You know the corporate goal is for a 20 percent return on investment for operating units, and your unit is not even close to that." Ross had a bad feeling that Smith had just fired a warning shot across his bow. There was an implicit threat underlying Smith's demands for improved performance. For the first time in his 20-year career at XCO, Ross felt that his job was on the line.

XCO was a U.S.-based multinational electronics enterprise with sales of $2 billion and operations in more than 10 countries. XCO China specialized in the mass production of printed circuit boards for companies in the cell phone and computer industries. It was a joint venture with Shanghai Electronic Corporation, a former state-owned enterprise that held 40 percent of the joint-venture equity (XCO held the rest). Although XCO held a majority of the equity, the company had to consult with its partner before making major investments or changing employment levels.

John Ross had been running XCO China for the past four years. He had arrived at XCO China after a successful career at XCO, which included extended postings in Mexico and Hungary. When he took the China position, Ross thought that if he succeeded he would probably be in line for one of the top jobs at corporate within a few years. He had known that he was taking on a challenge with XCO China, but nothing prepared him for what he found there. The joint venture was a mess. Operations were horribly inefficient.

Despite very low wage rates, productivity was being killed by poor product quality and lax inventory controls. The venture probably employed too many people, but XCO's Chinese partner seemed to view the venture as a job-creation program and repeatedly objected to any plans for cutting the workforce. To make matters worse, XCO China had failed to keep up with the latest developments in manufacturing technology, and it was falling behind competitors. Ross was determined to change this, but it had not been easy.

To improve operations, Ross had put in a request to corporate HR for two specialists from the United States to work with the Chinese production employees. It had been a disaster. One had lasted just three months before requesting a transfer home for personal reasons. Apparently, his spouse hated China. The other had stayed on for a year, but he had interacted so poorly with the local Chinese employees that he had to be sent back to the States. Ross wished that XCO's corporate HR department had done a better job of selecting and then training these employees for a difficult foreign posting, but in retrospect he had to admit that he wasn't surprised at the lack of cultural training—after all, he had never been given any.

After this failure, Ross had taken a different tack. He had picked four of his best Chinese production employees and sent them over to XCO's U.S. operations, along with a translator, for a two-month training program focusing on the latest production techniques. This had worked out much better. The Chinese had visited efficient XCO factories in the United States, Mexico, and Brazil and had seen what was possible. They had returned home fired up to improve operations at XCO China. Within a year they had introduced a Six Sigma quality control program and improved the flow of inventory through XCO's factory. Ross could now walk though the factory without being appalled by the sight of large quantities of inventory stacked on the floor, or bins full of discarded circuit boards that had failed postassembly quality tests. Productivity had improved, and after three tough years, XCO China had finally turned a profit.

Apparently, this was not good enough for corporate headquarters. Ross knew that improving performance further would be tough. The market in China had become very competitive. XCO was vying with many other enterprises to produce printed circuit boards for large multinational customers who themselves had assembly operations in China. The customers were constantly demanding lower prices, and it seemed to Ross that prices were falling almost as fast as XCO's costs. Moreover, Ross was limited in his ability to cut the workforce by the demands of his Chinese joint-venture partner. He had tried to explain all of this to Phil Smith, but Smith didn't seem to get it. "The man is just a number cruncher," thought Ross, "he has no sense of the market in China. He has no idea how hard it is to do business here. I have worked damn hard to turn this operation around, and I am getting no credit for it, none at all."

Source: This is a disguised case based on interviews undertaken by Charles Hill.

Introduction

This chapter continues our survey of specific functions within an international business by looking at international human resource management (HRM). **Human resource management** refers to the activities an organization carries out to use its human resources effectively.[1] These activities include determining the firm's human resource strategy, staffing, performance evaluation, management development, compensation, and labor relations. None of these activities is performed in a vacuum; all are related to the strategy of the firm. As we will see, HRM has an important strategic component.[2] Through its influence on the character, development, quality, and productivity of the firm's human resources, the HRM function can help the firm achieve its primary strategic goals of reducing the costs of value creation and adding value by better serving customer needs. See the Another Perspective below for a look at VW's top management style.

Human Resource Management
The activities an organization carries out to use its human resources effectively.

The strategic role of HRM is complex enough in a purely domestic firm, but it is more complex in an international business, where staffing, management development, performance evaluation, and compensation activities are complicated by profound differences between countries in labor markets, culture, legal systems, economic systems, and the like (see Chapters 2 and 3). For example,

Expatriate Manager
A citizen of one country appointed to a management position in another country.

- Compensation practices may vary from country to country, depending on prevailing management customs.
- Labor laws may prohibit union organization in one country and mandate it in another.
- Equal employment legislation may be strongly pursued in one country and not in another.

If it is to build a cadre of managers capable of managing a multinational enterprise, the HRM function must deal with a host of issues. It must decide how to staff key management posts in the company, how to develop managers so that they are familiar with the nuances of doing business in different countries, how to compensate people in different nations, and how to evaluate the performance of managers based in different countries. HRM must also deal with a host of issues related to expatriate managers. (An **expatriate manager** is a citizen of one country who is working abroad in one of the firm's subsidiaries.) It must decide when to use expatriates, determine whom to send on expatriate postings, be clear about why they are doing it, compensate expatriates appropriately, and make sure that they are adequately debriefed and reoriented once they return home.

The opening case described what can happen when the HRM function does not perform as well as it might. XCO sent two expatriates to XCO China to help the beleaguered boss of that unit, John Ross, but neither expatriate was successful. Apparently, the HR department had picked two employees who were well qualified from a technical perspective, but they were not suited in other ways to take a difficult foreign posting. This is not

Another Perspective

Top Management with an International Twist

What happens when a German-born, American-trained exec takes the helm at Volkswagen AG and is responsible for turning around the troubled (60 percent slide in profits since 2001) VW brand?

Wolfgang Bernhard is the exec, and he's been termed the "Wild West" manager. He belongs to a new generation of German executives who have worked in the United States and are challenging traditional management notions and styles.

At Bernhard's insistence, Volkswagen for the first time opened its European factories to American quality control experts and has begun resolving internal disputes over how to build new models by forcing hundreds of employees into the same room to debate. Specifically, Bernhard recently directed more than 200 VW employees to report to an auditorium a few miles from the headquarters, broke them into teams, and instructed them to figure out how to cut a planned SUV's cost by $2,500 per vehicle. He told them not to return to their workplace until they were done. Every evening around 6 p.m. he returned to the auditorium to watch and listen as the teams, sometimes working until midnight, presented their cost-cutting recommendations. After about four weeks, the employees met his target.

Bernhard said it was a team effort—another perspective on the VW factory turned ranch! (Stephen Power, "Top Volkswagen Executive Tries U.S.-Style Turnaround Tactics," *The Wall Street Journal*, July 18, 2006)

unusual. As we shall see, a large number of expatriates return home before their tour of duty is completed, often because while they have the technical skills to perform the required job, they lack the skills required to manage in a different cultural context, or because their spouses do not like the posting. To his credit, Ross came up with a solution to the problem: send Chinese employees to the United States and get them trained in the latest manufacturing techniques. The XCO case also illustrates another problem in international HRM: how to evaluate the performance of expatriate managers who are operating in very different circumstances from those found in the home country. It is apparent from the case that John Ross was being evaluated on the basis of the performance of his unit against corporatewide profitability criteria; but these criteria failed to account for the difficult conditions Ross inherited and the problems inherent in doing business in the Chinese market. The most skilled multinationals have found ways of dealing with this problem by adjusting performance appraisal criteria to take differences in context into account. XCO apparently did not do this.

In this chapter, we will look closely at the role of HRM in an international business. We begin by briefly discussing the strategic role of HRM. Then we turn our attention to four major tasks of the HRM function: staffing policy, management training and development, performance appraisal, and compensation policy. We will point out the strategic implications of each of these tasks. The chapter closes with a look at international labor relations and the relationship between the firm's management of labor relations and its overall strategy.

The Strategic Role of International HRM

LEARNING OBJECTIVE 1
Articulate the strategic role of human resource management in an international business.

A large and expanding body of academic research suggests that a strong fit between human resources practices and strategy is required for high profitability.[3] You will recall from Chapter 11 that superior performance requires not only the right strategy, but the strategy must also be supported by the right organization architecture. Strategy is implemented through organization. As shown in Figure 16.1 (which is based on Figure 11.5), people are the linchpin of a firm's organization architecture. For a firm to outperform its rivals in the global marketplace, it must have the right people in the right postings. Those people must be trained appropriately so that they have the skill sets required to perform their jobs effectively, and so that they behave in a manner that is congruent with the desired culture of the firm. Their compensation packages must create incentives for them take actions that are consistent with the strategy of the firm, and the performance appraisal systems the firm uses must measure the behavior that the firm wants to encourage.

As indicated in Figure 16.1, the HRM function, through its staffing, training, compensation, and performance appraisal activities, has a critical impact upon the people, culture, incentive, and control system elements of firm's organization architecture (performance appraisal systems are part of the control systems in an enterprise). Thus, HRM professionals have a critically important strategic role. It is incumbent upon them to shape these elements of a firm's organization architecture in a manner that is consistent with the strategy of the enterprise, so that the firm can effectively implement its strategy.

In short, superior human resource management can be a sustained source of high productivity and competitive advantage in the global economy. At the same time, research suggests that many international businesses have room for improving the effectiveness of their HRM function. In one study of competitiveness among 326 large multinationals, the authors found that human resource management was one of the weakest capabilities in most firms, suggesting that improving the effectiveness of international HRM practices might have substantial performance benefits.[4]

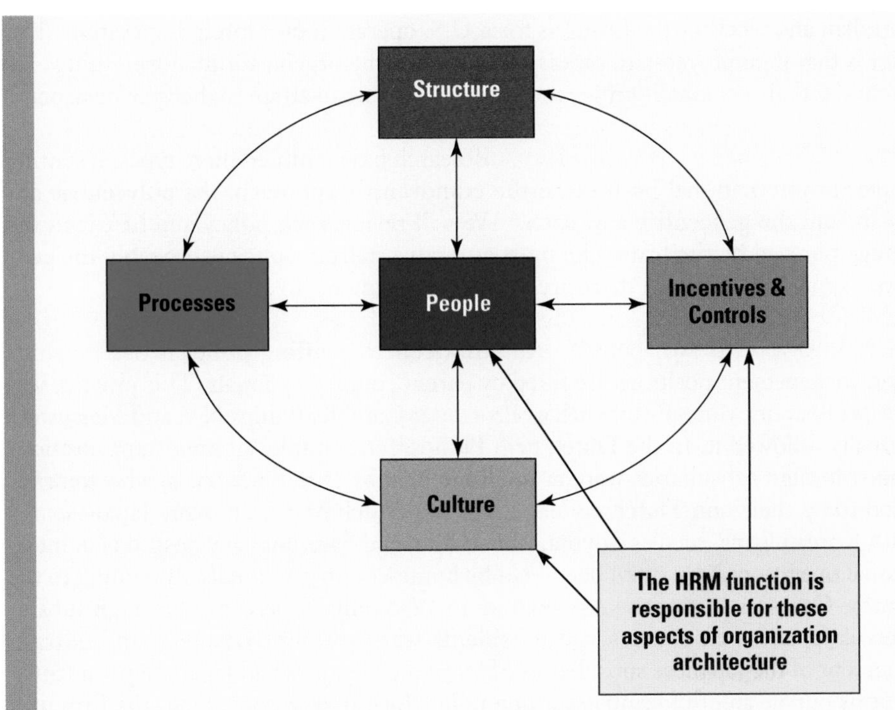

figure 16.1

The Role of Human Resources in Shaping Organization Architecture

In Chapter 11, we examined four strategies pursued by international businesses: localization strategy, international strategy, global standardization strategy, and transnational strategy. Firms that emphasize localization try to create value by emphasizing local responsiveness; international firms, by transferring products and competencies overseas; global firms, by realizing experience curve and location economies; and transnational firms, by doing all these things simultaneously. In this chapter, we will see that success also requires HRM policies to be congruent with the firm's strategy. For example, a transnational strategy imposes different requirements for staffing, management development, and compensation practices than a localization strategy. Firms pursuing a transnational strategy need to build a strong corporate culture and an informal management network for transmitting information and knowledge within the organization. Through its employee selection, management development, performance appraisal, and compensation policies, the HRM function can help develop these things. Thus, as we have noted, HRM has a critical role to play in implementing strategy. In each section that follows, we will review the strategic role of HRM in some detail.

Staffing Policy

LEARNING OBJECTIVE 2
Discuss the pros and cons of different approaches to staffing policy in an international business.

Staffing policy is concerned with the selection of employees for particular jobs. At one level, this involves selecting individuals who have the skills required to do particular jobs. At another level, staffing policy can be a tool for developing and promoting the desired corporate culture of the firm.[5] By **corporate culture**, we mean the organization's norms and value systems. A strong corporate culture can help a firm to implement its strategy. General Electric, for example, is not just concerned with hiring people who have the skills required for performing particular jobs; it wants to hire individuals whose behavioral styles, beliefs, and value systems are consistent with those of GE. This is true whether an American is being hired, an Italian, a German, or an

Staffing Policy An organization's strategy concerning the selection of employees for particular jobs.

Corporate Culture An organization's norms and value systems.

Ethnocentric Staffing Policy A staffing approach in which all key management positions are filled by parent-country nationals.

Australian and whether the hiring is for a U.S. operation or a foreign operation. The belief is that if employees are predisposed toward the organization's norms and value systems by their personality type, the firm will be able to attain higher performance.

TYPES OF STAFFING POLICY

Research has identified three types of staffing policies in international businesses: the ethnocentric approach, the polycentric approach, and the geocentric approach.[6] We will review each policy and link it to the strategy pursued by the firm. The most attractive staffing policy is probably the geocentric approach, although there are several impediments to adopting it.

The Ethnocentric Approach

An **ethnocentric staffing policy** is one in which all key management positions are filled by parent country nationals. This practice was widespread at one time. Firms such as Procter & Gamble, Philips NV, and Matsushita originally followed it. In the Dutch firm Philips, for example, all important positions in most foreign subsidiaries were at one time held by Dutch nationals, who were referred to by their non-Dutch colleagues as the Dutch Mafia. In many Japanese and South Korean firms, such as Toyota, Matsushita, and Samsung, key positions in international operations have often been held by home-country nationals. According to the Japanese Overseas Enterprise Association, in 1996 only 29 percent of foreign subsidiaries of Japanese companies had presidents who were not Japanese. In contrast, 66 percent of the Japanese subsidiaries of foreign companies had Japanese presidents.[7]

Firms pursue an ethnocentric staffing policy for three reasons. First, the firm may believe the host country lacks qualified individuals to fill senior management positions. This argument is heard most often when the firm has operations in less developed countries. Second, the firm may see an ethnocentric staffing policy as the best way to maintain a unified corporate culture. Many Japanese firms, for example, prefer their foreign operations to be headed by expatriate Japanese managers because these managers will have been socialized into the firm's culture while employed in Japan.[8] Procter & Gamble until recently preferred to staff important management positions in its foreign subsidiaries with U.S. nationals who had been socialized into P&G's corporate culture by years of employment in its U.S. operations. Such reasoning tends to predominate when a firm places a high value on its corporate culture.

Third, if the firm is trying to create value by transferring core competencies to a foreign operation, as firms pursuing an international strategy are, it may believe that the best way to do this is to transfer parent-country nationals who have knowledge of that competency to the foreign operation. Imagine what might occur if a firm tried to transfer a core competency in marketing to a foreign subsidiary without a corresponding transfer of home-country marketing management personnel. The transfer would probably fail to produce the anticipated benefits because the knowledge underlying a core competency cannot easily be articulated and written down. Such knowledge often has a significant tacit dimension; it is acquired through experience. Just like the great tennis player who cannot instruct others how to become great tennis players simply by writing a handbook, the firm that has a core competency in marketing, or anything else, cannot just write a handbook that tells a foreign subsidiary how to build the firm's core competency anew in a foreign setting. It must also transfer management personnel to the foreign operation to show foreign managers how to become good marketers, for example. The need to transfer managers overseas arises because the knowledge that underlies the firm's core competency resides in the heads of its domestic managers and was acquired through years of experience, not by reading a handbook. Thus, if a firm is to transfer a core competency to a foreign subsidiary, it must also transfer the appropriate managers.

Despite this rationale for pursuing an ethnocentric staffing policy, the policy is now on the wane in most international businesses for two reasons. First, an ethnocentric staffing policy limits advancement opportunities for host-country nationals. This can lead to resentment, lower productivity, and increased turnover among that group. Resentment can be greater still if, as often occurs, expatriate managers are paid significantly more than home-country nationals.

Second, an ethnocentric policy can lead to *cultural myopia*, the firm's failure to understand host-country cultural differences that require different approaches to marketing and management. The adaptation of expatriate managers can take a long time, during which they may make major mistakes. For example, expatriate managers may fail to appreciate how product attributes, distribution strategy, communications strategy, and pricing strategy should be adapted to host-country conditions. The result may be costly blunders. They may also make decisions that are ethically suspect simply because they do not understand the culture in which they are managing.[9] In one highly publicized case in the United States, Mitsubishi Motors was sued by the federal Equal Employment Opportunity Commission for tolerating extensive and systematic sexual harassment in a plant in Illinois. The plant's top management, all Japanese expatriates, denied the charges. The Japanese managers may have failed to realize that behavior that would be viewed as acceptable in Japan was not acceptable in the United States.[10]

Polycentric Staffing Policy
A staffing policy under which the firm recruits host-country nationals to manage subsidiaries in their own country, while parent-country nationals occupy key positions at corporate headquarters.

The Polycentric Approach

A **polycentric staffing policy** requires host-country nationals to be recruited to manage subsidiaries, while parent-country nationals occupy key positions at corporate headquarters. In many respects, a polycentric approach is a response to the shortcomings of an ethnocentric approach. One advantage of adopting a polycentric approach is that the firm is less likely to suffer from cultural myopia. Host-country managers are unlikely to make the mistakes arising from cultural misunderstandings to which expatriate managers are vulnerable. A second advantage is that a polycentric approach may be less expensive to implement, reducing the costs of value creation. Expatriate managers can be expensive to maintain.

A polycentric approach also has its drawbacks. Host-country nationals have limited opportunities to gain experience outside their own country and thus cannot progress beyond senior positions in their own subsidiary. As in the case of an ethnocentric policy, this may cause resentment. Perhaps the major drawback with a polycentric approach, however, is the gap that can form between host-country managers and parent-country managers. Language barriers, national loyalties, and a range of cultural differences may isolate the corporate headquarters staff from the various foreign subsidiaries. The lack of management transfers from home to host countries, and vice versa, can exacerbate this isolation and lead to a lack of integration between corporate headquarters and foreign subsidiaries. The result can be a "federation" of largely independent national units with only nominal links to the corporate headquarters. Within such a federation, the coordination required to transfer core competencies or to pursue experience curve and location economies may be difficult to achieve. Thus, although a polycentric approach may be effective for firms pursuing a localization strategy, it is inappropriate for other strategies.

The federation that may result from a polycentric approach can also be a force for inertia within the firm. After decades of pursing a polycentric staffing policy, food and detergents giant Unilever found that shifting from a strategic posture that emphasized localization to a transnational posture was very difficult. Unilever's foreign subsidiaries had evolved into quasi-autonomous operations, each with its own strong national identity. These "little kingdoms" objected strenuously to corporate headquarters' attempts to limit their autonomy and to rationalize global manufacturing.[11]

Geocentric Staffing Policy
A staffing policy under which the firm seeks the best people for key jobs throughout the company, regardless of nationality.

The Geocentric Approach

A **geocentric staffing policy** seeks the best people for key jobs throughout the organization, regardless of nationality. This

Another Perspective

Women in International Assignments

Would you send a woman expatriate to Saudi Arabia, Kuwait, Japan, or Korea? How are Western women expatriates doing in foreign cultures that have traditionally limited women's public roles? Women sent to these countries have met with substantial success. Their key challenge is to get the assignments! Once in place, women expatriates are successful. This is in part because once in the culture, women expatriates are seen first as expatriates who fall outside the local role for women. In addition, "expat" women also have salience in their new environment—they are noticed—and this can be a distinct business advantage. Locals often take pride in developing business relationships with women expatriates because by doing so they can suggest that the foreign stereotype of their culture is superficial and incomplete.

policy has a number of advantages. First, it enables the firm to make the best use of its human resources. Second, and perhaps more important, a geocentric policy enables the firm to build a cadre of international executives who feel at home working in a number of cultures. Creation of such a cadre may be a critical first step toward building a strong unifying corporate culture and an informal management network, both of which are required for global standardization and transnational strategies.[12] Firms pursuing a geocentric staffing policy may be better able to create value from the pursuit of experience curve and location economies and from the multidirectional transfer of core competencies than firms pursuing other staffing policies. In addition, the multinational composition of the management team that results from geocentric staffing tends to reduce cultural myopia and to enhance local responsiveness. Thus, other things being equal, a geocentric staffing policy seems the most attractive. See the Another Perspective for more details.

A number of problems limit the firm's ability to pursue a geocentric policy. Many countries want foreign subsidiaries to employ their citizens. To achieve this goal, they use immigration laws to require the employment of host-country nationals if they are available in adequate numbers and have the necessary skills. Most countries, including the United States, require firms to provide extensive documentation if they wish to hire a foreign national instead of a local national. This documentation can be time consuming, expensive, and at times futile. A geocentric staffing policy also can be expensive to implement. Training and relocation costs increase when transferring managers from country to country. The company may also need a compensation structure with a standardized international base pay level higher than national levels in many countries. In addition, the higher pay enjoyed by managers placed on an international fast track may be a source of resentment within a firm.

Summary The advantages and disadvantages of the three approaches to staffing policy are summarized in Table 16.1. Broadly speaking, an ethnocentric approach is compatible with an international strategy, a polycentric approach is compatible with a localization strategy, and a geocentric approach is compatible with both global standardization and transnational strategies. (See Chapter 11 for details of the strategies.)

While the staffing policies described here are well known and widely used among both practitioners and scholars of international businesses, some critics have claimed that the typology is too simplistic and that it obscures the internal differentiation of management practices within international businesses. The critics claim that within some international businesses, staffing policies vary significantly from national subsidiary to national subsidiary; while some are managed on an ethnocentric basis, others are managed in a polycentric or geocentric manner.[13] Other critics note that the staffing policy adopted by a firm is primarily driven by its geographic scope, as opposed to its strategic orientation. Firms that have a broad geographic scope are the most likely to have a geocentric mind-set.[14]

table 16.1

Comparison of Staffing Approaches

Staffing Approach	Strategic Appropriateness	Advantages	Disadvantages
Ethnocentric	International	Overcomes lack of qualified managers in host nation Unified culture Helps transfer core competencies	Produces resentment in host country Can lead to cultural myopia
Polycentric	Localization	Alleviates cultural myopia Inexpensive to implement	Limits career mobility Isolates headquarters from foreign subsidiaries
Geocentric	Global standardization and transnational	Uses human resources efficiently Helps build strong culture and informal management networks	National immigration policies may limit implementation Expensive

LEARNING OBJECTIVE 3
Explain why managers may fail to thrive in foreign postings.

EXPATRIATE MANAGERS Two of the three staffing policies we have discussed—the ethnocentric and the geocentric—rely on extensive use of expatriate managers. As defined earlier, expatriates are citizens of one country who are working in another country (John Ross, profiled in the opening case, was an expatriate). Sometimes the term *inpatriates* is used to identify a subset of expatriates who are citizens of a foreign country working in the home country of their multinational employer.[15] Thus, a citizen of Japan who moves to the United States to work at Microsoft would be classified as an inpatriate. With an ethnocentric policy, the expatriates are all home-country nationals who are transferred abroad. With a geocentric approach, the expatriates need not be home-country nationals; the firm does not base transfer decisions on nationality. A prominent issue in the international staffing literature is **expatriate failure**—the premature return of an expatriate manager to his or her home country.[16] Here we briefly review the evidence on expatriate failure before discussing a number of ways to minimize the failure rate.

Expatriate Failure
The premature return of an expatriate manager to his or her home country.

Expatriate Failure Rates Expatriate failure represents a failure of the firm's selection policies to identify individuals who will not thrive abroad.[17] The consequences include premature return from a foreign posting and high resignation rates, with expatriates leaving their company at about twice the rate of domestic managements.[18] Research suggests that between 16 and 40 percent of all American employees sent abroad to developed nations return from their assignments early, and almost 70 percent of employees sent to developing nations return home early.[19] Although detailed data are not available for most nationalities, one suspects that high expatriate failure is a universal problem. Some 28 percent of British expatriates, for example, are estimated to fail in their overseas postings.[20] The costs of expatriate failure are high. One estimate is that the average cost per failure to the parent firm can be as high as three times the expatriate's annual domestic salary plus the cost of relocation (which is affected by currency exchange rates and location of assignment).

Estimates of the costs of each failure run between $250,000 and $1 million.[21] In addition, approximately 30 to 50 percent of American expatriates, whose average annual compensation packages run to $250,000, stay at their international assignments but are considered ineffective or marginally effective by their firms.[22] In a seminal study, R. L. Tung surveyed a number of U.S., European, and Japanese multinationals.[23] Her results, summarized in Table 16.2, show that 76 percent of U.S. multinationals experienced expatriate failure rates of 10 percent or more, and 7 percent experienced a failure rate of more than 20 percent. Tung's work also suggests that U.S.-based multinationals experience a much higher expatriate failure rate than either European or Japanese multinationals.

Tung asked her sample of multinational managers to indicate reasons for expatriate failure. For U.S. multinationals, the reasons, in order of importance, were

1. Inability of spouse to adjust.
2. Manager's inability to adjust.
3. Other family problems.
4. Manager's personal or emotional maturity.
5. Inability to cope with larger overseas responsibilities.

Managers of European firms gave only one reason consistently to explain expatriate failure: the inability of the manager's spouse to adjust to a new environment. For the Japanese firms, the reasons for failure were

1. Inability to cope with larger overseas responsibilities.
2. Difficulties with new environment.
3. Personal or emotional problems.
4. Lack of technical competence.
5. Inability of spouse to adjust.

The most striking difference between these lists is that "inability of spouse to adjust" was the top reason for expatriate failure among U.S. and European multinationals but only the number five reason among Japanese multinationals. Tung comments that this difference is not surprising, given the role and status to which Japanese society traditionally relegates the wife and the fact that most of the Japanese expatriate managers in the study were men.

Since Tung's study, a number of other studies have consistently confirmed that the inability of a spouse to adjust, the inability of the manager to adjust, or other family

Expatriate Failure Rates

Source: Data from R. L. Tung, "Selection and Training of Personnel for Overseas Assignments," *Columbia Journal of World Business*, Spring 1981, pp. 68–78..

Recall Rate Percent	Percent of Companies
U.S. multinationals	
20–40%	7%
10–20	69
<10	24
European multinationals	
11–15%	3%
6–10	38
<5	59
Japanese multinationals	
11–19%	14%
6–10	10
<5	76

Management FOCUS

Managing Expatriates at Royal Dutch/Shell

Royal Dutch/Shell is a global petroleum company with joint headquarters in both London and The Hague in the Netherlands. The company employs more than 100,000 people, approximately 5,500 of whom are at any one time living and working as expatriates. The expatriates at Shell are a diverse group, made up of over 70 nationalities and located in more than 100 countries. Shell, as a global corporation, has long recognized that the international mobility of its workforce is essential to its success. By the early 1990s, however, Shell was finding it harder to recruit key personnel for foreign postings. To discover why, the company interviewed more than 200 expatriate employees and their spouses to determine their biggest concerns. The data were then used to construct a survey that was sent to 17,000 current and former expatriate employees, expatriates' spouses, and employees who had declined international assignments.

The survey registered a phenomenal 70 percent response rate, clearly indicating that many employees thought this was an important issue. According to the survey, five issues had the greatest impact on the willingness of an employee to accept an international assignment. In order of importance, these were (1) separation from children during their secondary education (the children of British and Dutch expatriates were often sent to boarding schools in their home countries while their parents worked abroad), (2) harm done to a spouse's career and employment, (3) failure to recognize and involve a spouse in the relocation decision, (4) failure to provide adequate information and assistance regarding relocation, and (5) health issues. The underlying message was that the family is the basic unit of expatriation, not the individual, and Shell needed to do more to recognize this.

To deal with these issues, Shell implemented a number of programs designed to address some of these problems. To help with the education of children, Shell built elementary schools for Shell employees where there was a heavy concentration of expatriates. As for secondary school education, it worked with local schools, often providing grants, to help them upgrade their educational offerings. It also offered an education supplement to help expatriates send their children to private schools in the host country.

Helping spouses with their careers is a more vexing problem. According to the survey data, half of the spouses accompanying Shell staff on assignment were employed until the transfer. When expatriated, only 12 percent were able to secure employment, while a further 33 percent wished to be employed. Shell set up a spouse employment center to address the problem. The center provides career counseling and assistance in locating employment opportunities both during and immediately after an international assignment. The company also agreed to reimburse up to 80 percent of the costs of vocational training, further education, or re-accreditation, up to $4,400 per assignment.

Shell also set up a global information and advice network known as "The Outpost" to provide support for families contemplating a foreign posting. The Outpost has its headquarters in The Hague and now runs 40 information centers in more than 30 countries. The center recommends schools and medical facilities and provides housing advice, and up-to-date information on employment, study, self-employment, and volunteer work.

Sources: E. Smockum, "Don't Forget the Trailing Spouse," *Financial Times,* May 6, 1998, p. 22; V. Frazee, "Tearing Down Roadblocks," *Workforce* 77, no. 2 (1998), pp. 50–54; C. Sievers, "Expatriate Management," *HR Focus* 75, no. 3 (1998), pp. 75–76; and J. Barbian, "Return to Sender," *Training,* January 2002, pp. 40–43.

problems remain major reasons for continuing high levels of expatriate failure (note that this was a problem at XCO China; see the opening case). One study by International Orientation Resources, an HRM consulting firm, found that 60 percent of expatriate failures occur due to these three reasons.[24] Another study found that the most common reason for assignment failure is lack of partner (spouse) satisfaction, which was listed by 27 percent of respondents.[25] The inability of expatriate managers to adjust to foreign postings seems to be caused by a lack of cultural skills on the part of the manager being transferred. According to one HRM consulting firm, this is because the expatriate selection process at many firms is fundamentally flawed, as appeared to be the case at XCO China. "Expatriate assignments rarely fail because the person cannot accommodate to the technical demands of the job. Typically, the expatriate selections are made by line managers based on technical competence. They fail because of family and personal issues and lack of cultural skills that haven't been part of the selection process."[26]

The failure of spouses to adjust to a foreign posting seems to be related to a number of factors. Often spouses find themselves in a foreign country without the familiar network of family and friends. Language differences make it difficult for them to make new friends. While this may not be a problem for the manager, who can make friends at work, it can be difficult for the spouse, who might feel trapped at home. The problem is often exacerbated by immigration regulations prohibiting the spouse from taking employment. With the recent rise of two-career families in many developed nations, this issue has become much more important. One survey found that 69 percent of expatriates are married, with spouses accompanying them 77 percent of the time. Of those spouses, 49 percent were employed before an assignment and only 11 percent were employed during an assignment.[27] Research suggests that a main reason managers now turn down international assignments is concern over the impact such an assignment might have on their spouse's career.[28] The accompanying Management Focus box, previous page examines how one large multinational company, Royal Dutch/Shell, has tried to come to grips with this issue.

Expatriate Selection One way to reduce expatriate failure rates is by improving selection procedures to screen out inappropriate candidates. In a review of the research on this issue, Mendenhall and Oddou state that a major problem in many firms is that HRM managers tend to equate domestic performance with overseas performance potential.[29] Domestic performance and overseas performance potential are *not* the same thing. An executive who performs well in a domestic setting may not be able to adapt to managing in a different cultural setting. From their review of the research, Mendenhall and Oddou identified four dimensions that seem to predict success in a foreign posting: self-orientation, others-orientation, perceptual ability, and cultural toughness.

1. *Self-orientation.* The attributes of this dimension strengthen the expatriate's self-esteem, self-confidence, and mental well-being. Expatriates with high self-esteem, self-confidence, and mental well-being were more likely to succeed in foreign postings. Mendenhall and Oddou concluded that such individuals were able to adapt their interests in food, sport, and music; had interests outside of work that could be pursued (e.g., hobbies); and were technically competent.
2. *Others-orientation.* The attributes of this dimension enhance the expatriate's ability to interact effectively with host-country nationals. The more effectively the expatriate interacts with host-country nationals, the more likely he or she is to succeed. Two factors seem to be particularly important here: relationship development and willingness to communicate. Relationship development refers to the ability to develop long-lasting friendships with host- country nationals. Willingness to communicate refers to the expatriate's willingness to use the host-country language. Although language fluency helps, an expatriate need not be fluent to show willingness to communicate. Making the effort to use the language is what is important. Such gestures tend to be rewarded with greater cooperation by host-country nationals.
3. *Perceptual ability.* This is the ability to understand why people of other countries behave the way they do; that is, the ability to empathize. This dimension seems critical for managing host-country nationals. Expatriate managers who lack this ability tend to treat foreign nationals as if they were home-country nationals. As a result, they may experience significant management problems and considerable frustration. As one expatriate executive from Hewlett-Packard observed, "It took me six months to accept the fact that my staff meetings would start 30 minutes late, and that it would bother no one but me." According to Mendenhall and

Oddou, well-adjusted expatriates tend to be nonjudgmental and nonevaluative in interpreting the behavior of host-country nationals and willing to be flexible in their management style, adjusting it as cultural conditions warrant.

4. *Cultural toughness.* This dimension refers to the relationship between the country of assignment and how well an expatriate adjusts to a particular posting. Some countries are much tougher postings than others because their cultures are more unfamiliar and uncomfortable. For example, many Americans regard Great Britain as a relatively easy foreign posting, and for good reason—the two cultures have much in common. But many Americans find postings in non-Western cultures, such as India, Southeast Asia, and the Middle East, to be much tougher.[30] The reasons are many, including poor health care and housing standards, inhospitable climate, lack of Western entertainment, and language difficulties. Also, many cultures are extremely male-dominated and may be particularly difficult postings for female Western managers.

Another Perspective

The Global Mind-Set

Some researchers suggest that a global mind-set, one characterized by cognitive complexity and a cosmopolitan outlook, is the fundamental attribute of a global manager. Such managers can deal with high levels of complexity and ambiguity and are open to the world. How do you develop these attributes? Often they are gained in early life, from a family that is bicultural, lives in foreign countries, or learns foreign languages as a regular part of family life.

Mendenhall and Oddou note that standard psychological tests can be used to assess the first three of these dimensions, whereas a comparison of cultures can give managers a feeling for the fourth dimension. They contend that these four dimensions, in addition to domestic performance, should be considered when selecting a manager for foreign posting. See the Another Perspective above. However, practice does not often conform to Mendenhall and Oddou's recommendations. Tung's research, for example, showed that only 5 percent of the firms in her sample used formal procedures and psychological tests to assess the personality traits and relational abilities of potential expatriates.[31] Research by International Orientation Resources suggests that when selecting employees for foreign assignments, only 10 percent of the 50 Fortune 500 firms they surveyed tested for important psychological traits such as cultural sensitivity, interpersonal skills, adaptability, and flexibility. Instead, 90 percent of the time employees were selected on the basis of their technical expertise, not their cross-cultural fluency.[32]

Mendenhall and Oddou do not address the problem of expatriate failure due to a spouse's inability to adjust. According to a number of other researchers, a review of the family situation should be part of the expatriate selection process (see the Management Focus on Royal Dutch/Shell for an example).[33] A survey by Windam International, another international HRM consulting firm, found that spouses were included in preselection interviews for foreign postings only 21 percent of the time, and that only half of them received any cross-cultural training. The rise of dual-career families has added an additional and difficult dimension to this long-standing problem.[34] Increasingly, spouses wonder why they should have to sacrifice their own career to further that of their partner.[35]

Training and Management Development

LEARNING OBJECTIVE 4
Articulate how management development and training programs can increase the value of human capital in an international business firm.

Selection is just the first step in matching a manager with a job. The next step is training the manager to do the specific job. For example, an intensive training program might be used to give expatriate managers the skills required for success in a foreign posting. However, management development is a much broader concept. It is intended to develop the manager's skills over his or her career with the firm. Thus, as part of a management

At Caterpillar, expatriate managers and their families receive culture and language training, as well as relocation assistance, before relocating to one of Caterpillar's global facilities. *Photo courtesy of Caterpillar Inc.*

development program, a manager might be sent on several foreign postings over a number of years to build his or her cross-cultural sensitivity and experience. At the same time, along with other managers in the firm, the person might attend management education programs at regular intervals. The thinking behind job transfers is that broad international experience will enhance the management and leadership skills of executives. Research suggests this may be the case.[36]

Historically, most international businesses have been more concerned with training than with management development. Plus, they tended to focus their training efforts on preparing home-country nationals for foreign postings. Recently, however, the shift toward greater global competition and the rise of transnational firms have changed this. It is increasingly common for firms to provide general management development programs in addition to training for particular posts. In many international businesses, the explicit purpose of these management development programs is strategic. Management development is seen as a tool to help the firm achieve its strategic goals, not only by giving managers the required skill set, but also by helping to reinforce the desired culture of the firm and by facilitating the creation of an informal network for sharing knowledge within the multinational enterprise.

With this distinction between training and management development in mind, we first examine the types of training managers receive for foreign postings. Then we discuss the connection between management development and strategy in the international business.

TRAINING FOR EXPATRIATE MANAGERS Earlier in the chapter we saw that the two most common reasons for expatriate failure were the inability of a manager's spouse to adjust to a foreign environment and the manager's own inability to adjust to a foreign environment. Training can help the manager and spouse cope with both these problems. Cultural training, language training, and practical training all seem to reduce expatriate failure. We discuss each of these kinds of training here.[37] Despite the usefulness of these kinds of training, evidence suggests that many managers receive no training before they are sent on foreign postings. One study found that only about 30 percent of managers sent on one- to five-year expatriate assignments received training before their departure.[38]

Cultural Training Cultural training seeks to foster an appreciation for the host country's culture. The belief is that understanding a host country's culture will help the manager empathize with the culture, which will enhance his or her effectiveness in dealing with host-country nationals. It has been suggested that expatriates should receive training in the host country's culture, history, politics, economy, religion, and social and business practices.[39] If possible, it is also advisable to arrange for a familiarization trip to the host country before the formal transfer, as this seems to ease culture shock. Given the problems related to spouse adaptation, it is important that the spouse, and perhaps the whole family, be included in cultural training programs.

Language Training English is the language of world business; it is quite possible to conduct business all over the world using only English. Notwithstanding the prevalence of English, however, an exclusive reliance on English diminishes an expatriate manager's ability to interact with host-country nationals. As noted earlier, a willingness to communicate in the language of the host country, even if the expatriate is far from fluent, can help build rapport with local employees and improve the manager's effectiveness. Despite this, one study of 74 executives of U.S. multinationals found that only 23 believed knowledge of foreign languages was necessary for conducting business abroad.[40] Those firms that did offer foreign language training for expatriates believed it improved their employees' effectiveness and enabled them to relate more easily to a foreign culture, which fostered a better image of the firm in the host country.

Practical Training Practical training is aimed at helping the expatriate manager and family ease themselves into day-to-day life in the host country. The sooner a routine is established, the better are the prospects that the expatriate and his or her family will adapt successfully. One critical need is for a support network of friends for the expatriate. Where an expatriate community exists, firms often devote considerable effort to ensuring the new expatriate family is quickly integrated into that group. The expatriate community can be a useful source of support and information and can be invaluable in helping the family adapt to a foreign culture.

REPATRIATION OF EXPATRIATES A largely overlooked but critically important issue in the training and development of expatriate managers is to prepare them for reentry into their home-country organization.[41] Repatriation should be seen as the final link in an integrated, circular process that connects good selection and cross-cultural training of expatriate managers with completion of their term abroad and reintegration into their national organization. However, instead of having employees come home to share their knowledge and encourage other high-performing managers to take the same international career track, expatriates too often face a different scenario.[42]

Often when they return home after a stint abroad—where they have typically been autonomous, well-compensated, and celebrated as a big fish in a little pond—they face an organization that doesn't know what they have done for the last few years, doesn't know how to use their new knowledge, and doesn't particularly care. In the worst cases, reentering employees have to scrounge for jobs, or firms will create standby positions that don't use the expatriate's skills and capabilities and fail to make the most of the business investment the firm has made in that individual.

Research illustrates the extent of this problem. According to one study of repatriated employees, 60 to 70 percent didn't know what their position would be when they returned home. Also, 60 percent said their organizations were vague about repatriation, about their new roles, and about their future career progression within the company; 77 percent of those surveyed took jobs at a lower level in their home organization than in their international assignments.[43] Not surprising, 15 percent of returning expatriates leave their firms within a year of arriving home, and 40 percent leave within three years.[44]

The key to solving this problem is good human resource planning. Just as the HRM function needs to develop good selection and training programs for its expatriates, it also needs to develop good programs for reintegrating expatriates back into work life within their home-country organization, for preparing them for changes in their physical and professional landscape, and for utilizing the knowledge they acquired while abroad. For an example of the kind of program that might be used, see the Management Focus on page 522 that looks at the repatriation program developed by Monsanto.

Management FOCUS

Monsanto's Repatriation Program

Monsanto is a global provider of agricultural products with revenues of $5 billion and 10,000 employees. At any one time, the company will have 100 mid- and higher-level managers on extended postings abroad. Two-thirds of these are Americans posted overseas; the remainder are foreign nationals employed in the United States. At Monsanto, managing expatriates and their repatriation begins with a rigorous selection process and intensive cross-cultural training, both for the managers and for their families. As at many other global companies, the idea is to build an internationally minded cadre of highly capable managers who will lead the organization in the future.

One of the strongest features of this program is that employees and their sending and receiving managers, or sponsors, develop an agreement about how this assignment will fit into the firm's business objectives. The focus is on why employees are going abroad to do the job and what their contribution to Monsanto will be when they return. Sponsoring managers are expected to be explicit about the kind of job opportunities the expatriates will have once they return home.

Once they arrive back in their home country, expatriate managers meet with cross-cultural trainers during debriefing sessions. They are also given the opportunity to showcase their experiences to their peers, subordinates, and superiors in special information exchanges.

However, Monsanto's repatriation program focuses on more than just business; it also attends to the family's reentry. Monsanto has found that difficulties with repatriation often have more to do with personal and family-related issues than with work-related issues. But the personal matters obviously affect an employee's on-the-job performance, so it is important for the company to pay attention to such issues.

This is why Monsanto offers returning employees an opportunity to work through personal difficulties. About three months after they return home, expatriates meet for three hours at work with several colleagues of their choice. The debriefing session is a conversation aided by a trained facilitator who has an outline to help the expatriate cover all the important aspects of the repatriation. The debriefing allows the employee to share important experiences and to enlighten managers, colleagues, and friends about his or her expertise so others within the organization can use some of the global knowledge. According to one participant, "It sounds silly, but it's such a hectic time in the family's life, you don't have time to sit down and take stock of what's happening. You're going through the move, transitioning to a new job, a new house, and the children may be going to a new school. This is a kind of oasis; a time to talk and put your feelings on the table." Apparently it works; since the program was introduced, the attrition rate among returning expatriates has dropped sharply.

Sources: C. M. Solomon, "Repatriation: Up, Down, or Out?" *Personnel Journal,* January 1995, pp. 28–34; and J. Schaefer, E. Hannibal, and J. O'Neill, "How Strategy, Culture and Improved Service Delivery Reshape Monsanto's International Assignment Program," *Journal of Organizational Excellence* 22, no. 3 (2003), pp. 35–40.

MANAGEMENT DEVELOPMENT AND STRATEGY Management development programs are designed to increase the overall skill levels of managers through a mix of ongoing management education and rotations of managers through a number of jobs within the firm to give them varied experiences. They are attempts to improve the overall productivity and quality of the firm's management resources.

International businesses increasingly are using management development as a strategic tool. This is particularly true in firms pursuing a transnational strategy, as increasing numbers are. Such firms need a strong unifying corporate culture and informal management networks to assist in coordination and control. In addition, transnational firm managers need to be able to detect pressures for local responsiveness, and that requires them to understand the culture of a host country.

Management development programs help build a unifying corporate culture by socializing new managers into the norms and value systems of the firm. In-house company training programs and intense interaction during off-site training can foster esprit de corps—shared experiences, informal networks, perhaps a company language or jargon—as well as develop technical competencies. These training events often include songs, picnics, and sporting events that promote feelings of togetherness. These rites of integration may include "initiation rites" wherein personal culture is stripped, company uniforms are donned (e.g., T-shirts bearing the company logo), and humiliation is inflicted (e.g., a pie in the face). All these activities aim to strengthen a manager's identification with the company.[45]

Bringing managers together in one location for extended periods and rotating them through different jobs in several countries helps the firm build an informal management network. Such a network can then be used as a conduit for exchanging valuable performance-enhancing knowledge within the organization.[46] Consider the Swedish telecommunications company L. M. Ericsson. Interunit cooperation is extremely important at Ericsson, particularly for transferring know-how and core competencies from the parent to foreign subsidiaries, from foreign subsidiaries to the parent, and between foreign subsidiaries. To facilitate cooperation, Ericsson transfers large numbers of people back and forth between headquarters and subsidiaries. Ericsson sends a team of 50 to 100 engineers and managers from one unit to another for a year or two. This establishes a network of interpersonal contacts. This policy is effective for both solidifying a common culture in the company and coordinating the company's globally dispersed operations.[47]

Performance Appraisal

LEARNING OBJECTIVE 5
Explain how and why performance appraisal systems might vary across nations.

Performance appraisal systems are used to evaluate the performance of managers against some criteria that the firm judges to be important for the implementation of strategy and the attainment of a competitive advantage. A firm's performance appraisal systems are an important element of its control systems, which is a central component of organization architecture (see Figure 16.1). A particularly thorny issue in many international businesses is how best to evaluate the performance of expatriate managers.[48] In this section, we look at this issue and consider some guidelines for appraising expatriate performance.

PERFORMANCE APPRAISAL PROBLEMS Unintentional bias makes it difficult to evaluate the performance of expatriate managers objectively. In many cases, two groups evaluate the performance of expatriate managers—host-nation managers and home-office managers—and both are subject to bias. The host-nation managers may be biased by their own cultural frame of reference and expectations. For example, Oddou and Mendenhall report the case of a U.S. manager who introduced participative decision making while working in an Indian subsidiary.[49] The manager subsequently received a negative evaluation from host-country managers because in India, the strong social stratification means managers are seen as experts who should not have to ask subordinates for help. The local employees apparently viewed the U.S. manager's attempt at participatory management as an indication that he was incompetent and did not know his job.

Home-country managers' appraisals may be biased by distance and by their own lack of experience working abroad. Home-office managers are often not aware of what is going on in a foreign operation. Accordingly, they tend to rely on hard data in evaluating an expatriate's performance, such as the subunit's productivity, profitability, or market share (recall from the opening case that this was a problem at XCO China). Such criteria may reflect factors outside the expatriate manager's control (e.g., adverse changes in exchange rates, economic downturns). Also, hard data do not take into account many less-visible soft variables that are also important, such as an expatriate's ability to develop cross-cultural awareness and to work productively with local managers. Due to such biases, many expatriate managers believe that headquarters management evaluates them unfairly and does not fully appreciate the value of their skills and experience. This could be one reason many expatriates believe a foreign posting does not benefit their careers. In one study of personnel managers in U.S. multinationals, 56 percent of the managers surveyed stated that a foreign assignment is either detrimental or immaterial to one's career.[50]

GUIDELINES FOR PERFORMANCE APPRAISAL Several things can reduce bias in the performance appraisal process.[51] First, most expatriates appear to believe more weight should be given to an on-site manager's appraisal than to an off-site manager's appraisal. Due to proximity, an on-site manager is more likely to evaluate the soft variables that are important aspects of an expatriate's performance. The evaluation may be especially valid when the on-site manager is of the same nationality as the expatriate, since cultural bias should be alleviated. In practice, home-office managers often write performance evaluations after receiving input from on-site managers. When this is the case, most experts recommend that a former expatriate who served in the same location should be involved in the appraisal to help reduce bias. Finally, when the policy is for foreign on-site managers to write performance evaluations, home-office managers should be consulted before an on-site manager completes a formal termination evaluation. This gives the home-office manager the opportunity to balance what could be a very hostile evaluation based on a cultural misunderstanding.

Compensation

LEARNING OBJECTIVE 6
Explain how and why compensation systems might vary across nations.

Two issues are raised in every discussion of compensation practices in an international business. One is how compensation should be adjusted to reflect national differences in economic circumstances and compensation practices. The other issue is how expatriate managers should be paid. From a strategic perspective, the important point is that whatever compensation system is used, it should reward managers for taking actions that are consistent with the strategy of the enterprise.

NATIONAL DIFFERENCES IN COMPENSATION Substantial differences exist in the compensation of executives at the same level in various countries. The results of a survey undertaken by Towers Perrin are summarized in Table 16.3, next page. This survey looked at average compensation for CEOs and manufacturing employees across 26 countries in the 2003–04 period for companies with annual sales of around $500 million.[52] The figures for CEOs include both base compensation and performance-related pay bonuses, but they do not include stock options. The figures for manufacturing employees refer to base pay and bonuses. As can be seen, wide variations exist across countries. The average compensation for a CEO in the United States was $2.25 million, compared with $456,937 in Japan and $249,075 in Taiwan. These figures underestimate the true differential because many U.S. executives earn considerable sums of money from stock option grants.[53]

National differences in compensation raise a perplexing question for an international business: Should the firm pay executives in different countries according to the prevailing standards in each country, or should it equalize pay on a global basis? The problem does not arise in firms pursuing ethnocentric or polycentric staffing policies. In ethnocentric firms, the issue can be reduced to that of how much home-country expatriates should be paid (which we will consider later). As for polycentric firms, the lack of managers' mobility among national operations implies that pay can and should be kept country-specific. There would seem to be no point in paying executives in Great Britain the same as U.S. executives if they never work side by side.

However, this problem is very real in firms with geocentric staffing policies. A geocentric staffing policy is consistent with a transnational strategy. One aspect of this policy is the need for a cadre of international managers that may include many different nationalities. Should all members of such a cadre be paid the same salary and the

Country	CEO Pay	Manufacturing Employee Pay
Argentina	$ 316,735	$ 6,937
Australia	694,638	31,543
Belgium	697,030	43,541
Brazil	545,024	8,861
Canada	889,898	36,283
China (Hong Kong)	746,417	20,932
China (Shanghai)	99,795	4,630
France	735,363	42,682
Germany	954,726	44,757
India	222,894	3,928
Italy	841,520	35,434
Japan	456,937	48,178
Malaysia	333,298	6,681
Mexico	966,759	15,312
Netherlands	675,062	36,860
New Zealand	449,414	23,068
Singapore	959,411	17,463
South Africa	538,290	7,453
South Korea	393,533	26,519
Spain	620,080	28,506
Sweden	700,290	39,816
Switzerland	1,190,567	60,193
Taiwan	249,075	17,144
United Kingdom	830,223	29,730
United States	2,249,080	51,121
Venezuela	401,799	9,849

table 

Compensation in 26 Countries

same incentive pay? For a U.S.-based firm, this would mean raising the compensation of foreign nationals to U.S. levels, which could be expensive. If the firm does not equalize pay, it could cause considerable resentment among foreign nationals who are members of the international cadre and work with U.S. nationals. If a firm is serious about building an international cadre, it may have to pay its international executives the same basic salary irrespective of their country of origin or assignment.

EXPATRIATE PAY The most common approach to expatriate pay is the balance sheet approach. According to Organizational Resources Consulting, some 80 percent of the 781 companies it surveyed in 2002 use this approach.[54] This approach equalizes purchasing power across countries so employees can enjoy the same living standard in their foreign posting that they enjoyed at home. In addition, the approach provides financial incentives to offset qualitative differences between assignment locations.[55]

figure 16.2

The Balance Sheet

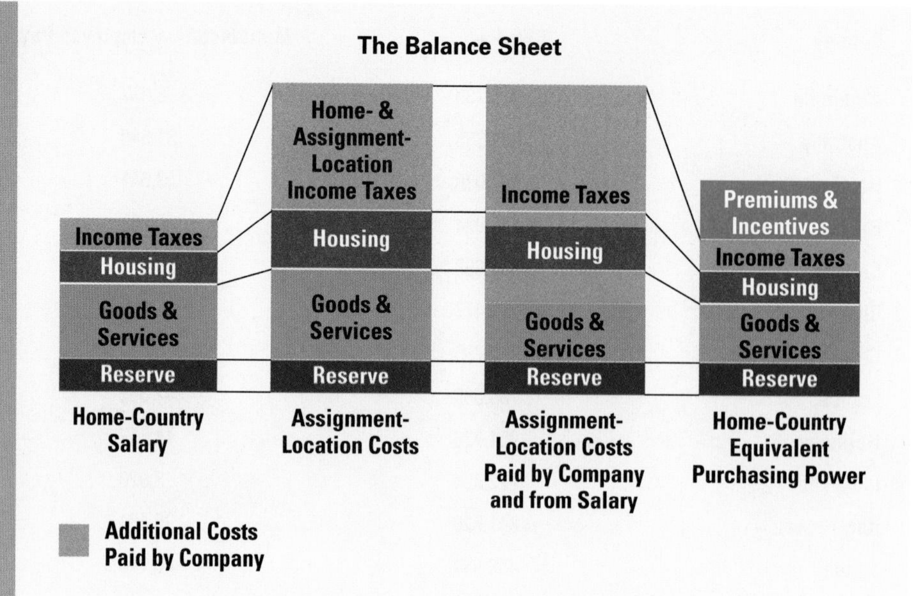

Figure 16.2 above shows a typical balance sheet. Note that home-country outlays for the employee are designated as income taxes, housing expenses, expenditures for goods and services (food, clothing, entertainment, etc.), and reserves (savings, pension contributions, etc.). The balance sheet approach attempts to provide expatriates with the same standard of living in their host countries as they enjoy at home plus a financial inducement (i.e., premium, incentive) for accepting an overseas assignment.

The components of the typical expatriate compensation package are a base salary, a foreign service premium, allowances of various types, tax differentials, and benefits. We shall briefly review each of these components.[56] An expatriate's total compensation package may amount to three times what he or she would cost the firm in a home-country posting. Because of the high cost of expatriates, many firms have reduced their use of them in recent years. However, a firm's ability to reduce its use of expatriates may be limited, particularly if it is pursuing an ethnocentric or geocentric staffing policy.

Base Salary An expatriate's base salary is normally in the same range as the base salary for a similar position in the home country. The base salary is normally paid in either the home-country currency or in the local currency.

Foreign Service Premium A foreign service premium is extra pay the expatriate receives for working outside his or her country of origin. It is offered as an inducement to accept foreign postings. It compensates the expatriate for having to live in an unfamiliar country isolated from family and friends, having to deal with a new culture and language, and having to adapt to new work habits and practices. Many firms pay foreign service premiums as a percentage of base salary, ranging from 10 to 30 percent after tax, with 16 percent being the average premium.[57]

Allowances Four types of allowances are often included in an expatriate's compensation package: hardship allowances, housing allowances, cost-of-living allowances, and education allowances. A hardship allowance is paid when the expatriate is being sent to a difficult location, usually defined as one where such basic amenities as health care, schools, and retail stores are grossly deficient by the standards of the expatriate's home country. A housing allowance is normally given to ensure that the expatriate can afford the same quality of housing in the foreign country as at home. In locations where housing is expensive (e.g., London, Tokyo), this allowance can be substantial—as much as 10 to 30 percent of the expatriate's total compensation package. A cost-of-living allowance ensures that the expatriate will enjoy the same standard of living in the foreign posting as at home. An education allowance ensures that an expatriate's children receive adequate schooling (by home-country standards). Host-country public schools are sometimes not suitable for an expatriate's children, in which case they must attend a private school.

Another Perspective

Will Tax Changes Force U.S. Expatriates Home and Change International Hiring Practices?

A new U.S. tax law, retroactive to January 2006, that cranks up the tax costs for Americans working abroad may send some packing their bags and could even change international hiring practices. This law hits hardest at Americans working in Russia, Hong Kong, and Singapore, where housing costs are high and local taxes are relatively low. The higher costs may also fall on some employers that guarantee that expatriates don't pay more in taxes in their countries of work than they would in the United States—a process known as *tax equalization*. These employers may rethink hiring expatriates. For those expatriates who are not offered tax equalization by their companies, the increased tax burden will fall directly on them. How much will this law shake up international hiring practices? Analysts believe the impact of the new tax law will vary widely, depending on company, employee salary, and country. (Cris Prystay and Tom Herman, "Tax Hike Hits Home for American Abroad," *The Wall Street Journal*, July 19, 2006)

Taxation Unless a host country has a reciprocal tax treaty with the expatriate's home country, the expatriate may have to pay income tax to both the home- and host-country governments. When a reciprocal tax treaty is not in force, the firm typically pays the expatriate's income tax in the host country. In addition, firms normally make up the difference when a higher income tax rate in a host country reduces an expatriate's take-home pay. See the Another Perspective at right for more on how a new U.S. law may make expatriate work more difficult.

Benefits Many firms also ensure that their expatriates receive the same level of medical and pension benefits abroad that they received at home. This can be costly for the firm, since many benefits that are tax deductible for the firm in the home country (e.g., medical and pension benefits) may not be deductible out of the country.

International Labor Relations

The HRM function of an international business is typically responsible for international labor relations. From a strategic perspective, the key issue in international labor relations is the degree to which organized labor can limit the choices of an international business. A firm's ability to integrate and consolidate its global operations to realize experience curve and location economies can be limited by organized labor, constraining the pursuit of a transnational or global standardization strategy. Prahalad and Doz cite the example of General Motors, which gained peace with labor unions by agreeing not to integrate and consolidate operations in the most efficient manner.[58] General Motors made substantial investments in Germany—matching its new investments in Austria and Spain—at the demand of the German metalworkers' unions.

One task of the HRM function is to foster harmony and minimize conflict between the firm and organized labor. With this in mind, this section is divided into three parts. First, we review organized labor's concerns about multinational enterprises. Second, we look at how organized labor has tried to deal with these concerns. And third, we look at how international businesses manage their labor relations to minimize labor disputes.

THE CONCERNS OF ORGANIZED LABOR Labor unions generally try to get better pay, greater job security, and better working conditions for their members through collective bargaining with management. Unions' bargaining power is derived largely from their ability to threaten to disrupt production, either by a strike or some other form of work protest (e.g., refusing to work overtime). This threat is credible, however, only insofar as management has no alternative but to employ union labor.

A principal concern of domestic unions about multinational firms is that the company can counter its bargaining power with the power to move production to another country. Ford, for example, clearly threatened British unions with a plan to move manufacturing to Continental Europe unless British workers abandoned work rules that limited productivity, showed restraint in negotiating for wage increases, and curtailed strikes and other work disruptions.[59]

Another concern of organized labor is that an international business will keep highly skilled tasks in its home country and farm out only low-skilled tasks to foreign plants. Such a practice makes it relatively easy for an international business to switch production from one location to another as economic conditions warrant. Consequently, the bargaining power of organized labor is once more reduced.

A final union concern arises when an international business attempts to import employment practices and contractual agreements from its home country. When these practices are alien to the host country, organized labor fears the change will reduce its influence and power. This concern has surfaced in response to Japanese multinationals that have been trying to export their style of labor relations to other countries. For example, much to the annoyance of the United Auto Workers (UAW), many Japanese auto plants in the United States are not unionized. As a result, union influence in the auto industry is declining.

THE STRATEGY OF ORGANIZED LABOR Organized labor has responded to the increased bargaining power of multinational corporations by taking three actions: (1) trying to establish international labor organizations, (2) lobbying for national legislation to restrict multinationals, and (3) trying to achieve international regulations on multinationals through such organizations as the United Nations. These efforts have not been very successful.

In the 1960s, organized labor began to establish international trade secretariats (ITSs) to provide worldwide links for national unions in particular industries. The long-term goal was to be able to bargain transnationally with multinational firms. Organized labor believed that by coordinating union action across countries through an ITS, it could counter the power of a multinational corporation by threatening to disrupt production on an international scale. For example, Ford's threat to move production from Great Britain to other European locations would not have been credible if the unions in various European countries had united to oppose it.

However, the ITSs have had virtually no real success. Although national unions may want to cooperate, they also compete with each other to attract investment from international businesses, and hence jobs for their members. For example, in attempting to gain new jobs for their members, national unions in the auto industry often court auto firms that are seeking locations for new plants. One reason Nissan chose to build its European production facilities in Great Britain rather than Spain was that the British unions agreed to greater concessions than the Spanish unions did. As a result of such competition between national unions, cooperation is difficult to establish.

A further impediment to cooperation has been the wide variation in union structure. Trade unions developed independently in each country. As a result, the structure and ideology of unions tend to vary significantly from country to country, as does the nature of collective bargaining. For example, in Great Britain, France, and Italy, many unions are controlled by left-wing socialists, who view collective bargaining through the lens of "class conflict." In contrast, most union leaders in Germany, the Netherlands, Scandinavia, and Switzerland are far more moderate politically. The

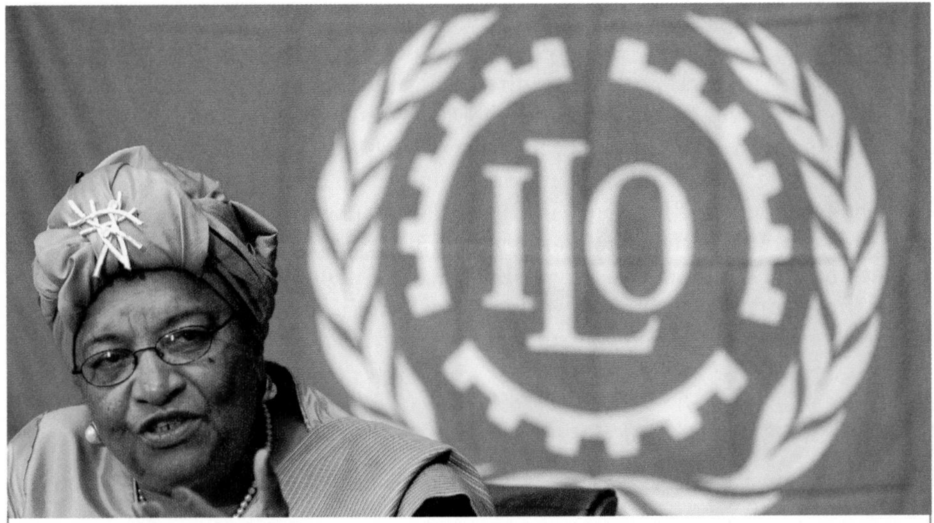

The International Labor Organization was set up to seek the promotion of social justice and internationally recognize human and labor rights. *Photo © International Labor Organization*

ideological gap between union leaders in different countries has made cooperation difficult. Divergent ideologies are reflected in radically different views about the role of a union in society and the stance unions should take toward multinationals.

Organized labor has also met with only limited success in its efforts to get national and international bodies to regulate multinationals. Such international organizations as the International Labor Organization (ILO) and the Organization for Economic Cooperation and Development (OECD) have adopted codes of conduct for multinational firms to follow in labor relations. However, these guidelines are not as far-reaching as many unions would like. They also do not provide any enforcement mechanisms. Many researchers report that such guidelines are of only limited effectiveness.[60]

APPROACHES TO LABOR RELATIONS International businesses differ markedly in their approaches to international labor relations. The main difference is the degree to which labor relations activities are centralized or decentralized. Historically, most international businesses have decentralized international labor relations activities to their foreign subsidiaries because labor laws, union power, and the nature of collective bargaining varied so much from country to country. It made sense to decentralize the labor relations function to local managers. The belief was that there was no way central management could effectively handle the complexity of simultaneously managing labor relations in a number of different environments.

Although this logic still holds, there is now a trend toward greater centralized control. This trend reflects international firms' attempts to rationalize their global operations. The general rise in competitive pressure in industry after industry has made it more important for firms to control their costs. Because labor costs account for such a large percentage of total costs, many firms are now using the threat to move production to another country in their negotiations with unions to change work rules and limit wage increases (as Ford did in Europe). Because such a move would involve major new investments and plant closures, this bargaining tactic requires the input of headquarters management. Thus, the level of centralized input into labor relations is increasing.

In addition, the realization is growing that the way work is organized within a plant can be a major source of competitive advantage. Much of the competitive advantage of Japanese automakers, for example, has been attributed to the use of self-managing teams, job rotation, cross-training, and the like in their Japanese plants.[61] To replicate their domestic performance in foreign plants, the Japanese firms have tried to replicate their work practices there. This often brings them into direct conflict with traditional work practices in those countries, as sanctioned by the local labor unions, so the Japanese firms have often made their foreign investments contingent on the local union accepting a radical change in work practices. To achieve this, the headquarters of many Japanese firms bargains directly with local unions to get union agreement to changes in work rules before committing to an investment. For example, before Nissan decided to invest in northern England, it got a commitment from British unions to agree to a change in traditional work practices. By its very nature, pursuing such a strategy requires centralized control over the labor relations function.

Key Terms

human resource management, p. 509

expatriate manager, p. 509

staffing policy, p. 511

corporate culture, p. 511

ethnocentric staffing policy, p. 512

polycentric staffing policy, p. 513

geocentric staffing policy, p. 514

expatriate failure, p. 515

Summary

This chapter focused on human resource management in international businesses. HRM activities include human resource strategy, staffing, performance evaluation, management development, compensation, and labor relations. None of these activities is performed in a vacuum; all must be appropriate to the firm's strategy. The chapter made these major points:

1. Firm success requires HRM policies to be congruent with the firm's strategy and with its formal and informal structure and controls.
2. Staffing policy is concerned with selecting employees who have the skills required to perform particular jobs. Staffing policy can be a tool for developing and promoting a corporate culture.
3. An ethnocentric approach to staffing policy fills all key management positions in an international business with parent-country nationals. The policy is congruent with an international strategy. A drawback is that ethnocentric staffing can result in cultural myopia.
4. A polycentric staffing policy uses host-country nationals to manage foreign subsidiaries and parent-country nationals for the key positions at corporate headquarters. This approach can minimize the dangers of cultural myopia, but it can create a gap between home- and host-country operations. The policy is best suited to a localization strategy.
5. A geocentric staffing policy seeks the best people for key jobs throughout the organization, regardless of their nationality. This approach is consistent with building a strong unifying culture and informal management network and is well suited to both global standardization and transnational strategies. Immigration policies of national governments may limit a firm's ability to pursue this policy.
6. A prominent issue in the international staffing literature is expatriate failure, defined as the premature return of an expatriate manager to his or her home country. The costs of expatriate failure can be substantial.
7. Expatriate failure can be reduced by selection procedures that screen out inappropriate candidates. The most successful expatriates seem to be those who have high self-esteem and self-confidence, can get along well with others, are willing to attempt to communicate in a foreign language, and can empathize with people of other cultures.

8. Training can lower the probability of expatriate failure. It should include cultural training, language training, and practical training, and it should be provided to both the expatriate manager and the spouse.
9. Management development programs attempt to increase the overall skill levels of managers through a mix of ongoing management education and rotation of managers through different jobs within the firm to give them varied experiences. Management development is often used as a strategic tool to build a strong unifying culture and informal management network, both of which support transnational and global standardization strategies.
10. It can be difficult to evaluate the performance of expatriate managers objectively because of unintentional bias. A firm can take a number of steps to reduce this bias.
11. Country differences in compensation practices raise a difficult question for an international business: Should the firm pay executives in different countries according to the standards in each country or equalize pay on a global basis?
12. The most common approach to expatriate pay is the balance sheet approach. This approach aims to equalize purchasing power so employees can enjoy the same living standard in their foreign posting that they had at home.
13. A key issue in international labor relations is the degree to which organized labor can limit the choices available to an international business. A firm's ability to pursue a transnational or global standardization strategy can be significantly constrained by the actions of labor unions.
14. A principal concern of organized labor is that the multinational can counter union bargaining power with threats to move production to another country.
15. Organized labor has tried to counter the bargaining power of multinationals by forming international labor organizations. In general, these efforts have not been effective.

Critical Thinking and Discussion Questions

1. What are the main advantages and disadvantages of the ethnocentric, polycentric, and geocentric approaches to staffing policy? When is each approach appropriate?
2. Research suggests that many expatriate employees encounter problems that limit both their effectiveness in a foreign posting and their contribution to the company when they return home. What are the main causes and consequences of these problems, and how might a firm reduce the occurrence of such problems?
3. What is the link between an international business's strategy and its human resource management policies, particularly with regard to the use of expatriate employees and their pay scale?
4. In what ways can organized labor constrain the strategic choices of an international business? How can an international business limit these constraints?

http://globalEDGE.msu.edu 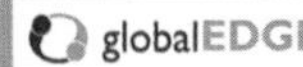 Research Task

Use the globalEDGE site (http://globalEDGE.msu.edu/) to complete the following exercises:

1. The U.S. Department of State prepares quarterly reports for *living costs abroad*. Using the most current report, identify the countries that are regarded as having a high cost of living and those that are perceived as risky. What are the living allowances and hardship differentials determined by the U.S. Department of State for those countries?
2. You work in the human resources department at the headquarters of a multinational corporation. Your company is about to send several American managers overseas as expatriates. Utilize resources available on the globalEDGE website regarding *expatriate* life to compile a short checklist of concerns and steps for your company to go through before sending its managers overseas.

Molex

Molex, a 70-year-old manufacturer of electronic components based in Chicago, is the world's second-largest manufacturer of electronic components. The company established an international division to coordinate exporting in 1967, opened its first overseas plant in Japan in 1970 and a second in Ireland in 1971. From that base, Molex has evolved into a global business that generated about 61 percent of its $1.84 billion in revenues outside of the United States. The company operates some 50 manufacturing plants in 21 countries and employs more than 16,000 people worldwide, with only one-third of them located in the United States. Molex's competitive advantage is based on a strategy that emphasizes a combination of low costs, excellent customer service, and the mass production of standardized products that are sold globally. Manufacturing sites are located in countries where cost conditions are favorable and major customers are close. Since the 1970s, a key goal of Molex has been to build a truly global company that is at home wherever in the world it operates and which proactively shares valuable knowledge across operations in different countries. The human resource management function of Molex has always played a central role in meeting this goal.

As Molex grew rapidly overseas, the HRM function made sure that every new unit did the same basic things. Each new entity had to have an employee manual with policies and practices in writing, new employee orientation programs, salary administration with a consistent grading system, written job descriptions, written promotion and grievance procedures, standard performance appraisal systems that were written down, and so on. Beyond these things, however, Molex views HRM as the most localized of functions. Different legal systems, particularly with regard to employment law, different compensation norms, different cultural attitudes to work, different norms regarding vacation, and so on, all imply that policies and programs must be customized to the conditions prevailing in a country. To make sure this occurs, Molex's policy is to hire experienced HRM professionals from other companies in the same country in which it has operations. The idea is to hire people who know the language, have credibility, know the law, and know how to recruit in that country.

Molex's strategy for building a global company starts with its staffing policy for managers and engineers. The company frequently hires foreign nationals who are living in the United States, have just completed MBAs, and are willing to relocate if required. These individuals will typically work in the United States for a while, becoming familiar with the company's culture. Some of them will then be sent back to their home country to work there. Molex also carefully screens its American applicants, favoring those who are fluent in at least one other language. Molex is unusual for a U.S. company in this regard. However, with more than 15 languages spoken at its headquarters by native speakers, Molex is committed to multilingual competency. There is also significant hiring of managers and engineers at the local level. Here, too, a willingness to relocate internationally and foreign language competency are important, although this time English is the preferred foreign language. In a sign of how multinational Molex's management has become, it is not unusual to see foreign nationals holding senior positions at company headquarters. In addition to Americans, individuals of Greek, German, Austrian, Japanese, and British origin have all sat on the company's executive committee, its top decision-making body.

To help build a global company, Molex moves people around the world to give them experience in other countries and to help them learn from each other. It has five categories of expatriates: (1) regular expatriates who live in a country other than their home country for three- to five-year assignments (there are approximately 50 of these at any one time), (2) "inpats" who come to the company's U.S. headquarters from other countries, (3) third-country nationals who move from one Molex entity to another (e.g., Singapore to Taiwan), (4) short-term transfers who go to another Molex entity for six to nine months to work on a specific project, and (5) medium terms who go to another entity for 12 to 24 months, again to work on a specific project.

Having a high level of intracompany movement is costly. For an employee making $75,000 in base salary, the total cost of an expatriate assignment can run as high as $250,000 when additional employee benefits are added in, such as the provision of schooling and housing, adjustments for higher costs of living, adjustments for higher tax rates, and so on. Molex also insists on treating all expatriates the same, whatever their country of origin, so a Singapore expatriate living in Taiwan is likely to be living in the same apartment building and sending his child to the same school as an American expatriate in Taiwan. This boosts the overall costs, but Molex believes that its extensive use of expatriates pays dividends. It allows individuals to understand the challenges of doing business in different countries, it facilitates the sharing of useful knowledge across different business entities, and it helps to lay the foundation for a common company culture that is global in its outlook.

Molex also makes sure that expatriates know why they are being sent to a foreign country, both in terms of their own career development and Molex's corporate goals. To prevent expatriates from becoming disconnected from their home office, the HRM department touches base with them on a regular basis through telephone, e-mail, and direct visits. The company also encourages expatriates to make home office visits so that they do not become totally disconnected from their base and feel like a stranger when they return. Upon return, they are debriefed and their knowledge gained abroad is put to use by, for example, placing the expatriates on special task forces.

A final component of Molex's strategy for building a cadre of globally minded managers is the company's in-house management development programs. These are open to a wide range of managers who have worked at Molex for three years or more. Molex uses these programs not just to educate its managers in finance, operations, strategy, and the like, but also to bring together managers from different countries to build a network of individuals who know each other and can work together in a cooperative fashion to solve business problems that transcend borders.

Sources: J. Laabs, "Molex Makes Global HR Look Easy," *Workforce,* March 1999, pp. 42–46; C. M. Solomon; "Foreign Relations," *Workforce,* November 2000, pp. 50–56; C. M. Solomon, "Navigating Your Search for Global Talent," *Personnel Journal,* May 1995, pp. 94–100; A. C. Poe, "Welcome Back," *HR Magazine,* March 2000, pp. 94–105; and Molex SEC Form 10K, 2004.

Case Discussion Questions

1. What multinational strategy is Molex pursuing: localization, international, global standardization, or transnational?
2. How would you characterize the approach to staffing used at Molex? Is this appropriate given its strategy?
3. Molex is successful in its use of expatriate managers. Why do you think this is the case? What can be learned from Molex's approach?
4. How does the human resource management function at Molex contribute toward the attainment of its multinational strategy?

glossary

Absolute advantage A country has an absolute advantage in the production of a product when it is more efficient than any other country at producing it.

Ad valorem tariff A tariff levied as a proportion of the value of an imported good.

Administrative trade policies Administrative policies, typically adopted by government bureaucracies, that can be used to restrict imports or boost exports.

Andean Pact A 1969 agreement between Bolivia, Chile, Ecuador, Colombia, and Peru to establish a customs union.

Antidumping policies Policies designed to punish foreign firms that engage in dumping and thus protect domestic producers from unfair foreign competition.

Arbitrage The purchase of securities in one market for immediate resale in another to profit from a price discrepancy.

Asia-Pacific Economic Cooperation (APEC) Made up of 21 member states whose goal is to increase multilateral cooperation in view of the economic rise of the Pacific nations.

Association of South East Asian Nations (ASEAN) Formed in 1967, an attempt to establish a free trade area between Brunei, Indonesia, Malaysia, the Philippines, Singapore, and Thailand.

Balance-of-payments accounts National accounts that track both payments to and receipts from foreigners.

Balance-of-trade equilibrium Reached when the income a country's residents earn from exports equals the money residents pay for imports.

Bandwagon effect When traders move like a herd, all in the same direction and at the same time, in response to each others' perceived actions.

Banking crisis A loss of confidence in the banking system that leads to a run on banks, as individuals and companies withdraw their deposits.

Barter The direct exchange of goods or services between two parties without a cash transaction.

Bill of exchange An order written by an exporter instructing an importer, or an importer's agent, to pay a specified amount of money at a specified time.

Bill of lading A document issued to an exporter by a common carrier transporting merchandise; it serves as a receipt, a contract, and a document of title.

Bretton Woods A 1944 conference in which representatives of 40 countries met to design a new international monetary system.

Business ethics Accepted principles of right or wrong governing the conduct of businesspeople.

Buyback When a firm builds a plant in a country and agrees to take a certain percentage of the plant's output as partial payment of the contract.

Capital flight Residents convert domestic currency into a foreign currency.

Caribbean Single Market and Economy (CSME) Unites six CARICOM members in agreeing to lower trade barriers and harmonize macro-economic and monetary policies.

CARICOM An association of English-speaking Caribbean states that are attempting to establish a customs union.

Caste system A system of social stratification in which social position is determined by the family into which a person is born, and change in that position is usually not possible during an individual's lifetime.

Central America Free Trade Agreement (CAFTA) The agreement of the member states of the Central American Common Market joined by the Dominican Republic to trade freely with the United States.

Central American Common Market A trade pact between Costa Rica, El Salvador, Guatemala, Honduras, and Nicaragua, which began in the early 1960s but collapsed in 1969 due to war.

Channel length The number of intermediaries that a product has to go through before it reaches the final consumer.

Channel quality The expertise, competencies, and skills of established retailers in a nation, and their ability to sell and support the products of international businesses.

Civil law system A system of law based on a very detailed set of written laws and codes.

Class consciousness A tendency for individuals to perceive themselves in terms of their class background.

Class system A system of social stratification in which social status is determined by the family into which a person is born and by subsequent socioeconomic achievements; mobility between classes is possible.

Code of ethics A business's format statement of ethical priorities.

Collectivism A political system that emphasizes collective goals as opposed to individual goals.

Command economy An economic system where the allocation of resources, including determination of what goods and services should be produced, and in what quantity, is planned by the government.

Common law A system of law based on tradition, precedent, and custom; when law courts interpret common law, they do so with regard to these characteristics.

Common market A group of countries committed to (1) removing all barriers to the free flow of goods, services, and factors of production between each other and (2) the pursuit of a common external trade policy.

Communist totalitarianism A version of collectivism advocating that socialism can be achieved only through a totalitarian dictatorship.

Communists Those who believe socialism can be achieved only through revolution and totalitarian dictatorship.

Comparative advantage The theory that countries should specialize in the production of goods and services they can produce most efficiently. A country is said to have a comparative advantage in the production of such goods and services.

Concentrated retail system A few retailers supply most of the market.

Confucian dynamism Theory that Confucian teachings affect attitudes toward time, persistence, ordering by status, protection of face, respect for tradition, and reciprocation of gifts and favors.

Contract A document that specifies the conditions under which an exchange is to occur and details the rights and obligations of the parties involved.

Contract law The body of law that governs contract enforcement.

Controls The metrics used to measure the performance of subunits and make judgments about how well managers are running those subunits.

Convention on Combating Bribery of Foreign Public Officials in International Business Transactions The covention obliges member states to make the bribery of foreign public officials a criminal offense.

Copyright Exclusive legal rights of authors, composers, playwrights, artists, and publishers to publish and dispose of their work as they see fit.

Core competence Firm skills that competitors cannot easily match or imitate.

Corporate culture Organization's norms and value systems.

Council of the European Union The ultimate decision-making body in the E.U.

Counterpurchase A reciprocal buying agreement.

Countertrade The trade of goods and services for other goods and services.

Countervailing duties Antidumping duties.

Country of origin effects The extent to which the place of manufacturing influences product evaluations.

Court of Justice Supreme appeals court for EU law.

Cross-cultural literacy Understanding how the culture of a country affects the way business is practiced.

Cross-licensing agreement An arrangement in which a company licenses valuable intangible property to a foreign partner and receives a license for the partner's valuable knowledge; reduces risk of licensing.

Cultural relativism The belief that ethics are culturally determined and that firms should adopt the ethics of the cultures in which they operate.

Culture The complex whole that includes knowledge, belief, art, morals, law, custom, and other capabilities acquired by a person as a member of society.

Currency board Means of controlling a country's currency.

Currency crisis Occurs when a speculative attack on the exchange value of a currency results in a sharp depreciation in the value of the currency or forces authorities to expend large volumes of international currency reserves and sharply increase interest rates to defend the prevailing exchange rate.

Currency speculation Involves short-term movement of funds from one currency to another in hopes of profiting from shifts in exchange rates.

Currency swap Simultaneous purchase and sale of a given amount of foreign exchange for two different value dates.

Current account In the balance of payments, records transactions involving the export or import of goods and services.

Customs union A group of countries committed to (1) removing all barriers to the free flow of goods and services between each other and (2) the pursuit of a common external trade policy.

D'Amato Act Act passed in 1996, similar to the Helms-Burton Act, aimed at Libya and Iran.

Democracy Political system in which government is by the people, exercised either directly or through elected representatives.

Deregulation Removal of government restrictions concerning the conduct of a business.

Dirty float A system under which a country's currency is nominally allowed to float freely against other currencies, but in which the government will intervene, buying and selling currency, if it believes that the currency has deviated too far from its fair value.

Draft See **Bill of exchange.**

Dumping Selling goods in a foreign market for less than their cost of production or below their "fair" market value.

Eclectic paradigm Argument that combining location-specific assets or resource endowments and the firm's own unique assets often requires FDI; it requires the firm to establish production facilities where those foreign assets or resource endowments are located.

Economic exposure The extent to which a firm's future international earning power is affected by changes in exchange rates.

Economic risk The likelihood that events, including economic mismanagement, will cause drastic changes in a country's business environment that adversely affect the profit and other goals of a particular business enterprise.

Economic union A group of countries committed to (1) the removal of all barriers to the free flow of goods, services, and factors of production between each other, (2) the adoption of a common currency, (3) the harmonization of tax rates, and (4) the pursuit of a common external trade policy.

Economies of scale Cost advantages associated with large-scale production.

Efficient market A market where prices reflect all available information.

Elastic When a small change in price produces a large change in demand.

Entrepreneurs Those who first commercialize innovations.

Ethical dilemma A situation in which there is no ethically acceptable solution.

Ethical strategy A course of action that does not violate a company's business ethics.

Ethical system Cultural beliefs about what is proper behavior and conduct.

Ethics officer An individual hired by a company to be responsible for making sure that all employees are trained to be ethically aware, that ethical considerations enter the decision-making process, and that employees follow the company's code of ethics.

Ethnocentric staffing policy A staffing approach within the MNE in which all key management positions are filled by parent-country nationals.

Ethnocentrism Behavior that is based on the belief in the superiority of one's own ethnic group or culture; often shows disregard or contempt for the culture of other countries.

European Commission Body responsible for proposing EU legislation, implementing it, and monitoring compliance.

European Free Trade Association (EFTA) A free trade association including Norway, Iceland, and Switzerland.

European Parliament Elected EU body that consults on issues proposed by European Commission.

European Union (EU) An economic group of 24 European nations; established as a customs union, it is moving toward economic union; formerly the European Community.

Exchange rate The rate at which one currency is converted into another.

Exclusive distribution channel A channel that outsiders find difficult to access.

Expatriate failure The premature return of an expatriate manager to the home country.

Expatriate manager A national of one country appointed to a management position in another country.

Experience curve Systematic production cost reductions that occur over the life of a product.

Experience curve pricing Aggressive pricing designed to increase volume and help the firm realize experience curve economies.

Export management company Export specialists who act as an export marketing department for client firms.

Export–Import Bank Agency of the U.S. government whose mission is to provide aid in financing and facilitate exports and imports; also referred to as the Ex–Im Bank.

Exporting Sale of products produced in one country to residents of another country.

External stakeholders Individuals or groups that have some claim on a firm such as customers, suppliers, and unions.

Externalities Knowledge spillovers.

Externally convertible currency Nonresidents can convert their holdings of domestic currency into foreign currency, but the ability of residents to convert the currency is limited in some way.

Factor endowments The extent to which a country is endowed with resources such as land, labor, and capital.

Factors of production Inputs into the productive process of a firm, including labor, management, land, capital, and technological know-how.

First-mover advantages Advantages accruing to the first to enter a market.

First-mover disadvantages Disadvantages associated with entering a foreign market before other international businesses.

Fisher effect Nominal interest rates (i) in each country equal the required real rate of interest (r) and the expected rate of inflation over the period of time for which the funds are to be lent (I); that is, $i = r + I$.

Fixed exchange rate A system under which the exchange rate for converting one currency into another is fixed.

Flexible machine cells Flexible manufacturing technology in which a grouping of various machine types, a common materials handler, and a centralized cell controller produce a family of products.

Flexible manufacturing technology (lean production) Manufacturing technology designed to improve job scheduling, reduce setup time, and improve quality control.

Floating exchange rate A system under which the exchange rate for converting one currency into another is continuously adjusted depending on the laws of supply and demand.

Flow of foreign direct investment The amount of foreign direct investment undertaken over a given time period (normally one year).

Folkways Routine conventions of everyday life.

Foreign Corrupt Practices Act U.S. law regulating behavior regarding the conduct of international business in the taking of bribes and other unethical actions.

Foreign debt crisis Situation in which a country cannot service its foreign debt obligations, whether private-sector or government debt.

Foreign direct investment (FDI) Direct investment in business operations in a foreign country.

Foreign exchange market A market for converting the currency of one country into that of another country.

Foreign exchange risk The risk that changes in exchange rates will hurt the profitability of a business deal.

Forward exchange When two parties agree to exchange currency and execute a deal at some specific date in the future.

Forward exchange rate The exchange rate governing forward exchange transactions.

Fragmented retail system Many retailers supply a market with no one having a major share.

Franchising A specialized form of licensing in which the franchiser sells intangible property to the franchisee and insists on rules to conduct the business.

Free trade The absence of barriers to the free flow of goods and services between countries.

Free trade area A group of countries committed to removing all barriers to the free flow of goods and services between each other, but pursuing independent external trade policies.

Freely convertible currency A country's currency is freely convertible when the government of that country allows both residents and nonresidents to purchase unlimited amounts of foreign currency with the domestic currency.

Fundamental analysis Draws on economic theory to construct sophisticated econometric models for predicting exchange rate movements.

Fundamental rights of stakeholders Basic rights of stakeholders, such as the right to information about products and working conditions, that should be considered when business decisions are made.

General Agreement on Tariffs and Trade (GATT) International treaty that committed signatories to lowering barriers to the free flow of goods across national borders and led to the WTO.

Geocentric staffing policy A staffing policy under which the firm seeks the best people for key jobs throughout the company, regardless of nationality.

Global learning The flow of skills and product offerings from foreign subsidiary to home country and from foreign subsidiary to foreign subsidiary.

Global web When different stages of value chain are dispersed to those locations around the globe where value added is maximized or where costs of value creation are minimized.

Globalization Trend away from distinct national economic units and toward one huge global market.

Globalization of markets Moving away from an economic system in which national markets are distinct entities, isolated by trade barriers and barriers of distance, time, and culture, and toward a system in which national markets are merging into one global market.

Globalization of production Trend by individual firms to disperse parts of their productive processes to different locations around the globe to take advantage of differences in cost and quality of factors of production.

Gold par value The amount of currency needed to purchase one ounce of gold.

Gold standard The practice of pegging currencies to gold and guaranteeing convertibility.

Greenfield investment Establishing a new operation in a foreign country.

Gross fixed capital formation Summarizes the total amount of capital invested in factories, stores, office buildings, and the like.

Gross national income (GNI) The yardstick for measuring economic activity of a country, this measures the total annual income of a nation's residents.

Group An association of two or more individuals who have a shared sense of identity and who interact with each other in structured ways on the basis of a common set of expectations about each other's behavior.

Hedging The process of insuring one's business against foreign exchange risk by using forward exchanges or currency swaps.

Helms-Burton Act Act passed in 1996 that allowed Americans to sue foreign firms that use Cuban property confiscated from them after the 1959 revolution.

Human Development Index (HDI) An attempt by the UN to assess the impact of a number of factors on the quality of human life in a country.

Human resource management Activities an organization conducts to use its human resources effectively.

Import quota A direct restriction on the quantity of a good that can be imported into a country.

Incentives The devices used to reward appropriate managerial behavior.

Individualism An emphasis on the importance of guaranteeing individual freedom and self-expression.

Individualism versus collectivism Theory focusing on the relationship between the individual and his or her fellows; in individualistic societies, the ties between individuals are loose and individual achievement is highly valued; in societies where collectivism is emphasized, ties between individuals are tight, people are born into collectives, such as extended families, and everyone is supposed to look after the interests of his or her collective.

Inefficient market One in which prices do not reflect all available information.

Inelastic When a large change in price produces only a small change in demand.

Infant industry argument New industries in developing countries must be temporarily protected from international competition to help them reach a position where they can compete on world markets with the firms of developed nations.

Inflows of FDI Flow of foreign direct investment into a country.

Innovation Development of new products, processes, organizations, management practices, and strategies.

Intellectual property Products of the mind, ideas (e.g., books, music, computer software, designs, technological know-how); intellectual property can be protected by patents, copyrights, and trademarks.

Internal stakeholders People who work for or own the business such as employees, directors, and stockholders.

Internalization theory The argument that firms prefer FDI over licensing in order to retaining control over know-how, manufacturing, marketing, and strategy or because some firm capabilities are not amenable to licensing.

International business Any firm that engages in international trade or investment.

International Fisher effect For any two countries, the spot exchange rate should change in an equal amount but in the opposite direction to the difference in nominal interest rates between countries.

International Monetary Fund (IMF) International institution set up to maintain order in the international monetary system.

International monetary system Institutional arrangements countries adopt to govern exchange rates.

International strategy Trying to create value by transferring core competencies to foreign markets where indigenous competitors lack those competencies.

International trade Occurs when a firm exports goods or services to consumers in another country.

ISO 9000 Certification process that requires certain quality standards must be met.

Joint venture Establishing a firm that is jointly owned by two or more otherwise independent firms.

Just distribution A distribution that is considered fair and equitable.

Justice theories Ethical approaches that focus on the attainment of a just distribution of economic goods and services.

Just-in-time (JIT) inventory Logistics systems designed to deliver parts to a production process as they are needed, not before.

Kantian ethics The belief that people should be treated as ends and never as means to the ends of others.

Lag strategy Delaying the collection of foreign currency receivables if that currency is expected to appreciate, and delaying payables if that currency is expected to depreciate.

Late-mover disadvantages Handicaps experienced by being a late entrant in a market.

Law of one price In competitive markets free of transportation costs and barriers to trade, identical products sold in different countries must sell for the same price when their price is expressed in the same currency.

Lead strategy Attempting to collect foreign currency receivables early when a foreign currency is expected to depreciate and paying foreign currency payables before they are due when a currency is expected to appreciate.

Lean production Flexible manufacturing technologies pioneered at Toyota and now used in much of the automobile industry.

Learning effects Cost savings from learning by doing.

Legal risk The likelihood that a trading partner will opportunistically break a contract or expropriate intellectual property rights.

Legal system System of rules that regulate behavior and the processes by which the laws of a country are enforced and through which redress of grievances is obtained.

Letter of credit Issued by a bank, indicating that the bank will make payments under specific circumstances.

Licensing Occurs when a firm (the licensor) licenses the right to produce its product, use its production processes, or use its brand name or trademark to another firm (the licensee); in return for giving the licensee these rights, the licensor collects a royalty fee on every unit the licensee sells.

Licensing agreement Arrangement in which a licensor grants the rights to intangible property to the licensee for a specified period and receives a royalty fee in return.

Local content requirement A requirement that some specific fraction of a good be produced domestically.

Localization strategy Increasing profitability by customizing the firm's goods and services so that they provide a good match to tastes and preferences in different national markets.

Location economies Cost advantages from performing a value creation activity at the optimal location for that activity.

Location-specific advantages Advantages that arise from using resource endowments or assets that are tied to a particular foreign location and that a firm finds valuable to combine with its own unique assets (such as the firm's technological, marketing, or management know-how).

Logistics The procurement and physical transmission of material through the supply chain, from suppliers to customers.

Maastricht Treaty Treaty agreed to in 1991, but not ratified until January 1, 1994, that committed the 12 member states of the European Community to a closer economic and political union.

Make-or-buy decisions Whether a firm should make or buy component parts.

Managed-float system System under which some currencies are allowed to float freely, but the majority are either managed by government intervention or pegged to another currency.

Market economy An economic system in which the interaction of supply and demand determines the quantity in which goods and services are produced.

Market segmentation Identifying groups of consumers whose purchasing behavior differs from others in important ways.

Marketing mix Choices about product attributes, distribution strategy, communication strategy, and pricing strategy that a firm offers its targeted markets.

Masculinity versus femininity Theory of the relationship between gender and work roles. In masculine cultures, sex roles are sharply differentiated and traditional "masculine values" such as achievement and the effective exercise of power determine cultural ideals; in feminine cultures, sex roles are less sharply distinguished, and little differentiation is made between men and women in the same job.

Mass customization The production of a variety of end products at a unit cost that could once be achieved only through mass production of a standardized output.

Mercantilism An economic philosophy advocating that countries should simultaneously encourage exports and discourage imports.

MERCOSUR Pact between Argentina, Brazil, Paraguay, and Uruguay to establish a free trade area.

Minimum efficient scale The level of output at which most plant-level scale economies are exhausted.

Mixed economy Certain sectors of the economy are left to private ownership and free market mechanisms, while other sectors have significant government ownership and government planning.

Moore's Law The power of microprocessor technology doubles and its costs of production fall in half every 18 months.

Moral hazard Arises when people behave recklessly because they know they will be saved if things go wrong.

Moral imagination Standing in the shoes of a stakeholder and asking how a proposed decision will affect that stakeholder.

Mores Norms seen as central to the functioning of a society and to its social life.

Multinational enterprise (MNE) A firm that owns business operations in more than one country.

Multipoint competition Arises when two or more enterprises encounter each other in different regional markets, national markets, or industries.

Multipoint pricing Occurs when a pricing strategy in one market may have an impact on a rival's pricing strategy in another market.

Naive immoralism The belief that if a manager of a multinational sees that firms from other nations are not following ethical norms in a host nation, that manager should not either.

Noblesse oblige A French term referring to the honorable and benevolent behavior required of persons of noble birth.

Noise The amount of other messages competing for a potential consumer's attention.

Nonconvertible currency A currency is not convertible when both residents and nonresidents are prohibited from converting their holdings of that currency into another currency.

Norms Social rules and guidelines that prescribe appropriate behavior in particular situations.

North American Free Trade Agreement (NAFTA) Free trade area between Canada, Mexico, and the United States.

Offset A buying agreement similar to counterpurchase, but the exporting country can then fulfill the agreement with any firm in the country to which the sale is being made.

Offshore production FDI undertaken to serve the home market.

Oligopoly An industry composed of a limited number of large firms.

Operations The various value-creation activities a firm undertakes.

Optimal currency area One where similarities between the economic structure of countries make it feasible to adopt a single currency.

Organization architecture The totality of a firm's organization, including formal organizational structure, control systems and incentives, organizational culture, processes, and people.

Organization culture The values and norms shared among an organization's employees.

Organizational structure The three-part structure of an organization, including its formal division into subunits such as product divisions, its location of decision-making responsibilities within that structure, and the establishment of integrating mechanisms to coordinate the activities of all subunits.

Outflows of FDI Flow of foreign direct investment out of a country.

Paris Convention for the Protection of Industrial Property International agreement to protect intellectual property; signed by 96 countries.

Patent Grants the inventor of a new product or process exclusive rights to the manufacture, use, or sale of that invention.

Pegged exchange rate Currency value is fixed relative to a reference currency.

People The employees of an organization, its recruiting, compensation, and retention strategies, and the type of people who work at the organization.

Personal ethics The generally accepted principles of right and wrong governing the conduct of individuals.

Pioneering costs Costs an early entrant bears that later entrants avoid, such as the time and effort in learning the rules, failure due to ignorance, and the liability of being a foreigner.

Political economy The political, economic, and legal systems of a country.

Political risk The likelihood that political forces will cause drastic changes in a country's business environment that will adversely affect the profit and other goals of a particular business enterprise.

Political system System of government in a nation.

Political union A central political apparatus that coordinates economic, social, and foreign policy.

Polycentric staffing policy A staffing policy in an MNE in which host-country nationals are recruited to manage subsidiaries in their own country, while parent-country nationals occupy key positions at corporate headquarters.

Power distance Theory of how a society deals with the fact that people are unequal in physical and intellectual capabilities. High power distance cultures are found in countries that let inequalities grow over time into inequalities of power and wealth; low power distance cultures are found in societies that try to play down such inequalities as much as possible.

Predatory pricing Reducing prices below fair market value as a competitive weapon to drive weaker competitors out of the market ("fair" being cost plus some reasonable profit margin).

Price elasticity of demand A measure of how responsive demand for a product is to changes in price.

Private action The theft, piracy, blackmail, and the like by private individuals or groups.

Privatization The sale of state-owned enterprises to private investors.

Processes The manner in which decisions are made and work is performed within any organization.

Product liability Involves holding a firm and its officers responsible when a product causes injury, death, or damage.

Product safety laws Set certain safety standards to which a product must adhere.

Production Activities involved in creating a product.

Production possibility frontier (PPF) The various output possibilities a country can produce from its resource pool.

Profit growth The percentage increase in net profits over time.

Profitability A ratio or rate of return concept.

Property rights Bundle of legal rights over the use to which a resource is put and over the use made of any income that may be derived from that resource.

Public action The extortion of income or resources of property holders by public officials, such as politicians and government bureaucrats.

Pull strategy A marketing strategy emphasizing mass media advertising as opposed to personal selling.

Purchasing power parity (PPP) An adjustment in gross domestic product per capita to reflect differences in the cost of living.

Push strategy A marketing strategy emphasizing personal selling rather than mass media advertising.

Quota rent Extra profit producers make when supply is artificially limited by an import quota.

Regional economic integration Agreements among countries in a geographic region to reduce and ultimately remove tariff and nontariff barriers to the free flow of goods, services, and factors of production between each other.

Relatively efficient market One in which few impediments to international trade and investment exist.

Religion A system of shared beliefs and rituals concerned with the realm of the sacred.

Representative democracy A political system in which citizens periodically elect individuals to represent them in government.

Righteous moralism The belief that a multinational's home-country standards of ethics are the appropriate ones for companies to follow in foreign countries.

Rights theories A twentieth century theory that recognizes that human beings have fundamental rights and privileges that transcend national boundaries and cultures.

Right-wing totalitarianism A political system in which political power is monopolized by a party, group, or individual that generally permits individual economic freedom but restricts individual political freedom, including free speech, often on the grounds that it would lead to the rise of communism.

Sight draft A draft payable on presentation to the drawee.

Single European Act A 1997 act, adopted by members of the European Community, that committed member countries to establishing an economic union.

Six Sigma Statistically based methodology for improving product quality.

Smoot-Hawley Act Enacted in 1930 by the U.S. Congress, this tariff erected a wall of barriers against imports into the United States.

Social democrats Those committed to achieving socialism by democratic means.

Social mobility The extent to which individuals can move out of the social strata into which they are born.

Social responsibility The idea that businesspeople should consider the social consequences of economic actions when making business decisions.

Social strata Hierarchical social categories often based on family background, occupation, and income.

Social structure The basic social organization of a society.

Socialism A political philosophy advocating substantial public involvement, through government ownership, in the means of production and distribution.

Society Group of people who share a common set of values and norms.

Source effects When the receiver of the message evaluates the message based on the status or image of the sender.

Specialized asset An asset designed to perform a specific task, whose value is significantly reduced in its next-best use.

Specific tariff Tariff levied as a fixed charge for each unit of good imported.

Spot exchange rate The exchange rate at which a foreign exchange dealer will convert one currency into another that particular day.

Staffing policy Strategy concerned with selecting employees for particular jobs.

Stakeholders The individuals or groups that have an interest, stake, or claim in the actions and overall performance of a company.

Stock of foreign direct investment The total accumulated value of foreign-owned assets at a given time.

Strategic alliances Cooperative agreements between two or more firms.

Strategic commitment A decision that has a long-term impact and is difficult to reverse, such as entering a foreign market on a large scale.

Strategic pricing Pricing aimed at giving a company a competitive advantage over its rivals.

Strategic trade policy Government policy aimed at improving the competitive position of a domestic industry or domestic firm in the world market.

Strategy Actions managers take to attain the firm's goals.

Subsidy Government financial assistance to a domestic producer.

Sullivan principles A twofold approach to doing business in apartheid South Africa, comprising passive resistance to apartheid laws and attempts to influence the abolition of apartheid laws.

Switch trading The use of a specialized third-party trading house in a countertrade arrangement.

Tariff A tax levied on imports.

Tariff rate quota The process of applying a lower tariff rate to imports within the import quota than those over the quota.

Technical analysis Uses price and volume data to determine past trends, which are expected to continue into the future.

Theocratic law system A system of law based on religious teachings.

Theocratic totalitarianism A political system in which political power is monopolized by a party, group, or individual that governs according to religious principles.

Time draft A promise to pay by the accepting party at some future date.

Timing of entry Entry is early when a firm enters a foreign market before other foreign firms and late when a firm enters after other international businesses have established themselves.

Total quality management (TQM) Management philosophy that takes as its central focus the need to improve the quality of a company's products and services.

Totalitarianism Form of government in which one person or political party exercises absolute control over all spheres of human life and opposing political parties are prohibited.

Trade creation Trade created due to regional economic integration; occurs when high-cost domestic producers are replaced by low-cost foreign producers in a free trade area.

Trade diversion Trade diverted due to regional economic integration; occurs when low-cost foreign suppliers outside a free trade area are replaced by higher-cost foreign suppliers in a free trade area.

Trademark Designs and names, often officially registered, by which merchants or manufacturers designate and differentiate their products.

Transaction exposure The extent to which income from individual transactions is affected by fluctuations in foreign exchange values.

Translation exposure The extent to which the reported consolidated results and balance sheets of a corporation are affected by fluctuations in foreign exchange values.

Transnational strategy Attempting to simultaneously achieve low costs through location economies, economies of scale, and learning effects while also differentiating product offerings across geographic markets to account for local differences and fostering multidirectional flows of skills between different subsidiaries in the firm's global network of operations.

Treaty of Rome The 1957 treaty that established the European Community.

Tribal totalitarianism A political system in which a party, group, or individual that represents the interests of a particular tribe (ethnic group) monopolizes political power.

Turnkey project A project in which a firm agrees to set up an operating plant for a foreign client and hand over the "key" when the plant is fully operational.

Uncertainty avoidance Extent to which cultures socialize members to accept ambiguous situations and to tolerate uncertainty.

United Nations An international organization made up of 189 countries headquartered in New York City, formed in 1945 to promote peace, security, and cooperation.

United Nations Convention on Contracts for the International Sale of Goods (CIGS) A set of rules governing certain aspects of the making and performance of commercial contracts between sellers and buyers who have their places of businesses in different nations.

Universal Declaration of Human Rights A United Nations document that lays down the basic principles of human rights that should be adhered to.

Universal needs Needs that are the same all over the world, such as steel, bulk chemicals, and industrial electronics.

Utilitarian approaches to ethics These hold that the moral worth of actions or practices is determined by their consequences.

Value creation Performing activities that increase the value of goods or services to consumers.

Values Abstract ideas about what a society believes to be good, right, and desirable.

Voluntary export restraint (VER) A quota on trade imposed from the exporting country's side, instead of the importer's; usually imposed at the request of the importing country's government.

Wholly owned subsidiary A subsidiary in which the firm owns 100 percent of the stock.

World Bank International institution set up to promote general economic development in the world's poorer nations.

World Intellectual Property Organization An international organization whose members sign treaties to agree to protect intellectual property.

World Trade Organization (WTO) The organization that succeeded the General Agreement on Tariffs and Trade (GATT) as a result of the successful completion of the Uruguay Round of GATT negotiations.

Zero-sum game A situation in which an economic gain by one country results in an economic loss by another.

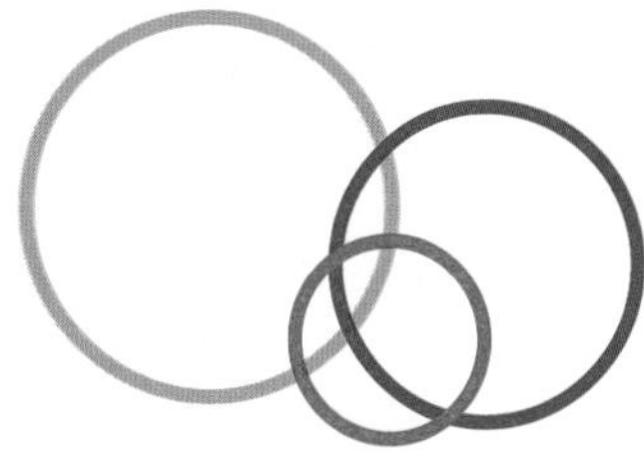

endnotes

Chapter 1

1. World Trade Organization, trade statistics database, accessed June 2006 at http://stat.wto.org/Home/WSDBHome.aspx.
2. Thomas L. Friedman, *The World Is Flat* (New York: Farrar, Straus and Giroux, 2005).
3. Ibid.
4. T. Levitt, "The Globalization of Markets," *Harvard Business Review,* May–June 1983, pp. 92–102.
5. U.S. Department of Commerce, "A Profile of U.S. Exporting Companies, 2000–2001," February 2003; report available at www.census.gov/foreign-trade/aip/index.html#profile.
6. Ibid.
7. C. M. Draffen, "Going Global: Export Market Proves Profitable for Region's Small Businesses," *Newsday,* March 19, 2001, p. C18.
8. B. Benoit and R. Milne, "Germany's Best Kept Secret, How Its Exporters Are Betting the World," *Financial Times,* May 19, 2006, p. 11.
9. See F. T. Knickerbocker, *Oligopolistic Reaction and Multinational Enterprise* (Boston: Harvard Business School Press, 1973); and R. E. Caves, "Japanese Investment in the U.S.: Lessons for the Economic Analysis of Foreign Investment," *The World Economy* 16 (1993), pp. 279–300.
10. I. Metthee, "Playing a Large Part," *Seattle Post-Intelligencer,* April 9, 1994, p. 13.
11. D. Pritchard, "Are Federal Tax Laws and State Subsidies for Boeing 7E7 Selling America Short?" *Aviation Week,* April 12, 2004, pp. 74–75.
12. D. Barboza, "An Unknown Giant Flexes Its Muscles," *The New York Times,* December 4, 2004, pp. B1, B3.
13. W. M. Bulkeley, "IBM to Export Highly Paid Jobs to India," *The Wall Street Journal,* December 15, 2003, pp. B1, B3.
14. R. B. Reich, *The Work of Nations* (New York: A. A. Knopf, 1991).
15. United Nations, "The UN in Brief," www.un.org/Overview/brief.html.
16. J. A. Frankel, "Globalization of the Economy," National Bureau of Economic Research, working paper no. 7858, 2000.
17. J. Bhagwati, *Protectionism* (Cambridge, MA: MIT Press, 1989).
18. F. Williams, "Trade Round Like This May Never Be Seen Again," *Financial Times,* April 15, 1994, p. 8.
19. W. Vieth, "Major Concessions Lead to Success for WTO Talks," *Los Angeles Times,* November 14, 2001, p. A1; and "Seeds Sown for Future Growth," *The Economist,* November 17, 2001, pp. 65–66.
20. United Nations, *World Investment Report, 2005.*
21. Ibid.
22. World Trade Organization, *International Trade Trends and Statistics, 2005* (Geneva: WTO, 2006); and WTO press release, "World Trade for 2005: Prospects for 2006," April 11, 2006, available at www.wto.org.
23. United Nations, *World Investment Report, 2005;* and UN Conference on Trade and Development, "Data Shows Foreign Direct Investment Climbed Sharply in 2005," UNCTAD press release, January 23, 2006.
24. World Trade Organization, *International Trade Statistics, 2005* (Geneva: WTO, 2005); and United Nations, *World Investment Report, 2005.*
25. United Nations, *World Investment Report, 2005.*
26. Moore's Law is named after Intel founder Gordon Moore.
27. Frankel, "Globalization of the Economy."
28. J. G. Fernald and V. Greenfield, "The Fall and Rise of the Global Economy," *Chicago Fed Letters,* April 2001, pp. 1–4.
29. Data compiled from various sources and listed by CyberAtlas at http://cyberatlas.internet.com/big_picture.
30. www.forrester.com/ER/Press/ForrFind/0,1768,0,00.html.
31. For a counterpoint, see "Geography and the Net: Putting It in Its Place," *The Economist,* August 11, 2001, pp. 18–20.
32. Frankel, "Globalization of the Economy."
33. Data from Bureau of Transportation Statistics, 2001.
34. Fernald and Greenfield, "The Fall and Rise of the Global Economy."
35. Data located at www.bts.gov/publications/us_international_trade_and_freight_transportation_trends/2003/index.html.

36. N. Hood and J. Young, *The Economics of the Multinational Enterprise* (New York, Longman, 1973).

37. United Nations, *World Investment Report, 2005.*

38. Ibid.

39. Ibid.

40. S. Chetty, "Explosive International Growth and Problems of Success among Small and Medium Sized Firms," *International Small Business Journal,* February 2003, pp. 5–28.

41. R. A. Mosbacher, "Opening Up Export Doors for Smaller Firms," *Seattle Times,* July 24, 1991, p. A7.

42. "Small Companies Learn How to Sell to the Japanese," *Seattle Times,* March 19, 1992.

43. Holstein, "Why Johann Can Export, but Johnny Can't."

44. N. Buckley and A. Ostrovsky, "Back to Business—How Putin's Allies Are Turning Russia into a Corporate State," *Financial Times,* June 19, 2006, p. 11.

45. J. E. Stiglitz, *Globalization and Its Discontents* (New York: W. W. Norton, 2003); J. Bhagwati, *In Defense of Globalization* (New York: Oxford University Press, 2004); and Friedman, *The World Is Flat.*

46. See, for example, Ravi Batra, *The Myth of Free Trade* (New York: Touchstone Books, 1993); William Greider, *One World, Ready or Not: The Manic Logic of Global Capitalism* (New York: Simon and Schuster, 1997); and D. Radrik, *Has Globalization Gone Too Far?* (Washington, DC: Institution for International Economics, 1997).

47. James Goldsmith, "The Winners and the Losers," in *The Case against the Global Economy,* eds. J. Mander and E. Goldsmith (San Francisco: Sierra Club, 1996); and Lou Dobbs, *Exporting America* (New York: Time Warner Books, 2004).

48. D. L. Bartlett and J. B. Steele, "America: Who Stole the Dream," *Philadelphia Inquirer,* September 9, 1996.

49. For example, see Paul Krugman, *Pop Internationalism* (Cambridge, MA: MIT Press, 1996).

50. Peter Gottschalk and Timothy M. Smeeding, "Cross-National Comparisons of Earnings and Income Inequality," *Journal of Economic Literature* 35 (June 1997), pp. 633–87; and Susan M. Collins, *Exports, Imports, and the American Worker* (Washington, DC: Brookings Institution, 1998).

51. B. Milanovic and L. Squire, "Does Tariff Liberalization Increase Wage Inequality?" *National Bureau of Economic Research,* working paper no. 11046, January 2005; and B. Milanovic, "Can We Discern the Effect of Globalization on Income Distribution?" *World Bank Economic Review,* 19, 2005, pp. 21–44.

52. "A Survey of Pay. Winners and Losers," *The Economist,* May 8, 1999, pp. 5–8.

53. Jared Bernstein, Elizabeth C. McNichol, Lawrence Mishel, and Robert Zahradnik, "Pulling Apart: A State by State Analysis of Income Trends," *Economic Policy Institute,* January 2000.

54. See Krugman, *Pop Internationalism;* and D. Belman and T. M. Lee, "International Trade and the Performance of U.S. Labor Markets," in *U.S. Trade Policy and Global Growth,* ed. R. A. Blecker (New York: Economic Policy Institute, 1996).

55. See Robert Lerman, "Is Earnings Inequality Really Increasing? Economic Restructuring and the Job Market," brief no. 1 (Washington, DC: Urban Institute, March 1997).

56. M. Forster and M. Pearson, "Income Distribution and Poverty in the OECD Area," *OECD Economic Studies* 34 (2002).

57. Bernstein et al., "Pulling Apart."

58. E. Goldsmith, "Global Trade and the Environment," in *The Case against the Global Economy,* eds. J. Mander and E. Goldsmith (San Francisco: Sierra Club, 1996).

59. P. Choate, *Jobs at Risk: Vulnerable U.S. Industries and Jobs under NAFTA* (Washington, DC: Manufacturing Policy Project, 1993).

60. Ibid.

61. B. Lomborg, *The Skeptical Environmentalist* (Cambridge: Cambridge University Press, 2001).

62. H. Nordstrom and S. Vaughan, *Trade and the Environment, World Trade Organization Special Studies No. 4* (Geneva: WTO, 1999).

63. Figures are from "Freedom's Journey: A Survey of the 20th Century. Our Durable Planet," *The Economist,* September 11, 1999, p. 30.

64. For an exhaustive review of the empirical literature, see B. R. Copeland and M. Scott Taylor, "Trade, Growth and the Environment," *Journal of Economic Literature,* March 2004, pp. 7–77.

65. G.M. Grossman and A. B. Krueger, "Economic Growth and the Environment," *Quarterly Journal of Economics* 110 (1995), pp. 353–78.

66. Krugman, *Pop Internationalism.*

67. R. Kuttner, "Managed Trade and Economic Sovereignty," in *U.S. Trade Policy and Global Growth,* ed. R. A. Blecker (New York: Economic Policy Institute, 1996).

68. Ralph Nader and Lori Wallach, "GATT, NAFTA, and the Subversion of the Democratic Process," in *U.S.*

Trade Policy and Global Growth, ed. R. A. Blecker (New York: Economic Policy Institute, 1996), pp. 93–94.

69. Lant Pritchett, "Divergence, Big Time," *Journal of Economic Perspectives* 11, no. 3 (Summer 1997), pp. 3–18.
70. Ibid.
71. W. Easterly, "How Did Heavily Indebted Poor Countries Become Heavily Indebted?" *World Development,* October 2002, pp. 1677–96; and J. Sachs, *The End of Poverty* (New York, Penguin Books, 2006).
72. See D. Ben-David, H. Nordstrom, and L. A. Winters, *Trade, Income Disparity and Poverty. World Trade Organization Special Studies No. 5* (Geneva WTO, 1999).
73. William Easterly, "Debt Relief," *Foreign Policy,* November–December 2001, pp. 20–26.
74. Jeffrey Sachs, "Sachs on Development: Helping the World's Poorest," *The Economist,* August 14, 1999, pp. 17–20.
75. World Trade Organization, *Annual Report 2003* (Geneva: WTO, 2004).
76. Easterly, "Debt Relief."

Chapter 2

1. Although as we shall see, there is not a strict one-to-one correspondence between political systems and economic systems. A. O. Hirschman, "The On-and-Off Again Connection between Political and Economic Progress," *American Economic Review* 84, no. 2 (1994), pp. 343–48.
2. For a discussion of the roots of collectivism and individualism, see H. W. Spiegel, *The Growth of Economic Thought* (Durham, NC: Duke University Press, 1991). A discussion of collectivism and individualism can be found in M. Friedman and R. Friedman, *Free to Choose* (London: Penguin Books, 1980).
3. For a classic summary of the tenets of Marxism details, see A. Giddens, *Capitalism and Modern Social Theory* (Cambridge: Cambridge University Press, 1971).
4. J. S. Mill, *On Liberty* (London: Longman's, 1865), p. 6.
5. A. Smith, *The Wealth of Nations, Vol. 1* (London: Penguin Book), p. 325.
6. R. Wesson, *Modern Government—Democracy and Authoritarianism,* 2nd ed. (Englewood Cliffs, NJ: Prentice Hall, 1990).
7. For a detailed but accessible elaboration of this argument, see Friedman and Friedman, *Free to Choose.* Also see P. M. Romer, "The Origins of Endogenous Growth," *Journal of Economic Perspectives* 8, no. 1 (1994), pp. 2–32.
8. T. W. Lippman, *Understanding Islam* (New York: Meridian Books, 1995).
9. "Islam's Interest," *The Economist,* January 18, 1992, pp. 33–34.
10. Rodney Wilson, "Islamic Banking," *Economic Record,* September 2002, pp. 373–74; and M. El Qorchi, "Islamic Finance Gears Up," *Finance and Development,* December 2005, pp 46–50.
11. This information can be found on the UN's Treaty Web site at http://untreaty.un.org/ENGLISH/bible/englishinternetbible/partI/ch apterX/treaty17.asp.
12. International Court of Arbitration, www.iccwbo.org/index_court.asp.
13. D. North, *Institutions, Institutional Change, and Economic Performance* (Cambridge: Cambridge University Press, 1991).
14. P. Klebnikov, "Russia's Robber Barons," *Forbes,* November 21, 1994, pp. 74–84; C. Mellow, "Russia: Making Cash from Chaos," *Fortune,* April 17, 1995, pp. 145–51; and "Mr Tatum Checks Out," *The Economist,* November 9, 1996, p. 78.
15. K. van Wolferen, *The Enigma of Japanese Power* (New York: Vintage Books, 1990), pp. 100–5.
16. P. Bardhan, "Corruption and Development: A Review of the Issues," *Journal of Economic Literature,* September 1997, pp. 1320–46.
17. K. M. Murphy, A. Shleifer, and R. Vishny, "Why Is Rent Seeking So Costly to Growth?" *American Economic Review* 83, no. 2 (1993), pp. 409–14.
18. Transparency International, "Global Corruption Report, 2005," www.transparency.org, 2005.
19. www.transparency.org.
20. J. Coolidge and S. Rose Ackerman, "High Level Rent Seeking and Corruption in African Regimes," World Bank policy research working paper no. 1780, June 1997; Murphy et al., "Why Is Rent Seeking So Costly to Growth?"; M. Habib and L. Zurawicki, "Corruption and Foreign Direct Investment," *Journal of International Business Studies* 33 (2002), pp. 291–307; J. E. Anderson and D. Marcouiller, "Insecurity and the Pattern of International Trade," *Review of Economics and Statistics* 84 (2002), pp. 342–52; and T. S. Aidt, "Economic Analysis of Corruption: A Survey," *The Economic Journal* 113 (November 2003), pp. 632–53.
21. Details can be found at www.oecd.org/EN/home/0,,EN-home-31-nodirectorate-no-nono-31,00.html.
22. Dale Stackhouse and Kenneth Ungar, "The Foreign Corrupt Practices Act: Bribery, Corruption, Record Keeping and More," *Indiana Lawyer,* April 21, 1993.

23. For an interesting discussion of strategies for dealing with the low cost of copying and distributing digital information, see the chapter on rights management in C. Shapiro and H. R. Varian, *Information Rules* (Boston: Harvard Business School Press, 1999). Also see Charles W. L. Hill, "Digital Piracy," *Asian Pacific Journal of Management,* forthcoming, 2007.

24. Douglass North has argued that the correct specification of intellectual property rights is one factor that lowers the cost of doing business and, thereby, stimulates economic growth and development. See North, *Institutions, Institutional Change, and Economic Performance.*

25. International Federation of the Phonographic Industry, *The Commercial Music Industry Global Piracy Report, 2005,* www.ifpi.org.

26. Business Software Alliance, "Third Annual BSA and IDC Global Software Piracy Study," May 2006, www.bsa.org.

27. Ibid.

28. "Trade Tripwires," *The Economist,* August 27, 1994, p. 61.

29. World Bank, *World Development Indicators Online, 2006.*

30. A. Sen, *Development as Freedom* (New York: Alfred A. Knopf, 1999).

31. G. M. Grossman and E. Helpman, "Endogenous Innovation in the Theory of Growth," *Journal of Economic Perspectives* 8, no. 1 (1994), pp. 23–44; and Romer, "The Origins of Endogenous Growth."

32. W. W. Lewis, *The Power of Productivity* (Chicago: University of Chicago Press, 2004).

33. F. A. Hayek, *The Fatal Conceit: Errors of Socialism* (Chicago: University of Chicago Press, 1989).

34. James Gwartney, Robert Lawson, and Walter Block, *Economic Freedom of the World: 1975–1995* (London: Institute of Economic Affairs, 1996).

35. North, *Institutions, Institutional Change, and Economic Performance.* See also Murphy et al., "Why Is Rent Seeking So Costly to Growth?"; and K. E. Maskus, "Intellectual Property Rights in the Global Economy," *Institute for International Economics,* 2000.

36. Hernando de Soto, *The Mystery of Capital: Why Capitalism Triumphs in the West and Fails Everywhere Else* (New York: Basic Books, 2000).

37. Hirschman, "The On-and-Off Again Connection between Political and Economic Progress"; and A. Przeworski and F. Limongi, "Political Regimes and Economic Growth," *Journal of Economic Perspectives* 7, no. 3 (1993), pp. 51–59.

38. Ibid.

39. For details of this argument, see M. Olson, "Dictatorship, Democracy, and Development," *American Political Science Review,* September 1993.

40. For example, see Jared Diamond's Pulitzer Prize–winning book, *Guns, Germs, and Steel* (New York: W. W. Norton, 1997). Also see J. Sachs, "Nature, Nurture and Growth," *The Economist,* June 14, 1997, pp. 19–22; and J. Sachs, *The End of Poverty* (New York: Penguin Books, 2005).

41. Sachs, "Nature, Nurture and Growth."

42. "What Can the Rest of the World Learn from the Classrooms of Asia?" *The Economist,* September 21, 1996, p. 24.

43. J. Fagerberg, "Technology and International Differences in Growth Rates," *Journal of Economic Literature* 32 (September 1994), pp. 1147–75.

44. See The Freedom House Survey Team, "Freedom in the World: 2005" and associated materials, www.freedomhouse.org.

45. "Russia Downgraded to Not Free," Freedom House press release, December 20, 2004, www.freedomhouse.org.

46. Freedom House, "Democracies Century: A Survey of Political Change in the Twentieth Century, 1999," www.freedomhouse.org.

47. L. Conners, "Freedom to Connect," *Wired,* August 1997, pp. 105–6.

48. F. Fukuyama, "The End of History," *The National Interest* 16 (Summer 1989), p. 18.

49. S. P. Huntington, *The Clash of Civilizations and the Remaking of World Order* (New York: Simon & Schuster, 1996).

50. Ibid., p. 116.

51. United States National Counterterrorism Center, *Reports on Incidents of Terrorism,* 2005, April 11, 2006.

52. S. Fisher, R. Sahay, and C. A. Vegh, "Stabilization and the Growth in Transition Economies: the Early Experience," *Journal of Economic Perspectives* 10 (Spring 1996), pp. 45–66.

53. M. Miles et al *2006 Index of Economic Freedom* (Washington, DC: Heritage Foundation, 2006).

54. International Monetary Fund, *World Economic Outlook: Focus on Transition Economies* (Geneva: IMF, October 2000).

55. J. C. Brada, "Privatization Is Transition—Is It?" *Journal of Economic Perspectives,* Spring 1996, pp. 67–86.

56. See S. Zahra et al., "Privatization and Entrepreneurial Transformation," *Academy of Management Review* 3, no. 25 (2000), pp. 509–24.

57. N. Brune, G. Garrett, and B. Kogut, "The International Monetary Fund and the Global Spread of Privatization," *IMF Staff Papers* 51, no. 2 (August 2004), pp. 195–219.

58. Fischer et al., "Stabilization and the Growth in Transition Economies."

59. J. Sachs, C. Zinnes, and Y. Eilat, "The Gains from Privatization in Transition Economies: Is Change of Ownership Enough?" CAER discussion paper no. 63 (Cambridge, MA: Harvard Institute for International Development, 2000).

60. J. Nellis, "Time to Rethink Privatization in Transition Economies?" *Finance and Development* 36, no. 2 (1999), pp. 16–19.

61. M. S. Borish and M. Noel, "Private Sector Development in the Visegrad Countries," *World Bank,* March 1997.

62. For a discussion of first-mover advantages, see M. Liberman and D. Montgomery, "First-Mover Advantages," *Strategic Management Journal* 9 (Summer Special Issue, 1988), pp. 41–58.

63. S. H. Robock, "Political Risk: Identification and Assessment," *Columbia Journal of World Business,* July–August 1971, pp. 6–20.

Chapter 3

1. See R. Dore, *Taking Japan Seriously* (Stanford, CA: Stanford University Press, 1987).

2. Data come from J. Monger, "International Comparison of Labor Disputes in 2003," *Labor Market Trends,* April 2005, pp. 159–69.

3. E. B. Tylor, *Primitive Culture* (London: Murray, 1871).

4. Geert Hofstede, *Culture's Consequences: International Differences in Work-Related Values* (Beverly Hills, CA: Sage Publications, 1984), p. 21.

5. J. Z. Namenwirth and R. B. Weber, *Dynamics of Culture* (Boston: Allen & Unwin, 1987), p. 8.

6. R. Mead, *International Management: Cross-Cultural Dimensions* (Oxford: Blackwell Business, 1994), p. 7.

7. Edward T. Hall and M. R. Hall, *Understanding Cultural Differences* (Yarmouth, ME: Intercultural Press, 1990).

8. Edward T. Hall and M. R. Hall, *Hidden Differences: Doing Business with the Japanese* (New York: Doubleday, 1987).

9. "Iraq: Down but Not Out," *The Economist,* April 8, 1995, pp. 21–23.

10. S. P. Huntington, *The Clash of Civilizations* (New York: Simon & Schuster, 1996).

11. M. Thompson, R. Ellis, and A. Wildavsky, *Cultural Theory* (Boulder, CO: Westview Press, 1990).

12. M. Douglas, *In the Active Voice* (London: Routledge, 1982), pp. 183–254.

13. M. L. Dertouzos, R. K. Lester, and R. M. Solow, *Made in America* (Cambridge, MA: MIT Press, 1989).

14. C. Nakane, *Japanese Society* (Berkeley: University of California Press, 1970).

15. Ibid.

16. For details, see M. Aoki, *Information, Incentives, and Bargaining in the Japanese Economy* (Cambridge: Cambridge University Press, 1988); and Dertouzos et al., *Made in America.*

17. For an excellent historical treatment of the evolution of the English class system, see E. P. Thompson, *The Making of the English Working Class* (London: Vintage Books, 1966). See also R. Miliband, *The State in Capitalist Society* (New York: Basic Books, 1969), especially Chapter 2. For more recent studies of class in British societies, see Stephen Brook, *Class: Knowing Your Place in Modern Britain* (London: Victor Gollancz, 1997); A. Adonis and S. Pollard, *A Class Act: The Myth of Britain's Classless Society* (London: Hamish Hamilton, 1997); and J. Gerteis and M. Savage, "The Salience of Class in Britain and America: A Comparative Analysis," *British Journal of Sociology,* June 1998.

18. Adonis and Pollard, *A Class Act.*

19. Y. Bian, "Chinese Social Stratification and Social Mobility," *Annual Review of Sociology* 28 (2002), pp. 91–117.

20. N. Goodman, *An Introduction to Sociology* (New York: HarperCollins, 1991).

21. R. J. Barro and R. McCleary, "Religion and Economic Growth across Countries," *American Sociological Review,* October 2003, pp. 760–82.

22. M. Weber, *The Protestant Ethic and the Spirit of Capitalism* (New York: Charles Scribner's Sons, 1958, original 1904–1905). For an excellent review of Weber's work, see A. Giddens, *Capitalism and Modern Social Theory* (Cambridge: Cambridge University Press, 1971).

23. Weber, *The Protestant Ethic and the Spirit of Capitalism,* p. 35.

24. A. S. Thomas and S. L. Mueller, "The Case for Comparative Entrepreneurship," *Journal of International Business Studies* 31, no. 2 (2000), pp. 287–302; and S. A. Shane, "Why Do Some Societies Invent More than Others?" *Journal of Business Venturing* 7 (1992), pp. 29–46.

25. See S. M. Abbasi, K. W. Hollman, and J. H. Murrey, "Islamic Economics: Foundations and Practices," *International Journal of Social Economics* 16, no. 5 (1990),

pp. 5–17; and R. H. Dekmejian, *Islam in Revolution: Fundamentalism in the Arab World* (Syracuse, NY: Syracuse University Press, 1995).

26. T. W. Lippman, *Understanding Islam* (New York: Meridian Books, 1995).
27. Dekmejian, *Islam in Revolution.*
28. M. K. Nydell, *Understanding Arabs* (Yarmouth, ME: Intercultural Press, 1987).
29. Lippman, *Understanding Islam.*
30. The material in this section is based largely on Abbasi et al., "Islamic Economics."
31. "Islam's Interest," *The Economist,* January 18, 1992, pp. 33–34.
32. For details of Weber's work and views, see Giddens, *Capitalism and Modern Social Theory.*
33. See, for example, the views expressed in "A Survey of India: The Tiger Steps Out," *The Economist,* January 21, 1995.
34. See R. Dore, *Taking Japan Seriously;* and C. W. L. Hill, "Transaction Cost Economizing as a Source of Comparative Advantage: The Case of Japan," *Organization Science* 6 (1995).
35. C. C. Chen, Y. R. Chen, and K. Xin, "Guanxi Practices and Trust in Management," *Organization Science* 15, no. 2 (March–April 2004), pp. 200–10.
36. See Aoki, *Information, Incentives, and Bargaining*; and J. P. Womack, D. T. Jones, and D. Roos, *The Machine That Changed the World* (New York: Rawson Associates, 1990).
37. For examples of this line of thinking, see M. W. Peng and P. S. Heath, "The Growth of the Firm in Planned Economies in Transition," *Academy of Management Review* 21 (1996), pp. 492–528; M. W. Peng, *Business Strategies in Transition Economies* (Thousand Oaks, CA: Sage, 2000); and M. W. Peng and Y. Luo, "Managerial Ties and Firm Performance in a Transition Economy," *Academy of Management Journal,* June 2000, pp. 486–501.
38. This hypothesis dates back to two anthropologists, Edward Sapir and Benjamin Lee Whorf. See E. Sapir, "The Status of Linguistics as a Science," *Language* 5 (1929), pp. 207–14; and B. L. Whorf, *Language, Thought, and Reality* (Cambridge, MA: MIT Press, 1956).
39. The tendency has been documented empirically. See A. Annett, "Social Fractionalization, Political Instability, and the Size of Government," *IMF Staff Papers* 48 (2001), pp. 561–92.
40. D. A. Ricks, *Big Business Blunders: Mistakes in Multinational Marketing* (Homewood, IL: Dow Jones-Irwin, 1983).
41. Goodman, *An Introduction to Sociology.*
42. M. E. Porter, *The Competitive Advantage of Nations* (New York: Free Press, 1990).
43. Ibid., pp. 395–97.
44. G. Hofstede, "The Cultural Relativity of Organizational Practices and Theories," *Journal of International Business Studies,* Fall 1983, pp. 75–89; and G. Hofstede, *Cultures and Organizations: Software of the Mind* (New York: McGraw-Hill, 1997).
45. For a more detailed critique, see R. Mead, *International Management: Cross-Cultural Dimensions* (Oxford: Blackwell, 1994), pp. 73–75.
46. For example, see W. J. Bigoness and G. L. Blakely, "A Cross-National Study of Managerial Values," *Journal of International Business Studies,* December 1996, p. 739; D. H. Ralston, D. H. Holt, R. H. Terpstra, and Y. Kai-Cheng, "The Impact of National Culture and Economic Ideology on Managerial Work Values," *Journal of International Business Studies* 28, no. 1 (1997), pp. 177–208; and P. B. Smith, M. F. Peterson, and Z. Ming Wang, "The Manager as a Mediator of Alternative Meanings," *Journal of International Business Studies* 27, no. 1 (1996), pp. 115–37.
47. G. Hofstede and M. H. Bond, "The Confucius Connection," *Organizational Dynamics* 16, no. 4 (1988), pp. 5–12; and G. Hofstede, *Culture's Consequences: Comparing Values, Behaviors, Institutions and Organizations across Nations* (Thousand Oaks, CA: Sage, 2001).
48. R. S. Yeh and J. J. Lawerence, "Individualism and Confucian Dynamism," *Journal of International Business Studies* 26, no. 3 (1995), pp. 655–66.
49. For evidence of this, see R. Inglehart. "Globalization and Postmodern Values," *The Washington Quarterly,* Winter 2000, pp. 215–28.
50. Mead, *International Management,* chap. 17.
51. "Free, Young, and Japanese," *The Economist,* December 21, 1991.
52. Namenwirth and Weber, *Dynamics of Culture;* and Inglehart, "Globalization and Postmodern Values."
53. G. Hofstede, "National Cultures in Four Dimensions," *International Studies of Management and Organization* 13, no. 1, pp. 46–74.
54. See Inglehart, "Globalization and Postmodern-Values." For updates, go to http://wvs.isr.umich.edu/index.html.
55. Hofstede, "National Cultures in Four Dimensions."
56. Hall and Hall, *Understanding Cultural Differences.*
57. See Aoki, *Information, Incentives, and Bargaining;* Dertouzos et al., *Made in America;* and Porter, *The Competitive Advantage of Nations,* pp. 395–97.

58. For empirical work supporting such a view, see Annett, "Social Fractionalization, Political Instability, and the Size of Government."

Chapter 4

1. S. Greenhouse, "Nike Shoe Plant in Vietnam Is Called Unsafe for Workers," *The New York Times*, November 8, 1997; and V. Dobnik, "Chinese Workers Abused Making Nikes, Reeboks," *Seattle Times*, September 21, 1997, p. A4.
2. Thomas Donaldson, "Values in Tension: Ethics away from Home," *Harvard Business Review*, September–October 1996.
3. Robert Kinloch Massie, *Loosing the Bonds: The United States and South Africa in the Apartheid Years* (New York: Doubleday, 1997).
4. Not everyone agrees that the divestment trend had much influence on the South African economy. For a counterview, see Siew Hong Teoh, Ivo Welch, and C. Paul Wazzan, "The Effect of Socially Activist Investing on the Financial Markets: Evidence from South Africa," *Journal of Business* 72, no. 1 (January 1999), pp. 35–60.
5. Andy Rowell, "Trouble Flares in the Delta of Death; Shell Has Polluted More than Ken Saro Wiwa's Oroniland in Nigeria," *The Guardian*, November 8, 1995, p. 6.
6. H. Hamilton, "Shell's New World Wide View," *Washington Post*, August 2, 1998, p. H1.
7. Rowell, "Trouble Flares in the Delta of Death."
8. Peter Singer, *One World: The Ethics of Globalization*. (New Haven, CT: Yale University Press, 2002).
9. Garrett Hardin, "The Tragedy of the Common," *Science* 162, 1, p. 243–48.
10. Richard T. De George, *Competing with Integrity in International Business* (Oxford: Oxford University Press, 1993).
11. Details can be found at www.oecd.org/EN/home/0,,EN-home-31-nodirectorate-no-nono-31,00.html.
12. Bardhan Pranab, "Corruption and Development," *Journal of Economic Literature* 36 (September 1997), pp. 1320–46.
13. A. Shleifer and R. W. Vishny, "Corruption," *Quarterly Journal of Economics*, no. 108 (1993), pp. 599–617; and I. Ehrlich and F. Lui, "Bureaucratic Corruption and Endogenous Economic Growth," *Journal of Political Economy* 107 (December 1999), pp. 270–92.
14. P. Mauro, "Corruption and Growth," *Quarterly Journal of Economics*, no. 110 (1995), pp. 681–712.
15. Detailed at www.iit.edu/departments/csep/PublicWWW/codes/coe/Bus_Conduct_Dow_Corning(1996).html.
16. S. A. Waddock and S. B. Graves, "The Corporate Social Performance-Financial Performance Link," *Strategic Management Journal* 8 (1997), pp. 303–19.
17. Daniel Litvin, *Empires of Profit* (New York: Texere, 2003).
18. Details can be found at BP's Web site, www.bp.com.
19. This is known as the "when in Rome perspective." Donaldson, "Values in Tension."
20. De George, *Competing with Integrity in International Business.*
21. Saul W. Gellerman, "Why Good Managers Make Bad Ethical Choices," in *Ethics in Practice: Managing the Moral Corporation*, ed. Kenneth R. Andrews (Cambridge, MA: Harvard Business School Press, 1989).
22. David Messick and Max H. Bazerman, "Ethical Leadership and the Psychology of Decision Making," *Sloan Management Review* 37 (Winter 1996), pp. 9–20.
23. Robert Bryce, *Pipe Dreams: Greed, Ego and the Death of Enron* (New York: Public Affairs, 2002).
24. Milton Friedman, "The Social Responsibility of Business Is to Increase Profits," *The New York Times Magazine*, September 13, 1970. Reprinted in Tom L. Beauchamp and Norman E. Bowie, *Ethical Theory and Business*, 7th ed. (Upper Saddle River, NJ: Prentice Hall, 2001).
25. Friedman, "The Social Responsibility of Business Is to Increase Profits," p. 55.
26. For example, see Donaldson, "Values in Tension." See also Norman Bowie, "Relativism and the Moral Obligations of Multination Corporations," in Beauchamp and Bowie, *Ethical Theory and Business.*
27. For example, see De George, *Competing with Integrity in International Business.*
28. Details can be found at www.bp.com/sectiongenericarticle.do?category1d=79&contentId=2002369#2014689.
29. This example is often repeated in the literature on international business ethics. It was first outlined by Arthur Kelly in "Case Study—Italian Style Mores." Printed in Thomas Donaldson and Patricia Werhane, *Ethical Issues in Business* (Englewood Cliffs, NJ: Prentice Hall, 1979).
30. See Beauchamp and Bowie, *Ethical Theory and Business.*
31. Thomas Donaldson, *The Ethics of International Business* (Oxford: Oxford University Press, 1989).
32. Found at www.un.org/Overview/rights.html.
33. Donaldson, *The Ethics of International Business.*
34. See Chapter 10 in Beauchamp and Bowie, *Ethical Theory and Business.*

35. John Rawls, *A Theory of Justice,* rev. ed. (Cambridge, MA: Belknap Press, 1999).

36. Joseph Bower and Jay Dial, "Jack Welch: General Electrics Revolutionary," Harvard Business School Case 9-394-065, April 1994.

37. For example, see R. Edward Freeman and Daniel Gilbert, *Corporate Strategy and the Search for Ethics* (Englewood Cliffs, NJ: Prentice Hall, 1988); Thomas Jones, "Ethical Decision Making by Individuals in Organizations," *Academy of Management Review* 16 (1991), pp. 366–95; and J. R. Rest, *Moral Development: Advances in Research and Theory* (New York: Praeger, 1986).

38. Ibid.

39. See E. Freeman, *Strategic Management: A Stakeholder Approach* (Boston: Pitman Press, 1984); C. W. L. Hill and T. M. Jones, "Stakeholder-Agency Theory," *Journal of Management Studies* 29 (1992), pp. 131–54; and J. G. March and H. A. Simon, *Organizations* (New York: Wiley, 1958).

40. Hill and Jones, "Stakeholder-Agency Theory"; and March and Simon, *Organizations.*

41. De George, *Competing with Integrity in International Business.*

42. The code can be accessed at United Technologies Web site, www.utc.com/profile/ethics/index.htm.

43. Colin Grant, "Whistle Blowers: Saints of Secular Culture," *Journal of Business Ethics,* September 2002, pp. 391–400.

Chapter 5

1. H. W. Spiegel, *The Growth of Economic Thought* (Durham, NC: Duke University Press, 1991).

2. M. Solis, "The Politics of Self-Restraint: FDI Subsidies and Japanese Mercantilism," *The World Economy* 26 (February 2003), pp. 153–70.

3. S. Hollander, *The Economics of David Ricardo* (Buffalo: University of Toronto Press, 1979).

4. D. Ricardo, *The Principles of Political Economy and Taxation* (Homewood, IL: Irwin, 1967; first published in 1817).

5. For example, R. Dornbusch, S. Fischer, and P. Samuelson, "Comparative Advantage: Trade and Payments in a Ricardian Model with a Continuum of Goods," *American Economic Review* 67 (December 1977), pp. 823–39.

6. B. Balassa, "An Empirical Demonstration of Classic Comparative Cost Theory," *Review of Economics and Statistics,* 1963, pp. 231–38.

7. See P. R. Krugman, "Is Free Trade Passé?" *Journal of Economic Perspectives* 1 (Fall 1987), pp. 131–44.

8. P. Samuelson, "Where Ricardo and Mill Rebut and Confirm Arguments of Mainstream Economists Supporting Globalization," *Journal of Economic Perspectives* 18, no. 3 (Summer 2004), pp. 135–46.

9. P. Samuelson, "The Gains from International Trade Once Again," *Economic Journal* 72 (1962), pp. 820–29.

10. S. Lohr, "An Elder Challenges Outsourcing's Orthodoxy," *The New York Times,* September 9, 2004, p. C1.

11. P. Samuelson, "Where Ricardo and Mill Rebut and Confirm Arguments of Mainstream Economists Supporting Globalization," *Journal of Economic Perspectives* 18, no. 3 (Summer 2004), p. 143.

12. See A. Dixit and G. Grossman, "Samuelson Says Nothing about Trade Policy," Princeton University, 2004, from www.princeton.edu/~dixitak/home.

13. J. Bhagwati, A. Panagariya, and T.N. Sirinivasan, "The Muddles over Outsourcing," *Journal of Economic Perspectives* 18, no. 4 (Fall 2004), pp. 93–114.

14. For example, J. D. Sachs and A. Warner, "Economic Reform and the Process of Global Integration," *Brookings Papers on Economic Activity,* 1995, pp. 1–96; J.A. Frankel and D. Romer, "Does Trade Cause Growth?" *American Economic Review* 89, no. 3 (June 1999), pp. 379–99; and D. Dollar and A. Kraay, "Trade, Growth and Poverty," working paper, Development Research Group, World Bank, June 2001. Also, for an accessible discussion of the relationship between free trade and economic growth, see T. Taylor, "The Truth about Globalization," *Public Interest,* Spring 2002, pp. 24–44.

15. Sachs and Warner, "Economic Reform and the Process of Global Integration."

16. Ibid., pp. 35–36.

17. R. Wacziarg and K.H. Welch, "Trade Liberalization and Growth: New Evidence," National Bureau of Economic Research working paper series, no. 10152, December 2003.

18. Frankel and Romer, "Does Trade Cause Growth?"

19. A recent skeptical review of the empirical work on the relationship between trade and growth questions these results. See Francisco Rodriguez and Dani Rodrik, "Trade Policy and Economic Growth: A Skeptics Guide to the Cross-National Evidence," National Bureau of Economic Research working paper series, no. 7081, April 1999. Even these authors, however, cannot find any evidence that trade hurts economic growth or income levels.

20. B. Ohlin, *Interregional and International Trade* (Cambridge: Harvard University Press, 1933). For a summary, see R. W. Jones and J. P. Neary, "The

Positive Theory of International Trade," in *Handbook of International Economics,* eds. R. W. Jones and P. B. Kenen (Amsterdam: North Holland, 1984).

21. W. Leontief, "Domestic Production and Foreign Trade: The American Capital Position Re-Examined," *Proceedings of the American Philosophical Society* 97 (1953), pp. 331–49.
22. R. M. Stern and K. Maskus, "Determinants of the Structure of U.S. Foreign Trade," *Journal of International Economics* 11 (1981), pp. 207–44.
23. See H. P. Bowen, E. E. Leamer, and L. Sveikayskas, "Multicountry, Multifactor Tests of the Factor Abundance Theory," *American Economic Review* 77 (1987), pp. 791–809.
24. D. Trefler, "The Case of the Missing Trade and Other Mysteries," *American Economic Review* 85 (December 1995), pp. 1029–46.
25. D.R. Davis and D.E. Weinstein, "An Account of Global Factor Trade," *American Economic Review,* December 2001, pp. 1423–52.
26. R. Vernon, "International Investments and International Trade in the Product Life Cycle," *Quarterly Journal of Economics,* May 1966, pp. 190–207; and R. Vernon and L. T. Wells, *The Economic Environment of International Business,* 4th ed. (Englewood Cliffs, NJ: Prentice Hall, 1986).
27. M. B. Lieberman and D. B. Montgomery, "First-Mover Advantages," *Strategic Management Journal* 9 (Summer 1988), pp. 41–58; and W. T. Robinson and Sungwook Min, "Is the First to Market the First to Fail?" *Journal of Marketing Research* 29 (2002), pp. 120–28.
28 J. R. Tybout, "Plant and Firm Level Evidence on New Trade Theories," National Bureau of Economic Res-earch working paper series, no. 8418, August 2001; paper available at www.nber.org. Also see S. Deraniyagala and B. Fine, "New Trade Theory versus Old Trade Policy: A Continuing Enigma," *Cambridge Journal of Economics* 25 (November 2001), pp. 809–25.
29. A. D. Chandler, *Scale and Scope* (New York: Free Press, 1990).
30. Krugman, "Does the New Trade Theory Require a New Trade Policy?"
31. M. E. Porter, *The Competitive Advantage of Nations* (New York: Free Press, 1990). For a good review of this book, see R. M. Grant, "Porter's Competitive Advantage of Nations: An Assessment," *Strategic Management Journal* 12 (1991), pp. 535–48.
32. B. Kogut, ed., *Country Competitiveness: Technology and the Organizing of Work* (New York: Oxford University Press, 1993).
33. Porter, *The Competitive Advantage of Nations,* p. 121.
34. Lieberman and Montgomery, "First-Mover Advantages." See also Robinson and Min, "Is the First to Market the First to Fail?"; W. Boulding and M. Christen, "First-Mover Disadvantage," *Harvard Business Review,* October 2001, pp. 20–21; and R. Agarwal and M. Gort, "First-Mover Advantage and the Speed of Competitive Entry," *Journal of Law and Economics* 44 (2001), pp. 131–59.
35. C. A. Hamilton, "Building Better Machine Tools," *Journal of Commerce,* October 30, 1991, p. 8; and "Manufacturing Trouble," *The Economist,* October 12, 1991, p. 71.

Chapter 6

1. For a detailed welfare analysis of the effect of a tariff, see P. R. Krugman and M. Obstfeld, *International Economics: Theory and Policy* (New York: HarperCollins, 2000), chap. 8.
2. Y. Sazanami, S. Urata, and H. Kawai, *Measuring the Costs of Protection in Japan* (Washington, DC: Institute for International Economics, 1994).
3. J. Bhagwati, *Protectionism* (Cambridge, MA: MIT Press, 1988); and "Costs of Protection," *Journal of Commerce,* September 25, 1991, p. 8A.
4. The study was undertaken by Kym Anderson of the University of Adelaide. See "A Not So Perfect Market," *The Economist; Survey of Agriculture and Technology,* March 25, 2000, pp. 8–10.
5. R. W. Crandall, *Regulating the Automobile* (Washington, DC: Brookings Institution, 1986).
6. Krugman and Obstfeld, *International Economics.*
7. G. Hufbauer and Z. A. Elliott, *Measuring the Costs of Protectionism in the United States* (Washington, DC: Institute for International Economics, 1993).
8. Bhagwati, *Protectionism;* and "Japan to Curb VCR Exports," *The New York Times,* November 21, 1983, p. D5.
9. Alan Goldstein, "Sematech Members Facing Dues Increase; 30% Jump to Make Up for Loss of Federal Funding," *Dallas Morning News,* July 27, 1996, p. 2F.
10. N. Dunne and R. Waters, "U.S. Waves a Big Stick at Chinese Pirates," *Financial Times,* January 6, 1995, p. 4.
11. John Broder, "Clinton to Impose Ban on 58 Types of Imported Guns," *The New York Times,* April 6, 1998, p. A1.
12. Bill Lambrecht, "Monsanto Softens Its Stance on Labeling in Europe," *St. Louis Post-Dispatch,* March 15, 1998, p. E1.
13. Peter S. Jordan, "Country Sanctions and the International Business Community," *American Society*

of International Law Proceedings of the Annual Meeting 20, no. 9 (1997), pp. 333–42.

14. "Waiting for China; Human Rights and International Trade," *Commonwealth,* March 11, 1994; and "China: The Cost of Putting Business First," *Human Rights Watch,* July 1996.
15. "Brazil's Auto Industry Struggles to Boost Global Competitiveness," *Journal of Commerce,* October 10, 1991, p. 6A.
16. For reviews, see J. A. Brander, "Rationales for Strategic Trade and Industrial Policy," in *Strategic Trade Policy and the New International Economics,* ed. P. R. Krugman (Cambridge, MA: MIT Press, 1986); P. R. Krugman, "Is Free Trade Passé?" *Journal of Economic Perspectives* 1 (1987), pp. 131–44; and P. R. Krugman, "Does the New Trade Theory Require a New Trade Policy?" *World Economy* 15, no. 4 (1992), pp. 423–41.
17. "Airbus and Boeing: The Jumbo War," *The Economist,* June 15, 1991, pp. 65–66.
18. For details see Krugman, "Is Free Trade Passé?"; and Brander, "Rationales for Strategic Trade and Industrial Policy."
19. Krugman, "Is Free Trade Passé?"
20. This dilemma is a variant of the famous prisoner's dilemma, which has become a classic metaphor for the difficulty of achieving cooperation between self-interested and mutually suspicious entities. For a good general introduction, see A. Dixit and B. Nalebuff, *Thinking Strategically: The Competitive Edge in Business, Politics, and Everyday Life* (New York: W. W. Norton & Co., 1991).
21. Note that the Smoot-Hawley Act did not cause the Great Depression. However, the beggar-thy-neighbor trade policies that it ushered in certainly made things worse. See Bhagwati, *Protectionism.*
22. Ibid.
23. World Bank, *World Development Report* (New York: Oxford University Press, 1987).
24. World Trade Organization, "World Trade 2005, Prospects 2006," WTO press release, April 11, 2006.
25. Frances Williams, "WTO—New Name Heralds New Powers," *Financial Times,* December 16, 1993, p. 5; and Frances Williams, "Gatt's Successor to Be Given Real Clout," *Financial Times,* April 4, 1994, p. 6.
26. W. J. Davey, "The WTO Dispute Settlement System: The First Ten Years," *Journal of International Economic Law,* March 2005, pp. 17–28.
27. Information provided on WTO Web site, www.wto.org/english/tratop_e/dispu_e/dispu_status_e.htm.
28. Frances Williams, "Telecoms: World Pact Set to Slash Costs of Calls," *Financial Times,* February 17, 1997.
29. G. De Jonquieres, "Happy End to a Cliff Hanger," *Financial Times,* December 15, 1997, p. 15.
30. Jim Carlton, "Greens Target WTO Plan for Lumber," *The Wall Street Journal,* November 24, 1999, p. A2.
31. Kari Huus, "WTO Summit Leaves Only Discontent," MSNBC, December 3, 1999, www.msnbc.com.
32. Data at www.wto.org/english/tratop_e/adp_e/adp_e.htm.
33. *Annual Report by the Director General 2003* (Geneva: World Trade Organization, 2003).
34. Ibid.
35. Ibid.
36. World Trade Organization, *Annual Report 2002* (Geneva: WTO, 2002).
37. A. Tanzer, "Pill Factory to the World," *Forbes,* December 10, 2001, pp. 70–72.
38. S. C. Bradford, P. L. E. Grieco, and G. C. Hufbauer, "The Payoff to America from Global Integration," in *The United States and the World Economy: Foreign Policy for the Next Decade,* C. F. Bergsten, ed. (Washington, DC: Institute for International Economics, 2005).
39. World Bank, *Global Economic Prospects 2005* (Washington, DC: World Bank, 2005).
40. W. Vieth, "Major Concessions Lead to Success for WTO Talks," *Los Angeles Times,* November 14, 2001, p. A1; and "Seeds Sown for Future Growth," *The Economist,* November 17, 2001, pp. 65–66.
41. "The WTO under Fire—The Doha Round," *The Economist,* September 20, 2003, pp. 30–32.
42. "Punitive Tariffs Are Approved on Imports of Japanese Steel," *The New York Times,* June 12, 1999, p. A3.

Chapter 7

1. United Nations, *World Investment Report, 2000* (New York and Geneva: United Nations, 2001).
2. United Nations, *World Investment Report, 2005;* and "Data Shows Foreign Direct Investment Climbed Sharply in 2005," UN Conference on Trade and Development, press release, January 23, 2006.
3. World Trade Organization, *International Trade Statistics, 2005* (Geneva: WTO, 2005); and United Nations, *World Investment Report, 2005.*
4. United Nations, *World Investment Report, 2005.*
5. Ibid.
6. Ibid.
7. Ibid.
8. Ibid; and "Data Shows Foreign Direct Investment Climbed Sharply in 2005."

9. "World FDI Flows Grew an Estimated 6% in 2004," UN Conference on Trade and Development, press release.

10. United Nations, *World Investment Report, 2005.*

11. Ibid.

12. See D. J. Ravenscraft and F. M. Scherer, *Mergers, Selloffs and Economic Efficiency* (Washington, DC: The Brookings Institution, 1987); and A. Seth, K. P. Song, and R. R. Pettit, "Value Creation and Destruction in Cross-Border Acquisitions," *Strategic Management Journal* 23 (2002), pp. 921–40.

13. For example, see S. H. Hymer, *The International Operations of National Firms: A Study of Direct Foreign Investment* (Cambridge, MA: MIT Press, 1976): A. M. Rugman, *Inside the Multinationals: The Economics of Internal Markets* (New York: Columbia University Press, 1981); D. J. Teece, "Multinational Enterprise, Internal Governance, and Industrial Organization," *American Economic Review* 75 (May 1983), pp. 233–38; C. W. L. Hill and W. C. Kim, "Searching for a Dynamic Theory of the Multinational Enterprise: A Transaction Cost Model," *Strategic Management Journal* 9 (special issue, 1988), pp. 93–104; A. Verbeke, "The Evolutionary View of the MNE and the Future of Internalization Theory," *Journal of International Business Studies* 34 (2003), pp. 498–501; and J. H. Dunning, "Some Antecedents of Internalization Theory," *Journal of International Business Studies* 34 (2003), pp. 108–28.

14. J. P. Womack, D. T. Jones, and D. Roos, *The Machine that Changed the World* (New York: Rawson Associates, 1990).

15. The argument is most often associated with F. T. Knickerbocker, *Oligopolistic Reaction and Multinational Enterprise* (Boston: Harvard Business School Press, 1973).

16. The studies are summarized in R. E. Caves, *Multinational Enterprise and Economic Analysis*, 2nd ed. (Cambridge, UK: Cambridge University Press, 1996).

17. See R. E. Caves, "Japanese Investment in the US: Lessons for the Economic Analysis of Foreign Investment," *The World Economy* 16 (1993), pp. 279–300; B. Kogut and S. J. Chang, "Technological Capabilities and Japanese Direct Investment in the United States," *Review of Economics and Statistics* 73 (1991), pp. 401–43; and J. Anand and B. Kogut, "Technological Capabilities of Countries, Firm Rivalry, and Foreign Direct Investment," *Journal of International Business Studies*, 1997, pp. 445–65.

18. K. Ito and E. L. Rose, "Foreign Direct Investment Location Strategies in the Tire Industry," *Journal of International Business Studies* 33 (2002), pp. 593–602.

19. H. Haveman and L. Nonnemaker, "Competition in Multiple Geographical Markets," *Administrative Science Quarterly* 45 (2000), pp. 232–67; and L. Fuentelsaz and J. Gomez, "Multipoint Competition, Strategic Similarity and Entry into Geographic Markets," *Strategic Management Journal* 27 (2006), pp. 447–57.

20. For the use of Vernon's theory to explain Japanese direct investment in the United States and Europe, see S. Thomsen, "Japanese Direct Investment in the European Community," *The World Economy* 16 (1993), pp. 301–15. Also see Z. Gao and C. Tisdell, "Foreign Investment and Asia, Particularly China's Rise in the Television Industry: The International Product Life Cycle Reconsidered," *Journal of Asia-Pacific Business* 6, no. 3 (2005), pp. 37–50.

21. J. H. Dunning, *Explaining International Production* (London: Unwin Hyman, 1988).

22. P. Krugman. "Increasing Returns and Economic Geography," *Journal of Political Economy* 99, no. 3 (1991), pp. 483–99.

23. J. M. Shaver and F. Flyer, "Agglomeration Economies, Firm Heterogeneity, and Foreign Direct Investment in the United States," *Strategic Management Journal* 21 (2000), pp. 1175–93.

24. J. H. Dunning and R. Narula, "Transpacific Foreign Direct Investment and the Investment Development Path," *South Carolina Essays in International Business*, May 1995.

25. W. Shan and J. Song, "Foreign Direct Investment and the Sourcing of Technological Advantage: Evidence from the Biotechnology Industry," *Journal of International Business Studies*, 1997, pp. 267–84.

26. For some additional evidence see L. E. Brouthers, K. D. Brouthers, and S. Warner, "Is Dunning's Eclectic Framework Descriptive or Normative?" *Journal of International Business Studies* 30 (1999), pp. 831–44.

27. For elaboration, see S. Hood and S. Young, *The Economics of the Multinational Enterprise* (London: Longman, 1979); and P. M. Sweezy and H. Magdoff, "The Dynamics of U.S. Capitalism," *Monthly Review Press*, 1972.

28. C. Forelle and G. Hitt, "IBM Discusses Security Measure in Lenovo Deal," *The Wall Street Journal*, February 25, 2005, p. A2.

29. For an example of this policy as practiced in China, see L. G. Branstetter and R. C. Freenstra, "Trade and Foreign Direct Investment in China: A political Economy Approach," *Journal of International Economics* 58 (December 2002), pp. 335–58.

30. M. Itoh and K. Kiyono, "Foreign Trade and Direct Investment," in *Industrial Policy of Japan*, ed. R. Komiya,

M. Okuno, and K. Suzumura (Tokyo: Academic Press, 1988).

31. R. E. Lipsey, "Home and Host Country Effects of FDI," National Bureau of Economic Research, working paper no. 9293, October 2002; and X. Li and X. Liu, "Foreign Direct Investment and Economic Growth," *World Development* 33 (March 2005), pp. 393–413.
32. X. J. Zhan and T. Ozawa, *Business Restructuring in Asia: Cross Border M&As in Crisis Affected Countries* (Copenhagen: Copenhagen Business School, 2000); I. Costa, S. Robles, and R. de Queiroz, "Foreign Direct Investment and Technological Capabilities," *Research Policy* 31 (2002), pp. 1431–43; B. Potterie and F. Lichtenberg, "Does Foreign Direct Investment Transfer Technology across Borders?" *Review of Economics and Statistics* 83 (2001), pp. 490–97; and K. Saggi, "Trade, Foreign Direct Investment and International Technology Transfer," *World Bank Research Observer* 17 (2002), pp. 191–235.
33. K. M. Moden, "Foreign Acquisitions of Swedish Companies: Effects on R&D and Productivity," Stockholm: Research Institute of International Economics, 1998, mimeo.
34. "Foreign Friends," *The Economist,* January 8, 2000, pp. 71–72.
35. A. Jack, "French Go into Overdrive to Win Investors," *Financial Times,* December 10, 1997, p. 6.
36. "Foreign Friends."
37. G. Hunya and K. Kalotay, *Privatization and Foreign Direct Investment in Eastern and Central Europe* (Geneva: UNCTAD, 2001).
38. P. R. Krugman and M. Obstfeld, *International Economics: Theory and Policy* (New York: Harper Collins, 1994), chap. 9. Also see P. Krugman, *The Age of Diminished Expectations* (Cambridge, MA: MIT Press, 1990).
39. United Nations, *World Investment Report, 2002* (New York and Geneva: United Nations, 2002).
40. R. Ram and K. H. Zang, "Foreign Direct Investment and Economic Growth," *Economic Development and Cultural Change* 51 (2002), pp. 205–25.
41. United Nations, *World Investment Report, 1998* (New York and Geneva: United Nations, 1997).
42. United Nations, *World Investment Report, 2000.*
43. R. B. Reich, *The Work of Nations: Preparing Ourselves for the 21st Century* (New York: Alfred A. Knopf, 1991).
44. This idea has been articulated, although not quite in this form, by C. A. Bartlett and S. Ghoshal, *Managing across Borders: The Transnational Solution* (Boston: Harvard Business School Press, 1989).
45. P. Magnusson, "The Mexico Pact: Worth the Price?" *BusinessWeek*, May 27, 1991, pp. 32–35.
46. C. Johnston, "Political Risk Insurance," in *Assessing Corporate Political Risk,* ed. D. M. Raddock (Totowa, NJ: Rowman & Littlefield, 1986).
47. M. Tolchin and S. Tolchin, *Buying into America: How Foreign Money Is Changing the Face of Our Nation* (New York: Times Books, 1988).
48. S. Rai, "India to Ease Limits on Foreign Ownership of Media and Tea," *The New York Times,* June 26, 2002, p. W1.
49. L. D. Qiu and Z. Tao, "Export, Foreign Direct Investment and Local Content Requirements," *Journal of Development Economics* 66 (October 2001), pp. 101–25.
50. United Nations, *World Investment Report, 2003.*
51. See R. E. Caves, *Multinational Enterprise and Economic Analysis* (Cambridge, UK: Cambridge University Press, 1982).
52. For a good general introduction to negotiation strategy, see M.H. Bazerman, *Negotiating Rationally* (New York: Free Press, 1992); A. Dixit and B. Nalebuff, *Thinking Strategically: The Competitive Edge in Business, Politics, and Everyday Life* (New York: W. W. Norton, 1991); and H. Raiffa, *The Art and Science of Negotiation* (Cambridge, MA: Harvard University Press, 1982).

Chapter 8

1. Information taken from World Trade Organization Web site and current as of March 2006, www.wto.org.
2. Ibid.
3. The Andean Pact has been through a number of changes since its inception. The latest version was established in 1991. See "Free-Trade Free for All," *The Economist,* January 4, 1991, p. 63.
4. D. Swann, *The Economics of the Common Market,* 6th ed. (London: Penguin Books, 1990).
5. See J. Bhagwati, "Regionalism and Multilateralism: An Overview," Columbia University discussion paper 603, Department of Economics, Columbia University, New York; A. de la Torre and M. Kelly, "Regional Trade Arrangements," International Monetary Fund occasional paper 93, Washington, DC,, March 1992; J. Bhagwati, "Fast Track to Nowhere," *The Economist,* October 18, 1997, pp. 21–24; Jagdish Bhagwati, *Free Trade Today* (Princeton and Oxford: Princeton University Press, 2002); and B. K. Gordon, "A High Risk Trade Policy," *Foreign Affairs* 82, no. 4 (July–August 2003), pp. 105–15.
6. N. Colchester and D. Buchan, *Europower: The Essential Guide to Europe's Economic Transformation in*

1992 (London: The Economist Books, 1990); and Swann, *Economics of the Common Market.*

7. A. S. Posen, "Fleeting Equality, The Relative Size of the EU and US Economies in 2020," the Brookings Institution, September 2004.
8. Swann, *Economics of the Common Market;* Colchester and Buchan, *Europower;* "The European Union: A Survey," *The Economist,* October 22, 1994; "The European Community: A Survey," *The Economist,* July 3, 1993; and the European Union Web site, http://europa.eu.int.
9. E. J. Morgan, "A Decade of EC Merger Control," *International Journal of Economics and Business,* November 2001, pp. 451–73.
10. "The European Community: A Survey."
11. "One Europe, One Economy," *The Economist,* November 30, 1991, pp. 53–54; and "Market Failure: A Survey of Business in Europe," *The Economist,* June 8, 1991, pp. 6–10.
12. Alan Riley, "The Single Market Ten Years On," *European Policy Analyst,* December 2002, pp. 65–72.
13. See C. Wyploze, "EMU: Why and How It Might Happen," *Journal of Economic Perspectives* 11 (1997), pp. 3–22; and M. Feldstein, "The Political Economy of the European Economic and Monetary Union," *Journal of Economic Perspectives* 11 (1997), pp. 23–42.
14. "One Europe, One Economy"; and Feldstein, "The Political Economy of the European Economic and Monetary Union."
15. Feldstein, "The Political Economy of the European Economic and Monetary Union."
16. "Time for Europhoria?" *The Economist,* January 4, 2003, p. 58.
17. "The Passing of the Buck?" *The Economist,* December 4, 2004, pp. 78–80.
18. Details regarding conditions of membership and the progression of enlargement negotiations can be found at http://europa.eu.int/comm/enlargement/index.htm.
19. "What Is NAFTA?" *Financial Times,* November 17, 1993, p. 6; and S. Garland, "Sweet Victory," *BusinessWeek,* November 29, 1993, pp. 30–31.
20. "NAFTA: The Showdown," *The Economist,* November 13, 1993, pp. 23–36.
21. N. C. Lustog, "NAFTA: Setting the Record Straight," *The World Economy,* 1997, pp. 605–14.
22. R. H. Ojeda, C. Dowds, R. McCleery, S. Robinson, D. Runsten, C. Wolff, and G. Wolff, "NAFTA—How Has It Done? North American Integration Three Years after NAFTA," North American Integration and Development Center at UCLA, December 1996.
23. W. Thorbecke and C. Eigen-Zucchi, "Did NAFTA Cause a Giant Sucking Sound?" *Journal of Labor Research,* Fall 2002, pp. 647–58; G. Gagne, "North American Free Trade, Canada, and U.S. Trade Remedies: An Assessment after Ten Years," *The World Economy,* 2000, pp. 77–91; and G.C. Hufbauer and J. J. Schott, *NAFTA Revisited: Achievements and Challenges* (Washington DC: Institute for International Economics, 2005).
24. All trade figures from U.S. Department of Commerce Trade Stat Express, http://tse.export.gov.
25. J. Cavanagh et al., "Happy Ever NAFTA?" *Foreign Policy,* September–October 2002, pp. 58–65.
26. "The Business of the American Hemisphere," *The Economist,* August 24, 1991, pp. 37–38.
27. "NAFTA Is Not Alone," *The Economist,* June 18, 1994, pp. 47–48.
28. "Murky MERCOSUR," *The Economist,* July 26, 1997, pp. 66–67.
29. See M. Philips, "South American Trade Pact under Fire," *The Wall Street Journal,* October 23, 1996, p. A2; A. J. Yeats, *Does MERCOSUR's Trade Performance Justify Concerns about the Global Welfare-Reducing Effects of Free Trade Arrangements? Yes!* (Washington, DC: World Bank, 1996); and D. M. Leipziger et al., "MERCOSUR: Integration and Industrial Policy," *The World Economy,* 1997, pp. 585–604.
30. "Another Blow to MERCOSUR," *The Economist,* March 31, 2001, pp. 33–34.
31. "Lula Lays Out MERCOSUR Rescue Mission," *Latin America Newsletters,* February 4, 2003, p. 7.
32. "A Free Trade Tug of War," *The Economist,* December 11, 2004, p. 54.
33. "CARICOM Single Market Begins," *EIU Views,* February 3, 2006.
34. M. Esterl, "Free Trade Area of the Americas Stalls," *The Economist,* January 19, 2005, p. 1.
35. M. Moffett and J. D. McKinnon, "Failed Summit Casts Shadow on Global Trade Talks," *The Wall Street Journal,* November 7, 2005, p. A1.
36. "Every Man for Himself: Trade in Asia," *The Economist,* November 2, 2002, pp. 43–44.
37. "Aimless in Seattle," *The Economist,* November 13, 1993, pp. 35–36.
38. G. de Jonquieres, "APEC Grapples with Market Turmoil," *Financial Times,* November 21, 1997, p. 6; and G. Baker, "Clinton Team Wins Most of the APEC Tricks," *Financial Times,* November 27, 1997, p. 5.
39. M. Turner, "Trio Revives East African Union," *Financial Times,* January 16, 2001, p. 4.

40. United Nations, *World Investment Report,* various issues (New York and Geneva: United Nations).

41. P. Davis, "A European Campaign: Local Companies Rush for a Share of EC Market While Barriers Are Down," *Minneapolis–St. Paul City Business,* January 8, 1990, p. 1.

42. "The Business of Europe," *The Economist,* December 7, 1991, pp. 63–64.

43. T. Horwitz, "Europe's Borders Fade," *The Wall Street Journal,* May 18, 1993, pp. A1, A12; "A Singular Market," *The Economist,* October 22, 1994, pp. 10–16; and "Something Dodgy in Europe's Single Market," *The Economist,* May 21, 1994, pp. 69–70.

44. E. G. Friberg, "1992: Moves Europeans Are Making," *Harvard Business Review,* May–June 1989, pp. 85–89.

Chapter 9

1. For a good general introduction to the foreign exchange market, see R. Weisweiller, *How the Foreign Exchange Market Works* (New York: New York Institute of Finance, 1990). A detailed description of the economics of foreign exchange markets can be found in P. R. Krugman and M. Obstfeld, *International Economics: Theory and Policy* (New York: HarperCollins, 1994).

2. Bank for International Settlements, *Tri-annual Central Bank Survey of Foreign Exchange and Derivatives Market Activity, April 2004* (Basle, Switzerland: BIS, March 2005).

3. Ibid.

4. Ibid.

5. M. Dickson, "Capital Gain: How London Is Thriving as It Takes on the Global Competition," *Financial Times,* March 27, 2006, p. 11.

6. For a comprehensive review see M. Taylor, "The Economics of Exchange Rates," *Journal of Economic Literature* 33 (1995), pp. 13–47.

7. Krugman and Obstfeld, *International Economics.*

8. M. Friedman, *Studies in the Quantity Theory of Money* (Chicago: University of Chicago Press, 1956). For an accessible explanation, see M. Friedman and R. Friedman, *Free to Choose* (London: Penguin Books, 1979), chap. 9.

9. Juan-Antino Morales, "Inflation Stabilization in Bolivia," in *Inflation Stabilization: The Experience of Israel, Argentina, Brazil, Bolivia, and Mexico,* ed. Michael Bruno et al. (Cambridge, MA: MIT Press, 1988); and The Economist, *World Book of Vital Statistics* (New York: Random House, 1990).

10. For reviews and recent articles see H. J. Edison, J. E. Gagnon, and W. R. Melick, "Understanding the Empirical Literature on Purchasing Power Parity," *Journal of International Money and Finance* 16 (February 1997), pp. 1–18; J. R. Edison, "Multi-Country Evidence on the Behavior of Purchasing Power Parity under the Current Float," *Journal of International Money and Finance* 16 (February 1997), pp. 19–36; K. Rogoff, "The Purchasing Power Parity Puzzle," *Journal of Economic Literature* 34 (1996), pp. 647–68; D. R. Rapach and M. E. Wohar, "Testing the Monetary Model of Exchange Rate Determination: New Evidence from a Century of Data," *Journal of International Economics,* December 2002, pp. 359–85; and M. P. Taylor, "Purchasing Power Parity," *Review of International Economics,* August 2003, pp. 436–56.

11. M. Obstfeld and K. Rogoff, "The Six Major Puzzles in International Economics," National Bureau of Economic Research working paper no. 7777, July 2000.

12. Ibid.

13. See M. Devereux and C. Engel, "Monetary Policy in the Open Economy Revisited: Price Setting and Exchange Rate Flexibility," National Bureau of Economic Research working paper no. 7665, April 2000. See also P. Krugman, "Pricing to Market When the Exchange Rate Changes," in *Real Financial Economics,* ed. S. Arndt and J. Richardson (Cambridge, MA: MIT Press, 1987).

14. For a summary of the evidence, see the survey by Taylor, "The Economics of Exchange Rates."

15. R. E. Cumby and M. Obstfeld, "A Note on Exchange Rate Expectations and Nominal Interest Differentials: A Test of the Fisher Hypothesis," *Journal of Finance,* June 1981, pp. 697–703; and L. Coppock and M. Poitras, "Evaluating the Fisher Effect in Long-Term Cross-Country Averages," *International Review of Economics and Finance* 9 (2000), pp. 181–203.

16. Taylor, "The Economics of Exchange Rates." See also R. K. Lyons, *The Microstructure Approach to Exchange Rates* (Cambridge, MA: MIT Press, 2002).

17. See H. L. Allen and M. P. Taylor, "Charts, Noise, and Fundamentals in the Foreign Exchange Market," *Economic Journal* 100 (1990), pp. 49–59; and T. Ito, "Foreign Exchange Rate Expectations: Micro Survey Data," *American Economic Review* 80 (1990), pp. 434–49.

18. For example, see E. Fama, "Forward Rates as Predictors of Future Spot Rates," *Journal of Financial Economics,* October 1976, pp. 361–77.

19. L. Kilian and M. P. Taylor, "Why Is It So Difficult to Beat the Random Walk Forecast of Exchange Rates?" *Journal of International Economics* 20 (May 2003), pp. 85–103; and R. M. Levich, "The Efficiency of Markets for Foreign Exchange," in *International Finance,* ed. G. D. Gay and R. W. Kold (Richmond, VA: Robert F. Dane, Inc., 1983).

20. J. Williamson, *The Exchange Rate System* (Washington, DC: Institute for International Economics, 1983); and R. H. Clarida, L. Sarno, M. P. Taylor, and G. Valente, "The Out of Sample Success of Term Structure Models as Exchange Rate Predictors," *Journal of International Economics* 60 (May 2003), pp. 61–84.
21. Kilian and Taylor, "Why Is It So Difficult to Beat the Random Walk Forecast of Exchange Rates?"
22. Rogoff, "The Purchasing Power Parity Puzzle."
23. C. Engel and J. D. Hamilton, "Long Swings in the Dollar: Are They in the Data and Do Markets Know It?" *American Economic Review,* September 1990, pp. 689–713.
24. J. R. Carter and J. Gagne, "The Do's and Don'ts of International Countertrade," *Sloan Management Review,* Spring 1988, pp. 31–37.
25. "Where There Is a Will," *Trade Finance,* October 2003, pp. 1–2.
26. D. S. Levine, "Got a Spare Destroyer Lying Around?" *World Trade* 10 (June 1997), pp. 34–35; and Dan West, "Countertrade," *Business Credit,* April 2001, pp. 64–67.
27. For details on how various firms manage their foreign exchange exposure, see the articles contained in the special foreign exchange issue of *Business International Money Report,* December 18, 1989, pp. 401–12.
28. Ibid.
29. S. Arterian, "How Black & Decker Defines Exposure," *Business International Money Report,* December 18, 1989, pp. 404, 405, 409.

Chapter 10

1. Updates can be found at the IMF Web site, www.imf.org.
2. The argument goes back to eighteenth-century philosopher David Hume. See D. Hume, "On the Balance of Trade," reprinted in *The Gold Standard in Theory and in History,* ed. B. Eichengreen (London: Methuen, 1985).
3. R. Solomon, *The International Monetary System, 1945–1981* (New York: Harper & Row, 1982).
4. International Monetary Fund, *World Economic Outlook, 2005* (Washington, DC: IMF, May 2005).
5. For an extended discussion of the dollar exchange rate in the 1980s, see B. D. Pauls, "U.S. Exchange Rate Policy: Bretton Woods to the Present," *Federal Reserve Bulletin,* November 1990, pp. 891–908.
6. R. Miller, "Why the Dollar Is Giving Way," *BusinessWeek,* December 6, 2004, pp. 36–37.
7. For a feel for the issues contained in this debate, see P. Krugman, *Has the Adjustment Process Worked?* (Washington, DC: Institute for International Economics, 1991); "Time to Tether Currencies," *The Economist,* January 6, 1990, pp. 15–16; P. R. Krugman and M. Obstfeld, *International Economics: Theory and Policy* (New York: HarperCollins, 1994); J. Shelton, *Money Meltdown* (New York: Free Press, 1994); and S. Edwards, "Exchange Rates and the Political Economy of Macroeconomic Discipline," *American Economic Review* 86, no. 2 (May 1996), pp. 159–63.
8. The argument is made by several prominent economists, particularly Stanford's Robert McKinnon. See R. McKinnon, "An International Standard for Monetary Stabilization," *Policy Analyses in International Economics* 8 (1984). The details of this argument are beyond the scope of this book. For a relatively accessible exposition, see P. Krugman, *The Age of Diminished Expectations* (Cambridge, MA: MIT Press, 1990).
9. A. R. Ghosh and A. M. Gulde, "Does the Exchange Rate Regime Matter for Inflation and Growth?" *Economic Issues,* no. 2 (1997).
10. "The ABC of Currency Boards," *The Economist,* November 1, 1997, p. 80.
11. International Monetary Fund, *World Economic Outlook, 1998.*
12. Ibid.
13. See P. Carroll and C. Torres, "Mexico Unveils Program of Harsh Fiscal Medicine," *The Wall Street Journal,* March 10, 1995, pp. A1, A6; and "Putting Mexico Together Again," *The Economist,* February 4, 1995, p. 65.
14. World Trade Organization, *Annual Report, 1997,* vol. II, table III, p. 69.
15. J. Ridding and J. Kynge, "Complacency Gives Way to Contagion," *Financial Times,* January 13, 1998, p. 8.
16. J. Burton and G. Baker, "The Country That Invested Its Way into Trouble," *Financial Times,* January 15, 1998, p. 8.
17. P. Shenon, "The Suharto Billions," *The New York Times,* January 16, 1998, p. 1.
18. World Bank, *1997 World Development Report* (Oxford: Oxford University Press, 1998), table 11.
19. Ridding and Kynge, "Complacency Gives Way to Contagion."
20. Burton and Baker, "The Country That Invested Its Way into Trouble."
21. "Bitter Pill for the Thais," *Straits Times,* July 5, 1997, p. 46.
22. World Bank, *1997 World Development Report,* table 2.
23. International Monetary Fund, press release no. 97/37, August 20, 1997.
24. T. S. Shorrock, "Korea Starts Overhaul; IMF Aid Hits $60 Billion," *Journal of Commerce,* December 8, 1997, p. 3A.

25. See J. Sachs, "Economic Transition and Exchange Rate Regime," *American Economic Review* 86, no. 92 (May 1996), pp. 147–52; and J. Sachs, "Power unto Itself," *Financial Times,* December 11, 1997, p. 11.
26. Sachs, "Power unto Itself."
27. Martin Wolf, "Same Old IMF Medicine," *Financial Times,* December 9, 1997, p. 12.
28. Sachs, "Power unto Itself."
29. P. Gumbel and B. Coleman, "Daimler Warns of Severe '95 Loss Due to Strong Mark," *The New York Times,* June 29, 1995, pp. 1, 10; and M. Wolf, "Daimler-Benz Announces Major Losses," *Financial Times,* June 29, 1995, p. 1.

Chapter 11

1. More formally, ROIC = Net profit after tax/Capital, where capital includes the sum of the firm's equity and debt. This way of calculating profitability is highly correlated with return on assets.
2. T. Copeland, T. Koller, and J. Murrin, *Valuation: Measuring and Managing the Value of Companies* (New York: John Wiley & Sons, 2000).
3. The concept of consumer surplus is an important one in economics. For a more detailed exposition, see D. Besanko, D. Dranove, and M. Shanley, *Economics of Strategy* (New York: John Wiley & Sons, 1996).
4. However, P = V only in the special case where the company has a perfect monopoly, and where it can charge each customer a unique price that reflects the value of the product to that customer (i.e., where perfect price discrimination is possible). More generally, except in the limiting case of perfect price discrimination, even a monopolist will see most consumers capture some of the value of a product in the form of a consumer surplus.
5. This point is central to the work of Michael Porter, *Competitive Advantage* (New York: Free Press, 1985). See also P. Ghemawat, *Commitment: The Dynamic of Strategy* (New York: Free Press, 1991), chap. 4.
6. M. E. Porter, *Competitive Strategy* (New York: Free Press, 1980).
7. M. E. Porter, "What Is Strategy?" *Harvard Business Review,* On-point Enhanced Edition article, February 1, 2000.
8. Porter, *Competitive Advantage.*
9. D. Naidler, M. Gerstein, and R. Shaw, *Organization Architecture* (San Francisco: Jossey-Bass, 1992).
10. G. Morgan, *Images of Organization* (Beverly Hills, CA: Sage Publications, 1986).
11. Empirical evidence does seem to indicate that, on average, international expansion is linked to greater firm profitability. For some recent examples, see M. A. Hitt, R. E. Hoskisson, and H. Kim, "International Diversification, Effects on Innovation and Firm Performance," *Academy of Management Journal* 40, no. 4 (1997), pp. 767–98; and S. Tallman and J. Li, "Effects of International Diversity and Product Diversity on the Performance of Multinational Firms," *Academy of Management Journal* 39, no. 1 (1996), pp. 179–96.
12. This concept has been popularized by G. Hamel and C. K. Prahalad, *Competing for the Future* (Boston: Harvard Business School Press, 1994). The concept is grounded in the resource-based view of the firm; for a summary, see J. B. Barney, "Firm Resources and Sustained Competitive Advantage," *Journal of Management* 17 (1991), pp. 99–120; and K. R. Conner, "A Historical Comparison of Resource-Based Theory and Five Schools of Thought within Industrial Organization Economics: Do We Have a New Theory of the Firm?" *Journal of Management* 17 (1991), pp. 121–54.
13. J. P. Womack, D. T. Jones, and D. Roos, *The Machine That Changed the World* (New York: Rawson Associates, 1990).
14. M. E. Porter, *The Competitive Advantage of Nations* (New York: Free Press, 1990).
15. Example is based on C. S. Trager, "Enter the Mini-Multinational," *Northeast International Business,* March 1989, pp. 13–14.
16. See R. B. Reich, *The Work of Nations* (New York: Alfred A. Knopf, 1991); and P. J. Buckley and N. Hashai, "A Global System View of Firm Boundaries," *Journal of International Business Studies,* January 2004, pp. 33–50.
17. D. Barboza, "An Unknown Giant Flexes Its Muscles," *The New York Times,* December 4, 2004, pp. B1, B3.
18. G. Hall and S. Howell, "The Experience Curve from an Economist's Perspective," *Strategic Management Journal* 6 (1985), pp. 197–212.
19. A. A. Alchain, "Reliability of Progress Curves in Airframe Production," *Econometrica* 31 (1963), pp. 697–93.
20. Hall and Howell, "The Experience Curve from an Economist's Perspective."
21. For a full discussion of the source of economies of scale, see D. Besanko, D. Dranove, and M. Shanley, *Economics of Strategy* (New York: John Wiley & Sons, 1996).
22. This estimate was provided by the Pharmaceutical Manufacturers Association.
23. "Matsushita Electrical Industrial in 1987," in *Transnational Management,* eds. C. A. Bartlett and S. Ghoshal (Homewood, IL: Richard D. Irwin, 1992).

24. See J. Birkinshaw and N. Hood, "Multinational Subsidiary Evolution: Capability and Charter Change in Foreign Owned Subsidiary Companies," *Academy of Management Review* 23 (October 1998), pp. 773–95; A. K. Gupta and V. J. Govindarajan, "Knowledge Flows within Multinational Corporations," *Strategic Management Journal* 21 (2000), pp. 473–96; V. J. Govindarajan and A. K. Gupta, *The Quest for Global Dominance* (San Francisco: Jossey Bass, 2001); T. S. Frost, J. M. Birkinshaw, and P. C. Ensign, "Centers of Excellence in Multinational Corporations," *Strategic Management Journal* 23 (2002), pp. 997–1018; and U. Andersson, M. Forsgren, and U. Holm, "The Strategic Impact of External Networks," *Strategic Management Journal* 23 (2002), pp. 979–96.

25. S. Leung, "Armchairs, TVs and Espresso: Is It McDonald's?" *The Wall Street Journal,* August 30, 2002, pp. A1, A6.

26. C. K. Prahalad and Yves L. Doz, *The Multinational Mission: Balancing Local Demands and Global Vision* (New York: Free Press, 1987). Also see J. Birkinshaw, A. Morrison, and J. Hulland, "Structural and Competitive Determinants of a Global Integration Strategy," *Strategic Management Journal* 16 (1995), pp. 637–55.

27. J. E. Garten, "Wal-Mart Gives Globalization a Bad Name," *BusinessWeek,* March 8, 2004, p. 24.

28. Prahalad and Doz, *The Multinational Mission.* Prahalad and Doz actually talk about local responsiveness rather than local customization.

29. T. Levitt, "The Globalization of Markets," *Harvard Business Review,* May–June 1983, pp. 92–102.

30. K. Belson, "In U.S., Cell Phone Users Are Often All Talk," *The New York Times,* December 13, 2004, pp. C1, C4.

31. W.W. Lewis, *The Power of Productivity* (Chicago: University of Chicago Press, 2004).

32. C. J. Chipello, "Local Presence Is Key to European Deals," *The Wall Street Journal,* June 30, 1998, p. A15.

33. Bartlett and Ghoshal, *Managing across Borders.*

34. Ibid.

35. T. Hout, M. E. Porter, and E. Rudden, "How Global Companies Win Out," *Harvard Business Review,* September–October 1982, pp. 98–108.

36. See K. Ohmae, "The Global Logic of Strategic Alliances," *Harvard Business Review,* March–April 1989, pp. 143–54; G. Hamel, Y. L. Doz, and C. K. Prahalad, "Collaborate with Your Competitors and Win!" *Harvard Business Review,* January–February 1989, pp. 133–39; W. Burgers, C. W. L. Hill, and W. C. Kim, "Alliances in the Global Auto Industry," *Strategic Management Journal* 14 (1993), pp. 419–32; and P. Kale, H. Singh, H. Perlmutter, "Learning and Protection of Proprietary Assets in Strategic Alliances: Building Relational Capital," *Strategic Management Journal* 21 (2000), pp. 217–37.

37. L. T. Chang, "China Eases Foreign Film Rules," *The Wall Street Journal,* October 15, 2004, p. B2.

38. B. L. Simonin, "Transfer of Marketing Know-How in International Strategic Alliances," *Journal of International Business Studies,* 1999, pp. 463–91; and J. W. Spencer, "Firms' Knowledge Sharing Strategies in the Global Innovation System," *Strategic Management Journal* 24 (2003), pp. 217–33.

39. C. Souza, "Microsoft Teams with MIPS, Toshiba," *EBN,* February 10, 2003, p. 4.

40. M. Frankel, "Now Sony Is Giving Palm a Hand," *BusinessWeek,* November 29, 2000, p. 50.

41. P. Kale, H. Singh, and H. Perlmutter, "Learning and Protection of Proprietary Assets in Strategic Alliances: Building Relational Capital," *Strategic Management Journal* 21 (2000), pp. 217–37.

42. R. B. Reich and E. D. Mankin, "Joint Ventures with Japan Give away Our Future," *Harvard Business Review,* March–April 1986, pp. 78–90.

43. J. Bleeke and D. Ernst, "The Way to Win in Cross-Border Alliances," *Harvard Business Review,* November–December 1991, pp. 127–35.

44. E. Booker and C. Krol, "IBM Finds Strength in Alliances," *B to B,* February 10, 2003, pp. 3, 27.

45. W. Roehl and J. F. Truitt, "Stormy Open Marriages Are Better," *Columbia Journal of World Business,* Summer 1987, pp. 87–95.

46. McQuade and Gomes-Casseres, "Xerox and Fuji-Xerox."

47. See T. Khanna, R. Gulati, and N. Nohria, "The Dynamics of Learning Alliances: Competition, Cooperation, and Relative Scope," *Strategic Management Journal* 19 (1998), pp. 193–210; and Kale, Singh, and Perlmutter, "Learning and Protection of Proprietary Assets in Strategic Alliances"

48. Kale, Singh, and Perlmutter, "Learning and Protection of Proprietary Assets in Strategic Alliances."

49. Hamel, Doz, and Prahalad, "Collaborate with Your Competitors"; Khanna, Gulati, and Nohria, "The Dynamics of Learning Alliances"; and E. W. K. Tang, "Acquiring Knowledge by Foreign Partners from International Joint Ventures in a Transition Economy: Learning by Doing and Learning Myopia," *Strategic Management Journal* 23 (2002), pp. 835–54.

50. Hamel, Doz, and Prahalad, "Collaborate with Your Competitors."

51. B. Wysocki, "Cross-Border Alliances Become Favorite Way to Crack New Markets," *The Wall Street Journal,* March 4, 1990, p. A1.
52. Hamel, Doz, and Prahalad, "Collaborate with Competitors," p. 138.

Chapter 12

1. For interesting empirical studies that deal with the issues of timing and resource commitments, see T. Isobe, S. Makino, and D. B. Montgomery, "Resource Commitment, Entry Timing, and Market Performance of Foreign Direct Investments in Emerging Economies," *Academy of Management Journal* 43, no. 3 (2000), pp. 468–84; and Y. Pan and P. S. K. Chi, "Financial Performance and Survival of Multinational Corporations in China," *Strategic Management Journal* 20, no. 4 (1999), pp. 359–74. A complementary theoretical perspective on this issue can be found in V. Govindarjan and A. K. Gupta, *The Quest for Global Dominance* (San Francisco: Jossey-Bass, 2001). Also see F. Vermeulen and H. Barkeme, "Pace, Rhythm and Scope: Process Dependence in Building a Profitable Multinational Corporation," *Strategic Management Journal* 23 (2002), pp. 637–54.
2. This can be reconceptualized as the resource base of the entrant, relative to indigenous competitors. For work that focuses on this issue, see W. C. Bogner, H. Thomas, and J. McGee, "A Longitudinal Study of the Competitive Positions and Entry Paths of European Firms in the U.S. Pharmaceutical Market," *Strategic Management Journal* 17 (1996), pp. 85–107; D. Collis, "A Resource-Based Analysis of Global Competition," *Strategic Management Journal* 12 (1991), pp. 49–68; and S. Tallman, "Strategic Management Models and Resource-Based Strategies among MNEs in a Host Market," *Strategic Management Journal* 12 (1991), pp. 69–82.
3. For a discussion of first-mover advantages, see M. Lieberman and D. Montgomery, "First-Mover Advantages," *Strategic Management Journal* 9 (summer 1988, special issue), pp. 41–58.
4. J. M. Shaver, W. Mitchell, and B. Yeung, "The Effect of Own Firm and Other Firm Experience on Foreign Direct Investment Survival in the United States, 1987–92," *Strategic Management Journal* 18 (1997), pp. 811–24.
5. S. Zaheer and E. Mosakowski, "The Dynamics of the Liability of Foreignness: A Global Study of Survival in the Financial Services Industry," *Strategic Management Journal* 18 (1997), pp. 439–64.
6. Shaver, Mitchell, and Yeung, "The Effect of Own Firm and Other Firm Experience on Foreign Direct Investment Survival in the United States."
7. P. Ghemawat, *Commitment: The Dynamics of Strategy* (New York: Free Press, 1991).
8. R. Luecke, *Scuttle Your Ships before Advancing* (Oxford: Oxford University Press, 1994).
9. Isobe, Makino, and Montgomery, "Resource Commitment, Entry Timing, and Market Performance"; Pan and Chi, "Financial Performance and Survival of Multinational Corporations in China"; and Govindarjan and Gupta, *The Quest for Global Dominance.*
10. Christopher Bartlett and Sumantra Ghoshal, "Going Global: Lessons from Late Movers," *Harvard Business Review,* March–April 2000, pp. 132–45.
11. This section draws on numerous studies, including C. W. L. Hill, P. Hwang, and W. C. Kim, "An Eclectic Theory of the Choice of International Entry Mode," *Strategic Management Journal* 11 (1990), pp. 117–28; C. W. L. Hill and W. C. Kim, "Searching for a Dynamic Theory of the Multinational Enterprise: A Transaction Cost Model," *Strategic Management Journal* 9 (special issue on strategy content, 1988), pp. 93–104; E. Anderson and H. Gatignon, "Modes of Foreign Entry: A Transaction Cost Analysis and Propositions," *Journal of International Business Studies* 17 (1986), pp. 1–26; F. R. Root, *Entry Strategies for International Markets* (Lexington, MA: D. C. Heath, 1980); A. Madhok, "Cost, Value and Foreign Market Entry: The Transaction and the Firm," *Strategic Management Journal* 18 (1997), pp. 39–61; K. D. Brouthers and L. B. Brouthers, "Acquisition or Greenfield Start-Up?" *Strategic Management Journal* 21, no. 1 (2000), pp. 89–97; X. Martin and R. Salmon, "Knowledge Transfer Capacity and Its Implications for the Theory of the Multinational Enterprise," *Journal of International Business Studies,* July 2003, p. 356; and A. Verbeke, "The Evolutionary View of the MNE and the Future of Internalization Theory," *Journal of International Business Studies,* November 2003, pp. 498–515.
12. For a general discussion of licensing, see F. J. Contractor, "The Role of Licensing in International Strategy," *Columbia Journal of World Business,* Winter 1982, pp. 73–83.
13. See E. Terazono and C. Lorenz, "An Angry Young Warrior," *Financial Times,* September 19, 1994, p. 11; and K. McQuade and B. Gomes-Casseres, "Xerox and Fuji-Xerox," Harvard Business School case no. 9-391-156.
14. O. E. Williamson, *The Economic Institutions of Capitalism* (New York: Free Press, 1985).
15. J. H. Dunning and M. McQueen, "The Eclectic Theory of International Production: A Case Study of the International Hotel Industry," *Managerial and Decision Economics* 2 (1981), pp. 197–210.

16. Andrew E. Serwer, "McDonald's Conquers the World," *Fortune,* October 17, 1994, pp. 103–16.

17. For an excellent review of the basic theoretical literature of joint ventures, see B. Kogut, "Joint Ventures: Theoretical and Empirical Perspectives," *Strategic Management Journal* 9 (1988), pp. 319–32. More recent studies include T. Chi, "Option to Acquire or Divest a Joint Venture," *Strategic Management Journal* 21, no. 6 (2000), pp. 665–88; H. Merchant and D. Schendel, "How Do International Joint Ventures Create Shareholder Value?" *Strategic Management Journal* 21, no. 7 (2000), pp. 723–37; H. K. Steensma and M.A. Lyles, "Explaining IJV Survival in a Transitional Economy though Social Exchange and Knowledge Based Perspectives," *Strategic Management Journal* 21, no. 8 (2000), pp. 831–51; and J. F. Hennart and M. Zeng, "Cross Cultural Differences and Joint Venture Longevity," *Journal of International Business Studies,* December 2002, pp. 699–717.

18. D. G. Bradley, "Managing against Expropriation," *Harvard Business Review,* July–August 1977, pp. 78–90.

19. J. A. Robins, S. Tallman, and K. Fladmoe-Lindquist, "Autonomy and Dependence of International Cooperative Ventures," *Strategic Management Journal,* October 2002, pp. 881–902.

20. Speech given by Tony Kobayashi at the University of Washington Business School, October 1992.

21. A. C. Inkpen and P. W. Beamish, "Knowledge, Bargaining Power, and the Instability of International Joint Ventures," *Academy of Management Review* 22 (1997), pp. 177–202; and S. H. Park and G. R. Ungson, "The Effect of National Culture, Organizational Complementarity, and Economic Motivation on Joint Venture Dissolution," *Academy of Management Journal* 40 (1997), pp. 279–307.

22. Inkpen and Beamish, "Knowledge, Bargaining Power, and the Instability of International Joint Ventures."

23. See Brouthers and Brouthers, "Acquisition or Greenfield Start-up?"; and J. F. Hennart and Y. R. Park, "Greenfield versus Acquisition: The Strategy of Japanese Investors in the United States," *Management Science,* 1993, pp. 1054–70.

24. This section draws on Hill, Hwang, and Kim, "An Eclectic Theory of the Choice of International Entry Mode."

25. C. W. L. Hill, "Strategies for Exploiting Technological Innovations: When and When Not to License," *Organization Science* 3 (1992), pp. 428–41.

26. See Brouthers and Brouthers, "Acquisition or Greenfield Start-Up?"; and J. Anand and A. Delios, "Absolute and Relative Resources as Determinants of International Acquisitions," *Strategic Management Journal,* February 2002, pp. 119–34.

27. United Nations, *World Investment Report, 2005* (New York and Geneva: United Nations, 2005).

28. Ibid.

29. For evidence on acquisitions and performance, see R. E. Caves, "Mergers, Takeovers, and Economic Efficiency," *International Journal of Industrial Organization* 7 (1989), pp. 151–74; M. C. Jensen and R. S. Ruback, "The Market for Corporate Control: The Scientific Evidence," *Journal of Financial Economics* 11 (1983), pp. 5–50; R. Roll, "Empirical Evidence on Takeover Activity and Shareholder Wealth," in *Knights, Raiders and Targets,* ed. J. C. Coffee, L. Lowenstein, and S. Rose (Oxford: Oxford University Press, 1989); A. Schleifer and R. W. Vishny, "Takeovers in the 60s and 80s: Evidence and Implications," *Strategic Management Journal* 12 (Winter 1991, special issue), pp. 51–60; T. H. Brush, "Predicted Changes in Operational Synergy and Post-Acquisition Performance of Acquired Businesses," *Strategic Management Journal* 17 (1996), pp. 1–24; and A. Seth, K. P. Song, and R. R. Pettit, "Value Creation and Destruction in Cross-Border Acquisitions," *Strategic Management Journal* 23 (October 2002), pp. 921–40.

30. J. Warner, J. Templeman, and R. Horn, "The Case against Mergers," *BusinessWeek,* October 30, 1995, pp. 122–34.

31. "Few Takeovers Pay Off for Big Buyers," *Investors Business Daily,* May 25, 2001, p. 1.

32. S. A. Christofferson, R. S. McNish, and D. L. Sias, "Where Mergers Go Wrong," *The McKinsey Quarterly* 2 (2004), pp. 92–110.

33. D. J. Ravenscraft and F. M. Scherer, *Mergers, Selloffs, and Economic Efficiency* (Washington, DC: Brookings Institution, 1987).

34. See P. Ghemawat and F. Ghadar, "The Dubious Logic of Global Mega-mergers," *Harvard Business Review,* July–August 2000, pp. 65–72.

35. R. Roll, "The Hubris Hypothesis of Corporate Takeovers," *Journal of Business* 59 (1986), pp. 197–216.

36. "Marital Problems," *The Economist,* October 14, 2000.

37. See J. P. Walsh, "Top Management Turnover following Mergers and Acquisitions," *Strategic Management Journal* 9 (1988), pp. 173–83.

38. B. Vlasic and B.A. Stertz, *Taken for a Ride: How Daimler-Benz Drove Off with Chrysler* (New York: HarperCollins, 2000).

39. See A.A. Cannella and D.C. Hambrick, "Executive Departure and Acquisition Performance," *Strategic Management Journal* 14 (1993), pp. 137–52.

40. P. Haspeslagh and D. Jemison, *Managing Acquisitions* (New York: Free Press, 1991).

41. Ibid.

Chapter 13

1. R. A. Pope, "Why Small Firms Export: Another Look," *Journal of Small Business Management* 40 (2002), pp. 17–26.

2. S. T. Cavusgil, "Global Dimensions of Marketing," in *Marketing,* eds. P. E. Murphy and B. M. Enis (Glenview, IL: Scott, Foresman, 1985), pp. 577–99.

3. S. M. Mehta, "Enterprise: Small Companies Look to Cultivate Foreign Business," *The Wall Street Journal,* July 7, 1994, p. B2.

4. P. A. Julien and C. Ramagelahy, "Competitive Strategy and Performance of Exporting SMEs," *Entrepreneurship Theory and Practice,* 2003, pp. 227–94.

5. W. J. Burpitt and D. A. Rondinelli, "Small Firms' Motivations for Exporting: To Earn and Learn?" *Journal of Small Business Management,* October 2000, pp. 1–14; and J. D. Mittelstaedt, G. N. Harben, and W. A. Ward, "How Small Is Too Small?" *Journal of Small Business Management* 41 (2003), pp. 68–85.

6. Small Business Administration, "The State of Small Business 1999–2000: Report to the President," 2001, www.sba.gov/advo/stats/stateofsb99_00.pdf.

7. A. O. Ogbuehi and T. A. Longfellow, "Perceptions of U.S. Manufacturing Companies Concerning Exporting," *Journal of Small Business Management,* October 1994, pp. 37–59; and U.S. Small Business Administration, "Guide to Exporting," www.sba.gov/oit/info/Guide-to-Exporting/index.html.

8. R. W. Haigh, "Thinking of Exporting?" *Columbia Journal of World Business* 29 (December 1994), pp. 66–86.

9. F. Williams, "The Quest for More Efficient Commerce," *Financial Times,* October 13, 1994, p. 7.

10. See Burpitt and Rondinelli, "Small Firms' Motivations for Exporting"; and C. S. Katsikeas, L. C. Leonidou, and N. A. Morgan, "Firm Level Export Performance Assessment," *Academy of Marketing Science* 28 (2000), pp. 493–511.

11. M. Y. Yoshino and T. B. Lifson, *The Invisible Link* (Cambridge, MA: MIT Press, 1986).

12. L. W. Tuller, *Going Global* (Homewood, IL: Business One Irwin, 1991).

13. Haigh, "Thinking of Exporting?"

14. M. A. Raymond, J. Kim, and A. T. Shao. "Export Strategy and Performance," *Journal of Global Marketing* 15 (2001), pp. 5–29; and P. S. Aulakh, M. Kotabe, and H. Teegen, "Export Strategies and Performance of Firms from Emerging Economies," *Academy of Management Journal* 43 (2000), pp. 342–61.

15. J. Francis and C. Collins-Dodd, "The Impact of Firms' Export Orientation on the Export Performance of High-Tech Small and Medium Sized Enterprises," *Journal of International Marketing* 8, no. 3 (2000), pp. 84–103.

16. For a review of the conditions under which a buyer has power over a supplier, see M. E. Porter, *Competitive Strategy* (New York: Free Press, 1980).

17. *Exchange Agreements and Exchange Restrictions* (Washington, DC: International Monetary Fund, 1989).

18. Some argue that countertrade is a way of reducing the risks inherent in a traditional money-for-goods transaction, particularly with entities from emerging economies. See C. J. Choi, S. H. Lee, and J. B. Kim, "A Note of Countertrade: Contractual Uncertainty and Transactional Governance in Emerging Economies," *Journal of International Business Studies* 30, no. 1 (1999), pp. 189–202.

19. J. R. Carter and J. Gagne, "The Dos and Don'ts of International Countertrade," *Sloan Management Review,* Spring 1988, pp. 31–37; and W. Maneerungsee, "Countertrade: Farm Goods Swapped for Italian Electricity," *Bangkok Post,* July 23, 1998.

20. Estimates from the American Countertrade Association at www.countertrade.org/index.htm. See also D. West, "Countertrade," *Business Credit* 104, no. 4 (2001), pp. 64–67; and B. Meyer, "The Original Meaning of Trade Meets the Future of Barter," *World Trade* 13 (January 2000), pp. 46–50.

21. Carter and Gagne, "The Dos and Don'ts of International Countertrade."

22. Maneerungsee, "Countertrade."

23. For details, see Carter and Gagne, "Dos and Don'ts"; J. F. Hennart, "Some Empirical Dimensions of Countertrade," *Journal of International Business Studies,* 1990, pp. 240–60; and West, "Countertrade."

24. D. J. Lecraw, "The Management of Countertrade: Factors Influencing Success," *Journal of International Business Studies,* Spring 1989, pp. 41–59.

Chapter 14

1. B. C. Arntzen, G. G. Brown, T. P. Harrison, and L. L. Trafton, "Global Supply Chain Management at Digital Equipment Corporation," *Interfaces* 25 (1995), pp. 69–93; and Diana Farrell, "Beyond Offshoring," *Harvard Business Review,* December 2004, pp. 1–8.

2. D. A. Garvin, "What Does Product Quality Really Mean," *Sloan Management Review* 26 (Fall 1984), pp. 25–44.

3. See the articles published in the special issue of the *Academy of Management Review on Total Quality Management* 19, no. 3 (1994). The following article provides a good overview of many of the issues involved from an academic perspective: J. W. Dean and D. E. Bowen, "Management Theory and Total Quality," *Academy of Management Review* 19 (1994), pp. 392–418. Also see T. C. Powell, "Total Quality Management as Competitive Advantage," *Strategic Management Journal* 16 (1995), pp. 15–37.
4. For general background information, see "How to Build Quality," *The Economist,* September 23, 1989, pp. 91–92; A. Gabor, *The Man Who Discovered Quality* (New York: Penguin, 1990); P. B. Crosby, *Quality Is Free* (New York: Mentor, 1980); and M. Elliot et al., "A Quality World, a Quality Life," *Industrial Engineer,* January 2003, pp. 26–33.
5. G. T. Lucier and S. Seshadri, "GE Takes Six Sigma beyond the Bottom Line," *Strategic Finance,* May 2001, pp. 40–46.
6. M. Saunders, "U.S. Firms Doing Business in Europe Have Options in Registering for ISO 9000 Quality Standards," *Business America,* June 14, 1993, p. 7.
7. G. Stalk and T. M. Hout, *Competing against Time* (New York: Free Press, 1990).
8. Farrell, "Beyond Offshoring"; and M. A. Cohen and H. L. Lee, "Resource Deployment Analysis of Global Manufacturing and Distribution Networks," *Journal of Manufacturing and Operations Management* 2 (1989), pp. 81–104.
9. P. Krugman, "Increasing Returns and Economic Geography," *Journal of Political Economy* 99, no. 3 (1991), pp. 483–99; and J. M. Shaver and F. Flyer, "Agglomeration Economies, Firm Heterogeneity, and Foreign Direct Investment in the United States," *Strategic Management Journal* 21 (2000), pp. 1175–93.
10. For a review of the technical arguments, see D. A. Hay and D. J. Morris, *Industrial Economics: Theory and Evidence* (Oxford: Oxford University Press, 1979). See also C. W. L. Hill and G. R. Jones, *Strategic Management: An Integrated Approach* (Boston: Houghton Mifflin, 2004).
11. See P. Nemetz and L. Fry, "Flexible Manufacturing Organizations: Implications for Strategy Formulation," *Academy of Management Review* 13 (1988), pp. 627–38; N. Greenwood, *Implementing Flexible Manufacturing Systems* (New York: Halstead Press, 1986); J. P. Womack, D. T. Jones, and D. Roos, *The Machine That Changed the World* (New York: Rawson Associates, 1990); and R. Parthasarthy and S. P. Seith, "The Impact of Flexible Automation on Business Strategy and Organizational Structure," *Academy of Management Review* 17 (1992), pp. 86–111.
12. B. J. Pine, *Mass Customization: The New Frontier in Business Competition* (Boston: Harvard Business School Press, 1993); S. Kotha, "Mass Customization: Implementing the Emerging Paradigm for Competitive Advantage," *Strategic Management Journal* 16 (1995), pp. 21–42; and J. H. Gilmore and B. J. Pine II, "The Four Faces of Mass Customization," *Harvard Business Review,* January–February 1997, pp. 91–101.
13. M. A. Cusumano, *The Japanese Automobile Industry* (Cambridge, MA: Harvard University Press, 1989); T. Ohno, *Toyota Production System* (Cambridge, MA: Productivity Press, 1990); and Womack, Jones, and Roos, *The Machine That Changed the World.*
14. P. Waurzyniak, "Ford's Flexible Push," *Manufacturing Engineering,* September 2003, pp. 47–50.
15. K. Ferdows, "Making the Most of Foreign Factories," *Harvard Business Review,* March–April 1997, pp. 73–88.
16. This argument represents a simple extension of the dynamic capabilities research stream in the strategic management literature. See D. J. Teece, G. Pisano, and A. Shuen, "Dynamic Capabilities and Strategic Management," *Strategic Management Journal* 18 (1997), pp. 509–33.
17. T. S. Frost, J. M. Birkinshaw, and P. C. Ensign, "Centers of Excellence in Multinational Corporations," *Strategic Management Journal* 23 (November 2002), pp. 997–1018.
18. C. W. L. Hill, "Globalization, the Myth of the Nomadic Multinational Enterprise, and the Advantages of Location Persistence," University of Washington, School of Business, working paper, 2001.
19. J. Solomon and E. Cherney, "A Global Report: Outsourcing to India Sees a Twist," *The Wall Street Journal,* April 1, 2004, p. A2.
20. The material in this section is based primarily on the transaction cost literature of vertical integration; for example, O. E. Williamson, *The Economic Institutions of Capitalism* (New York: Free Press, 1985).
21. For a review of the evidence, see Williamson, *The Economic Institutions of Capitalism.* See also L. Poppo and T. Zenger, "Testing Alternative Theories of the Firm: Transaction Cost, Knowledge-Based, and Measurement Explanations for Make-or-Buy Decisions in Information Services," *Strategic Management Journal* 19 (1998), pp. 853–78.
22. A. D. Chandler, *The Visible Hand* (Cambridge, MA: Harvard University Press, 1977).
23. For a review of these arguments, see C. W. L. Hill and R. E. Hoskisson, "Strategy and Structure in the Multiproduct Firm," *Academy of Management Review* 12 (1987), pp. 331–41.

24. C. W. L. Hill, "Cooperation, Opportunism, and the Invisible Hand," *Academy of Management Review* 15 (1990), pp. 500–13.

25. See R. Narasimhan and J. R. Carter, "Organization, Communication and Coordination of International Sourcing," *International Marketing Review* 7 (1990), pp. 6–20; and Arntzen et al., "Global Supply Chain Management at Digital Equipment Corporation."

26. H. F. Busch, "Integrated Materials Management," *IJPD & MM* 18 (1990), pp. 28–39.

27. T. Aeppel, "Manufacturers Cope with the Costs of Strained Global Supply Lines," *The Wall Street Journal,* December 8, 2004, p. A1.

Chapter 15

1. For evidence on the importance of marketing and R&D in the performance of a multinational firm, see M. Kotabe, Srini Srinivasan, and P. S. Aulakh, "Multinationality and Firm Performance: The Moderating Role of R&D and Marketing Capabilities," *Journal of International Business Studies* 33, no. 1 (2002), pp. 79–97.

2. See R. W. Ruekert and O. C. Walker, "Interactions between Marketing and R&D Departments in Implementing Different Business-Level Strategies," *Strategic Management Journal* 8 (1987), pp. 233–48; and K. B. Clark and S. C. Wheelwright, *Managing New Product and Process Development* (New York: Free Press, 1993).

3. T. Levitt, "The Globalization of Markets," *Harvard Business Review,* May–June 1983, pp. 92–102. Copyright © 1983 by the Harvard Business School Publishing Corporation. Reprinted by permission. All rights reserved.

4. For example, see S. P. Douglas and Y. Wind, "The Myth of Globalization," *Columbia Journal of World Business,* Winter 1987, pp. 19–29; C. A. Bartlett and S. Ghoshal, *Managing across Borders: The Transnational Solution* (Boston: Harvard Business School Press, 1989); V. J. Govindarajan and A. K. Gupta, *The Quest for Global Dominance* (San Francisco: Jossey Bass, 2001); and J. Quelch. "The Return of the Global Brand," *Harvard Business Review,* August 2003, pp. 1–3.

5. J. Tagliabue, "U.S. Brands Are Feeling Global Tension," *The New York Times,* March 15, 2003, p. C3.

6. D. B. Holt, J. A. Quelch, and E. L. Taylor, "How Global Brands Compete," *Harvard Business Review,* September 2004.

7. J. T. Landry, "Emerging Markets: Are Chinese Consumers Coming of Age?" *Harvard Business Review,* May–June 1998, pp. 17–20.

8. C. Miller, "Teens Seen as the First Truly Global Consumers," *Marketing News,* March 27, 1995, p. 9.

9. This approach was originally developed in K. Lancaster, "A New Approach to Demand Theory," *Journal of Political Economy* 74 (1965), pp. 132–57.

10. V. R. Alden, "Who Says You Can't Crack Japanese Markets?" *Harvard Business Review,* January–February 1987, pp. 52–56.

11. T. Parker-Pope, "Custom Made," *The Wall Street Journal,* September 26, 1996, p. 22.

12. "RCA's New Vista: The Bottom Line," *BusinessWeek,* July 4, 1987, p. 44.

13. N. Gross and K. Rebello, "Apple? Japan Can't Say No," *BusinessWeek,* June 29, 1992, pp. 32–33.

14. "After Early Stumbles P&G Is Making Inroads Overseas," *The Wall Street Journal,* February 6, 1989, p. B1.

15. C. Matlack and P. Gogoi, "What's This? The French Love McDonald's?" *BusinessWeek,* January 13, 2003, pp. 50–51.

16. Z. Gurhan-Cvanli and D. Maheswaran, "Cultural Variation in Country of Origin Effects," *Journal of Marketing Research,* August 2000, pp. 309–17.

17. See M. Laroche, V. H. Kirpalani, F. Pons, and L. Zhou, "A Model of Advertising Standardization in Multinational Corporations," *Journal of International Business Studies,* 32 (2001), pp. 249–66; and D. A. Aaker and E. Joachimsthaler, "The Lure of Global Branding," *Harvard Business Review,* November–December 1999, pp. 137–44.

18. "Advertising in a Single Market," *The Economist,* March 24, 1990, p. 64.

19. D. Waller, "Charged Up over Competition Law," *Financial Times,* June 23, 1994, p. 14.

20. R. G. Matthews and D. Pringle, "Nokia Bets One Global Message Will Ring True in Many Markets," *The Wall Street Journal,* September 27, 2004, p. B6.

21. R. J. Dolan and H. Simon, *Power Pricing* (New York: Free Press, 1999).

22. B. Stottinger, "Strategic Export Pricing: A Long Winding Road," *Journal of International Marketing* 9 (2001), pp. 40–63; and S. Gil-Pareja "Export Process Discrimination in Europe and Exchange Rates," *Review of International Economics,* May 2002, pp. 299–312.

23. These allegations were made on a PBS *Frontline* documentary telecast in the United States in May 1992.

24. Y. Tsurumi and H. Tsurumi, "Fujifilm–Kodak Duopolistic Competition in Japan and the United States," *Journal of International Business Studies* 30 (1999), pp. 813–30.

25. G. Smith and B. Wolverton, "A Dark Moment for Kodak," *BusinessWeek,* August 4, 1997, pp. 30–31.

26. R. Narisette and J. Friedland, "Disposable Income: Diaper Wars of P&G and Kimberly-Clark Now Heat Up in Brazil," *The Wall Street Journal,* June 4, 1997, p. A1.

27. J. F. Pickering, *Industrial Structure and Market Conduct* (London: Martin Robertson, 1974).

28. S. P. Douglas, C. Samuel Craig, and E. J. Nijissen, "Integrating Branding Strategy across Markets," *Journal of International Marketing* 9, no. 2 (2001), pp. 97–114

29. The phrase was first used by economist Joseph Schumpeter in *Capitalism, Socialism, and Democracy* (New York: Harper Brothers, 1942).

30. S. Kotabe, S. Srinivasan, and P. S. Aulakh. "Multinationality and Firm Performance: The Moderating Role of R&D and Marketing," *Journal of International Business Studies* 33 (2002), pp. 79–97.

31. See D. C. Mowery and N. Rosenberg, *Technology and the Pursuit of Economic Growth* (Cambridge, UK: Cambridge University Press, 1989); and M. E. Porter, *The Competitive Advantage of Nations* (New York: Free Press, 1990).

32. W. Kuemmerle, "Building Effective R&D Capabilities Abroad," *Harvard Business Review,* March–April 1997, pp. 61–70; and C. Le Bas and C. Sierra, "Location versus Home Country Advantages in R&D Activities," *Research Policy* 31 (2002), pp. 589–609.

33. "When the Corporate Lab Goes to Japan," *The New York Times,* April 28, 1991, sec. 3, p. 1.

34. D. Shapley, "Globalization Prompts Exodus," *Financial Times,* March 17, 1994, p. 10.

35. E. Mansfield. "How Economists See R&D," *Harvard Business Review,* November–December, 1981, pp. 98–106.

36. Ibid.

37. G. A. Stevens and J. Burley, "Piloting the Rocket of Radical Innovation," *Research Technology Management* 46 (2003), pp. 16–26.

38. K. B. Clark and S. C. Wheelwright, *Managing New Product and Process Development* (New York: Free Press, 1993); and M. A. Shilling and C. W. L. Hill, "Managing the New Product Development Process," *Academy of Management Executive* 12, no. 3 (1998), pp. 67–81.

39. O. Port, "Moving Past the Assembly Line," *Business Week Special Issue: Reinventing America,* 1992, pp. 177–80.

40. K. B. Clark and T. Fujimoto, "The Power of Product Integrity," *Harvard Business Review,* November–December 1990, pp. 107–18; Clark and Wheelwright, *Managing New Product and Process Development;* S. L. Brown and K. M. Eisenhardt, "Product Development: Past Research, Present Findings, and Future Directions," *Academy of Management Review* 20 (1995), pp. 348–78; and G. Stalk and T. M. Hout, *Competing against Time* (New York: Free Press, 1990).

41. Shilling and Hill, "Managing the New Product Development Process."

42. C. Christensen. "Quantum Corporation—Business and Product Teams," Harvard Business School case no. 9-692-023.

43. R. Nobel and J. Birkinshaw, "Innovation in Multinational Corporations: Control and Communication Patterns in International R&D Operations," *Strategic Management Journal* 19 (1998), pp. 479–96.

44. Information comes from the company's Web site; also see K. Ferdows, "Making the Most of Foreign Factories," *Harvard Business Review,* March–April 1997, pp. 73–88.

Chapter 16

1. P. J. Dowling and R. S. Schuler, *International Dimensions of Human Resource Management* (Boston: PSW-Kent, 1990).

2. J. Millman, M. A. von Glinow, and M. Nathan, "Organizational Life Cycles and Strategic International Human Resource Management in Multinational Companies," *Academy of Management Review* 16 (1991), pp. 318–39.

3. See Peter Bamberger and Ilan Meshoulam, *Human Resource Strategy: Formulation, Implementation, and Impact* (Thousand Oaks, CA: Sage, 2000); P. M. Wright and S. Snell, "Towards a Unifying Framework for Exploring Fit and Flexibility in Human Resource Management," *Academy of Management Review* 23 (October 1998), pp. 756–72; and B. A. Colbert, "The Complex Resource-Based View: Implications for Theory and Practice in Strategic Human Resource Management," *Academy of Management Review* 29 (July 2004), pp. 341–60.

4. R. Colman, "HR Management Lags behind at World Class Firms," *CMA Management,* July–August 2002, p. 9.

5. E. H. Schein, *Organizational Culture and Leadership* (San Francisco: Jossey-Bass, 1985).

6. H. V. Perlmutter, "The Tortuous Evolution of the Multinational Corporation," *Columbia Journal of World Business* 4 (1969), pp. 9–18; D. A. Heenan and H. V. Perlmutter, *Multinational Organizational Development* (Reading, MA: Addison-Wesley, 1979); D. A. Ondrack, "International Human Resources Management in European and North American Firms," *International Studies of Management and Organization* 15 (1985), pp. 6–32; and T. Jackson, "The Management of People across Cultures: Valuing People Differently," *Human Resource Management* 41 (2002), pp. 455–75.

7. V. Reitman and M. Schuman, "Men's Club: Japanese and Korean Companies Rarely Look Outside for People to Run Their Overseas Operations," *The Wall Street Journal,* September 26, 1996, p. 17.

8. S. Beechler and J. Z. Yang, "The Transfer of Japanese Style Management to American Subsidiaries," *Journal of International Business Studies* 25 (1994), pp. 467–91. See also R. Konopaske, S. Warner, and K. E. Neupert, "Entry Mode Strategy and Performance: The Role of FDI Staffing," *Journal of Business Research,* September 2002, pp. 759–70.

9. M. Banai and L. M. Sama, "Ethical Dilemma in MNCs' International Staffing Policies," *Journal of Business Ethics,* June 2000, pp. 221–35.

10. Reitman and Schuman, "Men's Club."

11. C. A. Bartlett and S. Ghoshal, *Managing across Borders: The Transnational Solution* (Boston: Harvard Business School Press, 1989).

12. S. J. Kobrin, "Geocentric Mindset and Multinational Strategy," *Journal of International Business Studies* 25 (1994), pp. 493–511.

13. P. M. Rosenzweig and N. Nohria, "Influences on Human Resource Management Practices in Multinational Corporations," *Journal of International Business Studies* 25 (1994), pp. 229–51.

14. Kobrin, "Geocentric Mindset and Multinational Strategy."

15. M. Harvey and H. Fung, "Inpatriate Managers: The Need for Realistic Relocation Reviews," *International Journal of Management* 17 (2000), pp. 151–59.

16. S. Black, M. Mendenhall, and G. Oddou, "Toward a Comprehensive Model of International Adjustment," *Academy of Management Review* 16 (1991), pp. 291–317; J. Shay and T. J. Bruce, "Expatriate Managers," *Cornell Hotel & Restaurant Administration Quarterly,* February 1997, pp. 30–40; and Y. Baruch and Y. Altman, "Expatriation and Repatriation in MNCs—A Taxonomy," *Human Resource Management* 41 (2002), pp. 239–59.

17. M. G. Harvey, "The Multinational Corporation's Expatriate Problem: An Application of Murphy's Law," *Business Horizons* 26 (1983), pp. 71–78.

18. J. Barbian, "Return to Sender," *Training,* January 2002, pp. 40–43.

19. Shay and Bruce, "Expatriate Managers." Also see J. S. Black and H. Gregersen, "The Right Way to Manage Expatriates," *Harvard Business Review,* March–April 1999, pp. 52–63: and Baruch and Altman, "Expatriation and Repatriation in MNCs."

20. N. Foster, "The Persistent Myth of High Expatriate Failure Rates," *Journal of Human Resource Management* 8 (1997), pp. 177–205.

21. Barbian, "Return to Sender."

22. Black, Mendenhall, and Oddou, "Toward a Comprehensive Model of International Adjustment."

23. R. L. Tung, "Selection and Training Procedures of U.S., European, and Japanese Multinationals," *California Management Review* 25 (1982), pp. 57–71.

24. C. M. Solomon, "Success Abroad Depends upon More than Job Skills," *Personnel Journal,* April 1994, pp. 51–58.

25. C. M. Solomon, "Unhappy Trails," *Workforce,* August 2000, pp. 36–41.

26. Solomon, "Success Abroad."

27. Solomon, "Unhappy Trails."

28. M. Harvey, "Addressing the Dual-Career Expatriation Dilemma," *Human Resource Planning* 19, no. 4 (1996), pp. 18–32.

29. M. Mendenhall and G. Oddou, "The Dimensions of Expatriate Acculturation: A Review," *Academy of Management Review* 10 (1985), pp. 39–47.

30. I. Torbiorin, *Living Abroad: Personal Adjustment and Personnel Policy in the Overseas Setting* (New York: John Wiley & Sons, 1982).

31. R. L. Tung, "Selection and Training of Personnel for Overseas Assignments," *Columbia Journal of World Business* 16 (1981), pp. 68–78.

32. Solomon, "Success Abroad."

33. S. Ronen, "Training and International Assignee," in *Training and Career Development,* ed. I. Goldstein (San Francisco: Jossey-Bass, 1985); and Tung, "Selection and Training of Personnel for Overseas Assignments."

34. Solomon, "Success Abroad."

35. Harvey, "Addressing the Dual-Career Expatriation Dilemma"; and J. W. Hunt, "The Perils of Foreign Postings for Two," *Financial Times,* May 6, 1998, p. 22.

36. C. M. Daily, S. T. Certo, and D. R. Dalton, "International Experience in the Executive Suite: A Path to Prosperity?" *Strategic Management Journal* 21 (2000), pp. 515–23.

37. Dowling and Schuler, *International Dimensions of Human Resource Management.*

38. Ibid.

39. G. Baliga and J. C. Baker, "Multinational Corporate Policies for Expatriate Managers: Selection, Training, and Evaluation," *Advanced Management Journal,* Autumn 1985, pp. 31–38.

40. J. C. Baker, "Foreign Language and Departure Training in U.S. Multinational Firms," *Personnel Administrator,* July 1984, pp. 68–70.

41. A 1997 study by the Conference Board looked at this in depth. For a summary, see L. Grant, "That Overseas Job Could Derail Your Career," *Fortune,* April 14, 1997, p. 166. Also see J. S. Black and H. Gregersen, "The Right Way to Manage Expatriates," *Harvard Business Review,* March–April 1999, pp. 52–63.

42. J. S. Black and M. E. Mendenhall, *Global Assignments: Successfully Expatriating and Repatriating International Managers* (San Francisco: Jossey-Bass, 1992); and K. Vermond, "Expatriates Come Home," *CMA Management,* October 2001, pp. 30–33.

43. Ibid.

44. Figures from the Conference Board study. For a summary, see Grant, "That Overseas Job Could Derail Your Career."

45. S. C. Schneider, "National v. Corporate Culture: Implications for Human Resource Management," *Human Resource Management* 27 (Summer 1988), pp. 231–46.

46. I. M. Manve and W. B. Stevenson, "Nationality, Cultural Distance and Expatriate Status," *Journal of International Business Studies* 32 (2001), pp. 285–303; and D. Minbaeva et al., "MNC Knowledge Transfer, Subsidiary Absorptive Capacity, and HRM," *Journal of International Business Studies* 34, no. 6 (2003), pp. 586–604.

47. Bartlett and Ghoshal, *Managing across Borders.*

48. See G. Oddou and M. Mendenhall, "Expatriate Performance Appraisal: Problems and Solutions," in *International Human Resource Management,* ed. Mendenhall and Oddou (Boston: PWS-Kent, 1991); Dowling and Schuler, *International Dimensions;* R. S. Schuler and G. W. Florkowski, "International Human Resource Management," in *Handbook for International Management Research,* ed. B. J. Punnett and O. Shenkar (Oxford: Blackwell, 1996); and K. Roth and S. O'Donnell, "Foreign Subsidiary Compensation Strategy: An Agency Theory Perspective," *Academy of Management Journal* 39, no. 3 (1996), pp. 678–703.

49. Oddou and Mendenhall, "Expatriate Performance Appraisal."

50. "Expatriates Often See Little Benefit to Careers in Foreign Stints, Indifference at Home," *The Wall Street Journal,* December 11, 1989, p. B1.

51. Oddou and Mendenhall, "Expatriate Performance Appraisal"; and Schuler and Florkowski, "International Human Resource Management."

52. Towers Perrin, *Towers Perrin Worldwide Total Remuneration Study, 2003–2004,* www.towersperrin.com.

53. R. C. Longworth, "U.S. Executives Sit on Top of the World," *Chicago Tribune,* May 31, 1998, p. C1.

54. Organizational Resource Counselors, *2002 Survey of International Assignment Policies and Practices,* March 2003.

55. C. Reynolds, "Compensation of Overseas Personnel," in *Handbook of Human Resource Administration,* ed. J. J. Famularo (New York: McGraw-Hill, 1986).

56. M. Helms, "International Executive Compensation Practices," in *International Human Resource Management,* ed. M. Mendenhall and G. Oddou (Boston: PWS-Kent, 1991).

57. G. W. Latta, "Expatriate Incentives," *HR Focus* 75, no. 3 (March 1998), p. S3.

58. C. K. Prahalad and Y. L. Doz, *The Multinational Mission* (New York: Free Press, 1987).

59. Ibid.

60. Schuler and Florkowski, "International Human Resource Management."

61. See J. P. Womack, D. T. Jones, and D. Roos, *The Machine That Changed the World* (New York: Rawson Associates, 1990).

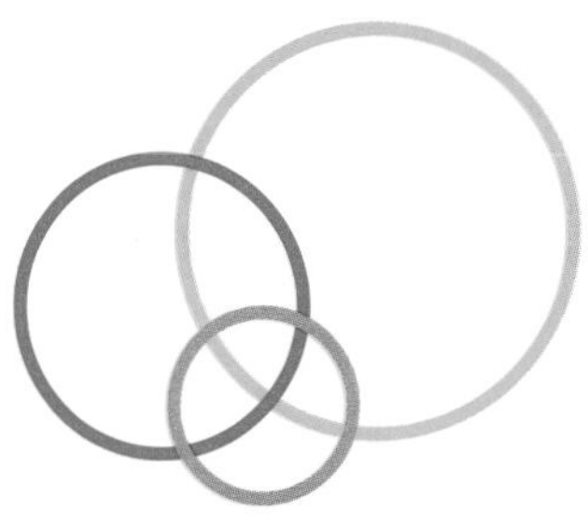

name index

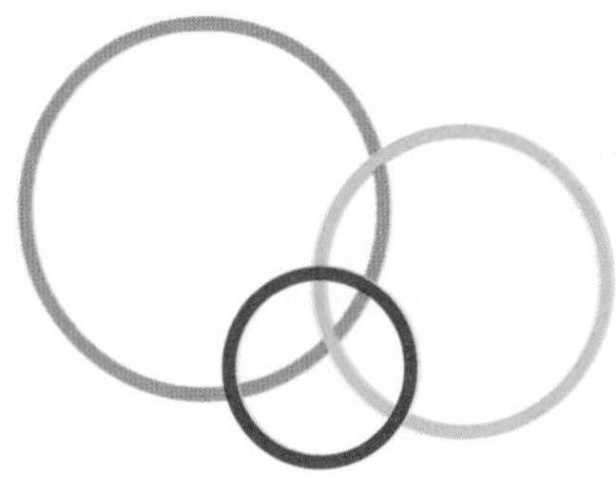

subject index

Scale: 1 to 111,922,000 — 0, 1000, 2000 Miles; 0, 1000, 2000, 3000 Kilometers

Note: All world maps are Robinson projection.

NORTH SEA
NORWAY
SWEDEN
BALTIC SEA
ESTONIA
0 100 Miles
0 100 Kilometers
DENMARK
LATVIA
RUSSIA
LITHUANIA
NETHERLANDS
BELARUS
GERMANY
POLAND
BELGIUM
CZECH REPUBLIC
UKRAINE
LUXEMBOURG
SLOVAKIA
FRANCE
LIECHTENSTEIN
MOLDOVA
SWITZERLAND
AUSTRIA
HUNGARY
SLOVENIA
ROMANIA
CROATIA
SAN MARINO
BOSNIA-HERZEGOVINA
BLACK SEA
MONACO
SERBIA
BULGARIA
ITALY
MONTENEGRO
ALBANIA
MACEDONIA
GREECE
TURKEY
MEDITERRANEAN SEA
MALTA
TIC OCEAN
NORWAY
SWEDEN
FINLAND
R U S S I A
KAZAKSTAN
MONGOLIA
NORTH PACIFIC OCEAN
UZBEKISTAN
KYRGYZSTAN
TURKMENISTAN
TAJIKISTAN
NORTH KOREA
TURKEY
JAPAN
SOUTH KOREA
TUNISIA
CYPRUS
SYRIA
LEBANON
IRAQ
IRAN
AFGHANISTAN
C H I N A
ISRAEL
JORDAN
KUWAIT
NEPAL
BHUTAN
LIBYA
EGYPT
BAHRAIN
QATAR
PAKISTAN
SAUDI ARABIA
MYANMAR (BURMA)
Tropic of Cancer
I N D I A
TAIWAN
UNITED ARAB EMIRATES
OMAN
NIGER
ERITREA
BANGLADESH
LAOS
CHAD
SUDAN
YEMEN
THAILAND
VIETNAM
PHILIPPINES
MARSHALL ISLANDS
NIGERIA
DJIBOUTI
CAMBODIA (KAMPUCHEA)
PALAU
UGANDA
ETHIOPIA
SRI LANKA
SOMALIA
BRUNEI
MICRONESIA
MALDIVES
MALAYSIA
KIRIBATI
Equator
RWANDA
SINGAPORE
I N D O N E S I A
NAURU
DEM. REP. OF THE CONGO
KENYA
BURUNDI
SEYCHELLES
PAPUA NEW GUINEA
SOLOMON ISLANDS
TANZANIA
MALAWI
TUVALU
COMOROS
INDIAN OCEAN
EAST TIMOR
ANGOLA
MOZAMBIQUE
ZAMBIA
VANUATU
FIJI
MADAGASCAR
MAURITIUS
Tropic of Capricorn
NAMIBIA
BOTSWANA
A U S T R A L I A
ZIMBABWE
SWAZILAND
SOUTH AFRICA
LESOTHO
NEW ZEALAND
MAURITANIA
MALI
NIGER
NEGAL
BURKINA FASO
GUINEA
BENIN
SIERRA LEONE
IVORY COAST
GHANA
NIGERIA
LIBERIA
TOGO
300 Miles
Kilometers
0 100 Miles
0 100 Kilometers
RUSSIA
CASPIAN SEA
BLACK SEA
GEORGIA
AZERBAIJAN
ARMENIA
TURKEY
AZERBAIJAN
IRAN

ACRONYM	PROPER NAME
ADB	Asian Development Bank
AfDB	African Development Bank
AFIC	Asian Finance and Investment Corporation
AFTA	Asian Free Trade Agreement
ASEAN	Association of Southeast Asian Nations
ATPA	Andean Trade Preference Act
BIS	Bank for International Settlements
BOP	Balance of Payments
CIM	Computer-Integrated Manufacturing
CIS	Commonwealth of Independent States
CISG	UN Convention on Contracts for the International Sale of Goods
CEMA	Council for Mutual Economic Assistance
CRA	Country Risk Assessment
DB	Development Bank
DC	Developed Country
DFIs	Development Finance Institutions
DISC	Domestic International Sales Corporation
EBRD	European Bank for Reconstruction and Development
ECOWAS	Economic Community of West African States
EMU	Economic and Monetary Union
EEA	European Economic Area
EFTA	European Free Trade Association
EMs	Export Management Companies
EMCF	European Monetary Cooperation Fund
EMS	European Monetary System
EPO	European Patent Organization
ETC	Export Trading Company
ETUC	European Trade Union Confederation
EU	European Union
FCPA	Foreign Corrupt Practices Act
FDI	Foreign Direct Investment
FSC	Foreign Sales Corporation
FTAA	Free Trade Agreement of the Americas
FTZ	Foreign Trade Zone
Fx	Foreign Exchange
G7	Group of Seven
GATT	General Agreement on Tariffs and Trade
GC	Global Company
GDP	Gross Domestic Product
GNP	Gross National Product
GSP	Generalized System of Preferences
IAC	International Anti-counterfeiting Coalition
IC	International Company
IDA	International Development Association
IDB	Inter-American Development Bank
IEC	International Electrotechnical Commission
IFC	International Finance Corporation
IMF	International Monetary Fund
IPLC	International Product Life Cycle
IRC	International Revenue Code
ISA	International Seabed Authority
ISO	International Organization for Standardization
ITA	International Trade Administration
JIT	Just-in-Time
JV	Joint Venture
LAIA	Latin American Integration Association (formerly LAFTA)
LDC	Less Developed Country
LIBOR	London Interbank Offer Rate
LOST	Law of the Sea Treaty
MERCOSUR	Free Trade Agreement between Argentina, Brazil, Paraguay, and Uruguay
MNC	Multinational Company
MNE	Multinational Enterprise
NAFTA	North American Free Trade Agreement
NATO	North Atlantic Treaty Organization
NIC	Newly Industrializing Country
NTBs	Nontariff Barriers
OECD	Organization for Economic Cooperation & Development
OPEC	Organizational of Petroleum Exporting Countries
PPP	Purchasing Power Parity
PRC	People's Republic of China
PTA	Preferential Trade Area for Eastern and Southern Africa
SACC	Southern African Development Coordination Conference
SBA	Small Business Administration
SBC	Strategic Business Center
SBU	Small Business Unit
SDR	Special Drawing Rights
SEZ	Special Economic Zone
TQM	Total Quality Management
UN	United Nations
UNCTAD	UN Conference on Trade and Development
VAT	Value Added Tax
VER	Voluntary Export Restraint
VRAs	Voluntary Restraints Agreements
WEC	World Energy Council
WIPO	World Intellectual Property Organization
WTO	World Trade Organization

COUNTRY	CAPITAL
Afghanistan	Kabul
Albania	Tirana
Algeria	Algiers
Andorra	Andorra la Vella
Angola	Luanda
Antigua and Barbuda	St. John's
Argentina	Buenos Aires
Armenia	Yerevan
Australia	Canberra
Austria	Vienna
Azerbaijan	Baku
Bahamas	Nassau
Bahrain	Manama
Bangladesh	Dhaka
Barbados	Bridgetown
Belarus	Minsk
Belgium	Brussels
Belize	Belmopan
Benin	Porto-Novo
Bhutan	Thimphu
Bolivia	La Paz
Bosnia and Herzegovina	Sarajevo
Botswana	Gaborone
Brazil	Brasilia
Brunei	Bandar Seri Begawan
Bulgaria	Sofia
Burkina Faso	Ouagadougou
Burundi	Bujumbura
Cambodia	Phnom Penh
Cameroon	Yaounde
Canada	Ottawa
Cape Verde	Praia
Central African Republic	Bangui
Chad	N'Djamena
Chile	Santiago
China	Beijing
Colombia	Bogota
Comoros	Moroni
Congo	Brazzaville
Congo (formerly Zaire)	Kinshasa
Costa Rica	San Jose
Cote d'Ivoire	Yamoussoukro
Croatia	Zagreb
Cuba	Havana
Cyprus	Nicosia
Czech Republic	Prague
Denmark	Copenhagen
Djibouti	Djibouti
Dominica	Roseau
Dominican Republic	Santo Domingo
Ecuador	Quito
Egypt	Cairo
El Salvador	San Salvador
Equatorial Guinea	Malabo
Eritrea	Asmara
Estonia	Tallinn
Ethiopia	Addis Ababa
Fiji	Suva
Finland	Helsinki
France	Paris
Gabon	Libreville
The Gambia	Banjul
Georgia	Tbilisi

COUNTRY	CAPITAL
Germany	Berlin
Ghana	Accra
Greece	Athens
Grenada	St. George's
Guatemala	Guatemala City
Guinea	Conakry
Guinea-Bissau	Bissau
Guyana	Georgetown
Haiti	Port-au-Prince
Honduras	Tegucigalpa
Hungary	Budapest
Iceland	Reykjavik
India	New Delhi
Indonisia	Jakarta
Iran	Tehran
Iraq	Baghdad
Ireland	Dublin
Israel	Jerusalem
Italy	Rome
Jamaica	Kingston
Japan	Tokyo
Jordan	Amman
Kazakhstan	Astana
Kenya	Nairobi
Kiribati	Tarawa
Korea, North	Pyongyang
Korea, South	Seoul
Kuwait	Kuwait City
Kyrgyzstan	Bishkek
Laos	Vientiane
Latvia	Riga
Lebanon	Beirut
Lesotho	Maseru
Liberia	Monrovia
Libya	Tripoli
Liechtenstein	Vaduz
Lithuania	Vilnius
Luxembourg	Luxembourg
Macedonia, The Former Yugoslav Republic of	Skopje
Madagascar	Antananarivo
Malawi	Lilongwe
Malaysia	Kuala Lumpur
Maldives	Male
Mali	Bamako
Malta	Valletta
Marshall Islands	Majuro
Mauritania	Nouakchott
Mauritius	Port Louis
Mexico	Mexico City
Micronesia	Palikir
Moldova	Chisinau
Monaco	Monaco
Mongolia	Ulaanbaatar
Montenegro	Podgorica
Morocco	Rabat
Mozambique	Maputo
Myanmar	Rangoon
Namibia	Windhoek
Nauru	Yaren
Nepal	Kathmandu
The Netherlands	Amsterdam
New Zealand	Wellington
Nicaragua	Managua
Niger	Niamey
Nigeria	Abuja
Norway	Oslo
Oman	Muscat

COUNTRY	CAPITAL
Pakistan	Islamabad
Palau	Koror
Panama	Panama City
Papua New Guinea	Port Moresby
Paraguay	Asuncion
Peru	Lima
Philippines	Manila
Poland	Warsaw
Portugal	Lisbon
Qatar	Doha
Romania	Bucharest
Russia	Moscow
Rwanda	Kigali
Saint Kitts and Nevis	Basseterre
Saint Lucia	Castries
Saint Vincent and the Grenadines	Kingstown
San Marino	San Marino
Sao Tome and Principe	Sao Tome
Saudi Arabia	Riyadh
Senegal	Dakar
Serbia	Belgrade
Seychelles	Victoria
Sierra Leone	Freetown
Singapore	Singapore
Slovakia	Bratislava
Slovenia	Ljubljana
Solomon Islands	Honiara
Somalia	Mogadishu
South Africa	Pretoria
Spain	Madrid
Sri Lanka	Colombo
Sudan	Khartoum
Suriname	Paramaribo
Swaziland	Mbabane
Sweden	Stockholm
Switzerland	Bern
Syria	Damascus
Taiwan	Taipei
Tajikistan	Dushanbe
Tanzania	Dar-es-Salaam
Thailand	Bangkok
Togo	Lome
Tonga	Nuku'alofa
Trinidad and Tobago	Port-of-Spain
Tunisia	Tunis
Turkey	Ankara
Turkmenistan	Ashgabat
Tuvalu	Funafuti
Uganda	Kampala
Ukraine	Kiev
United Arab Emirates	Abu Dhabi
United Kingdom	London
United States of America	Washington, DC
Uruguay	Montevideo
Uzbekistan	Tashkent
Vanuatu	Vila
Vatican City	
Venezuela	Caracas
Vietnam	Hanoi
Western Samoa	Apia
Yemen	Sanaa
Zambia	Lusaka
Zimbabwe	Harare

ISBN 0-07-321054-4